Poverty and Income Distribution

Poverty and Income Distribution

SECOND EDITION

EDWARD N. WOLFF

A John Wiley & Sons, Ltd., Publication

This edition first published 2009
© 2009 Edward N. Wolff

Blackwell Publishing was acquired by John Wiley & Sons in February 2007. Blackwell's publishing program has been merged with Wiley's global Scientific, Technical, and Medical business to form Wiley-Blackwell.

Registered Office
John Wiley & Sons Ltd, The Atrium, Southern Gate, Chichester, West Sussex, PO19 8SQ, United Kingdom

Editorial Offices
350 Main Street, Malden, MA 02148-5020, USA
9600 Garsington Road, Oxford, OX4 2DQ, UK
The Atrium, Southern Gate, Chichester, West Sussex, PO19 8SQ, UK

For details of our global editorial offices, for customer services, and for information about how to apply for permission to reuse the copyright material in this book please see our website at www.wiley.com/wiley-blackwell.

The right of Edward N. Wolff to be identified as the author of this work has been asserted in accordance with the Copyright, Designs and Patents Act 1988.

Wiley also publishes its books in a variety of electronic formats. Some content that appears in print may not be available in electronic books.

Designations used by companies to distinguish their products are often claimed as trademarks. All brand names and product names used in this book are trade names, service marks, trademarks or registered trademarks of their respective owners. The publisher is not associated with any product or vendor mentioned in this book. This publication is designed to provide accurate and authoritative information in regard to the subject matter covered. It is sold on the understanding that the publisher is not engaged in rendering professional services. If professional advice or other expert assistance is required, the services of a competent professional should be sought.

Library of Congress Cataloging-in-Publication Data

Wolff, Edward N.
   Poverty and income distribution / Edward N. Wolff.—2nd ed.
      p. cm.
   Rev. ed. of: Economics of poverty inequality and discrimination / Edward Nathan Wolff. c1997.
   Includes bibliographical references and index.
   ISBN 978-1-4051-7660-6 (hbk. : alk. paper)   1. Poverty—United States.   2. Poor—United States.
3. Income distribution—United States.   I. Wolff, Edward N. Economics of poverty inequality and discrimination.   II. Title.
   HC110.P6W648 2008
   305.5′690973—dc22

                                                                                            2008032203

A catalogue record for this book is available from the British Library.

Set in 10.5/12pt Times by Graphicraft Limited, Hong Kong
Printed in Singapore by Fabulous Printers Pte Ltd

SKYF09BB606-2145-4DD8-A6C8-EBAF35265E57_011922

Contents

Preface   xiv

Chapter 1   Introduction: Issues and Scope of Book   1

1.1   Recent trends in living standards   1
    1.1.1   Income and earnings stagnate while poverty remains unchanged   1
    1.1.2   Inequality rises sharply   4
    1.1.3   Middle-class debt explodes   5
    1.1.4   What has happened to tax rates?   6
    1.1.5   Rising profits is the key   7
    1.1.6   Yet schooling has continued to rise   8
    1.1.7   Some conclusions   11
1.2   Causes of rising inequality   12
    1.2.1   Skill-biased technology change   12
    1.2.2   The shift to services   13
    1.2.3   Declining unionization   13
    1.2.4   Globalization   13
    1.2.5   Downsizing and outsourcing   13
    1.2.6   Public policy changes   14
1.3   General description of the textbook   14
Notes   17

Part I   Inequality, Poverty, and Mobility: Measurement and Trends   19

Chapter 2   Income, Earnings, and the Standard of Living   21

2.1   Introduction   21
2.2   The composition of personal income in the United States   22
2.3   The standard of living   24
    2.3.1   Real versus nominal   25
    2.3.2   Trends in living standards in the United States   26
2.4   Factor shares   29
    2.4.1   Historical studies on factor shares*   31

2.5	International comparisons of living standards	32
	2.5.1 Per capita income	32
	2.5.2 The Human Development Index	33
2.6	Household production and well-being	35
	2.6.1 Defining household work	37
	2.6.2 The market cost approach	37
	2.6.3 The opportunity cost approach	38
	2.6.4 Empirical work on household production	38
2.7	Summary	39
2.8	References, bibliography, and data sources	40
2.9	Discussion questions and problem set	42

Appendix 2.1 An introduction to the National Income and Product Accounts* 44

A2.1.1	The relation to the national accounts	46
A2.1.2	The sources of personal income	47
A2.1.3	The derivation of factor shares	48
A2.1.4	Miscellaneous issues in national accounting	49
	A2.1.4.1 Treatment of international trade	49
	A2.1.4.2 National income at factor costs	51
	A2.1.4.3 The treatment of capital gains	51
Notes		52

Chapter 3 Income Inequality: Its Measurement, Historical Trends, and International Comparisons 55

3.1	Introduction	55
3.2	A review of basic statistics	55
	3.2.1 Mean, variance, and standard deviation	56
	3.2.2 Distributions	56
	3.2.3 Percentile ranking	59
3.3	Inequality measures	60
	3.3.1 Concentration measures	61
	3.3.2 Coefficient of variation	61
	3.3.3 The Lorenz curve	63
	3.3.4 Gini coefficient	64
	3.3.5 Log variance of income*	66
	3.3.6 The Theil entropy index*	67
	3.3.7 Atkinson's measure*	69
	3.3.8 Lorenz dominance*	70
3.4	Time trends in income inequality in the United States	70
3.5	International comparisons of inequality	74
	3.5.1 Inequality comparisons among high-income countries	74
	3.5.2 The Kuznets curve	80
	3.5.3 The world distribution of income*	84
3.6	Summary	85
3.7	References and bibliography	86
3.8	Discussion questions and problem set	90
Notes		91

Chapter 4   Poverty: Definitions and Historical Trends   93

4.1   Introduction   93
4.2   The measurement of poverty   93
      4.2.1   The official U.S. poverty standard   94
      4.2.2   Absolute versus relative poverty thresholds   95
      4.2.3   Subjective poverty lines   96
      4.2.4   Other concepts of poverty   99
4.3   Measurement of poverty incidence   99
      4.3.1   The poverty rate and the poverty gap ratio   99
      4.3.2   Composite measures of poverty*   100
4.4   Poverty trends in the United States   101
      4.4.1   Composition of the poor   103
4.5   Other dimensions of poverty   107
      4.5.1   Poverty spells and the permanence of poverty   107
      4.5.2   The underclass   108
      4.5.3   International comparisons of poverty rates   109
4.6   Other issues in the measurement of poverty   112
      4.6.1   Equivalence scales   113
      4.6.2   Choice of a price index   114
      4.6.3   The treatment of taxes   115
      4.6.4   The treatment of noncash government benefits   116
      4.6.5   The role of household wealth   119
      4.6.6   Consumption-based measures of poverty   120
      4.6.7   The accounting period   121
      4.6.8   Other issues   122
4.7   Summary   123
4.8   References and bibliography   125
4.9   Discussion questions and problem set   130
Notes   132

Chapter 5   Household Wealth   134

5.1   Introduction   134
5.2   What is household wealth?   135
      5.2.1   Wealth and well-being   135
      5.2.2   Marketable wealth   136
      5.2.3   Other definitions of household wealth   140
5.3   Historical time-series data on household wealth and its
      composition   141
      5.3.1   Trends in average wealth   142
      5.3.2   Changes in wealth composition   143
      5.3.3   Homeownership rates   146
5.4   Wealth inequality in the United States   147
      5.4.1   Methods used to estimate wealth inequality   148
      5.4.2   Long-term trends in household wealth inequality in the
              United States   150
      5.4.3   Changes in wealth inequality, 1962–2004   154
      5.4.4   The *Forbes* 400   166

5.5   International comparisons of household wealth distribution   167
    5.5.1   Comparisons of long-term time trends   167
    5.5.2   Comparisons of recent trends   168
5.6   Summary   171
5.7   References and bibliography   172
5.8   Discussion questions and problem set   176
Notes   177

Chapter 6   Economic Mobility   180

6.1   Introduction   180
6.2   Mobility measures   180
    6.2.1   Measuring intergenerational mobility   180
    6.2.2   The Shorrocks measure and other measures of lifetime mobility   181
6.3   Mobility over the time   184
    6.3.1   Income mobility   184
    6.3.2   Earnings mobility   188
    6.3.3   Other dimensions of mobility   189
6.4   Intergenerational mobility   189
    6.4.1   Results for the United States   190
    6.4.2   Mechanisms of transmission   194
    6.4.3   International comparisons   195
6.5   Wealth mobility   197
6.6   Summary   198
6.7   References and bibliography   200
Notes   204

Part II   Explanations of Inequality and Poverty   205

Chapter 7   The Labor Force, Employment, and Unemployment   207

7.1   Introduction   207
7.2   Basic concepts of the labor force, employment, and unemployment   208
    7.2.1   Employment   208
    7.2.2   Unemployment   209
    7.2.3   The labor force   209
    7.2.4   Estimating employment statistics   209
7.3   Labor force participation rates   210
    7.3.1   LFPR by gender, race, and age   211
    7.3.2   Two-earner households   216
    7.3.3   Educational attainment of the labor force   217
7.4   The industrial and occupational composition of employment   219
7.5   Measures of unemployment and historical trends   221
7.6   The incidence of unemployment   226
    7.6.1   Jobless rates by demographic characteristic   226
    7.6.2   Unemployment by industry, occupation, and region   229
7.7   Types of unemployment   232
    7.7.1   Frictional unemployment   232
    7.7.2   Seasonal unemployment   233

7.7.3	Structural unemployment	234
7.7.4	Deficient demand (Keynesian) unemployment	235
7.7.5	The debate over the causes of unemployment	236
7.8	Summary	238
7.9	References and bibliography	240
7.10	Discussion questions	243
Notes		243

Chapter 8   The Role of Education and Skills   246

8.1	Introduction	246
8.2	The human capital model	247
8.2.1	The rate of return to human capital	248
8.2.2	On-the-job training	251
8.2.3	Additional implications of the human capital model	254
8.3	Earnings, schooling, and experience	258
8.3.1	Rates of return to schooling	260
8.3.2	Lifetime earnings	267
8.4	The schooling–earnings function*	269
8.4.1	The extended earnings function*	272
8.5	Ability and earnings	273
8.5.1	Estimates of the ability effect*	275
8.5.2	The nature vs. nurture controversy	276
8.6	Productivity and earnings	279
8.6.1	Experience, productivity, and earnings	279
8.6.2	Other interpretations of the relation between schooling and earnings	281
8.7	Earnings inequality and human capital*	286
8.8	Summary and concluding remarks	288
8.9	References and bibliography	291
8.10	Discussion questions and problem set	296
Notes		297

Chapter 9   Unions, Dual Labor Markets, and Structural Models of Earnings   301

9.1	Introduction	301
9.2	The role of labor unions	303
9.2.1	A brief history of trade unionism in the United States	303
9.2.2	Trends in union membership	305
9.2.3	The economic role of labor unions	310
9.2.4	The effect of unions on wages: The evidence	315
9.3	Segmented labor markets	319
9.3.1	Internal labor markets	319
9.3.2	The dual labor market model	322
9.3.3	An evaluation of labor market segmentation	325
9.4	Industrial composition and earnings inequality*	326
9.4.1	State and regional differences in inequality	326
9.4.2	Regional differences in income levels	328
9.4.3	Industrial composition and rising earnings inequality of the 1980s	329

9.5   Industry wage differentials*   331
      9.5.1   Explanations of inter-industry wage differences   331
      9.5.2   Recent trends and efficiency wage theory   336
9.6   Occupational wage differentials   339
      9.6.1   Historical studies   339
      9.6.2   Trends in the United States in the twentieth century   340
      9.6.3   Rising skewness at the top   342
9.7   Summary and concluding remarks   343
9.8   References and bibliography   346
9.9   Discussion questions   352
Notes   353

**Chapter 10   The Role of Savings and Intergenerational Transfers in Explaining
Wealth Inequality**   355

10.1   Introduction   355
10.2   The basic lifecycle model   356
       10.2.1   Age–wealth profiles   357
       10.2.2   Longitudinal analyses*   359
       10.2.3   Simulation and regression analysis*   361
10.3   Extensions of the lifecycle model   363
       10.3.1   The role of uncertainty about death and lifetime annuities 364
       10.3.2   The role of pension and social security wealth   364
       10.3.3   The bequest motive   366
       10.3.4   Precautionary savings and liquidity constraints   371
10.4   Intergenerational equity   372
       10.4.1   Social security annuity and transfer wealth   372
       10.4.2   Private intergenerational transfers   375
       10.4.3   Generational accounting   376
10.5   Summary and overall assessment   377
10.6   References and bibliography   379
10.7   Discussion questions   385
Notes   385

Chapter 11   Sources of Rising Earnings Inequality*   386

11.1   Introduction   386
11.2   Skill-biased technological change   387
11.3   The IT "revolution"   389
11.4   Growing international trade and immigration   390
11.5   The shift to services   393
11.6   Institutional factors   394
11.7   Outsourcing and downsizing   395
11.8   Changes in the distribution of schooling and ability   395
11.9   Time trends in key explanatory variables   396
11.10 Econometric results   405
11.11 Summary and concluding remarks   408
11.12 References and bibliography   410
Appendix 11.1   Data sources and methods   416
Notes   417

Part III   Discrimination   419

Chapter 12   Discrimination: Meaning, Measurement, and Theory   421

12.1   Introduction   421
12.2   The meaning of discrimination   423
        12.2.1   The Blinder–Oaxaca decomposition*   424
        12.2.2   Pre-labor market discrimination   425
12.3   Theories of discrimination: an overview   429
12.4   Taste for discrimination   430
12.5   Statistical discrimination   434
12.6   The racial stigma model   436
12.7   The Marxian model   437
12.8   Overcrowding model of occupational segregation   438
12.9   Summary   440
12.10   References and bibliography   441
Notes   443

Chapter 13   Racial Discrimination: Progress and Reversal for Black Americans   445

13.1   Introduction   445
13.2   Trends and status report on racial inequality   446
        13.2.1   The earnings gap: have African American workers made gains on whites? 446
        13.2.2   Labor force participation and unemployment   449
        13.2.3   Family income, poverty, and wealth   453
        13.2.4   Hispanics   457
13.3   Migration from the South   460
13.4   Progress in educational attainment   461
        13.4.1   The role of educational gains on the earnings gap*   463
        13.4.2   Quality of schooling*   464
        13.4.3   Returns to schooling for blacks and whites   465
        13.4.4   Hispanic Americans   468
13.5   Changes in family structure among black Americans   469
13.6   Public policy and discrimination   471
        13.6.1   Public policy programs   472
        13.6.2   The effectiveness of the anti-discrimination programs   474
13.7   Summary and conclusion   478
13.8   References and bibliography   480
13.9   Discussion questions and problem set   485
Notes   486

Chapter 14   The Gender–Wage Gap and Occupational Segregation   488

14.1   Introduction   488
14.2   The wage gap and labor force participation trends   488
        14.2.1   Time trends   490
        14.2.2   Labor force participation patterns   491
        14.2.3   Explanations of the rising LFPR of women*   492
14.3   Explanations of the wage gap   494
        14.3.1   Human capital differences   494
        14.3.2   Occupational segregation   503

14.4 The role of public policy   509
    14.4.1 The effectiveness of the anti-discrimination programs   509
    14.4.2 Comparable worth   511
14.5 Other issues*   513
    14.5.1 Effects of wives' earnings on family income inequality   513
    14.5.2 The feminization of poverty   514
    14.5.3 International comparisons   516
14.6 Summary   517
14.7 References and bibliography   518
14.8 Discussion questions and problem set   525
Notes   525

Part IV The Role of Public Policy on Poverty and Inequality

527

Chapter 15 Public Policy and Poverty Alleviation

529

15.1   Introduction   529
15.2   A brief history of income maintenance programs   529
    15.2.1 Early developments   530
    15.2.2 The New Deal   530
    15.2.3 Post-war developments   532
    15.2.4 Housing assistance   533
    15.2.5 Public expenditures on major federal programs   534
15.3   Unemployment insurance (UI)   536
    15.3.1 A brief description of the UI system   536
    15.3.2 Time trends in UI benefits   538
    15.3.3 Incentive effects of the UI system   540
15.4   The social security system   541
    15.4.1 Determination of the social security benefit   542
    15.4.2 Incentive effects on labor supply   546
15.5   The welfare system   546
    15.5.1 The workings of AFDC and TANF   547
    15.5.2 Incentive effects of the welfare system   550
15.6   Work programs   554
    15.6.1 Effectiveness of the work programs   555
15.7   The minimum wage   556
15.8   Conclusion and overall assessment of government programs   559
    15.8.1 Effects on poverty   560
    15.8.2 Proposals for reform   562
15.9   References and bibliography   564
15.10 Discussion questions and problem set   570
Notes   571

Chapter 16 The Redistributional Effects of Public Policy

574

16.1 Introduction   574
16.2 Equality as a social goal   574
    16.2.1 Arguments in favor of promoting equality   574
    16.2.2 Arguments against promoting equality   577

16.3	The structure of tax systems	579
	16.3.1 Proportional, progressive, and regressive tax structures	579
	16.3.2 Inequality measures and the tax system	583
	16.3.3 Vertical versus horizontal equity	586
16.4	Distributional consequences of the U.S. tax system	587
	16.4.1 Tax schedules for the personal income tax	587
	16.4.2 Effective tax rates for the personal income tax	591
	16.4.3 The payroll tax	593
	16.4.4 Other federal taxes	594
	16.4.5 State and local government taxes	595
	16.4.6 The overall tax bite?	596
	16.4.7 International comparisons of taxation	598
	16.4.8 The overall effective tax rate structure in the United States	600
16.5	The negative income tax and the EITC	608
16.6	The distributional effects of government expenditures	611
16.7	Summary and conclusion	616
16.8	References and bibliography	619
16.9	Discussion questions and problem set	622
Notes		623
Index		627

* Section contains more advanced material or special topics that may be omitted without losing continuity in the book.

Preface

This book developed as an outgrowth of my own course, "Poverty and Income Distribution," which I have taught at New York University on and off since 1977. The textbook incubated over many years. Because of a scarcity of textbooks in the field in the 1970s, I developed my own set of lecture notes, which I later distributed to students. Over time, with feedback from students (the course typically had 40 students per semester), the lecture notes eventually evolved into this textbook. In this way, the textbook was constantly subjected to student reaction. Sections whose exposition was unclear were refined and rewritten. Topics that did not seem of interest to students were dropped and new ones added. The data used in the book were periodically updated.

The book also changed focus over the years. In the late 1970s, there were only inklings of the dramatic changes that were to befall the U.S. economy. The original focus of the course was on the measurement of inequality and poverty and explanations of inequality. Since the only well-developed models of inequality at that time were for labor markets, the course also had a heavy dose of labor economics. Moreover, at that time, the most widely used and most fully articulated model was human capital theory, so that considerable space was also devoted to this topic.

However, by the late 1980s, when the writing of this book began in earnest, the three-fold malady of falling real wages, stagnating living standards, and widening income disparities had become apparent. In addition, poverty rates, which had leveled off in the 1970s, began rising again in the 1980s. The numbers themselves tell a dramatic story. As a result, the book began to emphasize the actual statistics themselves as a way of telling the story of these disturbing changes in the U.S. economy (and other economies as well).

Some economists who teach in this field may feel that the book has, perhaps, an overdose of statistical evidence. Moreover, it is admittedly much harder to examine students on statistics than on economic theory. However, my own feeling is that numeracy is crucial in its own right. It is important to give students a feel for the actual magnitudes involved. If nothing else, an awareness of these figures will help students become more knowledgeable citizens and help them better understand the statistics that are periodically reported in our major newspapers and magazines.

The book maintains a strong emphasis on the role of labor markets. There are two reasons for this. First, about three-quarters of personal income arises from labor activities. Second, many public policy programs, most notably social security, are linked either directly or indirectly to labor market activities. This may create some overlap between this text and traditional labor economics, but the stress here is different – much more on the relation between labor activity and inequality. In my treatment of the human capital model, for example, the stress is on the determination of earnings differences between individuals. The book also provides a wider coverage of models of the labor market than is found in more traditional labor economics courses. Institutional models are given particular attention – such as internal and dual labor market theory, inter-industry wage differentials and efficiency wage theory, and structural models – because of the recent stress on the demand side of the labor market as a source of earnings inequality.

A section of the book is devoted to the inequality of household wealth, which is my own research specialty. As it turns out, changes in inequality are much more dramatic in terms of household wealth than in terms of income. Indeed, it appears that changes in income inequality become magnified in terms of wealth disparities. There is again a heavy emphasis on the statistical evidence, though a chapter in this section treats the determinants of wealth differences between families. The major focus is on lifecycle theory, since it is still the primary model on this subject. However, there is also a lengthy discussion on the role of inheritances, because they also play an important role in explaining disparities in wealth holdings among households and also raise some crucial ethical issues.

Discrimination is also another persistent problem, which seems unlikely to disappear over the next several decades, and a whole section of the book concentrates on this issue. This issue has grown in leaps and bounds in Europe as it deals with the economic problems of its immigrants and the less than ideal intergenerational mobility of these immigrants' children and grand-children. The news in the United States is particularly distressful for African American families, who after making some progress in closing the income gap relative to white families between the early 1960s and the mid-1970s now find their relative incomes at the same level as in the early 1960s. Poverty rates also remain much higher for blacks than for whites. The role of public policy, particularly affirmative action, in explaining the changing fortunes of minorities is given considerable emphasis. This subject is especially topical today in light of recent decisions by the Supreme Court and recent attempts by members of Congress to dismantle the system.

The last part of the book treats the role of public policy on both poverty and income inequality. This tends to be the section of the course that elicits the most student interest and participation. Because of the political discourse on this subject and the emotions it raises, I have found it particularly useful to "lay out the facts." The first chapter of this part examines the social security system and the welfare system in some detail. Most students are surprised by the fact that the resources devoted to the former are many times those spent on welfare. The second chapter describes the workings of the U.S. tax system. Here, too, there is considerable surprise that the overall tax burden has changed relatively little over time and that the tax system as a whole appears to favor neither the rich nor the poor and, as a whole, is distributionally neutral.

International comparisons also play an important role in this book. It becomes clear throughout the text that among the industrialized countries of the world the United States is really a special case both in terms of the level of inequality and the degree of increase of inequality since the 1980s. It also becomes apparent that U.S. poverty rates are exceptionally high when compared to countries at similar levels of development.

The book also extensively documents and discusses inequality and poverty trends in advanced countries (Canada, Europe, and East Asia) other than the United States and in less developed countries as well. We show that inequality is a problem in Europe as well and that the level of inequality is strikingly high in some European countries. Moreover, both income and wealth inequality have been increasing in other advanced countries. However, the "welfare states" in many European countries have considerably lowered both poverty and inequality relative to what it would have been without such extensive income transfers. Economic discrimination in Europe and various East Asian countries, particularly with regard to gender, is quite high (and worth examining in some detail). Some developing countries are catching up with the advanced countries both in terms of per capita income and according to a broader measure of average well-being called the Human Development Index. It also appears that the world distribution of income inequality follows the inverted U-shape of the so-called Kuznets curve.

The textbook serves as a self-contained course on income distribution and poverty, with additional emphasis on issues of discrimination. It is designed mainly for undergraduates who have had a full-year economics principles course but does not require any economics beyond this level. A statistics course is helpful but not necessary, since several sections on basic statistics are also included. There are some sections of the book which contain discussion of econometric studies and more advanced mathematical treatments of inequality measurement. However, these sections (which are starred) are optional and can be skipped without interfering with the continuity of the text.

The principal audience of the textbook is likely to be undergraduate economics students. However, the book can also be used as a core text in a masters level economics course on the same topic and as a primary or secondary text in a similar course in sociology, political science, or public administration (either undergraduate or masters level). Moreover, there are sections of the book that would be suitable for a Ph.D. level course in economics, sociology, political science, or public administration. The book can also serve as a supplementary textbook in courses in labor economics, discrimination, and public policy.

On the basis of my past experience, an instructor should be able to cover Chapters 1–6, 8, and 12–16, excluding the starred sections, in a full one-semester undergraduate course. The material in these chapters is almost completely self-contained. I have also included both discussion questions and numerical problem sets at the end of most chapters. I find that the problem sets are very helpful for the students in mastering the various measures developed in the textbook (such as the Gini coefficient).

Finally, this version of the textbook benefited greatly from the excellent and thorough comments supplied by reviewers. Since they have agreed to be identified, I would like to thank them for their help:

Charles L. Ballard, Michigan State University
Keith Bender, University of Wisconsin-Milwaukee
Dean Lillard, Cornell University
Thomas Odegaard, Baylor University
Lars Osberg, Dalhousie University

Wendy Rayack, Wesleyan University
Michael Sattinger, SUNY Albany
Frank Thompson, University of Michigan
Jennifer Warlick, Notre Dame

Edward Wolff
ew1@nyu.edu

Chapter 1

Introduction: Issues and Scope of Book

1.1 RECENT TRENDS IN LIVING STANDARDS

In this section, the author presents his *own* views about the development of the U.S. economy over the last 50 years. Please note that other researchers may differ in their opinions about these recent developments in U.S. living standards. A number of new terms are also introduced here. These will be formally defined in the ensuing five chapters. However, this section may serve as a way of motivating readers to delve more deeply into the subject matter of this book.

1.1.1 Income and earnings stagnate while poverty remains unchanged

The early years of the twenty-first century have witnessed a struggling middle class despite robust growth in the overall U.S. economy. During the first part of the George W. Bush administration, from 2001 to 2005, the economy (GDP in real dollars) expanded by 14 percent despite a brief recession in 2001, and labor productivity (real GDP divided by full-time equivalent employees) grew at an annual pace of 2.2 percent. Both figures are close to their post-World War II highs for similar periods.

Despite the booming economy, the most common metric used to assess living standards, real median family income (the income of the average family, found in the middle of the distribution when families are ranked from lowest to highest in terms of income), actually *fell by 3 percent*.[1] From 1973 to 2005 its total percentage gain amounted to 6 percent. In contrast, between 1947 and 1973, median family income almost exactly doubled (see Figure 1.1).

Mean (or *average*) family income likewise doubled between 1947 and 1973 and then increased by 21 percent from 1973 to 2005. This is less than the increase over the preceding quarter-century but greater than the rise in median family income. The disparity between the two reflects rising inequality since the early 1970s (see below).

Another troubling problem is poverty. Between 1959 and 1973, there was great success in reducing poverty in the United States, with the overall poverty rate declining by more than half, from 22.4 to 11.1 percent (see Figure 1.2). After that, the poverty rate has stubbornly refused to go any lower. After 1973, it trended upward to 15.1 percent in 1993, then fell back to 11.3 percent in 2000, only slight above its low point, but then rose again to 12.6 percent in 2005.

Another indicator of the well-being of lower income families is the share of total income received by the bottom quintile group (20 percent) of families (see Figure 1.3). Their share rose from 5 percent in 1947 to 5.7 percent in 1974, its high point. Since then it fell off rather sharply to

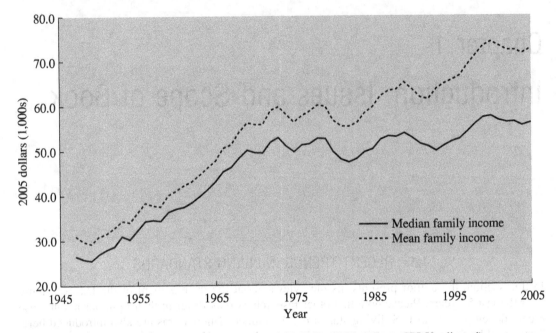

Figure 1.1   Median and average family income, 1947–2005 (2005 dollars, CPI-U adjusted)

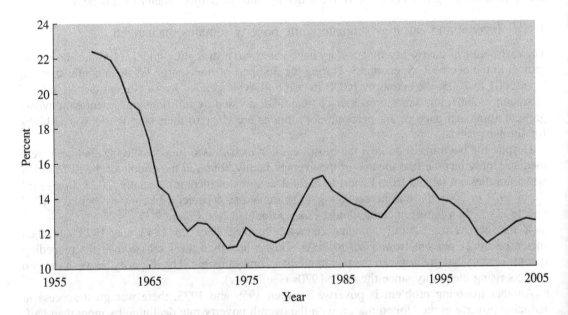

Figure 1.2   The official U.S. poverty rate, 1959–2005

4 percent in 2005. A related statistic is the mean income of the poorest 20 percent of families (in 2005 dollars), which shows the *absolute* level of well-being of this group (the share of income shows the *relative* level of well-being). Their average income more than doubled between 1947 and 1974 but then gained almost *nothing more* by 2005.

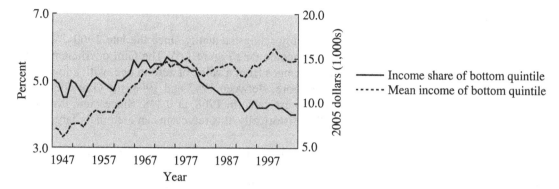

Figure 1.3 The share and mean income of the bottom quintile, 1947–2005

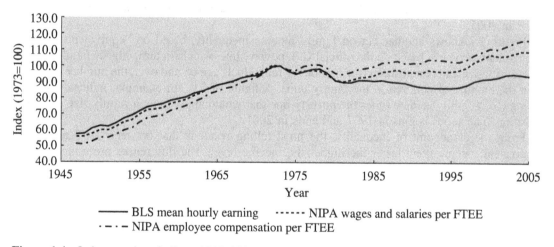

Figure 1.4 Labor earnings indices, 1947–2005 (1973=100)

The main reason for stagnating family incomes and recalcitrant poverty is the failure of wages to rise significantly. From 1973 and 2005 real wages were *down* by 6 percent (see Figure 1.4).[2] This contrasts with the preceding years, 1947 to 1973, when real wages grew by 75 percent. Indeed, in 2005, the hourly wage was $16.11 per hour, about the same level as in 1966 (in real terms).

Two other measures of worker pay are shown in Figure 1.4.[3] The results are fairly consistent among these alternative series. Average wages and salaries per full-time equivalent employee (FTEE) grew by 2.3 percent per year from 1947 to 1973 and then by only 0.3 percent per year from 1973 through 2005; and average employee compensation per FTEE increased by 2.6 percent per year during the first of these two periods and then by 0.5 percent per year in the second.

Despite falling real wages, living standards were maintained for a while by the growing labor force participation of wives, which increased from 41 percent in 1970 to 57 percent in 1988.[4] However, since 1989, married women entered the labor force more slowly and by 2005 their labor force participation rate had increased to only 61 percent, and with it occurred a slowdown in the growth of real living standards.

1.1.2   Inequality rises sharply

The United States has also experienced sharply rising inequality since the late 1960s. We will first look at the Gini coefficient for family income (see Figure 1.5). The Gini coefficient is the most widely used measure of inequality and ranges from a value of zero to one, with a low value indicating less inequality and a high value more. Between 1947 and 1968, the Gini coefficient generally trended downward, reaching its lowest value in 1968, at 0.348. Since then, it trended upward, reaching a value of 0.440 in 2005.[5] Historically, this represents an extremely large surge in income inequality.

A second index, the share of total income received by the top 5 percent of families, has a similar time trend. It first declined from 17.5 percent in 1947 to 14.8 percent in 1974 but then rose sharply to 21.1 percent in 2005, its highest value in the postwar period (see Figure 1.6).[6] A third index is the ratio of the average income of the richest 5 percent of families to that of the poorest 20 percent. It measures the spread in income between these two groups. This index generally dipped between 1947 and 1974, from 14.0 to 10.4, and then almost doubled to a value of 20.7 in 2005.

Figure 1.7 shows another cut on family income inequality, based on "equivalent income." Equivalent income is based on the official U.S. poverty line, which, in turn, adjusts family income for family size and composition (the number of individuals age 65 and over, the number of adults, and the number of children in the family unit). A figure of 3.0, for example, indicates that the income of a family is three times the poverty line that would apply to their family size and composition. The series begins in 1967 and ends in 2001.[7]

From the standpoint of inequality, the most telling result is that between 1973 and 2001, equivalent income grew faster the higher the income level. The differences are quite marked.

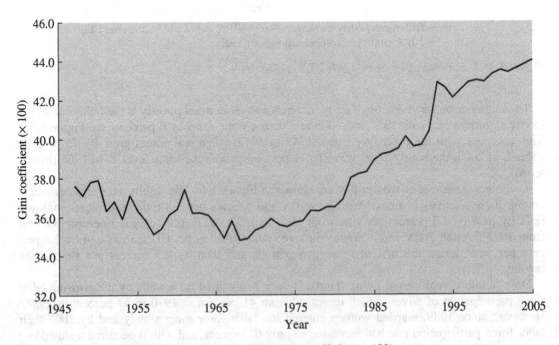

Figure 1.5   Income inequality trends, 1947–2005 (Gini coefficient × 100)

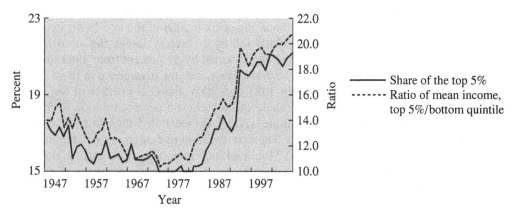

Figure 1.6 Income shares of the top 5 percent and bottom quintile, 1947–2005

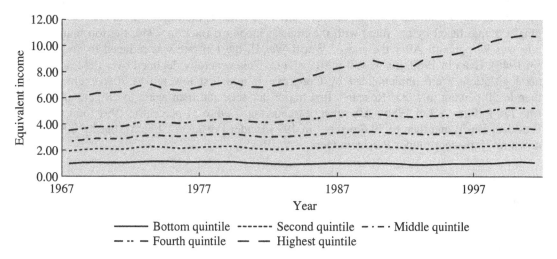

Figure 1.7 Trends in equivalent income by income quintile, 1967–2001

Equivalent income increased by 53 percent among families in the highest quintile, 25 percent in the fourth quintile, 16 percent in the middle quintile, 5 percent in the second quintile, and a *negative* 5 percent in the bottom quintile.

1.1.3 Middle-class debt explodes

Another dimension of well-being is household wealth. Wealth is a stock measure and indicates the value of assets owned by a household (such as housing and real estate, a business, bank accounts, money market funds, stocks, bonds) less outstanding debt (both mortgage and consumer debt). Wealth is an indicator of well-being independent of the direct financial income it provides. There are three reasons. First, owner-occupied housing provides services directly to their owner. Second, wealth is a source of consumption, independent of the direct money income it provides, because assets can be converted directly into cash and thus provide for immediate consumption needs. Third, the availability of financial assets can provide liquidity to a family in times of economic stress, such as occasioned by unemployment, sickness, or family break-up.

Median household wealth grew rapidly in real terms from 1983 to 2001, rising by 24 percent.[8] Much of this increase can be traced to the booming stock market of the late 1990s in the United States. However, from 2001 to 2004, it actually fell by 1 percent, despite the robust real estate market. Mean real wealth, on the other hand, skyrocketed by 65 percent from 1983 to 2001 and then rose by another 6 percent from 2001 to 2004. Here, too, the divergence in these two series indicates rising wealth inequality. Between 1983 and 2004, the Gini coefficient for household wealth climbed from 0.80 to 0.82 and the share of the richest 5 percent from 56 to 59 percent.

Nowhere is the middle-class squeeze more vividly demonstrated than in their rising debt. There are two ratios that are typically used. The first, the ratio of debt to net worth, jumped from 37 percent in 1983 to 62 percent in 2004. Middle-class households, experiencing slow growth in incomes, expanded their debt in order to maintain their consumer spending (see Chapter 5 for more discussion of household wealth).

1.1.4   What has happened to tax rates?

Trends in marginal tax rates of personal income tax are explained here, since these also affect the well-being of families (see Figure 1.8).[9] The first series is the top marginal tax rate (the marginal tax rate faced by tax filers with the highest income). Back in 1944, the top marginal tax rate was 94 percent! After the end of World War II, the top rate was reduced to 86.5 percent (in 1946). Even in 1960, it was still at 91 percent. This generally declined over time, as various tax legislations were implemented by Congress. It was first lowered to 70 percent in 1966, then to 50 percent in 1983 (Reagan's first major tax act), and then again to 28 percent in 1986 (the Tax Reform Act of 1986). After that, it trended upward to 31 percent in 1991 (under the first President Bush) and then to 39.6 percent in 1993 (under President Clinton), but by 2005 it was down to 35 percent (under President George W. Bush).

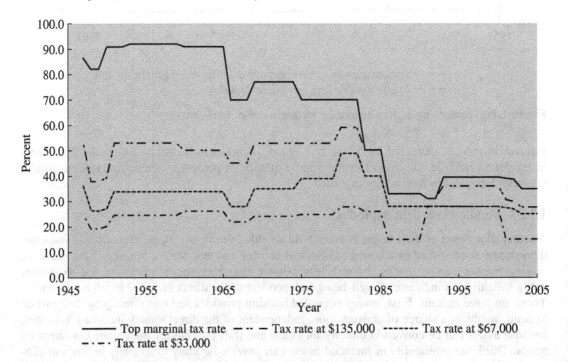

Figure 1.8   Marginal tax rates, selected income levels, 1946–2005 (1995 dollars)

The second series shows the marginal tax rate faced by filers with an income of $135,000 in 1995 dollars. This income level typically includes families at the ninety-fifth percentile (the top 5 percent). This series generally has the same trajectory as the top marginal tax rate. The last two series show the marginal tax rates at $67,000 and $33,000, respectively, both in 1995 dollars. The time patterns are quite a bit different for these than the first two. The marginal tax rate at $67,000 (about the sixtieth percentile) was relatively low in 1946, at 36 percent, generally trended upward, reaching 49 percent in 1980 and then declined to 25 percent by 2005. The marginal tax rate at $33,000 (about the thirtieth percentile) was also relatively low in 1946, at 25 percent, but it actually increased somewhat over time, reaching 28 percent in 1991, and then dropped to 15 percent from 2001 onward.

All in all, tax cuts over the postwar period have generally been more generous for high income taxpayers, particularly those at the top of the income distribution. From 1946 to 2005, the top marginal tax rate fell by 60 percent, the marginal rate at $135,000 by 47 percent, the marginal rate at $67,000 by 31 percent, and the rate at $33,000 by 39 percent.

1.1.5 Rising profits is the key

Where did the increased output go after the early 1970s if median income grew so slowly? To understand this, we must consider the relation between productivity and earnings. In particular, the historical connection between labor productivity growth and real wage growth appears to have broken down after 1973.

From 1947 to 1973, average real worker compensation (a broader concept than wages, including social insurance and fringe benefits) grew almost in tandem with the overall labor productivity growth (see Figure 1.9).[10] While the latter averaged 2.4 percent per year, the former ran at 2.6 percent per year. Labor productivity growth plummeted after 1973. The period from 1973 to 1979, in particular, witnessed the slowest growth in labor productivity during the postwar period, 0.5 percent per year, and the growth in real employee compensation per worker actually turned negative during this time. From 1979 to 2005, the U.S. economy experienced a modest reversal

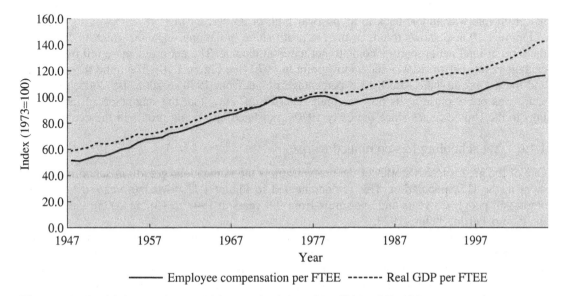

Figure 1.9   Real labor earnings and labor productivity, 1947–2005 (1973=100)

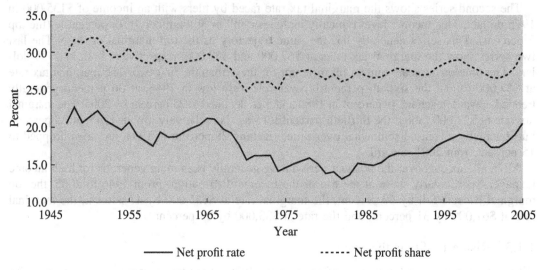

Figure 1.10   Trends in the net rate of profit and the net profit share, 1947–2005

in labor productivity growth, which averaged 1.3 percent per year, while the growth in real employee compensation per worker (full-time equivalent employee) ran at 0.6 percent per year.

If productivity rose faster than earnings after 1973, where did the excess go? The answer is increased profitability in the United States. The basic data are from the National Income and Product Accounts of the U.S. Bureau of Economic Analysis (BEA). For the definition of net profits, I use the BEA's definition of total gross property-type income, including corporate profits, interest, rent, and half of proprietors' income.[11] The net rate of profit is defined as the ratio of total net property income to total private net fixed capital. The net profit rate declined by 7.5 percentage points between 1947 and its low point in 1982 (see Figure 1.10). The trend then reversed itself and the net profit rate climbed by 7.4 percentage points from 1982 to 2005. By 2005, the net profit rate was almost back to its postwar high of 23 percent in 1948.

Figure 1.10 also shows trends in the net profit share in national income, which is defined as the ratio of total net property income to net national income. The net profit share fell by 4.8 percentage points between 1947 and its low point in 1970 (see Figure 1.10). The trend then reversed and the net profit share rose by 5.3 percentage points from 1970 to 2005. By 2005, the profit share was pretty close to its postwar high. The results show that the stagnation of labor earnings in the United States since the early 1970s translated into rising profits in the economy.

1.1.6   Yet schooling has continued to rise

One of the great success stories of the postwar era is the tremendous growth in schooling attainment in the U.S. population. This is documented in Figure 1.11.[12] Median years of schooling among all people 25 years and over grew from 9.0 years in 1947 to 13.7 in 2005, with most of the gain occurring before 1973.

Trends are even more dramatic for the percentage of adults (age 25 and over) who completed high school and college (see Figure 1.12). The former grew from 33 percent of all adults in 1947 to 86 percent in 2005. Progress in high school completion rates was as strong after 1973 as before. The percent of college graduates in the adult population soared from 5.4 percent in 1947 to 28.3 percent in 2005. In this dimension, progress was actually greater after 1973 than before.

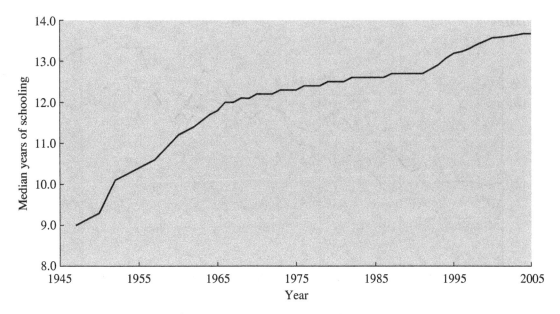

Figure 1.11 Median years of schooling completed by people 25 years and over, 1947–2005

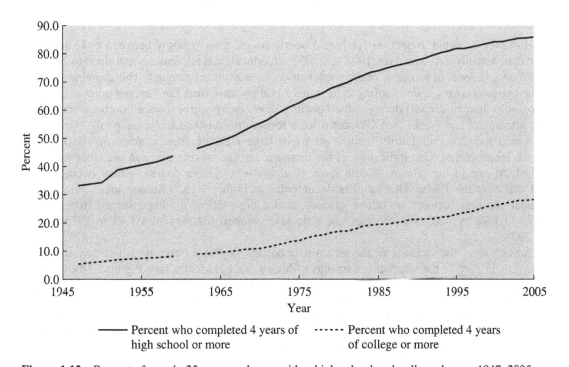

——— Percent who completed 4 years of
high school or more

- - - - - Percent who completed 4 years
of college or more

Figure 1.12 Percent of people 25 years and over with a high school and college degree, 1947–2005

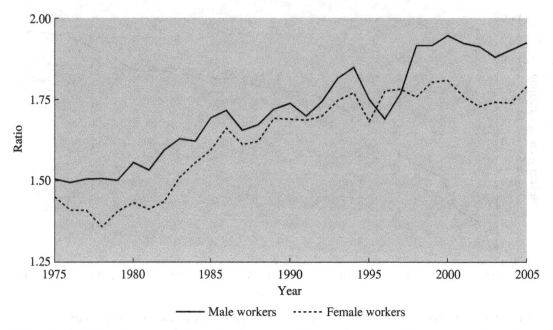

Figure 1.13   Ratio of mean annual earnings between college graduates and high school graduates by gender, 1975–2005 (includes all workers 18 years and over with earnings)

However, as noted in Section 1.1.1, real hourly wages grew strongly between 1947 and 1973 and then actually *declined* from 1973 to 2005. Yet, educational attainment continued to rise after 1973 and, indeed, in terms of college graduation rates even accelerated. The growing discordance between wages and schooling constitutes a real paradox from the vantage point of standard economic (human capital) theory, which posits a direct and positive association between schooling attainment and wages (see Chapter 8 for a formal treatment of human capital).

Rising inequality of family income stems in large measure from changes in the structure of the labor market. One indication of the dramatic changes taking place in the labor market is the sharp rise in the returns to education, particularly a college degree, which occurred during and after the 1980s. This trend is documented in Figure 1.13.[13] Among males, the ratio in annual earnings between a college graduate and a high school graduate surged from 1.50 in 1975 to 1.92 by 2005. For females, the ratio also climbed sharply, from 1.45 in 1975 to 1.79 in 2005.

Among men, the increase in the return to a college degree relative to a high school degree was due, in part, to the stagnating earnings of high school graduates (see Figure 1.14). Between 1975 and 2005, their annual earnings in constant dollars gained less than 4 percent, while the earnings of men with a bachelor's degree (but not further schooling) increased by 22 percent. The biggest increase in earnings occurred among males with an advanced degree (master's or higher), who saw their annual incomes grow by 32 percent. Among males who did not graduate high school, earnings plummeted by *11 percent*.

Another indicator of the country's success in education is the dramatic decline in the inequality of schooling in the United States. According to the human capital model, there is a direct and proportional relationship between earnings inequality and the variance of schooling (see Chapter 8). If the dispersion of schooling declines, so should earnings inequality.

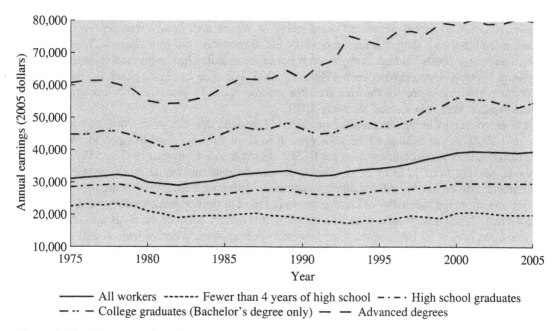

Figure 1.14 Mean annual earnings by educational attainment level, 1975–2005 (2005 dollars)

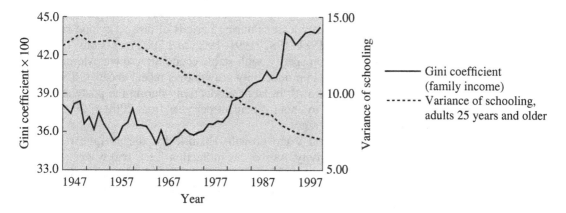

Figure 1.15 Family income inequality and the variance of schooling, 1947–2000

Yet, as shown in Figure 1.15, while income inequality has risen since the late 1960s, the variance of schooling of adults 25 years and older (computed from CPS data) trended sharply downward since 1950. In fact, the variance of schooling fell by almost half from 1950 to 2000 (from 12.5 to 6.9).[14] The simple correlation between the two series is, in fact, *negative*, −0.78. This finding leads to another paradox – namely, the growing discord between the inequality of income and the inequality of human capital.

1.1.7 Some conclusions

The last quarter of the twentieth century and the first few years of the twenty-first century saw slow growing earnings and income among the middle class in the United States. In addition, the poverty rate failed to decline further and income inequality climbed substantially. In contrast, the early postwar period witnessed rapid gains in wages and family income for the middle class, in addition to a sharp decline in poverty, and a moderate fall in inequality. The "booming 1990s and early 2000s" did not bring much relief to the middle class, with median family income growing by only 4 percent between 1989 and 2005. Personal tax rates generally fell over the postwar period but more for the rich than the middle class. In sum, the U.S. middle class has not prospered very much since the early 1970s.

The stagnation of living standards among the middle class over the years from the mid-1970s to the mid-2000s is attributable to the slow growth in labor earnings over this period. While average earnings (employee compensation per FTEE) almost doubled between 1947 and 1973, it gained only 16 percent from 1973 to 2005. This happened despite substantial progress in educational attainment. Moreover, in spite of notable success in reducing educational disparities within the U.S. population, the inequality of income not only failed to decline but actually rose sharply since the early 1970s. These results suggest a growing disconnect between earnings and schooling.

The main reason for the stagnation of labor earnings appears to derive from a shift of national income away from labor and towards capital, particularly since the early 1980s. Over this period, overall profitability rose substantially, almost back to postwar highs. While business gained from rising profits, workers did not experience much progress in terms of earnings.

1.2   CAUSES OF RISING INEQUALITY

The turnaround in inequality during the 1980s, 1990s, and early 2000s is particularly puzzling in light of the strong economic growth during the Reagan, George Bush, Clinton, and George W. Bush years. Normally, income inequality lessens during periods of prosperity and rises during economic downturns. Except for the 1981–1982, 1991–1992, and 2002 recessions, these two and a half decades were ones of general prosperity, with stable economic growth. Moreover, the U.S. economy also experienced a reversal in productivity growth over recent decades. The period from 1973–1979 witnessed the slowest growth in labor productivity during the postwar period. However, productivity growth recovered to about 2 percent per year from 2000 to 2005, which is quite close to its twentieth-century average.

Another anomaly is the pattern of real wage growth. Historically, the average real wage moved in line with average labor productivity. As we saw in Section 1.1.1, real wages remained virtually unchanged during the years from 1973 to 2005. This is understandable during the 1973–1979 period, when productivity was almost at a standstill, but not during the ensuing years, when productivity growth picked up.

The recent rise of inequality in light of sustained economic growth in the United States has spawned a considerable amount of literature. Why is inequality rising in this country? Is it also rising in other countries, and, if so, to the same degree? Much of the rest of this book will return to these issues when we look at the various factors that affect income inequality. It is, perhaps, useful at this point to mention the major factors that have been considered in these studies.

1.2.1   Skill-biased technology change

Perhaps the leading argument is that the period from 1980 to 2005 witnessed a major technological revolution led by widespread computerization and the consequent penetration of information technology into the whole economy. This change has skewed the income distribution by placing a high premium on college-educated and skilled labor while reducing the demand for semi-skilled and unskilled workers. One important piece of evidence is that the rate of return to a college education (the wage premium paid to a college graduate relative to a high school graduate) approximately doubled over the decades of the 1980s and 1990s (see above and Chapter 8).

1.2.2   The shift to services

One of the notable changes in the composition of the labor force during the postwar period is the shift of jobs from goods-producing industries to services. The share of employment in services grew from 43 percent in 1950 to 74 percent in 2003. All of the employment growth during the 1980s and 1990s occurred in the service sector. Some have argued that the dispersion of earnings is greater in services than goods-producing industries because of the greater mix of professional and managerial jobs with relatively low-skilled clerical and manual work (see Chapters 7 and 9).

1.2.3   Declining unionization

The proportion of the workforce represented by unions peaked in 1954, at 25.4 percent, and at 34.7 percent as a fraction of the nonfarm labor force. After 1954, the trend was downward, and by 2006, only 12 percent were union members. Part of the reason for the decline in union representation is the de-industrialization that has occurred over the last couple of decades, because manufacturing industries in particular have had high unionization rates. Unions have historically negotiated collective bargaining agreements with narrow wage differentials between different types of jobs. This is one reason why the dispersion of earnings in manufacturing has tended to be lower than that of service industries. As a result, the decline in unions has led to widening differentials in the overall wage structure (see Chapter 9).

1.2.4   Globalization

The increasing trade liberalization of the 1970s, 1980s, and 1990s has been cited as another factor. Imports into the U.S. economy have grown from 5.5 percent of GDP in 1970 to 14 percent in 2003, while the share of exports grew from 5.5 to 9.5 percent. According to standard trade theory, as trade increases, there is a growing tendency of factor prices – particularly, wages – to equalize across countries. This can take the form of rising wages among our trading partners as well as declining wages in our own labor force. As imports of manufactured products produced in low-income countries such as Indonesia, China, Thailand, Mexico, and Brazil increases, downward pressure is placed on the wages of unskilled and semi-skilled workers in U.S. manufacturing industries. This process explains both the falling average real wage of U.S. workers (see above) as well as the increasing gap between blue-collar workers and professionals who work in industries such as law, medicine, education, and business services that are well shielded from imports (also see Chapter 9).

A related aspect of globalization is increasing immigration into the United States. The share of foreign-born workers in the U.S. labor force grew from 11 percent in 1996 to 15 percent in 2006.[15] Insofar as foreign-born workers tend to be, on average, less skilled and less educated than native-born workers, immigration has increased the *relative* supply of low-skilled workers and therefore has helped to increase the wage gap between high-skill and low-skill employees in the United States (see Chapter 11 for more discussion).

1.2.5   Downsizing and outsourcing

Another suspect is the corporate restructuring that has taken place during the 1980s and 1990s. This process has taken two forms. First, permanent employees have gradually been replaced by part-time, temporary, and "leased" employees. Second, a number of important corporate functions such as maintenance, cafeteria services, legal services, and data processing that were traditionally performed by in-house employees have been outsourced (substituted for) by purchasing these operations from other companies. Both processes have reduced the relative number of permanent employees in large corporations. Corporate employees have traditionally enjoyed high wages, high benefits, job security, career-ladder type jobs, and good working conditions. This set of job characteristics is referred to as an internal or primary labor market. In contrast, wages tend to be low in secondary jobs found in part-time employment and small businesses. The shift of employment out of the primary labor force to the secondary labor market may have been another factor accounting for rising income inequality (see Chapter 9).

1.2.6 Public policy changes

The social safety net that has provided some degree of income maintenance to the low income population has gradually frayed during the 1980s, 1990s, and early 2000s. Welfare benefits have been falling in real terms (the average benefit in 1993 was down by 45 percent from 1970, before the change in the welfare system), and the percent of unemployed workers who receive unemployment compensation has also declined. Moreover, the minimum wage fell by 43 percent in real terms between its peak in 1968 and 2005. This has helped put downward pressure on the wages of unskilled workers and may account, in part, for the growing wage disparities between the unskilled and skilled workers and the decline in the average real wage since 1973 (see Chapter 15).

In contrast, changes in the tax code over the last two decades appear to have generally favored the rich over the middle class and the poor. As we saw in Section 1.1.4, the Tax Act of 1981 and the Tax Reform Act of 1986 lowered the tax rate paid by the rich (the top marginal tax rate) from 70 percent in 1980 to 28 percent in 1986, though it since rose to 39.6 percent in 1993 and then fell again to 35 percent in 2005. The biggest increase in taxes has been from the social security tax, which primarily affects middle-class taxpayers. However, some changes in the tax code have hurt the rich, including a tightening of tax loopholes, and some changes have benefited the poor, particularly the introduction of the Earned Income Tax Credit. Overall, however, it appears that the redistributional effects of the tax system – that is, the degree to which the rich are taxed more heavily than the poor – have lessened since the beginning of the 1980s. We shall analyze these changes more closely in Chapter 16.

1.3 GENERAL DESCRIPTION OF THE TEXTBOOK

Is the standard of living still rising in the United States? Is inequality increasing or declining? Has poverty in this country attenuated or is it growing? What groups have fared well and what groups have done poorly? Is race and gender discrimination still a problem today? How unequal a country are we in comparison to other industrialized countries? Should we be concerned about inequality and poverty in our country? What factors are responsible for inequality? What role has public policy played? What is happening to the status and well-being of U.S. citizens relative to citizens in other countries? How are people in developing countries faring in the international race to achieve economic growth? What factors cause poverty to persist and what policies are successful in breaking the cycle of persistent poverty? How are racial and gender wealth gaps perpetuated and what forces have been responsible for altering the economic success or failure of women and African Americans? These and related questions will provide the general focus of the textbook.

This is organized into four parts. Part I treats the definition and measurement of income, wealth, inequality, poverty, and mobility and presents a statistical portrait of each. Part II investigates some of the factors responsible for poverty and inequality. These include the role of labor force participation and labor markets in explaining differences in earnings among individuals as well as savings and bequest behavior. Part III explores the role of race and gender discrimination in accounting for differences in income and poverty rates. Part IV considers the effect of public policy in both reducing inequality and alleviating poverty. Here, it should be noted that discussion of public policy is not confined to Part IV but occurs throughout the textbook, particularly in Chapters 13 and 14 on discrimination.

Chapter 1 introduced the subject of inequality and poverty by presenting an overview of recent trends in living standards, inequality, and poverty in the United States. It also includes the plan of the textbook. Chapter 2 discusses how income and, more generally, the standard of living, are measured. Basic concepts of national income accounting are discussed, as well as the measurement of personal income and alternative measures of personal well-being. The definition of factor shares and the role of household production are also highlighted. Historical trends for the United States are discussed. International comparisons of per capita income, as well as the United Nations' Human Development Index, are also presented. The last part investigates various explanations of the distribution of income between factors (the wage and profit share).

Chapter 3 develops basic measures of income inequality, and presents a statistical overview. Standard measures of inequality are developed, including the coefficient of variation, the Gini coefficient, the Theil entropy index, and the Atkinson index (the latter two for advanced students). Particular attention is accorded to the rise in U.S. income inequality in more recent years. International comparisons are also included, which indicate that the United States is the highest in terms of income concentration in the industrialized world. The Kuznets curve and the world distribution of income are also discussed.

Chapter 4 presents a broad overview of issues in poverty. Three basic concepts of poverty are developed – absolute, relative, and subjective poverty lines. More recent issues in the measurement of poverty are canvassed, such as including noncash government benefits in the definition of family income and the use of consumption expenditure data to measure poverty incidence. Trends in poverty rates are discussed, which show declining poverty from 1960 to the early 1970s and a cyclical movement after that. The poverty data also show a much higher incidence of poverty among minorities than among white Americans. Particular attention is also paid to the changing composition of the poor in the United States, such as the "feminization of poverty," its rising incidence among children, and the development of an "underclass." International comparisons are also presented, which generally indicate a much higher incidence of poverty in the United States than other industrialized countries.

Another major factor in accounting for differences in family well-being is household wealth. Chapter 5 first introduces the concept of household wealth. Important methodological issues are then discussed, including the definition of wealth, the role of retirement income, and the availability of data sources. The next section presents evidence on long-term time trends in household wealth concentration in the United States and several European countries. More recent trends in U.S. wealth inequality are emphasized. The composition of household wealth is considered next, including trends in homeownership rates. Several economists have proposed composite measures of income and wealth as a better indicator of well-being than income alone, and several alternative measures are presented.

An important dimension of well-being that is often overlooked is mobility. In Chapter 6, two types of mobility are discussed. The first, lifetime mobility, concerns the degree to which an individual's (or family's) relative position in the income distribution changes over time. This may serve as an important offset to rising income inequality if lifetime mobility has risen as well. The second, intergenerational mobility, concerns the degree to which an individual's relative rank in the income distribution is correlated with that of his (or her) parents'. Intergenerational mobility reflects the fluidity (or lack thereof) of the class structure of a society. Statistics on mobility in income, earnings, and wealth will be presented. Evidence will also be presented on changes over time in both lifetime and intergenerational mobility in the United States as well as comparisons with other advanced countries.

Part II canvasses alternative explanations for both the existence of and change over time in both inequality and poverty. The first group of chapters looks at the role of the labor market as a source of income differences among individuals. Chapter 7 introduces concepts of the labor force, employment, and unemployment. It discusses trends in labor force participation patterns (who works and who does not), the composition of employment (the decline of manufacturing and the shift to services), and unemployment patterns (particularly by demographic characteristic). This chapter also discusses causes of unemployment, including frictional unemployment, structural unemployment, and demand-deficient unemployment.

Chapter 8 introduces the human capital model, with its emphasis on the role of both schooling and on-the-job training in the determination of relative earnings. It then summarizes empirical work in the human capital tradition, which shows that schooling and experience play a major role in the determination of relative earnings. The value of a college education is highlighted. The recent rise in the returns to education, experience, and skills is also given emphasis, as well as explanations for this occurrence. The next section treats the role of ability as a factor in determining wages and salaries and summarizes empirical work on the effect of ability on earnings. Other interpretations of the schooling–earnings relation are also considered, including job screening, the role of family background and schooling as a socializing mechanism. The contribution of human capital variables to overall earnings inequality is analyzed at the end of the chapter.

Chapter 9 surveys institutional factors accounting for differentials in labor earnings. The role of unions is discussed. After a brief history of the trade union movement in the United States and trends in union membership, the chapter considers the economic role of unions. The first section of the chapter concludes with an analysis of whether unions have been effective in raising their members' earnings. The second part looks at the role of both internal labor markets and segmented labor markets in explaining earnings differences. Are there rigidities in wage structures within organizations (internal labor markets)? Are there really well-defined segments in the labor market? Do these barriers help explain the persistence of earnings differences between certain groups?

The third section of Chapter 9 looks at structural explanations for inequality in earnings. It first considers the role of industrial mix in earnings inequality and then analyzes industry differences in wages and salaries. Do some industries pay more than others and why (efficiency wage theory)? It also looks at occupational wage differences – particularly, their increasing spread in recent years.

The accumulation of household wealth depends not only on income but also on savings behavior, capital appreciation, and gifts and inheritances. Moreover, wealth is the direct source of property income, which is an important factor in accounting for disparities in family income. Chapter 10 considers some of the factors accounting for differences in wealth among families. The first of these is the role of age. Since individuals work only part of their life, they have a strong incentive to accumulate wealth for their retirement years. The standard model of this is the lifecycle model, which is extensively discussed. Other factors, such as gifts and inheritances and capital appreciation, also play a role in wealth accumulation, and these too are treated in Chapter 10.

As noted above, the last 30 years in the United States have been characterized by a sharp increase in income inequality, and particularly inequality in labor earnings. Chapter 11 (optional) surveys the various explanations that have been put forward to explain the rise in earnings inequality. These include: (i) skill-biased technological change, favoring highly educated over less educated workers; (ii) growing international trade, which has caused the relative wages of low-skilled workers to fall; (iii) the shift of employment to services, which are characterized by a greater dispersion of earnings than goods producers; (iv) declining unionization, which has widened wage differentials between different types of jobs within an industry; (v) a declining minimum wage in real terms, which has put downward pressure on the wages of low-skilled jobs; (vi) corporate restructuring and downsizing in the 1980s and 1990s that may have widened earnings differentials within firms; and (vii) the role of education and ability.

Another major factor that explains differences in earnings and income between groups in our society is discrimination. This topic is covered in Part III. Chapter 12 discusses what discrimination means and how it is measured. Alternative models of discrimination are presented: taste for discrimination; statistical discrimination; the stereotype model; the Marxian model; and the over-crowding model of occupational segregation.

Chapter 13 considers evidence on trends in racial discrimination. Have blacks and Hispanics gained on (non-Hispanic) whites in terms of wages, employment patterns, education, family income and wealth, and poverty incidence over the postwar period? It considers the principal factors in explaining changes in the economic status of black families, including migration from the South, gains in education, and changes in black family structure. The role and effectiveness of anti-discrimination government programs are also treated.

Chapter 14 considers gender discrimination. Has the female/male wage gap declined since the end of World War II, and have women made gains in penetrating traditionally male occupations? This chapter discusses the major factors in explaining changes in the gender wage gap, including the sharp rise in female labor force participation rates, human capital differences, and occupational segregation. It also investigates the effectiveness of anti-discrimination programs, with particular attention paid to issues of comparable worth.

Have government programs made a difference on inequality and poverty in the United States? Part IV considers the role of public policy on poverty and income inequality. Chapter 15 focuses on the low-income population. It begins with a brief history of the social welfare system and the development of income maintenance programs in the United States. It then considers, in succession, how the unemployment insurance program, the social security system, and the welfare system function. The chapter also discusses manpower programs, the minimum wage statute, and housing programs. It ends with an overall assessment of whether these programs have been effective in reducing poverty in the United States.

Chapter 16 begins by raising the issue of why social equity may be an important social concern. It then looks at the redistributional effects of government tax and expenditure policy. Is the tax system progressive, regressive, or neutral? What are the relative magnitudes of the different government transfer programs and have they made a significant dent on inequality? What groups benefit from government expenditures and what are the distributional consequences of them? The chapter also discusses the negative income tax and the earned income tax credit and presents statistics on the extent of taxation in the United States in comparison with other advanced economies.

NOTES

1 *Source*: U.S. Census Bureau, *Detailed historical income and poverty tables from the March Current Population Survey 1947–2005*, available at http://www.census.gov/hhes/www/income/histinc/histinctb.html. Figures are in 2005 dollars unless otherwise indicated. The standard consumer price index – the CPI-U – which the U.S. Bureau of Labor Statistics (BLS) has been computing since 1947

is used to convert to 2005 dollars since this is the standard consumer price index used by the U.S. Census Bureau for the period from 1947 to the present.

Another deflator that is sometimes used is the personal consumption expenditure (PCE) deflator from the National Income and Product Accounts (NIPA). This deflator is based on price changes using product weights derived from household consumption in the NIPA. This deflator generally shows a smaller rise in consumer prices over time than the CPI-U. However, I follow here the convention of the U.S. Census Bureau and use the CPI instead of the PCE deflator.

2   These figures are based on the BLS hourly wage series for production and nonsupervisory workers in private, nonagricultural industries. *Source*: U.S. Council of Economic Advisers, *Economic Report of the President, 2007*. This is the most widely used wage series. The BLS converts nominal wage figures to constant dollars on the basis of the consumer price index (CPI-U).

3   These two are the NIPA wages and salaries per full-time equivalent employee (FTEE) and employee compensation (the sum of wages and salaries and employee benefits) per FTEE. Both series are deflated to constant dollars using the CPI-U price index. *Source*: http://www.bea.gov/national/index.htm.

4   *Source*: U.S. Census Bureau, *Statistical Abstract, 2007*.

5   *Source*: U.S. Census Bureau, *Detailed historical income and poverty tables from the March Current Population Survey 1947–2005* (see note 1). These figures are based on unadjusted data.

6   I use the term "postwar" to refer to the time period after World War II (1946 and after).

7   *Source*: U.S. Census Bureau, *Detailed historical income and poverty tables from the March Current Population Survey 1947–2005* (see note 1). The average income-to-poverty ratios are computed by dividing the mean income of families in each quintile (as ranked by family income) by the mean poverty threshold of the families in that quintile.

8   *Source*: Federal Reserve Board's *Survey of Consumer Finances*, which is done every three years starting in 1983 to 2004 (the last year currently available).

9   The marginal tax rate is the additional amount of taxes paid on an additional dollar of income. Rates quoted here are for married couples, filing jointly. *Source*: http://www.irs.gov/.

10 Results are shown for employee compensation per FTEE. *Source*: U.S. Bureau of Economic Analysis, National Income and Product Accounts, http://www.bea.gov/bea/dn/nipaweb/SelectTable.asp.

11 The definition excludes the capital consumption allowance (CCA) – that is, depreciation of the fixed capital stock.

12 *Source*: U.S. Census Bureau, *Detailed historical income and poverty tables from the March Current Population Survey 1947–2005* (see note 1). Adults refer to persons 25 years and over in the non-institutional population (excluding members of the Armed Forces living in barracks).

13 The figures are for annual earnings, which are not adjusted for hours worked or the experience level of the workers. *Source*: U.S. Census Bureau, *Detailed historical income and poverty tables from the March Current Population Survey 1947–2005* (see note 1) for the data in Figure 1.13, as well as the next two figures.

14 Because of a change in the educational attainment categories used by the U.S. Census Bureau, it is not possible to update the variance of schooling series beyond 2000.

15 *Source*: Migration Policy Institute, http://www.migrationinformation.org/USFocus/display.cfm?ID=638.

Part I
Inequality, Poverty, and Mobility: Measurement and Trends

Chapter 2

Income, Earnings, and the Standard of Living

2.1 INTRODUCTION

Is average income still rising in the United States? Does the United States still have the highest standard of living in the world? This chapter addresses these two issues and focuses, more generally, on how income and standard of living are measured. It begins with a discussion of national income accounting and the measurement of personal income. It also presents historical trends for the United States and comparisons of income levels with other countries. These topics are important for two reasons. First, in order to measure income inequality, it is necessary to determine what income is. Likewise with poverty – to provide an operational definition of poverty status, it is necessary to come up with an adequate concept of income. Second, trends in average income are just as important (perhaps more important) for well-being as changes in the inequality of income.

The major source of personal income is work. People earn a **wage** or **salary** for the time that they work. Wages and salaries – or, more broadly speaking, **labor earnings** – account for most of the **personal income** received in the United States and other developed countries today.

There are several other sources of personal income. One of the most common is **interest** income which comes from savings accounts, government bonds, corporate securities, and the like. Another form of personal income is **dividends** that are received from corporate stock ownership. Owners of small, unincorporated businesses receive **business income**. Real estate often yields **rental income**. Retirees who have participated in a pension plan receive **pension benefits**. There are also **transfer payments** from the government. The most common source is **social security income** (more technically called "Old Age and Survivors Insurance" or OASI), which is also received by retired workers. Other forms are **unemployment insurance benefits** paid to workers who are temporarily out of work and **welfare payments**, which are given to destitute families.

In Section 2.2, we define what is meant by personal income. Several tables are presented on the composition of personal income. Section 2.3 introduces the concept of the **standard of living**. Alternative measures of the average well-being of a society are discussed. Such indices are found to be sensitive to the choice of welfare unit – the individual versus the family, for example – and the choice of income concept – before-tax versus after-tax income, for example. Several tables are presented showing the change in average welfare levels in the United States over time.

In Section 2.4, the book shifts gears to a somewhat different concern – namely, factor shares or the functional distribution of income. Here the concern is with the form in which income is received – whether as wages and salaries or as income from property. Historical data are presented on trends in the wage and profit share from 1850 to the present.

Section 2.5 looks at the standard of living from an international perspective. Tables are presented which compare the United States to other countries. Two alternative measures are used. The first is based on income per capita in **purchasing power parity** terms. The second uses the United Nations' **Human Development Index** (HDI), a composite index of per capita income, life expectancy, and education.

Section 2.6 treats another dimension of well-being – household production. This concept refers to unpaid activities which occur within the household and provide direct utility to the family such as cooking, cleaning, child care and home repair. These activities often substitute for market production. A summary is given in Section 2.7. References and a bibliography are provided in Section 2.8, and discussion questions and a problem set in Section 2.9.

Appendix 2.1 presents a brief introduction to the **National Income and Product Accounts** (Section A2.1.1). The **national accounts**, as they are called for short, provide an overall conceptual framework for relating national income to the total product that the nation produces – that is, **gross domestic product** or **GDP**. In Section A2.1.2, we discuss the relation of personal income to national income. Section A2.1.3 shows how factor shares are derived from the national accounts. Section A2.1.4 raises a few technical issues on the measurement of income.

2.2   THE COMPOSITION OF PERSONAL INCOME IN THE UNITED STATES

In this book, we are interested primarily in **personal income** – that is, income received by families and individuals.[1] Let us look at time trends in the U.S. economy. Table 2.1 shows the percentage composition of personal income for selected years since 1929. The first component is total labor earnings. This is the sum of not only wages and salaries received by employees but also of employer-paid fringe benefits, such as health insurance, life insurance, and pension contributions. Since these benefits are paid directly by the employer, they are not included in the employee's pay check but still form part of total employee compensation.[2]

The second component is called proprietors' earnings. There are many businesses which are operated by single individuals (or partnerships) and are unincorporated. Income received by such self-employed individuals is considered personal income. These proprietors own farms, stores, and other small businesses.

The third component is the rental income received by individuals. This income comes from real estate and rental property owned by individuals (as opposed to corporations).[3] The next is dividends paid to owners of corporate stock. The fifth component is interest income which individuals receive on time and savings accounts, government bonds and other securities, corporate bonds, and other financial instruments. The last component is transfer payments to families and individuals. There are two types. The first and by far the major component is government transfers. The most common of these are social security payments, unemployment benefits, veterans' benefits, and family assistance payments – mainly Aid to Families with Dependent Children until 1996 and then Temporary Assistance to Needy Families after that (we shall discuss these transfer programs more fully in Chapter 15). The second component consists of transfers from businesses to individuals, notably private pension benefits.

The data on personal income in Table 2.1 show some interesting trends. The proportion of personal income that derives from labor earnings (including employer contributions for pensions and insurance) increased from 60 percent in 1929 to about two-thirds in 1960 and then declined to 60 percent in 1990 and remained at this level through 2005.[4] Proprietors' income and other forms of self-employment earnings accounted for 17 percent of total personal income in 1929,

Table 2.1 The percentage composition of total personal income by income source, 1929–2005

Year	Total labor earnings[a]	Total proprietors' earnings[b]	Rental income[c]	Dividends	Personal interest income	Transfer payments[d]	Total income
1929	60.4	17.1	5.8	6.9	8.2	1.8	100
1940	64.2	16.2	3.5	5.2	6.8	4.0	100
1950	64.9	17.0	3.4	3.9	4.2	6.7	100
1960	67.1	12.7	3.7	3.2	6.1	7.2	100
1970	67.1	9.6	2.6	3.0	8.5	9.2	100
1980	62.9	7.8	1.4	2.9	12.4	12.6	100
1990	60.0	7.8	1.0	3.5	15.5	12.2	100
2000	60.3	8.6	1.8	4.5	12.0	12.9	100
2005	60.1	9.5	0.7	5.6	9.2	14.9	100

Addendum: Supplements to wages and salaries as a percent of total wages and salaries

Year	All supplements[e]	All supplements less employer contributions for social insurance
1929	1.4	1.2
1940	4.6	3.2
1950	5.6	3.6
1960	8.7	5.3
1970	11.9	7.6
1980	19.9	13.4
1990	34.9	21.2
2000	32.4	19.7
2005	40.6	24.1

a   This is defined as the sum of wage and salary disbursements plus other labor income plus employer contributions for employee pensions and insurance funds less employer contributions for social insurance, and the excess of accruals over wage disbursements.
b   With inventory valuation and capital consumption adjustments.
c   With capital consumption adjustments.
d   This item includes transfers from private businesses such as private pension benefits.
e   This is defined as the sum of employer contributions for social insurance and to private pension, health and welfare funds; workmen's compensation, and a few miscellaneous items.
Source: Council of Economic Advisers, *Economic Report of the President, 1994*, U.S. Government Printing Office, Washington, 1994; *Economic Report of the President, 2007*, Table B-29, http://www.gpoaccess.gov/eop/tables07.html.

declined rather sharply to 8 percent in 1980, but then rebounded somewhat to 9.5 percent by 2005. The downward trend primarily reflected the decline in the ownership of small, unincorporated farms as agriculture became more mechanized and large farms became more efficient to run. The more recent increase is due to rising incomes of *partnerships* such as law and medical practices and investment banking.

Also showing a decline is rental income, which fell from 5.8 percent of total personal income in 1929 to 0.7 percent in 2005. Dividends dropped from 6.9 percent in 1929 to 2.9 percent in 1980 but then recovered to 5.6 percent in 2005. The recovery largely reflected the booming stock market of the 1990s. Interest income as a proportion of total personal income declined from 8 percent in 1929 to 4 percent to 1950, climbed back up to 15 percent in 1990, but then fell again to 9 percent in 2005. Transfer payments (both from the government such as social security benefits and from private businesses such as pension benefits) show the most dramatic change. A little under 2 percent of total income in 1929, it rose almost steadily to 15 percent in 2005. This trend largely reflects the growth in social security benefits. (This component will be treated in greater detail in Chapter 15.)

The category labor earnings includes not only wages and salaries but also fringe benefits such as employer contributions for employees' health insurance, life insurance, pension funds, and the like. One of the most important developments in the U.S. economy since 1929 is the increasing proportion of total labor compensation that has taken the form of fringe benefits and other supplements to wages and salaries. The first column of the Addendum to Table 2.1 shows all fringe benefits including employer contributions to social insurance (social security), as a percent of wages and salaries.[5] This ratio has increased almost continuously over time from 1.4 percent in 1929 to 20 percent in 1980 and then exploded to 41 percent in 2005. The second column shows the ratio of all fringe benefits, excluding employer contributions for social insurance, to wages and salaries. This ratio has also increased dramatically over time, from 1 percent in 1929 to 24 percent in 2005.

2.3 THE STANDARD OF LIVING

Up until now, we have been discussing total flows, such as total personal income. Yet, what is really important for welfare is not the total output of a nation's economy but its average level of output, since this better indicates how well off the average citizen is. For example, if two economies have the same total personal income and the first has half the population of the second, then it is apparent that the average citizen in the first country is better off.

Having said this, it is still not obvious what is the best way to measure the average standard of living. Since any measure of an average level is a ratio, there are two considerations: what is the best measure of the numerator and what is the best measure of the denominator? There are four common measures for the numerator: gross domestic product (GDP); net national product (NNP); total personal income; and total personal disposable income. Let us consider the relative merits of each. GDP shows the total (final) product that a nation produces in the course of a year. This measure includes not only the personal consumption of households but also investment and government expenditure (and the excess of exports over imports). Personal consumption provides immediate benefits to individuals and families. Investment expenditure, on the other hand, is not consumed by individuals or families and therefore does not directly improve their current well-being. However, by expanding the capital stock, investment can increase future production and therefore future consumption possibilities. Because of this, investment expenditure can be considered as contributing indirectly to future personal welfare.

Government expenditure can be considered as partly consumption and partly investment. For example, the police, fire, sanitation, power generation, educational, recreational, and public transit services provided by governments directly benefit individuals and families. Moreover, the road and highway construction, research and development, sewerage construction, and other forms of "social overhead expenditure" provided by the government sector expand the national capital stock and increase the potential for future consumption. Therefore, government expenditure can also be considered as contributing to either current personal well-being or future well-being. Thus, GDP is usually considered the most comprehensive measure of the contribution of a nation's economy to either the current or future well-being of its members.

Compared to GDP, NNP is usually considered a superior measure of a nation's annual output since, in theory at least, it controls for the fact that part of the capital stock wears out each year.

The GDP measure has the somewhat unfortunate property that the faster the capital stock wears out, the greater the value of GDP. The difference between GDP and NNP is depreciation – or, more technically, the capital consumption allowance. Since there is no widely agreed upon definition or measure of depreciation, the GDP measure is used more frequently than NNP, and we will also follow this convention.[6]

Total personal income measures that portion of national income that accrues directly to families. This measure is also referred to as before-tax family (or personal) income, because it includes the income and the personal taxes paid by individuals and families. Personal income is a better measure of current personal well-being than GDP or NNP, since it essentially excludes the investment portion of the national product. However, since this measure does include a portion of taxes and therefore implicitly a portion of government spending, it is not a very pure measure of private welfare. Therefore, another measure has been devised, called personal disposable income, which equals total personal income less personal income tax and other tax payments. Personal disposable income is a better measure of current well-being from (private) consumption than personal income.

As far as the denominator is considered, there are two common candidates. The first is the number of people living in a country. This is normally called a per capita measure. The second is the number of families (or households).[7] The choice of concept depends on one's judgment as to which is the appropriate welfare unit. For many purposes, the individual is considered the relevant unit, and output per capita the relevant measure of the average standard of living, since it is individuals who think and feel and who experience utility. However, it is also true that consumption is an activity that is usually performed jointly by the members of a family or household. For example, a house is shared by family members. There are certain "economies of consumption" realized in a family unit from the individual members sharing common resources. Therefore, as a unit of consumption, the family is usually considered the appropriate concept, and the family unit is usually used in conjunction with personal income.

One problem with the use of the family unit as a measure of welfare is that family income provides different levels of welfare to families of different sizes. A family income of $50,000 provides a higher standard of living to a family of two than a family of four. As a result, some researchers have used a measure of family income adjusted for family size, called **equivalent income**. This concept lies in between per capita income and family income and is probably the best indicator of well-being. (We shall discuss this concept in more detail in Chapter 4.)

2.3.1   Real versus nominal

Before looking at actual trends in the standard of living, it is first necessary to make another distinction – in this case, between "real" and "nominal" income. **Nominal income**, also called **income in current dollars**, records income in the actual values of that year. **Real income**, also called **income in constant dollars** or constant prices, adjusts the nominal income value for changes in prices over time. For example, if the price of bread rises between two years, the output value of bread in current dollars will increase even though there may be no corresponding increase in the number of loaves that are produced. Thus, it is important to distinguish between the current dollar value of output and real output, particularly if we are interested in how the economy has grown over time.

To measure real output, we convert the prices of each year into the prices of an (arbitrarily) chosen base period. This conversion is done by dividing output in current dollars for year x by the price index for year x. For example, actual data for the U.S. economy are shown below:

Year	GDP in current dollars (billions)	Price index [2000=100]	GDP in 2000 dollars (billions)
1995	7,398	92.1	8.032
2000	9,817	100.0	9,817
2005	12,456	112.7	11,049

To convert 1995 GDP in nominal dollars to GDP in 2000 dollars, we would divide $7,398 billion by 0.921, which yields $8,032 billion; and to convert 2005 GDP into 2000 prices, we divide $12,456 billion by 1.127, which yields $11,049 billion. This procedure is the best way of comparing the real output of different years.[8]

2.3.2 Trends in living standards in the United States

Table 2.2 shows four alternative measures of the average standard of living for the period 1929 to 2005 (also see Figures 2.1 and 2.2). The first column shows the growth of GDP per capita in

Table 2.2 GDP and personal disposable income per capita, median family income, mean hourly earnings, and median equivalent family income, 1929–2005

Year	GDP per capita[a] (2005$)	Personal disposable income per capita[a] (2005$)	Median family income (2005$)	Mean hourly earnings[c] (2005$)	Median equivalent family income[d]
1929	9,833	6,865			
1933	6,698	4,950			
1939	9,236	6,397			
1950	13,402	8,759	26,905	10.74	
1960	15,603	10,184	37,080	13.63	
1967	19,766	12,670	46,386	15.49	2.67
1973	23,093	15,409	53,008	17.16	3.15
1989	31,815	21,778	53,885	15.33	3.43
2001	39,073	27,905	56,731	15.99	3.68
2005	41,984	30,458	56,145	16.11	
Average annual growth rates (percent)					
1929–1939	−0.6	−0.7			
1939–1950	3.4	2.9			
1950–1973	2.4	2.5	2.9	2.0	2.8 [1967–73]
1973–2005	1.9	2.1	0.2	−0.2	0.6 [1973–01]

a   *Source*: Council of Economic Advisers, *Economic Report of the President, 1994*, U.S. Government Printing Office, Washington, 1994; *Economic Report of the President, 2007*, Table B-31, http://www.gpoaccess.gov/eop/tables07.html.
b   *Source*: U.S. Census Bureau, http://www.census.gov/hhes/income/histinc/f05.html. The CPI-U deflator is used to convert to constant dollars.
c   Hourly earnings are for total private nonagricultural production and nonsupervisory workers. The figures are adjusted for overtime in manufacturing and inter-industry employment shifts. *Source*: Council of Economic Advisers, *Economic Report of the President, 1994*, U.S. Government Printing Office, Washington, 1994; *Economic Report of the President, 2007*, Table B-47, http://www.gpoaccess.gov/eop/tables07.html.
d   Expressed as a ratio to the poverty line. *Source*: U.S. Census Bureau, *Detailed historical income and poverty tables from the March Current Population Survey 1947–1998*, http://www.census.gov/hhes/www/income/income.html/.

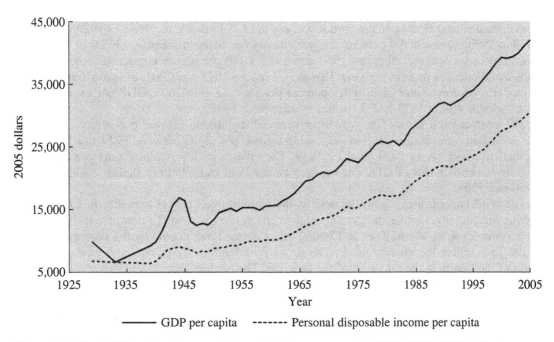

Figure 2.1   Real GDP and real personal disposable income per capita 1929–2005 (2005 dollars)

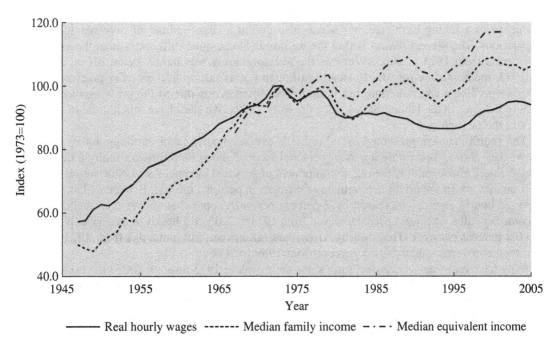

Figure 2.2   Average hourly wages, median family income, and median equivalent income, 1947–2005 (1973=100)

constant (2005) dollars.[9] Between 1929 and 1933, the period of the Great Depression, real GDP per capita declined by 32 percent, and it was not until 1940 that it regained its 1929 high. From 1939 to 1950, it grew at 3.4 percent per year, mainly due to the stimulating effects of World War II on the U.S. economy. Between 1950 and 1973, GDP per person continued to increase at a substantial rate, 2.4 percent per year. However, between 1973 and 2005, the growth in GDP per capita slowed down somewhat to 1.9 percent per year. Still, in 2005, GDP per capita was 4.3 times what it was in 1929 and 3.1 times as high as in 1950.

The next column shows the growth in personal disposable income per person. Here, too, we see a fairly precipitous drop in disposable income per capita between 1929 and 1933 and a gradual rise back to its 1929 level by 1939. The growth in disposable income per capita was slightly lower than that of GDP per capita between 1939 and 1950 but slightly higher between 1950 and 2005.

The third column uses family income as the welfare (well-being) measure. In addition, the median income level rather than the average or mean level is used. To compute the mean family income level, as we shall see in Chapter 3, we divide total income by the number of family units. To compute the median income level, we rank families by income and pick the income level of the family at the midpoint of the ordering. The median income level gives a better indication of what the average family receives than mean income level. Its growth pattern differs from that of GDP or personal disposable income per capita. Between 1950 and 1973, median family income grew by 2.9 percent per year, greater than the other two measures. Over this period, family size was substantially increasing as a result of the "baby boom" and therefore population was increasing quite a bit faster than the number of families. However, between 1973 and 2005, median family income increased very sluggishly, at only 0.2 percent per year.

Why do the trends between personal disposable income per capita and median family income differ so much since the early 1970s? There are two reasons. First, the number of families increased much more rapidly than the number of individuals in the United States. This was partly a consequence of a falling birth rate, but it was also due to a large number of divorces and marital separations. The second reason is that the *median* behaved quite differently than the *mean* over the period from 1973 to 2005. Whereas the average family was hardly better off in 2005 than in 1973, mean income rose fairly steadily (though not as fast as in the earlier postwar period). This seems like a contradiction, but it isn't. The difference is due to the growing *inequality* in family incomes in the United States since the early 1970s. We shall have much more to say about this in the next chapter.

The fourth measure presented in Table 2.2 is average hourly labor earnings. Labor earnings, as we saw above, forms only a part of personal income and is therefore not really a measure of well-being.[10] However, it is the major component of personal income. As a result, trends in wages and salaries are an important determinant of changes in personal income. Between 1950 and 1973, average hourly earnings increased by 2 percent per year, somewhat slower than median family income but still a significant pace. However, from 1973 to 2005, real hourly wages actually *declined*, by 0.2 percent per year. They fell by 11 percent (altogether, not annually) from 1973 to 1989, but then recovered slightly, by 5 percent from 1989 to 2005.

Why have real wages been declining since their peak in 1973 through 2005? Economists have several explanations, which we shall discuss in later chapters (see Chapters 8 and 9). However, we can explain why real wage trends differ from those of median family income. First, median family income has not fallen as much since 1973, because the number of two-earner families has been rising. In particular, the proportion of wives who have joined the labor force has risen dramatically over the last two decades (see Section 7.3). This is the principal explanation why family incomes have not fallen, despite the decline in real labor earnings. The second reason is that, as we saw from Table 2.1, other forms of income have been increasing faster than labor earnings. In particular, property income and, most importantly, transfer income have both been rising relative to labor income. This factor helps explain why personal income per capita has actually been rising since the early 1970s, while real wages have been falling.

The last measure in Table 2.2 is median equivalent family income, expressed as a ratio to the poverty line (also see Figure 2.2). As noted above, this measure adjusts family income for the size of the family. This series begins only in 1967 and ends in 2001. Between 1967 and 1973, this index grew by 2.8 percent per year – at about the same rate as median (unadjusted) family income. From 1973 to 1989, it rose at 0.5 percent per year. In comparison, median family income remained virtually unchanged. The difference reflected the fact that average family size fell over this period. Between 1989 and 2001, median equivalent family income rose by 7 percent (in total), slightly more than unadjusted median family income.

2.4   FACTOR SHARES

Factor shares or the **class distribution of income** refers to whether income is received in the form of wages or profits, irrespective of who gets it. A family may receive both salary income and some form of income from profits, such as dividends, interest, or rent. We are interested here in the source of the income, not its final disposition.

It is interesting to note that historically the term "income distribution" referred to the division of income between classes or factors. David Ricardo, writing in the early part of the nineteenth century, went so far as to argue that the primary aim of political economy (the original name for the field of economics) should be precisely to understand the factors that determined the distribution of income between classes.[11] The interest in this subject was to a great extent dictated by the politics of the early nineteenth century in Britain which focused on class relations (for example, whether a particular piece of legislation would benefit farmers, manufacturers, or workers) rather than individual welfare. Karl Marx's economic writings also focused on the class shares of income and were tied to his interest (and support) of class struggle. Many social democratic governments today actively pursue a policy of increasing labor's share in national income.

With the development of neoclassical theory, which began in the latter part of the nineteenth century, income distribution continued to be viewed as the apportionment of the national income between classes, though the mechanisms they analyzed were quite different from the earlier classical writers. It was only in the twentieth century that attention shifted to the allocation of income among individuals or families – the so-called **size distribution of income**. Today, the unqualified term "income distribution" typically refers to the size distribution of income. Class shares, on the other hand, are referred to as the **functional distribution of income**, since income is divided according to the factors in the production function.

It is also interesting to note that for the classical economists, the analysis of income distribution focused on "classes"– typically, the capitalists, workers, and, in some cases, the landowners. Income distribution was viewed as a consequence of historical forces and struggles between these social classes. With the neoclassical revolution in economic theory, income was seen as a return to a factor of production. Hence, income distribution became synonymous with "factor shares" – the share of the total product received by each factor. By its very structure, income distribution theory became, as a result, embedded in production theory.[12]

One of the earliest attempts to estimate the functional distribution of income was made by King in 1919. His estimates cover the period from 1850 to 1910 (see Table 2.3). In the 1850–1860 period, 37 percent of the national income was received by employees in the form of labor compensation (almost entirely wages) and 42 percent was received by proprietors (mainly self-employed

Table 2.3 Estimates of the functional distribution of income (factor shares) in the United States, 1850–2005 (percent)

Period and source	Employee compensation	Proprietor income		Other property income	Total labor	Total property
		Labor	*Profit*			
A. King's data[a]						
1850–1860	36.5	41.6			78.1	21.9
1860–1870	42.9	35.8			78.7	21.3
1870–1880	50.1	26.4			76.5	23.5
1880–1890	52.5	23.0			75.5	24.5
1890–1900	50.4	27.3			77.7	22.3
1900–1910	47.2	28.8			76.0	24.0
B. Johnson's data[b]						
1900–1909	55.0	14.4	9.2	21.4	69.4	30.6
1910–1919	53.2	14.9	9.3	22.6	68.1	31.9
1920–1929	60.5	11.2	6.4	22.0	71.7	28.4
1930–1939	66.8	9.7	5.3	18.1	76.5	23.4
1940–1949	64.3	10.9	6.0	18.7	75.2	24.7
C. Grant's data[c]						
1899–1909	49.1					
1909–1919	46.4					
1919–1929	49.5					
D. NIPA data[d]						
1950–1959	63.7	6.4	6.4	23.6	70.0	30.0
1960–1969	66.3	5.2	5.2	23.3	71.5	28.5
1970–1979	69.1	4.4	4.4	22.0	73.5	26.5
1980–1989	69.4	3.7	3.7	23.3	73.1	26.9
1990–1999	67.9	4.1	4.1	23.9	72.0	28.0
2000–2005	67.9	4.4	4.4	23.2	72.3	27.7

a   The original source is King, W.I. (1919). *The Wealth and Income of the People of the United States.* New York. The figures are as reported in Johnson, D.G. (1954). The functional distribution of income in the United States, 1850–1952. *Review of Economics and Statistics,* **36**(2), 175–82, p. 179.

b   *Source:* Johnson, D.G. (1954). The functional distribution of income in the United States, 1850–1952. *Review of Economics and Statistics,* **36**(2), 175–82, p. 178.

c   *Source:* Grant, A. (1963). Issues in distribution theory: The measurement of labor's relative share, 1899–1929. *Review of Economics and Statistics,* **45**(3), 273–9, p. 279. The figures are the share of employee compensation in business production only.

d   *Source:* Council of Economic Advisers, *Economic Report of the President, 1994,* U.S. Government Printing Office, Washington, 1994; *Economic Report of the President, 2007,* Tables B-28 and B-29, http://www.gpoaccess.gov/eop/tables07.html. Proprietors' income was split in half into a labor and property component.

farmers). In King's methodology, proprietor income was classified as labor income, and the sum of employee compensation and proprietors' income constituted the labor share. In 1850–60, the wage share was 78 percent of the national income, while the property share was only 22 percent. According to King's estimates, employee compensation as a share of national income rose quite sharply between 1850 and 1910 and the share of proprietors' income correspondingly fell, reflecting the shift of workers from the farm to the factory. However, together the labor share remained almost unchanged between 1850 and 1910.

Estimates were later made by Johnson (1954) for the period from 1900 to 1949. It is instructive to compare his estimates for 1900 to 1909 with those of King for 1900 to 1910. Using different data sources and a slightly different measure of national income, Johnson's figure on the share of employee compensation in national income was higher than King's and the share of proprietor income correspondingly lower. Moreover, Johnson broke proprietor income into two components – estimated compensation to the labor input of the proprietor and a profit on the capital invested in the business. Taken together, Johnson's estimated wage share in this period was 69 percent, compared with King's 76 percent.

Johnson's calculations show a moderate rise in the wage share from 69 percent to 75 percent between 1900 and 1950. The share of employee compensation in total income rose over the period from 55 percent to 64 percent, while the share of proprietor income fell. Between 1900 and 1949, the property income share fell from 31 percent to 25 percent. This was largely due to the proportion of interest and rent in national income, which declined from 15 percent to 6 percent. The share of corporate profits in national income, on the other hand, rose from 7 percent to 13 percent.

An alternative estimate of the wage share for the early part of the twentieth century was made by Grant (1963). He restricted his estimate of national income to the product of the business sector only (excluding the government sector and imputed rent to owner-occupied housing). Moreover, he included all of proprietor income as property income. His computations, shown in Table 2.3, indicate an almost constant ratio of employee compensation in national income in the period from 1899 to 1929.

My own estimates are also shown for the period from 1950 to 2005 on the basis of the National Income and Product Accounts. Employee compensation as a percent of total national income rose significantly from 63.7 percent in the 1950–1959 period to 69.4 percent in the years 1980–1989 but then fell to 67.9 percent in the years 2000–2005. If we append this series to Johnson's data, the estimates show an almost continuous rise in the share of employee compensation in national income since 1900, followed by a slight decline in the 1990s and early 2000s. On the other hand, proprietor income as a proportion of national income fell precipitously from 12.8 percent in the 1950–1959 period to 7.4 percent in the decade of the 1980s, though it then increased to almost 9 percent in the first half of the 2000s. I assumed that the apportionment of the income of the self-employed into a labor component and a profit component remained constant over the 1950–2005 period and was equal to 50 percent. On the basis of this assumption, the total labor share rose from 70 percent in the 1950s to 73.5 percent in the 1970s but then tailed off to 72.3 percent in the first half of the 2000s. Correspondingly, the share of total property income in national income fell from 30 percent in the 1950s to 26.5 percent in the 1970s but then recovered somewhat to 27.7 percent in the years 2000 to 2005.[13]

2.4.1   Historical studies on factor shares[*]

There have been several important historical studies of the wage and profit share. Hotson (1963) investigated the labor share in the Canadian economy over the period 1926 to 1960. Hotson's measure of the wage and profit share was based on the average mark-up over wage costs in the business economy. The mark-up is the difference between the wages a business pays and the price it charges for its output. If material inputs are ignored, the mark-up is essentially equivalent to property income – corporate profits, rents, and interest. Hotson found that the average mark-up on wages in the business economy remained very stable between 1926 and 1960.

Lecaillon and Germidis (1975) conducted a cross-national study intended to link the level of development of a country to the wage share in national income. The nations considered in the study included underdeveloped, developing, and industrialized ones. The major finding is that a greater fraction of the active labor force was employed as wage labor rather than self-employed in more developed economies (as measured by per capita income), than in less developed ones. As a result, the share of employee compensation in national income generally increases with development and the share of proprietors' income falls. This result is consistent with the statistical results for the United States over the last century. A secondary finding is that the relation between the share of employee compensation in national income and the ratio of wage and salary workers to the active labor force is nonlinear (actually parabolic). As the latter ratio approaches unity, the employee compensation share asymptotically approaches a constant less than one (0.70 in their study).

Wolff (2003) reported that profitability in the United States was rising since the early 1980s and by 1997 was at its highest level since its postwar peak in the mid-1960s, and the profit share, by one definition, at its highest point. He examined the role of the change in the profit share and capital intensity, as well as structural change, on movements in the rate of profit between 1947 and 1997. He found that the recovery of the profit rate in the 1980s and 1990s could be traced to a rise in the profit share in national income, a slowdown in capital-labor growth on the industry level, and employment shifts to relatively labor-intensive industries. Duménil and Lévy (2000) also provided time trends on the profit rate for Germany, the United Kingdom, and particularly France. All three countries, like the United States, showed declines in profitability from 1960 to the early 1980s and a sharp reversal through the late 1990s.

Ellis and Smith (2007) found that the growth in profits was strong in many developed economies in the 1990s and early 2000s, and the profit share (the share of factor income going to capital) in the early 2000s was high compared with earlier historical experience. Profit shares trended upwards since about the mid-1980s in most developed economies for which comparable data are available. These include France, Canada, the United States, Spain, Denmark, Japan, Norway, New Zealand, Sweden, Belgium, the United Kingdom, and the Netherlands. There are a number of possible explanations but the authors argue that the preferred explanation is that ongoing technological progress has increased the rate of obsolescence of capital goods. This induces a greater rate of turnover in both capital and employment, which puts firms in a stronger bargaining position relative to a labor force that now faces more frequent job losses on average. Firms can therefore reap a larger fraction of the economic surplus created by market frictions, which raises the measured profit share. This effect is stronger where labor market institutions are more rigid. There is also a positive relationship between the trend in the profit share and the extent of product market regulation. These explanations appear to fit the data better than alternatives raised in the literature.

2.5   INTERNATIONAL COMPARISONS OF LIVING STANDARDS

2.5.1   Per capita income

Does the United States still have the highest standard of living in the world? Have other countries been gaining? These and related issues have been a focus of recent policy debates in the United States and other countries around the world. Fortunately there are some recent data available to provide an answer to this set of questions.

For the period 1960–2003, the Penn World Tables have provided excellent data on per capita GDP for 188 countries (see Summers & Heston, 1988, for a description of the data). The figures for different countries are made comparable by an adjustment in terms of relative purchasing power parity (PPP), which reflects differences in the actual cost of living among countries, rather than currency exchange rates. They are expressed in units that Summers and Heston call "2000 international dollars" and the statistics are referred to as real GDP per capita, or RGDPL. These figures permit a comparison of the performance of the less developed countries, the middle income countries, and other groupings with that of the leading industrial countries.[14]

Comparative data for selected countries are shown in Table 2.4 for 1960, 1990, and 2003. The countries are ranked by their 2003 GDP per capita. Let us first look at the 2003 figures. According to the Penn World Tables, Luxembourg ranked first in terms of GDP per capita (RGDPL), *41 percent* ahead of the United States.[15] The United States was second followed very closely by Norway (98 percent of the U.S. level), then Switzerland (83 percent) and Ireland (81 percent). Denmark, Australia, Canada, Hong Kong, and Austria were all about 80 percent of the U.S. level. The United Kingdom's RGDPL was at 75 percent of the U.S. level, France at 74 percent, Germany at 72 percent, and Japan at 69 percent. The standard of living in South Korea and Portugal was half that of the United States.

Among the "third-world countries," Chile was the richest, at 35 percent of the U.S. level, while Mexico was at 23 percent and Brazil at 21 percent. Average income in the People's Republic of China was 14 percent of the U.S. level and in India only 9 percent. Among the poorest countries in the world were Pakistan at 7 percent, Bangladesh at 6 percent, and Nigeria at 4 percent of the U.S. RGDP.

A comparison of the 1960 and 2003 figures does show that many countries of the world were "catching up" with the United States in average income. This can be seen in Column 7, where a ratio greater than unity indicates that a country's RGDP was increasing relative to the United States' between 1960 and 1990. Luxembourg, Norway, Ireland, Hong Kong, Singapore, Japan, Taiwan, Korea, and Spain all made sizeable gains on the United States over this period. Luxembourg's RGDPL relative to the RGDPL in the United States increased by 43 percent; Norway's by 36 percent, Ireland's by 96 percent, Hong Kong's by 317 percent, Singapore's by 240 percent, and Japan's by 94 percent. Austria, France, Belgium, Finland, Italy, and Israel made more modest gains on the United States. Average income in Portugal gained by 68 percent on the U.S. level, Greece by 42 percent, the Czech Republic by 68 percent, and Thailand by 250 percent. China's RGDPL increased by *417 percent* relative to the U.S. level. India's standard of living rose by 28 percent relative to the U.S. level.

However, many countries fell even further behind the United States over this period. These include Switzerland, Chile, and Mexico, which suffered modest losses relative to the United States, and Venezuela, Peru, and Nigeria, which had sizable losses. Some very poor countries, including the Philippines and Bangladesh, also lost relative to the United States between 1960 and 2003.[16]

2.5.2   The Human Development Index

The Human Development Index (HDI) was developed by the United Nations and has been computed annually for 177 countries of the world since 1990. The motivation for the measure is to look beyond GDP to a broader definition of well-being. The HDI is a composite index of three dimensions of human development: living a long and healthy life (measured by life expectancy); being educated (measured by adult literacy and enrolment at the primary, secondary, and tertiary level); and having a decent standard of living (measured by PPP adjusted per capita income). The index is not in any sense a comprehensive measure of human development. It does not, for example, include indicators for human rights, democracy or inequality. Its purpose is to provide a broader perspective on human progress than GDP or personal income.

Table 2.4   Real GDP per capita (RGDPL) for selected countries, 1960, 1990, and 2003 (figures are in 2000 "international dollars")

Country	1960 dollar value (1)	RGDPL percent of U.S. (2)	1990 dollar value (3)	RGDPL percent of U.S. (4)	2003 dollar value (5)	RGDPL percent of U.S. (6)	1960–2003 catch-up rate [Col(6)/Col(2)] (7)
Luxembourg	12,888	99	32,033	118	49,261	141	1.43
United States	13,030	100	27,174	100	34,875	100	1.00
Norway	9,375	72	23,992	88	34,013	98	1.36
Switzerland	15,254	117	27,447	101	28,792	83	0.71
Ireland	5,380	41	13,462	50	28,247	81	1.96
Denmark	11,354	87	22,201	82	27,970	80	0.92
Australia	10,781	83	20,425	75	27,872	80	0.97
Canada	10,577	81	21,772	80	27,845	80	0.98
Hong Kong	3,264	25	22,003	81	27,656	79	3.17
Austria	8,495	65	22,220	82	27,567	79	1.21
Singapore	4,211	32	19,472	72	27,004	77	2.40
Netherlands	10,485	80	20,973	77	26,154	75	0.93
Sweden	10,955	84	21,713	80	26,138	75	0.89
United Kingdom	10,353	79	19,865	73	26,044	75	0.94
France	8,605	66	21,296	78	25,663	74	1.11
Belgium	8,051	62	20,645	76	25,262	72	1.17
Germany	8,860	68	21,279	78	25,189	72	1.06
Japan	4,632	36	21,640	80	24,036	69	1.94
Finland	7,674	59	19,883	73	23,786	68	1.16
Italy	7,103	55	19,532	72	22,924	66	1.21
New Zealand	12,104	93	17,171	63	22,197	64	0.69
Israel	6,526	50	16,538	61	20,715	59	1.19
Spain	4,965	38	15,396	57	20,642	59	1.55
Taiwan	1,491	11	11,284	42	19,886	57	4.98
Korea, Republic of	1,544	12	9,591	35	17,595	50	4.26
Portugal	3,677	28	13,621	50	17,333	50	1.76
Greece	4,156	32	12,004	44	15,787	45	1.42
Czech Republic	3,257	25	13,498	50	14,642	42	1.68
Chile	5,022	39	7,143	26	12,141	35	0.90
Argentina	7,859	60	8,231	30	10,172	29	0.48
South Africa	4,886	37	7,723	28	8,835	25	0.68
Mexico	3,695	28	6,877	25	7,939	23	0.80
Thailand	1,086	8	4,845	18	7,275	21	2.50
Brazil	2,670	20	6,834	25	7,204	21	1.01
Venezuela	5,968	46	7,484	28	6,251	18	0.39
Colombia	2,806	22	5,442	20	6,095	17	0.81
Turkey	2,264	17	4,768	18	5,634	16	0.93
China	445	3	1,678	6	4,970	14	4.17
Egypt	1,451	11	3,384	12	4,759	14	1.23
Peru	3,048	23	3,523	13	4,351	12	0.53
Indonesia	1,099	8	2,917	11	4,121	12	1.40
Philippines	2,037	16	3,209	12	3,576	10	0.66
India	870	7	1,897	7	2,990	9	1.28
Pakistan	803	6	2,197	8	2,592	7	1.21
Bangladesh	1,042	8	1,581	6	2,155	6	0.77
Nigeria	1,096	8	1,060	4	1,223	4	0.42

Source: Penn World Tables, Version 6.2, http://pwt.econ.upenn.edu/php_site/pwt62/pwt62_form.php (countries are ranked by 2003 RGDPL).

The life expectancy index is life expectancy at birth relative to a maximum life expectancy of 85 years. The education index measures a country's relative achievement in both adult literacy and combined primary, secondary, and tertiary gross enrolment. First, an index for adult literacy and one for combined gross enrolment are calculated. Then these two indices are combined to create the education index, with two-thirds weight given to adult literacy and one-third weight to combined gross enrolment. The GDP index is calculated using adjusted GDP per capita (in PPP-adjusted US dollar equivalents). In the HDI income serves as a surrogate for all the dimensions of human development not reflected in a long and healthy life and in knowledge. Income is adjusted because achieving a respectable level of human development does not require unlimited income. As a result, the logarithm of income is used. The HDI is then calculated as the simple arithmetic average of the three indices.[17]

Results for 2006 are shown in Table 2.5. It is of note that Norway ranks first in terms of HDI. Norway held the top position for six straight years. Before Norway, Canada was in first place from 1994 to 2000, and Japan and Canada alternated for the top spot from 1990 to 1993. Norway's first-place ranking compares to its fourth-place ranking in terms of GDP per capita. The difference is due to its high scores on both life expectancy and education. The United States was in eighth place in 2006, behind Norway, Iceland, Australia, Ireland, Sweden, Canada, and Japan. The United States' eighth place compares to a second-place ranking in GDP per capita. Here, too, the difference in the two ranks is attributable to the United States' poor showing on life expectancy (its performance on education is only slightly below that of Norway).

The HDI of Australia, Sweden, and Japan ranks well above their corresponding GDP per capita ranking (a difference of 11 in each case). Other notable differences are for Austria and Denmark, which rank 14th and 15th, respectively, in terms of HDI but seventh and eighth, respectively, in terms of GDP per capita, and Hong Kong which has a rank of 12 in GDP per capita but 22 in terms of HDI. Argentina, Poland, Chile, and Venezuela rank much higher in HDI than GDP per capita. Russia ranks 65 in HDI, compared to 59 in GDP per capita, while China ranks 81 in HDI and 90 in GDP per capita.

2.6   HOUSEHOLD PRODUCTION AND WELL-BEING

The contribution of household production to gross national product (GNP) is a well-established problem from the earliest days of national accounting (for example, Mitchell, 1921, considered this issue). Household work such as cooking, child care, home repairs, and cleaning increases the flow of goods and services and therefore of the national product and economic welfare. The value of such production is not included in the standard National Income and Product Accounts. However, the value of such work is quite sizable, and its inclusion in the NIPA could have far-reaching implications for the level and distribution of national income, and the growth of economic welfare over time. For example, the increasing participation of wives in the labor force means that they will have less time for household work. As a result, the use of traditional family income measures might lead to an *overstatement* of the growth of living standards over time, since part of the gains in labor earnings will be offset by a loss of home production.

There have been many attempts to estimate the value of household work. Estimates range from about 20 percent of GNP to over half. The estimates depend on the methodology used to measure the value of household work. There are two approaches that are commonly used. The first is based on the market price of services which the household provides. The second is based on the opportunity cost of the person performing the household work – the actual or potential earnings foregone by the individual performing the household work.

Table 2.5 The United Nations' Human Development Index (HDI) for selected countries, 2006

Country	HDI rank	HDI value	GDP per capita (PPP US$, 2004)	
			rank	value
Norway	1	0.965	4	38,454
Iceland	2	0.960	5	33,051
Australia	3	0.957	14	30,331
Ireland	4	0.956	3	38,827
Sweden	5	0.951	16	29,541
Canada	6	0.950	10	31,263
Japan	7	0.949	18	29,251
United States	8	0.948	2	39,676
Switzerland	9	0.947	6	33,040
Netherlands	10	0.947	9	31,789
Finland	11	0.947	15	29,951
Luxembourg	12	0.945	1	69,961
Belgium	13	0.945	11	31,096
Austria	14	0.944	7	32,276
Denmark	15	0.943	8	31,914
France	16	0.942	17	29,300
Italy	17	0.940	20	28,180
United Kingdom	18	0.940	13	30,821
Spain	19	0.938	22	25,047
New Zealand	20	0.936	25	23,413
Germany	21	0.932	19	28,303
Hong Kong, China (SAR)	22	0.927	12	30,822
Israel	23	0.927	23	24,382
Greece	24	0.921	27	22,205
Singapore	25	0.916	21	28,077
Korea, Republic of	26	0.912	31	20,499
Czech Republic	30	0.885	34	19,408
Hungary	35	0.869	39	16,814
Argentina	36	0.863	46	13,298
Poland	37	0.862	48	12,974
Chile	38	0.859	56	10,874
Mexico	53	0.821	60	9,803
Russian Federation	65	0.797	59	9,902
Brazil	69	0.792	64	8,195
Venezuela	72	0.784	89	6,043
Thailand	74	0.784	65	8,090
China	81	0.768	90	5,896
Turkey	92	0.757	70	7,753
Indonesia	108	0.711	116	3,609
India	126	0.611	117	3,139
Nigeria	159	0.448	158	1,154

Source: United Nations, *Human Development Report, 2006*, http://hdr.undp.org/hdr2006/statistics/ (countries are ranked by their 2006 HDI value). The source for GDP per capita is the Penn World Tables (see notes to Table 2.4).

2.6.1   Defining household work

In both approaches, it is first necessary to define what is meant by home production. The definition of economic activity that underlies the NIPA is based on market transactions. Since household work is not paid for through a market transaction, it is excluded from the NIPA definition of economic activity. There are two more general definitions of economic activity that have been employed by economists working on this issue. The most comprehensive concept defines economic activity to include virtually all household activities, including leisure, which yield a utility to household members. A second, more restrictive concept defines economic activity to include only household production for which there is a clear market alternative – that is, which results in a good or service which could be purchased from the market. Cooking, for example, would fall in this category, since one could purchase a meal at a restaurant.

The latter definition is normally used in these studies, since the former would lead to serious problems in measuring household activity (how do you assign a value to TV watching?). Activities which are typically included in household work are meal preparation and cleanup, house cleaning, gardening, laundry, home repairs, child care and child teaching, medical care, bill paying, and shopping.

Once the list of household activities to include in household production is decided upon, it is still necessary to decide on how to measure their *quantity*. In principle, the amount of household work can be evaluated as a flow of inputs or a flow of outputs. However, there are virtually no data on output flows (for example, the number of meals served in a year by the average family). As a result, most researchers in this field have measured quantity in terms of the amount of *time spent* on the activity. Such data are usually based on *time use studies*, where a family is asked to fill in a diary indicating how it allocates its time during a typical week. The latter approach also has problems. First, almost all household activities require nonlabor inputs. For example, cooking requires a stove and utensils; and mowing the lawn requires a lawn mower. In principle, the value of nonlabor inputs should also be included in the valuation, but these are difficult to measure and are usually excluded. Second, two or more household activities may occur simultaneously. For example, babysitting is often combined with cooking, cleaning, or dishwashing. It is difficult to divide the time up between such concurrent activities. In practice, individuals are asked their primary activity during each time interval.

2.6.2   The market cost approach

When a household hires someone to perform household work, there is a cost involved – namely, the prevailing wage of the service performed. Thus, if a babysitter is engaged to look after the children, the family must pay the babysitter a given hourly wage. If a gardener is hired to care for the garden, the family must pay the gardener a given fee. In this approach, household work performed by family members is valued according to the going market wage for the given activity. As a result, the valuation of household production will vary, depending on the activity performed. It will likely be higher for repairing a car than vacuuming the house. There are, of course, difficult problems in making this type of valuation. First, such estimates are very sensitive to the type of occupation the researcher chooses as the appropriate market replacement. Second, even if one selects the proper market replacement, it is still necessary to determine the equivalent wage rate. For example, if a person paints his (or her) own house, should the work be valued at the wage rate of an experienced union painter, a non-union painter, or a general laborer?

2.6.3   The opportunity cost approach

In this approach, it is assumed that an individual allocates time until the net return to an additional hour is equal in alternative employments. Since one use of time is to work for pay, in equilibrium the marginal value of an hour of housework should equal the marginal return to an additional hour of paid work. According to this argument, housework should be valued at the going market wage for the individual performing the work. As a result, different activities performed by a household member will be assigned the same hourly value, irrespective of the type of activity. For example, babysitting and house painting are given the same valuation. On the other hand, the same work performed by two different household members will generally receive different valuations, depending on the respective wages that the individual can command in the market.

There are a number of problems with this approach. First, since it is an equilibrium concept, it may not apply to persons who desire fewer or more hours of paid work or who are involuntary unemployed. For example, it can be argued that the opportunity cost of an unemployed painter is lower than that of a painter actively working. Second, the opportunity cost of individuals *not* in the labor force cannot be directly determined. For example, retirees do not normally have an opportunity wage available from paid work. In most applications it is assumed that every individual has an opportunity wage.

2.6.4   Empirical work on household production

Because the valuation of household production is normally based on special time use surveys, which appear intermittently, there are no annual time series data available on the total magnitude of household services. However, there have been estimates performed for several years by Murphy (1978) for the United States. On the basis of the market cost approach, he calculated that the total value of household production amounted to 37 percent of the official GNP figure for 1960 and 34 percent for 1970. According to the opportunity cost calculations, household output increased GNP by 38 percent in 1960 and 37 percent in 1970. Thus, according to both indices, there was a slight decline in the relative value of household work during the 1980s, a trend which reflected the increased labor force participation of married women. Adler and Hawrylyshyn (1978) made similar calculations for Canada in 1961 and 1971. On the basis of the market cost method, the value of household work amounted to 40 percent of GNP in 1961 and 41 percent in 1971; according to opportunity cost calculations, the proportion fell from 44 percent in 1961 to 40 percent in 1971.

Later studies (Chadeau, 1985; Fitzgerald & Wicks, 1990; Bonke, 1992; Goldschmidt-Clermont, 1993) all confirm the earlier results. Based on newer data for the United States, as well as several other industrialized countries, such as Denmark, France, Germany, Switzerland, and Great Britain in the 1980s, these researchers have consistently found that the value of household work amounts to between 40 and 50 percent of GDP. Wolff and Zacharias (2007) computed that the value of household production as a proportion of *total personal income* was 61.7 percent in the United States in 2001. This ratio was up slightly from 60.6 percent in 1989.

Another interesting dimension is afforded by looking at who contributes to household labor. On the basis of the market cost approach, Murphy (1978) found that housewives provided 55 percent of the total value of household services in 1970; married men provided 16 percent, single women 23 percent, and single men 6 percent. Similar percentages were obtained from the opportunity cost approach. Thus, altogether, women were responsible for 78 percent of total household production and men only 22 percent. Estimates for 2001, provided by Wolff and Zacharias

(2007), show that men's share of total household production has risen since 1970 because of the increased labor force participation of women (particularly wives). In 2001, women accounted for 73 percent of total household production and men for 27 percent.

Another interesting issue is how household production affects overall inequality. Though we have not formally introduced the concept of inequality (see the next chapter), it is useful to consider this issue here. The central idea is that a trade-off exists between market work and household work, particularly in the case of wives. Thus, if women (especially wives) spend more time in the labor market, they will have less time for household production. The addition of household production to (normal) household income should thus reduce measured inequality.

Bonke (1992) found this to be the case for both Denmark and the United States in 1987. Adding household production to before-tax income resulted in a 10 percent reduction in measured inequality (using the Gini coefficient) in the case of Denmark and a 16 percent reduction in the case of the United States.[18] Jenkins and O'Leary (1996) analyzed a similar issue for the United Kingdom using the British 1986 Family Expenditure Survey. They calculated that adding household production valued on the basis of housekeeper wage equivalents to money income resulted in a 36 percent reduction in measured inequality (using the Gini coefficient) and adding household production valued at opportunity cost resulted in an 18 percent reduction. Using the 2003 American Time Use Survey (ATUS), Frazis and Stewart (2006) found similar results for the United States, with the addition of household production causing a 21 percent reduction in the Gini coefficient.[19]

2.7 SUMMARY

The national accounts use a double-entry bookkeeping system in order to maintain an identity between total income and total product. This system is the basis of our measures of GDP and national income. Personal income is a component of national income. It consists of wage and salary earnings, proprietors' earnings, rental income, dividends, interest income, and government transfer payments.

The main component of personal income is labor earnings, historically between 60 and 67 percent. Proprietors' income accounted for 17 percent of total personal income in 1929 but was only 9.5 percent in 2005. Rental income has also declined in importance, from 5.8 percent in 1929 to 0.7 percent in 2005, while dividends also fell from 6.9 percent in 1929 to 2.9 percent in 1980 but then bounced back to 5.6 percent in 2005. Interest income has amounted to as low as 4.2 percent of personal income (in 1950) and as high as 15.5 percent (in 1990) but in 2005 amounted to only 9.2 percent of total personal income. Transfer payments show the most dramatic change, rising from 2 percent of income in 1929 to 14.9 percent in 2005.

There are different ways of measuring the standard of living. Three were presented in this chapter: (i) GDP per capita; (ii) personal disposable income per capita; and (iii) median family income. The first is based on total national output, including investment and government expenditures, while the second uses only after-tax personal income as the base. The third is based on pre-tax personal income but uses the family as the unit of welfare instead of the individual and reflects the income of the average family rather than mean income. A related index is average labor earnings, since this is the main component of personal income.

Two important findings were reported in this chapter. The first is that mean hourly wages, after increasing by 2 percent per year from 1950 to 1973, have fallen since then. Real wages fell by 6 percent (altogether, not annually) between 1973 and 2005. The second is the marked slowdown in the growth of median family income in real terms after 1973. Between 1950 and 1973, it grew by 2.9 percent per year, faster than real wages. However, over the years 1973 to

1989, median family income remained virtually unchanged and between 1989 and 2005 inched up by only 4 percent. The reasons that median family income remained constant over the 1973–1989 period, while real wages fell, are (i) the number of two-earner families rose and (ii) nonlabor income – property and transfer income – increased faster than labor income. However, since 1989, the growth in both two-earner families and nonlabor income has slowed down.

In contrast, real GDP per capita increased at 2.4 percent per year between 1950 and 1973, and continued to grow between 1973 and 2005, though at a somewhat slower rate of 1.9 percent per year. Likewise, real personal disposable income per capita rose at 2.5 percent per year from 1950 to 1973 and at 2.1 percent per year from 1973 to 2005. There are two reasons why both GDP and personal disposable income per capita continued to grow at a reasonable clip after 1973 while median family income sputtered. The first is that the number of families has been increasing more rapidly than the number of individuals. The second is that income inequality has been rising since the early 1970s, so that mean income has grown faster than median income.

Median equivalent family income showed positive albeit very modest growth between 1973 and 2001 of 17 percent in total, compared to a 7 percent increase in median unadjusted family income. The difference is due to the fact that average family size fell over this period.

This chapter also investigated differences in per capita income among countries of the world on the basis of purchasing power parity (PPP) rates. The figures indicate that in 2003, the United States had the second highest living standard in the world, behind Luxembourg. Norway was close to the United States, while Germany's per capita income was 72 percent of the U.S. level and Japan's was 69 percent. Per capita income in the United Kingdom was 75 percent of the U.S. level, while Mexico's was only 23 percent. The statistics also indicate that a majority of the industrialized countries of the world have been closing the income gap between themselves and the United States from 1960 to 2003, whereas underdeveloped countries have been falling further behind.

An alternative ranking is provided by the United Nations' Human Development Index (HDI). In 2006, Norway was first in terms of HDI while the United States ranked only eighth. Iceland, Australia, Ireland, Sweden, Canada, and Japan all ranked ahead of the United States.

Attention was also given to the economy-wide division of national income between labor and property. It was found that the labor share increased between 1900 and the 1970s but has then fallen between the 1980s and early 2000s. This is consistent with the fact that real wages fell from 1973 through 2005.

2.8   REFERENCES, BIBLIOGRAPHY, AND DATA SOURCES

References and bibliography

Adler, H.J. & Hawrylyshyn, O. (1978). Estimates of the value of household work Canada, 1961 and 1971. *Review of Income and Wealth*, **24**, December, 333–55.

Baumol, W., Batey Blackman, S.A. & Wolff, E.N. (1989). *Productivity and American Leadership: The Long View*. Cambridge, MA: MIT Press.

Bonke, J. (1992). Distribution of economic resources: implications of including household production. *Review of Income and Wealth*, ser. 38, no. 3, September, 281–94.

Chadeau, A. (1985). Measuring household activities: some international comparisons. *Review of Income and Wealth*, ser. 31, no. 1, March.

Clark, J.B. (1891). Distribution as determined by the law of rent. *Quarterly Journal of Economics*, **5**, April, 289–318.

De Serres, A., Scarpetta, S. & De La Maisonneuve, C. (2001). Falling wage shares in Europe and the United States: How important is aggregation bias? *Empirica*, **28**(4), 375–401.

Duménil, G., Glick, M. & Rangel, J. (1987). The rate of profit in the United States. *Cambridge Journal of Economics*, **11**(4), 331–59.

Duménil, G. & Lévy, D. (2000). *Costs and Benefits of Neoliberalism. A Class Analysis*. Paris: CEPREMAP, mimeo, May.

Duménil, G. & Lévy, D. (2002). The profit rate: Where and how much did it fall? Did it recover? (USA 1948–1997), *Review of Radical Political Economics*, **34**, 437–61.

Eisner, R. (1989). *The Total Incomes System of Accounts*. Chicago: University of Chicago Press.

Ellis, L. & Smith, K. (2007). The global upward trend in the profit share. Bank for International Settlements (BIS) Working Paper No. 231, Basel, Switzerland, July.

Fitzgerald, J. & Wicks, J. (1990). Measuring the value of household output: A comparison of direct and indirect approaches. *Review of Income and Wealth*, **36**, June, 129–41.

Frazis, H. & Stewart, J. (2006). How does household production affect earnings inequality? Evidence from the American Time Use Survey. U.S. Bureau of Labor Statistics, Washington, DC, April.

Goldschmidt-Clermont, L. (1993). Monetary valuation of non-market productive time: Methodological considerations. *Review of Income and Wealth*, ser. 39, no. 4, December, 419–34.

Grant, A. (1963). Issues in distribution theory: The measurement of labor's relative share, 1899–1929. *Review of Economics and Statistics*, **45**(3), 273–9.

Gollin, D. (2002). Getting income shares right. *Journal of Political Economy*, **110**(2), 458–74.

Guscina, A. (2006). Effect of globalization on labor's share in national income. IMF Working Paper 06/294, Washington, DC.

Hotson, J.H. (1963). The constancy of the wage share: The Canadian experience. *Review of Economics and Statistics*, **45**(1), 84–91.

Jenkins, S.P. & O'Leary, N.C. (1996). Household income plus household production: The distribution of extended income in U.K. *Review of Income and Wealth*, ser. 42, no. 4, December, 401–20.

Johnson, D.G. (1954). The functional distribution of income in the United States, 1850–1952. *Review of Economics and Statistics*, **36**(2), 175–82.

Jorgenson, D.W., Landefeld, J.S. & Nordhaus, W.D. (eds.) (2006). *A New Architecture for the U.S. National Accounts*. Chicago: University of Chicago Press.

Juster, F.T. & Stafford, F. (1985). *Time, Goods, and Well-Being*. Institute for Social Research, University of Michigan, Ann Arbor.

Kalecki, M. (1971). Class struggle and the distribution of national income. *Kyklos*, **24**(1), 1–9.

King, W.I. (1919). *The Wealth and Income of the People of the United States*. New York.

Krueger, A.B. (1999). Measuring labor's share. *American Economic Review Papers and Proceedings*, **89**(2), 45–51.

Lecaillon, J. & Germidis, D. (1975). Economic development and the wage share in national income. *International Labor Review*, **3**(5), 393–409.

Leontief, W. (1966). *Input-Output Economics*. New York: Oxford University Press.

Leontief, W. (1977). *Studies in the Structure of the American Economy*. White Plains, NY: International Arts and Sciences Press (now M.E. Sharpe, Inc.).

Mitchell, W. (1921). *Income in the United States: Its Amount and Distribution, 1909–1919*. New York: National Bureau of Economic Research.

Murphy, M. (1978). The value of nonmarket household production: Opportunity cost versus market cost estimates. *Review of Income and Wealth*, **24**, September, 243–55.

Murphy, M. (1982). Comparative estimates of the value of household work in the United States for 1976. *Review of Income and Wealth*, **28**, March, 29–43.

National Bureau of Economic Research (1964). *The Behavior of Income Shares: Selected Theoretical and Empirical Issues*. New York: National Bureau of Economic Research.

Parker, R.H. & Harcourt, G.C. (1969). *Readings in the Concept and Measurement of Income*. Cambridge: Cambridge University Press.

Ruggles, N. & Ruggles, R. (1970). *The Design of Economic Accounts*. New York: National Bureau of Economic Research.

Tobin, J. & Nordhaus, W. (1971). *Economic Growth*. National Bureau of Economic Research Colloquium V. New York: National Bureau of Economic Research.

Weisskopf, T.E. (1979). Marxian crisis theory and the rate of profit in the Postwar U.S. Economy. *Cambridge Journal of Economics*, **3**, 341–78.

Wolff, E.N. (1986). The productivity slowdown and the fall in the U.S. rate of profit, 1947–76. *Review of Radical Political Economy*, **18**(1&2), 87–109.

Wolff, E.N. (2003). What's behind the recent rise in profitability in the US? *Cambridge Journal of Economics*, **27**(4), 479–99.

Wolff, E.N. & Zacharias, A. (2007). The Levy Institute measure of economic well-being: United States, 1989–2001. *Eastern Economic Journal*, **33**(4), 443–70.

Young, A.T. (2005). One of the things we know that ain't so: Why US labor's share is not relatively stable. University of Mississippi, mimeo, August.

Data sources for the U.S. economy

Council of Economic Advisers, *Economic Report of the President*. Washington, DC: U.S. Government Printing Office. These volumes are available annually.

Survey of Current Business. Every year, the July issue of this publication contains detailed information on the National Income and Product Accounts.

U.S. Census Bureau (1973). *Long Term Economic Growth 1860–1970*. Washington, DC: U.S. Government Printing Office, June.

U.S. Census Bureau (1975). *Historical Statistics of the United States, Colonial Times to 1970*, Part 2. Washington, DC: U.S. Government Printing Office.

U.S. Census Bureau. *Statistical Abstract of the United States*, available annually, http://www.census.gov/compendia/statab/.

U.S. Census Bureau. *Census of Population, Subject Reports*. Various publications are available for each of the decennial censuses, http://www.census.gov/main/www/cen2000.html.

U.S. Census Bureau. *Current Population Reports*. Available annually, http://www.census.gov/hhes/www/income/income.html.

U.S. Bureau of Labor Statistics. *Employment and Earnings*. Washington DC: U.S. Government Printing Office. Available annually, http://www.bls.gov/bls/wages.htm.

International data sources

Kravis, I., Heston, A. & Summers R. (1978). *International Comparisons of Real Product and Purchasing Power*. Baltimore: World Bank.

Maddison, A. (1982). *Phases of Capitalist Development*. Oxford: Oxford University Press.

Maddison, A. (1991). *Dynamic Forces in Capitalist Development*. Oxford: Oxford University Press.

Maddison, A. (1995). *Monitoring the World Economy, 1820–1992*. Paris: OECD.

Maddison, A. (2001). *The World Economy: A Millennial Perspective*. Paris: OECD.

Maddison, A. (2003). *The World Economy: Historical Statistics*. Paris: OECD.

Penn World Tables: http://pwt.econ.upenn.edu/.

Summers, R. & Heston, A. (1984). Improved international comparisons of real product and its composition, 1950–1980. *Review of Income and Wealth*, **30**, June, 207–62.

Summers, R. & Heston, A. (1988). A new set of international comparisons of real product and prices: Estimates for 130 countries, 1950–1985. *Review of Income and Wealth*, ser. 34, March 1–26.

Summers, R. & Heston, A. (1991). The Penn World Table (Mark V): An expanded set of international comparisons. *Quarterly Journal of Economics*, **106**, 327–36.

United Nation's Human Development Index: http://hdr.undp.org/en/statistics/.

World Bank. *World Development Report*. New York: Oxford University Press. Available annually.

World Bank. *World Tables*. Baltimore: Johns Hopkins University Press. Available annually.

2.9 DISCUSSION QUESTIONS AND PROBLEM SET

1   Explain the difference between gross output and gross domestic product (GDP).
2   Why were time trends different for GDP per capita and median family income between 1973 and 2005?
3   What are the components of personal income? What has been the biggest change in the composition of personal income in the United States since 1929?
4   Explain the two methods used to value household work in relation to national accounts.
5   Explain why the definition of income used in the national income and product accounts excludes capital gains.

6   Suppose GDP and the price index for the United States are as follows:

Year	GDP in current dollars (billions)	Price index [2000=100]
1995	1,800	90
2000	2,000	100
2005	2,400	120

Calculate GDP in 2000 dollars for each of the 3 years. Calculate GDP in 1995 dollars for each of the 3 years.

7   Suppose median income in current (nominal) dollars and the CPI price index for the United States are as follows:

Year	Median income in current dollars (billions)	CPI price index [1990=100]
1980	24,000	75
1990	30,000	100
2000	40,000	125

Calculate median income in 2000 (real) dollars for each of the 3 years.

8   Suppose GDP in current (nominal) dollars and the GDP price index for the United States are as follows:

Year	GDP in current dollars (trillions)	Price index [2000=100]
1990	6.0	80
2000	10.0	100
2005	15.0	125

Calculate GDP in 2005 (real) dollars for each of the 3 years.

9   Suppose the input–output structure of Country X looks like this:

Input–output table of Country X	Intermediate users			Final demand			
Sectors and value added	Raw materials	Metal products	Food & clothing	Consumption	Investment	Government	Totals
Raw materials	7	9	6	2	0	0	
Metal products	3	6	1	13	5	4	
Food & clothing	0	0	0	21	0	4	
Wages & salaries	8	9	11				
Gross profits	4	5	5				
Indirect (business) taxes	2	3	2				
Totals							

(a) Compute the total (gross) output of each industry on both the output side and the input side.
(b) Show that GDP equals total final demand and also total value added.

Appendix 2.1　An Introduction to the National Income and Product Accounts*

The National Income and Product Accounts (NIPA or "national accounts," for short) is an overall accounting statement of the performance of the economy over a given time period (usually a calendar year). Perhaps, the most common measure from the national accounts is GDP, which shows the total output produced by a nation's economy in the course of a year. Other important measures are net national product (NNP), national income, personal income, and personal disposable income. All these measures appear quarterly (every three months) and are usually reported in major newspapers. In the context of this book, an understanding of national accounts is important for two reasons. First, it allows the student to understand the connection between the production side of the economy and the sources of personal income. Second, national accounting is necessary to understand how factor shares are defined and measured.

The development of national accounts began during the 1930s. Their principal architects were the Russian-born economist Simon Kuznets and the British economist, Richard Stone, who were awarded Nobel prizes for this achievement. Today, almost all the nations of the world publish official national accounts. In the United States, they are compiled by the Bureau of Economic Analysis, which is part of the Department of Commerce.

Perhaps, the easiest way to understand the national accounts is through another accounting device – **input–output analysis** – which was also developed during the 1930s and by another Russian-born economist, Wassily Leontief (he also received a Nobel prize for this achievement). An input–output system records the sales of goods not only to **final users** but also to **intermediate users**. These intermediate users are the producing industries of an economy, such as agriculture, mining, construction, manufacturing, transportation, and services. The transactions are recorded in a matrix form, so that each column of the inter-industry portion of the matrix shows the **inputs** required to produce a given level of output. The columns thus represent the technology of production. The rows of the matrix indicate how much each industry sells to other industries and final consumers. The rows thus show the distribution of the sales of each industry. In addition, beneath the inter-industry portion of the matrix are rows showing the wages paid out and the gross profits received in each sector.

Table 2.6 presents a simplified input–output view of the economy (the figures in the table are only illustrative). There are only three producing sectors (or industries). The first sector produces raw materials, such as iron ore, wood, and other basic materials. These are **intermediate goods** because they are used exclusively by other industries to produce their output. The second sector produces metal products. Some metal products like bolts and screws are intermediate goods since

Table 2.6   An illustrative input–output table of the economy

| Sectors and value added | Intermediate users | | | Final demand | | | |
	Raw materials	Metal products	Food & clothing	Consumption	Investment	Government	Totals
Raw materials	3	11	7	0	0	0	21
Metal products	2	4	1	13	5	7	32
Food & clothing	0	0	0	15	0	4	19
Wages & salaries	9	7	6				22
Gross profits	6	8	4				18
Indirect (business) taxes	1	2	1				4
Totals	21	32	19	28	5	11	
Employment	1000	500	600				2100
Capital	65	80	35				180

Memo: GDP = 28 + 5 + 11 = 22 + 18 + 4 = 44 (below the line).
All figures are in millions of dollars, except for employment which is in number of workers.

they are inputs into other industries, while others such as a stainless steel flatware are **final goods**, since they are purchased by households for their private consumption. The third sector produces food and clothing, which are consumption or final goods.

Let us first look at the columns of the three sectors. The total or gross output of the raw materials sector is $21 million. To produce this, the sector purchased $3 million of raw materials (trees, for example, are required to produce lumber) and $2 million worth of metal products. In addition, 1,000 workers were employed, who were paid a total of $9 million, and $65 million worth of capital was used. Capital consists of plant and equipment, which are distinguished from intermediate inputs in that they last much longer than the production period (for example, when trees are transformed into lumber, the original trees no longer exist, whereas the circular saws used to cut the lumber continue to function).

The total direct cost was $14 million (3 + 2 + 9). In addition, $1 million were paid out in **indirect business taxes**, such as sales and excise taxes. The remaining entry in the column is **gross profits**, which amounted to $6 million. This item is often regarded as a **return on capital**. For this sector, the return on capital was 9.2 percent (6 divided by 65). It should now be apparent that the total value of output equals the sum of all the inputs used plus gross profits plus indirect business taxes.

The total output of the metal products industry is $32 million. To produce this, the industry used $11 million worth of raw materials and $4 million worth of metal products. It hired 500 workers, who were paid $7 million, paid out $2 million in indirect business taxes, and made $8 million in gross profits. Since its capital was worth $80 million, its rate of return was 10 percent (8/80). The major input into the food and clothing sector was raw materials, which amounted to $7 million out of a total output of $19 million. Metal products worth $1 million were also purchased, and $6 million in wages and $1 million in indirect business taxes were paid out. The gross profits in this sector totaled $4 million, or 11.4 percent on the capital stock.[20]

The rows of the matrix show where the output produced in each sector is sold. Thus, of the $21 million worth of raw materials produced, $3 million were sold to other raw material producers, $11 million to the metal products industry, $7 million to the food and clothing industry, and none to final demand. It should be noted that the row total for each sector must, by construction, equal the column total.[21] The metal products industry sells its output to both intermediate and final users. Of the $32 million produced, $7 million were sold to other industries and $25 million to final demand. In this table, final demand is divided into three components: **household consumption**; **investment**; and **government expenditure**.[22] Metal products are purchased by all three sources of final demand. Consumers purchased $13 million worth of housewares, appliances, and other metal products; $5 million worth of equipment and machinery were purchased for investment; and $7 million worth of defense hardware, filing cabinets, and the like were bought by the government. Finally, food and clothing were sold exclusively to final users. Households bought $15 million worth and $4 million dollars worth were bought by the government (for police and armed force uniforms, food for troops, and the like).

A2.1.1   THE RELATION TO THE NATIONAL ACCOUNTS

Let us now see how the input–output table can be used to generate the national accounts. It is first important to distinguish between **gross output** and **final output**. The gross output (or, more technically, the gross domestic output) of a sector is the total value of the goods produced in the sector. This is recorded in both the first three column totals and the first three row totals. However, it should be apparent that the value of the gross output of a sector includes the value of goods produced by other industries during the period. Thus, the sum of gross output (in this case, $21 + 32 + 19 = 72$) does not really represent anything, since the output of raw materials and metal products is *double-counted*. What is meaningful is the sum of the final output of the economy, since there is no double-counting involved. In this case, total household consumption was $28 million, total investment $5 million, and total government expenditure $11 million. The grand total was $44 million. The sum of final output is very familiar; it is called gross domestic product or GDP.

There are three components on the income side of the ledger: (i) wages and salaries, which summed to $22 million; (ii) gross profits, which amounted to $18 million; and (iii) indirect business taxes, which equaled $4 million. These three components taken together are also referred to as **value added**, since they represent the net addition to the value of the inter-industry inputs added by the **factors of production**. These three components are also income flows, since they are received by households, firms, and the government, respectively. The sum of value added equals $44 million, which is identical to GDP. (This should not be too surprising, since the inter-mediate flows are subtracted from both the column totals and row totals to arrive at their respective totals.) This, in fact, is the ingenious feature of the NIPA, that total product and total income must always be equal. This means that one can either look at income statements or product accounts to get a measure of the total output produced by the economy.

It is also possible to derive net national product (NNP) from these accounts. As indicated above, the full value of the capital stock is not included in the value of the final product or value added, since it is not fully consumed during the production period. In fact, in any given period, some portion of the capital stock wears out (machines and buildings do not last forever). This portion of the capital stock that is consumed during a period is called **depreciation**. The actual measure of "true economic depreciation" is a subject of much controversy. However, for national income accounting purposes, the measure is usually based on computations done by corporations for business income tax purposes. The Internal Revenue Service provides guidelines for depreciation, and these entries, called **capital consumption allowances**, are used as the basis of the measure of depreciation.

In Table 2.6, depreciation is included in the gross profits entry. The difference between gross profits and depreciation is referred to as **net profits**. On the product side, the corresponding concept to depreciation is **replacement investment**. That is to say, the investment done by an economy during a given period consists of two parts: the first to replace worn out plant and equipment and the second to expand the capital stock. This second portion is referred to as **net investment**. NNP is thus equal to the sum of household consumption plus government expenditures plus *net investment* (plus exports less imports), which in turn equals the sum of labor earnings plus indirect business taxes plus *net profits*.

NNP is a conceptually superior measure of the total final product of an economy than GDP since it excludes that portion of new investment that is required simply to maintain the capital stock at its existing level.[23] However, because of the difficulty of measuring true economic depreciation, GDP is the concept most often used to measure the overall performance of an economy.

A2.1.2   THE SOURCES OF PERSONAL INCOME

In this book, we are interested primarily in personal income – that is, income received by families and individuals. Let us return to Table 2.6. As we noted above, the sum of national income must, of necessity, equal the sum of national product. However, it does not necessarily follow that the individual components of income equal the "corresponding" components of final demand. For example, total wages and salaries in Table 2.6 are $22 million, but total household consumption is higher, at $28 million. Gross profits are $18 million but total investment is only $5 million, while indirect business taxes total $4 million but government spending is $11 million. The reason for these differences is that the value added categories of income do not really indicate the final recipient of the income. For example, income taxes are paid on wages and are remitted to the government. This is also true of a portion of the gross profits received by business. Moreover, part of the gross profits of firms is disbursed to individuals in the form of dividends and interest payments. Finally, part of the taxes received by the government is transferred to individuals in the form of social security benefits and the like.

In Table 2.7, we show how the value added income categories can be schematically related to the final recipients of income. There are three different classes of recipients: (i) households; (ii) businesses; and (iii) governments. In our example, workers received $22 million in wages

Table 2.7   The relation of value added to the income of households, businesses, and the government: an illustrative example

	Final recipients Households	Businesses	Government	Total
Value-added components (and transfers)				
1. Wage & salaries	18	0	4 (personal income taxes)	22
2. Gross profits	5 (dividends)	4	9 (corporate income taxes)	18
3. Indirect business taxes	0	0	4	4
4. Transfers	7	0	−7	0
Total income	30	4	10	44
Total spending[a]	28	5	11	44
Net savings (deficit)	2	−1	−1	0

a   From the final demand columns of Table 2.6.

and salaries. Of this, we will assume that they paid $4 million in personal income taxes to the government. Gross profits received by businesses were $18 million. Of this, business paid $9 million in corporate income taxes and other business taxes to the government, leaving $9 million for the firms. Of this $9 million, business distributed $5 million to households in the form of dividends and retained $4 million, which represents the sum of undistributed firm profits and depreciation claimed by the businesses.

Finally, the government received $4 million in the form of indirect business taxes. It also collected $4 million of personal income taxes and $9 million in corporate taxes. The total receipts of government were thus $17 million. From this, the government transferred $7 million to households in the form of social security and other benefits. This transaction is recorded as a negative 7 for the government and a (positive) 7 for households.

Notice that the row totals are identical to those of the corresponding value added rows in Table 2.6. Moreover, since transfer payments always appear as a negative for one sector and a positive for another, on net the sum of transfer payments must equal zero. The sum of value added still remains $44 million.

Let us now look at the column totals. The first column records the various sources of personal income. The first is wages and salaries; the second consists of dividends distributed from businesses; and the third source in this example is transfer payments received from the government. The sum of household income was $30 million. This is referred to as personal disposable income, because the income taxes paid by families have already been subtracted, and this is the amount of money over which households have discretionary control. If we add back in the income taxes, we obtain what is called personal income, which totaled $34 million.[24]

In the second column of Table 2.7, the retained earnings of businesses (including depreciation allowances) totaled $4 million. In the third column, the net receipts of the government after transfer payments amounted to $10 million. The sum of personal disposable income plus business retained earnings plus government net receipts is $44 million, identical to total value added.

Let us now compare the income of these three segments of the economy with the final demand columns of Table 2.6. The personal disposable income of households amounted to $30 million, whereas total household consumption was $28 million. The difference of $2 million dollars is referred to as **personal savings**. Businesses, moreover, invested $5 million in new plant and equipment but their retained earnings were only $4 million. The government spent $11 million on goods and services, yet its net receipts were only $10 million. The government, in other words, ran a deficit of $1 million.

We may wonder how the business sector was able to invest $5 million when its retained earnings were only $4 million, and how the government managed to spend $11 million when its receipts were only $10 million? The answer lies in the fact that households saved $2 million. Thus, either directly through the purchase of corporate stocks and bonds and government securities or indirectly through deposits in banks, which in turn bought corporate and government securities, personal savings were used to finance the business and government deficits.

A2.1.3 THE DERIVATION OF FACTOR SHARES

Table 2.8 illustrates how the wage and profit shares are estimated, as discussed in Section 2.4 above. We begin with the broadest concept of national output, which is GDP. Subtracting from this the capital consumption allowance (depreciation), we obtain NNP. If indirect business taxes (and nontax liability) are then subtracted and several other minor adjustments are made, national income (NI) is obtained. NI shows the total income generated in the economy and valued at their source or factor (see Section A2.1.4 below for more details on measuring national income).

Table 2.8 Accounting framework for measuring factor shares

	Sources		
1. Persons	*2. Corporations*	*3. Other*	
Wages and supplements Proprietors' income: Wage portion			Wage share
Proprietors' income: Profit portion Rental income	Corporate profits	Net interest	Profit share — National income
Indirect business tax and notax liabilities Business transfers Current surpluses less subsidies of government enterprises			NNP
Capital consumption allowance			GDP

There are three sources of national income: (i) persons (including unincorporated businesses and nonprofit institutions); (ii) corporations; and (iii) net interest in the economy.[25] Households receive three kinds of income from factors employed: (i) wages, salaries, and supplements on their labor; (ii) proprietors' income on the equity invested in unincorporated businesses; and (iii) rental income on land and other real estate. Corporations receive one form of income, profits, on their invested capital. The last component of NI is net interest in the economy. The wage share consists mainly of wages and fringe benefits. The property income or profit share consists mainly of rental income, corporate profits, and net interest. Proprietors' income is a hybrid category, since part of the income is from the proprietors' labor and the remainder is pure profit on the invested capital. The labor portion is included in the wage share and the profit portion in the property income share.

A2.1.4 MISCELLANEOUS ISSUES IN NATIONAL ACCOUNTING

A2.1.4.1 Treatment of international trade

In defining GDP, as in Section A2.1.1 above, we skipped over two separate issues. The first is the treatment of imports and exports. Imports consist of goods and services that are produced outside a given country (in our case, the United States) but purchased by industries or residents of the United States. Exports are goods or services produced in the United States but purchased by industries or residents of other countries. Let us return to a simplified input–output framework to show how these are handled (Table 2.9). There are two domestic (that is, U.S.) industries, A and B. Each purchases inputs from each other and, in addition, each purchases inputs imported from abroad to produce its respective output. The value of the imported inputs is recorded in a separate row, labeled "imports."[26] The cost of producing a domestic product includes not only the cost of domestic inputs and value added but also the cost of imported inputs. This is

Table 2.9 An illustrative input–output table with imports and exports

Sectors and value added	Domestic industries		Final demand			Total output
	Industry A	Industry B	Domestic[a]	Exports	Imports	
Industry A	4	7	1	3	0	15
Industry B	2	3	10	5	0	20
Imports	1	4	3	0	−8	0
Value added	8	6				14
Total output	15	20	14	8	−8	

Memo: GDP = 14 + 8 − 8 = 8 + 6 = 14

a Domestic final demand is defined as the sum of domestic consumption, investment, and government expenditures.

apparent in the computation of the column sums for total output in industries A and B. Moreover, imports are also purchased directly by final consumers for personal consumption, investment, and government expenditure. Examples of these are Japanese cars and West German machinery. This is shown by an entry in the import row in final demand. Finally, part of the output produced in the United States, such as U.S. computers and U.S. wheat, is exported to other countries. These transactions are recorded in a separate column of final demand.

GDP is a production concept and is defined as the total final output produced in a given nation. Therefore, goods and services produced abroad but consumed in a given nation are excluded from the value of GDP. This is done by subtracting the total value of imports, shown in the import column of final demand. In the example here, the total amount of imports is 8 and, as a result, there is a −8 in the import column. On the other side of the ledger, exports are included in GDP since they are part of final output produced by a country. The fact that these goods and services are purchased abroad indicates only the disposition of the final product. Thus, GDP is defined to equal the sum of consumption, investment, government expenditure, and exports less imports. In the example here, GDP equals 14, which is the same, as it should be, as total value added.

The second issue is somewhat more subtle and ultimately stems from the fact that in NIPA total income must equal the total product. The problem arises because there are residents (and corporations) in a country that own income-producing property abroad. For example, an American may own stock in British Petroleum or Telefonos de Mexico. As a result, part of the income received each year by Americans comes from foreign production. The converse is also true – namely, that foreigners own stock in U.S. companies and therefore part of the value added generated in the United States is remitted abroad (that is, sent out of the country). The actual physical production that takes place in a given country is not the same as the income its citizens receive, so that two different concepts of "national product" have developed.

The first, which we called GDP, measures the total final output produced in a nation defined as a particular geographic area. The second is called GNP, and refers to the total income received by residents or corporations of a given country. To compute GNP it is necessary to subtract out from domestically generated value added (GDP) any dividends or other payments remitted abroad and add in any remittances from foreign countries received by U.S. residents or corporations.[27] In order to adjust the product side of the accounts a fictitious final product is created, called "the rest of the world sector," which is equal to the net remittances from abroad and added to the domestically produced final product to balance the accounts.[28]

A2.1.4.2   National income at factor costs

All production is performed by factors of production – labor, capital, land, and other natural resources. (Intermediate inputs, which are also inputs in the production process, are themselves produced by factors of production and therefore reducible to them.) From this point of view, all income must originally accrue to these basic factors, in the form of wages, interest, profits, and rent. National income at factor costs, or "national income" for short, in this regard, is the total sum of payments to these factors.

The relation between GDP and national income is as follows: First, since national income is the sum of compensation to factors, depreciation is excluded since it is a cost of production, not part of the return to capital. Second, indirect business taxes, such as sales taxes, and other payments to the government not levied on factor income are also excluded. The reason is that such indirect taxes are simply added on to the price of a product and are not paid out of profits or wages. On the other hand, income and social security taxes would be included in national income, since they are assessed directly on factor income such as wages and profits. Thus, national income at factor costs equals GDP less depreciation less indirect business taxes and similar payments to the government.

A2.1.4.3   The treatment of capital gains

Another concept of personal income is used by the Internal Revenue Service (IRS) for the computation of income taxes. The major difference with the NIPA definition of personal income is the inclusion of capital gains on the sale of property. A capital gain is the difference between the sale price of property, such as a house, land, or stock shares, and its original purchase price.[29] From the standpoint of the IRS, a capital gain on a sale represents money income to the seller and should therefore be subject to taxes like any other form of income. However, from the standpoint of NIPA, the inclusion of capital gains in income would violate the identity between total income and total product, because there is no production corresponding to the capital gain.

Take the simple case of housing prices increasing from general inflation. A person will receive a capital gain on the sale of the house, and yet the house itself may have remained completely unchanged from the time of purchase. From the standpoint of the overall economy, no new product has been created and therefore no additional income generated. Yet from the individual's standpoint, he or she could have bought a corporate bond with the same money which was used to pay for the house. In a world of perfect capital markets, the interest the person receives on the bond would be equal to the capital gain made on the house. From the standpoint of the IRS, it would make no sense to tax interest on corporate bonds if capital gains were not taxed, since an individual could switch wealth out of corporate bonds and into housing.[30]

A major political issue of recent years in the United States is the tax treatment of capital gains. Historically, capital gains have been subject to a lower tax rate than other components of personal income in the federal tax system. As of 2007, the maximum federal income tax on capital gains was only 15 percent, compared to a top marginal tax rate of 35 percent on all other income. However, many Republicans argue that the tax rate should be made still lower (if not actually eliminated), because capital gains taxation discourages savings and therefore investment. Moreover, they argue that a large portion of capital gains is illusory insofar as it merely reflects overall price inflation. If a house doubles in value over 10 years and all other prices double as well, then the house is no more valuable today than it was 10 years ago, since its value would purchase the same goods. Several Republican leaders have also advocated that capital gains be "indexed" for changes in the overall price level.

However, as we shall see in Chapter 5, wealth is very unequally distributed in the United States, and capital gain income is highly concentrated among the wealthy. As a result, many Democrats argue that the main beneficiaries of a reduction of capital gains taxation would be the rich, who already enjoyed major tax reductions on their income during the 1980s and early 2000s. They argue against a reduction in capital gains taxes on the basis of equity in the tax system. (See Chapter 16 for more discussion of the federal tax system.)

NOTES

1   See Appendix 2.1 for a discussion about how personal income is related to GDP.
2   An adjustment has also been made to exclude both the employee's and the employer's contribution for social insurance (mainly the social security contribution). The reason for the exclusion is that these contributions are transferred to other households in the form of social security benefits and the like. If we included both the social security contributions and benefits as part of personal income, we would essentially be counting the same flow twice.
3   There is a second part to this income category, which is "rent" imputed to owner-occupied homes. Since families that own their own homes do not (by definition) pay rent, the services received from owner-occupied housing would not be reflected in the national accounts. In order to make owner-occupied housing consistent with rental housing, NIPA estimates the market rental for owner-occupied housing and includes this "imputed rent" in national income. This imputation results in a better measure of national income. To make the income and product accounts balance, NIPA then includes imputed rent on the product side as a measure of the output of the "rental and real estate" sector.
4   Please note that this trend is *not* inconsistent with the trend reported in Chapter 1 that labor's share in *national income* fell between 1990 and 2005.
5   Both employee and employer make equal contributions to the social security system. The employee's share is usually referred to as the employee's social security tax and is treated, like income taxes, as a tax on wages and salaries. It is therefore considered as part of wages and salaries, not as a supplement. See Chapter 16 for more details.
6   There are a host of other issues connected with the measurement of average well-being. One that has been a subject of much recent discussion is that GDP may not accurately reflect the total final product that an economy produces. There are really two separate issues involved. The first is that certain goods and services classified as final products are really intermediate products. Some items suggested for this category are defense spending, since it serves primarily to protect the resources and production facilities of a country, and work-related personal consumption expenditures such as commuting expenses. The second is that some activities that are not included in GDP should be added to measure welfare. One example is household work such as cooking, cleaning, and do-it-yourself activities. These activities increase personal welfare and act as substitutes for services provided by restaurants, repair shops and the like that are paid for and therefore included in GDP. See Section 2.7 and Tobin and Nordhaus (1971) for further discussion.
7   The U.S. Census Bureau defines a family as two or more related individuals (as well as "partners") sharing a common living unit. A household is defined as individuals (related or otherwise) sharing a common living unit. A household may consist of one person.
8   As with many other statistical questions, there are alternative ways to construct price indices. The problem would be very simple to solve if the economy produced only one product (and the "quality" of this product did not change over time). However, once there is more than one product, then the selection of the appropriate combination of output weights (as they are called) to use to construct the price index can make some difference in the measure of inflation. Also see Chapter 1 for a discussion of the consumer price index (CPI).
9   The GDP deflator is used to convert from nominal to real dollars. The GDP deflator is a composite index of price indices for the components of GDP, such as household consumption, investment, and government spending.
10   However, labor earnings do constitute the vast majority of income for the vast majority of families.

11   In his case, there were three classes of interest: (i) workers; (ii) capitalists; and (iii) landowners. Karl Marx, writing in the mid-nineteenth century, also focused a large part of his work on the determinants of the division of income between workers and capitalists.

12   Because of the very high concentration of property ownership in the United States and other advanced industrialized countries, there is also a clear relationship between movements in factor shares and income inequality. See Chapters 3 and 5 for more details. Also, see Appendix Section A2.1.3 for the derivation of factor shares from national accounts.

13   See Chapter 1, Section 1.1 for more discussion of trends in the wage and profit shares in the United States. Also, note that the use of period averages here shows a different time trend than the year-by-year data used in Chapter 1, which does show a sharp increase in the profit share from 1985 to 2005.

14   There are two major problems in making cross-national comparisons of average living standards, especially between developed nations and underdeveloped ones. The first is that in underdeveloped countries, many items that contribute to the standard of living are not exchanged (such as food grown by the household) and therefore are not counted in the official national accounts statistics. The second is that people in different countries often consume very different commodities. For these two reasons, the official foreign exchange rate between two countries' currencies rarely reflects the relative cost of maintaining comparable living standards. Instead, PPP indices have been developed to capture differences in actual costs of living for international comparisons of well-being.

15   It should be noted that GDP per capita is a ratio. It can be high either because of a large numerator and/or because of a small denominator. In the case of Luxembourg, its high GDP per capita is due to a very small population.

16   See Baumol, Batey Blackman, and Wolff (1989), Chapter 5, for more discussion of the "catch-up" or "convergence" phenomenon.

17   The use of equal weights in combining the three indices has been criticized since this assumption is simply arbitrary. Other weighting (such as giving GDP per capita a weight of, say, 50 percent) would result in different composite scores and country rankings.

18   The Gini coefficient is a measure of inequality. We will define the Gini coefficient formally in Chapter 3.

19   This calculation was performed while excluding so-called secondary child care (that is, child care that was done while the parent was performing some other task like cooking) from the definition of household production. When secondary child care is included, the reduction of the Gini coefficient amounted to 28 percent.

20   The columns of the input–output matrix have another interpretation. Suppose we divide the interindustry entries in the matrix by their column total and designate this new matrix by the letter *a*:

$$a = \begin{matrix} 0.14 & 0.34 & 0.37 \\ 0.10 & 0.13 & 0.05 \\ 0.00 & 0.00 & 0.00 \end{matrix}$$

The *a* matrix, which is called the direct coefficient matrix, shows the technology of production used in each industry. For example, in the first industry, 14 cents worth of raw materials is required for each dollar of output, while in the third industry 37 cents is required. These coefficients are useful in projecting changes in industrial output that would result from changes in the pattern of demand.

21   What about about unsold goods produced by an industry? These are technically referred to as *inventories* and are recorded as a form of investment.

22   The two components missing from final demand are exports and imports, where the latter is recorded as a negative flow (see Section 2.8).

23   GDP actually has the somewhat ironic property that the faster capital goods are worn out the higher the value of GDP is! Students should try to construct an example to show why this is so.

24   To simplify the discussion, it was assumed that personal income taxes were paid only on wages and salaries. In actuality, income taxes are paid on total personal income, including dividends and some kinds of transfer payments.

25   Households receive interest income on savings accounts, corporate bonds, government securities and the like and pay interest on mortgages and consumer debt. The difference between what they receive and pay out is the net interest income of households. Likewise, corporations and the government sector both receive interest income and pay out interest on their debt. Each of these sectors has a net interest income. The sum of the net interest of households, corporations, and government is the net interest in the economy. If there is no interest received from or paid abroad, then the three sectors should cancel out, and economy-wide net interest should be zero. Because of imputations of interest to the financial sector, the net interest in the economy has historically been positive, though, until recently, relatively small.

26   In actual input–output accounting, imports are divided into two groups. The first are "competitive imports," which are imports that are directly substitutable for some domestic product, such as Saudi Arabian oil for U.S. oil or Japanese steel for U.S. steel. Competitive imports are added into the same row as their domestic substitutes and then subtracted in the import column of final demand. The second are "noncompetitive imports," which are those for which there are no comparable U.S. products, such as Colombian coffee. These are recorded in a separate import row.

27   The major flow consists of profits made by foreign subsidiaries of U.S. companies that are remitted to the parent company.

28   For the United States, GNP and GDP have historically been very close, and this distinction is not usually stressed. However, for many smaller economies, the two measures can differ substantially, and GDP is the preferred concept of national output since it measures the actual production taking place in a country.

29   Technically, capital gains refer to the difference between sale price and purchase price of property held for a predefined minimum period of time. Otherwise, the IRS calls this an "ordinary gain."

30   There is a secondary issue involved with capital gains. IRS taxes only realized capital gains – that is, gains on the actual sale of property. But the market value of unsold property may also increase. Such increases, called unrealized capital gains, are not taxed by the IRS.

Chapter 3

Income Inequality: Its Measurement, Historical Trends, and International Comparisons

3.1 INTRODUCTION

In Chapter 2, we developed the concept of mean earnings and median income. These measures are useful in tracking changes in the well-being of the average worker and the average family. This chapter focuses on the distribution or inequality of income. What does income inequality mean? Quite simply, it means that different people or families receive different amounts of income. In this chapter, our focus is on how great these differences are – that is, what the *dispersion* of income looks like. The term income distribution refers to a way of recording the differences in what people receive, and of measuring the overall dispersion of income.

Readers might wonder why inequality *per se* is an important issue to address. There is, of course, the issue of fairness and justice, which we shall consider more fully in Chapter 16 (see Section 16.2). However, even from a narrow economic viewpoint, some argue that inequality is necessary to provide incentives for hard work and savings (that is, the existence of inequality may indicate that the market is working efficiently). On the other hand, some argue that inequality may be socially bad because it is correlated with potentially bad outcomes for society such as poverty, unequal access to health care or police protection, increases in the crime rate, and the like. We shall address these issues more fully in subsequent chapters.

This chapter is primarily concerned with the measurement of income inequality. However, it will also investigate whether the United States has become more equal or unequal in terms of income distribution over time and how it compares to other countries in terms of income inequality. Section 3.2 presents a brief review of basic statistics. Section 3.3 develops the measurement of income inequality in some detail. Historical data on U.S. income inequality are shown in Section 3.4, while Section 3.5 presents comparisons between the United States and other countries. A summary is provided in Section 3.6.

3.2 A REVIEW OF BASIC STATISTICS

We begin with the concept of a *sample*. In most studies, it is too costly to survey a full population (such as the United States). Therefore, only a small percentage of the population is actually surveyed. In most cases, the sample is *randomly* drawn from the full population. In this way, it is hoped to be representative of the population, and the statistics estimated from the sample to be close to the actual population values.[1]

3.2.1 Mean, variance, and standard deviation

The two most common statistics used to describe a sample are the mean and variance. The mean is a measure of the central tendency of a sample. In studying income distribution, a primary concern is the average level of income since it reflects the average level of well-being of the population, as discussed in Chapter 2. Suppose the sample size consists of n observations. Let X_1 refer to the first observation, X_2 to the second, and so on to X_n for the nth observation. The sample mean, $\bar{X}$, is defined as

$$\bar{X} = (X_1 + X_2 + \ldots + X_n)/n \tag{3.1}$$

where the three dots (...) mean "and so on to." An alternative expression is given by:

$$\bar{X} = \sum_{i=1}^{n} X_i/n \tag{3.2}$$

where the symbol Σ, which is the Greek letter "sigma," means "summation of X_i from $i = 1$ to $i = n$." Equations (3.1) and (3.2) are identical.

Another important concern about a sample is the **dispersion** of its values. The dispersion of income also has important implication for the well-being of a population.[2] The most common measure of dispersion is the **variance** of a sample. The sample variance, s^2, is given by:

$$s^2 = \sum_{i=1}^{n} (X_i - \bar{X})^2/(n - 1) \tag{3.3}$$

The term $(X_i - \bar{X})$ is called the deviation from the sample mean of each observation X_i and measures the discrepancy (difference) between the observation and the center of the sample. The more dispersed a sample is, the greater these deviations are and the higher the variance statistic. The reason that the deviations are squared is that the sum of the algebraic value of the deviations will always equal zero.[3]

The sum of squared deviations is then divided by $n - 1$ to yield an estimate of the average squared deviation from the mean of the sample.[4] Without dividing by $n - 1$, the variance statistic would tend to increase merely as the sample size increased. The variance is also referred to as the mean squared deviation from the mean, and is probably the most common indicator of sample dispersion.

An alternative measure, which is directly derived from the sample variance, is the sample standard deviation, denoted by σ (or SD) and defined as the square root of the variance. Its advantage over the variance measure is that it is of the same exponential order as the mean, since the variance is the average *squared* deviation and the standard deviation is the square root of this. As a result, it is meaningful to make a direct comparison between the standard deviation and mean of a distribution, and one inequality measure, the coefficient of variation, is the ratio of the two, as we shall see below.

3.2.2 Distributions

So far the term "distribution" has been used rather loosely, but there is a technical meaning to it. A distribution, or more formally a **frequency distribution**, refers to the frequency with which observations on a given variable fall within predefined categories of values for that variable.

In the case of income, these categories are ranges of income, or **income classes**. In a sense, a frequency distribution is simply a convenient way of presenting statistical results for a variable with a wide range of values and for a sample with many observations.

Panel A of Table 3.1 presents data on the actual frequency distribution of family income in the United States in 2005. In that year, there were a little over 114 million households in the country. Note first of all that the income classes are all defined to be mutually exclusive. Also note that the ranges of income that define each income class can differ in width. There are 16

Table 3.1 Size distribution of household income in the United States by income class and percentile, 2005

A. Size distribution of income

Income class	Frequency (in 1,000s)	Percentage frequency	Cumulative percentage frequency	Mean income ($)	Total income (million $)	Percentage of total income	Cumulative percentage of income
Under $5,000	3,731	3.3	3.3	1,306	4,873	0.1	0.1
$5,000 to $9,999	5,670	5.0	8.2	7,702	43,668	0.6	0.7
$10,000 to $14,999	7,332	6.4	14.6	12,405	90,952	1.3	1.9
$15,000 to $24,999	14,139	12.4	27.0	19,753	279,288	3.9	5.8
$25,000 to $37,499	16,536	14.5	41.4	30,930	511,462	7.1	12.8
$37,500 to $49,999	13,498	11.8	53.2	43,420	586,078	8.1	20.9
$50,000 to $62,499	12,054	10.5	63.8	55,805	672,675	9.3	30.2
$62,500 to $74,999	8,977	7.8	71.6	68,451	614,480	8.5	38.7
$75,000 to $87,499	7,421	6.5	78.1	80,667	598,633	8.3	47.0
$88,000 to $99,499	5,313	4.6	82.8	93,185	495,093	6.8	53.8
$100,000 to $114,999	4,804	4.2	87.0	106,838	513,263	7.1	60.9
$115,000 to $129,999	4,232	3.7	90.7	120,405	509,579	7.0	67.9
$130,000 to $149,999	3,096	2.7	93.4	137,450	425,499	5.9	73.8
$150,000 to $199,999	4,031	3.5	96.9	170,091	685,637	9.5	83.2
$200,000 to $249,999	1,529	1.3	98.2	218,999	334,849	4.6	87.9
$250,000 and above	2,023	1.8	100.0	434,757	879,513	12.1	100.0
All households	114,384	100.0		63,344	7,245,540	100.0	

B. Cumulative percentage of income by percentile

Percentile	Cumulative number of households (in 1,000s)	Percentile income level ($)	Cumulative percentage of income
10	11,438	11,345	1.0
20	22,877	19,178	3.4
30	34,315	27,253	7.0
40	45,754	36,000	12.0
50 (median)	57,192	46,326	18.5
60	68,630	57,660	26.6
70	80,069	71,997	36.8
80	91,507	91,705	49.6
90	102,946	134,102	67.4
95	108,665	166,000	77.8
99	113,240	293,359	91.3
100	114,384		100.0

Table 3.1   (*Continued*)

C. Income shares by quintile

Quintile	Percentage share of total income
Bottom	3.4
Second	8.6
Middle	14.6
Fourth	23.0
Top	50.4
All	100.0

D. Other statistics

1. Median income	$46,326
2. Mean income	$63,344
3. Standard deviation of income	$66,741
4. Coefficient of variation	1.054
5. Gini coefficient	0.469
6. Log variance of income	1.624
7. Theil's "entropy" index	0.393
8. Atkinson index (0.5)	0.188
9. Atkinson index (0.8)	0.300
10. Atkinson index (1.5)	0.640

Source: http://pubdb3.census.gov/macro/032006/hhinc/toc.htm.

income classes in this distribution. The first 15 are referred to as **close-ended** classes, since specific limits are denoted for these, while the last is called an **open-ended** class, since there is no defined upper limit. The first column of Table 3.1 shows the frequency with which the income observations fall into the designated classes. This distribution is also referred to as the **size distribution of income**, since it shows the frequency of income by size of income (as opposed to the "functional distribution" of income, which shows the shares of income received by labor and capital).

The second column shows the percentage frequency distribution. This is computed by dividing the actual frequency by the total number of households. Thus, for example, 5.0 percent of all incomes fell in the $5,000–$9,999 income class, and 14.5 percent fell in $25,000–$37,499 income class. This income class is referred to as the *modal class*, since it has the largest frequency of observations. (The **mode** of a distribution is the income level with the largest frequency of cases.) The next column shows the cumulative percentage frequency. This is computed by summing the percentage frequency of the particular income class with those of lower income classes. The cumulative percentage frequency thus shows the proportion of the sample receiving income at or below a given income class. For example, 8.2 percent of households received income below $10,000, and 53.2 percent below $50,000.

It is also possible to present the relative frequency distribution in graphical form, as shown in Figure 3.1. The vertical axis of the graph shows the percentage of the population in each income class, and the horizontal axis represents the income level. Here the midpoint of each income interval is used to represent the income class. The shape of this graph is very typical for an income distribution. Most of the observations are crowded on the left side of the graph, and the

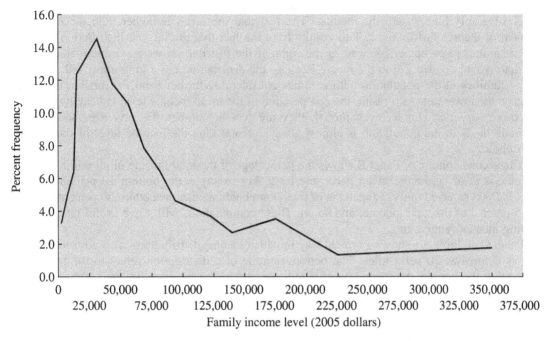

Figure 3.1   Size distribution of income for U.S. households, 2005 (based on the midpoint of each income class)

distribution peaks on the left side. The part of the distribution between zero income and the peak is referred to as the **lower tail** of the distribution. The right side, or **upper tail**, of the distribution is thinner and much longer than the lower tail. The basic shape of the distribution is referred to as **asymmetrical** or **skewed to the right**. A symmetrical distribution is one in which a vertical line drawn through the center of the distribution yields a mirror image of the two sides. An asymmetrical distribution is one in which this is not true, where one side is longer or thinner or otherwise differently shaped than the other. An asymmetrical distribution in which one tail is longer than the other is also called a **skewed** distribution, and the direction of **skewness** is the side where the tail is longer. The point where the curve changes from being concave to the origin to convex to the origin is called the *inflection point*. After the inflection point, the curve asymptotically approaches the income axis.

3.2.3   Percentile ranking

An alternative way of presenting the same data as in Panel A of Table 3.1 is in terms of percentile ordering, shown in Panel B. Percentiles are computed by first ordering the sample in terms of income from lowest to highest. The *n*th percentile is the income level such that *n* percent of the sample has income less than or equal to this level. In this case, 10 percent of U.S. households (or 11.4 million) had incomes less than or equal to $11,345 in 2005; 20 percent of families had incomes less than or equal to $19,178; and 50 percent of the sample had income less than or equal to $46,326. There is a special name for the 50th percentile, which is the **median**, since it is the middle income level of the distribution. Half of the sample is at or below this level, and the other half has income greater than this level. The median income, as we noted in Chapter 1, represents the level of well-being of the *average household*.

The **mean** (or **average**) income level of households in 2005 was $63,344 (see Panel D), which is considerably higher than the median. The fact that the mean is higher than the median is typical of income distributions. This results from the fact that the income distribution is asymmetrical and, in particular, skewed to the right. If the distribution were symmetrical, then the median would be identical to the mean. Because the distribution has a long upper tail, there are some families in the population with incomes considerably further from the median than families on the lower tail. As a result, the computation of the mean income level is heavily weighted by these very rich people, even though they are few in number. The average income level of households in the population is almost always greater than the income level of the average household.

The second column of Panel B shows the percentage of the total income of all families whose income is at or below the given percentile level. For example, the bottom 10 percent of families in 2005 received (only) 1.0 percent of total household income; the bottom 50 percent received 18.5 percent of the total income; and so on. These computations will prove useful later in computing inequality measures.

Panel C of Table 3.1 shows a typical way in which income distributions are analyzed. A quintile is defined as 20 percentiles. The bottom quintile of a distribution refers to the bottom 20 percent of the sample; the second quintile to those ranked between the 20th and 40th percentile; and so on to the top (or fifth) quintile. The share of total income is computed for each quintile. The bottom quintile of U.S. households received 3.4 percent of total income; the second quintile, 8.6 percent; and the top quintile, 50.4 percent. The fact that the quintile shares are so different is one indication of considerable income inequality in the United States.

3.3   INEQUALITY MEASURES

Economists have developed many measures of income inequality (see, for example, Sen, 1973, for a good review). In this section, we discuss the most common measures currently in use. Before doing so, it is helpful to discuss some of the properties that economists feel are desirable in an inequality index. As Sen (1973) discussed, there are several of these properties but the two most important from our perspective are **scale independence** and the **transfer principle**.

Scale independence requires that the inequality measure be *invariant* to uniform proportional changes. In other words, if each family's income changes by the same proportion (for example, when inflation affects every family's income to the same degree) then inequality should not change. In formal terms, for a given inequality index I and any scalar $a > 0$, $I(\mathbf{y}) = I(a\,\mathbf{y})$, where $\mathbf{y}$ is family income. The intuition behind this principle is that inequality is a *relative* measure. If inflation occurs and every family's income goes up by the same percent as the price index, then most of us would intuitively feel that the relative standing of families has not altered and we would not want our inequality index to change. Likewise if every family's income increases by the same percentage in *real terms*, most of us would again feel that relative positions had not altered and inequality is unchanged.[5]

The transfer principle, which is technically referred to as the Pigou–Dalton transfer principle (from Dalton, 1920, and Pigou, 1912) requires the inequality measure to rise (or at least not fall) when income is transferred from a poorer to a richer person and to fall (or at least not rise) when income is transferred from a richer to a poorer person. There are two restrictions in this case. First, mean income must remain unchanged. Second, there cannot be "rank reversal," whereby the rank or relative position of two persons change places. In technical terms, consider the vector $\mathbf{Y}'$ which is a transformation of the vector $\mathbf{Y}$ obtained by a transfer c from y_j to y_i, where $y_i > y_j$, and $y_i + c > y_j - c$, then the transfer principle is satisfied if and only if $I(\mathbf{Y}') \geq I(\mathbf{Y})$.

The intuition behind this principle is that if a poor family becomes better off by receiving an income transfer from a rich family and a rich family worse off, then the position of the poor family will improve *relative* to the rich family. This principle is also (humorously) referred to as the "Robin Hood principle." Most people would feel that inequality has been reduced as a result of this transfer, and we would say that income has been *redistributed* from the rich to the poor. This principle stands behind the progressive tax and transfer systems that characterize most Western countries.

3.3.1 Concentration measures

The simplest summary statistic on income inequality is the concentration ratio. This measures the percentage of total income received by the richest individuals – typically, the top 20 percent (quintile) of the income distribution, the top 10 percent (decile), the top 5 percent, or the top 1 percent. If there were perfect equality, each person by assumption would receive the same income and each percentile of the distribution would have 1 percent of total income. If there is inequality, then upper percentiles will receive more of total income than lower ones.

Panel C of Table 3.1 illustrates this point. The upper quintile of U.S. households in 2005 received 50.4 percent of total income, while the bottom quintile received only 3.4 percent. The second quintile received more than the lowest, the third more than the second, and the fourth more than the third. If there were perfect equality, each quintile would have received 20 percent of the total income. Since the difference in quintile shares is great, overall inequality is large.

Looking at overall quintile (or decile) shares is probably the best way to analyze the overall income distribution. However, sometimes it is convenient to use a single summary statistic. The usual way of doing this is to compute the percentage of the total income that accrues to the top income classes. There are four common measures. The first is the share of total income going to the top quintile, which in 2005 was 50.4 percent. The second is the share of income received by the top decile (10 percent), which was 32.6 percent. (This is computed from Panel B of Table 3.1 by subtracting the share of income going to the bottom 90 percent – 67.4 percent – from 100 percent.) The third is the share of the top 5 percent, which in 2005 was 22.2 percent, and the fourth is the share received by the top 1 percent, which was 8.7 percent.

Though these summary measures are very convenient and easy to compute, they reflect only the upper part of the distribution. Changes in the bottom part of the distribution – say, a redistribution of income from the middle classes to the lower class – would not be captured by these measures. Therefore, most researchers prefer to use summary inequality measures that reflect the full income distribution.

3.3.2 Coefficient of variation

The coefficient of variation, CV, is defined as the ratio of the standard deviation of income, $SD(Y)$, to mean income, $\bar{Y}$

$$CV = SD(Y)/\bar{Y} \tag{3.4}$$

As discussed in Section 3.2, the standard deviation of income is a measure of its dispersion. Why then divide the standard deviation of income by mean income? The reason is that a summary inequality measure should be a relative measure and, in particular, one that allows comparison between income distributions at different times and in different countries. It can be shown statistically that the standard deviation of a distribution moves proportionally with the mean of the distribution. This can be proved formally as follows. Suppose there are two distributions of income, Y and Z, where $Z_i = aY_i$ for every observation i and a is a constant (scalar). Then, from Equation (3.2),

$$Z = \sum_{i=1}^{n} Z_i/n = \sum_{i=1}^{n} aY_i/n = a\sum_{i=1}^{n} Y_i/n = a\bar{Y}$$

Moreover, from Equation (3.3),

$$\begin{aligned} \text{Var}(Z) &= \sum (Z_i - \bar{Z})^2/(n-1) \\ &= \sum (aY_i - a\bar{Y})^2/(n-1) \\ &= a^2 \sum (Y_i - \bar{Y})^2/(n-1) \\ &= a^2 \, \text{Var}(Y) \end{aligned}$$

Therefore,

$$SD(Z) = [\text{Var}(Z)]^{.5} = a\,SD(Y)$$

and

$$CV(Z) = SD(Z)/\bar{Z} = a\,SD(Y)/a\bar{Y} = CV(Y)$$

As a result, price inflation by itself would cause the standard deviation of income to rise over time. Dividing $SD(Y)$ by $\bar{Y}$ *standardizes* the measure of income inequality and makes it invariant to changes in the overall price level. The coefficient of variation is thus a scale-free index and obeys the principle of scale independence.

The coefficient of variation of income for the United States in 2005 is equal to 66,741/63,344 = 1.054. The coefficient of variation of income is typically close to 1. If there is perfect equality in income, then the standard deviation is equal to 0, and the CV also equals 0. At the other extreme, when all the income goes to one person, the CV approaches infinity (that is, increases without limit). One criticism of this measure is that it is unbounded.

Another criticism of this index is that the mean and standard deviation capture only two aspects ("moments") of an income distribution. If income were distributed normally,[6] this information would be sufficient to fully describe such a distribution. Instead, income distributions are generally skewed to the right. This third moment of the distribution – its skewness – is not captured by the CV. Since income is concentrated in the upper tail of the distribution, changes in its thickness and its overall shape affect the inequality of income.

A third criticism is that the CV is more sensitive to changes in the upper tail of the income distribution than the middle or lower tails. This can be seen by noting that the standard deviation is calculated by taking the sum of *squared* deviations from the mean. Consider the case where the sample mean is $20,000. Suppose the income of a person with $100,000 increases by $1,000. Then, the squared deviation increases by $161,000,000. On the other hand, if the income of a person with $8,000 increases by $1,000, the squared deviation rises by only $25,000,000. The same transfer of $1,000 has a much larger effect on the CV when it occurs in the upper tail of the distribution than at the bottom or middle.

This logic also enables us to see that the CV obeys the transfer principle. In the example above, the variance will fall by 186(161 + 25) million from a transfer of $1,000 from an income of

$100,000 to an income of $8,000 (recall that the mean stays unchanged). This will occur whenever the transfer occurs between an income above the mean to one below the mean. Suppose the transfer occurs on the same side of the mean – say, from an income of $18,000 to one of $8,000. Then the variance would change by 5,000,000 – 25,000,000 or by *–20,000,000*.

3.3.3 The Lorenz curve

The Lorenz curve is a graphical technique used to represent the relative size distribution of income (see Figure 3.2). We first draw a square. The horizontal dimension (axis) of the box represents the cumulative percentage of families (ordered from lowest to highest income), and the vertical dimension represents the cumulative percentage of income received by these families. A line connecting the opposite corners of the box between the points (0,0) and (1,1) is referred to as the 45° (degree) line, because in trigonometric terms it is 45° from the horizontal and vertical axes. It represents the Lorenz curve of perfect income equality, since if everyone receives the same income, the cumulative percent of income will exactly equal the cumulative percent of recipients. If there is less than perfect equality in income, the Lorenz curve will fall below the 45° line, because the lowest P percent of the income recipients will necessarily receive less than P percent of the total income.

The Lorenz curve for the U.S. income distribution in 2005 is shown in Figure 3.2. All Lorenz curves start at the (0,0) point (0 percent of the population receives 0 percent of total income) and end at the (1,1) point (100 percent of the population receives 100 percent of income). In between, the 2005 curve passes through the point (0.10,0.010), since, from Table 3.1, the poorest 10 percent of U.S. families received 1.0 percent of total income; the point (0.50,0.185), since the bottom half received 18.5 percent of total income; and the point (0.90,0.674), since the bottom 90 percent obtained 67.4 percent of total income (or, alternatively, the top 10 percent earned 32.6 percent).

Lorenz curves can be used to compare income distributions and assess the relative degree of income inequality. Two hypothetical nonintersecting curves are illustrated in Figure 3.3(a), referring to Country A and Country B. In this case, we can say unambiguously that Country A has less income inequality than Country B. To see why, select any percentile rank in the cumulative distribution of families, say point P, then draw a vertical line and note where it intersects curves A and B – in this case, at points a and b, respectively. As shown, a is greater than b. This means

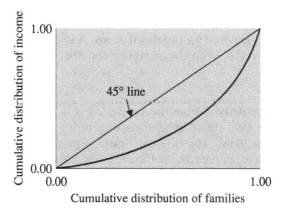

Figure 3.2 Lorenz curve for 2005 household income (based on percentile data from Table 3.1)

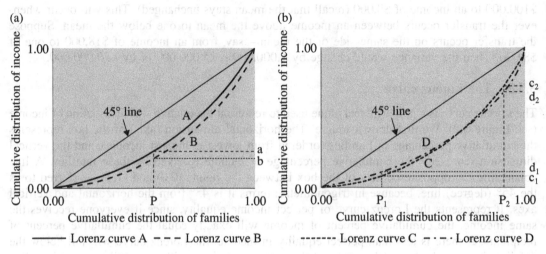

Figure 3.3   Illustrative Lorenz curves. (a) Nonintersecting. (b) Intersecting

that the poorest *P* percent of families have a *greater* share of income in Country A than in Country B. Since the two curves do not intersect, this is true of every point P. This implies that at *every* percentile level, income is less concentrated in Country A than in Country B, and, hence, Country B has greater income inequality than Country A.

In Figure 3.3(b) the two Lorenz curves cross. The comparative degree of income inequality between the two countries, C and D, is ambiguous in this case. Consider two points on the horizontal axis, P_1 and P_2, and their corresponding points on the Lorenz curves for countries C and D. At point P_1, d_1 is greater that c_1, which means that the poorest P_1 percent of families has a greater share of income in Country D than in Country C. However, at point P_2, c_2 is greater than d_2, which implies that the poorest P_2 percent has a greater share of income in Country C than in Country D. In Country C the upper income class has a smaller share of total income than in Country D, but the lower income class also has a smaller share. In this case, there is no direct way of assessing the relative degree of inequality between the two countries based on a comparison of Lorenz curves alone.[7]

In the case of nonintersecting Lorenz curves, a graphical representation can give a convenient and unambiguous way of ranking income inequality between two countries or at two points in time. However, graphs by themselves do not allow us to say, quantitatively, how much or little difference there is in equality between the two distributions. A summary measure of income inequality is desirable in order to make comparisons among countries or over time.

3.3.4   Gini coefficient

One very common measure derived from the Lorenz curve is the Gini coefficient, which was devised by Corrado Gini in 1912 (the English translation of his original work, which was written in Italian, was published in 1936). The Gini coefficient is proportional to the *area* between the 45° line and the Lorenz curve. In the case of Figure 3.3(a), Country A would have a larger Gini coefficient than Country B, reflecting its higher degree of inequality. A Lorenz curve further from the 45° line will always have a larger Gini coefficient, as it should. In the case of intersecting Lorenz curves, as in Figure 3.3(b), the Gini coefficient will in general provide a measure which will rank one of the two countries as having greater inequality. However, although the Gini coefficient will provide an unambiguous ranking, there is some disagreement among economists about whether it is a meaningful measure in such a situation.[8]

The computation of the Gini coefficient from the 2005 U.S. family income distribution data is illustrated in Figure 3.4. The area A between the 45° line and the Lorenz curve is equal to 0.5 (the area of the lower right triangle, which equals half the area of the square) less the area H underneath the Lorenz curve:

$$A = 0.5 - H$$

The area H can be approximated by dividing it into trapezoids. One such trapezoid H_i is illustrated in Figure 3.4. The base of trapezoid H_i is equal to the difference between P_i, the cumulative percentage of income recipients up through income class i, and P_{i-1}, and thus to the percent of recipients in income class i, or f_i (f stands for percent frequency). The shorter length of the trapezoid is equal to z_{i-1}, the cumulative percentage of income up through income class $i - 1$, and the longer length is equal to z_i. From elementary geometry, the area of a trapezoid is equal to its base multiplied by half the sum of its lengths:

$$H_i = f_i(z_{i-1} + z_i)/2$$

The area under the Lorenz curve is then given by:

$$H = \sum_{i=1}^{t} H_i = \sum_{i=1}^{t} f_i(z_{i-1} + z_i)/2$$

for t income classes, where z_0 is defined as equal to 0. The area A is then given by:

$$A = [(1 - \sum_{i=1}^{t} f_i(z_{i-1} + z_i)]/2$$

The Gini coefficient G is then derived by selecting a constant by which to multiply A so that G ranges from 0 to 1. To select the constant, note that complete equality is given by the 45° line, and in this case A would equal 0 (since H would equal 0.5). The other extreme – total inequality of income – would occur if one person received all the total income of a country. Then the Lorenz "curve" would be described by the lower horizontal axis and the right vertical axis of the square. In this case, H would equal 0 and A would equal 0.5. To standardize G, we thus use a factor of 2:

$$G = 2A$$

and, therefore,

$$G = 1 - \sum_{i=1}^{t} f_i(z_{i-1} + z_i) \tag{3.5}$$

Perfect equality would thus yield a value of 0 for G, and complete inequality a value of 1. In the case of the 2005 U.S. family income distribution shown in Table 3.1, the Gini coefficient is equal to 0.469.[9]

One important characteristic of the Gini coefficient is that it is more sensitive to changes in the middle of the distribution than at either extreme. This is apparent by noting that from Equation

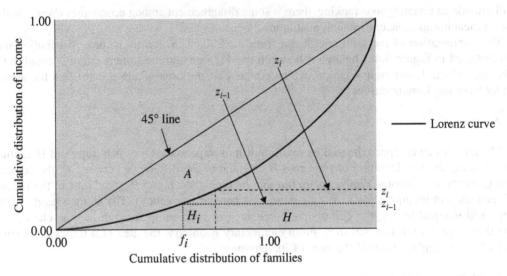

Figure 3.4 Computation of the Gini coefficient based on the U.S. 2005 household income distribution

(3.5) the cumulative share of income is, in effect, weighted by the percent of people in each income class. Since most people are in the middle-income classes and very few at either end, changes in the middle portion of a given dollar amount have a greater impact in the computation of G than at the two extremes.

The Gini coefficient also satisfies the two basic principle of inequality measures discussed above. First, it is scale independent. This can be seen by the fact that multiplying every family's income by the same constant c will leave z_i unchanged, since total income in income class i and overall total income will both increase by factor c. Second, the Gini coefficient satisfies the transfer principle. This can be seen by noting that a transfer of income from a richer person to a poorer person will cause the Lorenz curve to shift inward. Thus, both the area A and G will decline.

3.3.5 Log variance of income*

The so-called "log variance of income" is actually the variance of the logarithm of income. We noted above that while the variance of income is a good measure of dispersion, it is not a good measure of relative income inequality since it, as well as the standard deviation of income, tends to increase with mean income. The coefficient of variation corrects for this by dividing the standard deviation of income by the mean. There is an alternative way of correcting for this property, which is to use the logarithm of income instead of actual income. The variance of the logarithm of income can be shown to be scale-free (that is, independent of proportional changes in income), as follows. Let $Z_i = aY_i$ for each person i, where a is a constant and Y_i is income. Then:

$$\ln(Z_i) = \ln(a) + \ln(Y_i)$$
$$= a' + \ln(Y_i)$$

where "ln" stands for the natural logarithm and a' is a constant. Therefore:

$$\mathrm{Var}(\ln(Z)) = \mathrm{Var}(\ln(Y) + a') = \mathrm{Var}(\ln(Y)) \tag{3.6}$$

since the variance of the sum of a random variable and a constant is equal to the variance of the random variable. Thus, like the coefficient of variation, the log variance is an index of *relative* income dispersion. The log variance of income for the United States in 1989 was 1.624.

There is another justification for using the log variance measure. The common shape of an income distribution conforms somewhat closely to the log-normal distribution. A random variable has a log-normal distribution when the logarithm of the variable is normally distributed. A log-normal distribution can be fully characterized by its mean and its variance. If income has a log-normal distribution, its relative dispersion is fully captured by the log variance measure.

There are four criticisms of this index. First, if income does not conform closely to a log-normal distribution, then its skewness and the concentration of income in the upper tail is not adequately reflected in this measure. Second, its range of values, like that of the coefficient of variation, is unbounded.

Third, this measure violates the principle of transfers. In particular, if the same dollar amount is transferred from a very rich person to a rich person (both of whom with incomes significantly above mean income), the log variance will generally increase instead of declining. The reason is that changes in the logarithm of income depend on percentage changes in income, rather than changes in absolute dollar amounts.[10] A $1,000 change in income represents a larger percentage change for a rich person than for a very rich person. As a result, the decrease in the log variance from the loss of income to the richer of the two persons is actually less in absolute value than the increase in the log variance from the gain of income to the less rich individual.

A fourth and related criticism is that the log variance measure is more sensitive to changes of income in the lower part of the income distribution than the upper part. The reason is similar. A decrease of $1,000 in income of a low-income person will produce a larger increase in the log variance than a $1,000 increase in the income of a high-income person.

3.3.6 The Theil entropy index*

The Theil entropy index of inequality is given by the following formula:

$$T = (1/n) \sum_{i=1}^{n} (Y_i/\bar{Y}) \ln(Y_i/\bar{Y}) \tag{3.7}$$

where n is the size of the population, Y_i is the income of individual i, and $\bar{Y}$ is the mean income of the population. The rationale for this index stems from information theory. The underlying idea is that more surprising events have more information value. If an event is completely predictable, it has no information value; when it is less predictable, it has information content. When income is equally distributed or nearly so, income for any individual is predictable. When income is unequally distributed, however, it is less easy to predict the income of a randomly chosen individual, and a message which indicates what that individual's income is has information content.

The formal derivation is as follows. Suppose that there are n mutually exclusive events which may occur with probability π_i, $i = 1, \ldots, n$, with $0 < \pi_i < 1$ and $\sum \pi_i = 1$. According to information theory, if a particular event is very rare, then the information value of a message saying it has occurred is valuable, while the information value of very common events is rated low. If $h(\pi_i)$ is a function that assigns an information value to the event, it will be decreasing in π_i. Another provision of this theory is that the information content of knowing that two statistically independent events i and j have taken place should be the sum of the values of the separate messages. Since the probability of i and j both occurring is $\pi_i \cdot \pi_j$, then it follows that the function h must have the property that

$$h(\pi_i \cdot \pi_j) = h(\pi_i) + h(\pi_j)$$

A function which has this property and which is decreasing in π is:

$$h(\pi_i) = -\ln(\pi_i)$$

The expected information content ("entropy" or "disorder") of the whole system is given by the sum of $h(\pi_i)$ weighted by the respective probabilities:

$$S = \sum_{i=1}^{n} \pi_i h(\pi_i) = -\sum_{i=1}^{n} \pi_i \ln(\pi_i)$$

The maximum possible value of this function S is $\sum_i (1/n)h(1/n)$, which occurs when all events are equally likely. This can be proved by setting the first derivative of function S to zero and solving for $\pi_1 = \pi_2 = \ldots = \pi_n$ subject to the condition that $\lambda(\sum \pi_i - 1) = 0$ where λ is the Lagrange multiplier. The greater "disorder" – that is, differing probabilities – which occurs, the more the value of S falls below the maximum. A function which expresses this relation is the entropy index E given by:

$$E = \sum_{i=1}^{n} [(1/n)h(1/n) - \pi_i h(\pi_i)] = \sum_{i=1}^{n} \pi_i \ln(\pi_i) - \ln(1/n)$$

The function E will be higher the more disorder exists in the system.

The analogy between "disorder" and income inequality provides the rationale for using index E as the basis of an inequality index. In fact, the Theil function T is exactly equivalent to E if income shares $s_i = Y_i/(n\bar{Y})$, $i = 1, \ldots, n$, are substituted for the probabilities. The proof is that

$$E = \sum_{i=1}^{n} (Y_i/n\bar{Y}) \cdot \ln(Y_i/n\bar{Y}) - \ln(1/n) = (1/n) \sum_{i=1}^{n} (Y_i/\bar{Y}) \cdot [\ln(Y_i/\bar{Y}) + \ln(n) - \ln(n)]$$

because $\sum Y_i/\bar{Y} = n$.

The Theil index is the only index which satisfies the following three desirable characteristics of an inequality measure: (i) scale-free; (ii) the principle of transfers; and (iii) decomposability into between-group inequality and within-group inequality. The first property is apparent from the fact that a proportional increase in income will leave the ratio $Y_i/\bar{Y}$ unchanged.[11]

The third property can be shown as follows:

$$T = \sum_g s_g T_g + (1/n) \sum_g n_g(\bar{Y}_g/n\bar{Y}) \ln(\bar{Y}_g/\bar{Y}) \tag{3.8}$$

where g is the number of groups, n_g is the number of individuals in group g, $\bar{Y}_g$ is the mean income for group g, and $s_g = (n_g\bar{Y}_g/n\bar{Y})$ is the income share of group g. The first term of Equation (3.8) is a weighted sum of the Theil indices of each group (that is, a weighted sum of *within-group* inequality), where the weight for each group g is group g's share of total income. The second terms represents the *between-group* inequality, which is calculated by the Theil formula, as if each group were treated as an individual.[12]

The Theil index for the United States in 2005 is 0.393. There are two criticisms of the Theil index. First, in contrast to the Gini coefficient and the coefficient of variation, the Theil formula has no intuitive interpretation with regard to inequality. Second, like the Gini coefficient, the

Theil index is more sensitive to changes in the middle of the income distribution than in the lower or upper tails. The reason is that, like the Gini coefficient, the center of the distribution has a much larger weight in the calculation of the Theil index because of its large concentration of income recipients.

3.3.7 Atkinson's measure*

Atkinson (1970) developed a family of inequality indices in order to explicitly introduce value judgments into the measurement of inequality. His index is given as follows:

$$A = 1 - [(1/n) \sum_{i=1}^{n} (Y_i/\bar{Y})^{(1-\varepsilon)}]^{[1/(1-\varepsilon)]} \tag{3.9}$$

Atkinson notes that inequality measures implicitly involve value judgments, and argues that these value judgments should be made explicit in choosing an inequality measure. Such a judgment should take the form of introducing a specific social welfare function, and, in particular, specifying society's degree of inequality aversion. In his formulation, this amounts to the price that society is willing to pay in order to decrease income inequality.

Atkinson argues that if we are considering taking one dollar from a rich person and giving a certain proportion x to a poor person (the remainder being lost in the process), society ought to ask: "At what level of x do we cease to regard the redistribution as desirable?" If all the income transferred from the rich person actually gets to the poor individual (that is, $x = 1$), then any society which is in the least concerned about inequality will consider this redistribution as socially desirable. If only a small fraction of the dollar is actually received by the poor individual, then only a society which is particularly concerned about inequality will consider the transfer as socially desirable. The value of x is chosen so that society is indifferent between the actual degree of its inequality and a distribution in which everyone receives the same level of income but average income is only x percent of the actual average income.

Atkinson's measure of inequality requires a specification of ε, the degree of inequality aversion, where $x = 1/2^{\varepsilon}$. The choice of a high value of ε (a low value of x) implies a high degree of inequality aversion and, in particular, a concern for the share of the bottom portion of the income distribution. In contrast, the choice of a relatively low value of ε implies that society has a low degree of inequality aversion and is particularly concerned with changes in the upper portion of the income distribution. The value of the Atkinson index for the United States in 2005 is 0.188 for an ε value of 0.5; 0.300 for an ε value of 0.8; and 0.640 for an ε value of 1.5.[13]

The major advantage of this measure is that it overcomes the ambiguity in relative inequality when Lorenz curves cross. The reason is that our choice of ε determines whether we are more concerned with inequality at the top of the distribution or inequality at the bottom. Thus, the Atkinson index gives an *unambiguous* ranking in inequality between countries or at different points in time, even when Lorenz curves cross (see Section 3.3.3 above).

This measure has been criticized on two grounds. First, it is very difficult to determine society's value of ε (its degree of inequality aversion). Thus, typically, a researcher will use different values of ε in computing the Atkinson index (as we did for the United States in 2005). The value of the Atkinson index is very sensitive to the value of ε, as we have just seen. Moreover, different values of ε will often produce different trends in the Atkinson index, as well as different rank orders among countries.

Second, there is a certain internal inconsistency in the Atkinson index. The formula for the index implies that total social utility is the sum of individual utility levels (that is, the index is additively separable), and that individual utility depends *only* on individual incomes. But if individual utility depends only on individual income, why would society be concerned with the *relative* distribution of income and why would it have any aversion to income inequality in general?

3.3.8   Lorenz dominance*

Although the measures discussed above generally fulfill scale independence and the transfer principle (with the exception of the log variance), it is still possible that they will rank two distributions in different ways because of their differing sensitivity to incomes in different parts of the distributions. When rankings are ambiguous, the alternative method of stochastic dominance can be used. Two concepts of stochastic dominance are presented below. **First-order stochastic dominance** is sensitive to the mean value of a distribution and therefore cannot be used to rank inequality, though it is useful in comparisons of social welfare. It is presented first because it is logically prior to **Lorenz dominance**, which gives unambiguous comparisons of inequality across distributions.

First-order stochastic dominance is defined as follows: Consider two income distributions y_1 and y_2 with cumulative distribution functions (CDFs) $F(y_1)$ and $F(y_2)$. If $F(y_1)$ lies nowhere above and at least somewhere below $F(y_2)$ then distribution y_1 displays first-order stochastic dominance over distribution y_2: $F(y_1) \leq F(y_2)$ for all y. Hence in distribution y_1 there are no more individuals with income less than a given income level than in distribution y_2 for all levels of income. Alternatively, we can use the inverse function $y = F^{-1}(p)$ where p is the share of the population with income less than a given income level. First-order dominance is attained if $F_1^{-1}(p) \geq F_2^{-1}(p)$ for all p. In other words, the share of the population with incomes less than a given level in the first distribution is greater than or equal to that in the second at all income levels.

In order to rank distributions in terms of inequality alone (rather than welfare), a second concept known as Lorenz dominance is applied. If the Lorenz curve, the plot of cumulative income shares against cumulative population shares, of distribution y_1 lies nowhere below and at least somewhere above the Lorenz curve of distribution y_2 then y_1 Lorenz dominates y_2. Any inequality measure that satisfies the Pigou–Dalton transfer principle will rank the two distributions in the same way as the Lorenz curves.

3.4   TIME TRENDS IN INCOME INEQUALITY IN THE UNITED STATES

One important social issue that has occupied both policy makers and the public at large is whether inequality in the United States has been declining or rising over time, and how U.S. inequality compares to that of other countries. There are good reasons for believing that greater economic equality is a social good (see Section 16.1 for a discussion). Therefore, any movement towards increasing income equality might be viewed as a beneficial development for U.S. society.

The earliest inequality statistics based on official government data date back to 1913, the first year federal income taxes were paid in the United States. Table 3.2 shows the share of total income received by the top 1, 5, and 10 percent of tax units (filers) in the United States for selected years between 1913 and 1948. These results are based on Internal Revenue Service (IRS) tax return data. The unit of observation is the tax return unit. In these years, most families and unrelated individuals filed a single tax return, so that the tax return unit tends to correspond to the family unit (this is the most common unit used in income distribution analysis).

Between 1913 and 1948, there was a clear trend towards greater equality in the distribution of income. Except for 1929, all three concentration measures fell almost continuously over time

Table 3.2 The percentage share of total income received by the top percentiles of tax units, 1913–1948

Year	Top 1 percent	Top 5 percent	Top 10 percent
1913	15	—	—
1920	12.3	22.1	30.6
1929	14.5	26.1	—
1933	12.1	24.7	—
1940	11.9	22.7	32.1
1945	8.8	17.4	23.7
1948	8.4	17.6	24.8

Source: Kuznets, S. (1953). *Shares of Upper Income Groups in Income and Savings.* New York: National Bureau of Economic Research. The statistics are based on IRS tax data.

Table 3.3 Quintile shares of family personal income, 1935–1950

Year	Quintile					Total
	Bottom	Second	Third	Fourth	Top	
1935	4.1	9.2	14.1	20.9	51.7	100.0
1941	4.1	9.5	15.3	22.3	48.8	100.0
1944	4.9	10.9	16.2	22.2	45.8	100.0
1946	5.0	11.1	16.0	21.8	46.1	100.0
1947	5.0	11.0	16.0	22.0	46.0	100.0
1950	4.8	11.0	16.2	22.3	45.7	100.0

Source: Goldsmith, S., Jaszi, G., Kurtz, H. & Liebenberg, M. (1954). Size distribution of income since the mid-thirties. *Review of Economics and Statistics*, **36**(1).

for the indicated years. The share of income received by the top 1 percent fell almost by half, from 15 percent of all income in 1913 to 8 percent in 1948. The share of total income received by the top 5 percent declined from 26 percent in 1929 to 18 percent in 1948, and the share of the top 10 percent from 32 percent in 1940 to 25 percent in 1948. The share of income received by the top income groups fell considerably between 1913 and 1948. Even so, the income distribution was still far from perfect equality in 1948, with the top 1 percent having one-twelfth of all income; the top 5 percent with one-sixth; and the top 10 percent with one-quarter.

Table 3.3 presents a more complete picture of the change in the size distribution of income between 1935 and 1950. In this case, the income distribution is broken down by quintile shares. The share of total income received by the top quintile declined from 52 percent to 46 percent of total income between 1935 and 1950. This is consistent with the results of the previous table, which show a decline in the concentration of income in the top group. Analyzing the other quintile shares will enable us to see which groups gained at the expense of the top quintile. The fourth quintile's share of total income increased from 20.9 percent to 22.3 percent, for a net gain of 1.4 percentage points, while the third quintile gained 2.1 percentage points and the second quintile 1.8 percentage points. The bottom quintile's share of total income rose by only 0.7 percentage points, from 4.1 percent to 4.8 percent of total income.

Between 1935 and 1950, there was a movement toward greater equality in income distribution. However, the redistribution occurred mainly between the top group and the middle-income

Table 3.4   The percentage share of total income by income type received by the top percentile, 1917–1948

Year	Employee compensation	Self-employment income	Dividends	Interest	Rent	Property income[a]
1917	6.6	9.2	72.4	44.6	14.9	49.9
1920	5.8	13.8	72.4	32.6	14.9	42.2
1925	6.2	15.6	67.9	28.7	17.2	41.0
1929	6.2	16.2	66.0	31.1	17.2	44.5
1933	7.3	11.9	55.9	20.6	16.0	31.5
1940	6.4	14.8	63.2	23.7	13.0	37.7
1943	3.8	23.4	52.3	22.7	9.8	29.7
1945	3.4	23.0	—	—	9.1	28.0
1948	3.8	15.2	53.6	15.8	12.8	31.1

a   Total property income is defined as the sum of dividends, interest, and rent.
Source: Kuznets, S. (1953). *Shares of Upper Income Groups in Income and Savings*. New York: National Bureau of Economic Research. The statistics are based on IRS tax data.

classes (quintiles two through four). The relative position of the lower income classes changed very little during this period. This has very important implications concerning the elimination of poverty, as we shall see in the next chapter.

Table 3.4 shows a somewhat more detailed picture of the decline in inequality during the interwar period in the United States. In this table, the income received by the top 1 percent of tax return units is decomposed by type of income and compared to the total income from that source. Table 3.2 shows that the share of total income received by the top percentile declined from 15 percent to 8 percent between 1913 and 1948. Here, we can see that this decline characterized all income types, except self-employment (entrepreneurial and small business) income. Employee compensation, dividends, interest, rent, and total property income received by the top percentile all declined as a share of the total income of that type.

Another interesting aspect of this table is the *relative* sizes of the income shares by type of income. Note, first of all, that the top 1 percent received only a relatively small share of total wages and salaries (that is, employee compensation). This is not the major source of their income. Second, the top 1 percent received over half of total dividends over this period, and in 1917 and 1920 it was almost three-quarters of all dividends. Third, the top percentile received about 15 percent of all self-employment and rental income over this period, though the share tended to fluctuate considerably from year to year. Fourth, their share of interest income showed the most substantial decline over this period, falling from 45 percent of total interest to 16 percent. Fifth, in 1917 this group received half of all property income (that is, dividends from stock shares; interest from savings accounts and securities; and rent from rental property). By 1948, this ratio had fallen to about a third which, though lower than its 1917 level, was still quite substantial. Thus, the falling share of the top groups in total income between the two world wars was due largely to the widening ownership of income-producing property (see Chapter 5 for more discussion of wealth trends).

Figure 3.5 carries the story from the beginning of the postwar period through 2005. The Gini coefficient is used here as the measure of income inequality, and the unit of observation is the family. In the period between 1947 and 1968, there was a modest downward trend in income inequality, with the Gini coefficient falling from 0.376 to 0.348. The share of total income received

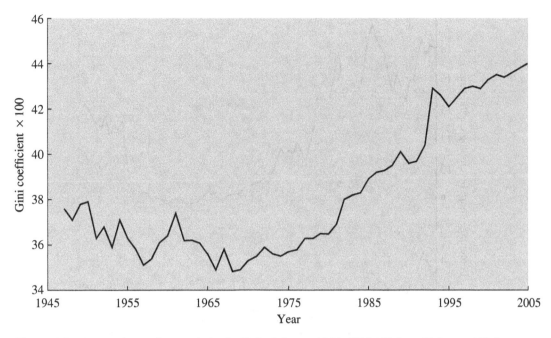

Figure 3.5 Income inequality trends in the United States, 1947–2005 (Gini coefficient × 100 for family income)

by the top 5 percent also declined from 17.5 percent to 15.6 percent. However, the trend was not uniform over these years, and, indeed, the Gini coefficient fluctuated back and forth between about 0.35 and 0.38. From 1968 (when the Gini coefficient reached its lowest value of 0.348) to 2005, there was a clear upward trend in inequality. The Gini coefficient rose almost continuously over these years, and by 2005 reached a value of 0.440, considerably greater than its value at the end of World War II. Most of the increase occurred after 1975, when its value was 0.357.[14]

The share of the top 5 percent also increased sharply between 1968 and 2005, from 15.6 percent to 21.1 percent. Though it appears that the large increase in income inequality was driven exclusively by the top end of the distribution getting much richer, Burkhauser *et al.* (1999, 2007a) argued that that the increases in inequality over the 1990s were also driven by the middle of the income distribution getting richer – not just increases among the "super rich."

More details on the top end of the distribution are given in Figure 3.6 on the basis of the work of Saez and Piketty (2003). These are based on IRS tax return data and tend to closely follow the methodology developed by Kuznets (1953). The advantage of using IRS tax data is that they provide a very large sample and give details on income values in excess of $1,000,000. (The CPS data, on the other hand, have been most recently top-coded at $100,000 – that is, incomes above $100,000 are simply listed as "$100,000 or more.") The series extends from 1913 to 1998.

The recent increase in the share of the top end now appears very dramatic. After falling from a high of 19.6 percent in 1928, the share of the top 1 percent dwindled to a low point of 7.7 percent in 1973. In 1987 the share was up to 10.7 percent and it then skyrocketed to 14.6 percent in 1998. The IRS data have a big enough sample size to permit an estimate of the share of the top 0.01 percent (that is, one-hundredth of 1 percent). It shows a very similar trend. After falling from a peak of 3.23 percent in 1928 to 0.50 percent in 1973, it increased more than *five-fold* to reach 2.57 percent in 1998.

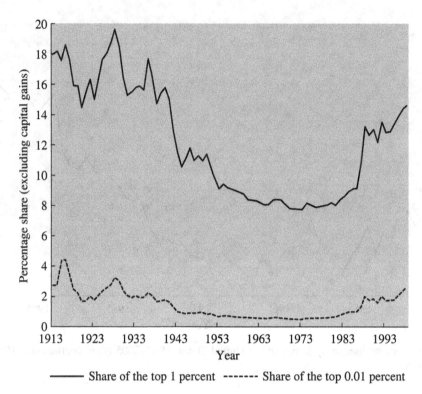

Figure 3.6   The income share of the top 1 percent in the United States, based on income tax data, 1913–1998
Source: Saez, E. & Piketty, T. (2003). Income inequality in the United States, 1913–1998. *Quarterly Journal of Economics*, **118**, 1–39, Table A1.

3.5   INTERNATIONAL COMPARISONS OF INEQUALITY

3.5.1   Inequality comparisons among high-income countries

We now consider U.S. income inequality in the light of the experiences of other countries. Such an analysis provides some perspective on whether inequality in the United States is high or low, since inequality measures *per se* provide very little guidance. We shall consider various indices of U.S. income inequality in comparison with those of other countries at similar levels of development, and also with those countries at lower levels of development.

Table 3.5 provides some comparative data on 12 highly developed economies. These results are taken from one of the earliest comparative income studies (Sawyer, 1976). In this study, no attempt was made to make the income concepts in the various countries comparable, so that these results have to be interpreted with some caution.

Raw data on income distribution in the 12 nations were first converted into decile shares, and Gini coefficients were computed from the decile shares. Two different computations were performed. The first was on income before income taxes were paid, and the second on income after income taxes were paid. Let us look at the pre-tax levels of inequality first. The three countries with the greatest amount of pre-tax inequality were France, the United States, and West Germany, in that order. All had Gini coefficients considerably above the average level for these

Table 3.5 Income inequality in selected industrialized countries, around 1970 (Gini coefficient)

Country	Year	Pre-tax income	Post-tax income
1. Australia	1966–7	0.313	0.312
2. Canada	1969	0.382	0.354
3. France	1970	0.416	0.414
4. West Germany	1973	0.396	0.383
5. Italy	1969	—	0.398
6. Japan	1969	0.335	0.316
7. Netherlands	1967	0.385	0.354
8. Norway	1970	0.354	0.307
9. Spain	1973–4	—	0.355
10. Sweden	1972	0.346	0.302
11. United Kingdom	1973	0.344	0.318
12. United States	1972	0.404	0.381
Average	—	0.366	0.350

Source: Sawyer, M. (1976). Income distribution in OECD countries. *OECD Economic Outlook: Occasional Studies*, July, Tables 5 and 6.

12 countries. Also high were the Netherlands and Canada. Considerably below this group was Norway, followed by Sweden, the United Kingdom, Japan, and Australia, which had the lowest level of pre-tax inequality.

The post-tax levels of income inequality were all lower than the respective pre-tax levels. This is as should be expected, since most income tax systems are **progressive**, which means that people with higher income pay a higher *proportion* of their income in the form of taxes. This implies that the share of after-tax income received by the top income group is smaller than its share of before-tax income, and conversely for the lower income groups. As a result, the after-tax Gini coefficient is lower than the before-tax Gini coefficient for each of the countries.[15]

However, as is evident from Table 3.5, the degree of progressivity of the tax system varies considerably across countries. France had the highest post-tax level of income inequality, and, in fact, the tax system had very little effect on income inequality in France. Italy had the second highest level of after-tax inequality, followed by West Germany and the United States. In the case of West Germany and the United States, the tax system had a moderate impact on reducing overall income inequality. Spain, the Netherlands, and Canada all ranked in the middle. For the Netherlands and Canada, the tax system made a fairly substantial contribution to reducing income inequality. The United Kingdom, Japan, Australia, Norway, and Sweden had the lowest levels of after-tax income inequality. For the two most equal countries, Norway and Sweden, the tax system had the biggest effect on reducing the level of income inequality among the 12 countries.

Tables 3.6 and 3.7 show the results of two studies which rely on the Luxembourg Income Study (LIS) database. This originally consisted of surveys which were conducted in the late 1970s and early 1980s in 10 industrialized countries. In the case of the LIS data, considerable effort has been made to make the income concepts and the unit of observation consistent among the various country samples.

The results of Table 3.6, interestingly, are fairly consistent with the earlier Sawyer study. The table shows the quintile shares for seven countries based on a 1989 study by O'Higgins, Schmaus, and Stephenson. They are computed for both gross (before-tax) income and net (after

Table 3.6 The distribution of income among advanced countries about 1980 (based on the LIS data)

Income concept	Percentage share of income by quintile					Gini coefficient
	Lowest	Second	Third	Fourth	Top	
A. Distribution of family gross income among quintiles of families						
Canada	4.6	11.0	17.7	25.3	41.4	0.374
U.S.A.	3.8	9.8	16.6	25.3	44.5	0.412
U.K.	4.9	10.9	18.2	25.3	40.8	0.365
Germany[a]	4.4	10.2	15.9	22.6	46.9	0.414
Sweden	6.6	12.3	17.2	25.0	38.9	0.329
Norway	4.9	11.4	18.4	25.5	39.8	0.356
Israel	4.5	10.5	16.5	24.9	43.6	0.395
B. Distribution of family net income among quintiles of families						
Canada	5.3	11.8	18.1	24.6	39.7	0.348
U.S.A.	4.5	11.2	17.7	25.6	41.0	0.370
U.K.	5.8	11.5	18.2	25.0	39.5	0.343
Germany[a]	5.0	11.5	15.9	21.8	45.8	0.389
Sweden	8.0	13.2	17.4	24.5	36.9	0.292
Norway	6.3	12.8	18.9	25.3	36.7	0.311
Israel	6.0	12.1	17.9	24.5	39.5	0.338
C. Distribution of family equivalent gross income among quintiles of persons						
Canada	6.7	12.6	17.5	24.0	39.2	0.327
U.S.A.	5.1	11.4	17.1	24.2	42.1	0.371
U.K.	7.9	13.0	17.9	23.7	37.5	0.297
Germany[a]	7.2	12.1	16.0	21.3	43.4	0.352
Sweden	9.4	14.6	18.5	23.3	34.3	0.249
Norway	8.1	13.6	17.9	23.4	37.0	0.289
Israel	6.1	10.3	15.9	23.7	44.0	0.382
D. Distribution of family equivalent net income among quintiles of persons						
Canada	7.6	13.3	17.9	23.8	37.4	0.299
U.S.A.	6.1	12.8	18.1	24.4	38.6	0.326
U.K.	9.0	13.5	18.0	23.4	36.1	0.273
Germany[a]	7.5	12.7	16.1	20.7	43.0	0.340
Sweden	10.6	16.1	19.1	23.1	31.1	0.205
Norway	9.9	14.8	18.4	22.9	34.1	0.243
Israel	7.5	11.7	16.8	23.7	40.3	0.333

Panels A and B weight each family unit equally, while Panels C and D weight each individual equally. Income units are ranked by family gross income in Panel A, by family net income in Panel B, by gross equivalent income in Panel C, and by net equivalent income in Panel D.

a   The German data are affected by a relatively large number of zero and negative incomes in the sample. A revised Gini coefficient is used which excludes income units with such incomes.

Source: O'Higgins, M., Schmaus, G. & Stephenson, G. (1989). Income distribution and redistribution: A microdata analysis for seven countries. *Review of Income and Wealth*, ser. 35, no. 2, 107–32, Table 2.

payroll and income tax) income. In Panels A and B, each family unit is weighted equally, while Panels C and D weight each family by the number of individuals living in the family unit. Income units are ranked by family gross income in Panel A, by family net income in Panel B, by gross equivalent income in Panel C, and by net equivalent income in Panel D, where equivalent income adjusts family income for differences in family size.[16]

Table 3.7 The inequality of income among advanced countries about 1980 (based on the LIS and using alternative measures)

Country	Gini coefficient	Coefficient of variation	Theil index	Atkinson index ($\varepsilon = .8$)	($\varepsilon = .5$)
United States	.330 (1)	.600 (2)	.182 (1)	.186 (1)	.099 (1)
Australia	.314 (2)	.584 (4)	.165 (2)	.151 (2)	.087 (2)
Netherlands	.302 (5)	.596 (3)	.159 (3)	.151 (2)	.083 (3)
Canada	.306 (3)	.569 (6)	.157 (4)	.144 (4)	.083 (3)
Switzerland	.292 (6)	.603 (1)	.154 (5)	.143 (5)	.079 (5)
United Kingdom	.303 (4)	.574 (5)	.153 (6)	.128 (6)	.078 (6)
Israel	.292 (6)	.564 (7)	.142 (7)	.114 (7)	.071 (7)
Germany	.280 (8)	.556 (8)	.134 (8)	.106 (8)	.066 (8)
Norway	.255 (10)	.484 (9)	.114 (9)	.105 (9)	.060 (9)
Sweden	.264 (9)	.474 (10)	.114 (9)	.104 (10)	.060 (9)

Countries are ranked from highest (U.S.A.) to lowest (Sweden) in terms of median disposable income. The rank order for each measure is shown in parentheses.
Source: Buhmann, B., Rainwater, L., Schmaus, G. & Smeeding, T.M. (1988). Equivalence scales, well-being, inequality, and poverty: Sensitivity estimates across ten countries using the Luxembourg Income Study (LIS) database. *Review of Income and Wealth*, ser. 34, no. 2, 115–42, Table 5.

By all four income concepts, the United States and Germany rank highest in terms of income inequality. Canada, the United Kingdom, Norway, and Israel form the middle group. Sweden is distinctly lower than any of the other countries in terms of family or individual income inequality. It is also of interest how the inequality levels differ among the four concepts. The difference between Panels A and B reflect the effects of the tax system (income and payroll taxes) on the size distribution of income. All seven countries show a reduction in inequality after taxes are netted out. The largest reduction in percentage terms is for Israel and the second largest is for Norway. The difference between Panels A and C (also between Panels B and D) reflects the adjustment of family income for family size. In so far as smaller families have lower income, this adjustment should make for greater equality. Indeed, this is the case for all countries with the exception of Israel, with Sweden showing the greatest reduction in percentage terms.

Table 3.7 shows five overall inequality measures for 10 advanced countries on the basis of a 1988 study by Buhmann, Rainwater, Schmaus, and Smeeding. The interesting aspect of this table is how inequality rankings vary by the measure used. It is a good illustration of the sensitivity of inequality to measure used. By four of the five indices, the United States ranked highest in terms of income inequality, and second according to the fifth index (the coefficient of variation). Indeed, according to the first four of these indices, there was a considerable gap in inequality between the United States and the second-ranked country. Australia, the Netherlands, Canada, Switzerland, the United Kingdom, Israel, and Germany comprised a middle group, with a fairly narrow range of inequality among them. Norway and Sweden were distinctly more equal than the other eight countries. However, for some countries (besides the United States), the rankings are quite sensitive to the index used. Canada ranked third most unequal according to the Gini coefficient but sixth according to the coefficient of variation (which is particularly sensitive to the share of the top incomes). Switzerland, on the other hand, ranked first according to the coefficient of variation but only sixth by the Gini coefficient. The Netherlands was second-most unequal by the Atkinson measure ($\varepsilon = .8$) but fifth by the Gini coefficient.

Results compiled by Atkinson, Rainwater, and Smeeding (1995) on the basis of more recent LIS data are shown for 11 advanced countries in Table 3.8. These later computations also have

Table 3.8   The ratio of the 90th to the 10th percentile of income (based on the LIS data, 1979–1987)

Country	Year	Ratio of percentile to median income (%)		Ratio of P90 to P10
		P10	P90	
Australia	1981	46.0	186.3	4.05
	1985	46.5	186.5	4.01
Belgium	1985	59.3	162.5	2.74
	1988	58.5	163.2	2.79
Canada	1981	44.9	182.7	4.07
	1987	45.8	184.2	4.02
Finland	1987	58.9	152.7	2.59
	1990	57.0	156.2	2.74
France	1979	53.6	186.5	3.48
	1984	55.4	192.8	3.48
The Netherlands	1979	64.8	176.1	2.72
	1984	61.5	175.0	2.85
New Zealand	1983/84	53.2	189.6	3.56
	1987/88	53.6	186.6	3.48
Norway	1979	57.0	158.1	2.77
	1986	55.3	162.2	2.93
Sweden	1981	61.5	150.9	2.45
	1987	55.6	151.5	2.72
United Kingdom	1979	50.9	179.7	3.53
	1986	51.1	194.1	3.79
United States	1979	38.1	187.6	4.93
	1986	34.7	206.1	5.94

P10 shows the ratio of the income of the 10th percentile to the median income of that country, and P90 shows the ratio of the income of the 90th percentile to the median income of that country.
Source: Atkinson, A.B., Rainwater, L. & Smeeding, T.M. (1995). *Income Distribution in Advanced Economies: The Evidence from the Luxembourg Income Study (LIS)*. Paris: OECD, Table 5.

the advantage of showing changes over the 1980s in the degree of inequality in the various countries. The calculations use a different indicator of inequality than the ones we have developed so far. The authors first compute the ratio of the income of the 10th percentile to the median income of that country (P10) and then the ratio of the income of the 90th percentile to the median income (P90). A small value for P10 indicates that the poor in the country have a relatively low level of income in comparison to the average family in that country. In 1986, among the 11 countries, the United States had the lowest value for P10, 34.7, meaning that the family ranked in the 10th percentile of the U.S. income distribution earned only 34.7 percent of the U.S. median income. In contrast, in the Netherlands in 1984, the 10th percentile received an income that was 61.5 percent of the median income in the Netherlands.

Conversely, a high value for P90 indicates that the rich in the country are particularly relatively well off in comparison to the average family. In 1986, the United States had the highest value of P90, 206.1, meaning that the 90th percentile received an income 2.061 times the median income of the United States The lowest value of P90 was found for Sweden in 1987, a value of 151.5.

A high value of P90 and a low value of P10 both reflect a high degree of income inequality. A useful summary measure of overall inequality is the ratio of P90 to P10. In the late 1980s,

Table 3.9 The ratio of the 90th to the 10th percentile of income and the Gini coefficient from the LIS data, around 2000

| Country | Year | Ratio of percentile to median income (%) | | Ratio of P90 to P10 | Gini coefficient |
		P10	P90		
Luxembourg	2000	66	215	3.24	0.260
Sweden	2000	57	168	2.96	0.252
Norway	2000	57	159	2.80	0.251
Netherlands	1999	56	167	2.98	0.248
Germany	2000	54	173	3.18	0.252
France	1994	54	191	3.54	0.288
Belgium	2000	53	174	3.31	0.277
Poland	1999	52	188	3.59	0.293
Canada	2000	48	188	3.95	0.302
United Kingdom	1999	47	215	4.18	0.345
Italy	2000	44	199	4.48	0.333
Israel	2001	43	216	5.01	0.346
Ireland	2000	41	189	4.57	0.323
United States	2000	39	210	5.45	0.368
Russia	2000	33	276	8.37	0.434
Mexico	2002	33	309	9.36	0.471

P10 shows the ratio of the income of the 10th percentile to the median income of that country, and P90 shows the ratio of the income of the 90th percentile to the median income of that country.
Source: Smeeding, T.M. (2005). Public policy, economic inequality, and poverty: The United States in comparative perspective. *Social Science Quarterly*, **86**(Supplement), 955–83, Figure 1.

the United States had by far the highest degree of inequality among the 11 countries – a ratio of 5.94 – followed by Canada at 4.02 and Australia at 4.01. The lowest inequality was recorded in Sweden at 2.72, followed by Finland at 2.74 and Belgium at 2.79.

It is also interesting to compare changes in the ratio over time within country. Here, too, the United States had by far the largest increase of inequality, from a ratio of 4.9 in 1979 to 5.9 in 1986. Changes were much smaller for other countries. Moreover, of the 11 countries in the sample, seven showed an increase in inequality, three showed a decline, and one showed no change.

More recent data from the LIS are shown in Table 3.9 (Smeeding, 2005). Both the P90/P10 ratio and the Gini coefficient are used as inequality measures and the data are for the year 2000 or so. This table also includes some middle-income countries like Mexico and Russia. The countries are ranked by their P10 value (highest to lowest). Among the high-income countries, the United States again ranked first in terms of inequality, with a P90/P10 ratio of 5.45 (Israel is second at 5.01) and a Gini coefficient of 0.368[17] (Israel is again second, at 0.346). However, compared to the two middle-income countries in the table, Russia and Mexico, the United States seems to be fairly equal. Russia had a P90/P10 ratio of 8.4 in 2000, Mexico had a ratio of 9.4 in 2002, and the United States had a ratio of (only) 5.4 in 2000. Mexico had the highest Gini coefficient (0.47), Russia the second highest (0.43), and the United States the third highest (0.37). There were some interesting changes over time. The United Kingdom became more unequal between 1986 and 1999 (P90/P10 ratios of 3.79 and 4.18, respectively), as did Sweden, Belgium and the Netherlands, but Canada and Norway became slightly more equal.

3.5.2 The Kuznets curve

When we now consider relative income inequality for countries at all levels of development, the pattern of inequality that ensues follows a well-known pattern referred to as the Kuznets curve. This idea was originally put forward by Simon Kuznets in a 1955 article. In this paper, he speculated that in the course of economic development, the level of income inequality normally rises during the early phase, levels off during the intermediate phase, and then declines during the later stages of development. This speculation, now referred to as the Kuznets' hypothesis, thus proposes an inverted U-shaped relation between income inequality and the level of development, where the latter is most often measured by the level of per capita income.

Kuznets based this speculation on an analysis of time-series data for the United States, England, and Germany and of cross-sectional data involving these three countries as well as Ceylon, India, and Puerto Rico. For the United States, he found that share of income received by the bottom two quintiles of the income distribution (i.e., the bottom 40 percent) rose from 13.5 percent in 1922 to 18 percent in about 1950, while the share of the top 5 percent declined from 31 to 20 percent and that of the top quintile from 55 to 44 percent during the same period. In the United Kingdom, the share of the top 5 percent declined from 46 percent of total income in 1880 to 43 percent in about 1910, to 33 percent in 1929, and to 24 percent in 1947. On the other side, the share of the bottom 85 percent of the income distribution rose from about 41 percent in 1880 to 55 percent in 1947. In Prussia, income inequality increased slightly from 1875 to 1913; in Saxony there was almost no change from 1880 to 1913; while for Germany as a whole, income inequality fell sharply between 1913 and the 1920s but then returned to pre-World War I levels during the 1930s.

Various explanations or models have been put forward to try to account for the Kuznets' relation. Kuznets himself in his 1955 article suggested a dualistic model (a "traditional" and a "modern" sector) to explain the movement of inequality with development, and most of the subsequent models have taken this form. The basic logic of this approach as originally suggested by Kuznets is as follows. Most underdeveloped countries are characterized by a very large share of the labor force employed in the low-income, slow-growing, "traditional" sector of the economy, which is primarily agrarian. In the early phase of development, income inequality tends to rise because both the population and the labor force shift into the faster growing, high-income "modern" sector of the economy. It is the disparity in mean incomes between these two sectors which causes income inequality to rise. Income inequality is further heightened as the mean income in the modern sector increases more rapidly than the mean income in the traditional sector (which, by some accounts, actually falls in absolute terms). Moreover, the movement towards greater overall inequality is further intensified if the modern sector also has the property of greater within-sector inequality than the traditional sector.

In the later phase of development, several factors operate to moderate and eventually reverse the increase in income inequality. First, as the modern sector expands, it absorbs an increasingly higher proportion of the labor force and population, and this shift in proportions between the traditional and modern sectors will by itself reduce income inequality. Second, the absorption of an increasing share of the labor force and population in the modern sector will also reduce population pressure in the traditional sector and thereby cause income differences between the traditional and modern sectors to narrow. Third, there are also forces that serve to reduce income inequality *within* the modern sector. These include the expansion of the educational system and the creation of a skilled labor force, which results in a more equal distribution of skills within the labor force and hence greater equality of labor earnings within the modern sector. The increased skill level of the labor force combined with the development of trade unions also cause the share of income going to labor to increase, further reducing income inequality within the modern sector.

Table 3.10 presents relative income distribution figures for a selection of countries at various levels of development in the late 1970s through the mid-1980s. These data were collected by the World Bank. The countries are organized into four groups, depending on the country's per capita income level. However, no attempt was made to make the underlying income concepts consistent. Moreover, in some cases, the income shares correspond to per capita income, in other cases to family income, and for some countries, to consumption expenditure rather than income.

Table 3.10 Income distribution comparisons for countries at various levels of development, 1978–1987

Country	1985 GDP per capita[a] [U.S.=100]	Year	Percentage share of household income[b]					
			Lowest quintile	Second quintile	Middle quintile	Fourth quintile	Highest quintile	Top 10%
A. Low-income countries								
Bangladesh[c]	5.0	1981–82	9.3	13.1	16.8	21.8	39.0	24.9
India	4.5	1983	8.1	12.3	16.3	22.0	41.4	26.7
Pakistan[d]	8.1	1984–85	7.8	11.2	15.0	20.6	45.6	31.3
Ghana[c]	—	1987	6.5	10.9	15.7	22.3	44.6	29.1
Sri Lanka[e]	11.2	1985–86	4.8	8.5	12.1	18.4	56.1	43.0
Indonesia	—	1987	8.8	12.4	16.0	21.5	41.3	26.5
Average	6.0		7.6	11.4	15.3	21.1	44.7	30.3
B. Lower-middle-income countries								
Philippines[d]	10.8	1985	5.5	9.7	14.8	22.0	48.0	32.1
Cote d'Ivoire[c]	10.2	1986	5.0	8.0	13.1	21.3	52.7	36.3
Morocco[d]	13.1	1984–85	9.8	13.0	16.4	21.4	39.4	25.4
Guatemala	—	1979–81	5.5	8.6	12.2	18.7	55.0	40.8
Botswana	16.1	1985–86	2.5	6.5	11.8	20.2	59.0	42.8
Jamaica[c]	—	1988	5.4	9.9	14.4	21.2	49.2	33.4
Colombia[e]	—	1988	4.0	8.7	13.5	20.8	53.0	37.1
Peru[c]	—	1985	4.4	8.5	13.7	21.5	51.9	35.8
Costa Rica[e]	—	1986	3.3	8.3	13.2	20.7	54.5	38.8
Poland[e]	24.5	1987	9.7	14.2	18.0	22.9	35.2	21.0
Malaysia[e]	—	1987	4.6	9.3	13.9	21.2	51.2	34.8
Brazil	—	1983	2.4	5.7	10.7	18.6	62.6	46.2
Average	14.9		5.2	9.2	13.8	20.9	51.0	35.4
C. Upper-middle-income countries								
Hungary[e]	31.2	1983	10.9	15.3	18.7	22.8	32.4	18.7
Yugoslavia[e]	29.2	1987	6.1	11.0	16.5	23.7	42.8	26.6
Venezuela[e]	—	1987	4.7	9.2	14.0	21.5	50.6	34.2
Average	30.2		7.2	11.8	16.4	22.7	41.9	26.5
C. High-income economies								
Spain[f]	46.0	1980–81	6.9	12.5	17.3	23.2	40.0	24.5
Israel	—	1979	6.0	12.1	17.8	24.5	39.6	23.5
Singapore	—	1982–83	5.1	9.9	14.6	21.4	48.9	33.5
Hong Kong	61.7	1980	5.4	10.8	15.2	21.6	47.0	31.3
New Zealand[f]	60.9	1981–82	5.1	10.8	16.2	23.2	44.7	28.7
Australia[f]	71.1	1985	4.4	11.1	17.5	24.8	42.2	25.8
United Kingdom[f]	66.1	1979	5.8	11.5	18.2	25.0	39.5	23.3
Italy[f]	65.6	1986	6.8	12.0	16.7	23.5	41.0	25.3
Belgium[f]	64.7	1978–79	7.9	13.7	18.6	23.8	36.0	21.5

Table 3.10   *(Continued)*

| Country | 1985 GDP per capita[a] [U.S.=100] | Year | Percentage share of household income[b] | | | | | |
			Lowest quintile	Second quintile	Middle quintile	Fourth quintile	Highest quintile	Top 10%
Netherlands[f]	68.2	1983	6.9	13.2	17.9	23.7	38.3	23.0
France[f]	69.3	1979	6.3	12.1	17.2	23.5	40.8	25.5
Canada[f]	92.5	1987	5.7	11.8	17.7	24.6	40.2	24.1
Denmark[f]	74.2	1981	5.4	12.0	18.4	25.6	38.6	22.3
Germany, Fed. Rep[f]	73.8	1984	6.8	12.7	17.8	24.1	38.7	23.4
Finland[f]	69.5	1981	6.3	12.1	18.4	25.5	37.6	21.7
Sweden[f]	76.9	1981	8.0	13.2	17.4	24.5	36.9	20.8
United States[f]	100.0	1985	4.7	11.0	17.4	25.0	41.9	25.0
Norway[f]	84.4	1979	6.2	12.8	18.9	25.3	36.7	21.2
Japan[f]	71.5	1979	8.7	13.2	17.5	23.1	37.5	22.4
Switzerland[f]	—	1982	5.2	11.7	16.4	22.1	44.6	29.8
Average	63.0		6.2	12.0	17.4	23.9	40.5	24.8

a   Conversion to U.S. dollars is based on the United Nations' International Comparison purchasing power parity deflators. The data are preliminary Phase V results.
b   These estimates should be treated with caution since they are based on different income concepts (see notes c, d, and e below).
c   Per capita expenditure.
d   Household expenditure.
e   Per capita income.
f   OECD member.
Source: World Bank (1990). *World Development Report 1990*, Table 30. New York: Oxford University Press.

Despite these drawbacks, the results are highly suggestive. The most equal countries in the world in terms of having the lowest concentration share of income among the top percentiles were the high-income ones, including the United States and other OECD countries. The average share of the top quintile of this group was 41 percent and that of the top 10 percent was 25 percent. The low-income economies, including India, Pakistan, and Indonesia, were the second-most equal group in this dimension. However, in terms of having the largest share of income going to the poorest groups, the low-income countries ranked above the high-income ones (7.6 percent of total income earned by the bottom quintile versus 6.2 percent). Their average per capita income was only 6 percent of the U.S. level. The average share of the top quintile of these countries was 45 percent and that of the top decile was 30 percent.

The most unequal countries are the lower-middle-income group, which includes the Philippines, Colombia, Peru, Poland, and Brazil. Their average per capita income was about 15 percent of the U.S. level in 1985. The average share of income of the top quintile of countries in this group was 51 percent, compared to an average share of 41 percent for the advanced economies. Their average share of the top decile was 35 percent, compared to 25 percent for the high-income countries. For Brazil, which appears to be the most unequal country in the world, the share of the top quintile was 63 percent and that of the top decile was 46 percent. In the main, the figures presented here do show an inverted U-shaped relation between per capita income and inequality and thus give strong support to the Kuznets' hypothesis.

Table 3.11 updates the international comparisons to around the year 2000. The data are once again from the World Bank. In this case, both the Gini coefficient and the P90/P10 ratio are

Table 3.11   Income distribution comparisons for countries at various levels of development, around 2000

Country	Year	y/c	Income (y) or consumption (c) inequality	
			Gini index	P90/P10 ratio
A. Low-income countries				
Bangladesh	2000	y	0.31	3.9
Ghana	1999	c	0.41	7.3
India	1999/2000	c	0.33	—
Indonesia	2000	c	0.34	—
Nigeria	2003	c	0.41	7.3
Pakistan	2001	c	0.27	3.1
Sri Lanka	2002	c	0.38	5.0
Average			0.35	5.3
B. Lower-middle-income countries				
Philippines	2000	c	0.46	—
Cote d'Ivoire	2002	c	0.45	6.8
Morocco	1998	c	0.38	5.3
Guatemala	2000	y	0.58	16.8
Jamaica	2001	c	0.42	5.9
Colombia	1999	y	0.54	15.0
Peru	2000	c	0.48	14.6
Costa Rica	2000	y	0.46	9.7
Poland	2002	c	0.31	4.0
Malaysia	1997	y	0.49	—
Brazil	2001	y	0.59	16.3
Average			0.47	10.5
C. Upper-middle-income countries				
Hungary	2002	c	0.24	3.0
Slovenia	1998	c	0.28	—
Turkey	2002	c	0.37	5.7
Venezuela	2000	y	0.42	7.9
Average			0.33	5.5
C. High-income economies				
Spain	2000	y	0.35	4.7
Israel	2001	y	0.31	4.3
Singapore	1998	y	0.43	—
New Zealand	1997	y	0.37	—
Australia	1994	y	0.32	4.9
United Kingdom	1999	y	0.34	5.0
Italy	2000	c	0.31	4.3
Belgium	2000	y	0.26	3.2
Netherlands	1999	y	0.29	3.9
France	1994	y	0.31	—
Canada	2000	y	0.33	4.5
Denmark	1997	y	0.27	—
Germany	2000	y	0.28	3.6
Finland	2000	y	0.25	3.1
Sweden	2000	y	0.25	3.2
United States	2000	y	0.38	6.3
Norway	2000	y	0.27	3.0
Japan	1993	y	0.25	—
Switzerland	1992	y	0.31	—
Average			0.31	4.1

Source: World Bank (2006). *World Development Report 2006*, Table A2, pp. 280–1. New York: Oxford University Press.

provided. Here, too, the underlying data come from both income and consumption surveys. For statistical reasons, consumption surveys tend to show less inequality than income surveys.

Roughly the same pattern emerges as in the 1970s and 1980s. The high-income countries again rank lowest in terms of both the Gini coefficient (an average of 0.31) and the P90/P10 ratio (an average of 4.1). The second-most equal group in terms of the Gini coefficient were the upper-middle-income countries (an average of 0.33), though this group was third in terms of the P90/P10 ratio. The low-income countries had levels of inequality very similar to the upper-middle-income group. This group was slightly more unequal according to the Gini coefficient (an average Gini coefficient of 0.35) but slightly more equal by the P90/P10 ratio (an average value of 5.3). Once again the lower-middle-income countries stand out as being far more unequal than any of the other three groups. Their average Gini coefficient was 0.47 and their average P90/P10 ratio was 10.5, more than twice that of any other country group. Brazil once again tops the list of all countries in terms of inequality.

3.5.3   The world distribution of income*

Several economists have attempted to combine the income distributions of individual countries into an estimate of the world (or global) distribution of income. There are three factors that determine the world income distribution. The first is the degree of income inequality within a country. We discussed this in the Section 3.5.2 and saw large disparities in the degree of inequality among different countries. The second and equally important factor is the differences in per capita income among countries (see Section 2.6.1). Here, too, we saw even greater disparities in per capita income among countries than in their degree of within-country inequality. The third is the share of world population in each country. More populous countries will have a larger effect (weight) on the world distribution of income.

The Theil decomposition is useful to see how these three factors affect the world income distribution:

$$T = \sum_g s_g T_g + (1/n) \sum_g n_g(\bar{Y}_g/n\bar{Y}) \ln(\bar{Y}_g/\bar{Y})$$

where the subscript g now represents individual countries. The term T_g refers to within-country inequality; the term $\bar{Y}_g$ refers to the average (per capita) income of the country; the term n_g refers to the population of the country; and the term s_g to the share of total income in country g. The change over time in world inequality would likewise depend on the same three factors: (i) how inequality changes within country; (ii) how per capita income in the country grows relative to other countries; and (iii) how fast the population of the country grows relative to the world population.

There are, of course, formidable data problems involved in constructing the world income distribution. Many countries have no size distribution. Of those that do, some are based on income data and others on consumption data. As a result, there are a number of ways to estimate the global income distribution. One procedure is to use national household income (or expenditure) surveys providing direct income information by quantiles for individual countries to construct world income distributions over time (see, for example, Milanovic, 2005). A short period of data collection is one limitation of this approach. A second approach is to use the mean income or GDP per capita for individual countries together with Gini coefficients as the measures of income dispersion within the country, and make an assumption of log-normality to construct the income distribution for individual countries. A third approximation is to use the known actual income distribution of representative countries and apply it to other countries with geographical and economic similarities but with missing data (Bourguignon & Morrisson, 2002). A fourth approach is to use aggregate GDP data and within-country income share to assign a level of income to each person in the world to estimate the global income distribution (see Sala-i-Martin, 2006).

The world income or expenditure distribution using the first approach at the individual level was used by Milanovic (2005). This study was based on household surveys from 91 countries for 1988 and 1993. Income and expenditure were adjusted by purchasing power parity (PPP) between countries. Inequality measured by the Gini coefficient increased from 0.63 in 1988 to 0.66 in 1993. The change is robust to changes in the sample of countries, PPP adjustment, and inequality measure (Gini coefficient and Theil).

Milanovic also found that differences in the economic growth, the demographic growth, and changes in the domestic income distribution are the main factors contributing to the world income inequality. The main factors leading toward greater inequality include the high economic performance of the European countries and its divergence from Anglo-Saxon countries; the poor growth performances of both rural China and India in conjunction with their very high populations; and the slow growth of sub-Saharan Africa. The major equalizing factors are the convergence in per capita income among the European countries; the catching up of the European countries to the United States in terms of per capita income; and the high growth rates of the Asian "Tigers" and of urban China since the 1980s.

Sala-i-Martin (2006) used aggregate GDP data and within-country income shares, although in some cases estimated income shares for the period 1970–1998 to assign a level of income to each person in the world. He then estimated the kernel density function for the worldwide distribution of income, as well as poverty rates for individual countries. In contrast to Milanovic, his main finding is a reduction in global inequality between 1970 and 2000. He calculated that the worldwide Gini coefficient fell from 0.653 to 0.637 over this period, and the Theil index from 0.812 to 0.783. Using the same data he also estimated the poverty rates and headcounts for 125 countries. Using $1 per day and $2 per day poverty lines he found that the worldwide poverty rates declined over this period. Asia was a great success, especially after 1980. Latin America reduced poverty substantially in the 1970s but progress stopped in the 1980s and 1990s. The worst performer was Africa, where poverty rates increased substantially over the last 30 years: the number of $1/day poor in Africa increased by 175 million between 1970 and 1998, and the number of $2/day poor increased by 227 million.

3.6 SUMMARY

Different inequality measures have their distinctive advantages and disadvantages. The concentration shares are indicative of the level of inequality at the top of the income distribution. The coefficient of variation is more sensitive to changes at the top of the income distribution than at the middle or bottom. Both the Gini and Theil coefficients are more responsive to changes in the middle ranges of the distribution than at either tail. The log variance measure is more sensitive to movements in the lower portion of the distribution. The Atkinson index specifies parametrically the portion of the distribution of interest but the measure is sensitive to the value of the parameter.

The chapter presented data on time trends in income inequality in the United States. Inequality fell rather dramatically in the United States from the early part of this century through World War II. This was followed by a moderate decline from the late 1940s through the late 1960s. However, this trend was reversed after this point. Inequality increased gradually from the late 1960s through the mid-1970s, and then rose sharply from the mid-1970s through the mid-2000s.

The rise of income inequality in the United States since the 1970s is one of the most important social changes in the country's postwar development. This is particularly so in light of the major reduction in inequality that occurred during the first half of this century. This conclusion may seem surprising in light of the major efforts put forward by the federal government to redistribute income in favor of the lower income classes. More discussion of this will appear in Chapters 15 and 16.

This reversal in inequality trends has been coupled with a stagnation in real income growth since the mid-1970s, as we saw in Chapter 1. As a result, income stagnation and rising inequality have become a major concern of public policy today in the United States.

From an international perspective, the United States is today characterized by the highest level of income inequality among industrialized countries. This holds for both before-tax income and after-tax income. The fact that the United States still had the highest per capita income in the world in 2005 (with the exception of Luxembourg) implies that the Kuznets curve is not always followed as countries develop. The only countries which appear to be distinctly more unequal than the United States are the lower-middle income group, including Colombia, Peru, and, particularly, Brazil.

3.7   REFERENCES AND BIBLIOGRAPHY

The measurement of inequality

Aitcheson, J. & Brown, J.A.C. (1957). *The Lognormal Distribution*. Cambridge: Cambridge University Press.

Amiel, Y. & Cowell, F.A. (1999). *Thinking about Inequality*. Cambridge: Cambridge University Press.

Arrow, K.J. (1963). *Social Choice and Individual Values*. New York: John Wiley & Sons, Inc.

Atkinson, A.B. (1970). On the measurement of inequality. *Journal of Economic Theory*, **2**, 244–63.

Atkinson, A.B. (ed.) (1973). *Wealth and Income Inequality*. Harmondsworth, England: Penguin.

Atkinson, A.B. (1983). *The Economics of Inequality*. Oxford: Oxford University Press.

Atkinson, A.B. & Bourguignon, F. (1987). Income distribution and differences in needs. In G.R. Feiwel (ed.), *Arrow and the Foundations of the Theory of Economic Policy*, chapter 12. London: Macmillan.

Atkinson, A.B. & Jenkins, S. (1984). The steady-state assumption and the estimation of distributional and related models. *Journal of Human Resources*, **19**(3), 358–76.

Berrebi, Z.M. & Silber, J. (1985). Income inequality indices and deprivation, a generalization. *Quarterly Journal of Economics*, **100**, 807–10.

Berrebi, Z.M., & Silber, J. (1987). Dispersion, asymmetry and the Gini index of inequality. *International Economic Review*, **28**, 331–8.

Blackorby, C. & Donaldson, D. (1978). Measures of relative equality and their meaning in terms of social welfare. *Journal of Economic Theory*, **19**, 59–80.

Blinder, A.S. (1974). *Towards an Economic Theory of Income Distribution*. Cambridge, MA: MIT Press.

Bourguignon, F. (1979). Decomposable inequality measures. *Econometrica*, **47**, 901–20.

Chakravarty, S.R. (1988). Extended Gini indices of inequality. *International Economic Review*, **29**, 147–56.

Champernowne, D.G. (1953). A model of income distribution. *Economic Journal*, **63**, 318–51. (Reprinted in Champernowne, 1973, Appendix 6.)

Champernowne, D.G. (1973). *The Distribution of Income Between Persons*. Cambridge: Cambridge University Press.

Champernowne, D.G. & Cowell, F.A. (1990). *Inequality and Income Distribution*. Cambridge: Cambridge University Press.

Cowell, F.A. (1977). *Measuring Inequality*. Oxford: Phillip Allan.

Cowell, F.A. (1999). Estimation of inequality indices. In J. Silber (ed.), *Income Inequality Measurement: From Theory to Practice*. Kluwer.

Cowell, F.A. (2000). Measurement of inequality. In A.B. Atkinson & F. Bourguignon (eds.), *Handbook of Income Distribution*, Volume 1 (pp. 87–166). Amsterdam: North-Holland.

Creedy, J. (1985). *The Dynamics of Income Distribution*. Oxford: Blackwell.

Dalton, H. (1920). The measurement of inequality of incomes. *Economic Journal*, **30**, September, 348–61.

Danziger, S., Haveman, R. & Smolensky, E. (1977). The measurement and trend of inequality: Comment. *American Economic Review*, **67**, June, 505–12.

Dixon, P.M., Weiner, J., Mitchell-Olds, T. & Woodley, R. (1987). Bootstrapping the Gini coefficient of inequality. *Ecology*, **68**, 1548–51.

Formby, J.P., James Smith, W. & Buhong, Z. (1999). The coefficient of variation, stochastic dominance and inequality: A new interpretation. *Economic Letters*, **62**(3), 319–23.

Foster, J.E. & Sen, A. (1997). On economic inequality after a quarter century. In J.E. Foster & A. Sen (eds.), *On Economic Inequality*, expanded edition. Oxford: Clarendon Press.

Gastwirth, J.L. (1971). A general definition of the Lorenz curve. *Econometrica*, **39**, 1037–9.

Gastwirth, J.L. (1972). The estimation of the Lorenz curve and Gini index. *Review of Economics and Statistics*, **54**, 306–16.

Gini, C. (1936). On the measure of concentration with special reference to income and wealth. Abstracts of papers presented at the Cowles Commission Research Conference on Economics and Statistics, Colorado College Press, Colorado Springs.

Gottschalk, P. & Smeeding, T. (1997). Cross-national comparisons of earning and income inequality. *Journal of Economic Literature*, **35**, 633–87.

Harrison, A.J. (1981). Earnings by size, a tale of two distributions. *Review of Economic Studies*, **48**, 621–31.

Jenkins, S. (1991). The measurement of income inequality. In L. Osberg (ed.), *Economic Inequality and Poverty: International Perspectives*. Armonk, NY: M.E. Sharpe Inc.

Jenkins, S.P. (1994). Accounting for inequality trends: Decomposition analysis for the UK 1971–1986. *Economica*, **61**, 1–35.

Jenkins, S.P. & Micklewright, J. (2007). New directions in the analysis of inequality and poverty. ECINEQ Working Paper 2007-71, June, http://www.ecineq.org/milano/WP/ECINEQ2007-71.pdf.

Kakwani, N.C. (1980). *Income, Inequality and Poverty, Methods of Estimation and Policy Applications*. Oxford: Oxford University Press.

Lambert, P.J. (1993). *The Distribution and Redistribution of Income*. Manchester, UK: Manchester University Press.

Levy, F. & Murnane, R. (1992). Earnings levels and earnings inequality: A review of recent trends and proposed explanations. *Journal of Economics Literature*, **30**, 1333–81.

Lydall, H.F. (1968). *The Structure of Earnings*. Oxford: Clarendon Press.

Lydall, H.F. (1976). Theories of the distribution of earnings. In A.B. Atkinson (ed.), *The Personal Distribution of Incomes*, chapter 1. London: Allen and Unwin for the Royal Economic Society.

Mills, J.A. & Zandvakili, S. (1997). Statistical inference via bootstrapping for measures of inequality. *Journal of Applied Econometrics*, **12**, 133–50.

Osberg, L. (1984). *Economic Inequality in the United States*. Armonk, NY: M.E. Sharpe Inc.

Paglin, M. (1975). The measurement and trend of inequality: A basic revision. *American Economic Review*, **65**, September, 598–609.

Pareto, V. (1897). *Cours d'Economie Politique*. Lausanne: Rouge.

Pen, J. (1971). *Income Distribution: Facts, Theories, Policies*. New York: Praeger.

Pigou, A.C. (1912). *Wealth and Welfare*. London: Macmillan.

Pigou, A.C. (1932). *The Economics of Welfare*, 4th edn. London: Macmillan.

Sahota, G.S. (1978). Theories of personal income distribution: A survey. *Journal of Economic Literature*, **16**, 1–55.

Sen, A. (1973). *On Economic Inequality*. New York: Norton.

Schultz, R.R. (1951). On the measurement of income inequality. *American Economic Review*, March, 107–22.

Shorrocks, A.F. (1980). The class of additively decomposable inequality measures. *Econometrica*, **48**, 613–25.

Taubman, P. (1978). *Income Distribution and Redistribution*. Reading, MA: Addison-Wesley.

Yntema, D. (1933). Measures of the inequality in the personal distribution of wealth or income. *Journal of the American Statistical Association*, **28**, 423–33.

Income distribution statistics for the United States

Benus, J. & Morgan, J.N. (1975). Time period, unit of analysis and income concept in the analysis of income distribution. In J.D. Smith (ed.), *The Personal Distribution of Income and Wealth*, NBER Studies in Income and Wealth, Vol. 39 (pp. 209–24). New York: Columbia University Press.

Budd, E.C. (1970). Postwar changes in the size distribution of income in the U.S. *American Economic Review*, **60**(2), 247–60.

Burkhauser, R.V., Butler, J., Feng, S. & Houtenville, A. (2004). Long term trends in earnings inequality: What the CPS can tell us. *Economic Letters*, **82**, 295–9.

Burkhauser, R.V., Crews, A.D., Daly, M.C. & Jenkins, S.P. (1999). Testing the significance of income distribution changes over the 1980s business cycle: A cross-national comparison. *Journal of Applied Econometrics*, **14**(3), 253–72.

Burkhauser, R.V., Feng, S. & Jenkins, S.P. (2007a). Using the P90/P10 index to measure US inequality trends with current population survey data: A view from inside the Census Bureau vaults. IZA Discussion Paper No. 2839, June.

Burkhauser, R.V., Oshio, T. & Rovba, L. (2007b). Winners and losers over the 1990s business cycles in Germany, Great Britain, Japan, and the United States. *Schmollers Jahrbuch: Journal of Applied Social Science Studies*. **127**(1), 75–84.

Cowell, F.A. (1984). The structure of American income inequality. *Review of Income and Wealth*, ser. 30, 351–75.

Danziger, S. & Taussig, M.K. (1979). The income unit and the anatomy of income distribution. *Review of Income and Wealth*, ser. 25, 365–75.

Danziger, S. & Gottschalk, P. (1995). *America Unequal*. Cambridge, MA: Harvard University Press.

Danziger, S. & Gottschalk, P. (2005). Inequality of wage rates, earnings, and family income in the United States, 1975–2002. *Review of Income and Wealth*, ser. 51, no. 2, 231–54.

Dew-Becker, I. & Gordon, R.J. (2005). Where did the productivity growth go? Inflation dynamics and the distribution of income. NBER Working Paper No. 11842, December.

Feenberg, D.R. & Poterba, J.M. (1993). Income inequality and the incomes of very high-income taxpayers: Evidence from tax returns. In J. Poterba (ed.), *Tax Policy and the Economy*, Vol. 7 (pp. 145–77), Cambridge, MA: MIT Press.

Feenberg, D.R. & Poterba, J.M. (2000). The income and tax share of very high-income households, 1960–1995. *American Economic Review Papers and Proceedings*, **90**(2), 264–70.

Feng, S., Burkhauser, R.V. & Butler, J.S. (2006). Levels and long-term trends in earnings inequality: Overcoming current population survey censoring problems using the GB2 distribution. *Journal of Business and Economic Statistics*, **24**(1), 57–62.

Goldsmith, S., Jaszi, G., Kurtz, H. & Liebenberg, M. (1954). Size distribution of income since the mid-thirties. *Review of Economics and Statistics*, **36**(1).

Hayes, K.J., Slottje, D.J., Nieswiadomy, M., Redfearn, M. & Wolff, E.N. (1994). Productivity and income inequality growth rates in the U.S. In J.H. Bergstrand, T.F. Cosimano, J.W. Houck & R.G. Sheehan (eds.), *The Changing Distribution of Income in an Open U.S. Economy* (pp. 299–327). North-Holland.

Internal Revenue Service. *Statistics of Income: Individual Income Tax Returns*, from 1948 to the present. Washington, DC: U.S. Government Printing Office, http://www.irs.gov/taxstats/indtaxstats/index.html.

Kuznets, S. (1953). *Shares of Upper Income Groups in Income and Savings*. New York: National Bureau of Economic Research.

Menderhausen, H. (1946). Changes in income distribution during the great depression. *Studies in Income and Wealth*. New York: National Bureau of Economic Research.

Miller, H.P. (1966). *Income Distribution in the U.S., 1960*. U.S. Census Bureau Monograph, Washington, DC: U.S. Government Printing Office.

Miller, H.P. (1971). *Rich Man, Poor Man*. New York: Thomas V. Crowell.

Regev, T. & Wilson, D. (2007). Changes in income inequality across the U.S. *FRBSF Economic Letter*, Number 2007-28, September 21, 1–3.

Saez, E. & Piketty, T. (2003). Income inequality in the United States, 1913–1998. *Quarterly Journal of Economics*, **118**, 1–39.

Radner, D.B. & Hinrichs, J.C. (1974). Size distribution of income in 1964, 1970, and 1971. *Survey of Current Business*, **50**, 19–31.

Schultz, T.P. (1969). Secular trends and cyclical behavior of income distribution in the U.S., 1944–1965. *Six Papers on the Size Distribution of Income and Wealth*. New York: National Bureau of Economic Research.

Soltow, L. (1965). The share of lower income groups in income. *Review of Economics and Statistics*, **47**, November, 429–33.

Taussig, M.K. (1977). Trends in inequality of well-offness in the United States since World War II. *Conference on the Trend in Income Inequality in the U.S.* Madison, WI: Institute for Research on Poverty.

U.S. Bureau of the Census. *Current Population Reports*, Series P-60 (Consumer Income). Washington, DC: U.S. Government Printing Office, various issues and dates, http://www.census.gov/hhes/.

International comparisons of income inequality

Acemoglu, D. & Ventura, J. (2002). The world income distribution. *Quarterly Journal of Economics*, **117**(2), 659–94.

Atkinson, A.B., Rainwater, L. & Smeeding, T.M. (1995). *Income Distribution in Advanced Economies: The Evidence from the Luxembourg Income Study (LIS)*. Paris: OECD.

Bergson, A. (1984). Income inequality under Soviet socialism. *Journal of Economic Literature*, **22**, September, 1052–99.

Berry, A. (1985). On trends in the gap between rich and poor in less developed countries: Why we know so little. *Review of Income and Wealth*, ser. 31, no. 4, 337–54.

Berry, A. (1987). Evidence on relationships among alternative measures of concentration: A tool for analysis of LDC inequality. *Review of Income and Wealth*, ser. 33, no. 4, 417–29.

Bourguignon, F. & Morrisson, C. (2002). Inequality among world citizens: 1820–1992. *American Economic Review*, **92**(4), 727–47.

Buhmann, B., Rainwater, L., Schmaus, G. & Smeeding, T.M. (1988). Equivalence scales, well-being, inequality, and poverty: Sensitivity estimates across ten countries using the Luxembourg Income Study (LIS) database.

Review of Income and Wealth, ser. 34, no. 2, 115–42.

Deininger, K. & Squire, L. (1996). A new data set measuring income inequality. *World Bank Economic Review*, **10**(3), 565–91.

Dowrick, S. & Akmal, M. (2005). Contradictory trends in global income inequality: A tale of two biases. *Review of Income and Wealth*, ser. 51, no. 2, 201–29.

Heshmati, A. (2004). The world distribution of income and income inequality, (August). IZA Discussion Paper No. 1267, http://ssrn.com/abstract=583121.

Jones, C.I. (1997). On the evolution of the world income distribution. *Journal of Economic Perspectives*, **11**(3), 19–36.

Kuznets, S. (1955). Economic growth and income inequality. *American Economic Review*, **45**(1), 1–28.

Lecaillon, J., Paukert, F., Morrison, C. & Germidis, D. (1984). *Income Distribution and Economic Development, an Analytical Survey*. Geneva: International Labor Organization.

Li, H., Squire, L. & Zou, H. (1998). Explaining international and intertemporal variations in income inequality. *Economic Journal*, **108**(466), 26–43.

Luxembourg Income Study (LIS) (2002). Datasets from various countries, http://www.lisproject.org/.

Milanovich, B. (2005). *Worlds Apart: Global and International Inequality 1950–2000*. Princeton, NJ: Princeton University Press.

O'Higgins, M., Schmaus, G. & Stephenson, G. (1989). Income distribution and redistribution: A microdata analysis for seven countries. *Review of Income and Wealth*, ser. 35, no. 2, 107–32.

Radner, D.B. (1985). Family, income, age, and size of unit: selected international comparisons. *Review of Income and Wealth*, ser. 31, no. 2, 103–26.

Ravallion, M. (2003). Inequality convergence. *Economics Letters*, **80**, 351–6.

Sala-i-Martin, X. (2002). The world distribution of income. NBER Working Paper No. 8905, May.

Sala-i-Martin, X. (2006). The world distribution of income: falling poverty and . . . convergence, period. *Quarterly Journal of Economics*, **121**(2), 351–97.

Sawyer, M. (1976). Income distribution in OECD countries. *OECD Economic Outlook*: *Occasional Studies*, July.

Smeeding, T.M. (2005). Public policy, economic inequality, and poverty: The United States in comparative perspective. *Social Science Quarterly*, **86**(Supplement), 955–83.

World Bank. *World Development Report*. New York: Oxford University Press, published annually.

Yotopoulos, P.A. (1989). Distributions of real income within countries and by world income classes. *Review of Income and Wealth*, ser. 35, no. 4, 357–76.

3.8   DISCUSSION QUESTIONS AND PROBLEM SET

1   Some economists use the ratio of mean to median income as an index of inequality. Explain why this would be an appropriate measure. What are the problems with this measure?

2   Explain why the concentration ratio is not a comprehensive measure of income inequality.

3   If the Lorenz curves for Country A and Country B cross, how do you interpret their relative inequality levels?

4   One desirable property of an inequality measure is that it satisfies the principle of scale independence (that is, is a scale-free index).

    (a)   Define what is meant by the principle of scale independence.

    (b)   Show why the Gini coefficient satisfies the principle of scale independence.

    (c)   Show why the coefficient of variation satisfies the principle of scale independence.

5   Prove why the slope of the Lorenz curve is increasing at every point.

6   Suppose a country has the following income distribution:

Income class	Number of families	Average income ($)
1	50,000	5,000
2	100,000	10,000
3	50,000	15,000

    (a)   Define and compute the coefficient of variation.

    (b)   Draw the Lorenz curve.

    (c)   Define and calculate the Gini coefficient.

7   Suppose Country A and Country B have the following income distribution:

Income class	Country A		Country B	
	Percent of families	Percent of total income	Percent of families	Percent of total income
1	15	5	15	3
2	20	10	20	8
3	20	15	20	12
4	20	20	20	20
5	15	25	15	25
6	10	25	10	32

    (a)   Draw the Lorenz curve for each country.

    (b)   Which country is more unequal and why?

8   Suppose Country A has the following cumulative distribution of income:

Cumulative percent of families	Cumulative percent of total income
20	5
40	15
50	27
60	30
80	50
90	65
95	80

Compute the quintile shares. What is the share of total income of the top 10 percent of families and of the top 5 percent of families?

9   Suppose a country has the following income distribution:

Income class	Number of families	Average income ($)
1	500	10,000
2	1,500	30,000
3	1,000	50,000
4	1,000	60,000
5	500	80,000
6	500	100,000

(a)   Draw the Lorenz curve (show all computations and points on the Lorenz curve).
(b)   Compute the quintile shares.
(c)   Compute the income share of the top 10 percent of families.
(d)   Compute the ratio of the mean income of the top quintile to the mean income of the bottom quintile.

10*   Suppose that there are 50 people in a village and one person receives all the income and the other 49 have nothing. Calculate the coefficient of variation (CV). Then show that CV can be made even greater by increasing the sample size while maintaining the assumption that one person continues to receive all the income.

NOTES

1   Another type of sampling technique is called *a stratified sample*, in which some subgroups of a population are sampled more heavily than others. This is a common technique used for analyses of wealth distribution, since a very small part of the population usually holds a very high percentage of the total wealth. In stratified samples, the overall population *weights* (that is, shares) must be known in advance from other sources in order to construct overall population statistics. See Chapter 5 for more discussion of stratified samples.

2   This is also true of other variables. Take temperature, for example. New York City and San Francisco have about the same annual mean temperature, but the dispersion in temperature over the year is much greater in New York City. Even though the mean values are close, the fact that the dispersion is greater in New York City means that it has many more unpleasant (that is, hot or cold) days than San Francisco.

3   The proof is as follows:

$$\sum_{i=1}^{n}(X_i - \bar{X}) = \sum_{x=1}^{n}X_i - \sum_{x=1}^{n}\bar{X} = n\bar{X} - n\bar{X} = 0$$

4   For statistical reasons, it can be shown that division by $n - 1$ rather than by n yields an unbiased estimate of the population variance.

5   This is not to say that this principle is universally accepted. It could be argued that absolute changes are just as important as percentage changes and that an inequality measure should be invariant to *absolute* changes of income. See Cowell (1999) for more discussion of this point.

6   A normal distribution is the standard bell-shaped curve. Many natural, psychological, and social phenomena such as height and weight have a normal distribution.

7   This example illustrates why caution should be used when applying concentration measures such as the share of the upper 1, 5, or 10 percent of the income distribution as summary measures of income inequality.

8   In particular, if the value judgment is such that people are more concerned about the poor having too little than the rich having too much, then Country C should be considered to be more unequal than Country D, since the poor have a smaller share of total income in C than in D. If, on the other hand, the objection is that the rich have too high a share of total income, then Country D would be considered to have greater inequality. See Section 3.3.7 for more discussion.

9   An alternative formulation of the Gini coefficient based on individual data is given by:

$$G = \sum_{i=1}^{n}\sum_{j=1}^{n}|Y_i - Y_j|/(2\bar{Y}n^2)$$

where Y_i is the income of individual i, n is the number of individuals, and $\bar{Y}$ is mean income.

10   In terms of calculus,

$$d(\ln Y) = dY/Y$$

where dY/Y is the percentage change in income.

11   The proof that the Theil index satisfies the transfer principle is rather complicated and beyond the scope of this book. See Amiel and Cowell (1999) for a proof.

12   According to this decomposition, inequality can be thought of as affected by three factors: (i) the proportion of the population in different groups; (ii) inequality within groups; and (iii) the variation of the group means around the overall mean.

13   To see how the Atkinson measure depends on the value of ε, consider the case when $\varepsilon = 0$. Then, $A = \Sigma(Y_i/\bar{Y})$, which is most sensitive to high values of Y_i since $(Y_i/\bar{Y})$ has the biggest weight from high incomes. Conversely, if ε is high, say, $\varepsilon = 2$, then $A = [\Sigma(\bar{Y}/Y_i)]^{-1}$, and low incomes would have the greatest weight in the A index.

14   Feng et al. (2006) argue that the sharp upward rise in inequality in labor earnings in 1993 was due almost exclusively to a change in top-coding of the CPS. While there was some increase in the Gini coefficient in the period from 1993 to 2005, it was not nearly as dramatic as the official CPS Gini calculations would lead one to believe. Feng et al. (2006) pointed out that the same problems probably existed for family income.

15   The structure of the U.S. tax system and its impact on inequality will be discussed more fully in Chapter 16. For the moment, the student might try to prove that a proportional tax on income leaves the Gini coefficient unaffected.

16   See Chapter 4 for a discussion of equivalence classes and equivalent income.

17   The figure of 0.368 differs from the Gini coefficient calculated from CPS data for that year because of the difference in the income concept used in this study.

Chapter 4
Poverty: Definitions and Historical Trends

4.1   INTRODUCTION

Chapter 3 developed indices of overall income inequality, which measure disparities of income among all segments of society. However, there is particular concern among policy makers and the public at large about the status of the low-income population. Have the number of poor increased or declined over time? Are the poor materially better off today than they were 20 or 50 years ago? These questions have led to the development of metrics which attempt to capture both the extent and intensity of poverty in a country. Ever since the New Deal was launched in the 1930s, much of public policy in the United States has been directed at alleviating poverty. The success or failure of these programs, particularly the welfare system, has been a primary focus of recent intense political debate.

It is worthy of note that the United States is still today the only country with an "official" poverty line. Why did the United States bother to develop a poverty standard? What is to be learned from analyzing poverty data year after year? The official poverty standard serves three basic functions. First, it provides a historical record of living standards. Second, it identifies who is poor for the purpose of designing government policies. Third, it allows the researcher and other interested observers to evaluate the effectiveness of public policies aimed at alleviating poverty.

This chapter discusses the measurement of poverty, presents statistics on trends in poverty and the composition of the poverty population, and analyzes some of the causes of poverty. Section 4.2 treats the definition of poverty and the poverty line. Section 4.3 discusses different measures of the incidence of poverty. Poverty trends for the United States are highlighted in Section 4.4. Section 4.5 presents empirical findings on the composition of the poor, the permanence of poverty, the extent of the underclass, and international differences in poverty incidence. In Section 4.6, other issues in measuring poverty are considered, such as the treatment of taxes and noncash government benefits. A summary is presented in Section 4.7. In Chapter 15, we shall consider in some detail the public policy measures that have been developed in the United States to alleviate poverty and evaluate their successes and failures.

4.2   THE MEASUREMENT OF POVERTY

The problem of defining and measuring poverty has been a subject of considerable research and debate over the last two decades. Two issues must be decided. The first is the identification of the poor and the second is the aggregation of the individuals who fall into the poverty population into an overall index of poverty.

4.2.1   The official U.S. poverty standard

It is helpful to discuss first how the poverty line is defined in the official U.S. government statistics. The official measure of the poverty line was developed by Mollie Orshansky in 1965 for the Social Security Administration. The index provided a range of income cutoffs adjusted for such factors as family size, farm versus nonfarm residence, age of the family head, and the number of children under 18. The threshold levels were designed to specify in dollar terms what a minimally "decent" level of consumption or "needs" would be for families of different types. The estimates were based primarily on food requirements. The Department of Agriculture estimated what constituted a minimally nutritionally sound diet (what it called the "economy food plan"). In 1955 the Department of Agriculture conducted a Survey of Food Consumption and determined that families of three or more individuals spent approximately one-third of their income on food. The poverty level of these families was then set at three times the cost of the minimally decent diet.[1] For families of two individuals and persons living alone, the cost of this diet was multiplied by a slightly higher factor than three in order to adjust for the relatively larger fixed expenses (particularly housing) of these smaller households.

Until 1969, annual revisions of these poverty thresholds were based on price changes of the items included in the economy food plan. After 1969, the poverty lines were adjusted each year according to changes in the overall consumer price index (CPI), instead of the cost of food alone. The poverty line of farm households was originally set at 70 percent of the corresponding nonfarm level because of the cheaper cost of food for farm families. In 1969 farm thresholds were raised to 85 percent of the corresponding nonfarm levels, and in 1981 a separate farm threshold was eliminated altogether.[2]

Table 4.1 shows the official **poverty lines** in current dollars for selected family types in 2005.[3] In 2005, a family of four was classified as poor if its income fell below $19,971, while a two-person family was consider poor if its income did not exceed $12,755. It is interesting to note that the poverty line does not rise proportionally with family size. The reason is that many consumption items, such as housing and furniture, can be shared among family members. Thus, a

Table 4.1   Official poverty thresholds for families by size of family, in current dollars, 2005

One person (unrelated individual)	9,973
Under 65	10,160
65 and over	9,367
Two persons	12,755
Householder under 65	13,145
Householder 65 and over	11,815
Three persons	15,577
Four persons	19,971
Five persons	23,613
Six persons	26,683
Seven persons	30,249
Eight persons	33,610
Nine persons or more	40,288

Weighted average thresholds.
Source: http://www.census.gov/hhes/www/poverty/poverty.html.

house or an apartment required for a family of four does not have to be twice as large as one for a couple (there is no reason to have two kitchens, for example). As a result, there are **economies of consumption** built into the poverty thresholds. On the other hand, food and clothing needs tend to rise proportionally with family size, so that the poverty threshold does increase with the size of family. Moreover, the poverty line is lower for individuals aged 65 and over than for those under 65. This was due to the fact that the food plan costs calculated for the aged families were lower than those for the non-aged families.

There are several points of interest to note about the official poverty definition. First, the definition of the poverty line is based on the *family* as the basic consumer unit. Second, the underlying assumption is that the well-being of families (and also single individuals living alone) is related to their ability to purchase consumption goods and services. A family is considered poor if its consumption level falls below some pre-established minimal standard. This is referred to as a **needs-based** definition of poverty. However, since it is easier to measure income than consumption in a household survey, the U.S. Census Bureau relies on family income in order to *actually* measure poverty.

Third, the income a family receives is used to measure its ability to consume. As a result, family income levels are used to define the poverty standard. Fourth, the poverty thresholds for different family sizes ($12,755 for a two-person family and $19,971 for a family of four) are referred to as **equivalence classes** or **equivalent income**. The assumption is that $12,755 is required to satisfy the same level of needs for a two-person family as $19,971 for a family of four. In this sense, the two incomes are equivalent in terms of the standard of living that can be attained.

4.2.2   Absolute versus relative poverty thresholds

The official U.S. poverty lines are adjusted each year to reflect the change in the cost of living. Since they are fixed in real terms, the official thresholds are said to be **absolute** poverty thresholds. There are two major criticisms of the absolute poverty line. First, in so far as it is an absolute poverty standard, the determination of what the necessities of life and what a minimum family diet should be is itself **relative**. Indeed, it is relative to a particular society at a particular time. As far as food requirements are concerned, nutritional needs depend in great measure on how active a person is, what kind of climate he or she lives in, the type of housing, and whether the standard is defined to simply ensure prolongation of life or to maintain a given standard of health. The estimated caloric intake for an adult man or woman can vary considerably depending on these factors.

Moreover, even given a minimal level of calories, it is possible to fulfill this requirement very cheaply if one could live on potatoes and raw vegetables alone. However, given the general dietary practices of the U.S. population, most of us would judge such a standard unreasonably low and would include poultry, some kinds of meat, and even some forms of dessert in a minimal diet. When it comes to other consumption items, the determination of what is a necessity is very much conditioned by the standards of a particular society. Today, indoor plumbing, a telephone and electricity are considered basic necessities of life, while in 1900 or so this was certainly not the case. Even an absolute poverty standard depends on what is considered socially acceptable at a given point in time.

Second, such absolute poverty standards would, as a result, provide some very misleading statistics on poverty over a long stretch over time. For example, according to our current poverty standards, almost the entire U.S. population in 1880 would have been recorded as living below the poverty line. On the other hand, by current standards almost no one living in the year 2090 would be likely to show up below the poverty line.

As a result of these criticisms, many economists have recommended that the official poverty line be set equal to a certain percentage of median family income – say, 45 percent or 50 percent.

Any family falling below this income level would be classified as poor. The poverty line would be adjusted each year to reflect increases in the cost of living and changes in the *real* standard of living. Such a poverty line is referred to as a **relative poverty standard**, because it is tied to and changes with the average real standard of living. A relative poverty measure has the advantage that it adjusts for changes in what people perceive to be necessities and the requirements of a decent living standard.

According to Danziger, Haveman, and Plotnick (1986), the official poverty threshold for a family of four stood at 46 percent of the median income in 1965, compared to 37 percent in 1983. If a relative poverty line was adopted at 46 percent of median income, they calculated that the poverty rate would have risen by 1.3 percentage points between 1965 and 1983. In comparison, the official poverty rate declined by 2.1 percentage points. In 1993, the poverty line for a four-person family was 40 percent of median family income, so that the discrepancy in poverty rates calculated from the official and relative measures would be somewhat less pronounced. By 2005, the ratio had fallen to only 36 percent of median family income, so that the relative poverty rate in 2005 using a 46 percent ratio would have been even higher. Between 1993 and 2005, while the official poverty rate fell by 2.5 percentage points, the relative poverty rate using the 46 percent ratio would have *risen by 2.6 percentage points*.[4]

Calculations by Ruggles (1990, Table 4.3) show that between 1967 and 1972 the relative poverty threshold would have increased 12 percent faster than the official (absolute) poverty threshold, when real median family income was growing rapidly (see Table 2.2 and Figure 2.2). However, between 1972 and 1987, the relative poverty line increased by only 2 percent relative to the official one, because real income growth was stagnant over these years. In periods when real incomes are growing very slowly, the difference in time trends between a relative poverty line and an absolute poverty standard is very small.

The relative poverty line too is subject to criticism. One is that by a relative poverty standard the percentage of poor in the population would most likely remain fairly constant over time. As long as the overall income distribution retains the same basic shape over time (for example, the decile shares remain unchanged), then the percentage of families below 45 or 50 percent of the median would also remain constant. Such a result would mean that as the bottom of the income distribution became better off in real terms from economic growth, their poverty categorization would remain unchanged.[5]

A second is that by a relative poverty standard a family may have all its material needs met and still be classified as "poor." This categorization may conflict with our intuitive idea of what it means to be deprived. Indeed, the concept of a relative poverty standard is intertwined with concepts of social justice of the sort that Amartya Sen incorporated in the so-called Sen index of poverty incidence (see Section 4.3.2 below).

4.2.3 Subjective poverty lines

Public opinion surveys have been conducted annually in the United States asking individuals what they consider to be an adequate amount of income to get by with. The income levels given in response have increased over time but not as fast as median income. This suggests that the average person thinks of poverty in terms of a mixture of an absolute and a relative poverty line.

This type of approach, based on individuals' own evaluation or perception of income adequacy, has been formalized in what are referred to as subjective poverty lines. This technique was originally developed by Dutch economists in Leyden and is also referred to as the Leyden Poverty Line (see Hagenaars & van Praag, 1985, or Hagenaars, 1986, for a summary). The underlying idea is that to discover the minimum amount of income or consumption that individuals require to maintain what they consider to be an adequate standard of living, then they should be asked directly. For the Leyden Poverty Line, the poverty line measure is based on survey responses to the following type of question (the so-called "Income Evaluation Question"):

Please try to indicate what you consider to be an appropriate amount of money for each of the following cases? Under my (our) conditions I would call an after-tax income of

$_____ very bad
$_____ bad
$_____ insufficient
$_____ sufficient
$_____ good
$_____ very good

Of particular interest to the researchers is what they called the "just sufficient" level of income, defined as the midpoint between "insufficient" and "sufficient" income. As might be anticipated, the response to such a question tends to vary with the level of an individual's income. The higher the person's income, the greater is the amount of income considered necessary for a minimal standard of living. The Dutch group found that the elasticity of the poverty line estimate with respect to income is about 0.6 (that is, individuals raise their estimate of a "just sufficient" amount of income by 0.6 percent for each additional percent of income that they have). This variation appears due to the fact that estimates of needs depend directly on the usual consumption habits of families with a given level of income. Moreover, as with the standard poverty line, the estimate of needs varies directly with the size of the family unit (larger families require greater income to meet a "just sufficient" level of consumption).

It is of interest that the elasticity of the subjective poverty line with respect to income lies intermediate to that of the absolute and relative poverty lines. For the former, the elasticity of the poverty line with respect to actual income is zero (that is, the poverty line is fixed in absolute terms). For the latter, the elasticity is one – that is, the relative poverty line rises *at the same rate* as (median) income. The subjective poverty line, based on experimental evidence, is right in between these two extremes. In many ways, it is a more intuitively satisfying measure than the other two because whereas most people believe that what we consider basic needs increases as income rises, it should increase at a lower rate than average income.

This approach has a certain amount of intuitive appeal, since poverty is in actuality a socially determined state, and poverty thresholds represent the opinion of some group of policy-makers of what constitutes a minimally decent standard of living. Since the responses to the question of what is a sufficient income increases with income, but not to the same degree, subjective measures may constitute an adequate compromise between absolute and relative poverty lines.

4.2.3.1   Formal derivation of the Leyden poverty line*

In this procedure, it is assumed that of the six responses indicated above (very bad, bad, insufficient, sufficient, good, and very good) each represents equal divisions (quantiles) of individual welfare or utility. Since the interval is divided into six categories, the "just sufficient" income level corresponds to the 50th percentile of the distribution. On the basis of the individual's response to this question, an individual welfare function can be derived, relating actual income levels to utility or welfare levels (this is also referred to as a "cardinal utility" function).

Formally, it is assumed that individuals evaluate income levels y according to a (cardinal) utility function $U(y)$. If a certain welfare (or utility) level δ is chosen, then the income level $y_{\delta,i}$ can be determined for each individual i which satisfies:

$$U(y_{\delta,i}) = \delta$$

The function U will be monotonically increasing in y (the higher the individual's income level, the greater the amount of income the individual will deem necessary to reach a certain utility level δ). In other words,

$$y_{\delta,i} = f(y_i, fs_i, \delta)$$

where the function f is increasing in y_i. The income level $y_{\delta,i}$ is also an increasing function of family size fs_i.

The welfare level δ^* is then chosen which corresponds to the "just sufficient" income level (midway between the answers "insufficient" and "sufficient" of the Income Evaluation Question). The "national poverty line" y^* is then defined as the solution to the following equation

$$Y^* = f(y^*, fs, \delta^*)$$

The basic idea is that for low-income individuals, the just sufficient income level will be above their actual income level. Conversely, for middle- and high-income individuals, their just sufficient income will be below their actual income level. At some income level, y^*, between the low- and middle-income levels, the just sufficient income level recorded by the respondent will be exactly equal to y^*. The poverty level is then defined as that level of income which someone with *that level of income* will deem just sufficient for an adequate living standard. The poverty threshold will also vary according to family size.

One more technical assumption is needed to be solved for the national poverty level – namely, that the individual welfare function is lognormal. It can then be shown that:

$$\ln y_{\delta,i} = \mu_i + \mu_\delta \sigma_i \tag{4.1}$$

where μ_i is the mean of the lognormal welfare distribution for individual i, σ_i is the standard deviation of the distribution, and μ_δ is the percentile of the standard normal distribution corresponding to welfare level δ. Moreover, empirically it has been found that

$$\mu_i = \beta_0 + \beta_1 \ln fs_i + \beta_2 \ln y_i \tag{4.2}$$

The coefficients β_0, β_1 and β_2 can be estimated econometrically with the addition of a stochastic error term to the equation. As indicated above, the coefficient of $\ln y$, the income elasticity of the poverty threshold, is normally found to be less than unity.

Substituting (4.1) into (4.2), we obtain:

$$\ln y_{\delta,i} = \beta_0 + \beta_1 \ln fs_i + \beta_2 \ln y_i + \mu_\delta \sigma_i \tag{4.3}$$

The parameter σ_i is then fixed at the national average, σ^*. The national poverty line y^* is then found by setting the welfare level equal to δ^* and solving

$$\ln y^* = \beta_0 + \beta_1 \ln fs + \beta_2 \ln y^* + \mu_{\delta^*} \sigma^* \tag{4.4}$$

The solution, y^*, is illustrated in Figure 4.1 for a given family size fs. People whose income is less than y^* are counted as poor, while people whose income is greater than or equal to y^* are considered nonpoor.

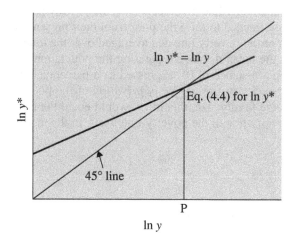

Figure 4.1   Solution of national poverty line based on subjective poverty line

4.2.4   Other concepts of poverty

Another approach that is widely used in the human rights literature and underpins the United Nations' Human Development Index (discussed in Section 2.5.2) is the so-called **capability approach**. The capability approach is a conceptual framework developed by Amartya Sen and Martha Nussbaum for evaluating society in terms of human well-being or welfare. This approach stresses "functional capabilities" or "substantive freedoms," such as the ability to live to old age, engage in economic transactions, or participate in political activities. These are developed in terms of the substantive freedoms people have reason to value, instead of utility (happiness) or access to resources (such as income, consumption, or wealth). Poverty is understood as "capability-deprivation." It is noteworthy that the emphasis is not only on how human beings actually function but also on their having the *capability* to function in important ways if they so wish. Someone could be deprived of such capabilities by ignorance, government oppression, lack of financial resources, or the like. The approach is first fully articulated in Sen (1985) and discussed in Nussbaum and Sen (1993). Applications to development are discussed in Sen (1999), Nussbaum (2000), Alkire (2002) and Clark (2002, 2005).

4.3   MEASUREMENT OF POVERTY INCIDENCE

4.3.1   The poverty rate and the poverty gap ratio

Once the actual poverty thresholds are decided upon, there still remains the question of how the overall poverty rate is to be defined. The most common measure is called the **head count ratio**. On the basis of the poverty lines, family units are first classified as poor or nonpoor. The head count is the number of *individuals* in families below the poverty line. The ratio of this count to the total population is defined as the **poverty rate**.

The head count measure of poverty measures the extent or incidence of poverty. However, it has been criticized because it does not adjust for the relative *severity* or *intensity* of poverty among the poor – that is, for how much the income of the poor falls short of the poverty line. As a result, another index is the **poverty gap ratio** (also called the **income deficiency index**), defined as the average ratio between the amount of income by which a poor family falls short of the poverty line and its actual poverty line. In other words, the poverty gap ratio expresses the amount of money which would be needed to raise the poor from their present incomes (Y) to the poverty line (Z_p) as a proportion of the poverty line and averaged over the total population. Alternatively, the poverty gap ratio is the mean distance separating the population from the poverty line (with the nonpoor being given a distance of 0), expressed as a percentage of the poverty line. It thus measures the *depth* of poverty or the *degree of privation* of the poor.

For families of the same family size, this index would equal the ratio of the average shortfall of income below the poverty line to the poverty line itself. In the more general case, the poverty gap ratio R is given by:

$$R = (1/q) \sum_{i=1}^{q} [(Z_{pi} - Y_i)/Z_{pi}] \tag{4.5}$$

where the summation is performed for poor families only, Z_{pi} denotes the poverty line for family i, Y_i the income (or expenditure) of the ith poor household (or individual), and q is the number of households whose incomes are below the poverty line.[6] If all or most poor families had incomes close to the poverty threshold, the poverty gap ratio would be low; if all or most had incomes considerably below the poverty line, this index would be high.[7] In particular, the poverty gap ratio varies from 0 (if all poor families had incomes just equal to the poverty line) to 1 (if all poor families had zero income).

4.3.2   Composite measures of poverty*

Other indices have been devised which reflect both the number of poor and the poverty gap. Each by itself is somewhat inadequate. The head count measure does not indicate the severity of poverty. The poverty gap ratio does not indicate the number of individuals who are poor. One such alternative measure was proposed by Sen (1976), which combines these two dimensions of poverty as well as the degree of income inequality *among the poor*. The Sen index S of poverty incidence is given by:

$$S = H[R + (1 - R)G] \tag{4.6}$$

where H is the head count measure of the poverty rate, R is the poverty gap ratio (as before), and G is the Gini coefficient of inequality among poor people only. The poverty gap measure captures the absolute (average) deprivation of the poor population. The Gini coefficient captures their relative deprivation and also reflects the extent of extreme poverty in the population of the poor. According to this measure, the poverty incidence is greater the greater the proportion of individuals in poverty, the greater the shortfall in income below the poverty line, and the greater the degree of inequality among the poor. This can be proved by taking the partial derivatives of Equation (4.6), as follows:

(i) $\partial S/\partial H = R + G(1 - R) > 0$ since $R > 0$ and $R < 1$.
(ii) $\partial S/\partial R = H(1 - G) > 0$ since $H > 0$ and G is always less than unity.
(iii) $\partial S/\partial G = H(1 - R) > 0$ since $H > 0$ and R is always less than unity.

An alternative index was proposed by Foster, Greer, and Thorbecke (1984). Their class of poverty indices P_α takes the following form:

$$P_\alpha = (1/N) \sum_{i=1}^{q} [(Z_p - Y_i)/Z_p]^\alpha \tag{4.7}$$

where, as above, Z_p denotes the poverty line, Y_i the expenditure or income of the ith poor household (or individual), N the total number of households, and q the number of households whose incomes are below the poverty line. This index is based on measuring the gap between the poverty line and the income of the poor as a fraction of the poverty line $[Z_p - Y_i]/Z_p$, raising it to a power α and then summing over all poor units. Not only does the index take into account the prevalence and intensity of poverty, it may also be used to reflect the degree of inequality among the poor by varying the value of the α parameter.

Thus, in the case when $\alpha = 0$, the index becomes $P_0 = q/N$, which is the head count index. It reflects the proportion of total population lying below the poverty line. This measure is indifferent to the intensity of poverty of the poor and is sensitive only to their number and reflects the prevalence of poverty.

Alternatively, with $\alpha = 1$, the poverty index becomes:

$$P_1 = (1/N) \sum_{i=1}^{q} [(Z_p - Y_i)/Z_p] = R'$$

where R' is similar to the poverty gap ratio except the summation is divided by N instead of by q. This index gives a good measure of the intensity of poverty since it reflects how far the poor are from the poverty line. It may also be used to show the amount of income, under perfect targeting, that needs to be transferred to the poor to close the poverty gap in order to eradicate poverty. However, P_1 is insensitive to income distribution among the poor. Income transfers among the poor will leave P_1 unchanged. For this to be reflected in the index, greater weight has to be given to the poorest units. This can be achieved by setting $\alpha = 2$.

If $\alpha = 2$, the poverty index becomes

$$P_2 = (1/N) \sum_{i=1}^{q} [(Z_p - Y_i)/Z_p]^2$$

P_2 is the mean squared proportionate poverty gap. This index is not as easy to interpret as P_0 and P_1. However, it has the advantage of reflecting the degree of inequality among the poor, in the sense that the greater the inequality of distribution among the poor and thus the severity of poverty, the higher is P_2.[8]

4.4   POVERTY TRENDS IN THE UNITED STATES

Figure 4.2 shows poverty rate statistics from 1959 to 2005 for the whole population and by race and Hispanic origin. These are head count rates based on the official U.S. poverty lines for those years. For the full population, the reduction in the poverty rate has been quite dramatic. In 1959, 22 percent of individuals in the population were recorded as living below the poverty line. In 1973, the poverty rate had fallen to 11 percent, its lowest point since these statistics were first recorded. The major reduction in the poverty rate occurred between 1964 and 1969. This dramatic change happened during the same period that President Lyndon Johnson waged his "*War on Poverty*," but more on this in Chapter 15. After 1969 the overall poverty rate changed very little in the United States, until 1980, when it rose to 13 percent. The rate climbed during the recession of the early 1980s, peaking at 15 percent in 1983. After 1983, the poverty rate fell again, reaching 13 percent in 1989. However, after the recession of the early 1990s the poverty rate again rose, to 15.1 percent in 1993. During the boom of the 1990s, the poverty rate fell, reaching a low of 11.3 percent in 2000. On the other hand, over the early 2000s, the poverty rate climbed again, reaching 12.6 percent in 2005.

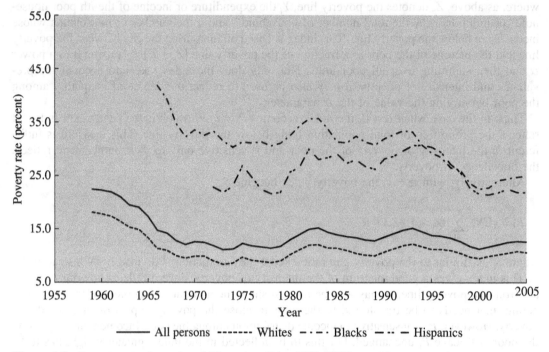

Figure 4.2   Poverty rates by race and Hispanic origin, 1959–2005

The poverty rate for white individuals was somewhat lower than for the full population. In 1959, 18.1 percent of white persons were classified as poor, compared to 22.4 percent for the full population; in 1973 the poverty rate for whites was 8.4 percent, compared to 11.1 percent overall; in 1993, it was 12.2 percent, compared to 15.1 percent for the full population; and in 2005, the respective poverty rates were 10.6 and 12.6 percent. The poverty trends for whites mirrored the overall rate, with a gradual reduction between 1959 and 1964, a sharp drop between 1964 and 1968, almost no change until 1979, a steep rise between 1979 and 1983 followed by a moderate decline until 1989, a gradual increase during the early 1990s, a steep decline during the late 1990s, and a moderate increase during the 2000s.

The poverty rate among the black population has been averaging about *two and a half* to *three* times that of whites, and this ratio was maintained fairly consistently since 1959. In 1959 *over half* the black persons in the United States fell into the poverty category. By 1966 the poverty rate had fallen to 42 percent, by 1969 to 32 percent, and by 1978 to 31 percent. The rate increased during the early 1980s, declined again to 31 percent in 1989, was back to 33 percent in 1993, fell to 22.5 percent in 2000, *its low point*, and then climbed back to almost 25 percent in 2005.

In 1973 a new category was added to the official poverty statistics, which was for Hispanic families (originally families with Spanish surnames and later those who identified themselves as of Latin origin). Their poverty rate has tended to be about twice the overall rate. It increased from 22 percent in 1973 to 27 percent in 1975, declined to 22 percent in 1979, increased to 29 percent in 1985, then fell to 26 percent in 1989, rose to 31 percent in 1993, fell to 21.5 percent in 2000, where it pretty much remained until 2005.

However, it should be noted that even though the *incidence* of poverty is much greater among black persons than white persons, about *two-thirds* of the poor people in the United States have been white since the early 1960s. The reason, as might be evident, is that whites constitute the vast majority (close to 90 percent) of the U.S. population.

4.4.1 Composition of the poor

Besides race, poverty incidence also differs substantially by age, class, and family type, as shown in Figures 4.3 and 4.4. The U.S. Census Bureau first draws a distinction between "families," which consist of two or more individuals living together related by blood or marriage,[9] and all others who are referred to as "unrelated individuals." Families are then divided into two types, "male-headed families," consisting of married couples and single men, and "female-headed families," comprising unmarried women with children and without a husband present.[10] It is first of interest to look at time trends for people in families as opposed to the full population. The poverty rate among the former is about 2 percentage points lower than poverty rate among the full population but the time trends are essentially the same.[11] Poverty incidence has also been considerably higher among female-headed families than male-headed ones. In 1973, their poverty rate was over *six* times greater than for male-headed families, and in 1993 and 2005, about *five* times as great. The poverty rate among female-headed families did not change very much between 1973 and 1993 (37.5 percent then compared to 38.7 percent in 1993) but fell rather steadily to 31.1 percent in 2005.

The poverty rate among adults in age group 18 to 64 has been consistently lower than that for the general population. In 1959, their poverty rate was 17.0 percent, compared to 22.4 percent overall; in 1993 it was 12.4 percent, compared to 15.1 percent for the whole population; and in 2005, it was 11.1 percent versus 12.6 percent. On the other hand, the poverty rate among children (under 18) has been consistently higher than the poverty rate for adults. Moreover, between 1973 and 1993, the incidence of poverty increased much more rapidly among children than among

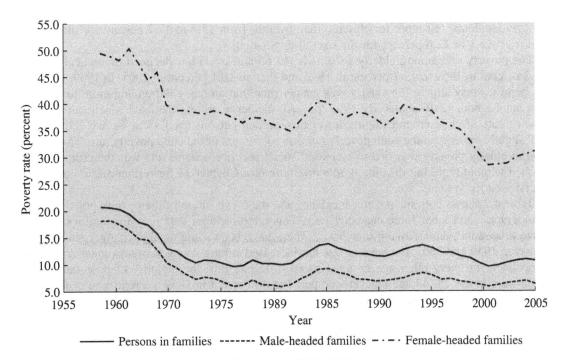

Figure 4.3 Poverty rates of persons by family type, 1959–2005

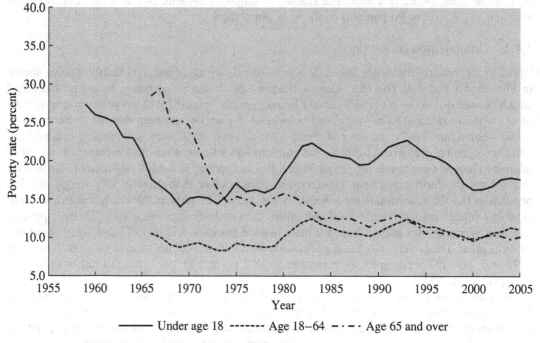

Figure 4.4 Poverty rates of persons by age group, 1959–2005

adults. Over these years, the poverty rate for children increased from 14.4 to 22.7 percent, whereas the overall poverty rate increased from 11.1 to only 15.1 percent. However, from 1993 to 2005, poverty incidence fell more for children than overall, from 22.7 to 17.7 percent for the former and from 15.1 to 12.6 percent for the overall population.

The poverty rate among elderly persons (aged 65 and over) has declined dramatically, from 35.2 percent in 1959 to 12.2 percent in 1993 and then to 10.1 percent in 2005. In 1959, the incidence of poverty among the elderly was greater than that among children and more than twice that among nonelderly adults. By 1993, poverty incidence among the aged was about half the poverty rate of children and slightly lower than among persons aged 18 to 64. By 2005 it was still slightly lower than the adult poverty rate and 57 percent of the child poverty rate. This reduction in elderly poverty was tied to increased social security benefits and was therefore accomplished without requiring the elderly to work more (see Chapter 15 for further discussion of the social security system).[12]

Table 4.2 shows both the poverty incidence and the composition of the poverty population by demographic and labor force characteristics. This table includes data only for families (two or more related individuals living together).[13] There have been some notable changes since 1959. Between 1959 and 2005, the poverty rate has increased among young families (under 25), while it declined for every other age group. However, despite this, the majority of poor families in 2005 were in the 25–44 age bracket, compared to 40 percent in 1959 – a reflection of the large number of baby-boom families in this age group.

As noted above, the poverty rate for female-headed females did not change much between the late 1960s and the late 1980s but then declined somewhat by the mid-2000s. Still, by 2005, female-headed families constituted over *half* of all poor families, compared to less than one-quarter in 1959. The reason for this is the rapid growth in the number of female-headed households in the

Table 4.2   Poverty rates for families and the composition of poverty among families by selected household characteristic and year, 1959–2005

Family characteristics	Poverty rate for group (in percent)					Percent of total poor[a]				
	1959	1969	1978	1989	2005	1959	1969	1978	1989	2005
A. All families	18.5	9.7	9.1	10.3	9.9	100.0	100.0	100.0	100.0	100.0
B. Age										
14–24	26.9	14.8	18.5	30.4	28.8	7.5	10.6	13.4	12.8	13.9
25–44	16.5	8.4	10.2	12.0	12.7	39.8	36.5	48.6	55.8	52.3
45–54	15.0	6.5	6.7	6.3	6.5	17.3	14.0	13.8	10.9	14.8
55–64	15.9	8.0	6.0	7.4	5.8	13.1	13.3	10.7	10.2	9.4
65 & over	30.0	17.7	8.4	6.6	5.9	22.4	25.5	13.5	10.4	9.4
C. Sex										
Male	15.8	6.9	5.3	5.9	5.7	77.0	63.5	49.7	48.3	47.2
Female	42.6	32.6	31.4	32.2	28.7	23.0	36.5	50.3	51.7	52.8
D. Size of family										
2 persons	19.6	10.9	8.0	8.2	8.2	34.3	38.7	34.2	33.4	36.9
3 persons	12.8	7.5	8.6	9.8	10.5	15.1	16.1	21.1	22.2	24.1
4 persons	12.7	6.8	8.1	10.1	9.4	14.0	13.5	18.4	20.9	18.5
5 persons	18.3	8.0	10.7	13.5	13.2	13.1	10.3	12.3	11.8	11.8
6 persons	24.2	11.3	13.9	12.1	16.0	8.5	7.9	6.7	6.2	4.8
7 or more persons	45.6	21.6	22.8	32.3	25.4	15.1	13.5	7.3	5.6	3.9
E. Employment status										
Not in labor force	40.8	26.7	20.9	21.1	16.9	38.8	52.7	52.4	51.5	43.4
Unemployed	33.7	18.0	24.9	31.7	27.0	6.7	4.2	8.0	9.9	8.4
Employed	12.8	5.3	4.9	5.6	6.6	54.5	43.1	39.7	38.5	48.2
F. Work experience										
Did not work	45.2	31.0	24.0	23.4	18.6	30.5	44.7	50.3	50.8	51.8
Part of the year	26.9	16.5	16.4	19.0						
Whole year, part-time	10.6	3.7	2.7	3.5						
Part year or part-time					15.4	38.0	34.0	33.6	33.0	30.0
Full-time, whole year	9.4	3.2	2.4	2.9	3.4	31.5	21.3	16.1	16.2	18.2
G. Educational attainment[b]										
No years of schooling			33.4	45.6				2.3	1.8	
Elementary: less than 8			20.3	25.5				18.2	14.1	
Elementary: 8 years			12.2	15.9				10.8	7.0	
High school: 1–3 years			14.4	19.2				20.7	20.2	
Less than 4 years of high school					24.2					34.4
High school: 4 years			6.6	8.9	11.9			23.0	30.5	36.4
College: 1 or more years			3.4	3.6				11.6	13.6	
(i) College: less than bachelor's degree					7.8					21.6
(ii) Bachelor's degree or more					2.6					7.4
H. Residence										
Farm	42.8	17.5	10.9	9.6	7.4	17.8	8.5	4.2	2.0	1.9
Nonfarm	15.7	9.3	9.1	10.3	10.0	82.2	91.5	95.8	98.0	98.1

Table 4.2   *(Continued)*

Family characteristics	Poverty rate for group (in percent)					Percent of total poor[a]				
	1959	*1969*	*1978*	*1989*	*2005*	*1959*	*1969*	*1978*	*1989*	*2005*
I. Residence										
Central cities	13.7	9.8	12.7	14.9	13.7	25.2	32.1	37.6	41.8	41.7
Suburbs	9.6	5.3	5.3	6.4	7.3	16.7	20.0	23.1	29.7	39.0
Rural	28.2	14.8	10.8	12.5	11.2	58.1	47.9	39.3	28.5	19.3
Addendum										
Mean income deficit (2005$)	7,899	6,812	7,099	7,827	8,125					
Average poverty gap ratio	0.431	0.375	0.415	0.462	0.375					

These figures are supplemented with the author's calculation from the *2005 Current Population Survey*.
All variables refer to the household head unless otherwise noted. Please note that this series refers to *family* poverty rates.
a   Note that the distribution shares do not sum to unity for some groupings, because of the exclusion of certain subgroups.
b   Includes only families with household heads 25 and over. In 2005, all schooling levels less than four years of high school are combined into a single group.
Sources: 1959–78: U.S. Census Bureau, *Current Population Reports*, Series P-60, No. 124; *Characteristics of the Population Below the Poverty Level: 1978*, July, 1980; U.S. Census Bureau, *Current Population Reports*, Series P-60, No. 166, *Money Income and Poverty Status in the United States: 1989*, September, 1990; http://pubdb3.census.gov/macro/032006/rdcall/3_000.htm; and 2006 CPS Annual Demographic Survey, http://pubdb3.census.gov/macro/032006/pov/toc.htm.

population since the late 1950s.[14] This phenomenon has been referred to as the *feminization of poverty*, which refers to the growth in the proportion of poor people who are found in female-headed families (as opposed to the increase in the incidence of poverty within this group).

Poverty rates also vary with the size of the family, even though the poverty line is adjusted for family size. In 2005, in particular, poverty incidence increased almost directly with family size. Very large families (seven or more persons) have had particularly high poverty rates (25.4 percent in 2005), because there are "many more mouths to feed." The major change since 1959 is that the poverty rate for two-person families has declined dramatically. This is mainly a reflection of declining poverty among elderly couples, who make up a large proportion of two-person families.

As we might expect, poverty incidence varies with employment status and work experience. The incidence of poverty is much higher among families whose prime earner is unemployed or not in the labor force than among those in which he or she is employed. Interestingly, while the poverty rate has fallen since 1969 for families whose prime earner is not in the labor force, poverty incidence has increased among those whose prime earner is unemployed. Part of the reason, as we shall discuss in Chapter 15, is that government benefits for unemployed workers have deteriorated since the early 1970s. Despite this increase, families with an unemployed household head constituted only a very small proportion of poor families in 2005. A little over 40 percent of the poor were families whose household head was not in the labor force and almost half were those whose household head was employed.

The poverty rate for families in which the household head worked full time (35 hours per week or more) and for the whole year has been very low since 1969 (3.4 percent in 2005). The poverty rate for families whose prime earner worked only part of the year or part time was much higher in 2005 (15 percent). In 2005, while a little over half of poor families consisted of those whose household head did not work, 30 percent were composed of those in which the household head worked only part of the year and/or part time, and the remaining 18 percent of those whose household head worked full time for the full year. These are the so-called "working poor" who make up almost half of poor families.

Moreover, as to be expected, poverty rates varied inversely with the level of education of the household head. Despite this, 34 percent of the poor in 2005 consisted of families in which the household head had attended high school (but not beyond), 36 percent of those whose household head had graduated high school (but did not attend college), and 22 percent of those whose household head had attended some college but did not receive a Bachelor's degree.

The poverty rate among farm families has declined enormously, from 43 percent in 1959 to 7.4 percent in 2005. In 2005, they constituted only 2 percent of the poverty population, compared to 18 percent in 1959. Poverty incidence was also higher for urban and rural dwellers than suburbanites. However, one of the most dramatic changes since 1959 is that the proportion of poor families living in rural areas declined from 58 percent to 19 percent in 2005, while the proportion living in urban areas (central cities) increased from 25 to 42 percent. This is one of the reasons for more recent concerns about urban poverty.

The last two rows in Table 4.2 show the mean income deficit (the mean poverty gap) and the poverty gap ratio. The income deficit is defined as the difference between the income of a family in poverty and its corresponding poverty line. The mean income deficit is the average of this for all families below the poverty line. In constant dollar terms, this statistic fell between 1959 and 1969, but by 2005 it was above its 1959 level. The poverty gap ratio (see Section 4.3.1) also declined between 1959 and 1969, from 0.43 to 0.38, then rose between 1969 and 1989, but then fell again in 2005. By 2005, it had fallen to 0.38, about the same as in 1969. So, even though the poverty rate (head count) had fallen by half between 1959 and 2005, there was almost no change in either the poverty rate or the *severity* of poverty for those below the poverty line, as measured by the poverty gap, from 1969 to 2005.

4.5 OTHER DIMENSIONS OF POVERTY

4.5.1 Poverty spells and the permanence of poverty

The official poverty definition is based on annual income flows. The *duration* of poverty is another important dimension to the problem of poverty. It is likely that a family that is poor for only a few months or a year experiences much less hardship than one that has been poor for many years. There is no official or even widely accepted definition as to what constitutes **permanent** or **chronic** poverty as opposed to **temporary** poverty. This is normally a research question, and economists have used different definitions in the past.

One of the first researchers to study this issue was Duncan (1984). He used the Panel Study of Income Dynamics (PSID), a panel survey that began in 1969, to study this issue and estimated that only 20 to 25 percent of individuals classified as poor on the basis of the annual poverty definition were poor in eight out of the 10 years between 1969 and 1978. Coe (1978) defined persistent poverty to occur if the family's income was below the poverty line in *every* year between 1967 and 1975 and estimated that only about 12 percent of the annual poverty population would fall into this group. Hill (1981), using the same definition for the 10 years from 1969 to 1978, estimated that only about 6 percent of the official poverty group would be classified as persistently poor.

Rodgers and Rodgers (1993) found that between the late 1970s and the mid-1980s not only did the overall poverty rate increase but poverty became more chronic and less transitory in nature.

Using the PSID, they calculated that chronic poverty characterized 42.8 percent of the average-annual poverty population during the 1975–1979 period and 47.1 percent during the 1982–1986 period. The rise in the proportion of the poor population who found themselves in permanent poverty rose among most demographic subgroups as well.

Another way of addressing this issue is to measure the **duration** of poverty spells. Bane and Ellwood (1986) in one of the first papers on this subject also used the PSID to examine movements into and out of poverty. They found that among nonelderly people who were classified in poverty status in a given year, about 45 percent left poverty within one year; 70 percent exited poverty within 3 years; and 87 percent within 8 years. Yet, somewhat paradoxically, about half of the nonelderly poor at any given time are in the midst of a long spell of poverty. The reason for this apparent inconsistency is that the chronic poor remain in the poverty population year after year, while the temporary poor are only classified as part of the poverty population for a short period of time, and are then replaced by other short-term poor.

They also found that the most common reason for a nonelderly family falling into poverty was a change in family composition, from the birth of a child, separation or divorce, or the establishment of a separate household unit (43 percent of poor families); while the second most important cause was a decline in the earnings of the head of the family (38 percent). Exits were typically caused by the same events in the reverse direction, such as marriage or an increase in earnings of the family head.

The composition of the permanently poor is also of interest. Hill (1981) calculated that 61 percent of the permanently poor between 1969 and 1978 were black; 49 percent were unmarried with children; 59 percent were nonelderly female, 22 percent were elderly female, and 4 percent elderly men; and 32 percent were disabled.

A later study by Stevens (1994) updated some of the earlier Bane and Ellwood results. She found that mobility out of poverty fell between 1970 and 1987, particularly among female-headed households. This means that poverty has become a more permanent condition among the poor, particularly among unwed mothers. Moreover, she found that half of all individuals who exited poverty fell back into poverty within 5 years. The tendency to experience repeated spells of poverty increased between 1970 and 1987 among families headed by white (though not black) females.

Using the Survey of Income and Program Participation (SIPP), Hisnanick (2007) calculated poverty duration over the period from 1996 to 1999. He found that half of all poor families exited poverty within 2 years and 57 percent exited within 3 years. The exit rates are quite a bit lower than those found by Bane and Ellwood (1986) over the 1970s and 1980s, once again pointing to the growing persistence of poverty in the United States. Hisnanick found very little difference in exit rates between married-couple families and single-parent families.

4.5.2   The underclass

A related issue is the existence of an "underclass" in the United States. Michael Harrington's classic 1962 book, *The Other America*, first brought widespread attention to the "culture of poverty." He described this in terms of the sense of hopelessness, depression, loss of self-esteem, and pessimism for the future among the poor. William Julius Wilson's 1987 book, *The Truly Disadvantaged*, focused attention on what he called "dysfunctional" social behavior among disadvantaged people living in inner-city "ghetto" areas. This is associated with a whole set of social problems, such as welfare dependency, dropping out of school, crime, drug culture, teenage pregnancy, almost permanent joblessness, and the presence of families headed largely by females. Wilson argued that, paradoxically, this may have occurred due to the success of anti-discrimination efforts that enabled successful blacks to move from the inner city areas, leaving a virtually homogeneous poor population behind. Whatever the reasons, the notion of an underclass is that there is a subset of the poor who have very different values, aspirations, and attitudes from the middle class, and these characteristics produce behavior that prevents them from escaping poverty.

The underclass has been defined in various ways, and estimates of their size depend critically on the definition used. Most definitions use as one criterion residence in a low-income area (usually measured as an area where the poverty rate is 40 percent or greater). U.S. Census data identify which areas fall into this category. On the basis of this criterion, only about 7 percent of the poverty population would be considered as belonging to the underclass, and only about 15 percent of poor blacks (and about 5 percent of the black population as a whole). On the other hand, by whatever gauge is used, the size of the underclass appears to have grown. During the 1970s, the number of poor people living in low-income areas increased by 36 percent, while the overall number of poor grew by only 8 percent (see Sawhill, 1988, pp. 1108–1109 for more discussion).

Ricketts and Sawhill (1988), using a similar definition, estimated that the number of people in the underclass in 1980 was roughly four times the number in 1970. They found that the underclass was disproportionately minority and concentrated primarily in large urban areas, especially in the mid-Atlantic and Midwest. In a follow-up study Ricketts and Sawhill (2006) found that the underclass, after growing dramatically in the 1970s, edged up further in the 1980s but fell very sharply in the 1990s (although not back to its 1970 level). The main reasons for the decline were a reduction in the number of census tracts with high levels dropping out of high school and high levels of welfare dependency. The smaller number of tracts with high public assistance is likely a consequence of the welfare reforms of 1996 and the resulting drastic fall in caseloads (see Chapter 15 for more discussion). The number of tracts with a high proportion of female heads continued to rise over the 1990s, though at a slower pace than earlier, while the number with a high proportion of men not in the labor force remained about the same. New York and Detroit showed the greatest reduction in the number of underclass tracts, followed by Chicago, Philadelphia, and Los Angeles. All racial and ethnic groups showed declines with whites and non-Hispanic blacks doing somewhat better than Hispanics.

4.5.3   International comparisons of poverty rates

There have been several attempts to compare poverty rates among countries. The main difficulty is that poverty line definitions vary considerably across nations, so that it would make little sense to make comparisons on the basis of official definitions in different places. One way of getting around this problem is to use a relative poverty line, defined as some percentage of the median income in a country. This has the virtue of providing the same standard across countries. Another difficulty in such comparisons is that different countries use different equivalence class adjustments, particularly for different family sizes, for their official poverty rates. An appropriate international comparison of poverty rates must also employ the same equivalence class adjustments in different countries.

A study by Smeeding *et al.* (1985) made both sets of adjustments. Their relative poverty line was set at one-half the median income for the country. They standardized the equivalence classes by family size on the basis of the official U.S. poverty lines. The calculations were based on the Luxembourg Income Study (LIS), which included data from the late 1970s and early 1980s.

Results are shown in Table 4.3 on both poverty rates and poverty gap ratios for seven countries for which the requisite data were available. The results are very interesting in placing U.S. poverty in an international perspective. The United States had the highest poverty rates of any

Table 4.3 International comparisons of poverty rates and the poverty gap ratio for selected countries, about 1980

Country	Total	Elderly families	One-parent families	Two-parent families	Other families
A. Percentage of persons who are poor					
Canada	12.1	11.5	37.5	11.0	8.5
Israel[a]	14.5	23.8	11.8	14.9	5.5
Norway	4.8	4.6	12.6	3.4	5.7
Sweden	5.0	0.1	9.2	5.0	7.0
United Kingdom	8.8	18.1	29.1	6.5	4.1
United States	16.9	20.5	51.7	12.9	9.8
West Germany	6.0	9.3	18.1	3.9	5.4
B. Percentage poverty gap ratio among persons living in poverty					
Canada	33.9	18.8	37.0	30.5	41.8
Israel[a]	16.3	13.4	13.7	20.4	13.3
Norway	40.8	48.3	27.7	29.2	47.6
Sweden	40.0	45.2	33.4	28.2	43.2
United Kingdom	16.0	10.9	17.7	10.8	24.3
United States	39.9	29.1	43.0	33.3	50.6
West Germany	30.6	28.5	31.4	23.2	48.4

Income is based on income after transfers (post-transfer income). Poverty is defined as families or persons in families with equivalent income below one-half of median family equivalent income.

Families are defined as two or more persons living together who are related by blood, marriage or adoption, or single (unrelated) individuals. More than one family may occupy one household.

Elderly families are those headed by a person age 65 or older. Single-parent families are nonelderly families with only one natural parent present and children under age 18.

Two-parent families are nonelderly families with two natural parents and children under age 18.

Other families are mainly nonelderly childless couples and nonelderly single individuals.

Totals may not equal sums across rows owing to rounding errors.

a   Israeli figures are for urban populations only.

Source: Smeeding, T.M., Rainwater, L., Rein, M., Hauser, R. & Schaber, G. (1985). Income Poverty in Seven Countries: Initial Estimates from the LIS Database. In T.M. Smeeding, M. O'Higgins & L. Rainwater, *Poverty, Inequality and Income Distribution in Comparative Perspective*. Washington, DC: Urban Institute Press.

of the seven countries. It was about twice that of the United Kingdom's, two and a half times that of West Germany, and over three times that of Norway and Sweden. Differences between the United States and other countries were particularly acute for one-person families. The fact that the United States had the highest relative poverty rate is perhaps not too surprising because the United States also had the highest level of inequality and the relative poverty rate is higher when the share of the lower tail of the income distribution is lower. The poverty gap was also very high for the United States, though several other countries, including Sweden and Norway, also showed similar levels.

The results of an updated study for around the year 2000 are shown in Table 4.4. As was the case around 1980, the United States still had the highest overall poverty rate using a relative poverty standard. Ireland now ranked second, followed by Italy, the United Kingdom, and Canada. The two Nordic countries, Sweden and Finland, ranked lowest in terms of the overall poverty rate. For elderly families, Ireland was now the highest, with the United States in second place and the United Kingdom in third place. Ireland also ranked highest for one-parent families (with

Table 4.4 International comparisons of poverty rates (head counts) using a relative and absolute measure for selected countries, around 2000

Country	All families	Elderly families	One-parent families (with children)	Two-parent families (with children)	Nonelderly families without children
A. Relative poverty line[a]					
United States	17.0	28.4	41.4	13.2	11.2
Ireland	16.5	48.3	45.8	10.8	13.1
Italy	12.7	14.4	20.1	15.1	8.4
United Kingdom	12.4	23.9	30.5	9.1	8.4
Canada	11.4	6.3	32.0	10.1	11.9
Germany	8.3	11.2	33.2	4.4	8.7
Belgium	8.0	17.2	21.8	4.3	5.9
Austria	7.7	17.4	17.9	5.1	7.0
Netherlands	7.3	2.0	30.7	7.6	6.4
Sweden	6.5	8.3	11.3	2.2	9.8
Finland	5.4	10.1	7.3	2.2	7.6

B. Absolute poverty line using U.S. poverty standard[b]

Country	Overall	Elderly	Children
United States	8.7	9.2	12.4
United Kingdom	12.4	16.1	17.5
Canada	6.9	1.1	9.0
Germany	7.6	7.1	9.1
Belgium	6.3	8.6	7.2
Austria	5.2	7.4	5.8
Netherlands	7.2	1.7	10.4
Sweden	7.5	7.3	5.8
Finland	6.7	8.6	4.6

a The relative poverty line is measured as 50 percent of median adjusted disposable income. Adjusted disposable income is given as $DP/s^{.05}$, where DP is disposable income and s is family size.
b PPP is used to convert national currency to U.S. dollars.
Source: Smeeding, T.M. (2006). Poor people in rich countries: The United States in comparative perspective. *Journal of Economic Perspectives*, **20**(1).

children) and for nonelderly families without children and the United States was again second highest. For two-parent families (with children), Italy now ranked highest in the relative poverty rate but the United States was again second. The two Nordic countries, as well as Germany and Belgium, had extremely low relative poverty rates for two-parent families.

A new addition to this table is the calculation of national poverty rates on the basis of the U.S. official poverty lines. Overall, the United Kingdom had the highest (absolute) poverty rate of the nine countries shown, and the United States was second highest. Among the elderly and among children, the same pattern held with the United Kingdom the highest and the United State second highest. Canada was lower than the United States, particularly in terms of poverty among the elderly.

Another approach for measuring poverty on an international basis has been taken by the World Bank. It has two standards. The first is to use $2.00 per capita per day to classify persons as poor or not poor. The second is to use $1.00 per capita per day. This is the World Bank's definition of severe (or extreme) poverty. The World Bank converts national currencies to U.S. dollars on

Table 4.5 International comparisons of poverty rates using the World Bank definition of poverty by region, 1987 and 1998

Region	One dollar per day		Two dollars per day	
	1987	*1998*	*1987*	*1998*
East Asia	26.6	14.7	67.0	48.7
(excluding China)	23.9	9.5	62.9	44.3
Eastern Europe and Central Asia	0.2	3.8	3.6	20.7
Latin American and Caribbean	15.3	12.1	35.5	31.7
Middle East and North Africa	4.3	2.1	30.0	29.9
South Asia	44.9	44.0	86.3	83.9
Sub-Saharan Africa	46.6	48.1	76.5	78.0
Total	28.3	23.5	61.0	56.1
Total (excluding China)	28.5	25.6	58.2	57.9

The standard used is $1 (and $2) per day at 1985 PPP per capita.
Source: Chen, S. & Ravallion, M. (2001). How Did the Poorest Fare in the 1990s? *Review of Income and Wealth*, ser. 47, no. 3, Table 2, p. 290.

the basis of its PPP exchange rates. The standard is set for 1985 and adjusted each year for inflation. This standard can then be applied to countries at all levels of development. As may be apparent, this standard is a form of absolute poverty line.

Results of a study by two World Bank economists are shown in Table 4.5. Computations were performed for both 1987 and 1998 to see whether any progress was made over the decade of the 1990s. The most striking finding is that for the world as a whole there was a sizable reduction in poverty. The world poverty rate fell from 61.0 percent in 1987 to 56.1 percent in 1998 on the basis of the $2.00 per day standard and from 28.3 to 23.5 percent on the basis of the $1.00 per day standard. A large part of the reduction in world poverty was due to the phenomenal growth in per capita income in China (and its huge share of the world population). However, even excluding China, we find a reduction in world poverty, though not as dramatic.

There were also important regional differences in both poverty levels and trends. The highest levels of poverty were found in Sub-Saharan Africa and South Asia (notably India). East Asia was second highest in terms of poverty incidence and Eastern Europe and the Middle East the lowest (North American and Western Europe is excluded from this table).

With regard to time trends, between 1987 and 1998 a big reduction in poverty was recorded in East Asia (with and without China included). Modest reductions occurred in Latin America and the Caribbean, the Middle East and North Africa, and South Asia. However, there was a slight rise in poverty in Sub-Saharan Africa and a very large increase in Eastern Europe and Central Asia. The latter trend reflects the collapse of many of the economies of the former Soviet republics and Eastern Europe after central planning ended.

4.6   OTHER ISSUES IN THE MEASUREMENT OF POVERTY

There has been continuing controversy over the last three decades on the proper way to measure poverty. In Section 4.2, we discussed alternative ways of setting the poverty threshold. Three such proposals were put forward: an absolute poverty line; a relative poverty line; and a subjective poverty line.

The measurement problems treated in this section discuss the absolute poverty standard used in the official U.S. measure. The first two issues that are addressed concern the adjustment of the poverty line for differences in family size and the indexation of the poverty threshold over time for changes in the price level.

Once the poverty lines are decided, several questions arise as to the correct measure of resource availability used to determine whether the poverty standard is met. The official U.S. statistics are based on annual family money income before taxes. The third issue considered here is the treatment of taxes and the fourth is whether noncash government benefits, such as food stamps, housing subsidies, Medicare, and Medicaid, should be included in family income.

Families may also have other resources available besides (current) income to provide for their consumption needs. In particular, many families own assets, such as houses, savings accounts, bonds, and other financial assets. The fifth issue discussed below is the incorporation of household wealth in a measure of family resources used to measure poverty.

Because of taxes, noncash government benefits, and the availability of savings and service flows from housing and consumer durables, annual income may not be a good measure of the actual consumption level enjoyed by a household over the course of a year. A sixth issue concerns the use of actual family consumption instead of income in order to measure poverty status.

The official poverty calculations are based on *annual income*. A seventh issue concerns the choice of the accounting period. Some researchers have suggested that a shorter accounting period be used, such as a month, while others have suggested two- or three-year periods. As will be seen below, the measured poverty rate is quite sensitive to the period of analysis chosen. Several other measurement issues are considered in the last part of this section.[15]

4.6.1 Equivalence scales

In constructing poverty thresholds for different family sizes and types, one must implicitly determine what levels of income are "equivalent" for them in terms of the needs that are satisfied. For example, according to the official U.S. poverty thresholds for 2005, a family of three requires $15,577 to obtain a minimally adequate standard of living, while a family of four requires $19,971 (see Table 4.1). These two incomes are considered equivalent for their respective family size. The full set of adjustment factors for different family sizes and types is referred to as an **equivalence scale**.

It is assumed that larger families require greater income to achieve the same standard of living as a smaller one, but that there are also economies of consumption as household size increases. The official U.S. poverty lines were set on the basis of food requirements. It was then assumed that other consumption needs varied more or less in the same proportion.

However, the resulting official poverty thresholds have a rather irregular pattern with respect to family size. The poverty line for a family of three is set 22 percent greater than for a two-person family; while the threshold for a four-person family is 28 percent greater than for three persons. The threshold is set 13 percent greater for a six-person family than for five persons and also 13 percent greater for a family of seven than one of six. If there are economies of scale in consumption, then the differential between a two-person and three-person family should be *greater* than that between a four-person and three-person one. Moreover, it is not clear why the differential between a seven- and six-person family is the same as that between a six- and five-person family.

Another anomalous feature is that the poverty threshold for elderly couples is set lower than for nonelderly ones (the difference is 8 percent for the 2005 thresholds). Whereas it is true that the food plan costs calculated for elderly persons were lower than nonelderly ones (this was found in the original 1955 Survey of Food Consumption), it is unlikely that other needs are correspondingly less. This is particularly true for medical expenses, which are much higher for elderly people.

Ruggles (1990) calculated that the poverty rate for elderly persons in 1984 would have been 12.7 percent, instead of the official rate of 10.3 percent, if the same poverty threshold were used for elderly people as for the nonelderly. My calculations for 2005 indicate that the elderly poverty rate would have been 11.3 percent instead of the actual rate of 10.1 percent if the nonelderly poverty threshold was used. Moreover, it is likely that consumption needs vary among all *age* groups, not just between the elderly and nonelderly, so that equivalence class adjustments could be performed for young and middle-aged households as well as elderly ones.[16]

Because of the irregularities in the official U.S. poverty thresholds, researchers usually prefer to use other equivalence scales. One of the most common in the literature is of the form:

$$Y_E = Y/N^\varepsilon \tag{4.8}$$

where Y is family income, Y_E is equivalent family income, and ε is a parameter set between 0 and 1 (typically 0.5). If ε equals 0, then equivalent income is equal to family income; and if ε equals 1, then equivalent income equals per capita income. This equivalence scale incorporates economies of consumption on a consistent basis (that is, the rate of increase in equivalent income declines with family size).

Recently, the preferred equivalence scale used by researchers is one recommended by the National Academy of Sciences in its 1995 report on measuring poverty (see Short (2001) or Citro & Michael (1995) for more information). For single parents the scale is $(A + 0.8 + 0.5 \times (C - 1))^{0.7}$, where A is the number of adults and C is the number of children. All other families use the formula $(A + 0.5 \times C)^{0.7}$.

4.6.2 Choice of a price index

The official U.S. poverty thresholds have been adjusted each year (after 1969) by the national consumer price index (CPI-U). The use of the CPI has been questioned by researchers for three reasons. First, the CPI is based on the consumption expenditure patterns of the average household (actually, the average *urban* household). Since the consumption patterns of low-income families may differ from those of the average family (in particular, they consume a higher proportion of food, housing, and other necessities), it is not clear that the CPI is the most appropriate deflator for indexing the poverty thresholds. If the prices of food, housing, and other necessities rise at different rates than other consumption items, then the use of the CPI may be an inaccurate index of the actual change of purchasing power of the poor.

Second, for technical reasons, the CPI has been shown to have a bias with regard to the treatment of housing expenses. In particular, before 1983, the housing price index was based on the actual change in the price of new houses that were purchased on the market. However, only a small proportion of households buy a new house in a given year. For the vast majority of homeowners, the cost of housing depends on (usually fixed) mortgage rates, real estate taxes, utilities, and maintenance costs, while for renters, it depends on rents and utilities.[17] This problem was particularly acute during the late 1970s and early 1980s, when the price of new housing was rising much faster than the costs of these other items.

In 1983, the Bureau of Labor Statistics (BLS) changed its treatment of housing costs in the construction of the CPI. Instead of using new housing prices, the BLS substituted the change in the *rental* prices of housing. This series was felt to be more representative of the actual change in housing costs faced by most consumers.

There are other problems with the standard CPI-U discussed in Chapter 1. In particular, the CPI-U has recently been criticized for overstating the rate of inflation. As a result, the BLS has been providing a new consumer price series, called the CPI-U-RS. The CPI-U-RS series makes quality adjustments for housing units and consumer durables such as automobiles and personal computers and employs a geometric mean formula to account for consumer substitution within CPI item categories. As a result, the CPI-U-RS deflator is not subject to the same criticisms as the CPI-U series. Indeed, the Current Population Survey (CPS) data are now normally deflated to constant dollars using the new CPI-U-RS price index.

While the CPI-U-RS deflator incorporates quality and other adjustments, the adjustments are made only from *1978* to the present. The CPI-U index is used for years prior to 1978. The CPI-U-RS shows a much slower rate of inflation after 1973 than the CPI-U: 288 versus 238 percent. If we use the CPI-U-RS deflator, then "real" median family income grew by 22 percent between 1973 and 2000, in comparison to the 6 percent growth rate on the basis of the CPI-U deflator. The U.S. Census Bureau is still required by statute to use the CPI-U in computing the official poverty rates for the United States. However, my own calculations show that the poverty rate would have *fallen by 2.8 percentage points* between 1973 and 2005 if the CPI-U-RS were used. In contrast, using the CPI-U, the overall official poverty rate *increased by 1.5 percentage points*.

A third problem with the use of the national CPI in adjusting poverty thresholds over time is that the cost of living may vary considerably around the country. It requires less income to attain the same standard of living in rural Mississippi in comparison to New York City. As a result, the official statistics likely overstate poverty in Mississippi and understate it in New York. Many researchers have proposed the use of state or local CPI indices to determine poverty rates in different localities.

4.6.3 The treatment of taxes

The official poverty measure is based on before-tax income. Economists believe that a better measure of resource availability is the actual amount of money families have to spend to meet their needs. This argument suggests that the resource measure should be based on *disposable* or *after-tax income*. This is particularly important for two reasons. First, the tax burden of low-income households has risen over time in the United States since the early 1960s, when the poverty population paid almost no income taxes because of the system of personal exemptions and the standard deduction. The trend over time was mainly due to so-called "bracket creep." Personal income tax schedule brackets tended to be fixed in nominal terms over time, so that inflation forced low-income households into higher marginal tax brackets even though there was no change in their real income (see Chapter 16 for a discussion of the U.S. tax system). As a result, by the early 1980s, tax liability started at incomes that were considerably below the poverty line. Also, the increase in the payroll tax has added to the burden of the low-income population. By 1984, a family of four earning poverty-level income was paying about 10 percent of its income in the form of payroll and income taxes (see Sawhill, 1988, p. 1079). However, the Tax Reform Act of 1986 substantially lowered the personal income tax burdens of low-income families, and today income tax brackets are indexed for inflation.

Second, if the actual taxes paid differ among different demographic groups, then comparisons of poverty rates across groups may also be misleading. This is particularly germane to comparisons of families of different sizes, since the number of income tax exemptions rise with the size of the family. This issue also affects poverty rate comparisons between elderly and nonelderly families, because the former receive an extra tax exemption and a major source of their income, social security income, is exempted from most income tax.

Ruggles (1990, Table 4.1) calculated the effects of excluding federal income taxes and payroll taxes from family income on the poverty rate. She found that the poverty rate for all individuals would have increased from its actual level of 13.6 percent in 1986 to 14.6 percent, or by one percentage point. Moreover, the poverty gap ratio would have increased by 4 percent. The changes are relatively small, because even though the tax burdens of low-income households have increased over time, they are still small relative to total family income. However, by 2005, there was virtually no change in the overall poverty rate from excluding social security and both federal and state income taxes from family income.[18] The main reason why there is no effect is that the federal income tax now includes a tax credit for low-income families called the Earned Income Tax Credit (EITC). See Chapter 16 for more discussion.

4.6.4   The treatment of noncash government benefits

The official poverty line is based on family *money* income. As a result, the poverty line reflects *cash* government benefits such as social security benefits but not *noncash* government benefits such as Medicaid. When the poverty line was first established in the early 1960s, noncash government benefits were virtually nonexistent. However, since that time, the Food Stamp Program, Medicare, and Medicaid were established, and these programs considerably augmented the amount of resources available to low-income households. If, in addition, housing subsidies and school lunches are included, total noncash benefits to poor households more than doubled between 1970 and 1986 and accounted for almost two-thirds of total assistance to the poor (see Sawhill, 1988, p. 1078).

Most researchers now agree that noncash benefits should be included in the measure of family income used to determine poverty status. A number of studies have constructed new measures of the poverty rate based on the inclusion of noncash benefits, and the U.S. Census Bureau publishes an alternative series of poverty rates on the basis of adjustments originally estimated by Smeeding (1982).

Despite this general agreement, there still remains the difficult question of how such in-kind benefits should be valued. One approach is to value them at their **market value** – that is, the price the consumer must pay to obtain the same item in the private market. However, such noncash benefits are not directly *fungible* – that is, they cannot be used like cash to purchase any commodity that the individual wishes. Consequently, their value to the individual may be less than their market value, since the person does not have discretion over how to spend the benefits. In fact, the recipient may be forced to consume too much medical care, for example, and not enough clothing.

Food stamps have been shown to be fairly fungible (indeed, many business will accept them in lieu of cash even for nonfood purchases). As a result, their value to the recipient may be close to their face value. The main problem in valuation is the treatment of medical expenses. If actual medical benefits received were added to cash income, this would have the paradoxical result of implying that sicker persons are better off than healthier ones. An alternative approach is to value medical benefits at their **insurance value** – that is, how much medical insurance a person would have to pay to achieve the same level of medical care. However, for elderly people, the insurance costs would be very high to replace Medicare and Medicaid. Indeed, studies have shown that adding the insurance value of these two programs to the incomes of the elderly would, by itself, be sufficient to lift almost all the elderly poor out of poverty! Moreover, medical benefits have very limited fungibility, so that their value to the recipient is likely to be considerably less than their insurance equivalent.

Despite these reservations, if we totally disregard the growth of medical benefits (as well as other noncash benefits) for low-income families over time, we will understate the improvement of their well-being. As a result, one compromise proposal put forward by Aaron (1985) is a two-tiered poverty measure. For the first, the value of "cash-like" government benefits, such as food stamps, would be added to the family income measure. For the second, the availability of adequate medical coverage would be considered. If the person passed the poverty threshold based on the first measure but failed to have adequate medical coverage, the person would be classified as poor. A person would have to surpass both criteria to be considered nonpoor.

Some alternative calculations of the poverty rate made by the U.S. Census Bureau calculations are shown in Table 4.6. Two valuations are provided. In the first set, noncash benefits are valued at their private market value equivalent. For food stamps, this was set equal to the face value of the food coupons. For medical expenses, this was calculated as the actual medical expenditures paid out by the government divided by the number of individuals covered by the various programs. For housing subsidies, this was defined as the difference between the market rent for the housing unit and the actual rent paid by the recipient of the housing subsidy.

The second valuation is based on **recipient value**, which theoretically reflects the recipient's own valuation of the noncash benefit received. This was estimated in a fairly complex manner by comparing the expenditure patterns of the benefit recipient with a comparable family which did not receive the benefit. By comparing the expenditure patterns of the latter on similar items (food, medical care, and housing), the Census Bureau was able to impute a value of these benefits to the recipient.

The results clearly indicate that including the value of noncash government benefits in family income significantly lowers the measured poverty rate. The official poverty rate for the total population was 13.4 percent for 1987. When food and housing benefits are included at market value, the measured poverty rate falls to 12.0 percent; and when the market value of all medical benefits are added, the rate declines to 8.5 percent. A similar pattern is observed for other years and for valuation at recipient value. It is also of interest that valuation at recipient value produces a smaller decline in the poverty rate than market value. This is particularly true for medical benefits, whose recipient value is much smaller than its market value.

However, interestingly, the inclusion of noncash benefits in family income does not appear to alter the *trends* in the poverty rate. By all measures, the poverty rate increased between 1979 and 1983 and then declined thereafter to 1987. This was true for all families, and for whites, blacks, and Hispanic households separately.

A more elaborate calculation is shown in Table 4.7 for both 1989 and 2005. This table shows the effects of both including government transfers and netting out taxes on the measurement of the poverty rate. It has several steps. For all persons, the official poverty rate for 1989 was 12.8 percent. If all government transfer payments are excluded from income, the poverty rate jumps to 20.0 percent. The adjustment for income taxes and payroll taxes paid, as was discussed above, has very little effect on the measured poverty rate. When non-means-tested government cash transfers, such as social security benefits, are added back to income, the measured poverty rate falls by 6.4 percentage points to 13.9 percent. The inclusion of Medicare benefits, valued at market value, reduces the poverty rate by another 0.5 percentage points; the inclusion of means-tested government transfers, particularly Aid to Families with Dependent Children (AFDC), reduces it by a further 0.9 percentage points; and the addition of the value of Medicaid, also at market value, by still another 0.8 percentage points. Finally, the inclusion of other noncash government transfers, particularly food stamps and housing subsidies, results in a further drop of 1.3 percentage points.[19]

In 2005, the pattern is very much the same (it is only by coincidence that the official poverty rates are very close in the 2 years). One difference is that federal income tax *lowered* the poverty rate much more in 2005 than in 1989. The reason is that the addition of the EITC by itself lowered the poverty rate by 1.3 percentage points in 2005. On the other hand, the addition of

Table 4.6   Alternative measures of the poverty rate from adding noncash government benefits to income, 1979–1987 (percent)

Year	All races	Whites	Blacks	Hispanics
A. Official poverty index				
1979	11.7	9.0	31.0	21.8
1980	13.0	10.2	32.5	25.7
1981	14.0	11.1	34.2	26.5
1982	15.0	12.0	35.6	29.9
1983	15.2	12.1	35.7	28.0
1984	14.4	11.5	33.8	28.4
1987	13.4	10.4	32.4	28.0
B. Valuing food and housing benefits only at market value				
1979	9.7	7.8	23.5	17.4
1980	11.1	9.0	25.6	21.5
1981	12.3	9.9	28.9	22.8
1982	13.4	10.9	30.7	26.5
1983	13.9	11.3	30.6	25.6
1984	12.9	10.5	28.8	25.5
1987	12.0			
C. Valuing food and housing benefits only at recipient value				
1979	10.0	7.9	24.7	17.9
1980	11.4	9.2	26.5	22.2
1981	12.6	10.1	30.0	23.6
1982	13.7	11.1	31.7	27.2
1983	14.1	11.4	31.7	25.9
1984	13.2	10.7	30.1	26.0
1987	12.4			
D. Valuing food, housing, and all medical benefits at market value				
1979	6.8	5.6	14.9	12.0
1980	7.9	6.6	16.2	15.2
1981	9.0	7.4	19.7	16.8
1982	10.0	8.3	21.5	20.5
1983	10.3	8.7	21.2	19.9
1984	9.7	8.0	20.5	19.9
1987	8.5			
E. Valuing food, housing, and all medical benefits at recipient value				
1979	9.0	7.1	22.2	16.6
1980	10.4	8.4	24.2	20.5
1981	11.7	9.3	27.9	22.2
1982	12.7	10.3	29.3	26.1
1983	13.1	10.6	29.2	24.6
1984	12.2	9.8	28.3	24.7
1987	11.0			

Source: U.S. Census Bureau (1988). *Noncash Benefits: 1987*. U.S. Government Printing Office, Washington, DC.

Table 4.7 The effect of taxes and government transfers on the poverty rate, 1989 and 2005 (in percent)

Line		Component	All races	1989			2005 All races
				Whites	*Blacks*	*Hispanics*	
	A. 1989						
1		Official poverty rate	12.8	10.0	30.7	26.2	12.6
2	(1)	less govt. transfers	20.0	17.2	38.2	31.3	20.3
3	(2)	plus capital gains	19.9	17.2	38.1	31.0	20.3
4	(3)	plus health insurance supplements to labor earnings	19.4	16.7	37.3	29.9	19.7
5	(4)	less social security payroll taxes	20.3	17.6	38.3	32.5	20.6
6	(5)	less federal income tax[a]	20.1	17.3	37.8	31.7	19.0
7	(6)	less state income tax	20.3	17.5	38.3	31.8	19.0
8	(7)	plus non-means-tested govt. cash transfers	13.9	11.0	32.8	28.3	12.0
9	(8)	plus Medicare[b]	13.4	10.5	31.8	27.7	11.7
10	(9)	plus school lunches	13.4	10.5	31.7	27.7	11.6
11	(10)	plus means-tested govt. cash transfers	12.5	9.9	29.3	26.0	11.0
12	(11)	plus Medicaid[b]	11.7	9.3	27.7	24.3	10.5
13	(12)	plus other noncash govt. transfers	10.4	8.3	23.9	21.5	9.6
14	(13)	plus net imputed rent to owner-occupied housing	8.9	6.9	21.2	19.4	8.9

a   Includes federal earned income tax credit.
b   Based on market value valuation (see text for details).
Source: U.S. Census Bureau, Current Population Reports, Series P-60. No. 169-RD, *Measuring the Effect of Benefits and Taxes on Income and Poverty: 1989*, U.S. Government Printing Office, Washington, DC, September, 1990; and same title, March 2007.

the net imputed rent to owner-occupied housing had a larger effect in 1989. The net result is that the adjusted poverty rate was 8.9 percent in 2005 (line 14), exactly the same as in 1989.

In a sense, the results provide an answer to the often-asked question of why the poverty rate seems to remain so high after the huge increase in government spending on anti-poverty programs. Part of the answer is that much of the improvement in the well-being of low-income families is not captured in our standard poverty measure. However, once we include the value of noncash government benefits, the poverty rates are, in fact, much lower than they were 20 years ago.

4.6.5   The role of household wealth

Families may have access to consumption over and above their income if they have accumulated wealth. This may take two forms. First if they have accumulated financial savings, they can draw on this during periods when their income is low. Second, families also receive consumption "services" from housing that they may own or from consumer durables, such as automobiles. If poverty is thought of as a deprivation of resources to acquire an adequate amount of consumption services, then it might make sense to include a wealth dimension in the measure of family resources used to construct the poverty rate.[20]

Several studies have attempted to do this. Usually, wealth is converted into an income flow by assuming a fixed rate of return (5 or 7 percent, for example) or converted into a lifetime annuity (that is, a constant income flow over the remaining lifetime of the individual so that the person's wealth is completely exhausted at the end of life). In addition, an implicit rent on owner-occupied housing is also computed. This is typically estimated as a set rate of return on the gross or net value of the home. In my own work (Wolff, 1990), I used a 5 percent rate of return and found that including an annuity along with household income reduced the estimated poverty rate by 8 percent in 1983 and the further addition of imputed rent on homes reduced it by another 8 percent. Weisbrod and Hansen (1968) and Moon (1977) obtained similar results. The drop in the poverty rate was substantially greater for elderly families, because they had higher wealth (and also a higher ratio of wealth to current income) than younger families. Similar calculations for 1962 showed an even higher percentage drop in the measured poverty rate (26 percent decline in 1962 compared to 16 percent in 1983) because of the declining wealth holdings of low-income families. Updated calculations performed by the author on the basis of the 2004 Survey of Consumer Finances (SCF) indicated a poverty rate of 9.6 percent when both an annuity flow from non-home wealth and imputed rent to owner-occupied housing were added to money income.[21] This compares to the official rate of 12.7 percent, a 3.1 percentage point difference. The larger effect of adding both an annuity flow and imputed rent to money income in 2004 compared to 1983 reflects the higher level of wealth in 2004, even among low-income households.

Another approach to treating the relation between wealth and poverty is evidenced in the work of Caner and Wolff (2004, 2007), who helped develop the notion of *asset poverty*. A household is considered to be asset-poor if its access to wealth-type resources is insufficient to enable the household to meet its basic needs for three months. Using the PSID data for years 1984–2001, they estimated the level and severity of asset poverty. They found first of all that asset poverty rates are almost double those of standard income-based poverty rates. Second, despite a sharp decline in the official income-based poverty rate, the asset poverty rate barely changed over this period. It was 26.4 percent in 1984 and 26.8 percent in 2001. Moreover, the severity of asset poverty increased during this period as indebtedness went up sharply. The asset poverty gap ratio almost doubled from 61.5 percent in 1984 to 106.3 percent in 2001.

According to their analysis, the aging of the population would have pulled the overall asset poverty rate down by a few percentage points, but increases in poverty rates among the younger groups kept the rate unchanged. During the period, the likelihood of being asset-poor decreased for those who were college graduates or married with children, whereas it increased for those who were white, working or homeowners. There was also much more persistence in asset poverty than in income poverty. Persistence was the highest among blacks, the elderly, single mothers, and those with low education. They also found that lifetime events, such as changes in the job market, marital and homeownership status were correlated with transitions into and out of asset poverty.

4.6.6   Consumption-based measures of poverty

We have already discussed four reasons why before-tax money income may not be an adequate measure of the resources available to the low-income population. First, tax payments reduce the amount of income that can be used for consumption. Second, government noncash benefits may add to family resources. Third, families can draw from accumulated savings. Fourth, housing and consumer durables provide service flows that can directly benefit households. A fifth reason is that families can borrow money (go into debt) in order to finance their consumption expenditures. A sixth is that families can receive transfers from other people in the form of gifts or bequests. As a result, income may be a poor proxy for consumption, particularly among families with low income.

A related argument comes from the permanent income hypothesis developed by Friedman (1957). He argued that income consists of two parts: permanent income, which represents the normal flow of resources to the family; and transitory income, which is subject to random fluctuations over time. Households base their consumption patterns on permanent income, rather than their actual income. The lower tail of the income distribution is likely to contain a disproportionate number of households who have experienced a temporary reduction in income. As a result, low-income households generally have high ratios of consumption to income in order to maintain their normal standard of living.

Because of the problems with an income-based measure of poverty, Slesnick (1993) developed new indices of poverty using actual expenditure data drawn from the Consumer Expenditure Survey. His main conclusion was that consumption-based measures of poverty are substantially lower than the official income-based poverty rates. His estimate of the poverty rate for 1989 was 8.4 percent, compared to the official figure of 12.8 percent. The time trends were also different. Whereas the official numbers show poverty declining between 1960 and 1973 and then generally rising, his consumption-based index showed a general downward trend from 1960 to 1989. Moreover, the divergence between the official rate and the consumption-based poverty rate widened over time. He concluded that poverty in the United States had declined much more over the postwar period than the official figures had indicated.

In a more recent study, Meyer and Sullivan (2006) reached the same conclusion. They used a very similar method and updated their comparison of income-based and consumption-based poverty to 2004. Using the National Academy of Sciences two-parameter equivalence scale (see Section 4.6.1 above), they calculated that the income-based poverty rate declined from 15.3 percent in 1983 to 11.6 percent in 2004 or by 3.7 percentage points. Consumption-based poverty rates, computed from the Consumer Expenditure Survey, were uniformly lower by 2 to 3 percentage points than the income-based poverty rates in all years from 1983 to 2004. Moreover, they estimated that the consumption-based poverty rate fell from 13.8 percent in 1983 to 9.2 percent in 2004, or by 4.6 percentage points.

A similar conclusion was reached by Meyer and Jencks (1993) on the basis of a somewhat different approach. They argued that poverty measures should reflect whether families have adequate food, shelter, clothing, medical care, and education. They evaluated the welfare level of the low-income population using actual measures of material well-being such as food and clothing expenditures, housing conditions (the presence of indoor plumbing, for example), access to automobiles, telephones, televisions, health status, and access to medical and dental care. Unlike the official poverty figures, they found no evidence of the deterioration in the living conditions of the poor during the 1980s, and concluded that anti-poverty programs have been effective in providing for the basic needs of the low-income population.

Though consumption-based measures tend to show lower poverty than income measures, many researchers feel that the latter are still superior as a measure of needs. The main reason is that a family's consumption can be high at a point in time while its income is low if the family goes into debt. Indeed, as we shall see in Chapter 5, the decade of the 2000s in the United States is characterized by a pronounced explosion in debt, particularly among lower income households. Many analysts in this field feel that consumption maintained by debt is not sustainable over time since the debt will eventually have to be repaid.

4.6.7 The accounting period

The official poverty rate calculation is based on annual family income. If a family's total income for the year falls short of the poverty threshold (also based on annual income), the family is classified as poor. However, income flows tend to be very uneven over time. As a result, it is much more likely for a family to experience an income shortfall for a short period of time than an extended one. Such setbacks may be associated with sudden or temporary changes in a family's condition, such as divorce or separation, a period of unemployment, death or disability of a worker in the family, or the birth of a child. Thus, the choice of accounting period can make a crucial difference in both the measure of the poverty rate and an understanding of the causes and remedies for poverty.

Let us first consider the use of accounting periods longer than one year. To examine such an issue, one must rely on a panel survey, which covers the same set of families on a continuing basis. One such database is the PSID, which has followed a sample of about 5,000 families since 1968. A study by Duncan (1984), based on the PSID, found that only a very small proportion (2.6 percent) of the *total* sample population would be classified as poor in eight out of the 10 years between 1969 and 1978. On the other hand, 24 percent of the population fell into poverty for at least one year over this period. Thus, as we saw in Section 4.5.1 above, the number of long-term poor is much smaller than the poverty population identified in a calendar year. If we use an accounting period longer than a year to define poverty, our estimate of the poverty rate will be correspondingly lower.

Let us now look at the other side of the question, the use of accounting periods shorter than one year. It is first of interest to note that eligibility to many government welfare programs, such as Temporary Assistance to Needy Families (TANF), is based on monthly income statements rather than annual income. These program designers were aware of the importance of short-term poverty, since even a temporary shortfall of income for many families may require immediate relief.

Research on this issue was done by Ruggles (1990) on the basis of the Survey of Income and Program Participation, which provides monthly income data. Four indices were computed using 1984 data: (i) the percent of poor on the basis of the official annual income definition; (ii) the percent whose monthly income fell below the official poverty threshold in monthly terms (the annual threshold divided by 12) for all 12 months; (iii) the percent whose monthly income fell below the official poverty threshold for at least one month; and (iv) the average of the monthly poverty rates. She found sharp differences in the measures. The official poverty index yielded a 11.0 percent poverty rate in this sample. In contrast, only 5.9 percent of individuals were poor in all 12 months (the second index), while 26.2 percent were poor in at least one month (the third index). The average monthly poverty rate (the fourth index), in turn, was 13.7 percent. It is of interest that the proportion of poor based on the average of monthly rates was higher than the annual poverty index, because of the high proportion of individuals who fall into poverty in at least one month.

In a more recent study, Iceland (2003) updated Ruggles' results using panel data from SIPP over the period from 1996 to 1999. On the basis of the SIPP data (and summing monthly incomes), he computed an annual poverty for 1999 of 10.1 percent. He then estimated that 19.5 percent of individuals were poor two or more months in 1999. The average monthly poverty rate in 1999 was calculated at 12.8 percent. Finally, he found that only 2.0 percent of individuals were poor on a monthly basis for the 48 months between 1996 and 1999.

Measures of poverty are thus quite sensitive to the period that we consider appropriate in determining what constitutes deprivation of a "minimally adequate standard of living." The majority of poor people are in poverty for relatively short periods rather than over long stretches of time.

4.6.8   Other issues

Another issue of measurement is the unit of analysis or the choice of the recipient unit. The official poverty line is based on the family unit. This choice is mainly due to the fact that a large amount of resource sharing occurs within the family unit. Thus, even though children do not typically earn any income themselves, they still have access to their parents' income. The same argument holds for nonworking wives. As a result, an individual's poverty status has traditionally depended on the total income of the family unit.

However, the nuclear family may have access to resources outside its immediate members. This is particularly so in the case of divorce if former wives receive alimony or their children receive child support from their father. In such a case, children may have access to resources from a father who no longer lives with them. Moreover, there still exists among certain segments of our population the "extended family system." In this regard, a nuclear family may receive assistance from the mother's or father's parents or other relatives. This may be particularly so in times when a family is experiencing economic hardship. Though these issues are of direct interest, it has proven very difficult to obtain precise estimates of how they might affect the measured poverty rate.[22]

Another issue concerns the value of leisure or nonmarket time (see Section 2.6.1). Low-income families, whose father and mother are both working full time, may have relatively little time left over for home production or child care. In some sense, such a family is materially worse off than another family unit with the same money income but whose mother does not work and can devote more time to nonmarket activity. It would also be of interest to adjust poverty measures for the welfare loss stemming from the unavailability of time for home production.

A related issue concerns the existence of some family or household units with low incomes, such as college students, who may be classified as poor according to the official poverty index but who expect low incomes to be temporary until they begin their lifetime career. Therefore, Garfinkel and Haveman (1977) took another approach to measure poverty, on the basis of what they call "earnings capacity." This measure is defined on the basis of 2,000 hours worked per year and on the wage that would be expected, given the person's schooling and occupation. Such a measure eliminates many young individuals, with a high level of education and temporarily low incomes, from the ranks of the poor. However, low-skilled workers, who sometimes work more than 2,000 hours per year ("moonlighting" with two jobs or working excessive overtime) in order to compensate for low wages, do enter the ranks of poor, even if their annual earnings are above the poverty threshold.

4.7   SUMMARY

There are three common ways of setting the poverty line in common use: (i) an absolute standard; (ii) a relative standard; and (iii) a subjective standard. The official U.S. poverty threshold is based on an absolute poverty standard, which remains fixed over time in real terms. The relative poverty line is set as a fixed percentage of the median income, which may change over time if median income changes in real terms. The subjective poverty line is based on respondents' answers to questions regarding what they consider an adequate standard of living.

The official poverty index for the United States is based on annual before-tax cash income received by the family unit. Alternative ways have also been proposed to modify the existing poverty standard, and studies have shown that measures of poverty are sensitive to the criteria for both the poverty threshold and the definition of income used. Among the modifications that have been used are as follows: First, different equivalence class adjustments have been employed to differentiate the poverty thresholds among families of different sizes and types. Second, after-tax income has been proposed as a better measure of family resources than before-tax income, which is used in the official definition. Measured poverty incidence has generally been slightly greater with after-tax income. Third, noncash government benefits – particularly, food stamps, Medicaid and Medicare benefits, and housing allowances – have also been added to family income. Such adjustments result in a considerably lower measure of poverty incidence, though the time trend in poverty rates, at least since 1979, does not seem to be affected. Fourth, including a return on household wealth in the definition of income lowers the measured poverty rate by 10 to 20 percent. Fifth, using monthly income instead of annual income produces a higher poverty rate, whereas using income for several years as the base produces a lower rate.

Actual poverty trends for the United States show a gradual reduction between 1959 and 1964, a pronounced drop between 1964 and 1968, almost no change until 1979, a steep rise between 1979 and 1983, a moderate decline to 1989, a subsequent increase to 1993 followed again by a sharp reduction until 2000, and then another upward trend until 2005. The poverty rate in 2005 was 12.6 percent, the same level as in 1970. Poverty rates have been about two and half to three times as high for black persons as whites, and two and a half times as high for Hispanic individuals as whites. Poverty rates in the United States are considerably higher than other industrialized (OECD) countries.

Poverty rates for children have been considerably greater than those for adults. Between 1973 and 1993, the poverty rate among children increased faster than the adult rate. During the 1980s and early 1990s, one-fifth or more of children were poor, though their poverty rate dropped to 17.6 percent in 2005. The big success story over the last three and a half decades has been the elderly, whose poverty rate fell from 35 percent in 1959, considerably above the overall rate, to 10 percent in 2005, below the overall poverty rate and even below the rate for nonelderly adults.

Poverty incidence is five to six times greater for female-headed families than for male-headed ones. Though the poverty rate for female-headed households has not changed very much since the 1960s, more than half of all poor families were headed by a female in 2005, compared to less than one-quarter in 1959. The reason is the rapid growth in the total number of female-headed households in the United States since the late 1950s. Although poverty incidence is much higher in families where the household head did not work, almost half of the poor in 2005 were in families in which the head *did* work.

Another dimension of poverty is its duration or "permanence." Only about 10 to 20 percent of poor families would be called permanently poor. About half of all poor families exit poverty within a year. The underclass, defined by residence in a low-income area, comprises only about 5 to 7 percent of all the poor. However, this proportion has increased since the 1970s, since today over 40 percent of poor families live in urban areas, compared to 25 percent in 1959.

The analysis of the determinants of poverty is really part of the analysis of income determination, a subject which will occupy us for most of the remainder of the text. There are many complex issues involved in what causes poverty, and these are best left for later treatment. However, it is possible at this point to make some general observations on the incidence and implications of poverty. Age seems to have an important bearing on poverty status. One might expect that poverty among young people is due to the difficulty of finding a good job and therefore temporary since better jobs are usually reserved for more experienced workers. On the other hand, the aged poor are often trapped in their poverty status since well-paying jobs are usually unavailable to them due to laws, custom, or their lack of work capacity. Therefore, poverty occurring in old age is usually more serious than for those who are younger.

Families headed by females have a very high incidence of poverty. The major reason is that the demands of child care often make the mother unavailable for work. Unwed mothers often become dependent on public assistance, though recently there has been some effort to make day-care facilities and training programs available to single parents to allow them to work.

Children have recently had a very high incidence of poverty. Many of them live in single-parent households. There is also a high incidence of poverty in families with a large number of children. The mere fact that a family has many children means that the same income must be spread over more people.

Poverty status is very closely related to employment status. For those not in the labor force or unemployed, the incidence of poverty is very high. There are a number of reasons why an adult might not be in the labor force. One, just discussed, is that the person might be a single parent, whose time is tied up in child care. Other causes include sickness, disability, and old age. Unemployment may be due to a recession or to the fact that an individual may be unskilled or uneducated or lack the necessary skills to meet job requirements. Racial and gender discrimination may prevent a person from obtaining a job.

Many families in poverty are the working poor. This may be a consequence of part-time or part-year work or a result of working in a low-wage job. In 2005, someone working full time and full year at the minimum wage would not earn enough income to keep a family of four above the poverty line. The incidence of low-wage employment is particularly high among persons with limited schooling and skills, unattached individuals, females, minorities, and employees in seasonal or service industries. This issue leads directly to the question of the determination of earnings with which Part II of the book is concerned.

We might wonder what explains the stagnancy of the poverty rate since 1973 despite robust economic growth in the period 1980 through 2005. An analysis by Hoynes, Page, and Stevens (2006) provides some insights. Relative to the large decline that was experienced during the 1960s, they found that U.S. poverty rates changed very little between 1975 and 2005. Part of the reason is that the relationship between poverty and the macro-economy (growth and the level of unemployment) weakened over time. However, in spite of this, changes in labor market opportunities still impact changes in the poverty rate rather well. Changes in female labor supply should have reduced the poverty rate further, but an increase in the share of families headed by women worked in the opposite direction to raise the poverty rate. Other factors that are often cited in the literature such as changes in the number and composition of immigrants and changes in the generosity of anti-poverty programs did not turn out to be important in their analysis.

4.8 REFERENCES AND BIBLIOGRAPHY

Aaron, H. (1967). The foundations of the "War on Poverty" reexamined. *American Economic Review*, **57**(4), 1229–40.

Aaron, H. (1978). *Politics and the Professors: The Great Society in Perspective*. Washington, DC: Brookings Institution.

Aaron, H. (1985). Comments on "Evaluation of Census Bureau Procedures for the Measurement of Noncash Benefits". In *Conference on the Measurement of Noncash Benefits*, Vol. 1, U.S. Census Bureau, Washington, D.C., pp. 57–62.

Alkire, S. (2002). *Valuing Freedoms: Sen's Capability Approach and Poverty Reduction*. Oxford: Oxford University Press.

Anderson, M. (1978). *The Political Economy of Welfare Reform in the United States*. Palo Alto, CA: Hoover Institute Press.

Anderson, W.H.L. (1964). Trickling down: The relationship between economic growth and the extent of poverty among American families. *Quarterly Journal of Economics*, **78**(4), 511–24.

Atkinson, A.B. (1987a). Income maintenance and social insurance: A survey. In A. Auerbach & M. Feldstein (eds.), *Handbook of Public Economics*, Vol. 2 (Chapter 13, pp. 779–889). Amsterdam: North Holland.

Atkinson, A.B. (1987b). On the measurement of poverty. *Econometrica*, **55**, 749–64.

Bane, M.J. & Ellwood, D. (1986). Slipping into and out of poverty: The dynamics of spells. *Journal of Human Resources*, **21**(1), 1–23.

Bassi, L. & Ashenfelter, O. (1986). The effect of direct job creation and training programs on low-skilled workers. In S.H. Danziger & D.H. Weinberg (eds.), *Fighting Poverty* (pp. 133–51). Cambridge, MA: Harvard University Press.

Beach, C. (1977). Cyclical sensitivity of aggregate income inequality. *Review of Economics and Statistics*, **59**(1), 56–66.

Blackburn, M.L. (1994). International comparisons of poverty. *American Economic Review Papers and Proceedings*, **84**(2), 371–4.

Blank, R. (1997). *It Takes a Nation: A New Agenda for Fighting Poverty*. Princeton, NJ: Princeton University Press.

Blank, R. (2002). Evaluating welfare reform in the United States. *Journal of Economic Literature*, **40**(4), 1105–66.

Blinder, A. (1980). The level and distribution of economic well-being. In M. Feldstein (ed.), *The American Economy in Transition* (pp. 415–79). Chicago: University of Chicago Press.

Blinder, A. & Esaki, H. (1978). Macroeconomic activity and income distribution in the postwar United States. *Review of Economics and Statistics*, **60**(4), 604–9.

Browning, E.K. & Johnson, W.R. (1984). The trade-off between equality and efficiency. *Journal of Political Economy*, **92**(2), 175–203.

Burtless, G. (1986). Public spending for the poor: Trends, prospects and economic limits. In S.H. Danziger & D.H. Weinberg, *Fighting Poverty* (pp. 18–49). Cambridge, MA: Harvard University Press.

Burtless, G. (1994). In-kind transfers and the trend in poverty. In D.J. Besharov & L. Lenkowsky (eds.), *Understanding Poverty and Dependence*. New York: Free Press.

Burtless, G. & Smeeding, T. (2001). The level, trend, and composition of poverty. In S.H. Danziger & D.H. Weinberg, *Fighting Poverty* (pp. 27–68). Cambridge, MA: Harvard University Press.

Cancian, M. & Reed, D. (2001). Changes in family structure. In S.H. Danziger & R. Haveman (eds.), *Understanding Poverty*. New York: Russell Sage Foundation.

Caner, A. & Wolff, E.N. (2004). Asset poverty in the United States, 1984–99: Evidence from the Panel Study of Income Dynamics. *Review of Income and Wealth*, ser. 50, no. 4, 493–518.

Caner, A. & Wolff, E.N. (2006). The persistence of asset poverty in the United States, 1984–2001. In M.V. Lane (ed.), *Trends in Poverty and Welfare Alleviation Issues* (Chapter 3, pp. 51–80). Nova Science.

Chen, S., Datt, G. & Ravallion, M. (1994). Is poverty increasing in the developing world? *Review of Income and Wealth*, ser. 40, no. 4, 359–76.

Chen, S. & Ravallion, M. (2001). How did the poorest fare in the 1990s? *Review of Income and Wealth*, ser. 47, no. 3, 283–300.

Citro, C.F. & Michael, R.T. (eds.) (1995). *Measuring Poverty: A New Approach*. Washington, DC: National Academy Press.

Clark, D.A. (2002). *Visions of Development: A Study of Human Values*. Cheltenham, UK: Edward Elgar.

Clark, D.A. (2006). Capability approach. In D.A. Clark (ed.), *The Elgar Companion to Development Studies*. Cheltenham, UK: Edward Elgar.

Clark, S., Hemming, R. & Ulph, D. (1981). On indices for the measurement of poverty. *Economic Journal*, **91**, 515–26.

Coe, R. (1978). Dependency and poverty in the short and long run. In G.J. Duncan & J.N. Morgan (eds.), *Five Thousand American Families: Patterns of Economic Progress* (Vol. VI, pp. 273–96). Ann Arbor, MI: Institute for Social Research.

Conley, D. (1999). *Being Black, Living in the Red: Race, Wealth and Social Policy in America*. Berkeley: University of California Press.

Corcoran, M. *et al.* (1985). Myth and reality: The causes and persistence of poverty. *Journal of Policy Analysis and Management*, **4**(4), 516–36.

Cowell, F.A. (1988). Poverty measures, inequality and decomposability. In D. Bos, M. Rose & C. Seidl (eds.), *Welfare and Efficiency in Public Economics*. Heidelberg: Springer Verlag.

Danziger, S.H. (1987). Recent trends in poverty and the antipoverty effectiveness of income transfers. In S.H. Danziger & K. Portney (eds.), *The Distributional Impacts of Public Policy* (pp. 33–45). London: Macmillan.

Danziger, S.H. & Gottschalk, P. (1986). Do rising tides lift all boats? The impact of secular and cyclical changes in poverty. *American Economic Review*, **76**(2), 405–10.

Danziger, S.H. & Gottschalk, P. (1987). Earnings inequality, the spatial concentration of poverty, and the underclass. *American Economic Review*, **77**(2), 211–15.

Danziger, S.H. & Gottschalk, P. (1995). *America Unequal*. Cambridge, MA: Harvard University Press and Russell Sage Press.

Danziger, S.H. & Gottschalk, P. (2004). *Diverging Fortunes: Trends in Poverty and Inequality*. New York: Russell Sage Foundation.

Danziger, S.H., Haveman, R. & Plotnick, R. (1981). How income transfer programs affect work, savings, and the income distribution: A critical review. *Journal of Economic Literature*, **19**(3), 975–1028.

Danziger, S.H., Haveman, R. & Plotnick, R. (1986). Antipoverty policy: Effects on the poor and the nonpoor. In S.H. Danziger & D.H. Weinberg, *Fighting Poverty* (pp. 50–77). Cambridge, MA: Harvard University Press.

Danziger, S.H. & Plotnick, R. (1982). The war on income poverty: Achievements and failures. In P. Sommers (ed.), *Welfare Reform in America* (pp. 31–52). Boston: Kluwer-Nijhoff.

Danziger, S.H. & Weinberg, D.H. (1986). *Fighting Poverty*. Cambridge, MA: Harvard University Press.

Deaton, A.S. & Muellbauer, J. (1980). *Economics and Consumer Behavior*. Cambridge: Cambridge University Press.

Dooley, M. & Gottschalk, P. (1984). Earnings inequality among males in the United States: Trends and the effect of labor force growth. *Journal of Political Economy*, **92**(1), 59–89.

Dooley, M. & Gottschalk, P. (1985). The increasing proportion of men with low earnings in the United States. *Demography*, **22**(1), 25–34.

Duncan, G. (1984). *Years of Poverty, Years of Plenty*. Ann Arbor, MI: University of Michigan Press.

Duncan, G. & Hoffman, S.D. (1988). The use and effects of welfare: A survey of recent evidence. *Social Service Review*, **62**, 238–57.

Duncan, O., Featherman, D. & Duncan, B. (1972). *Socioeconomic Background and Achievement*. New York: Seminar Press.

Ellwood, D. & Summers, L. (1986). Poverty in America: Is welfare the answer or the problem? In S.H. Danziger & D.H. Weinberg, *Fighting Poverty* (pp. 78–105). Cambridge, MA: Harvard University Press.

Fisher, F.M. (1987). Household equivalence scales and interpersonal comparisons. *Review of Economic Studies*, **54**, 519–24.

Fisher, G.M. (1992). The development and history of the poverty thresholds. *Social Security Bulletin*, **55**(4).

Foster, J. & Shorrocks, A.F. (1988). Poverty orderings. *Econometrica*, **56**, 173–77.

Foster, J.E., Greer, J. & Thorbecke, E. (1984). A class of decomposable poverty indices. *Econometrica*, **52**, 761–6.

Freeman, R. & Hall, B. (1987). Permanent homelessness in America? *Population Research Policy Review*, **6**, 3–27.

Freeman, R.B. & Wise, D.A. (eds.) (1982). The youth labor market problem: Its nature, causes and consequences. NBER Conference Report. Chicago: University of Chicago Press.

Friedman, M. (1957). *A Theory of the Consumption Function*. Princeton, NJ: Princeton University Press for the National Bureau of Economic Research.

van der Gaag, J. & Smolensky, E.e (1982). True household equivalence scales and characteristics of the poor in the United States. *Review of Income and Wealth*, **28**(1), 17–28.

Garfinkel, I. & Haveman, R. (1977). *Earnings Capacity, Poverty, and Inequality*. New York: Academic Press.

Glazer, N. (1986). Education and training programs and poverty. In S.H. Danziger & D.H. Weinberg, *Fighting Poverty* (pp. 152–73). Cambridge, MA: Harvard University Press.

Gottschalk, P. & Danziger, S.H. (1984). Macroeconomic conditions, income transfers, and the trend in poverty. In D.L. Bawden (ed.), *The Social Contract Revisited* (pp. 185–215). Washington, DC: Urban Institute Press.

Gottschalk, P. & Danziger, S.H. (1985). A framework for evaluating the effects of economic growth and transfers on poverty. *American Economic Review*, **75**(1), 153–61.

Gottschalk, P. & Danziger, S.H. (1995). *America Unequal*. Cambridge, MA: Harvard University Press.

Gramlich, E.M. (1974). The distributional effects of higher unemployment. *Brookings Papers on Economic Activity*, **2**, 293–336.

Grogger, J. & Karoly, L.A. (2005). *Welfare Reform: Effects of a Decade of Change*. Cambridge, MA: Harvard University Press.

Hagenaars, A.J.M. (1986). *The Perception of Poverty*. Amsterdam: North-Holland.

Hagenaars, A.J.M. & van Praag, B.M.S. (1985). A synthesis of poverty line definitions. *Review of Income and Wealth*, ser. 31, no. 2, 139–54.

Hagenaars, A.J.M. & de Vos, K. (1988). The definition and measurement of poverty. *Journal of Human Resources*, **23**(2), 211–21.

Harrington, M. (1962). *The Other America*. New York: Macmillan.

Harrison, B. & Bluestone, B. (1988). *The Great U-Turn: Corporate Restructuring and the Polarization of America*. New York: Basic Books.

Haveman, R. (1987). *Poverty Policy and Poverty Research: The Great Society and the Social Sciences*. Madison, WI: University of Wisconsin Press.

Haveman, R. & Wolff, E.N. (2004). The concept and measurement of asset poverty: Levels, trends and composition for the U.S., 1983–2001. *Journal of Economic Inequality*, **2**(2), 145–69.

Haveman, R. & Wolff, E.N. (2005). Who are the asset poor? Levels, trends and composition, 1983–1998. In M. Sherraden (ed.), *Inclusion in the American Dream: Assets, Poverty, and Public Policy* (pp. 61–86). New York: Oxford University Press.

Henle, P. & Ryscavage, P. (1980). The distribution of earned income among men and women, 1958–77. *Monthly Labor Review*, **103**(4), 3–10.

Hill, M.S. (1981). Some dynamic aspects of poverty. In M.S. Hill, D.H. Hill & J.N. Morgan (eds.), *Five Thousand American Families: Patterns of Economic Progress* (Vol. IX, pp. 93–120). Ann Arbor, MI: Institute for Social Research.

Hines, J., Hoynes, H. & Krueger, A. (2001). Another look at whether a rising tide lifts all boats. In A. Krueger & R. Solow (eds.), *The Roaring Nineties: Can Full Employment Be Sustained*. New York: Russell Sage Foundation.

Hirsch, B. (1980). Poverty and economic growth: Has trickle down petered out? *Economic Inquiry*, **18**(1), 151–8.

Hisnanick, J.J. (2007). The dynamics of low income and persistent poverty among U.S. families. *Journal of Income Distribution*, **16**(1), 114–31.

Hoynes, H.W., Page, M.E. & Huff Stevens, A. (2006). Poverty in America: Trends and explanations. *Journal of Economic Perspectives*, **20**(1), 47–68.

Hurst, E., Luoh, M.C. & Stafford, F.P. (1998). The wealth dynamics of American families, 1984–94. *Brookings Papers on Economic Activity*, **1**, 267–337.

Iceland, J. (2003). *Dynamics of Economic Well-Being, Poverty 1996–1999*, Current Population Reports, P70-91. U.S. Census Bureau, Washington, DC.

Jargowsky, P.A. & Sawhill, I.V. (2006). The decline of the underclass. The Center on Children and Families (CCF) Brief No. 36, The Brookings Institution, Washington, DC, January.

Jencks, C. (ed.) (1972). *Inequality*. New York: Basic Books.

Lampman, R. (1984). *Social Welfare Spending: Accounting for Changes from 1950 to 1978*. New York: Academic Press.

Lampman, R. & Smeeding, T. (1983). Inter-family transfers as alternatives to government transfers to persons. *Review of Income Wealth*, **29**(1), 45–66.

Lazear, E. & Michael, R. (1980). Family size and the distribution of real per capita income. *American Economic Review*, **70**(1), 91–107.

Mayer, S.E. (1993). Living conditions among the poor in four rich countries. *Journal of Population Economics*, **6**, 261–86.

Mayer, S.E. & Jencks, C. (1993). Recent trends in economic inequality in the United States: Income versus expenditures versus material well-being. In D.B. Papadimitriou & E.N. Wolff (eds.), *Poverty and Prosperity in the USA in the Late Twentieth Century*. London: Macmillan.

Meyer, B.D. (2004). The effects of welfare and tax reform: The material well-being of single mothers in the 1980s and 1990s. *Journal of Public Economics*, **88**, 1387–420.

Meyer, B.D. (2003). Measuring the well-being of the poor using income and consumption. *Journal of Human Resources*, **38**, 1180–220.

Meyer, B.D. & Sullivan, J.X.S. (2006). Three decades of consumption and income poverty. National Poverty Center (NPC) Working Paper No. 06-35, Ann Arbor, MI, September.

McMahon, P.J. & Tschetter, J.H. (1986). The declining middle class: a further analysis. *Monthly Labor Review*, **109**(9), 22–7.

Moon, M. (1977). *The Measurement of Economic Welfare: Applications to the Aged*. New York: Academic Press.

Murray, C. (1984). *Losing Ground: American Social Policy, 1950–1980*. New York: Basic Books.

Nussbaum, M.C. (2000). *Women and Human Development: The Capabilities Approach.* Cambridge: Cambridge University Press.

Nussbaum, M.C. & Sen, A. (eds.) (1993). *The Quality of Life.* Oxford: Clarendon Press.

Orshansky, M. (1965). Counting the poor: Another look at the poverty profile. *Social Security Bulletin*, **28**(1), 3–29.

Plant, M. (1984). An empirical analysis of welfare dependence. *American Economic Review*, **74**(4), 673–84.

Plotnick, R. (1984). The redistributive impact of cash transfers. *Public Finance Quarterly*, **12**(1), 27–50.

Ravallion, M., Datt, G. & van de Walle, D.E. (1991). Quantifying absolute poverty in the developing world. *Review of Income and Wealth*, ser. 37, no. 4, 345–61.

Ricketts, E.R. & Sawhill, I.V. (1988). Growth of the underclass, 1970–80. *Journal of Human Resources*, **25**(1), 137–45.

Rodgers, J.R. & Rodgers, J.L. (1993). Chronic poverty in the United States. *Journal of Human Resources*, **28**(1), 25–54.

Ruggles, P. (1990). *Drawing the Line.* Washington, DC: Urban Institute Press.

Sawhill, I.V. (1988). Poverty in the United States: Why is it so persistent. *Journal of Economic Literature*, **26**(3), 1073–119.

Seidl, C. (1988). Poverty measurement: A survey. In D. Bos, M. Rose & C. Seidl (eds.), *Welfare and Efficiency in Public Economics.* Heidelberg: Springer-Verlag.

Sen, A. (1976). Poverty: An ordinal approach to measurement. *Econometrica*, **44**(2), 219–32.

Sen, A. (1979). Issues in the measurement of poverty. *Scandinavian Journal of Economics*, 285–307.

Sen, A. (1979). Utilitarianism and welfarism. *Journal of Philosophy*, **LXXVI**(9), 463–89.

Sen, A. (1985). *Commodities and Capabilities.* Oxford: Oxford University Press.

Sen, A. (1999). *Development as Freedom.* New York: Knopf.

Shapiro, T.M. & Wolff, E.N. (eds.) (2001). *Assets for the Poor: Benefits of Spreading Asset Ownership.* New York: Russell Sage Foundation.

Sherraden, M. (1991). *Assets and the Poor: A New American Welfare Policy.* New York: M.E. Sharpe.

Short, K. (2001). Experimental poverty measures:

1999. *U.S. Census Bureau, Current Population Reports*, P60-216, U.S. Government Printing Office, Washington, DC.

Slesnick, D.T. (1992). Aggregate consumption and savings in the postwar United States. *Review of Economics and Statistics*, **74**(4), 585–97.

Slesnick, D.T. (1993). Gaining ground: Poverty in the postwar United States. *Journal of Political Economy*, **101**(1), 1–38.

Slesnick, D.T. (2001). *Consumption and Social Welfare.* Cambridge: Cambridge University Press.

Smeeding, T. (1977). The antipoverty effectiveness of in-kind transfers. *Journal of Human Resources*, **127**(3), 360–78.

Smeeding, T. (1982). Alternative methods for valuing selected in-kind benefits and measuring their effect of poverty. U.S. Census Bureau, Technical Paper 50. Washington, DC: U.S. Government Printing Office.

Smeeding, T. (2006). Poor people in rich countries: The United States in comparative perspective. *Journal of Economic Perspectives*, **20**(1), 69–90.

Smeeding, T. & Moon, M. (1980). Valuing government expenditures: The case of medical care transfers and poverty. *Review of Income and Wealth*, ser. 26, no. 3, 305–24.

Smeeding, T., Rainwater, L., Rein, M., Hauser, R. & Schaber, G. (1985). Income poverty in seven countries: Initial estimates from the LIS database. In T. Smeeding, M. O'Higgins & L. Rainwater (eds.), *Poverty, Inequality and Income Distribution in Comparative Perspective.* Washington, DC: Urban Institute Press.

Stevens, A.H. (1994). The dynamics of poverty spells: Updating Bane and Ellwood. *American Economic Review Papers and Proceedings*, **84**(2), 34–7.

Stevens, A.H. (1999). Climbing out of poverty, falling back in: Measuring the persistence of poverty over multiple spells. *Journal of Human Resources*, **34**(3), 557–88.

Triest, R. (1998). Has poverty gotten worse? *Journal of Economic Perspectives*, **12**(1), 97–114.

Valletta, R.G. (2006). The ins and outs of poverty in advanced economies: Government policy and poverty dynamics in Canada, Germany, Great Britain, and the United States. *Review of Income and Wealth*, ser. 52, no. 2, 261–84.

Watts, H. (1986). Have our measures of poverty become poorer? In *Focus* (Institute for Research on Poverty), **9**(2), 18–23.

Weinberg, D. (1985). Filling the poverty gap: Multiple transfer program participation. *Journal of Human Resources*, **20**(1), 64–89.

Weinberg, D. (1987). Filling the poverty gap, 1979–1984: Multiple transfer program participation. *Journal of Human Resources*, **22**(4), 563–73.

Weisbrod, B.A. & Hansen, L.W. (1968). An income-net worth approach to measuring economic welfare. *American Economic Review*, **58**(5), 1315–29.

Wilson, W.J. (1987). *The Truly Disadvantaged: The Inner City, the Underclass, and Public Policy*. Chicago: University of Chicago Press.

Wilson, W.J. & Neckerman, K. (1986). Poverty and family structure: The widening gap between evidence and public policy issues. In S.H. Danziger & D.H. Weinberg, *Fighting Poverty* (pp. 232–59). Cambridge, MA: Harvard University Press.

Wolff, E.N. (1990). Wealth holdings and poverty status in the U.S. *Review of Income and Wealth*, ser. 36, no. 2, 143–65.

Poverty statistics

Dalaker, J. (2005). *Alternative Poverty Estimates in the United States: 2003*. U.S. Census Bureau. Current Population Reports P60-227.

U.S. Census Bureau. Current Population Reports, Series P-60-166, *Money Income and Poverty Status in the United States*. Washington, DC: U.S. Government Printing Office, various years.

U.S. Census Bureau (1982). *Characteristics of the Population Below the Poverty Level: 1980*, Current Population Reports, Series P-60-133. Washington, DC: U.S. Government Printing Office.

U.S. Census Bureau (1987). *Estimates of Poverty Including the Value of Noncash Benefits: 1986*, Technical Paper 57. Washington, DC: U.S. Government Printing Office.

U.S. Census Bureau (1987). *Money Income and Poverty Status of Families and Persons in the United States, 1986*, Current Population Reports, Series P-60-157. Washington, DC: U.S. Government Printing Office.

U.S. Census Bureau (1990). *Measuring the Effect of Benefits and Taxes on Income and Poverty: 1989*, Current Population Reports, Series P-60. No. 169-RD. Washington, DC: U.S. Government Printing Office.

U.S. Census Bureau (1995). *Income, Poverty, and Valuation of Noncash Benefits: 1993*, Current Population Reports, Series P-60-188. Washington, DC: U.S. Government Printing Office, February.

U.S. Census Bureau (2000). Historical Poverty Tables – Current Population Survey, May 30. http://www.census.gov/hhes/income/histinc/histpovtb.html.

U.S. Census Bureau (2000). Current Population Survey (CPS) – Definitions and Explanations, last revised November 2. http://www.census.gov/population/www/cps/cpsdef.html.

U.S. Census Bureau (2007). *Measuring the Effect of Benefits and Taxes on Income and Poverty: 2005*, Current Population Reports, No. P60-232. Washington, DC: U.S. Government Printing Office, March.

4.9   DISCUSSION QUESTIONS AND PROBLEM SET

1   Discuss in what sense a subjective poverty line represents a "compromise" between an absolute and relative poverty standard.

2   Define the poverty gap ratio and the head count measure of poverty. What are the advantages and disadvantages of each?

3   Explain the apparent paradox that only a small percentage of individuals entering poverty will remain poor for a long period of time, yet about half of the poor at a given point in time are in the midst of a long spell of poverty.

4   Explain why a monthly poverty index would yield a higher average poverty rate over the course of a year than the official measure based on annual income.

5   What is the difference between market value and recipient value in evaluating noncash government benefits as part of family income?

6 Why does a consumption-based measure of poverty give a lower estimate of the overall poverty rate than one based on income?

7 Suppose a country has the following income distribution:

Income class	Number of families	Average income ($)
2	500	8,000
2	1,500	12,000
4	1,000	15,000
4	1,000	25,000

Suppose the official poverty lines are $10,000 for a family of two and $16,000 for a family of four. Also, suppose that median family income for a family of two is $30,000 and median family income for a family of four is $40,000.

(a) Compute the head count poverty rate.
(b) Compute the poverty gap ratio.
(c) Suppose that the relative poverty line is set at 45 percent of median family income. Compute the head count poverty rate on the basis of the relative poverty line.

8 Suppose a country has the following income distribution:

Income class	Number of families	Average income ($)
2	2,000	8,000
2	4,000	20,000
4	2,000	10,000
4	7,500	40,000

Also, suppose the poverty lines are as follows:

Family size	Poverty lines ($)
2	10,000
4	15,000

(a) Compute the head count poverty rate.
(b) Compute the poverty gap ratio.

9 Suppose that the following data characterize the United States for a two-person family:

	1995	1996
1. Official poverty rate	15.0%	16.0%
2. Official poverty line	$10,000	
3. Relative poverty line	$10,000	
4. Subjective poverty line	$10,000	
5. Median family income (current dollars)	$20,000	$21,000
6. Consumer price index (CPI)	100	110

Compute the following:
(a)   The official poverty line for a family of two in 1996.
(b)   The relative poverty line for a family of two in 1996.
(c)   The subjective poverty line in 1996 if elasticity of the subjective poverty line with respect to median family income is 0.6.

10   Suppose the official poverty rate in 1997 is 13 percent and the average of the official poverty rates from 1987 to 1997 is 11 percent. How would the measure of the poverty rate change if we used each of the following accounting periods (briefly explain your answers):
(a)   The percent whose monthly income fell below the official poverty threshold in monthly terms (the annual threshold divided by 12) for all 12 months in 1997.
(b)   The percent whose monthly income fell below the official poverty threshold in monthly terms for at least one month during 1997.
(c)   The average of the monthly poverty rates in 1997 from (b).
(d)   The proportion of the population that would be classified as poor on the basis of the official poverty threshold in eight out of the 11 years between 1987 and 1997.

11   Suppose that the following data characterize the United States:
(i)   The official poverty line for a family of four in 1997 is $16,000.
(ii)   Median income for four-person families is $40,000 in 1997.
(iii)   The average income of four-person families below the poverty line in 1997 is $10,000.
(iv)   The CPI increases by 3 percent between 1997 and 1998.
(v)   Median income for four-person families grows by 5 percent between 1997 and 1998.
Compute the following:
(a)   The poverty gap ratio for a family of four in 1997.
(b)   The official poverty line for a family of four in 1998.
(c)   The relative poverty line for a family of four in 1997 and 1998 if the relative poverty line is set at 40 percent of median family income.
(d)   The subjective poverty line in 1998 if the subjective poverty line is $10,000 in 1997 and the elasticity of the subjective poverty line with respect to median family income is 0.6.

NOTES

1   Some researchers have claimed that this finding is exaggerated and that low-income families actually spent only about one-fifth of their income on food. Using a one-fifth ratio would cause the official poverty thresholds to be higher than they currently are.
2   Another distinction contained in the original poverty lines was for male-headed versus female-headed families. The thresholds for the former were set at a slightly higher level than that for the latter, because men were assumed to have higher dietary requirements. These two categories were eliminated in 1981 in the official poverty lines.
3   Poverty lines also vary by the number of children in a household. For simplicity, I show only average thresholds by size of family.
4   Computations for 1993 and 2005 were performed by the author from the corresponding Current Population Survey data for those years.
5   From another point of view, however, this may not necessarily be a criticism. If indeed poverty is a relative phenomenon and a family *perceives* itself as poor in relation to the average standard of living, then it may make sense to say that the percentage of poor remains constant over time as long as the relative income distribution remains unchanged. From this point of view, reducing poverty becomes tantamount to reducing overall income inequality!
6   In some formulations, Y_i refers to the income of the ith poor *individual* and q is the total number of poor individuals.

7   A related measure is the *poverty gap squared*. One problem with the poverty gap ratio is that it ignores the variations in income among the poor, since the poverty gap is an average. This can be rectified by squaring the poverty gap ratio. Squaring individual poverty gaps means that the larger gaps count for more than the smaller gaps, and hence the measure is more sensitive to the *severity* of poverty in a population.

8   Another nice feature of this class of poverty indices is that they are additive – that is, they permit the summing up of poverty indices for various subgroups in the population.

9   More recently, the U.S. Census Bureau has considered co-habitating "partners" of the same or opposite sex as families.

10 The U.S. Census Bureau defines the head of a household to be the husband in the case of a married couple. Thus, by definition, female-headed families are those consisting of a mother with children and without a husband present.

11 That is to say, the poverty rate among unrelated individuals is quite a bit higher than among families.

12 Medicare benefits also showed a tremendous surge since the mid-1960s, but this increase is not captured in standard poverty measures (see Section 4.6.4).

13 Note that Figure 4.1 shows poverty rates for *persons*, so that the overall rates differ between the two tables.

14 See Chapters 13 and 14 for more discussion of this trend.

15 Also, see Isabel Sawhill's 1988 survey article, Patricia Ruggles' 1990 book, *Drawing the Line*, and the National Academy of Sciences' 1995 report (Citro & Michael, 1995) for more discussion of these issues.

16 See Deaton and Muellbauer (1980), for example, for a comprehensive treatment of equivalence scales.

17 During the mid- and late 2000s, many fixed-rate mortgages were replaced by so-called "sub-prime" mortgages. These are mortgages that require little in the way of down payments and are usually characterized by a low introductory interest rate (a "teaser rate"), which then balloons to a very high interest rate after 2 or 3 years. In 2007, these mortgages hurt many primarily low-income homeowners who found that they were unable to repay the loan and lost their home to foreclosure.

18 U.S. Census Bureau (2007).

19 There are several other technical adjustments that are made. First, realized capital gains on assets that are sold, which is not normally counted as part of "Census income," is added to family income (see Chapter 2). In addition, health insurance premiums paid by employers for their wage and salary workers are also estimated and added to family income. Both these adjustments have a negligible effect on the measured poverty rate. A still further adjustment is the inclusion of net imputed rent of owner-occupied housing. This is an estimation of the value of services provided to homeowners by the houses that they own. (Technically, it is defined as the equity in the house multiplied by the average rate on high-grade municipal bonds less imputed property taxes. See Section 4.6.5 for further discussion of "wealth adjustments" to the poverty definition.) Another interesting point is that the subtraction of federal income taxes actually reduces the measured poverty rate for families. This is due to the fact that some low-income families receive Earned Income Tax Credits (EITC), which increases their after-tax income. Also, see Chapter 15 for more discussion of government transfer programs to the poor.

20 A related issue is that some families may be "poor" because they record a large accounting loss from their business. Wolff (1990) estimated that only 4 to 5 percent of the poverty population in 1983 would fall into this group.

21 Technically speaking, I excluded the regular property income reported in the SCF in order to avoid double-counting.

22 On the other side of the ledger is the fact that official poverty data are based on a *household* survey. As a result, the *homeless* are, by construct, excluded from the official poverty count. Another large group that is excluded are residents of institutions such as prisons, nursing homes, and the like.

Chapter 5
Household Wealth

5.1 INTRODUCTION

In Chapter 3, we saw how income inequality is high in the United States by world standards and has been growing there, as well as in many European countries. But income is only an annual flow of economic resources. Economists believe that wealth – the stock of economic resources – may be a better indicator of the long-term economic well-being of a household. As it turns out, the United States also has the most unequal distribution of wealth in the industrialized world and wealth inequality has become more severe over the past 25 years or so. These trends are of particular social concern because, as we shall see below, only a small fraction of the U.S. population has benefited from the rapid growth of the 1990s and 2000s. The poor, in particular, have had difficulty buying a home and accumulating savings necessary for retirement and as a safety net. We shall address the issue of why wealth inequality has been growing in the United States and why the U.S. wealth distribution is more unequal than in other advanced countries.

In this chapter, we switch focus from household income to household wealth. Wealth represents a *stock* of accumulated assets; income represents a flow of current output. Families not only receive income over the course of a year but also save part of their income in the form of housing, savings accounts, stocks, bonds, and the like. Such accumulated savings are referred to as **wealth**. Wealth, like income, has an important bearing on the well-being of families and individuals. This chapter develops the concept of household wealth, discusses some of the problems inherent in its measurement, and presents statistics on changes in both average wealth holdings among households and the inequality of wealth holdings over time.

What determines the distribution of wealth? The principal way households accumulate wealth is through savings. Therefore, in order to understand why the distribution of wealth has changed over time, or why wealth differs among households at any given time, we must understand savings behavior. In Chapter 10, we investigate the process of household wealth accumulation – that is, savings. We consider different models of savings behavior and evaluate the available evidence.

Section 5.2 develops the concept of household wealth, and discusses several methodological issues involved in its definition and measurement. The household portfolio composition for 1983 to 2004 is also shown. Section 5.3 presents statistics showing historical change in both household wealth and its composition. Two issues are of particular interest. First, have average wealth holdings increased faster or slower than average income? Second, what are the major forms in which wealth is accumulated by households – such as housing, stocks, and bank deposits – and has their relative importance changed over time? Changes in homeownership rates are also shown.

In Section 5.4, we investigate changes in household wealth inequality in the United States. We begin with a discussion of some of the methodological issues involved in estimating the size distribution of household wealth. The next subsection shows long-term trends in U.S. wealth concentration covering the period from 1922 to 1998. The third subsection of Section 5.4 shows more detailed estimates of changes in wealth inequality from 1962 to 2004. We also look at changes in average wealth over this period, differences in the composition of wealth by wealth and age class, and the relation between family income and family wealth.

Section 5.5 draws international comparisons of household wealth inequality. The first part of this section shows long-term time trends on household wealth inequality for Sweden, the United Kingdom, and the United States. Comparisons of more recent measures of household wealth inequality are presented for Canada, France, Sweden, the United Kingdom, the United States, and several other advanced economies. A summary of the chapter is provided in Section 5.6.

5.2 WHAT IS HOUSEHOLD WEALTH?

5.2.1 Wealth and well-being

Why are we interested in household wealth? Most studies use income as a measure of family well-being. Though certain forms of income are derived from wealth, such as interest from savings accounts and bonds, dividends from stock shares, and rent from real estate, income and wealth are by no means identical. Many kinds of income, such as wages and salaries and transfer payments, are not derived from household wealth, and many forms of wealth, such as owner-occupied housing, produce no corresponding income flow.

Moreover, family wealth by itself is also a source of well-being, independent of the direct financial income it provides. There are six reasons. First, some assets, particularly owner-occupied housing, provide services directly to their owner. This is also true for **consumer durables**, such as automobiles. Such assets can substitute for money income in satisfying economic needs. Families with the same money income but differing amounts of housing and consumer durables will have different levels of welfare.

Second, wealth is a source of consumption, independent of the direct money income it provides. With the possible exception of consumer durables, assets can be converted directly into cash and thus provide for immediate consumption needs. Wealth ownership also allows a family to obtain **lines of credit** to borrow against. This is particularly true for the equity in owner-occupied housing, because second mortgages and home equity loans are a major source of credit.

Third, the availability of financial assets can provide liquidity to a family in times of economic stress (such as occasioned by unemployment, sickness, or family break-up). In this sense, wealth is a source of economic security for the family over and above the income that it directly provides.

Fourth, as the work of Conley (1999) has shown, wealth is found to affect household behavior over and above income. This is particularly the case when accounting for behavioral differences between races. In particular, Conley argues that it is impossible to understand the persistence of racial inequality in the United States without examining black/white differences in wealth ownership. Conley set out to establish the need to go beyond the standard socioeconomic status or SES indicators (education, occupation and income) in order to understand the causes of black/white inequality. He shows, for example, that the SES indicators by themselves do not adequately explain differences in educational performance between black and white students, but when wealth is included as an explanatory factor, much of the remaining gap in educational performance is accounted for.

Fifth, as Spilerman (2000) has argued, wealth-generated income does not require the same trade-offs with leisure as earned income. There is no cost in the form of the foregone alternative use of time in the case of wealth. Moreover, unlike labor market earnings, the income flow generated by wealth does not decline with illness or unemployment. In fact, it is constantly renewable.

Sixth, large fortunes can be a source of economic and social power that is not directly captured in annual income. Large accumulations of financial and business assets can confer special privileges to their holders. Such large fortunes are often transmitted to succeeding generations, thus creating family "dynasties."

Thus, wealth holdings provide another dimension to household welfare over and above income flows. As we shall see in Section 5.4, attempts have been made to create a more comprehensive measure of well-being that incorporates information on both family income and wealth.

5.2.2   Marketable wealth

The conventional definition of household wealth includes assets and liabilities that have a current market value and that are directly or indirectly marketable. In the Survey of Consumer Finances (SCF) conducted by the Federal Reserve Board of Washington on a triennial basis,[1] marketable wealth (or net worth) is defined as the current value of all marketable or fungible assets less the current value of debts. Net worth is thus the difference in value between total assets and total liabilities or debt. Total assets are defined as the sum of: (i) the gross value of owner-occupied housing; (ii) other real estate owned by the household; (iii) cash and demand deposits; (iv) time and savings deposits, certificates of deposit, and money market accounts; (v) government bonds, corporate bonds, foreign bonds, and other financial securities; (vi) the cash surrender value of life insurance plans; (vii) the cash surrender value of pension plans, including IRAs, Keogh, and 401(k) plans;[2] (viii) corporate stock and mutual funds;[3] (ix) net equity in unincorporated businesses; and (x) equity in trust funds. Total liabilities are the sum of: (i) mortgage debt; (ii) consumer debt, including auto loans; and (iii) other debt. All told, in 2004, total household wealth in the United States amounted to $48.3 trillion and average household wealth to $430,500.

This measure reflects wealth as a store of value and therefore a source of potential consumption and is used in conjunction with a standard national accounting framework. This concept probably best reflects the level of well-being associated with a family's holdings. Thus, only assets that can be readily converted to cash (that is, "fungible" ones) are included. As a result, consumer durables such as automobiles, televisions, furniture, household appliances, and the like, are excluded here, since these items are not easily marketed or their resale value typically far understates the value of their consumption services to the household. Also excluded is the value of future social security benefits the family may receive upon retirement (usually referred to as "social security wealth"), as well as the value of retirement benefits from private pension plans ("pension wealth"). Even though these funds are a source of future income to families, they are not in their direct control and cannot be marketed.

Table 5.1 presents the portfolio composition for the household sector in the United States from 1983 to 2004. These results are based on the SCF. The portfolio composition of household wealth shows the forms in which households save. Assets are divided into three main groups. The first, **tangible assets**, include stocks of real goods that are both "reproducible," such as houses, and "non-reproducible," such as land. The major tangible asset owned by households is **owner-occupied housing** (houses that are lived in by their owners).[4] In 2004, this was the most important household asset in the breakdown shown in Table 5.1, accounting for 33 percent of total

Table 5.1 Portfolio composition of household wealth, 1983–2004 (percent of gross assets)

Wealth component	1983	1989	1998	2001	2004
Principal residence (gross value)	30.1	30.2	29.0	28.2	33.5
Other real estate (gross value)[a]	14.9	14.0	10.0	9.8	11.5
Unincorporated business equity[b]	18.8	17.2	17.7	17.2	17.1
Liquid assets[c]	17.4	17.5	9.6	8.8	7.3
Pension accounts[d]	1.5	2.9	11.6	12.3	11.8
Financial securities[e]	4.2	3.4	1.8	2.3	2.1
Corporate stock and mutual funds	9.0	6.9	14.8	14.8	11.9
Net equity in personal trusts	2.6	3.1	3.8	4.8	2.9
Miscellaneous assets[f]	1.3	4.9	1.8	1.8	1.8
Total	100.0	100.0	100.0	100.0	100.0
Debt on principal residence	6.3	8.6	10.7	9.4	11.6
All other debt[g]	6.8	6.4	4.2	3.1	3.9
Total debt	13.1	15.0	15.0	12.5	15.5
Memo (selected ratios in percent):					
Debt/equity ratio	15.1	17.6	17.6	14.3	18.4
Debt/income ratio	68.4	87.6	90.9	81.1	115.0
Net home equity/total assets[h]	23.8	21.6	18.2	18.8	21.8
Principal residence debt/house value	20.9	28.6	37.0	33.4	34.8
Stocks, directly or indirectly owned/total assets[i]	11.3	10.2	22.6	24.5	17.5

a In 2001 and 2004, this equals the gross value of other residential real estate plus the *net equity* in non-residential real estate.
b Net equity in unincorporated farm and nonfarm businesses and closely-held corporations.
c Checking accounts, savings accounts, time deposits, money market funds, certificates of deposits, and the cash surrender value of life insurance.
d IRAs, Keogh plans, 401(k) plans, the accumulated value of defined contribution pension plans, and other retirement accounts.
e Corporate bonds, government bonds (including savings bonds), open-market paper, and notes.
f Gold and other precious metals, royalties, jewelry, antiques, furs, loans to friends and relatives, future contracts, and miscellaneous assets.
g Mortgage debt on all real property except principal residence; credit card, installment, and other consumer debt.
h Ratio of gross value of principal residence less mortgage debt on principal residence to total assets.
i Includes direct ownership of stock shares and indirect ownership through mutual funds, trusts, and IRAs, Keogh plans, 401(k) plans, and other retirement accounts.
Source: Own computations from the 1983, 1989, 1998, 2001, and 2004 Survey of Consumer Finances.

assets. The second component consists of land, apartment buildings, other rental property, and other real estate held by households. This group made up 12 percent of all assets. The third is unincorporated business equity, which refers to small businesses (such as a farm or a store) owned directly by individuals, in contrast to corporations which are owned through stock shares. A person's equity in an unincorporated business is the value of the business. Business equity comprised another 17 percent of total assets.

The second major group is referred to as **financial assets**. These are assets which function as money or are readily convertible to money. The first component includes cash, demand deposits (checking accounts), time and savings deposits, money market funds, and certificates of deposit (CDs). It also includes the "cash surrender value" of life insurance funds. Certain life insurance plans (called "full life insurance") allow individuals to contribute to a savings funds, and the amount the individual can withdraw from this savings fund is referred to as its cash surrender value. Collectively they are referred to as **liquid assets**, and comprised 7 percent of total assets in 2004. The second consists of **pension accounts** like Individual Retirement Accounts (IRAs), so-called Keogh plans, 401(k) plans, and the accumulated value of other defined contribution pension plans and other retirement accounts. These plans constitute savings such as savings accounts. However, they are especially designed to allow workers to save for retirement by providing tax-deferred savings (that is, the money put into these accounts are not subject to income taxes until the person retires and withdraws the money). In 2004, pension accounts made up almost 12 percent of total household assets.[5]

The third component, called **financial securities**, includes bonds, notes, and financial securities issued mainly by corporations and the government. Such securities are "promissory notes," by which the borrower agrees to pay back the lender a certain amount of money (the principal plus interest), at a certain date. In 2004, they amounted to only 2 percent of total household assets.

The third major group of assets consists of **equities** or ownership rights. The first component of this group is corporate stock and mutual funds. A corporate stock certificate issued by a company represents ownership of a certain percentage of the company's assets. A mutual fund is a package provided by a financial entity such as a bank that includes a portfolio of stocks and other financial instruments such as bonds. Its chief advantage is that it helps to diversify the risk associated with individual stock (and bond) movements over time. In 2004, stocks and mutual funds amounted to almost 12 percent of total assets. The second item in this group, net equity in personal trusts (or "trust fund equity" for short) refers to bank deposits, securities, corporate stock, and other financial instruments, which are held in a special legal arrangement called a trust fund. In a typical trust, the actual assets are managed by a specially named administrator (often a bank), and the income earned from the assets in the trust are remitted to individual beneficiaries. Trust funds held for individuals are counted as part of household wealth. In 2004, they comprised only 3 percent of total assets.

On the liability side, the major form of household debt is home mortgages. A mortgage is a loan issued normally by a bank and usually for a period of 15 to 30 years that is used to finance the purchase of real property, particularly houses to live in. In 2004, mortgage debt comprised 75 percent of total household debt.[6] The remaining 25 percent consisted of other household debt, including automobile and other consumer loans and credit card debt. Together, total household debt amounted to 16 percent of the value of total household assets.

Five other entries are shown in the bottom of Table 5.1. The first of these is the **debt–equity** ratio, which is defined as the ratio of total debt to net worth. This figure was 18.4 percent in 2004. The second is the ratio of total debt to personal income. In 2004, it amounted to 115 percent. Both of these ratios indicate how burdensome personal debt is in relation to personal resources to pay it off. The third is home equity, defined as the gross value of owner-occupied housing less outstanding mortgage debt. This represents the amount of money a family could net from the sale of the house (after paying off its outstanding mortgage balance). Home mortgages amounted to 35 percent of the value of owner-occupied housing (the fourth entry in this group). As a result, home equity made up a smaller proportion of total assets than the gross value of owner-occupied housing – 22 percent versus 33 percent. Stocks can be owned either directly (like shares of IBM) or indirectly through mutual funds, trusts, IRAs, Keogh plans, 401(k) plans, and other retirement accounts. The last row shows the total amount of stocks owned either directly or indirectly as a share of total assets. In 2004, the figure was 17.5 percent, which was considerably more than the total value of corporate stock and mutual funds as a share of total assets.

In sum, the principal household asset in 2004 was owner-occupied housing, which comprised almost exactly a third of total assets. However, net home equity amounted to only 22 percent of total assets. Financial assets as a group were 21 percent of total assets, while other real estate and unincorporated business equity were 29 percent. The other major component, corporate stock and mutual funds, comprised 12 percent of total assets, and stocks directly or indirectly owned made up 17 percent. The ratio of total debt to total assets was 15.5 percent.

There have been some notable changes in the composition of household wealth over the period between 1983 and 2004. The first is the steep rise in the share of gross housing wealth in total assets. After fluctuating between 28.2 and 30.4 percent from 1983 to 2001, the ratio jumped to 33.5 percent in 2004. There are two factors behind this. The first is the rise in the homeowner-ship rate. According to the SCF data, the homeownership rate, after falling from 63.4 percent in 1983 to 62.8 percent in 1989, picked up to 67.7 percent in 2001 and then to 69.1 percent in 2004. The second is the sharp rise in housing prices. Between 2001 and 2004, the median house price for existing one-family homes rose by 17.9 percent in real terms.[7] The rise in housing prices by itself would have caused the share of housing in total assets to rise by 5.05 percentage points instead of the actual 5.2 percentage points.

A second and related trend is that net equity in owner-occupied housing (the difference between the market value and outstanding mortgages on the property), after falling almost continuously from 23.8 percent in 1983 to 18.2 percent in 1998, picked up to 18.8 percent in 2001 and 21.8 percent in 2004. The difference between the two series (gross versus net housing values as a share of total assets) is attributable to the changing magnitude of mortgage debt on home-owner's property, which increased from 21 percent in 1983 to 37 percent in 1998, fell back to 33 percent in 2001, and then rose again to 35 percent in 2004. Moreover, mortgage debt on prin-cipal residence climbed from 9.4 to 11.6 percent of total assets between 2001 and 2004. The fact that net home equity as a proportion of assets increased between 2001 and 2004 thus reflected the strong gains in real estate values over these years.

Third, overall indebtedness first increased, with the debt–equity ratio leaping from 15.1 per-cent in 1983 to 19.4 percent in 1995, before falling off to 17.6 percent in 1998 and 14.3 percent in 2001. However, from 2001 to 2004, it jumped to 18.4 percent, close to its previous 1992 high. Likewise, the ratio of debt to total income first surged from 68 percent in 1983 to 91 percent in 1995, leveled off in 1998, declined to 81 percent in 2001, and then skyrocketed to *115 per-cent* in 2004, its high for this period. If mortgage debt on principal residence is excluded, then the ratio of other debt to total assets fell off from 6.8 percent in 1983 to 3.1 percent in 2001 but then rose to 3.9 percent in 2004. One implication is that over the 1990s and early 2000s families have been using tax-sheltered mortgages and home equity loans rather than consumer loans and other forms of consumer debt to finance normal consumption.

A fourth change is that pension accounts rose from 1.5 to 11.8 percent of total assets. This increase largely offset the decline in total liquid assets, from 17.4 to 7.3 percent, so that it is reas-onable to conclude that households have to a large extent substituted tax-free pension accounts for taxable savings deposits.

Fifth, the proportion of total assets in the form of other (nonhome) real estate fell off sharply, from 15 percent in 1983 to 10 percent in 2001, but then increased to 11.5 percent. The change from 2001 to 2004 to a large extent reflected rising real estate prices. Financial securities fell from 4.2 to 2.3 percent of total assets between 1983 and 2004. Unincorporated business equity fell slightly as a share of gross wealth over this period. The share of corporate stock and mutual funds in total assets rose rather briskly from 9.0 in 1983 to 14.8 percent in 1998, stayed at 14.8 percent in 2001, and then plummeted to 11.9 percent in 2004. If we include the value of stocks indirectly owned through mutual funds, trusts, IRAs, 401(k) plans, and other retirement accounts, then the value of total stocks owned as a share of total assets more than doubled from 11.3 percent in 1983 to 24.5 percent in 2001 and then tumbled to 17.5 percent in 2004. The rise during the 1990s reflected the bull market in corporate equities as well as increased stock owner-ship, while the decline in the early 2000s was a result of the fall in the stock market over this period as well as a small drop in stock ownership. The change in stock prices by itself would have caused the share of total stocks in assets to fall by only 2.9 percentage points, compared to the actual decline of 7.0 percentage points. Most of the decline in the share of stocks in total assets was due to sales of stocks and withdrawals from stock funds.

5.2.3   Other definitions of household wealth

A theme that regularly emerges in the literature on household wealth is that there is no unique concept or definition of wealth that is satisfactory for all purposes. One concept that is broader than marketable wealth is the sum of marketable wealth and consumer durables. Consumer durables such as automobiles, televisions, furniture, household appliances, and the like provide consumption services directly to the household. However, they are not easily marketed and the resale value of these items typically far understates the value of their consumption services to the household, so that consumer durables are often excluded from marketable wealth.

How much are consumer durables relative to total household wealth? The SCF includes a valu-ation of the automobiles owned by households but no other major consumer durables. In 2004, the average value of autos owned by households was $17,350, which equaled 3.3 percent of total assets (including the value of autos). Another source of data on consumer durables is the Federal Reserve Board's Flow of Funds. In 2004, according to this source, total consumer durables amounted to $3.57 trillion or 7.7 percent of the total assets owned by households.

A second concept, which is more narrow than marketable wealth, is *financial wealth*, defined as marketable net worth minus net equity in owner-occupied housing, where net equity is defined as the difference between the value of the property and the outstanding mortgage debt on the property. Financial wealth is a more "liquid" concept than marketable wealth, since one's home is difficult to convert into cash in the short term. It thus reflects the resources that may be directly available for consumption or various forms of investments in the short term. In 2004, total house-hold financial wealth was $35.8 trillion, 74 percent of marketable wealth.

One of the major developments since the end of World War II has been the enormous growth in both public and private pension systems. Even though such pension funds are not in the direct control of individuals or families, they are a source of future income to families and thus may be perceived as a form of family wealth. Moreover, as Feldstein (1974) has argued, insofar as families accumulate "traditional" wealth to provide for future consumption needs, the growth of such pension funds may have offset private savings and hence traditional wealth accumulation.

A wider definition of household wealth will thus add some valuation of pension rights, from both public and private sources, to marketable wealth. Such a measure provides a better gauge of potential future consumption. **Augmented household wealth** (or "augmented wealth") is defined as the sum of household marketable wealth, social security wealth, and pension wealth. Social security wealth is defined as the present discounted value of the stream of future social security benefits, and pension wealth as the present discounted value of future pension benefits.[8] As is apparent from the definitions, these two forms of wealth are not fungible or marketable, since individuals cannot convert these assets into cash.[9]

What is the rationale for including these two forms of wealth? The main motivation is that from the standpoint of an individual a future guaranteed flow of income is in many ways like owning a financial asset. Indeed, there are marketable assets called "annuities" which have pre-cisely the characteristic of providing a steady stream of income after a certain time (or age) is reached. The anticipated social security (or pension) benefits that an individual will receive after retirement is comparable to such an annuity. From the individual's point of view, then, a

Table 5.2   Mean and total augmented wealth, 1983, 1989, and 2001 (in thousands, 2001 dollars)

					Percentage change	
	1983	*1989*	*2001*	*1983–89*	*1989–2001*	*1983–2001*
A. Mean values						
1. Net worth (NW)	231.0	264.6	380.1	14.6	43.7	64.6
2. Pension wealth (PW)	73.9	57.3	94.8	−22.5	65.6	28.3
3. Social security wealth (SSW)	127.2	123.4	139.5	−3.0	13.1	9.7
4. Retirement wealth (RW)	201.2	180.7	234.4	−10.2	29.7	16.5
5. Augmented wealth (AW)	428.8	459.2	561.0	7.1	22.2	30.8
B. Total values (trillions)						
1. Net worth (NW)	19.4	24.6	40.5	27.0	64.5	108.9
2. Pension wealth (PW)	6.2	5.3	10.1	−14.1	89.6	62.8
3. Social security wealth (SSW)	10.7	11.5	14.9	7.5	29.4	39.2
4. Retirement wealth (RW)	16.9	16.8	25.0	−0.4	48.5	47.9
5. Augmented wealth (AW)	36.0	42.7	59.7	18.7	39.9	66.1

RW = PW + SSW.
AW = NWX + RW; where NWX equals NW less defined contribution person accounts.
Source: Author's computations from the 1983, 1989, and 2001 Surveys of Consumer Finances.

guaranteed stream of future pension or social security benefits may be as much a form of wealth as money put into a savings account that will be drawn on after retirement.[10]

In 2004, total marketable net worth amounted to $40.5 trillion. According to my estimates, total pension wealth (PW) in 2004 was $10.2 trillion and total social security wealth (SSW) was $14.9 trillion (see Table 5.2).[11] Together, retirement wealth (RW) amounted to $25 trillion or 62 percent of marketable net worth, and augmented wealth (AW) equaled $59.7 trillion. Social security wealth by itself was thus larger than any other component of household wealth, including owner-occupied housing and liquid assets. As we shall see in Section 5.4, the large size of social security wealth has important implications for differences in the distribution of marketable household wealth and augmented household wealth.[12]

It is also of interest that between 1983 and 2001, both PW and SSW have grown slower than marketable net worth. While average net worth increased by 65 percent over this period, average PW grew by 28 percent and average SSW by 10 percent. Altogether, AW rose by 31 percent from 1983 to 2001. As we shall see in the next section, this is rather different from the earlier part of the century when AW outdistanced net worth in terms of growth.

5.3   HISTORICAL TIME-SERIES DATA ON HOUSEHOLD WEALTH AND ITS COMPOSITION

There are two major historical time series available on aggregate household wealth in the United States: (i) For the period 1900–1958, household balance sheet data are available in Goldsmith, Brody and Mendershausen (1956) and Goldsmith, Lipsey and Mendelsen (1963). (ii) For the period 1946 to the present, complete balance sheet data are contained in the Flow of Funds Accounts of the Board of Governors of the Federal Reserve System (these are published quarterly).

Unfortunately, the wealth data contained in these two sources are not entirely consistent with each other, thus necessitating several adjustments to make them comparable. First, there are several differences in the categorization of assets between the various data sources. These differences do not affect the wealth totals, only the composition among asset categories. Second, there are some differences in the definition of household wealth. Third, there are methodological differences. For example, the two series treat trust fund equity and pensions differently. Fourth, for the overlapping period, 1946–1958, the data contained in the earlier two Goldsmith works have since been revised by the Federal Reserve Board. Complete details on the adjustments can be found in Wolff (1989).

5.3.1 Trends in average wealth

The combined estimates are shown in Table 5.3 for selected years between 1900 and 1992 (see also Figure 5.1). These figures are based on national balance sheet estimates and, as a result, will generally differ from those based on household survey data such as the SCF. The basic data have been converted to figures on average wealth per household in constant (1992) dollars. Between 1900 and 1992, average marketable wealth increased by a factor of 2.3, or by 0.9 percent per year. However, the growth was not uniform over the period. Between 1900 and 1929, it grew at a substantially higher rate, 1.4 percent per year. During the Depression and World War II years of 1929 to 1949, average household wealth actually declined in real terms, altogether by 7 percent. During the high growth period of the 1950s and 1960s, its growth accelerated to 1.9 percent per year, its highest level to date. Then, during the ensuing slow growth period from 1969 to 1989, the growth in mean wealth per household slowed to 0.8 percent per year. Between 1989 and 1992, it again declined in real terms, by 1.1 percent per year.

In comparison, between 1900 and 1992, real GNP per household rose by a factor of 2.6, or 1.0 percent per year, faster than average wealth holdings. Personal disposable income per household grew slightly more, by 1.1 percent per year, over the same period. However, with the

Table 5.3 Mean marketable net worth, augmented net worth, GNP, and personal disposable income per household, 1900–1992 (1992 dollars)

Year	Marketable net worth	Pension wealth	Social security wealth	Augmented net worth	Personal disposable income	GNP
1900	92,609	0	0	92,609	16,065	24,064
1929	137,404	576	0	137,980	23,073	34,612
1949	127,921	3,570	33,411	164,903	25,773	37,936
1969	187,366	16,747	82,861	286,974	37,714	55,613
1989	224,751	43,789	96,120	364,659	44,399	62,658
1992	217,428	45,337	94,688	357,453	44,414	61,513
Annual rate of growth (in percent)						
1900–29	1.36			1.37	1.25	1.25
1929–49	−0.36	9.12		0.89	0.55	0.46
1949–69	1.91	7.73	4.54	2.77	1.90	1.91
1969–89	0.83	4.38	0.44	1.05	0.59	0.58
1989–92	−1.1	1.16	−0.50	−0.67	0.01	−0.61
1900–92	0.93			1.47	1.11	1.02

Sources: Wolff, E.N. (1989). Trends in aggregate household wealth in the U.S., 1900–1983. *Review of Income and Wealth*, ser. 35(1), 1–30; Wolff, E.N. (1994). Trends in household wealth in the U.S., 1962–1983 and 1983–1989. *Review of Income and Wealth*, ser. 40(2), 143–74; *Economic Report of the President, 1994*, and author's computations from the 1989 and 1992 Survey of Consumer Finances.

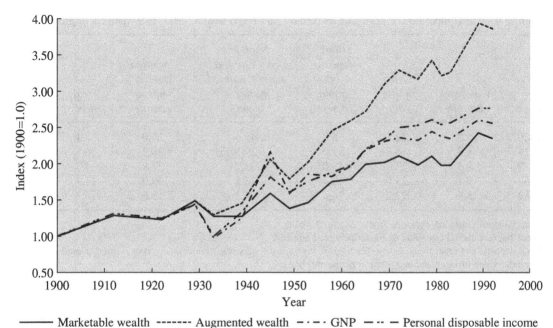

Figure 5.1 Marketable and augmented wealth, GNP, and personal disposable income per household, 1900–1992

exception of the 1929–1949 and 1989–1992 periods, wealth has grown at the same rate or faster than personal disposable income and GNP. Between 1949 and 1969, all three increased at virtually the same rate. From 1969 to 1989, average household wealth rose by 0.8 percent per year while disposable income and GNP per household increased by 0.6 percent per year.

Augmented household wealth grew considerably faster than personal disposable income or marketable wealth. Between 1900 and 1992, augmented wealth per household increased by a factor of 3.9, compared to a 2.3-fold increase in average marketable wealth and a 2.8-fold increase in average disposable income. Average pension wealth mushroomed from virtually zero in 1900 to over $45,000 in 1992, and average social security wealth from zero in 1937 (when the social security system started up) to over $94,000. Even in 1949, pension wealth amounted to only 3 percent of marketable wealth and social security wealth to 26 percent, compared to 21 percent and 44 percent, respectively, in 1992.

Insofar as the standard of living is reflected in both family income and family wealth holdings, differences in growth rates between the two will affect our measurement of changes in well-being. If wealth grows faster than income, then our usual income-based measures will understate the true growth in the standard of living. Such differences are particularly marked between personal disposable income and augmented net worth. Insofar as families are deferring more and more income to their retirement years, the growth in current income will increasingly understate the growth in well-being.

5.3.2 Changes in wealth composition

The portfolio composition of household wealth is important for several reasons. First, it shows the forms in which households save. Do households save for direct consumption, as, for example, in the form of housing and automobiles? Do families save for precautionary reasons, as, for

Table 5.4 The composition of aggregate marketable household wealth, 1900–1989 (percent of gross assets)

Year	Consumer durables	Gross house value	Bank deposits & other liquid assets	Nonhome real estate & unincorporated business equity	Corporate stock & financial securities	Total debt	Home equity
1900	5.8	22.6	5.0	46.6	20.0	4.1	21.4
1929	6.8	16.8	7.9	29.5	38.9	6.8	15.4
1949	8.3	23.7	13.0	33.2	21.8	5.7	22.3
1969	9.1	25.0	13.4	23.5	29.0	11.7	18.4
1989	8.6	27.2	16.4	28.1	19.6	14.3	18.9

Miscellaneous assets are excluded from household wealth.
Gross house value: Gross value of owner-occupied housing.
Bank deposits and other liquid assets: Cash, currency, demand deposits, time deposits, money market funds, cash surrender value of insurance and pension plans, and IRAs.
Nonhome real estate and unincorporated business equity: Gross value of other real estate plus net equity in unincorporated farm and nonfarm businesses.
Corporate stock and financial securities: Corporate stock, including mutual funds; corporate bonds, government bonds, open-market paper, notes, and other fixed-interest financial securities; and net equity in personal trusts and estates.
Total debt: Mortgage, installment, consumer, and other debt.
Home equity: Gross value of owner-occupied housing less apportioned mortgage debt (split proportionally between owner-occupied housing and other real estate).
Sources: Wolff, E.N. (1989). Trends in aggregate household wealth in the U.S., 1900–1983. *Review of Income and Wealth*, ser. 35(1), 1–30; Wolff, E.N. (1994). Trends in household wealth in the U.S., 1962–1983 and 1983–1989. *Review of Income and Wealth*, ser. 40(2), 143–74.

example, in the form of demand deposits or time and savings deposits? Do they save for retirement, as in insurance plans, IRAs, or the like? Or do they save mainly for investment purposes, as in financial securities and corporate stock? This disposition of household wealth has implications for theories of household savings, as we shall discuss in Chapter 10.

Second, this information indicates how much financial capital is available for investment purposes by the business sector of the economy. If households save mainly to finance their own consumption, particularly in housing, then only a relatively small proportion of total household savings will be available for new investment by the business sector. On the other hand, if savings take mainly the form of financial instruments, then a considerable amount of capital will become available to the business community. Third, these data have a bearing on the theory of risk and portfolio selection (which assets are purchased) among families. Assets differ in both their expected yield and their attendant risk. A body of theory has been developed in economics to explain how families trade off expected returns on assets and risk.

Historical time trends on wealth composition are shown in Table 5.4 (also see Figures 5.2 and 5.3). These figures are based on national balance sheet estimates and, as a result, will generally differ from those based on household survey data like the Survey of Consumer Finances (and shown in Table 5.1). Moreover, the national balance sheet data include consumer durables while the SCF data exclude them.

The results show that there have been important changes in the composition of household wealth over the twentieth century. Consumer durables rose from 6 percent of total assets in 1900 to 9 percent in 1989. Perhaps, somewhat surprisingly, (gross) owner-occupied housing increased only moderately as a proportion of gross assets, from 23 percent in 1900 to 27 percent in 1989.

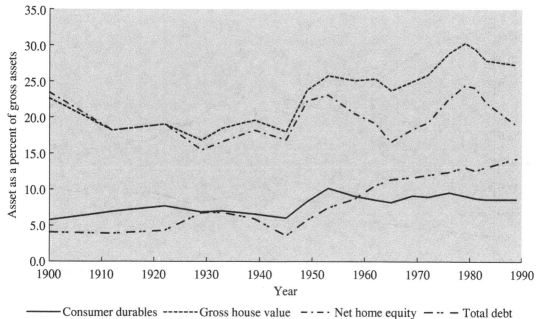

Figure 5.2   U.S. portfolio composition: durables, housing, and debt, 1900–1989

In fact, the increase was not continuous throughout the period. Between 1900 and 1912, owner-occupied housing fell from 23 to 18 percent of total assets and then remained at this level until 1945. Thereafter, the proportion rose almost continuously to 30 percent in 1979, and then fell off to 27 percent in 1989.

The trend in home equity (the difference between the gross value of owner-occupied housing and mortgage debt) was somewhat different. Home equity remained relatively constant as a proportion of total assets from 1912 to 1945, at about 17 percent, increased to 23 percent in 1953, and then fell off to 19 percent by 1989. What is particularly striking is the difference in trend between gross house value and net home equity. The two figures remained quite close from 1900 to 1949, indicating relatively little mortgage debt on homes, and then diverged more and more thereafter, indicating a rising proportion of mortgage debt to home value. Home mortgage debt grew from 5 percent of the gross value of owner-occupied housing at the beginning of the century to 31 percent by 1989.

This tendency is also reflected in increasing total household debt. Total debt as a proportion of total assets remained at about 4 to 6 percent of total assets from 1900 to 1949 and then rose rather steadily over the postwar period, reaching 14 percent in 1989. The ratio of debt other than home mortgages to total assets grew from 2.9 percent in 1900 to 6.1 percent by 1989.

Bank deposits and other liquid assets showed relatively steady growth as a share of total assets, climbing from 5 percent in 1900 to 16 percent in 1989. In contrast, over the same period non-home real estate and unincorporated business equity fell almost continuously as a proportion of assets, from 47 to 28 percent. Most of the decrease is accounted for by the declining importance of small owner-run farms in the U.S. economy. The share of unincorporated farm business equity in total assets alone fell from 27 percent in 1900 to 5 percent in 1989.

The most volatile element in the household portfolio is corporate stock and financial securities. Between 1900 and 1929 their share in total assets almost doubled, from 20 to 39 percent,

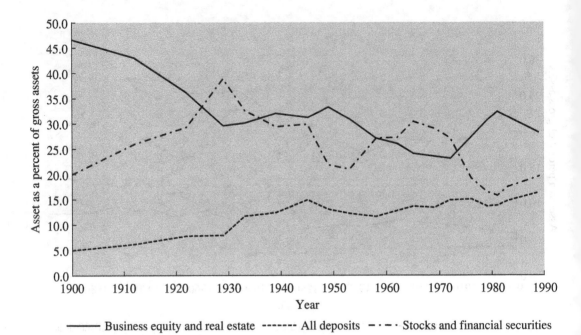

Figure 5.3   U.S. portfolio composition: business equity, stocks and deposits, 1900–1989

then fell off to 22 percent in 1949, increased to 29 percent in 1969, and then declined to 16 percent in 1979 before rising again to 20 percent in 1989. The rise and fall of this component is largely explained by movements in the stock market, which had peaks in 1929, 1969, and 1989.

In sum, over the twentieth century, U.S. households have invested more of their wealth in consumer durables. Home equity has remained relatively constant as a share of total assets. Among investment type assets, household have substituted more liquid and less risky assets such as bank deposits and money market funds for risky, illiquid assets such as small business equity and non-home real estate. Changes in the share of corporate stock and financial securities in the household portfolio tend to follow movements in the stock market. Finally, the rising ratio of liabilities to assets suggests the greater willingness of households to take on debt, as well as the greater accessibility of mortgages on real property and the greater availability of consumer credit.

5.3.3   Homeownership rates

Table 5.5 shows statistics on the homeownership rate, the percentage of housing units that are owner-occupied (that is, owned by their occupants). The data cover the years from 1920 to 2005. One of the more remarkable trends in the twentieth century has been the increasing proportion of U.S. families owning their own homes. For the full population, the homeownership rate increased from 46 percent in 1920 to 48 percent in 1930, fell to 44 percent during the Great Depression, and then rose almost continuously to 65 percent in 1975. However, since 1975, the homeownership rate has increased at a more modest pace. It actually fell by a full percentage point between 1975 and 1985 but by 1991 was back to its 1975 level. It then rose from 64.2 percent in 1991 to 68.8 percent in 2005, with most of the gain occurring between 1995 and 2001.

Table 5.5 also shows separate statistics by race. Time trends were quite similar for whites and nonwhites. Among nonwhite families, in fact, the homeownership rate almost doubled between

Table 5.5 Homeownership trends in the United States, 1920–2005 (percent of housing units that are owner-occupied)

Year	All races	Whites	Nonwhites
1920	45.6	48.2	23.9
1930	47.8	50.2	25.2
1940	43.6	45.7	23.6
1950	55.0	57.0	34.9
1960	61.9	64.4	38.4
1970	62.9	65.4	42.1
1975	64.6	67.4	43.8
1980	64.4	67.8	44.2
1985	63.5	66.8	42.8
1991	64.2	67.9	43.2
1995	65.0	69.2	44.8
2001	68.0	73.2	49.7
2005	68.8	72.7	50.6

Source: U.S. Census Bureau. *Statistical Abstract of the United States: 2007* (127th edition). Washington, DC.

1920 and 1975. The homeownership rate for this group reached 44 percent in 1980, fell to 43 percent in 1991, but then surged to 51 percent in 2005. However, the homeownership rate among nonwhite families still remains considerably below that of white families.

Homeownership is often considered a key determinant of middle-class status. After increasing rapidly for many years, the percentage of U.S. families owning their own home has risen modestly since 1975. These results are the basis of the concern expressed in recent years about the greater difficulty of a family owning its own home and thus gaining entry to the middle class.

5.4 WEALTH INEQUALITY IN THE UNITED STATES

There are now official estimates of the size distribution of household income in the United States (as well as almost all other industrialized countries). The U.S. Census Bureau conducts an annual survey in March, the Current Population Survey (CPS), which provides detailed information on individual and household earnings and income.[13] On the basis of these data, the U.S. Census Bureau constructs its estimates of both family and household income inequality. Moreover, the Current Population Surveys have been conducted in the United States since 1947. As a result, there exists a consistent time series on household income distribution for the United States which covers more than six decades.

Unfortunately, there do not exist comparable data on the size distribution of household wealth for the United States or, for that matter, for any other country. There are no official household surveys conducted on an annual basis for this purpose. As a result, researchers in this field have had to make estimates of household wealth inequality from a variety of sources, which are sometimes inconsistent. Compounding this problem is the fact that household wealth is much more heavily concentrated in the upper percentiles of the distribution than income. Thus, unless surveys or data sources are especially designed to cover the top wealth groups in a country, it is quite easy to produce biased estimates of the size distribution of wealth, which understate the true level of inequality. The net result is that estimates of household wealth distribution are more problematic than those of income distribution.

In this section, we shall first discuss the methods researchers have used to measure inequality in household wealth (Section 5.4.1). We shall then look at long-term time trends in wealth concentration in the United States (Section 5.4.2) and then more recent changes (Section 5.4.3).

5.4.1   Methods used to estimate wealth inequality

There have been four principal sources of data for developing household wealth estimates: (i) estate tax data; (ii) household survey data; (iii) wealth tax data; and (iv) income capitalization technique. Each has its characteristic advantages and disadvantages.

5.4.1.1   Estate tax data

Estate tax data was the first major source of data used for wealth analysis. When someone dies, the person's assets are said to comprise his or her estate, and estate tax records are actual tax returns filed for probate. Such data have a great degree of reliability, since they are subject to scrutiny and audit by the state. Their main limitation (in the United States at least) is that the threshold for filing is relatively high, so that only a small proportion of estates (typically, 1 percent or so) are required to file returns.[14]

Another difficulty with this data source is that the sample consists of decedents. Since most researchers are interested in distribution of wealth among the *living* population, a technique based on *mortality multipliers* is used to infer the distribution of wealth among the actual population. If mortality rates were the same for each group, then the wealth of decedents would constitute a representative sample of the living population, and researchers could use the estate data directly. However, mortality rates are much greater for older people than younger ones, so that different "weights" must be given to the estates filed by decedents of different ages. Mortality rates are also higher for men than for women (that is, women, on average, live longer than men), and also higher for black individuals than whites. As a result, estates are assigned a weight based on the inverse of the group's mortality rate (one divided by the mortality rate), and these are then used to generate the size distribution of wealth in the living population.

Estimates of wealth inequality based on this technique are, as might be expected, quite sensitive to the precision of the mortality multipliers. The estimates can have a very large standard error, particularly for the young, since there are very few of them in the sample. This means that the results are very sensitive to who happens to die in a given year and may therefore not be very reliable for young adults. There are two other problems associated with this technique. First, insofar as mortality rates are inversely correlated with wealth (that is, the rich tend to live longer), the resulting multipliers can be biased.[15] Most studies do try to correct for this problem by using mortality rates for the wealthy that are lower than for the population as a whole due to the longer expected life span of the wealthy.

Second, the distribution of wealth estimated by this technique is for individuals, rather than for families. Changing ownership patterns within families (for example, joint ownership of the family's house) can affect estimated wealth concentration. As noted by Atkinson (1975) and Shorrocks (1987), marital customs and relations have changed over the last century. Married women now inherit more wealth and have higher wealth levels in 2000 than they did in 1900 or 1930. This reduces individual concentration even if household wealth inequality does not change. For example, between 1929 and 1953, Lampman (1962) reported that the percentage of married women among top wealth-holders increased from 9 percent to 18 percent. As a result, since most researchers are interested in the distribution of family wealth rather than individual wealth, additional imputations must be performed to infer family wealth from estimates of individual wealth holdings.[16]

Another problem with this data source is underreporting and nonfiling for tax avoidance. Though the returns are subject to audit, the value of cash on hand, jewelry, housewares, and business assets is difficult to ascertain. Their value is typically understated in order to reduce the tax liability of the estate. Moreover, *inter vivos* transfers (that is, transfers of wealth between living individuals), particularly in anticipation of death, can bias estimates of household wealth among the living. If older people pass on wealth to their children just before they die, then their estates would tend to under-represent the wealth of comparably aged individuals still living.

Estate tax data have been extensively used by Atkinson and Harrison (1978) and Shorrocks (1987) for the United Kingdom; and Lampman (1962), Smith (1984, 1987), Wolff and Marley (1987), and, most recently, Kopczuk and Saez (2004) for the United States. The long-term time series on wealth concentration for the United Kingdom and the United States are based on estate tax data (see Section 5.4.2).

5.4.1.2 Household survey data

Household surveys are questionnaires that are given to a sample of households in a population. Their primary advantage is to provide considerable discretion to the interviewer about the information requested of respondents. Their major drawbacks are that information provided by the respondent can be inaccurate (response error) and the information requested may not be provided (nonresponse problems). Another problem is that because household wealth is extremely skewed, the very rich (the so-called "upper tail" of the distribution) are often considerably under-represented in random samples. An alternative is to use stratified samples, based typically on income tax returns, which oversample the rich. However, studies indicate that response error and nonresponse rates are considerably higher among the wealthy than among the middle class. Moreover, there are problems in "weighting" the sample in order to reflect the actual population distribution. Results based on two major wealth surveys for the United States, the 1962 Survey of Financial Characteristics of Consumers (SFCC) and the SCF for various years, are presented in Section 5.4.3.

5.4.1.3 Wealth tax data

A third source is wealth tax return data, which is available in a number of European countries such as Germany, Sweden, and Switzerland. These countries assess taxes not only on current income but also on the stock of household wealth. Though there is typically a threshold for paying wealth taxes, population coverage can be considerably greater than that of estate tax returns. However, the measurement problems are similar to those of estate tax data. The filer has a great incentive to understate the value of his or her assets, or even not to report them at all, for tax avoidance. Moreover, the assets subject to tax do not cover the full range of household assets (for example, consumer durables, pensions, and life insurance policies are often excluded). In addition, the observational unit is the tax return unit, which does not directly correspond to the family unit. Wealth tax data have been used extensively by Spånt (1987) for an analysis of wealth trends in Sweden (see Section 5.4.3).

5.4.1.4 Income capitalization technique

The fourth source of wealth data is based on the *income capitalization* technique, which is usually applied to a sample of income tax returns. The earliest use of this technique on U.S. data was a 1939 study by Stewart. In this procedure, certain income flows, such as dividends, rents, and interest, are converted into corresponding asset values based on the average asset yield. For example, dividends are capitalized into corporate stock holdings by dividing dividends reported in an income tax return by the average ratio of dividends to corporate stock in the economy as a whole. This technique when applied to a large sample of tax returns can provide an estimate of the size distribution of wealth.

This source also suffers from a number of problems. First, only assets with a corresponding income flow are covered in this procedure. Thus, owner-occupied housing, consumer durables, and idle land cannot be directly captured. Also, in the United States, state and local bonds cannot be estimated, because this source of interest income is exempt from federal income taxes. Second, the estimation procedure rests heavily on the assumption that asset yields are uncorrelated with asset levels (that is, for example, that large stock holders will receive the same average return on their stock holdings as small stock holders). Any actual correlation between asset holdings and yields can produce biased estimates. Third, the observational unit is based on the tax return. Various assumptions must be made in order to construct family wealth estimates from tax unit wealth.

5.4.2   Long-term trends in household wealth inequality in the United States

This section pieces together the existing information to document the historical trends. Data on the size distribution of household wealth in the United States are available principally from estate tax records and household surveys. A reasonably consistent series of estate tax records for the very wealthy collected from national estate tax records exists for selected years between 1922 and 1981. Comparative estimates of household wealth inequality are also provided from seven surveys conducted by the Federal Reserve Board, in 1962, 1983, 1986 (a special follow-up of the 1983 survey), 1989, 1992, 1995, and 1998. These are based on stratified samples and are reasonably consistent over time. In addition, a figure for 1969 is obtained from the MESP dataset of that year and one for 1979 from the Income Survey and Development Program (ISDP) of that year.

Wolff (1995, 2002) put these data together to construct a time series on wealth concentration in the United States. The resulting series is shown in Figure 5.4. The figures show a high concentration of wealth throughout the period from 1922 to 1998. A quarter or more of total wealth was owned by the top 1 percent in each of these years except 1976 and 1981. A comparison of the two endpoints reveals similar concentration figures: 37 percent in 1922 and 35 percent in 1998. However, this comparison hides important trends over the period.

Between 1922 and 1929 there was a substantial increase in wealth concentration, from 37 percent to 44 percent. Wealth inequality in 1929 was at its highest point over this period (and

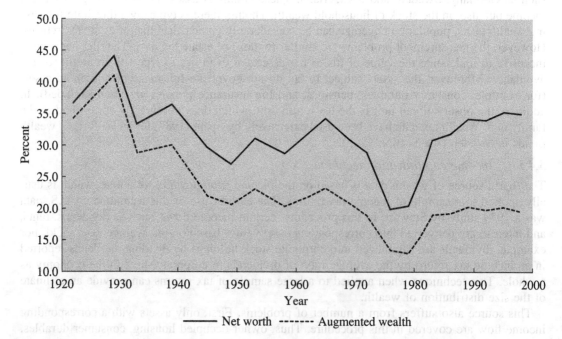

Figure 5.4   Share of wealth owned by the top 1 percent of U.S. households, 1922–1998

probably over the twentieth century). The Great Depression saw a sizable drop in inequality, with the share of the top percentile falling to 33 percent, but by 1939, the concentration level was almost the same as it was in 1922. There followed a substantial drop in inequality between 1939 and 1945, a result of the leveling effects of World War II, and a more modest decline between 1945 and 1949.

The share of wealth held by the richest 1 percent of households showed a gradual upward trend from 27 percent in 1949 to a peak of 34 percent in 1965. There followed a rather pronounced fall in wealth inequality lasting until 1979. Between 1965 and 1972, the share of the top percentile fell from 34 to 29 percent, and then from 29 to 20 percent between 1972 and 1976. The main reason for the decline in concentration over this four-year period is the sharp drop in the value of corporate stock held by the top wealth-holders. The total value of corporate stock owned by the richest 1 percent fell from $491 billion in 1972 to $297 billion in 1976 (see Smith, 1987). Moreover, this decline appears to be attributable to the steep decline in share prices, rather than a divestiture of stock holdings.

Wealth inequality appears to have bottomed out some time during the late 1970s. A sharp increase in wealth concentration occurred between 1979 and 1981, from a 21 to a 25 percent share, again from 1981 to 1983, from a 25 to a 31 percent share, and then again between 1983 and 1989, from 31 to 34 percent. A further though more modest rise is evident in the 1990s, to 35 percent in 1998. This sharp rise in the concentration of household wealth paralleled the growth in income inequality evident during the 1980s and 1990s.[17]

Figure 5.4 also shows the trend in the share of augmented household wealth owned by the top 1 percent of wealth-holders as ranked by augmented wealth. The addition of pension and social security wealth has had a significant effect on measured wealth inequality. Because of the growth over time in pension and social security wealth, particularly the latter, in relation to marketable wealth, the gap between the marketable wealth and the augmented wealth series widened over time, from 2 percentage points in 1922 to 15 percentage points in 1998. However, the time paths are almost identical. Wealth concentration based on augmented wealth showed a sharp increase between 1922 and 1929; a substantial decline from 1929 to 1933 followed by an increase between 1933 and 1939; a significant decrease between 1939 and 1945; a fairly flat trend from 1945 through 1972; a sharp decline from 1972 to 1976; and then a substantial rise between 1979 and 1998. The increase during the 1980s and 1990s (1979 to 1998) is more muted on the basis of augmented wealth, 7 percentage points, in comparison to marketable wealth, 15 percentage points.

5.4.2.1 *Comparisons with income inequality*

Wealth inequality is today and has historically been extreme and substantially greater than income inequality. Indeed, the top 1 percent of wealth-holders has typically held over one-quarter of household wealth, in comparison to an 8 or 9 percent share of income received by the top percentile of the income distribution.

Figure 5.5 shows the share of total family income held by the top 5 percent of families as ranked by income. The basic data source is the Current Population Report series on shares of income held by families that runs from 1947 to 1998. The earlier data, from 1922 to 1949, are from Kuznets' (1953) series on the percentage share of total income received by the top percentiles of tax units. This series is benchmarked against the Census figure for 1949.

Though wealth inequality is more extreme than that of income, has its historical course mirrored the time pattern of income inequality? Income inequality, as measured by the share of the top 5 percent, increased between 1922 and 1929, from 21 to 25 percent, declined rather steadily during the Depression years, reaching a 22 percent share in 1939, and then fell precipitously during World War II, bottoming out at 17 percent in 1945. There was a slight decline between 1945 and 1953, from 17 to 16 percent, but then income inequality remained virtually flat until

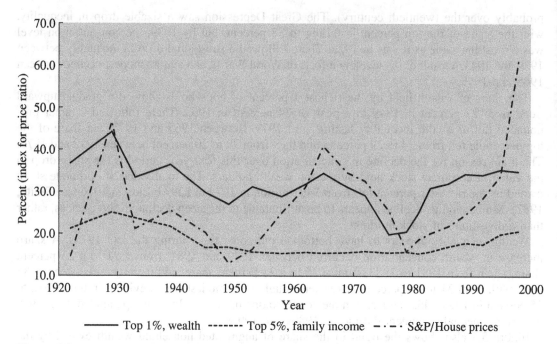

Figure 5.5   Wealth inequality, income inequality, and the ratio of stock prices to housing prices

1981. Between 1981 and 1989, there ensued a fairly sharp rise in income inequality, from a 15 to a 18 percent share, and then from 1989 to 1998 a further increase to 21 percent.

A comparison of trends in income inequality and wealth inequality during the 1980s and 1990s might prove illuminating at this point, particularly since the rise in the former has received so much attention in both professional economic journals and the mass media. There are several points of interest. First, the evidence presented above indicates that the level of wealth concentration was at a high point in 1998. The time series on income inequality indicates exactly the same result for the concentration of household income. Second, the run up in wealth inequality that characterized the 1980s and 1990s was almost unprecedented in the twentieth century except for the 1920s. A similar finding can be reported for income inequality, which either declined or remained stable over the century except for the 1920s, 1980s, and 1990s.

It is hard to provide a direct comparison on the degree of increase in inequality for the two series, because of limitations on data availability and differences in the apparent timing of the rise of each. The Gini coefficient for wealth inequality shows an increase from 0.80 in 1983 to 0.83 in 1989, whereas, on the basis of the Current Population Report series, the Gini coefficient for income inequality rose from 0.414 to 0.431 over the same period. The share of wealth held by the top 5 percent of wealth-holders increased from 56 to 59 percent over these years, whereas the share of total income received by the top 5 percent of income recipients moved upward from 16 to 18 percent. Thus, over this period, both wealth and income inequality increased. Moreover, even if we move the clock backward to 1977, when income inequality began its recent ascent, we find that the Gini coefficient for income inequality increased by only 0.29, from 0.402 to 0.431, and the share of the top 5 percent by only 2.1 percentage points, from 15.8 to 17.9 percent. Moreover, from 1989 to 1998, wealth inequality increased only very modestly, with the share of the top 1 percent of wealth-holders rising by 0.7 percentage points, while income inequality grew very vigorously, with the share of the top 5 percent of income recipients advancing by almost 3 percentage points.

As is apparent, the time paths of wealth inequality and income inequality have been similar but certainly not identical over the period from 1922 to 1998. Both showed a sharp rise from 1922 to 1929 followed by declines from 1929 through 1945 and increases from 1981 to 1998, but income inequality was generally stable during the intervening years while wealth inequality fell sharply during the 1970s. What can explain the discrepancy in these patterns?

5.4.2.2 *Movements in stock and housing prices*

One variable that appears to explain much of the additional variation in movements in wealth inequality is the ratio of stock prices to housing prices. The rationale is that stocks are an asset held primarily by the upper wealth classes, whereas housing is the major asset of the middle classes (see below). If stock prices increase relative to housing prices, the share of wealth held by the top wealth groups will rise, and conversely.

This price ratio (indexed to a value of 15 in 1922 in order to fit to Figure 5.5) shows a time path very similar to that of wealth inequality. The ratio more than trebled between 1922 and 1929, corresponding to the tremendous growth in wealth inequality; fell by half between the 1929 "Crash" and 1933, as wealth inequality declined; and then increased by about 20 percent between 1933 and 1939 as the stock market partially recovered, which helped cause a rise in wealth inequality. The price ratio then fell by almost half between 1939 and 1949, because of a rapid inflation in housing prices, which, in turn, partly accounted for the pronounced decline in wealth inequality.

The ratio of stock to housing prices more than trebled between 1949 and 1965, fueled mainly by rapidly rising stock values, and this movement corresponded to a rise in wealth inequality. Between 1965 and 1979, this ratio fell by almost two-thirds, with most of the decline occurring after 1972. Before 1972 the main culprit was rising house prices but after 1972 the principal reason was a stagnating stock market. This period was also characterized by a dramatic decline in wealth inequality. Between 1979 and 1989, the price ratio increased by more than half, as the stock market flourished, and a sharp increase in wealth inequality was also recorded over this decade. From 1989 to 1998, the ratio skyrocketed by two and a half times, though wealth inequality inched up very modestly.

Econometric analysis reveals that the dominant factor in explaining changes in wealth concentration is income inequality. A regression performed by this author of a wealth inequality index, measured by the share of marketable wealth held by the top 1 percent of households (WLTH) on income inequality, by the share of income received by the top 5 percent of families (INC), and the ratio of stock prices (the Standard & Poor index) to housing prices (RATIO), with 21 data points between 1922 and 1998 yields:

$$\text{WLTH} = 5.10 + 1.27 \text{ INC} + 0.26 \text{ RATIO}, R^2 = 0.64, N = 21$$
$$\quad\ (0.9)\quad\ (4.2)\qquad\quad (2.5)$$

with *t*-ratios shown in parentheses.[18] Both variables are statistically significant (INC at the 1 percent level and RATIO at the 5 percent level) and with the expected (positive) sign. Also, the fit is quite good, even for this simple model.

The dominant factor in explaining changes in wealth concentration is income inequality. However, the movement in the ratio of stock to housing prices explains most of the increase in wealth inequality between 1949 and 1965 and the subsequent decline between 1965 and 1979 (particularly between 1972 and 1976). What about the 1980s and 1990s? From the regression results, almost two-fifths (39 percent) of the increase in wealth concentration between 1981 and 1998 is attributable to the increase in income inequality and 29 percent to the increase of stock prices relative to housing prices. The remaining 29 percent is left unexplained.

5.4.3   Changes in wealth inequality, 1962–2004

Eight household wealth surveys conducted by the Federal Reserve Board – the 1962 Survey of Financial Characteristics of Consumers (SFCC) and the 1983, 1989, 1992, 1995, 1998, 2001, and 2004 Survey of Consumer Finance – provide the basis of a detailed comparison of household wealth inequality in those years. All eight surveys use similar methodology. Each is stratified by income – that is, each oversamples high-income households. The original survey data from the 1962 SFCC and the 1983, 1989, 1992, and 1995 SCF were then adjusted so that the surveys are consistent in wealth concept and align to national balance sheet totals for that year (see Wolff, 1987a, 1994, 2001, 2006, and 2007 for details on the adjustment procedures).

5.4.3.1   Changes in average wealth holdings

We begin by looking at trends in real wealth over the period from 1962 to 2004 (all figures are reported in 2004 dollars). As shown in Table 5.6, average household wealth grew at an average annual rate of 1.8 percent between 1962 and 1983 and then at 2.3 percent between 1983 and 1989. Between 1989 and 2004, growth again accelerated, to 2.8 percent per year. By 2004, the average wealth of households was about $430,500, almost triple that of 1962. Average financial wealth grew faster than marketable wealth in the 1983–1989 period (2.7 versus 2.3 percent per year), reflecting the increased importance of bank deposits, financial assets, and equities in the overall household portfolio over this period. On the other hand, financial wealth grew slower than marketable wealth between 1962 and 1983, 1.4 versus 1.8 percent per year, and at about the same rate from 1989 to 2004, 2.8 percent per year. Thus, the acceleration in the growth of financial wealth between the 1962–1983 and the 1989–2004 periods was even greater than marketable net worth.

Average household income also grew faster in the 1983–1989 period than the 1962–1983 period. Its annual growth accelerated from 1.5 to 2.4 percentage points. However, growth slowed down to 1.4 percent per year in the years 1989 to 2004. Average income grew more slowly than average wealth, except for the 1983–1989 period.

The trend in median household wealth gives a contrasting picture to the growth of mean wealth. Median household wealth grew more slowly than mean household wealth in all three periods, but the difference was much more marked in the later periods – 1.9 percentage points in 1989–2004 and 1.1 percentage points in 1983–1989 – than for the 1962–1983 period, 0.2 percentage points. The results for the later periods, in particular, also imply that the upper wealth classes enjoyed

Table 5.6   Average and median real household wealth and income, 1962–2004 (in thousands, 2004 dollars)

Wealth concept	1962	1983	1989	1998	2004	Annual rate of growth			
						1962–1983	1983–1989	1989–2004	1962–2004
Means									
Marketable net worth	168.2	246.4	282.3	313.2	430.5	1.82	2.27	2.81	2.24
Financial net worth	133.8	178.8	210.7	246.0	319.4	1.38	2.74	2.77	2.07
Income	35.3	48.2	55.6	60.1	68.8	1.48	2.40	1.41	1.59
Medians									
Marketable net worth	45.0	63.3	67.7	70.3	77.9	1.63	1.13	0.93	1.31
Financial net worth	12.1	13.7	16.1	20.6	18.2	0.56	2.76	0.81	0.96
Income	33.9	39.6	44.0	45.1	42.0	0.75	1.76	−0.32	0.51

Source: Figures are calculated from the 1962 Survey of Financial Characteristics of Consumers and the 1983, 1989, 1998, and 2004 Survey of Consumer Finances.

a disproportionate percentage of the total wealth increase over the period – a finding consistent with rising wealth inequality during these periods. Median financial wealth grew more slowly than mean financial wealth in both the 1962–1983 and the 1989–2004 periods but at about the same pace in 1983–1989. Median household income increased at a slower pace than mean income in all three periods, and the difference was greatest for the 1989–2004 years (when median income actually declined in real terms).

5.4.3.2 Trends in wealth inequality

The results of Table 5.7 point to sharply rising wealth inequality in the 1980s. The most telling finding is that the share of marketable net worth of the top 1 percent (the "super-rich") increased

Table 5.7 Gini coefficient and percentage shares of total wealth and income by percentile group and quintile, 1962, 1983, 1989, 1998, and 2004

Year	Gini coefficient	Top 0.5%	Next 0.5%	Next 4.0%	Next 5.0%	Next 10.0%	Bottom 80.0%	All
			*Percentage share of wealth (income) held by*					
A. Marketable net worth								
1962	0.80	25.9	7.5	21.2	12.4	14.0	19.1	100.0
1983	0.80	26.2	7.5	22.3	12.1	13.1	18.7	100.0
1989	0.83	26.9	10.5	21.6	11.6	13.0	16.5	100.0
1998	0.82	26.5	11.6	21.3	11.5	12.5	16.6	100.0
2004	0.83	25.3	9.0	24.6	12.3	13.4	15.3	100.0
Percent of total net worth increase accruing to each group[a]								
1962–1983		26.9	7.6	24.7	11.8	11.2	17.9	100.0
1983–2004		24.2	11.0	27.6	12.6	13.8	10.9	100.0
B. Financial net wealth								
1962	0.88	31.5	8.8	23.8	12.9	12.7	10.4	100.0
1983	0.89	34.0	8.9	25.1	12.3	11.0	8.7	100.0
1989	0.93	34.6	12.3	23.9	11.6	11.0	6.6	100.0
1998	0.89	32.3	15.0	21.0	11.4	11.2	9.1	100.0
2004	0.90	31.6	10.6	26.7	12.0	11.6	7.5	100.0
Percent of total financial wealth increase accruing to each group[a]								
1962–1983		41.4	9.4	29.0	10.4	6.1	3.7	100.0
1983–2004		28.9	12.6	28.4	11.8	12.2	6.1	100.0
C. Household income								
1961	0.43	5.7	2.7	11.3	10.2	16.1	54.0	100.0
1982	0.48	9.2	3.7	13.3	10.3	15.5	48.1	100.0
1988	0.52	13.4	3.2	13.3	10.4	15.2	44.5	100.0
1997	0.53	12.6	4.0	14.4	10.2	15.0	43.8	100.0
2003	0.54	13.0	4.0	15.0	10.9	14.9	42.1	100.0
Percent of total income increase accruing to each group[a]								
1961–1982		18.8	6.4	18.8	10.3	13.7	32.1	100.0
1982–2003		27.3	5.4	21.6	13.3	12.9	19.5	100.0
D. Augmented wealth[b]								
		Top 1 percent						
1962	0.59	21.9		16.1				
1983	0.57	19.0		17.4				
1989	0.63	23.8		18.4				
2001	0.66	23.4		20.3				

Table 5.7   (*Continued*)

Year	Percentage share of wealth (income) held by quintile					
	Top	Fourth	Middle	Second	Bottom	All
A. Net worth						
1962	81.0	13.4	5.4	1.0	−0.7	100.0
1983	81.3	12.6	5.2	1.2	−0.3	100.0
1989	83.5	12.3	4.8	0.8	−1.5	100.0
1998	83.4	11.9	4.5	0.8	−0.7	100.0
2004	84.7	11.3	3.8	0.7	−0.5	100.0
B. Financial net wealth						
1962	89.6	9.6	2.1	0.0	−1.4	100.0
1983	91.3	7.9	1.7	0.2	−1.0	100.0
1989	93.4	7.4	1.7	0.0	−2.5	100.0
1998	90.9	8.3	1.9	0.1	−1.2	100.0
2004	92.5	7.3	1.2	2.5	−3.5	100.0
C. Household income						
1962	46.0	24.0	16.6	9.9	3.5	100.0
1983	51.9	21.6	14.1	8.6	3.7	100.0
1989	55.5	20.7	13.2	7.6	3.1	100.0
1998	56.2	20.5	12.8	7.6	2.9	100.0
2004	57.9	19.9	12.1	7.4	2.8	100.0
D. Augmented wealth[b]						
1962	62.5	17.6	10.5	6.4	3.1	100.0
1983	61.7	17.4	10.8	6.7	3.3	100.0
1989	68.0	17.2	9.4	4.5	0.8	100.0
2001	69.3	15.9	8.5	4.5	1.7	100.0

a   The computation was performed by dividing the total increase in wealth (income) of a given group by the total increase of wealth (income) for all households over the period, under the assumption that the number of households in each group remained unchanged over the period. It should be noted that the families found in each group (such as the top 1.5 percent) may be *different* in each year.

b   Augmented wealth is the sum of marketable net worth, pension wealth, and social security wealth. It is assumed in these calculations that average social security benefits will grow at 2 percent per year in real terms. Estimates are not yet available for 2004.

Source: Figures are calculated from the 1962 Survey of Financial Characteristics of Consumers and the 1983, 1989, 1998, 2001, and 2004 Survey of Consumer Finances.

by 3.6 percentage points between 1983 and 1989. In 1989, this group owned 37.4 percent of total household wealth, compared to 33.8 percent in 1983. The share of the next 9 percent (the "rich") declined somewhat. The share of the bottom 80 percent declined by 2.2 percentage points, from 18.7 percent of total wealth to 16.5 percent.

An examination of the quintile shares reveals that while the top 20 percent increased their share of total wealth by 2.2 percentage points, the fourth quintile lost 0.3 percentage points, the middle lost 0.4, the second lost 0.4, and the bottom 1.2. The bottom quintile had negative net worth on average (their debts outweighed their assets). This is true for both 1983 and 1989 (as well as 1962). Another indicator of overall inequality, the Gini coefficient, also shows a sizable increase over the period, from 0.80 to 0.83.

Data are also presented for 1962. The estimated inequality figures for 1962 and 1983 are very similar. The Gini coefficient was 0.80 for both 1962 and 1983; the share of the top 1 percent of wealth-holders was 33.4 percent in 1962 and 33.7 percent in 1983; and the share of the top 5 percent was 54.6 percent in 1962 and 55.6 percent in 1983.[19] Between 1989 and 2004, wealth inequality again remained relatively static. The Gini coefficients were the same in the two years (0.83). The share of the top 1 percent did fall rather sharply, from 38.1 to 34.3 percent. However, the share of the top 5 percent was exactly the same in the two years, 58.9 percent. The share of the top 20 percent increased by more than 1 percentage point; that of the fourth quintile fell by 1 percentage point, as did the share of the middle quintile; the share of the second quintile was largely unchanged; and that of the bottom quintile was up by 1 percentage point.

Another dimension is afforded by looking at the distribution of financial net worth, defined as net worth less the equity in owner-occupied housing. Financial wealth is distributed even more unequally than total household wealth. In 1989, the top 1 percent of families as ranked by financial wealth owned 47 percent of total financial wealth, in contrast to a 37 percent share of marketable net worth among the top 1 percent of marketable wealth-holders (also compare the Gini coefficients of 0.83 for total net worth and 0.93 for financial wealth in 1989). The top quintile (as ranked by financial wealth) accounted for 93 percent of total financial wealth, and the second quintile accounted for nearly all the remainder.

The concentration of financial wealth increased at about the same degree as that of net worth between 1983 and 1989. The share of the top 1 percent of financial wealth-holders increased by 4 percentage points, from 43 percent of total financial wealth to 47 percent, and the Gini coefficient rose from 0.89 to 0.93. The share of the bottom 80 percent of financial wealth-holders fell from 8.7 percent to 6.6 percent. The concentration of financial net worth also increased slightly between 1962 and 1983, with the share of the top 1 percent rising from 40 to 43 percent and that of the top quintile from 90 to 91 percent, and the Gini coefficient nudging up from 0.88 to 0.89. In contrast to net worth, the inequality of financial wealth fell substantially from 1989 to 2004. The share of the top 1 percent plummeted by 5 percentage points, from 47 to 42 percent; that of the top 5 percent fell from 71 to 69 percent; that of the top quintile from 93 to 92 percent; and the Gini coefficient declined from 0.93 to 0.90.

Comparable results on household income distribution are shown in Panel C in Table 5.7, where families are ranked in terms of income to calculate the percentile shares. These data confirm that the concentration of income also increased between 1982 and 1988.[20] Most of the relative income gain accrued to the top half of 1 percent of income recipients, whose share grew by a "whopping" 4.2 percentage points. Almost all the loss in income was sustained by the bottom 80 percent of the income distribution, with the loss fairly evenly spread over the bottom four quintiles. The Gini coefficient also showed a sharp increase, from 0.48 to 0.52.[21] There was also a large increase in income inequality between 1962 and 1983, with the Gini coefficient rising from 0.43 to 0.48 and the share of the top 1 percent increasing from 8 to 13 percent and that of the top quintile from 46 to 52 percent. According to Census data, almost all of this increase occurred after 1973.

In contrast to both net worth and financial wealth, the inequality in income continued to grow from 1988 to 2003. The share of the top 1 percent rose from 16.6 to 17 percent; that of the top 5 percent from 30 to 32 percent; that of the top quintile from 56 to 58 percent; and the Gini coefficient rose from 0.52 to 0.54.

It is also illuminating to contrast the relative level of income and wealth inequality. Wealth is distributed *much more unequally* than income. As shown in Figure 5.6, the Lorenz curve for family income in 2004 lies considerably inside the Lorenz curve for wealth. The share of the top 1 percent of wealth-holders in 2004 was 34 percent, while that for the top 1 percent of income recipients was 17 percent. The top quintile of wealth-holders owned almost 85 percent of total

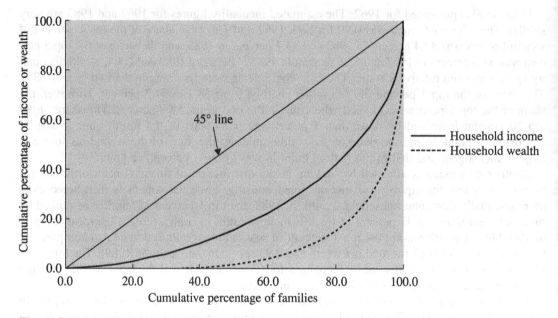

Figure 5.6   Lorenz curves for household income and household wealth, 2004

household wealth while the top quintile of income recipients accounted for 58 percent of total family income. The Gini coefficient for wealth in 2004 was 0.83, compared to 0.54 for income.

Another way of highlighting the changing distribution of wealth is to look at the proportion of the total increase in real household wealth accruing to each percentile group. This is calculated by computing the increase in total wealth of each percentile group and dividing this figure by the total increase in household wealth. If a group's wealth share remains constant over time, then the percentage of the total wealth growth received by that group will equal its share of total wealth. If a group's share of total wealth increases (decreases) over time, then it will receive a percentage of the total wealth gain greater (less) than its share in either year. However, it should be noted that in the calculations shown in Table 5.7, the households found in each group (say the top quintile) may be different in the two years.[22]

The calculations show that the top 1 percent of wealth-holders together accounted for 35 percent of the growth of total household wealth between 1983 and 2004, and the top quintile for 89 percent of the total wealth gain. Only 1.9 percent of the total wealth growth accrued to the middle quintile, and the bottom two quintiles accounted collectively for a *loss* of 0.7 percent of the total wealth growth – a loss of over $300 billion of wealth in 2004 dollars. In contrast, over the 1962–1983 period, each percentile and quintile group enjoyed some share of the overall wealth growth, and the gains were roughly in proportion to the share of wealth held by the group in 1962.

Gains in the overall growth in financial wealth were distributed even more unevenly than in marketable net worth. Between 1983 and 2004, 42 percent of the growth accrued to the top 1 percent, 94 percent to the top quintile, 7 percent to the fourth quintile, 0.7 percent to the middle quintile, and –1.3 percent to the bottom two quintiles. Results for 1962–1983 show that while gains in financial wealth were distributed more unevenly than those in marketable net worth over the period, they were distributed more equally than gains in financial wealth over the 1983–1989 period.

A similar calculation using the income data reveals that 33 percent of the total real income gain between 1983 and 2004 accrued to the top 1 percent of income recipients. This is still substantial, though considerably less than the proportional gain among the top 1 percent of wealth-holders.

A little over 80 percent of income growth went to the top quintile of income recipients, 13 percent to the fourth quintile, 4.2 percent to the middle, and only 2 percent to the bottom two quintiles. The distribution of income gains was more equal over the 1962–1983 period, with the top quintile receiving 68 percent of the growth, the second quintile 5.0 percent, and the bottom quintile 4.3 percent.

Pension and social security wealth were also imputed to the household balance sheet. Pension wealth is defined as the present value of discounted future pension benefits. Social security wealth is defined as the present value of the discounted stream of future social security benefits. Panel D in Table 5.7 shows results on the distribution of augmented household wealth, defined as the sum of marketable wealth plus pension and social security wealth. The addition of retirement wealth to traditional wealth causes a marked reduction in measured inequality. The Gini coefficient for augmented wealth was 0.57 and the share of the top 1 percent was 19 percent in 1983, compared to a Gini coefficient of 0.80 and a 34 percent share of the top 1 percent for marketable wealth in the same year.

A comparison of the 1962 SFCC and the 1983 SCF also reveal the growing importance of both social security and pension wealth. Without retirement wealth, measured wealth inequality was almost identical in the two years – Gini coefficients of 0.80 and a share of the top percentile of 33 percent and 34 percent, respectively. With social security and pension wealth included in the household portfolio, measured inequality is found to decline between the two years, from a Gini coefficient of 0.59 to 0.57 and with the share of the top percentile falling from 22 to 19 percent. The share of wealth of the top two quintiles also fell while the share of the bottom three rose.

Between 1983 and 1989, the inequality of augmented wealth showed a substantial increase, with the share of the top 1 percent rising from 19 to 24 percent and the Gini coefficient from 0.57 to 0.63. This growth in inequality mirrored that of marketable net worth. However, from 1989 to 2001, the inequality of augmented wealth showed another large gain, with the Gini coefficient climbing from 0.63 to 0.66.[23] This trend contrasts with the inequality of marketable net worth, which showed a slight decline over these years. The difference is primarily due to the rapid growth of pension wealth over this period, which is more unequally distributed than social security wealth (see Wolff, 2007, for more discussion of this issue).

5.4.3.3 *Portfolio composition by wealth and age class*

There are also marked differences in the assets owned by different wealth classes. Some assets are more concentrated in the hands of the rich and others are more dispersed among families of different wealth levels. Table 5.8 shows the proportion of total assets held by different wealth classes in the United States in 2004.

In 2004 the richest 1 percent of households held about half of all outstanding stock, financial securities, trust equity, and business equity, and 37 percent of nonhome real estate. The top 10 percent of families as a group accounted for about 80 to 85 percent of stock shares, bonds, trusts, business equity, and nonhome real estate. Moreover, despite the fact that 49 percent of households owned stock shares either directly or indirectly through mutual funds, trusts, or various pension accounts, the richest 10 percent of households accounted for 79 percent of the total value of these stocks, only slightly less than its 85 percent share of directly owned stocks and mutual funds.

In contrast, owner-occupied housing, deposits, life insurance, and pension accounts were more evenly distributed among households. The bottom 90 percent of households accounted for 62 percent of the value of owner-occupied housing, 39 percent of deposits, 43 percent of life insurance cash value, and 42 percent of the value of pension accounts. Debt was the most evenly distributed component of household wealth, with the bottom 90 percent of households responsible for 73 percent of total indebtedness.

Table 5.8 Percent of total assets held by wealth class, 2004

Asset type	Top 1.0%	Next 9.0%	Bottom 90.0%	All	Share of top 10%						
					1983	1989	1992	1995	1998	2001	2004
A. Investment assets											
Stocks and mutual funds	44.8	40.6	14.6	100.0	90.4	86.0	86.3	88.4	85.1	84.5	85.4
Financial securities	63.8	24.1	12.1	100.0	82.9	87.1	91.3	89.8	84.1	88.7	87.9
Trusts	47.7	33.9	18.5	100.0	95.4	87.9	87.9	88.5	90.8	86.7	81.5
Business equity	61.9	28.4	9.7	100.0	89.9	89.8	91.0	91.7	91.7	89.6	90.3
Nonhome real estate	36.8	42.6	20.6	100.0	76.3	79.6	83.0	78.7	74.9	78.5	79.4
Total for group	50.3	35.3	14.4	100.0	85.6	85.7	87.6	87.5	86.2	85.5	85.6
Stocks, directly or indirectly owned[a]	36.7	42.0	21.2	100.0	89.7	80.8	78.7	81.9	78.7	76.9	78.8
B. Housing, liquid assets, pension assets, and debt											
Principal residence	9.8	28.2	62.0	100.0	34.2	34.0	36.0	31.7	35.2	37.0	38.0
Deposits[b]	20.8	40.1	39.1	100.0	52.9	61.5	59.7	62.3	51.0	57.2	60.9
Life insurance	21.4	36.0	42.7	100.0	33.6	44.6	45.0	44.9	52.8	46.0	57.3
Pension accounts[c]	13.5	44.8	41.7	100.0	67.5	50.5	62.3	62.3	59.8	60.4	58.3
Total for group	12.2	33.5	54.3	100.0	41.0	43.9	45.2	42.5	44.0	45.9	45.7
Total debt	7.2	19.9	73.0	100.0	31.8	29.4	37.5	28.3	27.0	25.9	27.0

Households are classified into wealth class according to their net worth. Brackets for 2004 are:
Top 1 percent: net worth of $6,191,500 or more.
Next 9 percent: net worth between $811,000 and $6,191,500.
Bottom 90 percent: net worth less than $811,000.
a   Includes direct ownership of stock shares and indirect ownership through mutual funds, trusts, and IRAs, Keogh plans, 401(k) plans, and other retirement accounts.
b   Includes demand deposits, savings deposits, time deposits, money market funds, and certificates of deposit.
c   IRAs, Keogh plans, 401(k) plans, the accumulated value of defined contribution pension plans, and other retirement accounts.
Source: Author's computations from the Survey of Consumer Finances.

There was relatively little change between 1983 and 2004 in the concentration of asset ownership, with three exceptions. First, the share of total stocks and mutual funds held by the richest 10 percent of households declined from 90 to 85 percent over this period, and their share of stocks directly or indirectly owned from 90 to 79 percent. Second, the proportion of total pension accounts held by the top 10 percent fell from 68 percent in 1983 to 51 percent in 1989, reflecting the growing use of IRAs by middle-income families, and then rebounded to 58 percent in 2004 from the expansion of 401(k) plans and their adoption by high-income earners. Third, the share of total debt held by the top 10 percent also fell from 32 to 27 percent.

There are marked class differences in how middle-class families and the rich invest their wealth, and Table 5.9 shows the proportion of the total assets of each wealth class held in different asset types. The richest 1 percent of households (as ranked by wealth) invested over three-quarters of their savings in investment real estate, businesses, corporate stock, and financial securities in 2004. Corporate stocks, either directly owned by the households or indirectly owned through mutual funds, trust accounts, or various pension accounts, comprised 21 percent. Housing accounted for only 11 percent of their wealth (and net equity in housing 9 percent), liquid assets another 5 percent, and pension accounts another 5 percent. Their ratio of debt to net worth was 4 percent, their ratio of debt to income was 61 percent, and the ratio of mortgage debt to house value was 17 percent.

Table 5.9 Composition of household wealth by wealth class, 2004 (percent of gross assets)

Asset	All households	Top 1 percent	Next 19 percent	Middle three quintiles
Principal residence	33.5	10.9	32.2	66.1
Liquid assets (bank deposits, money market funds, and cash surrender value of life insurance)	7.3	5.1	8.6	8.5
Pension accounts	11.8	5.3	16.0	12.0
Corporate stock, financial securities, mutual funds, and personal trusts	17.0	26.9	16.3	4.2
Unincorporated business equity, other real estate	28.6	49.3	25.4	7.9
Miscellaneous assets	1.8	2.6	1.5	1.4
Total assets	100.0	100.0	100.0	100.0
Memo (selected ratios in percent)				
Debt/equity ratio	18.4	3.8	12.0	61.6
Debt/income ratio	115.0	61.4	107.0	141.2
Net home equity/total assets[a]	21.8	9.0	24.2	34.7
Principal residence debt/house value	34.8	17.1	24.9	47.6
All stocks/total assets[b]	17.5	21.3	19.8	7.5
Ownership rates (percent)				
Principal residence	69.1	97.4	96.8	78.2
Mobile home	4.3	0.0	0.7	5.9
Other real estate	18.1	78.9	47.0	13.6
Vacation homes	6.3	40.0	15.9	4.6
Pension assets	49.7	82.7	80.6	51.4
Unincorporated business	11.5	72.3	29.6	8.1
Corporate stock, financial securities,[c] mutual funds, and personal trusts	32.1	84.8	73.0	27.1
Stocks, directly or indirectly owned[b]	48.6	93.3	87.1	47.9
(1) $5,000 or more	36.4	93.2	82.9	32.2
(2) $10,000 or more	31.1	92.9	78.2	25.3

Households are classified into wealth class according to their net worth. Brackets for 2004 are:

Top 1 percent: net worth of $6,191,500 or more.

Next 19 percent: net worth between $406,450 and $6,191,500.

Quintiles 2 through 4: net worth between $500 and $406,450.

a   Ratio of gross value of principal residence less mortgage debt on principal residence to total assets.

b   Includes direct ownership of stock shares and indirect ownership through mutual funds, trusts, and IRAs, Keogh plans, 401(k) plans, and other retirement accounts.

c   Financial securities exclude U.S. government savings bonds in this tabulation.

Source: Author's computations from the 2004 Survey of Consumer Finances.

Among the next richest 19 percent of U.S. households, housing comprised 32 percent of their total assets (and net home equity 24 percent), liquid assets another 9 percent, and pension assets 16 percent. Forty-two percent of their assets took the form of investment assets – real estate, business equity, stocks, and bonds – and 20 percent was in the form of stocks directly or indirectly owned. Debt amounted to 12 percent of their net worth and a bit over 100 percent of their income, and the ratio of mortgage debt to house value was 25 percent.

In contrast, two-thirds of the wealth of the middle three quintiles of households was invested in their own home in 2004. However, home equity amounted to only 35 percent of total assets, a reflection of their large mortgage debt. Another 21 percent went into monetary savings of one form or another and pension accounts. Together housing, liquid assets, and pension assets accounted for 87 percent of the total assets of the middle class. The remainder was about evenly split among nonhome real estate, business equity, and various financial securities and corporate stock. Stocks directly or indirectly owned amounted to only 8 percent of their total assets. The ratio of debt to net worth was 62 percent, substantially higher than for the richest 20 percent, and their ratio of debt to income was 141 percent, also much higher than the top quintile. Finally, their mortgage debt amounted to almost half the value of their principal residences.

Almost all households among the top 20 percent of wealth holders owned their own home, in comparison to 78 percent of households in the middle three quintiles. Though this homeownership rate looks large, 6 percent of households in the middle three quintiles reported having a mobile home as their primary residence. Over three-quarters of very rich households (in the top percentile) owned some other form of real estate (40 percent owned a vacation home), compared to 47 percent of rich households (those in the next 19 percent of the distribution) and only 14 percent of households in the middle 60 percent. Eighty-three percent of the very rich owned some form of pension asset, compared to 81 percent of the rich and 51 percent of the middle. A somewhat startling 72 percent of the very rich reported owning their business. The comparable figures are 30 percent among the rich and only 8 percent of the middle class.

Among the very rich, 85 percent held corporate stock, mutual funds, financial securities or a trust fund, in comparison to 73 percent of the rich and 27 percent of the middle. Ninety-three percent of the very rich reported owning stock either directly or indirectly, compared to 87 percent of the rich and 48 percent of the middle. If we exclude small holdings of stock, then the ownership rates drop off sharply among the middle three quintiles, from 48 percent to 32 percent for stocks worth $5,000 or more and to 25 percent for stocks worth $10,000 or more.

The rather staggering debt level of the middle class in 2004 raises the question of whether this is a recent phenomenon or whether it has been going on for some time. The overall debt–equity ratio in 2004 was still below its peak value in 1995, while the overall debt–income ratio has been generally trending upward since 1983 and actually took a big jump from 2001 to 2004.

Differences are also interesting by age class (see Table 5.10). Gross owner-occupied housing was the most important asset among families under 35 years old, comprising 57 percent of their gross assets. However, the proportion declined almost systematically with age, from 57 percent for the youngest age group to 26 percent for age group 65 to 74, though it did rise to 34 percent for the oldest age group (75 and over).[24] On the other hand, net home equity as a proportion of gross assets shows little variation by age class, comprising 22 percent overall and about the same for each age group (except the oldest where it gets up to 31 percent). Liquid assets accounted for a larger share of the assets of the elderly (age 65 and over) than the nonelderly (10.7 versus 6.6 percent), while the value of nonhome real estate and business equity was considerably more important for families under 65, accounting for 30 percent of their gross assets compared to 26 percent for the elderly.

Financial securities, stocks, and trust equity increased systematically with age. All together, these assets comprised 14 percent of the assets of families under 65 and 24 percent of those of the elderly. Debt shows the opposite pattern, declining in importance with age, from 103 percent of net worth for the youngest group to only 4 percent for the oldest. The debt–equity ratio was 24 percent for families under 65 and only 5 percent for the elderly. The debt–income ratio also declined monotonically with age. The ratio was 125 percent among nonelderly families and 60 percent among the elderly.

Table 5.10 Composition of household wealth by age class, 2004 (percent of gross assets)

Asset	All	Under 35	35–44	45–54	55–64	65–74	75 & over
Principal residence	33.5	57.1	42.0	33.3	27.8	26.0	33.5
Liquid assets (bank deposits, money market funds, and cash surrender value of life insurance)	7.3	7.1	6.6	5.9	6.7	8.3	13.7
Pension accounts	11.8	8.1	9.6	12.8	14.7	12.8	6.4
Corporate stock, financial securities, mutual funds, and personal trusts	17.0	4.4	11.0	13.4	18.9	23.8	24.6
Unincorporated business equity, other real estate	28.6	22.1	29.9	32.3	30.5	27.1	19.0
Miscellaneous assets	1.8	1.0	0.9	2.3	1.5	2.0	2.7
Total assets	100.0	100.0	100.0	100.0	100.0	100.0	100.0
Memo (selected ratios in percent)							
Debt/equity ratio	18.4	103.2	37.6	21.9	10.6	5.5	4.2
Debt/income ratio	115.0	144.5	146.9	124.1	89.4	64.1	54.7
Net home equity/total assets[a]	21.8	18.8	19.9	19.6	21.2	22.6	31.4
Principal residence debt/house value	34.8	67.1	52.7	41.0	23.8	13.0	6.4
All stocks total assets[b]	17.5	6.1	13.1	15.5	20.8	23.4	17.7
Homeownership rate	69.1	41.5	68.6	77.3	79.1	81.2	85.1

Households are classified into age class according to the age of the household head.
a   Ratio of gross value of principal residence less mortgage debt on principal residence to total assets.
b   Includes direct ownership of stock shares and indirect ownership through mutual funds, trusts, and IRAs, Keogh plans, 401(k) plans, and other retirement accounts.
c   Financial securities exclude U.S. government savings bonds in this tabulation.
Source: Author's computations from the 2004 Survey of Consumer Finances.

5.4.3.4   Relation between income and wealth

It is often believed that income and wealth are almost interchangeable as measures of family well-being. That is to say, many believe that families with high income almost always (or, indeed, necessarily) have high wealth, and low-income families have low wealth. However, this is not the case. Some tabulations prepared by Radner and Vaughan (1987) for the year 1979 show that the two distributions are not identical (see Table 5.11).

In Table 5.11, if income and wealth were perfectly correlated, then each element of the diagonal of the matrix would equal 20 percent and the off-diagonal terms would all be zero. There was generally a strong positive correlation between income and wealth. For example, in the bottom income quintile, 41 percent (8.1/20.0) of the households were in the bottom net worth quintile, while only 7 percent (1.3/20.0) were in the top net worth quintile. In the top income quintile, only 5 percent were in the bottom net worth quintile, while 45 percent fell in the top net worth quintile.

However, the correlation is far from perfect and there was still a substantial amount of dispersion of wealth by income group. No net worth quintile contained more than 44 percent of the households in the corresponding income quintile. Moreover, in the three middle-income quintiles, each net worth quintile had at least 10 percent of the households in the income quintile. Thus, income and wealth, while positively correlated, were distributed rather differently among households. Wealth thus represents another dimension of well-being over and above income.

Updated calculations for 2001 based on the SCF are also shown in Table 5.11. The results are very similar to those for 1979. If anything the correlation between income and wealth appears

Table 5.11 The joint distribution of households among net worth and income quintiles, 1979 and 2001 (percent of households in the income and net worth quintile)

Income quintile	Net worth quintile					
	1	*2*	*3*	*4*	*5*	*All*
A. 1979[a]						
1	8.1	4.8	3.5	2.2	1.3	20
2	5.5	4.5	3.5	3.5	2.9	20
3	3.6	4.9	5.0	3.5	3.1	20
4	2.0	4.5	4.6	5.1	3.8	20
5	0.9	1.2	3.4	5.6	8.9	20
All	20	20	20	20	20	100
B. 2001[b]						
1	8.4	5.1	3.9	2.0	0.5	20
2	5.1	5.1	3.8	3.7	1.7	20
3	3.9	5.5	4.4	3.7	3.0	20
4	2.0	3.3	5.3	5.1	4.3	20
5	0.5	1.0	2.6	5.4	10.5	20
All	20	20	20	20	20	100

a *Source*: Radner, D.B. & Vaughan, D.R. (1987). Wealth, income, and the economic status of aged households. In E. Wolff (ed.), *International Comparisons of the Distribution of Household Wealth*, Table 5.6. New York: Oxford University Press. The underlying data are from the 1979 Income Survey Development Program (ISDP) file.
b *Source*: Author's computations from the 2001 Survey of Consumer Finances. Income quintiles are by money income (MI).

a bit higher, with a somewhat higher percentage of households in the bottom income quintile who were also in the bottom net worth quintile and, likewise, a somewhat higher percentage of households in the top income quintile who were also in the top net worth quintile. For 2001, the correlation coefficient between income and wealth was only 0.53.

There have been several attempts to combine the income and wealth dimension into a single index of household well-being. The most common technique is to convert the stock of wealth into a flow and add that flow to current income. In this approach, wealth is converted into a lifetime *annuity* for the expected remaining life of the family. The annuity is defined as a stream of annual payments which are equal over time and which will fully exhaust the stock of initial wealth. (This is like a fixed-rate mortgage with constant payments, except in reverse!) This annuity is then added to obtain an "augmented" measure of family income.[25] The interesting issue is whether the distribution of augmented income is more or less unequal than that of money income.

Four examples of this approach are presented in Table 5.12. The first, by Weisbrod and Hansen (1968), is based on the 1962 SFCC. The original data show that the share of the top two income classes was 5 percent of total money income in 1962, and that of the bottom income class was 20 percent. They then used both a 4 percent and a 10 percent annuity rate on household net worth, and calculated that the share of the top two income classes increased from 5 percent to 8 percent at a 4 percent annuity rate and to 10 percent at a 10 percent rate, while the share of the bottom income class fell from 20 percent to 18 percent and 17 percent, respectively. The inclusion of a wealth annuity in income thus increased measured income inequality.

The second study, by Taussig (1973), made use of the 1967 Survey of Economic Opportunity (SEO) database. Taussig computed Gini coefficients on the basis of money income and the sum of money income and a 6 percent annuity on household wealth. When the annuity was added to

Table 5.12 The distribution of income before and after the inclusion of a wealth annuity

	Income class							
Income concept	*Under $3,000*	*$3,000– $4,999*	*$5,000– $7,499*	*$7,500– $9,999*	*$10,000– $14,999*	*$15,000– $24,999*	*$25,000 & over*	*All*

A. Calculations from the 1962 Survey of Financial Characteristics of Consumers[a]
Percentage distribution

Money income	20	19	27	17	13	4	1	100
+ Annuity at 4%	18	17	25	17	15	6	2	100
+ Annuity at 10%	17	16	24	16	17	7	3	100

	Age group						
Income concept	*All*	*Under 25*	*25–34*	*35–44*	*45–54*	*55–64*	*65 & over*

B. Calculations from the 1967 Survey of Economic Opportunity[b]
Gini coefficient

Money income	0.36	0.32	0.26	0.28	0.32	0.39	0.45
+ Annuity at 6%	0.39	0.32	0.28	0.32	0.37	0.44	0.48

C. Calculations from the 1989 Survey of Consumer Finances[c]

	Age group				
Income concept	*All*	*18–34*	*35–54*	*55–69*	*70 & over*

Gini coefficient

Income	0.52	0.44	0.48	0.57	0.57
+ Annuity at 3%	0.54	0.45	0.50	0.60	0.60

D. Calculations from the 2001 Survey of Consumer Finances[d]
Gini coefficient

Income	0.55	0.43	0.53	0.60	0.56
+ Annuity and imputed rent	0.59	0.47	0.57	0.64	0.60

a *Source*: Weisbrod, B.A. & Hansen, W.L. (1968). An income-net worth approach to measuring economic welfare. *American Economic Review*, 58, 1315–29.

b *Source*: Taussig, M.K. (1973). *Alternative Measures of the Distribution of Economic Welfare.* Princeton University Industrial Relations Section Monograph.

c Source: *Source*: Author's computations from the 1989 Survey of Consumer Finances.

d *Source*: Wolff, E.N. & Zacharias, A. (2007). Household Wealth and the Measurement of Economic Well-Being in the United States. *Journal of Economic Inequality*, forthcoming, Table 8, from the 2001 Survey of Consumer Finances. The annuity value is based on historical rate of return data on household assets.

current money income, the measured Gini coefficient for all families rose from 0.36 to 0.39. Inequality also increased for all age groups, though the disequalizing effect was considerably stronger for older age groups.

A similar technique is used in Panel C of Table 5.12, on the basis of the 1989 SCF. As in the Taussig results, the Gini coefficient increased for all families, from 0.52 to 0.54, when a wealth annuity was added to money income. Measured inequality rose for all age groups, though the increase was greater for older age groups. Panel D shows results for 2001 using the 2001 SCF. Actual historical rates of return are used to calculate the annuity value and imputed rent to owner-occupied housing is also included (see Wolff & Zacharias, forthcoming, for more details). In this case, there was a substantial rise in measured inequality from the addition of an annuity value (and imputed rent), from a Gini coefficient of 0.55 to 0.59. Most of the increase reflected the large rise in the value of household wealth over the period from 1989 to 2001. Differences in measured inequality between money income and the sum of money income and income from wealth were similar across age groups.

All four sets of results indicate that the distribution of income becomes more unequal once the returns to wealth are included as part of total income. The disequalizing effects were not great in the earlier studies (before 1989). There are two reasons for this. First, though family income and wealth were positively correlated, they were not perfectly correlated, so that there were families with low income but high wealth and also some with high income but low wealth. Second, the annuity payments were small relative to current money income, typically on the order of 10 percent on average. As a result, their inclusion in augmented income did not alter the overall distribution very much. Moreover, annuities were much smaller for younger families than older ones, both because younger ones have lower wealth and because they have a longer remaining life expectancy. As a result, wealth annuities had a more disequalizing effect for older households than younger ones. Results for the year 2001, on the other hand, show a much more substantial equalizing effect. The main reason for the greater impact is that the annuity flow from wealth became much larger in 2001, 37 percent compared to 10 percent or less.

5.4.4   The *Forbes* 400

Every October, *Forbes* magazine compiles a list of what it estimates to be the 400 wealthiest individuals in the United States.[26] According to Kennickell (2006b), these people probably represent the segment of wealthy families best known to the public in general. However, on the basis of the limited documentation available, it is not clear how consistent the *Forbes* methodology is either over time or even within a given year. The estimates probably represent educated guesses ("guesstimates"), with a variety of inputs. Probably the largest sources of potential error in the *Forbes* figures are in the assignment of ownership of assets spread within a family and the valuation of assets that may not be publicly traded such as unincorporated businesses and investment real estate.

According to Kennickell's calculations based on the data reported in *Forbes*, the wealth held by the 400 wealthiest individuals grew by widely varying amounts over the period from 1989 to 2004 (the period covered in Kennickell's paper). The annual growth rate in real terms of the average wealth of the *Forbes* 400 was 0.5 percent from 1989 to 1992 and 3 percent per year from 1992 to 1995. Over the next 5 years, the annual growth rate hit a high of 34 percent in 1997 due to the sharp rise in value of high-technology stocks and a low of 12 percent in 2000 due to declining prices of high-technology stocks. Their average wealth then turned sharply negative – negative 23 percent in 2001 and negative 9.3 percent in 2002 as a result of the general collapse in stock prices over these years. The growth rate then turned positive in 2003, 7 percent, and in 2004, 2.2 percent. From 1989 to 2004, the average real wealth of the *Forbes* 400 grew by an average annual rate of 6.4 percent.

Within the *Forbes* 400, there were substantial differences in the wealth held by members of the group. The highest wealth in 2004 reported by *Forbes* was $51 billion. In contrast, the highest value was "only" $7.7 billion (in 2004 dollars) in 1989. The highest of the period was for Bill Gates at $96.3 billion (in 2004 dollars) in 1999 due to the extremely high share price of

Microsoft stocks. The minimum wealth to make it into the *Forbes* 400 was $750 million in 2004. In 1989, the minimum was $405 million (in 2004 dollars). The ratio of the highest value to the lowest value rose almost continuously over time from 19 in 1989 to a peak of 136 in 1999 – about seven times the ratio in 1989 – and then declined almost continuously to 68 in 2004.

Kenickell estimated that from 1989 to 1995, the total wealth of the *Forbes* 400 as a proportion of total household ranged from 1.5 to 1.7 percent. Then, following the pattern of growth in the top rank of the *Forbes* 400, the proportion jumped to 2.5 percent in 1998, before declining somewhat in both 2001 and 2004. In 2004 the fraction was 2 percent.

Because membership in the *Forbes* 400 changes over time, these changes refer to the top sliver of the wealth distribution, not the wealth of individual families. However, since it is possible to identify the *Forbes* 400 by name, it is also possible to trace the dynamics of their membership. As shown in Kennickell (2006a) for the period from 1989 to 2001, of the 400 people in the 2001 list, 230 were not present in the 1989 list. Persistence in the list was highest for people who were in the wealthiest 100 of the people in this group, 45 were in the same group in 1989 and 23 others were elsewhere in the list.

5.5   INTERNATIONAL COMPARISONS OF HOUSEHOLD WEALTH DISTRIBUTION

The availability of comparable household wealth data in other countries is quite limited. Besides the United States, the data required to calculate measures of household wealth inequality appear to be available for only 17 other countries, at least as identified by Davies *et al.* (2007).[27]

5.5.1   Comparisons of long-term time trends

There are two other countries apart from the United States for which long-term time series are available on household wealth inequality: the United Kingdom and Sweden. The most comprehensive data exist for the United Kingdom. The data are based on estate duty (tax) returns and use mortality multipliers to obtain estimates of the wealth of the living. Estimates are for the adult population (that is, individuals, not households). Figures are available on an almost continuous basis from 1923 to 1990.

The Swedish data are available on a rather intermittent basis from 1920 through 1990. The data are based on actual wealth tax returns. Tax return data are subject to error, like other sources of wealth data. The principal problem with tax return information is under-reporting due to tax evasion and legal tax exemptions. However, some assets, such as housing and stock shares, are extremely well covered, because of legal registration requirements in Sweden. Also, the deductibility of interest payments from taxable income makes it likely that the debt information is very reliable. On the other hand, bank accounts and bonds are not subject to similar tax controls, and it is likely that their amounts are under-reported.

Figure 5.7 shows comparative trends among the three countries.[28] For the United Kingdom, there was a dramatic decline in the degree of individual wealth inequality from 1923 to 1974 but little change thereafter. The share of the top 1 percent of wealth-holders fell from 59 percent in 1923 to 20 percent in 1974. However, between 1974 and 1990, there was only a relatively minor reduction in the concentration of household wealth, from a 20 percent share of the top percentile to 18 percent.

In Sweden, as in the United Kingdom, there was a dramatic reduction in wealth inequality between 1920 and the mid-1970s. Based on the years for which data are available, the decline appears to be a continuous process between 1920 and 1975. Over this period, the share of the

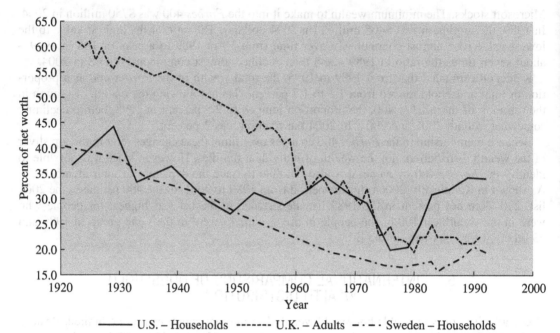

Figure 5.7   Share of marketable net worth held by top 1 percent of wealth-holders, Sweden, United Kingdom, and the United States, 1920–1992

top percentile declined from 40 to 17 percent of total household wealth. Between 1975 and 1985, there was virtually no change in the concentration of wealth. However, between 1985 and 1990, there was a sharp increase in wealth inequality, with the share of the top percentile increasing from 17 to 21 percent, a level similar to that of the early 1960s.

Comparisons among the three countries are rather striking. In all three countries, there was a fairly sizable reduction in wealth concentration between the early 1920s and the late 1970s, though the pattern appears much more cyclical in the United States than in the other two countries. However, during the 1980s, the United States showed an extremely sharp increase in wealth inequality, whereas the trend was almost flat in the United Kingdom. In Sweden, wealth inequality remained relatively constant between the late 1970s and mid-1980s and then showed a fairly substantial jump in the late 1980s.

5.5.2   Comparisons of recent trends

More recent trends in household wealth inequality are highlighted in Table 5.13. In addition to Sweden, the United Kingdom, and the United States, time-series data are also available for Canada and France. Again, it should be stressed that the data sources differ among the countries. To emphasize this point, I have presented the time series as an index, with the initial year of the series set to 100.

The results rather dramatically point out the difference between the U.S. experience and that of the other countries. As noted above, in the United States there was a very substantial increase in wealth inequality dating from the late 1970s. The degree of wealth inequality appears to have almost doubled between 1976 and 1989 and was about a quarter higher in 1989 than in 1972. In the United Kingdom, wealth concentration shows a sizable decline between 1972 and 1975 (perhaps, not unrelated to the similar decline in the United States) but it shows a further though

Table 5.13 Share of marketable net worth held by top percentiles of wealth-holders and Gini coefficients for the size distribution of household wealth, 1970–1992 (index, initial year of series = 100)

Year	Share of top 1 percent			Share of top 10% Canada	Gini coefficient		
	U.S.	U.K.	Sweden		U.K.	Canada	France
1970		100	100	100		100	
1972	100	106					
1975		77	91				100
1976	68	82			100		
1977		73		95	100	96	
1978		73	89		97		
1979	71	71			98		
1980		65			98		99
1981	85	75			98		
1983	106	83	95		98		
1984		75	84	96	97	96	
1985		75	89		98		
1986	110	75			100		100
1988		71	99				
1989	123	71					
1990		75	111				
1992	117		105				

Source: Wolff, E.N. (1996). International comparisons of wealth inequality. *Review of Income and Wealth*, ser. 42, no. 4, 433–51.

more moderate decline between 1975 and 1981 and then stabilizes until 1990, the last date of the series. In Sweden, there was a downward trend from 1970 to 1985, which was followed by a relatively sharp increase in 1990. In 1990, the level of wealth concentration was about 10 percent greater than in 1970.

The Canadian data are derived from the (Canadian) Survey of Consumer Finances, administered by Statistics Canada. The survey estimates suggest that wealth inequality in Canada showed a modest decline between 1970 and 1977 and then remained virtually unchanged between 1977 and 1984. There is thus no evidence of rising wealth inequality in Canada between the 1970s and mid-1980s. The last column of Table 5.13 shows results for France for 1975, 1980, and 1986 based on household surveys. The results of the three surveys show virtually no difference in wealth inequality in the three years.

More recent data are shown in Table 5.14. Wealth inequality is also much higher in the United States than in the other six countries. The Gini coefficient for wealth in the United States in 1998 is 0.82, compared to 0.73 in Canada in 1999, 0.64 in Germany in 1998, 0.61 in Italy in 2000, and 0.52 in Finland. Similar disparities exist with regard to the share of top wealth-holders. In the United States, the top 10 percent held 71 percent of all wealth in 1998, compared to a share of 56 percent in Canada in 1999, 42 percent in Germany in 1998, and 49 percent in Italy in 2000. Moreover, the shares of wealth held by the fourth and middle quintiles as well as the bottom 40 percent in Canada, Germany, and Italy are considerably higher than the corresponding shares in the United States. The Swedish data show percentile ratios. As a comparison to the U.S. data in 1998, for example, the P90/P50 ratio for the latter was 7.9, compared to 2.9 for Sweden. Indeed, the P10/P50 ratio was actually negative for the United States, compared to 0.08

Table 5.14   The size distribution of wealth (net worth) in selected OECD countries, 1983–2001

Year	Gini coefficient	P10/ P50	P90/ P50	Top 1.0%	Top 5.0%	Top 10.0%	Top 20.0%	4th 20.0%	3rd 20.0%	Bottom 40.0%	All
						Percentage share of wealth held by:					
A. United States											
1983	0.799			33.8	56.1	68.2	81.3	12.6	5.2	0.9	100.0
1989	0.832			37.4	58.9	70.6	83.5	12.3	4.8	−0.7	100.0
1992	0.823			37.2	60.0	71.8	83.8	11.5	4.4	0.4	100.0
1995	0.828			38.5	60.3	71.8	83.9	11.4	4.5	0.2	100.0
1998	0.822	−0.049	7.829	38.1	59.4	71.0	83.4	11.9	4.5	0.2	100.0
2001	0.826			33.4	59.2	71.5	84.4	11.3	3.9	0.3	100.0
B. Canada											
1984	0.691					51.8	69.3	19.7	9.1	1.8	98.1
1999	0.727					55.7	73.1	18.4	7.5	1.1	99.0
C. Germany											
1973	0.748					(NA)	78.0	13.5	5.7	2.8	97.2
1983	0.701					48.8	70.1	23.5	5.5	0.9	99.1
1988	0.668					45.0	66.9	24.7	7.4	1.0	99.0
1993	0.622					40.8	61.0	26.3	10.4	2.3	97.7
1998	0.640					41.9	63.0	25.9	9.5	1.6	98.4
D. Italy											
1989	0.553			10.6	27.3	40.2	57.9				
1995	0.573			10.7	29.0	42.1	59.5				
2000	0.613			17.2	36.4	48.5	63.8				
E. Sweden											
1983		0.012	2.716								
1985		0.069	2.639								
1992		0.055	3.058								
1995		0.088	2.887								
1997		0.080	2.916								
F. Finland											
1987	0.470										
1994	0.487										
1998	0.523										

Source: Wolff, E.N. (ed.) (2006b). *International Perspectives on Household Wealth*. Cheltenham, England: Edward Elgar.

for Sweden. By 2000 or so, Finland was by far the most equal of the five countries with comparable data, followed by Italy, Germany, Canada, and then the United States.

It is also of interest that wealth inequality rose in the United States, Canada, Italy, and Finland while it declined sharply in Germany. The Gini coefficient rose by 0.027 in the United States between 1983 and 2001, by 0.036 in Canada from 1984 to 1999, and by 0.060 in Italy between 1989 and 2000. In Germany, in contrast, it plummeted by 0.108 from 1973 to 1998 (and by 0.061 from 1983 to 1998).

5.6 SUMMARY

Marketable household wealth (or net worth) is defined as the sum of owner-occupied housing and other real estate; consumer durables; cash, checking, time and other savings accounts; bonds and other financial instruments; corporate stock; equity in unincorporated businesses; and trust fund equity; less mortgage and other debt. In 2004 owner-occupied housing comprised 33 percent of total marketable assets, net home equity 22 percent, financial assets (including corporate stock and bonds) as a group 17 percent, unincorporated business equity 17 percent, and nonhome real estate 12 percent. The ratio of total debt to net worth was 18 percent.

Two other concepts of household wealth were developed in this chapter. The first is financial household wealth, defined as fungible net worth minus net equity in owner-occupied housing. The second is augmented household wealth, defined as the sum of household marketable wealth, social security wealth, and pension wealth. In 2004, financial household wealth comprised 74 percent of marketable wealth, while in 2001 (the latest date available) augmented wealth was 48 percent greater than marketable wealth.

Between 1900 and 1992, real marketable wealth per household grew by 0.9 percent per year while average household income increased by 1.1 percent per year. Augmented wealth per household has grown faster than either marketable wealth or income per household, averaging 1.5 percent per year between 1900 and 1992.

Over the years from 1900 to 1992, households invested more of their wealth in consumer durables. Though the homeownership rate increased from 46 percent in 1920 to 65 percent in 1991, home equity remained relatively constant as a share of total assets. Households also substituted liquid assets such as bank deposits and money market funds for business equity and nonhome real estate. Changes in the share of corporate stock and financial securities in the household portfolio tended to follow movements in the stock market. The ratio of liabilities to total assets increased from 4 to 14 percent.

Four principal data sources have been used to develop measures of household wealth inequality: (i) estate tax data; (ii) household survey data; (iii) wealth tax data; and (iv) income capitalization technique. Each has its characteristic strengths and weaknesses.

Long-term trends in U.S. wealth concentration have been estimated from estate tax and household survey data. The share of marketable wealth owned by the top 1 percent of wealth-holders showed a sharp increase between 1922 and 1929; a substantial decline from 1929 to 1933 followed by an increase between 1933 and 1939; a significant decrease between 1939 and 1945; a fairly flat trend from 1945 through 1972; a sharp decline from 1972 to 1976; and then a rise of 15 percentage points between 1976 and 1998. Two important factors in explaining trends in the concentration of wealth are changes in income inequality and movements in the ratio of stock prices to housing prices.

The share of augmented wealth owned by the top 1 percent was lower than the comparable share of marketable wealth and the gap grew over time, from 2 percentage points in 1922 to 15 percentage points in 1998. However, time trends of the two are similar, though the increase in the share of augmented wealth between 1976 and 1998 was smaller on the basis of augmented wealth, 6 percentage points.

An examination of data from the Survey of Consumer Finances over the years 1983 to 2004 highlights the sharp increase in wealth inequality during the 1980s and its subsequent stability during the 1990s and early 2000s. The share of marketable net worth of the top 1 percent increased by almost 4 percentage points between 1983 and 1989 while the share of the bottom 80 percent declined by over 2 percentage points. The Gini coefficient was up by 0.03 points between 1983 and 1989 but experienced no change from 1989 to 2004. However, mean household wealth increased much more rapidly over the years from 1983 to 2004 than median household wealth. The top 1 percent of wealth-holders together accounted for 35 percent of the growth of total household wealth between 1983 and 2004 and the top quintile for almost 90 percent of the total wealth gain.

Wealth is distributed more unequally than income. The share of the top 1 percent of wealth-holders in 2004 was 34 percent, while the share of the top 1 percent of income recipients was 17 percent. The Gini coefficient for wealth in 2004 was 0.83, compared to 0.54 for income. Though household wealth and income are positively correlated, there is still a considerable amount of dispersion of wealth by income class. Adding an annuity value of wealth to income makes the distribution of income more unequal, particularly for older households, but the differences were not great, except recently, for 2001.

There are considerable differences in the assets owned by different wealth classes. The top 10 percent of wealth-holders accounted for almost 90 percent of stock shares, bonds, trusts, and business equity, and 80 percent of nonhome real estate in 2004. The bottom 90 percent of families accounted for over 60 percent of the value of owner-occupied housing, almost 40 percent of deposits, and over 70 percent of household debt. The debt-equity ratio was much greater among poorer households than richer ones and larger for younger families than older ones.

Comparisons of long-term wealth inequality trends among Sweden, the United Kingdom, and the United States show a substantial reduction in wealth concentration in all three countries between the early 1920s and the late 1970s. During the 1980s, both the United States and Sweden showed a sharp increase in wealth inequality, whereas little change was apparent for the United Kingdom, Canada, and France. During the 1990s wealth inequality rose in Canada, Italy, and Finland, was stable in the United States, and declined sharply in Germany. Wealth inequality appeared to be considerably greater in the United States during the 1980s and 1990s than in Canada, Finland, France, Germany, Italy, Sweden, and the United Kingdom.

5.7   REFERENCES AND BIBLIOGRAPHY

Aggregate household wealth

Board of Governors of the Federal Reserve System (1986). Flow of funds section. *Balance Sheets for the U.S. Economy, 1946–1985*. Washington, DC: Board of Governors of the Federal Reserve System.

Board of Governors of the Federal Reserve System (various years). *Flow of Funds Accounts of the U.S.* Washington, DC: Board of Governors of the Federal Reserve System.

Board of Governors of the Federal Reserve System (2007). *Z.1 Release: Flow of Funds Accounts of the U.S: Annual Flows and Outstandings*. http://www.federalreserve.gov/releases/Z1/Current/data.htm.

Curtin, R.T., Thomas Juster, F. & Morgan, J.N. (1989). Survey estimates of wealth: An assessment of quality. In R.E. Lipsey & H. Tice (eds.), *The Measurement of Saving, Investment, and Wealth*, Studies of Income and Wealth, Vol. 52. Chicago: Chicago University Press.

Goldsmith, R.W. (1962). *National Wealth of the United States in the Postwar Period*. Princeton, NJ: Princeton University Press.

Goldsmith, R.W. (1985). *Comparative National Balance Sheets*. Chicago: University of Chicago Press.

Goldsmith, R.W., Brady, D.S. & Mendershausen, H. (1956). *A Study of Saving in the United States*, III. Princeton, NJ: Princeton University Press.

Goldsmith, R.W. & Lipsey, R.E. (1963). *Studies in the National Balance Sheet of the United States*, I. Princeton, NJ: Princeton University Press.

Goldsmith, R.W., Lipsey, R.E., & Mendelson, M. (1963). *Studies in the National Balance Sheet of the United States*, II. Princeton, NJ: Princeton University Press.

Internal Revenue Service (1976). *Statistics of Income – 1972, Personal Wealth, U.S.* Washington, DC: Government Printing Office.

Kendrick, J.W., Lee, K.S. & Lomask, J. (1976). *The National Wealth of the United States: By Major Sectors and Industry.* New York: The Conference Board.

Musgrave, J.C. (1986). Fixed reproducible tangible wealth in the United States: Revised estimates. *Survey of Current Business*, **66**(1), 51–75.

Projector, D. & Weiss, G. (1966). *Survey of Financial Characteristics of Consumers.* Federal Reserve Technical Papers.

Ruggles, R. & Ruggles, N. (1982). Integrated economic accounts for the United States, 1947–1980. *Survey of Current Business*, **62**, 1–53.

Wolff, E.N. (1990). Trends in aggregate household wealth in the U.S., 1900–83. *Review of Income and Wealth*, ser. 35, no. 1, 1–29.

The distribution of household wealth

Atkinson, A.B. (1975). The distribution of wealth in Britain in the 1960s – the estate duty method reexamined. In J.D. Smith (ed.), *The Personal Distribution of Income and Wealth*, NBER, Studies in Income and Wealth, vol. 39. New York: Columbia University Press.

Atkinson, A.B. & Harrison, A.J. (1978). *Distribution of Personal Wealth in Britain.* Cambridge: Cambridge University Press.

Avery, R.B., Elliehausen, G.E. & Kennickell, A.B. (1988). Measuring wealth with survey data: An evaluation of the 1983 Survey of Consumer Finances. *Review of Income and Wealth*, ser. 34, no. 4, 339–71.

Avery, R.B. & Kennickell, A.B. (1991). Household saving in the U.S. *Review of Income and Wealth*, ser. 37, no. 4, 409–32.

Avery, R.B. & Kennickell, A.B. (1994). U.S. household wealth: Changes from 1983 to 1986. In E.N. Wolff (ed.), *Research in Economic Inequality*, Vol. 4. Greenwich, CT: JAI Press.

Board of Inland Revenue (1992). *Inland Revenue Statistics, 1992.* London: HMSO.

Bucks, B.K., Kennickell, A.B. & Moore, K.B. (2006). Recent changes in U.S. family finances: Evidence from the 2001 and 2004 Survey of Consumer Finances. *Federal Reserve Bulletin*, **92**, www.federalreserve.gov/pubs/bulletin/2006/financesurvey.pdf.

Caner, A., Wolff, E.N. & Zacharias, A. (2005). Household wealth, public consumption and economic well-being in the United States. *Cambridge Journal of Economics*, **29**, 1073–90.

Cartwright, W.S. & Friedland, R.B. (1985). The President's Commission on Pension Policy Household Survey 1979: Net wealth distribution by type and age for the United States. *Review of Income and Wealth*, ser. 31, no. 3, 285–308.

Canterbury, E.R. & Nosari, E.J. (1985). The *Forbes* 400: The determinants of super-wealth. *Southern Economic Journal*, **51**, 1073–982.

Conley, D. (1999). *Being Black, Living in the Red: Race, Wealth and Social Policy in America.* Berkeley: University of California Press.

Davies, J.B. (1993). The distribution of wealth in Canada. In E.N. Wolff (ed.), *Research in Economic Inequality*, Vol. 4, Studies in the Distribution of Household Wealth (pp. 159–80). Greenwich, CT: JAI Press.

Davies, J.B., Sandström, S., Shorrocks, A. & Wolff, E.N. (2007). Estimating the level and distribution of global household wealth. WIDER Working Paper, October.

Feldstein, M. (1974). Social security, induced retirement, and aggregate capital accumulation. *Journal of Political Economy*, **82**(September/October), 905–26.

Feldstein, M. (1976). Social security and the distribution of wealth. *Journal of the American Statistical Association*, **71**, 800–7.

Gale, W.G. & Pence, K.M. (2005). Household wealth accumulation in the 1990s: The role of demographic factors, unpublished manuscript, October.

Gallman, R.E. (1969). Trends in the size distribution of wealth in the nineteenth century. In L. Soltow (ed.), *Six Papers on the Size Distribution of Wealth and Income.* New York: National Bureau of Economic Research.

Greenwood, D.T. (1983). An estimation of U.S. family wealth and its distribution from microdata, 1973. *Review of Income and Wealth*, ser. 29, 23–43.

Greenwood, D.T. (1987). Age, income, and household size: Their relation to wealth distribution in the United States. In E.N. Wolff (ed.), *International Comparisons of the Distribution of Household Wealth.* New York: Oxford University Press.

Greenwood, D.T. & Wolff, E.N. (1989). Relative wealth holdings of the young and old: The

United States, 1962–1983. In T. Smeeding, J. Palmer & B. Torrey (eds.), *The Well-Being of Children and the Elderly*. Washington, DC: Urban Institute Press.

Harbury, C.D. & Hitchens, D.M.W.N. (1987). The influence of relative prices on the distribution of wealth and the measurement of inheritance. In E.N. Wolff (ed.), *International Comparisons of the Distribution of Household Wealth*. New York: Oxford University Press.

Haveman, R., Wolfe, B., Finnie, R. & Wolff, E.N. (1989). The well-being of children and disparities among them over two decades: 1962–1983. In T. Smeeding, J. Palmer & B. Torrey (eds.), *The Well-Being of Children and the Elderly*. Washington, DC: Urban Institute Press.

Jianakoplos, N.A., Menchik, P.L. & Irvine, F.O. (1989). Using panel data to assess the bias in cross-sectional inferences of life-cycle changes in the level and composition of household wealth. In R.E. Lipsey & H. Tice (eds.), *The Measurement of Saving, Investment, and Wealth*, Studies of Income and Wealth, Vol. 52. Chicago: Chicago University Press.

Kennickell, A.B. (2006a). A rolling tide: Changes in the distribution of wealth in the U.S., 1989–2001. In E.N. Wolff, (ed.), *International Perspectives on Household Wealth* (pp. 9–88). Cheltenham, England: Edward Elgar.

Kennickell, A.B. (2006b). Currents and undercurrents: Changes in the distribution of wealth, 1989–2004. Federal Reserve Board, January.

Kenickell, A.B. & Shack-Marquez, J. (1992). Changes in family finances from 1983 to 1989: Evidence from the Survey of Consumer Finances. *Federal Reserve Bulletin*, Board of Governors of the Federal Reserve System, **78**(1), 1–18.

Kennickell, A.B. & Woodburn, R.L. (1992). Estimation of household net worth using model-based and design-based weights: Evidence from the 1989 Survey of Consumer Finances, mimeo. Federal Reserve Board, April.

Kennickell, A.B. & Woodburn, R.L. (1999). Consistent weight design for the 1989, 1992, and 1995 SCFs, and the distribution of wealth. *Review of Income and Wealth*, ser. 45, no. 2, 193–215.

Kessler, D. & Masson, A. (1987). Personal wealth distribution in France: Cross-sectional evidence and extensions. In E.N. Wolff (ed.), *International Comparisons of the Distribution of Household Wealth*. New York: Oxford University Press.

Kessler, D. & Wolff, E.N. (1991). A comparative analysis of household wealth patterns in France and the United States. *Review of Income and Wealth*, ser. 37, no. 3, 249–66.

Kopczuk, W. & Saez, E. (2004). Top wealth shares in the United States, 1916–2000: Evidence from estate tax returns. *National Tax Journal*, **57**(2), 445–87.

Lansing, J.B. & Sonquist, J. (1969). A cohort analysis of changes in the distribution of wealth. In L. Soltow (ed.), *Six Papers on the Size Distribution of Income and Wealth*. New York: National Bureau of Economic Research.

Lampman, R. (1962). *The Share of Top Wealth-Holders in National Wealth, 1922–56*. Princeton, NJ: Princeton University Press.

Projector, D. & Weiss, G. (1966). *Survey of Financial Characteristics of Consumers*. Washington, DC: Federal Reserve Board Technical Papers.

Radner, D.B. & Vaughan, D.R. (1987). Wealth, income, and the economic status of aged households. In E.N. Wolff (ed.), *International Comparisons of the Distribution of Household Wealth*. New York: Oxford University Press.

Schwartz, M. (1983). Trends in personal wealth 1976–1981. *Statistics of Income Bulletin*, **3**, 1–26.

Schwartz, M. (1984–85). Preliminary estimates of personal wealth, 1982: Composition of assets. *Statistics of Income Bulletin*, **4**, 1–17.

Schwartz, M. & Johnson, B. (1990). Estimates of personal wealth, 1986. *Statistics of Income Bulletin*, **9**, 63–78.

Shorrocks, A.F. (1975). The age-wealth relationship: A cross-section and cohort analysis. *Review of Economics and Statistics*, **57**, 155–63.

Shorrocks, A.F. (1987). U.K. wealth distribution: Current evidence and future prospects. In E.N. Wolff (ed.), *International Comparisons of the Distribution of Household Wealth*. New York: Oxford University Press.

Smith, J.D. (1974). The concentration of personal wealth in American, 1969. *Review of Income and Wealth*, ser. 20, no. 2.

Smith, J.D. (1984). Trends in the concentration of personal wealth in the United States 1958–1976. *Review of Income and Wealth*, ser. 30, 419–28.

Smith, J.D. (1987). Recent trends in the distribution of wealth in the U.S.: Data, research problems, and prospects. In E.N. Wolff (ed.), *International Comparisons of the Distribution of Household Wealth*. New York: Oxford University Press.

Smith, J.D., & Franklin, S. (1974). The concentration of personal wealth, 1922–1969. *American Economic Review*, **64**(2) 162–7.

Soltow, L. (1971). Economics inequality in the United States from the period from 1860 to 1970. *Journal of Economic History*, **31**, 822–39.

Spånt, R. (1986). Wealth distribution in Sweden: 1920–1983. In E.N. Wolff (ed.), *International Comparisons of the Distribution of Household Wealth*. New York: Oxford University Press.

Spilerman, S. (2000). Wealth and stratification processes. *American Review of Sociology*, **26**, 497–524.

Statistics Sweden (1992). *Income Distribution Survey in 1990*. Orebro, Sweden: SCB Publishing Unit.

Steuerle, C.E. (1984). Realized income and wealth for owners of closely held farms and businesses: A comparison. *Public Finance Quarterly*, **12**, 407–24.

Stewart, C. (1939). Income capitalization as a method of estimating the distribution of wealth by size group. *Studies in Income and Wealth*, **3**. New York: National Bureau of Economic Research.

Taussig, M.K. (1973). *Alternative Measures of the Distribution of Economic Welfare*. Princeton University Industrial Relations Section Monograph.

Weisbrod, B.A. & Hansen, W.L. (1968). An income-net worth approach to measuring economic welfare. *American Economic Review*, **58**, 1315–29.

Williamson, J.G. & Lindert, P.H. (1980). Long-term trends in American wealth inequality. In J.D. Smith (ed.), *Modeling the Distribution and Intergenerational Transmission of Wealth*. Chicago: Chicago University Press.

Wolfson, M.C. (1979). Wealth and the distribution of income, Canada 1969–70. *Review of Income and Wealth*, ser. 25, 129–40.

Wolff, E.N. (1979). The distributional effects of the 1969–1975 inflation on household wealth holdings in the United States. *Review of Income and Wealth*, ser. 25, no. 2.

Wolff, E.N. (1980). Estimates of the 1969 size distribution of household wealth in the U.S. from a synthetic database. In J.D. Smith (ed.), *Modeling the Distribution and Intergenerational Transmission of Wealth*. Chicago: Chicago University Press.

Wolff, E.N. (1983). The size distribution of household disposable wealth in the United States. *Review of Income and Wealth*, ser. 29, 125–46.

Wolff, E.N. (ed.) (1987). *International Comparisons of the Distribution of Household Wealth*. New York: Oxford University Press.

Wolff, E.N. (1987a). Estimates of household wealth inequality in the U.S., 1962–1983. *Review of Income and Wealth*, ser. 33, 231–56.

Wolff, E.N. (1987b). The effects of pensions and social security on the distribution of wealth in the United States. In E. Wolff (ed.), *International Comparisons of the Distribution of Household Wealth*. New York: Oxford University Press.

Wolff, E.N. (1989). Trends in aggregate household wealth in the U.S., 1900–1983. *Review of Income and Wealth*, ser. 35, no. 1, 1–30.

Wolff, E.N. (1990a). Methodological issues in the estimation of the size distribution of household wealth. *Journal of Econometrics*, **43**(1/2), 179–95.

Wolff, E.N. (1990b). Wealth holdings and poverty status in the United States. *Review of Income and Wealth*, ser. 36, no. 2, 143–65.

Wolff, E.N. (1991). The distribution of household wealth: Methodological issues, time trends, and cross-sectional comparisons. In L. Osberg (ed.), *Economic Inequality and Poverty: International Perspectives* (pp. 92–133). Armonk, NY: M.E. Sharpe.

Wolff, E.N. (1992a). Methodological issues in the estimation of retirement wealth. In D.J. Slottje (ed.), *Research in Economic Inequality*, Vol. 2 (pp. 31–56). Greenwich, CT: JAI Press.

Wolff, E.N. (1992b). Changing inequality of wealth. *American Economic Review Papers and Proceedings*, **82**(2), 552–8.

Wolff, E.N. (1994). Trends in household wealth in the United States, 1962–1983 and 1983–1989. *Review of Income and Wealth*, ser. 40, no. 2, 143–74.

Wolff, E.N. (1995). *TOP HEAVY: A Study of Increasing Inequality of Wealth in America*. New York: The Twentieth Century Fund Press. Updated and expanded edition (1996). New York: The New Press; Newly updated and expanded edition (2002). New York: The New Press.

Wolff, E.N. (1996). International comparisons of wealth inequality. *Review of Income and Wealth*, ser. 42, no. 4, 433–51.

Wolff, E.N. (1998). Recent trends in the size distribution of household wealth. *Journal of Economic Perspectives*, **12**(3), 131–50.

Wolff, E.N. (1999). The size distribution of wealth in the United States: A comparison among recent household surveys. In J.P. Smith & R.J. Willis (eds.), *Wealth, Work, and Health: Innovations in Measurement in the Social Sciences* (pp. 209–232). Ann Arbor, MI: University of Michigan Press.

Wolff, E.N. (2000). Who are the rich? A demographic profile of high-income and high-wealth Americans. In J. Slemrod (ed.), *Does Atlas Shrug? The Economic Consequences of Taxing the Rich* (pp. 74–113). Cambridge, MA: Harvard University Press.

Wolff, E.N. (2001). Recent trends in wealth ownership, from 1983 to 1998. In T.M. Shapiro & E.N. Wolff (eds.), *Assets for the Poor: The Benefits of Spreading Asset Ownership* (pp. 34–73). Russell Sage Press.

Wolff, E.N. (2002). Income, wealth, and late-life inequality in the U.S. In S. Crystal & D. Shea (eds.), *Annual Review of Gerontology and Geriatrics*, Vol. 22 (pp. 31–58). New York: Springer.

Wolff, E.N. (2006a). Changes in household wealth in the 1980s and 1990s in the U.S. In E.N. Wolff, (ed.), *International Perspectives on Household Wealth* (pp. 107–50). Cheltenham, England: Edward Elgar.

Wolff, E.N. (ed.) (2006b). *International Perspectives on Household Wealth*. Cheltenham, England: Edward Elgar.

Wolff, E.N. (2007a). The tansformation of the American pension system. In T. Ghilarducci & J. Turner (eds.), *Work Options for Mature Americans* (pp. 175–211). Notre Dame, IN: University of Notre Dame Press.

Wolff, E.N. (2007b). Recent trends in household wealth in the U.S.: Rising debt and the middle class squeeze. Levy Institute Working Paper No. 502, June.

Wolff, E.N. & Marley, M. (1989). Long-term trends in U.S. wealth inequality: Methodological issues and results. In R.E. Lipsey & H. Tice (eds.), *The Measurement of Saving, Investment, and Wealth*, Studies of Income and Wealth, Vol. 52. Chicago: Chicago University Press.

Wolff, E.N. & Zacharias, A. (2007). Household Wealth and the Measurement of Economic Well-Being in the United States. *Journal of Economic Inequality*, forthcoming.

5.8   DISCUSSION QUESTIONS AND PROBLEM SET

1   Which is more equal, the distribution of wealth among individuals or the distribution of wealth among families? Why?

2   How is estate tax data used to obtain estimates of the concentration of household wealth? Briefly explain two problems associated with the use of estate tax data for this purpose.

3   Why might movements in stock prices relative to housing prices be associated with changes in wealth inequality?

4   Briefly describe trends since 1920 in wealth concentration in the United States on the basis of marketable wealth and augmented wealth. Why is inequality in marketable wealth greater than that of augmented wealth?

5   List the major components of household wealth. Which are more concentrated in the portfolios of the rich and which are more evenly dispersed among the general population?

6   Suppose average household wealth by type is given by:

	Mean value ($)
Assets	
Owner-occupied housing (gross value)	122,650
Other real estate (gross value)	42,642
Unincorporated business equity	74,644
Liquid assets	38,222
Pension accounts	53,667
Financial securities	9,960
Corporate stock and mutual funds	64,152
Net equity in personal trusts	20,706
Miscellaneous assets	8,016
Liabilities	
Debt on owner-occupied housing	41,009
All other debt	13,503
Household income	39,820

Compute the following statistics:
(a) Mean net worth
(b) The overall debt-equity ratio
(c) The ratio of overall debt to household income
(d) Net equity in owner-occupied housing as a ratio to total assets
(e) The ratio of net equity in owner-occupied housing to the total value of owner-occupied housing

7 Suppose mean income and wealth by income class is indicated as follows:

Income class	*Mean income ($)*	*Mean wealth ($)*
1	30,000	40,000
2	50,000	120,000
3	100,000	500,000

Compute the share of income in each income class. Suppose that a 3 percent annuity based on net worth is added to income in each income class. Re-compute the share of income in each income class with the added annuity flow (assume that households remain in the same income class after the annuity value is added to income). Redo the calculations for an annuity of 5 percent.

NOTES

1 The latest survey year is 2007. The data will become publicly available in early 2009.
2 Both 401(k) and Keogh plans are forms of tax-deferred retirement accounts.
3 Mutual funds are investment accounts in which a financial institution (such as a bank) holds a portfolio of stocks and other financial instruments such as bonds.
4 Technically speaking, Table 5.1 shows the value of principal residences only (that is, the main house a family lives in). A family may also own other homes such as vacation houses in which it lives part of the year.

5   See Section 5.2.3 for a more extended treatment of pensions in household wealth.
6   Another recent phenomenon (as of 2008) was the issuance of so-called "sub-prime" mortgages. These were mortgages that required little in the way of down payments and little corroboration of the ability of the mortgagee to repay the loan. These mortgages were also characterized by a low introductory interest rate (a "teaser rate"), which then ballooned to a very high interest rate after 2 or 3 years. In 2008, these mortgages hurt many homeowners who found that they were unable to repay the loan and lost their home to foreclosure (that is, repurchase by the bank or lending institution).
7   *Source*: Table 943 of the *2007 Statistical Abstract*, U.S. Census Bureau, http://www.census.gov/compendia/statab/.
8   See Section 8.2 for the procedure used to compute the present value of a stream of future income.
9   The exceptions are certain forms of pension plans that allow workers to convert their accumulated pension contributions into cash at any point in time (their so-called "cash surrender value"), and IRA and Keogh plans, that are also currently convertible to cash. These forms of pension wealth are already included in marketable wealth.
10 The imputation of both pension and social security wealth involves a large number of steps. These are presented in greater detail in Section 10.7.
11 Figures for 2004 are not available as of this time.
12 In the Flow of Funds accounts of the Federal Reserve Board, the reserves (assets) of pension funds are also included as part of household wealth. These funds are accumulated by corporations and the government in order to pay pension benefits for their workers when they retire. In 2004, they amounted to 23 percent of total household assets (excluding pension reserves). Technically speaking, these reserves are not part of marketable household wealth since households have no control over the assets in these funds and cannot directly draw on these funds. On the other hand, these reserves are held for the benefit of individuals and therefore have some of the characteristics of a trust fund.
13 The name of the March survey is now the Annual Social and Economic Supplement (ASEC).
14 In the United Kingdom the threshold is considerably lower, so that the majority of estates file tax returns. This is also true for some states in the United States, as well as Washington, DC, which have their own estate tax requirements.
15 See Jianakoplos, Menchik and Irvine (1989) for some evidence on the correlation between wealth and life expectancy.
16 These typically involve making assumptions about marriage patterns – in particular, the correlation between the wealth holdings of spouses (whether, for example, rich husbands tend to be married to rich wives or poor wives). This relationship is called *assortative mating*.
17 This trend is confirmed in the estate tax figures. According to Schwartz (1984–85), the share of total personal wealth held by the top 2.8 percent of the nation's adult population was 28 percent in 1982, and, according to Schwartz and Johnson (1990), the share held by the top 1.6 percent of the adult population was 28.5 percent in 1986.
18 A *t*-ratio is an indicator of statistical significance. Typically, if its value is greater than 2.0, then the coefficient passes the test of statistical significance.
19 This is not to say that there was no change in inequality between 1962 and 1983. Results reported in Section 5.4.2 indicate that wealth concentration, while remaining relatively constant between 1962 and 1973, fell sharply between 1973 and the mid-1970s and then increased substantially between the late 1970s and 1983.
20 Income figures are for the previous calendar year of the survey (for example, 1982 in the case of the 1983 SCF).
21 The SCF data show a much higher degree of income inequality than does the CPS. According to the U.S. Census Bureau (http://www.census.gov/hhes/www/income/income.html) the Gini coefficient for all households was 0.43 and the share of the top quintile was 46.3 in 1988, compared to figures of 0.52 and 55.5 percent, respectively, from the SCF. The difference is to be expected, since the SCF has a high-income supplement and does not "top-code" income figures, as is done in the CPS.
22 This method of calculating the wealth gains by group is slightly distorted because it reflects both the increase in the average wealth of a group and the increase in the number of households in that group.

For example, a group whose average wealth shows no increase but whose number of households does increase will be accorded a positive share of the overall wealth growth over the period. Though there is no simple analytical way of separating out the effects of the growth in average wealth from that in the number of families, the same calculation can also be performed holding the number of households in each group constant over time. This method is used for the results presented in Table 5.7.

23 Figures on augmented wealth are not yet available for 2004.

24 The reason is that pension accumulations and businesses were a relatively smaller part of the portfolio of the oldest age group compared to age group 65 to 74.

25 Technically, property income is first subtracted from current money income so that there is no double counting of the returns from household wealth.

26 See the October 2004 issue of *Forbes* for details on the methodology. The *Forbes* data for recent years are available at www.forbes.com; the earlier data are only available in the printed version of the magazine.

27 These include Australia, Canada, China, Denmark, Finland, France, Germany, India, Indonesia, Ireland, Italy, Japan, New Zealand, Norway, Spain, South Korea, Sweden, Switzerland, and the United Kingdom. With the exception of Sweden and the United Kingdom, these estimates are available only since 1980 or later for these countries.

28 The U.S. series is based on marketable wealth for the household unit. See Section 5.4.2 and Wolff (2002) for details. Sources for the United Kingdom are Shorrocks (1987) and *Inland Revenue Statistics, 1992*, Series C. Results are based on marketable wealth for adult individuals. Sources for Sweden are Spånt (1987) and Statistics Sweden (1992). The unit is the household; and wealth is valued at market prices.

Chapter 6
Economic Mobility

6.1 INTRODUCTION

An important dimension of well-being that is often overlooked in the inequality literature is mobility. There is a common myth that the United States is the "land of opportunity" where anyone, no matter whether the person began life rich or poor, can get ahead with enough effort and drive. Is this statement true? Is this statement more or less true about other advanced economies of the world? Is the United States truly a "classless" society or does it matter whether your family of birth is rich or poor? Do incomes at one point of time reflect lifetime differences in well-being or do incomes tend to even out over lifetime?

There are two types of mobility discussed in the pertinent literature. The first, lifetime mobility, concerns the degree to which an individual's (or family's) relative position in the income distribution changes over time. This may serve as an important offset to rising income inequality if lifetime mobility has risen as well. The second is intergenerational mobility, which concerns the degree to which an individual's relative rank in the income distribution is correlated with that of his (or her) parent's. (The apt phrase used is that "the apple does not fall far from the tree.") Intergenerational mobility reflects the fluidity (or lack thereof) of the class structure of a society.

There are four issues also commonly discussed about mobility. The first is how great is it? The second is how much has it changed over time and in *which* direction? The third is how one country (like the United States) stacks up in comparison to other countries. The fourth is the mechanism (or mechanisms) underlying mobility (or immobility).

In Section 6.2, the measurement of mobility is explored. Section 6.3 considers the findings of the mobility of income and earnings over time. Section 6.4 surveys the literature both on intergenerational mobility in the United States and comparisons with other countries. Section 6.5 discusses wealth mobility. A summary is provided in Section 6.6.

6.2 MOBILITY MEASURES

6.2.1 Measuring intergenerational mobility

We start with the measurement of intergenerational mobility because it is more straightforward than that of lifetime mobility. The standard procedure is based on a regression analysis framework.

Following Bowles and Gintis (2002), let the subscript p refer to parental measures such as income and let y stand for an individual's economic position (such as the person's income). We can estimate the degree of intergenerational *elasticity* β using the following regression equation:

$$y - \bar{y} = \beta(y_p - \bar{y}) + \varepsilon \tag{6.1}$$

where economic status in the two generations (say, income) is adjusted so that its mean value, $\bar{y}$, is constant across generations and ε is a random error term assumed to be uncorrelated with y_p. Let us focus on the intergenerational correlation of income. Equation (6.1) indicates that the deviation of the offspring's income from the mean is β times the deviation of the parent's income from the (same) mean value plus an error term. Typically, the variable y stands for the logarithm of income (or earnings, wealth, etc.) In this case, β measures the intergenerational income elasticity – that is, the percentage change in the offspring's income relative to a 1 percent change in the parent's income. The influence of mean economic status of the parents on that of the offspring is given by $1 - \beta$. This term is also called *regression to the mean*, since it indicates that the offspring may expect to be closer to the mean than its parents by the fraction $1 - \beta$.[1]

We can also define the *intergenerational correlation coefficient* ρ as:

$$\rho = \beta \sigma_{yp}/\sigma_y \tag{6.2}$$

where σ_y is the standard deviation of y (say, income) and σ_{yp} is the standard deviation of income of the parents' generation. In the case where y is the logarithm of income, then σ_y is the log variance of income, a standard measure of income inequality (see Section 3.3.5 for a discussion of this measure). In the case when inequality is the same in the two generations ($\sigma_{yp} = \sigma_y$), then $\rho = \beta$. However, when inequality rises between the two generations, the income elasticity β exceeds the correlation coefficient ρ, and conversely when inequality is lower for the offspring generation. Effectively, the intergenerational correlation coefficient ρ is affected by changes in the distribution of income while the intergenerational elasticity is not affected by inequality changes. In addition, ρ^2 measures the proportion of the variance in the offspring's income that is linearly associated with the income of the parents' generation. We will see that both ρ and β have been used in the literature on intergenerational mobility.

6.2.2 The Shorrocks measure and other measures of lifetime mobility

6.2.2.1 Standard measures

Since the pioneering work by Shorrocks (1978b), several different mobility indicators have been developed in order to quantify the observed movement of income over time from the beginning of a period to the end of a period.[2] Several economists have developed an axiomatic approach to the measurement of mobility to compare the different measures on the basis of their properties.[3] A common trait of all the indices that have been used so far is that they show no mobility if all the individual incomes remain unchanged over time.

Income mobility may be analyzed either in absolute terms or in relative terms. Let y_1 be the income level of a given person at time $t1$ and y_2 be the income level of the same person at time $t2$. *Absolute mobility* is measured as a function of the changes in the individual income levels – that is $(y_2 - y_1)$ – regardless of the ranking of the persons in the initial distribution and in the final one. On the other hand, *relative mobility* refers to changes in the positions over time in the income distribution. In this case, a person's relative rank can change even if the person's actual income does not change as long as the income of the other individuals varies over time.

The first measure we consider is the so-called Shorrocks R measure of mobility. The basic intuition of the Shorrocks R measure is that if there is income mobility over time, then incomes will even out over time and the inequality of income averaged over a period will be lower than that of annual income. Shorrocks (1978a) developed a measure of mobility by the degree to which income equalization occurs in the long run. In this regard, he derived a mobility indicator (actually, a "rigidity index") that results from a comparison between the inequality in average incomes over the long term and a weighted average of income inequality in each of the separate time periods. Since long-term inequality decreases as the degree of mobility increases, a large difference between the two terms denotes a high degree of mobility.

In the simplest case, suppose we consider incomes in two different years, $t1$ and $t2$. Then, the Shorrocks rigidity index is given as follows:

$$R = \frac{I(y_1 + y_2)}{[\mu_1 I(y_1) + \mu_2 I(y_2)]/(\mu_1 + \mu_2)} \tag{6.3}$$

where $I(y_1)$ is the degree of income inequality at time $t1$ (for example, the Gini coefficient), $I(y_2)$ is inequality at time $t2$, and μ_i is mean income at time i ($i = 1, 2$). The inequality indices $I(y_1)$ and $I(y_2)$ are each weighted by the mean income of that year relative to the overall mean income over all years. The index R is equal to one if there is no mobility or perfect rigidity – that is, if inequality of average income over the long term is equal to that of the incomes of each year. The index R is equal to zero if there is complete mobility – that is, if mobility results in a complete equalization of average incomes over the long term.

Fields (1999) classified the Shorrocks R index among the measures of mobility that reflect movements in individual income shares. If the incomes of all the individuals vary proportionately, and consequently the relative incomes do not change, this index shows no mobility since income shares remain unchanged. If, on the other hand, individuals change position over time, the R index will indicate mobility since income shares will also change over time.

Related mobility measures that are based on the association between income in the base year and income in the last year are the correlation coefficient ρ between the incomes of the two years and the Spearman correlation coefficient ρ_s between the income ranks of the two years:

ρ = Correlation (y_1, y_2)
ρ_s = Correlation $[r(y_1), r(y_2)]$

where $r(y_1)$ is the income rank of individuals in year $t1$ and $r(y_2)$ is the income rank if individuals in year $t2$.

A high value of the correlation coefficient shows persistence over time in income and therefore a low degree of mobility. In fact, that is the reason why ρ is often referred to as an "immobility" index. In addition, the ρ index indicates zero mobility if all incomes change by an additive and/or multiplicative constant. The Spearman correlation coefficient, on the other hand, measures relative position in the income distribution and is therefore a relative mobility measure. It indicates mobility only if individuals change income ranks over time.

The Fields–Ok index (see Fields & Ok, 1996) is defined as the average absolute change in individual incomes, expressed in logarithmic terms:

$$FO = \sum_{i=1}^{N} |\ln(y_{2i}) - \ln(y_{1i})|/N \tag{6.4}$$

where "ln" stands for the natural logarithm and the symbol "|" indicates the absolute value. This index satisfies several axiomatic properties, including the decomposability condition. In particular, the FO index can be written as the sum of two components:

$$FO = \sum_{i=1}^{N} [\ln(y_{2i}) - \ln(y_{1i})]/N + 2 \sum_{i \in L} [\ln(y_{1i}) - \ln(y_{2i})]/N \tag{6.5}$$

where L is the set of individuals whose income fell between the two periods (the "losers"). The first term measures the effect of overall economic growth on income changes over time. The second term effectively measures the effect on mobility that comes from income transfers from the losers, under the assumption that total income remains unchanged.

The Fields–Ok index is defined as a function of individual changes in (absolute) income. The logarithmic transformation relates to *percentage* changes in income. In contrast, the formulation in terms of absolute difference allows mobility to be treated in a symmetric fashion – that is, gains and losses are treated in the same way, without taking into account the direction of the change. On the basis of this index, mobility is positive each time at least one person's income changes, even if this income change does not result in a change in the relative position of the person in the income distribution or in the share of total income that each individual receives.

6.2.2.2   *More advanced mobility indices**

More advanced measures of mobility usually start from the so-called *transition matrix* **P** from time $t1$ to $t2$ (and hence require some matrix algebra). It is first necessary to group incomes by income class. This can be done in terms of percentiles (say, deciles or quintiles) or in terms of predetermined cut-off values (for example, different percentages of the mean or median). The ijth element of the matrix is the number of individuals who have passed ("transited") from income class i at time $t1$ to income class j at time $t2$.

The main diagonal of the matrix shows the "stayers" – that is, those individuals who have remained in their initial income class and consequently have not changed their relative position. Outside the main diagonal are the "movers" – that is, those individuals who have transited from one income class to another between time $t1$ and time $t2$. This movement can have an upward or downward direction, depending on whether the person improves his (or her) relative position.

If the entries of the transition matrix are the row relative frequencies (interpreted as conditional probabilities), the values on the main diagonal indicate the probability of remaining in the income class, while the off-diagonal entries indicate the probability of transitioning from one income class to another. The higher the transition probabilities are, the greater will be overall mobility as embodied in the matrix. A mobility measure based on such a transition matrix will depend, among other things, on the number of income classes and consequently on their size. Such indexes measure mobility according to a relative concept because they register changes in the income ranking that allow individuals to cross the boundary values. Such measures will show no mobility when changes in incomes occur that have no effects on movements between income classes or else when all the incomes change proportionately or by a constant amount (see Table 6.1 for an example of a transition matrix).

The first of these indices is the Shorrocks index (1978b). It measures mobility on the basis of a transition matrix through the calculation of the *trace* of the matrix. The actual formula is given by:

$$S = [n - \text{tr}(\mathbf{P})]/(n - 1) \tag{6.6}$$

where n is the number of the income classes and, consequently, the number of rows and column in matrix $\mathbf{P}$ and tr($\mathbf{P}$) is the trace of the matrix. The trace of a square matrix is the sum of the elements on the principal diagonal. The index ranges from zero to $n/(n-1)$ and it goes up as mobility increases. In particular, if everyone changes income classes between the two periods, then the diagonal of the matrix contains only zeroes and as a result tr($\mathbf{P}$) = 0. In this case, mobility is at its highest level and $S = n/(n-1)$. On the other hand, if everyone stays in his (or her) original income class, there is no mobility over time. The diagonal of matrix $\mathbf{P}$ contains only ones, tr($\mathbf{P}$) = n, and, as a result, $S = 0$.

Another measure of mobility derives from the *eigenvalues* of matrix $\mathbf{P}$.[4] In the case when there is no mobility and all the elements of the diagonal are equal to one, the eigenvalues of the $\mathbf{P}$ matrix are also all equal to one, as is the determinant. This suggests that the variability of the eigenvalues of the transition matrix $\mathbf{P}$ may be a good indicator of the degree of mobility. A simple way to measure this is by the standard deviation of the eigenvalues: $\sigma(\lambda_i)$, where λ_i is the ith eigenvalue of matrix $\mathbf{P}$. The lack of variability indicates zero mobility. As the variability of the eigenvalues increases, so does the degree of mobility.

Another mobility indicator, B, was developed by Bartholomew (1982) on the basis of the transition matrix $\mathbf{P}$. The index is as follows:

$$B = \sum_{i=1}^{n} \sum_{j=1}^{n} p_{ij} |i - j| \tag{6.7}$$

B is thus given as the weighted mean of the total relative frequencies p_{ij}, where the weights are the distances between income classes, $|i - j|$. In the case of zero mobility, all the elements of the diagonal equal one and the elements off the diagonal are zero, so that $B = 0$. As the degree of mobility gets greater, the B index likewise increases. However, unlike the S index discussed above, the B index has no upper bound.

6.3   MOBILITY OVER THE TIME

6.3.1   Income mobility

As suggested in the discussion of the Shorrocks R measure, income mobility over time is an important social issue because it can offset rises in (annual) income inequality. In particular, if there is income mobility over time, then incomes will even out over time and the inequality of income averaged over a period will be lower than that of annual income. Thus, the rise in income inequality reported for the United States in Chapters 1 and 3 may not be an important social problem if there has been a corresponding increase in income mobility over the same period. Some of the studies we will look at here will consider whether mobility increased or declined over time in the United States.

Hungerford (1993) provided one of the first comparative studies on income mobility in the United States over two consecutive periods. In particular, he used PSID data to examine income mobility in the period 1969 to 1976 ("the 1970s") and the period 1979 to 1986 (the "1980s"). He divided the income distributions of each year into deciles. His main conclusion was that overall mobility within the income distribution appeared to be about the same in the 1970s as in the 1980s.

He calculated that 77 percent of all individuals moved from one decile to another between 1969 and 1976. Of these, 30 percent moved only within one decile and another 17 percent moved within two deciles. All in all, about 70 percent of all individuals either remained in their original decile or moved within two deciles during the 1970s. Results were quite similar for the 1980s

Table 6.1 Transition matrix by income quintile in the United States, 1975–1995

1979 quintile	1995 quintile						
	Bottom quintile	Second quintile	Middle quintile	Fourth quintile	Top quintile	Top 1%	Total of five quintiles
Bottom quintile	46.1	26.9	15.1	8.2	3.8	0.0	100.0
Second quintile	25.9	25.6	24.7	18.7	5.1	0.0	100.0
Middle quintile	11.9	22.2	28.0	24.0	13.9	0.0	100.0
Fourth quintile	8.6	15.4	22.4	29.9	23.7	1.0	100.0
Top quintile	7.6	9.9	9.8	19.3	53.4	36.9	100.0
Top 1%	2.1	11.4	1.8	6.8	68.8	29.9	

The figures show the probability of attaining each income quintile in 1995 based on the taxpayer's income quintile in 1979.
Source: Carroll, R., Joulfaian, D. & Rider, M. (2007). Income mobility: The recent American experience, Table 2. Andrew Young School of Public Policy, Working Paper 07-18, March. The data source is IRS individual tax returns.

as well. For example, in both the 1969–1976 period and the 1979–1986 period, the same percentage, 27 percent, remained in their original decile.

In a later study, Carroll, Joulfaian, and Rider (2007) used a panel of individual income tax returns for the period 1979 to 1995 to examine patterns of income mobility in the United States. These data came from actual federal income tax returns filed by individuals. Income tax data are probably more reliable than survey data because they are subject to audit by the Internal Revenue Service (IRS). The IRS created a special sample of such tax returns which linked the same individuals (or couples) over time. The authors divided these years into two periods: 1979–1986 and 1987–1995. They also limited the sample to individuals in age group 30–44 in 1979 or 47–61 in 1995.

Table 6.1 shows the transition matrix over the whole 1979–1995 period. It is first of note that mobility was particularly restricted at the bottom and top of the income distribution. In particular, 46 percent of the taxpayers found in the bottom quintile in 1979 were still in the bottom quintile in 1995, while 53 percent of the taxpayers in the top quintile in 1979 remained in the top quintile in 1995. Even more striking is that 30 percent of taxpayers who were in the top 1 percent in 1979 were still in the top 1 percent in 1995, and more than two-thirds of taxpayers who were in the top 1 percent in 1979 wound up in the top quintile in 1995. On the other hand, virtually no taxpayer from the bottom four quintiles in 1979 made it to the top 1 percent in 1995. Mobility was more fluid in the middle. Among those in the middle three quintiles in 1979, over 70 percent wound up in a different quintile (both up and down) by 1995.

To compare mobility over the two time periods, the authors used as their mobility index 100 minus the trace of the relative frequency matrix. (The measure is similar to Equation (6.6).) For the full 1979–1995 period, their mobility index was equal to 63 (that is, 63 percent of the observations in the sample were in different quintiles in 1995 than the one in which they started in 1979). Their mobility index for the 1979–1986 period was 56 and that for the 1987–1995 period was somewhat smaller, at 54. They concluded that there was a slight decline in mobility over these two time periods.

Bradbury and Katz (2002) used the PSID to compute family income transition matrices for three decades in the United States: 1969–1979, 1979–1989, and 1989–1998. Their results are very striking and clearly indicate a decline in income mobility over these three decades (see Table 6.2). The probability of a family in the lowest income quintile at the beginning of the period remaining

Table 6.2 Transition matrix by family income quintile in the United States, 1969–1979, 1979–1989, and 1989–1998

Quintile in first year	Quintile in second year					
	Bottom quintile	Second quintile	Middle quintile	Fourth quintile	Top quintile	Total
A. 1969–1979						
Bottom quintile	49.4	24.5	13.8	9.1	3.3	100.0
Second quintile	23.2	27.8	25.2	16.2	7.7	100.0
Middle quintile	10.2	23.4	24.8	23.0	18.7	100.0
Fourth quintile	9.9	15.0	24.1	27.4	23.7	100.0
Top quintile	5.0	9.0	13.2	23.7	49.1	100.0
B. 1979–1989						
Bottom quintile	50.4	24.1	15.0	7.4	3.2	100.0
Second quintile	21.3	31.5	23.8	15.8	7.6	100.0
Middle quintile	12.1	23.3	25.0	24.6	15.0	100.0
Fourth quintile	6.8	16.1	24.3	27.6	25.3	100.0
Top quintile	4.2	5.4	13.4	26.1	50.9	100.0
C. 1989–1998						
Bottom quintile	53.3	23.6	12.4	6.4	4.3	100.0
Second quintile	25.7	36.3	22.6	11.0	4.3	100.0
Middle quintile	10.9	20.7	28.3	27.5	12.6	100.0
Fourth quintile	6.5	12.9	23.7	31.1	25.8	100.0
Top quintile	3.0	5.7	14.9	23.2	53.2	100.0

The figures show the probability of attaining each income quintile in the second year based on the family's income quintile in the first year.
Source: Bradbury, K. & Katz, J. (2002). Women's labor market involvement and family income mobility when marriages end. *New England Economic Review*, Q4, 41–74. The data source is the PSID.

in the bottom quintile at the end of the period rose from 49.4 percent in the 1969–1979 period to 50.4 percent in the 1979–1989 period and then to 53.3 percent in the 1989–1998 period. Likewise, the likelihood of a family in the top income quintile at the beginning of the period staying in the top quintile at the end of the period rose from 49.1 percent in the first period to 50.9 percent in the second and then to 53.2 percent in the third period. The results indicated an increasing rigidity in the class structure over these three periods, though particularly during the 1990s. The Shorrocks index of economic mobility (see Equation (6.6)) also declined over the three periods, from 0.80 in 1969–1979 to 0.79 in 1979–1989, and then to 0.74 in 1989–1998.

There are a few studies that presented international comparisons of income mobility over time. Aaberge *et al.* (2002) used a sample of four countries – Denmark, Norway, Sweden, and the United States – to compare income mobility over time. Their approach in this study was to compare inequality measures for annual income with those for incomes averaged over a period of time (in this case, 10 years, from 1980 to 1990). They looked at three measures of resources – earnings, market income, and disposable income. They found very large differences between the three Scandinavian countries and the United States. For earnings, the Gini coefficient for the average earnings over the 10 years from 1980 to 1990 was 0.22 in Denmark, 0.23 in Sweden, and 0.26 in Norway, whereas it was 0.38 in the United States. A similar result was obtained for both market income (a Gini coefficient of 0.20 in Sweden and 0.22 in Denmark, compared to 0.37 in the United States) and disposable income (a Gini coefficient of 0.16 in Sweden and 0.20

Table 6.3   Income mobility indices over time for Denmark, Norway, Sweden, and the United States

Country	*Earnings*	*Market income*	*Disposable income*
A. 1980–1990			
Denmark	0.080	0.076	0.078
Norway	0.069	—	—
Sweden	0.073	0.115	0.154
United States	0.065	0.097	0.092
B. 1986–1990			
Denmark	0.057	0.046	0.054
Norway	0.053	0.070	0.075
Sweden	0.045	0.071	0.097
United States	0.051	0.062	0.060

The figures refer to the authors' mobility index *M* (Equation (6.8)).
Source: Aaberge, R. *et al.* (2002). Income inequality and income mobility in the Scandinavian countries compared to the United States. *Review of Income and Wealth*, **48**(4), 443–69, Table 2.

in Denmark, compared to 0.30 in the United States). They noted that the rank order of countries with regard to their Gini coefficient for the average earnings over the 10 years was very similar to that for annual income.

They also looked at the difference between the weighted *average* Gini coefficient over the time period and the Gini coefficient of the *average income* over the period. The measure that they actually used was:

$$M = 1 - G \Big/ \sum_{t=1}^{T} (\mu_t/\mu)G_t \qquad (6.8)$$

where G is the Gini coefficient for the average income over the period, G_t is the Gini coefficient for income at time t, μ_t is average income at time t, T is the number of time periods and μ is the average income over the whole period. This measure is closely related to the Shorrocks R measure of immobility (see Equation (6.3)). Results are shown in Table 6.3. As can be seen, there is no clear pattern that emerges from the table regarding inter-country differences in mobility. Denmark had the most mobility in earnings over the 1980–1990 period and the United States the least, while Sweden had the highest mobility with regard to both market income and disposable income and Denmark the least. However, the differences in mobility among the countries were not very large. Moreover, the rank order was different for earnings and incomes averaged over the four years from 1986 to 1990. The authors concluded that the four countries had similar levels of income and earnings mobility over this time period at least.

Maasoumi and Trede (2002) used the generalized entropy mobility measure to compare income mobility in Germany and the United States. The generalized entropy mobility measure is a generalized version of the mobility *M* index (Equation (6.8)) developed by Aaberge *et al.* (2002). They compared the United States and Germany over the period from 1984 to 1989. For the United States, they used the PSID. For Germany, they used the GSOEP, which is very similar in structure to the PSID. Their income concept was household income net of taxes but including government transfers. Their main finding was that mobility was considerably higher in Germany than in the United States. They divided their sample by age group and computed a mobility index of 0.39 for Germany and only 0.21 for the United States for age group 16 to 25; mobility indices of 0.30 and 0.15, respectively, for age group 26 to 35; and indices of 0.20 and 0.12, respectively, for age group 36 to 50.

6.3.2 Earnings mobility

One of the first studies on U.S. earnings mobility was conducted by Gottschalk (1997). He used PSID data and looked at earnings mobility over the period 1974 to 1992. His results are shown in Table 6.4. It is difficult to infer from the transition matrix whether mobility was low or high in the United States over this period. In order to do this, we need to compare transition matrices over different time periods or summary measures of mobility for different time periods. However, it is of note that mobility was particularly restricted at the bottom and top of the income distribution. Over 40 percent of the individuals found in the bottom quintile in 1974 wound up in the bottom quintile in 1991, while over half of the people in the top quintile in 1974 were still in the top quintile in 1991. The situation was more fluid in the middle. Among those in the middle three quintiles in 1974, about two-thirds moved to a different quintile (both up and down) by 1991. Interestingly, the mobility patterns for earnings were very similar to those for family income shown in the previous section (see Table 6.1).

Gittleman and Joyce (1996) used matched cross-sectional data from the Current Population Survey (CPS) to examine patterns of short-term earnings mobility over the period from 1967 to 1991. Using actual identifiers from the annual Demographic files of the CPS over these years, they were able to calculate earnings changes over two-year periods. Their main finding was that there was no evidence that short-term earnings mobility either increased over this time period or declined. In particular, they concluded that mobility trends did not offset the rise in the inequality of (annual) earnings over these years.

Buchinsky and Hunt (1999) used data on annual earnings and hourly wages derived from the National Longitudinal Survey of Youth (NLSY) over the period from 1979 to 1991. The sample included only individuals in age group 14 to 21 in 1979. They measured mobility using Equation (6.8) for three successive three-year periods: 1981–1984, 1984–1987, and 1988–1991. Their principal finding was of a significant decline in mobility over these three periods. The mobility M index for hourly wages fell from 23.5 in 1981–1984 to 19.6 in 1984–1987 and 13.5 in 1988–1991. The M index for annual earnings also fell from 24.6 in 1980–1983 to 19.2 in 1983–1986 and then to 14.6 in 1987–1990. These results, however, have to be interpreted cautiously since their sample included only young workers.

Table 6.4 Transition matrix by earnings quintile in the United States, 1974–1991

	1991 quintile					
1974 quintile	*Bottom quintile*	*Second quintile*	*Middle quintile*	*Fourth quintile*	*Top quintile*	*Total*
Bottom quintile	42.1	22.8	14.3	13.0	7.8	100.0
Second quintile	28.7	36.0	19.3	9.2	6.7	100.0
Middle quintile	14.7	20.6	32.1	20.5	12.0	100.0
Fourth quintile	9.7	12.0	24.2	32.4	21.7	100.0
Top quintile	3.1	7.3	10.2	25.4	53.9	100.0

The figures show the probability of attaining each income quintile in 1991 based on the person's income quintile in 1974. *Source*: Gottschalk, P. (1997). Inequality, income growth and mobility: The basic facts. *Journal of Economic Perspectives*, **11**(2), 21–40, Table 1. The data source is the PSID.

Kopczuk, Saez, and Song (2007) used Social Security Administration (SSA) longitudinal earnings micro-data since 1937 to analyze changes in mobility in the United States.[5] The SSA data are based on quarterly earnings reports filed for all employees covered by the social security system since the system started in 1937. This data source is therefore the longest continuous panel data file on earnings in the United States (and probably the world). The data are also very accurate since they are based on administrative records. However, one drawback is that the wages are capped at the maximum taxable wage base for each year (see Chapter 16 for more discussion of social security taxes).

Their major conclusion was that short-term and long-term (rank-based) mobility among all workers was quite stable since 1950, following a temporary surge during World War II. Therefore, the trend of annual earnings inequality was very close to that of inequality of longer term earnings. Mobility at the top was also very stable and did not mitigate the dramatic increase in annual earnings concentration since the 1970s.

Among the top 1 percent of earners in 2004, 38 percent were also among the top 1 percent 10 years earlier in 1994, about 36 percent were in percentiles 95–99, 15 percent were in percentiles 80–95, and only 11 percent were found in the bottom 80 percent of the earnings distribution. The share of the top 1 percent coming from the other parts of the earnings distribution were remarkably stable from about 1950 to 2004. The share of workers remaining in each of the quintiles after one year was virtually unchanged between 1950 and 2003. For example, 61 percent of workers in the bottom quintile remained in the bottom quintile from 1953 to 1954 and 60 percent in the bottom quintile in 2003 were still in the bottom quintile in 2004.

However, there were striking differences among different demographic groups. There was a substantial increase in upward mobility over a career for women and a marked decline for men. Indeed, the offsetting effects of the two trends were responsible for the relative stability in overall mobility over these years.

6.3.3   Other dimensions of mobility

Parrado, Caner, and Wolff (2007) investigated occupational and industrial mobility in the United States over the period from 1969 to 1993. Using PSID data, they compared the degree of both occupational and industrial mobility of individuals over the years 1969–1980 to that of years 1981–1993. They found that workers changed both occupations and industries more frequently in the later period. Occupational mobility for men ranged from 15 to 20 percent per year during the first period and from 20 to 25 percent per year over the second. This result indicated an increase in both occupational and industrial mobility between the 1970s and 1980s. Kambourov and Manovskii (2004) also reported similar findings of rising occupational and industrial mobility in the United States between the same two periods.

Parrado, Caner, and Wolff (2007) also found that for men occupational and industrial changes were associated with lower earnings, though this effect lessened somewhat over time, while for women the results were mixed. Their results also indicated that older and better paid men were less likely to shift occupation or industry.

6.4   INTERGENERATIONAL MOBILITY

Perhaps, from a political standpoint, the issue of intergenerational mobility is even more charged with passion than lifetime mobility. Whether the children of poor parents can succeed in a country ("rags to riches") is indicative of how free and open a society is to newcomers. This is particularly germane to the large number of immigrants that came to the United States during the 1990s and 2000s.

There are two methodological issues of note in this literature. The first is the role of measurement error. Many of the studies, particularly the early ones, relied on "recall information" from the respondent. Thus, after asking the respondent the family's earnings and income, some surveys also asked them to indicate their parents' earnings and income at the same (or similar) age. Such recall, as might be expected, is subject to a great deal of error. Results reported for the earlier studies relied on this technique but did not correct for measurement error. As we shall see, when measurement error is corrected, estimates of intergenerational correlation change markedly.

Second, later studies were able to use surveys (or administrative records) that linked "real" information of parents and children. The basic example of such a survey is the PSID, which as of 2007 has been going on for some 40 years and links information of parents with those of (adult) children who have moved out of the original family and formed separate households. Still, even with this better information, it turns out that estimates of intergenerational correlations are very sensitive to the length of time used to measure both parental and children resources. In the case of income, for example, estimates of intergenerational correlations are generally much higher when the incomes of both parent and child are averaged over several years than when incomes for a single year are used. This makes sense since income averaged over several years is a better indicator of permanent income than is the income of a single year.

6.4.1   Results for the United States

We begin first with a survey of the literature on intergenerational mobility in the United States. As reported in Mulligan (1997) and Solon (1999), the consensus estimate of the income correlation between parents and their children in the United States is in the range of 0.4 to 0.6, once measurement errors in survey data are accounted for. This is quite high, since it indicates that about half of the income of children is "explained" by the income received by their parents.

Bowles, Gintis, and Groves (2005) pointed out in the "Introduction" to their edited volume that the early studies in the United States tended to find very low intergenerational correlations in the economic status of parents and children. For example, Becker and Tomes (1979) reported correlations in the neighborhood of 0.15 between parents' and son's income or earnings. Becker (1988) in his presidential address to the American Economics Association concluded that "low earnings as well as high earnings are not strongly transmitted from fathers to sons."

More recent studies estimate much higher intergenerational correlations than those first reported by Becker and Tomes. Mazumder (2005a), for example, showed that the low correlations found in the early studies were largely attributable to measurement error, particularly when individuals were asked to recall the income of their parents. When the measurement error was corrected, intergenerational correlations from these earlier studies were then estimated to be in the range of 0.3 to 0.4.[6]

Two articles appeared in the *American Economic Review* in June, 1992, which generated a great deal of interest in the subject. The first by Solon (1992) used the PSID with linkages between parents and grown children. The study focused on father–son correlations in earnings, hourly wage rates, and family incomes. His main sample included 348 father–son pairs. The sons in the sample were children from the original 1968 PSID households who reported positive annual earnings for 1984. The son sample was restricted to the cohort born between 1951 and 1959. This restriction implied that the sons were at least 25 years of age in 1984.

Solon also used different measures of fathers' earnings. These included single-year measures, two-year averages, three-year averages, four-year averages, and five-year averages. Using single-year annual earnings, he estimated intergenerational correlation coefficients in the range of 0.25 to 0.29 but with five-year average earnings, the estimated correlation coefficient jumped to 0.41. He argued that the latter was the best estimate because the five-year average was closer to the variable of most interest, permanent income. He also found that a correction for measurement error (on the basis of instrumental variables regression) resulted in an even higher estimate of intergenerational correlation, 0.53 for both earnings and income. He concluded that intergenerational mobility was much lower than previously thought.

The second by Zimmerman (1992) looked at the correlation in lifetime earnings between fathers and sons, using data from the National Longitudinal Survey (NLS). The NLS is a panel survey that began in 1966 with about 5,000 respondents. Using father–son pair matches, Zimmerman was able to isolate 876 father–son pairs for his analysis. He compared "father data" for year 1965 with "son data" for year 1981. He estimated a range of intergenerational correlation coefficients of income and earnings which were corrected for measurement error. He found that the estimated intergenerational correlation coefficients were of the order of 0.4. This estimate was similar to that of Solon and considerably higher than the intergenerational correlations originally reported by Becker and Tomes.

Harding *et al.* (2005) presented estimates of intergenerational associations in economic status. They provided estimates of the income elasticity of child income relative to parental income instead of correlation coefficients. These were estimated from a regression of offspring outcomes such as income (in logarithmic form) on the corresponding parental outcomes (deviations from the mean were used in the actual regression equation). They reported rather high intergenerational elasticities – 0.29 for years of schooling, 0.34 for labor earnings, 0.43 for annual income, and 0.50 for wealth.

Harding *et al.* (2005) also found that parent–child income correlations fell somewhat between 1961 and 1999. This suggests that the degree of intergenerational mobility in the United States may actually have increased a bit between the 1960s and 1990s.

Mazumder (2005b) used the U.S. Social Security Administration longitudinal earnings file. This dataset contains the complete earnings records of workers who have contributed to the social security system since its start-up in 1937 (see Chapter 15 for more discussion of the social security system). He argued that the social security earnings records provide the most accurate data on worker earnings of any dataset (household surveys such as the PSID are based on responses made by interviewees). Also, the social security file contains the longest longitudinal data on earnings for the United States. Since intergenerational correlations should be based on lifetime earnings rather than annual earnings, this data source provided the opportunity to obtain a reasonably good estimate of the latter. As a result, Mazumder (2005b) estimated even higher intergenerational income elasticities when incomes of both parent and child were averaged over two or more years. In fact, the intergenerational elasticity of labor earnings reached 0.65 when 16 years of earnings data were averaged.

Another fascinating finding, reported by Hertz (2005), is that the degree of intergenerational transmission of economic status varied with the position of the parents in the income distribution. Using PSID data, Hertz first found that the overall intergenerational correlation of income was 0.42. However, dividing the parents' income distribution into deciles, he found much stronger intergenerational connects at both the bottom and the top on the income distribution (his so-called "twin peaks"). A child born into the top decile had a 30 percent chance of attaining the top decile and a 44 percent chance of reaching the top quintile. On the other hand, a child born in the bottom decile had 32 percent chance of also winding up in the bottom decile and a 51 percent chance of winding up in the bottom quintile. Hertz also reported dramatic differences in mobility by race, with the rate of persistence in the bottom of the distribution much greater for blacks than for whites. It was also likely that different mechanisms were at work at

Table 6.5 Transition matrix between parents' income quintile in 1967–1971 and children's income quintile in 1994–2000 in the United States

Parental income quintile (1967–1971)	Bottom quintile	Second quintile	Middle quintile	Fourth quintile	Top quintile	Top 5 percent
Bottom quintile	41.5	24.0	15.5	13.2	5.9	1.1
Second quintile	22.6	25.8	23.1	18.5	10.0	1.5
Middle quintile	18.7	25.8	24.1	19.6	16.9	1.8
Fourth quintile	11.1	19.0	20.7	25.1	24.0	5.6
Top quintile	6.1	11.1	17.2	23.7	41.9	14.2
Top 5 percent	2.9	9.0	15.5	21.5	51.1	21.7

The figures show the probability of attaining each income quintile in 1994–2000 based on the parents' income quintile in 1967–1971.
Source: Hertz, T. (2006). Understanding mobility in America. Center for American Progress, Washington, DC, April 26, Table 3. The data source is the PSID.

different parts of the distribution, with wealth inheritance playing a much greater role at the top and vulnerability to illness and violence being much more important at the bottom.

In a follow-up paper, Hertz (2006) used data from the PSID which links parents with their (grown) children's families. He calculated a transition matrix, which is shown in Table 6.5. The matrix shows the probability of a child whose parents' household income placed them in a given income quintile in 1967–1971 landing up in each income quintile in 1994–2000. If there were no inter-generational correlation of income, then the figures in each quintile square would equal 20 percent. (In the case of the last column, which shows the top 5 percent, the figures in this column would all equal 5 percent in the absence of any intergenerational correlation of income.)

The "twin-peaks" phenomenon shows up very clearly here. The probability of a child whose parents were in the bottom income quintile in 1967–1971 winding up in the bottom income quintile in 1994–2000 was 41.5 percent, whereas the probability of a child whose parents were in the top income quintile winding up in the bottom income quintile was only 6.1 percent. Indeed, if the parents were in the top 5 percent of the income distribution in the late 1960s, the probability of the child landing in the bottom income quintile was less than 3 percent. Conversely, the probability of a child whose parents were in the top quintile in 1967–1971 winding up in the top income quintile in 1994–2000 was 41.9 percent, whereas the probability of a child whose parents were in the bottom income quintile reaching the top income quintile was only 5.9 percent. In fact, if the parents were in the top 5 percent of the income distribution, then the child had over a 50 percent chance of reaching the top 10 percent of his (or her) generation's income distribution and more than a 20 percent chance of reaching the top 5 percent.

Hertz also noted that children born in the middle quintile of parental household income had about the same chance of ending up in a lower quintile than their parents as they did of advancing to a higher quintile. Their probability of attaining the top 5 percent of the income distribution for their generation was less than 2 percent.

Hertz also looked at racial differences in immobility. He found that African American children who were born in the bottom quartile were almost *twice* as likely to remain there when they became adults as white children, whose parents had the same income, and *four times* less likely to reach the top quartile. In this analysis he found that differences in mobility for African Americans and whites persisted even after controlling for family background characteristics like education and for the child's education and health.

Jencks (1990) took another approach to the subject of intergenerational mobility by looking into occupational mobility. Occupational mobility is usually measured by the extent to which parents and their children are in jobs with the same (or similar) socioeconomic standing or prestige. Prestige ratings sometimes depend on the responses made by people who are surveyed and sometimes on ratings provided by sociologists who work on the subject. The socioeconomic status of an occupation is usually a composite measure of the average income and educational levels of people who work in the occupation. Jencks reported that estimates of intergenerational occupational mobility based on prestige ratings typically fell into the range of 0.35 to 0.45. This range is very similar to intergenerational correlations between father's income and either son's income or son's earnings.

Several papers have looked at whether mobility has increased or declined in the United States over time. Most of the studies used data from two points of time. Levine and Mazumder (2002) used three different datasets to examine this issue. The first was the General Social Survey (GSS), which contains data on the earnings of the respondent and that of his or her parents. They focused on the elasticity of son's labor earnings with respect to his parents' income and looked at data for sons born from 1940 to 1956 (cohort 1) and sons born from 1951 to 1966 (cohort 2). They found a very large increase in their estimated intergenerational elasticity (a decline in mobility), from 0.12 to 0.49 for sons from married parents and from 0.17 to 0.66 for all sons. They also used the National Longitudinal Survey (NLS) for men born between 1944 and 1952 (cohort 1) and for men born between 1957 and 1965 (cohort 2). They also reported a rise in the intergenerational elasticity of sons' earnings with respect to parental income, from 0.23 to 0.39 for sons from married parents and from 0.24 to 0.33 for all sons. This increase was more moderate than that estimated from the GSS.

The third dataset was the PSID. Here, the findings were just the opposite. They computed intergenerational elasticities for sons born from 1946 to 1954 (cohort 1) and for those born between 1957 and 1965 (cohort 2). In this case, the estimated elasticity fell from 0.45 to 0.29 for sons from married parents and from 0.37 to 0.29 among all sons. Corcoran (2001) also used the PSID but looked at the son's income with respect to his parents' income. The first birth cohort was sons born from 1953 to 1960 and the second cohort was sons born from 1961 to 1968. She also found a decline in the intergenerational elasticity, from 0.26 to 0.18.

Hauser (1998) made use of the GSS to examine the elasticity of son's income with respect to parental income. His time series extended over four cohorts born between 1922 and 1963. His main conclusion was that there was no discernible time trend in estimated elasticities. Fertig (2003) returned to the PSID and constructed elasticity estimates of sons' earnings with respect to parents' income for five cohorts born from 1945 to 1972. In contrast to Hauser, she found a statistically significant and substantial decline in the estimated elasticity, from 0.50 to 0.22.

Mayer and Lopoo (2005) were among the first to examine *continuous time trends* in intergenerational earnings mobility in the United States. They used data from the PSID which links parents with their grown children and looked at the relationship between son's income and that of his parents. They compiled estimates of intergenerational elasticities of (the logarithm of) sons' income with respect to (the logarithm of) their parents' income for sons born between the years 1949 and 1965.

Their main finding was that the elasticity first increased over time, peaked for the birth cohorts born in the mid-1950s and then declined over time. They estimated an intergenerational elasticity of 0.35 for sons born between 1949 and 1952, an elasticity of 0.47 for sons in the 1953–1956 birth cohort, and an elasticity of 0.28 for sons born between 1962 and 1965. Overall, there appeared to be a downward trend over the full 16-year period. However, the authors cautiously concluded that no inference could be made about the overall time trends in earnings mobility because the change over time was not statistically significant.

Lee and Solon (2006) reached similar conclusions on the basis of PSID data. They looked at cohorts born between 1952 and 1975. However, in their study, unlike previous ones, they looked at intergenerational income elasticities for both sons and *daughters* over the period from 1977 to 2000. Their measure of parental resources was a three-year average of log income for the time when the child was 15–17 years old. For the child, they used log annual family income in years ranging from 1977 to 2000 and at ages ranging from 25 to 48. Their estimates showed a rise in the intergenerational elasticity for sons from 0.34 in 1977 to 0.52 in 1982, followed by a decline to 0.36 in 1990, and then a rebound to 0.49 in 2000. For daughters, the intergenerational elasticity first increased from 0.05 in 1977 to 0.53 in 1985, remained fairly steady at this level through 1991, and then fell to 0.46 in 2000. They concluded that there was no statistically significant upward or downward trend in intergenerational mobility for either sons or daughters.

Aaronson and Mazumder (2008) constructed an even longer time series on intergenerational economic mobility in the United States, from 1940 to 2000. Their method was to use U.S. decennial Census data and match men in the Census to "synthetic" parents in the prior generation. Their measure of economic mobility was based on the relationship between adult men's log annual earnings and the logarithm of annual family income in the previous generation. They found that mobility was relatively low in 1940 but then increased from 1940 to 1980. It then declined sharply during the 1980s and continued to decline in the 1990s. One set of estimates, using family income, showed that the intergenerational elasticity (for men aged 40 to 44) was 0.40 in 1950, 0.32 in 1980, 0.46 in 1990, and 0.58 in 2000. Another set, using personal income per capita, showed a decline in the intergenerational elasticity for men aged 40 from 0.59 in 1940 to 0.34 in 1980 and then an increase to 0.57 in 2000. From their results, it appears that mobility in the year 2000 was back to where it was in the 1940s.

6.4.2   Mechanisms of transmission

There is no clear consensus on the mechanism or mechanisms by which economic success (or failure) is transmitted from generation to generation. Several studies have tried to look inside the "black box" to determine how economic status is transmitted from one generation to another. Three key factors are often cited in this literature. The first is genetics and is often related to the inheritance of "native intelligence." The second is through education and other forms of human capital acquisition. The third is through family background and the advantages (or disadvantages) that are associated with a family's socioeconomic status.[7]

Hertz (2005) pointed to the inheritance of financial wealth as one mechanism (also see Section 6.5 below). Groves (2005) focused on the genetic and cultural transmission of cognitive skills and noncognitive personal traits between generations. Bowles, Gintis, and Groves (2005) concluded in their "Introduction" that the combined inheritance process operating through superior cognitive performance and the educational attainment of rich parents accounted for no more than half of the intergenerational transmission of income. On the other hand, the genetic transmission of IQ appeared to be quite unimportant. Groves (2005) explicitly introduced personality variables from the NLS in modeling the intergenerational transmission of economic status. She found that the personality variables accounted for a larger fraction of intergenerational transmission than does IQ. Duncan *et al.* (2005) also looked at the intergenerational transmission of personality traits and their relation to the transmission of economic status between parent and child and reached a similar conclusion.[8]

One important method to analyze the intergenerational transmission mechanism is to use a sample of both fraternal and identical twins. This allows the researcher to separate out genetic from environmental influences on intergenerational correlations of income or other outcomes. Björklund, Jäntti, and Solon (2005) used the Swedish Twin Registry, which is the population of all twins born in Sweden between 1926 and 1967 – in all 54,890 pairs – to analyze this issue. Though the exact influences of the two factors were sensitive to the model specification, they concluded that the genetic component of earnings variation accounted for about 20 percent of earnings inequality among men and about 10 percent among women. Moreover, on the basis of comparing identical twin brothers to fraternal twin brothers, they found that the largest sibling correlation in earnings was a correlation of 0.36 between identical twins who grew up in the same home environment. This result implied that about 64 percent of the variation in earnings was explained neither by genetic nor by environmental resemblance.

Several studies have looked into the connection between parental educational achievement and that of their children. Almost universally, these studies find a very strong intergenerational correlation between the two. However, the actual transmission mechanism is hard to determine and these studies have tried to understand what it is.

Hertz (2006) reported in his study of intergenerational correlations of income in the United States on the basis of the PSID that the educational attainment of the child was the main explanatory variable in a regression of the child's household income on parental income. He calculated that this factor alone accounted for 30 percent of the intergenerational correlation in household income per capita. Race was the second most important factor, accounting for 13 percent of the intergenerational correlation in income, and the health status of the child was third, explaining 8 percent of the intergenerational correlation of income.

Black, Devereux, and Salvanes (2005) used Norwegian data to analyze the intergenerational correlation of educational achievement.[9] They looked at two alternative hypotheses. The first, which they called the "selection story," argues that the type of parent who has more education and earns a higher salary has the type of child who will do so as well, regardless of other factors (perhaps because of genetic inheritance). The second, the "causation story" argues that obtaining more education makes one a different type of parent and thus leads children to have better educational outcomes. In a standard (OLS) regression of child's education on parental education, they estimated a statistically significant coefficient of about 0.2. However, they found little evidence of a causal connection between father's education and children's years of schooling. They did find a significant causal relationship between a mother's education and that of her son's but none between the former and her daughter's education. They concluded that the selection hypothesis provided the best explanation of the intergenerational correlation in education attainment.

Chevalier (2004) engaged in a similar type of analysis using British data. Chevalier found a large positive effect of a mother's education on her child's educational attainment but no significant effect emanating from the father's education. Plug (2004) used data on adopted children to investigate the causal link between parental education and that of their children. He argued that if adopted children are randomly placed with parents, the relationship between parental education and that of their children cannot simply reflect genetic factors. Plug found a positive effect of the father's years of schooling on that of the child but no significant effect from the mother's schooling. Restuccia and Urrutia (2004) constructed a simulation model of the U.S. economy using macro and demographic data. They surmised that about a half of the intergenerational correlation in earnings was accounted for by parental investment in education, particularly early education.

6.4.3 International comparisons

One of the first international comparisons of intergenerational mobility was undertaken by Björklund and Jäntti (1997). They compared the United States and Sweden using comparable data and focused

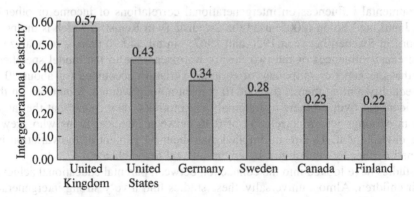

Figure 6.1 Intergenerational elasticity of son's earnings relative to father's earnings
Source: Solon, G. (2002). Cross-country differences in intergenerational earnings mobility. *Journal of Economic Perspectives*, **16**(3), 59–66

on father–son correlations in labor earnings. The U.S. data were from the PSID. The authors used a five-year average of the logarithm of fathers' earnings from 1967 to 1971 and data on sons' earnings from 1987. For Sweden, they used the Swedish Level of Living Survey, which is a panel survey that has been conducted since 1968 and was originally based on a representative sample of 6,000 Swedish individuals aged 15 to 75. The sample was then re-interviewed in 1974, 1981, and 1991. Their main result was that the intergenerational correlation of sons' income and father's income was 0.226 for Sweden and 0.329 for the United States. In other words, earnings mobility was about 50 percent greater in Sweden than in the United States.

Solon (2002) provided a survey of estimates of the intergenerational elasticity of sons' labor earnings relative to their father's earnings for six advanced countries including the United States. The studies were conducted mainly on data from the 1990s. His results are shown in Figure 6.1. The United Kingdom stood out at the top of the list, with an intergenerational elasticity of 0.57 (that is, the United Kingdom had the lowest mobility). The United States was second, with an intergenerational elasticity of 0.43. Germany and Sweden were next in line, with intergenerational elasticities of 0.34 and 0.28, respectively. Canada and Finland were at the bottom (that is, had the greatest mobility), with intergenerational elasticities of 0.23 and 0.22, respectively.

In a far-reaching study, Corak (2004) organized a new set of studies on intergenerational income mobility for nine advanced industrial countries including the United States. His principal findings are summarized in Corak (2006) and shown in Figure 6.2. Each study used national data to investigate the intergenerational elasticity of sons' labor earnings relative to their fathers' earnings. The data were mainly for the 1990s and early 2000s in each country.

The studies also found a very similar ranking of countries in terms of intergenerational mobility as Solon (2002) had reported. The differences among countries were also striking. The United States had the second highest intergenerational elasticity at 0.47, slightly below the United Kingdom at 0.50. The United Kingdom and the United States were the two countries with the least intergenerational mobility. France also had a sizable intergenerational elasticity, at 0.41, which also indicated a low level of intergenerational mobility. There was then a large gap between the top three and the middle two, Germany and Sweden, whose intergenerational income elasticities were 0.32 and 0.27, respectively. There was again a large gap between the middle two countries and the bottom four. The four most mobile countries were Denmark, Norway, Finland, and Canada. Their intergenerational elasticities ranged from 0.15 to 0.19, which were much lower than the other countries, particularly the United Kingdom and the United States.

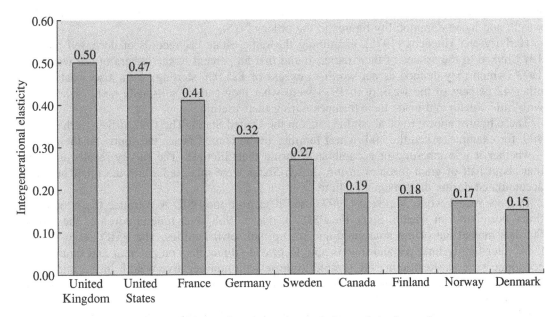

Figure 6.2 Intergenerational elasticity of son's earnings relative to father's earnings
Source: Corak, M. (2006). Do poor children become poor adults? Lessons for public policy from a cross-country comparison of generational earnings mobility. *Research on Income Inequality*, **13**(1), 143–88

6.5 WEALTH MOBILITY

How do bequests and gifts affect wealth inequality among younger households? It is hard to answer this question directly because of the relative paucity of information on direct gifts and transfers. However, we can look at the question of intergenerational *mobility* in wealth. How likely is it that a child of poor parents will become wealthy over his or her lifetime?

Several studies have tried to examine this issue. Some have looked at the intergenerational correlation of wealth, between parents and children. These are based on a "coefficient of immobility," whose value ranges from zero to one. A value of zero indicates that there is no intergenerational correlation of wealth (all individuals are equally likely to amass wealth, independently of their parent's wealth) and a value of one indicates a perfect correlation between parent and children wealth (wealthier children have wealthier parents).

Menchik (1979), using probate records of men who died in Connecticut in the 1930s and 1940s, which were matched to probate records of their children, calculated a coefficient of immobility of 0.7. In contrast, the corresponding figure for income immobility between generations was only 0.25. In a later study, using data from the National Longitudinal Surveys of Mature Men between 1966 and 1981, Jianakoplos and Menchik (1997) calculated an immobility coefficient of 0.67. Both these estimates indicated a very low degree of intergenerational wealth mobility. Kearl and Pope (1986) relied on data from a registry of Mormons in Utah during the nineteenth century which gave information on family wealth holdings. They estimated an intergenerational wealth correlation of 0.26.

Harbury and Hitchens (1979) and Atkinson, Maynard, and Trinder (1983) examined estate tax records of deceased males in 1973 from the United Kingdom which linked the estate of the deceased with that of his father (the study was conducted only for males). The two studies found both wealth and income immobility figures in the order of 0.5.

Harbury and Hitchens (1976), examining the same estate tax records of deceased males in 1973 linked to the estates of their father, found that 58 percent of the fathers of the wealthy in 1973 (which they defined as net worth in excess of £25,000 sterling) were also wealthy. The other 42 percent of the wealthy in 1973 were what they called "self-made men," who started with little wealth and made their fortunes during their lifetime.

These figures appear to be about the same in the United States. The 1992 survey of the *Forbes 400*, for example, asked the 400 richest families in the United States the source of their wealth – whether it was inherited or accumulated during their lifetime. The survey results suggested that about half of great fortunes in the United States were inherited while the other half were accumulated during the person's lifetime.

In more recent work, Mulligan (1997) used data from the PSID to estimate the intergenerational correlation of wealth. Since the PSID began in 1968, over time children of the original families moved out of the household and set up their own families. The PSID keeps track of these inter-family linkages and thus is able to provide direct data on parental and (adult) child economic success. Restricting the sample to those with non-negative wealth in the mid-1980s, Mulligan estimated the elasticity of the logarithm of wealth between parents and their children to lie in the range of 0.32 to 0.43.

Charles and Hurst (2003) also used data from the PSID to look at the intergenerational correlation of wealth. They also relied on the intergenerational linkages in the PSID. They restricted the sample to parent–child pairs where a child was between ages 25 and 65 in the 1999 survey, where the parent was not retired in 1984, and where the parents were part of the survey in both 1984 and 1999. These restrictions resulted in a sample size of 1,648 parent–child pairs.

Charles and Hurst compared the wealth holdings of the children in 1999 with those of their parents in 1984. There was about a 15-year age difference between the two groups. Their major result was that the intergenerational correlation of wealth was between 0.23 and 0.50 when the sample was adjusted for age differences. This figure was somewhat lower than previous estimates on the subject reported above. However, they argued that this intergenerational relationship was large because they focused only on households that had not received bequests from their parents (though some had received *inter-vivos* gifts from their parents). They also found that permanent income explained less than half of the intergenerational correlation of wealth. However, using measures of time preference and risk aversion included in the PSID, they found that a sizable intergenerational persistence in preferences for saving did explain a significant proportion of the intergenerational correlation in wealth.

These studies do indicate that individuals can accumulate significant wealth through savings and entrepreneurial activity. Yet, it is hardly a fair game, with children of the rich much more heavily favored to win. The degree of intergenerational persistence of wealth appears to be even higher than that of earnings or income.

6.6   SUMMARY

This chapter has surveyed the recent evidence on both mobility over time and mobility between generations. Estimates often vary depending on the data source used and the time period covered. From a methodological point of view, it appears that estimates of intergenerational correlations become higher the better the data that are used and the more controls that are used for measurement error. Moreover, using income (and other resource measures such as earnings) averaged over longer periods of time yields higher correlation coefficients for both income over time and for income between generations.

The evidence generally suggests a decline in income mobility over time in the United States from the 1970s to the 1990s. Hungerford (1993), using the PSID, found no time trend in mobility between 1969–1976 and between 1979–1986. Carroll, Joulfaian, and Rider (2007), using a panel of individual income tax returns, found a small decline in income mobility between 1979–1986 and between 1987–1995. Bradbury and Katz (2002) used the PSID to compute family income transition matrices for three decades in the United States: 1969–1979, 1979–1989, and 1989–1998. Their results clearly indicate a decline in income mobility over these three decades, particularly in the 1990s.

There is no universal evidence of a significant time trend, either up or down, in earnings mobility over time in the United States from 1950 to 2004. Kopczuk, Saez, and Song (2007), using SSA longitudinal earnings, found no significant upward or downward trend in earnings mobility. Gittleman and Joyce (1996), using matched cross-sectional CPS data, reached a similar conclusion about trends in short-term earnings mobility from 1967 to 1991.

Likewise, there is no solid evidence of a significant time trend, either up or down, in intergenerational correlations in the United States. Aaronson and Mazumder (2008) provided the most recent evidence which suggested that intergenerational income mobility increased substantially from 1940 to 1980 and then nosedived from 1980 to 2000, almost back to where it was in 1940. On the other hand, both Mayer and Lopoo (2005) and Lee and Solon (2006) concluded that there was no significant upward or downward trend.

On the other hand, there are striking differences among countries in the degree of intergenerational mobility. From Corak (2006), the United States had the second-highest intergenerational elasticity at 0.47, slightly below the United Kingdom at 0.5. France also had a sizable intergenerational elasticity, at 0.41. There was then a large gap between the top three and the middle two, Germany and Sweden, whose intergenerational income elasticity was about 0.3. Another large gap loomed between these two and Denmark, Norway, Finland, and Canada, whose intergenerational elasticities ranged from 0.15 to 0.19. It is also of note that Denmark, Finland, and Norway rank among the lowest countries in terms of inequality, and the United Kingdom and particularly the United States rank among the highest in terms of inequality (see Chapter 3 for further details). Thus, there was no apparent trade-off between high income inequality and high intergenerational income mobility.

Whether or not parents leave inheritances for altruistic motives, it is still the case that inheritances play a large role in the process of wealth accumulation. Moreover, intergenerational transfers are not distributed equitably among younger families. How do bequests and gifts affect intergenerational wealth mobility? Studies for the United States indicate that there is a very strong correlation between an individual's wealth and that of his or her parents – on the order of 70 percent in some studies. Moreover, half of all large fortunes in the United States appeared to be inherited. These results suggest that individuals can accumulate significant wealth over their lifetime through savings and entrepreneurial activity, but a person is much more likely to be rich if his or her parents are also rich.

One general area of weakness of these studies on mobility is that they do not generally discuss or analyze the reasons that cause mobility to change over time or that account for inter-country differences. It is likely that lifecycle factors, the accumulation of general and specific human capital, changes in family composition, immigration patterns, and the like all play a role in explaining why individuals might change relative position in the earnings or income distribution over time. We will discuss these factors more fully in Part II of this book.

6.7   REFERENCES AND BIBLIOGRAPHY

Aaberge, R., Björklund, A., Jäntti, M., Palme, M., Pedersen, P.J., Smith, N. & Wennemo, T. (2002). Income inequality and income mobility in the Scandinavian countries compared to the United States. *Review of Income and Wealth*, **48**(4), 443–69.

Aaronson, D. & Mazumder, B. (2008). Intergenerational economic mobility in the United States, 1940 to 2000. *Journal of Human Resources*, **43**(1), 139–72.

Atkinson, A.B. (1983). The measurement of economic mobility. In A.B. Atkinson (ed.), *Social Justice and Public Policy*. London: Wheatsheaf.

Atkinson, A.B., Bourguignon, F. & Morrisson, C. (1992). *Empirical Studies of Earnings Mobility*. Chur, Switzerland: Harwood.

Atkinson, A.B., Maynard, A.K. & Trinder, C.G. (1983). *Parents and Children*. London: Heinemann.

Bartholomew, D.C. (1982). *Stochastic Models for Social Processes*, 3rd Edition. New York: John Wiley & Sons, Inc.

Becker, G.S. (1988). Family economics and macro behavior. *American Economic Review*, **78**, 1–13.

Becker, G.S. & Tomes, N. (1979). An equilibrium theory of the distribution of income and intergenerational mobility. *Journal of Political Economy*, **87**, 1153–89.

Becker, G.S. & Tomes, N. (1986). Human capital and the rise and fall of families. *Journal of Labor Economics*, **4**, S1–S39.

Behrman, J.R. & Rosenzweig, M.R. (2002). Does increasing women's schooling raise the schooling of the next generation? *American Economic Review*, **92**(1), 323–34.

Björklund, A. (1993). A comparison between actual distributions of annual and lifetime income: Sweden 1951–89. *Review of Income and Wealth*, **39**(4), 377–86.

Björklund, A. & Jäntti, M. (1997). Intergenerational income mobility in Sweden compared to the United States. *American Economic Review*, **87**(5), 1009–18.

Björklund, A., Jäntti, M. & Lindquist, M.J. (2007). Family background and income during the rise of the welfare state: Brother correlations in income for Swedish men born 1932–1968. IZA Discussion Paper No. 3000, Bonn, Germany, August.

Björklund, A., Jäntti, M. & Solon, G. (2005). Influences of nature and nurture on earnings variation. In S. Bowles, H. Gintis & M.O. Groves (eds.), *Unequal Chances: Family Background and Economic Success* (pp. 145–64). Princeton, NJ: Princeton University Press.

Black, S.E., Devereux, P.J. & Salvanes, K.G. (2005). Why the apples doesn't fall far: Understanding intergenerational transmission of human capital. *American Economic Review*, **95**(1), 437–49.

Blanden, J., Goodman, A., Gregg, P. & Machin, S. (2004). Changes in intergenerational mobility in Britain. In M. Corak (ed.), *Generational Income Mobility in North America and Europe* (pp. 122–46). Cambridge: Cambridge University Press.

Blanden, J., Gregg, P. & Macmillan, L. (2007). Accounting for intergenerational income persistence: Noncognitive skills, ability and education. *Economic Journal*, **117**, C43–C60.

Bowles, S. & Gintis, H. (2002). The inheritance of inequality. *Journal of Economic Perspectives*, **16**(3), 3–30.

Bowles, S., Gintis, H. & Groves, M. (eds.) (2005). *Unequal Chances: Family Background and Economic Success*. Princeton, NJ: Princeton University Press.

Bowlus, A.J. & Robin, J.-M. (2004). Twenty years of rising inequality in US lifetime labor income values. *Review of Economic Studies*, **71**(3), 709–43.

Bradbury, K. & Katz, J. (2002). Women's labor market involvement and family income mobility when marriages end. *New England Economic Review*, Q4, 41–74.

Buchinsky, M. & Hunt, J. (1999). Wage mobility in the United States. *Review of Economics and Statistics*, **81**(3), 351–68.

Buchinsky, M., Fields, G., Fougre, D. & Kramarz, F. (2005). Francs and ranks: Earnings mobility in France, 1967–1999. CEPR Discussion Paper 9.

Burkhauser, R.V. & Poupore, J.G. (1997). A cross-national comparison of permanent inequality in the United States and Germany. *Review of Economics and Statistics*, **79**(1), 10–17.

Burkhauser, R.V., Holtz-Eakin, D. & Rhody, S.E. (1997). Labor earnings mobility and inequality in the United States and Germany during the growth years of the 1980s. *International Economic Review*, **38**(4), 775–94.

Carroll, R., Joulfaian, D. & Rider, M. (2007). Income mobility: The recent American experience. Andrew Young School of Public Policy, Working Paper 07-18, March.

Chadwick, L. & Solon, G. (2002). Intergenerational income mobility among daughters. *American Economic Review*, **92**(1), 335–44.

Charles, K.K. & Hurst, E. (2003). The correlation of wealth across generations. *Journal of Political Economy*, **111**(6), 1155–82.

Chevalier, A. (2004). Parental education and child's education: A natural experiment. IZA Discussion Paper No. 1153, Bonn, Germany.

Corak, M. (ed.) (2004). *Generational Income Mobility in North America and Europe*. Cambridge: Cambridge University Press.

Corak, M. (2006). Do poor children become poor adults? Lessons for public policy from a cross-country comparison of generational earnings mobility. *Research on Income Inequality*, **13**(1), 143–88.

Corcoran, M. (2001). Mobility, persistence, and the consequences of poverty for children: Child and adult outcomes. In S. Danziger & R. Haveman (eds.), *Understanding Poverty*. New York: Russell Sage Foundation.

Couch, K.A. & Dunn, T.A. (1997). Intergenerational correlations in labor market status: A comparison of the United States and Germany. *Journal of Human Resources*, **32**(1), 210–32.

Dardanoni, V. (1993). Measuring social mobility. *Journal of Economic Theory*, **61**, 372–94.

Dearden, L., Machin, S. & Reed, H. (1997). Intergenerational mobility in Britain. *Economic Journal*, **107**, 47–66.

Duncan, G., Kalil, A., Mayer, S.E., Tepper, R. & Payne, M.R. (2005). The apple does not fall far from the tree. In S. Bowles, H. Gintis & M.O. Groves (eds.), *Unequal Chances: Family Background and Economic Success* (pp. 23–80). Princeton, NJ: Princeton University Press.

Ermisch, J., Francesconi, M. & Siedler, T. (2006). Intergenerational mobility and marital sorting. *Economic Journal*, **116**(513), 659–79.

Ferrie, J.P. (2005). The end of American exceptionalism? Mobility in the United States since 1850. *Journal of Economic Perspectives*, **19**(3), 199–215.

Fertig, A.R. (2003). Trends in intergenerational earnings mobility. Center for Research on Child Wellbeing, Princeton University, Working Paper No. 01-23.

Fields, G.S. (1999). Income mobility: concepts and measures. In N. Birdsall & C. Graham (eds.), *New Markets, New Opportunities? Economic and Social Mobility in a Changing World*. Washington, DC: Brookings Institution Press.

Fields, G.S. & Ok, E. (1996). The meaning and measurement of income mobility. *Journal of Economic Theory*, **71**, 349–77.

Fields, G.S. & Ok, E. (1999a). The measurement of income mobility. In J. Silber (ed.), *Handbook of Income Inequality Measurement*. Dordrecht: Kluwer Academic.

Fields, G.S. & Ok, E. (1999b). Measuring movements of incomes. *Economica*, **66**, 455–71.

Geweke, J. & Keane, M. (2000). An empirical analysis of income dynamics among men in the PSID: 1968–1989. *Journal of Econometrics*, **96**, 293–356.

Gittleman, M. & Joyce, M. (1995). Earnings mobility in the United States, 1967–1991. *Monthly Labor Review*, **118**(9), 3–13.

Gittleman, M. & Joyce, M. (1996). Earnings mobility and long-run inequality: An analysis using matched CPS data. *Industrial Relations*, **35**, 180–96.

Gottschalk, P. (1997). Inequality, income growth and mobility: The basic facts. *Journal of Economic Perspectives*, **11**(2), 21–40.

Gottschalk, P. & Moffit, R. (1994). The growth of earnings instability in the U.S. labor market. *Brookings Papers on Economic Activity*, no. 2, 217–72.

Gottschalk, P. & Spolaore, E. (2002). On the evaluation of economic mobility. *Review of Economic Studies*, **69**, 191–208.

Grawe, N. (2006). Life-cycle bias in estimates of intergenerational earnings persistence. *Labour Economics*, **13**(5), 551–70.

Groves, M.O. (2005). Personality and the intergenerational transmission of economic status. In S. Bowles, H. Gintis & M.O. Groves (eds.), (1983). *Unequal Chances: Family Background and Economic Success* (pp. 208–31). Princeton, NJ: Princeton University Press.

Haider, S. (2001). Earnings instability and earnings inequality of males in the United States: 1967–1991. *Journal of Labor Economics*, **19**(4), 799–836.

Haider, S. & Solon, G. (2006). Life-cycle variations in the association between current and lifetime income. *American Economic Review*, **96**(4), 1308–20.

Harbury, C.D. & Hitchens, D.M.W.N. (1976). The inheritances of top wealth leavers: Some further evidence. *Economic Journal*, **86**, 321–6.

Harbury, C.D. & Hitchens, D.M.W.N. (1979). *Inheritance and Wealth Inequality in Britain*. London: Allen and Unwin.

Harding, D.J., Jencks, C., Lopoo, L.M. & Mayer, S.E. (2005). The changing effect of family background on the incomes of American adults. In S. Bowles, H. Gintis & M.O. Groves (eds.), *Unequal Chances: Family Background and Economic Success* (pp. 100–44). Princeton, NJ: Princeton University Press.

Harper, B. (1995). Male occupational mobility in Britain. *Oxford Bulletin of Economics and Statistics*, **57**, 349–69.

Hauser, R. (1998). Intergenerational economic mobility in the United States: Measures, differentials and trends. University of Wisconsin, Madison, mimeo.

Haveman, R. & Wolfe, B. (1995). The determinants of children's attainments: A review of methods and findings. *Journal of Economic Literature*, **33**, 1829–78.

Hertz, T. (2005). Rags, riches, and race. In S. Bowles, H. Gintis & M.O. Groves (eds.), *Unequal Chances: Family Background and Economic Success* (pp. 165–91). Princeton, NJ: Princeton University Press.

Hertz, T. (2006). Understanding mobility in America. Center for American Progress, Washington, DC, April 26.

Hertz, T. (2007). Trends in the intergenerational elasticity of family income in the United States. *Industrial Relations*, **46**(1), 22–50.

Holtz-Eakin, D., Rosen, H.S. & Weathers, R. (2000). Horatio Alger meets the mobility tables. NBER working Paper No. 7619, March.

Huggett, M., Ventura, G. & Yaron, A. (2007). Sources of lifetime inequality. NBER Working Paper No. 13224, July.

Hungerford, T. (1993). U.S. income mobility in the seventies and eighties. *Review of Income and Wealth*, **39**, 403–17.

Jencks, C. (1990). What is the true rate of social mobility? In R.L. Breiger (ed.), *Social Mobility and Social Structure*. New York: Cambridge University Press.

Jianakoplos, N.A. & Menchik, P.L. (1997). Wealth mobility. *Review of Economics and Statistics*, **79**(1), 18–31.

Kambourov, G. & Manovskii, I. (2004). Rising occupational and industry mobility in the United States: 1968–1993. Institute for the Study of Labor (IZA) Discussion Paper No. 1110, Bonn, Germany.

Kearl, J. & Pope, C. (1986). Unobservable family and individual contributions to the distributions of income and wealth. *Journal of Labor Economics*, **4**(3), S48–S79.

Kopczuk, W., Saez, E. & Song, J. (2007). Uncovering the American dream: Inequality and mobility in social security earnings data since 1937. NBER Working Paper No. 13345, August.

Laitner, J. (1997). Intergenerational and inter-household economic links. In M.R. Rosenzweig & O. Stark (eds.), *Handbook of Population and Family Economics* (pp. 189–238). Amsterdam: Elsevier Science.

Lee, C.-I. & Solon, G. (2006). Trends in intergenerational mobility. NBER Working Paper No. 12007, January.

Levine, D. & Mazumder, B. (2002). Choosing the right parents: Changes in the intergenerational transmission of inequality – Between 1980 and the early 1990s. Federal Reserve Bank of Chicago, Working Paper No. 2002-08.

Maasoumi, E. (1998). On mobility. In D. Giles & A. Ullah (eds.), *The Handbook of Economic Statistics* (pp. 119–76). New York: Marcel Dekker.

Maasoumi, E. & Trede, M. (2001). Comparing income mobility in Germany and the United States using generalized entropy mobility measures. *Review of Economics and Statistics*, **83**(3), 551–9.

Maasoumi, E. & Zandvakili, S. (1986). A class of generalized measures of mobility with applications. *Economic Letters*, **22**(1), 97–102.

Maasoumi, E. & Zandvakili, S. (1990). Generalized entropy measures of mobility for different sexes and income levels. *Journal of Econometrics*, **43**(1–2), 121–33.

Mayer, S.E. & Lopoo, L.M. (2004). What do trends in the intergenerational economic mobility of sons and daughters in the United States mean? In M. Corak (ed.), *Generational Income Mobility in North America and Europe* (pp. 90–121). Cambridge, UK: Cambridge University Press.

Mayer, S.E. & Lopoo, L.M. (2005). Has the intergenerational transmission of economic status changed? *Journal of Human Resources*, **40**(1), 169–85.

Mazumder, B. (2005a). The apple falls even closer to the tree than we thought. In S. Bowles, H. Gintis & M.O. Groves (eds.), *Unequal Chances: Family Background and Economic Success* (pp. 80–99). Princeton, NJ: Princeton University Press.

Mazumder, B. (2005b). Fortunate sons: New estimates of intergenerational mobility in the United States using social security earnings data. *Review of Economics and Statistics*, **87**(2), 235–55.

Menchik, P.L. (1979). Inter-generational transmission of inequality: An empirical study of wealth mobility. *Economica*, **46**, 349–62.

Moffitt, R. & Gottschalk, P. (2002). Trends in the transitory variance of earnings in the US. *Economic Journal*, **112**, C68–C73.

Moscarini, G. & Vella, F. (2008). Occupational mobility and the business cycle. NBER Working Paper No. 13819, January.

Mulligan, C.B. (1997). *Parental Priorities and Economic Inequality*. Chicago: University of Chicago Press.

Mulligan, C.B. (1999). Galton versus the Human capital approach to inheritance. *Journal of Political Economy*, **107**(6), 184–224.

Parrado, E., Caner, A. & Wolff, E.N. (2007). Occupational and industrial mobility in the United States. *Labour Economics*, **14**(3), 435–55.

Plug, E. (2004). Estimating the effect of mother's schooling on children's schooling using a sample of adoptees. *American Economic Review*, **94**(1), 358–68.

Restuccia, D. & Urrutia, C. (2004). Intergenerational persistence of earnings: The role of early and college education. *American Economic Review*, **94**(5), 1354–78.

Schiller, B.R. (1977). Relative earnings mobility in the United States. *American Economic Review*, **67**(5), 926–41.

Shorrocks, A.F. (1978a). Income inequality and income mobility. *Journal of Economic Theory*, **19**, 376–93.

Shorrocks, A.F. (1978b). The measurement of mobility. *Econometrica*, **46**(5), 1013–24.

Shorrocks, A.F. (1988). Aggregation issues in inequality measurement. In W. Eichorn (ed.), *Measurement in Economics*. New York: Springer Verlag.

Solon, G. (1992). Intergenerational income mobility in the United States. *American Economic Review*, **82**, 393–408.

Solon, G. (1999). Intergenerational mobility in the labor market. In O.C. Ashenfelter & D. Card (eds.), *Handbook of Labor Economics*, Vol. 3A. Amsterdam: Elsevier.

Solon, G. (2002). Cross-country differences in intergenerational earnings mobility. *Journal of Economic Perspectives*, **16**(3), 59–66.

Solon, G., Corcoran, M., Gordon, R. & Laren, D. (1991). A longitudinal analysis of sibling correlations in economic status. *Journal of Human Resources*, **26**(3), 509–34.

Sommers, D. & Eck, A. (1977). Occupational mobility in the labor force. *Monthly Labor Review*, **100**, 3–26.

Van Kerm, P. (2004). What lies behind income mobility? Reranking and distributional change in Belgium, Western Germany and the USA. *Economica*, **71**(282), 223–39.

Zimmerman, D.J. (1992). Regression toward mediocrity in economic status. *American Economic Review*, **82**(3), 409–29.

NOTES

1   That is to say, the lower the value of β, the closer the offspring's income is to the average of the general population. A pertinent example is with regard to the heights of sons in relation to the heights of fathers. Statistically, tall fathers tend to produce sons that are taller than average but the sons are, on average, less tall than their fathers. This is a good example of "regression to the mean."

2   In this section, although I use the term "income," the same formulation can be used for any measure of economic well-being.

3   An "axiomatic" approach derives an income mobility measure from first principles about what the desirable characteristics of such a measure might be. In the case of an income inequality measure, the scale independence principle and the transfer principle are often considered basic axioms in deriving such an inequality measure (see Chapter 3 for more discussion).

4   Please consult a standard textbook on linear algebra for a discussion of eigenvalues.

5   One of the earliest studies using this data source (then called the Longitudinal Employer Employee Data file) to study earnings mobility was Schiller (1977) for the period from 1957 to 1971.

6   The availability of longitudinal or panel data that connected parents with their grown offspring many years later enabled more accurate measurement of intergenerational correlations in income and other attributes.

7   A fourth is through the inheritance of wealth, which we will discuss in Section 6.5.

8   Also, see Section 8.6.2.2 for more discussion on the relation between family background and earnings.

9   They chose Norwegian data because during the 1960s there was a drastic change in compulsory schooling laws in Norway. This change allowed them to statistically "identify" the determinants of this process through a regression technique called "instrumental variables."

Part II
Explanations of Inequality and Poverty

Chapter 7

The Labor Force, Employment, and Unemployment

7.1 INTRODUCTION

One of the principal objectives of this book is to develop explanations as to why incomes differ among families and individuals. Since, as we saw in Chapter 2, labor earnings have accounted for between 60 and 70 percent of personal income in the United States since the end of World War II, much of the variation in family income derives from differences in pay. We are thus left with the question of why workers earn different amounts.

Part II focuses on the role of the labor market in the determination of relative earnings. We approach this issue in stages. Before analyzing the determinants of wages and salaries, it is first necessary to consider the issue of who works and who does not. We begin, in Chapter 7, with the definitions of the labor force, employment, and unemployment. We also discuss trends in labor force participation patterns, the composition of employment, and the incidence of unemployment. Alternative explanations of unemployment are also considered in this chapter.

This chapter lays out the basic groundwork for understanding changes in the composition of the labor force. Though the chapter is mainly factual in basis, it has clear connections with the major themes of the book – income inequality, poverty, and discrimination. Wherever possible, we will indicate the relation between labor force changes and the determinants of family income and poverty. For example, unemployment and labor force participation are relevant to low-income individuals and households. As we saw in Chapter 4, poverty incidence is much higher among the unemployed and the nonworking (nonelderly) population. As a result, public policy is often directed towards reducing unemployment and increasing labor force participation for these groups.

At upper levels, tax policy was reformed over the years to encourage labor force participation among individuals with high wage rates (to oppose the substitution effects of taxation instead of opposing the income effects of higher wage rates). Married women's labor force participation is also related to family income. In particular, wives' earnings have helped to keep family incomes from falling or declining as men's wages stagnated or even declined in real terms over time.

Section 7.2 introduces the concepts of the labor force, employment, and unemployment. Section 7.3 shows historical trends in labor force participation rates and rather dramatic changes in the demographic make-up of the labor force. Section 7.4 documents equally dramatic shifts in both the industrial and occupational composition of employment. Section 7.5 presents historical trends on the unemployment rate and average duration of unemployment. Distinctions are made according to the reasons for unemployment and some consideration is given to the "discouraged worker effect," as well as the relation between the unemployment rate and the vacancy rate. Section 7.6 documents considerable variation in the incidence of unemployment among age, gender, and racial groups, as well as by geographic region and occupation and industry of employment.

In Section 7.7, we discuss causes of unemployment. Four principal factors have been cited in the literature. The first, frictional unemployment, is ascribed to the lack of perfect information on job openings and the consequent search time required to find a new position. The second, seasonal unemployment, characterizes certain industries, such as agriculture and tourism, where employment occurs on an irregular basis. The third, structural unemployment, refers to an imbalance between job vacancies by skill type and the qualifications of individuals looking for work. The fourth, demand-deficient unemployment, arises when the aggregate demand for output is not sufficient to absorb the full labor force in production. Section 7.8 presents a summary of the chapter.

7.2   BASIC CONCEPTS OF THE LABOR FORCE, EMPLOYMENT, AND UNEMPLOYMENT

The population can be divided into two groups – those in the **labor force** and those not in the labor force. The former, in turn, can be subdivided into those at work or **employed** and the rest who are without a job or **unemployed**.

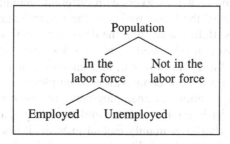

In the United States, the Bureau of Labor Statistics (BLS) of the Department of Labor is legally empowered to estimate and publish figures on both the size of the labor force and the unemployment rate each month. It is instructive to consider the definitions it uses for these concepts.

7.2.1   Employment

The BLS definition of employment includes not only individuals with a paid job who are working for someone else but also self-employed individuals working in their own business, profession, or farm, and unpaid family members working in a family business 15 hours or more per week. Homemakers and those engaged in volunteer work for a religious or charitable organization are not counted as employed.

In computing total employment, BLS counts each employed person only once. Those individuals who hold more than one job are counted only in the job in which they work the most hours. It should be noted that total employment will, in general, differ from the total number of jobs in an economy. The former is a count of persons while the latter is a count of the number of positions in the economy.

7.2.2   Unemployment

A person is considered unemployed if that person did not work during a given week but was both available for and actively looking for work. An individual who made a specific effort to find work within the preceding four-week period, such as by registering at a public or private employment agency, writing application letters, and canvassing for work, is considered to be looking for work. BLS also defines a person as unemployed who has been temporarily laid off from a job and is waiting to be recalled or who is scheduled to start a new job soon.

BLS divides the unemployed into four categories depending on the reason for being unemployed. (i) A person is a *job loser* if employment ended involuntarily because of firing or layoff and the search for a new job begins immediately. (ii) A person is a *job leaver* if the person quits or otherwise voluntarily terminates employment and begins to look for a new job immediately. (iii) A person is a *reentrant* if the person previously worked at a full-time job and was out of the labor force prior to looking for a new job. (iv) A person is a *new entrant* if the person has never worked at a full-time job.

7.2.3   The labor force

The *civilian labor force* is defined as the total of all civilians classified as either employed or unemployed. The *total labor force* includes, in addition, all members of the Armed Forces stationed either in the United States or abroad. The **unemployment rate** is defined as the ratio of the number of unemployed individuals to the number of individuals in the civilian labor force.

BLS divides all individuals 16 years of age or older who are not in the labor force into five categories: (i) engaged in housework; (ii) in school; (iii) unable to work because of long-term physical or mental illness; (iv) retired; and (v) other. The last group includes so-called "discouraged workers," individuals who have essentially given up looking for work because they believe that no jobs are available to them due to a lack of training or education or due to prevailing job market conditions. Some economists have argued that the unemployment count should include discouraged workers because they would work if suitable jobs were available and, as a result, the "true" unemployment rate may be considerably higher than the official unemployment rate.

Economists have raised several other concerns as well. First, both part-time and full-time workers are counted as employed workers. Yet, some part-time workers might be willing to work full time if the opportunity arose and are therefore, in a sense, unemployed, or at least underemployed. A second issue is the asymmetric treatment of housemakers and domestic servants. The former are classified as "not in the labor force," while the latter are classified as employed workers. Yet, both perform the same type of "work" – the only difference is that the latter are paid for it (by someone else) while the former are not.[1] A third issue is the treatment of students, who, it is true, do not perform paid labor, yet are engaged in an activity that may presumably increase their future productivity. By this interpretation, students can be considered as engaged in an investment activity and their time should be considered as work.[2] Third, people who are working illegally or who claim that they are searching for a job but are really not actively looking are now counted in the ranks of the unemployed but should not be so classified. Their inclusion in the unemployed pool will bias upward the unemployment rate.

7.2.4   Estimating employment statistics

BLS is charged with the task of publishing monthly statistics on employment and unemployment. The data are based on the Current Population Survey (CPS), which is conducted for the BLS by the U.S. Census Bureau. The monthly survey is based on a scientifically selected sample of households, which is representative of the civilian noninstitutional population of the United States.[3]

A brief history of the development of these statistics might prove illuminating. Before the 1930s, no official measurements of unemployment were provided. During the Great Depression, unemployment became a major and visible national problem and this spurred the development of statistics to measure unemployment. During the early 1930s, estimates of the unemployment rate began to appear on the basis of a wide assortment of indirect techniques, but these estimates showed wide discrepancies. As a result, many research groups, as well as the government, started experimenting with direct survey techniques to measure the labor force, employment, and unemployment. In these surveys, individuals were asked a series of questions in order to classify them by labor force or employment status. In most of these attempts, unemployment was defined as the number of individuals who were not working but were "willing and able to work." However, this concept of unemployment was unsatisfactory and vague, since it appeared to depend heavily on the attitudes and interpretation of the individuals who were interviewed.

By the late 1930s, a more exact set of concepts of the labor force, employment, and unemployment was developed to make the measurement more objective. By these new criteria, an individual's classification was to depend on the actual activity in which he or she was engaged during the survey period – that is, on whether the person was working, actively looking for work, or involved in some other activity. The conventions were adopted by the Works Progress Administration (WPA) in 1940 for the first national sample survey of households. The original survey was called the Monthly Report on Unemployment, and was administered by the WPA until 1943, when it was turned over to the Census Bureau. In 1943, the name of the survey changed to the Monthly Report on the Labor Force, and in 1948 it changed to its present name, the Current Population Survey (CPS). In 1959, the responsibility for analyzing and publishing the CPS employment statistics was transferred to the BLS, although the Census Bureau continues to administer the survey.

The CPS provides statistics on the civilian noninstitutional population who are 16 years or older. In addition to labor force statistics, the CPS also provides information on demographic, social, and economic characteristics of the population. The CPS is based on a monthly probability sample, which originally consisted of 47,000 households. In 1975 the survey was expanded to 58,000 households and in 2007 about 60,000 households were included. The time period covered in each monthly survey is a calendar week. The sample is designed to cover all states, which allows labor force statistics to be developed by state. In addition, the sample is designed to allow sufficient coverage of the largest 146 metropolitan areas, and labor force statistics are also published individually for each of these. Besides total employment, unemployment, and the labor force, the CPS also provides a wealth of monthly statistics on hours worked, earnings, the composition of the labor force, and the composition of the population.

7.3 LABOR FORCE PARTICIPATION RATES

The labor force participation rate, or **LFPR**, is defined as the proportion of a particular population group that is in the labor force. In the aggregate, this concept is of limited interest since the full population includes many groups who are not expected to work, such as children, the disabled, and the elderly. The usual participation rate statistics are those which show the labor force as a percent of the civilian noninstitutional population 16 years or older,[4] since it is from this population that the labor force is drawn. Generally speaking, the LFPR indicates the proportion of the population that could be at work that is in the labor force. Moreover, labor force participation is often disaggregated into smaller population groups, such as by gender, race, age, or education.

7.3.1 LFPR by gender, race, and age

Table 7.1 and Figure 7.1 show historical trends of both the size of the labor force and LFPR since 1900. Between 1900 and 2005, the civilian labor force grew from 28.5 million to 149.3 million workers, or by a factor of 7.9. The labor force doubled in size between 1900 and 1941 and then doubled again between 1941 and 1985. From 1985 to 2005 it grew by about one-quarter.

Over the years from 1900 to 2005, the overall LFPR also increased, from 56 to 66 percent. It remained virtually unchanged from 1900 to 1941, the start of U.S. involvement in World War II. During the war years, the LFPR increased to 63 percent and then fell to 57 percent in 1946. After 1946 there was a gradual upward trend in the LFPR.

Beginning in 1948, it is possible to identify separately the trends in LFPR by gender. In 1948, the LFPR for males was 87 percent and for females 33 percent. Between 1948 and 2005, there was an almost steady drop in the LFPR of males, from 87 to 73 percent. For females, the trend was exactly the opposite, with their LFPR increasing almost steadily from 33 to 59 percent. The increase in the aggregate LFPR in the postwar period was thus due to the increasing labor force participation of females, dominating the declining rate for males. In 1948, females accounted for 27 percent of the labor force, in 1977 for 41 percent, and in both 1993 and 2005 for 46 percent.

The top of Table 7.2 presents some detail on the age distribution of the labor force. In 1950, 19 percent of the labor force was under the age of 25; by 1977 the figure had risen to 24 percent; but in 2005 the figure was down to 15 percent. The percentage of the labor force in the prime working ages of 25 to 54 fell from 64 percent in 1950 to 61 percent in 1977, then increased to 72 percent in 1994, but retracted to 69 percent in 2005. These two trends largely reflect the

Table 7.1 The civilian labor force and labor force participation rates, 1900–2005

Year	Labor force (millions)[a]	Participation rate (percent)[b]		
		All	Male	Female
1900	28.5	55.5		
1910	36.9	57.4		
1920	41.7	55.6		
1930	48.8	55.0		
1940	56.2	56.0		
1950	62.2	59.2	86.4	33.9
1960	69.6	59.4	83.3	37.7
1970	82.8	60.4	79.7	43.3
1980	106.9	63.8	77.4	51.5
1990	125.8	66.5	76.4	57.5
2000	142.6	67.1	74.8	59.9
2005	149.3	66.0	73.3	59.3

a   Before 1948, the data refer to all members of the labor force 14 years of age or older; and for 1948 and after, to all labor force members 16 years or older.

b   Before 1948, the participation rate is defined as the ratio of the civilian labor force to the civilian noninstitutional population 14 years of age or older; and for 1948 and after, it refers to the same ratio for those 16 years of age or older.

Sources: U.S. Department of Commerce, Census Bureau (1975). *Historical Statistics of the United States: Colonial Times to 1970*, Bicentennial Edition, Part 1, Washington, DC; Council of Economic Advisers, *Economic Report of the President, 1994 and 2008.*

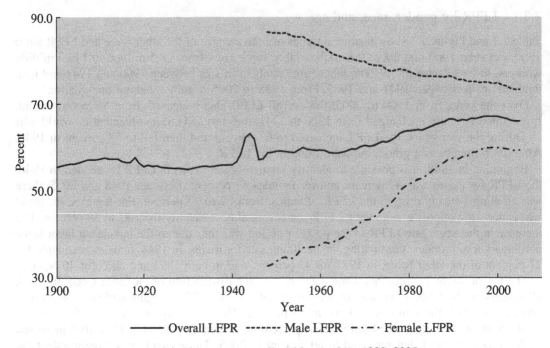

Figure 7.1   Labor force participation rates (overall and by gender), 1900–2005

Table 7.2   Percentage composition of the labor force by age, gender, and race, 1950–2005

Demographic group	Year					
	1950	*1970*	*1988*	*1994*	*2000*	*2005*
A. Age class						
Under 25	18.5	21.6	18.5	16.5	15.8	14.9
25–54	64.3	61.0	69.1	71.6	71.1	68.8
55–64	12.3	13.6	9.7	8.9	10.1	12.7
65+	4.9	3.9	2.7	2.9	3.0	3.5
Total	100.0	100.0	100.0	100.0	100.0	100.0
B. Race and gender						
White males	62.5[a]	55.6	47.9	48.3	47.8	47.9
Black males	6.6[a]	6.3	6.5	5.6	5.7	5.7
White females	26.8[a]	33.3	39.2	40.1	40.1	39.9
Black females	4.1[a]	4.9	6.4	5.9	6.4	6.5
Total	100.0[a]	100.0	100.0	100.0	100.0	100.0

a   1954.

Sources: Bureau of Labor Statistics (1990). *Handbook of Labor Statistics, 1989*, Bulletin 2340; and Bureau of Labor Statistics (1995). *Employment and Earnings*, January; www.data.bls.gov.

progression of the "baby boomers" first as new entrants into the labor force during the 1970s, then as middle-aged workers in the 1980s, and finally as older workers in the mid-2000s. During the 1980s, the number of new entrants, members of the "baby dearth generation," fell sharply.

Older workers declined rather steadily as a share of the labor force from 1950 to 1994. The proportion in age group 55–64 fell from 12 percent in 1950 to 9 percent in 1994, and the proportion 65 or older fell from 4.9 to 2.9 percent. This trend was largely a consequence, as we shall see in Chapter 15, of improved social security and other retirement benefits. However, from 1994 to 2005, the trend reversed with the share of age group 55–64 rising from 9 to 13 percent, as the baby boomers entered this age group. The share of age group 65 and over also rose slightly, from 2.9 to 3.5 percent, as the elderly population increased due to rising life expectancies.

There were also important changes in the racial and gender make-up of the labor force. White males, who constituted 63 percent of the labor force in 1954, fell to about half in 1985 and to 48 percent in 1994, where they remained through 2005. Black males comprised a fairly constant 6 to 7 percent of the labor force. White females, in contrast, increased their representation in the labor force, from 27 percent in 1954 to 40 percent in 2005, and black females also increased as a share of the labor force from 4.1 percent in 1954 to 6.5 percent in 2005.

Table 7.3, along with Figures 7.2 and 7.3, provide additional highlights of some of the important changes in the demographic make-up of the labor force. In this table, LFPRs are recorded separately by age group, gender, and race in 1954 and 2005. There are striking differences in the LFPR among white males in different age groups. In 1954, about half of 16–17-year-old white males were in the labor force, about 70 percent in the 18–19 age bracket, over 95 percent in the 25–54 age bracket, close to 90 percent in the 55–64 age group, and 40 percent of the elderly.

Between 1954 and 2005, the LFPR of white male teenagers showed a large decline (between 10 and 15 percentage points), while the LFPR of prime-age (25–54) white males showed a more modest decline (about 5 percentage points). The biggest change occurred for older men. Among white males aged 55 to 64, the participation rate began to decline in the early 1960s and dropped almost steadily from 89 percent in 1954 to 70 percent in 2005. This decline is attributable to the increase in social security and pension benefits available for early retirement. There was also an

Table 7.3 Civilian labor force participation rates by age, gender, and race groups, 1954 and 2005

Age group	White males		Nonwhite males			White females		Nonwhite females		
			Both	Black	Hispanic			Both	Black	Hispanic
	1954	2005	1954	2005	2005	1954	2005	1954	2005	2005
16–17	47.1	33.5	46.7	20.4	24.5	29.3	37.2	24.5	21.2	22.2
18–19	70.5	60.7	78.4	48.0	61.6	52.1	59.5	37.7	44.3	49.3
20–24	86.3	81.4	91.1	70.1	84.1	44.4	71.0	49.6	68.1	59.4
25–34	97.5	93.0	96.3	85.5	93.3	32.5	73.7	49.7	78.5	62.4
35–44	98.2	93.0	96.6	85.5	93.1	39.3	75.4	57.5	79.7	68.2
45–54	96.8	89.0	93.2	78.6	87.7	39.8	76.7	53.4	73.3	66.6
55–64	89.1	70.4	83.0	57.3	69.3	29.1	57.5	41.2	53.7	48.4
65+	40.4	20.0	41.2	17.1	20.1	9.1	11.4	12.2	11.4	9.3
Total	85.6	74.1	85.2	67.3	80.1	33.3	58.9	46.1	61.6	55.3

Sources: Bureau of Labor Statistics (1990). *Handbook of Labor Statistics 1989*, Bulletin 2340; Bureau of Labor Statistics (1995) *Employment and Earnings*, January; www.data.bls.gov.

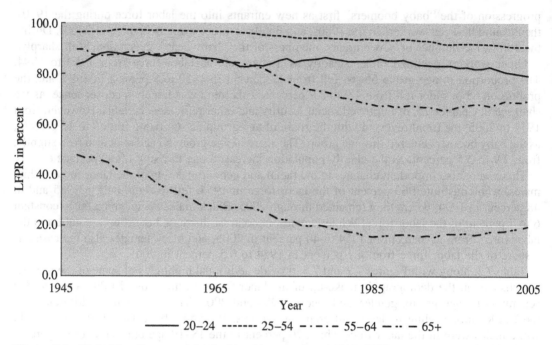

Figure 7.2   Male labor force participation rates by age group, 1947–2005

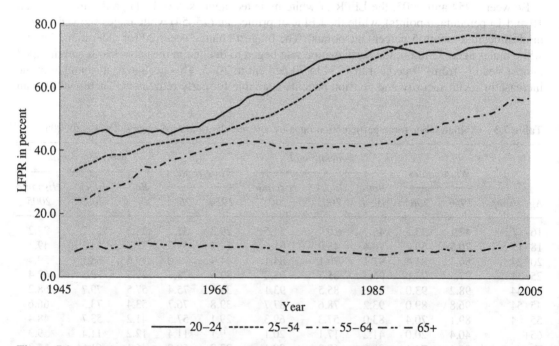

Figure 7.3   Female labor force participation rates by age group, 1947–2005

almost continuous drop in the LFPR of white males 65 and over, from 48 percent in 1947 to 20 percent in 2005. This is likewise a consequence of the continual improvement in retirement benefits over this period.

The LFPRs show the same pattern across age groups for nonwhite males, rising with age, peaking in the 25–54 age bracket, and then declining with age. However, historical trends differ between 1954 and 1977. Overall, the LFPR of nonwhite males dropped from 85 percent in 1954 to 71 percent in 1977 and then declined even more to 67 percent among black males in 2005. The decline in the LFPR of nonwhite teenagers was particularly marked, reflecting in part the increasing time spent in school. The drop in participation rates among prime-aged nonwhite males was also sharp. This change may, in part, be attributable to the discouraged worker effect – that is, the withdrawal from the labor force of individuals whose skills or schooling are insufficient to allow suitable employment.

Two other factors have been cited to explain the lower LFPR of nonwhite males relative to white males over the last two decades. The first is a higher incidence of disability among nonwhite males. The second is that a higher percentage of nonwhite males are single than white males, and participation rates tend to be lower among single men than among married men. It is also interesting to note that Hispanic males had about the same participation rates as white (non-Hispanic) males in 2005 (actually higher overall). We shall discuss differences in LFPR by race in more detail in Chapter 13.

The pattern of labor force participation by age group was considerably different for females than for males, and among white females there have been notable changes in the postwar period. Among white females, the labor force pattern of the 1950s was characterized by a peak participation rate in the 18–19 age bracket. The participation rate declined during the child-bearing years (ages 20–34), increased during the child-rearing years (35–54), and then declined again after age 54. This pattern generally characterized white female labor force behavior until the early 1960s. After this point, there was a rapid acceleration in labor force participation among all age groups, though particularly among those in the child-bearing and child-rearing age groups. Overall, the LFPR of white females increased from 33 percent in 1954 to 59 percent in 2005. By 2005, participation rates for white females had a very similar structure to those of men, rising with age, peaking in the 35–44 age group, and then declining with age.

The major reasons for this change in labor force behavior are, first, that a larger share of newly married women continued to work after marriage, and, second, that an increasing number of married women returned to work while their children were young. A number of explanations have been offered. The first is that the housewife's productivity in the home was greatly amplified by the greater availability of home appliances, processed foods, and various outside services such as child care, restaurants, and cleaning. As a result, much of the woman's time has been freed from housework, allowing more time for outside employment. A second reason is that there has been a secular decline in the average work week and a shorter work week has allowed an increasing number of married women to hold a full-time or part-time job while working in the home.

A third factor is the trend toward smaller families, which began in the 1950s, and the resultant reduction in child care responsibilities. A fourth reason is that traditional roles in U.S. society, particularly those for females, have undergone a major transformation since about 1980 and, as a result, it is more socially acceptable for married women to work. A fifth factor is that during the postwar period there has been a large increase in the demand for traditional female jobs, such as clerical, secretarial, teaching, nursing, and health care workers, coupled with rising real wages for these positions. Moreover, many occupations that were formerly largely closed to women such as law and medicine became much more open to female workers.

The labor force patterns of nonwhite females were considerably different from those of white females in 1954, and historical changes have been less pronounced. In 1954, the LFPR of nonwhite females by age group was similar to that of males, increasing with age, peaking in the 35–44 age bracket, and then declining with age. The overall LFPR for nonwhite females was 46 percent in 1954, compared to 33 percent for white females. Between 1954 and 2005, the LFPR rose from 46 percent for nonwhite females to 62 percent for black females (and 55 percent for Hispanic women). Upward trends characterized every age group, except teenagers and those 65 and over, but they were less pronounced than for white females. By 2005, both the overall LFPR and the pattern of LFPR by age group were very similar among nonwhite females and white females.

One seeming paradox is that despite the rising LFPR of women and the growing share of women in the labor force, their wages have been catching up to those of men, particularly since 1980. This development appears paradoxical from the point of view of labor demand since as the relative supply of a factor of production increases, its relative price (in this case, its relative wage) normally declines. However, as we shall see in Chapter 14, women's relative earnings rose because their average years of experience also increased and because they were able to enter occupations previously closed to them. Therefore, the composition of the female labor force shifted toward women who brought skills that were better rewarded in the labor market. In addition, more women decided to work because their earnings were rising. We shall return to the topic of gender differences in earnings and LFPR in more detail in Chapter 14.

7.3.2 Two-earner households

As noted above, one of the most striking changes in labor force behavior in the postwar period has been the large increase in participation rates among married women. This trend is highlighted in Table 7.4, which shows the number of families with two or more wage earners. Between 1954

Table 7.4 Number of families with two or more wage earners, 1954–2005

Year	All two-earner families		Husband–wife earners	
	Number (1,000s)	Percent of total families	Number (1,000s)	Percent of married couple families
1954	16,872	43.6		
1958	19,742	47.9		
1962	22,143	49.6		
1967	26,380	52.9	18,888	43.6
1972	28,706	53.0	21,279	45.7
1976	30,171	52.5	23,104	48.0
1979	32,949	55.0	25,595	52.1
1983	33,473	53.5	26,119	52.1
1987	37,085	56.5	29,369	56.6
1995	39,523	56.8	29,999	55.7
2000	42,134	57.1	31,095	56.2
2005	41,713	53.9	31,398	54.2

Sources: U.S. Census Bureau, Current Population Reports, Series P-60, Nos. 20, 24, 27, 30, 33, 35, 37, 39, 41, 43, 47, 51, 53, 59, 66, 75, 80, 85, 90, 97, 101, 105, 114, 118, 123; U.S. Department of Labor, Bureau of Labor Statistics (1990). *Handbook of Labor Statistics 1989*, Bulletin 2340; U.S. Census Bureau (1995). *Income, Poverty, and Valuation of Noncash Benefits: 1993*, Series P60-168, February; www.census.gov/hhes.

and 2005, the number of such families grew by almost two and a half times, whereas the total number of families grew by 85 percent. As a result, the proportion of families with two or more earners increased from 44 to 54 percent.

Results are also shown for the number of families in which both the husband and wife worked. Between 1967 and 1987, their number grew by 55 percent, and the proportion of married couple families in which both husband and wife worked increased from 44 to 57 percent. By the 1980s, the "typical" married family was one in which both spouses were at work. However, between 1987 and 2005 there was a slight decline in the share to 54 percent, as many wives withdrew from the labor force.

The growth in two-earner families helps to explain the apparent anomaly that while real wages have been declining since 1973, median family income has remained relatively constant, at least until 1989 (see Chapter 2 for more details). The increased labor force participation of wives has helped compensate for the falling income of their husbands. Moreover, the increasing presence of working wives in the labor force is one factor explaining the widening disparities of family income since the 1970s, particularly between married couples and single men and women. According to data from the U.S. Census Bureau, the median income of households with two earners was 85 percent greater than those with only one earner in 2005 ($72,687 versus $39,368).[5]

7.3.3   Educational attainment of the labor force

Another striking trend is the increasing educational attainment of the labor force, as documented in Table 7.5. The median years of schooling of the entire labor force increased from 10.9 years in 1952 to 12.7 years in 1982 and to 13.3 years in 1994.[6] In 1952, 38 percent of the labor force had not attended any high school, but by 2005 the proportion was only 4 percent. While 43 percent of workers had graduated high school in 1952, close to 90 percent of the labor force were high school graduates in 2005. In 1952, 16 percent of the labor force had attended some college, whereas over 60 percent did in 2005. By 2005, almost one-third of the labor force consisted of college graduates.[7]

The gains in educational attainment were even more pronounced among nonwhite males than in the labor force as a whole. In 1952, their median level of schooling was 7.2 years; in 1962 it had risen to 9.0 years; by 1977 it was 12.1 years; and in 1984, the median was 12.4 years for black males and 12.0 for Hispanic males.[8] In 1952, only 32 percent of the nonwhite male labor force had more than an elementary school education, whereas in 2005 the figure had risen to 97 percent for black males. Only 15 percent of the nonwhite male labor force had graduated from high school in 1952, compared to 86 percent for black males in 2005. While only 5 percent had attended some college in 1952, 48 percent of black male workers completed at least one year of college in 2005 and 19 percent had graduated from college.[9]

By 2005 the gap in educational attainment between black and white males had narrowed considerably. There are two reasons that explain this important development. The first is the greatly expanded educational opportunities provided to nonwhites beginning with the 1954 Supreme Court decision to desegregate public schools and continuing with federal legislation during the 1960s, particularly the Civil Rights Act of 1964, providing for increasing access to educational institutions for nonwhites. The second is the "drop-out" of many older, poorly educated black males from the labor force. The gains made by black men in educational performance is one principal reason why the gap in earnings between them and white men narrowed over the postwar period. See Chapter 13 for more discussion of racial differences in earnings and educational attainment.

Historical trends for white females also differ from those for white males. The median level of schooling of white females in the labor force was already 12.1 in 1952, considerably higher

Table 7.5 Educational attainment of the labor force, 1952–2005 (percentage distribution of workers by schooling level)

Year	Elementary school	High school 1–3 years	High school 4 years	College 1–3 years	College 4+ years	Total	Median years of schooling (years)
A. All workers							
1952	37.5	18.5	26.6	8.3	7.9	100.0	10.9
1972	15.2	16.6	40.0	14.0	14.1	100.0	12.5
1994	4.0	8.8	34.7	29.3	23.3	100.0	13.3
2005	3.5	6.4	29.7	27.4	32.9	100.0	—
B. White males							
1952	38.2	18.9	24.6	8.4	8.5	100.0	10.8
1972	16.0	16.1	36.8	14.9	16.3	100.0	12.5
1994	4.9	9.2	33.4	26.4	26.1	100.0	—
2005	4.7	7.9	30.8	27.4	29.2	100.0	—
C. Nonwhite males							
1952	68.1	15.0	9.5	3.4	1.9	100.0	7.2
1972	29.0	24.0	30.0	8.8	8.1	100.0	11.6
1994: Blacks	4.0	12.8	43.4	25.9	13.9	100.0	—
2005: Blacks	2.5	11.0	38.9	29.0	18.6	100.0	—
D. White females							
1952	26.3	18.4	36.9	9.6	8.3	100.0	12.1
1972	10.7	15.1	47.7	14.2	12.3	100.0	12.5
1994	2.9	7.7	35.1	31.0	23.4	100.0	—
2005	2.4	5.6	28.4	33.0	30.5	100.0	—
E. Nonwhite females							
1952	61.6	17.1	12.6	4.0	3.6	100.0	8.1
1972	19.8	24.2	37.2	10.5	8.3	100.0	12.2
1994: Blacks	2.1	10.8	38.6	32.5	16.0	100.0	—
2005: Blacks	1.4	9.2	33.3	34.0	22.1	100.0	—

Sources: Bureau of Labor Statistics (1979). *Handbook of Labor Statistics 1978*, Bulletin 2000; Bureau of Labor Statistics (1986). *Handbook of Labor Statistics 1985*, Bulletin 2217; Bureau of Labor Statistics (1990). *Handbook of Labor Statistics 1989*, Bulletin 2340; http://pubdb3.census.gov/macro/032006/perinc/new04_000.htm.

than that for white males. However, schooling levels grew more slowly for white females in the labor force, and by 1984 median years of schooling were identical for the two groups, 12.8 years.

Here, we must be careful in interpreting these trends. The increase in educational attainment of the white male labor force reflected the growth in schooling levels of the white male population as a whole during this period. In contrast, trends in educational attainment of the white female labor force reflected both increases in the educational attainment of white women as a whole as well as changes in their labor force participation behavior. In 1952, the typical pattern among white females was to work for a number of years after graduating high school until marriage and then drop out of the labor force. Older women with less schooling had already left the labor force.

Between 1952 and 2005, the LFPR among females of all age groups had increased considerably, and the educational composition of the white female labor force was more representative of the white female population as a whole. In particular, older women with less schooling either remained in the labor force or entered (reentered) the labor force during the 1970s, 1980s, and 1990s. The relatively slow increase in the schooling level of the white female labor force was thus a result of increases in educational attainment among white females as a whole, which were offset to a large extent by a growing percentage of less educated white women participating in the labor force.

Trends in schooling among the nonwhite female labor force were similar to those of nonwhite males. The median years of schooling rose from 8.1 years in 1952 to 10.5 in 1962 and to 12.6 in 1984 for black females and 12.3 years for Hispanic females. By 2005, the gap in schooling levels between nonwhite and white females in the labor force had narrowed substantially. Gains in schooling among nonwhite females in the labor force are attributable to, first, greatly expanded educational opportunities for nonwhites, and, second, to the exit from the labor force of a large number of poorly educated nonwhite females.

7.4   THE INDUSTRIAL AND OCCUPATIONAL COMPOSITION OF EMPLOYMENT

The structure of employment in the United States has changed substantially since the end of World War II, and this is indicative of the changing nature of work and industrial activity in the U.S. economy. Table 7.6 shows the distribution of employment among industries over the period 1950 to 2005. One of the most dramatic changes has been in agriculture, which accounted for 14 percent of employment in 1950 and only 2 percent in 2005. This relative decline has been going on for at least the last 100 years. In 1929, for example, the fraction of total employment accounted for by agriculture was 22 percent. The proportion fell to 14 percent in 1947, 8 percent in 1960, and 4 percent in 1978. The major decline in employment in the agricultural sector was from the exodus of owners of small farms and their families.[10]

The share of employment in mining also declined between 1950 and 2005, from 1.7 to 0.4 percent. The proportion of workers in construction, after remaining roughly constant at about 4 percent from 1950 to 1953, jumped to almost 10 percent in 2005. This recent trend reflected the housing boom of the early 2000s in the United States. Another major change occurred in manufacturing, whose share of total employment fell by more than 60 percent, from 29 percent in 1950 to 12 percent in 2005. In absolute terms, employment in manufacturing peaked in 1980

Table 7.6   Percentage distribution of employment by major industry, 1950, 1970, 1993, and 2005

Industry	1950	1970	1993	2005
Agriculture	13.7	4.7	2.7	1.6
Mining	1.7	0.8	0.5	0.4
Construction	4.5	4.8	4.0	7.9
Manufacturing	29.1	26.1	15.7	11.5
Transportation and public utilities	7.7	6.1	5.0	5.2
Wholesale and retail trade	17.9	20.2	22.8	15.1
Finance, insurance, and real estate	3.6	4.9	5.8	7.2
Services	10.2	15.5	26.7	35.8
Government	11.5	16.9	16.6	15.4
Total	100.0	100.0	100.0	100.0

Sources: Council of Economic Advisers, *Economic Report of the President, 1994, 2008*; *Statistical Abstract of the United States, 2008*.

at 20.3 million workers and then fell to 14.2 million in 2005. Much discussion has recently ensued over this development, which has been labeled by some as the "deindustrialization" of the United States. However, it should be noted that much of the decline in employment in manufacturing is due to the high (labor) productivity growth of this sector. In fact, manufacturing accounted for almost the same share of total output in the early 2000s as it did in the early 1950s.[11] The share of employment in transport and public utilities also fell over this period, from 7.7 to 5.2 percent. The proportion of total employment in wholesale and retail trade, after increasing from 18 to 23 percent between 1950 and 1993, slipped to 15 percent in 2005.

If the share of employment fell in the goods-producing sectors and in trade, where did it increase? The answer is the service sectors, which absorbed most of the growth of employment in the post-war period. The percent in finance, insurance, and real estate doubled from 3.6 to 7.2 between 1950 and 2005, the percent on government payrolls rose from 12 to 15, and the share in other services (personal and business) more than tripled from 10 to 36 percent. In sum, two major developments characterized the postwar period. The first was the shrinking share of workers employed in agriculture and manufacturing, and the second was the shift of the workforce out of goods-producing sectors and into services.

Another way of dividing up the labor force is by occupation. Occupations are indicative of the type of work a person does (accountants, teachers, truck drivers, laborers, etc.), while the industry classification is indicative of the type of product the worker produces. There is, of course, some correspondence between the occupation and industry categories. For example, some occupational groups such as "farm laborers" are found only in certain industries (in this case, agriculture). However, other occupational categories, such as clerical workers, are found in a large number of industries, so that occupational trends in employment may differ from industrial trends.

Table 7.7 shows the occupational distribution of employment from 1900 to 2005. Some of the changes have been quite dramatic. Professional and technical workers doubled as a share of

Table 7.7 Percentage distribution of employment by occupational group, 1900–2005

Occupational group	1900	1950	1970	1993	2005
Professional, technical, and similar	4.3	8.6	13.8	17.5	19.6
Administrators and managers except farm	5.8	8.7	10.2	12.9	13.4
Clerical	3.0	12.3	17.4	15.6	13.9
Sales	4.5	7.0	6.1	11.9	11.7
Craft and similar	10.5	14.2	12.8	11.2	10.8
Operatives	12.8	20.4	18.2	10.4	12.6
Laborers, nonfarm	12.5	6.6	5.0	3.9	—
Private household	5.4	2.6	2.0	0.8	
Service (except household)	3.6	7.8	10.5	13.1	
Private household and service					17.1
Farmers and farm managers	20.0	7.4	2.1		
Farm laborers	17.8	4.4	1.8		
Farmers, farm managers, farm laborers				2.8	0.8
Total	100.0	100.0	100.0	100.0	100.0

Sources: U.S. Department of Commerce, Census Bureau (1978). *Historical Statistics of the U.S.: Colonial Times to 1970*, Bicentennial Edition, Part 2, Washington, DC; Bureau of Labor Statistics (1979). *Handbook of Labor Statistics 1978*, Bulletin 2000; U.S. Census Bureau, *Statistical Abstract of the United States, 1994 and 2008*.

employment from 4.3 percent in 1900 to 8.6 percent in 1950 and more than doubled again to 19.6 percent in 2005. Managers and administrators also increased substantially as a proportion of the workforce, from 6 percent in 1900 to 13 percent in 2005. Clerical workers showed a sharp increase in their share, from 3 percent in 1900 to 16 percent in 1993, followed by a reduction to 14 percent in 2005. The trend in the late 1990s and early 2000s may reflect the widespread introduction of computers and information technology and the consequent displacement of clerical workers.

A much higher proportion of the labor force were also engaged as sales workers by 2005 in comparison with 1900, with most of the increase apparently occurring during the 1980s.[12] The other major increase occurred for service workers (excluding private household workers), whose share rose from 4 percent in 1900 to 13 percent in 1993. The share of total service workers in employment increased further between 1993 and 2005, from 13.9 to 17.1 percent.

The proportion of the labor force employed as craft workers and operatives (that is, machine and transportation operators) was about the same in 2005 as in 1900.[13] The other occupational categories all declined substantially as a share of employment. Nonfarm laborers (that is, unskilled workers except those employed on the farm) fell from 13 percent of employment in 1900 to 4 percent in 1993.[14] Domestic servants and other household workers declined as a proportion of the employed labor force from 5 percent in 1900 to only 1 percent in 1993. Finally, farmers, farm managers, and farm laborers fell from 38 percent of total employment in 1900 to only 1 percent in 2005. In sum, the twentieth century witnessed a huge reduction in the share of unskilled and farm labor as a share of total employment and a corresponding increase in the share of white-collar workers, including professional, managerial, clerical, and sales workers.

Changes in the occupational composition of the labor force are connected to shifts in the industrial pattern of employment. The relative decline of employment in goods-producing industries, which are particularly intensive in their use of blue-collar workers, is one reason for the relative decline in the number of craft workers, operatives, and laborers in the workforce since 1950. The shift to services helps to explain the postwar rise in the share of professionals, administrators, clerical workers, and sales workers in the labor force.

Employment shifts also help account for recent trends in real wages and the distribution of labor earnings. First, since wages tend to be higher in goods-producing industries – particularly, manufacturing – than in services, the shift to services is one factor responsible for the declining real wage in the United States since 1973. Second, the dispersion of earnings is generally higher in service industries than in goods-producing sectors, so that this change also accounts, in part, for the rising earnings inequality of the 1980s and 1990s. We shall return to these developments in Chapters 9 and 11 when we consider the relation between industrial patterns of employment and earnings differences.

7.5 MEASURES OF UNEMPLOYMENT AND HISTORICAL TRENDS

Figure 7.4 shows the U.S. unemployment rate for selected years from 1900 to 2005.[15] Between 1900 and 1947, peaks (high points) and troughs (low points) in the unemployment rate are shown. All years after 1947 are shown. The most striking result is the sharp cyclical changes in the unemployment rate. This is most evident during the Great Depression. In 1929, the number of unemployed was 1.6 million and the unemployment rate was 3.2 percent. By 1933, the number of unemployed reached its twentieth-century peak of 12.8 million and the unemployment rate hit 25.2 percent. The unemployment rate fell slowly during the 1930s, and it was not until 1942, after the United States had entered World War II, that the unemployment rate fell under 5 percent. In 1944, the unemployment rate reached its lowest point ever at 1.2 percent.

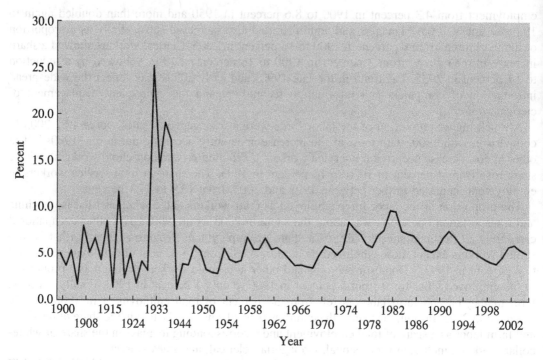

Figure 7.4   The U.S. unemployment rate, 1900–2005

By 1946, after the war had ended, the unemployment rate climbed back to 3.9 percent, and in the postwar period resumed its cyclical pattern. In 1982, the unemployment rate reached its highest level in the postwar period of 9.7 percent.[16] Moreover, for the first time since the Great Depression the number of unemployed exceeded 10 million. By the late 1980s, the unemployment rate had again fallen to the 5–6 percent range. During the 1992 recession, the unemployment rate climbed to 7.4 percent but by 2000 it was back down to 4 percent, a consequence of the technology boom years of the late 1990s. The unemployment rate increased to 6 percent in 2003 after a small recession but fell to 5.1 percent in 2005.

As noted in Section 7.2, the BLS (beginning in 1967) has categorized the unemployed into four groups depending on the reason for their joblessness: (i) *job losers*, workers who lose their job because they are fired (terminated due to poor work performance) or laid off (terminated because the job itself is eliminated); (ii) *job leavers*, those who voluntarily quit a job; (iii) *reentrants*, individuals who were previously in the labor force and are now reentering it; and (iv) *new entrants*, consisting of those who are entering the labor market for the first time. One striking result, as shown in Table 7.8, is that typically one-third to two-fifths of the unemployed consist of those who are newly entering or reentering the labor market. These are individuals who have not lost jobs but are looking for work for the first time or after an extended period of being outside the labor force.[17]

Individuals who involuntarily lost their jobs typically accounted for about half of the unemployed over the years 1967 to 2005. Of these, many were on "temporary layoff" – that is, subject to immediate recall by their employers. Workers who voluntarily quit their jobs typically accounted for about 10 percent of the unemployed.[18]

There is also a fairly strong relation between the reasons for unemployment and the overall jobless rate. In periods of low unemployment, such as 1967, 1970, 1973, and 2000, the proportion

Table 7.8 Percentage distribution of unemployment by reason for unemployment, selected years, 1967–2005

Year	Unemployment rate (percent)	Reason for unemployment (percent distribution)				Unemployment duration in weeks	
		Job losers	Job leavers	Re-entrants	New entrants	Mean	Median
1950	5.3					12.1	
1960	5.5					12.8	
1967	3.8	41.3	14.7	31.8	12.3	8.7	2.3
1970	4.9	44.2	13.4	30.0	12.3	8.6	4.9
1973	4.9	38.8	15.6	30.7	14.9	10.0	5.2
1976	7.7	49.7	12.2	26.0	12.1	15.8	8.2
1979	5.8	42.9	14.3	29.4	13.3	10.8	5.4
1982	9.7	58.7	7.9	22.3	11.1	15.6	8.7
1985	7.4	49.8	10.6	27.1	12.5	15.6	6.8
1988	5.5	46.1	14.7	27.0	12.2	13.5	5.9
1990	5.5	48.3	14.8	27.4	9.5	12.1	5.4
1992	7.4	56.4	10.4	23.7	9.5	17.9	8.8
1993	6.8	54.6	10.8	24.6	10.0	18.1	8.4
1995	5.6	46.9	11.1	34.1	7.8	16.6	8.3
2000	4.0	44.2	13.7	34.5	7.6	12.6	5.9
2001	4.7	51.1	12.3	29.9	6.7	13.1	6.8
2002	5.8	55.0	10.3	28.3	6.4	16.6	9.1
2003	6.0	55.1	9.3	28.2	7.3	19.2	10.1
2004	5.5	51.5	10.5	29.5	8.4	19.6	9.8
2005	5.1	48.3	11.5	31.4	8.8	18.4	8.9

Source: Council of Economic Advisers, *Economic Report of the President, 1994 and 2008.*

of the unemployed who were job losers was relatively low, while in periods of high unemployment, such as 1982 and 1992, layoffs increase and this becomes the primary cause of unemployment. Moreover, during economic downturns, the number of workers who voluntarily quit a job without having another job in line becomes much smaller, since the probability of finding a new job is much lower when the overall unemployment rate is high.

Another important dimension of joblessness is the **duration** of unemployment. This is the length of time during which an individual remains jobless. The economic impact of unemployment on family resources increases the longer someone is without a job. Short spells of unemployment cause relatively little economic hardship, while long periods of unemployment can be devastating to a family.

In 1948, 1953, and 1967, when the unemployment rate was under 4 percent, the mean duration of unemployment was less than 9 weeks. Moreover, over half the unemployed were out of work for less than 5 weeks. In high unemployment years, such as 1975, 1982, and 1992, the average duration of unemployment was over 14 weeks. Indeed, in 1983, it reached 20 weeks. Moreover, in these three years about a third of the unemployed were out of work for 15 weeks or more. This indicates that periods of high unemployment cause particular hardships on families, because not only are a lot of people out of work but many remain out of work for long periods of time.

It is also interesting to compare the *median* duration of unemployment with its mean duration. The median duration refers to the length of time out of work for the average unemployed worker (while the mean duration is the arithmetic average of unemployment spells of all workers unemployed at a point in time). Median duration was typically half of the mean duration. This indicates that most workers who are unemployed find new work in a relatively short period of time, while the "hard-core" unemployed may remain jobless for a considerable length of time. Even in 1983, half of all unemployed workers found work in 10 weeks or less. The reason that the mean duration was so high that year is that a substantial proportion of the unemployed remained out of work for 6 months or more.

The official unemployment rate is often considered to understate the "true" level of unemployment, because some of the unemployed are "hidden." There are two reasons for this. First, there are some individuals who would like to work but believe that no (suitable) jobs are available and therefore do not actively look for work. These individuals are referred to as "discouraged workers." Discouraged workers are not officially counted in either the ranks of the unemployed or in the labor force. Second, there are many part-time workers who would like to work full time but cannot because the requisite full-time jobs are not available. These individuals are officially counted as employed workers but should probably be considered "underemployed."

Table 7.9 provides estimates which adjust the unemployment rate for these two groups of individuals. The number of discouraged workers is added to both the labor force and the unemployment count in the adjusted unemployment rate. The part-time "unemployed" are already counted in

Table 7.9   The unemployment rate adjusted for discouraged and part-time unemployed workers, selected years, 1969–2005

Year	Official unemployment rate (percent)	Official number of unemployed workers (1,000s)	Number of discouraged workers (1,000s)	Number of part-time "unemployed" (1,000s)	Adjusted unemployment rate[a] (percent)
1969	3.5	2,831	574	2,056	6.7
1970	4.9	4,088	638	2,443	8.6
1971	5.9	4,993	774	2,675	9.9
1972	5.6	4,840	765	2,624	9.4
1973	4.9	4,304	679	2,519	8.4
1974	5.6	5,076	686	2,943	9.5
1975	8.5	7,830	1,082	3,748	13.5
1980	7.1	7,671			10.1
1985	7.2	8,313			10.6
1990	5.5	7,061			8.2
1994	5.4	7,112	400	4,400	10.9
2000	4.0	5,685	262	4,002	7.0
2005	5.1	7,580	436	5,212	8.9

a   This is defined as the ratio of the sum of the official number of unemployed workers plus the number of discouraged workers plus the number of part-time "unemployed" to the sum of the official labor force plus the number of discouraged workers.

Sources: 1969–1975: Bureau of Labor Statistics, *Employment and Training Report of the President, 1976*; 1980–1990: U.S. Department of Labor, *Report on the American Workforce, 1994*; 1994: Bureau of Labor Statistics news release of unemployment statistics for December, 1994.

the official labor force figure and are added to the ranks of the unemployed in the adjusted unemployment rate. The inclusion of discouraged workers and the part-time unemployed in the ranks of the unemployed makes a substantial difference in the unemployment rate calculation. In a special study conducted for 1969 to 1975, these adjustments added between 3 and 5 percentage points to the official unemployment rate. The main effect comes from including the part-time unemployed, which typically outnumber discouraged workers by four to one. Recently, the Bureau of Labor Statistics has included its own estimates of hidden unemployment. In 1994, the inclusion of discouraged workers and workers who worked part time because they could not find full-time jobs increased the unemployment rate from its official level of 5.4 percent to 9.0 percent. In 2005, while the official unemployment rate registered 5.1 percent, the adjusted unemployment rate was estimated to be 8.9 percent.[19]

Another issue of some importance is the relation between job vacancies and unemployment. It is quite possible for there to exist unemployed workers and job vacancies at the same time and in the same location. This is often due to mismatches between the skills required for the job openings and the (existing) skills of the unemployed workers. For example, while openings in technical fields may require very specific backgrounds, the qualifications may not be available among the ranks of the unemployed. Likewise, while vacancies may exist for unskilled jobs, unemployed workers who have received substantial training may not be willing to fill these positions.

A telling statistic is the ratio of the number of vacant positions available at a given point in time to the number of unemployed individuals. This variable is crucial in disentangling the effects of structural and frictional causes of unemployment from those of inadequate demand (Keynesian) unemployment (see Section 7.7 below). A high vacancy/unemployment ratio would suggest that there are plenty of jobs available relative to the number of people looking for work and that the primary reason for unemployment is that the skills of the job seekers are not in balance with the skills required for the vacant positions (structural unemployment) or that workers are in transition from one job to another (frictional unemployment). A low ratio, on the other hand, would suggest that there simply are not enough jobs available for those looking and the problem is an inadequate number of jobs (Keynesian unemployment).

In an analysis of job vacancies and unemployment, Abraham (1983) found that during the mid-1960s there were approximately 2.5 unemployed individuals per vacant job. During the early 1970s the ratio grew to 4.0 unemployed per vacancy, and in the late 1970s, 5.0 unemployed persons per vacant position. Abraham concluded that during the 1970s the main source of unemployment was an inadequate number of jobs being created relative to the number of people seeking work.[20]

There is a clear connection between unemployment and poverty. As we saw in Section 4.4, the poverty rate is five to six times greater in a family where the household head is unemployed than in one where he or she is employed (for example, 31.7 versus 5.6 percent in 1989). The incidence of poverty is also about four times as great in family in which the household head is not in the labor force as one in which the person is employed (for example, 21.1 versus 5.6 percent in 1989). As a result, discouraged workers who leave the workforce entirely also encounter a very high frequency of poverty.

The duration of unemployment also makes a difference with regard to both poverty and family income. From Section 4.4, the poverty rate among families in which the household head did not work at all is about eight times as great as one in which the household head worked the entire year (for example, 23.4 versus 3.2 percent in 1989) and about six times as great among families where the household head worked only part of the year compared to one where the person worked the full year (for example, 19.0 versus 3.2 percent in 1989). According to data from the U.S. Census Bureau's CPS,[21] the median income of households where the household head worked full time and full year was $63,610 in 2005, compared to $40,171 where the household head worked at a part-time job and $23,801 where the household head did not work at all.

7.6 THE INCIDENCE OF UNEMPLOYMENT

Substantial variation exists in the degree of unemployment experienced by different groups of workers. Unemployment rates vary by age, race, gender, experience level, region of the country, occupation, and industry. During periods of high unemployment, some groups may suffer particularly hard while others not at all. During periods of low overall unemployment, some groups may still experience a high incidence of joblessness. In some recessions, unemployment may be very high in certain regions of the country (such as the Midwest during the 1982–1983 downturn and California during the 1992 recession) but low in other parts of the country (the "sunbelt" in 1982 and the Midwest in 1992). The structure of unemployment may also vary across the business cycle and from one business cycle to another.

7.6.1 Jobless rates by demographic characteristic

Table 7.10 shows unemployment rates by age, gender, and race in 1957, 1977, and 1994. In 1957 and 1977, the unemployment rate was lower for white males than for white females. Indeed, the gap in unemployment rates between these two groups widened considerably over this 20-year stretch, from 0.7 to 1.8 percentage points. The increasing gap is largely due to the falling LFPR of white males and the rising participation rate of white females over this period. In particular, older white males who lost jobs dropped out of the labor force in greater numbers over time, thus reducing their unemployment rate, while the rising number of white females entering or reentering the labor force increased their overall jobless rate, since entrants and reentrants have a higher incidence of unemployment than experienced workers. However, by 1994, the jobless rate for the two groups was almost identical, as was the case in 2005.

The unemployment rate among black workers was more than double that of white males in all four years. This large difference is partly accounted for by differences in education and skills and partly by discrimination. As shown in Table 7.5, nonwhite workers had considerably less schooling than the white labor force in the 1950s. Though by the mid-1990s blacks in the labor force had just about caught up to whites in terms of median years of schooling, they still fell short with regard to the proportion who had graduated college.

An additional factor that has been cited to account for the difference in unemployment rates between whites and blacks is the high level of black migration, particularly out of the rural South. The argument is that new migrants to a region tend to experience greater unemployment than long-term residents, since the former are less aware of available jobs and have no job experience in the region. However, black migration from the South diminished considerably during the 1980s and 1990s, yet the large racial differential in unemployment rates continued to persist, suggesting that discrimination may account for a large part of the racial disparity. Moreover, the higher incidence of unemployment among black workers is an important factor accounting for the lower family income of black families relative to white ones (see Chapter 13 for more discussion).

Unemployment rates also show considerable variation among age groups. For all four race–gender groups, the highest unemployment rates were found among teenagers. The age group with the second highest unemployment rate was the 20–24-year-old group (with the exception of white males in 1957), followed by age group 25–34. Joblessness was lowest for those 35 and over.

Table 7.10   Unemployment rates by age, gender, and race, 1957, 1977, 1994 and 2005 (percent)

Age	White males	White females	Black[a] males	Black[a] females
A. 1957				
16–17	11.9	11.9	16.3	18.3
18–19	11.2	7.9	20.0	21.3
20–24	7.1	4.1	12.7	12.2
25–34	2.7	4.7	8.5	8.1
35–44	2.5	3.7	6.4	4.7
45–54	3.0	3.0	6.2	4.2
55–64	3.4	3.0	5.5	4.0
65+	8.2	3.5	5.0	4.3
All	3.6	4.3	8.3	7.3
B. 1977				
16–17	17.6	18.2	38.7	44.7
18–19	13.0	14.2	36.1	37.4
20–24	9.3	9.3	21.7	23.6
25–34	5.0	6.7	10.6	12.9
35–44	3.1	5.3	6.1	8.5
45–54	3.0	5.0	5.2	5.6
55–64	3.3	4.4	6.4	4.9
65+	4.9	4.9	8.3	3.6
All	5.5	7.3	12.4	14.0
C. 1994				
16–17	18.5	16.6	39.3	32.9
18–19	14.7	11.8	36.5	32.5
20–24	8.8	7.4	19.4	19.6
25–34	5.2	5.1	10.6	11.7
35–44	3.9	4.2	9.1	8.0
45–54	3.7	3.7	6.5	4.9
55–64	4.1	3.7	6.0	4.9
65+	3.7	3.9	8.2	4.4
All	5.4	5.2	12.0	11.0
D. 2005				
16–17	18.9	14.0	45.1	37.3
18–19	14.3	11.1	31.5	26.6
20–24	7.9	6.4	20.5	16.3
25–34	4.1	4.7	9.7	10.6
35–44	3.3	3.6	7.0	7.2
45–54	3.0	3.1	6.7	5.4
55–64	3.0	3.0	5.9	5.3
65+	3.1	3.2	7.1	6.6
All	4.4	4.4	10.5	9.5

a   Nonwhites in 1957.
Sources: U.S. Department of Labor, Bureau of Labor Statistics (1979). *Handbook of Labor Statistics, 1978*, Bulletin 2000; U.S. Department of Labor, Bureau of Labor Statistics (1990). *Handbook of Labor Statistics 1989*, Bulletin 2340; www.data.bls.gov.

The likelihood of unemployment tends to decline with age. The explanation is that teenagers who are largely new entrants in the labor force ordinarily experience a period of frictional unemployment while searching for a job (see the next section). In periods of layoff, teenagers are often the first to be let go, because they tend to have the least seniority. As workers age, they gain experience and are more likely to find a job that they find suitable. As a result, older workers are less vulnerable to layoffs because of their seniority and are less likely to quit because of dissatisfaction with their job. Moreover, if they do quit or lose their job, they are more likely to withdraw from the labor force than younger workers.[22]

Another striking result is the sharp increase in the unemployment rate among teenagers between 1957 and 1977 particularly among black youths. One explanation is that the number of teenagers entering the labor market between 1957 and 1977 increased considerably because of the postwar baby boom. The increase in the new teenager entrants was greater than the labor market could absorb. Indeed, during the 1982–1983 recession, the black youth unemployment rate climbed to close to 50 percent. By 1994 jobless incidence among young people had subsided somewhat, though by 2005 it was very high once again for 16–17-year-old black males.

Doeringer and Piore (1975) argued that the increasing unemployment rate among youths, particularly black youths, during the 1960s and 1970s reflected the closing down of employment opportunities in the primary labor market. This is evidenced, in part, by the low unemployment rates of prime-age males (mainly white males), which seem to imply that the primary labor market was essentially full during the 1970s. Youths entering the labor force were apparently forced into the secondary labor market. The high youth unemployment rate was thus partially attributable to the temporary nature of most secondary jobs and their concomitant high turnover. In addition, for those young people who did manage to find and hold onto jobs, the training they received was minimal and the advancement opportunities limited. Doeringer and Piore predicted that such early labor market experiences could eventually have unfortunate consequences as these young workers matured into prime-age workers.[23]

Shimer (2001), on the other hand, estimated the response of the unemployment rate and LFPR to exogenous variation in the youth share of the working age population. He found that, *ceteris paribus*, a 1 percent increase in the youth share increased the unemployment rate of young workers by more than 1 percent. It also raised the LFPR of young workers by about one-third of 1 percent for young workers.

The higher unemployment rates among younger workers are also reflected in a higher incidence of poverty. According to data from the U.S. Census Bureau's CPS, the poverty rate among families in age group 18–24 was 28.8 percent in 2005, compared to 12.7 percent for age group 25–44 and 6.5 percent for age group 45–54, and 5.8 percent for age group 55–64 (see Table 4.2).

Another striking difference in unemployment rates is by marital status. As shown in Table 7.11, single men experienced unemployment rates about double that among all males. This held true in both recessionary years and full-employment years. In contrast, married men faced unemployment rates that were only about two-thirds the rate for all men. Unemployment rates for men who were widowed, divorced, or separated were higher than the average male unemployment rate but lower than that for single men. One explanation of this difference in jobless rates is that married men, particularly those with children, have greater financial responsibilities and are thus likely to search harder for a job, accept a job position more quickly, and are less likely to quit a job than unmarried men. Moreover, an employer may prefer married men over unmarried men because the former are less likely to quit their jobs.[24]

The same pattern held among women. Married women experienced lower jobless rates than widowed, divorced, or separated females, and the latter group had lower unemployment rates than single (and never married) women. The differentials in unemployment rates by marital

Table 7.11 Unemployment rates by marital status, selected years, 1956–2005 (percent)

Marital status	1956	1961	1969	1975	1988	1994	2005
A. All	3.8	6.7	3.5	8.5	5.5	6.1	5.1
B. Males							
(i) All males	3.5	6.5	2.8	7.9	5.5	6.2	5.1
(ii) Single	7.7	13.1	8.0	16.1	9.9	11.0	9.5
(iii) Married, spouse present	2.3	4.6	1.5	5.1	3.3	3.7	2.8
(iv) Widowed, divorced or separated	6.2	10.3	4.0	11.0	7.0	7.4	5.6
C. Females							
(i) All females	4.3	7.2	4.7	9.3	5.6	6.0	5.1
(ii) Single	5.3	8.7	7.3	13.0	8.6	9.7	8.3
(ii) Married, spouse present	3.6	6.4	3.9	7.9	3.9	4.1	3.3
(iv) Widowed, divorced or separated	5.0	7.4	4.0	8.9	6.3	6.6	5.4

Sources: Bureau of Labor Statistics (1980). *Handbook of Labor Statistics 1979*, December, Bulletin 2070; *Economic Report of the President, 1984*; Bureau of Labor Statistics (1989). *Handbook of Labor Statistics 1990*, August, Bulletin 2340; *Monthly Labor Review*, statistical supplement; www.data.bls.gov.

status were not as pronounced among women as among men. The explanation is that unmarried women, particularly those with children to support, are likely to experience much greater financial pressure than married women. As a result, single women are more apt to be looking for a job than married ones. Moreover, married women who involuntarily lose their job often leave the labor force entirely, since there is usually another income in the family, and hence do not show up in the unemployment statistics. In contrast, single women who lose their job will generally have to search for a new one and will thus be counted among the unemployed.

Here, again, poverty rates tend to mirror the unemployment experience of different demographic groups. According to data from the U.S. Census Bureau's CPS, the poverty rate among husbands and wives living together was 5.9 percent in 2005, compared to 13.4 percent among single men, and 31.1 percent among female-headed households.[25]

7.6.2 Unemployment by industry, occupation, and region

The incidence of unemployment also shows large variation by industry of (last) employment. This is particularly true during recessionary times when certain industries are impacted more heavily than others. Comparative jobless rates are shown by major sectors of the economy for five low unemployment years and two recession years (1958 and 1975) in Table 7.12. The construction sector generally had the highest unemployment rate (in 1975 it reached 18.1 percent), followed generally by agriculture. The jobless rate among mining workers varied over time – below average in 1948, 1969, 1975, 1994, and 2005 and above average in 1988 and much higher than the overall rate in 1958. The jobless rate in manufacturing was about average during peak years but quite high during the two recession years 1958 and 1975.

The jobless rate in transportation and utilities tended to be below the national rate and that in the trade sector generally a bit above the overall rate. Both the finance, insurance, and real estate sector and the government sector had unemployment rates considerably below the overall level (about half the national rate in most years). Unemployment in the service sector had a counter-cyclical pattern, at or above the national level during prosperity and below the national level during economic downturns.

Table 7.12   Unemployment rates by industry for selected years, 1948–2005 (percent)

Industry	1948	1958	1969	1975	1988	1994	2005
All workers	3.8	6.8	3.5	8.5	5.5	6.1	5.1
Agriculture	5.5	10.3	6.0	10.3	5.2	11.3	8.3
Mining	3.0	10.9	2.8	4.0	7.9	5.4	3.1
Construction	8.7	15.3	6.0	18.1	10.6	11.8	7.4
Manufacturing	4.2	9.3	3.3	10.9	5.3	5.6	4.9
Transportation and public utilities	3.5	6.1	2.1	5.6	3.9	4.8	4.1
Wholesale and retail trade	4.7	6.8	4.1	8.7	6.2	7.4	4.9
Finance, insurance, and real estate	1.8	2.8	2.1	4.9	3.0	3.6	2.9
Services	4.8	5.7	3.5	7.1	4.9	6.1	5.4
Government	2.2	2.5	1.9	4.0	2.8	3.4	2.6

Based on industry of last employment.
Sources: Bureau of Labor Statistics (1980). *Handbook of Labor Statistics 1979*, December, Bulletin 2070; Bureau of Labor Statistics (1991). *Handbook of Labor Statistics 1990*, Bulletin 2340; *Monthly Labor Review*, March 1995, statistical supplement; U.S. Census Bureau, *Statistical Abstract of the United States, 2008*.

Table 7.13   Unemployment rates by occupation for selected years, 1958–2005 (percent)

Occupation	1958	1969	1975	1979	2000	2005
All workers	6.8	3.5	8.5	5.8	4.0	5.1
A. White-collar workers	3.1	2.1	4.7	3.3	—	—
(i) Professional and technical	2.0	1.3	3.2	2.4	1.9	2.4
(ii) Managers and administrators	1.7	0.9	3.0	2.1	1.6	2.2
(iii) Sales	4.1	2.9	5.8	3.9	4.1	5.0
(iv) Clerical	4.4	3.0	6.6	4.6	3.6	4.6
B. Blue-collar workers	10.2	3.9	11.7	6.9	—	—
(i) Craft and similar	6.8	2.2	8.3	4.5	4.3	5.8
(ii) Operatives	11.0	4.4	13.2	7.7	5.2	6.5
(iii) Nonfarm laborers	15.1	6.7	15.6	10.8	—	—
C. Service workers	6.9	4.2	8.6	7.1	5.2	6.4
D. Farmers and farm laborers	3.2	1.9	3.5	3.8	10.2	9.6

Based on occupation held in last job.
Sources: Bureau of Labor Statistics (1980). *Handbook of Labor Statistics 1979*, December, Bulletin 2070; U.S. Census Bureau, *Statistical Abstract of the United States, 2008*.

Unemployment rates also vary by occupation, as shown in Table 7.13.[26] The incidence of unemployment among white-collar workers was considerably lower than for blue-collar or service workers. Managers and administrators experienced the lowest rate of joblessness, about one-third of the overall rate. Professional and technical workers also enjoyed a very low rate of unemployment, slightly above that of managers. The incidence of joblessness among sales and clerical workers generally fell a bit below that for all workers.

The unemployment rate for blue-collar workers was greater than the overall rate. The differential was particularly wide during recession years, reflecting reduced demand for construction and manufactured products. There were considerable differences in the incidence of joblessness among the five blue-collar categories. Craft and skilled workers had the lowest unemployment rate in this group. The jobless rate for the skilled trades was about equal to the national average during economic downturns and fell below the national average during periods of prosperity. The jobless rate for operatives was considerably above the level for all workers, while that for the unskilled nonfarm labor was almost double the national rate. The incidence of unemployment among service workers was about the same level as the overall rate during times of high unemployment and somewhat greater than average during low unemployment periods. Farmers and farm laborers experienced jobless rates about half that for all workers until 1980 or so but about twice the overall rate in the 2000s.

The general pattern that emerges from Table 7.13 is that unemployment rates are considerably lower in occupations that require either substantial training, such as the craft trades, or high levels of schooling, such as the professions. An explanation of this comes from the internal labor market model (see Chapter 8). The argument is that firms invest more heavily in their primary labor force, who tend to be white-collar and skilled workers, than in their secondary labor force, who tend to be semiskilled and unskilled workers. As a result, during downturns, firms are likely to lay off their less skilled workers first. Another explanation of the difference in unemployment rates among skill groups is that unemployed skilled workers usually have an easier time finding a new job than jobless workers with little or no skills.

One reason for the higher unemployment rates of black workers is that they are disproportionately represented in the lower-skilled occupations, particularly as unskilled laborers and service workers. However, this is only part of the story, because even within occupations, black workers generally experience higher jobless rates than comparable white workers. This is also true between black workers and white workers with the same schooling, experience level, and on-the-job training. Differences in jobless rates are another aspect of labor market discrimination experienced by black workers (see Part III for more discussion).

Differences in industrial and occupational mix among regions of the country cause major differences in the jobless rate experienced by various localities in the United States. As shown in Table 7.14, in 1975, which was a recession year with a national unemployment rate of 8.5 percent, the unemployment rate was 9.5 percent in the Northeast, 7.7 percent in the South, 7.9 percent in the North Central states, and 9.2 percent in the West. The variation in jobless rates by state was even greater. The highest state unemployment rate was 11.2 percent in Massachusetts that year and the lowest was 3.6 percent in North Dakota. Even within regions of the country there were large differences in jobless rates. In the South, unemployment rates ranged from a low of 5.6 percent in Texas to a high of 10.7 percent in Florida, and in the West the range was from 4.2 percent in Wyoming to 12.1 percent in Arizona.[27]

In 1994, which was a relatively low unemployment year for the nation as a whole, there was again a large spread in jobless rates. The lowest rate of unemployment occurred in Nebraska, at 2.6 percent, and the highest in Louisiana, at 8.1 percent. The same was true for 2005, which was also a low unemployment year. The spread was from 3.4 percent in North Dakota to 6.7 percent in Alaska. In many cases, states that had high unemployment rates in one year experienced low unemployment in the other year. This was the case for Massachusetts, whose jobless rate was the second highest in 1975 but below average in 1994 and 2005, and Alaska, whose rate of joblessness was lower than average in 1975 but among the highest in 1994 and 2005. Such switches in a state's relative unemployment ranking may reflect changes in demand composition, particularly between a recession year and a boom year. Over the long term, these shifts often reflect changes in industrial composition, as, for example, in New Hampshire and Massachusetts, where light industries such as electronics have gradually replaced textiles and shoes.

Table 7.14 Unemployment rates by selected states, 1975, 1994, and 2005 (percent)

Occupation	1975	1994	2005
United States	8.5	6.1	5.1
A. Northeast	9.5		
Massachusetts	11.2	5.5	4.9
New Hampshire	9.0	3.8	3.7
New York	9.5	6.3	5.0
Pennsylvania	8.3	6.9	4.9
B. South	7.7		
Delaware	9.7	4.5	4.3
Florida	10.7	6.8	3.6
Oklahoma	7.2	5.7	4.6
Texas	5.6	5.5	5.4
C. North Central	7.9		
Illinois	7.1	5.0	5.6
Michigan	12.5	4.6	6.6
Nebraska	4.2	2.6	4.0
North Dakota	3.6	3.1	3.4
D. West	9.2		
Alaska	6.9	7.4	6.7
Arizona	12.1	6.1	4.8
California	9.9	7.7	5.3
Wyoming	4.2	4.5	3.6

Source: Bureau of Labor Statistics (1980). *Handbook of Labor Statistics 1979*, December, Bulletin 2070; *Monthly Labor Review*, March 1995, statistical supplement; *Statistical Abstract of the United States, 2008*.

7.7 TYPES OF UNEMPLOYMENT

What causes unemployment? This subject has occupied economic writings for the last hundred years. Today, economists typically identify four different types of unemployment: (i) frictional; (ii) seasonal; (iii) structural; and (iv) deficient aggregate demand. These distinctions are important because each type leads to a different form of policy remedy.

7.7.1 Frictional unemployment

Frictional unemployment refers to joblessness caused by a temporary lack of smoothness in job transitions. This type of unemployment often characterizes workers who have quit their job and are actively searching for a new one and to new entrants and reentrants to the labor force who are searching for a position. It is also associated with search time for a new job, since longer search time increases the amount of frictional unemployment. Frictional unemployment is related to cyclical movements in the economy and structural change. In principle, better job vacancy information and better employment markets could reduce the level of frictional unemployment. Since frictional unemployment arises when workers change jobs or enter the job market, this type of unemployment is viewed as "voluntary" insofar as workers quit one position to search for another.

Frictional unemployment occurs because the labor market is dynamic and constantly changing and information on available jobs is imperfect. As a result, it takes time for a jobless worker to find an appropriate new job. This is true even if the size of the labor force is unchanging, since some workers will leave the labor force while new people enter it. In addition, shifts in demand composition will cause some industries to lay off workers and others to look for new employees. Because information is imperfect, matches between individuals looking for work and employers seeking to hire cannot be instantly made. Thus, even if the aggregate demand for labor equals the aggregate supply, there may still be simultaneously present workers who are unemployed and job vacancies.

Because of frictional unemployment, there will still be some unemployment even when the economy is operating at "full employment." However, the level of frictional unemployment is particularly sensitive to the kinds of job placement services and institutional arrangements that exist in the labor market. In the United Kingdom, the unemployment rate was under 3 percent during much of the 1960s, and, in West Germany, it fell under 1 percent in both 1963 and 1973. The lower unemployment rates in these two countries may have partly reflected the fact that employers were required by law to register all job vacancies with the government. However, more recent evidence suggests that job registration may not be a cure-all for frictional unemployment because as of the first quarter of 2008 unemployment rates were higher in both Germany (8.0 percent) and the United Kingdom (5.2 percent) than in the United States (4.9 percent).[28]

7.7.2   Seasonal unemployment

Another source of joblessness is seasonal fluctuations in business activity. These are usually associated with climatic changes or seasonal changes in behavior. The most obvious example is agriculture, where the level of employment varies according to the weather and the growing seasons of different crops. This is particularly true during harvesting, when the demand for farm labor is very high. As a result, many workers migrate from one place to another to meet the harvesting schedule of crops in different regions of the country.

Another industry affected by weather conditions is construction in the Northeast and the Midwest. During winter months, construction slows down considerably in these states, as does its employment. Food processing is also directly affected by weather, as many fruits and vegetables must be canned soon after picking. The tourist industry is likewise extremely seasonal in nature. Buying habits also change over the seasons. This is particularly true in retailing, where a large proportion of activity is directly related to the Christmas season. (In many stores, one-third to nearly half the sales take place during December.) The garment industry is also affected by the seasonal change in fashions. Likewise, employment in the automobile industry usually falls during the summer, as the factories are retooled for the new model year.

Seasonal declines in employment in one industry or location do not necessarily produce a corresponding rise in joblessness. Migratory farm workers may, for example, continue to find employment by traveling south during harvesting season. Moreover, workers laid off in one industry due to seasonal factors may find work in another industry in a seasonal upswing. Some seasonal workers may quit the labor force after being laid off (for example, students working in the tourist trade during the summer returning to school in the fall or housewives employed in the retail trade during the Christmas season). However, seasonal shifts in employment may not be sufficient to offer employment to all workers laid off for seasonal reasons.

Seasonal employment may also arise due to shifts in the supply of labor. In particular, the labor force usually expands during the summer as students pour into the labor market looking for work and contracts during the fall as young people return to school.[29]

7.7.3   Structural unemployment

Another source of unemployment is from discrepancies that arise between the job skills required by existing industries and the job skills possessed by the labor force. Structural unemployment is usually a local phenomenon and arises from three principal causes. The first is shifts in the structure of product demand either across industries or across regions of the country. This will cause workers to be laid off in one industry (or locality) and vacancies to occur in another industry (or locality). In many cases, the new positions require skills different than those the displaced workers possess. In such cases, the displaced workers would remain jobless even though vacancies exist in their local labor market. A classic example is Appalachia in the 1960s, where the shift of jobs away from low-skilled positions left many uneducated residents jobless. This type of unemployment differs from frictional unemployment, because unemployment is not eliminated by continued search or better information. Structural unemployment is ultimately a result of a mismatch between the skills of the labor force in a given locality and the skills in demand.

A second cause of structural unemployment is technological change, which may render some kinds of specialized skills obsolete. The development of the automobile industry in the early part of this century, for example, made blacksmithing and related trades virtually obsolete. The widespread use of computers over the last two decades has displaced many kinds of clerical skills (telephone operators and stenographers, for example). Displaced workers with specialized skills may be unable to use them in other industries and may remain jobless because they have no suitable substitute skills. A related factor is globalization and changes in comparative advantage among countries. If a less developed country (like China) can produce certain manufactured products (like steel and cement) relatively cheaper than the United States, then these industries may decline in the United States. It should be noted, however, that technological change does not necessarily lead to structural unemployment or, indeed, to joblessness. Though technological change is normally labor saving (that is, it leads to the substitution of capital for labor), the reduced costs of production, if passed on to the consumer in lowered prices, will increase product demand and may also cause employment in the firm or industry to expand (depending on the elasticity of the product demand curve).

A third source of structural unemployment emanates from the supply side. Demographic changes and changes in the labor force participation rates may alter the composition of skills in the labor force. For example, during the 1970s, there was a large influx of young people (the baby-boom generation) and first-time female workers into the labor force. As a result, there was a higher concentration of less experienced and lower skilled workers in the labor force which were out of balance with the skills in demand by industry.

The existence of both frictional and structural unemployment may cause joblessness to occur even if the aggregate demand for labor is in balance with the aggregate supply of labor. This level of joblessness is referred to as the "full-employment" unemployment rate or the *natural rate of unemployment*. There has been some debate among macroeconomists in recent years about exactly what the natural rate is. However, most believe that the full-employment unemployment rate has risen since the late 1950s. Gordon (1981), for example, estimated that the natural rate of unemployment rate was 4.3 percent in 1957, 4.9 percent in 1968, and 5.6 percent in 1979. Analysis by Juhn, Murphy, and Topel (1991) led them to the conclusion that the natural rate may have settled at about 5 percent during the late 1980s, while Adams and Coe (1992) estimated a natural rate of 5.75 percent for the late 1980s.

There are two major reasons why the natural rate may have risen between the 1950s and the 1980s. The first is the growing proportion of females in the labor force, who, on average, had less experience and labor market skills than male workers. This increased the difficulty of job placements, particularly among new entrants and reentrants to the labor force. Second, there were significant changes in technology and industrial structure in the 1970s and 1980s from the widespread introduction of computers and information technology. This caused many skills to become obsolete, particularly in the clerical occupations, and increased the difficulty of matching skills among unemployed workers with those skills required by the new technology.

In more recent literature on this subject, attention shifted to the **NAIRU** – the non-accelerating inflation rate of unemployment. In this literature, the NAIRU is also called the "full-employment" unemployment rate, which is sometimes termed the "inflation-threshold unemployment rate": if actual unemployment falls below the NAIRU, the inflation rate is likely to rise quickly (accelerate). In this literature as well, the NAIRU is also referred to as the "natural rate of unemployment," although this term describes an estimated unemployment rate derived from the market's actual performance while the NAIRU is calculated from the Philips curve. The point at which the Philips curve, which relates unemployment to inflation, intersects the horizontal axis indicates the NAIRU. In terms of output, the NAIRU corresponds to potential output, the highest level of real GDP (or the "natural gross domestic product") that can be sustained at any one time.

The idea behind the natural rate hypothesis is that any given labor market structure must involve a certain amount of unemployment, including frictional unemployment associated with individuals changing jobs and possibly classical unemployment arising from real wages being held above the market-clearing level by minimum wage laws, trade unions, or other labor market institutions. Unexpected inflation might allow unemployment to fall below the natural rate by temporarily depressing real wages, but this effect would dissipate once expectations about inflation were corrected. Only with continuously accelerating inflation could rates of unemployment below the natural rate be maintained.

Others argued that the actual level of the natural rate could itself be the consequence of past macroeconomic events and the new historical norms that thereby became established. This process was referred to as hysteresis or path dependency, whereby the present state of affairs depends on the historical process by which it was reached. In this sense, there may be little that is "natural" about the natural rate of unemployment.[30]

The analysis supporting the natural rate hypothesis was controversial, and empirical evidence suggested that the natural rate varied over time in ways that could not easily be explained by changes in labor market structures. As a result the "natural rate" terminology was largely supplanted by that of the NAIRU, which referred to a rate of unemployment below which inflation would accelerate, but did not imply a prediction that the rate would be stable over time.

Mankiw and Ball (2002) considered the role of the NAIRU concept in business cycle theory. They argued that the exact value of the NAIRU is hard to measure, in part because it changes over time. They then investigated why the NAIRU fell in the United States during the 1990s. Their most promising hypothesis was that the decline in the NAIRU was attributable to the acceleration in productivity growth that occurred in the United States during the 1990s.[31]

7.7.4   Deficient demand (Keynesian) unemployment

A fourth major cause of unemployment is a decline in aggregate demand. Also referred to as cyclical unemployment, this type of joblessness occurs in business cycle downturns when the aggregate demand for products and, correspondingly, that for labor falls. One of Keynes' major contributions was to analyze this form of unemployment. The high unemployment rates of the Great Depression (reaching 25 percent) were attributable to deficient demand, as were the high unemployment rates associated with postwar recessions (primarily 1958 at 6.8 percent, 1961 at 6.7 percent, 1975 at 8.5 percent, 1982–1983 at 9.7 and 9.6 percent, and 1992 at 7.4 percent).

When aggregate demand falls, firms in industries with reduced demand respond in two ways. First, they may temporarily lay off workers. In many cases, such workers are subject to immediate recall by the company. Second, they may stop replacing employees who voluntarily quit the firm. For both reasons, the number of unemployed will increase, as will the unemployment rate. In principle, if wages were perfectly flexible, the real wage should fall in the face of such mounting unemployment and the jobless rate decline. Yet, in actuality, real wages are not downward flexible and the macroeconomic response to falling aggregate demand is rising unemployment.[32] From a standard neoclassical view of the labor market, this type of unemployment is inefficient since the wage will not fall to clear the labor market.

There are three major reasons why money wages at least may be quite rigid in the short run. First, collective bargaining agreements in unionized industries do not allow the employer to unilaterally reduce wages. This explanation, however, begs the question of why unions would prefer layoffs to a reduction in wages in the face of reduced demand. The rationale is that in most union agreements, the last hired are the first to be let go during layoffs. The most experienced workers are normally the last to be laid off. Therefore, most layoffs affect only a small percentage of union members and these are likely to be the newest ones. A reduction of wages, on the other hand, will affect all union members, including the most experienced. Union leaders, who are themselves likely to be drawn from the ranks of the most experienced, will tend to support their interests over those of the new members. As a result, unions will likewise favor a policy of layoffs over across-the-board wage reductions (see Medoff, 1979, for some evidence).

Second, in non-union firms, the employer will often favor a policy of layoffs over across-the-board wage reductions. The rationale comes from internal labor market theory. The argument is that because firms invest heavily in firm-specific training, they are reluctant to lose their most experienced employees. A wage reduction, even if temporary, might induce these workers to look for work in another firm or, if they stay, to reduce their morale and work effort. In contrast, a policy of laying off the least experienced employees would not be particularly detrimental to the firm, since these are precisely the employees in which the firm has invested least. Thus, from the non-unionized firm's point of view, layoffs would be a preferable alternative to an across-the-board reduction in wages.

Third, employees in a non-union firm may also prefer a layoff policy to a wage-reduction one. The argument comes from implicit contract theory. Assume that, on average, employees are risk-averse – that is, they prefer a stream of steady income that is fairly certain to one that is on average higher (that is, its expected value is greater) but is more uncertain (that is, subject to greater variability over time). Such employees might engage in an implicit contract (not an explicit one, as in the case of unionized workers) with their employer to the effect that most recent hires are laid off first in the case of economic downturns but wages will not be reduced and the experienced labor force will be kept on except in circumstances that threaten the firm with bankruptcy. This is essentially a form of insurance in which the employee, except for an initial period after he (she) is first hired, is generally guaranteed stable earnings over time. In exchange for such lower risk, the employees should be willing to accept a lower average wage. Thus, the employer is also on average better off, since the firm's labor costs would be reduced by such an (implicit) arrangement.[33]

7.7.5   The debate over the causes of unemployment

There is an extended debate among economists over the relative importance of these four causes of unemployment. Most economists do, however, believe that each of these four sources can exist at a given point in time and, indeed, they may all coexist simultaneously during certain periods. Frictional, seasonal, and structural unemployment can occur even when the aggregate demand for labor equals the aggregate supply. Frictional unemployment arises because members of the labor force may be out of work while searching for a (new) job. This type of unemployment is ultimately due to the fact that the job structure is constantly changing and information about job vacancies is imperfect. Seasonal unemployment arises from the seasonal nature of many industries and occupations. Structural unemployment is due to the possibility that imbalances may occur within certain occupational or geographical labor markets between supply and demand for labor. In contrast, demand-deficient unemployment reflects an imbalance in the aggregate labor market. Such joblessness is due to a drop in the aggregate demand for goods and services and thence for labor.

The disagreement among economists is not so much about the possibility that each of these types of unemployment may arise but about the *quantitative* importance of each in explaining the unemployment rate at a given point in time. This is not simply an academic debate since it will guide the choice of appropriate government policies to reduce the level of joblessness. If unemployment is largely frictional in nature, the appropriate policy response would be to improve information about job vacancies and employment placement services. If joblessness is largely structural in nature, the appropriate policy might be to encourage workers to move to locations where jobs are available or to retrain workers in skills that are in demand. If unemployment is due to deficient demand, the proper response is to pursue macroeconomic policies that increase aggregate demand. In a Keynesian world, these include increasing government spending and reducing taxes; in a monetarist world, these include increasing the rate at which the money supply grows and reducing the interest rate.

Most economists believe that the large cyclical swings in unemployment are due to changes in aggregate demand. The high unemployment rates during the early 1930s were due to deficient demand (see Figure 7.4). During the postwar period, the unemployment rate has fluctuated in a range from 2.9 percent in 1953 to 9.7 percent in 1983. The jobless rate has fallen below 4 percent in 1947, 1948, 1951, 1952, 1953, and 1966 to 1969. These were periods of high aggregate demand, which produced tight labor markets. (Not surprisingly, most were during the Korean War and the War in Vietnam.) The jobless rate climbed above 6 percent in 1958 and 1961, and above 8 percent in 1975 and 1982–1983. These were all recession years, caused by low aggregate demand.

During the low unemployment years, it is probably safe to say that almost all of it was due to frictional, seasonal, and structural unemployment. During the high unemployment years, these factors still played a role, though it is hard to determine exactly their relative importance.

"Structuralists" argue that two factors led to greater occupational and geographical imbalances in the labor market. The first is the introduction of computers and automation and the spread of information technology that caused the displacement of a large number of skilled and semi-skilled workers. The second was the increasing shift to services in the U.S. economy, which tended to make many goods-related skills obsolete. Killingsworth (1965) referred to this phenomenon as the "labor market twist," whereby the new jobs created called for educated labor while the workers displaced by automation were largely unskilled.

Frictional sources of unemployment have been receiving increasing emphasis since the 1970s. Motivated partly by the perceived failure of government fiscal and monetary policy to reduce unemployment, the "frictionalists" emphasized the search process as a major source of unemployment. They advanced the argument that most unemployment tends to be of short duration. Based on data from 1969 to 1975, it was found that in four of these years, over half the unemployed remained jobless for less than 5 weeks. Between 1948 and 1966, the average spell of unemployment was 5.5 weeks. Moreover, it was found that most unemployment was concentrated in relatively few individuals. For example, in 1973, when the annual unemployment rate stood at 4.9 percent, 13 percent of the experienced labor force had one or more periods of joblessness, and of these a third had two or more spells and a half of the latter group had three or more spells. The inference drawn was that unemployment was not an aggregate problem but was concentrated among relatively few workers who experienced frequent spells of unemployment of relatively short duration. These spells were interpreted as search periods.

By emphasizing the search process, the frictionalists made the workers and the institutions that fostered inflexibilities in reservation wages the primary culprits of unemployment. Joblessness was viewed as primarily "voluntary." Such institutional factors as union-induced wage rigidities, the minimum wage law, and the unemployment insurance system were also seen as responsible for unemployment since they served to prolong the job search process. The idea of a "natural" rate of unemployment surfaced in this literature. Moreover, as we discussed above, the natural rate was seen to rise during the 1960s and the 1970s due to the changing demographic composition of the labor force.

The debate between voluntary or frictional unemployment versus involuntary or demand-deficient unemployment can be resolved, in part, by looking at vacancy data. If unemployment were entirely due to frictional causes, then the number of vacancies should equal or exceed the number of workers looking for jobs. Indeed, the vacancies should match the unemployed workers both in terms of skill requirements and location (otherwise, we would have structural unemployment). If, on the other hand, the number of jobless workers exceeds the number of vacancies, this can be taken as an indicator of demand-deficient unemployment. One of the most careful studies of this issue was done by Abraham (1983), discussed in Section 7.4 above. She found that during the low-unemployment years, the ratio of unemployed individuals to job vacancies was about 2.5, and during the 1970s the ratio ranged from 4.0 to 5.0. This suggests that demand-deficient unemployment has become more important than frictional causes over time.

Moreover, even if there are frictional and structural sources for unemployment, it is still possible for Keynesian-type macroeconomic policies to reduce the jobless rate. In the case of frictional unemployment, stimulating aggregate demand will increase the number of job vacancies and thereby reduce the average search time of workers, *ceteris paribus*. In the case of structural unemployment, increasing aggregate demand will create additional job vacancies, some of which may match the skills and area of residence of the structurally unemployed. Macroeconomic policy, in conjunction with government retraining and relocation programs, could further facilitate labor market adjustments needed to remove imbalance between excess supplies of certain skills and excess demand for others.

7.8   SUMMARY

The overall labor force participation rate of a nation indicates the proportion of the population that could be at work that is in the labor force. It is one important determinant of the average income per capita of a country. We saw that for the United States, the civilian labor force grew from 28.5 million in 1900 to 149.3 million workers in 2005, or by a factor of 7.9. Over the same period, the overall LFPR increased from 56 to 66 percent, with most of the growth occurring after World War II. The trends were different for men and women. The male LFPR declined from 87 percent in 1948 to 73 percent in 2005, while the female LFPR rose from 33 to 59 percent over the same period. In 1948, females accounted for 27 percent of the labor force, while in 2005 for 46 percent.

During the 1960s and 1970s, the proportion of young workers in the labor force increased due to the large influx of baby boomers into the workforce. In the 1980s and early 1990s, the number of new entrants, members of the "baby-dearth generation," fell dramatically. Throughout the postwar period, the proportion of older workers in the labor force declined sharply.

The educational attainment of the labor force increased substantially during the postwar period. The median years of schooling for the whole labor force rose from 10.9 years in 1952 to 13.3 in 1994. The proportion of the labor force who had not attended high school fell from 38 percent in 1952 to 3.5 percent in 2005; the proportion who were high school graduates or better rose from 43 to 90 percent; and the proportion who had attended some college increased from 16 to 60 percent. For black men, the gains in educational attainment were particularly dramatic, with their median schooling level increasing from 7.2 years in 1952 to 12.4 years in 1984 and the proportion graduating from high school rising from 15 percent in 1952 to 86 percent in 2005.

There were important changes in the industrial and occupational composition of the labor force over the twentieth century. The proportion employed in agriculture fell dramatically. There was also a substantial shift in the composition of the workforce out of goods-producing sectors and into services. This was accompanied by a large reduction in the relative share of unskilled workers and farm workers in the labor force and a large increase in the relative share of white-collar workers, particularly professional, managerial, clerical, and sales workers.

The definition of the unemployment rate is the ratio of the number of unemployed to the total labor force. There have been sharp cyclical movements in the unemployment rate over the last hundred years. This is most evident during the Great Depression. In 1929, the unemployment rate was 3.2 percent but by 1933, it had climbed to 25.2 percent. The unemployment rate fell slowly during the 1930s, and in 1944, it reached its lowest point ever at 1.2 percent. By 1946, after the war had ended, the unemployment rate climbed back to 3.9 percent, and resumed its cyclical pattern. In 1982, the unemployment rate reached its highest level in the postwar period of 9.7 percent, by 2000 it had fallen to 4.0 percent and in 2005 it was at 5.1 percent.

Typically, about 33 to 40 percent of the unemployed consists of persons who are newly entering the labor market or reentering it. Individuals who involuntarily lost their jobs account for about half of the unemployed. The remaining 10 percent or so consist of workers who voluntarily quit their jobs.

There is considerable variation in jobless rates by demographic group. The unemployment rate for blacks has been about double that of whites. Among age groups, the unemployment rate was greatest for teenagers, generally second highest for the 20–24-year-old group, third highest for the 25–34 years range, and lowest for those 35 and over. The likelihood of unemployment tends to decline with experience.

Economists have identified four different causes of unemployment types: (i) frictional; (ii) seasonal; (iii) structural; and (iv) deficient aggregate demand. Frictional unemployment arises because members of the labor force may be out of work while searching for a (new) job. This type of unemployment is ultimately due to the fact that the job structure is constantly changing and information about job vacancies is imperfect. Seasonal unemployment arises from the seasonal nature of many industries and occupations. Structural unemployment is due to the possibility that imbalances may occur within certain occupational or geographical labor markets between supply and demand for labor. Demand-deficient unemployment reflects an imbalance in the aggregate labor market, and is due to a drop in the aggregate demand for goods and services and, as a result, for labor.

During low-unemployment periods, it is likely that all of it is due to frictional, seasonal, and structural unemployment. During the high unemployment years, these factors still play a role, but demand deficiency is likely the major factor.

Although the next two chapters of this textbook will focus on earnings differences as a source of income inequality, it should be emphasized that both labor force participation and unemployment also play a crucial role in inequality and, especially, poverty. As we saw in Chapter 4, the incidence of poverty is much higher in families whose adult members do not work than in those in which they are employed. A low labor force participation rate is a particularly acute problem among female-headed households, elderly families, and individuals with disabilities, chronic illnesses, and criminal records. A high incidence of unemployment is pervasive among teenagers and young families and individuals with low levels of schooling and training. The large differences in unemployment rates between white and black workers may also be due, in part, to racial discrimination. Special government programs may be called for to enable these groups to participate more fully in the labor market (see Chapter 15 for more discussion).

7.9   REFERENCES AND BIBLIOGRAPHY

Employment and labor force participation

Akerlof, G. & Main, B. (1981). Experience-weighted measure of employment and unemployment durations. *American Economic Review*, **71**, 1003–11.

Antos, J. & Mellow, W. (1978). The youth labor market: a dynamic overview. Bureau of Labor Statistics, February, mimeo.

Bailey, M. (1974). Wages and employment under uncertain demand. *Review of Economic Studies*, **41**, 37–50.

Baumol, W.J., Batey Blackman, S.A. & Wolff, E.N. (1989). *Productivity and American Leadership: The Long View*. Cambridge, MA: MIT Press.

Ben-Porath, Y. (1973). Labor force participation rates and the supply of labor. *Journal of Political Economy*, **81**, 697–704.

Bertola, G. (1999). Microeconomic perspectives on aggregate labor markets. In O. Ashenfelter & D. Card (eds.), *Handbook of Labor Economics*, Vol. 3C, (pp. 2985–3028). Amsterdam: North-Holland.

Bertola, G., Blau, F.D. & Kahn, L.M. (2002). Comparative analysis of labor market outcomes: Lessons for the U.S. from international long-run evidence. In A. Krueger & R. Solow (eds.), *The Roaring Nineties: Can Full Employment Be Sustained?* (pp. 159–218). New York: Russell Sage.

Bertola, G., Blau, F.D. & Kahn, L.M. (2007). Labor market institutions and demographic employment patterns. *Journal of Population Economics*, **20**(4), 833–67.

Blanchard, O. & Diamond, P. (1989). The Beveridge curve. *Brookings Papers on Economic Activity*, no. 1, 1–60.

Blanchard, O. & Diamond, P. (1992). The flow approach to labor markets. *American Economic Association Papers and Proceedings*, **82**(2), 354–9.

Blau, F.D. & Kahn, L.M. (1983). Unionism, seniority, and turnover. *Industrial Relations*, **23**, 362–73.

Blau, F.D. & Kahn, L.M. (2002). *At Home and Abroad: U.S. Labor-Market Performance in International Perspective*. New York: Russell Sage.

Bowen, W. & Finegan, T.A. (1969). *The Economics of Labor Force Participation*. Princeton, NJ: Princeton University Press.

Cain, G.G. (1966). *Married Women in the Labor Force: An Economic Analysis*. Chicago: University of Chicago Press.

Clark, K.B. & Summers, L.H. (1981). Demographic differences in cyclical employment variation. *Journal of Human Resources*, **16**(1), 61–79.

Davis, S., Haltiwanger, J. & Schuh, S. (1996). *Job Creation and Destruction*. Cambridge, MA: MIT Press.

Freeman, R.B. & Wise, D.A. (1982). *The Youth Labor Market Problem: Its Nature, Causes, and Consequences*. Chicago: University of Chicago Press.

Gordon, R. (1981). *Macroeconomics*. Boston: Little, Brown.

Gordon, R.J. & Hall, R.E. (1980–81). Arthur M. Okun, 1928–1980. *Brookings Papers on Economic Activity*, 1–5.

Heckman, J.J. & LaFontaine, P.A. (2007). The American high school graduation rate: Trends and levels. NBER Working Paper No. 13670, December.

National Commission on Employment and Unemployment Statistics (1979). *Counting the Labor Force*. Washington, DC: U.S. Government Printing Office.

Owen, J.D. (1986). *The American Work Force since 1920*. Lexington, MA: Heath-Lexington Books.

Stevenson, W. (1978). The relationship between early work experience and future employability. In A. Adams & G. Magnum (eds.), *The Lingering Crisis of Youth Unemployment*. Kalamazoo, MI: W.E. Upjohn Institute.

Unemployment

Abraham, K. (1983). Structural/frictional vs. deficient demand unemployment: Some new evidence. *American Economic Review*, **83**(4), 708–24.

Abraham, K. (1986). Structural/frictional vs. deficient demand unemployment: Reply. *American Economic Review*, **76**(1), 273–6.

Adams, A. & Magnum, G. (1978). *The Lingering Crisis of Youth Unemployment*. Kalamazoo, MI: W.E. Upjohn Institute.

Adams, C. & Coe, D. (1990). A systems approach to estimating the natural rate of unemployment and potential output for the United States. *IMF Staff Papers*, **37**(2), 232–93.

Akerlof, G. & Main, B. (1980). Unemployment spells and unemployment experience. *American Economic Review*, **70**, 885–93.

Azariadis, C. (1975). Implicit contracts and underemployment equilibria. *Journal of Political Economy*, **83**, 1183–202.

Ball, L.N. (1997). Disinflation and the NAIRU. In C. Romer & D. Romer (eds.), *Reducing Inflation: Motivation and Strategy* (pp. 167–85). Chicago: University of Chicago Press.

Ball, L.N. (1999). Aggregate demand and long-term unemployment. *Brookings Papers on Economic Activity*, no. 2, 189–236.

Becker, B. & Hills, S. (1980). Teenage unemployment: Some evidence on the long-run effects on wages. *Journal of Human Resources*, **15**, 354–72.

Benjamin, D. & Kochin, L. (1979). Searching for an explanation of unemployment in interwar Britain. *Journal of Political Economy*, **87**, 441–78.

Blanchflower, D.G. & Freeman, R.B. (eds). (2000). *Youth Employment and Joblessness in Advanced Countries*. Chicago: University of Chicago Press.

Blau, F.D. & Kahn, L.M. (2000). Gender and youth employment outcomes: The U.S. and West Germany, 1984–91. In D.G. Blanchflower & R.B. Freeman (eds.), *Youth Employment and Joblessness in Advanced Countries* (pp. 107–67). Chicago: University of Chicago Press.

Clark, K.B. & Summers, L.H. (1982). The dynamics of youth unemployment. In R. Freeman & D. Wise (eds.), *The Youth Labor Market Problem: Its Nature, Causes & Consequences*. Chicago: University of Chicago Press.

Corcoran, M. & Hill, M.S. (1985). Reoccurrence of unemployment spells among adult men. *Journal of Human Resources*, **20**, 165–83.

Doeringer, P.B. & Piore, M.J. (1975). Unemployment and the dual labor market. *The Public Interest*, **38**, 74–5.

Ehrenberg, R.G. (1980). The demographic structure of unemployment rates and labor market transition probabilities. *Research in Labor Economics*, **3**, 241–3.

Estrella, A. & Mishkin, F.S. (1999). Rethinking the role of NAIRU in monetary policy: Implications of model formulation and uncertainty. In J.B. Taylor (ed.), *Monetary Policy Rules* (pp. 405–30). Chicago: University of Chicago Press.

Feldstein, M. (1975). The importance of temporary layoffs: an empirical analysis. *Brookings Papers on Economic Activity*, 725–44.

Feldstein, M. (1976). Temporary layoffs in the theory of unemployment. *Journal of Political Economy*, **84**, 937–57.

Flaim, P. (1979). The effect of demographic change on the nation's unemployment rate. *Monthly Labor Review*, **102**, 13–23.

Flaim, P. (1990). Population changes, the baby boom and the unemployment rate. *Monthly Labor Review*, **113**, 3–10.

Freeman, R.B. & Holzer, H.J. (1986). *The Black Youth Unemployment Crisis*. Chicago: University of Chicago Press.

Gordon, R.J. (1984). Unemployment and potential output in the 1980s. *Brookings Papers on Economic Activity*, no. 2, 537–63.

Gordon, R.J. (1998). Foundations of the Goldilocks economy: Supply shocks and the time-varying NAIRU. *Brookings Papers on Economic Activity*, no. 2, 297–333.

Hall, R.E. (1970). Why is the unemployment rate so high at full employment? *Brookings Papers on Economic Activity*, no. 3, 369–402.

Hall, R.E. (2005). Employment fluctuations with equilibrium wage stickiness. *American Economic Review*, 95, 50–65.

Hurd, M. (1980). A compensation measure of the cost of unemployment to the unemployed. *Quarterly Journal of Economics*, 95, 225–44.

Johnson, G.E. & Layard, P.R.G. (1986). The natural rate of unemployment: explanation and policy. In O.C. Ashenfelter & R. Layard (eds.), *Handbook of Labor Economics*, Vol. II. New York: North-Holland.

Juhn, C., Murphy, K.M. & Topel, R.H. (1991). Why has the natural rate of unemployment increased over time? *Brookings Papers on Economic Activity*, no. 2, 75–126.

Killingsworth, C.C. (1965). Automation, jobs, and manpower: The case for structural unemployment. In G.L. Magnum (ed.), *The Manpower Revolution: Its Policy Consequences*. Garden City, NY: Doubleday.

Mankiw, N.G. & Ball, L. (2002). The NAIRU in theory and practice. *Journal of Economic Perspectives*, 16(4), 115–36.

Marston, S.T. (1976). Employment instability and high unemployment rates. *Brookings Paper on Economic Activity*, 169–203.

Mattila, J.P. (1974). Job quitting and frictional unemployment. *American Economic Review*, 64, 235–9.

Medoff, J. (1979). Layoffs and alternatives under trade unions in United States manufacturing. *American Economic Review*, 69, 380–95.

Mortensen, D.T. (1970). Job search, the duration of unemployment, and the Phillips curve. *American Economic Review*, 60, 847–62.

Mortensen, D.T. (1986). Job search and labor market analysis. In O.C. Ashenfelter & R. Layard (eds.), *Handbook of Labor Economics*, Vol. II. New York: North-Holland.

Mortensen, D.T. & Nagypal, E. (2005). More on unemployment and vacancy fluctuations. NBER Working paper No. 11692, October.

Mortensen, D.T. & Pissarides, C.A. (1994). Job creation and job destruction in the theory of unemployment. *Review of Economic Studies*, 61, 397–415.

Mortensen, D.T. & Pissarides, C.A. (1999a). Job reallocation and employment fluctuations. In M. Woodford & J.B. Taylor (eds.), *Handbook of Macro Economics*, Vol. 1 (pp. 1171–227). Amsterdam: Elsevier Science.

Mortensen, D.T. & Pissarides, C.A. (1999b). New developments in models of search in the labor market. In O.C. Ashenfelter & D. Card (eds.), *Handbook of Labor Economics*, Vol. 3 (pp. 2567–627). Amsterdam: Elsevier Science.

Nickell, S. (1997). Unemployment and labor market rigidities: Europe versus North America. *Journal of Economic Perspectives*, 11(3), 55–74.

Osberg, L., Apostle, R. & Clairmont, D. (1986). The incidence and duration of individual unemployment: Supply side or demand side? *Cambridge Journal of Economics*, 10, 13–33.

Osterman, P. (1978). Race differences in male youth unemployment. In U.S. Department of Labor, *Conference Report on Youth Unemployment: Its Measurement and Meaning*. Washington, DC: U.S. Government Printing Office.

Phelps, E.S. (1967). Phillips curves, expectations of inflation and optimal unemployment over time. *Economica*, 2, 22–44.

Phelps, E.S. (1968). Money-wage dynamics and labor market equilibrium. *Journal of Political Economy*, 76, 678–711.

Pissarides, C.A. (2000). *Equilibrium Unemployment Theory*, 2nd Edition. Cambridge, MA: MIT Press.

Rowthorn, B. & Glyn, A. (1990). The diversity of unemployment experience since 1973. *Structural Change and Economic Dynamics*, 1(1), 57–89.

Schwartz, A.R., Cohen, M.S. & Grimes, D.R. (1986). Structural/frictional vs. deficient demand unemployment: comment. *American Economic Review*, 76(1), 268–72.

Shimer, R. (1998). Why is the U.S. unemployment rate so much lower? In B. Bernanke & J. Rotemberg (eds.), *NBER Macroeconomics Annual*, Vol. 13. Cambridge, MA: MIT Press.

Shimer, R. (2001). The impact of young workers on the aggregate labor market. *Quarterly Journal of Economics*, 116(3), 969–1007.

Shimer, R. (2005). The cyclical behavior of equilibrium unemployment and vacancies. *American Economic Review*, 95(1), 25–49.

Sider, H. (1985). Unemployment duration and incidence. *American Economic Review*, 75(3), 461–72.

Staiger, D., Stock, J.H. & Watson, M.W. (2002). Prices, wages, and the U.S. NAIRU in the 1990s. In A. Krueger & R. Solow (eds.), *The Roaring Nineties: Can Full Employment Be Sustained?* New York: Russell Sage.

Summers, L.H. (1986). Why is the unemployment rate so very high near full employment? *Brookings Papers on Economic Activity*, 2, 339–83.

Summers, L.H. (1988). Relative wages, efficiency wages, and Keynesian unemployment. *American Economic Review Papers and Proceedings*, 78(2), 383–8.

Welch, F. (1977). What have we learned from empirical studies of unemployment insurance? *Industrial and Labor Relations Review*, 30, 451–61.

7.10   DISCUSSION QUESTIONS

1 Give three reasons why the LFPR of men and women appear to be converging over time.
2 Describe the principal changes in the occupational and industrial make-up of the labor force since 1950.
3 Explain why the mean duration of unemployment is higher than its median duration. What does this imply about the composition of the unemployed population?
4 Discuss three sources of structural unemployment.
5 Explain why and how the official unemployment rate might need adjustment for discouraged workers and part-time employment.
6 Explain why the natural rate of unemployment (or NAIRU) increased during the 1970s and 1980s in the United States and then declined in the 1990s.

NOTES

1 Also, as a result, the income of domestic servants is counted in GDP, while the work performed by housewives is not. This leads to the further anomaly that if every pair of housewives could arrange to pay each other a "salary" while continuing to perform the same work, the level of GDP would increase while the amount of work actually performed would remain unchanged. See Section 2.7 for estimates of household production.
2 See Section 8.2 for further discussion in the context of human capital theory.
3 Technically, the institutional population consists of members of the armed forces living in barracks, prison inmates, and residents of nursing homes, college dormitories, and other group institutions.
4 Until 1947, the relevant age group was those 14 years or older, but because of the change in child labor laws, the age bracket was raised to those 16 years or older at that time.
5 Source: http://www.census.gov/hhes/www/income/histinc/f12ar.html.
6 Because of a change in educational statistics, it is not possible to update this series to 2005.
7 As indicated in the notes to Table 7.5, the data sources are official U.S. government statistics, which were provided by the National Center for Educational Statistics. These numbers have recently been severely criticized by Heckman and LaFontaine (2007), who argued that there are important biases in the official government statistics. Their corrections to the data suggest that the "true" high school graduation rate was substantially lower than the official numbers indicate and that it was declining from 1968 to 2004.
8 More recent official government data for this series are not available.
9 Heckman and LaFontaine (2007), in contrast, argue that the differential in high school graduation rates between non-Hispanic whites and the two minority groups did not lessen between 1968 and 2004.
10 Another implication of their exodus was that the proportion of self-employed workers (and also unpaid family members) in the labor force has fallen considerably since the beginning of the twentieth century.

11   If a sector's output share remains constant and its labor productivity growth is greater than average, then its share of total employment must, of consequence, fall. This mechanism is often referred to as the "unbalanced growth" effect. See Baumol, Blackman, and Wolff (1989), Chapter 6, for more discussion.

12   The data show an increase in the share of sales workers from 6 percent in 1977 to 12 percent in 1988. However, these numbers should be interpreted with some caution, because the Census Bureau changed its classification of sales jobs during the 1980s.

13   The share of operatives in total employment actually showed a large increase from 13 percent in 1900 to 20 percent in 1950 but then a pronounced reduction to 13 percent in 2005.

14   Nonfarm laborers were not recorded as a separate category after the year 2000. The same is true for domestic servants.

15   Sources: U.S. Department of Labor, Employment and Training Administration, *1976 Employment and Training Report of the President*, Transmitted to Congress 1976, U.S. Government Printing Office; U.S. Department of Labor, Bureau of Labor Statistics, *Handbook of Labor Statistics 1978*, Bulletin No. 2000, June 1979; and *Economic Report of the President, 1994 and 2008*. The labor force, employment, and unemployment are defined for those 14 years or older for 1900–1960, and after that for those 16 years or older. In both cases, the statistics include only the civilian labor force. The definition of employment and unemployment was modified somewhat in 1957. As a result, approximately 200,000 to 300,000 workers who were formerly classified as employed were reclassified as unemployed.

16   This was the average unemployment rate for that year. The unemployment rate peaked in November and December of 1982 at 10.7 percent.

17   In some countries, new entrants and reentrants are not officially counted among the unemployed.

18   It should be noted that workers who voluntarily leave their jobs to take new ones or to leave the labor force entirely are not counted as unemployed.

19   Some economists have argued that a related problem in counting the unemployed is "disguised" unemployment, which refers to lower skill jobs held by workers whose skills or training would qualify them for higher positions. Official statistics on unemployment do not reflect this form of "underemployment." Overqualified workers may have been particularly prevalent during the Depression of the 1930s, when many college graduates, for example, held low-level clerical and sales jobs.

20   Also, see Schwartz, Cohen, and Grimes (1986) for comments on the Abraham study and Abraham (1986) for a reply. For more recent work on the subject, see Mortensen and Pissarides (1994 and 1999a), Hall (2005), Mortensen and Nagypal (2005), and Shimer (2005).

21   See: http://pubdb3.census.gov/macro/032006/hhinc/new01_001.htm.

22   Also, see Ehrenberg (1980) for an interesting analysis of sources of differences in unemployment rates between the various gender–race groups.

23   Several studies have attempted to assess the effect of youth unemployment on the eventual wages and career paths achieved in adulthood. Four earlier papers (Stevenson, 1978; Osterman, 1978; Antos & Mellow, 1978; and Becker & Hills, 1980) and several of the papers contained in Freeman and Wise (1982) and Freeman and Holzer (1986) tried to determine whether adult males who had experienced unemployment while teenagers had a higher probability of being unemployed and lower wages than adult males who had not. The results indicated that such long-lasting adverse effects were in evidence among black males but not among white males. For more recent papers on youth unemployment, see Blanchflower and Freeman (2000).

24   Also, married men are, on average, older than men who are single. As we saw from the previous table, jobless rates are lower among men 25 years and older than those under 25. However, econometric studies have generally found that, even after controlling for differences in age, married men have lower unemployment rates than singles.

25   Source: http://pubdb3.census.gov/macro/032006/pov/new02_100_01.htm.

26   The U.S. Bureau of Labor Statistics discontinued this series in the 1980s and 1990s but resumed it in 2000.

27   The U.S. Bureau of Labor Statistics generates a map of unemployment rates by county, which is a nice way to show that there are big differences even within states. See: http://www.bls.gov/lau/maps/aacnrt.pdf.

28   These statistics are from the following sources. UK: http://www.statistics.gov.uk/instantfigures.asp; Germany: http://www.destatis.de/jetspeed/portal/cms/Sites/destatis/Internet/EN/Content/Statistics/ TimeSeries/EconomicIndicators/NationalAccounts/Content100/vgr910a,templateId=renderPrint.psml; and United States: http://www.bls.gov/news.release/empsit.toc.htm.

29   Because of the importance of such seasonal fluctuations in output and employment, many official government statistics are seasonally adjusted to allow comparisons with other periods of the year. The student should not confuse seasonal fluctuations with cyclical fluctuations, since the former occur on a regular basis each year whereas the latter occur on an irregular basis depending on aggregate demand conditions.

30   See Ball (1999) and the commentary on his article.

31   See also Ball (1997 and 1999); Gordon (1998); Estrella and Mishkin (1999); and Staiger, Stock, and Watson (2002) for more discussion of the NAIRU and its implications.

32   Not only may the lack of flexible wages be a problem here. The Keynesian debt–deflation cycle implies that, if deficient aggregate demand increases the unemployment rate, a downward spiral could occur. In particular, consumption may also fall and the real value of debt may rise, putting further downward pressure on aggregate demand. In other words, falling prices may not always correct the high unemployment rates. The history of Japan in the 1990s showed some evidence of this.

33   This is true only in the case where the proportion of employees subject to layoffs is small. If it is large, the employer might be better off paying higher wages during good times and reducing wages during hard times. See Bailey (1974) and Azariadis (1975) for more detailed arguments.

Chapter 8
The Role of Education and Skills

8.1 INTRODUCTION

In Chapter 8 we next turn to the role of education and skills in the determination of earnings. Among the strong points of human capital theory is that it has observable and testable implications. One is that annual earnings should increase with both education and the experience level of the worker. Moreover, as we shall see in subsequent sections, the relation between earnings, schooling, and experience should assume a certain functional form. A vast amount of empirical research has gone into statistically estimating these earnings functions. A second implication of human capital theory that we shall consider here is that if people do not differ in terms of tastes, discount rates, and talents, the present value of lifetime earnings (net of educational expenses) for different educational groups should be equal. A third is that differences in earnings between workers should reflect differences in their productivity. A fourth implication is that the inequality of the overall earnings distribution should be related to the distribution of both schooling and experience levels among workers.

The last point, in particular, connects this chapter with major themes of the book – inequality and poverty. As we shall see below, both schooling and work experience play major roles in the determination of earnings and therefore of household incomes. Differences in educational attainment among individuals should have a direct bearing on overall inequality according to human capital theory. Indeed, how much the inequality of schooling contributed to overall income inequality was the subject of a 1972 book by Jencks *et al.* called *Inequality: A Reassessment of the Effect of Family and Schooling in America*. The rate of return to schooling is also of relevance since it reflects the spread of earnings between different educational groups (say, college graduates versus high school graduates). Moreover, low levels of schooling and the lack of work experience are often seen as major factors in accounting for family poverty (see Chapter 4).

It should also be stressed that the human capital model is purely a "supply-side" model. The occupational and industrial structure of labor demand is left completely blank. The human capital model might help explain the relative earnings advantage of individuals. However, in order to explain the size distribution of income among individuals, it is necessary to explain both the relative earnings ratios of individuals in equilibrium and the frequency distribution of individuals at each wage rate. The latter is left unexplained in human capital theory (see Section 8.2.3.4 for more discussion of this point). In Chapter 9, we shall investigate institutional and demand-side factors that might account for the size distribution of earnings among workers.

Chapter 8 begins by introducing the human capital model, with its emphasis on the role of both schooling and on-the-job training in the determination of relative earnings (Section 8.2). Section 8.3 summarizes empirical work in the human capital tradition, which shows that schooling and experience play a major role in the determination of relative earnings. The section presents basic statistical results on age–earnings profiles by schooling level for males and females and for different racial groups. It also presents estimates of the rate of return to schooling (Section 8.3.1). The times series for the United States extends from the mid-1950s to 2000. The value of a college education is highlighted. The recent rise in the returns to education, experience, and skills are also given emphasis, as well as explanations for this occurrence. Estimates from other countries are also shown. Section 8.3.2 presents figures on the present value of lifetime earnings for different educational and occupational groups.

Section 8.4 (which is optional) presents a more analytical treatment of the schooling–earnings function. It discusses how the schooling–earnings function is derived and presents econometric estimates of the rate of return to schooling. It also shows how the earnings function can be extended to include experience, and regression estimates of the extended earnings function.

Section 8.5 treats the role of ability as a factor in determining wages and salaries and summarizes empirical work on the effect of ability on earnings. Ability is viewed as an additional factor that along with schooling and experience jointly determine labor earnings. This section also reviews some of the studies that have attempted to assess the contribution of ability to earnings.

In Section 8.6, other interpretations of the schooling–earnings relation are also considered. It first assesses the relation between earnings and worker productivity. In the human capital model, schooling is believed to increase worker earnings, because it makes workers more productive. The same is true for experience on the job. This section first reviews evidence concerning the relation between experience and direct indicators of worker productivity on the job. It then considers other interpretations for the observed positive association between schooling and earnings. These include the screening model of schooling, education as a transmitter of family background, and schooling as a socializing mechanism.

The contribution of human capital variables to overall earnings inequality is analyzed in Section 8.7. The algebraic relationship between the two is first derived analytically. It then considers whether the recent rise in income inequality can be attributed in whole or in part to changes in the distribution of schooling and experience levels in the workforce. A summary is provided in Section 8.8.

8.2 THE HUMAN CAPITAL MODEL

Although elements of human capital theory can be traced back to Adam Smith's *Wealth of Nations* (written in 1776), its modern formulation is largely credited to Theodore Schultz, who coined the phrase in a 1961 article, and to Gary Becker, who produced the first systematic exposition of the model in a 1964 book, entitled *Human Capital*. The human capital model is actually an extension of the neoclassical model of wage determination to the long-run supply curve of labor. The emphasis here is on the determination of the marginal productivity of labor.

In the human capital model, each individual makes an investment decision about how much schooling and training to acquire. Both schooling and training are assumed to increase the productivity of the worker. The benefit of acquiring increased skills is to augment marginal productivity and (future) wages. However, there is a cost involved. An individual normally forgoes earnings while studying in school, as well as spending money on books, supplies, and tuition. A rational individual will therefore choose to invest in his (or her) human capital as long as the rate of return on investment is greater than the prevailing discount rate. The notion that the acquisition of skills is an investment decision is the central concept of human capital theory. One direct implication is that differences in human capital help explain why earnings differ among workers.

Section 8.2.1 introduces the basic human capital model, and develops the concept of the rate of return to human capital. Section 8.2.2 extends the human capital model to the acquisition of on-the-job training. Section 8.2.3 explores some additional implications of the human capital model.

8.2.1　The rate of return to human capital

Human capital theory is really a special application of capital theory. In the basic model, individuals are viewed as choosing between two possible courses of action: either working or investing in new skills. In the simplest form of the model, the choice is made between working and schooling. Schooling increases a person's skills, future productivity on the job, and future wage. There are two types of cost associated with schooling. The first are the *direct costs* of schooling – tuition, books, and supplies. The second is *forgone earnings* – the income that could have been earned if the person had been working instead of in school. This is also called the *opportunity cost* or the *indirect costs* of schooling.

How does an individual decide whether to continue in school? In human capital theory, the choice is viewed as an investment decision. The added skills acquired from schooling increase the person's stock of human capital. Like other capital, human capital commands a certain return in the marketplace, computed as the difference between the added income and its cost. If the rate of return is sufficiently high, the investor will undertake the investment by remaining in school. If the return is too low, the person will quit school and enter the labor force.

Consider the case of a high school graduate at age 18 deciding between college and work. Suppose he can earn $40,000 a year if he goes to work but can earn $52,000 with a four-year college degree. We will assume for now that his earnings do not change over time and that he retires at age 65. For the moment, we will also assume that a college education is free – that is, there are no tuition fees or expenses for books or supplies. These *age–earnings profiles* are illustrated in Figure 8.1. Note that if the person goes to college, he earns nothing between ages 18 and 22.

Should the person go to college? At first glance, it would seem to make sense. His lifetime earnings would be $2,288,000 [(65 − 22 + 1) × $52,000)], compared to $1,920,000 [(65 − 18 + 1) × $40,000] if he went directly to work. But this is not really the correct way to make the comparison.

Suppose the (real) market interest rate is 5 percent.[1] A person with $40,000 in 2005 could invest the money at 5 percent, and in 2006 the investment would be worth $42,000 (1.05 × $40,000). In other words, to have $42,000 next year, a person needs to invest only $40,000 today. The amount $40,000 is referred to as the *present value* of $42,000 in 2006, since this would be the value in 2005 of having $42,000 in 2006.

With a market interest rate of 5 percent (and perfect capital markets[2]), a rational person would be indifferent between $40,000 today and $42,000 next year. The reason is that if you had $40,000 today, you could invest it and earn $42,000 next year, or if you borrowed $40,000 today, you would have to pay back $42,000 next year. In other words, if you had $40,000 today, you could *exchange* it for $42,000 next year, and vice versa.

Thus, the correct way of comparing two alternative income streams is to look at their *present values*. Let V_h be the present value of the total lifetime earnings of the high school graduate:[3]

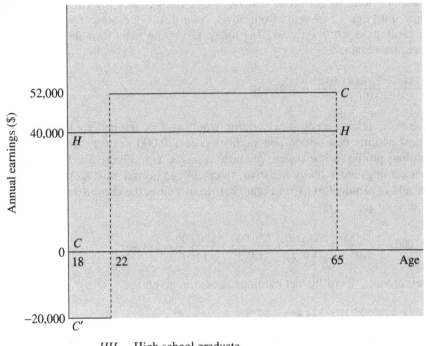

HH – High school graduate
CC – College graduate (no tuition or other college costs)
C′C – College graduate ($15,000 per year in college costs)

Figure 8.1   Hypothetical age–earnings profiles of a high school graduate and a college graduate

$$V_h = \$40,000 + \frac{\$40,000}{1.05} + \frac{\$40,000}{(1.05)^2} + \ldots + \frac{\$40,000}{(1.05)^{47}}$$

where $47 = 65 - 18$, the number of years to retirement at age 18. The 5 percent interest rate is also referred to as the **discount rate**, because this is the rate at which a person would discount future earnings. Algebraically, this summation is a geometric series with a ratio of $1/1.05$. Using the formula for a sum of a finite geometric series,[4] we obtain:

$$V_h = \frac{40,000 - 40,000/(1.05)^{48}}{1 - 1/1.05} = \$759,241$$

This means that an investment today of $759,241 at 5 percent per year will yield an income (annuity) stream of $40,000 per year over the next 48 years. At the end of this time period, the initial investment would be totally exhausted.

The present value of the lifetime earnings of the college graduate, V_c, is given by:

$$V_c = \frac{\$52,000}{(1.05)^4} + \frac{\$52,000}{(1.05)^5} + \ldots + \frac{\$52,000}{(1.05)^{47}}$$

Note that the first term in the series is divided by $(1.05)^4$, since the college graduate does not start working until age 22 (4 years from now). As a result, the present value of the graduate's first year's earnings is worth only $42,781 today. Using the same formula for the sum of a geometric series, we obtain:

$$V_c = \frac{42,781 - 42,781/(1.05)^{44}}{1 - 1/1.05} = \$793,404$$

Under these assumptions, a college education would still be the better choice.

Let us now assume that tuition and supplies cost $20,000 per year for a college education. The net earnings profile for the college graduate is now $C'C$ in Figure 8.1. From age 18 to 22, the person's net earnings are actually negative, since college tuition must be paid. After age 22, the earnings profile is identical to CC in Figure 8.1. In this case, the present value of the direct costs of 4 years of college, D_c, is:

$$D_c = \$20,000 + \frac{\$20,000}{1.05} + \frac{\$20,000}{(1.05)^2} + \frac{\$20,000}{(1.05)^3} + \frac{\$20,000}{(1.05)^4} = \$74,465$$

and the present value $V_{c'}$ of his net earnings stream is given by:

$$V_{c'} = V_c - D_c = \$759,241 - \$74,465 = \$718,939$$

$V_{c'}$ is now less than V_h, so in this case the rational choice would be to start work immediately after high school.

It should now be apparent that the present value calculation depends critically on the market interest rate. If the interest rate changes, so does the present value of the earnings profile. Suppose that the market interest rate falls to 3 percent. Then,

$$V_{h,.03} = \$40,000 + \frac{\$40,000}{1.03} + \frac{\$40,000}{(1.03)^2} + \ldots + \frac{\$40,000}{(1.03)^{47}} = \$1,040,988$$

The present value of the earnings stream increases when the interest rate falls from 5 to 3 percent. The reason is that future earnings are discounted less at a lower interest rate.

The same is true, of course, of the earnings stream for the college graduate. The interesting question is whether the present value of the earnings stream is still greater for the college graduate than for the high school graduate at the lower interest rate. Since the college graduate defers more of his earnings to the future than the high school graduate, the college graduate should be better off relative to the high school graduate from a drop in the interest rate because future earnings now count more. For earnings stream CC, then:

$$V_{c,.03} = \frac{\$52,000}{(1.03)^4} + \frac{\$52,000}{(1.03)^5} + \ldots + \frac{\$52,000}{(1.03)^{47}} = \$1,154,197$$

With a 3 percent market interest rate college becomes even more attractive (assuming no tuition costs) than working at age 18, since the ratio of present values V_c/V_h is now 1.11 ($1,154,197/$1,040,988), compared to 1.04 ($793,404/$759,241) at a 5 percent interest rate. The gain from going to college is greater at the lower interest rate.

What if the student had to pay $20,000 per year in college costs? At a 5 percent interest rate, it made sense to go straight to work after high school. At a 3 percent interest rate, $D_{c,.03} = \$76,572$

and $V_{c',.03} = \$1,077,625$. At a 3 percent interest rate, college would now be preferable to working even with college costs of $20,000 per year.

Let us now see what would happen if the market interest rate rises to 7 percent. $V_{h,.07} = \$587,664$ and $V_{c,.07} = \$575,499$. At a 7 percent market interest rate it would no longer make sense for the 18 year old to go to college even if it were free. The reason is that at the higher interest rate future earnings of the college graduate are discounted even more.

8.2.1.1 The internal rate of return

A somewhat different way of viewing the decision to go to college is to ask at what interest rate an 18 year old would be indifferent between college and working. This interest rate is called the *internal rate of return* (or just the "rate of return") to a college education. If the internal rate of return to college is greater than the market interest rate, then it would pay the 18 year old to invest in college. This decision-making process is analogous to a firm's choosing among alternative investment opportunities.

The internal rate of return is defined as the rate which would equalize the lifetime earnings of the high school and college graduate. In the case of free college tuition, the internal rate of return, r^* is given by:

$$V_{c,r^*} = V_{h,r^*}$$

or, as in the example above,

$$\sum_{t=4}^{47} \frac{\$52,000}{(1 + r^*)^t} - \sum_{t=0}^{47} \frac{\$40,000}{(1 + r^*)^t} = 0 \tag{8.1}$$

This equation has no simple analytical solution. However, we know that r^* must lie between 5 percent and 7 percent, because at 5 percent, lifetime earnings are greater for the college graduate while at 7 percent they are greater for the high school graduate. By trying different values of r^* in this range, we can obtain a solution, which is $r^* = 6.4$ percent.

8.2.2 On-the-job training

Another form of human capital investment is *on-the-job training*. For some jobs, formal training programs are provided by the company. Skilled trades, such as machinists, plumbers, and electricians, offer special apprenticeship programs, which allow a beginning worker to acquire the skills of the trade while working. The medical professions have required training programs for doctors – internships and residencies. Many companies also provide special training for junior executives and computer programmers. In other cases, workers are trained *informally* while on the job. This training is often done by the worker's supervisor or fellow workers. A newly hired factory worker must be taught how to operate equipment in the plant. A secretary must learn the procedures and forms used in a company.

On-the-job training increases a worker's productivity in much the same way as formal schooling. Moreover, like formal schooling, on-the-job training entails both direct and indirect costs. Direct costs include payments for the instructor, equipment, and materials used in the training program. The indirect (opportunity) cost is the forgone production resulting from the fact that the worker's time is absorbed in training instead of engaged in direct production.

The major difference between on-the-job training costs and those of formal schooling is that all or part of the former may be borne by the *firm*. In the standard neoclassical model of the labor market, it can be shown that in competitive equilibrium, the wage is equal to the worker's marginal value product. However, this condition may not hold if there are training costs involved.

Let us see what differences training costs would make. The standard neoclassical model implicitly assumes that production in each period is independent of other periods. However, if a firm trains a worker in one period and this affects the firm's output in subsequent periods, then this assumption no longer holds.

In particular, from the firm's point of view, the total revenue generated by a worker (its marginal revenue product, *MRP*) must be sufficient to recoup its total expenditure on the worker, including both wages (*w*) and the direct costs of training (*TC*). To simplify the discussion, suppose the firm operates in two periods and provides training in only the first period. Then, in equilibrium,

$$MRP_1 + MRP_2 = w_1 + w_2 + TC \qquad (8.2)$$

where the subscript refers to the time period.[5]

To see how this equation is interpreted, it is first necessary to distinguish between two kinds of on-the-job training – *specific training* and *general training*. Specific training is entirely firm-specific and nontransferable to other firms. There are several examples. One is training that familiarizes a new secretary in a company with the forms, coding procedures, filing procedures, and other organizational matters that are specific to that company. A second is training a new factory hire with the use of a very specific (perhaps, custom-made) piece of machinery. A third is military training in advanced weaponry or learning how to operate a tank. Specific training can be formally defined as that which increases the marginal productivity of the worker in the worker's own firm but which has no effect on the worker's potential productivity in other firms.

At the opposite extreme is general training, which is formally defined as training that increases the marginal productivity of the trainee both in the firm providing the training as well as in other firms that may hire the worker. There are several examples of general training. First, a plumber apprenticed to one firm will receive skills that can be transferred to other plumbing companies. Second, a programmer trained by one company can usually use the skills that are acquired in other companies. Third, surgeons who receive training in one hospital can use these skills in other hospitals or private practice. General training increases the worker's marginal product in the firm providing the training, as well as in competing firms.

Let us first consider the implications of firm-specific training. From the employer's point of view, specific training is very useful because it increases the employee's future productivity on the job. The employer would thus be willing to absorb the full training costs insofar as the return is greater than or equal to the cost of the training. On the other hand, from the *employee's* point of view, the wage that can be commanded in a competing firm is *not* changed by specific training (by assumption, it increases the worker's wage in *only* the firm in which the worker is employed). As a result, the employee cannot rely on a higher outside wage offer to increase the wage being paid by his current employer. Therefore, the employee is essentially *indifferent* with regard to specific training. However, the employee is *not* willing to pay for specific training by accepting a lower wage, since there is no direct benefit for him. For these reasons, it is the employer who winds up paying the costs of specific training.

In terms of Equation (8.2), the worker will accept a first period wage, w_1, that is no lower than her marginal revenue value product in that period, MRP_1. As a result, $w_1 = MRP_1$ and therefore

$$w_2 = MRP_2 - TC \text{ [specific training]} \qquad (8.3a)$$

In other words, the employer will recoup the costs of training by paying the worker a wage less than her marginal value product in period 2. This is the only condition under which a profit-maximizing firm would be willing to invest in an employee's specific training. Moreover, in the case of specific training, wages will *not* rise over time (at least not from this form of training).

In contrast, general training, by assumption, increases the worker's marginal product not only in the worker's own firm but also in competing firms. After the worker acquires general training, other firms would be willing to pay a wage equal to his higher marginal revenue product. The firm providing this type of training would also have to pay the higher wage, because otherwise the employee would change jobs. As a result, the firm has no incentive to pay for general training. However, the worker does have an incentive, since general training will increase his future productivity and therefore his future wage.

In terms of Equation (8.2), this argument implies that in the case of general training, w_2 must equal MRP_2. Therefore,

$$w_1 = MRP_1 - TC \text{ [general training]} \tag{8.3b}$$

In other words, the earnings of the worker would be reduced by the cost of the training while he was engaged in training. The *employee* would essentially wind up paying the cost of the training by receiving a lower wage during the training period, though he would make it up later in the form of higher wages. In contrast to specific training, general training will lead to a *rise* in wages over time, both from the lower wages paid during the training period and the higher wages later on from the enhanced productivity of the worker.

In summary, in the case of specific training, the employer absorbs all the costs of training, while in the case of general training the employee absorbs the cost. In both cases, the costs consist of direct costs paid for instruction, materials, and equipment; and indirect costs in the form of the forgone output of the worker while in training. For specific training, the wage equals the worker's marginal value product during the training period but is less than the worker's marginal value product in subsequent periods. For general training, the wage is less than the worker's marginal value product during the training period but equals the worker's marginal value product in subsequent periods.

In actual fact, most forms of training lie between these two extremes and are neither completely firm specific nor completely general. As a result, both the employee and the employer typically absorb portions of the training cost, though the relative proportions vary, depending on how general or specific the training is. This has important implications for the shape of the age–earnings profile, as we shall discuss below.

Moreover, in the case of specific training, there are two reasons why an employee might be very interested in it, even though it may not increase her current wage. The first is that the mere fact that an employer has invested in the worker's training makes the worker much more valued by the firm than a new hire. The firm will not want to jeopardize its investment by losing the employee. Therefore, specific training may significantly reduce the likelihood that an employer will discharge the worker. This has important implications regarding the structure of internal labor markets, as we shall see in Section 9.3.

Second, by raising the worker's marginal product in later periods, specific training may also increase her future wage. The reason is that the employee by threatening to quit the firm and hence causing the firm to lose its investment could induce the firm to pay more than the worker's opportunity cost in another firm. This is another implication of internal labor markets, as we shall see in Section 9.2.

8.2.3   Additional implications of the human capital model

8.2.3.1   Basic assumptions of the model

As in the neoclassical model, the derivation of the human capital model depends on five key assumptions: (i) perfect competition among firms and workers; (ii) perfect information and foresight on the part of both firms and workers; (iii) perfect rationality on the part of firms and employees; (iv) perfect capital markets; and (v) education yields no direct utility to the student.[6] A sixth assumption that is needed for the training model to hold is that that are no restrictions on access to training or to jobs that provide training opportunities.[7]

It might be instructive to consider cases when these assumptions fail to hold. With regard to perfect competition, though most occupations have free entry, a few do not. The most prominent example is doctors, where entry is restricted from limits placed on medical school openings. In this case, we would expect the internal rate of return in the medical professions to be higher than in other fields, because restrictions on entry will prevent people from entering this lucrative profession. Another result will be an excess demand for places in medical schools.[8]

Another important assumption of the human capital model is that capital markets are perfect – that is, everyone with the same risk of defaulting on their loan (that is, the same "risk class") can borrow money at the same interest rate to finance a college education. This assumption is particularly vital in the schooling model, since the cost of the investment in terms of both direct costs and forgone earnings can be quite high. Yet, capital markets for student loans are not perfect, since there are limitations on the amount that can be borrowed. Moreover, the cost of college financing differs among students – those from a rich family often have parents willing to pay for it, while those from poor families usually have to take out loans. Such imperfections in the capital market would mean that different students faced different market interest rates, depending on their circumstances (and for those who could not obtain funds, the interest rate would be effectively *infinite*). As a result, students with the same potential rate of return on a college education may make different schooling decisions, depending on the actual interest rate they faced. Consequently, there may be no tendency toward equilibrium in the schooling "market" (see the last Section 8.2.3.4 for more discussion of equilibrium in the human capital market).

The joint assumptions of perfect information and rationality may not always apply to high school seniors deciding on whether to attend college. How many of you have made the necessary calculations to decide to attend college or go to work? Moreover, if you had made these computations, how many of you would actually be guided by the results of your calculations?

Though very few students actually make the complicated calculations of the return to a college degree, most are aware of earnings differences between college graduates and high school graduates. Studies have shown that when differentials are high, a larger percentage of high school graduates go on to college than when differentials are small (see, for example, Freeman, 1976). Moreover, decisions about professional school, such as law, medicine, business, or engineering, are even more sensitive to the relative earnings of these professions (again see Freeman, 1976).

What if a student pursues education simply for its own sake (the love of learning perhaps)? Would this be considered irrational behavior according to the human capital market? The fifth assumption of the human capital model seems to rule out this possibility. However, this is only for analytical reasons in order to determine the schooling decision on the basis of expected labor earnings. Indeed, education has both an investment and a *consumption* component. Part of the reason that many students go to school is to acquire knowledge. An art history or music appreciation course may not have any direct relevance to a student's future career but may greatly add to the student's enjoyment of life later on. Thus, even if direct monetary rewards were not great from attending college, other "psychic" benefits could well justify the expenditure.

8.2.3.2 A theory of relative earnings

One immediate implication of the human capital schooling model is that *annual earnings* will differ according to the educational attainment of the worker. This follows directly from the human capital model, because schooling, by assumption, increases the marginal productivity of the worker. Moreover, an individual would not be willing to invest in additional schooling unless earnings were increased. Thus, we should find systematic differences in earnings between those with different amounts of schooling. In other words, schooling should help explain some of the variation in annual earnings among workers.

A second implication, which emerges from the on-the-job training model, is that labor earnings should be positively related to *work experience*. This result follows from the analysis of *general training*. During the training period, the worker's earnings are effectively reduced by the costs of the training. After the training period, the worker's marginal product and earnings both rise over time. Most workers obtain some form of on-the-job training, and it is normally a mixture of both specific and general skills. In addition, though formal training may last for only a short period of time, most workers continue to learn informally on the job. Therefore, for most workers, we would expect their productivity and earnings to rise with years of experience in the labor force.[9] As a result, years of experience is a second factor which should help account for the variation in labor earnings.

8.2.3.3 Policy implications

Human capital theory has had a strong influence on public policy throughout the world. Many public programs have emphasized the acquisition of human capital as one mechanism for combating poverty. As we demonstrated in Section 4.4.1, there is a strong correlation between low levels of schooling and poverty rates. As a result, many government programs have been implemented to increase the schooling and training of the low-income population. In the United States, special programs for poor children, such as *Head Start*, have been devised to prepare preschool children from poor families for elementary school education. Efforts have been made to reduce the drop-out rate among high school age students. Student loan programs have been designed to encourage college-age students from low-income families to attend college. For low-income adults, special manpower training programs have been developed to increase their marketable skills. In Section 15.6, we will discuss these programs in greater detail.

8.2.3.4 The formation of an equilibrium in the human capital market*

Let us return to the computation of the internal rate of return to schooling. Suppose it turns out that the internal rate of return to a college education is below the market interest rate. Why would anyone attend college?[10] Or, conversely, suppose the internal rate of return exceeded the market interest rate? Why would anyone go to work after high school? Both predictions are nonsensical, since they would imply that everyone should attend college or no one should attend college. Are there any mechanisms that ensure that an equilibrium is formed in the human capital market?

In fact, there are two such mechanisms at work. The first is market interest rate adjustments. We have implicitly assumed that it was fixed. Actually, it changes according to the supply of and demand for funds. Suppose the current market interest rate were lower than the rate of return to a college education. There would then be a great incentive to go to college. As a result, the quantity demanded of college loans would be high with many students seeking college loans, and the market interest rate would rise. In equilibrium, the interest rate would equal the internal rate of return. Conversely, if the internal rate of return to a college education were below the market interest rate, the quantity demanded of college loans would fall, and so would the interest rate.

The second mechanism involves changes in the earnings differential between high school and college graduates. We had implicitly assumed in Section 8.2.1 that they were fixed. However, suppose the return to a college education is very high. The market response would be an increase in the number of college students. As a result, the supply of college graduates would increase relative to the number of high school graduates in the labor market. The marginal product of a factor of production depends not only on its productivity but also on its supply. In general, the marginal product of a factor will decline as its use increases relative to other factors of production (the law of diminishing marginal returns). In this case, an increase in the number of college graduates relative to high school graduates would cause the earnings of the former to decline relative to the latter. A decline in the earnings differential would, in turn, cause the internal rate of return to a college education to fall, and in equilibrium it would be brought back in line with the market interest rate.

Equilibrium will then occur when the present value of the earnings streams of different educational levels are equal. This can come about from a change in the interest rate and/or a change in earnings differentials between educational groups. This also implies that in equilibrium the present value of *lifetime earnings* will be equal for all schooling groups (as long as the assumptions of the human capital model spelled out in Section 8.2.3.1 hold). This statement should not be confused with our previous discussion that annual earnings will differ systematically between levels of schooling. Indeed, the human capital model predicts that *annual* earnings will differ. What should be equalized is the present value of discounted lifetime earnings among workers. In the human capital model, then, the true measure of economic inequality is that of lifetime earnings, not annual earnings, since the latter may differ among workers with the same lifetime incomes.

In a sense, the human capital equilibrium may now be too rigid. In equilibrium, the present value of lifetime earnings net of training costs at different levels of schooling will be equal (as long as all the assumptions hold). However, this implies that individuals will be *indifferent* between going to college and working immediately after high school. In this sense, the human capital model is *indeterminate*, since there is no way to determine levels of schooling for individuals, the distribution of schooling, and therefore the distribution of labor earnings, because the latter depends on the distribution of human capital.

Becker (1967) suggested a solution to this problem by relaxing two of the assumptions of the human capital model. This can be conveniently represented in terms of the supply of and demand for schooling, as shown in Figure 8.2. Let us consider the supply curve first. Recall that one of the key assumptions of the human capital model is that there are perfect capital markets. This means that all students in the same risk class face the same interest rate when borrowing funds for their education. Suppose that this is not the case, and that different individuals face different costs in borrowing funds. Such differences in *opportunities* for acquiring human capital can be interpreted as differences in the *supply curve* for human capital.

Consider three different individuals, facing supply curves SC_1, SC_2, and SC_3 as shown in Figure 8.2. It should first be noted that the supply curves slope upward. This means that early years of schooling can be financed at relatively low costs – probably from family financing – and later years at higher costs – probably from taking out a loan. The cost of borrowing is related to the risk class an individual faces. Moreover, the risk of default is largely related to the tangible assets families can use to secure loans.[11]

Individual 1 faces the highest costs of acquiring funds, SC_1. This person comes from a poor family and cannot rely on family funds to finance much schooling. The interest rate becomes infinite at some point if he cannot get any loans. Individual 2, from a middle-income family, faces supply curve SC_2. Early years of schooling can be financed at relatively low costs from her family and later years with the help of low-cost government loans, and still later years through

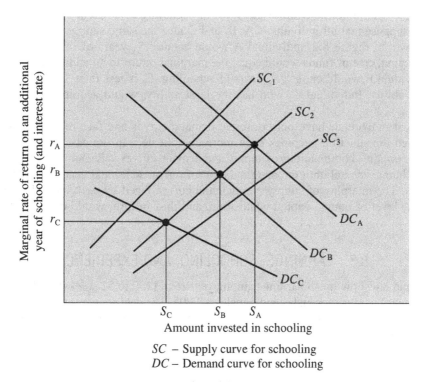

Figure 8.2   Supply and demand curves for schooling of three individuals

relatively high-cost bank loans. Individual 3, from a rich family, faces a lower supply curve for funds. She can rely on family resources for most of her school financing and on low-cost government loans for the remainder. To finance a given level of schooling, individual 1 must pay the highest interest rate, individual 2 the second highest, and individual 3 the lowest.

The demand curve for schooling depends largely on a person's ability.[12] In the basic model it is implicitly assumed that a given level of schooling will produce the same level of skill for everyone. Suppose that individuals differ in "native intelligence" and can convert a given level of schooling into different levels of skill.[13] This, in turn, implies that individuals with the same schooling attainment can earn different amounts. As a result, the *marginal rate of return* (additional earnings) from an additional year of schooling can differ among students.

These differences can be represented by a demand curve for schooling, as illustrated in Figure 8.2. It should first be noted that the demand curve slopes downward to the right. This means that there are diminishing returns to investment in schooling. Primary school generally provides the most essential and productive skills of work life (reading, writing, and arithmetic). High school and college supply more advanced literacy, reasoning, and mathematical skills, which, while still important, tend to have a smaller *incremental* impact on later productivity. As a result, the marginal return to schooling tends to decline with years of schooling.

Individual A has the most ability, and the corresponding demand curve, DC$_A$, is the highest of the three, indicating the greatest return for a given level of schooling. Individual B is of average ability, and the corresponding demand curve, DC$_B$, is in the middle. Individual C has the lowest ability and receives the lowest return for a given schooling investment. Thus, for a given schooling investment, individual A obtains the highest return, followed by B and C.

We can now determine the equilibrium level of schooling investment each individual would make. First, suppose that all individuals A, B, and C face the same supply curve for funds, SC_2. Then, as shown in Figure 8.2, individual A would acquire S_A years of schooling, since at this point the marginal cost of funds would equal the marginal return to an additional year of schooling, r_A. Individual B would choose S_B years of schooling. S_B is less than S_A, because individual B has lower ability. Individual C, who has the least ability, would acquire the lowest level of schooling, S_C.

Of course, if individuals have both different demand curves and face different supply curves for funds, then the situation becomes even more complicated. In the case of three individuals, there are nine possible combinations of supply and demand curves.[14] Each individual would invest in additional human capital until the marginal return from an additional year equaled his marginal cost of funds. The interplay of supply and demand curves faced by each individual would then determine the level of human capital acquisition, and this, in turn, would close the human capital model.[15]

8.3   EARNINGS, SCHOOLING, AND EXPERIENCE

Figures 8.3 and 8.4 show mean earnings among year-round (50 to 52 weeks), full-time (35 hours per week or more) workers for males and females in 2005. The data source is the Current Population Survey (CPS).[16] Human capital theory predicts that earnings will rise with schooling and experience. While educational attainment is very easy to establish on a survey questionnaire, it is difficult to obtain a good estimate of a person's total years of work experience (excluding time out of the labor force or out of a job). Therefore, age is often used as a "proxy" for experience, since work experience normally increases with a person's age.[17]

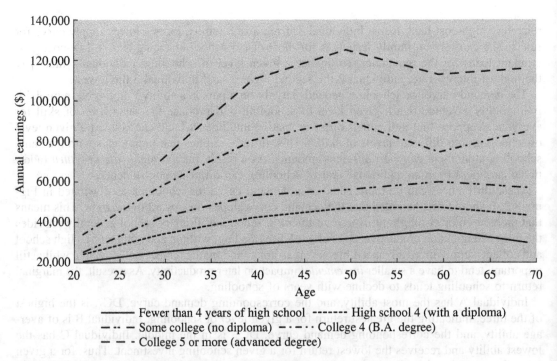

Figure 8.3   Age–earnings profiles, 2005: full-year, full-time male workers

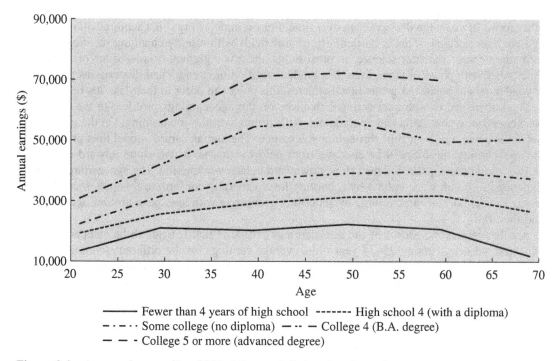

Figure 8.4   Age-earnings profiles, 2005: full-year, full-time female workers

In every case shown in the two figures, average earnings increased with schooling level. This conforms with the predictions of human capital theory. The relation between earnings and age is more complex. Becker (1964) presents three arguments why the age–earnings profile should slope upwards – that is, why earnings should initially increase with age. They all stem from the theory of on-the-job training. First, because working lives are finite, people will invest in their training as early as possible in their working life so that they will have a longer period in which to recoup their investment. This can be seen in Section 8.2.1, where the present value of life-time income is computed as the sum of discounted future earnings. An investment in human capital late in one's working life will increase earnings for only a few remaining years and there-fore will not add much to lifetime earnings.[18]

Second, because future earnings are discounted in computing the present value of lifetime earn-ings, the gains in labor earnings from an investment late in a person's working life has a much smaller weight in lifetime earnings than from an earlier investment. This is due to the fact that the discount factor increases exponentially with age (see Section 8.2.1). Therefore, earnings later in a person's working life count for less in computing lifetime earnings.

Third, because earnings normally increase with age due to early investments in human capital, the opportunity cost of investing in human capital likewise increases with age. The source of this increase is the rising penalty in forgone earnings. Early in life, when wages are low, the opportunity cost of one hour of training is also low. However, later in life, when one's earnings are higher, the opportunity cost of giving up an hour of pay for an hour of training is greater.[19] For these three reasons, then, workers will invest early in their on-the-job training, and earnings should therefore rise with their experience on the job and, on average, with their age.[20]

There is another part to the age–earnings relation. Mincer (1974) argues that human capital, like other forms of capital, will depreciate over time. For example, many skills acquired 30 or 40 years ago are now obsolete. This is particularly true of fields with rapidly changing technology, such as medicine and computer science. In most fields, there is a gradual obsolescence of skills over time. Also, with physical labor, there is a gradual attrition of strength and dexterity as people age beyond a certain point. For professional athletes, this point can occur in their late 20s or early 30s.

Thus, there are two counter-acting influences on the age–earnings profile. On the one hand, workers acquire new skills and upgrade old skills through on-the-job training. On the other hand, old skills depreciate over time through obsolescence. The human capital model thus predicts that the age–earnings profile will be concave from below – that is, it will slope upward during the early working years, peak, and then slope downward in later working life. The age–earnings profiles illustrated in Figures 8.3 and 8.4 by schooling level generally conform to this pattern.[21] For both males and females, mean earnings by schooling group rise with age, peak around age 50 to 60, and then fall.

Another interesting aspect of the age–earnings profile is that it tends to be steeper for more educated workers. Among 25–34 year olds, average earnings for the different schooling groups were relatively close. In the 35–44 age group, mean earnings were slightly more dispersed among schooling groups, and for the 45–54 and 55–64 age brackets, the dispersion increased even more. The reason for this increasing variation in earnings between schooling groups is the different rates of growth of earnings with age. The earnings profiles are decidedly flatter for the less educated than the more educated workers. This is true for both men and women.

An explanation for this is provided by Mincer (1970). He argues that the increasing steepness of the age–earnings profile with schooling level is due to a positive association between schooling and *post-schooling investment* (that is, on-the-job training). Higher educated workers will take jobs where there is ample opportunity to acquire new skills on the job. Less educated workers, on the other hand, tend to work in positions with little opportunity for on-the-job training. College graduates, for example, will generally work in professional and managerial jobs, while high school graduates may take clerical or semi-skilled jobs and those with less schooling even lower skilled positions. As a result, more educated workers will, on average, acquire more post-schooling investment and their earnings will rise more steeply over time than those with less schooling.[22]

8.3.1   Rates of return to schooling

Another way of comparing age–earnings profiles by schooling level is to compute rates of return to schooling. These estimates are typically made through a regression model in which the logarithm of earnings is regressed on the level of schooling. The actual regression model is derived in Section 8.4 below. Generally, these estimates are based on survey data of individual earnings and schooling.

This section considers studies covering data for the United States over the last half century or so. One of the earliest studies was conducted by Hanoch (1967) for white males using 1960 Census of Population data. His results are presented in Table 8.1. Each cell of the matrix shows the rate of return from completing the schooling level on the left margin of the table in comparison to completing the schooling level indicated at the top of the table. For example, among white males, the completion of 1 to 3 years of high school resulted in a 16 percent rate of return relative to 8 years of elementary school. From the diagonal of the matrix, graduating high school produced a 16 percent rate of return over 1 to 3 years of high school. Completing 1 to 3 years of college yielded a 7 percent rate of return over graduating high school, and graduating college a 12 percent rate of return over 1 to 3 years of college. The marginal rate of return to graduate

Table 8.1   Internal rates of return by schooling levels for white males in the non-South United States, 1959

Higher schooling level in each comparison	Lower schooling level in each comparison				
	Elementary 8	High school 1–3	High school 4	College 1–3	College 4
High school 1–3	0.16				
High school 4	0.16	0.16			
College 1–3	0.11	0.10	0.07		
College 4	0.12	0.11	0.10	0.12	
College 5+	0.10	0.10	0.09	0.10	0.07

Source: Hanoch, G. (1967). An economic analysis of earnings and schooling. *Journal of Human Resources*, **2**(3), 310–29.

Table 8.2   Internal rates of return to schooling for males, 1969

Higher educational level	Lower educational level		
	High school 4	College 1–2	College 3
A. 25 percent ability adjustment			
College 1–2	0.146		
College 3	0.115	0.082	
College 4	0.157	0.164	0.308
B. 15 percent ability adjustment			
College 1–2	0.156		
College 3	0.121	0.087	
College 4	0.168	0.176	0.341
C. No ability adjustment			
College 1–2	0.168		
College 3	0.129	0.094	
College 4	0.179	0.193	0.388

Source: Raymond, R. & Sesnowitz, M. (1975). The returns to investments in higher education: Some new evidence. *Journal of Human Resources*, **10**(2), 139–54.

school for white males was a relatively low 7 percent. In comparison to a high school degree, the rate of return to a four-year college degree was 10 percent, and 9 percent to graduate school.

One interesting pattern that emerges is that the rate of return to schooling generally declined with schooling level. For example, in the second column, the return to 4 years of high school (relative to 1 to 3 years of high school) was 16 percent, the return to 4 years of college was 11 percent, and that to 5 or more years of college was 10 percent. This is the pattern generally predicted by Becker (see Section 8.2.3.4).

Similar tabulations, provided by Raymond and Sesnowitz (1975), for all males in 1969, are shown in Table 8.2. These estimates are based on 1970 Census of Population data. They also include an "ability adjustment" to control for the fact that more educated individuals generally

Table 8.3   Rate of return to schooling indices for males, 1956–1979 [1956 = 100]

Year	Finishing high school (RORH)	Starting college (RORC)	Continuing college (RORCC)
1956	100.0	100.0	100.0
1957	108.8	96.3	100.1
1958	117.2	94.3	101.0
1959	125.1	93.9	102.7
1960	132.2	94.8	105.0
1961	138.4	96.7	107.9
1962	143.9	99.6	111.2
1963	148.4	102.8	114.6
1964	152.3	105.8	117.4
1965	155.4	108.7	120.0
1966	157.9	112.2	123.9
1967	160.0	114.3	126.1
1968	161.6	115.7	128.0
1969	163.0	115.5	128.4
1970	164.3	114.3	128.5
1971	165.5	111.8	127.8
1972	166.6	107.7	126.2
1973	168.0	102.2	124.2
1974	183.2	96.3	105.7
1975	190.6	95.5	106.1
1976	195.6	94.3	106.7
1977	198.3	93.9	109.0
1978	198.5	94.1	112.7
1979	196.0	94.9	117.9

RORH – return to completing the 4th year of high school versus having 1 to 3 years of high school.
RORC – return to starting college versus having completed the 4th year of high school.
RORCC – return to obtaining 4 or more years of college versus 1 to 3 years of college.
Source: Mattila, J.P. (1984). Determinants of male school enrollments: A time-series analysis. *Review of Economics and Statistics*, **64**(2), 242–51.

have greater natural ability than less educated ones (see Section 8.5 below). The Raymond and Sesnowitz figures are higher than those cited from Hanoch in the previous table. The newer estimates indicate that rate of return to attending college over graduating high school was 15–17 percent in 1969; and the return to graduating college over 3 years of college was 31–39 percent.

Part of the reason for the difference in estimates is that the rate of return to schooling tends to fluctuate over time in response to changes in both demand and supply conditions. A time series on estimated returns to both high school and college from 1956 to 1979 based on the work of Mattila (1984) is shown in Table 8.3 (also see Figure 8.5).[23] The data source is the Current Population Reports for the respective years. The returns are presented in index number form, where 1956 is set to 100.0. The data show a steady increase in the returns to a high school degree over 1 to 3 years of high school. In 1979, the return to 4 years of high school was almost twice that of 1956. In contrast, the return to a college degree (relative to 1 to 3 years of college) increased from 1956 through 1972, declined rather sharply between 1972 and 1974, remained low during

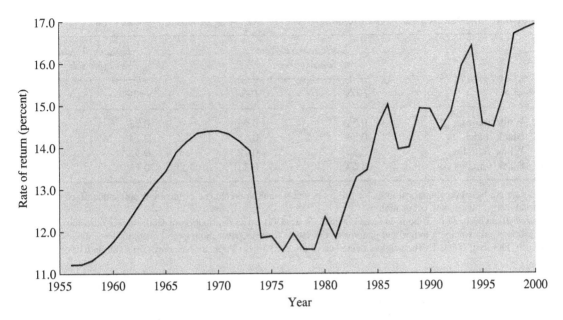

Figure 8.5   The rate of a return to a college degree (relative to a high school degree), 1955–2000

the mid-1970s, and then started to increase in the late 1970s. For college drop-outs (relative to high school graduates), returns fell during the mid-1950s, increased during the 1960s, and then declined again during the 1970s.

There was considerable discussion generated by the collapse in returns to a college education in the 1970s. Freeman (1976) documented both the rising returns to a college degree during the 1960s and its subsequent decline in the 1970s. He argued that during the 1960s, returns increased, despite a large increase in the number of college graduates, because of a rapidly growing demand for college graduates. This was due, in turn, to the growth in sectors and activities that were intensive in their use of college-educated workers. For example, in 1970, 31 percent of all employees in the financial sector had college degrees, compared to 6 percent in the automobile industry. If those industries that are intensive in their use of graduates, such as finance, grow rapidly, then the market demand for college graduates will increase. If these sectors grow slowly, then the market demand will likewise grow slowly.

During the 1960s, several sectors and activities which employed a high proportion of college graduates grew rapidly. These included finance, aerospace, research and development, and the education sector itself, which was very intensive in college manpower. Freeman calculated that between 1960 and 1969, college manpower-intensive sectors grew at 4.4 percent per year, while other sectors grew at only 2 percent per year. This large growth in demand caused the return to a college education to rise.

However, during the 1970s, these demand forces weakened, as the growth of the education, public administration, aircraft, and computer sectors fell off. College manpower-intensive sectors grew at only 2.8 percent per year from 1969 to 1974, while other sectors increased at 2.0 percent per year. Moreover, there was a large surge in the number of college graduates, as the baby-boom generation reached college age.

The result was an excess supply of college-educated workers relative to the demand, causing college-level earnings to drop relative to those of high school graduates. Among male year-round,

Table 8.4   Standardized earnings differentials between schooling groups, 1979 and 1988

Racial and gender Group	College 4 relative to high school 1–3		College 4 relative to high school 4	
	1979	*1988*	*1979*	*1988*
1. White males	0.51	0.66	0.28	0.38
2. Black males	0.56	0.58	0.34	0.41
3. White females	0.55	0.72	0.35	0.46
4. Black females	0.67	0.73	0.45	0.49

The data are based on annual earnings for full-time, year-round workers. The differentials are standardized for age, marital status, region, and occupation.
Source: Blackburn, M.L., Bloom, D.E. & Freeman, R.B. (1991). The distribution of labor market outcomes: measuring and explaining trends and patterns in the 1980s for selected demographic groups in the United States," mimeo, February, Table 3. The original data sources are the Current Population Surveys for 1980 and 1989.

full-time employees, college graduates earned 53 percent more than high-school graduates in 1969 but only 35 percent more in 1974. For recent graduates, the premium fell from 35 percent in 1969 to 16 percent in 1972. Moreover, for the class of 1972, only 45 percent of males with B.A. degrees were able to obtain professional jobs upon graduation, compared to 71 percent in 1968. The fraction of college graduates working as professionals or managers declined from 76 percent in 1969 to 68 percent in 1974.

During the 1980s, the picture changed once again. Comparisons between 1979 and 1988 based on work by Blackburn, Bloom, and Freeman (1991) are shown in Table 8.4. The figures show earnings differentials (rather than rates of return) between college graduates and high school-educated workers in the two years. The data are based on annual earnings for full-time, year-round workers. The differentials are standardized for age, marital status, region, and occupation. The original data sources are the Current Population Surveys for 1980 and 1989. The results show that the earnings of college graduates relative to both high school drop-outs and high school graduates increased from 1979 to 1988. This was true for all four demographic groups shown in the table – white males, black males, white females, and black females. Interestingly, the relative earnings of college graduates increased more for whites than for blacks over this period. Also, according to my figures, the rate of return to a college degree rose from 13.3 percent in 1979 to 16.4 percent in 1988 (see Figure 8.5).

The results are consistent with several other studies that have documented rising returns to a college education during the 1980s. Murphy and Welch (1993) calculated that the ratio of average hourly wages between white male college and high school graduates with 1 to 5 years of experience increased from 1.4 in 1978 to 1.8 in 1985 though it fell off slightly to 1.75 in 1990. Coleman (1993) also generally found large increases in the college earnings premium between 1980 and 1988 for workers with 1 to 5 years of experience – from 1.4 to 1.9 for white men, 1.6 to 1.9 for white women, and 1.7 to 2.0 for black men – though no change for black women (1.9 in both years).

The large relative gains of college graduates during the 1980s reflect both supply and demand factors. Though college enrollment rates did not decline appreciably during the 1980s, the number of people of college-age years did, as the "baby boom" gave way to the "baby dearth." Thus, the number of new college graduates declined during the 1980s. Moreover, many of the industries that experienced the most rapid rate of employment growth during the 1980s – including health, government, finance and banking, and business and professional services – were all intensive in their use of college graduates. Thus, both supply and demand factors helped fuel the growing returns to a college education.

During the 1990s, the return to a college education continued to rise. According to my calculations, the rate of return to a college degree increased from 16.4 percent in 1988 to 19.8 percent in 2000 (see Figure 8.5). However, during the early part of the 2000s decade, the return to college stabilized. The ratio of mean annual earnings between college and high school graduates was 1.9 in both 1988 and 2005 for men and 1.8 in both years for women.

The most prevalent view on the cause of rising return to a college degree in the 1990s is biased technological change. The argument is that the 25-year period from 1980 to 2005 or so witnessed a major technological revolution led by widespread computerization and the consequent diffusion of information technology (IT). This change skewed the income distribution by placing a high premium on college-educated and skilled labor while reducing the demand for less educated and skilled workers.

This argument was made by Bound and Johnson (1992) and Berman, Bound, and Griliches (1994), who identified the declining ratio of production to nonproduction workers *within industry* as the major determinant of changes in relative wages between skilled and unskilled workers. The fact that both the employment share and relative wages shifted in favor of nonproduction workers is evidence of biased technological change. Katz and Murphy (1992) also developed a model that accounted for changes in both the demand and supply of unskilled and skilled labor. Using CPS data over the period 1963 to 1987, they concluded that while the supply of college graduates fluctuated over time, there was a steady increase in the demand for skilled labor in the United States over the period.[24] Goldin and Katz (2007) updated these results to 2005. They estimated that during the 1980s and 1990s, the growth of the supply of college-educated workers slowed to 2.0 percent per year while demand for college graduates increased to about 3.5 percent per year. They argued that this discrepancy between the supply of and demand for college graduates explained the large increase in the return to a college degree observed during the 1980s and 1990s.

Table 8.5 presents comparisons of rates of returns to education for different regions of the world on the basis of work by Psacharopoulos (1985). The figures are based on a large number of country studies conducted mainly for the 1960s and the 1970s. The figures in Table 8.5 are averages of the returns computed for individual countries within each group. Two different sets of returns are calculated. The first is the social rate of return, based on the total cost of education, from both public and private sources, at each schooling level. The second, the private rate of return, is based on the costs of education to individual students, after the public subsidy to education is deducted.

The results indicate that for all regions of the world, social returns are greater to primary education than to secondary school, and greater to secondary than higher education. The main reason for the very high return to primary schooling is the substantial productivity differential between literate and illiterate workers. The data also show that returns to education are substantially higher for low-income regions of the world – Africa, Asia, and Latin America – than for middle-income and high-income countries. For example, the social return to a high school education was 70 percent higher in Africa than in the middle-income countries. The reason is the greater scarcity of human capital relative to physical capital in poor regions of the world. The figures also show that private returns are higher than social returns. The differences are particularly great for the poor regions of the world and for higher education in all regions. The differences reflect the greater public subsidy to education in poor countries than in richer ones, and the greater public subsidy for higher education than for lower levels of schooling.

Table 8.5   Average rates of return to education by region of the world and level of education

Region	Social returns			Private returns		
	Primary	Secondary	Higher	Primary	Secondary	Higher
A. 1960s and 1970s[a]						
Africa	0.26	0.17	0.13	0.45	0.26	0.32
Asia	0.27	0.15	0.13	0.31	0.15	0.18
Latin America	0.26	0.18	0.16	0.32	0.23	0.23
Middle Income	0.13	0.10	0.08	0.17	0.13	0.13
High income	—	0.11	0.09	—	0.12	0.12
B. Late 1990s and early 2000s[b]						
Sub-Saharan Africa	0.25	0.18	0.11	0.38	0.25	0.28
Asia	0.16	0.11	0.11	0.20	0.16	0.18
Latin America and the Caribbean	0.17	0.13	0.12	0.27	0.17	0.20
Europe, Middle East and North Africa[c]	0.16	0.10	0.10	0.14	0.14	0.19
OECD	0.09	0.09	0.09	0.13	0.11	0.12

a   *Source*: Psacharopoulos, G. (1985). Returns to education: A further international update and implications. *Journal of Human Resources*, **20**(4), 583–604, Table 1.
b   *Source*: Psacharopoulos, G. & Patrinos, H.A. (2002). Returns to investment in education: A further update. World Bank Policy Research Working Paper 2881, September, Table 1.
c   Non-OECD.

Comparable figures for the 1990s and early 2000s based on the work of Psacharopoulos and Patrinos (2002) are also shown in Table 8.5. The country categorization is a bit different than in the earlier data. However, the pattern of results is very similar. Returns to education are again higher for lower income countries than higher income ones; for lower levels of schooling in comparison to higher schooling levels; and for private returns in comparison to social returns.

8.3.1.1   Policy implications

If we accept the assumptions of the human capital model, then these rates of return could serve to give some guidance to social policy. For developing countries, particularly in Africa and Latin America, the implications are clear that underinvestment exists at all levels of education. This argument is documented by the fact that social returns to schooling are considerably higher than normal rates of return to investment in physical capital (plant and equipment). Primary school appears to be the top priority, since its social return exceeded that for secondary or college education. This also shows the importance of raising literacy rates in less-developed countries. The results also suggest that secondary schooling be given more priority than higher education in poorer countries. Interestingly, similar results of high rates of return to schooling were found for nonwhite males for the United States. This suggests that for the United States heavy investment is warranted in the education of black Americans, particularly at the secondary school level.

Results for advanced economies like the United States indicate that education is still a good investment, if not an "extraordinary" investment. Returns of the order of 10 to 12 percent are comparable to those obtained in private investment in physical capital. Returns to college, in particular, have been increasing during the 1980s and 1990s and are now as high as they were during the 1960s. This recommends the importance of continued investment in education in the United States.

8.3.2 Lifetime earnings

Another important implication of the human capital model is that the present value of the discounted stream of lifetime earnings ("lifetime earnings," for short) should be equal among schooling groups if the basic assumptions of the model are true (see Section 8.2). In actuality, many of the assumptions of the human capital do not hold. Capital markets are not perfect; because of trade unions and the like, the labor market is not perfectly competitive; and "native ability" may be correlated with schooling achievements (see Section 8.5 below). Any one of these three conditions would cause some inequality in lifetime earnings between schooling groups. However, for the human capital model to be at all reliable, there should be relatively small differences in lifetime earnings among these groups.

Four sets of estimates are presented on lifetime earnings in Table 8.6. The first, from Morgan and David (1963), was based on the 1959 Survey Research Center National Sample and showed lifetime earnings in 1959 dollars at different levels of educational attainment for white males. Differences in estimated lifetime earnings between schooling groups were quite small in this study. The percentage difference between lowest ($86,900) and highest ($101,700) was only 17 percent. Moreover, if we exclude the group with nonacademic training, lifetime earnings ranged from $91,000 to $102,000, a relatively narrow range.

The second set, from Lillard (1977), was derived from the NBER–Thorndike sample. This was a longitudinal or panel dataset, which followed the same set of individuals over time. In this

Table 8.6 Estimates of lifetime earnings by schooling group

A. Morgan and David (1963)[a]

Educational level	*Lifetime earnings ($)*
Grades 0–8	96,000
Grades 9–11	96,950
Grade 12	90,300
Grade 12 and nonacademic training	86,900
College, no degree	91,100
College, bachelor's degree	100,450
College, advanced degree	101,700

B. Lillard (1977)[b]

Ability level	*Years of schooling*								
	12	*13*	*14*	*15*	*16*	*17*	*18*	*19*	*20*
1. Discount rate = 0.03									
Low	252	251	252	254	255	256	257	258	259
Average	260	255	256	259	264	271	279	289	300
High	270	268	269	273	280	288	298	310	322
2. Discount rate = 0.05									
Low	163	159	156	154	152	151	149	147	146
Average	166	160	157	156	157	158	161	165	169
High	171	165	163	163	165	168	172	177	182

Table 8.6   *(Continued)*

C. 1989 Survey of Consumer Finances[c]

Educational level	White males	Nonwhite males	Females
Grades 0–11	895	653	454
High school 4	1,221	876	659
College 1–3	1,308	1,043	737
College 4	2,195	1,370	927
College 5+	2,770	2,341	1,248
Gini coefficients			
Annual earnings	0.50	0.41	0.40
Lifetime earnings	0.31	0.23	0.22

D. 1998 Survey of Consumer Finances[d]

Educational level	White males	Nonwhite males	Females
Grades 0–11	1,272	831	986
High school 4	2,395	983	1,056
College 1–3	3,176	1,507	943
College 4	3,222	1,342	1,921
College 5+	3,690	2,098	1,980
Gini coefficients			
Annual earnings	0.52	0.44	0.46
Lifetime earnings	0.26	0.28	0.33

a   *Source*: Morgan, J. & David, M. (1963). Education and income. *Quarterly Journal of Economics*, **77**(3), 423–37. Lifetime earnings is computed as the present value at age 15 of future earnings discounted at an interest rate of 4 percent, assuming 2,000 hours worked per year until age 65. Adjustments were made for differences in the social characteristics of workers, labor market condition, past mobility, and supervisory responsibility.

b   *Source*: Lillard, L.A. (1977). Inequality: Earnings vs. human wealth. *American Economic Review*, **67**(2), 42–53, Table 1. The figures show lifetime earnings in thousands of 1970 dollars by years of schooling, assuming full retirement at age 66 and with average values for social variables.

c   *Source*: Author's calculations from the 1989 Survey of Consumer Finances. The figures show lifetime earnings in thousands of 1989 dollars for individuals aged 35 in 1989 by years of schooling, assuming full retirement at age 65, a 1 percent growth rate in real earnings, and a 2 percent discount rate.

d   *Source*: author's calculations from the 1998 Survey of Consumer Finances. The figures show lifetime earnings in thousands of 1998 dollars for individuals aged 30 to 50 in 1998 by years of schooling, assuming full retirement at age 65, a 1 percent growth rate in real earnings, and a 2 percent discount rate.

case, men who were born between 1917 and 1925 and who volunteered for the Air Force in 1943 were surveyed in 1943 and one to four times more after that until 1970. On the basis of these data, lifetime earnings were estimated for each individual in the sample. Estimates were standardized for social and demographic factors, including parent's education, religion, and number of siblings, as well as an ability index based on the Armed Forces Qualification Test (AFQT).

The results show that there was variation in lifetime earnings between schooling groups even among individuals with the same ability level. However, here, again, the variation was not very great. One way of measuring the extent of variation is to compute the Gini coefficient for lifetime earnings. Lillard calculated a value of 0.19 for the Gini coefficient of lifetime earnings for the 4,699 individuals in the sample (the results were very similar for the different discount rates used in the analysis). In contrast, the Gini coefficient for annual earnings by age group averaged 0.28. Thus, inequality in lifetime earnings was about one-third less than that of annual earnings.[25]

My own calculations based on both the 1989 and 1998 Survey of Consumer Finances showed considerably more variation in lifetime earnings by schooling group than the previous sets. Among white males in 1989, there was an almost twofold difference between the lifetime earnings of college graduates and those of high school graduates. For nonwhite males, the ratio was 1.6 and for females, 1.4. In 1998, the ratio of lifetime earnings of college graduates to those of high school graduates was closer among white males (a ratio of 1.4) and nonwhite males (a ratio of 1.4) but greater among females (a ratio of 1.8). However, as in the other studies, the inequality of lifetime earnings was about a third to a half less than that of annual earnings.

In summary, these studies do show that there is variation in lifetime earnings among schooling groups. However, the variation in average lifetime earnings by schooling group was considerably smaller than that of average annual earnings, and inequality of lifetime earnings among all individuals was less than that of annual earnings.

These results have two important implications. First, they indicate that a substantial portion of the differences in annual earnings among individuals evens out over the lifetime. This is partly due to the fact that different educational groups start work at different ages and have different lifetime earnings trajectories. It is also a result of the fact that annual income has both a permanent and transitory component. The transitory component tends to wash out over the lifetime, so that the variation in permanent income among individuals is less than that of annual income.

Second, from a policy perspective, should we be unduly concerned with increases in the inequality of annual incomes if lifetime (or permanent) income is more equally distributed? It probably makes more sense to consider differences in lifetime income and resources as the more relevant measure of inequality for public policy, because this is what determines the long-term welfare of families. In this regard, it would be of interest to know whether inequality in lifetime income has also been rising in recent years.

8.4   THE SCHOOLING–EARNINGS FUNCTION*

Mincer (1970, 1974) contributed much of the basic work in deriving a specific functional relation between an individual's level of schooling and labor earnings. Following Mincer, let us assume that a worker with S years of schooling earns E_S per year and that earnings are constant over time. Assume also that the direct schooling costs are zero – that is, the only cost of schooling is forgone earnings – and that there is no further investment in human capital after the completion of schooling. If working life is n years and that the market rate of interest is r, then the present discounted value of the stream of future earnings, V_S, is given by:[26]

$$V_S = \sum_{t=S+1}^{S+n} E_S/(1 + r)^t \tag{8.4}$$

It is now convenient to convert Equation (8.4) into a continuous form. To do this requires some calculus. Instead of assuming that earnings are paid each year, we assume that they are received continuously over time. Therefore, the present value of lifetime earnings becomes:

$$V_S = \int_S^{S+n} E_S\, e^{-rt}\, dt \tag{8.5}$$

where $\int$ is the integral sign and e is the natural number.

Equation (8.5) can be solved to obtain[27]

$$V_S = E_S e^{-rS}(1 - e^{-rn})/r \tag{8.6}$$

The present value of earnings, $V_{S'}$, for a worker with S' years of schooling is given by:

$$V_{S'} = E_{S'} e^{-rS'}(1 - e^{-rn'})/r \tag{8.7}$$

where $E_{S'}$ is annual earnings (assumed constant over life) corresponding to S' years of schooling and n' is the person's working life in years.

By the assumptions of the human capital model, V_S must equal $V_{S'}$ in equilibrium. Therefore, from Equations (8.6) and (8.7),

$$E_S e^{-rS}(1 - e^{-rn})/r = E_{S'} e^{-rS'}(1 - e^{-rn'})/r \tag{8.8}$$

Rearranging terms, we obtain an expression for the relative annual earnings between the two workers:

$$\frac{E_S}{E_{S'}} = \frac{e^{-rS'}(1 - e^{-rn'})}{e^{-rS}(1 - e^{-rn})} \tag{8.9}$$

This ratio can be simplified under either of two conditions. First, if despite the fact that the two individuals have different amounts of schooling, they work the same number of years, then $n' = n$ and the two expressions in parentheses are equal. Second, if as recent data suggest, differences in working life are small and n and n' are large, then the difference in the value of the two expressions in parentheses is very small and can be conveniently ignored.[28] Under either condition, Equation (8.9) can be simplified to:

$$\frac{E_S}{E_{S'}} = e^{-r(S-S')} \tag{8.10}$$

If we now let S' be the zero schooling level and take the natural logarithms (ln) of both sides of Equation (8.10), we obtain:

$$\ln E_S = \ln E_0 + rS \tag{8.11}$$

Equation (8.11) is the basic earnings function of the human capital model.

Before considering the uses of the earnings Equation (8.11), let us consider three implications of Equation (8.10). First, the ratio $E_S/E_{S'}$ is greater than one if S is greater than S'. In other words, workers with more schooling should receive higher earnings. Second, the ratio $E_S/E_{S'}$ is a positive function of r. The higher the discount rate, the greater must be the increase in earnings to compensate for an additional year of schooling (and hence forgone earnings). This point was illustrated in the various numerical examples presented in Section 8.2. Third, the equation indicates that earnings differences are multiplicative between schooling levels. In other words, an additional year of schooling is associated with a certain *percentage* increase in earnings, rather than a certain absolute dollar amount. Or, by Equation (8.11), there is a log-linear relation between earnings and schooling.

Equation (8.11) lends itself very readily to econometric analysis. If E_i refers to the earnings of individual i and S_i the person's level of schooling, then the regression model becomes:

$$\ln E_i = b_0 + b_1 S_i + u_i \tag{8.12}$$

where b_0 and b_1 are parameter coefficients to be estimated and u_i is a random error term. The coefficient estimator b_1 is of particular interest, because it is the estimated rate of return to schooling (that is, it corresponds to the variable r in Equation (8.11)). The random error term u_i is supposed to pick up individual differences in earnings capacity, from differences in abilities, quality of schooling, family background, and the like.

Mincer (1974) applied this model to a sample of white, nonfarm male workers drawn from the 1960 Census of Population. As he noted, the equation was really incomplete because there was no variable for experience or other sources of post-schooling investment. Since the existence of on-the-job training or post-schooling investment will cause earnings to rise over time for each schooling group, the assumption of constant earnings E_S over time will be violated. However, Mincer found that after about 8 years of work experience, the average earnings of most schooling groups were close to their average lifetime value.[29] Therefore, choosing a sample of workers with 8 or so years of experience could provide a fairly valid test of the schooling model.

The results of these regressions are shown in Table 8.7, as well as those of an additional form with the logarithm of weeks worked (ln W) added.[30] The coefficient of schooling – that is, the estimated rate of return – was highly significant in each regression. The estimated rates of return ranged from 10 percent to 17 percent, which was similar to the range that Hanoch (1967) and Raymond and Sesnowitz (1975) found (see Tables 8.1 and 8.2). The coefficient of weeks worked was also highly significant. The coefficient of determination of the regression (R^2), which is the statistic that measures the amount of variation in the dependent variation explained by the independent variables of the regression, was very high for this type of individual data. For the forms

Table 8.7 Regressions of annual earnings on schooling and weeks worked for white, nonfarm males with 6 to 10 years of experience

Years of experience	Number of observations	Regression results		R^2
8	790	(1)	$\ln E = 6.36 + 0.162S$ (16.4)	0.306
		(2)	$\ln E = 2.14 + 0.115S + 1.27 \ln W$ (15.1) (21.0)	0.575
6–10	3,689	(3)	$\ln E = 6.75 + 0.133S$ 0.261 (36.1)	
		(4)	$\ln E = 2.07 + 0.104S + 1.31 \ln W$ (34.0) (43.4)	0.511
7–9	2,124	(5)	$\ln E = 6.30 + 0.165S$ 0.328 (26.5)	
		(6)	$\ln E = 1.89 + 0.121S + 1.29 \ln W$ (24.6) (30.6)	0.596

(1) ln E: natural logarithm of earnings; (2) S: schooling, (3) ln W: natural logarithm of weeks worked; and (4) R^2: coefficient of determination. Figures in parenthesis are t-ratios.
Source: Mincer, J. (1974). *Schooling, Experience, and Earnings*. New York: National Bureau of Economic Research, p. 53. The results are based on the 1/1,000 sample of the 1960 U.S. Census of Population.

without ln W, the R^2 ranged from 0.26 to 0.33, and in the forms with ln W, the range was 0.51 to 0.60.

8.4.1 The extended earnings function*

As Mincer (1974) noted, the schooling model is an incomplete specification for the human capital model, because no variable is included to reflect on-the-job training or other forms of post-school investment. Therefore, to complete the model, some variable or variables must be included to capture such training. Unfortunately, it is very difficult to observe the amount of training an individual receives, and most data sources include no such estimates. Actually, very few data sources have reliable estimates even of the amount of work experience someone has had. Therefore, a few additional assumptions must be made on the amount of post-school investment workers receive in order to obtain a form that can be estimated.

As Becker (1975) argued, investment in human capital should decline over the lifecycle, at least beyond an early stage, primarily because the pay-off period is limited (see Section 8.2 above). The actual form of the investment function cannot be directly predicted by the human capital model. However, Mincer (1974) proposed four possibilities. The one most widely used is discussed below.

Let k_X be the amount of time devoted to post-school investment at X years of experience. Then, the total amount of time devoted to post-school investment from the first year of work through X years of work, K_X, is given by:

$$K_X = \int_{t=0}^{X} k_t \, dt \tag{8.13}$$

For the same reason as the schooling model, earnings will increase exponentially with the total amount of post-school investment. Therefore, the logarithm of earnings of someone with S years of schooling and X years of experience is given by:

$$\ln E_{S,X} = \ln E_0 + rS + r'K_X \tag{8.14}$$

where r is the rate of return to schooling and r' is the rate of return to post-school investment.

Now, suppose post-school investment declines as a linear function of time. Then:

$$k_X = k_0 - (k_0/T)X \tag{8.15}$$

where T is the total period of post-school investment. In this case,

$$K_X = k_0 X - (k_0/2T)X^2 \tag{8.16}$$

and

$$\ln E_{S,X} = \ln E_0 + rS + r'k_0 X - (r'k_0/2T)X^2 \tag{8.17}$$

This relation is referred to as a *parabolic* earnings function because there is both an experience (X) and an experience-squared (X^2) term in the function. This implies that earnings will rise with experience for a time, level off, and then decline towards the end of the working life. The actual estimating form looks much simpler:

$$\ln E_i = b_0 + b_1 S_i + b_2 X_i + b_3 X_i^2 + u_i \tag{8.18}$$

Table 8.8 Regressions of annual earnings on schooling, experience, and weeks worked for white nonfarm, nonstudent males up to age 65

Regression results	R^2
(1) $\ln E = 7.58 + 0.070S$ (43.8)	0.067
(2) $\ln E = 6.20 + 0.107S + 0.081X - 0.0012X^2$ (72.3) (75.5) (55.8)	0.285

(1) $\ln E$: natural logarithm of earnings; (2) S: schooling; (3) X: experience; (4) $\ln W$: natural logarithm of weeks worked; and (5) R^2: coefficient of determination. Figures in parentheses are *t*-ratios.
Source: Mincer, J. (1974). *Schooling, Experience, and Earnings*. New York: National Bureau of Economic Research, p. 92. The results are based on the 1/1,000 sample of the 1960 U.S. Census of Population. The sample size is 31,093.

Mincer (1974) estimated this regression from a sample of 31,093 white, nonfarm, nonstudent males up to age 65 drawn from the 1960 Census of Population. The results are shown in Table 8.8. The first line shows the results of estimating the simple schooling equation on the full sample. Though the schooling variable is still significant at the 1 percent level, the R^2 is much lower than when the sample is restricted to a given number of years of experience (see Table 8.7). The second line shows the results of estimating the parabolic earnings function. The goodness of fit for the equation is 0.29, considerably higher than for the simple schooling model. The R^2 is actually comparable to the schooling equations in Table 8.7, which limit the sample to individuals with similar years of experience. Moreover, the schooling and experience variables are both still significant at the 1 percent level.

These results of Mincer, shown in Tables 8.7 and 8.8, have often been cited as confirmation of the human capital model. However, there are a number of criticisms of these results. First, including weeks worked as an explanatory variable for annual earnings will overstate the explanatory power of the model, since the real issue is difference in *compensation rates* explained by schooling achievement and experience.[31] As a result, the fair measure of the explanatory power of the model is between 26 and 33 percent which, though still high, leaves at least two-thirds of the variation unexplained. Jencks *et al.* (1972), for example, argued that the amount of unexplained variation was so large as to make schooling an *ineffective* weapon to reduce overall economic inequality. Second, the sample chosen was restricted to white males (employed in nonagricultural industries) in their prime working years. Most of the labor force – females, minorities, and agricultural workers – was therefore excluded in the test. Indeed, subsequent work has shown that the human capital earnings model does not work nearly as well for females as minorities as it does for white males (see, for example, Ishikawa & Ryan, 2002).

8.5 ABILITY AND EARNINGS

The idea of a positive association between ability and earnings is an intuitive one. People who are more able should be more productive on the job and therefore command higher pay in the workplace. In the neoclassical model, workers with more ability have higher marginal products and therefore command higher wages. Many early models of income distribution were based almost exclusively on the distribution of ability in the population.[32]

The main difficulty with these models is in defining "ability." If ability and productivity are simply synonymous, then we are left with a truism or tautology without explanatory content.

Unless we can explain what ability is or what determines it independently of what someone earns, we are left with a theory without economic content. In the old saw, "if you're so smart, why aren't you rich?", if "being rich" *means* "being smart," then there is no way of verifying that intelligence is positively related to labor earnings. We shall return to this point later.

In this section, we consider the relation between schooling, ability, and earnings. There are both theoretical and statistical issues involved. Suppose that ability affects productivity on the job and thereby pay, and ability also affects school performance. Then, how do we determine the independent effects of ability and schooling on a worker's productivity and earnings? More particularly, if we are in a human capital framework, how do we determine the rate of return to schooling independently of the return to ability? As will be seen, on the statistical level, this is equivalent to asking the question: How do we separate out the coefficients of schooling and ability on earnings? The failure to do this correctly will result in the commission of a potentially serious error in estimating the returns to education, called a specification bias.

In many models, ability is included along with schooling, experience, and other personal characteristics as independent determinants of a person's earnings. Unlike the traditional variables used in such models, there are two types of problems associated with the ability variable. First, as mentioned above, it is very difficult to define innate or natural ability and even more difficult to measure it. Most studies treat ability as synonymous with cognitive ability and measure it using standardized tests such as IQ or school achievement tests. But even with such tests, it very difficult to separate out "innate intelligence" from that produced by home environment or by schooling itself.

The second difficulty in the use of the ability variable is that ability may not only influence a person's earnings directly – that is, through its impact on job performance – but indirectly through its effect on schooling achievement. The path diagram shown in Figure 8.6 may help clarify the problem. Path (*a*) reflects the fact that ability may affect schooling attainment for two reasons. First, more able students will, in general, achieve a higher level of potential productivity from a given amount of schooling. Second, partly as a consequence of the first, the more able student will generally acquire more schooling than the less able student. Ability will, therefore, affect both a student's achievement from schooling and the level of schooling attained.

Ability will indirectly affect earnings via path (*b*) according to its effect on the amount of human capital acquired. Those with more human capital will, on average, command higher wages in the labor market. At the same time, by path (*c*), ability will directly affect earnings, independently of school-acquired skills. A worker with more ability may simply perform better on the job than someone who is less able.

Econometrically, the most straightforward way of assessing the independent effects of ability and schooling on earnings is to estimate two equations of the following form:

$$\ln E_i = a_0 + a_1 S_i \tag{8.19a}$$
$$\ln E_i = b_0 + b_1 S_i + b_2 A_i \tag{8.19b}$$

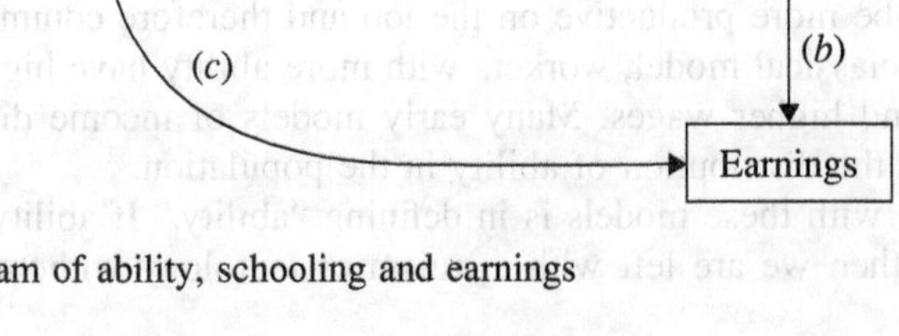

Figure 8.6   Path diagram of ability, schooling and earnings

where A_i is the ability level of individual i. Equation (8.19a) is the standard human capital earnings function, where the coefficient a_1 is the estimated rate of return to schooling. Equation (8.19b) includes an ability variable as an independent determinant of earnings.

If the model illustrated in Figure 8.6 is correct, then we would expect that schooling and ability will be positively correlated (related), since those with more ability will, on average, acquire more schooling. As a result, Equation (8.19a) will lead to an overstatement of the "true" impact of schooling on earnings, since part of the estimated effect of schooling on earnings is due to the greater ability of the more educated worker. The estimated rate of return to schooling from Equation (8.19a) will be biased upward – that is, is too high.[33] Equation (8.19b) corrects for this bias by including the ability variable. The coefficient b_1 is therefore a better estimate of the rate of return to schooling. b_1 will be lower than a_1, because part of the effect of schooling on earnings estimated in Equation (8.19a) will be properly attributed to ability. Becker (1964) thought that rates of return to schooling were probably overstated by about one-third because of the exclusion of an ability variable. However, there was no hard evidence available at that time on which to base this presumption. Since then, a number of studies have tried to estimate the size of the bias.

8.5.1 Estimates of the ability effect*

Several studies were based on the NBER–Thorndike sample. This sample consisted of men who had taken a battery of tests called the Armed Forces Qualification Test (AFQT), which were used to select candidates for the Army Air Force during World War II. These tests measured various abilities such as mathematical and reasoning skills, physical coordination, reaction to stress, and spatial perception. In 1955, a follow-up survey was conducted of 17,000 of those who took the test in 1943 to see how useful these tests were in predicting future vocational success. In 1969, the National Bureau of Economic Research conducted a follow-up survey to determine their vocational achievement in that year. About 4,700 of the original 17,000 responded to the follow-up questionnaire. This sample is useful for estimating Equation (8.19b) because the database provides observations on both schooling and ability.

Taubman and Wales (1974) conducted one of the first studies using the NBER–Thorndike sample. They found that the inclusion of all the ability measures in the model reduced the estimated rate of return to schooling by about 30 percent. This figure was quite close to Becker (1964)'s original guess. Looking more closely at the full range of ability measures provided by the AFQT, they also found that ability was a significant determinant of earnings for all schooling groups. Of the various measures of ability that they used, mathematical ability had the strongest effect on earnings.

As with the testing of many hypotheses in economics, results vary according to the sample of data and methodology used. Hause (1972, 1975), using the same NBER–Thorndike sample, found a smaller bias in estimating the rate of return to schooling, though his work concentrated primarily on measures of cognitive ability. Griliches and Mason (1972) also reported a relatively small effect of AFQT scores using a sample of World War II veterans. On the other hand, Hansen, Weisbrod, and Scanlon (1970) estimated a larger effect, a bias of about 50 percent, when the NBER–Thorndike sample was extended to include individuals who had taken but failed the AFQT.

Other data sources have also been used. Ashenfelter and Mooney (1968) compiled data on a sample of 1,322 Woodrow Wilson Fellows appointed between 1958 and 1960, with salary data reported for 1966. Adding SAT scores as their ability variable, the coefficient on the schooling variable declined very little. Wise (1975) used a sample consisting of college graduates working in a large corporation. He found that schooling level had a significant effect on a person's initial salary, but not on its rate of growth over time in the firm. On the other hand, school quality and class rank (interpreted as measures of ability) were very significant in affecting salary growth over time but not in the determination of starting salary. Similar results were reported by Solmon (1975) and Wachtel (1975), both using the NBER–Thorndike sample, and Jones and Jackson (1990) in a study of graduates in business administration.

Several more recent studies have relied on samples of twins to assess the relative contribution of ability to earnings. The advantage of using this type of data is that twins are much more likely to have similar innate ability (and family backgrounds) than a random sample of individuals. Ashenfelter and Rouse (1998) used such a special sample of twins collected during the summers of 1991, 1992, and 1993 at the Twinsburg Twins Festival, which is held annually in Twinsburg, Ohio. Based on the survey data collected from a sample of about 700 twins, they found only a marginally upward bias in the return to schooling estimated from conventional earnings equations like such as Equation (8.18).

A study of Australian twins by Miller, Mulvey, and Martin (1995) revealed an even stronger ability bias on estimated returns to schooling. They utilized data from the Australian Twin Register which was gathered in two surveys, in 1980–1982 and 1988–1989 and which contained a large sample of 3,808 twin pairs. Estimating standard earnings equations of the form (8.19a) and (8.19b), they estimated that fully one-third of the conventionally estimated returns to schooling was due to ability (and, in fact, one-third to shared family environment). Only the remaining one-third was due to schooling *per se*.

In sum, there is general agreement among economists about the importance of innate ability in the determination of earnings. Almost all agree that it affects earnings directly through its effect on job performance and indirectly through its effect on schooling achievement, although specific estimates do differ on its importance. On average, rates of return to schooling estimated without an ability variable included in the equation are probably overstated by about a third, as Becker had originally speculated.

The concern about the ability bias in estimating rates of return to education is not only of academic interest but can also have a direct bearing on public policy issues. As we discussed in Section 8.3.1.1, human capital theory has had and continues to have a direct bearing on social policy. This is particularly true for the emphasis on schooling as a mechanism to alleviate poverty and reduce inequality. Moreover, it has important implications for economic growth, since investment in human capital, along with that in physical capital, appear to be the two major determinants of output growth. As a result, accurate estimates of the rate of return to schooling do have direct relevance for public decisions regarding educational expenditures and, particularly, educational programs such as student loans. This concern will be addressed below, when we consider other interpretations of the relation between schooling and earnings.

8.5.2   The nature vs. nurture controversy

In our discussion of ability models, we have sidestepped one major and very contentious issue: What determines individual ability? Debate on this question has a long history, though it has heated up considerably over the last several decades. The central issue is whether ability, particularly intelligence, is genetically inherited or whether it is due to environment, particularly a child's family background. Much of the difficulty with resolving this issue is that, statistically, it is very hard to separate the influence of genetic factors from environment. The exception is the study of twins, where it is possible to control for genetic make-up.

Cyril Burt undertook one of the first studies of identical twins, some of whom were brought up in the same home, and some of whom were raised separately. He was also one of the earliest proponents of the "nature" view. The twin sample allows the most direct test of the heritability of ability, since identical twins have the same genetic make-up.[34] If identical twins raised in different environments achieve the same (or nearly the same) IQ score, then it is possible to attribute the determination of intelligence to heredity alone. If, on the other hand, pairs raised in different homes have different IQs, then the environment would be seen to have a major impact.[35] Burt determined from his study that genetic influences were paramount in determining intelligence. However, it was subsequently learned that Burt, who had already believed in the extreme importance of genetic make-up, simply falsified his data to obtain the desired result. Therefore, Burt's work has been completely discredited (see Kamin, 1974, or Hearnshaw, 1979, for more on Cyril Burt).

In more recent years, Jensen (1969, 1970), Shockley (1970), and Herrnstein and Murray (1994) resurrected the Burt position that genetic differences are the primary cause of differences in intelligence. Their work was particularly controversial, since it attributed a large part of the lower economic status achieved by blacks to genetic differences between blacks and whites. Much of their analysis was based on the rather strong assumption that gene pools evolved independently in the black and white populations. However, their work was generally criticized for its failure to control adequately for the effects of home environment versus genetic endowment in explaining both intelligence and economic performance.[36]

Taubman (1976) produced the first widely accepted study of the role of genetics versus home background on earnings. He surveyed 2,000 twins, including both identical and fraternal pairs, who were about 50 years old in 1950. Taubman's interest was to determine how much of the difference in earnings – not measured intelligence as Burt had done – could be attributed to family background and how much to intelligence. All of the twins in Taubman's samples were raised in the same home, so that family background could be controlled for. If genetics were very important in determining economic success, then identical twins should have earnings that were more similar than fraternal twins. For statistical reasons,[37] Taubman could compute only a range of possible effects, and concluded that between 18 and 41 percent of the variation in earnings was due to heredity. His overall conclusion was that environment was more important than heredity in the determination of earnings. In a later study, the econometrician Goldberger (1979), using the same data but making different though equally reasonable assumptions, concluded that *no* part of the difference in earnings was due to genetic differences.[38]

Studies by Lydall (1968) and Bowles and Nelson (1974) examined similar issues but relied on samples of the full population (rather than twins) which included measures of both home environment and intelligence. Lydall (1968) argued that family background and, in particular, the social class into which a child is born, largely influence measured intelligence. Intelligence testing always takes place after a child has reached a certain age, so that home environment and other environmental influences such as schooling cannot be directly separated out from heredity. Moreover, since most intelligence tests were couched in language, the literacy and the use of language in the home were very likely to make a difference in the child's measured intelligence. In this regard, socioeconomic class made an important difference.

Another indicator of intelligence is school achievement. Here, too, social class has a large impact, because of the greater emphasis on education that is characteristic of higher socioeconomic classes and because of the greater socialization of children into the work habits required in most school systems that is also characteristic of middle and upper classes. Social class also has a direct bearing on the quality of schooling received by the child. In his survey of various data on this issue, Lydall concluded that between 20 and 30 percent of measured intelligence could be attributed to the socioeconomic class of the parents.

Bowles and Nelson (1974) employed a recursive system to assess the role of socioeconomic background and intelligence in the determination of earnings. They estimated a four-equation

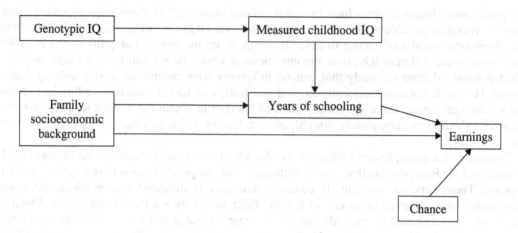

Figure 8.7 Path diagram of ability, socioeconomic background, schooling and earnings

system that is summarized in Figure 8.7. They argued that ability, as measured in their case by IQ, affects earnings directly and indirectly through its relation to years of schooling. However, they also argued that family background affects these relations in three ways. First, they distinguished between "genotypic IQ" or innate ability and measured childhood IQ. They argued that family background affected actual measured IQ, because parental literacy and education had a direct bearing on early childhood development. Second, family background had a direct bearing on schooling attainment, because financial resources differed among families as well as their emphasis on education. Third, family background affected earnings directly, because family connections and the like made an important difference in the jobs obtained.

Their principal findings were, first, that independent of socioeconomic background, measured childhood IQ exercised a substantial direct effect on schooling attainment but had a much smaller impact on income and occupational status. Second, considering both direct and indirect effects, variations in childhood IQ were less important than variations in socioeconomic background in determining schooling attainment, occupational status, and income. Third, the observed inter-generational transmission of educational and economic status was attributable primarily to the direct impact of education. Thus, even if IQ were largely hereditary, its role in explaining economic status was still relatively small.

In sum, the nature versus nurture controversy still remains unresolved. The reason is that statistically it is very difficult to control for all the genetic and environmental variables necessary to perform a conclusive test. Most social scientists take the view that both sets of factors are important in determining ability, particularly intelligence, as well as economic success. Perhaps, the vehemence with which this issue has been contested is due to the rather extreme policy implications some analysts have drawn. Some of those who support the heredity position have suggested that the only way to increase the average intelligence level of society and to reduce inequality is through eugenics – that is, the selective breeding of the population. Some have even suggested that this selection should be done on the basis of race. However, Goldberger (1979) pointed out that even *if* it could be shown that genetics were the primary factor in determining ability or intelligence, it did not follow that such genetically based handicaps could not be overcome. A good example is that someone born with poor eyesight can have this problem corrected through the acquisition of eyeglasses.[39]

8.6   PRODUCTIVITY AND EARNINGS

We have until now been rather reticent about an important linkage in the human capital model of earnings. Let us review Becker's argument, presented in Section 8.2, about the effect of increased schooling on labor earnings. There are two sides to the argument. On the one hand, the reason why a student would spend an extra year in school and forgo a year's worth of earnings is that the resultant wage will be higher after the extra year of school. On the other hand, the reason why a firm will pay more to a better-schooled worker is that the individual's *productivity* will be higher. This reflects a basic proposition of neoclassical theory that all factors of production are paid their marginal product. Therefore, from the firm's point of view, the only justification for paying a worker with greater schooling more is that his or her productivity is higher. The same argument must also hold for paying a higher wage for a worker with greater post-school investment, and, in general, for paying higher wages to those with greater human capital. Schematically, the "productivity linkage" can be illustrated as follows:

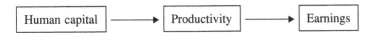

The evidence that has been presented in this chapter establishes a relation between human capital and earnings. Figures 8.3 and 8.4 on age–earnings profiles by schooling level and Mincer's regression results (Tables 8.7 and 8.8) establish a direct, positive relation between an individual's earnings and schooling and experience. However, these results do *not* establish the reason for this positive relation. Indeed, there may be other mechanisms or explanations for these observed relations.

8.6.1   Experience, productivity, and earnings

We shall first consider evidence concerning the relation between a worker's training and productivity on the job. There have been several studies which have tried to develop more or less direct measures of worker productivity on the job. The first, by Horowitz and Sherman (1980), examined the relations between the maintenance record of various ships in the U.S. Navy and the training and experience of maintenance personnel. Their measure of worker productivity was based on how well the ships were maintained. For this, the authors used the amount of "downtime" of the ship – that is, the amount of time it was laid up for repairs. The less downtime, the better maintained the ship was.

The authors examined the records of 91 navy vessels in 1972, 1973, and 1974. They also examined the personnel records of sailors who worked in the following maintenance occupations: boiler technician, machinist's mate, fire-control technician, gunner's mate, sonar technician, and torpedoman's mate. The economists were particularly interested in three characteristics of these sailors: length of service in the navy; sea experience; and the amount of advanced training. Through regression analysis, they were able to relate the personal characteristics of the crew members in these occupational categories to the ship's downtime. They found that all three characteristics were statistically significant. In other words, greater length of service in the navy, greater sea experience, and a greater amount of advanced training each led to improved ship maintenance. Therefore, the authors concluded that both experience and training had a positive effect on worker productivity.

However, a second study by Medoff and Abraham (1981) reached the opposite conclusion. They obtained personnel records from a large U.S. manufacturing firm. They selected a sample of white male managerial and professional employees from company records. Besides information on education, length of company service, age, current salary, and salary history, the personnel files also contained a performance rating for each worker. The performance evaluation was done by the employee's immediate superior, who was asked to rate the worker "both to his contributions in terms of the standards of his job and against others performing similar work at similar levels." The authors used this performance rating as a measure of the worker's productivity on the job. Of course, performance evaluations are, to some degree, subjective but the authors concluded that, on the whole, these performance ratings by one's superior were a fairly objective measure of how much each employee contributed in her work.

The authors then performed two types of regression analysis. First, they investigated the relation between experience in the company, earnings, and performance rating for their sample of employees in a given year. They found in their cross-sectional analysis that among managers and professionals performing tasks of similar difficulty, greater experience in the company was associated with significantly higher relative earnings, but *not* with higher rated performance. Second, they investigated the relation between the same three variables over time for employees staying in a given job. They found in their longitudinal analysis that among those managers and professionals remaining in a job, relative earnings rose but relative performance either remained constant or declined with the passage of time. They concluded that though earnings did rise with experience for their sample, growth in earnings was *not* due to higher productivity on the job.

In a later study, Medoff and Abraham (1983b) conducted a special survey to evaluate the effects of years of service in a firm and worker productivity on the probability of a worker being promoted in the firm. They surveyed personnel directors at 1,025 U.S. companies who were listed in the 1981 edition of Standard & Poor's Register (firms with 50 or more employees). They asked them, somewhat indirectly, about the importance of length of service in promotion decisions. They also obtained personnel records from two companies, which contained information on job promotion and performance ratings of the individual workers. They found, from both sources of data, that seniority, independently of job performance or productivity, played a significant role in promotion decisions. This was true for both union and non-union employees.

In a 1984 study, Maranto and Rodgers examined data on wage claims investigations of a state labor department to examine the effects of work experience on job performance. The main task of field investigators was to recover unpaid wages that employers allegedly owe to employees. Aggrieved employees were allowed to submit claims to this department in order to collect unpaid wages. The investigator's job was to convince employers to make legitimate payments to their workers. With practice and experimentation, investigators could be expected to increase the proportion of outstanding wage claims that were collected from employers. Using the proportion of wage claims that were collected as an index of the investigator's productivity, Maranto and Rodgers found that investigators did become significantly more productive during the first six years of their job tenure.

A 1985 study by Dunson examined a similar issue for a group of civilian middle managers and professionals in the Department of Defense. His productivity measure was a performance rating scheme employed by the Department of Defense. He found that more experienced workers were paid more than those with fewer years of experience but, once controlling for experience, performance ratings had no relation to worker pay.

A different approach was employed by James Brown in a 1989 study. The Michigan Panel Survey of Income Dynamics (PSID) asked respondents in 1976 and 1979 the following question: "On a job like yours, how long would it take the average new person to become fully trained and qualified?" On the basis of this question and corresponding information on length of experience in the current position, Brown could identify those workers who were currently in training, as well as the total time spent in training. His main finding was that wage growth within positions ceased with the completion of the training period. He concluded that on-the-job training explained a substantial proportion of the total wage growth experienced in a given job position.

Shaw and Lazear (2007) obtained special firm data from an auto glass company to examine the relationship between worker tenure in the company and the worker's productivity. Worker output was measured by the number of windshields installed per hour of work. They found a very steep learning curve at the beginning, with worker output 53 percent higher after one year of service compared to the time the worker was initially hired. In contrast, pay profiles were much flatter than output profiles in the first year and a half on the job. However, the pattern of productivity rising more rapidly than earnings reversed after two years of tenure on the job.

In sum, the various tests reported above of the relation between experience on the job and on-the-job productivity have been mixed. Some of the studies showed that job productivity is positively related to a worker's experience, and they concluded that training is responsible for the positive association between earnings and job experience. The others also found that earnings grow with experience, but found no evidence that this growth in earnings was due to higher productivity among more experienced workers.

8.6.2   Other interpretations of the relation between schooling and earnings

In the case of schooling, there have been several other theories proposed to explain the observed positive association between educational attainment and earnings. In this section, we consider three such interpretations of schooling: as a screening device; as a transmitter of family background; and as a socializing mechanism.

8.6.2.1   *Education as a screening device*

Since 1973, with the appearance of Kenneth Arrow's article "Higher Education as a Filter," several signaling or screening models have been developed in which schooling was viewed as an informational device. The underlying assumption of these models is that there is imperfect information in the labor market. In particular, while potential employees differ in their ability with regard to a particular job, employers have no direct way of (imperfect information in) assessing a prospective employee's productive abilities. Positions are therefore "allocated on the basis of imperfect indicators or surrogates for productive capability or potential," as Spence (1981) noted in his survey of the literature on the subject. Educational attainment is one of the primary sources of information used by a firm to gauge an employee's likely success on the job.

It is also assumed that beyond a certain point,[40] schooling does not improve an individual's productive capacity. Rather, it functions as a signaling device to identify pre-existing talents. A prospective employer who has no direct way of assessing an applicant's productive abilities uses educational attainment as an indicator of the employee's expected productivity. Thus, schooling functions as an *identification* device by indicating for prospective employers those (future) workers who are most likely to perform well in their jobs. In this sense, the educational system acts as a "screening" mechanism for prospective employees.[41]

Employers will therefore pay more to applicants with more schooling (or hire them in favor of less-educated applicants), not because (or solely because) education enhances their productivity but because it identifies the more productive workers. A necessary corollary of this argument, as Spence (1973) noted, is that for the job market to remain in equilibrium, the more educated workers will, in fact, have to demonstrate greater productivity on the job. Otherwise, it would not be rational for an employer to continue to use education as a screening device. Thus, the abilities that are necessary for superior school performance must be the same as those that are necessary for superior work performance.

This argument is directly contrary to human capital theory. In the human capital model, employers pay more to those employees with more schooling because education increases their productivity. Human capital theory thus views schooling as *productivity-augmenting*. In the screening model, schooling is viewed to provide information to a prospective employer about which students would likely perform better in a job, but schooling does not itself increase the individual's productivity.[42] The observed positive relation between schooling and earnings is then due to the identification or screening function of education, rather than to a productivity-augmenting process.

In both models, it still pays the individual student to seek greater schooling. In the human capital model, the reason for the greater earnings is higher productivity. In the screening model, the reason is to identify himself or herself as a potentially superior worker. In both models, then, a firm would be willing to pay a better educated worker a higher salary, though for very different reasons. In both models, moreover, schooling has a certain implied *private rate of return* for the individual student, since it increases the individual's earnings. The implications concerning the *social rate of return* are very different in the two models, as we will discuss in Section 8.8.

The problem then arises of how to discriminate between the human capital and the screening model. What kind of test can be devised in order to show that one is true and the other false (or, perhaps, neither is true)? In other words, is it possible to derive distinct testable hypotheses from the two models? If we can, then we will be able to determine empirically which of the two models better explains the observed relation between schooling and earnings.

Several ingenious attempts have been made over the years to discriminate between the two models. Layard and Psacharopoulos (1974) argued that if the screening hypothesis is true, then educational differentials in earnings should not rise with age, since employers should have better information about older employees' abilities. Instead, they found that earnings differences between workers of different schooling levels did increase with age, with earnings rising faster for more educated workers.

Wise (1975) made a similar argument. He argued that if college quality (selectivity) were used only as a screening device, then earnings should rise no faster over time for graduates of higher quality colleges than lower quality ones. Instead, using data on college graduates working in a large corporation, he found that after controlling for the undergraduate grade point average (GPA), earnings increased faster for those who had attended more selective colleges than less selective ones. Jones and Jackson (1990) reached similar conclusions on the basis of a sample of business school graduates.

Another approach was taken by Albrecht (1981), who compared the success of applicants for a given position between those inside an organization (the Internal Revenue Service office in San Francisco) with those outside the organization. He reasoned that the office would have better information on inside candidates than on outside ones. Therefore, if education were used as a screening device, schooling should have less bearing on the hiring decision of inside applicants than outside ones. He found no confirmation for this hypothesis.

Wolpin (1977) took another tack. His reasoning was that students planning to go into their own business will acquire less schooling than those planning to work for an employer, since the former will stay in school long enough to satisfy the needs of their work, whereas the latter will acquire additional schooling to signal a prospective employer. Wolpin made two predictions based on the screening hypothesis. First, self-employed workers will have a lower mean schooling than salaried workers. Second, the increment in earnings from schooling will be lower for self-employed than salaried employees. Using the NBER–Thorndyke sample and estimating separate earnings equations for salaried and self-employed workers, he found no confirmation of these predictions.

Kroch and Sjoblom (1994) developed a different test to discriminate between the two models. They argued that if the screening hypothesis were correct, then earnings should be related to *relative* schooling rank rather than to the absolute level of schooling as predicted by the human capital model. Using data from the PSID and the 1972 CPS Exact Match File, they estimated earnings regressions which included both schooling level and an individual's rank in the distribution of schooling for his or her age cohort as independent variables. Unfortunately, the tests were not conclusive, though the authors felt that evidence was slightly more in favor of the human capital model than the screening model.

Weiss (1995) argued in favor of the signaling model over the human capital model as an explanation of the positive relationship observed between wages and schooling. He found that almost all of the relationship between high school graduation and earnings can be explained by the lower likelihood of quitting and the lower rates of absenteeism of high school graduates compared to those who dropped out of high school. He argued that if perseverance is not directly observable by firms and that if firms desire this trait in their workers, then high school graduation will be "selected upon" by employers.

Though most of the empirical work to date seems to favor the human capital model over the screening model, these results must be interpreted with some caution. The main reason is that both models predict that the better educated will receive higher earnings *and* that the better educated will also be more productive on the job (Spence's corollary). The point of dispute is whether the additional schooling *causes* the increase in worker productivity by transmitting work-related skills or is merely correlated with it. Comparisons of job performance and earnings over time between workers of different educational attainment (or between those inside and those outside an organization) cannot discriminate between causation and correlation. Wolpin's tests avoid the pitfalls of the previous studies by selecting two groups – self-employed workers and salaried employees – whose behavior would differ under the screening model. However, for his test to be conclusive, the student must know ahead of time whether he or she will be self-employed or working for someone else.

Thus, in general, it has proven very difficult to devise a decisive test of the screening versus human capital hypothesis. A direct empirical test of this mechanism has so far proven allusive. This is why Blaug (1989, p. 334), for example, speaks of "the observational equivalence of human capital theory and screening models."

8.6.2.2   *Family background*

Another interpretation of the functioning of the educational system is that it helps maintain the class structure between generations. Children of rich parents become rich by hooking into the "old boys' network" and thereby developing the necessary contacts for high-paying jobs. Conversely, the children of poor parents are excluded from such contacts and wind up in poor-paying jobs. This view was developed by Bowles in four articles (1970, 1971, 1972, 1974) and later expanded into a book-length treatise in a work with Gintis (1976). The argument is similar to that of the signaling model. Employers screen prospective job candidates on the basis of their educational attainment. Moreover, schooling does not in itself enhance the productive skills of future workers. However, here, education is used to screen family background, rather than unobserved natural ability.

Bowles' 1972 paper highlighted the relation between earnings, socioeconomic status, and schooling. He argued that one of the primary objectives of the wealthy was to preserve their dominant position. This meant, in part, that a rich family would try to ensure that its children remain in the dominant class. Moreover, by preserving class background, the wealthy could better attempt to legitimate their position. If classes were stable between generations, a society might view one class as possessing power and authority and therefore entitled to it, while the subordinate class would become resigned to its lesser position. The preservation of class origins is one means of ensuring the maintenance of power by the rich.

From this point of view, the educational system is considered one means of preserving class background. Children from higher social classes are channeled into one part of the educational system and segregated from lower social classes. A kind of "old boys' network" is set up whereby children of rich parents meet other children of rich parents, and through these contacts are funneled onto the higher paying jobs. In more modern parlance, this relationship can be referred to as *social capital*. Conversely, the children of poorer parents never make these contacts and are thereby shut off from the upper slots in the job hierarchy.

To implement this model, Bowles estimated a recursive system of the form:

(i) $S_i = \alpha \mathbf{X}_i$

(ii) $E_i = \beta_0 S_i + \beta \mathbf{X}$

where S_i is years of schooling, E_i is annual income, $\mathbf{X}_i$ a vector of variables reflecting the respondent's socioeconomic background, and α and β are vectors of the corresponding coefficients. Among the variables used for socioeconomic background were: (i) the occupational status of the father or family head of the respondent; (ii) the educational attainment of the father or family head of the respondent; and (iii) the parents' annual income.

Bowles found that the socioeconomic status of a child's family was a statistically significant determinant of the child's educational attainment. Those from the upper social classes acquired much more schooling than those from poorer backgrounds. This suggests that schooling opportunity is strongly correlated with family background. Moreover, Bowles found that once family background was controlled for, schooling achievement explained relatively little about a person's earnings. A person's family background was a more important determinant of relative income (that is, explained more of the variation of income) than schooling achievement. Bowles concluded that "the educational system is a major vehicle for the transmission of economic status from one generation to the next" (p. S240).[43]

Several other economists have looked at the relationship between family background and earnings (or income). This work has tended to emphasize three effects: (i) parental resources; (ii) peer effects; and (iii) ability. Parental resources are useful for providing financial resources to students (both to pay tuition and other school fees and to provide extra services such as tutoring). Peer (or neighborhood) effects refer to the existence of positive externalities between students. If other students are rich and highly motivated, it is likely that a student will gain from her interaction with these other students. This effect is related to the first since richer parents can afford to live in richer communities and in better school districts. The third refers to the positive effects of family background on student achievement and even measured IQ, which we discussed in Section 8.5.2 above.[44]

Behrman and Taubman (1990) looked at the correlation between children's adult earnings and their parents' income. On the basis of the PSID, they calculated correlations of over 50 percent (also see Chapter 6 for more discussion of intergenerational mobility).

Other studies have relied on sibling or twin samples to assess the relative contribution of family background to earnings. The advantage of using this type of data is that individuals linked by family affiliation are more likely to have similar family backgrounds than a random sample of individuals. Ashenfelter and Zimmerman (1997) used a sample of siblings derived from the National Longitudinal Survey (NLS). They estimated that normal (ordinary least squares) estimates of the return to schooling using a standard Mincer-type equation (like Equation (8.18)) may be biased upward by about 25 percent by the omission of family background factors. However, interestingly, they also found that measurement error in both the schooling and earnings variables would lead to a downward bias in the estimated returns to schooling, also of about 25 percent. Thus, when corrected for both, the standard Mincer-type earnings equation yielded the "correct" rate of return to schooling. Altonji and Dunn (1996) also used data on sibling pairs from the NLS. In contrast to Ashenfelter and Zimmerman, they obtained mixed results on whether parental education raised the return to schooling among the offspring.

Zax and Rees (2002) used a special dataset called the Wisconsin Longitudinal Study of Social and Psychological Factors in Aspiration and Attainment (WLS) which had information on about 10,000 individuals. They were first interviewed in 1957 as high school seniors and then reinterviewed in 1964, 1975, and 1993. They were particularly interested in the importance of peers, friends, family, academic performance, and IQ measured in the last year of high school to earnings at ages 35 and 53. They found that all five effects were important and statistically significant. However, they found that the effect of IQ by itself was relatively smaller, but that of family background relatively large.

8.6.2.3 *Schooling as a socializing mechanism*

A third interpretation is that the schooling system, rather than developing the cognitive skills necessary for work, instead helps mold personality traits, such as discipline, subordination, the willingness to accept hierarchy and authority, punctuality, and motivation according to external rewards, which are needed in the factory and office. The social structure of the school mirrors that of the factory and office. Indeed, the school may be thought of as a prototypical workplace. According to this view, schools do transform future workers in productive ways, as the human capital model maintains. However, the mechanism is seen to be quite different.

Gintis (1971) and Bowles and Gintis (1976) argued that one function of the educational organization is to "replicate the relationships of dominance and subordinancy in the economic sphere" (Bowles & Gintis, 1976, p. 125). There is therefore a fairly direct correspondence between the social relations embodied in the school and that of the workplace. The social experience of the schooling process, and not merely the actual content of the subjects, is central to this function. The school system is considered a socializing mechanism. In particular, the educational organization tries to *inculcate* personality traits that are compatible with and required for work in the factory or office. In this way, a workforce that can fit into and function within the social organization of work is created.

Gintis argued that the social organization of schooling, "by requiring the student to function routinely and over long periods of time in role situations comprising specific situations on the part of the teacher, other students, and administrators tends to elicit uniformities of response codified in individual personality" (1971, p. 272). Moreover, "the system of grading, by rewarding certain classroom behavior patterns and penalizing others, tends to reinforce certain modes of individual response to social situations" (1971, p. 272). Gintis found that the following traits seemed to be positively rewarded in the educational process: perseverance, self-control, social leadership, suppression of aggression, sharing, deferred gratification, and responsibility. On the other hand, the following traits were negatively rewarded: independence and self-reliance, initiative, complexity of thought, originality, independence of judgment, and creativity.

Gintis summarized the personality traits that are positively reinforced in schooling as four types: (i) subordinancy; (ii) discipline; (iii) supremacy of cognitive over affective modes of response; and (iv) motivation according to external reward. First, subordinancy and the proper respect for authority are induced by the strict hierarchical structure of the school as embodied in the administrator–teacher–student relation. The teacher acts as an authority figure to the student, rewarding or penalizing him or her for actions, and the student comes to accept this loss of autonomy. Such behavior is required for a worker to function effectively in the bureaucratic organization of work. Second, the educational system rewards such traits as regularity, punctuality, and quiescence – in a word, discipline – in its students. Such traits are also of obvious value in the factory or office environment. Third, a rational matter-of-fact or cognitive way of reacting to a situation is rewarded in the school system as opposed to an emotional, personal, or irrational way of behaving. This trait is also desirable in the factory or office, where work is dehumanized and people are expected to act more like machines than emotional beings. Finally, students are trained to be motivated more by the external reward for an action (a "good grade," for example) than by the actual satisfaction from the action itself ("learning," for example). Such a mode of action is useful in the work world, where workers are motivated not by the intrinsic pleasure of the work process but rather by the promise of a raise or the threat of being fired.

In more recent work, Heckman and Vytlacil (2001) and Heckman and Krueger (2003) also emphasized the importance of the development of noncognitive skills in the schooling process. In particular, they argued that families are just as important as schools (if not more so) in the promotion of human capital. Moreover, they stressed the importance of the development of noncognitive skills such as work habits and attitudes for both success in school and success in the workplace.

In later work, Heckman (2008) argued that noncognitive ability was just as important as cognitive ability in shaping adult outcomes such as labor earnings. He reported the early emergence of differentials in abilities between children of advantaged families and children of disadvantaged (minority) families and found that family background played a crucial role in accounting for these ability differentials. Moreover, on a policy note, he argued in favor of the effectiveness of early interventions in offsetting these differential trends in ability formation between minority and nonminority families.

8.7   EARNINGS INEQUALITY AND HUMAN CAPITAL*

The human capital model lends itself directly to a theory of the inequality of labor earnings. This follows directly from Equation (8.11). Since the logarithm of earnings is proportional to the level of schooling, then the log variance of earnings is a linear function of the variance of schooling:

$$\ln (\text{Var } E) = r^2 \ln (\text{Var } S) \tag{8.20}$$

where ln is the natural logarithm, Var is the variance, and r is the rate of return to schooling.[45] As we discussed in Section 3.3, the log variance is often used directly as a measure of income inequality.

It is of interest to note that the schooling model provides one explanation for an asymmetric distribution of earnings. One of the almost universal characteristics of observed distributions of earnings is that they are skewed to the right (see Section 3.2). For many theories of income distribution, this has presented a paradox. For example, in a simple model of ability, earnings are assumed to proportional to a worker's ability. But most measures of ability, such as IQ, are shown to be normally and therefore symmetrically distributed.

Suppose schooling levels are normally distributed among the working population. Then, by Equation (8.11), earnings will be *log-normally* distributed, since the logarithm of earnings rises proportionally to the level of schooling. One characteristic of the lognormal distribution is that it is skewed to the right. More generally, if years of schooling has a symmetric distribution (though not necessarily normal), then earnings will be positively (rightward) skewed. Indeed, unless the distribution of schooling is highly skewed to the left, the distribution of earnings will have a positive skew (see Mincer, 1970).

We can also extend this model to include experience. If we use Equation (8.17) but ignore the X^2 term, then it follows that:

$$\ln (\text{Var } E) = r^2 \ln (\text{Var } S) + (r'k_0)^2 \ln (\text{Var } X) + 2c \text{ Cov}(S,X) \tag{8.21}$$

where r' is the rate of return to experience, k_0 and c are constants, and $\text{Cov}(S,X)$ is the covariance between schooling and experience.[46]

Have changes in the distribution of human capital played a role in explaining the rising income inequality of the 1980s and 1990s? The surface evidence does not appear to support this hypothesis. Empirically, it has been shown that when the average level of schooling is low, the distribution of schooling tends to be skewed to the right and the variance of schooling high. When average schooling levels rise, the skewness in the distribution of schooling becomes smaller and its variance declines.

Older cohorts (groups) of workers in the United States have had a low average schooling level and therefore a distribution of schooling skewed to the right. However, the schooling level of entering cohorts of workers has risen over time, thereby raising the average level of schooling in the workforce and lowering its dispersion. During the 1980s and 1990s, rising education should have lowered overall earnings inequality, rather than raising it.

Three studies – Mincer (1991 and 1997b) and Murphy and Welch (1992) – found that the declining number of college graduates entering the labor market during the 1980s – the "baby-boom" generation – played a role in explaining the rising premium to a college education. The reason is that a decline in the share of college graduates in the labor force will, *ceteris paribus*, cause the earnings differential between college graduates and high school graduates to increase (see Section 8.2). From the point of view of human capital theory, the key factor explaining rising earnings inequality is the steep rise in the rate of return to schooling, particularly a college degree. In terms of Equation (8.21), the explanation is that r^2 rose sharply, rather than that $\text{Var}(S)$ increased. In this regard, both studies noted that the change in the demographic composition of the labor force by itself could not account for the full increase in the return to education observed over the decade, and concluded that changes in the demand for educated workers was the principal cause of the rising return to schooling.

Wolff (2006) called attention to the apparent contradiction between rising income inequality and falling schooling inequality. As shown in Figure 8.8 the variance of schooling of adults 25 years and older, computed from CPS data, trended sharply downward since 1947, falling by 48 percent from its peak value of 13.1 in 1950 to 6.9 in 2000. The simple correlation between this series and the Gini coefficient for family income is -0.78.

However, evidence from numerous studies cited above indicates that the return to schooling has risen since the early 1970s. Figure 8.8 also shows a series for the rate of return to a college education from 1956 to 2000.[47] The rate of return does show a considerable rise from 1975 to 2000, from 11.9 to 16.9 percent. However, the return to a college education also climbed sharply from 11.2 percent in 1956 to its earlier peak of 14.4 percent in 1970 and then fell to 11.9 percent in 1974 before rising again. Nonetheless, the simple correlation between the rate of return to college and the Gini coefficient for family income is 0.64.[48] However, from Equation (8.20), the more critical variable of interest is the square of the rate of return to college *multiplied* by the variance of schooling ($r^2 \ln (\text{Var } S)$). On net, the correlation between the Gini coefficient for family income and $r^2 \ln (\text{Var } S)$ is *negative*, -0.23. This result would seem to contradict the human capital model of earnings inequality.

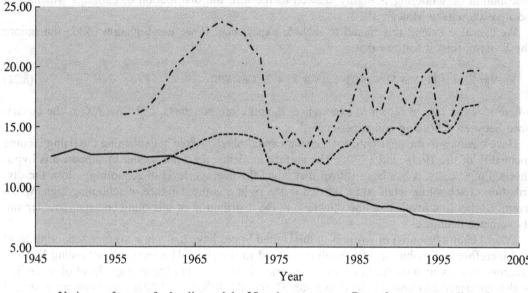

Legend:
——— Variance of years of schooling, adults 25 and over   ------- Rate of return to a college degree
– · – · Variance of schooling × rate of return squared

Figure 8.8   Trends in educational inequality and the return to schooling, 1947–2000

8.8   SUMMARY AND CONCLUDING REMARKS

The human capital model is an extension of neoclassical theory which derives the long-run supply curve of labor. In the model, each individual is viewed as making an investment decision about how much schooling and training to acquire. Both schooling and training increase the productivity of the worker and therefore future wages. However, the investment involves two types of costs: (i) indirect costs in the form of forgone earnings; and (ii) direct costs in the form of tuition, fees, and related expenses. The idea that the acquisition of skills is an investment decision is the central concept of human capital theory.

In the case of a college education, a high school senior would decide whether to continue in school or go to work by comparing the alternative lifetime earnings streams. Each earnings stream is converted into a present value by discounting future earnings at the market interest rate. The student would rationally choose the course of action which yielded the highest present value. An alternative calculation is based on the internal rate of return, which is defined as the discount rate which would equalize the lifetime earnings of the high school and college graduate. If the internal rate of return were higher than the market interest rate, the optimal choice would be to attend college.

Another form of human capital investment is on-the-job training. This also increases a worker's future productivity and entails both direct costs – payments for the instructor, materials, and the like – and indirect costs – the production forgone while the worker is training. The main difference between this form of human capital and schooling is that part of the costs may be borne by the employer instead of the individual.

Two kinds of training were distinguished. The first is firm-specific training, which increases the worker's productivity only in the firm where he is working. In this case, the employer absorbs all the costs of training but recoups it by paying a wage less than the worker's marginal value product after the training period. The second is general training, which provides skills that are transferable outside the firm. In this case, the employee pays the training cost in the form of a reduced wage while training but makes up for it in the form of higher wages later on.

Differences in human capital help explain why earnings vary among workers. There are two reasons. First, workers who attain a higher level of education will have higher productivity and will therefore command higher wages in the labor market. They also require higher wages to compensate them for the costs of additional schooling. Second, insofar as workers acquire general training while on the job, earnings should be positively correlated with years of work experience.

The evidence presented in this chapter provides strong support for the hypotheses that more educated workers receive greater earnings and that experience leads to greater earnings. These relations are confirmed by the age–earnings profiles shown in Figures 8.3 and 8.4, and the regression results presented in Tables 8.7 and 8.8. Moreover, the estimated rates of return to both schooling and experience are found to be quite high – in the neighborhood of 10 to 15 percent for the United States and even higher in less-developed countries. The rate of return to a college education, in particular, increased sharply during the 1950s and 1960s, fell dramatically in the 1970s, and increased substantially again during the 1980s and 1990s. This evidence has powerful implications for public policy, particularly the role of schooling in increasing income and reducing both poverty and income inequality.

However, there are several important qualifications to these results. The first concerns the role of ability. Insofar as students with more natural ability both do better in school and acquire more schooling, part of the estimated return to schooling can be due to ability rather than the skills acquired in the schooling process. Though the evidence varies, it appears that about one-third of the estimated return to schooling is due to ability differences among students.

Second, even after controlling for the effects of ability, it must still be established that not only is there a positive association between a worker's *productivity* on the job and educational attainment but also that it is the schooling process itself that has augmented the worker's productivity. The most damaging counterclaim comes from the screening model, where it is argued that schooling merely signals greater "innate" ability rather than produces additional skills. It is argued that employers cannot directly assess the productive ability of potential employees (that is, there is imperfect information in the labor market) and use schooling achievement to identify the potentially productive workers.

The screening model thus provides an explanation of the observed positive relation between schooling and earnings. If the screening argument is true, it raises some serious doubts about the social productivity of the education process. Empirically, it is very difficult to distinguish between the screening model and the human capital model, because in both the more educated must not only be more productive but demonstrate their greater productivity on the job for the labor market to be in equilibrium. Thus, the empirical implications of the human capital and screening models are almost identical. However, from our own casual observation we can think of examples where formal schooling seems to be specifically job related, such as vocational schools, secretarial schools, business schools, law schools, and medical schools. However, there are also examples of schooling whose content seems very far removed from any conceivable job the student is eventually likely to take. Some examples are high school social studies or a liberal arts college course in philosophy, literature, or linguistics. Yet, even in these subjects, it might still be the case that the critical thinking skills and writing competencies taught could be of great value on the job. On net, the truth probably lies in between the extreme forms of these two models. Some aspects of schooling do provide job-related skills, while others do not.

If the screening model is true in whole or even in part, then a discrepancy may arise between the "private" and "social" rate of return to schooling, where the former is the net benefit of schooling to the individual and the latter is its net benefit to society. The private return reflects the increased earnings to the individual from additional schooling. The social return, in contrast, reflects the increased stock of productive skills in the economy as a whole from its investment in schooling. If schooling serves merely as a signaling device, then society receives no benefit from the increased schooling that individuals acquire. As a result, the social return to schooling may be significantly lower than its private return. This distinction has important implications for economic policy. It may, for example, make little sense for society to spur on its rate of "human capital" formation on the basis of a high private return to education if the social return is low. Such a policy may be particularly misguided for a developing country where a large divergence may occur between the private and social returns to education.

Another interpretation of the role of schooling is that it serves to maintain socioeconomic status from one generation to another. The educational system provides a network of contacts, which enables children of rich families to obtain high-paying jobs, and excludes children from poor families. According to this view, schooling is also used as a signaling device, through screening is done on the basis of class background rather than innate ability. Earnings are not related to productivity or "what you know" but to "who you know"!

The evidence does indicate a significant intergenerational correlation in terms of both educational attainment and income. Yet, in criticism, the correlations are not perfect, and there is still a substantial amount of intergenerational mobility in terms of educational achievement and socioeconomic status. Some children of poor families do become rich and make it to the top levels of the corporate ladder and, conversely, children of rich parents often wind up in a lower economic stratum. The issue is how much mobility there actually is between generations and how much would constitute a refutation of this thesis (see Chapter 6 for more discussion of this issue).

Moreover, the fact that family background affects a person's schooling achievement and earnings can be and actually is incorporated in the human capital model. Becker (1967) talks of the family as one social mechanism by which human capital is produced. The type of influences, training, and instruction that a child receives in the home is viewed as a major source of human capital production, in addition to the schooling system. As a result, the human capital model would predict that children from rich family backgrounds acquire more capital in the home than those from poor families. The high correlation between family background and earnings is also consistent with the human capital model. In this case, too, it would be very difficult to distinguish empirically between the two explanations, and there is probably some truth in both views.

A third explanation is that the schooling process is a socializing mechanism, molding personality traits that allow a worker to perform effectively in the office or factory, rather than developing cognitive skills. In this regard, too, it is possible to think of cases where schooling provides very specific job-related skills, such as medical or law school, and of cases where it does not, such as social studies courses in grade school.

There is also conflicting evidence on the role of experience in generating higher earnings. The statistical data show that workers with more experience and seniority earn higher wages. However, it is not clear whether this is due to the greater productivity of older workers.

Human capital theory leads directly to a model of earnings inequality, where the degree of inequality is proportional to both the variance of schooling and the variance of experience. Changes in the distribution of schooling of the workforce during the 1980s did not play a direct role in explaining the rising income inequality over the decade, since the variance of schooling declined. However, the declining number of college graduates entering the labor force over this period has been found to be one factor accounting for the rising return to a college education.

8.9 REFERENCES AND BIBLIOGRAPHY

Human capital theory

Becker, G.S. (1964). *Human Capital: A Theoretical and Empirical Analysis*. New York: Columbia University Press and National Bureau of Economic Research; and 2nd edition (1975).

Becker, G.S. (1967). *Human Capital and the Personal Distribution of Income*. Ann Arbor, MI: University of Michigan Press.

Becker, G.S. (1974). A theory of social interactions. *Journal of Political Economy*, **82**(6), 1063–94.

Ben-Porath, Y. (1967). The production of human capital and the life-cycle of earnings. *Journal of Political Economy*, **57**.

Ben-Porath, Y. (1970). The production of human capital over time. In L. Hansen (ed.), *Education, Income, and Human Capital*. New York: Columbia University Press and National Bureau of Economic Research.

Blinder, A.S. & Weiss, Y. (1974). *Human Capital and Labor Supply: A Synthesis*. Princeton: Princeton University Press.

Fleischhauer, K.-J. (2007). A review of human capital theory: Microeconomics. University of St. Gallen Discussion Paper no. 2007-01, January, http://ssrn.com/abstract=957993.

Freeman, R. (1976). *The Overeducated American*. New York: Academic Press.

Ghez, G.R. & Becker, G.S. (1975). *The Allocation of Time and Goods over the Life Cycle*. Princeton: Princeton University Press and the National Bureau of Economic Research.

Haley, W.J. (1973). Human capital: The choice between investment and income. *American Economic Review*, **63**(5), 929–44.

Heckman, J.J. (1976). A life cycle model of earnings, learning and consumption. *Journal of Political Economy*, **84**(4), S11–S44.

Lucas, R.E.B. (1977). Is there a human capital approach to income inequality? *Journal of Human Resources*, **12**(3), 387–95.

Mincer, J. (1970). The distribution of labor incomes: A survey with special reference to the human capital approach. *Journal of Economic Literature*, **8**(1), 1–26.

Rosen, S. (1977). Human capital: A survey of empirical research. In R. Ehrenberg (ed.), *Research in Labor Economics*, Vol. 1 (pp. 3–39). Greenwich, CT: JAI Press.

Schultz, T.W. (1960). Capital formation by education. *Journal of Political Economy*, **68**(6), 571–83.

Schultz, T.W. (1961). Investment in human capital. *American Economic Review*, **51**(1), 1–17.

Schultz, T.W. (1971). *Investment in Human Capital: The Role of Education and of Research*. New York: The Free Press.

Smith, A. (1961). *The Wealth of Nations*. London: University Paperbacks, Nuthuen (originally published in 1776).

Education, experience and earnings

Barron, J.M., Berger, M.C. & Black, D.A. (1999). Do workers pay for on-the-job training? *Journal of Human Resources*, **34**(2), 235–52.

Becker, G.S. & Chiswick, B.R. (1966). Education and the distribution of income. *American Economic Review*, **56**(2), 358–69.

Berman, E., Bound, J. & Griliches, Z. (1994). Changes in the demand for skilled labor within U.S. manufacturing: Evidence from the Annual Survey of Manufactures. *Quarterly Journal of Economics*, **109**, 367–98.

Black, S.E. & Lynch, L.M. (1996). Human capital investments and productivity. *American Economic Review*, **86**(2), 263–7.

Blackburn, M.L., Bloom, D.E. & Freeman, R.B. (1991). The distribution of labor market outcomes: measuring and explaining trends and patterns in the 1980s for selected demographic groups in the United States, mimeo, February.

Borgans, L. & de Grip, A. (eds.) (2000). *The Overeducated Worker? The Economics of Skill Utilization*. Cheltenham, UK: Edward Elgar.

Bound, J. & Johnson, G.E. (1992). Changes in the structure of wages in the 1980s: An evaluation of alternative explanations. *American Economic Review*, **82**, 371–92.

Card, D. (2001). Estimating the returns of schooling: Progress on some persistent economic problems. *Econometrica*, **69**(5), 1127–60.

Chiswick, B.R. (1974). *Income Inequality*. New York: Columbia University Press and National Bureau of Economic Research.

Chiswick, B.R. & Mincer, J. (1994). Time series changes in personal income inequality in the

U.S. from 1939, with Projections to 1985. *Journal of Political Economy*, **80**(3), 534–7.

Coleman, M.T. (1993). Movements in the earnings–schooling relationship, 1940–88. *Journal of Human Resources*, **28**(2), 660–80.

Creedy, J. (1974). Income changes over the life-cycle. *Oxford Economic Papers*, **26**(3), 405–23.

Creedy, J. (1999). Lifetime versus annual income distribution. In J. Silber (ed.), *The Handbook of Income Inequality Measurement*, Vol. 71 (pp. 513–33). Boston: Kluwer Academic.

Frazis, H. & Steward, J. (1999). Tracking the returns to education in the 1990s. *Journal of Human Resources*, **34**(3), 629–41.

Freeman, R.B. (1976). *The Over-Educated American*. New York: Academic Press.

Friesen, P.H. & Miller, D. (1983). Annual inequality and lifetime inequality. *Quarterly Journal of Economics*, **98**(1), 139–55.

Goldin, C. & Katz, L.F. (2007). The race between education and technology: The evolution of U.S. educational wage differentials, 1890 to 2005. NBER Working Paper No. 12984, March.

Grubb, W.N. (1993). The varied economic returns to postsecondary education: New evidence from the class of 1972. *Journal of Human Resources*, **28**(2), 367–82.

Hancock, K. & Richardson, S. (1985). Discount rates and the distribution of lifetime earnings. *Journal of Human Resources*, **20**(3), 346–60.

Hanoch, G. (1967). An economic analysis of earnings and schooling. *Journal of Human Resources*, **2**(3), 310–29.

Hansen, W.L., Weisbrod, B.A. & Scanlon, W.J. (1970). Schooling and earnings of low achievers. *American Economic Review*, **50**(3), 409–18.

Hanushek, E.A. (1996). Measuring investment in education. *Journal of Economic Perspectives*, **10**(4), 9–30.

Heckman, J.J. (2008). Schools, skills, and synapses. NBER Working Paper No. 14064, June.

Heckman, J.J. & Krueger, A.B. (eds.) (2002). *Inequality in America. What Role for Human Capital Policies?* Cambridge, MA: MIT Press.

Ishikawa, M. & Ryan, D. (2002). Schooling, basic skills and economic outcomes. *Economics of Education Review*, **21**(3), 231–43.

Jencks, C., *et al.* (1972). *Inequality: A Reassessment of the Effect of Family and Schooling in America*. New York: Basic Books.

Johnson, G.E. & Stafford, F. (1973). Social returns to quantity and quality of schooling. *Journal of Human Resources*, **8**(2), 139–55.

Johnson, T. (1970). Returns from investment in human capital. *American Economic Review*, **50**(4), 546–60.

Kane, T.J. & Rouse, C.E. (1995). Comment on W. Norton Grubb "The Varied Economic Returns to Postsecondary Education: New Evidence from the Class of 1972." *Journal of Human Resources*, **30**(1), 205–21.

Katz, L.F. & Murphy, K.M. (1992). Changes in relative wages, 1963–1987: Supply and demand factors. *Quarterly Journal of Economics*, **107**(1), 35–78.

Krueger, A.B. & Lindahl, M. (2001). Education and Growth: Why and for whom? *Journal of Economic Literature*, **39**(4), 1101–36.

Lee, C. (2005). Rising family income inequality in the United States, 1968–2000: Impacts of changing labor supply, wages, and family structure. NBER Working Paper No. 11836, December.

Lillard, L.A. (1977). Inequality: Earnings vs. human wealth. *American Economic Review*, **67**(2), 42–53.

Marcotte, D.E. (2000). Continuing education, job training, and the growth of earnings inequality. *Industrial and Labor Relations Review*, **53**(4), 602–23.

Mattila, J.P. (1984). Determinants of male school enrollments: A time-series analysis. *Review of Economics and Statistics*, **64**(2), 242–51.

Mincer, J. (1958). Investment in human capital and the personal income distribution. *Journal of Political Economy*, August.

Mincer, J. (1962). On the job training: Costs, returns and some implications. *Journal of Political Economy*, October, 50–79.

Mincer, J. (1974). *Schooling, Experience, and Earnings*. New York: National Bureau of Economic Research.

Mincer, J. (1991). Human capital, technology, and the wage structure: What do time series show? NBER Working Paper No. 3581, January.

Mincer, J. (1997a). The production of human capital and the life cycle of earnings: Variation on a theme. *Journal of Labor Economics*, **15**(1), 26–47.

Mincer, J. (1997b). Changes in wage inequality, 1970–1990. *Research in Labor Economics*, **16**, 1–18.

Mincer, J. & Polachek, S. (1974). Family investments in human capital: Earnings of women. *Journal of Political Economy*, **82**(2), S76–S108.

Morgan, J. & David, M. (1963). Education and income. *Quarterly Journal of Economics*, **77**(3), 423–37.

Murphy, K.M. & Welch, F. (1992). The structure of wages. *Quarterly Journal of Economics*, **107**(1), 285–326.

Murphy, K.M. & Welch, F. (1993). Inequality and relative wages. *American Economic Review Papers and Proceedings*, **83**(2), 104–9.

Polachek, S.W. (2007). Earnings over the life-cycle: The Mincer earnings function and its applications. IZA Discussion Paper No. 3181, Bonn, Germany, November.

Psacharopoulos, G. (1985). Returns to education: A further international update and implications. *Journal of Human Resources*, **20**(4), 583–604.

Psacharopoulos, G. & Patrinos, H.A. (2002). Returns to investment in education: A further update. World Bank Policy Research Working Paper 2881, September.

Raymond, R. & Sesnowitz, M. (1975). The returns to investments in higher education: Some new evidence. *Journal of Human Resources*, **10**(2), 139–54.

Rosen, S. (1976). A theory of life earnings. *Journal of Political Economy*, **84**(4), 545–68.

Rumberger, R.W. (1987). The impact of surplus schooling on productivity and earnings. *Journal of Human Resources*, **22**(1), 24–50.

Shaw, K.L. (1984). A formulation of the earnings function using the concept of occupational investment. *Journal of Human Resources*, **19**(3), 319–40.

Weisbrod, B.A. & Karpov, P. (1968). Monetary returns to college education, student ability and college quality. *Review of Economics and Statistics*, **50**(4), 491–510.

Welch, F. (1970). Education in production. *Journal of Political Economy*, **78**(1), 35–59.

Wilkinson, B.W. (1966). Present values of lifetime earnings for different occupations. *Journal of Political Economy*, **74**(6), 556–72.

Wolff, E.N. (2006). *Does Education Really Help? Skill, Work, and Inequality*. New York: Oxford University Press.

Ability and earnings

Ammon, O. (1895). *Die Gesellschaftsordung und ihre naturlichen Grundlagen*. Jena.

Ashenfelter, O. & Krueger, A. (1994). Estimates of the economic returns to schooling from a new sample of twins. *American Economic Review*, **84**(5), 1157–73.

Ashenfelter, O. & Mooney, J.D. (1968). Graduate education, ability, and earnings. *Review of Economics and Statistics*, **50**(1), 76–86.

Ashenfelter, O. & Rouse, C. (1998). Income, schooling, and ability: Evidence from a new sample of twins. *Quarterly Journal of Economics*, **113**, 253–84.

Boissiere, M., Knight, J.B. & Sabot, R.H. (1985). Earnings, schooling, ability, and cognitive skills. *American Economic Review*, **75**(5), 1016–30.

Bound, J., Griliches, Z. & Hall, B.H. (1986). Wages, schooling and IQ of brothers and sisters: Do the family factors differ? *International Economic Review*, **27**(1), 77–105.

Bowles, S., Gintis, H. & Groves, M.O. (eds.) (2005). *Unequal Chances: Family Background and Economic Success*. Princeton, NJ: Princeton University Press.

Bowles, S. & Nelson, V. (1974). The "inheritance of IQ" and the intergenerational reproduction of economic inequality. *Review of Economics and Statistics*, **56**(1), 39–51.

Filer, R.K. (1981). The influence of effective human capital on the wage equation. In R.G. Ehrenberg (ed.), *Research in Labor Economics*, Vol. 4. (pp. 367–416). Greenwich, CN: JAI Press.

Goldberger, A.S. (1979). Heritability. *Economica*, **46**, 327–47.

Goldberger, A.S. & Manski, C.F. (1995). Review article: *The Bell Curve* by Herrnstein & Murray. *Journal of Economic Literature*, **33**, 762–76.

Griliches, Z. & Mason, W.M. (1972). Education, income, and ability. *Journal of Political Economy*, **80**(3), S74–S103.

Hansen, L., Weisbrod, B. & Scanlon, W. (1970). Schooling and earnings of low achievers. *American Economic Review*, **60**(3), 409–18.

Hause, J. (1972). Earnings profile: Ability and schooling. *Journal of Political Economy*, **80**(3), S108–S138.

Hause, J. (1975). Ability and schooling as determinants of lifetime earnings. In F.T. Juster (ed.), *Education, Income, and Human Behavior*. New York: McGraw-Hill.

Hearnshaw, L.S. (1979). *Cyril Burt, Psychologist*. Ithaca, NY: Cornell University Press.

Heckman, J.J. (1976). The common structure of statistical models of truncation, sample selection and limited dependent variables and a simple estimator for such models. *Annals of Economic and Social Measurement*, 5, 475–92.

Heckman, J.J. & Vytlacil, E. (2001). Identifying the role of cognitive ability in explaining the level of and change in the return to schooling. *Review of Economics and Statistics*, 83(1), 1–12.

Herrnstein, R. & Murray, C. (1994). *The Bell Curve*. New York: Basic Books.

Jensen, A.R. (1969). How much can we boost IQ and scholastic achievement. *Harvard Educational Review*, 39(1), 1–123.

Jensen, A.R. (1970). Learning ability, intelligence, and educability. In V.L. Allen (ed.), *Psychological Factors in Poverty*. Chicago: Markham.

Kamin, L.H. (1974). *The Science and Politics of IQ*. New York: John Wiley & Sons, Inc.

Lydall, H.F. (1968). *The Structure of Earnings*. Oxford: Clarendon Press.

Mandelbrot, B. (1962). Paretian distributions and income maximization. *Quarterly Journal of Economics*, 56, 57–85.

Miller, P., Mulvey, C. & Martin, N. (1995). What do twins studies reveal about the economic returns to education? A comparison of Australian and U.S. findings. *American Economic Review*, 85(3), 586–99.

Roy, A.D. (1950). The distribution of earnings and of individual output. *Economic Journal*, 60, 489–505.

Shockley, W. (1970). A "try simplest case" approach to the heredity-poverty-crime problem. In V.L. Allen (ed.), *Psychological Factors in Poverty*. Chicago: Markham.

Solmon, L.J. (1975). The definition of college quality and its impact on earnings. *Explorations in Economic Research*, 2(4), 537–89.

Taubman, P. (1976). The determinants of earnings: Genetics, family and other environments; a study of white male twins. *American Economic Review*, 66(5), 858–70.

Taussig, F.W. (1915). *Principles of Economics*. New York: Macmillan.

Wachtel, P. (1975). The effect of school quality on achievement, attainment levels, and lifetime earnings. *Explorations in Economic Research*, 2(4), 502–36.

Willis, R.J. & Rosen, S. (1979). Education and self-selection. *Journal of Political Economy*, 87(5), S7–S36.

Wise, D. (1975). Academic achievement and job performance. *American Economic Review*, 65(3), 350–66.

Age, earnings, and productivity

Abraham, K.G. & Farber, H.S. (1987). Job duration, seniority, and earnings. *American Economic Review*, 77(3), 278–97.

Altonji, J. & Williams, N. (2005). Do wages rise with job seniority? A re-assessment. *Industrial and Labor Relations Review*, 58(3), 370–97.

Altonji, J. & Shakotko, R. (1987). Do wages rise with job seniority? *Review of Economic Studies*, 54(3), 437–59.

Brown, J.N. (1989). Why do wages increase with tenure? On-the-job training and life-cycle wage growth observed within firms. *American Economic Review*, 79(5), 971–91.

Dunson, B.H. (1985). Pay, experience, and productivity: The government sector case. *Journal of Human Resources*, 20(1), 153–60.

Horowitz, S.A. & Sherman, A. (1980). A direct measure of the relationship between human capital and productivity. *Journal of Human Resources*, 15(1), 67–76.

Hutchens, R.M. (1989). Seniority, wages and productivity: A turbulent decade. *Journal of Economic Perspectives*, 3(4), 49–64.

Kotlikoff, L.J. & Gokhale, J. (1992). Estimating a firm's age-productivity profile using present value of lifetime earnings. *Quarterly Journal of Economics*, 107(431), 1215–42.

Lazear, E.P. (2001). The Peter principle: Promotions and declining productivity. NBER Working Paper No. 8094, January.

Maranto, C.L. & Rodgers, R.C. (1981). Does work experience increase productivity? A test of the on-the-job training hypothesis. *Journal of Human Resources*, 19(3), 341–57.

Medoff, J.L. & Abraham, K.G. (1980). Experience, performance, and earnings. *Quarterly Journal of Economics*, 95, 703–36.

Medoff, J.L. & Abraham, K.G. (1981). Are those paid more really more productive? The case of experience. *Journal of Human Resources*, **16**(2), 186–216.

Medoff, J.L. & Abraham, K.G. (1983a). Length of service, terminations and the nature of the employment relationship. NBER Working Paper No. 1086, March.

Medoff, J.L. & Abraham, K.G. (1983b). Years of service and probability of promotion. NBER Working Paper No. 1191, August.

Shaw, K. & Lazear, E.P. (2007). Tenure and output. NBER Working Paper No. 13652, November.

Other interpretations of the relation
between schooling and earnings

Albrecht, J. (1981). A procedure for testing the signaling hypothesis. *Journal of Public Economics*, **15**(1), 123–32.

Altonji, J.G. & Dunn, T.A. (1996). The effects of family characteristics on the return to education. *Review of Economics and Statistics*, **78**(4), 692–704.

Arrow, K. (1973). Higher education as a filter. *Journal of Public Economics*, **2**(3), 193–216.

Ashenfelter, O. & Zimmerman, D.J. (1997). Estimates of the return to schooling from sibling data: Fathers, sons, and brothers. *Review of Economics and Statistics*, **79**(1), 1–9.

Behrman, J.E. & Taubman, P. (1990). The intergenerational correlation between children's adult earnings and their parents' income: Results from the Michigan Panel Survey of Income Dynamics. *Review of Income and Wealth*, ser. 36, no. 2, 115–28.

Blaug, M. (1989). Review of *Economics of Education. Journal of Human Resources*, **24**(2), 331–5.

Bowles, S. (1970). Towards an educational production function. In W.L. Hansen (ed.), *Education, Income, and Human Capital*. New York: National Bureau of Economic Research.

Bowles, S. (1971). Unequal education and the reproduction of the social division of labor. *Review of Radical Political Economy*, **3**(4), 1–30.

Bowles, S. (1972). Schooling and inequality from generation to generation. *Journal of Political Economy*, **80**(3), S219–S251.

Bowles, S. (1974). The integration of higher education into the wage labor system. *Review of Radical Political Economy*, **6**(1), 100–33.

Bowles, S. & Gintis, H. (1974). The problem with human capital theory. *American Economic Review*, **65**(2), 74–82.

Bowles, S. & Gintis, H. (1976). *Schooling in Capitalist America*. New York: Basic Books.

Bowles, S., Gintis, H. & Osborne, M. (2001). The determinants of earnings: A behavioral approach. *Journal of Economic Literature*, **39**(4), 1137–76.

Gintis, H. (1971). Education, technology, and the characteristics of worker productivity. *American Economic Review*, **61**(2), 266–79.

Jones, E.B. & Jackson, J.D. (1990). College grades and labor market rewards. *Journal of Human Resources*, **25**(2), 253–66.

Kroch, E.A. & Sjoblom, K. (1994). Schooling as human capital or a signal. *Journal of Human Resources*, **39**(1), 156–80.

Lang, K. (1994). Does the human-capital/educational-sorting debate matter for development policy? *American Economic Review*, **84**(1), 353–8.

Layard, R. & Psacharopoulos, G. (1974). The screening hypothesis and the return to education. *Journal of Political Economy*, **82**(5), 985–98.

Lazear, E. (1977). Academic achievement and job performance: Note. *American Economic Review*, **67**(2), 252–4.

Riley, J. (1975). Competitive signaling. *Journal of Economic Theory*, **10**, 175–86.

Riley, J. (1976). Information, screening, and human capital. *American Economic Review*, **66**(2), 254–60.

Riley, J. (1979). Testing the educational screening hypothesis. *Journal of Political Economy*, **87**, S227–S251.

Ross, S., Taubman, P. & Wachter, M. (1981). Learning by observing the distribution of wages. In S. Rosen (ed.), *Studies in Labor Markets* (pp. 359–86). Chicago: Chicago University Press.

Saloner, G. (1985). Old boy networks as screening mechanisms. *Journal of Labor Economics*, **3**(3), 255–67.

Spence, M. (1973). Job market signaling. *Quarterly Journal of Economics*, **87**(3), 355–74.

Spence, M. (1981). Signaling, screening, and information. In S. Rosen (ed.), *Studies in Labor Markets*. Chicago: Chicago University Press.

Stiglitz, J. (1975). The theory of "screening", education, and the distribution of income. *American Economic Review*, **65**(3), 283–300.

Taubman, P. & Wales, T. (1973). Higher education, mental ability and screening. *Journal of Political Economy*, **81**(1), 28–55.

Taubman, P. & Wales, T. (1974). *Higher Education and Earnings*. New York: McGraw-Hill.

Weiss, A. (1984). Testing the sorting model of education. NBER Working Paper No. 1420, August.

Weiss, A. (1988). High school graduation, per-formance, and earnings. *Journal of Political Economy*, **96**(4), 785–820.

Weiss, A. (1995). Human capital vs. signaling explanations of wages. *Journal of Economic Perspectives*, **9**(4), 133–54.

Wolff, E.N. (1977). Schooling and occupational earnings. *Review of Income and Wealth*, Ser. 23, no. 3, 259–78.

Wolpin, K. (1977). Education and screening. *American Economic Review*, **67**(5), 949–58.

Zax, J.S. & Rees, D.I. (2002). IQ, academic per-formance, environment and earnings. *Review of Economics and Statistics*, **84**(4), 600–16.

8.10   DISCUSSION QUESTIONS AND PROBLEM SET

1   Discuss three reasons why, according to human capital theory, individuals will invest in schooling early in their life rather than later.

2   What is the characteristic shape of the age–earnings profile? From the standpoint of the human capital model, explain why it has the characteristic shape and why the peak is later for more highly educated workers.

3   Explain why the failure to control for differences in individual ability may lead to an overstatement of the returns to schooling.

4   Compare and contrast the implications of the human capital and screening models with regard to the relation between an individual's schooling level and the person's earnings and why. What are the implications for the social rate of return to schooling in each model?

5   Discuss three ways in which family background may affect educational attainment and earnings.

6   Explain why according to the human capital model general training will increase the worker's future earnings whereas specific training will not.

7   Why would fewer high school graduates go on to college if the (real) rate of interest increases?

8   Compute the present value of lifetime earnings at age 18 for a high school graduate who works immediately after graduating high school at age 18 and one who attends college for 4 years after graduating high school if the annual earnings of the former is $40,000 (assumed constant over time) and that of the college graduate is $50,000 (assumed constant over time) at:
   (a)   a 3, 5, and 7 percent rate of interest, with no direct costs of college
   (b)   a 3, 5, and 7 percent rate of interest, with college costing $10,000 per year.
   Explain in each of these cases whether it would make sense to attend college.

9   Assume that individuals start to work right after school (either high school or college) and retire at age 65. Compute the present value of lifetime earnings at age 18 for a high school graduate who works immediately after graduating high school at age 18 and one who attends college for 4 years after graduating high school if the annual earnings of the former is $40,000 (assumed constant over time) and that of the college graduate is $50,000 (assumed constant over time) at:
   (a)   a 3, 5, and 7 percent rate of interest, with no direct costs of college
   (b)   a 3, 5, and 7 percent rate of interest, with college costing $10,000 per year.
   Compute the internal rate of return to a college education in the case where
   (c)   there are no direct costs of college.
   (d)   college costs are $10,000 per year.

Suppose the earnings of high school graduates grow by 2 percent per year and those of college graduates by 3 percent per year. Compute the present value of lifetime earnings at age 18 for a high school graduate and for a college graduate if the annual earnings of the former starts at $40,000 and that of the college graduate starts at $50,000 at:

(e)   a 3, 5, and 7 percent rate of interest, with no direct costs of college

NOTES

1   The "nominal" interest rate is the interest rate actually recorded on a savings account or loan. The "real" interest rate is the difference between the nominal interest rate and the inflation rate. This is analogous to the difference between nominal growth rates of output and real growth rates of output, discussed in Chapter 2. Throughout this chapter, we will assume all interest rates are in real terms.

2   The assumption of perfect capital markets means that all people with the same risk of defaulting on their loan can lend or borrow money at the same interest rate.

3   It is assumed that the salary is paid at the beginning of the year.

4   A geometric series is one in which each term (except the first) is a fixed multiple of the preceding term. The formula for the sum S is given by:

$$S = (a - aq^n)/(1 - q)$$

where a is the first term of the series, q the ratio between one term and the next lower term, and n the number of terms.

5   Also, for simplicity, it is assumed that the discount rate is zero.

6   A related "technical" assumption is that the utility function is assumed to be additively separable.

7   Unequal access to training opportunities might, for example, result from labor market discrimination. See Chapters 12, 13, and 14 for more discussion of these issues.

8   The entry restrictions may also enable doctors to charge fees above what would be feasible in a competitive market. Medical schools could capture part of this "excess profit" by charging higher direct tuition fees. In fact, by raising direct costs of a medical education sufficiently high, medical schools could drive the internal rate of return to medical training back to a competitive level. However, because of competition for students among medical schools, medical schools are unable to do this, thus allowing doctors to capture the "rent" from restricted entry.

9   This is true up to a point. As we shall discuss in Section 8.3, after a certain age, human capital may actually start to depreciate, as skills become obsolete, and earnings may fall with experience after this point.

10   We shall assume that there are no consumption benefits to a college education.

11   Whereas financial or physical capital like a house can be used to secure a loan, human capital because it is embodied in a person cannot be repossessed or used to secure a loan.

12   It may also depend on differences in preferences for the non-pecuniary aspects of work that require training.

13   These differences could, for example, be reflected in school grades.

14   Actually, the supply and demand curves for human capital may not be entirely independent. For example, ability, as we argued, affects the demand curve for human capital. It may also affect the supply curve, if brighter students have a better chance of getting a scholarship and thereby lowering the cost of funding their schooling.

15   An alternative way of "closing" the model is to introduce the fact that young people may differ in their personal discount rate. Some individuals have a very strong preference for immediate gratification, while others are more willing to defer consumption. A student will leave school when the return to an additional year of schooling falls below her personal discount rate.

16   The specific source is: CPS Table P-32 Educational Attainment – Full-Time, Year-Round Workers 18 Years Old and Over by Mean Earnings, Age, and Sex: 2005.

17   This relation is more reliable for men than for women, since historically many mothers have left the labor force when their children were young and reenter it when their children are older. See Chapter 14 for further discussion of estimating female experience levels.

18   Another implication of this argument is that capital investment should rise as working life increases. The reason is that an investment in human capital can be recaptured over a longer period of time. This implies that, *ceteris paribus*, the internal rate of return to a given investment, C, will be higher. The internal rate of return r^* is approximately given by:

$$r^* = (k/C)[1 - (1 + r^*)^{-n}]$$

where k is the net increase in earnings resulting from the investment C and n is the number of years of working life. As n becomes larger, the term $(1 + r^*)^{-n}$ becomes smaller and therefore r^* becomes larger. In the limit, as n gets increasingly larger, r^* approaches k/C, the ratio of the net increment in earnings to the initial investment C. One reason for the average work life to increase is that the median life span is rising. This has particular relevance for developing countries where, according to the human capital model, decreasing mortality rates should cause increases in investment in education and training.

19   Another reason might be that individual's capacity for learning declines with age because of biological and psychological factors ("you can't teach an old dog new tricks"). This argument, however, is difficult to substantiate.

20   By this argument, one might wonder why workers do not complete all their human capital investment as quickly as possible, say before age 22. One answer comes from Ben-Porath (1967), who argues that the marginal cost curve of producing human capital is upward sloping within each period. For example, trying to cram all the training required to become a surgeon into, say, a one-year time span would be very expensive because the training costs would rise astronomically (even assuming that a person could absorb all the training in such a short time span.) Since individuals will invest until the marginal gain (in this case, the net increase in earnings) equals the marginal cost, they will tend to spread out their human capital investment to keep the cost down.

21   One technical qualification should be mentioned. The data shown here come from a "cross-sectional" sample – that is, one in which people of different ages are observed at a single point of time (in this case, 2005). The age–earnings profile predicted by the human capital model, on the other hand, refers to the time path of earnings of a single individual over time. A sample that includes such data is called a "longitudinal sample" or a "panel survey." Since no longitudinal data source now exists which traces a person's entire working life, most of the empirical tests are made on the basis of cross-sectional samples such as the 2005 Current Population Survey. However, it can be demonstrated that under general conditions if the longitudinal age–earnings profiles are concave downward, then the cross-sectional profiles will also be shaped concave downward.

22   Another implication is that earnings will peak later in life for the more educated workers. This is also generally confirmed by the data, particularly for males. Technically, it should also be noted that the argument implies that the actual *dollar increases* in earnings over time will be greater for the more educated than the less educated, because there is a positive correlation between the dollar value of the post-school investment and school investment. On the other hand, the *percentage increase* in earnings over time is much closer between schooling groups, because this depends on the amount of post-school investment *relative* to schooling investment.

23   The figures are updated to 2000 by this author on the basis of data on annual earnings from the Current Population Survey.

24   See Chapter 11 for an extended discussion of the skill-biased technological change hypothesis.

25   Calculations by Friesen and Miller (1983) produced similar results. In 1962, the Gini coefficient for annual income was 0.36 and that for lifetime earnings was 0.21.

26   As noted in Section 8.2.3.1, this formulation implicitly assumes perfect capital markets and, by implication, the lack of short-term liquidity constraints.

27   The solution is obtained by first noting that the integral of $E_S e^{-rt} dt$ is $-E_S e^{-rt}/r$ and then substituting first $S + n$ for t and then subtracting and substituting S for t.

28 As Mincer (1970) notes, the main reason why more educated workers receive higher annual earnings than less educated ones is the postponement of earnings early in life rather than a shorter pay-off period.

29 In more technical terms, the average earnings of a schooling group after about 8 years of experience tended to equal that amount of annual earnings in a constant income stream whose present value equals the present value of the actual stream of lifetime earnings. Mincer called this number of years the "overtaking years of experience."

30 Since the left-hand variable, logarithm of earnings, will vary with the number of weeks worked, this was considered a "natural" variable to add to the regression specification.

31 An alternative specification might have had the logarithm of weekly earnings ($\ln E/W$) as the dependent variable.

32 See, for example, Ammon (1895), Taussig (1915), Roy (1950), and Mandelbrot (1962).

33 Technically, this is called a "specification bias" or an "omitted variable" bias, since Equation (8.19a) is incorrectly specified by the exclusion of an ability variable. There is another, more subtle, error in estimation associated with this problem, which is called a "self-selection bias" or a "selectivity bias." This problem arises not from an omitted variable in the basic schooling model but rather from the fact that the sample itself is unrepresentative of the full population. For example, if we observe earnings for a sample of college graduates in a given year but have no information on their ability, their earnings will reflect both their schooling achievement and their unobserved ability. Presumably, because this group of people went on to finish college, their ability or set of talents is, on average, different than a sample of high school graduates. Therefore, the earnings the group of high school graduates would have received had they completed college would not be the same as the actual earnings received by the college graduates. In general, the earnings would be lower. On the other hand, the earnings actually received by the high school graduates would, in general, be different than the earnings the sample of college graduates would have received had they had gone to work immediately after graduating high school.

In the human capital model, such a computation of forgone earnings is necessary to estimate the rate of return to additional schooling (see Section 8.2). This argument indicates that such computations of the rate of return to schooling based on only the observed earnings of high school and college graduates is not really valid, and the error is called a selectivity bias because the sample of high school and college graduates select themselves based on, for us, unobserved attributes. Heckman (1976) and Willis and Rosen (1979) both developed statistical techniques for correcting this problem.

34 This is not 100 percent true, because there is the possibility of genetic mutation during the development of the embryo.

35 Since some statistical variation in IQ scores were expected even among twins raised in the same home, this variation was used as a control for the statistical analysis of twins raised apart.

36 Also, see Goldberger and Manski (1995) for a scathing review of the Herrnstein and Murray book.

37 In particular, his model was econometrically underidentified, so that additional assumptions were required to estimate the model.

38 It has also been pointed out that twins are not a very representative sample of the population as a whole. The major reason is that a twin on average probably gets less attention from parents and spends more time with siblings than other children. Therefore, it may not be possible to generalize results from twin studies to the full population.

39 See Chapter 6 and, in particular, Bowles, Gintis, and Groves (2005) for more recent literature and further discussion of the "nature versus nurture" debate in the context of intergenerational economic mobility.

40 It is usually noted that the basic skills learned in elementary and, perhaps, high school – particularly, reading, writing, and arithmetic – are necessary for most occupations. Subjects taught in more advanced schooling, particularly in college, are less relevant to the skills required in the workplace.

41 There is an analogy from the natural world. The (male) peacock has evolved over time to develop an enormous and beautiful feathered tail. This tail is very costly in terms of the amount of energy and metabolism required to maintain it. The argument is that the size of the tail performs no (known)

300 *Explanations of Inequality and Poverty*

biological function except to attract a mate (the female peahen). The peahen is attracted to a male with very large tail because the plumage *signals* that the male is healthy and virile. Thus, like schooling, the peacock's tail does not enhance the virility or health of the bird but merely signals that the bird is a "good catch."

42 The same argument may apply to self-employed workers since a degree (or certificate) may be useful as a signal to a prospective client.

43 In quantitative terms, Bowles estimated that 52 percent of the variation in schooling achievement was explained by the family background variables. Moreover, family background accounted directly for 13 percent of the variation of earnings and indirectly for another 15 percent via its impact on schooling achievement. On the other hand, once family background was controlled for, schooling achievement explained only 2 percent of the variation of earnings. Similar findings were reported in the Bowles and Nelson (1974) paper, discussed in Section 8.5.2.

44 A related factor is family stability. Research has shown that students in more stable families, particularly married couples, perform better in school than those with single parents.

45 Technically, it is necessary to assume that the rate of return to schooling is fixed.

46 Lucas (1977) criticized the human capital model of earnings inequality for lacking an appropriate specification of the demand side of the labor market. To correct this, Lucas introduced a production function which included human capital as a factor of production.

47 The source for 1956 to 1979 is Mattila (1984), which is based on the rate of return to 4 years of college relative to 4 years of high school for male workers. I extended the series to 2000 on the basis of CPS data on the ratio of annual earnings between male college graduates and male high school graduates. The rate of return was estimated using the standard internal rate of return to schooling formula under the assumption that the ratio in earnings between college and high school graduates remains constant over the life cycle and that college graduates begin work 4 years later, on average, then high school graduates.

48 The correlation between the square of the rate of return to college and the Gini coefficient for family income is 0.66.

Chapter 9
Unions, Dual Labor Markets, and Structural Models of Earnings

9.1 INTRODUCTION

Chapter 8 examined the role of individual (supply-side) characteristics in explaining differences in earnings among the working population. In this chapter and the next, we will focus on institutional and demand-side factors that might account for why workers earn different incomes. Institutional considerations are important for a number of reasons. First, they help to explain earnings differences and are thus a factor in accounting for income inequality. Second, several economists have argued that changes in the institutional framework of the labor market played an important role in accounting for *rising* earnings inequality in the United States since the early 1970s (see Chapter 11 for more details). Third, the presence of distinct labor segments as argued in dual labor market theory may be an important component in accounting for racial discrimination in the labor market.

We begin this chapter with a treatment of labor unions. These are associations of workers that try to improve the wages, fringe benefits, and working conditions of their members through collective bargaining and other means. By 2006, only 12 percent of all employees were represented by some form of union in the United States. This figure is considerably below that of many Western European countries, where the proportion of workers in unions reaches 90 percent. However, trade unions are still believed to have a significant effect on wages and employment in the United States.

Section 9.2 examines the economic role of trade unions and surveys the pertinent evidence on their role in the economy. Section 9.2.1 presents a brief history of trade unions in the United States. Section 9.2.2 looks at the growth in union membership and their occupational and industrial distribution. Section 9.2.3 discusses the functions performed by unions in the economy. Section 9.2.4 reviews evidence about the relative wages of union versus non-union workers and the relation of unions to the overall distribution of earnings.

Another important institutional feature is labor market segmentation. Section 9.3 develops the dual labor market model characterized by two distinct groups of workers. The **primary labor market** is found in large organizations where jobs require substantial training, provide security and steady advancement, and pay high wages and benefits. In the **secondary labor market**, jobs require little education and training and pay low wages, and worker turnover is high. Many people employed in the secondary market are trapped in a vicious cycle of low training, low wages, and chronic poverty. Both the decline in unionism and the rise in secondary employment are believed to have contributed to the rise of inequality in the United States since the early 1970s. Sections 11.6 and 11.7 present some evidence on this issue.

Structural models emphasize the role played by industrial composition, occupational mix, technology, regional characteristics, market structure, plant size, per capita income, and other institutional characteristics on earnings. They assume that the overall distribution of earnings is determined primarily by the job structure of an economy. Changes in the inequality of earnings occur chiefly when the job structure changes.

It is helpful to contrast structural models with human capital theory. In the latter, the distribution of earnings is determined by the distribution of human capital – that is, of schooling, experience, and ability. These are all characteristics of the supply of labor. Changes in supply characteristics of labor are held to be responsible for changes in the overall distribution of earnings. In contrast, structural theories stress the demand for labor. Changes in structural characteristics, such as the industrial mix of a region, affect the demand for labor. For example, a shift in consumer demand toward medical care and away from housing will affect the overall job structure (more doctors and nurses, and fewer carpenters, plumbers, and electricians) and thereby the distribution of labor earnings. A secondary theme is that human capital factors such as schooling and experience have less bearing on the overall distribution of income. Empirical research in this vein often considers the relative importance of structural characteristics and human capital factors in explaining the distribution of earnings.

The simplest type of structural model is the fixed coefficient manpower model. It is assumed that each industry has a characteristic technology, which determines the industry's job structure – that is, the number of workers of different types necessary to produce a unit of output. For example, to manufacture the Boeing 747 requires so many aeronautical engineers, welders, machinists, electricians, mechanics, and so on. Furthermore, it is assumed that the occupational mix in each industry is constant (fixed) over time, and that the relative wage rates paid to each occupation are also fixed. The overall distribution of earnings then becomes completely determined by the mix of industries in the economy. As the pattern of demand shifts over time, so will the industrial composition of the economy and, consequently, so will the overall occupational skill mix. In this model, the distribution of labor earnings becomes a function exclusively of the composition of output. This example represents the extreme form of the structural model. Other models allow for effects from changing labor supply on earnings.[1]

Structural elements permeate the internal labor market model, where it is claimed that the jobs within large organizations have well-defined entry ports, promotional ladders, and exit points. These structures are largely due to the kinds of technology in use and customary rules. The need for specific skills in an organization and the resulting requirements for on-the-job training lead to the formation of rigid job ladders and wage scales. This is reinforced by custom, since, once this structure is in place for a time, workers are apt to resist attempts to change it.

The formation of dual labor markets is also viewed as the outcome of structural forces. The 1890s and 1990s saw the structure of many industries becoming characterized by a dichotomization of firms. In the core were large corporations with a clearly delineated hierarchy of jobs, high capital intensity, and long production runs. On the periphery developed a competitive fringe of small firms, characterized by low capital intensity, short production runs, and a relatively unstructured job hierarchy. The duality of the job market developed as a reflection of differences in technology between the large monopolistic firms and the small competitive ones.

Section 9.4 considers the effects of industrial structure on earnings inequality. Several approaches are investigated, including the role of agricultural and service employment on the variation of income among states in the United States. There are significant and persistent industry differences in the wages paid even for the same kind of work. Section 9.5 explores some of the factors that play a role in causing such wage differences, including differences in industry productivity, market power, profitability, and firm size. A more recent approach, efficiency wage theory, offers the rationale that paying higher wages helps to raise a firm's profitability. Section 9.6 treats a related concern, the pattern of occupational wages over time. Studies have emphasized the role of increasing education and technological advances on changes in occupational skill differentials.

Section 9.7 presents a summary and considers the implications of structural change for rising earnings inequality in the United States since the 1970s. Three factors are relevant. The first is the continuing shift of employment shares out of goods-producing industries, particularly manufacturing, toward services. The second factor is a substantial widening of industry wage differentials since the 1970s. The third is a similar trend in occupational earnings, whose dispersions also rose over time since the early 1970s.

9.2   THE ROLE OF LABOR UNIONS

9.2.1   A brief history of trade unionism in the United States

Local craft unions first appeared in the United States in the 1790s. These associations were called "societies" or "bodies", and their membership consisted largely of skilled artisans in the towns and cities. These early unions were local and organized by trade, such as carpenters, printers, or shoemakers. The motivation for forming such unions was to promote better wages and fewer hours of work. Strikes were used by these workers as a means of inducing employers to meet their demands. However, this weapon was not always effective, because courts during that period often ruled that strikes were illegal.

The year 1827 marked the first attempt at the formation of *federations* of labor unions, which in this case was an organization of local unions in the city of Philadelphia across craft and industry lines. Such city-wide labor federations became more involved in political issues than in collective bargaining disputes. A National Trades' Union, representing an association of city federations, was formed in 1834, and one of its major objectives was to achieve a 10-hour day for federal government employees.

Both the number of trade unions and trade membership grew during the 1830s until the panic of 1837, when many local trade unions, as well as the National Trades' Union, disappeared. The ebb and flow of union membership in response to macroeconomic conditions was a recurring theme in U.S. trade union history until 1930. When the economy was prosperous, labor was scarce and profits were high, and, as a result, employers were more willing to meet union demands for higher wages and better working conditions. Union membership therefore grew during boom periods. During depressions, jobs were scarce and profits low and, as a result, employers were less willing to meet union demands and workers were more willing to work for lower wages. Unions therefore lost their effectiveness during downturns and union membership declined.

The 1850s saw the formation of the first *national* trade union, the National Typographical Union. This was followed in suit by the formation of national trade unions among machinists, locomotive engineers, stonecutters, cigar-makers, and blacksmiths. These national unions were formed along craft (or trade) lines and were originally loose associations of local trade unions, with bargaining still done on the local level. Soon, however, the national level of the union became predominant, with most of union policy set at this level.

The rationale for the formation of national unions was that product makers were becoming national in scope, a result of the tremendous improvements in communication and transportation, particularly through the building of canals and railroads. This development sufficiently lowered transportation costs so that goods produced in one part of the country could compete successfully with locally produced goods. As a result, goods made in low-wage areas could under-sell those produced in high-wage ones. Local unions could not successfully control wages, since these could be undermined by wage standards set in other parts of the country. National trade unions, on the other hand, could standardize wage rates across localities.

9.2.1.1   The formation of the American Federation of Labor (AFL)

Begun in 1881, the AFL soon rose to be the dominant labor organization on the U.S. scene, a position it has held to this day. It started as a loose federation of several national craft unions. Much of its success was due to its stress on economic activity, particularly wages, hours, and working conditions, rather than on political activity. The AFL granted a charter to each of its national unions which gave the union the exclusive right to organize workers within a particular occupation or trade.

The AFL was led by Samuel Gompers of the cigar-makers union, who served as its president from 1886 until 1925. The period 1897 to 1904 witnessed a dramatic increase in union membership from 447,000 to 2,073,000 members (see Rees, 1977). Much of this occurred in the railroads, mining, and building industries. This increase was partly due to the prosperity of the period and partly due to the successful use of collective bargaining between employers and unions.

After 1904, union membership continued to grow, but at a slower rate. One major reason was that in 1908, the Supreme Court in a case involving the Danbury (Connecticut) Hatters' Union ruled that it was illegal for the union to engage in a consumer boycott against non-union producers of hats. This decision was based on the Sherman Antitrust Act, passed in 1890, which prohibited "restraint of trade" in interstate commerce.[2]

The tight labor markets caused by World War I brought another spurt in union membership, and by 1920 membership had passed the 5 million mark. This increase was partly aided by the passage of the Clayton Act in 1914, which included clauses that exempted labor unions from the antitrust acts. A major event during this period was the passage of the Adamson Act in 1916, which set an 8-hour day for railroad employees. The 8-hour day quickly spread as a standard in other industries.

A recession in 1921 brought a sharp reduction in union membership, and despite prosperity from 1923 to 1929 membership stagnated. In 1929, membership stood at 3.5 million, compared to 5 million in 1920. One major reason was that companies were improving working conditions, wages, and benefits for non-unionized workers, partly as a means to forestall unionization.

9.2.1.2   The Great Depression and its aftermath

The depression that began in 1929 was a tremendous shock to the U.S. economy. By 1933 output had fallen by half and the unemployment rate stood at 25 percent. Unions were also adversely affected by this turn of events, with membership falling from 3.5 million in 1929 to 2.7 million in 1933.

The New Deal inaugurated with the election of Franklin Roosevelt was to have a major and lasting impact on industrial relations. In 1933, the National Industrial Recovery Act was enacted, which for the first time explicitly gave labor the legal right to organize into unions and to engage in collective bargaining with management. Though in 1935 the Supreme Court found the National Industrial Recovery Act unconstitutional, later that year a new law was passed, called the National Labor Relations Act or Wagner Act, which again made it legal for workers to organize and bargain collectively. The law also prohibited employers from blacklisting or otherwise discriminating against union members and provided an institutional mechanism, the National Labor Relation Board, for adjudicating complaints against management. In 1937, the

Supreme Court declared the Wagner Act constitutional, which further strengthened the union movement. Between 1933 and 1941, union membership increased from 2.7 million to 10.2 million (about 17 percent of the labor force in 1941).

Concomitant with the renewed vigor of the union movement were growing divisions within the AFL. The problem arose from the presence of two different principles used to organize workers – the trade (or craft) and the industry (irrespective of occupation). Almost all the early unions were organized around trades. The mining and clothing workers were organized according to the industry principle. As unionization penetrated new industries, such as automobiles and rubber, jurisdictional fights arose. A schism thus formed in the AFL, with the industrial unions breaking off and forming the Congress of Industrial Organizations (CIO), under the leadership of John Lewis. It was not until 1955 that the two groups came back together to form a single organization, the AFL-CIO.

During World War II, union membership leaped once again, from 10.2 million in 1941 to 14.3 million in 1945. After the war, unions demanded large wage increases, and a resulting wave of strikes swept across the country. Partially as a result of this, public sentiment seemed to shift against labor, and this led to the passage of the Taft–Hartley Labor–Management Relations Act of 1947. This Act shifted the balance of bargaining power back toward management by, for example, making unions as well as employers prosecutable for unfair labor practices and allowing the decertification of unions. The Taft–Hartley Act probably helped slow the growth of union membership, for by 1956 membership had grown to only 17.5 million workers.

9.2.2   Trends in union membership

Figure 9.1 summarizes the trends in union membership since 1930. Although the *number* of union members increased in almost every year since 1933, this was not true of the more telling statistic,

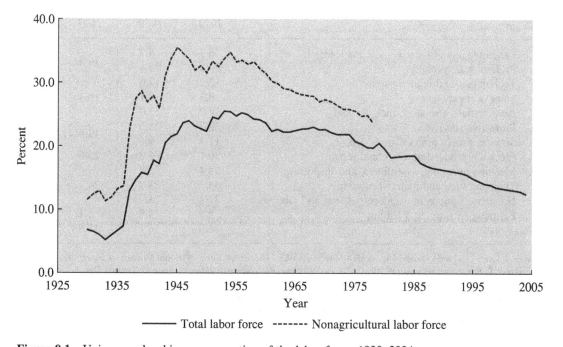

Figure 9.1   Union membership as a proportion of the labor force, 1930–2004

union membership as a percent of the labor force. In 1933, 5.2 percent of the total labor force and 11.3 percent of the nonagricultural labor force were represented by unions of one form or another.[3] This proportion increased in almost every year until 1954, when union membership as a fraction of the total labor force peaked at 25.4 percent and as a fraction of the nonfarm labor force at 34.7 percent. After 1954, the trend was basically downward. By 1960, the proportion stood at 23.6 percent of the total labor force and 31.4 percent of the nonfarm labor force; by 1978 at 19.7 percent of the total labor force and 23.6 percent of the nonfarm workforce; and at 16.6 percent of the total labor force in 1988, 15.8 percent in 1993, and 12.5 percent in 2004.

Table 9.1 provides details on trends in unionization by occupational group. The most heavily unionized occupations during the 1950s and 1960s were the blue-collar trades. Foremost among

Table 9.1   Union membership as a percent of the labor force by occupation, selected years, 1950–2006

Category	1950	1960
1. Professional, technical and kindred workers	11.9	10.6
2. Managers and administrators	0.3	0.5
3. Salesworkers	1.7	2.9
4. Clerical and kindred workers	17.6	12.5
5. Craftsmen and kindred workers	32.9	40.8
6. Operatives	82.4	73.6
7. Laborers, except farm	56.2	28.8
8. Farm laborers and foremen	1.2	2.2
9. Farmers and farm managers	—	—
10. Service workers	20.5	16.4
11. Private household workers	—	—
Overall	22.3	23.6

Category	1984	1989	1993	2006
1. Executive, administrative, and managerial	6.3	6.2	} 14.9	12.8
2. Professional specialty	23.4	22.4		
3. Technicians and related support	12.2	12.0	} 10.4	7.0
4. Sales occupations	6.3	5.1		
5. Administrative support, incl. clerical	14.0	13.0		
6. Protective service	38.7	38.3	} 13.8	11.0
7. Service, except protective service	11.7	9.6		
8. Precision production, craft, and repair	30.1	26.3	25.6	16.0
9. Machine operators, assemblers, and inspectors	35.4	28.8	} 24.7	17.0
10. Transportation and material moving	34.7	28.9		
11. Handlers, equipment cleaners, helpers, and laborers	27.4	23.9		
12. Farming, forestry, and fishing	5.5	3.8	5.1	—
Overall	18.5	16.4	15.8	12.0

Sources: Troy, L. (1965). *Trade Union Membership, 1892–1962*. New York: National Bureau of Economic Research); U.S. Census Bureau (1950). *U.S. Census of the Population: 1950*, IV, Special Reports Part I, Chapter C, Occupation by Industry. Washington, DC: U.S. Government Printing Office. U.S. Census Bureau. (1963). *U.S. Census of the Population: 1960*, Subject Reports, Occupation by Industry. Final Report PC(2)-72. Washington, DC: U.S. Government Printing Office; U.S. Bureau of Labor Statistics. (1985). *Employment and Earnings*, January. Washington, DC: U.S. Government Printing Office; U.S. Bureau of Labor Statistics. (1990). *Employment and Earnings*, January. Washington, DC: U.S. Government Printing Office; U.S. Census Bureau. *Statistical Abstract of the United States, 1994 and 2007*.

them were operatives such as machine operators and truck drivers (over 80 percent in 1950 and over 70 percent in 1960). Second in line were unskilled laborers such as assembly line workers (56 percent in 1950 and 29 percent in 1960). About a third of craftsmen and skilled workers were in unions in 1950, and this proportion increased to slightly over 40 percent in 1960. About a fifth of all service workers were represented by unions in 1950, and this proportion fell to 16 percent in 1960.

The white-collar occupations generally had lower union representation than blue-collar workers. Clerical workers were the most unionized white-collar group, at 18 percent in 1950 and 13 percent in 1960. Professional, technical, and kindred workers, including nurses, health technicians and teachers, were the second-most unionized group, at a little over 10 percent in 1950 and 1960. The other two white-collar occupational groups, managers and sales workers, had almost no union representation in the two years. Finally, it should be noted that farmers, agricultural workers, and private household workers also had almost no union members in 1950 and 1960.

Though the occupational classification scheme for the 1980s and 1990s differs from the earlier one, it is still possible to make some comparisons. Perhaps, the most dramatic change was the fall in union representation for the blue-collar trades. The unionization rate fell to about 25 percent among craft, operative, and unskilled workers by 1993 and to only 17 percent by 2006. Union representation for service workers also declined, to 14 percent in 1993 and to 11 percent in 2006.

A similar pattern is evident among the white-collar occupations. In 1989, 22 percent of professional specialties and 12 percent of technical trades were organized. In 1993, the unionization rate for professional and administrative workers was 15 percent but by 2006 it was down to 13 percent. Unionization among sales workers increased from 3 percent in 1960 to 5 percent in 1989. However, for the combined group of technicians, sales, and administrative support services, the unionization rate fell from 10 percent in 1993 to 7 percent in 2006. Unions also penetrated the agricultural sector, reaching 5.1 percent in 1993 though no comparable figure is available for 2006.

By and large, unions have maintained their strength in areas where they were strong by the close of World War II but have failed to penetrate new sectors of the economy with one major exception. This exception is the government and the nonprofit sector, including universities and hospitals, in which union membership increased dramatically in the 1960s and 1970s. This is particularly true for state and local government employees, where the passage of new laws giving them the right to organize and bargain collectively greatly aided the process. In 1956, as shown in Table 9.2, 5 percent of all union members worked for the government. By 1993, this proportion had grown to 42 percent and by 2006 to 48 percent. Moreover, the percent of public employees organized in unions grew from 11 percent in 1960 to 36 percent in 2006 (also, see Freeman, 1986, for more discussion).

There were other notable changes in the distribution of union membership. In 1956, half of union workers were found in manufacturing (and the other half in nonmanufacturing). However, by 1993, over three-quarters of organized workers were in nonmanufacturing and by 2006 almost 90 percent. Almost all the manufacturing sectors lost in terms of their relative share of union workers.

Among the nonmanufacturing sectors, the picture was mixed. Eight percent of union members were employed in transportation and utilities in 2006, down from 19 percent in 1956. The proportion of union workers employed in construction declined from 12 percent in 1956 to 7 percent in 2006. In contrast, 5 percent of union members were employed in the trade sector in 1956; by 1993 the proportion had reached 8 percent, though it slipped to 6 percent in 2006. The fraction of organized workers employed in services increased from 7 percent in 1956 to 9 percent in 1993 and then to 17 percent in 2006.

Table 9.2   Union membership by industry as a percent of total union membership, selected years, 1956–2006

Industry	1956	1960	1970	1978	1983	1993	2006
A. Nonmanufacturing industries	51.3	52.3	55.8	63.0	70.1	78.4	88.1
1. Mining and quarrying	2.9	3.3	1.8	2.0	1.0	0.6	0.3
2. Construction	11.7	12.6	12.5	13.6	6.4	5.6	7.1
3. Transportation	15.1	14.2	11.9	8.2			
4. Telephone and telegraph	2.4	2.3	2.4	2.6	12.3	11.6	8.0
5. Electric and gas utilities	1.8	1.5	1.5	1.6			
6. Wholesale and retail trade	4.9	4.7	7.6	8.1	8.9	8.2	6.3
7. Finance and insurance[a]	0.3	0.4	0.3	0.2	0.9	0.8	1.1
8. Services	6.7	7.1	6.3	9.4	8.0	9.2	17.1
9. Agriculture and fishing	0.4	0.3	0.1	0.2	0.3	0.1	0.2
10. Government	5.1	5.9	11.3	17.1	32.3	42.3	48.1
B. Manufacturing industries	48.8	47.6	44.2	37.0	29.9	21.6	11.9
11. Food, beverage, tobacco		5.8	4.7	3.0			
12. Clothing, textiles, leather		6.8	5.8	4.4			
13. Furniture, lumber, wood products, paper	4.6	4.2	3.9				
14. Printing and publishing		1.9	1.8	1.3			
15. Petrol, chemicals, rubber		3.0	3.4	2.7			
16. Stone, clay, glass		1.4	1.4	1.3			
17. Metals, machinery, equipment (except transportation equipment)		16.0	16.3	13.4			
18. Transportation equipment		7.3	5.5	5.2			
C. Total	100.0	100.0	100.0	100.0	100.0	100.0	
Addendum: Union membership as a percent of employment by industry							
1. Mining and quarrying					20.7	16.0	7.5
2. Construction					27.5	20.0	13.0
3. Transportation and utilities					42.4	30.5	23.2
4. Wholesale and retail trade					8.7	6.3	5.0
5. Finance, insurance and real estate				2.9	1.9	1.9	
6. Services					7.7	5.8	5.4
7. Agriculture and fishing					3.4	1.6	2.3
8. Government					36.7	37.7	36.2
9. Manufacturing					27.8	19.2	11.7
Total					20.1	15.8	12.0

a This sector includes real estate beginning 1968.
Sources: U.S. Bureau of Labor Statistics. *Handbook of Labor Statistics, 1978*; Washington, DC: U.S. Government Printing Office; U.S. Census Bureau. *Statistical Abstract of the United States, 1994 and 2007*. Washington, DC: U.S. Government Printing Office.

What is also striking is that the percent of employees organized in unions fell in every major sector between 1983 and 2006 except government (see the Addendum to Table 9.2). In mining, the proportion fell from 21 to 8 percent; in construction, from 28 to 13 percent; in transportation and utilities, from 42 to 23 percent; and in manufacturing, from 28 to 12 percent. The share of government workers represented by a union remained steady at around 36 to 37 percent.

In sum, in 2006 only 27 percent of all union membership was found in construction, transportation, utilities, and manufacturing, compared to almost 80 percent in 1956. On the other hand, three service sectors – trade, general services, and government – accounted for 17 percent of all union membership in 1956 and 72 percent in 2006. Within these services, public sector trade unions showed the most rapid gains.

9.2.2.1 The decline in trade unionism

Why has unionization fallen so sharply in the United States since the mid-1950s? Several studies have attempted to answer this question, and several factors have been identified as contributing to the process. The first was that since the end of World War II, employment has grown much more rapidly in the white-collar occupations, which were and have remained relatively less unionized than in the blue-collar trades, the traditional area of union strength. Dickens and Leonard (1985) found that about a third of the decline in the union membership rate was due to plant closures, layoffs, and slower growth in basic manufacturing industries. However, this explains only part of the trend, because the unionization rate of the core union sectors – mining, manufacturing, construction, and transportation – also fell, particularly in the 1970s (see below).

A second factor was that union organizing activity fell off since the 1950s, particularly during the 1970s. Dickens and Leonard (1985) found that the number of workers involved in new union certification elections declined during the 1970s, while the labor force grew. A third and related factor is the decline in the success rate of union organizing efforts. The success rate, defined as the number of eligible voters in union elections choosing unions as a percent of all eligible workers, also dropped between the mid-1950s and the early 1980s. However, Farber and Western (2001), after examining the data on unionization rates from 1973 to 1998, concluded that most of the decline in the union membership rate was attributable to differential employment growth rates among industries. On the other hand, changes in union organizing activity had relatively little effect.

Other factors include the deregulation of transportation industries; changes in public attitudes toward unions; increased government regulation of the labor market, substituting for union rules; change in labor relations of corporations to forestall unionization attempts, particularly increased anti-union activity; and changes in government industrial relations policies, particularly the Reagan administration's opposition to the air traffic controllers' strike in 1982. Freeman (1988) felt that increased corporate opposition to unionization attempts, including maintaining high wages and good benefits for non-union workers, was a major factor. Reder (1988) stressed the role of deregulation of key industries. Neumann and Rissman (1984) argued that government provision of services traditionally supplied by unions (particularly social welfare expenditures) played a major role in reducing union membership.

The experience of other industrialized countries was strikingly different in regard to unionization during the 1970s and 1980s (see Freeman, 1988). In several countries, the unionization rate (the percent of nonagricultural workers in unions) increased dramatically since 1970: in Denmark, from 66 to 98 percent in 1984/85; in Sweden, from 79 to 95 percent; and in Finland, from 56 to 85 percent. Other countries have experienced a moderate increase in or stable level of union density over this period, including Germany (37 to 42 percent), France (22 to 28 percent), Italy (39 to 45 percent), Canada (32 to 37 percent), Switzerland (31 to 35 percent), and the United Kingdom (51 to 52 percent). Among the industrialized countries, the United States experienced the largest decline in unionism during the 1970s and 1980s and had the lowest percentage of unionization by the mid-1980s (see Freeman, 1990, for more discussion). We shall return to this point in Section 9.3.

Table 9.3   Union density in selected industrialized countries, 1970–2003 (percent)

Year	1970	1980	1990	2003
United States	23.5	19.5	15.5	12.4
Canada	31.6	34.7	32.9	28.4
Australia	50.2	49.5	40.5	22.9
New Zealand	55.2	69.1	51.0	22.1
Japan	35.1	31.1	25.4	19.7
South Korea	12.6	14.7	17.6	11.2
European Union	37.8	39.7	33.1	26.3
Germany	32.0	34.9	31.2	22.6
France	21.7	18.3	10.1	8.3
Italy	37.0	49.6	38.8	33.7
UK	44.8	50.7	39.3	29.3
Ireland	53.2	57.1	51.1	35.3
Finland	51.3	69.4	72.5	74.1
Sweden	67.7	78.0	80.8	78.0
Norway	56.8	58.3	58.5	53.3
Denmark	60.3	78.6	75.3	70.4
Netherlands	36.5	34.8	24.3	22.3
Belgium	42.1	54.1	53.9	55.4
Spain	—	12.9	12.5	16.3
Switzerland	28.9	31.1	24.3	17.8
Austria	62.8	56.7	46.9	35.4
Hungary	—	—	—	19.9
Czech Republic	—	—	78.8	27.0
Slovak Republic	—	—	78.7	36.1
Poland	—	—	53.1	14.7

Source: Visser, J. (2006). Union membership statistics in 24 countries. *Monthly Labor Review*, **129**(1), 38–49, Table 3. The results are based on data adjusted to provide international consistency in definitions and coverage of union membership.

However, more recent data provided by Visser (2006) indicated that during the 1990s and early 2000s several other countries followed the pattern of de-unionization established by the United States during the 1980s. Comparisons of unionization rates for 24 industrialized countries over the period from 1970 to 2003 are shown in Table 9.3. These results are based on data adjusted to provide consistent definitions of union membership and coverage among the 24 countries. The unionization rate (density) continued to decline in the United States after 1990 and fell to 12.4 percent in 2003 from 19.5 percent in 1980. Of the 24 countries, only four – Belgium, Finland, Sweden, and Denmark – had higher rates of unionization in 2003 than in 1970. Indeed, for most countries union density was far lower in 2003 than in 1970 (in Australia, for example, it declined from 50 to 23 percent). By 2003, the unionization rate was actually lower in South Korea and France than in the United States.

9.2.3   The economic role of labor unions

Despite their recent decline, unions are still a major institution on the U.S. economic scene. On the surface, at least, their endurance would seem to indicate that unions provide important benefits for labor. The question then arises as to what unions actually do. What functions do they perform? What are their goals? We shall look at these issues in this section. In the next section, we shall present a more formal analysis of their economic function in the labor market. In Section 9.2.4, we shall investigate the evidence as to their success.

9.2.3.1 Union organization

Before discussing the functioning of unions, it is useful to provide a brief overview of their organization and structure. As noted in the previous section, there are, in general, two broad classes of unions. The first is the trade or craft union, which includes members of the same occupations or related occupations. Some craft unions may be localized in a single industry but most cut across industry lines. The second is the industrial union, which encompasses all workers in a particular industry, regardless of occupation or skill.

Unions are organized in several layers. The smallest unit is the *bargaining unit*, which consists of a group of employees who are exclusively represented by a union in collective bargaining over compensation, hours, and working conditions. The contract or collective agreement reached between the union and the employer governs the relationship between the employer and the employee with respect to these matters. In most cases, the bargaining unit is established as a result of an initial representation election, held by the National Labor Relations Board (NLRB). One type of bargaining unit in manufacturing consists of production and maintenance workers in a single plant. Perhaps more common in manufacturing is the single-employer unit, where the bargaining unit may include all the plants owned by a given firm, as in the automobile industry. In non-manufacturing sectors, the more typical bargaining unit cuts across employer lines and consists of employees in a particular industry, such as trucking, who are located in a specific geographic area.

The vertical structure of unions is usually in three layers – the local union at the bottom, the national union in the middle, and the federation (AFL-CIO) at the top. The local union is usually a subordinate unit to a national union. In industrial unions, the local union usually covers a geographic region such as a city or metropolitan area. In cases where the product market is restricted to a local geographic area, as in construction, local transit, restaurants, and entertainment, the local unions are usually the primary bargaining unit. In cases where the product market is national in scope, as in automobiles, the principal bargaining unit is usually the national union, and the function of the local union is usually confined to administering the collective agreement at that level.

The next level is the national union, which is typically the strongest and most important of the three levels. There are three reasons for this. First, the AFL-CIO normally grants the charter to a national union, which gives it the exclusive right to organize a given industry or craft. Second, because most product markets are national in scope, it is the national union that for strategic reasons does the bargaining in the industry or trade. Third, union dues are usually paid directly to the national union.

The top layer is the federation, which today is the AFL-CIO. The federation's primary function is to act as the spokesman for labor, particularly on the political scene. In many ways, the AFL-CIO acts as a lobby for labor in national politics. The federation does not engage in collective bargaining; this function is performed by the national unions. Its primary organizational power is its ability to grant jurisdictional charters to new unions.

9.2.3.2 Collective bargaining

The most important function performed by labor unions is to bargain collectively with employers to reach an agreement on the terms of employment of the members of the union. Agreements usually cover wages, hours, and working conditions, as well as other relevant matters, such as security clauses to prevent non-union members from being hired; seniority (i.e., length of service) policy, particularly in regard to wage differentials, the order of layoffs and recalls, and transfer policies; complaints and grievance procedures; and fringe benefits, including vacations, sick time, pensions, and health benefits. On the other side of the table, management is also concerned with work rules – that is, control over the productive process. These involve the freedom to assign workers to different jobs, control over machine speed, the right to introduce new technology in a plant, and the freedom to subcontract certain services, such as maintenance.

9.2.3.3   Strikes and other union weapons

The strike is by far the most powerful weapon a union has to win its negotiating demands. A strike is a decision made by a union to withhold labor from one or more workplaces. The usual reason for a strike is that an old contract has expired and negotiations with an employer have failed to provide a new contract. During a strike, workers do not receive wages or other employer-provided benefits, and the employer is stuck with idle plant and equipment. There is therefore a considerable cost associated with strikes. Strikes may also cause resources to lay idle in supplying and using industries (a strike in the railroad industry could idle steelworkers if there are no other means of shipping steel).

Once a strike is in effect, unions try to keep the pressure on employers by preventing any work from taking place in the plant or company. Until about 1940, employers often tried to break a strike by hiring new non-union employees to replace the strikers (so-called "scabs"). Unions, on the other hand, engaged in picketing and occasionally violence to stop the scabs from working. Since the start of World War II, employers have very rarely resorted to this tactic. In some basic service industries, such as telephones, supervisory personnel may keep service going during a strike but in most other industries operations are discontinued.

A strike ends when a settlement is reached between the union and employer, which normally takes the form of a new contract. The factors determining both the timing and terms of the settlement are complex. On the union side, the main determinant is the ability of the workers to hold out financially. Many large unions have strike funds for this purpose. On the other side, employers will lose money as their plant and equipment lie idle. If production is completely halted, they will continue to lose money during the strike.

There are other weapons in labor's arsenal besides the planned strike. There is the "wildcat strike," which often occurs spontaneously by a local union without authorization from above. Wildcat strikes are usually called in violation of an existing collective bargaining agreement. They are sometimes ignited by a local grievance against a particular employer (over safety conditions, for example) but sometimes they are motivated by dissatisfaction with the national union. The primary aim, in both cases, is to win added concessions for the workers. Another tactic is the "slowdown," whereby workers will purposely slow down the pace of work in order to reduce output. This tactic is also used to gain concessions from management.

Less direct tactics include the use of "union labels" and boycotts. A union label is often put on consumer goods made by a union in order to encourage consumers who are sympathetic with the goals of organized labor to buy only union goods. A "boycott" is the converse of this, for it attempts to discourage consumers from buying non-union products. These are, in general, weak weapons, although the United Farm Workers in California were fairly successful in using the boycott to help organize farm workers in grape and lettuce production in the 1970s.

9.2.3.4   Labor market impact of trade unions

The effect of a union on a labor market can perhaps be most easily understood by a comparison with the perfectly competitive labor market. In Figure 9.2, we have indicated the industry

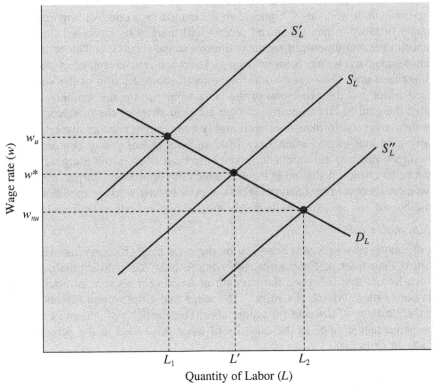

S_L — Supply curve for labor under perfect competition
S_L' — Supply curve for union labor
S_L'' — Supply curve for non-union labor
w^* — Wage under perfect competition
w_u — Wage for union labor
w_{nu} — Wage for non-union labor

Figure 9.2 Demand and supply curves for labor under perfection competition and under unionization

supply curve for labor under pure competition by S_L. The equilibrium wage in this situation will be w^* and the equilibrium quantity of labor L^*.

Suppose a union organizes the workers in this industry and negotiates a wage rate w_1, which is greater (as it hopefully should be) than the prevailing equilibrium wage w^*. The firms in the industry will therefore reduce employment until the quantity of labor is equal to L_1. However, at the wage rate w_u, workers will be willing to supply L_2 of labor. L_2 will be greater than the competitive equilibrium level L^*, since the higher wage w_u will attract additional workers to the industry.

The initial effect of unionization is to create an excess supply of labor in the industry – that is, a larger number of workers willing to work at the prevailing wage than the number actually hired. In a perfectly competitive situation, this excess supply would cause the wage to be bid down until w^* is reached. However, with a union present, the wage cannot be changed, since the union is a monopsonist. What happens to the excess workers? They either remain unemployed or find work in another sector of the economy. The eventual effect of unionization in this industry is then to *shift the supply curve of labor to the left*, as indicated by $S_{L'}$. In other words, the primary effect of a union is to *restrict* the supply of labor flowing into an industry, which thereby allows the union to maintain a wage level higher than the competitive one. An important side-effect is that the supply of labor in non-unionized sectors will thereby be increased (that is, the supply curve of labor in the non-unionized sector will move to the right, $S_{L'}$). This will lower the wage rate in the non-unionized sector, from w^* to w_{nu}. The wage rate advantage of unionized workers over non-unionized ones thus comes from *two* effects: the restriction of the supply of labor to the unionized sector and the expansion of the labor supply to the non-unionized sector.

Essentially, the goal of labor unions is to get a bigger share of the producer surplus (or firm profits) for their workers. In industries with highly competitive product markets, profit margins are generally slim and unions often have little success in improving compensation for their workers. In oligopolistic or monopolistic product markets, where profit margins are high, unions often stand a better chance in sharing in the economic rent (or producer surplus). Moreover, unions usually have more success in negotiating higher wages or cushier working conditions during periods of economic booms and less success in negotiating during periods of economic downturns.[4]

9.2.3.5   *Marshall's rules**

The effect of unions on wages was analyzed by the great English economist Alfred Marshall in his classic text *Principles of Economics* (8th edition, New York: Macmillan, 1920). Marshall analyzed four factors that influence the strength of unions (in his day, primarily craft unions), which today are called "Marshall's rules." The wage and employment effects of unionization depend on the *elasticity of demand* for union labor. The elasticity of demand ε is defined as the ratio of the percentage change in the quantity of labor demanded to the percentage change in the wage rate. In particular,

$\varepsilon = (\Delta L/L) \, / \, (\Delta dw/w)$

where "Δ" is the change, L is the quantity of labor demanded and w is the wage rate. In the case where two demand curves pass through a common point, then the flatter of the two is more *elastic* and the steeper of the two is more *inelastic*. In the case when the two curves do not pass through a common point, then calculations are necessary to determine the elasticity.[5]

For an elastic demand curve, a small change in the wage rate will cause a large change in the quantity of labor demanded. In the extreme case, when the demand curve is horizontal, its elasticity is infinite. For an inelastic demand curve, a large change in the wage rate will cause only a small change in the quantity demanded. In the extreme case, when the demand curve is vertical, its elasticity is zero.[6]

Marshall's basic principle is that the more inelastic the demand curve for union labor, the smaller the impact on employment of a given percentage change in the wage rate and therefore the larger wage gains are likely to come from unionization. The rationale is that if the demand curve is elastic, then unions will be hesitant to push for a large increase in wages for fear of losing many jobs and hence members. If the labor demand curve is inelastic, on the other hand, unions will push for much higher wages since the expected loss in jobs will be small. Union strength will then be higher the more inelastic the demand curve for its members.

The demand for labor is a "derived demand" and, in particular, depends on labor's substitutability with other factors of production and on the demand curve for the product of the firm. Marshall used the theory of derived demand for labor to determine the factors that affect the elasticity of labor. His four conditions or rules are as follows:

Rule 1   The demand curve for labor is more inelastic the more "essential" union labor is in the production process – that is, the less substitutable other factors of production are for union labor. This condition would characterize many of the skilled construction trades, such as plumbers, electricians, and masons, for whom it is difficult to substitute other types of labor or equipment. Unions should thus be strong in the craft trades.

Rule 2   The more inelastic the product demand curve, the more inelastic the demand curve for the union workers. If the *product* demand curve is inelastic, then a large increase in its price will cause only a small decrease in the quantity of the product sold. A large wage increase, translated into a large output price increase, would not substantially reduce output and therefore the employment of union members.

This condition has two interpretations. First, if a union has organized all the firms in a particular industry, then the relevant product demand curve is that of the industry. Second, if an industry is only partially organized, then the relevant product demand curve is that of the firm. As is the case in monopolistic competition, the demand curve for a firm's product is much more elastic than the industry demand curve, because the product of competing firms is easily substitutable. This factor helps to explain why unions that succeed in organizing only part of an industry are often quite weak. It also helps to account for phenomena such as "union labels" (see above), which is a way of persuading consumers to discriminate between union and non-union products (such as apparel) and thus make the demand curve for the union product more inelastic.

Rule 2 helps explain why unions are particularly prevalent in oligopolistic and monopolistic industries, since their product demand curve is generally inelastic. This condition also helps account for the rapid growth of unions in the public sector, because the government enjoys perhaps the greatest degree of monopolization of any industrial sector. Growing international competition has also slowly eroded the strong oligopoly position of many domestic manufacturing firms over the last three decades. This is particularly notable in automobiles, steel, and electronics, where imports have made striking gains. This has made the product demand curve in these industries more elastic and further weakened unions.

Rule 3   The demand for union labor is more inelastic the lower the share of union wages in the total cost of production. If the share is low, a large increase in union wages will cause only a small increase in the cost (and hence price) of the product. This principle is particularly important when the product demand curve is elastic, since by rule 2, if the demand curve is inelastic, the reduction in employment will be low even for a large increase in the product price. The third principle tends to reinforce the view that craft unions will be stronger than industrial unions, since craft trades normally account for a smaller percentage of total costs than industrial unions.

Rule 4   The demand curve for union labor is more inelastic the more inelastic are the supply curves of substitutable factors of production. If wages go up, firms will generally try to substitute other factors of production, such as non-union labor, machinery, and materials. If the supply curve of the other factors is inelastic, then the firm will have to pay higher prices for them and thus be more reluctant to substitute for union labor. This principle is particularly important when the first principle fails to hold – that is, when there are good technological substitutes for union labor. This condition may differ in the short run and long run. In the short run, capital equipment is sunk (that is, fixed) and its supply curve is inelastic. Over the long run, a company can buy new capital equipment and the supply curve of capital is more elastic. Union strength may therefore be greater in the short run than the long run.

9.2.4   The effect of unions on wages: The evidence

Marshall's four conditions offer direct implications of which occupations and industries unions are expected to have the most impact on wages. Table 9.4 shows the ratio of earnings between

Table 9.4 Median weekly earnings by union status and percent union members by occupation and industry, 1993 and 2006

Occupation or industry	Median weekly earnings ($), 1993		1993 earnings ratio	1993 Percent union members	2006 earnings ratio
	Union members	Non-union workers			
A. Occupation					
Managerial and professional	$696	$670	1.04	14.9	1.00
Technical, sales, and administrative support	509	408	1.25	10.4	1.22
Service occupations	478	265	1.80	13.8	1.58
Precision, production, craft, and repair	642	453	1.42	25.6	1.54
Operators, fabricators, and laborers	501	321	1.56	24.7	1.43
Farming, forestry, and fishing	436	264	1.65	5.1	—
B. Industry					
Mining	631	657	0.96	16.0	—
Construction	692	425	1.63	20.0	1.59
Manufacturing	505	448	1.13	19.2	1.09
Transportation and public utilities	640	516	1.24	30.5	1.26
Wholesale and retail trade	465	347	1.34	6.3	1.11
Finance, insurance, and real estate	484	490	0.99	1.9	0.89
Services	482	416	1.16	5.8	1.24
Government workers	602	498	1.21	37.7	1.21
Overall	575	426	1.35	15.8	1.27

Sources: U.S. Census Bureau, *Statistical Abstract of the United States, 1994, 2007.*

union and non-union employees in 1993 and 2006. It should be noted that these data do not adjust for any other factors that might influence earnings, such as schooling, experience, geographic region, and so on (see below). The biggest differential was found among service workers, among whom union members earned, on average, 80 percent more than non-union workers in 1993 and 58 percent more in 2006. Other large differences characterized farming, forestry, and fishing workers (65 percent in 1993); operators, fabricators, and laborers (56 percent in 1993 and 43 percent in 2006); and precision, craft, and repair workers (42 percent in 1993 and 54 percent in 2006). Unionized technical, sales, and administrative support workers averaged 25 percent more in earnings than their non-union counterparts in 1993 and 22 percent more in 2006. In managerial and professional jobs, there was almost no difference in earnings between union and non-union workers.

Panel B of Table 9.4 presents similar statistics by industry. The largest differential occurred in construction, where union members enjoyed a 63 percent advantage over non-union workers in 1993 and a 59 percent advantage in 2006. In wholesale and retail trade, the union workers earned 34 percent more in 1993 but only 11 percent more in 2006. In manufacturing, transportation and public utilities, services, and government, the union edge varied between 13 and 24 percent in 1993 and between 9 and 26 percent in 2006, while in mining and finance, insurance and real estate, there were no significant differences in earnings. Within the entire labor force, union members earned 35 percent more than non-union workers in 1993 and 27 percent more in 2006.

Econometric studies of union–non-union earnings disparities attempt to standardize the union and non-union samples for a variety of factors, such as schooling, experience, and skill differences, which might affect earnings independently of union membership. The most comprehensive and systematic review of this subject is Lewis (1963).[7]

The statistical studies on union wage effects generally show a lower union wage advantage than the estimates derived from the unadjusted data. The reason is that union workers tend to be more skilled and experienced than non-union ones. Throop (1968) adjusted earnings for differences in skill level between the unionized and non-unionized sectors. Using aggregate industry data, Throop found that with this adjustment, the union wage advantage fell to 22 percent in 1950 and 26 percent in 1960.

Weiss (1966), using 1960 Census of Population data, estimated a 20 percent union wage effect among male craftsmen and operatives. Stafford (1968) estimated a union wage effect between 18 and 52 percent for all wage and salary workers in the same year. Freeman and Medoff (1984, p. 46) presented several estimates of the union wage effect for the decade of the 1970s on the basis of the Panel Survey of Income Dynamics (PSID), the Current Population Survey (CPS), and the National Longitudinal Survey (NLS). These ranged from 21 to 32 percent.

There has also been considerable variation in the union–non-union wage spread over time. According to estimates provided by Pencavel and Hartsog (1984), the differential was particularly high during the 1920s (23 percent in 1920–1924 and 35 percent in 1925–1929), the 1930s (50 percent in 1930–1934 and 22 percent in 1935–1939), and the period 1955–1969 (about 20 percent), but small during the 1940s (under 5 percent) and the 1970s (under 8 percent). They estimated that over the years from 1920 to 1980, the union wage advantage averaged about 17 percent.[8]

Blanchflower and Bryson (2004), using CPS data, documented a noticeable downward trend in the union wage premium in the private sector over the period from 1973 to 2002. In the late 1970s, the union wage premium averaged about 21 percent in the private sector but fell to about 17 percent in the late 1990s and early 2000s. In contrast, the union wage premium showed a slight increase in the governmental sector over the same period. They also estimated that over the entire period from 1973 to 2002, the union wage gap averaged about 17 percent, which was very close to the Pencavel and Hartsog estimate.

9.2.4.1 The "threat effect"

One criticism that has been raised about many of the studies of union wage differentials concerns the implicit assumption that unionization in one sector will leave unchanged or even lower the wages of the non-unionized sector. This assumption is based on the model developed in Section 9.2.3.4 (Figure 9.2), where an increase in the wage of unionized labor causes a reduction of employment in the unionized sector, a resulting increase in the supply of workers to the non-unionized sectors, and thereby a fall in non-union wages. An alternative possibility is that unionization in one sector will induce employers in the non-unionized sector to *raise* wages because of the *fear or threat* of unionization. Companies may try to keep wages and benefits on a par with unionized companies in order to forestall the introduction of unions. Increases in wages in "key" organized industries may be imitated by the non-unionized sectors. If contagion to the non-union industries is widespread, the observed union/non-union wage differential may *understate* the true union wage effect because non-union wages may also rise from increased unionization (see Flanagan, 1976, for more discussion).

The threat effect has important implications because it suggests that unions may have effects on wages in not only the unionized but also the non-unionized sector as well. Moreover, the decline of unionism in the United States may depress wages among non-unionized workers because the threat of unionization has also subsided. Farber (2005) used CPS data over the 1977–2002 period to look at the threat effect. He found that estimates employing the predicted probability of union membership as a measure of the union threat effected showed no important link between the degree of the union threat and either the level of non-union wages or the union to non-union wage gap. His results tended to confirm earlier evidence on the threat effect which had been largely inconclusive (see Mitchell, 1980; Freeman & Medoff, 1981, 1984; and Neumark & Wachter, 1995).[9]

9.2.4.2 *Inequality of earnings*

Somewhat surprisingly, though unions generally raise the wages of their members relative to non-union workers, unionization may actually reduce overall earnings inequality. Lewis (1963) proposed four reasons for this. First, unions raise the earnings of production workers who are generally in unions relative to the higher wages of professional and managerial workers who are not generally found in unions. Second, unions tend to equalize wage rates for a given skill or occupational category both among firms and among different geographic locations. Third, unions tend to reduce the spread in wages among different classes of unionized workers within a company. Fourth, unions tend to even out wages within a skill or occupational class among individuals with different personal characteristics.

   The evidence seems to indicate that unionization reduces the inequality of earnings among all workers, although the effect is probably very modest. Freeman (1980), using data from the 1973, 1974, and 1975 Current Population Surveys, found that wage inequality among union workers was substantially smaller than among non-union workers. He also found that unions decreased the wage differential between unionized blue-collar workers and non-unionized white-collar workers. In two separate studies Hyclak (1979 and 1980) confirmed that unions tended to reduce overall inequality. In the first, he found a positive association between the extent of unionization and the level of earnings equality in metropolitan areas. In the second, he found a positive association between the degree of income equality and the degree of unionization across the states of the United States.

   Plotnick (1982), using a time series of CPS data, found that wage inequality among male workers was higher when the unionization rate was lower. Podursky (1983), using the 1971 CPS, found, as in previous studies, that collective bargaining agreements reduced the dispersion of income among union families. However, because union families tend to be found in the middle-income range, the union impact on overall family income inequality was negligible. Kahn and Curme (1987) argued that, because of the threat effect, non-union firms most at risk from unionization will raise the wages of workers who would benefit most from a union. As a consequence, the dispersion of non-union wages should be lower in sectors where the likelihood of unionization is greater. Using the 1979 CPS, they found confirmation that the inequality of earnings among non-union employees was lower in more highly unionized industries.

   Gittleman and Pierce (2007), using a special Bureau of Labor Statistics survey called the 2003 National Compensation Survey, determined that the union wage premium was lower for higher skilled workers than for lower skilled ones. They argued that this was result was consistent with the view that unions work to decrease wage skill differentials and thus help reduce earnings inequality within the firm.

   Freeman and Medoff (1984) concluded on the basis of their own work and those of other researchers that trade unionism in the United States reduced overall wage inequality by about 3 percent. This effect was primarily due to the demand of unions for standard rates of pay within and across establishments.

9.3   SEGMENTED LABOR MARKETS

Doeringer and Piore developed the dual labor market in their 1971 book. They argued there are effectively two distinct labor markets operating in the economy. In the primary labor market, training requirements are high. These jobs are largely career-type positions in large, highly structured organizations. There are fairly well-established entry positions and standard promotional ladders. These positions form an **internal labor market**. Wage policy for these positions is set by the organization and internal consistency in wage levels is usually considered more important than consistency with the external labor market. As a result, relative salaries at different positions remain fairly stable over time. Schooling and experience are important in determining the level at which a prospective employee is hired, but once in the internal labor market, they play a subordinate role in advancement.

The secondary labor market consists of jobs which require little or no training. These jobs offer low wages, and worker turnover is generally very high. The secondary labor market consists largely of marginal workers whose attachment to the labor force is tangential. Blacks and other minorities, females, students, teenagers, the aged, the disabled, part-time workers, and the poorly educated are considerably overrepresented in this market. These workers receive little on-the-job training and may, as a result, have low wages throughout their work life.

Section 9.3.1 presents a discussion of internal labor markets. Section 9.3.2 develops the dual labor market model. In section 9.3.3, some criticisms of the dual labor market model are addressed.

9.3.1   Internal labor markets

The term "internal labor markets" was coined by Clark Kerr in a 1954 article. He emphasized the importance of institutional rules in the operation of the labor market. Kerr argued that rules and procedures followed by large organizations set sharp boundaries between the internal and external labor market and, in particular, defined points of entry. Employees in an internal market do not compete directly against outside workers. Employers usually make the "admission decisions" determining who may enter the organization, though unions can exert some influence. Inside the internal market, labor mobility is largely dictated by organizational rules. Seniority plays a large role in advancement, particularly for production workers. Wage rates are set according to institutional rules and do not necessarily reflect supply and demand conditions in the external labor market.[10]

Doeringer and Piore (1971) revived the internal labor market model, though they emphasized the role of large organizations on wage setting and employment patterns. Doeringer and Piore define an internal labor market as "an administrative unit within which the pricing and allocation of labor is governed by a set of administrative rules and procedures." Ports of entry and exit mediate between the internal and external labor markets. Other jobs are filled by promotions and transfers and are thus shielded from the external labor market. In a sense, internal markets represent "industrial feudalism," where each "fiefdom" is relatively insulated from others. Doeringer and Piore estimated that about 80 percent of the employed labor force in the 1960s was located in internal labor markets.

9.3.1.1   The structure of internal labor markets

Internal labor markets are characterized by four factors: (i) ports of entry; (ii) exit ports; (iii) promotional ladders; and (iv) wage structure. With regard to the first factor, there are a well-defined and limited number of positions into which workers from the external labor market are hired. Internal labor markets also have specific rules relating to exit. These rules are designed to control involuntary movements out of the internal labor market. With the exception of the military, workers are always free to quit a job or leave a position. These are voluntary terminations. However, there are also involuntary terminations consisting of layoffs (both temporary and permanent), discharge for failure to perform one's work adequately, and compulsory retirement. Such work rules determine the various exit points in the job structure and the conditions under which the discharge can occur.

The third characteristic of internal markets is that they typically have well-defined promotional ladders. A promotional ladder indicates the normal progression of jobs through which advancement takes place. These ladders usually consist of related jobs requiring similar but increasingly more advanced skills. Promotion may depend on ability, but more often on seniority. The fourth characteristic is a relatively rigid wage structure, which does not respond or change much in relation to changes in outside conditions such as unemployment and shifting wage rates. Internal consistency in the wage structure is therefore considered more important than external consistency.

9.3.1.2   Rationale for internal labor markets

There are three factors primarily responsible for the development and structure of internal labor markets: (i) skill specificity; (ii) on-the-job training; and (iii) customary law. The first of these, skill specificity, is related to the concept of specific training developed in human capital theory by Gary Becker (see Chapter 8). Specific training is defined as training that has an effect on the productivity of a worker in a particular firm but which would not be useful in other firms. General training increases the marginal productivity of the worker by the same amount in the firm providing the training as in other firms. For Doeringer and Piore, on the other hand, the terms "specific" and "general" refer to skills and, in particular, to the frequency with which various skills can be used within different internal markets. A completely specific skill is one which is used within a single job classification in a single enterprise; a completely general skill is one which is required for every job in every company.

Skill specificity increases the proportion of training costs borne by the employer, as opposed to the worker. The reason for this is that as skills become more specific, it becomes increasingly difficult for the worker to use these skills in other employments. As a result, the worker has less incentive to invest in such training, and an increasingly higher proportion of the training cost will be borne by the employer, the more specific the skill (cf. Becker's argument for specific training in Chapter 8). A second implication is that skill specificity increases the absolute costs of such training. The reason is that the less often a particular skill is used in the labor market, the less frequently workers are trained in that skill and, as a result, economies of scale in such training cannot be obtained. Both of these effects enhance the importance of a stable workforce and give the employer an incentive to reduce worker turnover.

The second factor is the need for on-the-job-training. In the human capital literature, on-the-job training is viewed primarily as an extension of formal education with the major difference that the location of the investment in human capital is shifted to the workplace. In contrast, Doeringer and Piore emphasize the process of training, which they regard as very different from formal schooling. They find that the vast majority of blue-collar job skills are acquired on the job. Learning to operate a piece of equipment, for example, requires demonstration from fellow workers. A new employee in a repair or maintenance team will typically learn the job by serving as an assistant to a more experienced worker. Almost all the on-the-job training in a plant is informal. The "instructor" is usually the supervisor or an experienced worker. Participants in the training process thus spend part of their time in training and the rest in the production process.

The informal nature of on-the-job training is closely related to skill specificity. Such specificity leads to this type of training since the number of trainees for a particular job is typically small. Also, because skill specificity often takes the form of unrecorded knowledge, the transmission of such skills must come from those already working on the job, who are in possession of the required knowledge. Training also has an effect on skill specificity. On-the-job training makes possible increasing specificity in skills and further specialization in tasks. Skills can also change over time as they are passed from one worker to the next. Such a process leads to innovations and greater productivity. In addition, machine operators and maintenance staff often modify equipment on their own without written record, and this knowledge can be passed on to new employees by informal training.

The third factor leading to the formation of internal labor markets is custom. Custom is an unwritten set of rules at the workplace based primarily on past practice or precedent. These rules can govern a variety of aspects of the work relationship. Such customary practices grow out of a stable workforce in an internal labor market. Stable employment leads to the formation of social groups or communities in the workplace, and this, in turn, leads to the development of unwritten behavioral rules governing the interaction of members of the group. These boost morale and impart a stabilizing influence to workplace rules and, in particular, to those affecting wage and employment policy. One result is that such internal allocation rules create a fairly rigid wage structure in the internal market and one that is unresponsive to pressures from the external labor market.

The development of internal labor markets provides economic benefits to both the employees and the employer. Workers benefit from increased job and wage security and the likelihood of promotion. Because employers must invest resources in workers for the acquisition of specific skills, employers are reluctant to discharge workers and lose their investment. In addition, customary rules and work practices guarantee workers a considerable degree of job security and certainty in wage setting and help to maintain a relatively stable wage structure over time. Internal labor markets also have well-established paths for advancement. Movement up such promotional ladders is often based on seniority, which increases the prospects of advancement with age. A secondary benefit of internal labor markets is that they provide equity and due process for employees. These are important both for morale and to minimize grievances.

The employer also benefits from the existence of internal labor markets. The major advantage is the reduction in worker turnover. Because of skill specificity, the training costs borne by the employer may be substantial. Reducing turnover thus lowers overall training costs.

Employers reduce turnover by making job security and advancement depend on the worker's length of service (for example, layoffs are usually done in reverse order of seniority). Employers typically assign their most senior employees to those positions which have the most turnover cost. Also, this system provides an incentive for workers to train new employees, since there is no fear that the new workers will replace the established ones.

Internal labor markets, as a result, provide job security to workers and stability to employers. Insofar as such a system leads to reduced training and associated turnover costs, it lowers the cost of production and leads to efficiencies. However, this system can also lead to inefficiencies. This is particularly so when promotion chains come to be viewed as customary by employees and hence equitable. Promotion can then become based strictly on seniority, not ability, which tends to reduce efficiency. Another consequence is that employees may resist the introduction of new technology, because this tends to upset previously established work rules.

Internal labor markets also preserve a relatively rigid wage structure. This is so because any wage structure which exists for a period of time begins to take on a customary status. Such a wage structure is looked upon as normal and equitable by the workers. Any attempt to change the overall wage structure may therefore reduce worker morale or generate opposition in the form of strikes. Thus, short-run cost savings that employers can receive by hiring cheap "outside" labor may be far outweighed by the costs associated with a loss of worker morale.

Doeringer and Piore argued that the internal consistency of wages far outweighs their relation to the external labor market. Even at the entry ports, maintaining a regular relation between these wage rates and others in the internal structure receives a higher priority than responding to changing supply conditions of labor. Thus, even if a surplus of car mechanics develops in the external labor market, the entry wage for mechanics will not go down but will maintain its customary relation to other wages in the internal structure.

Internal markets thus help keep wage inequality low. The breakdown of internal labor markets that seems to have occurred since the late 1970s may be one factor explaining rising earnings inequality over this period. We will return to this point in Section 9.3.3.

9.3.2 The dual labor market model

Dual and segmented labor market theory may be said to date back to the work of John Stuart Mill (1848). He argued that there existed *noncompeting groups* within the labor market, which accounted for the persistence of wage differentials over long periods of time between industries, among occupations, and among firms within the same industry. These noncompeting groups were formed as the result of certain exogenous forces which erected barriers between various groups of workers in the labor force and prevented the long-run equalizing tendencies of the marketplace to occur over time. This caused mobility of labor between these segments of the labor force to be so limited that wage differences could remain over long stretches of time.

This theory was resurrected in the 1960s. One version, the dual labor market model, was developed by Doeringer and Piore (1971). They defined the primary market by four characteristics: First, wages and fringe benefits are high. Second, working conditions are safe and clean. Third, employment is stable and there are considerable opportunities for promotion. Fourth, there is equity in pay scales, due process in work rules, and channels available for grievances. These conditions characterize the internal labor market described above.

The secondary market is characterized by opposite traits. First, wages are low and fringe benefits almost nonexistent. Second, secondary jobs generally have poor working conditions. Third, there is relatively little job security and hence high turnover in secondary employment. Fourth, advancement opportunities are limited. Fifth, work rules are generally arbitrary and supervision can be autocratic. One example of secondary labor markets is the hiring hall for temporary labor found in urban areas. The work is unskilled; hiring is done on a first-come, first-served basis; and no assurance of continued employment is made. Other examples are janitorial jobs in large companies, menial jobs in the health industry, stitching jobs in the clothing industry, laboring jobs in construction or steel, wood yard work in paper mills, temporary packaging jobs in manufacturing, dishwashing, domestic work, and seasonal agricultural jobs such as fruit picking.

9.3.2.1 Rationale for a secondary labor market

We have seen why an internal labor market might be advantageous to both employee and employer alike. Why would a secondary labor market be beneficial? Some employees prefer unstable employment. One example is the working mother whose primary concern is her family and whose earnings go to supplement those of her husband. Many mothers expect to work for only short periods of time, either until another child is born or some purchase, like a car, can be made. For them, jobs which tolerate absenteeism or lateness may be quite desirable. Students are a second example. Their principal activity is school and they usually seek part-time, temporary, or summer employment. A third example is individuals who take on second jobs (i.e., "moonlight") in order to supplement their primary income.

From the employer viewpoint, the main advantage of secondary jobs is that they require little training. As a result, there is no incentive for the employer to build up a stable workforce for these jobs, and the employer is willing to trade off high turnover for low wages. Since little employer investment in training is required, the costs of turnover are relatively small. This is further reinforced by the fact that secondary jobs rarely carry termination benefits such as severance pay or unemployment insurance. Firms often view secondary jobs as an alternative to subcontracting. Instead of adjusting output to the temporary vicissitudes of demand by subcontracting out part of the work, the firm can adjust by expanding and contracting its secondary workforce.

9.3.2.2 The make-up and consequences of the secondary labor market

Doeringer and Piore identified four segments of the secondary labor force. The first are adults with stable but low-wage work experience. A large percentage of black workers are in this group, particularly black females, as well as Hispanics and recent immigrants. The second are teenagers with relatively little work experience. Urban black teenagers are particularly overrepresented in this group. The third are adults who, for health or other reasons, have a long history of job loss and absenteeism. The fourth consists of groups who face well-defined barriers to long-term stable employment. Besides mothers with young children, students working part time, and second job holders are the elderly, alcoholics and addicts, those who are poorly educated or illiterate, the disabled, and welfare recipients.

Though students and mothers with young children are in the secondary labor force temporarily and will eventually enter the primary workforce, the other groups often remain trapped in the secondary workforce. This entrapment may come about from race or gender discrimination, an unstable prior work history, the lack of appropriate educational credentials, a criminal record and the like. Once in the secondary job market, secondary employment can become a self-perpetuating phenomenon. Secondary jobs tend to be short-lived and the secondary workforce experiences high turnover. Secondary employment tends to be unpleasant, so that these workers develop a "bad" attitude about work. Due to the poor prospects for advancement, there is little incentive for developing a good work record and little opportunity for upgrading skills. Because of an unstable employment history, poor work habits, and the lack of skills, a secondary worker is unable to obtain employment in the primary labor market. This *feedback cycle* then becomes a vicious circle, where employers have little incentive to train these workers and these workers see little to be gained by training since their job prospects are so poor. Once in secondary employment, it becomes very difficult to pull out. From the viewpoint of dual labor market theory, this vicious cycle is the principal problem of the working poor.

9.3.2.3 Extensions of the dual labor market model

There are other versions of the dual labor market model. One interesting variant was developed by Reich, Gordon, and Edwards (1973), who divided the primary segment into "subordinate" and "independent" jobs. The former are fairly routinized positions like factory and office jobs. The latter are positions which require creative or problem-solving talents and are typically professional jobs.

Reich, Gordon, and Edwards argued that labor market segmentation arose out of a historical process in which economic and social forces encouraged the segregation of the labor market into distinct components, each with its own labor market characteristics and behavioral roles. Segmentation developed during the transition from competitive to monopoly capitalism in the 1890s and the first decade of the twentieth century. The same two decades saw the development of the large oligopolistic corporations that still dominate the U.S. economy today. These corporations felt threatened by the increasing militancy of the labor force. They argued that these large companies "actively and consciously fostered labor market segmentation in order to 'divide and conquer' the labor force" (p. 361). In addition, the competitive efforts of large companies to increase their market share led to a dichotomization of the industrial structure which reinforced the segmentation of the labor force.

The new form of organization taken by these large corporations consisted of bureaucratic control. Whole new structures of stratified jobs were introduced, with a clearly delineated hierarchy of positions. Power and control were exercised from the top of the hierarchy down through the ranks. Within the global corporation, internal labor markets were carved out in various pockets. Unions were often given authority to allocate jobs in selected internal labor markets in order to soften union resistance to this new form of organization. Ethnic and racial lines were often employed to separate groups of workers into different internal labor markets. More recently, education credentials were introduced to separate workers into different sectors of the job structure – particularly between blue-collar and white-collar jobs. These strategies were all conscious attempts on the part of the management of the large corporations to divide and segment the labor force.

Concomitant with these developments within the large corporation was the growing bifurcation in industrial structure. Giant corporations grew to occupy the monopolistic core of the U.S. economy. These large corporations were highly capital intensive and functioned effectively only when there was stable demand. On the periphery developed a competitive fringe of firms. These firms were typically small and had low capital intensity. Their function was to absorb fluctuations in demand which the large corporations could not. When demand rose rapidly, the large companies would subcontract part of the work to the smaller firms, and during periods of contraction the small firms would absorb most of the reduced demand.

The stable work environment of the monopoly core thus developed into the primary labor market. The instability that characterized the competitive fringe helped create the secondary labor market (also, see Gordon, 1972, for a fuller discussion).

Osterman (1975) provided empirical support for the Reich, Gordon, and Edwards' model. Osterman classified occupations into three segments: (i) primary sector consisting of upper tier jobs in which the employee had a great degree of autonomy and personal participation in the work process; (ii) primary sector consisting of lower tier jobs in which the employee had relatively little autonomy or participation in the work process; and (iii) secondary sector.

Osterman drew a sample of workers for each segment from the 1967 Survey of Economic Opportunity. His main interest was to ascertain whether the determinants of earnings were the same or different in each of the three segments. Human capital earnings functions were used: individual earnings were regressed on schooling, age, the square of age, race, weeks worked, hours worked per week, and industry dummy variables. Osterman found that human capital characteristics explained the variation of earnings very well for the upper tier of the primary segment ($R^2 = 0.48$), moderately well for the lower tier of the primary segment ($R^2 = 0.25$), but not at all for secondary workers. For the secondary segment, only the amount of time worked was found to be a statistically significant determinant of earnings. The implication is that there were very significant differences in the factors which determined earnings within these three segments, and this result, in turn, supported the existence of distinct labor market segments.

Later studies continued to provide strong empirical confirmation for the existence of distinct labor market segments, including Rumberger and Carnoy (1980) and Dickens and Lang (1985). Dickens and Lang also found that in the primary labor market, the wage profile was similar to that predicted by human capital theory, whereas in the secondary market, the wage profile was almost completely flat – that is, wages were almost completely independent of schooling and experience. They also found support for the hypothesis that there existed noneconomic barriers that prevented minorities from entering the primary labor segment.

Schochet and Rangarajan (2004) investigated the characteristics of low-wage workers and their labor market experiences from 1995 to 2000. The study was conducted using data from the 1996 longitudinal panel of the Survey of Income and Program Participation (SIPP). Though the paper was not explicitly on the "secondary labor market," the results were very telling.

Their approach for defining low-wage workers was to use the hourly wage at which a full-time worker would have annual earnings below poverty for a family of four. Using federal poverty guidelines, and assuming a full-time worker works 2,080 hours per year, they set the low-wage cutoff at $7.50 per hour in 1996, $7.72 in 1997, $7.91 in 1998, $8.03 in 1999, and $8.20 in 2000. They conducted the analysis using employed SIPP sample members who were between ages 16 and 64 and who were not enrolled in school.

They found that in 1996, less than one-third of all workers were low-wage workers. About 28 percent of all workers were low-wage workers, with hourly wages below $7.50 in 1996 dollars. Most workers (43 percent) were medium-wage workers, with wages between $7.50 and $15 per hour. About 29 percent were high-wage workers, with wages over $15 per hour. The share of low-wage workers decreased somewhat during the mid- to late 1990s as the unemployment rate declined.

Low-wage workers were disproportionately young, female, nonwhite, and with a high school degree or less. During the late 1990s, more than one-third of all employed females were in the low-wage labor market, compared to 22 percent of all employed males. About 84 percent of employed teenagers held low-wage jobs, compared to less than one-quarter of those between the ages of 30 and 60. About 56 percent of workers who did not finish high school were low-wage workers, compared to 36 percent of workers with a high school degree, and only about 14 percent of workers who completed college. Moreover, more than 40 percent of employed single parents with children in the sample were in the low-wage labor market, compared to 25 percent of married couples. In addition, workers who received public assistance in the past year were twice as likely as their counterparts to be in the low-wage labor market.

In 1996, nearly one-third of all low-wage workers were in service occupations, compared to only 10 percent of high-wage workers. Conversely, only 14 percent of low-wage workers were in professional and technical occupations, compared to 40 percent for other workers. Only about 6 percent of low-wage workers were unionized, compared to 16 percent of medium-wage and 25 percent of high-wage workers.

9.3.3   An evaluation of labor market segmentation

One problem in evaluating segmented labor market theory is that different versions use different principles with which to define segments. Some economists focused on the characteristics of the job – employment stability (Piore) or control over working time (Gordon), for example. Others classified workers by occupations and looked at occupational characteristics (Osterman). Others looked at divisions by industry – for example, large corporations versus small competitive firms (Reich, Gordon, and Edwards). Piore emphasized differences in technology as the basis of segmentation – large capital-intensive production processes which require long production runs versus small labor-intensive production processes which are adaptable to short production runs. Others attempted to combine both industrial and occupational characteristics as the basis of segmentation (Rumberger & Carnoy, 1980). Still others look to the existence of workers with loose labor market attachment as the basis of classifying secondary workers (Bluestone, 1970; Wachtel & Betsey, 1972; Wachter, 1972).[11]

Traditional economists often ask whether there are really distinct "segments" in the labor market or a continuum of job characteristics which differ among a spectrum of jobs. They also question whether the barriers which are posited between segments are, in fact, permanent or temporary. Along this line, Cain (1975, 1976) argued that segmented labor market theory can be viewed as a discussion of imperfections and temporary disequilibria in a neoclassical framework. Cain raised a number of "challenges" to dual labor market theory. First, is there really very little mobility of workers between segments of the labor market? If not, then dual labor market theory should be seriously questioned. Second, is labor market discrimination really a conscious attempt by employers to "divide and conquer" the workforce by creating artificial divisions? Cain felt that pre-labor market discrimination, due to segregated housing and schools and cultural differences, is a sounder explanation of occupational and wage differences between races and genders.

Third, Cain called into question the notion that unemployment and instability are intrinsic to certain (secondary) jobs. Rather, he argued that these phenomena can be more adequately explained by neoclassical theories of job search. Fourth, wage rigidities and protected labor markets can be easily interpreted within the neoclassical framework as market imperfections. In the long run, economic forces should erode such artificial barriers between labor market segments and make internal labor market wages more responsive to external labor market conditions.

Baker and Holmstron (1995), as well as Baker, Gibbs, and Holmstrom (1994a, 1994b) also take issue with internal labor market theory. They used personnel records of individual firms to analyze wage and career paths of managerial workers. Their main criticism is that their analysis did not generally conform to the Doeringer and Piore view of internal labor markets. In particular, they failed to find much evidence of standard ports of entry and exit in the firms that they looked at. Instead, substantial numbers entered at each level and exits were spread out evenly across levels. Moreover, in contradistinction to internal labor market theory, they found substantial variation in wages within each job level. Moreover, wages ranges of levels overlapped considerably. However, they did find a very distinct and stable hierarchy of jobs with clearly identified career ladders. Employees tended to advance along a few well-defined paths, usually one level at a time. There were very few lateral moves and essentially no demotions.

Despite the interpretation that labor market segments represent market imperfections, the point remains that there exist *qualitative* differences in the characteristics of jobs in the U.S. labor market. There are "good" jobs on the top and "bad" jobs on the bottom of the job ladder. The econometric evidence supports the existence of fundamental differences in factors which determine wages in the primary and secondary labor market segments. One can, of course, argue about the exact position of the line that separates the two segments, but this problem characterizes most classification systems in economics.

9.4   INDUSTRIAL COMPOSITION AND EARNINGS INEQUALITY*

9.4.1   State and regional differences in inequality

The first area of research to consider is how industrial composition on the regional level affects regional earnings. The models used in these studies generally assume that industries differ in average wages. If employment in a region is concentrated in a few industries, then wage dispersion will generally be low. If it is spread out over many industries, then inequality will typically be high. The greater the mix of industries with different wage levels, the greater will be the dispersion of income in a region. One special case occurs when there is a sector, such as agriculture, which pays low wages. Then income inequality will be greater in regions in which the proportion of the labor force employed in agriculture is greater.[12] The same argument applies for a high-wage sector such as finance.

The early studies on this topic were particularly interested in agricultural employment, since its share of total employment fell rapidly, from 14 to 5 percent between 1950 and 1970.

Al-Samarrie and Miller (1967) used five explanatory variables in their analysis: (i) the relative importance of agriculture in the state's economy measured by the proportion of the state's income originating in agriculture; (ii) the percent of property income in the total personal income of the state; (iii) median years of schooling of the adult population; (iv) the percent of nonwhites in the state's population; and (v) the extent of labor force participation in the state measured by the percent of the civilian population employed. A multiple regression was used. The data sources were the 1950 and 1960 Censuses of Population. For each year, over 80 percent of the state-to-state variation in income inequality was explained by these variables (that is, the R^2 exceeded 0.8).

The proportion of nonwhites in the population was the most important variable in the regression, and had a positive relation to inequality.[13] The second most important variable was the percent of income originating in agriculture, which also had a positive effect on inequality. This variable was less important in the 1960 regression than in the 1950 one, reflecting agriculture's decline as a source of income and employment in the U.S. economy. Median years of schooling was also a significant variable, and states with higher levels of schooling tended to have lower levels of income inequality.[14] Another interesting finding was that states with a high per capita income and a high degree of industrialization had less income inequality, on average, than states with low per capita income.[15]

Newhouse (1971) reported considerable variation in income distribution by state. He developed a model to relate the income distribution within a state to its industrial mix. He assumed that an industry's wage structure was invariant across geographic regions – that is, that local labor market conditions did not affect industry wages. He indicated three reasons for this. The first is that the technology within an industry is probably very similar across regions. The fact that factory jobs are very specialized as to industry, that technological information is highly disseminated around the nation, and that factories typically train the local labor force it hires to meet its skill needs imply that the skill mix of an industry will be uniform throughout the country.

This factor, however, is not sufficient to guarantee the same industry wage distribution across regions. It is also necessary to assume that there is no regional variation in pay for each job, which is the second reason. This condition will follow if an industry's output is sold in a national product market, because firms in different regions will face the same demand curve for their product, and the marginal revenue product of workers and thus the wage will be the same in each region. The third reason is that there are many industrial unions organized by product market, and during negotiations they try to eliminate regional differentials in wages.

The empirical application of the model relied on a combined factor analysis–multiple regression technique. The dependent variable was the proportion of income in each income class by state and the explanatory variables were the proportion of state employment in each of 31 industries. Newhouse reported that 88 percent of the variation in income distribution by state was explained by differences in the industrial mix of employment.

Smith and Jennings (1976) also looked at the effect of the industrial composition of employment on state income inequality. Their work is particularly interesting because it covers a much longer period than the other studies, 1920–1970. They computed the Gini coefficient in each state in 1920, 1950, 1960, and 1970. The model they used was somewhat different that the others we have so far considered. Rather than comparing the level of income inequality by state, they compared the *change* in the Gini coefficient over time. The change in income inequality within state was then regressed on the (weighted) change in sectoral employment in each state. For both the 1920–1950 period and the 1950–1960 period, the change in the distribution of employment between agriculture and nonagriculture was found to be a significant determinant of the change in state income inequality. However, by 1960, agricultural employment had become quite small in the U.S. economy, but employment in the service sector was becoming increasingly important (see Section 7.4). As a consequence, they found that for the 1960–1970 period, the change in the employment mix between the service and nonservice sector was the most important determinant of changes in income inequality.

Farbman (1973) investigated determinants of the degree of income concentration in the South. Using 1960 Census of Population data, he computed the Gini coefficient of income inequality for 1,156 counties in 12 Southern states. His model was similar to that of Al-Samarrie and Miller, except that his structural variable was the percent of the labor force employed in middle-level occupations, defined as craft, clerical, and operative (such as truck drivers) jobs. Farbman argued that the dispersion of earnings was very high both among professional and technical workers and among service and low-skilled workers. However, earnings in the middle-level occupations tended to have a relatively narrow dispersion. He found that this variable was statistically significant and the most important determinant of interregional inequality in the South.

9.4.2   Regional differences in income levels

Significant differences exist not only in regional inequality but also in regional income levels. In the United States before 1980, average incomes were generally higher in the Northern and Western states than in the South.

In a 1965 study, Williamson developed the argument that regional income differentials tend to widen over time as a nation develops, reach a maximum, and then decline during advanced stages of development. He argued that uneven development of regions is one cause of interregional differences in average incomes. Some regions industrialize more quickly than others, and, as a result, their per capita income rises faster than the stagnant regions. In the early stages of development, some regions will shoot rapidly ahead of others, causing large disparities in regional incomes. Eventually, through labor migration, capital migration, technological diffusion, and government policy, the backward regions will start to industrialize and their per capita income will begin to catch up with the leading regions. This is what happened during the 1970s and 1980s in the United States, when the "Sunbelt" caught up (and, in some cases, surpassed) the "Snowbelt."

Williamson used the percent of the labor force in a region employed in agriculture as the indicator of its level of development. On the basis of regional data for seven countries (Great Britain, Austria, Sweden, Brazil, Italy, Canada, and Finland), he found that per capita income was lower in regions with higher percentages of their labor force employed in agriculture. As the backward areas industrialized, their per capita income converged on the advanced regions.

Green (1969), expanding Williamson's analysis for the case of Canada, disaggregated the economy into three sectors: (i) agriculture; (ii) mining and manufacturing; and (iii) the service sector. In Canada the share of the labor employed in agriculture declined from 53 to 24 percent between 1890 and 1956, while the share in mining and manufacturing increased from 16 to 20 percent. However, by province there were considerable differences in both the share of employment in the three sectors and their trend over time.

He examined the industry mix by province in Canada over the period from 1890 to 1956 to determine how much of interregional differences in per capita income could be explained by differences in industrial composition. Between 1890 and 1929, provincial differences in the sectoral mix of employment widened considerably, and this was accompanied by a widening regional income gap. Between 1929 and 1956, there was some convergence in the industrial mix among the provinces, and this was associated with a decrease in income differentials among the regions. The main conclusion was that regional differences in income levels in Canada were largely due to the increasing concentration of mining and manufacturing in a few provinces.

Another interesting study of regional income differences was conducted by Scully (1969). One of his major objectives was to explain why wage rates in the manufacturing sector were higher in the North than in the South. Using the 1958 Census of Manufactures, he found that state-to-state variation in manufacturing wages was attributable to four factors: (i) the capital–labor ratio in the industry; (ii) the average schooling level of workers in the industry; (iii) nonwhites as a percent of the industry's labor force; and (iv) females as a percent of the industry's labor force.

He found that differences in the mean schooling level of workers and the proportion of non-whites played a significant role in explaining the higher wages in the North than the South. However, the most significant factor was the difference in industry composition between North and South. In 1958, high-wage manufacturing industries, such as machinery, equipment, and chemicals, tended to be concentrated in the North, while low-wage manufacturing industries, such as textiles, apparel, and lumber, tended to be concentrated in the South. This study also confirmed the importance of differences in industrial mix in accounting for wage differences between regions.

Hanushek (1973) also investigated interregional differences in earnings. He was particularly concerned with the relative importance of structural versus human capital factors in the deter-mination of regional earnings. He used a 1969 sample of males who had taken the Armed Forces Qualification Test (AFQT). He estimated a human capital earnings function, where the logarithm of earnings was regressed on years of schooling, years of experience, and ability (as measured by the AFQT). He computed separate earnings functions for 150 distinct regions. He found that the rate of return to human capital varied considerably by region.

He then considered to what degree differences in the mean earnings in each of these areas were due to differences in the average amount of human capital (as measured by years of school-ing, years of experience, and ability) and to differences in the rate of return to human capital among regions. His main result was that 80 percent of the interregional variation in earnings was attributable to differences in returns to human capital but less than 6 percent could be attributed to differences in human capital.

What causes differences in the return to human capital? He speculated that these differentials were largely due to differences in the industrial structure of a region. The industrial make-up of an area will determine its available employment opportunities, and this, in conjunction with the supply of human capital in the region, will determine the measured returns to human capital.

In a follow-up article, Hanushek (1981) used 1970 Census of Population data to estimate earnings functions for 341 regions of the country. As in the earlier paper, he found significant differences in regional earnings functions – both in the level and the shape of the earnings profile. Hanushek then used regression analysis to relate regional differences in earnings functions to structural dif-ferences in local labor markets, particularly differences in industrial mix and labor productivity. He used the proportion of the local workforce employed in manufacturing, construction, and government to measure industrial composition. His major finding was that variation in industrial make-up by region was significant in explaining differences in regional earnings functions.[16]

9.4.3   Industrial composition and rising earnings inequality of the 1980s

The sharp rise in earnings inequality during the 1980s and the continuing shift of employment out of goods-producing industries and into services rekindled interest in the role of industrial composition on income distribution. As reported in Section 7.4, the proportion of workers employed in industry fell from 43 percent in 1970 to 28 percent in 1993 and, correspondingly, the share in services rose from 57 to 72 percent.

Blackburn, Bloom, and Freeman (1990) were among the first investigators to argue that inter-industry employment shifts played a major role in explaining the rising return to education during the 1980s (which we discussed in Chapter 8). Using a decomposition analysis, they analyzed the effect of changes in employment patterns over 43 industries over the period 1979 to 1987 on the demand for workers of different educational levels. The calculated that about one-quarter to one-third of the rise in the premium associated with a college education could be attributed to shifts in employment by industry. A similar finding was reported by Bound and Johnson (1992) on the basis of 17 industries for the period 1979 to 1988.

Katz and Murphy (1992) concluded that inter-industry employment shifts played a major role in rising inequality. Between 1967 and 1987, industries which depended most heavily on college-educated manpower, such as professional, medical, and business services, finance, insurance, and real estate, and education and welfare, had the largest relative increases of employment and those that relied primarily on less-educated workers, such as manufacturing, agriculture, and mining, showed declines in their employment shares. This change in industrial composition shifted demand in favor of college-educated workers and against less-educated ones. They concluded that structural change accounted for a large part of the increase in the earnings of college graduates relative to other educational groups and to rising overall earnings inequality over the period.

Juhn (1999) extended the analysis of the effects of industrial change on earnings inequality to the period from 1940 to 1990. Using decennial Census of Population data, Juhn found that the demand for highly educated and skilled male workers increased no faster from changes in industrial composition during the 1980s than in the previous four decades. However, the peculiar feature of the 1980s is that the demand for male workers in the middle skill categories, such as found in manufacturing, contracted severely during the 1980s. Juhn concluded that it was the decline in medium skill jobs, rather than a sharp increase in highly skilled ones, that was primarily responsible for the rising wage inequality over this period.

Work by Mishel and Bernstein (1994) showed that industrial shifts were important in explaining the widening pay gap between white-collar and blue-collar workers. They first reported that hourly compensation (wages plus benefits) in 1993 averaged $20.22 in goods-producing industries and only $15.51 in services (see Table 9.5). Moreover, while employment grew by 38 percent in service industries between 1979 and 1993, it contracted by 12 percent among goods producers.

They then analyzed what would have happened to the pay of white-collar and blue-collar workers if the occupation and industry composition of employment had remained unchanged between 1980 and 1989 and compared this to the actual changes in pay for the two groups over the period. The difference is a measure of the effect of employment composition shifts on average pay. They estimated that employment shifts by themselves lowered the hourly compensation of blue-collar workers by 6.9 percent while it raised the hourly compensation of white-collar workers by 0.6 percent. They concluded that employment shifts were partly responsible for the widening gap in compensation between blue-collar and white-collar workers. Interestingly, they also found that employment shifts caused the average compensation among all workers to decline by 3.4 percent.

Karoly and Klerman (1994), using regional data for the United States, estimated that between 15 and 20 percent of the rise in male wage inequality between 1973 and 1988 was due to shifts in the industrial composition of the workforce. Murphy and Welch (1993) likewise attributed only 16 percent of the overall change in the demand for college-educated workers to changes in industrial shares.

Bernard and Jensen (2000) investigated inequality at the state level within the United States. They found that increases in inequality at the state level were strongly correlated with changes in industrial mix, particularly the loss of durable manufacturing jobs. Blum (2008) found an even larger effect. Using aggregate data on employment by industry in the United States over the 1970 to 1996 period, he calculated that about 60 percent of the relative increase in wages of skilled

Table 9.5 Employment growth by industry, 1979–1993

Industry	Employment (1,000s)		Percent growth in employment	Average hourly compensation in 1993
	1979	*1993*		
Goods producing	26,461	23,256	−12.1	$20.22
Manufacturing	21,040	18,003	−14.4	20.09
Construction	4,463	4,642	4.0	19.71
Mining	958	611	−36.2	—
Services	63,363	87,269	37.7	15.51
Transportation, utilities	5,136	5,787	12.7	24.07
Communications, finance, insurance, and real estate	4,975	6,712	34.9	20.37
General services	17,112	30,278	76.9	16.34
Trade	20,193	25,675	27.1	11.33
Government	15,947	18,816	18.0	—
Total	89,823	110,525	23.0	16.70

Source: Author's calculations from data presented in Mishel, L. & Bernstein, J. (1994). *The State of Working America 1994–95*. Armonk, NY: M.E. Sharpe.

workers over this period could be attributed to changes in the sectoral composition of the economy. He argued that in essence capital was reallocated to sectors where it was relatively complementary to skilled workers.

9.5 INDUSTRY WAGE DIFFERENTIALS*

In the last section, we considered a number of structural models which looked at the effect of industry mix on income inequality. In most of these, it was implicitly assumed that the wage structure within an industry remained stable over time. With fixed industry wage structure, the change in industrial composition would be entirely responsible for changes in the overall distribution of earnings. Three questions immediately arise. First, how stable are relative wages between industries over time? Second, what factors account for differences in earnings among industries? Third, if industry wage differentials do change over time, what factors are responsible for these changes?

9.5.1 Explanations of inter-industry wage differentials

Interest in these issues dates back to 1950. According to neoclassical price theory, in equilibrium, industries in the same location should pay the same wage to each type of labor. Wage differences between locations for a given skill should reflect only interregional differences in the cost of living. There should also be no difference in average industry wage levels except insofar as these are correlated with the skill mix (see Reder, 1962).

However, the early studies showed that industries in the same locality paid different wages for essentially the same work. Slichter (1950) reported that the wages of common labor in Cleveland ranged from 50 cents to $1.09 per hour in February, 1947. Dunlop (1957) found that the union scale for truck drivers in Boston in July, 1953, ranged from $1.27 to $2.49 per hour, depending on what was being transported. As Slichter (1950) noted, there appeared to be "regularities" in the inter-industry wage structure that did not appear to conform to neoclassical wage theory.

Several papers investigated how stable industry wage differentials remained over time. In one study based on Census of Manufactures data, Cullen (1956) concluded that the industry wage structure had remained remarkably stable over the first half of the twentieth century. Several tests were made. The first was the change in industry rankings with respect to their average wage paid over the period 1899 to 1950. Industries were ranked from lowest to highest on the basis of average pay. The result was clear that the rank order of industries changed very slowly over time.[17]

In the second, industries were divided into a high-wage and low-wage group. The 14 industries that comprised the high-wage group in 1899 were still members of that group in 1950. Moreover, 10 of the 15 low-paying industries in 1899 were still in the low-paying group in 1950.

The third set of tests was based on two measures of the dispersion of the industry wage structure: (i) the interquartile range divided by the median; and (ii) the high–low percent differential, defined as the median of the 21 industries forming the top 25 percent of the earnings distribution divided by the median of the 21 industries forming the bottom 25 percent of the earnings structure. Both measures remained remarkably stable over time. The interquartile range fell by only 7.3 percent over the entire period from 1899 to 1950 while the high–low percent differential declined by only 3.3 percent.[18]

Several factors have been proposed to account for differences in industry wages. These include industry productivity levels and productivity growth rates, employment growth rates, the share of labor costs in total value added, the degree of monopolization of an industry, the concentration ratio, market power, unionization, and the average firm size in an industry.

One of the earliest articles in this line of research was published by John Dunlop in 1948. He investigated changes in mean manufacturing wages by industry and found them to be significantly correlated with changes in worker productivity. One reason, he argued, was the use of piece-rate incentive schemes in many industries, whereby the worker is paid according to his (or her) output. He also suggested that the skill mix of an industry would affect the average wage it paid.

Slichter (1950) analyzed 1937 hourly wage data for 10 manufacturing industries. He observed that the hourly earnings of male unskilled workers were high in industries where the wages of semiskilled and skilled workers were also high. This result indicated that high-wage industries tended to pay above-average wages to all grades of labor. He found that the wage levels of unskilled male workers were high where the value added per worker was high, confirming the Dunlop result that wages were higher in industries with higher productivity. He also found that the wages of male unskilled workers were generally lower in industries where the labor costs were a higher share of sales revenue. His explanation was that management had to be much more careful in giving wage increases in industries where labor costs were a high percentage of total costs.

Garbarino (1950) looked at the effect of industry concentration and the extent of unionization on industry wages. He viewed the former as a measure of market power in the product market and the latter an indicator of market power in the labor market. He argued that in concentrated industries, workers should be able to capture part of the increase in productivity growth in the form of wage gains, since the firms had considerable market power. Moreover, in heavily unionized industries, workers should likewise be able to capture a portion of productivity growth in the form of increased wages because of the union's market power. In contrast, in industries with little market power in both the product and labor markets, wages would not rise from productivity gains. Using industry wage data for the period 1923–1945, Garbarino found that, as predicted, concentration and unionization were both significant and positive explanatory factors of industry wage movements. He also found that industries that were growing faster in terms of employment had higher than average wages increases.

Perlman (1956) followed up the work of Garbarino in investigating the relation between productivity growth and wage movements. His method was to replace the separate measures of industrial concentration and "physical" productivity growth with a single measure of "value productivity," defined as total sales in dollars per person-hour of work. There were two advantages to this approach. First, a more general concept of market power than industry concentration was reflected in this measure, including the effects of advertising and barriers to entry. Second, increases in the value productivity measure reflected both increases in physical productivity and the ability of an industry to absorb some of the increased physical productivity in the form of profits and/or wages.

In a perfectly competitive industry, increases in physical productivity would result in a proportional decline in the product price and hence no increase in the industry's profits or wages. Insofar as an industry has market power, it can appropriate part of the physical productivity gain in the form of increased profits and/or wages levels. The value productivity measure could thus be interpreted to reflect an industry's "ability to pay" higher wages. Using a sample of manufacturing industries at the two-digit SIC level, he found that wage increases were highly correlated with changes in the value productivity measure in both the 1937–1947 and 1947–1952 periods. This result provided strong confirmation about the positive effects of productivity growth and market power on industry wage growth.

Fabricant (1959) also looked at the relation between physical productivity and industry wages. He computed a (rank) correlation of 0.26 between industry productivity level and average industry labor compensation for a sample of 80 industries over the period from 1899 to 1947. This result, like Perlman's, indicated a positive relation between physical productivity and wages across industry, although Fabricant's coefficient was not quite significant at the 5 percent level. Fabricant also found a positive rank correlation coefficient of 0.21 between industry wages and the amount of labor employed in the industry for 33 industries for the period 1899 to 1953, though the coefficient was not statistically significant. This result thus weakly suggested that industries that were expanding more rapidly tended to pay higher wages.

In a major study published in 1960, Bowen also looked at the relation between wages and employment growth. Using a sample of 20 two-digit manufacturing industries over six subperiods between 1947 and 1959, he computed correlation coefficients between the percentage change in earnings and the percentage growth in employment. The coefficients were generally positive when unemployment was low. However, in periods of high unemployment, the results were mixed. Bowen's results indicated that during periods of labor scarcity, wage increases were highest in the industries expanding most rapidly. This result is consistent with neoclassical wage theory, which would explain such a result by an upward-sloping short-run supply curve for labor. However, during recessions, there was no evidence that wages increased less rapidly in those industries with the greatest reductions in employment. This result is not consistent with the neoclassical model.[19]

9.5.1.1 The later literature

The later literature on inter-industry wages differs from the earlier material in two important ways. First, it reflected the influence of human capital theory. In addition to such factors as productivity growth, employment growth, market power, the concentration ratio, unionization, and firm size, the later studies included measures of schooling and other forms of human capital in the list of variables used to explain industry wages. Second, most of the modern literature used multiple regression analysis to separate out the influence of the various factors on industry wages.

In a 1966 study, Weiss investigated the relation between earnings and industrial concentration. He argued that industries with greater concentration (a higher degree of monopolization) would pay higher wages, because more concentrated industries tend to have higher profits than less concentrated ones. Industries with high profits, whether from monopolization or some other cause, tend to attract trade unions, since potential wage gains are high. High labor earnings would then result from unionization or from the attempt by companies to forestall the introduction of unions. Low-profit companies, in contrast, would pay lower wages, because the threat of labor unions would be smaller and because such companies have smaller profits out of which to offer increased wages (see Section 9.2 above). One implication of this line of reasoning was that more concentrated industries would pay higher wages for labor of the same occupation or skill level.

Using 1960 Census of Population data, Weiss regressed the mean wages in each industry on the industry's concentration ratio,[20] its degree of unionization, and a set of other variables that affected the wages paid in an industry.[21] The sample was then divided by occupation group. The results showed that a higher concentration ratio led to higher mean wages for almost every occupational grouping. This relation, moreover, was statistically significant in almost every case.[22]

Weiss carried the analysis one step further by raising the issue of whether concentrated industries paying high wages attract "superior" workers. To answer this question, he added variables to the regression model measuring the human capital of the workers in each industry. These human capital variables were generally significant. Moreover, when they were introduced into the regression model, the concentration variable became statistically insignificant. Weiss concluded that the higher labor earnings associated with concentration in an industry could be explained by the higher level of human capital of these workers.[23]

A related study was conducted by Pugel in 1980. He argued that more concentrated industries paid higher wages because of greater "ability to pay" to achieve the firm's objectives. These goals can include the achievement of low turnover rates of the labor force, increasing worker morale to promote higher work performance, and the creation of a pool of available labor for periods of intense demand. Since concentrated industries are generally more profitable than competitive industries, they have the ability to pay higher wages in order to achieve these aims.

Pugel argued that, in fact, this argument is based on the relative profitability of different industries. It is true that more concentrated industries tend to have higher profit rates than less concentrated ones but that there are other elements of market power, besides concentration, that affect profitability. As a result, Pugel argued, economic profitability may be a better summary measure for analyzing the effects of market power on labor compensation.

Using a variety of data sources for 1968–1970, Pugel estimated two regression equations. In the first, the logarithm of the industry's mean hourly wages was regressed on the concentration ratio of the industry, its degree of unionization, the percent of the industry's labor force employed in large establishments, and various measures of employee human capital. In the second equation, the same set of variables was used except that industry profitability was substituted for the industry concentration ratio. The major finding was that industry profitability was a more significant determinant of industry wages than the concentration ratio. Pugel estimated that about 14 percent of the excess profits industries earn due to market imperfections were "returned" to workers in the form of higher wages. Another result was that the concentration ratio variable became statistically insignificant as a determinant of industry wages once the median years of schooling in the industry's labor force was included in the regression equation. This was similar to Weiss' finding. However, the profitability variable remained statistically significant even after the schooling variable was included in the equation.

Allen (1995) provided an update on inter-industry wage differentials. His analysis covered the period from 1890 to 1990, though for manufacturing only. He found that the dispersion of wages across industries was higher in 1990 than in any previous time in the twentieth century (at least through 1990). Using regression analysis, he estimated that the variables most strongly correlated with wage growth on the industry level were productivity growth, rising union density, rising capital intensity, and profit growth.

9.5.1.2 The effects of plant and firm size

In both the Weiss and Pugel studies, a variable was included in the model to reflect the size of firms or plants in industries. A study that focused on the effect of plant size on industry wages was conducted by Masters (1969). He argued that firms normally set minimum standards when hiring employees. A worker must usually demonstrate that he or she can meet these standards in order to be retained by the firm. The higher these minimum standards, the higher the wages the firm must be willing to pay.

Masters then argued that large plants will have higher standards than small plants. One reason is that in a large plant, the production process is subdivided into more tasks than in a small plant. Therefore, coordination is more difficult in a large plant and, as a result, more formal work rules and greater regimentation of the workforce is required. Higher wages must be paid to obtain workers who are willing to tolerate this greater regimentation. Second, larger plants will generally have more expensive capital equipment. To avoid damage, large plants will hire more dependable workers and thus set higher standards than small plants. Third, unionization is more likely at a large plant than at a small one because the potential gains in membership are greater. Therefore, a large plant may be willing to pay higher wages in order to avoid unionization.[24]

Masters tested these hypotheses using 1963 Census of Manufactures data for 417 manufacturing industries. In his regression model, the dependent variable was average hourly earnings for production workers. The plant size variable was the percentage of the total labor force of the industry working in establishments of 1,000 or more employees. After controlling for the industry's concentration ratio, the degree of unionization in the industry, and other industry characteristics, he found a positive and highly significant relation between industry wages and the plant size variable.

In a later study, Mellow (1981) investigated the relation between wages and firm size. Firm size is different from plant size, since a firm may own more than one plant (or establishment). A large firm could conceivably operate many small plants or establishments, though in actuality large firms tend to own large plants and small firms tend to own small plants. The reasons why large firms pay high wages are similar to those for why large plants and concentrated industries pay high wages: large firms usually have high profitability, are desirable targets for unionization, and tend to have high standards for hiring.

Using 1979 CPS data, Mellow regressed individual wages on various human capital variables as well as on variables indicating union status and the size of the firm in terms of employment. The database covered all workers, not just those in manufacturing. His principal finding was that employer size had a significant and independent effect on wages. This was true even after controlling for the worker's human capital and other measures of labor quality, as well as for industry concentration, unionization, and occupation/industrial status. The wage premium to employer size was found to be quite substantial. After other factors were controlled for, wages were 16 percent higher when employer size exceeded 1,000 employees, and 8 percent higher when employer size was in the 500–999 range, compared to the smallest employer size of 25 employees or fewer. This wage premium of large firms characterized all sectors of the economy.[25]

Leslie (1985) followed up some of the earlier literature on the effects of productivity growth on inter-industry wage differentials. He examined the behavior of real wages in 20 (two-digit) U.S. manufacturing industries over the period from 1948 to 1976. Among these industries, he found no significant relationship between the growth of real wages and an industry's rate of productivity growth (as measured by total factor productivity). He concluded that gains from productivity growth are shared by all industries, a result that is consistent with the competitive neoclassical model.

Troske (1999), using the Worker-Establishment Characteristic Database, examined six competing hypotheses to explain the employer size–wage premium: (i) complementarity between worker skill and physical capital; (ii) larger firms being managed by more skilled managers who hire more skilled workers; (iii) more skilled workers being matched together in larger plants; (iv) the greater likelihood of larger firms and plants employing sophisticated capital such as computers and, in turn, employing more skilled workers; (v) trade-off of higher wages for less monitoring of workers; and (vi) rent sharing between larger employers and their workers. Troske found that none of these hypotheses can fully explain the employer size–wage premium, though the matching or more skilled workers together in large plants accounted for about 20 percent of the wage premium and the capital–skill complementarity hypothesis accounted for about 45 percent of the wage premium.

9.5.2   Recent trends and efficiency wage theory

One of the more notable developments of the 1980s has been an end to the stability of industry wage differentials that prevailed since World War II. According to estimates provided by Krueger and Summers (1988) on the basis of 42 (two-digit) industries, the standard deviation of industry wage differentials increased by 30 percent between 1979 and 1984. On the other hand, the ranking of industries according to the wage premium that they paid changed very little over this period. Thus, the increasing dispersion of industry wage differences was a result of a *widening* of pre-existing differentials, rather than a reordering of high- and low-wage industries.

The figures shown in Table 9.6 confirm the same pattern. In 1985, the industry wage differential, defined as the percentage difference between the industry's average wage and the average wage in the whole economy, ranged from a low of −71 percent in agriculture to a high of 55 percent in electricity, gas, and water. In 1970, the differentials ranged from −68 percent in agriculture to 39 percent in construction. The dispersion of industry wage differentials (measured by the log variance) increased from 0.092 in 1970 to 0.118 in 1985, or by 29 percent. However, the ranking of industries in terms of wages was very close in the two years. The correlation coefficient of the industry wage differentials in the two years was 0.97 and the rank correlation coefficient was also 0.97.

More recent figures on inter-industry wage differentials in 1998 provided by Osburn (2000) showed a similar pattern. The wage premium was 32 percent in motor vehicles and equipment manufacturing in 1998, 29 percent in petroleum refining, 23 percent in aircraft manufacturing, 21 percent in chemicals, and 15 percent in household appliances manufacturing. The wage differential was −3 percent in apparel, −15 percent in footwear, −20 percent in tobacco manufacturing, and about −70 percent in retailing.

Partly in order to explain this new phenomenon, a new model of wage determination, called *efficiency wage theory*, was developed by a number of economists. Though there are some differences among versions of the theory, the common feature of efficiency wage theory is that paying higher wages helps to increase a firm's profitability. There are four factors cited to explain the benefits received by a firm from paying higher wages: (i) *the shirking model*: eliciting increased effort (especially if the monitoring costs of workers is high); (ii) *the turnover model*: reducing turnover costs; (iii) *the selection model*: attracting a higher quality workforce; and (iv)

Table 9.6 Industry wage differentials for the United States, 1970 and 1985

Industry	1970	1985	Percent change
Electricity, gas, and water	0.374	0.553	47.7
Mining	0.287	0.525	82.7
Basic metal products	0.317	0.484	52.8
Chemicals	0.310	0.429	38.3
Machinery and equipment	0.282	0.385	36.4
Transport, storage, and communication	0.251	0.344	37.2
Nonmetallic mineral products	0.155	0.253	63.6
Finance and insurance	0.091	0.227	149.0
Paper, printing, and publishing	0.178	0.198	11.2
Food, beverages, and tobacco	0.063	0.153	143.8
Construction	0.385	0.149	−61.3
Producers of government services	0.014	0.034	150.4
Real estate	0.003	0.015	334.7
Other manufactured products	−0.035	−0.038	7.7
Wood and wood products	−0.066	−0.065	−1.0
Community, social, and personal services	−0.365	−0.293	−19.8
Textiles	−0.260	−0.310	19.3
Wholesale and retail trade	−0.166	−0.314	88.9
Restaurants and hotels	−0.489	−0.484	−1.0
Agriculture	−0.682	−0.707	3.7
Inequality of industry wages[a]	0.092	0.118	28.6
Correlation with 1970		0.97	
Rank correlation with 1970		0.97	

a Inequality is measured by the unweighted variance of the logarithm of industry wage differentials d_i. The industry wage differential for industry i, d_i, is defined as the percentage difference between the industry's average wage and the average wage for the whole economy. The industries are ranked by the industry wage differential in 1985.
Source: Gittleman, M. & Wolff, E.N. (1993). International comparisons of inter-industry wage differentials. *Review of Income and Wealth*, ser. 39, no. 3, 295–312, computed from the OECD International Sectoral Data Base.

the sociological model: improving worker morale. Since the benefits of each of these factors will differ across industries, the theory implies that different industries will, in general, pay different wages for the same work.

The factors that receive the most attention vary by model. According to the shirking model, high wages will be paid in industries where monitoring is difficult and where it is costly if workers do not perform up to standard. Oi (1983), like Masters (1969), suggests that this would be the case in large establishments, where monitoring may be difficult. In addition, the cost of mistakes is likely to be large in industries with expensive equipment (which, in turn, may be related to the capital intensity of production or to situations where shirking by one worker affects the performance of other workers).

According to the turnover model, wages will be high in industries where the costs of training and therefore turnover are high. The selection model predicts high pay in industries where it is difficult to directly evaluate labor quality. The sociological model implies that wages will be high in industries where worker morale is important and where a firm's evident ability to pay would lead workers to perceive that they were being treated unfairly (see Dickens & Katz, 1987b, for more discussion).

These models, with the exception of the sociological model, predict that wage premia would differ across jobs within an industry depending on, for example, the ease of monitoring, the amount of firm- or industry-specific human capital needed, or differences in recruiting costs. In contrast, studies of industry wages typically find that industry wage differentials are almost the same among jobs within an industry. To reconcile the two, the theory often includes the additional consideration that the amount of effort supplied by workers may also depend on how fairly they feel they are being treated, which, in turn, depends on how other workers in the firm or industry are compensated and how firms are doing in terms of profitability (see for example, Akerlof, 1984). This last consideration may explain the "rent sharing" discussed above (high profit industries pay high wages), since a firm may fear that if workers perceive that they are not being fairly compensated, they may withhold effort.

In an influential paper, Krueger and Summers (1988) provided strong econometric evidence that industry wage differentials were statistically significant and persistent over time, even after controlling for differences in worker characteristics among industries. On the basis of the 1974, 1979, and 1984 Current Population Surveys, cross-sectional wage equations were estimated with industry (dummy) variables, as well as schooling levels, experience levels, demographic characteristics, and working conditions among workers. The authors found that, after controlling for these latter effects, the industry variables remained statistically significant and explained a substantial amount of the variation of earnings among workers. They concluded that industry wage differences could not be explained away by differences in worker attributes but, instead, appeared to depend on specific industry characteristics.

Krueger and Summers (1987) also provided a comprehensive analysis of industry wage differences in the United States and concluded that the industry wage structure reflected the sharing of rents with workers. These rents may be the result of monopoly power, returns to intangible assets, or returns to capital already in place. Where rents per worker (that is, profitability) were greatest, wage rates tended to be highest.

In a historical study of the introduction of a $5 per day wage rate in the Ford Motor Company in 1914, Raff and Summers (1987) found supporting evidence for efficiency wage theory. The new rate doubled the pay for most of the workers in the factory. The authors found strong evidence that the new wages, by increasing morale, lowered worker turnover, increased worker productivity, and, as a result, increased the profitability of the firm. Krueger and Summers (1988) also found that high industry wages were correlated with low worker turnover.

Bell and Freeman (1991), using industry wage data for the United States, reported a sharp increase in the dispersion of industry wages not only for the economy as a whole but also within manufacturing and services over the period 1970–1987. Using regression analysis, they calculated that about 60 percent of the rise in inter-industry wage dispersion can be attributed to changes in human capital (education and age) and occupational mix within industry. However, even after controlling for these effects, they found a positive and significant relation between changes in industry wages and increases in industry productivity. They concluded that strong links between wages and productivity reflected rent-sharing behavior of the type predicted by efficiency wage theory.

Levine (1992) used company data provided by 250 large U.S. manufacturers (mostly Fortune 500 companies) to analyze the relation between assessments made by managers of the relative wages paid to their workers and changes in worker productivity. Controlling for worker quality, he found a positive relation between relative wages and productivity. As predicted by efficiency wage theory, the resultant increase in productivity was sufficient to pay for the higher wages of the workers.

Chen and Edin (2002) used data on male workers in Swedish metalworking industries in 1985. He argued that if industry wage differences reflect efficiency wage factors, then these pay differences should have less explanatory power for piecework than for normal hourly pay. Their results, unfortunately, were not consistent with efficiency wage theory. In particular, they found that industry wage differentials were of equal importance for workers paid by piece rate as for workers who received pay based on time work.

9.6   OCCUPATIONAL WAGE DIFFERENTIALS

In the last section, we focused on differences in earnings among industries in the United States. Throughout this literature, it was assumed, either explicitly or implicitly, that, *ceteris paribus*, average industry wages should vary directly with the skill level of the industry. Indeed, in long-run equilibrium in a perfectly competitive neoclassical world, mean wage difference should reflect *only* differences in average skill levels. Of course, in actuality, this is not the case and other factors are important in accounting for occupational wage differences.

In this section, we are interested in differences in earnings between skill levels or *occupations*, which are also referred to as *skill margins*. There are three questions of particular interest. First, what factors account for differences in earnings between skill levels? Second, have skill margins remained roughly stable over time? Third, if not, what factors account for changes in wage differentials between skill levels?

The skill margin is defined as the ratio of the mean (or median) wage of skilled workers to that of unskilled workers. The skill margin is also referred to as the "skill differential" or as the "wage differential according to skill." The consensus seems to be that skill margins in the United States have narrowed from the turn of the century until 1950 or so. However, the decline in the skill differential over this period was not continuous, and during some shorter periods the skill margin has risen. From 1950 until 1980 or so, skill differentials tended to remain constant. However, during the 1980s, there is strong evidence that skill margins have been increasing.

9.6.1   Historical studies

Before examining the U.S. experience, let us first consider long-term historical studies of skill margins in other countries. In a series of papers, Phelps Brown and Hopkins (1955, 1956, and 1959) investigated the skill differential in Southern England over the period from 1300 to 1914 (see Phelps Brown, 1977, for summary of these studies). They found that the skill differential remained roughly constant at 1.5 over this entire period. This ratio was affected by special historical circumstances, such as the Black Death, which caused a doubling of the skill margin during the latter half of the fourteenth century, but the ratio returned to 1.5 by 1412.[26]

Phelps Brown also computed skill differentials for Germany, France, and United States in the period 1860 to 1910. The differentials were computed between a skilled manual worker and his helper or a laborer. The results did not indicate a coherent trend in wage differentials over this period.

From about 1914 through the 1960s, the pattern of wage differentials did change. It appears that in some countries, the skill margin narrowed significantly if we compare the skill ratio at the beginning and the end of the period. This was true of the United States and the United Kingdom. However, Canada and France did not display such a trend in skill differentials. Moreover, Ozanne (1968) argued that even in the United States there had not been a continual decline in skill margins but rather a series of troughs and peaks that other researchers isolated as trends. Phelps Brown acknowledged the erratic behavior of skill margins noted by Ozanne but claimed that the skill margin still exhibited a secular downward trend.

9.6.2   Trends in the United States in the twentieth century

Ober (1948) was one of the first to look systematically at skill differentials in the United States. The study examined the period from 1907 to 1947. Three skills classes were considered: skilled; semiskilled; and unskilled jobs. Semiskilled workers were further subdivided into two groups, depending on their degree of responsibility in identifying problems in the normal work process and repairing malfunctions, as were unskilled workers, depending on the physical arduousness of the work.

In 1947, wage rates for skilled occupations were, on average, 55 percent greater than unskilled wages; wages of the first tier of semiskilled workers were 35 percent greater, those of the second tier were 15 percent higher, and wages of unskilled jobs requiring heavy labor were 15 percent greater. He also found a pronounced narrowing of the skill differentials over the period. In 1907, skilled workers were earning twice that of unskilled workers, but by 1947 the ratio had fallen to 1.55. However, the trend was not uniform over these years. The greatest portion of this decline took place between 1907 and 1917. During the depression of the early 1930s, the trend reversed and skilled differentials widened, but by 1940 the skill differentials began to narrow again.

Reder (1955) argued that the cyclical movements observed for skill margins could be explained by changes in the supply and the demand for labor. During periods of expansion, such as wartime, gross shortages of labor arise, which cause wage rates for the most skilled to rise. The increase in pay for the most skilled jobs attracts new applicants, who were previously unable to overcome the strict barriers to these positions. Because of labor shortages, the existing standards are relaxed and previously unqualified workers are accepted for these jobs.

This process of substituting less skilled for more skilled workers causes a shortage of supply at the next lower grade of labor. As this process continues down the occupational ladder, each occupation is filled by personnel of a lower skill level until the lowest occupation level is reached, where further substitution of less for more skilled workers can no longer take place. The lowest grade of labor, the unskilled, would then experience a proportionately greater increase in the demand for their services, bidding up their wages relative to the skilled and resulting in a narrowing of the skill differentials.[27]

When the expansion eases, a reverse process of "downward bumping" occurs, which results in a relative increase in the supply of labor available for the lowest grade of labor and leads to a widening of wage differentials. Ober's results confirm this argument. Both World War periods were characterized by a dramatic narrowing of the skill differential while the depression of the 1930s saw a significant increase in the wage differential.

Both Reder and Phelps Brown argued that the skill differential had narrowed over the long term. Reder's explanation is that the laboring class was becoming better educated over time because of the increasing availability of schooling. The rising educational level of the working class increased the ease of substituting less skilled labor for more skilled workers. The supply of completely unskilled labor falls, due to the increased substitutability, and hence the relative wage of the unskilled increases, narrowing the wage differential.

Another reason for the long-run decline in the skill margin is the mechanization and specialization of skills. These tend to reduce the demand for the broadly skilled laborer who requires long periods of training to achieve that skill capability. The rise of the specialized worker, requiring shorter training periods, further increases skill substitutability. These two developments – the improvement in educational standards and increased mechanization – exert downward pressure on the wage of skilled workers and upward pressure on those of the unskilled.

Perlman (1958) disputed this interpretation of the effects of technological change on skill margins. First, he argued, there is not as much substitution between skill groups as there is substitution within the highly skilled group. As a result, the decline in the demand for one highly skilled occupation is likely to be accompanied by an increase in demand for another highly skilled group. This will cause the former's wage to fall and the latter's to rise but, on net, not affect the average wage of skilled workers as a group. Second, the reason why the wage differentials between broad skill groups remained relatively constant is that technological change results in an increased demand for "new skills" and a decreased demand for "old skills." This shift in the demand occurs across the full spectrum of the occupational ladder – at the highly skilled, semiskilled, and unskilled levels. As a consequence, there is no relative shift in demand among the three broad skilled groups and no resulting change in relative wage levels among the three groups.

Like Reder, Phelps Brown considered education to be the primary reason for the decline in the skill margin but took issue with Reder on the effects of technological change. The effect of technological change and innovation, according to Phelps Brown, is not as unambiguous as Reder implied. On the other hand, many skilled occupations are becoming less skilled due to mechanization. For example, craft workers can be replaced by semiskilled operatives due to automation – a process that is referred to as "deskilling." On the other hand, there is a decreasing number of jobs that can use completely unskilled labor. These two effects, he argued, would lead to a decline in the skill differential.

Ober had a different argument. He believed that there had been more mechanization of unskilled tasks in industry than of skilled tasks. This mechanization was primarily aimed at relieving labor of arduous lifting and loading tasks. These innovations, consisting of such devices as forklifts, hoists, and steam shovels, as well as improvements in the organization of production processes, made it possible to better compensate the unskilled. But more importantly, according to Ober, mechanization and organizational improvements made it possible for many unskilled operators to become specialized and move up to the semiskilled category. These effects helped reduce the skill differential.

Keat (1960) looked at the period 1903 to 1956, both peak years in the business cycle. He computed the coefficient of variation (see Chapter 3) among wage rates by occupation in each year. It showed a 42 percent decline for the full economy. He also calculated the coefficient of variation in occupational wages within each industry in 1903 and 1956. The measure declined in all but two industries, and the declines ranged from 27 to 78 percent.[28]

Relatively little work on skill margins has been done since the early 1960s. The major reason for this is the shift in the focus of labor economics to the human capital model and the consequent attention to differentials in earnings between *schooling groups*, as opposed to skill or occupational groups. However, a few studies have appeared since 1960, which focus primarily on the postwar period. Blackmore (1968) compared the earnings of skilled and unskilled workers in manufacturing. He found that the ratio in wages between these two groups fell from 2.1 in 1907 to 1.4 in 1953 but between 1953 and 1967 the skill margin remained virtually unchanged. Ward (1980) compared the wage levels of janitors to more skilled occupations in manufacturing establishments. She found that the skill margin remained stable from 1962 to 1967 and then narrowed slightly from 1967 to 1976.

Gittleman (1991) found that skill margins increased rather substantially between 1979 and 1987. On the basis of the 1973, 1979, and 1987 Current Population Surveys, he computed the standard deviation of earnings among full-time, full-year employees in 49 occupations in each year. He found that dispersion in occupational earnings first declined by 15 percent between 1973 and 1979 and then increased by 26 percent between 1979 and 1987.[29] On net, the dispersion in occupational earnings was higher in 1987 than in 1973. As with industry wage differentials, a sharp increase in occupational wage differentials occurred in the 1980s, after almost three and a half decades of relative stability.

9.6.3   Rising skewness at the top

In Chapter 3 (Section 3.4), we documented a sharp rise of inequality in the United States since the early 1970s. In particular, we saw that the average incomes and the share of income at the very top of the income distribution (the top 1 percent and even the top 0.1 and 0.01 percent) showed a dramatic rise over this period (see, for example, Piketty and Saez, 2006). Several papers investigated this phenomenon, which is often called the "winner-take-all" effect.

Two papers by Rosen (1981 and 1986) provided the theoretical underpinnings for this line of research.[30] His objective was to explain a peculiar feature of certain labor markets, such as sports and entertainment, wherein a relatively small number of "superstars" earn enormous compensation and dominate the activities of their fields. This is true despite the fact that the superstars may be only slightly more talented than the next rung of workers in their field, so that differences in pay between the top performers and the rest could exist even though there are only relatively small differences in productivity. Rosen essentially argued that a small difference in talent could make a huge difference in outcomes. This would be the case in competitive sports, where the most talented team or player would win the championship and the others would lose. In law, also, the difference between winning and losing a case could mean millions of dollars to the client.

Rosen also argued that such a market might be efficient because it would provide very large incentives to excel. Having a tournament with a very lucrative first prize will give all the participants something to aim for and may, as a result, elicit exceptional effort from the players. In a large corporation, for example, providing huge compensation for the top executive spot (the chief executive officer or CEO) will give workers a tremendous incentive to perform. This will be the case even if the top position goes to someone who is only marginally more talented than the other employees in a company (see Adler, 1985, for a different justification).

Frank and Cook (1995) claimed that a key feature of this argument was that winner-take-all markets are becoming more pervasive in the U.S. economy. Though these markets were historically features of entertainment, sports, and the arts, they are now found in law, journalism, medicine, consulting, investment banking, corporate management, publishing, design, and fashion. One pertinent statistic is that in 1993, CEOs of top corporations earned *120 times as much as the average worker*,[31] compared to 35 times as much in the mid-1970s. Another is that the number of workers earning more than $120,000 in 1990 dollars doubled between 1980 and 1990 (from 0.5 million to 1 million). Indeed, 40 percent of the growth in earnings was captured by the top 1 percent of earners between 1973 and 1993, a period when the median wage fell by 15 percent in real terms. Frank and Cook argued that the increasing prevalence of winner-take-all markets primarily accounted for the increasing concentration of income at the very top of the income distribution.

Gordon and Dew-Becker (2008) also focused attention at the increased skewness at the very top of the earnings distribution. They divided the very top of the distribution into three groups. The first consisted of market-driven superstars where audience magnification (through television, the Internet, and the like) allowed a performance to reach 1 or 10 million people. This process enhanced the earnings of the superstars in entertainment and sports. The second was composed of a market-driven segment consisting of occupations like lawyers and investment bankers, where competition for scarce talent has driven up the compensation for those at the top of their respective professions. For example, even though the most talented lawyer may be only slightly better than the lawyer on the second rung, the fact that the most talented lawyer is more likely to win a court case than the one just below may mean the difference in millions (and even billions) of dollars to a firm in a civil court case. The third segment consisted of top corporate officers (CEOs).

Their review of the CEO debate placed equal emphasis on the market in showering capital gains through stock options and a management power hypothesis which was based on numerous nonmarket aspects of executive pay. They argued that compensation of CEOs has accelerated substantially in recent years because of their potential effect on the stock prices of the firm in which they work.

9.7 SUMMARY AND CONCLUDING REMARKS

Unions and labor market segmentation both play an important role in wage determination. With regard to unionization, four general conclusions can be drawn. First, although there is some disparity about the relative wage effects of particular unions in different industries and trades, union workers tend to earn to earn 15 to 25 percent more than non-union employees, after controlling for other worker characteristics. Second, the union wage advantage has changed over time. It was high during the 1950s and 1960s but low during the 1970s. Moreover, it showed a rather noticeable decline between the late 1970s and the early 2000s, from about 21 to 17 percent.

Third, the relative wage effects of unions do tend to vary among individual industries and crafts according to Marshall's rules. The largest effect occurs in the construction trades, of the order of 30 to 40 percent, where, because of the specialized skills involved, the demand curve for union labor is inelastic. Among operatives and laborers, the union effect is in the order of 15 to 20 percent. The union effect in heavy manufacturing is smaller than in construction. In competitive industries such as clothing, unions have very little effect on relative wages. Fourth, unionization tends to reduce overall earnings inequality, though the effect is relatively small.

Has the decline of unionism in the United States been one factor responsible for declining real wages and rising earnings inequality over the last two decades? Time-series evidence for the United States does not appear to support this argument. Real wages have been falling or stagnant since 1973, while union membership as a proportion of the labor force peaked in 1954 and has been going down ever since. Moreover, unionism's decline predated the rise in earnings inequality since the mid-1970s. Still, two studies, Freeman (1993) and Card (1996), using time-series data for the United States, surmised that about one-fifth of the increase in wage inequality among male workers in the 1980s was attributable to declines in unionism, particularly among lower wage workers (also, see Chapter 11 for more discussion of this issue).

Several studies which examined international differences in earnings inequality among industrialized countries concluded that the degree of unionization played a major role. Freeman (1993) found that industrial wages in the 1980s were more dispersed in countries that were less heavily unionized, and that between 1978 and 1987, the change in inequality was negatively correlated with the initial level of unionization. Gittleman and Wolff (1993) also reported that those countries with low levels of unionization were the ones that experienced the greatest increase in industry wage inequality. Blau and Kahn (1996) concluded that the lower level of overall wage inequality among male workers found in other OECD countries in comparison to the United States in the 1980s was due, in part, to their greater degree of unionization and to their use of centralized systems of collective bargaining which extended the terms of union contracts to non-union workers.

Another important source of earnings differences among workers is found to lie in the existence of relatively distinct labor market segments. Workers employed in the primary labor market enjoy high wages, good fringe benefits, stable employment and advancement possibilities, good working conditions, and due process in work rules. The secondary market is characterized by low wages and almost nonexistent fringe benefits, little job security and high turnover, limited advancement opportunities, poor working conditions, and arbitrary work rules. In the primary labor market, the wage profile is similar to that predicted by human capital theory, with earnings higher for more educated workers and increasing over time with experience. In the secondary market, wages show little gain from increased schooling or experience. There is also evidence that there exist both economic and noneconomic barriers that prevent secondary workers from entering the primary labor segment.

Many secondary workers often remain trapped in the secondary workforce throughout their work lives. Secondary jobs tend to be short-lived and therefore the secondary workforce experiences high turnover. Because the prospects for advancement are limited, these is little incentive or opportunity for upgrading skills. Because of an unstable employment pattern and the lack of skills, a secondary worker is unable to obtain employment in the primary labor market. This cycle becomes a vicious circle, where employers have little incentive to train secondary workers and these workers have little motivation for training. As a result, many of these workers are unable to escape the secondary labor market.

The breakdown of internal labor markets and the rise in secondary employment that seem to have occurred since the late 1970s may be other factors explaining rising earnings inequality over this period. Internal markets, by standardizing wage differentials among different classes of labor, help keep wage differences low. Wage inequality may be positively related to the proportion of secondary workers in total employment, since these are generally the lowest paid members in the labor force.

Though there is no hard statistical evidence on this issue, anecdotal evidence seems to suggest that the industrial restructuring of the 1980s – particularly, the "downsizing" of the core manufacturing industries – may have reduced the scope of internal labor markets. Moreover, the number of so-called contingent workers – those who work part time or part year – rose as a share of total employment, from 14 percent in 1979 to 18 percent in 1994.[32] Though contingent workers are not identical with secondary employees, there is likely to be considerable overlap between the two groups. Circumstantial evidence thus seems to suggest that the primary labor market is shrinking and the secondary labor market is correspondingly rising (also, see Chapter 11 for more discussion).

This chapter also covered a wide range of topics that can be loosely grouped under the rubric of structural theories of income distribution. The unifying thread that runs through these works is the importance of the demand side of the labor market. In particular, these works have emphasized aspects of the labor market which reflect technology, industrial composition, market structure, plant size, and regional characteristics. Structural change, such as industrial shifts, affects the demand for labor and the distribution of wages.

The studies surveyed in Section 9.4 lend strong support to the argument that the industrial or occupational distribution of employment is a significant determinant of regional differences in both income inequality and average earnings. In the early studies, particular attention was given to the proportion of the labor force employed in agriculture. In the later ones, measures of the entire mix of industries in a region were employed.

The evidence presented in Section 9.5 generally supports the view that industry wage differentials have remained fairly stable over long periods of time in the United States, except since about 1980 or so, when they have widened. The earlier studies emphasized the importance of structural and institutional characteristics as determinants of industry wage differences. These include industrial concentration, market power, firm size, and unionization. The earlier literature also investigated other economic factors such as profitability, employment growth, and productivity in accounting for wage differences between industries. These factors were all generally found to be positively and significantly related to the industry wage level (or rate of wage growth).

The later literature, while continuing to include these factors as determinants of industry wages, added human capital as another determinant of industry wage differences. It was almost universally found that industries with higher average levels of human capital (particularly as measured by the mean or median level of schooling of the workers in the industry) had higher than average wages. Moreover, in some studies, though not in all, it was found that the concentration ratio and other structural variables became statistically insignificant as determinants of industry wages once human capital was included as an explanatory variable. However, when a variable measuring ability to pay was used to measure industry market power, this variable remained significant even when schooling was added as an independent factor.

More recent work on this subject has generally emanated from efficiency wage theory. The common thread in these models is that paying higher wages helps to increase a firm's profitability. The reasons are that higher wages may elicit increased effort, reduce worker turnover, attract a better quality workforce, and improve worker morale. These arguments help to explain the "rent sharing" observed across industries – namely, that high-profit industries typically pay high wages.

In Section 9.6, strong evidence was found that wage differentials according to skill level declined from the turn of the century to the 1950s. Estimates of the decline in the skill margin ranged from 24 to 31 percent. The period from 1950 to 1980 was characterized by relatively stable skill margins. Since 1980, skill margins have been widening

Three explanations were advanced for the secular trend in the skill margin. One focused on the supply side and attributed changes to the increasing level of education of the lower skilled portion of the workforce. On the one hand, this increased the ease of substituting less skilled for more skilled workers, and, on the other hand, decreased the supply of totally unskilled labor. Both forces would tend to narrow the spread in wages among the various skill levels. A second explanation stressed the demand side, and, in particular, the effects of technological change. Here, too, there are two effects. First, automation tends to reduce the demand for highly skilled workers who require many years of training. Second, the introduction of new technology is also accompanied by some upgrading of previously unskilled jobs, since even the lowest jobs on the hierarchy entail some training with advanced technology. These two forces would also tend to narrow skill differentials. A third explanation was institutional in nature and emphasized the effects of the social minimum and the legislated minimum wage. A secular increase in wage floors would also serve to lower the skill margins.

How do the findings reported in this chapter with regard to industrial composition, industry wage differentials, and occupational wage margins relate to growing inequality in labor earnings since the mid-1970s? All three effects appeared to play a role in explaining rising income inequality over this period. Several studies concluded that the shift in industrial composition over these years favored highly skilled and college-educated workers relative to low and medium skilled and less educated ones. This would account both for rising inequality and the increasing returns to a college education.

The dispersion in industry wage differentials remained almost unchanged from 1940 through the mid-1970s and then increased sharply, particularly during the 1980s. Changes in industry wages appeared to be strongly linked to industry productivity and profitability movements and reflected rent-sharing behavior of the type predicted by efficiency wage theory. Skill margins also remained remarkably stable between 1950 and the 1970s, and then showed a pronounced widening starting in the late 1970s. This trend was probably attributable to recent changes in technology which favor more educated workers and was related to the rising premium to a college education. Related work also found evidence of the growing tendency of the labor market to pay exceptionally high wages to superstars, even though their productivity may be only marginally superior to the next rung of workers.

9.8   REFERENCES AND BIBLIOGRAPHY

Unionization

Belman, D. & Voos, P.B. (2006). Union wages and union decline: Evidence from the construction industry. *Industrial and Labor Relations Review*, **60**(1), 67–87.

Blanchflower, D.G. (2007). International patterns of union membership. *British Journal of Industrial Relations*, **45**(1), 1–28.

Blanchflower, D.G. & Bryson, A. (2004). The union wage premium in the US and the UK. Centre for Economic Performance, London, England, February.

Blanchflower, D.G. & Freeman, R. (1992). Unionism in the U.S. and other advanced O.E.C.D. countries. *Industrial Relations*, **31**, 56–79.

Blau, F.D. & Kahn, L.M. (1996). International differences in male wage inequality: Institutions versus market forces. *Journal of Political Economy*, **104**, 791–837.

Boskin, M.J. (1972). Unions and relative real wages. *American Economic Review*, **62**(3), 466–72.

Bratsberg, B. & Ragan, J.F. Jr. (2002). Changes in the union wage premium by industry. *Industrial and Labor Relations Review*, **56**(1), 65–83.

Budd, J.W. (1996). Union wage determination in Canadian and U.S. manufacturing, 1964–1990. *Industrial and Labor Relations Review*, **49**(4), 673–89.

Card, D. (1996). The effect of unions on the distribution of wages: Redistribution or relabeling? *Econometrica*, **64**(4), 957–80.

Card, D. (2001). The effect of unions on wage inequality in the U.S. labor market. *Industrial and Labor Relations Review*, **54**(2), 354–67.

Curme, M.A., Hirsch, B.T. & Macpherson, D.A. (1990). Union membership and contract coverage in the United States, 1983–88. *Industrial and Labor Relations Review*, **44**(1), 5–33.

Dickens, W.T. & Leonard, J.S. (1985). Accounting for the decline in union membership, 1950–1980. *Industrial and Labor Relations Review*, **38**(3), 323–34.

DiNardo, J. & Lee, D.S. (2004). Economic impacts of new unionization on private

sector employers: 1984–2001. *Quarterly Journal of Economics*, **119**, 1383–441

Farber, H.S. (1987). The analysis of union behavior. In O. Ashenfelter & R. Layard (eds.), *Handbook of Labor Economics* (pp. 1039–89). Amsterdam: North Holland Elsevier.

Farber, H.S. (1990). The decline of unionization in the United States: What can be learned from recent experience? *Journal of Labor Economics*, **8**(1), S75–S105.

Farber, H.S. (2005). Non-union wage rates and the threat of unionization. *Industrial and Labor Relations Review*, **58**(3), 335–52.

Farber, H.S. & Western, B. (2001). Accounting for the decline of unions in the private sector, 1973–1998. *Journal of Labor Research*, **22**(3), 459–85.

Flanagan, R.J. (1976). Wage interdependence in unionized labor markets. *Brookings Papers on Economic Activity*, 3, 1976, 635–73.

Freeman, R. (1980). Unionism and the dispersion of wages. *Industrial and Labor Relations Review*, **35**, 3–23.

Freeman, R. (1981). The effect of trade unionism on fringe benefits. *Industrial and Labor Relations Review*, **34**, 489–509.

Freeman, R. (1986). Unionism comes to the public sector. *Journal of Economic Literature*, **24**, 41–86.

Freeman, R. (1988). Contraction and expansion: The divergence of private sector and public sector unionism in the United States. *Journal of Economic Perspectives*, **2**(2), 63–88.

Freeman, R. (1990). On the divergence of unionism among developed countries. In R. Brunetta & C. Dell' Aringa (eds.), *Labour Relations and Economic Performance*, (pp. 304–22). London: Macmillan.

Freeman, R. (1993). How much has de-unionization contributed to the rise in male earnings inequality. In S. Danziger & P. Gottschalk (eds.), *Uneven Tides: Rising Inequality in America* (pp. 133–63). New York: Russell Sage.

Freeman, R. & Medoff, J.L. (1981). The impact of the percentage organized on union and non-union wages. *Review of Economics and Statistics*, **63**(4), 561–72.

Freeman, R. & Medoff, J.L. (1984). *What Do Unions Do?* New York: Basic Books.

Gittleman, M. & Pierce, B. (2007). New estimates of union wage effects in the U.S. *Economics Letters*, **95**, 198–202.

Hildebrand, G.H. (1979). *American Unionism: An Historical and Analytical Survey*. Reading, MA: Addison-Wesley.

Hirsch, B.T. (2004). Reconsidering union wage effects: Surveying new evidence on an old topic. *Journal of Labor Research*, **25**(2), 233–6.

Hirsch, B.T. & MacPherson, D.A. (2003). Union membership and coverage database from the current population survey: Note. *Industrial and Labor Relations Review*, **56**(2), 349–54.

Hirsch, B.T. & Neufeld, J.L. (1987). Nominal and real wage differentials and the effects of industry and SMSA density: 1973–83. *Journal of Human Resources*, **22**(1), 138–48.

Hirsch, B.T. & Schumacher, E.J. (1998). Unions, wages, and skills. *Journal of Human Resources*, **33**(1), 201–19.

Hirsch, B.T. & Schumacher, E.J. (2001). Private sector union density and the wage premium: Past, present, and future? *Journal of Labor Research*, **22**(3), 487–518.

Hyclak, T. (1979). The effect of unions on earnings inequality in local labor markets. *Industrial and Labor Relations Review*, **33**(1), 77–84.

Hyclak, T. (1980). Unions and income inequality: Some cross state evidence. *Industrial Relations*, **19**(2), 212–15.

Kahn, L.M. (1998). Collective bargaining and the interindustry wage structure: International evidence. *Economica*, **65**, 507–34.

Kahn, L.M. (2000). Wage inequality, collective bargaining, and relative employment from 1985 to 1994: Evidence from fifteen OECD countries. *Review of Economics and Statistics*, **82**(4), 564–79.

Kahn, L.M. & Curme, M. (1987). *Review of Economics and Statistics*, **69**(4), 600–7.

Kokkelenberg, E.C. & Sockell, D.R. (1985). Union membership in the United States, 1973–81. *Industrial and Labor Relations Review*, **38**(4), 497–543.

Lewis, H.G. (1963). *Unionism and Relative Wages in the United States*. Chicago: University of Chicago Press.

Lewis, H.G. (1986). *Union Relative Wage Effects: A Survey*. Chicago: University of Chicago Press.

Mellow, W. (1981). Unionism and wages: A longitudinal analysis. *Review of Economics and Statistics*, **63**(1), 43–52.

Mitchell, D.J.B. (1980). *Union Wages and Inflation*. Washington, DC: Brookings Institution.

Mitchell, D.J.B. (1985). Shifting norms in wage determination. *Brookings Papers on Economic Activity*, **2**, 575–608.

Neumann, G.R. & Rissman, E.R. (1984). Where have all the union members gone? *Journal of Labor Economics*, **2**(2), 175–92.

Neumark, D. & Wachter, M.L. (1995). Union threat effects and non-union industry wage differentials. *Industrial and Labor Relations Review*, **49**(1), 20–38.

Oaxaca, R. (1975). Estimation of union/non-union differentials within occupational/regional subgroups. *Journal of Human Resources*, **10**, 529–36.

Parsley, C.J. (1980). Labor union effects on wage gains: A survey of recent literature. *Journal of Economic Literature*, **18**, 1–31.

Pencavel, J. & Hartsog, C.E. (1984). A reconsideration of the effects of unionism on relative wages and employment in the United States, 1920–80. *Journal of Labor Economics*, **2**(2), 193–232.

Plotnick, R.D. (1982). Trends in male earnings inequality. *Southern Economic Journal*, **48**(3), 724–32.

Podursky, M. (1983). Unions and family income inequality. *Journal of Human Resources*, **18**(4), 574–91.

Reder, M.W. (1988). The rise and fall of unions: The public sector and the private. *Journal of Economic Perspectives*, **2**(2), 89–110.

Rees, A. (1977). *The Economics of Trade Unions*, 2nd edition. Chicago: University of Chicago Press.

Stafford, F. (1968). Concentration and labor earnings: Comment. *American Economic Review*, **58**, 174–81.

Throop, A. (1968). The union–non-union wage differential and cost-push inflation. *American Economic Review*, **58**(1), 79–99.

Troy, L. (1965). *Trade Union Membership, 1892–1962*. New York: National Bureau of Economic Research.

U.S. Bureau of Labor Statistics (1979). *Handbook of Labor Statistics, 1978*, Bulletin No. 2000. Washington, DC: Government Printing Office, June.

U.S. Bureau of Labor Statistics, *Employment and Earnings*. Washington, DC: U.S. Government Printing Office, various years.

U.S. Census Bureau (1950). *U.S. Census of the Population: 1950*, IV, Special Reports Part I, Chapter C, Occupation by Industry. Washington, DC: U.S. Government Printing Office.

U.S. Census Bureau. (1963). *U.S. Census of the Population: 1960*, Subject Reports, Occupation by Industry. Final Report PC(2)-72. Washington, DC: U.S. Government Printing Office.

U.S. Census Bureau. *Statistical Abstract of the United States*. Washington, DC: U.S. Government Printing Office, various years.

Visser, J. (2006). Union membership statistics in 24 countries. *Monthly Labor Review*, **129**(1), 38–49.

Weiss, L. (1966). Concentration and labor earnings. *American Economic Review*, **56**, 96–117.

Wessels, W. (1994). Do unionized firms hire better workers?" *Economic Inquiry*, **32**(4), 616–29.

Wolman, L. (1936). *Ebb and Flow in Trade Unionism*. New York: National Bureau of Economic Research.

Segmented and internal labor market theory

Alexander, A.J. (1974). Income, experience, and the structure of internal labor markets. *Quarterly Journal of Economics*, **88**(350), 63–85.

Baker, G., Gibbs, M. & Holmstrom, B. (1994a). The internal economics of the firm: evidence from personnel data. *Quarterly Journal of Economics*, **109**(4), 881–919.

Baker, G., Gibbs, M. & Holmstrom, B. (1994b). The wage policy of a firm. *Quarterly Journal of Economics*, **109**(4), 921–55.

Baker, G. & Holmstrom, B. (1995). Internal labor markets: Too many theories, too few facts. *American Economic Review*, **85**(2), 255–9.

Bluestone, B. (1970). The tripartite economy: Labor markets and the working poor. *Poverty and Human Resources*, July–August, 15–35.

Bulow, J.I. & Summers, L.H. (1986). A theory of dual labor markets with application to industrial policy, discrimination, and Keynesian unemployment. *Journal of Labor Economics*, **4**, 376–414.

Cain, G. (1975). The challenge of dual and radical theories of the labor market to orthodox theory. *American Economic Review*, **65**(2), 16–22.

Cain, G. (1976). The challenge of segmented labor market theories to orthodox theory. *Journal of Economic Literature*, **14**(4), 1215–57.

Dickens, W.T. & Lang, K. (1985). A test of dual labor market theory. *American Economic Review*, **75**(4), 792–805.

Dickens, W.T. & Lang, K. (1988). The reemergence of segmented labor market theory. *American Economic Review Papers and Proceedings*, **78**(2), 129–34.

Doeringer, P.B. & Piore, M.J. (1971). *Internal Labor Markets and Manpower Analysis*. Lexington, MA: D.C. Heath.

Dunlop, J.T. (1957). Wage contours. In G.W. Taylor & F.C. Pierson (ed.), *New Concepts of Wages Determination*. New York: McGraw-Hill.

Elbaum, B. (1983). The internalization of labor markets: causes and consequences. *American Economic Review*, **73**(2), 260–5.

Gordon, D. (1972). *Theories of Poverty and Underemployment*. Lexington, MA: D.C. Heath.

Kerr, C. (1954). The Balkinization of labor markets. In E.W. Bakke (ed.), *Labor Mobility and Economic Opportunity*. Cambridge, MA: MIT Press.

Lazear, E.P. (1992). The job as a concept. In W.J. Bruns (ed.), *Performance Measurement, Evaluation, and Incentives* (pp. 183–215). Boston, MA: Harvard Business School Press.

Manwaring, T. (1984). The extended internal labour market. *Cambridge Journal of Economics*, **8**(2), June 1984, 161–87.

Mill, J.S. (1900). *Principles of Political Economy*, I, Revised Edition. New York: The Colonial Press (originally published in 1848).

Osterman, P. (1975). An empirical study of labor market segmentation. *Industrial and Labor Relations Review*, **28**(4), 508–23.

Osterman, P. (ed.) (1984). *Internal Labor Markets*. Cambridge, MA: MIT Press.

Piore, M.J. (1983). Labor market segmentation: To what paradigm does it belong? *American Economic Review*, **73**(2), 249–53.

Reich, M., Gordon, D.M. & Edwards, R.C. (1973). A theory of labor market segmentation. *American Economic Review*, **63**(2), 359–65.

Reich, M., Gordon, D.M. & Edwards, R.C. (1984). Segmented labour: Time series hypothesis and evidence. *Cambridge Journal of Economics*, **8**(1), 63–81.

Reynolds, L. (1951). *The Structure of Labor Markets: Wages and Labor Mobility in Theory and Practice*. Westport, CN: Greenwood Press.

Rumberger, R.W. & Carnoy, M. (1980). Segmentation in the U.S. labour market: Its effects on the mobility and earnings of whites and blacks. *Cambridge Journal of Economics*, **4**, 117–32.

Schochet, P. & Rangarajan, A. (2004). Characteristics of low-wage workers and their labor market experiences: evidence from the mid- to late 1990s. Final Report. Office of the Assistant Secretary for Planning and Evaluation, Department of Health and Human Services, April 30, http://aspe.hhs.gov/hsp/low-wage-workers04/execsum.htm#toc.

Theodos, B. & Bednarzik, R. (2006). Earnings mobility and low-wage workers in the United States. *Monthly Labor Review*, **129**, 34–47.

Wachtel, H.M. & Betsey, C. (1972). Employment at low wages. *Review of Economics and Statistics*, **54**(2), 121–9.

Wachter, M.L. (1972). A labor supply model for secondary workers. *Review of Economics and Statistics*, **54**(2), 141–51.

Industry wage differentials, occupational wage differentials, and structural and related models

Adler, M. (1985). Stardom and talent. *American Economic Review*, **75**(1), 208–12.

Aigner, D.J. & A.J. Heins (1967). On the determinants of income inequality. *American Economic Review*, **57**(1), 175–81.

Al-Samarrie, A. & Herman P. Miller (1967). State differentials in income concentration. *American Economic Review*, **57**(1), 59–72.

Allen, S.G. (1987). Relative wage variability in the United States, 1860–1983. *Review of Economics and Statistics*, **69**(4), 617–26.

Allen, S.G. (1995). Updated notes on the interindustry wage structure. *Industrial and Labor Relations Review*, **48**(2), 305–21.

Ashenfelter, O. & George E. Johnson (1972). Unionism, relative wages, and labor quality in U.S. manufacturing industries. *International Economic Review*, **13**, 488–503.

Barsky, C. (1977). Occupational wage levels cluster in petroleum refineries. *Monthly Labor Review*, June, 54–6.

Bernard, A.B. & Jensen, J.B. (2000). Understanding increasing and decreasing wage inequality. In R.C. Feenstra (ed.), *The Impact of International Trade on Wages* (pp. 227–68). Chicago: University of Chicago Press.

Bell, P. (1951). Cyclical variations and trends in occupational wage differentials in American industry since 1914. *Review of Economics and Statistics*, **33**(4), 329–37.

Blackburn, M.L., Bloom, D.E. & Freeman, R.B. (1990). The declining economic position of less skilled American men. In G. Burtless (ed.), *A Future of Lousy Jobs?* Washington, DC: The Brookings Institution.

Blackmore, D. (1968). Occupational wage relationships in metropolitan areas. *Monthly Labor Review*, December, 29–36.

Blum, B.S. (2008). Trade, technology, and the rise of the service sector: The effects on US wage inequality. *Journal of International Economics*, **72**, 441–58.

Bowen, W.G. (1960). *The Wage–Price Issue: A Theoretical Analysis*. Princeton, NJ: Princeton University Press.

Bound, J. & Johnson, G. (1992). Changes in the structure of wages in the 1960s: An evaluation of alternative explanations. *American Economic Review*, **82**(3), 371–92.

Brown, C. & Medoff, J. (1989). The employer size–wage effect. *Journal of Political Economy*, **97**(5), 1027–59.

Conlisk, J. (1967). Some cross-state evidence on income inequality. *Review of Economics and Statistics*, **49**(1), 115–18.

Cullen, D. (1956). The interindustry wage structure, 1899–1950. *American Economic Review*, **46**, 353–69.

Dalton, J.A. & Ford Jr., E.J. (1977). Concentration and labor earnings in manufacturing and utilities. *Industrial and Labor Relations Review*, **31**, 45–60.

Dunlop, J. (1948). Productivity and the wage structure. In *Income, Employment, and Public Polic. Essays in Honour of Alvin H. Hansen* (pp. 341–62), New York: W.W. Norton.

Dunlop, J. (1957). Wage contours. In G.W. Taylor & F.C. Pierson (eds.), *New Concepts of Wage Determination*. New York: McGraw-Hill.

Dunne, T. & Roberts, M.J. (1990). Wages and the risk of plant closures. U.S. Census Bureau Discussion Paper No. 90-6, July.

Evans, D.S. & Leighton, L.S. (1989). Why do small firms pay less? *Journal of Human Resources*, **24**(2), 299–318.

Fabricant, S. (1959). Basic facts on productivity change. Occasional Paper 63. New York: NBER.

Farbman, M. (1973). Income concentration in the Southern United States. *Review of Economics and Statistics*, **55**(3), 333–40.

Farbman, M. (1975). The size and distribution of family income in U.S. SMSAs, 1959. *Review of Income and Wealth*, ser. 21, no. 2, 217–38.

Frank, R.H. & Cook, P.J. (1995). *The Winner-Take-All Society*. New York: The Free Press.

Freeman, R.B. (1976). *The Over-Educated American*. New York: Academic Press.

Freeman, R.B. (1980). An empirical analysis of the fixed coefficient "manpower requirements" model, 1960–1970. *Journal of Human Resources*, **15**(2), 176–99.

Garbarino, J.W. (1950). A theory of interindustry wage structure variation. *Quarterly Journal of Economics*, **64**, 282–305.

Gittleman, M. (1991). Changes in the rate of return to education in the U.S., 1973–87: The role of occupational factors. mimeo, New York University, November.

Gittleman, M. & Wolff, E.N. (1993). International comparisons of inter-industry wage differentials. *Review of Income and Wealth*, ser. 39, no. 3, 295–312.

Gordon, R.J. & Dew-Becker, I. (2008). Controversies about the rise of American inequality: A survey. NBER Working Paper No. 13982, May.

Green, A.G. (1969). Regional inequality, structural change, and economic growth in Canada – 1890–1956. *Economic Development and Cultural Change*, **89**(2), 136–55.

Groshen, E.L. (1991). Five reasons why wages vary among employers. *Industrial Relations*, **30**(3), 350–81.

Hanushek, E.A. (1973). Regional differences in the structure of earnings. *Review of Economics and Statistics*, **55**(2), 204–13.

Hanushek, E.A. (1981). Alternative models of earnings determination and labor market structures. *Journal of Human Resources*, **16**(2), 238–59.

Haworth, C.T. & Reuther, C.J. (1978). Industrial concentration and interindustry wage determination. *Review of Economics and Statistics*, February, 85–95.

Juhn, C. (1999). Wage inequality and demand for skill: evidence from five decades. *Industrial and Labor Relations Review*, **52**(3), 424–43.

Karoly, L.A. & Klerman, J.A. (1994). Using regional data to reexamine the contribution of demographic and sectoral changes to increasing U.S. wage inequality. In J.H. Bergstrand, T.F. Cosimano, J.W. Houck & R.G. Sheehan (eds.), *The Changing Distribution of Income in an Open U.S. Economy* (pp. 183–216). Amsterdam: North-Holland.

Katz, L.F. & Murphy, K.M. (1992). Changes in relative wages, 1963–1987: Supply and demand factors. *Quarterly Journal of Economics*, **107**(1), 35–78.

Keat, P. (1960). Long run changes in occupational wage structure, 1900–1956. *Journal of Political Economy*, **68**(6), 584–00.

Kuznets, S. (1955). Economic growth and income inequality. *American Economic Review*, **45**(1), 1–28.

Lawson, T. (1982). On the stability of the interindustry structure of earnings in the U.K: 1954–1978. *Cambridge Journal of Economics*, **6**(3), 249–66.

Leslie, D. (1985). Real wage growth, technical change and competition in the labor market. *Review of Economics and Statistics*, **67**(4), 640–7.

Lydall, H.B., *The Structure of Earnings*, (Oxford: Clarendon Press), 1968.

Masters, S.H. (1969). An interindustry analysis of wages and plant size. *Review of Economics and Statistics*, **51**(3), 341–5.

Mellow, W. (1981). Employer size and wages. Bureau of Labor Statistics Working Paper No. 116, April.

Mishel, L. & Bernstein, J. (1994). *The State of Working America 1994–95*. Armonk, NY: M.E. Sharpe.

Murphy, K.M. & Welch, F. (1993). Industrial change and the rising importance of skill. In S. Danziger & P. Gottschalk (eds.), *Uneven Tides: Rising Inequality in America* (pp. 101–32). New York: Russell Sage.

Newhouse, J.P. (1971). A simple hypothesis of income distribution. *Journal of Human Resources*, **6**(1), 52–74.

Ober, H. (1948). Occupational wage differentials, 1907–1947. *Monthly Labor Review*, August, 127–34.

Osburn, J. (2000). Interindustry wage differentials: patterns and possible sources. *Monthly Labor Review*, 34–46.

Ozanne, R. (1968). *Wages in Practice and Theory: McCormick and International Harvester, 1860–1960.* Madison, WI: Union of Wisconsin Press.

Perlman, R. (1958). Value productivity and interindustry wage structure. *Industrial and Labor Relations Review*, **40**(2), 107–15.

Phelps Brown, E.H. (1977). *The Inequality of Pay*. Oxford: Oxford University Press.

Phelps Brown, E.H. & Hopkins, S.V. (1955). Seven centuries of building wages. *Economica*, **22**(87), 195–206.

Phelps Brown, E.H. & Hopkins, S.V. (1956). Seven centuries of the prices of consumables, compared with builders' wage rates. *Economica*, **23**(92), 296–314.

Phelps Brown, E.H. & Hopkins, S.V. (1957). Builders' wage rates, prices, and population: Some further evidence. *Economica*, **26**(101), 18–38.

Piketty, T. & Saez, E. (2006). The evolution of top incomes: A historical and international perspective. *American Economic Review*, **96**(2), 200–5.

Pugel, T.A. (1980). Profitability, concentration, and the interindustry variation in wages. *Review of Economics and Statistics*, **62**(2), 248–53.

Reder, M.W. (1955). The theory of occupational wage differentials. *American Economic Review*, **45**(5), 833–52.

Reder, M.W. (1962). Wage differentials: Theory of measurement. In *Aspects of Labor Economics*. Princeton, NJ: Princeton University Press.

Reder, M.W. (1968). The size distribution of earnings. In J. Marchal & B. Ducros (eds.), *The Distribution of National Income*. New York: St. Martin's Press.

Reder, M.W. (1969). A partial survey of the theory of income size distribution. In L. Soltow (ed.), *Six Papers on the Size Distribution of Wealth and Income*. New York: National Bureau of Economic Research.

Reilly, K.T. (1995). Human capital and information. The employer size–wage effect. *Journal of Human Resources*, **30**(1), 1–17.

Rosen, S. (1981). The economics of superstars. *American Economic Review*, **71**(5), 845–58.

Rosen, S. (1986). Prizes and incentives in elimination tournaments. *American Economic Review*, **76**(4), 701–15.

Sahota, G.S. (1978). Theories of personal income distribution: A survey. *Journal of Economic Literature*, **16**, 1–55.

Scully, G.W. (1969). Interstate wage differentials: A cross-section analysis. *American Economic Review*, **59**(5), 757–73.

Slichter, S. (1950). Notes on the structure of wages. *Review of Economics and Statistics*, **22**, 80–9.

Smith, D.M. & Jennings, E.J. (1976). The distribution of state income: differential growth of sectoral employment. *American Economic Review*, **66**(4), 717–22.

Tarling, R. & Wilkinson, F. (1982). Changes in the inter-industry structure of earnings in the post-war period. *Cambridge Journal of Economics*, **6**(3), 231–48.

Troske, K.R. (1999). Evidence on the employer size–wage premium from Worker-Establishment Matched Data. *Review of Economics and Statistics*, **81**(1), 15–26.

Weiss, L.W. (1966). Concentration and labor earnings. *American Economic Review*, **56**(1), 96–117.

Ward, V.L. (1980). Measuring wage relationships among selected occupations. *Monthly Labor Review*, May, 21–5.

Williamson, J.G. (1965). Regional inequality and the process of national development. *Economic Development and Cultural Change*, **13**(4), 3–84.

Williamson, J.G. (1976). The sources of American inequality, 1896–1948. *Review of Economics and Statistics*, **58**(4), 387–97.

Efficiency wage theory

Akerlof, G.A. (1984). Gift exchange and efficiency wages: Four views. *American Economic Review*, **74**, 79–83.

Bell, L. & Freeman, R.B. (1991). The causes of increasing interindustry wage dispersion in the United States. *Industrial and Labor Relations Review*, **44**(2), 275–87.

Chen, P. & Edin, P.-A. (2002). Efficiency wages and industry wage differentials: A comparison across methods of pay. *Review of Economics and Statistics*, **84**(4), 617–31.

Dickens, W.T. & Katz, L.F. (1987a). Inter-industry wage differences and industry characteristics. In K. Lang & J. Leonard (eds.), *Unemployment and the Structure of Labor Markets*. Oxford: Basil Blackwell.

Dickens, W.T. & Katz, L.F. (1987b). Inter-industry wage differences and theories of wage determination. NBER Working Paper No. 2271, June.

Heywood, J.S. (19). Labor Quality and the Concentration-Earnings Hypothesis. *Review of Economics and Statistics*, **68**(2), May 1986, 342–346.

Hodson, R. & England, P. (1986). Industrial structure and sex differences in earnings. *Industrial Relations*, **25**, 16–32.

Holzer, H., Katz, L.F. & Krueger, A.B. (1991). Job queues and wages. *Quarterly Journal of Economics*, **106**(3), 739–68.

Katz, L.F. (1986). Efficiency wage theories: A partial evaluation. In S. Fischer (ed.), *NBER Macroeconomics Annual 1986*. Cambridge, MA: MIT Press.

Katz, L.F. & Summers, L.H. (1989). Can inter-industry wage differentials justify strategic trade policy? *Brookings Papers on Economic Activity*, Microeconomics Annual, 209–75.

Keane, M.P. (1993). Individual heterogeneity and interindustry wage differentials. *Journal of Human Resources*, **28**(1), 134–61.

Krueger, A.B. & Summers, L.H. (1987). Reflections on the inter-industry wage structure. In K. Lang & J. Leonard (eds.), *Unemployment and the Structure of Labor Markets*. Oxford: Basil Blackwell.

Krueger, A.B. & Summers, L.H. (1988). Efficiency wages and the inter-industry wage structure. *Econometrica*, **56**, 259–94.

Lawrence, C. & Lawrence, R. (1985). Relative wages in U.S. manufacturing: An endgame interpretation. *Brookings Papers on Economic Activity*, 47–106.

Lawson, T. (1982). On the stability of the inter-industry structure of earnings in the U.K: 1954–78. *Cambridge Journal of Economics*, **6**(3), 249–66.

Levine, D.I. (1992). Can wage increases pay for themselves? Tests with a production function. *Economic Journal*, **102**, 1102–15.

Oi, W. (1983). Heterogeneous firms and the organization of production. *Economic Inquiry*, **21**, 147–71.

Raff, D.M.G. & Summers, L.H. (1987). Did Henry Ford pay efficiency wages? *Journal of Labor Economics*, **5**(4), 57–86.

Tarling, R. & Wilkinson, F. (1982). Changes in the inter-industry structure of earnings in the post-war period. *Cambridge Journal of Economics*, **6**(3), 231–48.

9.9   DISCUSSION QUESTIONS

1   Explain how the elasticity of demand for labor in a particular industry affects the potential strength of a union in that industry.

2   Discuss how unions affect the union/non-union wage differential through their impact on the labor supply. How does the so-called "threat effect" affect the union/non-union wage differential?

3   Briefly discuss Marshall's "four rules" with regard to the factors that influence the strength of unions. How are these rules related to actual union/non-union wage differential observed in the U.S. economy by industry?

4   Discuss three reasons why the unionization rate has declined in the United States since the early 1950s.

5   Explain why internal labor markets might help to maintain a low level of wage inequality.

6   Explain the role of industry concentration and industry profitability in the determination of industry wage differentials.

7   Discuss two reasons why larger firms might pay higher wages than smaller ones.

8   Efficiency wage theory develops four models to explain why the benefits a firm gains from paying higher wages. Briefly describe each of the models and discuss how each relates to the empirical evidence on industry wage differentials.

9   Summarize the evidence on the relation between changes in the industrial composition of employment and the rise of earnings inequality in the 1980s in the United States.

10 Discuss three reasons why wage differentials between different skill levels of workers (or occupations) might change over time.

NOTES

1   Freeman (1980) found that the fixed coefficient model predicted employment by occupation relatively well, accounting for about 45 percent of the change in employment by occupation between 1960 and 1970 at a detailed three-digit occupational level (about 300 occupations).

2   This interpretation of the antitrust act was not reversed by the Supreme Court until 1940.

3   Union membership as a percent of the nonfarm workforce has always been higher, because the agricultural sector has had very low union representation.

4   It might also be noted that when unions successfully raise wages for their members, there can be long-run effects on the rate at which firms adopt capital that substitutes for labor. As an example, the telephone operators' strike at AT&T in the 1950s was often credited as the major impetus for the development of automatic switching systems (thereby eliminating a whole occupation from the U.S. workforce). Therefore the long-run effects of raising labor costs may be the elimination of jobs for workers.

5   Strictly speaking, the elasticity is a point measure and its value normally varies along the demand curve. It should also be noted that the elasticity measure is negative in the case of a demand curve, since an increase in the wage rate will cause a decrease in employment, but the negative sign is normally dropped when citing an elasticity.

6   The dividing line between an elastic and inelastic demand curve is one of "unitary elasticity," which means an x percent change in the wage will cause an exactly x percent change in employment in the opposite direction.

7   For other surveys of the literature, see Parsley (1980) and Lewis (1986).

8   Also, see Freeman and Medoff (1984) for comparative estimates. The Freeman–Medoff figures are similar to those of Pencavel and Hartsog, except for the 1970s. Freeman and Medoff found a union wage advantage of 19 percent for the early 1970s and 30 percent for the late 1970s.

9   Another issue is the effect of unionization on total labor compensation, including fringe benefits. The consensus seems to be that the union effect on fringe benefits is even greater than that on wages (see Freeman, 1981, or Freeman & Medoff, 1984, for example).

10 Reynolds (1951) and Dunlop (1957) also developed early models of internal labor markets.

11 Another view is provided by Bulow and Summers (1986), who viewed segmentation as deriving from the employer's need to motivate workers. They argued that firms are willing to pay primary workers a wage premium in order to elicit effort. See Section 9.5.2 for more discussion of "efficiency wage theory."

12 That is to say, as long as agriculture accounts for less than half of total employment. Technically speaking, the degree of income inequality is a quadratic function of the percent employed in agriculture, first rising and then falling.

13 The degree of importance was measured by the beta coefficient, defined as the product of the regression coefficient and the standard deviation of the independent variable divided by the standard deviation of the dependent variable.

14 It was also found that income concentration was higher in states with lower rates of labor force participation and with a higher proportion of property income in the state's income, though the latter variable was significant only in 1950.

15 In related work, Aigner and Heins (1967) and Conlisk (1967), both using 1960 Census of Population data, also found that income inequality was lower in states with higher mean income. This result is consistent with the Kuznets hypothesis, which maintains that in the course of normal economic development countries are likely to experience widening economic inequality in the early stages and declining inequality in the latter stages. See Section 3.5 and Kuznets (1955) for details.

16 He also found that differences in the local cost of living and the local unemployment rate were also significant.

17 Using rank order in 1899 as the base, Cullen found that the rank correlation coefficient declined from 0.94 in 1904 to 0.66 in 1950.

18 Another important result that emerged from this study is that there is no evidence that unionization made the wage structure more rigid. The rate of change in the relative positions of industries, as measured by the rank correlation, was no greater in 1930–1950, a period of expanding unionization, than in prior years, when unionization was not expanding.

19 Also see Reder (1962) for a good review of the pre-1960 literature on industry wage differentials.

20 The concentration ratio was measured by the ratio of the sales accounted for by the top four firms in an industry to the total sales of the industry.

21 Other variables included the growth rate of employment in the industry, the percentage of employees in establishments with 250 or more employees, and a dummy variable to indicate the variability of employment in an industry over the business cycle.

22 The effect of unionization on the mean wage was generally positive. Moreover, it was generally stronger in less concentrated industries. This result was consistent with the original argument, which was that concentrated industries may pay high wages either because of the presence of unions or the *threat* of unionization. Thus, non-unionized companies that fear unionization will also pay high wages. See Section 9.2 for a discussion of the threat effect.

23 As with many other hypotheses in economics, there are contradictory findings in the empirical literature. Like Weiss (1966), Ashenfelter and Johnson (1972) found that the concentration ratio variable became statistically insignificant once variables reflecting human capital were included in the regression equation. On the other hand, Dalton and Ford (1977) found that the concentration ratio remained significant, while Haworth and Reuther (1978) found that it remained significant for a 1958 (recession year) sample but not for 1967.

24 A related argument is that large plants tend to have more layers in their job hierarchy than small plants. If wages go up with each rung of the job ladder at the same rate in small as in large plants and the bottom wage is the same in large plants and small ones, then, *ceteris paribus*, average wages will be higher in larger plants.

25 Later studies have also confirmed the effects of both plant and employer size on industry wages. See, for example, Evans and Leighton (1989), Brown and Medoff (1989), and Dunne and Roberts (1990).

26 Moreover, this 50 percent differential seemed to prevail over most of Europe during much of the period. There were a couple of notable exceptions, where the skill margin narrowed. This occurred in Valencia, Spain, in the late 1500s and in Augsburg, Germany, in the early 1700s. The reason for this decline in the skill differential was a large population increase.

27 This assumes that the unemployment rate is sufficiently low so that all the reserves of labor have been fully absorbed in production.

28 For males alone, the coefficient showed a decline of 40 percent.

29 For male workers alone, the corresponding figures are 14 percent and 30 percent.

30 Earlier variants of this model were formulated by Reder (1968, 1969).

31 By the early 2000s, the ratio is estimated to have risen to 400 to 1.

32 The source for these figures is the *Monthly Labor Review*, statistical appendices.

Chapter 10

The Role of Savings and Intergenerational Transfers in Explaining Wealth Inequality

10.1 INTRODUCTION

Individuals can acquire wealth by gifts, by inheritances, or by saving out of their own income. What explains differences in wealth among individuals and families? These questions are of relevance because they bear directly on the determinants of the inequality of wealth and equity in the distribution of household resources. As Chapter 5 discussed at some length, wealth is an important component of family well-being.[1]

One issue of particular concern throughout this literature is the relative importance of life-cycle savings – the tendency of individuals to build up assets as they grow older – versus inheritance in the accumulation of household wealth. Insofar as the former is the major determinant, then differences in household wealth can be viewed as the result of the "natural" process of aging and therefore are not a major concern of public policy. However, if inheritances play the major role, then issues of fairness and equity come to the fore.

The accumulation of household wealth depends not only on income but also on savings behavior, capital appreciation, and gifts and inheritances. Moreover, wealth is the direct source of property income, which is an important factor in accounting for disparities in family income. This chapter considers some of the factors accounting for differences in wealth among families. The first of these is the role of age. Since individuals work only part of their life, they have a strong incentive to accumulate wealth for their retirement years. In this chapter, we explore the standard lifecycle model that economists have developed to describe this behavior. Other factors, such as gifts, inheritances, and capital appreciation, also play a role in wealth accumulation, and these too are treated here.

Section 10.2 begins with a presentation of the basic lifecycle model. We then examine some of the evidence on the validity of the model, including age–wealth profiles (average wealth by age group), longitudinal analyses, simulation studies, and regression studies. There have been various attempts to expand the lifecycle model. Section 10.3 discusses four extensions of the model: (i) introduction of uncertainty about length of life; (ii) the role of retirement wealth; (iii) the bequest motive; and (iv) precautionary savings and liquidity constraints. Pertinent empirical studies are also reviewed.

Three topics on intergenerational equity are treated in Section 10.4. The first is the role the government plays, particularly through the social security system, in the distribution of public benefits across generations. We will see that the current system essentially transfers considerable wealth from today's working population to today's retirees. The second is the role of private transfers – in particular, bequests and gifts. We will present evidence that in many ways, private transfers offset the public transfer system by redistributing wealth from the elderly to the working population. The third topic, generational accounting, is an overall accounting of the taxes paid by each generation less the amount that generation receives from the government in the form of transfers and benefits. Section 10.5 provides a summary, as well as an overall assessment.

10.2   THE BASIC LIFECYCLE MODEL

The basic lifecycle model (LCM), developed by Modigliani and Brumberg (1954), assumes that households save in order to spread out their consumption uniformly over their lifetime. Since individuals normally work until age 65 or so but live into their 70s, 80s, and even longer, they will save during their working years to provide for consumption during retirement. This, in turn, implies that household wealth, defined as accumulated savings, will rise with age until retirement and then decline.

In the simplest form of the model, it is assumed that families earn the same amount in each year until retirement, that lifetime earnings are fully consumed over the lifetime, that age of retirement and longevity are known with certainty at the beginning of work life, and that the interest rate is zero. Under a certain class of utility functions, maximization of lifetime utility leads to a constant annual consumption over the lifetime. The savings pattern that results is a constant savings rate per year until retirement and a constant dissavings rate thereafter. The resulting age–wealth profile is an inverted "V" (see Figure 10.1). Net worth rises linearly with age until retirement and then declines with age in linear fashion.

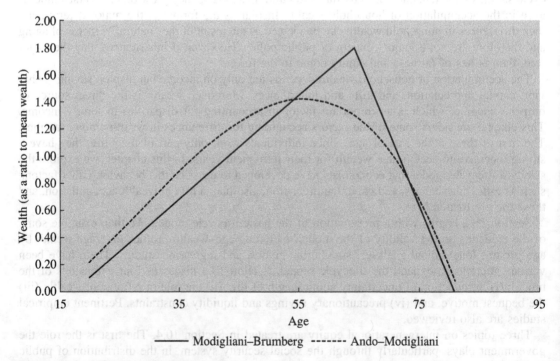

Figure 10.1 Lifecycle age–wealth profiles

Ando and Modigliani (1963) relaxed the assumption of a zero interest rate and assumed that it is positive and unchanging over time. The resulting profile is an inverted "U", with net worth rising with age until around retirement age and declining thereafter (again, see Figure 10.1). In both cases, the "hump-shaped" profile implies that wealth will decline after retirement, an issue which has received extensive empirical investigation.

10.2.1 Age–wealth profiles

We begin our survey of empirical work on the LCM with a consideration of age–wealth profiles, which show average wealth by age group. It should be noted at the outset that the LCM is a longitudinal model – that is, it describes the path of wealth accumulation for a given household as it ages over time. On the other hand, age–wealth profiles are "cross-sectional" – that is, they describe the wealth holdings of households of different ages at a *single* point in time. There are two biases that may arise from the use of cross-sectional profiles as a test of the LCM.

First, because real income typically increases over time, the cross-sectional age–wealth profile may be hump-shaped even though the longitudinal profile rises over time (see Shorrocks, 1975). This stems from the fact that if real incomes rise over time, lifetime income may be higher for younger age cohorts than older ones. As a result, in the cross-section (at a given point in time, say 2005), we may observe that 60 year olds have greater wealth than 70 year olds, even though the 70 year olds have greater wealth in 1995 than they had 10 years ago, when they were 60. As a result, accumulated wealth may peak among families in their 60s in the cross-section even if each age cohort has continued to save money over time.

Second, as Shorrocks (1987) notes, there exists a positive correlation between wealth and longevity, so that people who live longer will generally be wealthier than those who have become deceased. In this case, the cross-sectional profile may slope upward, particularly among the older age cohorts, even though the longitudinal profiles are hump-shaped. The two biases are offsetting, but the net effect of the two is not known (though see Bernheim, 1984 and 1987, for an analysis).

The early work on age–wealth profiles provided mixed results on the issue of whether families dissave after retirement. Lydall (1955), analyzing wealth data for the United Kingdom in 1953, found almost no difference in mean wealth between families in ages 55–64 and those 65 and over. Lansing and Sonquist (1969) reported that in 1953 average wealth was slightly greater for 63 year olds than 53 year olds in the United States, while in 1962 mean wealth among 62 year olds exceeded that among 52 year olds but was less than the average wealth of 72 year olds. Brittain (1978), using estate tax data for the United States, found wealth increasing with age among older Americans.

Table 10.1 shows age–wealth profiles based on more recent data for the United States. The wealth concept is marketable net worth. The first is computed from the 1962 Survey of Financial Characteristics of Consumers. It shows wealth rising steadily with age until age group 55–59, peaking at 1.7 times the overall mean for this age cohort, and then generally declining with age thereafter.

The second set of results is based on the 1983 Survey of Consumer Finances (also see Figure 10.2). The profile shows mean wealth rising steadily with age and peaking in the 65–69 age group at 2.3 times the overall mean and then falling sharply among older age groups. The third set is drawn from the 1989 Survey of Consumer Finances. The results are quite similar to the 1983 data. Wealth rises with age until the 65–69 age group, where the peak is 1.8 times the mean, followed by a steady decline thereafter. The final set is based on the 2004 Survey of Consumer finances. The same hump-shaped profile is in evidence but in this case peak wealth occurred for the 60–64 age group and the peak was 2.1 times the overall mean. It is also of note that the

Table 10.1   Age–wealth profiles for marketable net worth, 1962, 1983, 1989, and 2004 (mean wealth by age group as ratio to the overall mean)

Age group	1962 SFCC[a]	1983 SCF[b]	1989 SCF[c]	2004 SCF[d]
Under 25	0.13	0.14	0.11	0.05
25–34	0.44	0.35	0.32	0.18
35–44	0.79	0.78	0.71	0.65
45–54	1.05	1.70	1.47	1.21
55–59	1.74	1.78	1.46	1.73
60–64	1.25	1.83	1.71	2.13
65–69	1.65	2.29	1.75	1.47
70–74	1.44	1.52	1.47	1.69
75–79	1.34	1.25	1.37	1.26
80 and over	1.01	0.93	1.30	1.14
Mean	1.00	1.00	1.00	1.00

The statistics are for household wealth. Families are classified into age group according to the age of the head of household.
a   *Source*: 1962 Survey of Financial Characteristics of Consumers, adjusted to align with national balance sheet totals. See Wolff (1987b) for details.
b   *Source*: 1983 Survey of Consumer Finances, adjusted to align with national balance sheet totals. See Wolff (1987b) for details.
c   *Source*: 1989 Survey of Consumer Finances, adjusted to align with national balance sheet totals. See Wolff (1994) for details.
d   *Source*: 2004 Survey of Consumer Finances.

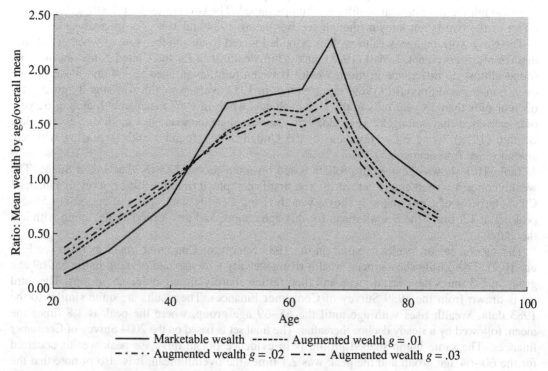

Figure 10.2   Age–wealth profiles, 1983

relative mean wealth of the younger age groups (under age 45) slipped rather sharply over time, from 1962 to 2004.

The age–wealth profiles do provide general support to the hump-shaped pattern predicted by the LCM. Wealth increases with age, peaks around age 65, and then declines with age. However, two anomalies appear. First, although wealth does decline among older age groups, it does not appear to approach zero, even for households aged 80 and over. This result is consistent with earlier tests of the LCM (see Friedman, 1982, and Hammermesh, 1984, for example).

Second, the data show that the cross-sectional age–wealth profiles became more hump-shaped over the 1962–1983 period and with higher mean wealth at the peak. However, the 1989 profile was flatter than the 1983 one and, indeed, was very close in shape to that of 1962. The age–wealth profile then became sharper in 2004, with peak wealth rising once again. These results suggest that age–wealth profiles are not static but can change quite substantially over time.

Table 10.2 shows the effect of adding pension wealth (PW) and social security wealth (SSW) to marketable net worth on the shape of the age–wealth profile (also see Figure 10.2). Pension wealth is defined as the present discounted value of future pension benefits. In similar fashion, social security wealth is defined as the present discounted value of the stream of future social security benefits (see Wolff, 1993 and 2007, for details on the estimation of PW and SSW).

Chapter 5 discussed at some length the concept of augmented household wealth. From the standpoint of an individual a future guaranteed flow of income is in many ways like owning a financial asset. Indeed, there are marketable assets called "annuities" which have precisely the characteristic of providing a steady stream of income after a certain time (or age) is reached. The anticipated social security (or pension) benefits that an individual will receive after retirement is comparable to such an annuity (we will have more to say about this below). In the context of the lifecycle model, the main motivation for saving is to guarantee a steady stream of income after retirement, so that social security (or pension) wealth may *substitute* for marketable wealth. One implication of this, as we will discuss below, is that there may be a *trade-off* between the accumulation of marketable wealth and that of retirement wealth.

When looking at the results, we should note that SSW (and PW) has been constructed to reflect conditional mortality rates, so that there is a built-in bias for its mean value to decline with age, particularly after age 70. In other words, since a person's remaining life expectancy declines as the person ages, the total value of his or her remaining social security wealth is also going to decline. Despite this, the net effect of including retirement wealth is a flattening of the age–wealth profile (compare the first two columns of Table 10.2, for example). The younger age cohorts gain relative to the older ones and peak wealth declines. Moreover, the greater the assumed rate of growth of future social security benefits (the parameter g), the more the younger groups gain and the more the peak flattens. However, all three measures of augmented wealth retain the basic hump shape of the LCM.

10.2.2   Longitudinal analyses*

Though cross-sectional age–wealth profiles generally follow the basic inverted U-shape predicted by the LCM, this cannot be taken as confirmation of the LCM. As noted above, Shorrocks (1975) demonstrated that if real income is growing over time, the cross-sectional age–wealth profile can be hump-shaped even though individuals continue to accumulate wealth over their lifetime (that is, the longitudinal age–wealth profile slopes upward). A hump-shaped cross-sectional wealth profile is a necessary but not sufficient condition to ensure a hump-shaped wealth profile over the lifetime.

Mirer (1979) used actual data on real earnings growth over time to adjust cross-sectional age–wealth profiles for differences in cohort earnings. Using a cross-sectional sample of individuals

Table 10.2   Age–wealth profiles for marketable and augmented household wealth, 1962 and 1983 (mean wealth by age group as ratio to the overall mean)

Age group	Marketable wealth	Augmented household wealth[a]		
		$g = .01$	$g = .02$	$g = .03$
A. 1962 SFCC[b]				
Under 25	0.13	0.23	0.28	0.37
25–34	0.44	0.50	0.54	0.61
35–44	0.79	0.81	0.83	0.86
45–54	1.05	1.09	1.09	1.09
55–59	1.74	1.63	1.59	1.54
60–64	1.25	1.31	1.28	1.23
65–69	1.65	1.61	1.56	1.49
70–74	1.44	1.35	1.29	1.22
75–79	1.34	1.13	1.07	1.01
80 and over	1.01	0.82	0.78	0.73
Mean	1.00	1.00	1.00	1.00
B. 1983 SCF[c]				
Under 25	0.14	0.27	0.32	0.38
25–34	0.35	0.56	0.60	0.67
35–44	0.78	0.92	0.96	1.00
45–54	1.70	1.44	1.42	1.38
55–59	1.78	1.65	1.61	1.54
60–64	1.83	1.63	1.57	1.49
65–69	2.29	1.82	1.73	1.62
70–74	1.52	1.30	1.23	1.15
75–79	1.25	0.96	0.91	0.84
80 and over	0.93	0.70	0.66	0.62
Mean	1.00	1.00	1.00	1.00

The statistics are for household wealth. Households are classified by age group by age of the head of household in 1962 and age of respondent in 1983.

a g is the assumed rate of growth of social security benefits over time.

b   *Source*: 1962 Survey of Financial Characteristics of Consumers, adjusted to align with national balance sheet totals. See Wolff (1987b) for details.

c   *Source*: 1983 Survey of Consumer Finances, adjusted to align with national balance sheet totals. See Wolff (1987b) for details.

over 65 in the United States and adjusting for actual differences in cohort earnings, he found no significant reduction in wealth with advancing age. In other words, even though age–wealth profiles were hump-shaped, the evidence indicated that elderly families did not dissave as they aged. In a follow-up piece, Mirer (1980) used a one-year panel from the 1963 and 1964 Federal Reserve Board Survey of Financial Characteristics of Consumers (the same families observed in the two years) and calculated a very small dissavings rate for the elderly – a median of 1.2 percent over the year – though it was not statistically significant.

Later work on the LCM used longitudinal (panel) data, which followed the same individuals over time. Diamond and Hausman (1984), using the National Longitudinal Sample of older men, found that individuals accumulated wealth up to retirement and then depleted it, though very few individuals in their sample had actually retired. Friedman (1982), using the Retirement History

Survey (RHS), which covered individuals from age 58 to 73 over a 10-year period, reported that individuals continued to save in the first four to six years after retirement and then dissaving began.

Hammermesh (1984) found from the RHS that spending on consumption items covered in this survey (food, housing, transportation, and health) declined in the first few years after retirement, a finding consistent with Friedman. This finding also confirmed earlier work of Danziger *et al.* (1982), based on the cross-sectional 1972–1973 Consumer Expenditure Survey, that the average ratio of consumption expenditures to after-tax income, declined with age after age 71. Blinder, Gordon, and Weiss (1983), also using the RHS and introducing a variable for lifetime earnings, found that conventionally measured wealth showed no tendency to decline with age among older people.

However, Hurd (1987, 1990), using evidence from the same source of data (the RHS), reached the opposite conclusion. In these papers, Hurd reported that the wealth of the elderly did decline over time, by 22 percent for singles and 2 percent for couples over the period 1969 to 1979. Later, Hurd (1992) concluded from the RHS that though family consumption declined after retirement as the family aged, so did its wealth.

Borsch-Supan (1992) reached a striking conclusion regarding the savings patterns of elderly German families. He found that although wealth holdings declined between families aged 60 and 70, they increased after age 70, and that very old (over age 80) had the highest savings rate among all age groups. He attributed this finding to two factors. First, the German social security system provided very generous annuities to aged pensioners as well as complete health coverage. Second, consumption expenditures actually declined after age 70, presumably reflecting the lessening needs for items such as clothing, transportation and travel, and food. This is similar to the results reported for U.S. households by Hammermesh (1984).

Banks, Blundell, and Tanner (1998) and Bernheim, Skinner, and Weinberg (2001) also found that consumption appeared to fall after retirement. Bernheim, Skinner, and Weinberg (2001) also argued that the standard lifecycle model failed to explain the heterogeneity (inequality) of retirement wealth found among households after the age of 65. On the other hand, Engen, Gale, and Uccello (1999) argued that the standard lifecycle model coupled with stochastic income shocks over the lifetime is not inconsistent with a large level of wealth inequality among retirees.

All in all, econometric studies have generally confirmed the age–wealth profile predicted by the lifecycle model, with only one or two exceptions. These findings provide further reinforcement to the cross-sectional studies which have also largely found the inverted U-shape profile of the LCM.

10.2.3 Simulation and regression analysis*

Simulation and regression techniques have also been used to assess the explanatory power of the lifecycle model. In simulation analysis, the researcher attempts to reproduce the actual characteristics of the wealth distribution on the basis of the LCM and assumed or estimated parameters of the model.

Atkinson (1971) used a simulation experiment to account for the concentration of household wealth. He started with the actual distribution of labor earnings in the United Kingdom and assumed that all wealth accumulation was due to lifecycle savings. He simulated that the basic LCM would predict that the top 10 percent of the population would hold only about 20 percent of total wealth, well below the actual concentration ratio of 60 to 70 percent. He then added the assumption that the top 10 percent of the distribution received equal inheritance shares. Even with this added assumption, he calculated that the top 10 percent would hold at most 30 percent of total wealth, still well below the actual share held by the top decile. He concluded that the simple LCM, even with the introduction of some inheritance effects, could not account for the actual concentration of household wealth.

Oulton (1976) generalized Atkinson's model to allow the age distribution, individual earnings functions, and the rate of return on assets to vary. Substituting the distribution of earnings estimated from the actual U.K. data into his model and assuming no inheritance, Oulton computed a maximum coefficient of variation of wealth of 0.75, which was substantially less than the actual value of 3.98. He also concluded that the LCM could not by itself adequately explain inequality in individual wealth holdings.

Two U.S. studies, White (1978) and Kotlikoff and Summers (1981), used simulation to determine whether the LCM could account for the aggregate accumulation of wealth observed in the U.S. economy. Both found that the LCM could explain only a very small proportion of observed household wealth in the United States. Kotlikoff and Summers, for example, used actual age–earnings profiles (showing average earnings by age group) and consumption rates by age group in the United States and calculated that lifecycle savings accounted for only about 20 percent of observed U.S. household wealth in 1974. The remainder, by implication, was due to inheritance and intergenerational transfers.

Wolff (1981 and 1988) used regression analysis to explore the explanatory power of the lifecycle model in accounting for differences in wealth holdings among households in the United States. The regressions were cross-sectional in nature, with observations on households of different ages at a given point in time. However, cohort effects were controlled for by the addition of a lifetime earnings variable. Results of the second paper are summarized in Table 10.3.

Table 10.3 Lifecycle regressions on marketable and augmented wealth, based on the 1983 Survey of Consumer Finances

Independent variable	Dependent variable					
	HW	AHW	HW	AHW	HW	AHW
Constant	−49.3	−19.0	−37.8	−4.9	−20.7	−66.0*
(1,000s)	(1.91)	(0.69)	(1.43)	(0.18)	(1.81)	(2.03)
$AGE^2/100$	1.91**	2.15**	1.58**	1.76**	0.55**	1.44*
	(6.20)	(6.58)	(5.03)	(5.48)	(9.72)	(11.00)
AGE^3	−2.05**	−2.26**	−1.64**	−1.68**	−0.58**	−1.78**
	(5.57)	(5.83)	(4.40)	(4.73)	(7.82)	(10.45)
LE			0.20**	0.21**	0.25**	0.33**
			(13.20)	(15.90)	(18.40)	(27.00)
R^2	0.012	0.015	0.037	0.051	0.122	0.198
Adj. R^2	0.012	0.015	0.036	0.050	0.120	0.192
F-test	25.9**	32.7**	54.6**	76.1**	235.8**	324.3**
Sample	All HH	All HH	All HH	All HH	Bot 95%	Bot 95%
Sample size	4,262	4,262	4,262	4,262	4,049	4,049

t-ratios are shown in parentheses.

* Significant at 5 percent level (2-tail test for coefficients; 1-tail test for F value).

** Significant at 1 percent level (2-tail test for coefficients; 1-tail test for F value).

HW – marketable household wealth; AHW – augmented household wealth, the sum of HW, pension wealth, and social security wealth (it is assumed that the annual rate of growth of future social security benefits is 2 percent); AGE – age of respondent; LE – lifetime earnings (it is assumed that the future the annual rate of growth of labor earnings is 1 percent).

Source: Wolff, E.N. (1988). Social security, pensions, and the lifecycle accumulation of wealth: Some empirical tests. *Annales d'Economie et de Statistique*, **9**, 199–216.

Various specifications were tried, including quadratic, cubic, and fourth power functions of age, as well as piece-wise linear functions. The best fit in terms of the adjusted R^2 was the cubic form, shown in Table 10.3.[2] In the first regression, with marketable wealth (HW) as the dependent variable, the coefficients of the two age variables had the predicted signs (the coefficient of AGE^2 was positive and that of AGE^3 was negative) and both were significant at the 1 percent level. However, the R^2 (the measure of the goodness of fit or the explanatory power of the equation) was very low, with a value of 0.012 (only about 1 percent of the variation of household wealth was explained by age). Regression results are also shown for augmented household wealth, AHW (second column). The R^2 for this regression form was 0.015.

As noted above, the use of cross-sectional data tends to produce a biased test of the (longitudinal) LCM if real earnings have been rising over time. The introduction of measures of lifetime earnings should control for this effect. Moreover, differences in lifetime earnings should also explain a substantial portion of the intra-cohort variation (differences among households of the same age) in household wealth.[3]

Results on the LCM with the inclusion of lifetime earnings (LE) are shown in the third and fourth columns of Table 10.3. The LE variable was highly significant, with t-statistics of 13.2 and 15.9. The inclusion of LE tripled the goodness of fit of the model. Even so, the extended model explained only 4 to 5 percent of the variation of wealth holdings among households.

The same equations were then estimated on a subset of the original sample, in which the upper 1 percent of the wealth distribution is excluded (columns 6 and 7 of Table 10.3).[4] The significance level of all the independent variables – the age terms and lifetime earnings – increased markedly. Moreover, the explanatory power of the model rose substantially. The R^2 increased from 0.037 to 0.122 for marketable wealth (HW) and from 0.051 to 0.198 for augmented wealth (AHW).

These results suggest that the explanatory power of the LCM in accounting for the variation of marketable wealth among all households was quite weak. This remained true even when differences in lifetime earnings among households were controlled for. When the concept of household wealth was expanded to include both social security and pension wealth (or, together, retirement wealth), the goodness of fit of the regression improved. As noted above, the inclusion of retirement wealth in household wealth was more consistent with the LCM than the use of marketable household wealth alone. However, as before, the explanatory power of the model was still very low (at most 5 percent of the variation of wealth explained), even when lifetime earnings were introduced into the model.

Perhaps, the most telling result is that the explanatory power of the LCM (particularly with lifetime earnings) was substantially greater (by a factor of three or four) when the sample was restricted to the bottom 95 percent of the wealth distribution. This held for all measures of household wealth. This result suggested that, although the LCM predicted household savings behavior well for the vast majority of households, it was not successful in explaining the wealth accumulation motives of the top wealth classes, who also happened to hold the majority of household wealth. It appears that the difference was due to dissimilarities in the strength of the bequest motive. One inference from these results that the top wealth classes likely form a distinct social class in the sense that their motivation for wealth accumulation is for political and economic power and social status. It also appears that this class is interested in the expansion of family wealth over the generations.

10.3   EXTENSIONS OF THE LIFECYCLE MODEL

The general findings that individuals did not totally exhaust their wealth at time of death and that many older individuals did not dissave (reduce their wealth) as they aged raise some questions about the validity of the LCM. The response was to modify the basic model, by relaxing one or more of its assumptions. There are four directions, in particular, that we shall review here: (i) uncertainty, particularly about length of life; (ii) the role of social security and pension wealth; (iii) introduction of a bequest motive; and (iv) precautionary savings and liquidity constraints. The first two topics are directly related, as we shall see. A related topic, intergenerational equity, will be treated in Section 10.4.

10.3.1   The role of uncertainty about death and lifetime annuities

In the basic LCM and the Ando–Modigliani version, it is assumed that length of life is known with certainty. However, individuals do not know when they will die. The introduction of uncertainty about length of life can affect the shape of the age–wealth profile, particularly the pattern of dissavings after retirement. Yaari (1965) was the first to analyze the effects of uncertainty on lifecycle behavior. He demonstrated that uncertainty by itself could lead to increased savings and a (non-altruistic) individual will always leave unintended bequests, because the individual will always have savings available for the possibility of living longer than expected.

Yaari then introduced annuities into his model. An annuity is a savings instrument that guarantees an individual a fixed annual income until death. At time of death, the value of this asset becomes zero. An example of this is a pension. Most pensions guarantee a retiree a fixed annual income until time of death (some will also continue the benefit for a surviving spouse). Such an asset removes most of the problems associated with uncertainty about death, since the pension provider assumes the risk about length of life. It thus has considerable advantages over a fixed-value asset such as a bond. Yaari demonstrated that if an annuity were available that was indexed for inflation, then the availability of such an indexed annuity would lead to reduced savings in other forms by older individuals and might lead to an exhaustion of wealth at death.

Following Yaari's line of reasoning, Kotlikoff and Spivak (1981) estimated on the basis of certain parameter values that individuals could leave up to a quarter of their wealth at age 55 unintentionally – that is, without directly planning that it should be left as a bequest to their spouse or children. Davies (1981) applied the same argument to explain the slow dissaving by individuals after retirement. In a lifecycle model with uncertain longevity, he demonstrated that consumption during retirement would be smaller than in a regime of complete certainty. Using Canadian data, he simulated the post-retirement consumption and savings pattern of Canadian families and found that savings would still be higher with uncertainty than with certainty about longevity, even with the availability of pensions (a form of annuity). He concluded that uncertainty about length of life could explain the slow dissaving of households after retirement. Using the same data, King and Dick-Mireaux (1982) did find that household wealth decreased after retirement but at a rate much slower than that predicted by the basic LCM. They attributed this discrepancy to uncertainty over lifetime and the bequest motive (see below).

10.3.2   The role of pension and social security wealth

The empirical work on household savings and social security dates from Feldstein's 1974 article, which used aggregate time-series data for the United States. He argued that social security should reduce household savings, since the need to put away money for retirement would be lessened if the government was guaranteeing future retirement benefits. He also argued that the payment of social security benefits would reduce household disposable income and therefore decrease savings.[5] He estimated that social security may have reduced personal savings by as much as 50 percent.

This provocative paper generated considerable work on the effects of social security on household savings. Cross-sectional evidence was generally mixed. Feldstein and Pellechio (1979), using the 1963 Survey of Financial Characteristics of Consumers, found a very strong offset of social security wealth for private wealth. Blinder, Gordon, and Weiss (1983), using the RHS, estimated that each dollar of social security wealth substituted for 39 cents of private wealth, though the estimated coefficient had a very large standard error and was quite unstable over alternative specifications. Diamond and Hausman (1984), using the National Longitudinal Survey of older men, estimated effects on private wealth from 30 to 50 cents per dollar of social security wealth. Kotlikoff (1979) found a significant negative tax effect of social security contributions on individual savings.

Leimer and Lesnoy (1982), using the same aggregate time-series data as Feldstein, found no negative effect of social security on private savings. However, Feldstein's (1982) reply reconfirmed his earlier results as did his 1983 study. Aaron (1982), in a review of the literature, surmised that the wide variation in results on this subject made it difficult to reach any definitive conclusion on the impact of social security on savings.

David and Menchik (1985) employed a special sample of probate records (estate tax records with information on the individual's wealth) matched to income tax records for Wisconsin males born between 1890 and 1899. They investigated the effect of social security benefits on household wealth by comparing the actual age–wealth profile of males in the sample with what would have been predicted from the LCM augmented with social security wealth. They found no evidence that the availability of social security benefits affected the accumulation of marketable wealth over time. They concluded on the basis of this sample that social security did not depress or displace saving in traditional assets and that individuals did not deplete their marketable wealth in old age.

Hubbard (1983), using 1979 and 1980 survey data collected by the U.S. President's Commission on Pension Policy (1980) and controlling for permanent income, found that both social security wealth and pension wealth had statistically significant negative effects on private wealth. Social security wealth was estimated to have a 33 cents per dollar offset on private wealth, while private pensions had a 16 cents per dollar offset. However, as he noted, the substitution effects were considerably less than the dollar-for-dollar reduction predicted in a standard lifecycle model.

Avery, Elliehausen, and Gustafson (1985) provided similar estimates based on the 1983 Survey of Consumer Finances (SCF). Their analysis was confined to households headed by persons 50 years of age or older who were in the labor force. Their computation of net social security and pension wealth is based on the difference between the present value of expected benefits less that of anticipated contributions into the respective systems. Standard mortality rates were used to calculate present values. For pensions, expected benefits were based on respondent information, while for social security, expected benefits were calculated on the basis of current and future social security rates. Current family income was included as an independent variable, though a measure of lifetime earnings or permanent income was not. They reported a substantial substitution between pension and non-pension wealth. A dollar increase in pension wealth offset non-pension wealth by 66 cents. However, coefficients for social security wealth were small in size and statistically insignificant, indicating little substitution between social security wealth and marketable wealth.

Wolff (1988), relying on the same 1983 Survey of Consumer Finance data, reached different conclusions. This study included estimates of gross pension and social security wealth, along with a measure of lifetime earnings, in a standard lifecycle regression, with marketable wealth as the dependent variable. No statistically significant substitution effect was found between marketable wealth and pension wealth. The substitution effect between social security wealth and marketable wealth was marginally significant for both the full sample and the bottom 95 percentiles, and the coefficient was less than half in both cases.

Another study of direct interest is that of Bernheim (1986). Using the RHS, he first divided his sample into retirees and non-retirees. He computed longitudinal age–wealth profiles for retirees, and found significant dissaving in traditional wealth after retirement. He then argued that, with annuities such as social security available, the proper concept of wealth is the sum of traditional wealth and the simple discounted value of private pension and social security benefits.[6] He found that augmented wealth showed little tendency to decline with age after retirement.

Several more recent studies have investigated whether social security and pension wealth displaced traditional wealth in the lifecycle pattern of accumulation.

A number of papers used the Health and Retirement Survey (HRS) to examine what proportion of total (augmented) household wealth is composed of pension and social security wealth. Gustman *et al.* (1997) found that in 1992, pensions, social security, and health insurance accounted for half of the wealth held by all households aged 51 to 61 in the HRS; for 60 percent of total wealth of HRS households who are in wealth percentiles 45 to 55; and for 48% of health for those in the 90th to 95th wealth percentiles. In a follow-up study, Gustman and Steinmeier (1998) used data from the HRS to examine the composition and distribution of total wealth for a group of 51–61 year olds. They focused on the role of pensions in forming retirement wealth. They found that pension coverage was widespread, covering two-thirds of households and accounting for one-quarter of accumulated wealth on average. Social security benefits accounted for another quarter of total wealth. They also reported that the ratio of wealth (excluding pensions) to lifetime earnings was the same for those individuals with pensions and for those without pensions. They concluded that pensions caused very limited displacement of other forms of wealth.

Several papers looked at the issue of whether Defined Contribution (DC) plans substituted for other forms of wealth and whether there was any net savings derived from DC plans.[7] Poterba, Venti, and Wise (1992, 1993, 1995), using SIPP data for 1984 and 1991, Poterba, Venti, and Wise (1998), using HRS data for 1993, and Poterba, Venti, and Wise (2001), using both macro national accounting data and micro HRS data, concluded that the growth of IRAs and 401(k) plans did not substitute for other forms of household wealth and, in fact, raised household net worth relative to what it would have been without these plans. They found no substitution of DC wealth for either Defined Benefit (DB) wealth or other components of household wealth.

In contrast, Gale in a series of papers, both by himself and with colleagues, found very little net savings emanating from DC plans. Gale (1998) concluded that when biases in estimation procedures in the previous literature on the subject are corrected, the offset of pension wealth on other forms of wealth can be very high. Using data from the 1984, 1987, and 1991 SIPP, Engen and Gale (1997) estimated that "at best" only a small proportion of 401(k) contributions represent net increments to household savings. In later work, Engen and Gale (2000) refined their analysis to look at the substitution effect by earnings groups. Using data from the 1987 and 1991 SIPP, they found that 401(k)s held by low earners more likely represented additions to net worth than 401(k)s held by high earners, who hold the bulk of this asset. Overall, only between 0 and 30 percent of the value of 401(k)s represent net additions to private savings. Kennickell and Sunden (1999) found a significant negative effect of both defined benefit plan coverage and social security wealth on non-pension net worth but concluded that the effects of defined contribution plans, such as 401(k) plans, on other forms of wealth were statistically insignificant.

10.3.3   The bequest motive

The LCM has also been generalized by introducing a bequest motive for households. If an individual wants to leave a bequest for children (or other heirs), the person will make sure that some wealth will be left at time of death. The bequest motive, like uncertain longevity, will therefore result in a nonzero net worth at time of death.

Modigliani and Brumberg recognized this possibility in their original paper. Later, Modigliani (1975) estimated that only somewhere between one-tenth and one-fifth of all (private) wealth could be traced to inheritances. This estimate was subsequently challenged – for example by White (1978) and Kotlikoff and Summers (1981), who put the estimated share much higher (see above). There have also been theoretical attempts to incorporate the bequest motive into a life-cycle model. For example, Menchik and David (1983) introduced the notion of intergenerational "altruism" to account for the willingness of parents to leave part of their wealth to their children.

Survey evidence on the importance of bequests is fairly consistent. Projector and Weiss (1966), on the basis of the 1963 Survey of Financial Characteristics of Consumers, reported that only 17 percent of families had received any inheritance. This compares with a figure of 18 percent, reported by Morgan *et al.* (1962). The Projector and Weiss study also found that only 5 percent of households had received a "substantial" proportion of their wealth from inheritance. However, this latter proportion did rise with household wealth, with 34 percent of families with net worth exceeding half a million dollars indicating a substantial bequest. Barlow, Brazer, and Morgan (1966) found from a 1964 Brookings study on the affluent, covering families with income of $10,000 or more, that only 7 percent of the sample mentioned gifts and inheritance alone as the source of most of their present assets. They estimated that about one-seventh of the total wealth of this group came from inheritance.

Menchik and David (1983) used probate records of men who died in Wisconsin between 1947 and 1978 to obtain an estimate of $20,000 (in 1967 dollars) for the mean bequest of all decedents in their sample. This figure includes not only intergenerational transfers but interspousal and other transfers as well. They also found no evidence that older individuals de-accumulated wealth. They attributed this to the presence of a bequest motive.

David and Menchik (1982) estimated that of this the average interspousal transfer was $15,800, with about one-half of all individuals dying while still married. Moreover, they computed that about 60 percent of all non-interspousal bequests went to children. Putting these figures together, a rough estimate can be obtained, that the average intergenerational bequest among decedents was $7,500 in 1967 dollars, which amounted to less than one-fifth of average household wealth in 1967 and about 10 percent of the average household wealth of families aged 65 or over.

Hurd and Mundaca (1989) analyzed data from both the 1964 Survey on the Economic Behavior of the Affluent and the 1983 Survey of Consumer Finances on the importance of gifts and inheritances in individual wealth holdings. Both surveys asked questions of the respondents about whether they had received gifts and inheritances and how much these transfers were worth. They found from the 1964 data that only 12 percent of households in the top 10 percent of the income distribution reported that more than half their wealth came from gifts or inheritances. The corresponding figure from the 1983 data was only 9 percent. They concluded that intergenerational transfers were not an important source of wealth, even for rich families.

A similar type of analysis was conducted on French data by Kessler and Masson (1979) (also, see Kessler & Masson, 1989). In a 1975 survey of 2,000 French families, the respondent was asked whether the family had received any significant inheritance (above $4,000) or gifts (above $2,000). Of all the households in the sample, 36 percent reported that they had already received some inheritance. Of the total wealth of the population, Kessler and Masson estimated that 35 percent originated from inheritances or gifts. Among those who had reported receiving an intergenerational transfer (who were about two and a half times richer than the average household), the corresponding proportion was 40 percent.

Table 10.4   Time trends in wealth transfers, 1989–1998 (1998 U.S. dollars)

	1989	1992	1995	1998
1. Percent of households receiving wealth transfers[a]	23.5	20.7	22.2	20.4
2. Present value of wealth transfers				
For recipients only[b]				
a. Mean	312.2	313.3	345.8	256.9
b. Median	51.8	50.0	51.9	54.5
3. Present value of wealth transfers as a percent of net worth	29.7	25.8	35.5	19.4

a   The figures record the proportion of households who indicate receiving a wealth transfer at any time before the
time of the survey.
b   The figures show the present value of all transfers as of the survey year which were received up to the time of
the survey and accumulated at a real interest rate of 3.0 percent.
Source: Author's computations from the 1989, 1992, 1995, and 1998 Survey of Consumer Finances.

Wolff (2002, 2003) used data from the 1989, 1992, 1995, and 1998 Survey of Consumer Finances which provided questionnaire information on inheritances and other wealth transfers received and the date of the transfer. On the basis of both the reported value of wealth transfers and the date of the transfer, Wolff computed the present value of all inheritances as of the survey year which were received up to the time of the survey by accumulating them at a real interest rate of 3.0 percent. The value of inheritances was then converted to 1998 dollars.

Results for the 1989 to 1998 period are shown in Table 10.4. In 1998, 20.4 percent of all households reported receiving a wealth transfer. This figure is comparable to those from previous U.S. surveys. The fraction receiving a wealth transfer declined from 23.1 percent in 1989 to 20.7 percent in 1992, rose to 22.2 percent in 1995, and then fell once again to 20.4 percent in 1998. In 1998, the mean present value of wealth transfers (in 1989 dollars) among recipients was $260,000 and the median was $54,500. The results of Table 10.4 also indicate a sharp decline in the mean present value of wealth transfers between 1989 and 1998 – almost 18 percentage points. The median value showed a moderate increase – by 5 percentage points.

The present value of wealth transfers received as a percent of the current net worth of households was 19.4 percent in 1998. This figure is comparable to previous estimates for U.S households. However, since net worth has risen during the 1990s and the wealth transfers have declined, this ratio has also fallen rather sharply, from 29.7 percent in 1989 to 25.8 percent in 1992 and 35.5 percent in 1995.

Blinder, Gordon, and Weiss (1983) also attempted a test of the importance of bequests, using the RHS. Their hypothesis was that if there is a strong bequest motive in accumulating wealth, it should imply that families with more children should have greater assets later in life than families with fewer children. Their results did not support this hypothesis, though it should be noted that *inter vivos* intergenerational transfers were not included. Hurd (1987), testing a similar hypothesis found that, in fact, families with more children have less wealth than smaller families and dissave the same fraction of wealth after retirement.

Hurd (1992) made an interesting test of the bequest motive. He argued that if families were motivated to accumulate in order to bequeath wealth, elderly couples who had children should show greater wealth and lower consumption (after controlling for income) than childless couples. On the basis of the RHS, he reported no significant difference in the consumption and wealth profiles between these two groups of elderly couples.

Though direct survey evidence and econometric tests on household survey data (or probate records) failed to show a significant effect of bequests on household wealth accumulation (except, perhaps, for the French studies), indirect test have. One model developed by Davies (1982) augmented the standard lifecycle model with a bequest motive. He began with the actual distribution of wealth in Canada in 1970. He then used actual data on the distribution of inheritances, mortality rates, and other factors to simulate the effects of inheritance on the distribution of wealth in Canada. He concluded that inheritances were a major source of wealth inequality in Canada.

In a follow-up paper, Davies and St-Hilaire (1987) used the same model to estimate the proportion of total wealth accumulation in Canada that could be traced to inheritances. Without cumulating interest on inheritances, they estimated that 35 percent of total household wealth was traceable to inheritances. With the interest on the inheritances added in, the proportion rose to 53 percent. Laitner (1992) calibrated a model incorporating both lifecycle saving and inheritance with U.S. data and estimated the share of inherited wealth in the range of 58 to 67 percent.

In another simulation analysis, Greenwood and Wolff (1992) investigated the importance of four sources of household wealth accumulation: (i) savings; (ii) capital appreciation on existing wealth holdings; (iii) inheritances; and (iv) *inter-vivos* transfers (gifts from living parents to their children). In the simulation, initial wealth holdings by age group, as reported in the 1962 SFCC, were updated annually until 1983 on the basis of savings rates computed from Consumer Expenditure Survey data and capital gains by individual asset type. On the basis of mortality rates by age cohort and age differences between generations, the study was able to simulate the transfer of inheritances between parents and children.

As shown in Table 10.5, it was estimated that 75 percent of the growth of overall household wealth between 1962 and 1983 arose from capital gains (appreciation) of existing wealth and

Table 10.5 Sources of wealth accumulation by birth cohort, 1962–1983

1983 Age class	Net worth[a]		Sources of wealth change, 1962–1983 (percent)			
	1962	1983	Savings[b]	Appreciation of wealth[c]	Inheritance[d]	Remaining gap
40–44	4.8	110.6	13	6	27	54
45–49	18.7	251.7	9	13	23	55
50–54	44.1	180.7	34	34	49	−16
55–59	60.8	230.0	34	41	38	−13
60–64	80.4	246.3	40	48	37	−25
65–69	93.6	339.0	32	39	21	8
70–74	101.6	203.5	44	76	22	−42
75–79	173.8	166.4	47	151	14	−112
80 and over	131.3	133.2	38	160	6	−105
All	95.6	142.5	25	75	—	—

a   Net worth in 1,000s, 1985 dollars, by birth cohort.
b   Includes appreciation of assets accumulated in savings.
c   Includes appreciation of assets received in inheritance.
d   Appreciation of initial wealth only.
Source: Greenwood, D.T. & Wolff, E.N. (1992). Changes in Wealth in the United States, 1962–1983: Savings, capital gains, inheritance, and lifetime transfers. *Journal of Population Economics*, **5**(4), 261–88. Calculations from simulations based on the 1962 SFCC and the 1983 SCF.

the remaining 25 percent from savings (income less consumption expenditures). However, there were striking differences by age cohort. First, as to be expected, savings were relatively more important than capital appreciation for younger age groups than older ones. Second, inheritances (including the capital appreciation on the assets in the bequest) accounted for a substantial portion of the wealth accumulation for households under the age of 65 in 1983. The proportion ranged between 23 percent for age class 45–49 in 1983 to 49 percent for age class 50–54. For ages 40–64 as a whole, 34 percent of the wealth accumulated over this 21-year period (1962–1983) could be traced to inheritances.[8]

Third, even with inheritances included in the model, the simulations systematically fell short of explaining the wealth of younger age groups but overstated that of older ones. For example, for age groups 40–44 and 45–49 (in 1983), we were able to account for only 45 percent of their total wealth accumulation, with 55 percent unaccounted for. On the other hand, for age groups over 69 years, their simulated wealth was much larger than their actual wealth holdings in 1983. What is the likely explanation? It appeared that *inter-vivos* transfers (gifts) were the missing factor. The wealth holdings of younger households in 1983 were much larger than that which could be explained by their savings, capital gains, and inheritances, while the wealth holdings of older households were much smaller than would have been the case if they kept all their wealth accumulation. The most reasonable explanation is that older parents have been transferring significant amounts of wealth to their (adult) children in the form of gifts. All told, it was estimated that inheritances and *inter-vivos* transfers together accounted for 40 percent of the wealth accumulation of age cohorts under the age of 65 between 1962 and 1983. Wolff (1999) in a follow-up study extended the period of analysis from 1962 through 1992. He estimated that over the lifetime, inheritances and *inter-vivos* gifts *each* contributed about one-third to the lifetime accumulation of wealth.

What accounts for this sizable discrepancy in results between the direct survey evidence (and regression analysis) and the simulation results in regard to the importance of intergenerational transfers in household wealth accumulation? The direct survey evidence suggests that no more than about 20 percent of household wealth is due to intergenerational transfers (though the figure is closer to one-third for French households). In contrast, the simulation models suggest that lifecycle savings explain only a small portion of total wealth accumulation. Kotlikoff and Summers' (1982) results suggest that only 20 percent of wealth accumulation was due to lifecycle savings, with the remainder presumably the result of intergenerational transfers.

This subject was the source of a lively debate between Modigliani (1988a, 1988b) and Kotlikoff (1988) and Kotlikoff and Summers (1988), with commentary by Blinder (1988) and Kessler and Masson (1989). There are three major differences between the two approaches. First, direct survey evidence is hampered by recall bias and underreporting. It is hard for people to remember the amount of inheritances received 5, 10, or, certainly, 20 years ago. As a result, many respondents may understate the value of inheritances received, and this may bias downward the direct survey evidence on the importance of inheritances.

Second, the treatment of the appreciation of inheritances is a crucial factor. Suppose a house was inherited 10 years ago and its value doubles over the decade. Should its contribution to current wealth be valued at its original value or at its now appreciated value? Modigliani appeared to favor the former method, in which the appreciation of inherited assets is counted as savings, while Kotlikoff and Wolff included the appreciation on the inheritance as part of the contribution of inheritances to current wealth. This issue is definitional – it depends on the accounting framework used – but the difference in the assessment can be quite substantial.

Third, the role of *inter-vivos* transfers is often overlooked in direct tests of the bequest motive. When asked about in direct surveys, gifts are particularly subject to recall error because, typically, there are no formal records made of these transfers. Moreover, as the Greenwood and Wolff simulations suggest, they may be a particularly important source of wealth for young households. In a survey of the literature on the subject, Davies and Shorrocks (1999) surmise that between 35 and 45 percent of household net worth may be traceable to inheritances and gifts.

10.3.4   Precautionary savings and liquidity constraints

Another way to modify the LCM is to introduce capital market imperfections into the model. These usually take one of two forms. The first is that the interest rate at which a consumer can borrow may differ from that at which he or she can lend (the borrowing rate is usually higher than the lending rate). A second is that due to credit market restrictions, a consumer cannot borrow all that he or she may desire. These two cases are usually referred to as a "liquidity constraint." In both cases, the implication is that the consumer cannot carry out his or her optimal lifetime consumption plan, and at some stage desired consumption will be constrained by current resources (in particular, by disposable income and the amount of financial assets). Moreover, since borrowing is constrained, the family will accumulate more wealth than a pure lifecycle model would predict. Tobin and Dolde (1971a, 1971b) provided the early theoretical foundations for this approach.

Several studies have suggested the importance of these liquidity constraints on wealth accumulation. Hubbard and Judd (1986, 1987a) developed a 55-period simulation model in which young consumers are constrained in terms of borrowing for nine years (age 20–29). They estimated that such liquidity constraints could increase aggregate savings by as much as one-third.

The age–wealth profiles shown in Table 10.1 indicate that even families under the age of 25 have, on average, accumulated positive net worth. As a result, only a fraction of young households may face a liquidity constraint. Lawrence (1983) used such an approach and found a smaller effect on aggregate savings from liquidity constraints.

A related argument is that consumers will accumulate precautionary savings (that is, saving for a rainy day). Individual consumers will accumulate a stock of assets in order to allay the uncertainties associated with their future stream of labor earnings – for example, those related to layoffs, job changing, sickness, and the like. In this sense, precautionary savings serve as insurance against potential earnings misfortunes. As a result, when young, families will accumulate more wealth than if their future income stream was known with certainty. This argument also leads to the hypothesis that consumers will accumulate more wealth than is strictly optimal from a pure lifecycle perspective. This motive will also yield a hump-shaped age–wealth profile even in the absence of the standard LCM retirement motive.

There is evidence that precautionary savings do explain a sizable fraction of the wealth accumulation observed among households. Zeldes (1989) modeled the uncertainty associated with future earnings. He argued that the fear of being liquidity constrained some time in the future (from a shortfall of income) may induce consumers to save more today. On the basis of simulation analysis, Zeldes found that the possibility of future liquidity constraints might raise total savings by as much as 25 percent. A similar analysis and result is reported by Skinner (1988).

Kotlikoff (1989, Chapter 6) explored the relation between household saving and uncertainty over future health expenses. He argued that in the absence of full health insurance, families will save as a hedge against uncertain future health expenses. Using simulation analysis, he found that the absence of complete health insurance could exert a substantial positive effect on personal savings. Palumba (1999) also argued that uncertainty about medical expenses could explain the high level of precautionary savings among the elderly and their failure to dissave significantly after retirement.

Caballero (1991) calculated from a simulation model that 60 percent of the observed wealth of U.S. households, net of the portion due to strictly lifecycle savings, could be attributed to precautionary savings. Jianakoplos, Menchik, and Irvine (1996) used data from the National Longitudinal Surveys (NLS) of men aged 45 to 49 in 1966 over the period 1966 to 1981 to examine determinants of household wealth. They also found that the standard lifecycle model was inadequate to explain the variation of wealth across households. However, once both precautionary and bequest motives were added to the model, the regression fit was considerably better.

Caroll (1994) developed a "buffer-stock" model of consumption, which emphasizes the importance of precautionary saving in the face of uncertain future income flows. In the standard lifecycle model, current consumption should depend not only on current income but on future expected income. However, Carroll found that consumption was closely related to current income but not to future expected income. On the other hand, he found that that the buffer-stock model, in which precautionary motives greatly reduce the willingness of prudent consumers to consume out of uncertain future income, did a much better job in predicting consumption than the standard lifecycle model.

Caroll and Samwick (1998) estimated that as much as 40 percent of aggregate financial (nonhousing, nonbusiness) wealth was held for precautionary motives. Gourinchas and Parker (2002) combined the lifecycle model with a buffer-stock model (that is, one with precautionary savings). Using synthetic cohort data derived from the Consumer Expenditure Surveys, they found that young consumers typically behave as buffer-stock agents, with precautionary savings the primary motive. However, around age 40, the typical household started to accumulate liquid assets for retirement and its behavior conformed most closely to the traditional lifecycle model. A similar set of findings on the importance of including a precautionary savings motive was reported by Attanasio *et al.* (1999).

10.4   INTERGENERATIONAL EQUITY

Part IV will provide a fuller account on issues of equity but here we want to focus on one particular aspect of this issue – the distribution of resources across generations. The government plays an important role, as do private transfers. In the previous section, we discussed bequests and *inter-vivos* transfers in the context of the LCM. In this section, we treat the issue in terms of the intergenerational distribution of resources.

10.4.1   Social security annuity and transfer wealth

Several studies have examined the intergenerational effects of the social security system. In this work, social security wealth is divided into two components: an *annuity* value and a *transfer* value. The annuity portion is defined as the benefit level the worker would receive on the basis of his (or her) contributions into the social security system (OASI) if the system were *actuarially fair*. The calculation is based on the worker's earnings history and social security contributions. The contributions are accumulated over the work life of the employee (with interest). The lump-sum amount is then converted into an annuity – that is, an annual stream of income based on the person's life expectancy. The transfer portion is the difference between the actual social security benefit the person receives or is expected to receive and the annuity value based on the person's contributions into the social security system.[9]

It is first of interest to examine the relative size of social security transfers and annuities and to determine whether the ratio has changed over time. Four sets of estimates are available. The

Table 10.6 Ratio of social security transfers to total social security benefits for households 65 and over, 1969, 1973, and 1983

Year	Source	Ratio
1969	MESP dataset[a]	0.85
1969	Hurd–Shoven (1985)[b]	0.80
1973	Burkhauser–Warlick (1981)[c]	0.73
1983	SCF dataset (treasury bill rate)[d]	0.66
1983	SCF dataset (portfolio rate)[d]	0.61

a *Source*: Wolff (1993), on the basis of the 1969 MESP file. The treasury bill rate is used as the discount rate.
b *Source*: Hurd and Shoven (1985), on the basis of the Retirement History Survey for 1969.
c *Source*: Burkhauser and Warlick (1981), on the basis of the 1973 Social Security Exact Match file.
d *Source*: Wolff (1993), on the basis of the 1983 SCF file. The treasury bill rate is based on the yield of 10-year U.S. treasury bills. The portfolio rate is calculated at 3.28 percent per year (in real terms) on the basis of the average portfolio holdings of U.S. households over the period 1962–1983.

first two are from Wolff (1993), based on a 1969 synthetic dataset of household wealth (called the MESP file) and the 1983 SCF. The third set is from Burkhauser and Warlick (1981), which is developed from the 1973 Social Security Exact Match file. Calculations are based on actual earnings and OASI histories. The fourth is from Hurd and Shoven (1985), on the basis of the RHS for 1969. Their calculations are based on actual earnings histories, although social security contributions are imputed.

As shown in Table 10.6, Burkhauser and Warlick calculated that overall, social security transfers amounted to 73 percent of total social security income for households 65 and over. Wolff's calculations yielded ratios of 0.85 for 1969 and 0.66 (treasury bill rate) and 0.61 (portfolio rate) for 1983, and Hurd and Shoven's estimate for 1969 was 0.80. Though the three methodologies differ, the results still strongly suggest that the transfer component of social security income was declining over time (that is, the annuity portion was rising).

These results together also indicate that social security transfers comprise a rather large (perhaps, surprisingly large) proportion of social security income. In other words, the benefits received from the social security system have far outweighed the annuity value of the social security contributions. The average retiree in 1983, for example, received twice as much in social security benefits as he or she contributed into the system. Thus, most of the social security benefits received by people who retired during the 1960s, 1970s, and 1980s have been a pure government transfer, over and above the actual contributions made into the system by the retirees.

More recent estimates made by Leimer (2007) of the Social Security Administration used a different methodology based on the actual earnings histories of workers who contributed to the social security system. He also used different assumptions regarding future earnings growth and several alternative interest rate assumptions. Though his results are not strictly comparable to the others reported above, it appears that by 2005 the ratio of social security transfers to social security benefits among households 65 and over had fallen to about 0.15. This represents a sharp drop from the 1980s.

Table 10.7 shows results on the ratio of social security transfers to social security benefits by age group in 1983. The most striking result is that the ratio of social security transfers to social security benefits among households under 65 is slightly *negative*, –0.08. This means that, on average, those who were under 65 in 1983 will contribute slightly more into the social security system than they will receive in benefits. The corresponding ratio among individuals who were

Table 10.7   The ratio of social security transfers to total social security benefits by age group, 1983

Age group	Ratio
18–30	−0.05
31–35	−0.52
36–40	−0.39
41–45	−0.26
46–50	−0.09
51–55	0.33
56–60	0.36
61–65	0.62
65–69	0.63
70–74	0.65
75–79	0.68
80 and over	0.73
Under 65	−0.08
65 and over	0.66

Source: Author's calculations from the 1983 SCF file. Calculations assume that real social security benefits will grow at 2 percent per year and use the treasury bill rate to discount social security contributions and benefits.

retired in 1983 is 0.66. They have received (or will receive) about twice as much in benefits as they contributed in the form of social security taxes.

The results by age group are also dramatic. Because of increasing OASI (social security) tax rates since the start-up of the system in 1937, the transfer component as a percent of the total social security benefit increased almost monotonically with age, from −0.52 for the 31–35 age group to 0.62 for the 61–65 age group. The latter ratio was almost identical to that for retirees aged 65–69. Workers who were age 50 or younger in 1983 were net losers in the social security system, contributing more into the system than they get out. Workers over 50 were net gainers, though the gains were relatively small, except for those in age group 61–65. The ratio of social security transfers to social security benefits was also found to increase with age group among the elderly. The ratio ranged from 0.63 for those in age group 65–69 to 0.73 for those 80 and over.

These results highlight one important aspect of intergenerational equity. The social security system provided the elderly population of the 1980s with benefits far in excess of their contribution into the social security system. Indeed, the figures presented above *understated* the full value of the transfer component, since additional benefits from Medicare were not included in the calculation. Insofar as it is a "pay-as-you-go" system (the benefits of the retired population in any given year is financed by the social security contributions of the working population of that year), this represented a major *transfer* of income between the nonelderly and the elderly. In other words, the working population of the 1980s was subsidizing their parents' generation via the social security system.

It is also clear that the transfer component of social security income was declining over time (that is, the annuity portion has been rising). There are two reasons for this. First, older beneficiaries paid into the social security system over a fewer number of years, since the system started up in 1937, and paid lower tax rates (OASI contribution rates for employees increased from 1 percent in 1937 to 4.8 percent in 1983). Second, Congress periodically increased OASI benefit levels for retirees over the last few decades.

In rather stark contrast, net social security transfers for the working population of the 1980s was actually negative. Those workers contributed more into the social security system than they received in the form of benefits. Under current law, today's working population will be net losers from the social security system.

10.4.2 Private intergenerational transfers

Whereas the retirees of the 1980s were the net beneficiaries of intergenerational transfers through the social security system, older people also transfer wealth to younger people – primarily their children – through gifts and bequests.

Barro (1974) argued that the two processes of intergenerational transfers were not independent. A deficit in the government budget implies that today's population is consuming more through government purchases than it is paying in the form of taxes. As a result, today's population is able to expand its public consumption over and above the amount it reduces its private consumption by paying taxes. Insofar as the government debt is transferred to future generations, the latter, in effect, are financing the consumption of today's population.

Barro (1974) argued that private transfers may, in fact, offset the burden of government debt on future generations. He argued that if families are *altruistic*, they would respond to today's government deficit by maintaining the same level of consumption that they would have had if they paid enough taxes to finance fully government expenditure and passing the full amount of this additional savings onto their children in the form of gifts and inheritances. These additional private transfers, in effect, enable their children's generations to pay for the added government debt. In this sense, private (intra-family) transfers should fully compensate for the public intergenerational transfers that flow from the children's generation to their parents'.

Several studies have tried to determine whether, in fact, families act "altruistically" toward their children. In several of these formulations, the parent is viewed to have a utility function which includes not only their own well-being but that of their children. Direct tests of such a specification are difficult to conduct. However, indirect tests are feasible, because testable implications can be drawn from models of altruism.

One set of implications concerns the division of estates among children. It is interesting to note that in some countries, such as France (and others that have adopted the Napoleonic code of law), equal division is prescribed by law (with a slight degree of leeway). However, in the United States and the United Kingdom (and other "common law" countries), the division of the estate is at the discretion of parents through their will. How do parents divide their estate?

According to the altruism model, the division of the estate should be "compensatory." This means that parents will leave less money to their more successful (richer) child and more money to their poorer offspring. Several studies have examined this issue. Tomes (1981), using questionnaire data taken from a survey in Cleveland, Ohio, found that most estates were *unequally* distributed among heirs. However, Menchik (1988) re-examined the same Cleveland data and concluded that the appearance of unequal division was simply the result of response error. Moreover, using probate records from Connecticut, Menchik (1980) reported that most parents divided their estate equally among their children. Joulfaian (1994), using a specially prepared file of estate data for the United States in 1982, linked to income tax records of the heirs, found that somewhat less than two-thirds of estates provided for equal division of bequests and the remaining third unequal division. Wilhelm (1996) concluded from the same data source that there was no evidence that the division of bequests could be interpreted as compensating differences in income among children.

Another prediction of the altruism model is that members of an extended family (including parents and adult children living in separate households) should fully share resources in the sense that the consumption of members of the extended family should be equal, independently of their individual incomes. Altonji, Hayashi, and Kotlikoff (1992) provided a test of this model using the Panel Study of Income Dynamics, in which parents are linked to adult children living in separate households. They found "overwhelming" evidence that such sharing did *not* occur. Instead, they find that the consumption of adult children (as well as parents) was significantly related to their income levels and the other direct resources at their disposal. The wealth of the parents had at most a modest effect on the consumption of the adult children.

Whether or not parents leave inheritances for altruistic motives or to offset the large public transfers from younger generations to older ones is still a matter of debate. However, what is clear from the various studies reviewed in this chapter is that inheritances play a large role in the process of wealth accumulation. Whereas it is the case that public transfers of wealth from younger generations to the elderly are distributed rather equitably among the elderly population (see Wolff, 1993, for details), it is certainly not the case with private transfers. The children of wealthy parents will, on average, receive much larger inheritances than the offspring of poorer parents. Bequests and gifts are thus not distributed equitably among younger families (see Chapter 6 for more discussion of intergenerational mobility).

10.4.3   Generational accounting

The notion of generational accounting was introduced by Auerbach, Gokhale, and Kotlikoff (1991) and Kotlikoff (1992). Generational accounts indicate the amount that each generation has paid plus the amount expected to be paid to the government in the form of taxes less the amount that generation has received and can be expected to receive from the government in the form of transfers and benefits. For example, in the case of the social security system, an individual will pay so much money into the social security system over his or her work life and will receive a certain amount in the form of social security benefits after retirement (see Section 10.4.1). By accumulating the payments and receipts over the lifetime and converting them to present value form (see Section 8.2 for the calculation of present values), the *net* amount – the difference between the payments and receipts – that the individual has paid into the system can be computed. If the same procedure is applied to all taxes and benefits and these amounts are summed over all individuals in an age group, then the net total payments for an age group (or generation) can be calculated.

The procedure outlined is, however, rather difficult to implement. First, retrospective data must be available in order to calculate past taxes paid and transfers received. Moreover, projections have to be made both about the future state of the economy (in particular, its real growth rate over time) and future tax and benefit legislation in order to arrive at future taxes and benefits. It is then necessary to choose an interest rate at which to obtain the present value of these two streams.

Auerbach, Gokhale, and Kotlikoff (1991) used SIPP data as the basis for their calculations. On the benefit side, they included OASDI (social security payments, including disability benefits), Medicare and Medicaid, AFDC (Aid to Families with Dependent Children, the principal federal welfare program), general welfare, and Food Stamps. On the tax side were personal income taxes, contributions to the social security system, sales taxes, and residential property taxes. There is also an assignment of government debt to future generations. A deficit in the government budget implies that today's population is consuming more through government purchases than it is paying in the form of taxes. As a result, today's population is able to expand its consumption (and reduce its savings). Insofar as the government debt is transferred to future generations, the latter, in effect, wind up financing the consumption of today's population.

Table 10.8 Net future government payments (in 1989 dollars) by birth cohort, 1989: future estimated tax payments less future estimated transfers and benefits

Age in 1989	Males	Females
0	73,700	36,400
10	116,800	60,400
20	169,100	85,500
30	194,500	90,900
40	176,200	78,200
50	114,100	41,000
60	18,900	−22,500
65	−31,800	−53,700
70	−42,700	−60,200
75	−41,500	−57,900
80	−35,600	−50,800
Future generations	89,500	44,200

Source: Auerbach, A.J., Gokhale, J. & Kotlikoff, L.J. (1991). Generational accounting. In D. Bradford (ed.), *Tax Policy and the Economy* (pp. 55–110). Cambridge, MA: MIT Press for the National Bureau of Economic Research, Tables 1 and 2. The interest rate is assumed to be 6 percent per year and the growth rate 0.75 percent per year.

The results, shown in Table 10.8, are quite striking. The figures show estimated future tax payments less government benefits received by age group in 1989 (past payments and benefits are *not* included in this calculation). They estimated that a male born in 1989 will pay $73,700 more to the government in taxes than he receives in benefits. The figures are even larger for adult males under the age of 50. For example, a man aged 30 in 1989 is expected to pay in $194,500 more than he receives from the government. In contrast, the figures for those 65 and over are negative, indicating that their future benefits are expected to exceed their future tax payments. Men aged 70 will have a net gain of $42,700. This largely reflects that fact that retirees can expect to pay relatively little in income taxes but will receive substantial social security and Medicare benefits.

The figures for younger females are lower than those for men, reflecting the fact that women had a lower labor force participation rate than men (see Chapter 7) and hence pay less in the way of taxes. On the other hand, among older persons, women will likely receive greater net benefits than men. This reflects the fact that women live longer, on average, than men (and hence have more years of social security benefits) and that even women who have never worked may receive social security benefits as a surviving spouse of a man who did work.

Another interesting result is that the authors estimate that future generations (those born after 1989) will actually have higher net payments to the government than someone born in 1989. This mainly reflects the increasing burden of the burgeoning government debt on future generations.

10.5 SUMMARY AND OVERALL ASSESSMENT

This chapter has provided an overview of the major sources of saving and wealth accumulation. We began with the lifecycle model (LCM). The LCM predicts that individuals will accumulate wealth over time until retirement age and then reduce their wealth holdings. Cross-sectional age–wealth profiles conformed to this prediction. However, longitudinal data (which follow the same individuals over their lifetime) provided mixed results. Some studies showed the elderly dissaving whereas others indicated little if any dissaving in older ages. One reason for this latter set of findings may be that the very old (over age 75) reduce their consumption expenditures as their needs decline. Moreover, there is no evidence that families draw down their wealth to near zero as they age.

How much does the LCM explain about the distribution of household wealth? Two simulation studies, based on data for the United Kingdom, concluded that the LCM could explain at most about one-quarter of the actual concentration of wealth of the top wealth-holders in Britain.

Regression analysis was used to explore the explanatory power of the LCM in accounting for differences in wealth holdings in a sample of U.S. households. The results reported in this chapter indicated that the basic LCM did yield statistically significant age coefficients with the predicted signs, but explained a very small part of the variation of household wealth (less than 2 percent). With the inclusion of lifetime earnings, the explanatory power of the model increased to at most 5 percent. However, when the sample was restricted to the bottom 95 percent of the wealth distribution (that is, the very wealthy were excluded), the explanatory power of the life-cycle model increased by a factor of four. These results suggest that, although the LCM predicts household savings behavior well for the vast majority of households, it is not successful in explaining the wealth accumulation motives of the top wealth classes who hold the majority of household wealth. It appears likely that the difference is due to the strength of the bequest motive of the very rich.

These results also suggest that tests of the lifecycle model depend very heavily on the sample used – particularly on how much of the upper tail of the distribution is captured in the sample. Analysis using data sources, such as the PSID, RHS, and SIPP, which focus almost exclusively on middle-income families, will give very different results than surveys like the SCF, which has a good representation of the very wealthy.

How much does the lifecycle model explain about wealth accumulation? Two U.S. studies concluded that the LCM could account for only a small part (in one study, only 20 percent) of the growth in household wealth over time.

Partly to overcome deficiencies in the predictive power of the basic lifecycle model, subsequent theoretical and empirical work has extended the LCM by modifying one or more of its basic premises. Four modifications were reviewed in this chapter: (i) uncertainty about length of life; (ii) the role of social security and pension wealth; (iii) the introduction of a bequest motive; and (iv) liquidity constraints and precautionary savings.

Estimates varied about the importance of each of these other factors. With regard to uncertainty about death, the theoretical work suggests that this factor might account for increased savings and, in particular, the non-exhaustion of wealth at death. One study found that up to a quarter of wealth could be explained by including this factor in the LCM.

Theoretical work indicates that the availability of social security and pension wealth should lead to a reduction in the accumulation of traditional (marketable) wealth. Several studies have found that social security and pension wealth reduced traditional savings, but others found no effect. In the former case, the estimated substitution effects were considerably less than the dollar-for-dollar reduction predicted in the standard lifecycle model.

The desire to leave bequests is another explanation for the slow dissaving (or positive saving) of elderly families and the non-exhaustion of wealth at time of death. Studies differ drastically about the importance of bequests in household wealth accumulation. Direct questionnaire evidence suggested that no more than about 20 percent of household wealth in the United States was due to intergenerational transfers. In contrast, simulation studies suggested that lifecycle savings explained only a small portion of total wealth accumulation (typically, 25 percent or less), with the remainder presumably the result of intergenerational transfers. The discrepancy in results can be traced to three factors: (i) recall error in direct surveys; (ii) the accounting framework, particularly, the treatment of the capital appreciation of inheritances; and (iii) the role of *inter-vivos* transfers.

The presence of liquidity (borrowing) constraints implies that a family will accumulate more wealth than a pure lifecycle model would predict. Precautionary savings serve as a self-insurance device against potential earnings misfortunes, and, as a result, consumers will accumulate more wealth than if their future income stream is known with certainty. Some studies estimated that liquidity constraints and precautionary saving could explain as much as one-third of total household wealth.

Issues of intergenerational equity were also raised in this chapter. The social security system was examined. It was found that the elderly population of the 1980s received more in social security benefits (about two times as much) than they paid into the system in the form of social security contributions. This represented a transfer of resources from younger Americans to older ones. In contrast, today's working population will fail to break even with respect to the social security system – that is, their expected benefits will not cover their contributions into the system.

In contrast, private transfers generally go in the opposite direction – from older people to their children. Barro argued that if parents are "altruistic," their bequests and gifts to their children should fully compensate for the public intergenerational transfers that flow from the children's generation to their parents'. However, microdata tests of altruism models generally proved inconclusive.

10.6 REFERENCES AND BIBLIOGRAPHY

Aaron, H.J. (1982). *Economic Effects of Social Security*. Washington, DC: Brookings Institution.

Abel, A.B. (1985). Precautionary saving and accidental bequests. *American Economic Review*, 75(5), 777–91.

Abel, A.B. (1987). Aggregate savings in the presence of private and social insurance. In R. Dornbusch, S. Fischer & J. Bossons (eds.), *Essays in Honor of Franco Modigliani* (pp. 131–57). Cambridge, MA: MIT Press.

Alessie, R., Kapteyn, A. & Melenberg, B. (1989). The effects of liquidity constraints on consumption: Estimation from household panel data. *European Economic Review*, 33(2/3), 547–55.

Altonji, J.G., Hayashi, F. & Kotlikoff, L.J. (1992). Is the extended family altruistically linked? Direct tests using micro data. *American Economic Review*, 82(5), 1177–98.

Ando, A. & Modigliani, F. (1963). The lifecycle hypothesis of saving: Aggregate implications and tests. *American Economic Review*, 53, 55–84.

Attanasio, O. & Weber, G. (1995). Is consumption growth consistent with intertemporal organization? Evidence from the Consumer Expenditure Survey. *Journal of Political Economy*, 103, 1121–57.

Attanasio, O., Banks, J., Meghir, C. & Weber, G. (1999). Humps and bumps in lifetime consumption. *Journal of Business and Economic Statistics*, 17(1), 22–35.

Auerbach, A.J., Gokhale, J. & Kotlikoff, L.J. (1991). Generational accounting. In D. Bradford (ed.), *Tax Policy and the Economy* (pp. 55–110). Cambridge, MA: MIT Press for the National Bureau of Economic Research.

Atkinson, A.B. (1971). The distribution of wealth and the individual lifecycle. *Oxford Economic Papers*, 23, 239–54.

Atkinson, A.B., Maynard, A.K. & Trinder, C.G. (1983). *Parents and Children*. London: Heinemann.

Avery, R.B., Elliehausen, G.E. & Gustafson, T.A. (1985). Pensions and social security in household portfolios: Evidence from the 1983 Survey of Consumer Finances. Federal Reserve Board Research Papers in Banking and Financial Economics, October.

Banks, J., Blundell, R. & Tanner, S. (1998). Is there a retirement-savings puzzle? *American Economic Review*, 88(4), 769–88.

Barlow, R., Brazer, H.E., & Morgan, J.N. (1966). *Economic Behavior of the Affluent.* Washington, DC: Brookings Institution.

Barro, R.J. (1974). Are government bonds net wealth? *Journal of Political Economy,* **48**(6), 1095–118.

Bernheim, B.D. (1984). Lifecycle annuity valuation. NBER Working Paper No. 1511, December.

Bernheim, B.D. (1986). Dissaving after retirement: Testing the pure lifecycle hypothesis. In Z. Bodie, J. Shoven & D. Wise (eds.), *Issues in Pension Economies.* Chicago: University of Chicago Press.

Bernheim, B.D. (1987). The economic effects of social security: Toward a reconciliation of theory and measurement. *Journal of Public Economics,* **33**(3), 273–304.

Bernheim, B.D., Skinner, J. & Weinberg, S. (2001). What accounts for the variation in retirement wealth among U.S. households? *American Economic Review,* **91**(4), 832–57.

Blinder, A.S. (1973). A model of inherited wealth. *Quarterly Journal of Economics,* **87**(4), 608–26.

Blinder, A.S. (1988). Comments on Chapters 1 and 2. In D. Kessler & A. Masson (eds.), *Modelling the Accumulation and Distribution of Wealth* (pp. 68–76). Oxford: Oxford University Press.

Blinder, A.S., Gordon, R. & Weiss, D. (1983). Social security bequests and the life-cycle theory of savings: Cross-sectional texts. In F. Modigliani & R. Hemming (eds.), *Determinants of National Saving and Wealth.* New York: St. Martin's Press.

Borsch-Supan, A. (1992). Saving and consumption patterns of the elderly: The German case. *Journal of Population Economics,* **5**, 289–303.

Brittain, J.A. (1978). *Inheritance and the Inequality of Material Wealth.* Washington, DC: Brookings Institution.

Browning, M. & Crossley, T.F. (2001). The life-cycle model of consumption and saving. *Journal of Economic Perspectives,* **15**(3), 3–22.

Burkhauser, R.V. & Warlick, J.L. (1981). Disentangling the annuity from the redistributive aspects of social security in the United States. *Review of Income and Wealth,* ser. 27, no. 4, 401–21.

Caballero, R.J. (1991). Earnings uncertainty and aggregate wealth accumulation. *American Economic Review,* **81**(4), 859–71.

Carroll, C.D. (1994). How much does future income affect current consumption? *Quarterly Journal of Economics,* **109**(1), 111–47.

Carroll, C.D. & Samwick, A.A. (1998). How important is precautionary saving? *Review of Economics and Statistics,* **80**(3), 410–19.

Danziger, S., Van der Gaag, J., Smolensky, E. & Taussig, M.K. (1983). The lifecycle hypothesis and the consumption behavior of the elderly. *Journal of Post Keynesian Economics,* **5**(2), 208–27.

David, M. & Menchik, P.L. (1982). Distribution of estates and its relationship to intergenerational transfers. Statistics of income and related administration record research: 1982, Department of the Treasury Internal Revenue Service, Statistics of Income Division, October.

David, M. & Menchik, P.L. (1985). The effect of social security on lifetime wealth accumulation and bequests. *Economica,* **52**, 421–34.

Davies, J.B. (1981). Uncertain lifetime, consumption and dissaving in retirement. *Journal of Political Economy,* **89**, 561–78.

Davies, J.B. (1982). The relative impact of inheritance and other factors on economic inequality. *Quarterly Journal of Economics,* **96**, 471–98.

Davies, J.B. (1999). Age, wealth inequality and life-cycle modelling. *Geneva Papers on Risk and Insurance,* **24**(1), 64–76.

Davies, J.B. & St-Hilaire, F. (1987). *Reforming Capital Income Taxation in Canada.* Ottawa: Economic Council of Canada.

Davies, J.B. & Shorrocks, A.F. (1999). The distribution of wealth. In A.B. Atkinson & F. Bourguignon (eds.), *Handbook on Income Distribution,* Vol. 1 (pp. 605–765). Amsterdam: Elsevier Science.

Diamond, P.A. & Hausman, J.A. (1984). Individual retirement and savings behavior. *Journal of Public Economics,* **23**, 81–114.

Engen, E.M. & Gale, W.G. (1997). Debt, taxes, and the effects of 401(k) plans on household wealth accumulation, mimeo. Brookings Institution, May.

Engen, E.M. & Gale, W.G. (2000). The Effects of 401(k) plans on household wealth:

Differences across earnings groups, mimeo. Brookings Institution, August.

Engen, E.M., Gale, W.G. & Uccello, C.E. (1999). The adequacy of household saving. *Brookings Papers on Economic Activity*, **2**, 65–165.

Feldstein, M.S. (1974). Social security, induced retirement and aggregate capital accumulation. *Journal of Political Economy*, **82**, 905–26.

Feldstein, M.S. (1976). Social security and the distribution of wealth. *Journal of the American Statistical Association*, **71**, 800–7.

Feldstein, M.S. (1982). Social security and private saving: Reply. *Journal of Political Economy*, **90**, 630–41.

Feldstein, M.S. (1983). Social security benefits and the accumulation of pre-retirement wealth. In R. Hemming & F. Modigliani (eds.), *Determinants of National Saving and Wealth*. London: Macmillan.

Feldstein, M.S. & Pellechio, A. (1979). Social security and household wealth accumulation: New microeconomic evidence. *Review of Economics and Statistics*, **61**, 361–8.

Friedman, J. (1982). Asset accumulation and depletion among the elderly. Paper presented at the Brookings Institution Conference on Retirement and Aging.

Gale, W.G. (1998). The effects of pensions on wealth: A re-evaluation of theory and evidence. *Journal of Political Economy*, **106**, 707–23.

Gourinchas, P.-O. & Parker, J. (2002). Consumption over the Lifecycle. *Econometrica*, **70**(1), 47–89.

Greenwood, D. (1987). Age, income, and household size: Their relation to wealth distribution in the United States. In E.N. Wolff (ed.), *International Comparisons of the Distribution of Household Wealth*. New York: Oxford University Press.

Greenwood, D.T. & Wolff, E.N. (1992). Changes in Wealth in the United States, 1962–1983: Savings, capital gains, inheritance, and lifetime transfers. *Journal of Population Economics*, **5**(4), 261–88.

Gustman, A.L., Mitchell, O.S., Samwick, A.A. & Steinmeier, T.L. (1997). Pension and social security wealth in the Health and Retirement Study. NBER Working Paper No. 5912, February.

Gustman, A.L. & Steinmeier, T.L. (1998). Effects of pensions on saving: Analysis with Data from the Health and Retirement Study. NBER Working Paper No. 6681, August.

Harbury, C.D. & Hitchens, D.M.W.N. (1976). The inheritances of top wealth leavers: Some further evidence. *Economic Journal*, **86**, 321–6.

Harbury, C.D. & Hitchens, D.M.W.N. (1979). *Inheritance and Wealth Inequality in Britain*. London: Allen and Unwin.

Hammermesh, D.S. (1984). Consumption during retirement: The missing link in the lifecycle. *Review of Economics and Statistics*, **66**(1), 1–7.

Hammermesh, D.S. & Menchik, P.L. (1987). Planned and unplanned bequests. *Economic Inquiry*, **25**, 55–66.

Heckman, J.J. (1976). The common structure of statistical models of truncation, sample selection and limited dependent variables and a simple estimator for such models. *Annals of Economic and Social Measurement*, **5**, 475–92.

Heckman, J.J. (1979). Sample selection bias as a specification error. *Econometrica*, **47**, 153–62.

Hubbard, R.G. (1983). Uncertain Lifetimes and the impact of social security on individual wealth holding, mimeo. Harvard University.

Hubbard, R.G. (1986). Uncertain lifetimes, pensions, and individual savings. In Z. Bodie, J. Shoven & D. Wise (eds.), *Issues in Pension Economies*. Chicago: University of Chicago Press.

Hubbard, R.G. (1984a). Do IRA's and Keoghs increase saving? *National Tax Journal*, **37**, 43–54.

Hubbard, R.G. (1984b). "Precautionary saving" revisited: Social security, individual welfare, and the capital stock. NBER Working Paper No. 1430, August.

Hubbard, R.G. (1995). Precautionary saving and social insurance. *Journal of Political Economy*, **103**, 360–99.

Hubbard, R.G. & Judd, K.J. (1986). Liquidity constraints, fiscal policy, and consumption. *Brookings Papers on Economic Activity*, **1**, 1–59.

Hubbard, R.G. & Judd, K.J. (1987a). Finite lifetimes, borrowing constraints, and short-run fiscal policy. NBER Working Paper No. 2158, January.

Hubbard, R.G. & Judd, K.J. (1987b). Social security and individual welfare: Precautionary saving, liquidity constraints, and the payroll

382   *Explanations of Inequality and Poverty*

7.

tax. *American Economic Review*, **77**(4), 630–46.

Hubbard, R.G., Skinner, J. & Zeldes, S.P. (1995). Precautionary saving and social insurance. *Journal of Political Economy*, **103**(2), 360–99.

Hurd, M.D. (1987). Savings of the elderly and desired bequests. *American Economic Review*, **77**(2), 298–312.

Hurd, M.D. (1989). Mortality, risk, and bequests. *Econometrica*, **57**(4), 779–813.

Hurd, M.D. (1990). Research on the elderly: Economic status, retirement, and consumption and saving. *Journal of Economic Literature*, **28**, 565–637.

Hurd, M.D. (1992). Wealth depletion and life-cycle consumption. In D.A. Wise (ed.), *Topics in the Economics of Aging* (pp. 135–60). Chicago: University of Chicago Press for the National Bureau of Economic Research.

Hurd, M.D. & Mundaca, G. (1989). The importance of gifts and inheritances among the affluent. In R.E. Lipsey & H. Stone Tice (eds.), *The Measurement of Saving, Investment, and Wealth*, Studies of Income and Wealth, Vol. 52 (pp. 737–63). Chicago: Chicago University Press.

Hurd, M.D. & Shoven, J.B. (1985). The distributional impact of social security. In D.A. Wise (ed.), *Pensions, Labor, and Individual Choice*. Chicago: Chicago University Press.

Irvine, I.J. (1981). The use of cross-section microdata in lifecycle models: An application to inequality theory in nonstationary economies. *Quarterly Journal of Economics*, **95**, 301–16.

Jappelli, T. & Pagano, M. (1989). Consumption and capital market imperfections: An international comparison. *American Economic Review*, **79**(5), 1088–105.

Jianakoplos, N.A., Menchik, P.L. & Irvine, F.O. (1989). Using panel data to assess the bias in cross-sectional inferences of life-cycle changes in the level and composition of household wealth. In R.E. Lipsey & H. Stone Tice (eds.), *The Measurement of Saving, Investment, and Wealth*, Studies of Income and Wealth, Vol. 52 (pp. 553–644). Chicago: Chicago University Press.

Jianakoplos, N.A., Menchik, P.L. & Irvine, F.O. (1996). Saving behavior of older households: Rate-of-return, precautionary and inheritance effects. *Economic Letters*, **50**(1), 111–20.

Joulfaian, D. (1994). The distribution and division of bequests in the U.S.: Evidence from the collation study. OTA Paper 71, US Department of the Treasury.

Kennickell, A.B. & Sunden, A.E. (1999). Pensions, social security, and the distribution of wealth, mimeo. Federal Reserve Board of Washington, December.

Kessler, D. & Masson, A. (1979). Les transferts intergenerationales: l'aide, la donation, l'heritage. *C.N.R.S. Report*, Paris.

Kessler, D. & Masson, A. (1989). Bequests and wealth accumulation: Are some pieces of the puzzle missing? *Journal of Economic Perspectives*, **3**(3), 141–52.

King, M.A. (1985). The economics of saving: A survey of recent contributions. In K.J. Arrow (ed.), *Frontiers of Economics* (pp. 227–94). Oxford: Basil Blackwell.

King, M.A. & Dick-Mireaux, L. (1982). Asset holdings and the lifecycle. *Economic Journal*, **92**, 247–67.

Kotlikoff, L.J. (1979). Testing the theory of social security and lifecycle accumulation. *American Economic Review*, **69**, 396–410.

Kotlikoff, L.J. (1989). *What Determines Savings?* Cambridge, MA: MIT Press.

Kotlikoff, L.J. (1988). Intergenerational transfers and savings. *Journal of Economic Perspectives*, **2**(2), 41–58.

Kotlikoff, L.J. (1992). *Generational Accounting*. New York: Macmillan.

Kotlikoff, L.J. & Smith, D.E. (1983). *Pensions in the American Economy*. Chicago: University of Chicago Press.

Kotlikoff, L.J. & Spivak, A. (1981). The family as an incomplete annuities market. *Journal of Political Economy*, **89**, 372–91.

Kotlikoff, L.J., Spivak, A. & Summers, L.H. (1982). The adequacy of savings. *American Economic Review*, **72**(5), 1056–69.

Kotlikoff, L.J. & Summers, L.H. (1981). The role of intergenerational transfers in aggregate capital accumulation. *Journal of Political Economy*, **90**, 706–32.

Kotlikoff, L.J. & Summers, L.H. (1988). The contribution of intergenerational transfers to total wealth: A reply. In D. Kessler & A. Masson (eds.), *Modelling the Accumulation and Distribution of Wealth* (pp. 53–67). Oxford: Oxford University Press.

Laitner, J. (1992). Random earnings differences, lifetime liquidity constraints, and altruistic intergenerational transfers. *Journal of Economic Theory*, **58**, 135–70.

Lansing, J.B. & Sonquist, J. (1969). A cohort analysis of changes in the distribution of wealth. In L. Soltow (ed.), *Six Papers on the Size Distribution of Income and Wealth*. New York: National Bureau of Economic Research.

Lawrence, E. (1983). Do transfers to the poor reduce savings? Mimeo.

Lee, C. (2001). Life-cycle savings in the United States, 1900–90. *Review of Income and Wealth*, ser. 47, no. 2, 165–79.

Leimer, D.R. (2007). Cohort-specific measures of lifetime social security taxes and benefits. ORES Working Paper Series No. 110, Social Security Administration, December.

Leimer, D.R. & Lesnoy, S.D. (1982). Social security and private saving: New time-series evidence. *Journal of Political Economy*, **90**, 606–21.

Lydall, H. (1955). The lifecycle, income, saving, and asset ownership. *Econometrica*, **46**, 985–1012.

Masson, A. (1986). A cohort analysis of age-wealth profiles generated by a simulation model of France (1949–1975). *Economic Journal*, **96**, 173–90.

Masson, A. (1988). Age, income, and the distribution of wealth: A lifecycle interpretation. *Annales d'Economie et de Statistique*, **9**.

Menchik, P.L. (1979). Inter-generational transmission of inequality: An empirical study of wealth mobility. *Economica*, **46**, 349–62.

Menchik, P.L. (1980). Primogeniture, equal sharing and the U.S. division of wealth. *Quarterly Journal of Economics*, **94**, 299–316.

Menchik, P.L. (1988). Unequal estate division: Is it altruism, reverse bequests, or simply noise. In D. Kessler & A. Masson (eds.), *Modelling the Accumulation and Distribution of Wealth* (pp. 105–16). Oxford: Oxford University Press.

Menchik, P.L. & David, M. (1983). Income distribution, lifetime saving and bequests. *American Economic Review*, **73**(4), 672–90.

Mirer, T.W. (1979). The wealth-age relationship among the aged. *American Economic Review*, **69**, 435–43.

Mirer, T.W. (1980). The dissaving behavior of the retired elderly. *Southern Economic Journal*, **46**(4), 1197–205.

Modigliani, F. (1975). The lifecycle hypothesis of saving, twenty years later. In M. Parkin (ed.), *Contemporary Issues in Economics* (pp. 2–36). Manchester: Manchester University Press.

Modigliani, F. (1988a). Measuring the contribution of intergenerational transfers to total wealth: Conceptual issues and empirical findings. In D. Kessler & A. Masson (eds.), *Modelling the Accumulation and Distribution of Wealth* (pp. 21–52). Oxford: Oxford University Press.

Modigliani, F. (1988b). The role of intergenerational transfers and lifecycle savings in the accumulation of wealth. *Journal of Economic Perspectives*, **2**(2), 15–40.

Modigliani, F. & Brumberg, R. (1954). Utility analysis and the consumption function: An interpretation of cross-section data. In K. Kurihara (ed.), *Post-Keynesian Economics*. New Brunswick: Rutgers University Press.

Morgan, J.N., David, M.H., Cohen, W.J. & Brazer, H.E. (1962). *Income and Welfare in the United States*. New York: McGraw-Hill.

Oulton, N. (1976). Inheritance and the distribution of wealth. *Oxford Economic Papers*, **28**, 86–101.

Palumbo, M. (1999). Uncertain medical expenses and precautionary saving near the end of the lifecycle. *Review of Economic Studies*, **66**(2), 395–421.

Poterba, J.M., Venti, S.F. & Wise, D.A. (1992). 401(k) plans and tax-deferred saving. NBER Working Paper 4181, October.

Poterba, J.M., Venti, S.F. & Wise, D.A. (1993). Do 401(k) contributions crowd out other personal savings. NBER Working Paper 4391, June.

Poterba, J.M., Venti, S.F. & Wise, D.A. (1995). Targeted retirement saving and the net worth of elderly Americans. *American Economic Review Papers and Proceedings*, **84**(2), 180–5.

Poterba, J.M., Venti, S.F. & Wise, D.A. (1998). 401(k) plans and future patterns of retirement saving. *American Economic Review Papers and Proceedings*, **87**(2), 179–84.

Poterba, J.M., Venti, S.F. & Wise, D.A. (2001). The transition to personal accounts and increasing retirement wealth: Micro and macro evidence. NBER Working Paper No. 8610, November.

President's Commission on Pension Policy. (1980). Preliminary findings on a nationwide survey on retirement income issues. Mimeo.

Projector, D. & Weiss, G. (1966). Survey of Financial Characteristics of Consumers. Federal Reserve Technical Papers, 1966.

Radner, D.B. & Vaughan, D.R. (1987). Wealth, income and the economic status of aged households. In E.N. Wolff (ed.), *International Comparisons of the Distribution of Household Wealth*. New York: Oxford University Press.

Sheshinski, E. & Weiss, Y. (1981). Uncertainty and optimal social security systems. *Quarterly Journal of Economics*, **96**, 189–206.

Shorrocks, A.F. (1975). The age–wealth relationship: A cross-section and cohort analysis. *Review of Economics and Statistics*, **57**, 155–63.

Shorrocks, A.F. (1987). U.K. wealth distribution: Current evidence and future prospects. In E.N. Wolff (ed.), *International Comparisons of the Distribution of Household Wealth*. New York: Oxford University Press.

Skinner, J.S. (1988). Risky income, lifecycle consumption, and precautionary savings. *Journal of Monetary Economics*, **22**, 237–55.

Tobin, J. & Dolde, W. (1971a). Monetary and fiscal effects on consumption. In *Consumer Spending and Monetary Policy: The Linkages*, Federal Reserve Bank of Boston Conference Series 5. Boston: Federal Reserve Bank of Boston.

Tobin, J. & Dolde, W. (1971b). Wealth, liquidity, and consumption. In *Consumer Spending and Monetary Policy: The Linkages*, Federal Reserve Bank of Boston Conference Series 5. Boston: Federal Reserve Bank of Boston.

Tomes, Nigel. (1981). The family, inheritance, and the intergenerational transmission of inequality. *Journal of Political Economy*, **89**, 928–58.

White, B.B. (1978). Empirical tests of the life-cycle hypothesis. *American Economic Review*, **68**, 547–60.

Wilhelm, M.O. (1996). Bequest behavior and the effect of heirs' earnings: Testing the altruistic model of bequests. *American Economic Review*, **86**(4), 874–92.

Wolff, E.N. (1981). The accumulation of household wealth over the life-cycle: A microdata analysis. *Review of Income and Wealth*, ser. **27**, 75–96.

Wolff, E.N. (ed.) (1987). *International Comparisons of the Distribution of Household Wealth*. New York: Oxford University Press.

Wolff, E.N. (1987a). The effects of pensions and social security on the distribution of wealth in the U.S. In E.N. Wolff (ed.), *International Comparisons of Household Wealth Distribution*. New York: Oxford University Press.

Wolff, E.N. (1987b). Estimates of household wealth inequality in the United States, 1962–83. *Review of Income and Wealth*, ser. **33**, 231–56.

Wolff, E.N. (1988). Social security, pensions, and the lifecycle accumulation of wealth: Some empirical tests. *Annales d'Economie et de Statistique*, **9**, 199–216.

Wolff, E.N. (1992). Methodological issues in the estimation of retirement wealth. In D.J. Slottje (ed.), *Research in Economic Inequality*, Vol. 2 (pp. 31–56). Greenwich, CT: JAI Press.

Wolff, E.N. (1993). The distributional implications of social security annuities and transfers on household wealth and income. In E.N. Wolff (ed.), *Research in Economic Inequality*, Vol. 4 (pp. 131–57). Greenwich, CT: JAI Press.

Wolff, E.N. (1994). Trends in household wealth in the United States, 1962–1983 and 1983–1989. *Review of Income and Wealth*, ser. 40, no. 2, 143–74.

Wolff, E.N. (1999). Wealth accumulation by age cohort in the U.S., 1962–1992: The role of savings, capital gains and intergenerational transfers. *Geneva Papers on Risk and Insurance*, **24**(1), 27–49.

Wolff, E.N. (2007). The retirement wealth of the baby boom generation. *Journal of Monetary Economics*, **54**(1), 1–40.

Yaari, M.E. (1965). Uncertain lifetime, life insurance, and the theory of the consumer. *Review of Economic Studies*, **32**, 137–58.

Zeldes, S.P. (1989). Optimal consumption with stochastic income: Deviations from certainty equivalence. *Quarterly Journal of Economics*, **104**, 275–98.

10.7 DISCUSSION QUESTIONS

1 Explain why a cross-sectional age–wealth profile may give a biased picture of the longitudinal age–wealth profile.

2 Why would uncertainty about death or the existence of liquidity constraints lead to positive wealth at the time of death in the context of the lifecycle model?

3 Discuss the arguments for why expected social security and pension benefits might displace private savings. What is the evidence on this issue? Why is this issue of relevance to the determination of the inequality of household wealth?

4 Summarize the available evidence on the respective roles of the lifecycle motive and the bequest motive in accounting for differences in household wealth among households.

5 Give three reasons why older generations have received higher *net* benefits from the social security system than younger ones have received or are likely to receive.

NOTES

1 Also see Chapter 5 for an extended discussion of the definition (or definitions) of household wealth, its measurement, and its distribution.

2 The quadratic form produces a symmetric (parabolic) age–wealth profile with respect to age whereas a cubic or higher power form yields an asymmetrical profile, which corresponds more closely to the age–wealth profiles illustrated in Figures 10.1 and 10.2. After some experimentation, it was found that the best fit was provided by a cubic form which included only an AGE^2 and AGE^3 term.

3 The inclusion of lifetime earnings also implicitly controls for the other source of bias noted by Shorrocks (1987), the sample selection effect induced by the positive correlation between wealth and longevity. The reason for this is the high positive correlation between wealth and lifetime earnings and, correspondingly, between lifetime earnings and life expectancy. As a result, the fact that richer families are overrepresented among the older age groups is controlled for by their higher lifetime earnings. Also, see Bernheim (1984), who found this sample selection bias relatively small in other tests of the LCM.

4 Technically, the truncation of the sample on the top and also on the bottom (see text) introduces a sample selection bias, since the error term is now also truncated. To correct for this truncation bias, Wolff used the two-stage procedure developed by Heckman (1976, 1979), which entails, first, the estimation of a probit model for high wealth-holders and, then, the inclusion of the inverse of the Mills' ratio in a second-stage regression of wealth on age and lifetime earnings. Also, see King and Dick-Mireaux (1982) for more details on this procedure.

5 Feldstein also argued that the availability of social security retirement income might induce workers to retire earlier than otherwise and this possibility might have a positive effect on private savings. No independent estimate of this effect on savings was provided.

6 As King and Dick-Mireaux (1982) argued, the use of actuarial values to compute retirement wealth builds in a tendency for total wealth to decline rapidly after retirement, because conditional life expectancy decreases with age.

7 As a reminder, defined contribution pension plans consist of Individual Retirement Accounts (IRAs), Keogh plans, 401(k) plans, and the like. These plans are like savings accounts. However, they are especially designed to allow workers to save for retirement by providing tax-deferred savings (see Chapter 5 for more details).

8 Even this figure might be an understatement of the actual importance of inheritance, because there was no information available on the sources of wealth before the calendar year 1962.

9 In effect, social security contributions are treated as if they are made into a "defined contribution" pension plan, the benefits from which are based directly on the contributions. See Burkhauser and Warlick (1981), Wolff (1987b), and Wolff (1993) for technical details on the imputation techniques used. Also, see Section 15.4 for a discussion of the so-called Social Security Trust Fund, which records the net balance between social security contributions received and benefits to be paid out.

Chapter 11
Sources of Rising Earnings Inequality*

11.1 INTRODUCTION

As we saw in Chapters 1 and 3, the period from 1970 to 2005 witnessed some dramatic changes in inequality in the United States. Inequality in the distribution of family income, which had remained virtually unchanged since the end of World War II until 1968, then increased sharply. The main source of the rising inequality of family income appears to stem from changes in the structure of the labor market.

Another indication of the dramatic changes taking place in the labor market was the sharp rise in the returns to education, particularly a college degree, which occurred in the United States since 1975, especially in the 1980s. As we discussed in Chapter 1, the ratio in annual earnings between male college graduates and male high school graduates climbed from 1.50 in 1975 to 1.92 in 2005. For females, the ratio grew from 1.45 in 1975 to 1.92 in 2005. Among men, the increase in the return to a college degree relative to a high school degree was due, in part, to the stagnating earnings of high school graduates. Between 1975 and 2003, their annual earnings in constant dollars gained only 4 percent, while the earnings of men with a bachelor's degree increased by 22 percent. The biggest increase in earnings occurred among males with an advanced degree (master's or higher), who saw their annual incomes surge by 31 percent. Among males who did not graduate college, earnings plummeted by 12 percent.

Another notable change was the widespread diffusion of computers in the United States since about 1970. Particular interest is focused on the post-1980 period, which saw a tremendous growth in the use of computers in production and which Freeman (1987) and others have termed a new "techno-economic paradigm," based on computer-driven information technology. The other principal focus of this chapter is the extent to which the computer revolution is responsible for the upsurge of inequality in the United States.

The chapter begins with a recapitulation of the various explanations that have been proposed to account for rising earnings inequality in the United States and their associated literatures. These include: (i) skill-biased technological change, favoring highly educated over less-educated workers (Section 11.2); (ii) the information technology revolution (Section 11.3); (iii) growing international trade and rising immigration, both of which may have caused the relative wages of low-skilled workers to fall (Section 11.4); (iv) the shift of employment to services, which are characterized by a greater dispersion of earnings than goods producers (Section 11.5); (v) declining unionization, which may have widened wage differentials between different types of jobs within an industry (Section 11.6); (vi) a declining minimum wage in real terms, which may have put downward pressure on the wages of low-skilled jobs (also Section 11.6); (vii) corporate restructuring and downsizing in the 1980s and 1990s, which may have widened earnings differentials within firms (Section 11.7); and (viii) changes in the distribution of schooling (Section 11.8).

Section 11.9 provides descriptive statistics on aggregate trends in the overall inequality of income and earnings and the dispersion of educational attainment in the population over the period from 1947 to 2000. Time trends on technological factors, computerization, international trade, and pertinent institutional factors are also reviewed. Section 11.10 presents some econometric time-series results on the effects of these technological, structural, and institutional factors, and trade openness on trends in income inequality in the United States. A summary and concluding remarks are provided in Section 11.11.

11.2 SKILL-BIASED TECHNOLOGICAL CHANGE

A considerable literature has now accumulated on factors that might have caused earnings inequality to rise since the early 1970s. At the outset, it is important to distinguish between three separate but related trends. The first is the actual rise in the dispersion of earnings among all workers (or among all male workers) in the economy. The second is the rising returns to schooling, particularly a college education over the same period. The third is the large increase of earnings dispersion within education–experience cells – that is, even after controlling for education and experience – over these years as well (see, for example, Levy & Murnane, 1992; or Juhn, Murphy, & Pierce, 1993). A successful model must be able to account for all three phenomena simultaneously. Several candidates have been put forward to explain these changes in earnings patterns.

The most prevalent view on the cause of rising wage inequality is biased technological change, due to the introduction of computers and the general diffusion of information technology (IT). The argument is that the period since 1970 or so witnessed a major technological revolution led by widespread computerization and the consequent diffusion of IT. This change skewed the income distribution by placing a high premium on college-educated and skilled labor while reducing the demand for semiskilled and unskilled workers. One important piece of evidence was that the rate of return to a college education (the wage premium paid to a college graduate relative to a high school graduate) almost doubled over the decade of the 1980s and 1990s, as noted in the Introduction.

This argument has been made by Bound and Johnson (1992) and Berman, Bound, and Griliches (1994), who identify the declining ratio of production to nonproduction workers *within industry* as the major determinant of changes in relative wages between skilled and unskilled workers. The fact that both the employment share and relative wages shifted in favor of nonproduction workers is evidence of biased technological change.

Work on the subject has been limited in three ways. First, most studies measure skills by the relative shares of production and nonproduction workers in total employment. This division does not constitute a particularly sharp distinction between skilled and unskilled jobs (Burtless, 1995, made a similar criticism). Second, because of available data, the analysis is generally confined to manufacturing, which accounted for only 15.3 percent of total employment in 1995. It may be precarious to make inferences to other sectors on the basis of results for manufacturing. Third, the measure of skill bias is indirect – that is, it is inferred from the rising share of nonproduction workers in conjunction with their rising relative earnings. Very few direct tests of skill-biased technological change exist.

Mincer (1991), using aggregate time-series data for the United States over the period 1963 to 1987, and Davis and Haltiwanger (1991), using data on production and nonproduction workers in U.S. manufacturing plants from 1963 to 1986, provided some of the early evidence to support this hypothesis. Mincer found that R&D expenditures per worker explained a significant amount of the year-to-year variation in educational wage differentials, while productivity growth was also a significant factor but had weaker explanatory power. Davis and Haltiwanger found that the employment shift toward nonproduction workers occurred disproportionately in large plants between 1977 and 1986, and this was accompanied by a sharp upgrading of worker education and occupational skill levels. Lawrence and Slaughter (1993) reached a similar conclusion, after eliminating international trade as a culprit in rising earnings inequality.

Katz and Murphy (1992) developed a model that accounted for changes in both the demand and supply of unskilled and skilled labor. Using CPS data over the period 1963 to 1987, they concluded that while the supply of college graduates fluctuated over time, there was a steady increase in the demand for skilled labor in the United States over the period. Goldin and Katz (2007a, 2007b) updated much of this work to cover the 1990s as well. They concluded that although skill-biased technological change generated rapid growth in the relative demand for more educated workers over the twentieth century, increases in the supply of skill from the rising educational attainment of the U.S. population more than kept pace for most of the century. However, since 1980, a sharp decline in the growth of skill supply occasioned by a slowdown in the rise of educational attainment was responsible for the rising returns to schooling over the 1980s and 1990s.

Berman, Bound, and Griliches (1994), using data from the Annual Survey of Manufactures over the period 1979 to 1987 for 450 manufacturing industries, found that over two-thirds of the increase in the ratio of nonproduction to production workers within manufacturing was due to the increased use of nonproduction workers within industry, and less than one-third to a reallocation of labor between industries. They inferred from this the existence of skill-biased technological change. Berman, Bound, and Machin (1998) also provided evidence that the increase in the share of skilled (nonproduction) workers in total employment occurred across a wide range of OECD countries. Yet, they also found that the trend decelerated in almost all OECD countries during the 1980s (with the notable exception of the United States). Allen (2001) concluded that technology variables accounted for 30 percent of the increase in the college wage premium over the period from 1979 to 1989. Juhn, Murphy, and Pierce (1993), using a time series of CPS data between 1963 and 1987, documented the rising variance of earnings within schooling and experience groups. They concluded that it was due to rising employer demand for and hence premium on unobservable skills.

In a more direct test of the effects of new technology on earnings, Adams (1997, 1999), using world patent and CPS earnings data for 24 manufacturing industries over the period 1979 to 1993, found that a rise in patenting activity was associated with a widening of the earnings gap between college and high school graduates. One direct test of skill-biased technological change was provided by Betts (1997) for Canadian manufacturing industries between 1962 and 1986. Using a cost share equation in which production and nonproduction workers were treated as separate inputs, he found evidence of bias away from production workers in 10 of the 18 industries used in the analysis.

A counter argument was presented by Howell (1997), who pointed out an important anomaly – namely, that while employment in low-skill jobs was declining relative to more skilled jobs, the proportion of low-wage workers was actually rising. He also found that the entire increase in the ratio of nonproduction to production workers since 1979 took place between 1980 and 1982; between 1983 and the early 1990s, the ratio remained essentially unchanged. Glynn (1998) found, after dividing U.S. workers into educational quartiles, that the employment position of the low-schooled workers sharply deteriorated between 1973 and 1981, when wage inequality grew slowly, but hardly declined at all after 1981, when wage inequality surged.

Mishel, Bernstein, and Schmitt (1997) argued that in order to explain the sharp rise in earnings inequality after 1979, the rate of bias in technological change must have accelerated during the 1980s. However, there is no evidence to this effect, and, indeed, the rate of conventionally measured productivity growth slowed down since the early 1970s. Murphy and Welch (1993b), after examining decennial Census of Population data on employment by occupation over the period 1940 to 1980 and CPS data for 1989 to 1991, found that there was a steady increase in the demand for skilled labor between 1940 and 1990 but no particular acceleration during the 1970s and 1980s. Juhn (1999), including 1990 Census of Population data, reported similar results.

In sum, while the skill-biased technological change has widespread support among labor economists as the dominant explanation of rising earnings inequality since the early 1970s, the evidence is still a bit mixed. I think that Goldin and Katz (2007a, 2007b) provide the most compelling evidence that skill-biased technological change has characterized the U.S. economy over almost the whole of the twentieth century and that the upsurge of inequality in the last three decades was most likely due to changes in the *supply* of college-educated workers rather than to an acceleration in the rate of skill-biased technological change.

11.3   THE IT "REVOLUTION"

Two relatively early papers have called the rapid introduction and diffusion of computers and associated IT a "technological revolution." Freeman (1987) termed this transformation as a new "techno-economic paradigm," based on microprocessor driven information technology. According to Freeman (1987, p. 51), IT has "emerged in the last couple of decades as a result of the convergence of a number of inter-related radical advances in the field of microelectronics, fibre optics, software engineering, communications and computer technology." He defined it "both as a new range of products and services, and as a technology which is capable of revolutionizing the processes of production and delivery of all other industries and services." David (1991) referred to "the paradigmatic shift" from electromechanical automation to information technologies.

One result of this technological revolution is a transformation of the skills required in the labor market. According to Freeman (1987, p. 66), the results of extensive research conducted by the Science Policy Research Unit (SPRU) of the University of Sussex showed that information technology "reduces the requirements for inspection and lower management (and clerical) employees, but increases the requirement for skilled systems designers and engineers and the level of responsibility for skills for maintenance."

Doeringer (1991, p. 166) wrote that "New information technologies may be particularly important for facilitating organizational adjustment" and referred to Osterman's (1986) finding that "a 10% increase in company computing power led to a 1% reduction in managerial employment." And in the plants that she observed, Zuboff (1988) noted that lower and middle managers were particularly "vulnerable" to deskilling and displacement by information technologies (pp. 284, 358–9). David (1991) argued that the shift to information technologies might entail major changes in the organizational structure of companies.

Wolff (2002) presented evidence on the "disruptive" effects of computerization on the labor market and the consequent structural adjustments that have ensued. On the basis of both time-series and pooled time-series, industry-level data for the period 1970 to 2000, the econometric results indicated that the coefficient of computerization as measured by the rate of growth of office, computing, and accounting equipment (OCA) per worker was statistically significant at the 1 percent level and that computerization was strongly and positively associated with the degree of occupational restructuring within an industry over time.

Several other papers have looked at the effects of computer usage or IT on earnings. Reich (1991) argued that U.S. workers were divided into two distinct groups – "symbolic analysts" who produce knowledge and new IT and ordinary clerical and production workers, who were outside the IT revolution. Globalization rewarded the first group of workers with increased earnings but depressed the earnings of the second group.

Krueger (1993) argued that pronounced declines in the cost of personal computers caused their widespread adoption in the workplace and shifted the production function in ways that favored more skilled workers. He also estimated the rate of return to computer usage at 15 to 20 percent. This finding was later challenged by DiNardo and Pischke (1997), who, using German household data, estimated a similar return to the use of pencils. They argued that computer use *per se* was not causing workers to earn a premium but rather was associated with unmeasured skills that were being rewarded in the workplace. Handel (1999) also showed that the returns to computers fell by half in cross-sectional estimates when other correlates, such as "reading news or magazine articles," were included as explanatory variables. However, in later work, Autor, Katz, and Krueger (1998) supplied new evidence that there was a substantial and increasing wage premium associated with computer use, despite a large growth in the number of workers with computer skills. However, Bresnahan (1999) argued, after a review of the pertinent literature, that there was no direct evidence that the actual use of IT (particularly personal computers) was associated with job enrichment. He concluded that "There is little complementarity between highly skilled workers and PC use, certainly not enough to affect skill demand."

11.4   GROWING INTERNATIONAL TRADE AND IMMIGRATION

The increasing trade liberalization, beginning in 1973 with the end of the Bretton Woods agreement and continuing through the 1980s and 1990s, is, perhaps, the second leading contender to explain rising inequality. Imports into the U.S. economy grew from 5.4 percent of GDP in 1970 to 14.0 percent in 2003, while the share of exports grew from 5.5 to 9.5 percent. According to standard trade theory, as trade increases, there is a growing tendency of factor prices – particularly, wages – to equalize across countries. This can take the form of rising wages among the United States' trading partners as well as declining wages among the U.S. labor force. As imports of manufactured products produced in low-income countries such as Indonesia, China, Thailand, Mexico, and Brazil increased, downward pressure was placed on the wages of unskilled and semiskilled workers in U.S. manufacturing industries. This process may explain both the falling average real wage of U.S. workers (see Chapter 2) as well as the increasing gap between blue-collar workers and professionals who work in industries such as law, medicine, education, and business services that are well shielded from imports.

A large literature has also accumulated on the effects of international trade on wage differentials. In the main, two different approaches have been used to analyze the linkage between trade and earnings inequality. The first is the factor content of trade model, advanced mainly by labor economists, which puts primary emphasis on the effective supplies of less skilled and more skilled labor (see, for example, Berman, Bound, and Griliches, 1994). Imports embody both unskilled and skilled labor, which when added to the domestic supply of these two factors, determines their effective supply. Because imports to the United States are generally less skill intensive than domestic production (see Wolff, 2003, for some empirical support), the opening of the domestic economy to imports augments the relative effective supply of low-skilled workers and lowers that of high-skilled workers and thereby puts downward pressure on the wages of the former relative to the latter.

The alternative view, advanced primarily by trade economists, derives from the Stolper–Samuelson theorem, an offshoot of the Heckscher–Ohlin model of international trade (see Wolff,

2003, for more discussion and associated references). The principal contention is that it is exogenous output prices, not endogenous factor quantities, that determine relative wages between skilled and unskilled workers (see, for example, Leamer, 1996). The Stolper–Samuelson theorem provides a direct linkage between factor prices and output prices which are set on the world market. The model shows that if two countries have the same technology and face the same (world) output prices, those two countries will have the same relative wage structure, regardless of the level of trade. Therefore, if trade with less skill-intensive under-developed countries is liberalized, the relative output price of the less skill-intensive products will fall in a country such as the United States, as will the relative wage paid to less-skilled workers. The movement of relative wages in the advanced country is thus linked to changes in relative output prices, not to the volume of trade.

Studies which emanate from the first theoretical approach, the factor content of trade, generally concluded that increased trade had a minimal effect on relative wage movements. The reason was that U.S. international trade was just too small to have much impact on wages or employment. Almost all of these studies estimated that the rising volume of imports in the United States accounted for no more than 20 percent of the shift in demand between low-skilled and high-skilled workers. Borjas, Freeman, and Katz (1992) estimated that rising trade flows explained at most 15 percent of the increase in the earnings differential between college graduates and high school graduates between 1980 and 1988. Bound and Johnson (1992), Bhagwati and Dehejia (1994), Krugman and Lawrence (1994), Bhagwati and Kosters (1994), Berman, Bound, and Griliches (1994), and Richardson (1995) also found very little effect of international trade on the divergence in compensation between more-skilled and less-skilled workers. However, Krugman and Lawrence (1994) did find that imports from developing countries significantly reduced employment of unskilled production workers in developed countries (see Freeman, 1995 and 2003, for reviews of these studies).

The notable exception is Wood (1991, 1994, 1998) who, using this approach, found large effects, with international trade accounting for as much as half of the decreased demand for low-skilled workers. Wood (1998, p. 57) concluded that "the main cause of the deteriorating situation of unskilled workers in developed countries has been the expansion of trade with developing countries." However, in later work, Wood and Anderson (1998) concluded that trade expansion during the 1980s had a greater effect on the acceleration in skill upgrading than on skill upgrading itself.

There is a wider range of estimates of the effects of international trade on relative wages in the United States devolving from the second approach. Lawrence and Slaughter (1993) found little effect of changes in output prices on the earnings structure during the 1980s. Sachs and Shatz (1994) constructed a special database detailing imports and exports of goods for 131 manufacturing industries and 150 trading partners. They estimated that the increase in net imports over the period 1978 to 1990 was associated with a drop of 7.2 percent in production jobs in manufacturing and only a 2.1 percent fall in nonproduction jobs in manufacturing. They surmised that these trends contributed to the widening wage gap between skilled and unskilled workers, though technology changes also played a role. Leamer (1996) estimated that trade effects were responsible for 40 percent of the decline in wages of less-skilled workers, but his model required long lags because he relied on price changes in the 1970s to account for changes of wages in the 1980s (also see Burtless, 1995, for reviews of the literature on trade and inequality).

Krugman (2000) offered one way of reconciling these two approaches. He argued that the relevant counterfactual to consider is what the prices of tradable goods and services (and therefore factor prices) would have been if trade had not increased. Using observed changes in commodity prices is inappropriate because such changes reflect a whole host of characteristics besides international trade. He proposed that the change in world prices depends critically on the *volume* of trade. If trade expanded less, than the impact on world prices would have been smaller. He then developed a CGE (computable general equilibrium) model of world prices on the basis of commonly accepted supply and demand elasticities with which to infer changes in the prices of tradables induced by trade expansion.

He concluded that world supply and demand would not have changed very much as long as trade increases were small relative to the world totals of such products. With the assumed price elasticities, prices would have had to adjust by only a small degree to absorb the resulting changes in world demand. Consequently, only a small proportion of actual changes in relative commodity prices and hence of factor prices reflected the expansion of world trade. Moreover, using simulated price changes in tradables yielded similar results even using the Stolper–Samuelson approach. However, in a more recent paper, Krugman (2008) was more agnostic with respect to his earlier conclusions and now argued that international factors may have had a larger effect on domestic wages in the 2000s than in the 1980s or 1990s.

There are several other studies that do not fit neatly into these two categories and that also investigated the effects of international trade on earnings. Murphy and Welch (1993a) found a close correspondence between changes in net imports over the 1967–1986 period among three industry groups, durables, nondurables, and services, and changes in employment patterns of less educated and more highly educated workers. In particular, they concluded that changes in trade patterns were largely responsible for the loss of low-skilled employment in U.S. manufacturing. Feenstra and Hanson (1996a, 1996b, 1999), using the NBER Manufacturing Productivity Database for the period 1979–1990, estimated in the first study that rising imports explained 15 to 33 percent of the increase in the wages of nonproduction workers relative to production workers during the 1980s in manufacturing, while in the third they found that foreign outsourcing of intermediate inputs and expenditures on high-technology capital, particularly computers, explained a substantial amount (a minimum of 35 percent) of the relative increase in the wages of nonproduction workers during the 1980s in manufacturing.

Borjas and Ramey (1994, 1995) argued that the impact of imports on wages and employment would be particularly pronounced in highly concentrated industries such as automobiles. Using SMSA-level data, they reported a strong negative correlation between the share of employment in high concentration import industries and the relative wages of less-skilled workers, both over time within cities and in a cross-section of cities. Bernard and Jensen (1997), using plant-level data, estimated that rising exports accounted for almost all of the rise in the wage differential between high-skilled and low-skilled workers.

A related argument is that immigration may have also increased the relative pool of low-skill workers over the last 20 years or so, likewise putting downward pressure on their relative wages. There is some evidence that locations which have a high number of immigrants are characterized by larger wage differentials between less-schooled and more-schooled workers than those with fewer immigrants. Using data from the 1980 Census of Population and from the Current Population Survey from 1980 to 1988, Borjas, Freeman, and Katz (1992) first reported that immigrants in 1980 were, on average, less educated than native-born male workers. For example, while 77 percent of native male workers had a high school diploma or better in 1980, only 60 percent of immigrants had the equivalent of a high school diploma. They argued that the immigration of male workers would lead to an increased supply of low-skill workers relative to high-skill workers. However, the effect on inequality was relatively small because the immigrant share of the labor force was not very large – varying from 6.9 percent in 1980 to 9.3 percent in 1988.

Later work on the subject has tended to confirm the Borjas, Freeman, and Katz (1992) findings that immigration had little effect on the overall distribution of wages. Altonji and Card (1991),

Butcher and Card (1991), Lalonde and Topel (1991), and Schoeni (1997) all found, for example, that immigration had little or no significant negative effect on natives' wages.

However, some studies found that immigration had sizable impacts on particular subpopulations of the United States. Borjas, Grogger, and Hansen (2006), using Census data from 1960 to 2000, estimated that the immigration influx between 1980 and 2000 accounted for as much as 20 to 60 percent of the decline of wages and 25 percent of the decline in employment among black males. Using CPS data, Orrenius and Zavodny (2007) found that an increase in the fraction of foreign-born workers in the labor force tended to lower the wages of native born in blue-collar occupations (but did not have an effect among natives in skilled occupations). A similar result was reported earlier by Camarota (1997) on the basis of data from the 1991 Current Population Survey. Borjas (2003) found that higher immigrant inflows within education and experience group, which Borjas used as a proxy for skill, have a negative association with the wages of native-born male workers, particularly for those who did not attend college.

11.5 THE SHIFT TO SERVICES

One of the notable changes in the composition of the labor force during the postwar period is the shift of jobs from goods-producing industries to services. The share of employment in services grew from 47 percent in 1947 to 74 percent in 2003. Almost all of the employment growth during the 1980s and 1990s occurred in the service sector (see Chapter 7 for more details). Some have argued that the dispersion of earnings is greater in services than goods-producing industries because of the greater mix of professional and managerial jobs with relatively low-skilled clerical and manual work, so that the employment shift will lead to rising inequality.

Bluestone and Harrison (1988a, 1988b), who were among the first to observe rising earnings inequality in the United States beginning in the 1970s, argued that the proximate cause of both rising inequality and the growth in low-wage employment was the deindustrialization of the U.S. economy, particularly the shift of workers out of high-wage manufacturing and towards low-wage service industries.

Various estimates of the effect of structural shifts in employment have been offered. Grubb and Wilson (1989), using Census of Population data for 1960 and 1980 and 14 economic sectors, calculated that almost two-thirds of the overall increase in earnings inequality (measured by the Theil coefficient) over this period could be explained by shifts in the sectoral composition of employment. However, Blackburn (1990), using CPS data and 41 industry classification, estimated that at most 20 percent of the increase in male earnings inequality between 1967 and 1985 could be attributed to the changing industrial composition of the labor force. Blackburn, Bloom and Freeman (1990), using a 43-industry classification, also estimated that about 20 percent of the increase in the earnings differential between white male college graduates and high school graduates was accounted for by shifts of employment among these industries.

Katz and Murphy (1992), dividing employment into 50 industries and three broad occupational groups, found that shifts in employment among both industries and occupations within those industries clearly favored more-educated workers relative to less-educated ones over the period 1947–1987. The demand for more-educated (and experienced) workers within industry/occupation cell accelerated during the 1980s, especially within manufacturing. Karoly and Klerman (1994), using regional data for the United States, estimated that between 15 and 20 percent of the rise in male wage inequality between 1973 and 1988 was due to shifts in the industrial composition of the workforce. Murphy and Welch (1993a) likewise attributed only 16 percent of the overall change in the demand for college-educated workers to changes in industrial shares.

Bernard and Jensen (2000) investigated inequality at the state level within the United States. They found that increases in inequality were strongly correlated with changes in industrial mix, particularly the loss of durable manufacturing jobs. Blum (2008) found an even larger effect. Using aggregate data on employment by industry in the United States over the 1970 to 1996 period, he calculated that about 60 percent of the relative increase in wages of skilled workers over this period could be attributed to changes in the sectoral composition of the economy. He argued that in essence capital was reallocated to sectors where it was relatively complementary to skilled workers.

Gittleman (1994) estimated that about one-third of the rising wage premium to a college education during the 1980s was attributable to shifts in occupational demand. Groshen (1991b), using a special panel survey of firms in Cleveland, Cincinnati, and Pittsburgh, also found that during the 1980s the main factor explaining rising inequality was the widening of occupational wage differentials.

11.6   INSTITUTIONAL FACTORS

Two institutional trends, in particular, have achieved prominence in the literature on rising inequality. The first of these is declining unionization. The proportion of the workforce represented by unions peaked in 1954, at 25.4 percent, and at 34.7 percent as a fraction of the nonfarm labor force. After 1954, the trend was downward, and by 2003 only 12.9 percent were union members. Unions have historically negotiated collective bargaining agreements with narrow wage differentials between different types of jobs. This is one reason why the dispersion of earnings in manufacturing has tended to be lower than that of service industries. The argument is that the decline in unions has led to widening differentials in the overall wage structure.

The second factor is the declining minimum wage in real terms. The federal minimum wage has fallen by 34 percent in real terms between its peak in 1968 and 2003.[1] This has put downward pressure on the wages of unskilled workers and may account, in part, for the growing wage disparities between unskilled and skilled workers and the decline in the average real wage since 1973. Gordon (1996) argued that the change in unionization and the minimum wage was part of a broader range of institutional changes in the 1980s in which U.S. corporate managers exerted increasing pressure on workers, partly in reaction to rising international competition.

Freeman (1993) argued that the decline of unions in the U.S. economy and/or the decline in the real value of the minimum wage since the late 1960s removed the "safety net" supporting the wage level of unskilled workers, thereby allowing it to fall. Blackburn, Bloom, and Freeman (1990) estimated that as much as 20 percent of the rising differential of earnings between college graduates and other educational groups between 1980 and 1988 might be due to de-unionization. He also found that changes in the minimum wage, on the other hand, had a minimal impact. Both Freeman (1993) and Card (1992) estimated that between 10 and 20 percent of the increased wage inequality among men was due to the decline in unionization.

Horrigan and Mincy (1993) attributed considerably under a third of the declining share of earnings received by the bottom quintile of wage earnings to the fall in the minimum wage. DiNardo, Fortin, and Lemieux (1996), using a semiparametric estimation technique on CPS data from 1979 to 1988, concluded that the decline in the real value of the minimum wage over this period accounted for up to 25 percent of the rise in male wage inequality and up to 30 percent of the rise in female wage inequality. Fortin and Lemieux (1997) estimated that about 30 percent of rising wage rate dispersion in the United States was due to the decline in the real value of the minimum wage. Lee (1999), using regional data drawn from the CPS together with regional minimum wage levels over the 1980s, concluded that the decline in the real minimum wage over the period accounted for as much as 70 percent of the rise in wage dispersion in the lower tail of the wage distribution among men and from 70 to 100 percent among women.

Card (2001), using CPS data for the period from 1973 to 1993, concluded that the decline in union membership accounted for 15 to 20 percent of the rise in male wage inequality. On the other hand, trends in unionization explained very little of the rise in female wage inequality. Card also found that the rise of unionization in the public sector substantially retarded the growth in wage inequality in this sector.

There is also cross-national evidence that points to the importance of unionization and the minimum wage in explaining inequality differences. Katz, Loveman, and Blanchflower (1995) found in a comparison of changes in wage inequality in the United States, Great Britain, Japan, and France, that in the case of France sharp rises in the national minimum wage and the strength of French labor unions prevented wage differentials from expanding between 1967 and 1987. Blau and Kahn (1996), using cross-national data for OECD countries, attributed a large part of the inter-country differences in wage inequality among men to differences in unionization patterns.

DiNardo and Lemieux (1997) compared the rise of wage inequality in Canada and the United States and estimated that two-thirds of the faster rise of inequality in the latter over the period 1981–1988 was due to a more severe decline in the rate of unionization. Koeniger, Leonardi, and Nunziata (2007) examined the effects of differences of labor market institutions such as unemployment insurance, unions, and minimum wages among 11 OECD countries and concluded that such institutional differences accounted for a large part of the change in wage inequality among these countries after controlling for time and country effects. Lemieux (2007) also concluded after an examination of several OECD countries that de-unionization played an important role in explaining the rise of wage inequality among English-speaking countries such as the United States.

11.7 OUTSOURCING AND DOWNSIZING

Another suspect is the corporate restructuring that occurred during the 1980s and 1990s. This process took two forms. First, permanent employees were replaced by part-time, temporary, and "leased" employees. Second, a number of important corporate functions such as maintenance, cafeteria services, legal services, and data processing that were traditionally performed by in-house employees were outsourced (substituted for) by purchasing these operations from other companies. Both processes have reduced the relative number of permanent employees in large corporations. Corporate employees have traditionally enjoyed high wages, high benefits, job security, career-ladder type jobs, and good working conditions. This set of job characteristics is referred to as an internal or primary labor market (see Doeringer & Piore, 1971). In contrast, wages tend to be low in secondary jobs found in part-time employment and small businesses. The shift of employment out of the primary labor force to the secondary labor market may have been another factor accounting for rising income inequality.

One paper that looked at this issue is Groshen and Levine (1998), who argued that declines in the extent of internal labor markets within U.S. industry might have led to both phenomena, since internal labor markets keep pay structure within a firm equitable and help maintain high wages. However, using data from 228 large Midwestern employers over the past four decades, they found no evidence of a weakening of internal labor markets over this period.

11.8 CHANGES IN THE DISTRIBUTION OF SCHOOLING AND ABILITY

There is an extensive literature dating back to Becker (1964, 1975) and Mincer (1974) which emphasize the importance of schooling and human capital as determinants of earnings. Another book of the same period is Freeman (1976) who argued that an oversupply of college graduates appeared during the 1970s due to both increased college enrollment resulting from the baby-boom generation coming of college age and a slackening of growth in industries that employed college-educated manpower. The human capital approach was criticized by Jencks (1972 and 1979), who stressed the importance of family background as a factor influencing both schooling attainment and success in the labor market.

Hernstein and Murray (1994) argued that genetic differences are the primary cause of differences in intelligence and earnings, particularly racial difference, though their evidence was relatively weak. Danziger and Gottschalk (1995) looked into causes of increasing poverty and inequality, particularly the role of economic growth and changes in the racial/ethnic composition of the population and family structure. They concluded that demographic changes played little role in explaining rising inequality in the 1970s and 1980s. Frank and Cook (1995) argued that the increasing prevalence of winner-take-all markets was the primary factor accounting for the increasing concentration of income at the very top of the income distribution.

Several other works have pointed to changes in schooling patterns or skill levels as proximate causes of rising inequality. Bishop (1991) argued that declines in the quality of U.S. education at the primary and secondary level, as evidenced by falling SAT scores, may have lowered the marketability of low-skill workers and therefore their relative wages. However, Jencks and Phillips (1998) found no evidence of a decline in test scores among 17 year olds between 1971 and 1986. Using data from the National Assessment of Educational Progress, they reported that both reading and math test scores had risen, both overall and among white and black students separately.

Blackburn and Neumark (1993) found that the rise in the return to education was concentrated among people with both high education and high ability. Levy, Murnane, and Willet (1995) used math ability at the end of high school as measure of cognitive ability and estimated that between 38 and 100 percent of the increase in the return to education for 24 year olds from 1978 to 1986 can be attributed to increasing returns to ability.

Grogger and Eide (1996) identified that as much as one-quarter of the rise in the male college wage premium in the 1980s was due to a shift away from low-skill college subjects such as education toward high-skill subjects, such as engineering. For women, the rise in the college premium was largely a result of the increase in the returns to math ability. However, Heckman and Vytlacil (2001), using nonparametric econometric techniques on data drawn from the National Longitudinal Sample of Youths (NLSY), found little evidence that the increase in the return to education was centered among those with the highest ability scores.

Bluestone (1990) called attention to the apparent inconsistency between rising earnings inequality and declining dispersion of schooling. He reported, on the basis of CPS data, that while wage inequality (measured by the variance of the logarithm of earnings) among full-time, full-year workers increased from 0.56 in 1963 to 0.63 in 1987, the coefficient of variation of their schooling levels fell from 0.27 to 0.20.

11.9   TIME TRENDS IN KEY EXPLANATORY VARIABLES

We next consider time trends in the major explanatory variables that have been proposed to account for rising earnings inequality in the United States. We look at trends in income inequality in the United States in the postwar period (see Figure 11.1). The first, based on the March Supplement to the Current Population Survey, is for family income and is the longest consistent series available, running from 1947 to 2003.[2] Inequality shows a slight downward trend from 1947 to 1968, with the Gini coefficient falling by 7 percent. The series bottoms out in 1968 and then

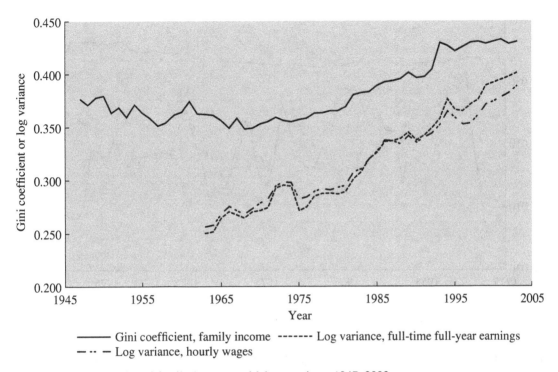

Figure 11.1 legend:
——— Gini coefficient, family income ------- Log variance, full-time full-year earnings
— ·· — Log variance, hourly wages

Figure 11.1 Inequality of family income and labor earnings, 1947–2003

rises thereafter, with the rate of increase accelerating after 1976. The 2003 Gini coefficient is 0.430, 0.082 points above its 1968 value.[3]

The other two series are for labor earnings, which are shorter in duration, running from 1963 to 2003. The first of these is the variance of the logarithm of earnings for full-time, full-year workers and the second is the variance of the logarithm of hourly wages. Both series are from Autor, Katz, and Kearny (2005) and are based on the March Current Population Survey.[4] Both show time trends very similar to the Gini coefficient for family income, rising from 0.25 in 1963 to 0.40 in 2003 in the case of the former and from 0.26 to 0.39 for the latter. The correlation coefficient between the Gini coefficient for family income and the log variance of earnings is 0.97 in the case of full-time, full-year workers and 0.96 for hourly earnings.

We are primarily interested in the inequality of labor earnings in this analysis. Unfortunately, the longest consistent time series for these series begins only in 1963 and does not cover the slight downward drift in inequality between the late 1940s and the late 1960s. However, because the two labor earnings inequality series are almost perfectly correlated with the family income inequality series, we shall use the latter in the regression analysis.

As discussed in Section 11.2, a leading argument is that skill-biased technological change is the major cause of rising earnings inequality. Figure 11.2 shows time trends in both labor productivity growth and total factor productivity (TFP) growth. TFP growth is defined as:

$$TFPGRTH_t = dY_t/Y_t - \alpha dL_t/L_t - (1 - \alpha)dK_t/K_t \qquad (11.1)$$

where Y_t is GDP (in 2000 dollars) at time t, L_t is the total labor input, K_t is the capital input, and α is the average wage share in over the period. The labor input is measured by persons engaged

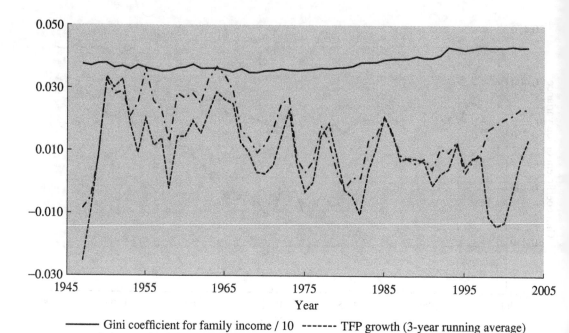

- Gini coefficient for family income / 10 ------- TFP growth (3-year running average)
- - · - · Labor productivity growth (3-year running average)

Figure 11.2   Family income inequality, labor productivity growth, and TFP growth, 1947–2003

in production (PEP) and the capital input by the fixed nonresidential net capital stock (in 2000 dollars). A second index of TFP growth was also used, with full-time equivalent employees (FTEE) as the measure of labor input. See Appendix 11.1 for details on data sources and methods.

These two technology indicators trend downward from the high growth period of 1947–1973 (annual growth rates of 2.4 and 1.7 percent per year, respectively) to the productivity slowdown of 1973–1979 (annual growth rates of 0.5 and 0.4 percent per year, respectively) before recovering in the 1979–2003 period (annual growth rates of 1.2 and 0.9 percent per year, respectively). Not surprisingly, the productivity growth rates are negatively correlated with income inequality but the correlations are very low (in absolute value): −0.21 and −0.07, respectively (see Table 11.1).

The second set of technological indicators are measures of R&D activity – the ratio of total R&D expenditures to GDP and the number of scientists and engineers engaged in R&D per 1,000 employees. As shown in Figure 11.3, these two variables track much better with movements in income inequality than does productivity growth. The ratio of total R&D to GDP rose between the early 1950s and the 1960s and then fell in the 1970s before rising again in the 1980s and 1990s. Its correlation with family income inequality is 0.29. In contrast, the number of scientists and engineers engaged in R&D per 1,000 employees increased between the late 1950s and early 1960s, leveled out and then fell in the early 1970s before rising sharply after 1976. It has a much higher correlation with income inequality −0.87.

Another potential source of bias in technological change might derive from investment in equipment and machinery – particularly computers – as we discussed in Section 11.3. Figure 11.4 shows time trends in both investment in equipment per worker and investment in OCA per worker. Equipment investment per PEP remained relatively flat between 1947 and 1961 and then tripled between 1961 and 2003. It is highly correlated with family income inequality, at 0.78.

Table 11.1 Correlation coefficients between the Gini coefficient for family income and technological, structural, and institutional variables

Variable	Period	Correlation with Gini coefficient for family income
A. Technology variables		
1. Labor productivity (GDP in 1992$/PEP) growth (3-year running average)	1947–2003	−0.21
2. TFP growth (3-year running average)	1947–2003	−0.07
3. Ratio of total industry R&D expenditures to GDP	1953–2003	0.29
4. Scientists and engineers per FTEE	1957–2003	0.87
B. Investment variables		
5. Equipment investment/PEP	1947–2003	0.78
6. Office, computing, & accounting machinery (OCA)/PEP	1947–2003	0.81
7. OCA plus communication equipment (OCACM)/PEP	1947–2003	0.84
C. Trade and immigration variables		
8. Total exports/GDP	1947–2003	0.74
9. Total imports/GDP	1947–2003	0.74
10. Total exports plus imports/GDP	1947–2003	0.75
11. Foreign-born workers/Total labor force	1950–2003	0.94
D. Structural and institutional variables		
12. Union members/Total labor force	1947–2003	−0.83
13. Minimum wage (2000$)	1947–2003	−0.50
14. Minimum wage/Average hourly wage	1947–2003	−0.66
E. Human capital variables		
15. Variance of schooling	1947–2000	−0.78
16. Rate of return to schooling	1956–2000	0.64
17. Variance of schooling × rate of return to schooling squared	1956–2000	−0.23
F. Control variables		
18. Civilian unemployment rate	1947–2003	0.27
19. Female-headed families/Total families	1947–2003	0.78
20. Property income/Total personal income	1947–2003	0.84

Investment in OCA per PEP grew slowly from 1947 to 1977 and then surged at an incredible pace thereafter, increasing by a factor of 221 between 1977 and 2003. It is apparent that the huge growth of OCA investment occurred after the upswing in income inequality. Despite this, OCA investment per employee is even more strongly correlated with family income inequality than is total equipment investment per worker – a coefficient of 0.81.[5]

A fourth factor, shown in Figure 11.5, measures trade intensity. The ratio of the sum of exports plus imports to GDP, after increasing slightly from 7.3 percent in 1950 to 9.4 percent in 1970, shot up to 23.5 percent in 2003. There is a sharp break in this series in the early 1970s, almost coincident with the rise in income inequality. The correlation of income inequality with the ratio of the sum of exports plus imports to GDP is very high, 0.75.[6] A fifth variable is the share of foreign-born workers in the total U.S. labor force.[7] It tends to track rather closely with time trends

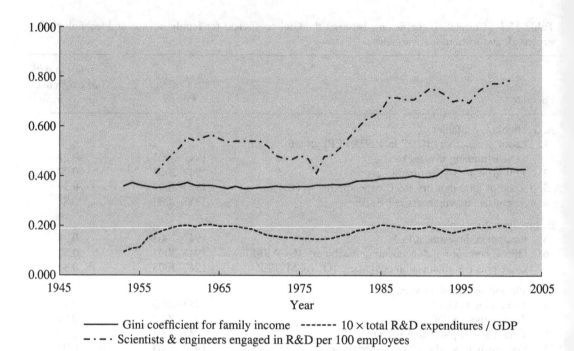

Figure 11.3   Family income inequality and R&D activity, 1953–2003

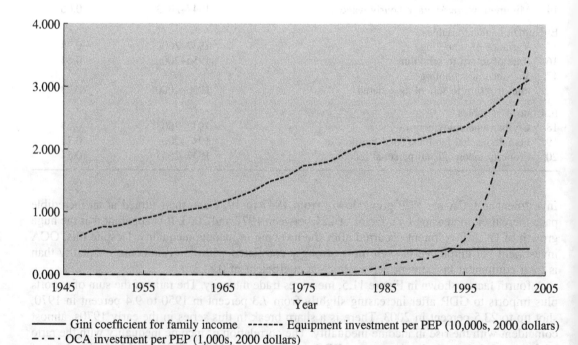

Figure 11.4   Family income inequality and investment in equipment and OCA per PEP, 1947–2003

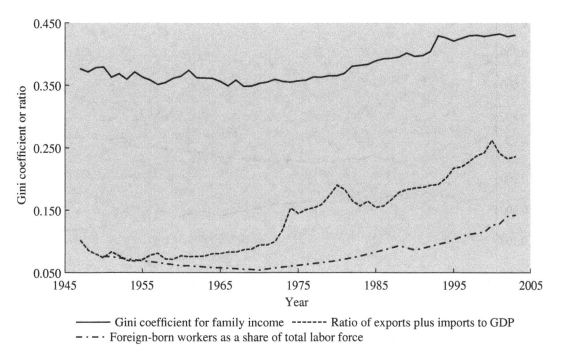

——— Gini coefficient for family income   ------- Ratio of exports plus imports to GDP
— · — · Foreign-born workers as a share of total labor force

Figure 11.5   Family income inequality, international trade intensity, and immigration, 1947–2003

in inequality, falling from 7.6 percent in 1950 to a low of 5.4 percent in 1970 and then rising to 14.1 percent in 2003. Its correlation with income inequality is extremely high, 0.94.

A sixth variable, shown in Figure 11.6, is the overall unionization rate. The proportion of the workforce represented by unions peaked in 1954, at 25.4 percent, and then diminished almost continuously to 12.9 percent in 2003. On the surface, the timing was different from the trend in inequality, which began its upward spiral in the late 1960s. Still, the correlation between the two series is very strong, −0.83. Another variable is the minimum wage in constant dollars, which peaked in 1968, the same year as income inequality bottomed out. The correlation between the two series is −0.50. A related variable is the ratio of the minimum wage to average hourly earnings. This also peaked in 1968, and its correlation with family income inequality is −0.66.

The next variable, shown in Figure 11.7, is the variance of schooling of adults 25 years or older, computed from CPS data. As discussed in Chapter 8, according to the standard human capital model, the variance of logarithm of earnings should be proportional to the product of the variance of schooling and the rate of return to schooling squared. This can be shown as follows. The basic earnings function of the human capital model is given by:

$$\ln E_S = c + rS$$

where $\ln$ is the natural logarithm, E_S is the annual earning of a worker with S years of schooling, r is the rate of return to schooling, and c is a constant. Since the logarithm of earnings is proportional to the level of schooling, then the log variance of earnings is a linear function of the variance of schooling:

$$\ln (\text{Var } E) = r^2 (\text{Var } S) \tag{11.2}$$

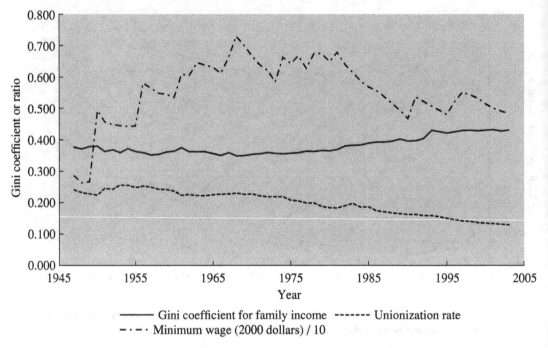

Figure 11.6   Family income inequality, the unionization rate, and the minimum wage, 1947–2003

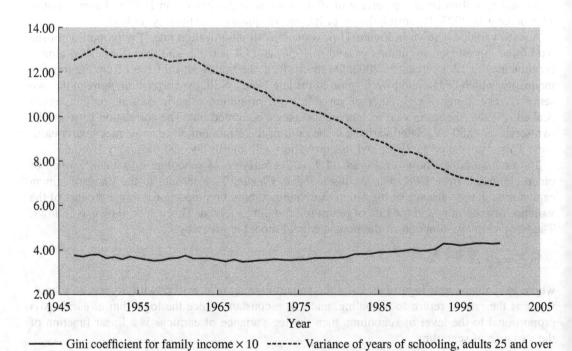

Figure 11.7   Family income inequality and the variance of schooling, 1947–2000

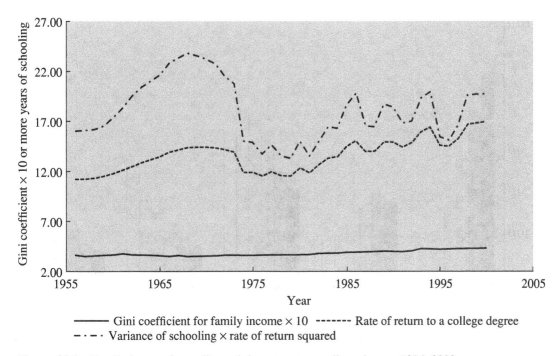

Figure 11.8 Family income inequality and the return to a college degree, 1956–2000

where Var is the variance, and r is the rate of return to schooling. As we discussed in Section 3.3, the log variance is often used directly as a measure of income inequality.

The variance of schooling has trended sharply downward since 1947, falling by 48 percent from its peak value of 13.1 in 1950 to 6.9 in 2000. The simple correlation between this series and the Gini coefficient for family income is −0.78.

However, evidence from numerous studies cited above indicates that the return to schooling rose since the early 1970s. Figure 11.8 shows a series for the rate of return to a college education from 1956 to 2000.[8] The rate of return does show a considerable rise from 1975 to 2000, from 11.9 to 16.9 percent. However, the return to a college education also climbed sharply from 11.2 percent in 1956 to its earlier peak of 14.4 percent in 1970 and then fell to 11.9 percent in 1974 before rising again. Nonetheless, the simple correlation between the rate of return to college and the Gini coefficient for family income is 0.64.[9] However, the correlation between the Gini coefficient for family income and the more critical variable, the square of the rate of return to college multiplied by the variance of schooling is *still* negative, −0.23.

As noted above, the dispersion in years of schooling among the adult population 25 years and over showed a dramatic decline between 1950 and 2000. The coefficient of variation plummeted by 19 percent from 1950 to 1970 and by another 32 percent from 1970 to 2000. Figure 11.9 shows the size distribution of schooling over the period 1950 to 2000. As is evident, not only has the dispersion of schooling fallen over the postwar period but its mean level has risen. The fraction of adults age 25 and over with less than 4 years of high school plunged from 66 percent in 1950 to 15 percent in 2000 and the proportion with 4 years of more of college skyrocketed from 6 to 27 percent. Over this period, moreover, the schooling distribution shifted from being skewed to the right to being skewed to the left.

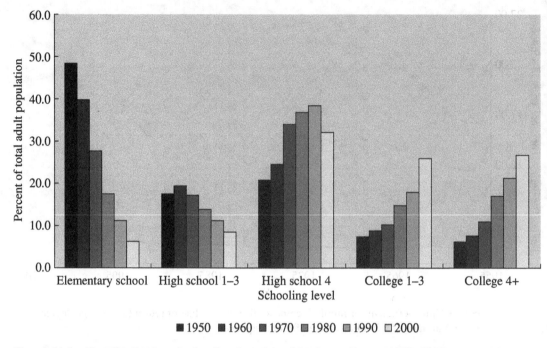

Figure 11.9   Size distribution of schooling for adults, 25 years and over, 1950–2000

While schooling grew steadily less unequal over these years, income inequality showed a different course. The Gini coefficient for family income inequality, after declining by 7 percent between 1950 and 1970, increased by 22 percent from 1970 to 2000 (Figure 11.8). Over the entire 1950–2000 period, the Gini coefficient for income inequality rose by 13 percent, while the coefficient of variation of schooling dropped by 45 percent (and the variance of schooling by 48 percent).

Moreover, in the regression analysis presented in the next section, we control for three factors that may account for much (if not most) of the deviation between income and earnings inequality. The first is the unemployment rate, which controls, in part, for the fact that some families receive zero labor income. Not surprisingly, its movement was cyclical over time, whereas family inequality trended rather continuously upward since the late 1960s. As a result, its correlation with family income inequality is rather low, only 0.27 (see Table 11.1). The second control variable is the number of female-headed families as a percentage of total families. It is included since this group has historically had the lowest level of family income of any family type, and a large part of its income has taken the form of government transfers. Its share has trended almost continuously upward since 1959, from 10 percent, to 19 percent in 2003. As result, it is strongly correlated with family income inequality – a correlation coefficient of 0.78.

The third variable in this group is personal property income, defined as the sum of rent, dividends, interest, and one-half of proprietors' income, as a share of total personal income. It is included, because it comprises part of the difference between family income and labor earnings (the other major part is government transfer income). Its time path is somewhat similar to family income inequality. This variable shows a slightly downward trend from 1947 to 1972 (from 21 to 18 percent) followed by an upward trajectory to 24 percent in 2003. As a result, its correlation coefficient with family income inequality is very high –0.84.

11.10 ECONOMETRIC RESULTS

To understand the effects of these various factors on trends in income inequality, I next turn to multivariate regression for the 1947–2000 period. The general estimating equation is given by:

$$GINIFAM_t = \beta_0 + \beta_1\ TFPGRT_t + \beta_2\ RDGDP_t + \beta_3\ EQPXINVPEP_t + \beta_4\ OCAINVPEP_t$$
$$+ \beta_5\ EXPGDP_t + \beta_6\ IMPGDP_t + \beta_7\ UNION_t + \beta_8\ MINWAGE_t$$
$$+ \beta_9\ IMMIGRANT_t + \beta_{10}\ VARSCHOOL_t \times SCHOOLRETSQ_t + u_t \qquad (11.3)$$

where $GINIFAM_t$ is the Gini coefficient for family income in year t, $TFPGRT_t$ is TFP growth in year t, $RDGDP_t$ is the ratio of R&D expenditures to GDP in year t, $EQPXINVPEP_t$ is investment in the total net stock of equipment and machinery less OCA per worker (PEP) in year t, $OCAINVPEP_t$ is investment in the net stock of OCA per worker in year t, $EXPGDP_t$ is the ratio of exports to GDP in year t, $IMPGDP_t$ is the ratio of imports to GDP in year t, $UNION_t$ is the unionization rate in year t, $MINWAGE_t$ is the minimum wage (in constant dollars) in year t, $IMMIGRANT_t$ is the ratio of immigrant workers to total employment in year t, $VARSCHOOL_t$ is the variance of schooling in year t, $SCHOOLRETSQ_t$ is square of the rate of return to schooling in year t, and u_t is a stochastic error term.[10]

With regard to the predictions for these variables, the literature cited above would suggest that, first of all, inequality should be positively associated with the technology and investment variables. Second, many researchers have argued that export or import competition may increase the wage gap between high- and low-paid workers, so that income inequality may be positively related to both export and import intensity. Third, since unions typically negotiate contracts involving relatively tight wage structures, then the argument here is that wage dispersion should be negatively associated with the degree of unionization.

Fourth, if an increase in the minimum wage raises the wages of the lowest paid workers (without affecting those of high-paid workers), then wage dispersion should be negatively associated with the minimum wage (in constant dollars). Fifth, if immigrants compete directly against low-wage U.S. workers, then inequality should be positively correlated with the share of immigrant workers in the total labor force. Sixth, inequality should be positively associated with the variable, the product of the variance of schooling, and the rate of return to schooling squared, as noted above. Seventh, as noted in the previous section, also included are control variables for the unemployment rate, the share of property income in total income, and the number of female-headed households as a share of total households.

A word should be added about lagged versus contemporaneous effects. It is likely that technological change affects wage dispersion with a lag, since it may take time for the job structure or pay structure to react to changes in the technology in use. A similar argument may apply to changes in international competition. As a result, *TFPGRT, RDGDP, EQPXOCAGRT, OCAGRT, INVOCAPEP, INVEQPXOCAPEP, EXPGDP*, and *IMPGDP* have been entered with a one-year lag.[11] On the other hand, it is likely that the minimum wage level, the distribution of employment between services and goods producers, the variance of schooling, and the return to schooling, as well as the unemployment rate, the property income share, and the share of female-headed households affect current income immediately. As a result, these variables are entered contemporaneously. The effect of the unionization rate is a bit ambiguous, because it may affect income concurrently or with a lag, so both forms were tried. The best fit is provided by the contemporaneous union rate.

Table 11.2 shows the results. With regard to the technology and investment variables, the most consistently significant one is OCA investment per worker lagged one period. The coefficient of

Table 11.2 Time-series regressions of family income inequality on technological, structural, and institutional variables, 1947–2000

Independent variables	Specification							
	(1)	(2)	(3)	(4)	(5)	(6)	(7)	(8)
Constant	0.422** (14.70)	0.445** (12.03)	0.435** (15.51)	0.425** (14.42)	0.460** (12.73)	0.439** (13.45)	0.459** (19.14)	0.448** (18.03)
Unemployment rate	0.214* (2.55)	0.211* (2.49)	0.203* (2.35)	0.244** (2.59)	0.233* (2.68)	.208* (2.39)	0.152 (1.49)	0.155# (1.69)
Unionization rate	-0.290* (2.33)	-0.354** (2.57)	-0.302** (2.68)	-0.271* (2.26)	-0.374** (2.83)	-0.260* (2.04)	-0.315** (3.49)	-0.326** (2.52)
OCA investment per worker (1 period lag)	0.023* (2.35)	0.027** (2.64)	0.027** (2.79)	0.026** (2.73)	0.027** (2.78)	0.024* (2.35)	0.032** (4.03)	0.031** (3.89)
Non-OCA equipment investment per worker (1 period lag)		-0.056 (0.97)						
Minimum wage (1995$)			-0.236 (1.32)	-0.225 (1.24)	-0.186 (1.03)	-0.194 (1.07)	-0.841** (3.15)	-0.832** (3.03)
TFP growth (3-year running average)								
Ratio of exports to GDP in current $ (1 period lag)				0.122 (1.18)	-0.189 (1.29)			
Variance of schooling						-0.141 (0.44)		
Variance of schooling × Rate of return to schooling squared							0.064 (1.27)	0.083 (1.41)
R^2	0.93	0.93	0.93	0.93	0.93	0.93	0.95	0.95
Adjusted R^2	0.92	0.93	0.93	0.92	0.93	0.92	0.94	0.95
Standard error	0.0063	0.0062	0.0061	0.0062	0.0062	0.0063	0.0060	0.0060
Durbin–Watson	1.94	1.96	2.04	2.11	2.06	2.06	1.93	1.95
Sample size	54	54	54	54	54	54	45	45
Period	1947–00	1947–00	1947–00	1947–00	1947–00	1947–00	1956–00	1956–00
Est. Tech.	AR(1)	AR(1)	AR(1)	AR(1)	AR(1)	AR(1)	AR(1)	IV,AR(1)

The dependent variable is the Gini coefficient for family income inequality (GINIFAM). The absolute value of the t-statistic is in parentheses below the coefficient. See Appendix 11.1 for data sources and methods.

AR(1): Autoregressive process, First-order: $u_t = e_t + r_t u_{t-1}$, where u_t is the error term of the original equation and e_t is a stochastic term assumed to be identically and independently distributed. IV: Instrumental variables. The instruments are as follows: (i) unemployment rate; (ii) investment in OCA per PEP; (iii) variance of schooling; (iv) minimum wage in 1995 dollars; and (v) ratio of exports to GDP.

* Significant at the 10 percent level. * Significant at the 5 percent level. ** Significant at the 1 percent level.

Significant at the 10 percent level.

this variable is positive and is significant at the 1 percent level in six of the eight cases shown and at the 5 percent level in the other two.[12] The coefficient of non-OCA equipment investment per worker is negative but not significant (Specification 2).

Both the annual rate of TFP growth (Specification 4) and the annual rate of labor productivity growth (result not shown) have positive coefficients but are not significant. Industry R&D as a share of GDP and the number of full-time equivalent scientists and engineers engaged in R&D per employee have positive coefficients but are not significant (results not shown).

Among the trade variables, the best fit is provided by exports as a percent of GDP, which has a negative coefficient but one that is not significant (Specification 5). The other trade variables, including imports as a share of GDP and the sum of exports and imports as a share of GDP, all have negative coefficients but are not significant. Likewise, the share of immigrant workers in total employment has a positive coefficient but is not statistically significant.

With regard to the institutional and structural variables, the most significant is the unionization rate, which has the predicted negative sign and is significant at the 1 or 5 percent level in seven of the eight cases and at the 10 percent level in the other. The minimum wage in constant dollars also has the predicted negative sign although its coefficient is not significant in the first six specifications but is significant at the 1 percent level in the last two. The reason for the latter result is the shorter time period used in the regression – 1956 to 2000, instead of 1947 to 2000.[13]

Among the control variables, the most consistent one is the civilian unemployment rate. It is included in the specification to control for the cyclical effects of the economy on inequality – inequality normally rises during a recession and declines during a recovery. The coefficient has the predicted positive sign and is significant at the 1 or 5 percent level in six of the eight cases and at the 10 percent level in a seventh.

With the exception of the unionization rate and the unemployment rate, the other structural and control variables are not statistically significant. The coefficients of both the number of female-headed families as a percentage of total families and personal property income as a share of total personal income have the predicted positive sign but neither is significant. Several other variables were also introduced. First, a positive coefficient is expected for the ratio of employment in service sectors to total employment, because earnings inequality in service sectors is in the main greater than earnings inequality in goods industries. The coefficient is found to be positive but not significant. Second, a positive coefficient is also expected for the ratio of white-collar to total employment, since mean earnings and the dispersion of earnings are greater among white-collar than blue-collar workers. The coefficient of this variable is likewise positive but is not significant. Third, the coefficient of the number of part-time workers as a percent of total employment is also not significant, with a value essentially equal to zero. The fourth is the change in the share of women in the labor force. The argument is that because of the increasing labor force participation of women and because of the historically lower wages of women, the increased share of women in the labor force may lead to an increase in the overall variance of earnings. However, this variable did not prove significant.

The results for OCA investment per worker, the unionization rate, and the unemployment rate are robust over a wide range of alternative specifications. Only a few of the regression equations are shown in Table 11.2.

The variance of schooling is added in Specification 6. Its coefficient is (perversely) negative but not statistically significant. The negative coefficient is extremely robust over a wide range of alternative specifications. In Specification 7, the theoretically preferred variable, the product of the variance of schooling and the rate of return to schooling squared, is included. The coefficient of this variance has the predicted positive sign but is not significant.

Because much of the theoretical work on rising earnings inequality (such as the skill-biased technological change hypothesis) posits that the same forces that have caused earnings inequality to increase have also caused the return to schooling to rise, it is likely that the rate of return to schooling is an endogenous variable. Therefore, specification 8 uses an instrumental variable (IV) estimation procedure, with the minimum wage in constant dollars and the ratio of exports to GDP as instruments in place of the rate of return variable.[14] The results are virtually identical to those of Specification 7, though now the coefficient of variance of schooling multiplied by the rate of return to schooling squared has a slightly higher coefficient value and t-statistic.

The goodness of fit for the eight equations shown in Table 11.2 is quite high – R^2 statistics ranging from 0.93 to 0.95 and adjusted-R^2 statistics from 0.92 to 0.94. The Durbin–Watson statistic is in the acceptable range – very close to 2.0.[15] It is also of note that the regression results for the various variables used in the analysis remain very robust among alternative specifications, including the use of lagged values for both the investment, technology, and trade variables.

To gauge the quantitative significance of this set of variables in accounting for changes in inequality over time, a growth accounting exercise (results not shown) was performed. The sample was divided into two periods – 1947–1968, when inequality declined, and 1968–2000, when inequality grew. The contribution of each factor is determined as the product of its regression coefficient and the change in the value of the variable over the period. Three different specifications were used.

Between 1947 and 1968, the Gini coefficient declined from 37.6 to 34.8 or by 2.8 points. By far, the largest positive contribution to the fall in inequality is made by the rise in the minimum wage, from $2.73 to $7.01 (in 1995 dollars) per hour. The increased minimum wage accounts for some 30 percent of the decrease in inequality. None of the other variables prove to be very important. However, some 90 percent of the decline remains unexplained by the variables used in the regressions.[16]

The regression results do a much better job in accounting for the rise in inequality between 1968 and 2000, when the Gini coefficient increased from 34.8 to 43.0 or by 8.2 points. In this case, the increase in OCA investment per worker makes the largest contribution, accounting for between 44 and 52 percent of the increased inequality. The second largest contributor is the sharp fall in the unionization rate from 23.0 to 13.4 percent. This decline explains between 30 and 42 percent of the rise in the Gini coefficient. The decline in the hourly minimum wage (in 2000 dollars), from $7.31 to $5.15, makes a small contribution in the first two growth accounting exercises but accounts for 22 percent of the decline in the third exercise. The unemployment rate plays a small role because it increased very modestly between 1968 and 1997, from 3.6 to 4.9 percent. The three-year running average of TFP growth also changed very little between the two years, from 0.91 to 0.84 percent per year. The increase in export intensity, from 5.0 to 11.8 percent of GDP, offset the increase in inequality by 1.22 points or 15 percent. The human capital variable, the variance of schooling times the rate of return to schooling squared, plays almost no role in explaining the rise in inequality. Though the rate of return to schooling increased over this period, the variance of schooling declined and the value of this variable also fell, 0.238 to 0.166. For these years, only between 10 and 20 percent of the rise in inequality is left accounted for (the "unexplained residual").

11.11 SUMMARY AND CONCLUDING REMARKS

This chapter documented three striking trends. First, inequality in the distribution of family income, which had remained virtually unchanged since the end of World War II until 1968, increased sharply since then. Second, in contrast, the dispersion (variance) of schooling within the adult population has declined dramatically since the early 1970s. Third, there also occurred a pronounced rightward shift in the distribution of schooling, with a very large decline in low-educated workers and a corresponding increase in highly educated workers.

The time-series regression and growth accounting results indicate that the largest effect on income inequality comes from OCA investment. In the time-series analysis, the coefficient of lagged investment in OCA per worker is positive and highly significant and the variable accounts for between 44 to 52 percent of the rise in income inequality between 1968 and 2000. Non-OCA equipment investment per worker, on the other hand, is found to have a positive but not significant relation to income inequality. According to the growth accounting decomposition, it has a very weak effect on changes in income inequality over time and OCA investment is the dominate element and heavily outweighs non-OCA investment in accounting for the rise in income inequality. These results tend to lend support to the skill-biased technological change hypothesis (see Section 11.2).

Unionization is also found to be an important explanatory variable in accounting for rising inequality. The unionization rate has a decidedly negative relation to income inequality. The effect is consistently strong in the time-series data. The decline in unionization is found to account for between 36 and 44 percent of the rise in family income inequality over the 1968–2000 period. Unions thus appear to retard the restructuring of jobs in the workplace and thereby help mitigate increases in both earnings and skill inequality. These results are also consistent with some of the findings in the earlier literature, including Blackburn, Bloom, and Freeman (1990), Freeman (1993), Gordon (1996), and DiNardo and Lemieux (1997) (see Section 11.6).

Export intensity is found to be negatively though not significantly related to income inequality. Import intensity, likewise, does not appear to play a substantial role in explaining trends in income inequality. The same is true with the share of immigrants in the U.S. labor force. These results are broadly consistent with most of the studies surveyed in Section 11.4.

In the time-series regressions, the dispersion of schooling is found to be negatively associated with income inequality though its coefficient is not significant. On the other hand, the coefficient of the variance of schooling multiplied by the rate of return to schooling squared has the positive sign predicted by the human capital model but is not statistically significant. The variable also played almost no role in accounting for the rise in income inequality between 1968 and 1997 because the value of the variable changed little over the period. These results seem to cast doubt on the importance of human capital explanations of rising inequality (see Section 11.8).

In the time-series regressions, the unemployment rate is found to be a highly significant determinant of income inequality. This result accords with most of the previous research on the subject (see Section 11.6). However, this variable played little role in accounting for the rise of inequality after 1968 because its value was almost the same in 2000 as in 1968. Though the minimum wage in real terms peaked in 1968, its coefficient has the predicted negative sign in the time-series regressions on income inequality but is generally not significant. The decline in the minimum wage after 1968 also played a fairly small role in explaining the rise in inequality after 1968. This finding seems to contradict some of the earlier research on the subject (also see Section 11.6).

TFP growth and labor productivity growth appear to have no statistically significant effect on income inequality. Likewise, R&D investment does not play a role with regard to income inequality. These results do not appear to be consistent with those of Mincer (1991) and Adams (1997, 1999), who both reported a positive association between R&D expenditures and educational wage differentials (see Section 11.2).

Two recent large-scale surveys of the literature are also of interest here, particularly since they appear to reach opposite conclusions. The first, Levy and Temin (2007), put much more emphasis on institutional changes as important in explaining increasing wage inequality, with skill-biased technical change working its effect in the context of de-unionization. To reach this conclusion, they contrasted conditions since 1980 in the United States with those in earlier postwar years. They argued that the income distribution in each period was strongly shaped by a set of economic institutions. The early postwar years were dominated by unions, a negotiating framework set in the automobile industry, and a high minimum wage – all parts of a general government effort to broadly distribute the gains from growth. In contrast, more recent years were characterized by reversals in all these dimensions. Other explanations for income disparities including skill-biased technical change and international trade were seen as factors operating within this broader institutional story.

The second, Gordon and Dew-Becker (2008), re-emphasized the importance of skill-biased technical change. They argued that there is little evidence on the effects of imports on inequality, and an ambiguous literature on immigration which implied a small overall impact on the wages of the average native American, though a significant downward effect on high-school drop-outs, On the other hand, the literature on skill-biased technical change was valuably enriched by a finer grid of skills, switching from a two-dimension to a three- or five-dimensional breakdown of skills. They argued that the three-way "polarization" hypothesis seems a plausible way of explaining differentials in wage changes.

11.12   REFERENCES AND BIBLIOGRAPHY

Acemoglu, D. (2002a). Cross-country inequality trends. NBER Working Paper No. 8832, March.

Acemoglu, D. (2002b). Technical change, inequality and labor market. *Journal of Economic Literature*, **40**, 7–72.

Adams, J.D. (1997). Technology, trade, and wages. NBER Working Paper No. 5940, February.

Adams, J.D. (1999). The structure of firm R&D, the factor intensity of production, and skill bias. *Review of Economics and Statistics*, **81**(3), 499–510.

Allen, S.G. (2001). Technology and the wage structure. *Journal of Labor Economics*, **19**(2), 440–83.

Altonji, J.C. & David Card (1991). The effects of immigration on the labor market outcomes of less-skilled natives. In J.M. Abowd & R.B. Freeman (eds.), *Immigration, Trade, and the Labor Market* (pp. 201–34). Chicago: University of Chicago Press.

Autor, D.H., Katz, L.F. & Kearny, M.S. (2005). Trends in U.S. wage inequality: Re-assessing the revisionists. Harvard Institute of Economic Research Discussion Paper Number 2095, October.

Autor, D.H., Katz, L.F. & Krueger, A.B. (1998). Computing inequality: How computers changed the labor market. *Quarterly Journal of Economics*, **113**(4), 1169–214.

Autor, D.H., Levy, F. & Murnane, R.J. (2002). Upstairs, downstairs: Computers and skills on two floors of a bank. *Industrial and Labor Relations Review*, **55**(3), 432–47.

Autor, D.H., Levy, F. & Murnane, R.J. (2003). The skill content of recent technological change: An empirical exploration. *Quarterly Journal of Economics*, **118**(4), 1279–334.

Bartel, A.P. & Lichtenberg, F.R. (1987). The comparative advantage of educated workers in implementing new technology. *Review of Economics and Statistics*, **69**, 1–11.

Becker, G.S. (1964). *Human Capital: A Theoretical and Empirical Analysis*. New York: Columbia University Press and NBER.

Becker, G.S. (1975). *Human Capital: A Theoretical and Empirical Analysis*, 2nd edition. New York: Columbia University Press and NBER.

Berman, E., Bound, J. & Griliches, Z. (1994). Changes in the demand for skilled labor within U.S. manufacturing: Evidence from the Annual Survey of Manufactures. *Quarterly Journal of Economics*, **109**, 367–98.

Berman, E., Bound, J. & Machin, S. (1998). Implications of skill-biased technological change: International evidence. *Quarterly Journal of Economics*, **113**(4), 1245–80.

Bernard, A.B. & Jensen, J.B. (1997). Exporters, skill upgrading, and the wage gap. *Journal of International Economics*, **42**, 3–31.

Bernard, A.B. & Jensen, J.B. (2000). Understanding increasing and decreasing wage inequality. In R.C. Feenstra (ed.), *The Impact of International Trade on Wages* (pp. 227–68). Chicago: University of Chicago Press.

Bernard, A.B. & Jensen, J.B. (2004). Exporting and productivity. *Oxford Review of Economic Policy*, **20**(3), 343–57.

Betts, J.R. (1997). The skill bias of technological change in Canadian manufacturing industries. *Review of Economics and Statistics*, **79**(1), 146–50.

Bhagwati, J. & Dehejia, V. (1994). Freer trade and wages of the unskilled: Is Marx striking again? In J. Bhagwati & M. Kosters, (eds.), *Trade and Wages: Leveling Wages Down?* Washington, DC: AEI Press.

Bhagwati, J. & Kosters, M. (eds.), *Trade and Wages: Leveling Wages Down?* Washington, DC: AEI Press.

Bishop, J. (1991). Achievement, Test Scores, and Relative Wages. in Marvin Kosters (ed.), *Workers and their Wages*, (Washington, DC: AEI Press), 1991, pp. 146–190.

Blackburn, M. (1990). What can explain the increase in earnings inequality among males? *Industrial Relations*, **29**(3), 441–56.

Blackburn, M., Bloom, D. & Freeman, R.B. (1990). The declining position of less-skilled American males. In G. Burtless (ed.), *A Future of Lousy Jobs?* (pp. 31–67). Washington, DC: Brookings Institution.

Blackburn, M. & Neumark, D. (1993). Omitted-ability bias and the increase in the return to schooling. *Journal of Labor Economics*, **11**(3), 521–44.

Blau, F.D. & Kahn, L.M. (1996). International differences in male wage inequality: Institutions versus market forces. *Journal of Political Economy*, **104**(4), 791–836.

Bluestone, B. (1990). The impact of schooling and industrial restructuring on recent trends in wage inequality in the United States. *American Economic Review Papers and Proceedings*, **80**(2), 303–7.

Bluestone, B. & Harrison, B. (1988a). *The Great U-Turn: Corporate Restructuring and the polarization of America.* New York: Basic Books.

Bluestone, B. & Harrison, B. (1988b). The growth of low-wage employment: 1963–86. *American Economic Review Papers and Proceedings*, **78**(2), 124–8.

Blum, B.S. (2008). Trade, technology, and the rise of the service sector: The effects on US wage inequality. *Journal of International Economics*, **72**, 441–58.

Borjas, G.J. (1994). The economics of immigration. *Journal of Economic Literature*, **32**, 1667–717.

Borjas, G.J. (1995). The economic benefits from immigration. *Journal of Economic Perspectives*, **9**(2), 3–22.

Borjas, G.J. (2003). The labor demand curve *is* downward sloping: Reexamining the impact of immigration on the labor market. *Quarterly Journal of Economics*, **118**, 1335–74.

Borjas, G.J., Freeman, R.B. & Katz, L.F. (1992). On the labor market effects of immigration and trade. In G.J. Borjas & R.B. Freeman (eds.), *Immigration and the Workforce: Economic Consequences for the United States and Source Areas.* Chicago: University of Chicago Press.

Borjas, G.J. & Ramey, V.A. (1994). The relationship between wage inequality and international trade. In J.H. Bergstrand, T.F. Cosimano, J.W. Houck & R.G. Sheehan (eds.), *The Changing Distribution of Income in an Open U.S. Economy* (pp. 217–41). Amsterdam: North-Holland.

Borjas, G.J. & Ramey, V.A. (1995). Foreign competition, market power, and wage inequality: Theory and evidence. *Quarterly Journal of Economics*, **110**, 1075–110.

Borjas, G.J., Grogger, J. & Hansen, G. (2006). Immigration and African-American employment opportunities: The response of wages, employment, and incarceration to labor supply shocks. NBER Working Paper No. 12518, September.

Bound, J. & Johnson, G.E. (1992). Changes in the structure of wages in the 1980s: An evaluation of alternative explanations. *American Economic Review*, **82**, 371–92.

Butcher, K.F. & Card, D. (1991). Immigration and wages: Evidence from the 1980s. *American Economic Review*, **81**, 292–6.

Bresnahan, T.F. (1999). Computerization and wage dispersion: An analytical reinterpretation. *Economic Journal*, **109**(456), 339–76.

Bresnahan, T.F., Brynjolfsson, E. & Hitt, L.M. (2002). Information technology, workplace organization, and the demand for skilled labor: Firm-level evidence. *Quarterly Journal of Economics*, **117**, 339–76.

Bresnahan, T.F. & Trajtenberg, M. (1995). General purpose technologies: engines of growth? *Journal of Econometrics, Annals of Econometrics*, **65**(1), 83–108.

Burkhauser, R.V., Butler, J.S., Feng, S. & Houtenville, A.J. (2004). Long term trends in earnings inequality: What the CPS can tell us. *Economics Letters*, **82**, 295–9.

Burtless, G. (1995). International trade and the rise in earnings inequality. *Journal of Economic Literature*, **33**, 800–16.

Camarota, S.A. (1997). The effect of immigrants on the earnings of low-skilled native workers: Evidence from the June 1991 Current Population Survey. *Social Science Quarterly*, **78**, 417–31.

Card, D. (1992). The effect of unions on the structure of wages: A longitudinal analysis. *Econometrica*, **64**, 957–79.

Card, D. (2001). The effect of unions on wage inequality in the U.S. labor market. *Industrial and Labor Relations Review*, **54**(2), 296–315.

Card, D. & John E. Dinardo, J.E. (2002). Skill Biased Technological Change and Rising Inequality: Some Problems and Puzzles. *Journal of Labor Economics*, **20**, pp. 733–83.

Card, D. & Lemieux, T. (2001). Can falling supply explain the rising return to college for younger men? A cohort-based analysis. *Quarterly Journal of Economics*, **116**, 705–46.

Danziger, S. & Gottschalk, P. (1995). *America Unequal*. Cambridge, MA: Harvard University Press for the Russell Sage Foundation.

David, P.A. (1991). Computer and dynamo: The modern productivity paradox in a not-too-distant mirror. In *Technology and Productivity: The Challenge for Economic Policy* (pp. 315–48). Paris: OECD.

Davis, S.J. & Haltiwanger, J. (1991). Wage dispersion between and within U.S. manufacturing plants, 1963–86. *Brookings Papers on Economic Activity: Microeconomics*, 115–80.

DiNardo, J.E., Fortin, N.M. & Lemieux, T. (1996). Labor market institutions and the distribution of wages, 1973–1992: A semi-parametric approach. *Econometrica*, **64**(5), 1001–44.

DiNardo, J.E. & Lemieux, T. (1997). Diverging male wage inequality in the United States and Canada, 1981–1988: Do institutions explain the difference. *Industrial and Labor Relations Review*, **50**(4), 629–51.

DiNardo, J.E. & Pischke, J.-S. (1997). The returns to computer use revisited: Have pencils changed the wage structure too? *Quarterly Journal of Economics*, **112**(1), 291–303.

Doeringer, P. (1991). *Turbulence in the American Workplace*. New York: Oxford University Press.

Doeringer, P.B. & Piore, M.J. (1971). *Internal Labor Markets and Manpower Analysis*. Lexington, MA: D.C. Heath.

Doms, M., Dunne, T. & Troske, K.B. (1997). Workers, wages, and technology. *Quarterly Journal of Economics*, **107**(1), 253–90.

Feenstra, R.C. & Hanson, G.H. (1996a). Foreign investment, outsourcing and relative wages. In R.C. Feenstra, G.M. Grossman & D.A. Irwin (eds.), *The Political Economy of Trade Policy*. Cambridge, MA: MIT Press.

Feenstra, R.C. & Hanson, G.H. (1996b). Globalization, outsourcing, and wage inequality. *American Economic Review*, **86**(2), 240–5.

Feenstra, R.C. & Hanson, G.H. (1999). The impact of outsourcing and high-technology capital on wages: Estimates for the United States, 1979–1990. *Quarterly Journal of Economics*, **114**(3), 907–40.

Ferguson, W.D. (1996). Explaining the rising wage-productivity gap of the 1980s: Effects of declining employment and unionization. *Review of Radical Political Economics*, **28**(2), 77–115.

Fortin, N.M. & Lemieux, T. (1997). Institutional changes and rising wage inequality: Is there a linkage? *Journal of Economic Perspectives*, **11**, 75–96.

Frank, R. & Cook, P. (1995). *The Winner-Take-All Society*. New York: The Free Press.

Freeman, C. (1987). Information technology and the change in techno-economic paradigm. In C. Freeman & L. Soete (eds.), *Technical Change and Full Employment*. Oxford: Basil Blackwell.

Freeman, R.B. (1976). *The Over-Educated American*. New York: Academic Press.

Freeman, R.B. (1993). How much has de-unionization contributed to the rise in male earnings inequality? In S. Danziger & P. Gottschalk (eds.), *Uneven Tides: Rising Inequality in America* (pp. 133–63). New York: Russell Sage.

Freeman, R.B. (1995). Are your wages set in Beijing? *Journal of Economic Perspectives*, 9(3), 15–32.

Freeman, R.B. (2003). Trade wars: The exaggerated impact of trade in economic debates. NBER Working Paper No. 10000, September.

Freeman, R.B. & Katz, L.F. (1991). Industrial wage and employment determination in an open economy. In J.W. Abowd & R.B. Freeman (eds.), *Immigration, Trade, and Labor Markets* (pp. 235–59). Chicago: NBER.

Gittleman, M. (1994). Earnings in the 1980s: An occupational perspective. *Monthly Labor Review*, July, 16–27.

Glynn, A. (1998). Low pay and employment performance. Centre for Economic Performance and Institute of Economics. Oxford University.

Goldin, C. & Katz, L.F. (1998). The origins of technology-skill complementarity. *Quarterly Journal of Economics*, 113, 693–732.

Goldin, C. & Katz, L.F. (2007a). The race between education and technology: The evolution of U.S. educational wage differentials, 1890 to 2005. NBER Working Paper No. 12984, March.

Goldin, C. & Katz, L.F. (2007b). Long-run changes in the U.S. wage structure: Narrowing, widening, polarizing. NBER Working Paper No. 13568, November.

Gordon, D.M. (1996). *Fat and Mean: The Corporate Squeeze of Working Americans and the Myth of Managerial "Downsizing"*. New York: Free Press.

Gordon, R.J. & Dew-Becker, I. (2008). Controversies about the rise of American inequality: A survey. NBER Working Paper No. 13982, April.

Grogger, J. & Eide, E. (1996). Changes in college skills and the rise in the college wage premium. *Journal of Human Resources*, 30(2), 280–301.

Groshen, E. (1991a). Source of intra-industry wage dispersion: How much do employers matter? *Quarterly Journal of Economics*, 106(3), 869–84.

Groshen, E. (1991b). Rising inequality in a salary survey: Another piece of the puzzle. Federal Reserve Bank of Cleveland Working Paper 9121.

Groshen, E. & Levine, D.I. (1998). The rise and decline (?) of U.S. internal labor markets. Federal Reserve Bank of New York Research Paper No. 9819.

Grubb, W.N. & Wilson, R.H. (1989). Sources of increase inequality in wages and salaries, 1960–80. *Monthly Labor Review*, April, 3–13.

Handel, M. (1999). Computers and the wage structure. Levy Economics Institute of Bard College Working Paper No. 285, October.

Heckman, J. & Vytlacil, E. (2001). Identifying the role of cognitive ability in explaining the level and change in the return to schooling. *Review of Economics and Statistics*, 83(1), 1–12.

Head, S. (2003). *The New Ruthless Economy: Work and Power in the Digital Age*. New York: Oxford University Press.

Helpman, E. & Trajtenberg, M. (1998). A time to sow and a time to reap: Growth based on general purpose technologies. In E. Helpman (ed.), *General Purpose Technologies and Economic Growth*. Cambridge, MA: MIT Press.

Hernstein, R. & Murray, C. (1994). *The Bell Curve*. New York: Basic Books.

Hirsch, B.T. & Macpherson, D.A. (1993). Union membership and coverage files from the Current Population Surveys: Note. *Industrial and Labor Relations Review*, 46(3), 574–78.

Horrigan, M.W. & Mincy, R. (1993). The minimum wage and earnings and income inequality. In S. Danziger & P. Gottschalk (eds.), *Uneven Tides: Rising Inequality in America*. New York: Russell Sage.

Howell, D. (1997). Institutional failure and the American worker: The collapse of low-skill wages. *Public Policy Brief*. Jerome Levy Economics Institute.

Jencks, C. (1972). *Inequality: A Reassessment of the Effect of Family and Schooling in America*. New York: Basic Books.

Jencks, C. (1979). *Who Gets Ahead?* New York: Basic Books.

Jencks, C. & Phillips, M. (1998). America's next achievement test. *American Prospect*, **40**, 44–53.

Juhn, C. (1999). Wage inequality and demand for skill: Evidence from five decades. *Industrial and Labor Relations Review*, **52**(3), 424–43.

Juhn, C., Murphy, K.M. & Pierce, B. (1993). Wage inequality and the returns to skill. *Journal of Political Economy*, **101**, 410–42.

Karoly, L.A. (1992). Changes in the distribution of individual earnings in the United States from 1967 to 1986. *Review of Economics and Statistics*, **74**(1), 107–15.

Karoly, L.A. & Klerman, J.A. (1994). Using regional data to reexamine the contribution of demographic and sectoral changes to increasing U.S. wage inequality. In J.H. Bergstrand, T.F. Cosimano, J.W. Houck & R.G. Sheehan (eds.), *The Changing Distribution of Income in an Open U.S. Economy* (pp. 183–216). Amsterdam: North-Holland.

Katz, A.J. & Herman, S.W. (1997). Improved estimates of fixed reproducible tangible wealth, 1929–95. *Survey of Current Business*, May, 69–92.

Katz, L.F., Loveman, G.W. & Blanchflower, D.G. (1995). A comparison of changes in the structure of wages in four OECD countries. In R.B. Freeman & L.F. Katz (eds.), *Differences and Changes in Wage Structures* (pp. 25–66). Chicago: National Bureau of Economic Research.

Katz, L.F. & Murphy, K.M. (1992). Changes in relative wages, 1963–1987: Supply and demand factors. *Quarterly Journal of Economics*, **107**(1), 35–78.

Kennan, J. (1995). The elusive effects of minimum wages. *Journal of Economic Literature*, **33**, 1950–65.

Koeniger, W., Leonardi, M. & Nunziata, L. (2007). Labor market institutions and wage inequality. *Industrial and Labor Relations Review*, **60**(3), 340–56.

Kokkelenberg, E.C. & Sockell, D.R. (1985). Union membership in the United States, 1973–81. *Industrial and Labor Relations Review*, **38**(4), 497–543.

Krueger, A.B. (1993). How computers have changed the wage structure: Evidence from microdata. *Quarterly Journal of Economics*, **108**, 33–60.

Krugman, P.A. (2000). Technology, trade, and factor prices. *Journal of International Economics*, **50**(1), 51–71.

Krugman, P.A. (2008). Trade and wages, reconsidered. Princeton University Working Paper, February.

Krugman, P.A. & Lawrence, R.Z. (1994). Trade, jobs and wages. *Scientific American*, 44–9.

Krusell, P., Ohanian, L., Rios-Rull, J.-L. & Violante, G. (2000). Capital-skill complementarity and inequality. *Econometrica*, **68**(5), 1029–53.

LaLonde, R.J. & Topel, R.H. (1991). Labor market adjustments to increased immigration. In J.M. Abowd & R.B. Freeman (eds.), *Immigration, Trade, and the Labor Market* (pp. 167–99). Chicago: University of Chicago Press.

Lawrence, R.Z. & Slaughter, M.J. (1993). Trade and US wages: Great sucking sound or hiccup. *Brookings Papers on Economic Activity: Microeconomics*, **2**, 161–210.

Leamer, E.E. (1984). *Sources of International Comparative Advantage*. Cambridge, MA: MIT Press.

Leamer, E.E. (1996). Wage inequality from international competition and technological change: Theory and country experience. *American Economic Review Papers and Proceedings*, **86**(2), 309–14.

Lee, D.S. (1999). Wage inequality in the United States during the 1980s: Rising dispersion or falling minimum wage? *Quarterly Journal of Economics*, **114**, 977–1023.

Levy, F. & Murnane, R. (1992). U.S. earnings levels and earnings inequality: A review of recent trends and proposed explanations. *Journal of Economic Literature*, **30**(3), 1333–81.

Levy, F. & Murnane, R. (1996). With what skills are computers a complement? *American Economic Review Papers and Proceedings*, **86**(2), 258–62.

Levy, F., Murnane, R. & Willett, J.B. (1995). The growing importance of cognitive skills in wage determination. *Review of Economics and Statistics*, **77**(2), 251–66.

Levy, F. & Temin, P. (2007). Inequality and institutions in 20th century America. NBER Working Paper No. 13106, May.

Lemieux, T. (2006). Increasing residual wage inequality: composition effects, noisy data, or rising demand for skill? *American Economic Review*, **96**(3), 461–98.

Lemieux, T. (2007). The changing nature of wage inequality. NBER Working Paper No. 13523, October.

Manacorda, M., Manning, A. & Wadsworth, J. (2006). The impact of immigration on the structure of male wages: Theory and evidence from Britain. IZA Discussion Paper No. 2352, Bonn, Germany, October.

Mincer, J. (1974). *Schooling, Experience, and Earnings*, (New York: National Bureau of Economic Research), 1974.

Mincer, J. (1991). Human capital, technology, and the wage structure: What do the time series show? NBER Working Paper No. 3581, January.

Mishel, L., Bernstein, J. & Schmitt, J. (1997). Did technology have any effect on the growth of wage inequality in the 1980s and 1990s? Economic Policy Institute, December.

Murphy, K.M. & Welch, F. (1991). The role of international trade in wage differentials. In M. Kosters (ed.), *Workers and their Wages* (pp. 39–69). Washington, DC: AEI Press.

Murphy, K.M. & Welch, F. (1993a). Industrial change and the rising importance of skill. In S. Danziger & P. Gottschalk (eds.), *Uneven Tides: Rising Inequality in America* (pp. 101–32). New York: Russell Sage.

Murphy, K.M. & Welch, F. (1993b). Occupational change and the demand for skill, 1940–1990. *American Economic Review Papers and Proceedings*, **83**(2), 122–26.

Orrenius, P.M. & Zavodny, M. (2007). Does immigration affect wages? A look at occupation-level evidence. *Labour Economics*, **14**(5), 757–73.

Osterman, P. (1986). The impact of computers on the employment of clerks and managers. *Industrial and Labor Relations Review*, **39**, 163–89.

Peri, G. & Sparber, C. (2007). Task specialization, comparative advantages, and the effects of immigration on wages. NBER Working Paper No. 13389, September.

Reich, R. (1991). *The Work of Nations: Preparing Ourselves for 21st Century Capitalism*. New York: Alfred Knopf.

Richardson, D.J. (1995). Income inequality and trade: How to think, what to conclude? *Journal of Economic Perspectives*, **9**, 33–55.

Sachs, J.D. & Shatz, H.J. (1994). Trade and jobs in U.S. manufacturing. *Brookings Papers on Economic Activity: Microeconomics*, **1**, 1–84.

Saint-Paul, G. (2008). *Innovation and Inequality: How Does Technical Progress Affect Workers?* Princeton, NJ: Princeton University Press.

Schoeni, R.F. (1997). The effects of immigration on the employment and wages of native workers: Evidence from the 1970s and 1980s, mimeo. Rand Corporation, Santa Monica, CA.

Wolff, E.N. (1996). Technology and the demand for skills. *OECD Science, Technology and Industry Review*, **18**, 96–123.

Wolff, E.N. (2002). Computerization and structural change. *Review of Income and Wealth*, **48**(2), 59–75.

Wolff, E.N. (2003). Skills and changing comparative advantage. *Review of Economics and Statistics*, **85**(1), 77–93.

Wood, A. (1991). How much does trade with the south affect workers in the north? *World Bank Research Observer*, **6**, 19–36.

Wood, A. (1994). *North-South Trade, Employment, and Inequality: Change Fortunes in a Skill-Driven World*. New York: Oxford University Press.

Wood, A. (1998). Globalization and the rise in labour market inequalities. *Economic Journal*, **108**, 1463–82.

Wood, A. & Anderson, E. (1998). Does Heckscher–Ohlin theory explain why the demand for unskilled labour in the north first accelerated than decelerated? Unpublished paper, Institute of Development Studies, University of Sussex, U.K.

Wozniak, G.D. (1987). Human capital, information, and the early adoption of new technology. *Journal of Human Resources*, **21**(1), 101–12.

Zuboff, S. (1988). *In the Age of the Smart Machine: The Future of Work and Power*. New York: Basic Books, 1988.

APPENDIX 11.1   DATA SOURCES AND METHODS

1   Gini coefficient for family income: U.S. Census Bureau, Current Population Survey, March Supplement, http://www.census.gov/ftp/pub/hhes/www/incpov.html.

2   Educational attainment: The source is: U.S. Census Bureau, *Current Population Reports*, available on the Internet. Adults refer to persons 25 years and over in the noninstitutional population (excluding members of the Armed Forces living in Barracks). The CPS data are provided on the Internet.

3   Output, investment, capital stock, and employment data

   (a)   Investment data refer to nonresidential fixed investment in constant (1992) dollars and GDP to GDP in constant (1992) dollars. Source: U.S. Bureau of Economic Analysis, National Income and Product Accounts, www.bea.gov/industry/.

   (b)   Capital stock figures are based on chain-type quantity indexes for net stock of fixed capital in 1992 dollars, year-end estimates. Equipment and structures, including information technology equipment, are for the private (nongovernment) sector only. Information processing and related equipment includes: (i) computers and peripheral equipment; (ii) other office and accounting machinery; (iii) communication equipment; (iv) instruments; and (v) photocopy and related equipment. Source: U.S. Bureau of Economic Analysis, CD-ROM NCN-0229, "Fixed Reproducible Tangible Wealth of the United States, 1925–97." This series is updated with data from http://www.bea.gov/bea/dn2/home/annual_industry.htm. For technical details, see Katz and Herman (1997).

   (c)   Investment flows by industry and by type of equipment or structures are for the private (nongovernment) sector only. The source is: U.S. Bureau of Economic Analysis, CD-ROM NCN-0229, "Fixed Reproducible Tangible Wealth of the United States, 1925–97." This series is updated with data from the internet at http://www.bea.gov/bea/dn2/home/annual_industry.htm.

   (d)   NIPA employee compensation: Figures are from the National Income and Product Accounts (NIPA): http://www.bea.gov/bea/dn2/home/annual_industry.htm. No adjustment is made for hours worked. Employee compensation includes wages and salaries and employee benefits. Proprietors' income is net income to self-employed persons, including partners in businesses and owners of unincorporated businesses.

   (e)   NIPA employment data: Figures are from the National Income and Product Accounts, available at: http://www.bea.gov/bea/dn2/home/annual_industry.htm. Full-time equivalent employees (FTEE) equals the number of employees on full-time schedules plus the number of employees on part-time schedules converted to a full-time basis. The number of full-time equivalent employees in each industry is the product of the total number of employees and the ratio of average weekly hours per employee for all employees to average weekly hours per employee on full-time schedules. Persons engaged in production (PEP) equals the number of full-time and part-time employees plus the number of self-employed persons. Unpaid family workers are not included.

4   Research and development expenditures performed by industry include company, federal, and other sources of funds. Company-financed R&D performed outside the company is excluded. Industry series on R&D and full-time equivalent scientists and engineers engaged in R&D per full-time equivalent employee run from 1957 to 1997. *Source*: National Science Foundation, Internet. For technical details, see National Science Foundation (1996). *Research and Development in Industry* (Arlington, VA: National Science Foundation), NSF96-304.

5 Unionization. Percent of labor force covered by unions. Estimates for 1950–1983 are the annual average number of dues paying members reported by labor unions. Estimates for 1983–2003 are annual averages from the Current Population Survey. Data exclude numbers of professional and public employee associations. *Sources*: (a) U.S. Department of Labor, Bureau of Labor Statistics (1979), *Handbook of Labor Statistics 1978*, Bulletin 2. Washington, DC: U.S. Government Printing Office; (c) U.S. Department of Labor, Bureau of Labor Statistics (1990). *Handbook of Labor Statistics 1989*, Bulletin 23. Washington, DC: U.S. Government Printing Office; and (d) E.E. Jacobs (ed.) (1998). *Handbook of U.S. Labor Statistics*, 2nd edition. Lanham, MD: Bernan Press. Sources for the industry-level data include in addition to the above: Kokkelenberg and Sockell (1985); Hirsch and Macpherson (1993), accompanying data files; and Bureau of Labor Statistics, Office of Employment Projections, Output and Employment database.

6 Minimum wage. *Source*: U.S. Census Bureau (1998). *Statistical Abstract of the United States: 1998*, 118th edition. Washington, DC: U.S. Government Printing Office.

7 Property income and personal income: U.S. Bureau of Economic Analysis, National Income and Product Accounts, http://www.bea.gov/bea/dn/nipaweb/index.asp.

8 Number of female householders and total number of families: U.S. Census Bureau, Current Population Survey, March Supplement, http://www.census.gov/hhes/www/income/histinc/f10ar.html.

9 Imports and exports: Source for the aggregate data: U.S. Bureau of Economic Analysis, National Income and Product Accounts, http://www.bea.gov/bea/dn/home/gdp.htm.

10 Service sector employment: Sectors include wholesale and retail trade; finance, insurance, real estate; personal and business services; and government. The employment concept is persons engaged in production (PEP). *Source*: U.S. Bureau of Economic Analysis, National Income and Product Accounts, http://www.bea.gov/bea/dn2/home/annual_industry.htm.

11 Foreign-born workers: The source is the U.S. Census Bureau, Current Population Survey and decennial Census of Population, http://www.census.gov/population/www/socdemo/foreign/reports.html.

NOTES

1 It should be noted that individual states also set minimum wages for employees in their states, and as of 2008 a majority of states have minimum wages that are above the federal level (details of state minimum wages are available at http://www.dol.gov/esa/minwage/america.htm).

2 *Source*: http://www.census.gov/hhes/www/income/histinc/f04.html.

3 Burkhauser, Butler, Feng, and Houtenville (2004) show that changes in the CPS rules, particularly with regard to top-coding, in the 1990s artificially increased measured earnings inequality. Nonetheless, the correlation coefficient between the standard CPS family inequality series and the new, consistent times series supplied by these authors is 0.991.

4 I would like to especially thank David Autor for supplying the data.

5 Indeed, OCACM (the sum of communications equipment and OCA) per PEP has an even higher correlation coefficient with family income inequality, 0.84.

6 The correlation of both export intensity and import intensity individually with income inequality is almost exactly the same, 0.74.

7 This variable was constructed from data from the U.S. Census Bureau Current Population Survey and decennial Census of the Population.

8 The source for 1956 to 1979 is Mattila (1984), which is based on the rate of return to 4 years of college relative to 4 years of high school for male workers. I extended the series to 2000 on the basis of CPS data on the ratio of annual earnings between male college graduates and male high school graduates (see Figure 1.13). The rate of return was estimated using the standard internal rate of return

    to schooling formula under the assumption that the ratio in earnings between college and high school graduates remains constant over the lifecycle and that college graduates begin work 4 years later, on average, then high school graduates.

9   The correlation between the square of the rate of return to college and the Gini coefficient for family income is 0.66.

10 The inclusion of an interactive term between the variance of schooling and the square of the rate of return to schooling follows directly from Equation (11.2).

11 Longer lags were also tried but the one-year lag seems to provide the best fit.

12 Also significant at the 1 or 5 percent level are computer investment per PEP and investment in OCACM per PEP.

13 Similar results hold for the ratio of the minimum wage to average hourly earnings of the workforce (results not shown). However, as noted in note 1, many states have minimum wages above the federal level. As a result, even though the federal minimum wage has been declining in real terms, the increases in many state minimum wages have mitigated this effect.

14 Both variables are highly correlated with the rate of return to schooling.

15 Another test that was performed is the Augmented Dickey–Fuller (DF) unit root test for nonstationarity in the dependent variable. The regression includes one lagged value of the dependent variable. The results are as follows:

Variables included	DF t-statistics	Critical value (1%)	Reject unit root?
No constant; no time trend	−5.003	−2.611	Yes
A constant; no time trend	−5.169	−3.571	Yes
A constant; a time trend	6.263	−4.158	Yes

Similar results are found using multiple lagged terms of the dependent variable.

16 The results for specification 8 (Panel C) cover the 1956–1968 period only, when the Gini coefficient was virtually unchanged. As a result, the growth accounting results are not very meaningful.

Part III
Discrimination

Chapter 12

Discrimination: Meaning, Measurement, and Theory

12.1 INTRODUCTION

In Part II, we looked at the functioning of the labor market and how it was responsible for differences in earnings among workers. In Part III, we consider another factor which causes earnings differences – discrimination. This has taken two predominant forms in the United States – racial and gender discrimination.

The terms "discrimination," "prejudice," and "racism" evoke considerable passions. Prejudice refers to attitudes, particular unfavorable feelings that an individual has toward another group of people. Discrimination refers to actions or outcomes which suggest that one group is treated unfairly compared to another. People who consciously feel that they are not prejudiced against a particular group may engage in actions that treat members of this group unfairly. Conversely, people who are prejudiced may consciously try to avoid treating another group unfavorably. In this and the next two chapters, we will focus mainly on discrimination, rather than on prejudice.

Racism is often used as a "loaded" term to encompass both prejudicial attitudes and discriminatory behavior. In its narrow usage, it refers to overt behavior on the part of individuals who engage in specific actions against another race – for example, racial taunts, assaults, and, in the extreme case, killings. The current usage refers to a set of attitudes and institutions that appear to produce unfavorable outcomes for a particular race. Some black leaders, for example, blame the low incomes and high poverty among black families on white racism. Because racism is very hard to define or identify, we shall avoid this term in our treatment of discrimination.

Some statistics on the racial income gap are shown in Tables 12.1 and 12.2. In 2005, the average income of black households was 62 percent that of white households. The ratio of median household income was slightly lower, 61 percent (recall that the median is the income of the household in the middle of the income distribution and the mean is the total income divided by the number of households). For families (two or more related individuals living in the same housing unit), the ratio in mean income was 60 percent and the ratio of median income was 56 percent. In 2005, black families still lagged considerably behind whites in terms of income.

Table 12.1 also shows that nonwhite households gained on whites between 1947 and 1967 (there are no separate statistics available for black households over this period). In 1947, the median income of nonwhite households was only 51 percent of white households; by 1967, the ratio had climbed to 62 percent. The data also indicate that the major gains were made between 1957 and 1967, a period that was characterized by a major civil rights movement (see Chapter 13

Table 12.1   Ratio of household and family income between blacks and whites, 1947–2005 (percent)

Year	Ratio of means	Medians
A. Household income: Ratio of nonwhite income to white income[a]		
1947	51	
1957	53	
1967	62	
B. Household income: Ratio of black income to white income[b]		
1967	63	58
1983	62	57
1989	63	59
1999	66	63
2005	62	61
C. Family income (families only): Ratio of black income to white income[b]		
1967	62	59
1983	61	56
1989	61	56
1999	63	59
2005	60	56

a   Ratio is between nonwhites and whites; Hispanic households are included and may be of any race.
b   Ratio is between blacks and whites; Hispanic households are excluded.
Sources: U.S. Census Bureau (1990). Population Reports, Series P-60-167, *Trends in Income: By Selected Characteristics: 1947 to 1988*. Washington, DC: U.S. Government Printing Office; U.S. Census Bureau (1990). Population Reports, Series P-60-168, *Money Income and Poverty Status in the United States: 1989*. Washington, DC: U.S. Government Printing Office; http://www.census.gov/hhes/www/income/histinc/histinctb.html.

Table 12.2   Ratio of median earnings of full-time, year-round workers between women and men, selected years, 1960–2005 (percent)

Year	Ratio of medians
1960	61
1967	58
1977	59
1983	64
1988	66
1993	72
1998	73
2005	77

Source: http://www.census.gov/hhes/www/income/histinc/p40.html.

for more discussion of this point). However, between 1967 and 2005, there was virtually no change in the relative position of black families. In 1967, the ratio of mean household income between black and white families was 63 percent, slightly higher than in 2005, and the ratio of median incomes was 58 percent, a little lower than in 2005.

Table 12.2 shows the ratio of median wage and salary income for full-time (those working 35 hours per week or more), full-year (those working 50 or more weeks per year) workers between females and males. In 2005, the average full-time female worker earned 77 percent that of male workers. However, female workers have made sizable gains on male workers. In 1967, the gender–earnings ratio was only *61 percent*; in 1983, it closed to 64 percent; and it reached 72 percent by 1993. Thus, female workers have made progress relative to male workers over this 45-year period but still remained behind in 2005.

These "raw" income ratios suggest the presence of both racial and gender discrimination but do not provide direct proof. In Section 12.2, we consider what discrimination means and how is it measured. Sections 12.3 to 12.8 present different views on the sources of labor market discrimination. A summary is provided in Section 12.9.

12.2 THE MEANING OF DISCRIMINATION

The data in Tables 12.1 and 12.2 indicate that black families have historically had lower incomes than white families and that female workers have earned less than men. Though there have been some gains made by blacks relative to whites (principally between the mid-1950s and the late 1960s) and women relative to men (primarily since 1967), the racial–income gap and the gender–wage gap were still quite substantial in 2005. Do these figures constitute *prima facie* evidence for the existence of gender and race discrimination in the U.S. labor market? The answer depends on what we mean by discrimination. As we have seen in previous chapters, there are many factors which explain why workers earn different amounts – schooling attainment, years of experience, ability, union status, industry of employment, occupation, and firm size. If one worker has more schooling than another, then it may be *justifiable* that the first earn more than the second.[1] If white males have, on average, more schooling than black males, then part of the difference in their average earnings may be attributable to difference in productivity. The mere existence of earnings differentials between two groups of workers does not, by itself, constitute proof of discrimination.

Labor economists view discrimination as the "unexplained" difference in earnings between two groups of workers. Economists will differ in the variables they use to control for earning differences. This depends on the model or theoretical framework they use. However, almost all include schooling, experience, and ability as explanatory factors. Proof of discrimination would require evidence that one group earns less than another even after controlling or standardizing for *all observed and unobserved* pertinent explanatory variables. Indeed, to prove employers discriminate against one group of workers in favor of another group, we need evidence that one group of workers earns less than another group even when we statistically control for *all factors* that affect a worker's productivity.

Employment discrimination may take one of two forms. First, workers with the same human capital – schooling, experience, ability, and so on – may be assigned different jobs because they are members of different groups. Women equally qualified with men may be assigned jobs lower down the job ladder – for example, college-educated females may be given administrative assistant jobs while college-educated men are given executive jobs. Second, workers with essentially the same job may receive different pay because they are from different groups. For example, female prison guards may receive lower pay than male prison guards who perform essentially the same work.

Labor market discrimination may take two other forms besides differences in pay. First, the incidence of unemployment may vary between groups. As we saw in Chapter 7, black workers have historically experienced much higher unemployment rates than white workers. Both hiring and lay-off decisions may reflect the prejudices of employers. Employers may give white workers preference in terms of hiring. Moreover, in times of economic downturns, black workers may be dismissed before white ones.

Second, labor force participation rates may differ between groups. As we discussed in Chapter 7, a person is classified as unemployed if he or she does not currently have a job but is actively looking for one. Persons without a job who are not actively seeking one are classified as not in the labor force. Individuals who search for a job for a long time but do not find one may simply "drop out" of the labor force. This phenomenon is referred to as the discouraged worker effect. The evidence presented in Chapter 7 indicates that the labor force participation rate of black men has recently been lower than that of white men of the same age. This is particularly true among older men (ages 45 to 64). This may also reflect discrimination against black workers.

12.2.1 The Blinder–Oaxaca decomposition*

The standard way of measuring discrimination in economics is through a regression model. The technique was originally developed by Blinder (1973) and Oaxaca (1973) and is referred to as the Blinder–Oaxaca decomposition. It has been a valuable tool for the analysis of wage gaps since its conception in the early 1970s. It decomposes the differences in earnings between two groups into two additive elements: one attributed to the existence of differences in observable characteristics between the two groups and the other attributed to differences in the returns (coefficients) to those characteristics. The decomposition is used to compare only pairs of groups: females and males, whites and African Americans, rural and urban residents, etc.

The Blinder–Oaxaca decomposition has the following form. Let the two groups be designated by 1 and 2. The income (or wage) gap between these two groups is given by:

$$\bar{y}_2 - \bar{y}_1$$

In the standard procedure, two regressions are estimated:

$$y_{2i} = \beta_2 \times x_{2i} + \varepsilon_{2i} \text{ and } y_{1i} = \beta_1 \times x_{1i} + \varepsilon_{1i} \quad (12.1)$$

where x represents a vector of observable characteristics, β the corresponding vector of coefficients (or returns to these characteristics) and ε is the residual term. The regressions are run separately on the two groups (say males and females). The x variables typically include characteristics such as education, experience (or age), ability (if available), urban/rural residence, union status, and the like. The estimators for expected income of each group can be then estimated as $\bar{y}_2 = \hat{\beta}_2 \bar{x}_2$ and $\bar{y}_1 = \hat{\beta}_1 \bar{x}_1$, respectively. The income gap can then be estimated as:

$$\bar{y}_2 - \bar{y}_1 = \hat{\beta}_2 \bar{x}_2 - \hat{\beta}_1 \bar{x}_1$$

which, after adding and subtracting $\hat{\beta}_1 \bar{x}_1$, becomes:

$$\bar{y}_2 - \bar{y}_1 = \hat{\beta}_2 (\bar{x}_2 - \bar{x}_1) + (\hat{\beta}_2 - \hat{\beta}_1) \bar{x}_1 \quad (12.2)$$

The first component $\hat{\beta}_2 (\bar{x}_2 - \bar{x}_1)$, denoted by Δ_x, is then interpreted as the part of the gap that is explained by differences in average observable characteristics of the individuals, such as years of schooling and age, and the second component, $(\hat{\beta}_2 - \hat{\beta}_1) \bar{x}_1$, denoted by Δ_β, is the part attributed to differences in the returns to those characteristics.

In the discrimination literature, the first component, Δ_x, is usually interpreted as the part of the income or wage gap that is attributable to "justifiable" differences, such as education and experience. The second component, Δ_β, is the part used to measure "discrimination." Of course, this inference has to be interpreted with some caution because it is usually the case that not all of the justifiable characteristics are encompassed by the vector **x**. Thus, the term Δ_β also reflects unobservable characteristics of the two groups (for example, differences in natural ability).

The decomposition is also sensitive to the choice of weights. An alternative decomposition is thus given by:

$$\bar{y}_2 - \bar{y}_1 = \hat{\beta}_1(\bar{x}_2 - \bar{x}_1) + (\hat{\beta}_2 - \hat{\beta}_1)\bar{x}_2 \tag{12.2'}$$

In this case, the coefficients from the group 1 regression are used in the first term and average values of characteristics of group 2 are used in the second term. It is also possible to use the average coefficients estimated from the two regressions in the decomposition.

The traditional notation of the Blinder–Oaxaca decomposition outlined above can also be expressed within a single regression. As developed by Ñopo (2007), let the dummy variable D_i indicate the group to which individual i belongs ($D_i = 0$ for those individuals i that belong to the base group and $D_i = 1$ for those individuals i that belong to the other group). Denoting by y_i the income (or other outcome) of individual i, the coefficient α_1 in the equation:

$$y_i = \alpha_0 + \alpha_1 D_i + \varepsilon_i$$

represents the income gap between the two groups (that is, $\alpha_1 = E[y|D = 1] - E[y|D = 0]$).[2] The Blinder–Oaxaca decomposition attempts to explain the α_1 coefficient (the gap) on the basis of observable characteristics. For that purpose, it is necessary to estimate the equation:

$$y_i = \beta_0 + \beta_1 x_i + \beta_2 D_i + \beta_3 x_i D_i + v_i$$

where D is the dummy variable introduced above, **x** is, as before, a vector of observable characteristics, β_1 and β_3 are the corresponding coefficients for those characteristics (β_1 for individuals of group 1 and $\beta_1 + \beta_3$ for individuals of group 2), β_0 and β_2 are the intercept coefficients, and v_i is a random error term. Then, α_1 can be expressed as:

$$\alpha_i = E[(\beta_0 + \beta_2) + (\beta_1 + \beta_3)x|D = 1] - E[\beta_0 + \beta_1 x|D = 0]$$

This expression can be rearranged to obtain:

$$\alpha_1 = \beta_1(E[\mathbf{x}|D = 1] - E[\mathbf{x}|D = 0]) + \beta_2 + \beta_3 E[\mathbf{x}|D = 1] \tag{12.3}$$
$$\alpha_1 = \Delta_x + \Delta_\beta$$

where now $\Delta_x \equiv \beta_1(E[\mathbf{x}|D = 1] - E[\mathbf{x}|D = 0])$ and $\Delta_\beta \equiv \beta_2 + \beta_3 E[\mathbf{x}|D = 1]$ and both can be interpreted in the same way as in the traditional decomposition. Δ_x is the portion of the wage gap that is explained by the difference in average characteristics of the individuals, while Δ_β is the component that remains unexplained and can be attributed to the existence of a combination of discrimination and unobservable characteristics.

12.2.2   Pre-labor market discrimination

In Part III, we shall principally investigate forms of labor market discrimination. However, there are other forms of discrimination that affect the socioeconomic status of minorities and females. One of the most pernicious forms is housing segregation.[3] In a 2002 study entitled *Racial and*

Ethnic Residential Segregation in the United States: 1980–2000, the U.S. Census Bureau found extensive residential racial segregation in the United States in the year 2000. The Census Bureau used a measure called the *dissimilarity index*. The dissimilarity index measures the percentage of a group's population that would have to change residence for each neighborhood to have the same percentage of that group as the metropolitan area overall. The index ranges from 0.0 (complete integration) to 1.0 (complete segregation). For the year 2000, the average value of the index for African Americans was 0.645, which means that almost two-thirds of black households would have to move to other neighborhoods to achieve complete racial integration. However this is an improvement over 1980 when the comparable statistic was 0.730. Thus there has been some progress in reducing racial housing segregation in the United States though it was still quite high in 2000.

Housing segregation has direct implications for access to quality schooling, as we shall see below. However, it also affects other aspects of economic success. The increasing concentration of poor black families in inner-city ghettos is seen by some social scientists as a primary reason for the high incidence of welfare dependency, dropping out of school, teenage pregnancy, almost permanent joblessness, the presence of families headed largely by females, drug trafficking, gang membership, and crime (see Wilson, 1987, for example). The lack of jobs and economic opportunity in inner-city ghettos often creates a sense of hopelessness, loss of self-esteem, and pessimism for the future among poor black families that leads to complete withdrawal from the labor market.

There are several reasons for the persistence of housing segregation over time. First, up until the 1950s, there were explicit Jim Crow laws in the South which forbade backs from living in white neighborhoods. Housing segregation in the South was not only *de facto* but *de jure* as well.[4] Second from the 1940s through the 1960s, there was a massive migration of black families from the South to northern cities.[5] During this period, blacks settled in these mainly white cities, like Boston, New York, Philadelphia, Chicago, St. Louis, and Detroit. As more and more blacks settled in these cities, racial tensions often grew and many white families left the cities for the surrounding suburbs (so-called "white flight"). This resulted in a large concentration of black families in inner-city areas in northern cities. The relatively low income of most black families as well as housing segregation prevented them from buying homes in the suburbs.

Third, though since the 1960s explicit laws prohibiting black families from settling in white neighborhoods have been declared unconstitutional, other means have been used. As incomes of black families grew and suburban housing became affordable to many of them, they often encountered an unwillingness on the part of white homeowners to sell to them. This was often due to an unofficial covenant among white homeowners in an area to exclude black families (and often other racial or ethnic minorities). Real estate brokers often colluded with white homeowners by "steering" prospective black home buyers away from all-white areas. Though this practice is illegal, it is very difficult to prove.

Fourth, zoning regulations adopted by wealthier white communities have also served to maintain housing segregation. These include restrictions on the minimum size of house lots, which keeps housing prices high and out of reach of middle-class black families. Many suburban communities also exclude most forms of low-income housing, both public and private, which prevents many black families from living there.

Fifth, the federal government itself actually exacerbated housing segregation through its public housing programs. The federal Public Housing Administration subsidized the construction of low-income rental apartments in inner cities throughout the country. To qualify for a lease, applicants were subjected to a maximum income level, which meant that black families were more apt to qualify than whites. Many of these inner-city housing projects were occupied almost exclusively by black families, which tended to reinforce existing patterns of housing segregation.

Another federal program, the Federal Housing Administration (FHA) was set up in 1938 to guarantee mortgage loans on residential housing. It helped to finance almost one-third of all new housing built during the postwar housing boom of the late 1940s and 1950s. Part of its original mandate was to ensure that properties in a community were occupied by the same racial and social groups (ostensibly to maintain social stability in a neighborhood). As a result, the FHA purposely helped retain existing patterns of housing segregation. Though President Kennedy issued an executive order in 1962 which outlawed the segregationist practices of the FHA, it was too late, since the racial pattern of suburban housing had been fairly well established by then.

A sixth source of housing segregation occurs in the credit market. To purchase a house, families almost always have to take out a mortgage loan. There is considerable evidence that banks and other credit providers have typically discriminated against black families in providing such mortgages. White and black families with identical income and earnings histories are often treated differently by banks. This often helps to exclude black families from white neighborhoods.

A related practice is "redlining," which means that certain sections of a city or town are "lined in red pencil" to indicate that they are "off limits" for mortgage loans. These areas are typically occupied by black families or members of other minority groups. This practice does not reinforce housing segregation but it does make it difficult for black and minority families to obtain better housing in their own (segregated) neighborhood. Discrimination may also apply to other forms of credit – such as car loans and credit cards. The availability of credit may affect a family's wealth. Evidence presented in the next chapter will show that black families have accumulated considerably less wealth than whites.[6]

Finally, a seventh reason for housing segregation may be *voluntary* segregation. We would observe housing segregation when people voluntarily choose to live with people of similar racial or ethnic background.

Pre-labor market discrimination refers to inequality of opportunity in the acquisition of schooling and other forms of human capital. For example, blacks in the South, up until 1960 or so, were often served by inferior schools and had less access to higher education than Southern whites. Though the earnings of Southern black males in comparison to white males might be attributable to their lower level of schooling, the fact that they received less schooling or lower quality schooling might itself be due to discrimination in schooling.

Today, unequal access to the same quality schooling often results from housing segregation. Black families (and Hispanic families) are often concentrated in segregated neighborhoods. Since school enrollment is usually allocated on a neighborhood basis, school children are often segregated into different schools on the basis of race. This is referred to as *de facto* segregation.

School busing is one strategy that has been used over the past 35 years to achieve some measure of racial parity among schools. However, such efforts occasionally meet with resistance from local communities. Moreover, legally, it is more difficult to effect school busing across local jurisdictional lines, so that wealthy white communities are often unreachable for inner-city black students.

To obtain an idea of the extent of school desegregation, a study was conducted by the (then) U.S. Department of Health, Education, and Welfare. It found that in 1976, 44 percent of minority students were enrolled in schools that were 80 percent or more minority, and another 23 percent in schools that were 50 to 80 percent minority. Effectively, only one-third of minority students were in schools that were less than 50 percent minority. Schools in 1976 were still largely segregated. Interestingly, the most segregated schools were found in the Northeast and the least segregated in the South and Border States.

Conditions did not change much between 1976 and 1992. In the later year, according to statistics compiled by Orfield (1993), 34 percent of black students were still found in schools that were 90 percent or more minority and another 32 percent in schools that were between 50 and 90 percent minority. As in 1976, only one-third of black students attended schools that were more than half nonminority. Segregation is even more marked for Hispanic students. In 1992, 34 percent were enrolled in schools 90 percent or more minority and another 39 percent in schools between 50 and 90 percent minority. Thus, only about one-quarter of Hispanic students attended integrated schools.

Orfield's later figures indicated very little change in the pattern of school segregation. For example, he found that in 1997, nearly 70 percent of African American students and 75 percent of Latino students attended predominantly minority schools, according to data gathered from the Civil Rights Project at Harvard University. More than one-third of the students in each group were in schools where 90 percent or more of their classmates were minorities. In contrast, the average white student was enrolled in a school where more than 8 in 10 of his or her classmates also were white.

Orfield and Lee (2006) updated these figures to the early 2000s. Their primary conclusion was that most schools were going through a process of *re-segregation*. Their report was based on the National Center for Education Sciences (NCES) Common Core of Data for 2003–2004 as well as historical data for analyzing trends. Multiracial schools were defined as schools in which at least one-tenth of the students are from three or more of the five major racial and ethnic groups: African American, Latino, Asian, Native American, and white.

Geographically, the most dramatic trends in re-segregation were seen in the South and the Border States for black students and increasing segregation for Latinos in the West. From 1991–2003, the number of black students attending majority nonwhite schools rose sharply across all regions. In the South, this percentage increased from 61 percent to 71 percent. Latinos constituted the largest minority and were increasingly segregated in regions where they were concentrated. Asians were the least segregated group of students and were most likely to attend multiracial schools.

From 1991 to 2003, the percentage of students of every race in multiracial groups increased. Segregation was no longer black and white but increasingly multiracial. Attendance in multiracial schools varied by region, with more than half of black and Asian students attending these schools in the West and about two-fifths of Latino students attending these schools in the Border region. States where the largest shares of students attend multiracial schools include the three largest states – California, Texas, and Florida – and one state, Nevada, in which the Latino population was climbing very rapidly.

Is school segregation in and of itself bad? There are three problems that result from school segregation: (i) financial; (ii) peer group; and (iii) family effects. First, different schools within the same locality may be allocated different resources depending on the racial make-up of the school. This was particularly true in the South before 1960, where educational expenditures per pupil were lower for black schools, though it is less true today. Even today schools in *different communities* spend very different amounts on education per pupil, depending on the wealth of the community. Insofar as white communities are generally richer than those occupied by minorities, their school expenditures will be higher.[7]

Second, many studies have shown that the performance of minority children is correlated with the racial composition of a school. Black students, in particular, are found to achieve better in schools that are racially mixed because of the peer group effect. One reason for this is that black students from poor neighborhoods often develop value systems that are quite different than white students from affluent areas. The exposure of black pupils to more education-oriented values often helps improve their school performance.[8] Third, a related factor is the family effect. Insofar as minority students come from families with less education and resources, it is likely that they will have less in the way of parental inputs into the educational process.

It is interesting that most recent studies have failed to find much difference between white and black students in regard to input measures of education, such as expenditures per pupil, teacher–student ratios, and other indices of school resources. However, most studies find clear racial differences in "measured output" from schooling. One telling statistic is from a report issued by the National Center for Educational Statistics in 1979. It found that among 9 year olds, black students scored 12 percent lower in a standardized math test and 11 percent lower in reading, while among high school graduates, the differentials had widened to a 20 percent gap in math scores and a 16 percent gap in reading comprehension. A second is based on a study conducted by the Office of Education (see Congressional Budget Office, 1977). Using a reading test consisting of such items as street signs, telephone directories, and the like given to 17-year-old high school students, it classified 42 percent of blacks in this group as functionally illiterate, compared to only 8 percent of the white students.

In an updated study, Krueger, Rothstein, and Turner (2005) looked at racial differences in the National Assessment of Education Progress (NAEP) scores from 1970 to 2000. In 1970, the average black student scored one standard deviation below the average white student in both reading and math.[9] They found a substantial decline in the racial achievement gap in the early part of this period, from 1970 to about 1990. However, after 1990 there was essentially no further progress in reducing the test gap. In 2000, the racial test difference was three-quarters of a standard deviation in reading and even higher in math.

A third is racial and ethnic differences in the educational attainment of persons 25 years or older. According to data from the U.S. Census Bureau (2007), 29 percent of white males 25 or older completed 4 years of college or more in 2005, compared to 16 percent of black males and only 12 percent of Hispanic males in this age group. Comparable statistics on college completion rates among females 25 years or older are 27 percent for white women, 19 percent among black women, and 12 percent among Hispanic women.

These differences in educational output cannot fail to affect the relative labor market performance of whites, blacks, and Hispanics. In the next chapter, we will look at more detail into the educational attainment of the black, white, and Hispanic population, and how it has changed over time.

A more subtle form of pre-labor market discrimination evolves from *sex stereotyping*. As we shall see in Chapter 14, the main source of differences in earnings between men and women is that they tend to work in different occupations. This phenomenon is referred to as *occupational segregation*. A large proportion of female workers have traditionally been found in teaching, nursing, secretarial jobs, and clerical jobs. The source of this pattern is not clearly understood. However, it appears to stem, at least in part, to different socialization patterns that boys and girls experience. Exposure to television and societal norms leads to different role models for boys and girls and, this, in turn, may lead to different job preferences. We shall return to this issue in Chapter 14.[10]

12.3   THEORIES OF DISCRIMINATION: AN OVERVIEW

How do we explain both the existence and the apparent persistence of discrimination? If we consider the strictly constructed neoclassical model of the labor market, discrimination makes no sense. Suppose two male workers from different groups have exactly the same marginal productivity but the first is paid a wage equal to his marginal product and the latter is paid a lower wage. If there were perfect competition among employers, then a profit-maximizing firm would realize that it could increase its profits by paying the second worker slightly more than his current wage but still less than the person's marginal product. With perfect information, all employers would realize this and a bidding war would ensue until the wage of the second worker was brought in line with the first's. Thus, if all the assumptions of the neoclassical model held, discrimination could occur only in the short run, until the labor market was brought into equilibrium.

In this chapter, we consider five models that try to account for the existence of discrimination in the labor market. In each, one or more of the assumptions of the neoclassical model are changed. The first, developed by Becker (1957), assumes that employers may have a **taste for discrimination** – that is, gain utility from hiring one type of worker over another. In this model, employers maximize utility rather than monetary profits. This leads to wage differentials between the two groups, depending on how prejudiced employers are and the relative size of the minority population. The result is that white workers are paid more than equally productive black workers.

The second, the **statistical theory of discrimination**, assumes that employers do not have complete information about the true productive abilities of potential employees. Employers rely on past information or data (thus the term statistical discrimination) to form expectations about the likely productivity of job candidates. In so doing, they often group prospective employees according to their race or gender and *screen* on these characteristics (see Section 8.6.2.1 for a discussion of the screening model in its relation to education). On the basis of past performance, employers may view minority and female workers as less capable than white male workers with similar credentials and pay them less.

The third is a Marxian **divide and conquer** model, which argues that the division of the national product between the capitalists and the workers is a result of the class struggle. It is in the interests of the capitalist class to prevent the workers from forming a cohesive and unified political front. One means is a divide and conquer strategy, whereby capitalists strive to create divisions within the working class. Another way is to segment workers within the workplace on the basis of race and gender. White male workers are assigned the elite positions while minorities and females are shunted into the low-paying ones. This policy creates internal friction within the working class and prevents the formation of a united class.

The fourth is the **racial stigma** model developed by Loury (1998 and 2002). The central focus of the argument is around interracial social interactions that occur under conditions of uncertainty, the evolution of racial stereotypes resulting from such interactions, and a prominent role played by racial stigma in biasing the socially cognitive processes by which racial conventions are formed. Such negative stereotyping may become self-fulfilling and thus "confirm" the original prejudices.

The fifth is the **overcrowding model**, usually applied to gender discrimination. Either because of employer discrimination or gender differences in job preference, males and females are segregated into two groups of occupations. Though such segregation by itself need not cause gender differences in wages, pay differences may result if job opportunities in the female occupations are low relative to those in the male occupations.

12.4   TASTE FOR DISCRIMINATION

This model, developed by Becker (1957, 1971) assumes that employers have a "taste for discrimination." Because of prejudice, some employers may prefer hiring one group of workers to another. The prejudice may take the form of a desire to maintain social distance from another race or may stem from a belief in what jobs constitute appropriate social roles for women.

In economic terms, prejudice means that an employer is willing to pay a premium for one type of worker over another with exactly the same productive capabilities. Formally, the model assumes that two groups of workers have the same skills and are perfect substitutes in the production process. Employers who harbor prejudice against a minority group will hire these workers only at a wage discount sufficient to compensate for the disutility of working with them.

Becker defines employer i's "discrimination coefficient" d_i for a minority worker as the percentage difference between the worker's marginal product and the "value" or utility of the worker to employer i. Suppose MP_m is the marginal product produced by a minority worker. Then the value of this worker to a particular employer i is given by $MP_m(1 + d_i)$, where $-1 <= d_i <= 0$, and this is also the wage employer i would be willing to pay the minority worker.[11]

It should be noted that discrimination coefficients d_i will generally differ among employers. If an employer is prejudiced against minority workers, then d_i would be negative for *this employer*, and this employer will pay less for a minority worker than a white worker of the same skills. If, for example, both workers have marginal product MP^*, then employer i will pay the white worker a wage $w^* = MP^*$ but the minority worker only $w^*(1 + d_i)$.[12] The more prejudiced an employer is, the more negative the value of d_i. However, some employers may not be prejudiced at all, and for them d_i will be zero.

Because the degree of prejudice will generally differ among employers, the actual market degree of discrimination will depend on *both* the *distribution* of individual discrimination coefficients d_i and the *size of the minority population*. This can be seen with the aid of Figure 12.1. The vertical axis shows the ratio of the wage paid to a minority worker to the wage paid to a white

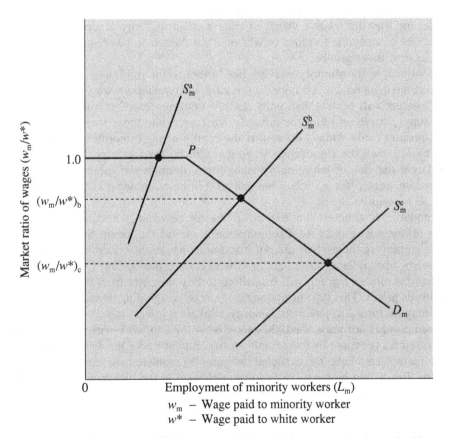

w_m – Wage paid to minority worker
w^* – Wage paid to white worker

Figure 12.1 The formation of an equilibrium wage differential between minority and white workers in the Becker model

worker with the same productive capabilities, and the horizontal axis shows the employment level of minority workers. Let us first consider the demand curve for minority workers, indicated by the "kinked line" labeled D_m. The demand curve is formed by arranging wage offers made by employers in order of the size of the offer.[13] This is equivalent to ordering employers in reverse order of their discrimination coefficients d_i.

The left part of the line is horizontal, at a wage rate ratio of 1.0. This portion represents the employers who harbor no prejudice ($d_i = 0$) and are willing to pay minority workers the same as white workers (of equal productivity). The demand curve then slopes downward (at point P), indicating that beyond this point all other employers have some taste for discrimination (d_i is less than zero). Some of these are only mildly prejudiced and thus willing to hire minority workers at only a slight "discount." The further to the right along the demand curve, the more discriminatory the employer and the lower the wage the employer is willing to pay for a minority worker.

Three alternative supply curves for minority workers are shown in this diagram – S_{ma}, S_{mb}, and S_{mc}. If the size of the minority workforce is small (S_{ma}), then the supply curve may intersect the demand curve at its horizontal portion. In this case, the market equilibrium will be at 1.0 – that is, minority workers will be paid exactly the same wage as white workers. This is true even though some (or even most) of the employers are prejudiced against minority workers. Despite this, there are a sufficient number of nonprejudiced employers (with zero values of d_i) willing to hire the total supply of minority workers at the same wage as white workers. This case may help account for why the relative wages of certain small minority groups, such as the Chinese or Japanese, are comparable to those of whites, even though some or many employers may be prejudiced against these groups.

If the supply curve for minority workers lies further to the right, as S_{mb}, then it will intersect the demand curve in its downward slope. In this case, the equilibrium wage ratio between minority and white workers will be less than unity. Employers represented on the demand curve to the left of the supply curve will hire the minority workers, while those found to the right will not hire any minorities (only white workers). If the supply of the minority labor force is larger, as illustrated by S_{mc}, then the equilibrium wage gap will be even greater. The wage ratio will be lower the larger the size of the minority labor force, because the value of d_i for the marginal employer whose wage offer will clear the market will be more negative and therefore the equilibrium wage w_m will be lower.

In this model, it is assumed that employers do not necessarily maximize money profits but rather their utility, where taste for discrimination is one of the parameters. Becker also argues that even if employers themselves are not discriminatory, profit-maximizing firms may engage in discriminatory behavior if customers or coworkers are prejudiced. Customers who are prejudiced against a minority group will be willing to buy products from them only at a discount (that is, a lower price). This type of prejudice can arise in retailing or service jobs. In this case, employers may be forced to pay their minority workers a lower wage.

If white employees are prejudiced, they may be willing to work with minority workers only if they are offered a premium by their employer to compensate for the disutility of having minority coworkers. In such a case, the expected outcome is complete race segregation of firms, since an integrated firm would be more costly to run (because of the higher wages to white workers) than an all-white or all-minority company.

This model was criticized by Arrow (1973) because it fails to account for the long-term persistence of discrimination in the labor market under conditions of perfect competition. We illustrate the argument in Figure 12.2. Consider the case of a competitive industry. The initial market demand curve for minority workers is given by D_{m1}, with a kink at P, and the supply curve for

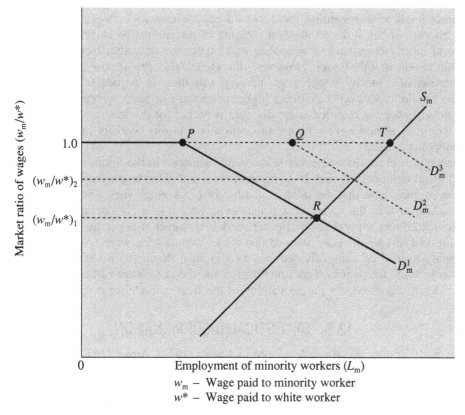

Figure 12.2 The movement over time in the wage differential between minority and white workers in the Becker model

minority workers is given by S_m. The initial equilibrium wage ratio is thus given by $(w_m/w^*)_1$. Firms which lie to the right of point R on the demand curve D_{m1} will hire only white workers, and firms to the left will hire minority workers.

Since the less prejudiced employers (with a lower d_i) are willing to hire minority workers at their lower wage, their wage costs will be lower and their profits will therefore be greater than those employers who have a high d_i and hire only white workers.[14] Firms which hire minority workers are at a competitive advantage and should expand faster than firms that hire only white workers. Over time, the demand curve for minority workers will shift to D_{m2} (with a kink at point Q), and the new equilibrium wage ratio will become $(w_m/w^*)_2$, higher than the previous level. The shifting out of the demand curve D_m is due to the change in the relative size of firms – in particular, the relative growth of the nondiscriminatory firms. Over the long run, the nondiscriminators should win out and dominate the industry, and the market wage ratio between minority and white workers should eventually approach unity (at point T).[15] In a sense, the market rewards the progressive employers – the ones who do not exhibit prejudice against minority groups.

Becker also argues that in a competitive industry there would be forces that would reduce the level of discrimination over time. In a monopolistic industry, on the other hand, free entry is excluded and therefore discrimination against minorities may persist over time. Becker therefore predicted that the degree of wage discrimination against minorities would be higher in a monopolistic industry than a competitive one.

In his 1971 book, Becker presented some evidence to support his argument. While his model has a direct implication regarding the observed pay differential between white and minority workers, the use of pay differentials as a measure of discrimination is difficult because of the influence of other factors such as schooling and experience on wages (see the Chapter 13 for further discussion of this issue). However, this model also provides a hypothesis regarding the proportion of minority workers an industry will hire. In particular, less discriminatory employers should, *ceteris paribus*, hire a higher percentage of black workers than a discriminatory employer (since the required wage discount is higher for the latter). By implication, competitive industries should have a higher proportion of minority workers in a given type of job than monopolistic ones.

To analyze this proposition, Becker selected 38 industries in the South in 1940, 10 of which he described as monopolistic and 28 as competitive. He divided employment into eight occupational groups and found that the relative number of black employees was greater in the competitive industries than the monopolistic ones in seven out of eight occupational groups. This result provided direct support to the Becker model. However, a paper by Franklin and Tanzer (1970) disputed this result. They showed that if the 38 industries were ordered by their degree of monopoly instead of being divided into two groups, there was no statistically significant correlation between the degree of monopolization and the percentage of black employees in the industry. This cast some doubt on the validity of the Becker model of discrimination.

12.5   STATISTICAL DISCRIMINATION

A second model of discrimination, developed by Phelps (1972), Arrow (1972a, 1972b, 1973), and Aigner and Cain (1977), relies on the role of imperfect information in employment decisions. Two key assumptions are introduced: (i) employers cannot determine the true productivity of a prospective employee; (ii) employers have a preconceived notion of the relative productivity of two groups of workers, say whites and minorities. Suppose that employers believe minority workers to be less productive than white workers with other characteristics that are identical, such as education and experience. Then employers will screen job candidates on race, assign a lower probability of success to a minority applicant, and therefore be less likely to hire a minority employee or be willing to hire the person only at a lower wage. In either case, minority workers will receive, on average, lower earnings than comparably "qualified" white workers. The same argument can be used to explain lower earnings for female workers.

In contrast to the Becker model, employers are assumed to be profit-maximizers. Moreover, there is no reliance here on the formation of exogenous tastes. Instead, the model is based on subjective probabilities about how productive different kinds of workers are. But this begs the question of where such subjective evaluations or "stereotypes" come from in the first place.

Phelps (1972) provides an ingenuous solution. He argues that the current assessment of relative productive capability is likely to be based on past experience. Suppose that out of pure prejudice or because of existing social norms, employers in the past hired white workers for the more skilled jobs and minorities for the less skilled ones. White workers also received higher wages, enjoyed superior working conditions, and obtained more training than minority workers. As a consequence, minority workers might show slower growth of productivity over time due to limited training and might even become discouraged and leave the firm. Employers might then base their current assessment of the likely success of different groups of workers on their previous "statistical" experience with them. In this case, we have a self-fulfilling prophecy, whereby initially incorrect signals or evaluations lead to discriminatory actions which actually result in creating productivity differences between races. Thus, reliance on past (incorrect) information leads to actions which corroborate the past information.[16]

The statistical discrimination model does a better job than the Becker model in explaining why competition does not eventually eliminate discrimination. In Becker's model, those employers who are nondiscriminatory should eventually prevail over the employers who do discriminate. In the statistical discrimination model, discrimination is due to imperfect information which can persist over long periods of time. If men believe that a woman would never make a good president and a woman is never given the opportunity to become president and disprove this misconception, then there is no reason why this misconception should go away.

This is not, of course, to say that such erroneous ideas can never disappear. Sometimes, extraordinary events are necessary for this to happen. This often happens in tight labor markets (periods of low unemployment) when there are shortages of qualified white males and companies are forced to hire minority and female workers to fill skilled jobs normally reserved for white males. During World War II, for example, when there was a shortage of male workers for skilled factory jobs, many women were hired for these positions. "Rosie the Riveter" became a national symbol for the success of women in these traditionally male jobs. In this case, when World War II ended and the veterans returned from Europe and the Far East, these factory jobs were restored to the men, and women returned to their traditional role as homemaker.

Another famous example is the hiring of the black baseball player Jackie Robinson by the (then) Brooklyn Dodgers in 1947. Major League baseball had until that time been a completely segregated sport. Many owners were afraid that fans would not come to the stadium to see black players. However, Robinson was an exceptional player and helped the Dodgers win several pennants during the early 1950s. Fans did come to see the Dodgers play because they were more interested in a winning team than in the color of the ball players. The success of the Brooklyn Dodgers and Jackie Robinson opened the way for the integration of professional baseball.

These smart employers will then hire minorities and females into the skilled jobs at their lower prevailing market wages, increase their profit, and expand more rapidly than their "ignorant" competitors. Over time, nondiscriminatory employers will eventually dominate the industry and discriminatory differences in earnings should be eliminated.[17] Look at professional basketball where white players are now a distinct minority.

It may require extraordinary circumstances to break through statistical discrimination. This form of discrimination may thus provide a rationale for **affirmative action** – a government program designed to induce employers to hire more minorities and females into traditionally white male jobs (a program that we will discuss in more detail in the next two chapters). In the context of this model, affirmative action may be seen as one way of breaking the vicious cycle of self-fulfilling prophecy based originally on prejudice and race and sex stereotypes. By providing minority and female workers with the same opportunity for decent wages, good working conditions, and adequate training as white males, this program may enable these groups to perform equally to white males in the workplace. Companies may, as a result, reassess their statistical evaluation of the relative likelihood of success of these groups and help end the use of race or gender as a screening device.[18]

Further work on the statistical discrimination model has tended to highlight some of the incentive effects on racial minorities. Lundberg and Startz (1983) emphasized the effects of statistical discrimination on human capital acquisition. In particular, they argued that the lower returns to human capital investment for African Americans will, in general, lead to underinvestment by African Americans in schooling and training. The result is group discrimination because "groups with equal average initial endowments of productive ability do not receive equal average compensation in equilibrium" (Lundberg & Startz, 1983, p. 342).[19]

Lang (1986) argued that differences in communication behavior (the use of language, speaking, and listening) between blacks and whites, together with the fact that most employers are white males, can lead to a situation of less reliable information about minority job applicants. Cornell and Welch (1996) formally demonstrated that in equilibrium this type of interaction will lead employers to treat white workers more favorably even when they have no pre-existing discriminatory preferences. Neumark (1999) provided econometric evidence about the reliability of labor market information concerning minorities and females. His estimates indicated that employers had inferior information about female new hires than male new hires but about the same information regarding minorities relative to white new hires.

Lundberg and Startz (2004) expanded their work on statistical discrimination by examining the relationship between imperfect information and segregation. Using a search model, they showed that racial signaling leads to a pattern of racially segregated transactions, which in turn perpetuate the informational asymmetries. Minority groups necessarily suffer more from segregation than whites since the degree to which transactions opportunities are curtailed depends on the size of the group as well as the informational "distance" between racial groups. This process is self-reinforcing because the contact between the majority group and the minority group diminishes as the distance between the two racial groups increases. In other words, as the minority group becomes more and more segregated from the majority group, the ability of the majority to learn about the true capabilities of minority workers also lessens over time.

12.6   THE RACIAL STIGMA MODEL

A fourth model of discrimination is the racial stigma model developed by Loury (1998 and 2002). The model applies to racial discrimination, particularly against African American males. The argument focuses on racial stereotypes and the racial stigma resulting from such stereotyping. Such negative stereotyping may become self-fulfilling and thus "confirm" the original prejudices.[20] As will become apparent, the Loury model has striking similarities with statistical discrimination models.

Loury argues that it is "natural" for people to classify others by their observable physical, class, and other characteristics in order to deal with a social environment characterized by uncertainty. This cognitive process by which other people are classified into separate groups and by which properties are assigned to these groups leads to the formation of rules of thumb in dealing with other people. Each individual will treat observed subjects on the basis of the classification scheme each has developed. Insofar as an individual classifies others by race, an individual will discriminate in their interactions with other people on the basis of race.

When the perceived information signaled by race is relevant to a particular social situation, an individual will attribute perceived group characteristics to the subject he or she is dealing with. This "virtual social identity" for the subject may have little relationship to the actual traits of the subject. This analysis is very similar to the statistical discrimination model discussed above. The individual will, in general, consider both the group characteristics relevant to the subject's "group" and the subject's individual characteristics as well. For example, in a hiring decision, an employer may consider both the group characteristics of an African American male job candidate in addition to the particular attributes of the candidate and may refuse to hire an African American job candidate with comparable qualifications to a white job applicant.

The next step in Loury's model differentiates his model from standard statistical discrimination models. Loury goes on to argue that the differential treatment of "similar" subjects by an agent (such as an employer) creates *incentive structures* that depend on the agent's cognitive classification scheme. Such differential incentives result in different behavioral responses. Often, the behavioral response may actually confirm the initial beliefs of the agent even though the initial beliefs were ungrounded. Through this type of feedback mechanism, the initial erroneous beliefs become perpetuated. In equilibrium, the initial prejudice regarding racial stereotypes becomes reinforced in spite of the lack of an initial inherent relationship between the racial classifications and actual behavior. Loury feels that this self-reinforcing mechanism is the main reason for the perpetuation of racial inequality in the United States.

Loury gives several examples of this mechanism at work. In one example, suppose that an employer observes workers during a probationary training period, that the employer can observe only the mistakes that the trainee makes but not the effort expended by the trainee, and that for legal or institutional reasons, it is much more difficult to dismiss an employee once the training period is over. Moreover, suppose that due to prejudice the employer believes that an African American trainee will exert less effort during the training period than a "comparable" white trainee. The employer may therefore set up a lower threshold of "tolerable" mistakes for the African American trainee, after which the trainee is dismissed. As a result, the likelihood of the African American trainee being hired is lower than that of the comparable white trainee.

Loury then argues that the African American trainee is likely to respond to this difference in treatment. In particular, if the standard to which the black trainee is held is harsher, the black trainee may rationally decide that the extra cost of exerting effort during the training period does not outweigh the expected benefit. The resulting reduction in effort on the part of the black trainee will lead to an increase in the number of mistakes made by the black trainee, and this result will confirm the initial belief of the employer. The employer will then feel justified in imposing a more stringent standard on the black trainee than the white trainee by the "resulting" evidence concerning racial differences in the effort expended during the period of training. As in the statistical discrimination model, the observed results give justification to the employer in his (her) initial beliefs regarding racial differences in ability.

Another example is with regard to schooling decisions. In particular, if African Americans perceive widespread discounting of their worth as potential employees, the incentive for the accumulation of human capital through acquiring more schooling and training is thereby diminished. This, in turn, will confirm the negative stereotype held by prospective employers. In the Loury model, this self-reinforcing mechanism creates a "stigma" effect for African American workers.[21]

Loury (2002) appeared to soften his position on affirmative action. In particular, he argued that it is not simply racial discrimination that keeps African Americans from achieving their goals, but rather the more complex reality of racial stigma, which concerns who, at the deepest cognitive level, they are understood to be. Loury argued that the image white Americans have of black Americans as less than full citizens influences policy far more than who African Americans are in reality. He concluded that the employment of color-blind policies will not address widespread racial inequalities because they do not take into account either the external or internal harm done to African Americans from a protracted history during which bias against blacks was the norm. This argument might provide a rationale for introducing affirmative action in order to *undo* both the psychological and financial harm that past discrimination created among African Americans.

12.7 THE MARXIAN MODEL

A model of discrimination also derives from Marxian economic theory. The central assumption of Marxian thought is that there are two major classes in a capitalist society, the capitalists and the workers. The division of the national product between these two classes is a result of "class struggle." This battle takes both an economic form, as in collective bargaining and strikes, as well as a political form, as in the development of labor parties in many Western European countries and lobbying in the United States. It is generally in the interests of the capitalist class to prevent the workers from forming a cohesive and unified political party or economic front. One way of accomplishing this is a **divide and conquer** strategy, whereby the capitalists try to create divisions within the working class. Such a strategy could weaken working-class consciousness and solidarity and enable the capitalists to obtain a larger share of the national output.

As developed by Reich (1977, 1978, 1981a, 1981b, 1988), this line of argument continues that one effective way of fragmenting the workforce is on the basis of race and gender. Occupational segregation therefore comes about wherein minorities and whites are given different jobs, as are males and females. Antagonism develops between groups of workers on the basis of visible differences of race and gender. White workers see minority workers as a threat to their jobs. The interest of white workers is to prevent minority workers from taking over their jobs. Minority workers see white workers as preventing them from advancing. The interest of minority workers is to occupy the jobs formerly reserved for white workers. The same sort of antagonism develops between male and female workers. The result is that workers see other groups of workers as their primary enemy instead of uniting against the capitalists. In consequence, workers' bargaining power against capitalists is reduced, and capitalists receive higher profits.[22]

This model is consistent with the persistence of discrimination over time. It is in the interest of the capitalists to maintain discriminatory pay differentials between races and genders. It is also in the interests of the white male workers to maintain their hegemony. Both capitalists and white males benefit from continued racism and sexism. Moreover, by co-opting one segment of the working class, the capitalists have managed to maintain control over the economy.

But why don't workers "get smart" and realize that the workforce as a whole would benefit from eliminating antagonisms along race and gender lines and presenting a united front to the capitalists? Marxian work has not provided a compelling argument as to why a more unified working class has failed to form in the United States whereas it has formed in other advanced industrial economies.[23]

12.8　OVERCROWDING MODEL OF OCCUPATIONAL SEGREGATION

The overcrowding model of occupational segregation, originally developed by Bergmann (1974) and later extended by Stevenson (1975), Blau and Hendricks (1979), and Blau (1984b), is principally applicable to gender discrimination. It is assumed that there are separate male jobs and female jobs in the workplace. Occupational segregation by itself need not result in pay differentials between male and female workers. However, the model assumes that there are far fewer female occupations than male occupations. Women enter only the female occupations, which increases the supply of workers to the female sector and correspondingly lowers the supply of workers to the male sector. Since job opportunities in female occupations are small relative to the supply of female labor, wages in female jobs are artificially lowered. Likewise, the lower supply of workers in male jobs artificially raises wages in male occupations. As a result, females with the same qualifications as male workers will receive lower wages.[24]

This argument can be illustrated by means of Figure 12.3. Two occupations are available to the labor force – secretaries (s) and truck drivers (t). We assume that the two occupations require identical human capital, so that the demand curve for each (D_s, D_t) is the same.[25] With no job discrimination, women and men can work freely in each job, so that the supply curves are identical (S_s, S_t). Under perfect competition, the wages for secretaries and truck drivers are the same (w_c) and both males and females may be employed in each occupation.

(a)   (b)

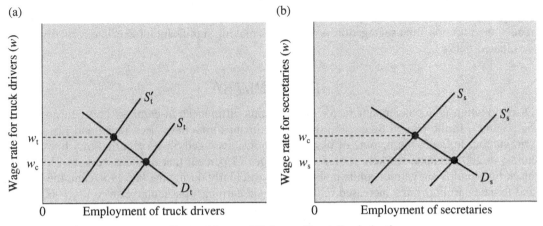

c – Competitive equilibrium without discrimination
s – Secretaries
t – Truck drivers
D – Demand curve
S – Competitive supply curve
S' – Supply curve with discrimination

Figure 12.3   The formation of wage equilibria for male and female jobs in the overcrowding model

Now, suppose that only females are allowed to work as secretaries, whereas male workers have a wide range of job opportunities. As a result, there are more females competing for secretarial jobs than males for truck driver positions. The supply curve for truck drivers therefore shifts to the left (S'_t) and that for secretaries shifts to the right (S'_s). The new equilibrium wage for truck drivers (w_t) is now higher than that for secretaries (w_s).[26]

This model raises a number of questions. First, what is the source of the occupational segregation? Bergmann in her 1974 article, following the work of Becker, assumes that employer preference or preconceptions of "sex-appropriate" roles causes the segregation of male and female labor into separate occupations.

Job segregation may also reflect gender preferences. Family upbringing and general socialization processes may create sex-role models for different types of occupations. Young women may voluntarily decide to develop skills and choose jobs that are consistent with traditional sex roles. The schooling system, starting even in primary school, may encourage boys to pursue certain career paths and girls to pursue others. In secondary school and college, this may take the form of encouraging males to take science and math and females to concentrate in the humanities.

Another important question is why "female" jobs tend to be overcrowded relative to male occupations. As we shall see in Chapter 14, female employment was historically concentrated in six or seven occupations, whereas male workers are dispersed over a much wider range of jobs. It is not clear what historical mechanism funneled females into such a relatively small number of potential job opportunities.

Another issue is the long-term persistence of occupational segregation. Here, too, there is no clear explanation of the factors that maintain occupational segregation by gender in the face of competitive pressures. In the case of employer discrimination, there is always the potential that a "smart" employer will hire cheaper but equally productive female labor in traditionally male occupations and reap the extra profits. A more compelling argument for the persistence of sex segregation is that it emanates primarily from the early socialization process and sex stereo-typing. However, as we shall see in Chapter 14, the 1980s and 1990s have witnessed a large reduction in occupational segregation, with females making significant inroads into formerly male-dominated fields.

12.9 SUMMARY

Discrimination is another major factor that explains differences in earnings between groups in our country. In the United States, the two predominant forms have been racial and gender dis-crimination. In 2005, the income of black households averaged 62 percent that of white house-holds; in 2005, female workers earned, on average, 77 percent that of male workers. However, black households did gain on white households, particularly during the late 1950s and the 1960s; and female earnings have increased relative to male earnings, particularly since the 1960s.

Differences in income between whites and minorities and between males and females do not of themselves constitute evidence of discrimination. Economists view discrimination as the "un-explained" difference in earnings between these groups. Though they may differ to some degree in what factors they consider relevant or "justifiable" in explaining earnings differences, almost all would include schooling and experience. Proof of discrimination would entail evidence that one group continues to earn less than another even after controlling or *standardizing* for pertin-ent explanatory variables.

This chapter considered several alternative views of the sources of labor market discrimina-tion. The Becker model derives from "tastes for discrimination" among employers. The equi-librium wage for minority workers is shown to depend on both the distribution of prejudicial preferences among employers and the size of the minority workforce. The Arrow–Phelps stat-istical discrimination model is based on imperfect information and screening. On the basis of past "statistical" experience with minority or female workers, employers are led to believe that they are less productive or reliable than "comparable" white male employees. They pay the minority and female workers lower wages and provide them with less training than white male employees, a result that leads to lower productivity gains for both minority and female workers and thus confirms the employers' original prejudices.

The Loury racial stigma model focuses on racial stereotypes and the racial stigma resulting from such stereotyping. Employers classify prospective employees by their observable physical, class, and racial characteristics in order to deal with an environment characterized by uncertainty. The behavioral response of minority workers may actually confirm the initial beliefs of the employer even though the initial beliefs were unfounded. Through this type of feedback mechanism, the initial erroneous beliefs become perpetuated. Such negative stereotyping may thus become self-fulfilling and thus "confirm" the original prejudices.

The Marxian "divide and conquer" model is based on the view that capitalists attempt to create divisions within the working class. One way of accomplishing this objective is to seg-ment workers on the basis of race and gender. White male workers are given the high-paying jobs while minorities and females are consigned to low-paying ones. This stratagem creates inter-nal friction within the working class, reduces class unity, and thereby increases the profits of the capitalist class.

The overcrowding model, usually applied to gender discrimination, rests on the assumption that male and female workers are typically segregated into male and female occupations. Because female opportunities are more limited than those of male workers, there is an oversupply of workers to the female occupations and a restricted supply to the male occupations. This raises the wages of male workers relative to females.

12.10 REFERENCES AND BIBLIOGRAPHY

Aigner, D. & Cain, G.G. (1977). Statistical theories of discrimination in labor markets. *Industrial Labor Relations Review*, **30**, 175–87.

Altonji, J.G. & Pierret, C.R. (2001). Employer learning and statistical discrimination. *Quarterly Journal of Economics*, **106**(1), 313–50.

Arrow, K.J. (1972a). Models of job discrimination. In A.H. Pascal (ed.), *Racial Discrimination in Economic Life* (pp. 83–102). Lexington, MA: D.C. Heath.

Arrow, K.J. (1972b). Some mathematical models of race in the labor market. In A.H. Pascal (ed.), *Racial Discrimination in Economic Life* (pp. 187–204). Lexington, MA: D.C. Heath.

Arrow, K.J. (1973). The theory of discrimination. In O. Ashenfelter & A. Rees (eds.), *Discrimination in Labor Markets*. Princeton, NJ: Princeton University Press.

Bayer, P.J. (2006). Separate when equal? Racial inequality and racial segregation. Yale Economics Applications and Policy Discussion Paper No. 9, May.

Becker, G.S. (1957). *The Economics of Discrimination* (2nd edition, 1971) Chicago: University of Chicago Press.

Bergmann, B.P. (1974). Occupational segregation, wages and profits when employers discriminate by race or sex. *Eastern Economic Journal*, April–July, 103–10.

Bergmann, B.P. (1976). Reducing the pervasiveness of discrimination. In E. Ginzberg (ed.), *Jobs for Americans* (pp. 120–41). Englewood Cliffs, NJ: Prentice-Hall.

Blau, F.D. (1972). Women's place in the labor market. *American Economic Review*, **62**(2), 161–6.

Blau, F.D. (1977). *Equal Pay in the Office*. Lexington, MA: D.C. Heath.

Blau, F.D. (1984a). Discrimination against women: Theory and evidence. In W. Darity, Jr. (ed.), *Labor Economics: Modern View* (pp. 53–89). Boston, MA: Kluwer-Hijhoff.

Blau, F.D. (1984b). Occupational segregation and labor market discrimination. In B.F. Reskin (ed.), *Sex Segregation in the Workplace: Trends, Explanations, Remedies*. Washington, DC: National Academy Press.

Blau, F.D. & Hendricks, W.E. (1979). Occupational segregation by sex: Trends and prospects. *Journal of Human Resources*, **14**(2), 197–210.

Blinder, A. (1973). Wage discrimination: Reduced form and structural estimates. *Journal of Human Resources*, **7**(4), 436–55.

Cain, G.G. (1986). The economic analysis of labor market discrimination: A survey. In O. Ashenfelter & R. Layard (eds.), *Handbook of Labor Economics*, Vol. 1. New York: North-Holland.

Coate, S. & Loury, G. (1993). Will affirmative-action policies eliminate negative stereotypes? *American Economic Review*, **83**(5), 1220–40.

Congressional Budget Office (1977). *Inequalities in the Educational Experiences of Black and White Americans*. Washington, DC: Government Printing Office.

Cornell, B. & Welch, I. (1996). Culture, information, and screening discrimination. *Journal of Political Economy*, **104**(3), 542–71.

Cymrot, D.J. (1985). Does competition lessen discrimination: Some evidence. *Journal of Human Resources*, **20**(4), 605–12.

D'Amico, T. (1987). The conceit of labor market discrimination, *American Economic Review*, **77**(2), 31–5.

Darity, W.A. (1982). The human capital approach to black-white earnings inequality: Some unsettled questions. *Journal of Human Resources*, **17**(1), 72–93.

Dickinson, D. & Oaxaca, R. (2006). Statistical discrimination in labor markets: An experimental analysis. NEP Working Paper, November.

Doeringer, P.B. & Piore, M.J. (1971). *Internal Labor Markets and Manpower Analysis*. Lexington, MA: Lexington Books.

Fairlie, R. (2005). An extension of the Blinder–Oaxaca decomposition technique to Logit and Probit models. *Journal of Economic and Social Measurement*, **30**, 305–16.

Franklin, R. & Tanzer, M. (1970). Traditional microeconomic analysis of racial discrimination: A critical view and alternative approach. In D. Mermelstein (ed.), *Economics: Mainstream Readings and Critiques*. New York, Random House.

Hacker, A. (1992). *Two Nations: Black and White, Separate, Hostile, Unequal*. New York: Scribners.

Havet, N. & Sofer, C. (2007). Why do women's wages increase so slowly throughout their career? A dynamic model of statistical discrimination. GATE Working Paper No. 07-22, Ecully, France, October.

Jaynes, G.D. (1989). *Branches without Roots*. New York: Oxford University Press.

Kaas, L. (2006). Does equal pay legislation reduce labour market inequality? IZA Discussion Paper No. 2421, Bonn, Germany, November.

Krueger, A., Rothstein, J. & Turner, S. (2005). Race, income, and college in 25 years: The continuing legacy of segregation and discrimination. NBER Working Paper No. 11445, June.

Kozol, J. (1991). *Savage Inequalities: Children in American Schools*. New York: Crown.

Lang, K. (1986). A language theory of discrimination. *Quarterly Journal of Economics*, 101(2), 363–82.

Lemann, N. (1992). *The Promised Land*. New York: Vintage.

Lloyd, C.B. (ed.) (1975). *Sex, Discrimination, and the Division of Labor*. New York: Columbia University Press.

Loury, G.C. (1998). Discrimination in the post-civil rights era: Beyond market interactions. *Journal of Economic Perspectives*, 12(2), 117–26.

Loury, G.C. (2002). *The Anatomy of Racial Inequality*. Cambridge, MA: Harvard University Press.

Loury, G.C. (2003). Racial stigma: Toward a new paradigm for discrimination theory. *American Economic Review*, May, 334–7.

Lundahl, M. & Wadensjo, E. (1984). *Unequal Treatment: A Study in the Neo-Classical Theory of Discrimination*. New York: New York University Press.

Lundberg, S.J. (1991). The enforcement of equal opportunity laws under imperfect information: Affirmative action and alternatives. *Quarterly Journal of Economics*, 106(1), 309–26.

Lundberg, S.J. & Startz, R. (1983). Private discrimination and social intervention in competitive labor markets. *American Economic Review*, 73(3), 340–7.

Lundberg, S.J. & Startz, R. (2004). Information and racial exclusion. IZA Working Paper No. 1389, Bonn, Germany, November.

Marshall, R. (1974). The economics of racial discrimination: A survey. *Journal of Economic Literature*, 12, 849–71.

Massey, D.S. (2007). *Categorically Unequal*. New York: Russell Sage Foundation.

Massey, D.S. & Denton, N.A. (1993). *American Apartheid: Segregation and the Making of the Underclass*. Cambridge, MA: Harvard University Press.

Neumark, D. (1999). Wage differentials by wage and sex: The role of taste discrimination and labor market information. *Industrial Relations*, 38(3), 414–45.

Ñopo, H. (1997). An extension of the Blinder–Oaxaca decomposition to a continuum of comparison groups. IZA Discussion Paper No. 2921, July.

Oaxaca, R. (1973). Male–female wage differentials in urban labor market. *International Economic Review*, 14(3), 693–709.

Oaxaca, R. & Ransom, M. (1994). On discrimination and the decomposition of wage differentials. *Journal of Econometrics*, 61(1), 5–21.

Orfield, G. (1993). *The Growth of Segregation in American Schools*. Alexandria, VA: National School Boards Association.

Orfield, G. & Lee, C. (2006). *Racial Transformation and the Changing Nature of Segregation*. Cambridge, MA: The Civil Rights Project of Harvard University.

Papke, L. (2005). The effects of spending on test pass rates: Evidence from Michigan. *Journal of Public Economics*, 89, 821–39.

Phelps, E.S. (1972). The statistical theory of racism and sexism. *American Economic Review*, 62, 659–61.

Raphael, S. (2002). The anatomy of racial inequality. *Journal of Economic Literature*, 40, 1202–14.

Reich, M. (1977). The economics of racism. In D.M. Gordon (ed.), *Problems in Political Economy*, 2nd edition. Lexington, MA: D.C. Heath.

Reich, M. (1978). Who benefits from racism? The distribution among whites of gains and losses from racial inequality. *Journal of Human Resources*, 13.

Reich, M. (1981a). Changes in the distribution of benefits from racism in the 1960's. *Journal of Human Resources*, 16(2), 314–21.

Reich, M. (1981b). *Racial Inequality*. Princeton, NJ: Princeton University Press.

Reich, M. (1988). Postwar income differences: Trends and theories. In G. Mangrum &

P. Phillips (eds.), *Three Worlds of Labor Economics*. White Plains, NY: M.E. Sharpe.

Roemer, J.E. (1978). Differentially exploited labor: A Marxian theory of discrimination. *Review of Radical Political Economics*, **10**(2), 43–53.

Roemer, J.E. (1979). Divide and conquer: Micro-foundations of a Marxian theory of wage discrimination. *Bell Journal of Economics*, **10**(2), 695–705.

Schwab, S. (1986). Is statistical discrimination efficient? *American Economic Review*, **76**(1), 228–34.

Stevenson, M.H. (1975). Relative wages and sex segregation by occupation. In C.B. Lloyd (ed.), *Sex, Discrimination, and the Division of Labor*. New York: Columbia University Press.

Stiglitz, J.E. (1973). Approaches to the economics of discrimination. *American Economic Review*, **63**, 287–95.

Stiglitz, J.E. (1974). Theories of discrimina-tion and economic policy. In G.M. von Furstenberg, A.R. Horowitz & B. Harrison (eds.), *Patterns of Racial Discrimination*, Vol. II. Lexington, MA: Lexington Books.

Thurow, L.C. (1969). *Poverty and Discrimination*. Washington, DC: Brookings.

U.S. Census Bureau (2002). *Racial and Ethnic Residential Segregation in the United States: 1980–2000*. Washington, DC: U.S. Government Printing Office.

U.S. Census Bureau (2007). *Statistical Abstract of the United States, 2007*, 127th edition. Washington, DC: U.S. Government Printing Office.

Wachter, Michael (199). Primary and second-ary labor markets: A critique of the dual approach. *Brookings Papers on Economic Activity*, **3**, 637–94.

Wilson, W.J. (1987). *The Truly Disadvantaged: The Inner City, the Underclass, and Public Policy*. Chicago: University of Chicago Press.

NOTES

1   Moreover, as we shall discuss, it is also possible that racial differences in schooling levels may them-selves reflect discrimination.

2   The symbol "E" refers to the expected value of the expression.

3   Also, see Massey (2007) for more detailed discussion of the issues addressed in this section of the book.

4   The term *de jure* refers to a matter of law whereas *de facto* refers to a matter of fact (or actuality). Jim Crow practices also included prohibitions of blacks from working in certain trades, school seg-regation, and restrictions on the use of public facilities (for example, blacks were not allowed to drink water from "white" drinking fountains and blacks had to sit in the back of public buses).

5   This northward migration had actually been going on since the beginning of the twentieth century (see Lemann, 1992).

6   Another recent phenomenon is the issuance of so-called "sub-prime" mortgages. These are mortgages that require little in the way of down payments and little corroboration of the ability of the mortgagee to repay the loan. These mortgages are also characterized by a low introductory interest rate (a "teaser rate"), which then balloons to a very high interest rate after two or three years. In 2007, these mort-gages hurt many homeowners who found that they were unable to repay the loan and lost their home to foreclosure. The evidence also indicated that minorities were harder hit by these loan instruments than whites.

7   However, it should be noted that many states have changed their funding formulas in aid to local schools in an effort to reduce the disparities in total expenditures per pupil between poor and rich communities (see Papke, 2005).

8   See the Chapter 13 for more discussion of this topic and citations of relevant studies.

9   See Chapter 3 (Section 3.2) for the definition of standard deviation.

10   Also, see D'Amico (1987) for an interesting discussion of labor market and pre-labor market dis-crimination in the case of differences in success between black males born in the United States and those who immigrated to the United States from the West Indies.

11   It is assumed that there is a single wage for white workers and a single wage for minority workers.

12   It is also equivalent to argue that the employer will pay a minority worker with marginal product MP^* the same wage as a less productive white worker, with marginal product $MP^*(1 + d_i)$.

13   Technically, it is assumed that the total employment in a given type of work is fixed and that the equilibrium wage rate for white workers is fixed (and, in particular, is independent of the number of white workers employed).

14   Recall that, by assumption, minority workers are as productive as white workers. Since their wages are lower, a firm that hires minority workers will have a greater profit than those that hire only white workers.

15   This result assumes that there are at least a few employers in the industry who do not discriminate. If there are not, then presumably with reasonably open and competitive capital markets, minority-owned businesses may be able to move into such an industry to take advantage of the profit potential associated with minority workers. This suggests, by the way, that promoting minority-owned businesses may be one way to alleviate unfair wage discrimination against minority workers.

16   Also, see Bergmann (1976) and Blau (1977) for related arguments of feedback effects on pay discrimination.

17   There is an analogous argument with respect to insurers. If one group is thought to be a greater risk than another (female drivers as compared to male, perhaps) based on incorrect information, then a "smart" insurance company should eventually discover this and expand its profit by readjusting its rates. In long-run equilibrium, the rate structure should reflect the true relative risk of different classes of individuals.

18   A related argument derives from the dual labor market model (see Section 9.2). It is assumed that a firm's labor force is roughly divided into two segments. The first, the primary labor force, consist of workers who are expected to be long-term employees of a company. The second, the secondary labor force, consist of more marginal employees whose tenure with the company is expected to be short-lived. Companies invest more heavily in and pay higher wages to their primary workers than to the secondary workers. Employers may be predisposed to believe that both minority and female workers are less likely to remain long-term employees and therefore track them into the lower-paying, secondary jobs.

19   They also argued that as long as the marginal cost of human capital investment is increasing for each individual, this equilibrium is not socially efficient because the cost of training the marginal white worker will exceed the cost of training the marginal African American worker.

20   Also see Raphael (2002) for a critical appraisal of the Loury model.

21   See the interesting discussion of the relation between statistical discrimination and affirmative action provided by Coate and Loury (1993), who suggest that affirmative action may induce employers to patronize minority workers which, in turn, may undercut their incentive to acquire additional skills.

22   Some statistical evidence supporting this hypothesis is presented in Reich (1978).

23   Another interesting issue is why individual employers do not break away from the pack and hire cheaper minority and female labor. An interesting game theoretic analysis is developed by Roemer (1978, 1979), in which it is shown that there are bargaining equilibria in which both white and minority workers are worse off and employers are better off than would be the case without worker divisions. Moreover, the equilibria are stable over time, and because of the bargaining structure, market forces cannot overcome the discriminatory equilibrium wages.

24   Another implication of the model is that employers will use more labor-intensive techniques for the female jobs and capital-intensive ones for male jobs. The lower female wages will then be associated with a lower marginal productivity of female workers. Male and female workers with the same human capital will generally have different pay and different productivity on the job.

25   Moreover, we assume that the number of jobs available in each occupation is the same at a given wage rate.

26   This model is quite similar in structure to the one used to explain the differential in pay between union and non-union workers. See Section 9.2 for details.

Chapter 13

Racial Discrimination: Progress and Reversal for Black Americans

13.1 INTRODUCTION

In 1944, the Swedish economist Gunnar Myrdal published a major study of race relations in the United States, entitled *The American Dilemma: The Negro Problem and Modern Democracy*. In this book, he posed the "dilemma" between the alleged commitment to equal opportunity within the United States and actual discrimination against black Americans. Is such discrimination compatible with a democratic society?

Since the publication of this famous work, there have been many important changes in race relations and the economic status of black Americans. The story, as it unfolds, will show three decades of progress of blacks, from about 1940 through 1970, followed by three and a half decades of relative stagnation in both labor earnings and family incomes. Moreover, the 1980s and 1990s have witnessed a sharp decline in the employment of black men, as well as rising inequality within the black community.

In Section 13.2 we review the basic evidence on the progress of black Americans. We begin with a comparison of the labor earnings of white and black Americans. We then look at changes over time in labor force participation patterns among blacks. Family incomes of blacks and whites are considered next, as well as differences in poverty incidence. Some comparative data are then presented on the wealth holdings of the two groups. Finally, because Hispanic Americans represent a large and growing minority in the United States, we also consider similar trends for this group.

The next four sections consider reasons for the advances made by black Americans in the two decades or so following World War II and the later reversal of fortunes. One reason for their early gains was a massive migration out of the then low-wage South to the high-wage North, particularly since 1945 (Section 13.3). A second reason for their economic progress was steady gains in schooling attainment made by African Americans (Section 13.4). A third development has been the growth in the number of female-headed households in the black community, particularly since 1970, which has largely been responsible for the deterioration in incomes among African American families (Section 13.5).

Public policy measures enacted to reduce racial discrimination have also made important contributions to progress among black families. Section 13.6 discusses the two major programs, the Civil Rights Act of 1964 and President Lyndon Johnson's 1965 Executive Order 11246. This section also presents evidence about the effectiveness of these programs. A summary is provided in Section 13.7.

13.2   TRENDS AND STATUS REPORT ON RACIAL INEQUALITY

13.2.1   The earnings gap: Have African American workers made gains on whites?

We begin with a consideration of differences in wages and salaries between blacks and whites (Table 13.1). Earnings ratios are shown by age and schooling group for full-year, full-time employees in 2004. This enables us to **standardize** or control for differences in human capital between blacks and whites. A ratio of 1.0 would indicate identical earnings for blacks and whites.

The ratio in median earnings among all full-time, full-year male workers was 68 percent in 2004 (Panel A). When we standardize by education, the ratios are higher. Among males who attended high school but did not receive a degree, the ratio was 76 percent, while among high school graduates, the ratio was 74 percent. For those who attended college but did not receive a B.A., the ratio in earnings between blacks and white males was around 78 percent. Among those with a B.A. degree or more, the ratio was 76 percent. There is relatively little systematic difference in the earnings gap by age group.[1]

Earnings ratios are also shown between black and white females who worked full-time, full-year (Panel B). Among all females, the ratio in median annual earnings was 0.83, compared to 0.68 among all males. The earnings differential was noticeably smaller by educational group. The earnings ratio varied from a low of 0.88 among female workers without a high school degree to 0.91 among those with some college. Among younger women (ages 25–34), the earnings ratios were even higher by educational group (a range of 0.93 to 0.98). There appears to be less evidence of discrimination against black women relative to white women than of black men relative to white men. However, as we will see in Chapter 14, both white and black females still earn less than male workers (also, see Chapter 14 or more discussion of earnings differences between black and white women).

Table 13.1   The ratio of median annual earnings between black and white workers, classified by gender, education, and age, 2004

Education	25–34	35–44	45–54	55–64	All ages (25+)
A. Black males/White males					
Less than a high school graduate	0.75	0.83	0.77	—	0.76
High school graduate[a]	0.75	0.76	0.76	0.81	0.74
Some college, no B.A.	0.82	0.77	0.80	—	0.78
College, B.A. or more	0.80	0.75	0.69	0.76	0.76
All schooling levels	0.71	0.71	0.69	0.69	0.68
B. Black females/White females					
Less than a high school graduate	0.98	0.93	0.72	—	0.88
High school graduate[a]	0.96	0.90	0.86	0.91	0.90
Some college, no B.A.	0.93	0.92	0.92	0.93	0.91
College, B.A. or more	0.93	0.82	0.98	0.99	0.89
All schooling levels	0.85	0.82	0.84	0.89	0.83

a   Includes equivalency (GED) degrees.
Source: http://pubdb3.census.gov/macro/032005/perinc/new03_139.htm. Earnings data are for year-round (defined as those who worked 50 or more weeks), full-time (defined at those who work 35 or more hours per week) employees. Hispanics are excluded from this table.

13.2.1.1 Changes over time

The results of Table 13.1 show that among full-time, full-year workers, black males earned about a quarter less than white males in 2004, after standardizing for human capital, while black females made about 10 percent less than white females in terms of annual earnings. It is next of interest to see whether the race–earnings gap widened or narrowed over time. Since part of the overall gains in earnings made by blacks is attributable to their increasing educational attainment (as we shall see in Section 13.4 below), it is again necessary to control for educational attainment when we make these earnings comparisons.

Table 13.2 shows the ratio of earnings between blacks and whites from 1939 to 2004 (also see Figures 13.1(a) and (b)). The results are quite dramatic. In 1939, black males typically earned about half that of white males. Between 1939 and 1984, the earnings gap was steadily reduced, so that by 1984, the ratio of earnings between black and white males averaged 77 percent across educational groups. The earnings gap narrowed at all educational levels over this period.

After 1984, black males continued to make relative progress at some educational levels but either made no further gains or fell behind at others. The race–earnings gap stayed the same for those with less than a high school degree and further narrowed among workers with a high school degree. By 2004, the earnings ratio between black and white males had increased to 0.73 for the latter. However, among those who attended college but did not graduate and among college graduates, the earnings ratio fell somewhat. Among college graduates, the ratio slipped from 74 percent in 1984 to 72 percent in 2004.

The progress of black female workers relative to white female workers was even more dramatic than that of black males. Like black males, black females typically earned about half that of their white counterpart in 1939. However, unlike black males, their relative progress was steady throughout the period from 1939 to 1984, and by 1984, they had generally reached earnings parity with (or exceeded) white females of the same educational level. Unfortunately, from 1984

Table 13.2 The ratio of mean annual earnings between black and white workers, for males and females, classified by education, 1939–2004

Education	1939	1949	1959	1969	1979	1984	1992	2004
A. Black males/White males								
Elementary 0–8	0.48	0.56	0.60	0.70	0.78	0.86	0.81	—
High school 1–3	0.53	0.63	0.63	0.73	0.82	0.83	0.82	0.83
High school 4	0.57	0.60	0.61	0.71	0.71	0.66	0.72	0.73
College 1–3	0.50	0.53	0.62	0.75	0.75	0.77	0.75	0.76
College 4+	0.51	0.52	0.54	0.68	0.70	0.74	0.71	0.72
B. Black females/White females								
Elementary 0–8	0.43	0.54	0.54	0.67	0.95	1.08	0.94	—
High school 1–3	0.50	0.68	0.67	0.88	1.17	1.05	0.91	0.88
High school 4	0.53	0.69	0.73	0.92	1.03	0.99	0.97	0.90
College 1–3	0.56	0.72	0.85	1.15	1.09	1.06	0.94	0.97
College 4+	0.64	0.93	0.94	1.14	1.14	1.11	1.01	0.97

Sources: Jaynes, G.D. (1990). The labor market status of black Americans: 1939–1985. *Journal of Economic Perspectives*, **4**(4), 9–24.; U.S. Census Bureau (1993). Current Population Reports, Series P60-184, *Money Income of Households, Families, and Persons in the United States: 1992*. Washington, DC: U.S. Government Printing Office; http://pubdb3.census.gov/macro/032005/perinc/new03_139.htm.

(a)

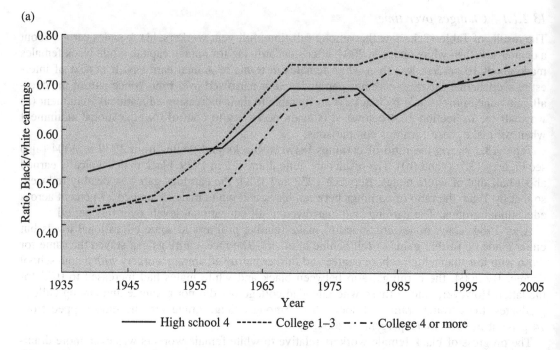

(b)

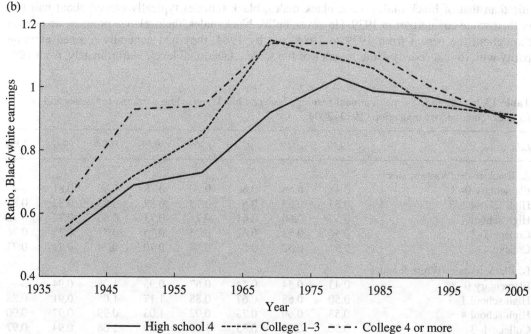

Figure 13.1   The ratio of annual earnings between (a) black and white males by education and (b) black and white females by education, 1939–2005

to 2004, the earnings ratio declined, so that by 2004 black women were making about 7 percent less than white women with the same schooling.

13.2.2 Labor force participation and unemployment

Section 13.2.1 has documented the fact that black Americans have made considerable progress relative to white Americans in terms of labor earnings. For black males, most of the gains were made by 1984, though with some slow advances thereafter. Black females, on the other hand, had reached virtually parity with white females in terms of earnings by 1984, though they slipped backwards a bit in the early 2000s.

However, there is another aspect of this story – the proportion of working-age adults with jobs. This, in turn, has two dimensions, as we saw in Chapter 7: (i) the labor force participation rate – the percentage of working-age individuals who are in the labor force; and (ii) the unemployment rate – the proportion of the labor force currently without a job but looking for work. In both dimensions, black males have fared much more poorly than white males, particularly since 1970.[2]

Table 13.3 presents labor force participation rates (LFPR) by race. Let us first consider differences by educational attainment for men aged 25 to 34 (Panel A). In 1940, black and white males had almost identical levels of labor force participation. This remained generally true until the 1960s. After this, the LFPR of black men fell substantially below that of white men. This occurred at all levels of schooling, except among college graduates, and was particularly marked at lower levels of educational attainment. In 1992, the LFPR of black males with no more than an elementary school education was 48 percent, compared to 85 percent for white males of the same schooling level – a difference of 37 percentage points. The difference was 19 percentage points (76 percent versus 95 percent) among high school graduates, and 9 percentage points (86 versus 95 percent) among those who attended but did not complete 4 years of college.

Panel B of Table 13.3 shows LFPR by age group for black and white males from 1955 to 2005 (also see Figure 13.2(a)). The same trends are evident. In 1955, the overall LFPR of black and white males was identical, at 85 percent. Since that time, the LFPR of both black and white males declined but after 1970 they declined considerably faster for black men. Among white men, the LFPR fell from 85 percent in 1955 to 74 percent in 2005. The decline was particularly marked for white men aged 55 to 64, whose LFPR decreased from 88 to 71 percent. Among black men, the overall LFPR fell from 85 percent in 1955 to 63 percent in 1994 – 11 percentage points below the corresponding rate for white men. The decline occurred for all age groups, though it was particularly sharp among those 55 to 64 in age (down to 54 percent). By 2005, the LFPR of black men was lower than that of white men in *all age groups*, with differences ranging from 10 to 17 percentage points.

The experience of women was just the opposite of men (see Panel C of Table 13.3 and Figure 13.2(b)). Between 1955 and 2005, the overall LFPR of both black and white women increased – the former from 46 to 61 percent and the latter from 35 to 59 percent. The increase occurred for all age groups. The most telling difference is that a higher percentage of black women than white women have historically been in the labor force. In 1955, the LFPR of black females was 46 percent, compared to 35 percent for white females – a difference of 11 percentage points. However, the difference has narrowed over time and by 2005 was reduced to only 2 percentage points.

Not all people in the labor force are employed at any given time, and there are also noticeable differences in the incidence of unemployment between black and white workers (also see

Table 13.3   Labor force participation rates by race, gender, schooling, and age (percent)

A. Black and white males by educational attainment, ages 25–34

Education	1940		1960		1980		1992	
	Black	White	Black	White	Black	White	Black	White
Elementary 0–8	95	95	92	91	66	76	48	82
High school 1–3	95	97	94	96	75	90	77	87
High school 4	97	98	95	98	86	95	76	93
College 1–3	93	95	91	94	89	94	86	95
College 4+	98	96	96	96	93	96	97	96

B. Black and white males by age group

Age	1955		1970		1980		1994		2005	
	Nonwhite	White	Nonwhite	White	Black	White	Black	White	Black	White
25–34	96	98	94	97	91	96	86	94	82	92
35–44	96	98	93	97	89	96	86	94	83	93
45–54	94	97	88	95	83	92	79	90	74	90
55–64	83	88	79	83	62	73	55	66	54	71
All ages	85	85	77	80	70	79	69	76	63	74

C. Black and white females by age group

Age	1955		1970		1980		1994		2005	
	Nonwhite	White	Nonwhite	White	Black	White	Black	White	Black	White
25–34	51	33	58	43	71	65	72	75	78	76
35–44	56	40	60	50	68	65	76	78	81	75
45–54	55	43	60	54	61	60	71	75	71	77
55–64	41	32	47	43	45	41	45	49	56	60
All ages	46	35	50	43	53	51	59	59	61	59

Sources: Jaynes, G.D. (1990). The labor market status of black Americans: 1939–1985. *Journal of Economic Perspectives*, **4**(4), 9–24; U.S. Census Bureau (1993). Current Population Reports, Series P60-184, *Money Income of Households, Families, and Persons in the United States: 1992*. Washington, DC: U.S. Government Printing Office; worksheets provided by the U.S. Bureau of Labor Statistics: http://www.bls.gov/web/cpseea13.pdf. and ttp://pubdb3.census.gov/macro/032005/perinc/new03_139.htm. Note that before 1977, figures were provided for only nonwhites as a group.

Chapter 7). As shown in Table 13.4, the overall unemployment rate of black men has typically been about two and a half to three times that of white men. This relationship has not changed very much over the postwar period, as figures for 1955, 1975, 1994, and 2005 indicate. The unemployment incidence has been greater for black men in comparison to white men at every age level. However, recently (since the late 1970s), unemployment has been particularly high among young black males, under the age of 20.[3]

The picture is rather similar among females. Black females have also had substantially higher unemployment rates than white women, typically about double. This relationship has also

(a)

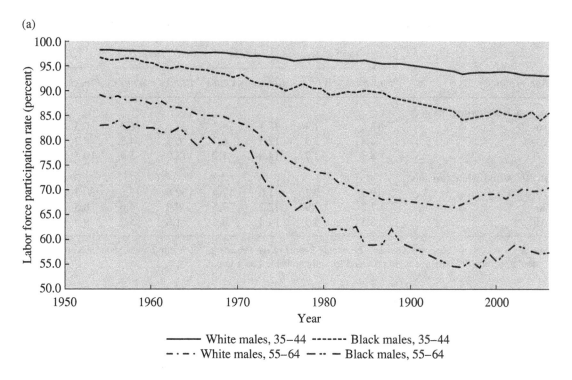

(b)

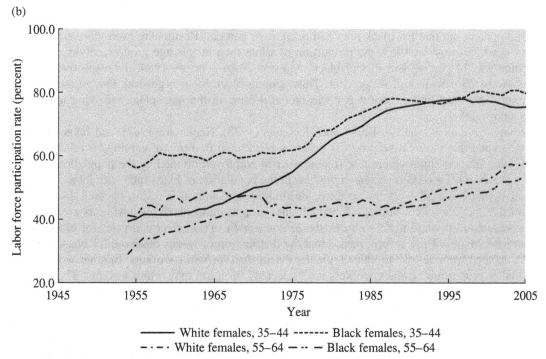

Figure 13.2 Labor force participation rates of (a) black and white males by age and (b) black and white females by age, 1954–2005

Table 13.4   Unemployment rates by race, gender, and age group, 1955, 1975, 1994, and 2005

Age group	1955		1975		1994		2005	
	Nonwhites	*Whites*	*Blacks*	*Whites*	*Blacks*	*Whites*	*Blacks*	*Whites*
A. Black and white males								
16–19	13.4	11.3	38.1	18.3	37.6	16.3	36.3	16.1
20+	8.4	3.3	12.5	6.2	10.3	4.8	9.2	3.8
All	8.8	3.7	14.8	7.2	12.0	5.4	10.5	4.4
B. Black and white females								
16–19	19.2	9.1	41.0	17.4	32.6	13.8	30.3	12.3
20+	7.7	3.9	12.2	7.5	9.8	4.6	8.5	3.9
All	8.5	4.3	14.8	8.6	11.0	5.2	9.5	4.4

Sources: Council of Economic Advisers, *Economic Report of the President, 1995*; http://www.gpoaccess.gov/eop/.
Note that before 1972, figures were provided for only nonwhites as a group.

remained relatively unchanged over the postwar period. As with black males, black females have experienced higher unemployment rates in every age group than white females. Here, too, differences are particularly marked among females under the age of 20.

One way of summarizing the differences in both LFPR and unemployment rates is to consider the number of persons of both races who earned zero labor income. According to calculations made by Jaynes (1990), in 1959, 5 percent of white men and 8 percent of black men aged 25 to 54 received no labor earnings. In 1984, the corresponding proportion for white men was still 5 percent but that for black men had risen to 16 percent. Results are even more striking for men aged 55 to 64. In 1959, the proportion of white men in this age group receiving no labor income was 14 percent and that of black men was 20 percent; by 1984, the respective proportions were 26 percent and *42 percent*. Thus, among black men in general, though particularly among older black men, there was a substantial decline in the percentage receiving income in the labor market.

Some economists, such as Butler and Heckman (1978), Heckman (1987), and Jaynes (1990), have argued that the relative progress made by black men in terms of earnings is related to the reduction in their employment rate (the number of employed divided by the population).[4] Their interpretation is based upon a *selectivity bias* in the population of black men with jobs. The argument is that low-skill workers have trouble finding jobs and, as a result, become discouraged and leave the labor force entirely. Since a higher proportion of black male workers are low skill in comparison to white male workers, the *discouraged worker effect* is greater for black males than white males. This, in turn, means that the distribution of wages observed for black workers is "truncated from below" to a much greater extent than for white workers. In other words, only a smaller proportion of black workers are "selected" for a job than white workers. The average labor earnings of black male workers thus appears higher than it would if all black workers (or if the same proportion of black workers as white workers) had a job.

One implication of this hypothesis is that gains made by black males since 1970 are *overstated* by using earnings data alone as the measure of labor market success. One way of showing the difference is to compare the average weekly earnings of black males (with a job) to the average earnings of black males of working age (20 to 65), including those with a job and those without a job. According to calculations made by Jaynes (1990), the weekly earnings of black male workers relative to those of white male workers increased by 53 percent between 1939 and 1959 and by 24 percent from 1959 to 1979. The corresponding figures for earnings per black male of working age are much lower, 36 and 14 percent respectively. These results led many to believe that gains made by black male workers were much more modest since 1960 than earnings data alone indicate. On the other hand, this argument does not apply to black women, since their employment rate is comparable to that of white women. A similar calculation shows almost no difference between the growth in the average weekly earnings of black women relative to white women and the growth in average earnings per female of working age.

13.2.3 Family income, poverty, and wealth

The last two sections considered only the labor income of individuals. However, family income is the key concept for understanding changes in well-being or the standard of living. As we saw in Chapter 2, family income includes not only wages and salaries but also property income (such as interest, rent, and dividends) as well as transfer income (such as social security benefits, welfare payments, and unemployment insurance). Also, the family is a different unit of observation than the individual. A family may have more than one person working or it may not have anyone working. Trends in family income may, as a result, be different than those for individual labor earnings.

What has happened to the income of black families relative to white families? Figure 13.3 shows the trends in the ratio of median family income between the two groups from 1947 to 2005.[5] In 1947, the ratio of median income was 51 percent. There was some increase in this ratio between 1947 and 1952 but by 1958 the ratio had returned to 51 percent. After that point, the trend was mostly upward, reaching a peak of 62 percent in 1975. But the relative income of

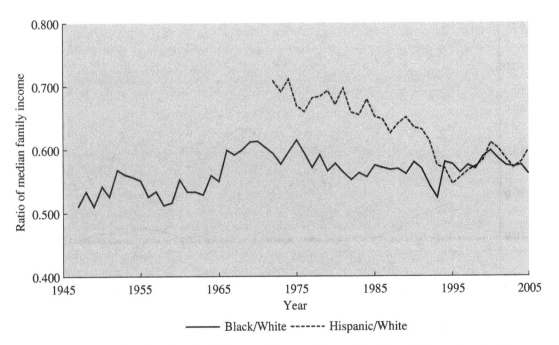

Figure 13.3 The ratio of median family income between black and white and Hispanic and white families, 1947–2005

black families then declined to 52 percent in 1993, about the same ratio as in 1959. During the "Clinton years," the situation improved markedly for African Americans and by the year 2000 the ratio reached 0.60. This was about the same ratio as in 1976, though still a little below its peak value of 0.62 in 1975. During the George W. Bush years, their relative position deteriorated once again and in 2005 the ratio fell to 0.56, about the same as in 1980. Indeed, in absolute terms (constant dollars), the median income of black families was the same in 2005 as it was in 1998.

The trend in median family income seem at odds with changes over time in the wages and salaries of black workers, both male and female, which continued to gain on white workers during the late 1970s and into the 1980s, albeit rather slowly. There are two reasons for the difference. First, as we discussed above, there was also a large increase in the number of working-age black males who were without a job from 1970 onward. Second, there was a significant change in the composition of black households, with a large increase in the number of families headed by females (with no husband present). We shall say more about this in Section 13.5 below.

As shown in Figure 13.4, black families have historically had a much higher poverty rate than white families. In 1959 (the earliest date for which such data are available), 55 percent of black families had incomes below the poverty line, compared to 18 percent of white families. Since that time, poverty has declined for both races. Among black families, the poverty rate reached 30 percent in 1974. However, after 1974, the poverty rate among African Americans turned upward. By 1983, it had risen to 36 percent. It fell to 31 percent in 1989 but by 1993 rose again to 33 percent. During the Clinton years, African Americans made steady income gains and by 2000 their poverty rate fell to 22 percent, their *lowest point ever*. During the George W. Bush administration, the trend reversed again and by 2005 their poverty rate had returned to 25 percent.[6]

Another aspect of family well-being is its holdings of household wealth (see Table 13.5). Let us first consider the homeownership rate (the percentage of housing units that are owned by their

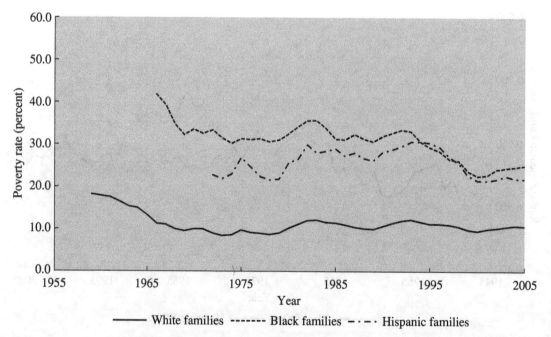

Figure 13.4   Poverty rates by race and Hispanic origin, 1959–2005 (percent of persons below poverty line)

Table 13.5 Homeownership rates by race, 1920–2005 (percent of housing units that are owner occupied)

Year	All races	Whites	Blacks and others	Ratio black/white
1920	45.6	48.2	23.9	0.50
1930	47.8	50.2	25.2	0.50
1940	43.6	45.7	23.6	0.52
1950	55.0	57.0	34.9	0.61
1960	61.9	64.4	38.4	0.60
1970	62.9	65.4	42.1	0.64
1980	64.4	67.8	44.2	0.65
1991	64.2	67.9	43.2	0.64
1995	64.7	69.4	46.8	0.67
2000	67.4	71.3	46.3	0.65
2004	69.0	75.8	50.1	0.66

Sources: U.S. Census Bureau (1994). *Statistical Abstract of the United States: 1994* (114th Edition). Washington, DC: U.S. Government Printing Office; U.S. Census Bureau (2007). *Statistical Abstract of the United States: 2007* (127th Edition). Washington, DC: U.S. Government Printing Office.

occupant), which almost doubled among nonwhite families between 1940 (24 percent) and 1991 (43 percent). Between 1991 and 2004 their homeownership rate continued to rise and reached 50 percent in 2005. There was a particularly large increase in the early 2000s.[7] The ratio of home-ownership rates between nonwhites and whites also increased, from 52 percent in 1940 to 64 percent in 1991, reaching parity with relative income levels of that year. Between 1991 and 2005 there was a modest increase in the ratio to 0.66. However, increases in nonwhite homeowner-ship rates in relative terms were confined mainly to the 1940s and the 1960s. Racial differences in homeownership rates, besides reflecting racial disparities in family income, may also be account-able by discrimination in housing and mortgage lending that was discussed in Chapter 12.

Nonwhite families also made substantial gains on whites in terms of net worth between the early 1960s and the early 1990s (see Table 13.6). Between 1962 and 1992, the ratio of mean wealth between nonwhite and white families grew from 13 percent to 37 percent, while the ratio of medians increased from 4 percent to 17 percent. However, from 1992 to 2004 there was no further change in the ratio of mean wealth between the two groups and the ratio of median wealth actually fell from 0.17 to 0.12.

Another concern is the fact that the wealth of nonwhite families averaged *only 19 percent* that of white families in 2004, compared to 65 percent for income, and the ratio of median net worth was only 10 percent, reflecting the large number of nonwhite families with zero or negative net worth. Why is the racial gap in wealth so much greater than that in income? One explanation emphasizes the role played by intergenerational transfers in household wealth accumulation. The argument is that inheritances and gifts play a crucial role in the accumulation of family wealth. Some economists estimate that up to 80 percent of the wealth owned by families today may have originated from such transfers (see Chapter 10 for more discussion).

Some evidence of this is provided in three papers. The first, by Blau and Graham (1990), exam-ined the sources of black–white differences in wealth holdings. Using econometric techniques on the National Longitudinal Survey, Blau and Graham were able to explain only about one-quarter of the difference in wealth holdings between black and white households on the basis of family income, age, and other demographic characteristics. They speculated that differences in

Table 13.6   Ratio in household income and wealth of blacks to whites, 1962–2005

Year	Ratio of means	Medians
A. Household income[a]		
1967	0.62	0.59
1983	0.62	0.57
1989	0.63	0.59
1992	0.63	0.58
1995	0.65	0.63
1998	0.63	0.62
2001	0.65	0.66
2004	0.65	0.65
B. Household net worth[b]		
1962	0.12	0.04
1983	0.19	0.07
1989	0.17	0.03
1992	0.19	0.17
1995	0.17	0.12
1998	0.18	0.12
2001	0.14	0.10
2004	0.19	0.10

a   *Sources*: U.S. Census Bureau (1990a). Current Population Reports, Series P-60, No. 168, *Money Income and Poverty Status in the United States: 1989*. Washington, DC: U.S. Government Printing Office; http://www.census.gov/hhes/www/income/histinc/inchhtoc.html#5. Hispanic households are excluded.

b   *Sources*: Author's calculations from the 1962 Survey of Financial Characteristics of Consumers and the 1983, 1989, 1992, 1995, 1998, 2001, and 2004 Survey of Consumer Finances. Hispanic households are excluded.

inheritances may play an important role in explaining the rest of the discrepancy, because income differences between blacks and whites were much greater in older generations.

Menchik and Jianakoplos (1997) were able to rigorously test this hypothesis using data from a more recent version of the National Longitudinal Survey and the 1989 Survey of Consumer Finances. Both datasets contain information on inheritances received, as well as the income and wealth of respondents. They found that racial differences in inheritances accounted for between 10 and 20 percent of the black–white differences in average wealth holdings. Together with income and demographic differences, they were able to account for close to half of the interracial wealth gap.

The third paper, by Gittleman and Wolff (2004), used the PSID from 1984 to 1994 to look at the sources of interracial wealth difference. They found that over this period white families received, on average, 13 times as much in inheritances as black families. Moreover, they calculated that 20 percent of the difference in the net change in mean household wealth between black and white families between 1984 and 2004 was attributable to differences in inheritances received.

If inheritances play an important role in wealth accumulation, then the much larger wealth of white families in comparison to nonwhites today may reflect differences in income and wealth of preceding generations. Though the wealth gap between nonwhite and white families has narrowed over the last 30 years, it remains higher than the income gap because it reflects the larger racial income gap of the parents and grandparents of today's families. If this is so, then it may take several generations for the wealth gap between blacks and whites to narrow to the same level as the income gap.

Another finding of note is that the inequality of income among black Americans was quite a bit higher than among whites. Calculations performed by the U.S. Census Bureau (1993) on the basis of 1992 Current Population Survey show that while the bottom 20 percent of white families accounted for 4.9 percent of all the income of the white community, the bottom quintile of black families received only 3.0 percent of the total income of the black community. Moreover, the top 20 percent of white families received 43.8 percent of the total income of white families, compared to a 48.8 percent share of the top quintile of black families.

In 2005, the Gini coefficient for household income among black families was 0.486, in comparison to a Gini coefficient of 0.462 among white households. The share of total income received by the top 5 percent in 2005 was 22.1 percent among both black and white households, while the share of the bottom quintile was 3.6 percent among the latter but only 2.8 percent among the former.[8] Moreover, calculations performed by Jaynes (1990) indicate that the inequality in labor earnings among males was rising much faster for blacks than whites. The Gini coefficient for white males increased from 0.37 in 1959 to 0.39 in 1984, while that for black males rose from 0.50 to 0.59.

13.2.4 Hispanics

Another important racial minority in the United States are Hispanics – those of mainly Caribbean or Latin American origin. Most of the Hispanic population in the United States came originally from Mexico, Puerto Rico, and Cuba, though today there are also significant numbers from South America and Central America. The U.S. Census Bureau has provided separate statistics on Hispanics since 1972. There is some difficulty in classifying people of Hispanic origin. The Census Bureau originally used Spanish surname as the basis of its classification but more recently has based this grouping on the self-identification of the respondent. In most tabulations, Hispanics can be of any race – that is, white or black.

By most indices, Hispanic families have fared somewhat better than black families but significantly worse than white families. As shown in Figure 13.3, the median income of Hispanic families was generally greater than that of black families, though noticeably lower than that of whites. In 2005, the median family income of Hispanics was 7 percent greater than that of black families but only 60 percent the level of white families. The ratio of median family income between Hispanic and white families declined from a peak of 71 percent in 1974 to a low of 55 percent in 1995 but then rebounded to 60 percent in 2005. This pattern reflects, in part, the large surge in Hispanic immigration during the 1990s and early 2000s (see Chapter 11 for more discussion).[9]

The incidence of poverty has likewise been substantially greater for Hispanic families than whites though generally somewhat lower than among African American families (see Figure 13.4). In 2005, the poverty rate for individuals of Hispanic origin was 21.8 percent, in comparison to 10.6 percent for whites and 24.9 percent for African Americans. The poverty rate for Hispanics rose from 22 percent in 1973 to 30 percent in 1982, declined to 26 percent in 1989, rose back up to 31 percent in 1994 but then declined again to 22 percent in 2005.

Table 13.7 provides some comparative data on earnings of Hispanic and white males in 2005 by age and educational attainment. Hispanic males have earned lower wages and salaries than white males and have also fared somewhat worse than black males. Among full-time, full-year workers, Hispanic males earned, on average, 61 percent the wages of white employees (compared to 68 percent for black male employees). However, when standardized by educational levels, the earnings ratios were noticeably higher, ranging from 76 to 82 percent across all educational groups. This result already indicates that a large part of the earnings gap between Hispanic and white workers is due to differences in educational attainment. Hispanic males also

Table 13.7   The ratio of median annual earnings between Hispanic and white male workers, classified by education and age, 2005

Education	25–34	35–44	45–54	55–64	All ages (25+)
Less than a high school graduate	0.81	0.88	0.96	—	0.79
High school graduate[a]	0.79	0.75	0.78	0.83	0.76
Some college, no B.A.	0.92	0.82	0.84	0.87	0.82
College, B.A. or more	0.92	0.69	0.77	0.87	0.77
All schooling levels	0.64	0.60	0.61	0.63	0.61

a   Includes equivalency (GED) degrees.
Source: http://pubdb3.census.gov/macro/032005/perinc/new03_139.htm. Earnings data are for year-round (defined as those who worked 50 or more weeks), full-time (defined as those who work 35 or more hours per week) employees.

Table 13.8   Labor force participation rates for Hispanic and white (non-Hispanic) individuals by age and gender, 1980, 1988, and 2005 (percent)

Age group	1980		1988		2005	
	Hispanic	White	Hispanic	White	Hispanic	White
A. Hispanic and white males						
16–17	45	54	39	49		
18–19	75	74	70	71		
20–24	88	87	89	87		
25–34	93	96	93	95	93	92
35–44	94	96	94	95	93	93
45–54	92	92	89	92	88	90
55–64	74	73	69	68	69	71
65+	21	19	17	17		
All, 16+	81	79	82	77	80	74
B. Hispanic and white females						
16–17	30	47	32	48		
18–19	50	65	56	66		
20–24	57	71	62	75		
25–34	54	65	61	73	62	76
35–44	55	65	62	75	68	75
45–54	55	60	58	69	67	77
55–64	35	41	42	44	48	60
65+	6	8	7	8		
All, 16+	47	51	53	56	55	59

Sources: U.S. Bureau of Labor Statistics (1990). *Handbook of Labor Statistics 1989*, Bulletin 2340. Washington, DC: U.S. Government Printing Office; http://data.bls.gov/PDQ/outside.jsp?survey=ln.

earned about the same as black males of the same educational attainment. Also, when standardized by schooling level, younger Hispanic males (ages 25 to 44) generally did considerably better relative to white workers of the same age group than older Hispanic workers (ages 45 to 64).

Table 13.8 shows both LFPR and unemployment rates for Hispanic and white Americans. In 1980, 1988, and 2005, Hispanic males had a higher overall LFPR than white males. However,

Table 13.9 Unemployment rates for Hispanic and white (non-Hispanic) individuals by age and gender, 1977, 1988, and 2005 (percent)

Age group	1977 Hispanic	1977 White	1988 Hispanic	1988 White	2005 Hispanic	2005 White
A. Hispanic and white males						
16–17	24.4	17.6	29.5	16.1	19.4	16.1
18–19	18.2	13.0	19.5	12.4		
20–24	12.2	9.3	9.2	7.4		
25–34	8.2	5.0	7.0	4.6		
35–44	4.9	3.1	5.9	3.4		
45–54	5.4	3.0	6.1	3.2		
55–64	6.8	3.3	6.7	3.3		
65+	10.4	4.9	6.9	2.2		
All, 16+	9.0	5.5	8.1	4.7	5.4	4.4
B. Hispanic and white females						
16–19					17.3	12.3
16–17	31.0	18.2	24.5	14.4		
18–19	23.0	14.2	18.9	10.8		
20–24	12.3	9.3	10.7	6.7		
25–34	9.7	6.7	7.2	4.5		
35–44	7.9	5.3	6.2	3.7		
45–54	10.7	5.0	5.9	3.1		
55–64	10.2	4.4	4.6	2.5		
65+	3.2	4.9	3.0	2.6		
All, 16+	11.9	7.3	8.3	4.7	6.9	4.4

Sources: U.S. Bureau of Labor Statistics (1990). *Handbook of Labor Statistics 1989*, Bulletin 2340. Washington, DC: U.S. Government Printing Office; http://data.bls.gov/PDQ/outside.jsp?survey=ln.

when standardized by age, the LFPR of the two groups are almost identical. (The higher overall LFPR of Hispanic men is due to the fact that a higher percentage of them fall within the prime working ages of 25 to 54 than white males.) Moreover, the LFPR of Hispanic males was noticeably higher than those of black males in all three years. For both these reasons, it seems unlikely that the type of selectivity bias discussed above in comparing the earnings of black and white men would affect the comparison of earnings between Hispanic and white males.

Though LFPR were about equal between Hispanic and (non-Hispanic) white males, unemployment rates of Hispanic males were about twice as great in both 1977 and 1988 (see Table 13.9). This was true for almost every age group. The relative difference in unemployment rates was particularly high among older men (45 and over). However, by 2005 the unemployment rates among Hispanic men were only slightly greater than among white men. It is also to be noted that unemployment among Hispanic males was less than that of black males in the three years (an overall rate of 8.1 percent in 1988 for the former in comparison to 11.7 percent for the latter, and 5.4 percent for the former in 2005 compared to 10.5 percent among the latter).

Among females, the LFPR of Hispanics was lower than that of whites, though the differences narrowed somewhat between 1980 and 1988. This was true for every age group. Hispanic women also experienced a higher incidence of unemployment than white women. This pattern characterized every age group. Interestingly, the unemployment rate among Hispanic women was almost the same as among Hispanic men in 1988 and only slightly greater in 2005.

13.3 MIGRATION FROM THE SOUTH

Work on racial discrimination has focused on the progress and eventual reversal of fortunes of black Americans. There are four factors that are predominantly responsible for changes in the economic status of black families: (i) outmigration from the South; (ii) progress in schooling; (iii) break-up of the black family unit; and (iv) public policy measures. In this section, we shall focus on the first issue.

At the time of the Civil War, and almost until 1900, 90 percent of black Americans lived in the South, mainly in rural areas. The preponderance of Southern blacks was employed in agriculture. By 1940 the proportion of blacks in the South had declined to 77 percent, in 1960 to 60 percent, and in 1980 to 53 percent, where it remained in 1990.[10] This change represents one of the greatest population migrations in the history of the United States.

Much of the change was driven by the prospects of higher wages in the North (and to some extent, the West). The shifting of the black population out of the low-wage South to the high-wage non-South was one of the major factors accounting for their relative wage gains between 1940 and 1960.

To see how this works, we will use a simple arithmetic example to illustrate the importance of *weighted averages*. Suppose the black/white earnings ratio is 0.4 in the South and 0.7 in the North, and, for simplicity, that whites earn the same in the South as in the North. Also, suppose that about 80 percent of black employees worked in the South, as was the case in 1940. Then, the country-wide average ratio of black to white earnings would be 0.46 $[0.8 \times 0.4 + (1 - 0.8) \times 0.7]$.

Suppose now that the proportion of blacks working in the South declines from 80 percent to 60 percent (as it did by 1960). Then, even if there were no change in the race–wage ratio in the South and the North, the new black/white earnings ratio would increase to 0.52 $[0.6 \times .4 + (1 - 0.6) \times 0.7]$. Thus, migration from the South to the North could be an important factor in explaining the relative wage gains made by black workers.

Actually, the explanation is a bit more complicated, because the wages of both white and black workers were initially higher in the North and there were changes of the wage gap within region over time. In fact, there are four separate effects involved, as the following data (for weekly wages) suggest (O'Neill, 1990, p. 30):

Black/White earnings ratios for male workers

	1940	1960
South	0.424	0.576
Non-South	0.669	0.740
Overall	0.489	0.637

The first, as we just described, is the migration effect, resulting from the higher wages in the North than the South. The second is also a migration effect but derives from the fact that the ratio of earnings between black and white workers was higher in the non-South than the South. This together with the higher overall wage levels in the North gave an extra boost to black earnings from migrating to the North.

The third results from the gradual convergence in overall wage levels between the South and the North, which occurred between 1940 and 1980. Because a larger proportion of blacks continued to live in the South (despite their outmigration) than of whites, this tended to raise the average earnings of blacks relative to whites. Fourth, within each region (but particularly the South, as the numbers above indicate) the black/white earnings ratio rose. This also helped narrow the overall gap between black and white earnings.

A study by Gwartney (1970b) analyzed the importance of the migration effect. He reported that in 1939 the income of nonwhite males 25 to 64 years of age residing in urban areas was 41 percent of the level of the equivalent group of white males in the South and 58 percent in the North. In 1959, the corresponding figures were 47 percent in the South and 64 percent in the North. He calculated that the outmigration of blacks from the South by itself raised the ratio of earnings between the two groups by 3 to 4 percentage points over this period.

Among females, Gwartney reported impressive gains for nonwhites relative to whites between 1949 and 1967, though very little gain during the 1940s. Earnings of nonwhite females relative to white females increased by 21 percent during the 1950s and 27 percent during the 1960s. He found that about a third of this gain was due to the migration of nonwhites to the North and the remainder to the increasing educational attainment and earnings by educational level of nonwhite females relative to white females.

In a more recent study, Vigdor (2006) indicated that the black/white earnings gap has historically been larger in the South than in other regions of the United States. However, since 1970, the male annual earnings gap outside the South increased quite sharply while the racial earnings gap in the South narrowed. In fact, according to the 2000 U.S. Census, there was significantly lower racial inequality in the South than in the non-South in 2000. Vigdor examines three possible explanations for this trend: (i) changing patterns of selective migration (that is, which African Americans moved between regions); (ii) labor market trends including reduced discrimination and the decline of manufacturing employment; and (iii) reductions in school segregation and school resource disparities in the South relative to the North. He found that selective migration can explain about 40 percent of the South's relative advance, and virtually all of the relative advance after 1980. Before 1980, the decline in the racial earnings gap could be attributed in large part to reduced industrial segregation and other labor market advances in the South. Relative improvements in school quality for Southern blacks explained at most 20 percent of the overall trend.

13.4 PROGRESS IN EDUCATIONAL ATTAINMENT

Perhaps, one of the most remarkable developments in the postwar period was the gradual convergence in educational attainment levels between black and white Americans. This, in turn, has been largely a result of the implementation of strong governmental programs to eliminate racial discrimination in this important social dimension.

In the antebellum South, the education of slaves was forbidden by law, so that by 1865, the vast majority of Southern blacks were virtually illiterate. After the Civil War, schools for black children were established in the South. By 1880, about one-third of black children were enrolled in schools, compared to about two-thirds of white children, most of whom lived outside the South (see Smith, 1984, and O'Neill, 1990, for more discussion).

Systematic data on schooling attainment date from 1940. Table 13.10 shows the percent of adults (25 years or older) who have completed high school and college. It is first instructive to see the tremendous gains in schooling made by black Americans. In 1940, only 7 percent of black male adults had completed high school, but, by 2005, the fraction had risen to 81 percent. In 1940, slightly more than 1 percent of all black male adults had graduated from college, whereas in 2005 the proportion stood at 16 percent. Similar gains were made by black women. The proportion that completed high school grew from 8 percent in 1940 to 81 percent in 2005, and the fraction who graduated from college increased from 1 to 19 percent.

Table 13.10 Educational attainment of persons 25 years and older by race, Hispanic origin, and gender, 1940–2005

Year	Male			Female			All
	White	Black[a]	Hispanic[b]	White	Black[a]	Hispanic[b]	
A. Percent who have completed 4 years of high school or more							
1940	24.2	6.9		28.1	8.4		24.5
1947	33.2	12.7		36.7	14.5		33.1
1959	44.5	19.6		47.7	21.6		43.7
1970	57.2	32.4		57.6	34.8		55.2
1974	63.6	39.9	38.3	63.0	41.5	34.9	61.2
1980	71.0	51.1	46.4	70.1	51.3	44.1	68.6
1989	78.6	64.2	51.0	78.2	65.0	50.7	76.9
1993	81.8	69.6	52.9	81.3	71.1	53.2	80.5
1997	82.9	73.5	54.9	83.2	76.0	54.6	82.1
2001	84.4	79.2	55.5	85.1	78.5	58.0	84.1
2005	85.2	81.1	58.0	86.2	81.2	58.9	85.2
B. Percent who have completed 4 years of college or more							
1940	5.9	1.4		4.0	1.2		4.6
1947	6.6	2.4		4.9	2.6		5.4
1959	11.0	3.8		6.2	2.9		8.1
1970	15.0	4.6		8.6	4.4		11.0
1974	17.7	5.7	7.1	10.6	5.3	4.0	13.3
1980	22.1	7.7	9.7	14.0	8.1	6.2	17.0
1989	25.4	11.7	11.0	18.5	11.9	8.8	21.1
1993	25.7	11.9	9.8	19.7	12.4	8.7	24.8
1997	27.0	12.5	10.6	22.3	13.9	10.1	23.9
2001	28.7	15.3	10.8	24.0	16.1	11.4	26.2
2005	29.4	16.1	11.8	26.7	18.8	12.1	27.6

a The data are for blacks and other races from 1940 to 1959, for blacks only from 1970 to 1989.
b Persons of Hispanic origin may be of any race.
Sources: U.S. Census Bureau (1991). Current Population Reports, Series P-20(451, *Educational Attainment in the United States: March 1989 and 1988*. Washington, DC: U.S. Government Printing Office; U.S. Census Bureau. *Statistical Abstract of the United States, 1994 and 2007*. Washington, DC: U.S. Government Printing Office.

Schooling attainment was increasing for all Americans, so that it is useful to consider the gains made by blacks in comparison to those made by whites. In 1940, while 7 percent of black male adults finished high school, 24 percent of white male adults graduated high school – more than a three-fold difference. By 2005, the respective proportions were 81 and 85 percent – only a 4 percentage point difference. Likewise, in 1940, 6 percent of white male adults completed college, compared to 1.4 percent of black male adults – a four-fold difference. In 2005, the respective figures were 29 percent and 16 percent – an 83 percent difference. Similar trends are evident for black and white females.

Since educational attainment for all adults reflects the experience of different age cohorts over time, it is perhaps more telling to look at the educational performance of young adults. According to data from the 1992 and 2006 Current Population Survey (see reference in Table 13.2), 85 percent of black males aged 25 to 34 graduated from high school, compared to 86 percent of white males in the same age group in 1992. The respective figures for 2005 were both 85 percent. The respective proportions for college graduates (bachelor's degree or better) were 12 percent and 28 percent in 1992 and 18 percent and 27 percent in 2005. Similar differences are evident between young black and white females.

The schooling attainment of Americans of Hispanic origin also increased. According to the data in Table 13.10, both the percent of Hispanics who graduated high school and college increased substantially between 1974 and 2005. Yet, even by 2005, there was a sizable difference between Hispanics and whites in the percent of adults who had graduated high school (58 percent for Hispanic males versus 85 percent for white males) and who had graduated college (12 percent and 29 percent, respectively). A similar gap exited between white and Hispanic women. It is also of note that even in 2005 Hispanics lagged far behind African Americans in educational attainment.

Thus, from the end of World War II to the present, the educational attainment of black Americans has been catching up to that of white Americans. This is particularly evident for the percent of adults who graduated from high school. However, there was still a sizable gap in college graduation rates between whites and blacks in 2005, though much smaller than 50 years ago. This difference was particularly important during the 1980s, because other evidence (Chapter 11) suggests that demand patterns for workers have been favoring the college educated relative to high school graduates. Moreover, Hispanic Americans still lagged white Americans and African Americans in both high school graduation rates and college graduation rates.

13.4.1   The role of educational gains on the earnings gap*

Several studies have investigated the effects of the convergence of educational attainment between blacks and whites on the racial earnings gap. Gwartney (1970a), using 1960 Census of Population data, reported that in 1959 the ratio of nonwhite to white median income was 58 percent for males living in urban areas. He estimated that differences in educational attainment accounted for 9 to 12 percentage points of the income difference, while differences in scholastic achievement accounted for another 12 to 18 percentage points. He concluded that in 1959 about half of the income disparity between nonwhite and white males was attributable to differences in educational attainment and achievement on scholastic aptitude tests.[11]

Rasmussen (1970) analyzed the change in the relative income of nonwhite men over the period from 1939 to 1964. On the basis of Census of Population data, his figures indicated that the ratio of nonwhite to white incomes increased from 0.41 in 1939 to 0.54 in 1948 and then to 0.57 in 1964. On the basis of regression analysis on the 1948–1964 data, he found that, once cyclical fluctuations are removed,[12] the trend increase in the income ratio was about 1 percentage point every 3 years, or a gain of 0.052 over the 1948–1964 period. Of the 5.2 percentage point gain, 3.7 points could be attributed to rising educational attainment of nonwhite males relative to white males, with the remaining 1.5 percentage points the residual. Rasmussen concluded that the improvement in the relative position of nonwhite males over the 1948–1967 period was primarily due to their improved educational achievement. He also suggested that the reduction in the earnings gap was also partly attributable to a decline in discrimination against nonwhites (the unexplained residual).

A different conclusion was reached by Ashenfelter (1970), who investigated the 1950–1966 period. He found little relative gain in the incomes of nonwhite males. For full-time employees, for example, the income ratio was 0.635 in 1955 and 0.632 in 1966. He estimated that over this period, the average quality of the nonwhite labor force, as estimated by its educational attainment, was growing at a rate of 0.6 to 0.7 percent per year, while that of the white labor force was growing at about 0.3 to 0.4 percent per year. Thus, in contradistinction to Rasmussen, Ashenfelter concluded that the relative increase in schooling for nonwhite males explained the total increase and more in the change in the earnings gap. Thus, he surmised, that there was actually a slight increase in discrimination against nonwhite males over this period, which depressed their relative earnings between 0.1 and 0.4 percentage points per year.

On the other hand, among females, he found a significant reduction in the degree of discrimination. There was a substantial rise in the income of black women relative to white women. In 1955, for example, the ratio was 0.57 and in 1964 it was 0.71. Moreover, though there were gains in the educational attainment of black women relative to white women, these gains accounted for only a small part of the closing of the earnings gap. He concluded that a secular decline in discrimination against black females accounted for a gain of 3.0 percentage points per year in the earnings ratio between nonwhite and white female workers.

O'Neill and O'Neill (2005) analyzed the Decennial Census of Population data and the National Longitudinal Survey of Youth (NLSY79) for the year 2000. They concluded that remaining differences in schooling levels and scholastic test scores (see the next section below) explained almost all of the earnings gap between black and white males, as well as between black and white females. They calculated that in 2000 there was a 34 percent earnings gap between black and white men. Using the Armed Forces Qualifying Test (AFQT) as their test score measure, they found that the mean percentile AFQT score for black men was 24, compared to 55 for white men. When they included controls for both schooling levels and AFQT scores in their regression model (as well as several other factors such as geographic location and age), the earnings gap fell to only 6.2 percent. Thus, they concluded that 82 percent of the racial earnings gap in 2000 could be attributed to productivity-related factors, with the remaining 18 percent was due to discrimination and other factors.

13.4.2   Quality of schooling*

Not only do differences in schooling attainment affect relative earnings between blacks and whites but so do differences in schooling *quality*. Defining and measuring schooling quality is a difficult task, and economists have used both resources devoted to schooling (an "input" measure) and schooling achievement, as reflected in achievement test scores (an "output" measure), as indices of school quality.

As we noted above, by the latter part of the nineteenth century, school enrollment rates for blacks were about half the level of whites. Moreover, as O'Neill (1990) reports, there was also a large difference in quality between schools attended by black and white children. Part of this was due to the fact that almost 90 percent of blacks lived in the South. The Civil War brought great destruction to the Southern economy, and the South could not devote many resources to schooling. In 1880, expenditures on schooling per person were *three* times as great in the North as in the South.

The other part was due to the fact that schooling systems were segregated in the South, with Southern states devoting more resources to white schools than to black schools. Even in 1920 it was estimated that Southern black children had one-third fewer school days than Southern white children. Similar discrepancies existed in teacher salaries and student–teacher ratios.

However, by 1953, most of the disparity in resources devoted to black and white schools had disappeared. In that year, the length of school term for black Southern students was 96 percent that of white Southern students; the teacher–student ratios were almost equal in black and white schools; and teacher salaries in black schools stood at 90 percent of the corresponding white level.[13] By 1965, the Coleman Report (1966) reported that differences in resources devoted to black and white schools were negligible.

Although black–white differences in educational attainment declined substantially over time, significant differences in education achievement remain. These are reflected in differentials in achievement test scores, which, in turn, are likely to be related to remaining differences in school quality and to differences in family background.

Data on achievement test results date from World War I and stem from the AFQT administered by the military for testing recruits. The results of these tests indicate that the difference in test scores between white and Southern black draftees of the same educational level was very large around 1918. According to O'Neill (1990), among men who had attended 4 years of elementary school, Southern blacks scored, on average, only 36 percent the level of white men. On the other hand, the median score of Northern black draftees at the fourth grade level was 85 percent of the level scored by white males. Such differences likely reflect the very inferior schools attended by Southern blacks during the early part of the twentieth century and the better schools attended by Northern blacks.

The differentials in test scores did narrow for a time. During the mid-1950s, the ratio of mean test scores between (both Southern and Northern) black males and white males of the same schooling level who took the test had risen to about 50 percent. However, according to the O'Neill study, between the 1950s and the 1980s, there was relatively little additional gain of black test scores on white ones. This, of course, seems surprising in light of the other evidence presented above that school resources devoted to black students were quickly converging on those for white students.

In a more recent study, Krueger, Rothstein, and Turner (2005) looked at racial differences in the National Assessment of Education Progress (NAEP) scores from 1970 to 2000. In 1970, the average black student scored one standard deviation below the average white student in both reading and math. They found a substantial decline in the racial achievement gap in the early part of this period, from 1970 to about 1990. However, after 1990 there was essentially no further progress in reducing the test gap. In 2000, the racial test difference was three-quarters of a standard deviation in reading and even higher in math.

We have no good explanation of why test scores of black males with the same educational attainment as white males have remained lower, even up to the present. Part of it may reflect the role of family background. White children have, on average, better educated parents than black children, and educational performance of students is positively related to the education of parents (see Section 8.6.2 for a discussion of the role of family background on educational attainment). Card and Rothstein (2007) used SAT scores of black and white students in the period 1998 to 2001 across different metropolitan areas. Their main finding was that the black–white test score gap was higher in more segregated cities. They concluded that neighborhood effects (that is, where people live) mattered more than school composition in explaining the racial test score gap.

13.4.3 Returns to schooling for blacks and whites

Another way of characterizing differences in schooling quality and achievement is through the returns to education (see Chapter 8). As has been noted, the greater average educational attainment of white males relative to black males has been one major source of earnings inequality between the two groups. A related source is the lower *rate of return* to schooling for blacks – that is, the fact that black males receive less gain in earnings from additional years of schooling than white males. A number of studies have investigated this phenomenon. Three early studies (Hanoch (1967), Thurow (1969), and Weiss (1970)) all found on the basis of 1960 Census of Population data that the returns to schooling for nonwhites were generally lower and considerably more erratic than those for whites.

Weiss and Williamson (1972) looked at the same issue with 1967 data for the United States, and some interesting changes were found. They discovered a significant shift in the earnings function for blacks between 1960 and 1967. In particular, schooling for black males in 1967 appeared to generate returns that were as large as those received by white males in that year. This increased payoff occurred at almost every educational level.

Welch (1973a) reached somewhat different conclusions, though he also used the 1960 Census of Population data and the same 1967 data. His major finding was that black males who entered the workforce in more recent periods fared better relative to white males than earlier entrants. Part of the reason for this was a convergence in educational level by race for younger workers. For example, black males in the labor force with 1 to 4 years of experience averaged 11.1 years of schooling, in comparison to a white average of 12.8, while for those with 13 to 25 years of experience, blacks averaged 8.8 years of schooling and whites 11.4. Moreover, there was a significant gain in the return to schooling for younger blacks in comparison to older blacks. In fact, in 1967 the rate of return to schooling was higher for young blacks than for young whites, while the rate of return to schooling for older blacks was significantly lower than for older whites.

In addition, the rate of return to schooling for the same cohort or "vintage" remained unchanged between 1960 and 1967.[14] Thus, the overall gains made by blacks in the payoffs to schooling between 1960 and 1967 was due to a "vintage effect" – namely, that younger blacks who had high rates of return to schooling were entering the labor force, while older blacks with very low returns to schooling were retiring from the labor force. Welch concluded that the reason for the gains in returns to schooling made by young blacks relative to young whites during the 1960s was most likely due to a decline in discrimination.

With the appearance of 1970 Census of Population data, several studies were conducted to ascertain whether blacks had improved their relative economic position over the decade of the 1960s. Freeman (1973b) reported a continued narrowing of the income gap between whites and blacks. For females, the income ratio between blacks and whites rose from 0.57 in 1960 to 0.86 in 1970; for males it rose from 0.58 to 0.64; and for males aged 20 to 24, it increased from 0.67 to 0.82. Among college graduates, rough equality in starting salaries between black and white males and between black and white females was attained by 1970. Moreover, he estimated that by 1970 the rate of return to a college education was actually somewhat greater for black graduates than for white graduates.

Haworth, Gwartney, and Haworth (1975) found that the median earnings ratio between non-white and white males aged 25 to 64 increased from 0.57 to 0.66 between 1960 and 1970, or by 17 percent. They asked whether this gain was from the increased productivity of blacks during this period or reduced discrimination. They found three main contributory factors to the gain made by blacks during the 1960s. First, between 6 and 8 percentage points of this gain was attributable to the retirement from the labor force of older nonwhites with low productivity combined with the entry of younger better-prepared nonwhites (the "vintage effect"). Second, an additional 2 percentage points was due to relative gains in the productivity of nonwhites, particularly from greater schooling. Third, the remaining 6 percentage points was attributable to a relative gain made by nonwhites in the payoff to schooling and other forms of human capital, and this gain, they concluded, was most likely due to a lessening of employment discrimination against blacks.

In a third study, Smith and Welch (1977) also found that the relative income of black males significantly improved during the 1960s. All experience and schooling groups shared in these gains. However, though all black schooling and experience groups improved on average relative to their white counterparts, the largest gains were made by the most educated and the most recent entrants and the smallest by the least educated and the oldest cohorts. Significant gains were also made in the level of schooling completion of black males relative to white males.

Further evidence on the vintage effect was garnered by Duncan and Hoffman (1983) for the 1970s. Using the PSID, they found that among males of ages 25 to 54, the ratio in mean hourly wages between blacks and whites increased from 64 percent in 1967 to 75 percent in 1978. For ages 25 to 34, the hourly wage ratio increased from 72 percent to 81 percent. They found that almost half of the relative earnings gain among all black workers was due to the departure from the labor market of older, less well-paid black workers, and the improved relative earnings position of young black males entering the labor force.

Interestingly, they found little effect on relative earnings from the increased educational attainment of younger black males. The reason is that even though the black workers in entering cohorts were better educated than older black men, so also were entering cohorts of white males relative to older white males. As a result, the net contribution of increasing schooling among black males to relative earnings was negligible. However, the continuing improvement in the quality of schools attended by black males was likely responsible for the increasing relative earnings of the youngest black workers (relative to the youngest white workers) entering the labor force.

Card and Krueger (1992) concurred with these findings. Their focus was on the change in the quality of schooling in 18 segregated Southern states between 1915 and 1966. They constructed various measures of schooling quality, including data on student–teacher ratios, annual teacher pay, and length of term for both white and black schools in these states. They found that schooling quality in the South increased substantially over this period, particularly after the 1954 Supreme Court school desegregation decision of *Brown v. Board of Education of Topeka, Kansas* (see Section 13.6). Card and Krueger estimated that about 20 percent of the narrowing of the black–white earnings gap between 1960 and 1980 could be ascribed to improvements in the relative quality of black schools in the South.

Bound and Freeman (1991) reported that advances made by black males, particularly younger ones, reversed during the 1980s. Their sample consisted of young males with fewer than 10 years of "potential experience" (workers in their twenties and early thirties).[15] They calculated that the percentage difference in earnings between blacks and whites in this sample, after controlling for differences in education and experience, increased from 6 percent in 1976 to 18 percent in 1989. In other words, the relative earnings of young black men declined substantially during the 1980s, even after controlling for changes in human capital. The authors do not feel that changes in school quality were responsible for the reversal. Rather, they put stress on changes in technology and resulting shifts in industrial and occupational demand patterns, particularly those emanating from the decline in the U.S. manufacturing base ("structural effects," as discussed in Chapter 9).

O'Neill (1990), using data from the National Longitudinal Survey of Youths, which has information on earnings, education, and AFQT scores, investigated the role of academic achievement on the earnings gap between black and white males. Her main result was that AFQT scores exerted a significant effect on earnings, even after holding schooling level constant. Moreover, the effect of AFQT scores was greater for black males than white males.[16]

O'Neill then analyzed the effects of difference in achievement test results on the black–white wage gap for males aged 22 to 29 in 1987. Before adjustment for any characteristics, the ratio in hourly wages between blacks and whites stood at 82.9 percent. When adjustments were made for different regions of residence, schooling levels, and potential work experience, the ratio increased to 87.7 percent. When AFQT test results were added, the wage ratio increased to 95.5 percent.

She concluded that difference in skills, as reflected in achievement test results, between black and white workers was a major source of the remaining wage gap between the two groups. Such skill differentials appeared to have taken on added importance during the 1980s by the apparent shift in demand patterns favoring the more highly skilled workers. This change helps to account for the failure of the earnings of black men to gain on those of white men during the 1980s.[17]

13.4.4   Hispanic Americans

Research on the economic status of Americans of Hispanic origin is more limited. This is partly because the Census Bureau introduced a separate category for this group only in 1972.[18] Three main factors have been cited to explain the earnings gap between Hispanic and non-Hispanic whites. The first is educational differences (discussed above). The second is the role of English proficiency (or the lack thereof) on earnings differences between Hispanic Americans and white non-Hispanic Americans. The third concerns the effects of immigration on Hispanic incomes.

Three early studies that look at this issue are Reimers (1983) and McManus (1985 and 1990). They reached somewhat different conclusions. The first study used data from the 1976 Survey of Income and Education. The sample was large enough so that Reimers was able to divide the Hispanic population into five groups by country of origin: (i) Cuba; (ii) Mexico; (iii) Puerto Rico; (iv) South and Central America; and (v) others. The purpose of the study was to determine what proportion of the lower wages received by Hispanic males relative to non-Hispanic white males was due to explainable differences in labor market characteristics, such as education, (potential) work experience, region of residence, U.S. military service, disability status, date of immigration to the United States, race, and fluency in English, and what portion was a residual and thus presumably due to discrimination.

Results varied by country of origin among the Hispanic population. For Hispanics of Cuban and Mexican origin, differences in labor market characteristics explained almost their entire wage gap relative to white, non-Hispanic males. Among Hispanics from Puerto Rico, Central and South America, and other places, differences in labor market characteristics accounted for at most half the difference in wages, with the remainder presumably due to discrimination. Interesting, the lack of English language skills was found to explain part of the Hispanic/non-Hispanic wage gap but not a very substantial part.

The second study, by McManus (1985), used the same data as Reimers and controlled for essentially the same labor market characteristics – education, work experience, region of residence, race, ethnicity, and place of birth. One interesting difference in McManus's specification is that he also included a variable measuring proficiency in Spanish, as well as proficiency in English. He found a much larger effect on the Hispanic/non-Hispanic wage gap from the lack of proficiency in English, which explained about one-third of the wage difference. He also calculated that almost all of the difference in wages usually associated with ethnicity, nativity, and time in the United States can be explained by the lack of English proficiency. Differences in labor market characteristics, as well as discrimination, accounted for the remaining gap. He also found that men who were proficient in both English and Spanish (bilingual proficiency) earned more than those who were proficient in English alone.

In a follow-up study, McManus (1990) found that the wage gap between Hispanics who are proficient in English and Hispanics who lack English-speaking skills was much lower if they lived in areas that were largely populated by Hispanics and much higher in other areas. The wage gap was 11 percent if they resided in areas that were at least 75 percent Hispanic and 26 percent if the areas were only 10 percent or less Hispanic.

More recent work has tended to look at the progress of Hispanic workers in terms of the economic effects of immigration. Some results compiled by Borjas (1994) are rather startling. In 1970, immigrants from Mexico aged 25 to 34 who were newly arrived in the United States earned, on average, 27 percent less than Mexican-American natives. In 1990, the difference had expanded to 34 percent. For other Hispanic immigrants (in age group 25–34), the differential also widened, from 16 to 28 percent. One factor explaining this change is that the educational attainment of arriving Hispanic immigrants was falling over time relative to that of native-born Hispanics.

O'Neill and O'Neill (2005) analyzed the Decennial Census of Population data and the National Longitudinal Survey of Youth (NLSY79) for the year 2000. They found that differences in educational attainment and scholastic test scores, as well as language proficiency and immigrant assimilation, explained almost all of the earnings gap between Hispanic and white non-Hispanic males and that between Hispanic and white non-Hispanic females. They calculated that in 2000 there was a 20 percent earnings gap between Hispanic and white non-Hispanic men. They also found that Hispanics, on average, scored about 20 percentile points lower in the AFQT than non-Hispanic whites. In their regression analysis, they controlled for English language proficiency (self-reported) and the number of years since migrating to the United States as well as schooling and AFQT test scores. When they included these factors in their regression model (as well as several other factors such as geographic location and age), the earnings gap fell to virtually zero (statistically insignificant). Thus, they concluded that almost all of the Hispanic/non-Hispanic white earnings gap in 2000 could be attributed to productivity-related factors.

13.5   CHANGES IN FAMILY STRUCTURE AMONG BLACK AMERICANS

Though there has been substantial catch-up between blacks and whites in terms of labor earnings for employed workers, buoyed largely by the rising educational levels of young black workers entering the labor market and rising returns to education, large differences persist between black and white family incomes. As we noted above, the ratio of median family incomes between blacks and whites peaked in 1975, at 62 percent, and declined thereafter, reaching 56 percent in 2005. One reason, as we discussed above, is the drop-out of black male workers, particularly older ones, from the labor force. A second, and equally important, reason is the changing composition of the black family. Indeed, as early as 1965, Patrick Moynihan called attention to the dramatic changes in family structure that were occurring within the black community (see Office of Policy Planning and Research, 1965).[19]

Table 13.11 highlights some of the changes in the structure of both black and white families since 1960. Because of the availability of Census data on which these tabulations are based, results are shown for both men and women in age group 15 to 44. There have been some dramatic changes in the living arrangements of black families since 1960. In 1960, over half of all black women (in age group 15 to 44) were married, but by 2005 the figure had fallen to 25 percent. Trends are similar for black men: the proportion of this group married fell from 48 percent in 1960 to 27 percent in 2005. The most pronounced changes occurred during the 1970s, with changes during the 1980s, 1990s, and early 2000s relatively modest by comparison. The main reason for this change was that the percent of both black women and men who never married rose substantially: among black women, from 28 percent in 1960 to 58 percent in 2005, and among black men, from 40 to 62 percent. As a result, the proportion of female-headed households (with no husband present) rose from 31 percent of all family units in 1970 to 45 percent in 2005.

Such changes in the marital arrangements of black adults had similar implications for the living arrangements of black children. The most notable change is that the proportion of children living with two parents fell from two-thirds in 1960 to slightly over a third (35 percent) in 2005. Moreover, the proportion of black children living with a parent who had never married skyrocketed from 2 percent in 1960 to almost 35 percent in 2005. Over the same period, the proportion of black children born to a single mother rose from 23 percent to more than 60 percent.

When we compare family incomes between blacks and whites, the important issue is not so much the absolute change in the composition of black families but its change relative to that of white families. There were similar trends in the living arrangements of white families but the magnitude of these changes was not nearly as great. Between 1960 and 2005, the proportion of

Table 13.11   Composition of families by type and race, 1960–1988 (percent)

Family type	1960	1970	1980	1988	2005
A. Black families					
1. Percent of black women, 15–44[a]					
i. Married, spouse present	51.4	44.4	31.2	29.1	25.0
ii. Divorced, separated, widowed	20.3	18.1	20.9	18.7	17.1
iii. Never married	28.3	37.5	47.9	52.2	57.9
2. Percent of black men, 15–44[a]					
i. Married, spouse present	47.7	42.2	33.1	30.9	27.0
ii. Divorced, separated, widowed	12.3	10.1	10.8	10.9	11.0
iii. Never married	40.0	47.7	56.1	58.2	62.0
3. Percent of black children living with					
i. Married couple	67.0	58.5	42.2	38.6	35.1
ii. Divorced, separated, or widowed parent	19.8	27.3	32.7	24.7	20.4
iii. Never married parent	2.1	4.5	13.1	29.3	34.6
iv. Not with a parent	11.1	9.7	12.0	7.4	9.8
4. Percent of black families who have					
i. Female householder, no husband present	—	30.5	41.7	43.5	45.4
ii. All others	—	69.5	58.3	56.5	54.6
B. White families					
1. Percent of white women, 15–44[a]					
i. Married, spouse present	69.1	64.1	56.5	54.5	52.6
ii. Divorced, separated, widowed	6.9	6.1	10.7	12.5	12.7
iii. Never married	24.0	29.8	32.8	33.0	34.7
2. Percent of white men, 15–44[a]					
i. Married, spouse present	61.8	58.6	50.9	48.5	46.3
ii. Divorced, separated, widowed	4.5	3.6	6.8	9.0	9.1
iii. Never married	33.7	37.8	42.3	42.5	44.6
3. Percent of white children living with					
i. Married couple	90.9	89.5	82.7	78.9	73.6
ii. Divorced, separated, or widowed parent	7.1	8.5	14.0	15.5	15.7
iii. Never married parent	0.1	0.2	1.1	3.4	7.4
iv. Not with a parent	1.9	1.8	2.2	2.2	3.4
4. Percent of white families who have					
i. Female householder, no husband present	8.9	9.5	11.9	13.0	14.5
ii. All others	91.1	90.5	88.1	87.0	85.5

a   Ages 18–44 in 2005.
The sum of percentages in each panel is 100 percent.
Sources: Ellwood, D.T. & Crane, J. (1990). Family change among black Americans: What do we know? *Journal of Economic Perspectives*, **4**(4), 65–84; U.S. Census Bureau (1990a). Current Population Reports, Series P-60, No. 168, *Money Income and Poverty Status in the United States: 1989*. Washington, DC: U.S. Government Printing Office; U.S. Census Bureau. *Statistical Abstract of the United States, 2007*; http://pubdb3.census.gov/macro/032006/perinc/new02_000.htm.

white women in age group 15 to 44 who were married fell from 69 to 53 percent, but the main reason was an increase in divorce and separation, not a decline in marriages. For them, also, the most dramatic change was during the 1970s. Similar trends are evident for white men. Still, in 2005, the percent of white women who were married was more than double the percent of black women (53 percent versus 25 percent), and the percent of black female-headed households was three times the proportion among white households (45 percent versus 15 percent).

Perhaps, the most telling difference between black and white families is the living arrangements of children. The percent of white children living with two parents declined from 91 percent in 1960 to 74 percent in 2005. However, in 2005, the proportion of children living with two parents was more than double for white families (74 percent) than black families (35 percent). Moreover, the proportion of white children living with a never married parent was much lower (7 percent) than for black children (35 percent). Perhaps, these changes more than anything else help explain why black family income has not kept up with white family income (see Ellwood & Crane, 1990, for a more extended treatment of these changes).

These implications are reflected in both data on poverty and family incomes. In 2005, the poverty rate (based on family count) among black female-headed households (no husband present) was 36.2 percent, compared to 8.3 percent among black married-couple families (more than a *four-fold* difference). The comparable statistics for white (non-Hispanic) families were 21.5 percent for female-headed households and 3.3 percent for married-couple households.[20] Among black female-headed households with children, the poverty rate was an astounding 42 percent. Likewise, within the black population, the median income of female-headed households was much lower than married-couple households – $22,598 versus $56,191 in 2005, for a ratio of 40 percent.[21] Within the (non-Hispanic) white population, the difference in median incomes between the two household groups was smaller – $36,539 versus $70,417, for a ratio of 52 percent. As a result, the ratio of median family incomes between black and (non-Hispanic) white families was higher among married-couple families, 80 percent, than among female-headed households, 62 percent. Thus, among both black and white families, there is a close correspondence between incomes and poverty status and marital status. The lower overall median income and higher overall poverty rates for black families than white families are due, in large measure, to a higher percentage of female-headed households in the black population.

Three reasons have been advanced to help explain this large increase in the number of female-headed households in the black community. The first is the large increase in unemployment rates among black youths. As we can see from Table 13.4, the unemployment rate among black men under the age of 20 almost tripled between 1955 and 1975, from 13 to 38 percent, and has remained at about this level ever since. Second, the incarceration rate of young black men has also increased. In 1992, about half a million black males were serving time in jail or prison and an approximately equal number were on parole. These two facts, taken together, suggest that the availability of marriageable black men who are capable of supporting a family is small relative to the number of black women who desire a family. The third is that blacks have a more matriarchal culture than whites, so that there is less social disapprobation attached to a single mother raising children on her own.[22]

13.6   PUBLIC POLICY AND DISCRIMINATION

Spurred in large measure by the civil rights movement of the 1950s and 1960s, the federal government instituted several major programs to combat discrimination since 1960. In this section, we shall briefly describe some of the major efforts undertaken by the federal government (Section 13.6.1), particularly as they relate to labor market discrimination. In Section 13.6.2, we shall consider evidence about whether these programs have been effective in reducing discrimination against black Americans.

13.6.1 Public policy programs

Most of the cornerstone legislation and executive orders were put into place during the 1960s. However, there was a major decision issued by the Supreme Court in 1954, which is considered to be a major stimulus to the subsequent programs enacted by the legislative and executive branches of the U.S. government.

13.6.1.1 Brown v. Board of Education of Topeka, Kansas, 1954

Before 1954, the rule on segregated schools (and other public facilities) was based on the 1896 Supreme Court case, *Plessy v. Ferguson*. In this landmark decision, the Court upheld the constitutionality of racial segregation in public accommodations under the doctrine of "separate but equal." "Separate but equal" is a set phrase denoting the system of segregation that justifies giving different groups of people separate facilities or services with the declaration that the quality of each group's public facilities remain equal. Blacks were entitled to receive the same public services such as schools, bathrooms, and water fountains, but the "separate but equal" doctrine mandated different facilities for the two groups. In actual fact, the facilities and social services exclusive to African Americans were of lower quality than those reserved for whites; for example, many African American schools received less public funding per student than nearby white schools. "Separate but equal" remained standard doctrine in U.S. law until its final repudiation in the 1954 Supreme Court decision.

In this landmark case, the Supreme Court of the United States ruled that segregated schools are inherently unequal and therefore unconstitutional. As we discussed in Section 13.4 above, the evidence was ambiguous about whether, in fact, schools attended by black children were receiving fewer resources than those attended by white students. However, the Supreme Court argued that segregated schools were by their very nature *inherently* unequal, creating a feeling of inferiority (a "badge of inferiority") among the black children who attended them. Even spending the same number of dollars per pupil in black schools as in white schools could never create equal educational opportunity for black children.[23] As Chief Justice Earl Warren argued in the decision, public education has become fundamental to political participation in society. "It is required in the performance of our most basic public responsibilities, even service in the armed forces. It is the very foundation of good citizenship. Today it is a principal instrument in awakening the child to cultural values, in preparing him for later professional training, and in helping him to adjust normally to his environment."[24]

The Supreme Court, in effect, took a psychological and sociological viewpoint on the issue of equality in educational opportunity. The mere act of segregation would create low esteem among black children and, as a result, they would likely perform more poorly and have lower expectations and aspirations than white children.

This decision led to major efforts to integrate schools around the nation, most notably (and most politically explosive) through school busing. However, the preponderance of subsequent evidence indicates that the *academic performance* of black children was enhanced by school integration (see, for example, the study of the Congressional Budget Office, 1977). Part of the improved performance of black children was from their exposure to white children whose academic motivation was stronger and whose educational and employment goals were greater. Black students were more motivated in school by the belief that their opportunities were greater and that there was a payoff to success in school.

Subsequent Supreme Court decisions softened the requirements of the *Brown* decision. In *Milken v. Bradley*, 1974, the Supreme Court found that federal courts lack the power to impose inter-district remedies for school segregation absent an interdistrict violation or interdistrict effects. The District court found that the Detroit schools had been deliberately segregated, and that any Detroit-only remedy would make the Detroit schools system more identifiably black, thereby increasing the flight of whites from the city, and the system. The Court ordered a desegregation plan encompassing 53 suburban school districts surrounding Detroit. The Court of Appeals affirmed after noting that any less comprehensive solution would result in an all-black school system surrounded by practically all-white suburban school systems. However, the Supreme Court reversed this decision and stated that federal courts lacked judicial power to impose school desegregation remedies that cut across jurisdictional lines. In a later case *Adarand v. Pena*, 1995, the Supreme Court held that all federal racial classifications were subject to strict scrutiny, and this is the main reason for the recent rollback of affirmative action in universities, and schools nationwide.[25]

13.6.1.2 Executive Order 10925, 1961

Issued by President John Kennedy, this order was the first to require federal contractors (firms that receive procurement contracts from the federal government) to take affirmative action to alleviate discrimination and to provide specific penalties, including the termination of a contract, if the company failed to do so. Though the intent was notable, this order was not effectively enforced.

13.6.1.3 Equal Pay Act, 1963

A 1963 amendment was made to the Fair Labor Standards Act of 1938 which required that females receive the same pay as men for the same work. Known as the "Equal Pay Act," this amendment was designed to eliminate wage differentials based solely on gender. We shall discuss this act in more detail in the next chapter.

13.6.1.4 Civil Rights Act of 1964

The major piece of federal legislation prohibiting labor market discrimination was Title VII of the Civil Rights Act of 1964. Title VII states that it is illegal for an employer to discriminate against any individual on the basis of sex, race, color, religion, or national origin in regard to employment opportunities or compensation. The law originally applied to private businesses, labor unions, and employment agencies. In 1972, it was amended to apply to all levels of government and educational institutions and to all firms and unions with at least 15 members. This piece of legislation was one of the cornerstones of Lyndon Johnson's War on Poverty (see Chapter 4).

This law intended to end discriminatory hiring practices as well as pay differentials based on race or gender. The Civil Rights Act set up the Equal Employment Opportunity Commission (EEOC) to administer and enforce the provisions of Title VII. The EEOC's original role was to seek voluntary compliance by employers on a case-by-case basis. Such voluntary compliance took the form of a consent agreement where the employer agreed to refrain from further discrimination and to correct any underrepresentation of females or minorities. With a 1977 amendment, the EEOC was given the added power of taking court action on behalf of complainants. However, with its somewhat limited budget, the EEOC has usually suffered under an enormous backlog of cases.[26]

13.6.1.5 Executive Order 11246, 1965

This Executive Order was issued by President Johnson and was designed to prevent discrimination by employers holding contracts with the federal government. This order forbids any federal contractor with a contract of $50,000 or more and 50 or more employees from discriminating on the basis of race, sex, religion, or national origin and it also requires them to take *affirmative action* to remedy any underrepresentation. The Office of Federal Contract Compliance (OFCC) of the Department of Labor was set up to enforce this order. In 1968, the OFCC established the requirement that the contractors must develop a written affirmative action plan containing target goals and a timetable to meet these goals in order to remedy deficiencies in equal opportunity employment. By 1972, standardization procedures were set up to identify underutilization of minorities and females in specified job categories and to issue progress reports on meeting goals.

The 1965 Executive Order, unlike its 1961 predecessor, has had considerable effect on the development of affirmative action plans by government contractors. Moreover, the requirement to develop a specific affirmative action plan has often led to the establishment of numerical goals for the hiring of minority workers into specific job categories. This, in turn, has led to the charge that *quotas* were being used to enforce the provisions of the order, and there is continuing controversy today over this charge. On the one hand, many have contended that unless specific numerical targets are issued and enforced, the Executive Order would lack teeth and be virtually unenforceable. On the other hand, the requirement of numerical standards for *equal opportunity* often leads to reliance on *equal results*, rather than equal opportunity. Indeed, some have contended that affirmative action plans tend to promote "reverse discrimination" (that is, preference for minority workers over white workers). Public policy makers are still unsure whether it is possible to enforce equality of opportunity except through the stipulation of numerical goals.

The OFCC has considerably more power than the EEOC. Under Title VII of the Civil Rights Act of 1964, affirmative action can be ordered only by a court and only after an employer has been found guilty of a legal violation. The OFCC, on the other hand, can order that an affirmative action plan be drawn up without the intervention of the court, and can require the cancellation of all government contracts in the event of noncompliance. However, few government contracts have been canceled by the OFCC and, like the EEOC, the OFCC relies mainly on voluntary compliance by the offending employer.

13.6.2   The effectiveness of the anti-discrimination programs

Title VII of the Civil Rights Act of 1964 and Executive Order 11246 are the two major legal instruments implemented to end employment discrimination. Since enforcement of both has and continues to be lax, and reliance is made on voluntary compliance, it might be thought that its effects on reducing discrimination have also been slight. Yet, the preponderance of the evidence, though there are some dissenters, suggests just the opposite – namely, that employment discrimination against blacks has decreased since 1960 and this has been due, in part, to affirmative action programs.

13.6.2.1   *Civil Rights Act of 1964*

Freeman (1981a, 1981b) examined the effects of the Civil Rights Act of 1964 on differences in racial earnings between 1964 and 1975. He concluded that significant gains were made by black workers after 1964. In the first of the two papers, he found that the ratio of mean annual earnings between black and white male workers increased from 0.59 in 1964 to 0.73 in 1975 and the ratio for year-round full-time workers increased from 0.68 to 0.78. Younger workers made the most gain. By 1975, the ratio of median income between black and white year-round full-time workers was 0.85 for those in the 20–24 age group, 0.81 for those aged 25–34, and 0.70 for those aged 45–54. Among females, virtual parity had been reached between black and whites by 1975. Moreover, among college graduates of both sexes, virtual parity in starting salaries between blacks and whites had been reached by 1970.

Freeman then separated out the influences of schooling, experience, home environment, and other productivity-related and background characteristics on the black–white earnings differential from the effect of labor market discrimination (the residual). He found a continuing reduction in the importance of labor market discrimination as an explanation of black–white earnings differences since 1964. Among the young, in particular, he calculated that background characteristics such as parents' education, became a more important impediment to achieving black–white economic equality than labor market discrimination. Finally, he argued that, though blacks had made economic gains relative to whites prior to 1964, the *rate of gain* accelerated after 1964, and this fact he attributed to the Civil Rights Act and other government anti-discrimination initiatives. In a follow-up study, Freemen (1981b) concluded that the relative gains made by blacks during the early 1970s were not dissipated during the sluggish economy of the late 1970s. Looking at data for 1979, he estimated that the relative earnings gains made by black workers between 1964 and 1975 were maintained through 1979, though no improvement was made beyond the 1975 level.

Smith (1978) disputed the conclusions of the Freeman studies. He also found major advances made by black workers relative to white workers between 1960 and 1975. He presented two reasons for the gains made by blacks. The first is the vintage effect. Younger cohorts of black workers enter the labor market with larger stocks of human capital relative to white workers than older black cohorts did when they began work. This resulted in a convergence in the degree of educational attainment between black and white workers. A second factor is the narrowing of regional wage differentials between the non-South and South, which has a large proportion of the black population. He concluded that the gains made by black workers were due to these two effects, and the Civil Rights Act of 1964 did little to cause the improved position of blacks.

Brown (1982), in an assessment of the conflicting evidence, asserted that most of the reported findings indicated that the economic position of blacks improved more rapidly since 1964 than would have been expected on the basis of past trends, general business conditions, or the increased educational attainment of blacks. However, the evidence does not demonstrate that this gain made by blacks was due to the work of the EEOC or the OFCC.

Two other studies argued that the Civil Rights Act had little effect on the relative gains made by black workers since the 1960s. Indeed, they both disputed that blacks had, in fact, made gains since 1964. The first, by Lazear (1979), claimed that the finding that the wage differential between young black and white workers disappeared by 1972 is illusory. He argued that the full compensation a worker receives is the sum of the monetary wage plus the amount of on-the-job training (OJT) the worker receives. His results indicated that the Civil Rights Act led employers to give blacks higher monetary wages but lower OJT.

Computations made by Lazear showed that the total compensation differential between non-whites and whites remained about constant between 1960 and 1974 while the wage differential narrowed. This meant that young black workers were effectively being short-changed in the amount of OJT they received. As a result, as the cohort ages, the earnings of white workers would increase even more rapidly than in the past relative to black workers of the same age. He concluded that government anti-discrimination programs may have produced parity in starting salaries between black and white workers but had no effect on differences in lifetime earnings.

Hylton (1984), in a comment on the Lazear paper, disputed the results reported in the paper. Estimates of lifetime earnings depend on both the current wage of a person and the slope of the age–earnings profile (that is, the rate of growth of earnings with age) over the person's work life (see Section 7.1). He used the National Longitudinal Survey to re-estimate the slope of the age–earnings profiles for both black and white workers. His main result was that there was no statistical difference in the slope coefficients for black and white workers. As a result, he inferred that the gap in lifetime earnings between black and white workers did narrow after 1964.

The second argument is the censuring or drop-out argument. Butler and Heckman (1978) argued that the observed relative increase in the earnings of black male workers was a statistical artifact which essentially reflected a decrease in the labor force participation rate of black men (a decline that Freeman himself found puzzling in light of supposed increases in the demand for black workers resulting from the government anti-discrimination programs). They argued that along with government anti-discrimination programs came an expansion of welfare programs during the 1960s, which served to draw discouraged black male workers out of the labor force in large numbers (hence the decrease in their labor force participation rates). Since these discouraged workers were largely low-wage workers, their exodus from the workforce resulted in a rise in the observed black to white average earnings ratio. They concluded that once controlling for such labor market drop-outs, the apparent effect of government anti-discrimination programs in reducing the black–white earnings gap disappeared.

Several later papers re-examined the Butler–Heckman censuring argument. Brown (1984) used cross-sectional data to recalculate the black–white earnings ratio correcting for drop-outs from the labor force. Even after this adjustment, the black–white ratio of median earnings still showed an increase after 1964, though the corrected trend was only half as large for black males as the uncorrected trend and somewhere between half and four-fifths as large for black females.

Vroman (1986), using the March 1978 Current Population Survey and earnings history records compiled by the Social Security Administration, also examined the labor market drop-out effect over the 1964–1973 period. He drew three main conclusions from his study. First, although labor market reduction was greater among black males than white males, there was no acceleration of this trend after 1964, the period of improvement in the black–white earnings ratio. Second, both black and white men were receiving increased government transfers over this period, and no unusually large increase was observed for black men between 1964 and 1973. Third, the sample selection explanation based on increasing welfare availability for black men for the increased black–white earnings ratio over this period was not supported by the data.

Chandra (2000) re-examined the same issue on the basis of U.S. Decennial Census data over the period 1940 to 1990. He employed the same method as used by Brown (1984). Using this new data source and the longer period of data, she essentially reached the same conclusion as Brown. The results supported the selective withdrawal hypothesis about lower skilled black men but also confirmed the conclusion that the civil rights legislation of the 1960s played an important role in improving the wages of black men during the 1960s.

What about the 1980s? As we discussed in Section 13.2, most studies found that the earnings of black workers, both male and female, had made substantial progress relative to white workers during the 1960s and 1970s. However, during the 1980s, further gains were slight, and, indeed, for some educational groups, the relative earnings of black workers actually declined.

Some economists contended that the failure of black workers to make further progress during the 1980s was due to the lack of commitment on the part of the Reagan and Bush administrations to enforce Title VII of the Civil Rights Act. However, in a careful analysis of the data, Smith (1993) found that the lack of further progress of black male workers could be explained almost entirely by labor market changes. First, during the 1980s, as we saw in Section 13.4 above, there was a slowdown in the narrowing of racial disparities in educational attainment. Second, there was a large increase in the return to education, particularly to a college degree (see Chapter 8). These two factors together explained most of the lack of further closure of the racial wage gap during the 1980s.

Juhn (2003) also examined the "drop-out effect" issue but for later years. Her technique was to impute wages to nonworkers among the black males who dropped out of the labor force. She found that when nonworkers are accounted for by this calculation, real wage growth among prime-age African American males is reduced by approximately 40 percent over the years 1969 to 1998, and black–white wage convergence is reduced by approximately one-third. However, even this correction still led to the conclusion of a continued reduction in the racial wage gap.

Chay (1998) took a different approach. He first noted that the Equal Employment Opportunity Act (EEOA) of 1972 extended civil right coverage to employers with 15–24 employees (who had been excluded in the 1964 Civil Rights Act). This new law set up a "natural experiment" in which the new smaller employers covered by the new act could be compared to other employers still not covered. Using CPS data for 1979, he concluded that the extension of the EEOA in 1972 had a positive impact on the wages and employment of African American workers.

13.6.2.2 Affirmative action programs

A series of studies, carried out by Leonard (1984a, 1984b, 1984c, 1985a, 1985b, 1986, 1990), examined the impact of affirmative action plans on the labor market success of minority workers. The focus was on the effectiveness of Executive Order 11246. Since this order applies only to federal contractors, one way of assessing its impact is to compare the progress of minority workers at firms with federal contracts with establishments that did not have affirmative action obligations. Leonard found that the share of both black male and black female employment in total employment rose significantly faster among federal contractors in comparison to noncontractors between 1974 and 1980. The difference remained statistically significant even after controlling for other factors such as establishment size, region of the country, industry, occupational structure, and corporate structure. He estimated that the difference in the employment growth of black males relative to white males was 0.82 percent per year faster among federal contractors than among noncontractors. Similar effects were also reported by Ashenfelter and Heckman (1976) and Heckman and Wolpin (1976).

Leonard also found that compliance reviews played a significant role in black employment growth over and above that from the requirement of an affirmative action plan. A compliance review (or audit) consists of an actual audit of an employer's hiring record by the OFCC, with a timetable drawn up for remedying any underrepresentation of minority workers. Leonard found that employment growth for black males was twice that in firms undergoing compliance review than among federal contractors generally.

The earlier studies of both Ashenfelter and Heckman (1976) and Heckman and Wolpin (1976) indicated that while affirmative action increased their rate of growth of black employment, it did not increase the share of black employees in the skilled occupations before 1974. Leonard, working with later data, did find an increasing share of black employees in the skilled occupations among federal contractors from 1974 to 1980. The growth in skilled black employment was significantly greater among federal contractors than noncontractors.

Though affirmative action did spur employment growth among blacks during the 1970s, Leonard discovered that the picture changed in the 1980s. Examining data for the period between 1980 and 1984, he found that employment growth among black males was actually somewhat slower among federal contractors than among noncontractors. Differences were even more marked for black females. Leonard attributed this reversal in the effectiveness of affirmative action to a reduced commitment of the Reagan administration to push for compliance. Examining the whole decade of the 1980s in a later study, Leonard (1996) confirmed his earlier conclusion that there was no consistent pattern of success in reducing employment discrimination as a result of government efforts over this decade.[27]

13.7   SUMMARY AND CONCLUSION

Since 1940, black Americans made considerable progress relative to white Americans in terms of labor earnings. For black males, most of the gains were made by 1969, with some slow advances thereafter. Still, by 2004, black male workers earned, on average, only about two-thirds the incomes of white male workers. Moreover, the LFPR of black men declined both in absolute terms, from 85 percent in 1955 to 63 percent in 2005, and relative to the LFPR of white males, which was 74 percent in 2005. Black males also suffered from unemployment rates two and a half to three times as great as white males. As a result, the proportion of males of working age with zero labor earnings was much higher among black males than white males. In 1984, for example, it was three times as high among blacks (16 percent) as among whites (5 percent). In summary, while black males made progress in closing the earnings gap after 1950, they retrogressed in terms of employment rates.

In contrast, black females had reached virtual parity with white females in terms of earnings by 1980, though their relative earnings declined somewhat between 1980 and 2004. Moreover, a higher proportion of black women have historically been in the labor force than white women, though the difference virtually disappeared by 1992 (58 percent for both groups). However, the unemployment rate among black women has typically been about twice the level of that for white women.

Though black workers, both males and females, have generally gained on whites in terms of labor earnings throughout the years since 1940, the same has not been true for family income. The ratio of median family income between black and white families increased from 51 percent in 1958 to 62 percent in 1975 but subsequently fell to 56 percent in 2005. Racial disparities in wealth holdings are even greater than income differences, though they have narrowed somewhat since the 1960s. In 1959, 55 percent of black families had incomes below the poverty line but by 1974 it was down to 30 percent. After 1974, the poverty rate among African Americans turned upward and reached 36 percent in 1983. During the 1990s, African Americans made steady income gains because of a tight labor market and by 2000 their poverty rate fell to 22 percent, their *lowest point ever.* During the early 2000s the trend reversed again and by 2005 their poverty rate had returned to 25 percent. In sum, African Americans made substantial progress in terms of income and poverty during the 1960s and 1990s, but they tended to lose out during the 1980s and 2000s.

What explains the progress of black families relative to white families from 1940 to the mid-1970s? There are five main factors. The first is the outmigration of black families from the low-wage South to the high-wage North. The second is the very significant catch-up in educational attainment between blacks and whites. By 2005, 85 percent of both black males and white males aged 25 to 34 were high school graduates. The third was the improvement in the quality of schools attended by black children. Though this had been going on for some time, since the beginning of the twentieth century, the 1954 Supreme Court case of *Brown v. Board of Education of Topeka, Kansas*, appears to have given added impetus to the process.

The fourth is the vintage effect. Entry-level cohorts of black male workers made substantial gains on earnings of white males up until the late 1970s. Older black males did not. Part of their failure to gain on white males was due to the lower quality of education and their lower labor market experience, differences which reflected past discrimination against blacks. The retirement of older black males from the labor force and their replacement by young black males, with more and better education, is one factor that has reduced the black–white earnings differential.

The fifth was the enactment and implementation of several federal programs to combat discrimination. The two most important of these were the Civil Rights Act of 1964, which created the Equal Employment Opportunity Commission, and Executive Order 11246, issued by President Johnson in 1965, which created the OFCC and required the development of affirmative action plans. Despite the apparent anemic enforcement efforts of the EEOC and the OFCC, many studies have shown that blacks made gains in terms of both earnings and employment as a consequence of these programs from the mid-1960s through the 1970s. The likely reason is increased awareness of discrimination by employers and their sense of a moral imperative to lessen discrimination.

What explains the subsequent decline in the relative fortunes of black families since the mid-1970s? One factor is that academic achievement among black males, as measured by standardized achievement test scores, failed to advance on white males of the same educational level. This is also reflected in the fact that the returns to schooling for blacks, particularly young black workers, failed to increase during the 1980s though it had increased during the 1960s and 1970s. This effect was compounded by structural shifts in the labor market favoring college graduates who have performed well in school and disfavoring low-skilled workers. Some researchers, in fact, attributed almost all of the remaining racial earnings gap to the difference in scholastic achievement between blacks and whites.

A second factor, as noted above, is the falling LFPR of black men, particularly after 1970 and particularly among older black men. The third is the substantial increase in the percentage of female-headed households (with no husband present) among the black population, particularly since 1970. The proportion of black children living with two parents fell from 59 percent in 1970 to 35 percent in 2005. The decline in the black–white ratio of median family income since the 1970s is closely correlated with the rising percentage of black female-headed families. The fourth is that the effectiveness of affirmative action appeared to have dissipated during the 1980s, though some researchers disagree.

Hispanic families have fared somewhat better than black families but significantly worse than non-Hispanic white families according to most indices. In 2005, the median family income of Hispanics was 7 percent greater than that of black families but only 60 percent the level of white families. In the same year, the poverty rate for individuals of Hispanic origin was 22 percent, in comparison to 11 percent for whites and 25 percent for blacks. Moreover, the ratio of median family income between Hispanic and white families declined fairly steadily over time, from a peak of 71 percent in 1974.

Among all full-time, full-year workers, Hispanic males earned, on average, 61 percent the wages of white non-Hispanic employees in 2005. However, when standardized by age and educational levels, the earnings ratios were substantially higher, ranging from 76 to 82 percent. A large part of the earnings gap between Hispanic and non-Hispanic white workers was due to differences in educational attainment, which have not narrowed as much as between blacks and whites, and differences in scholastic test scores, which were smaller than between black and white males. The lack of fluency in English, as well as immigrant status, also played an important role in explaining the relatively lower earnings of Hispanic men.

Has labor market discrimination against blacks and Hispanics ended? Probably not, but the preponderance of evidence does suggest that it has lessened considerably since the 1950s. This result, interestingly, is consistent with several of the models of discrimination discussed in the previous chapter, including Becker's taste for discrimination model and the Arrow–Phelps statistical discrimination model. There has also been substantial progress in providing equal educational resources to black children as those received by white children. A significant hurdle that still remains for achieving full racial equality between young blacks and whites devolves from differences in parental resources. Insofar as parental background and income affect schooling performance, today's black students will continue be at a disadvantage relative to white students.

Moreover, the larger wealth holdings of older whites relative to older black Americans will continue to place young black households at a disadvantage in the wealth accumulation process.

13.8   REFERENCES AND BIBLIOGRAPHY

Akin, J.S. & Garfinkel, I. (1977). School expenditures and the economic returns to schooling. *Journal of Human Resources*, **12**, 460–81.

Akin, J.S. & Garfinkel, I. (1980). The quality of education and cohort variation in black–white earnings differentials: Comment. *American Economic Review*, **70**, 186–91.

Alexis, M. (1998). Assessing 50 years of African American economic status, 1940–1990. *American Economic Review Papers and Proceedings*, **88**(2), 368–75.

Ashenfelter, O. (1970). Changes in labor market discrimination over time. *Journal of Human Resources*, **5**(4), 403–29.

Ashenfelter, O. (1974). Comments. In M.D. Intriligator & D.A. Kendrick (eds.), *Frontiers of Quantitative Economics*, Vol. II. New York: American Elsevier.

Ashenfelter, O., Collins, W.J. & Yoon, A. (2004). Evaluating the role of Brown vs. Board of Education in school equalization, desegregation, and the income of African Americans. Princeton Law and Public Affairs Working Paper No. 05-001, November.

Ashenfelter, O. & Heckman, J. (1976). Measuring the effect of an antidiscrimination program. In O. Ashenfelter & J. Blum (eds.), *Evaluating the Labor Market Effects of Social Programs*. Princeton, NJ: Princeton University Press.

Ashenfelter, O. & Rees, A. (ed.) (1973). *Discrimination in Labor Markets*. Princeton, NJ: Princeton University Press.

Baldwin, M.L. & Johnson, W.G. (1996). The employment effects of wage discrimination against black men. *Industrial and Labor Relations Review*, **49**(2), 302–16.

Bell, D. (1972). Occupational discrimination as a source of income differences: Lessons of the 1960s. *American Economic Review*, **62**(2), 363–72.

Bergman, B.P. (1971). The effect on white income of discrimination in employment. *Journal of Political Economy*, **79**, 294–313.

Black, D., Haviland, A., Sanders, S. & Taylor, L. (2006). Why do minority men earn less? A study of wage differentials among the highly educated. *Review of Economics and Statistics*, **88**(1), 300–13.

Blau, F.D. & Graham, J.W. (1990). Black–white differences in wealth and asset composition. *Quarterly Journal of Economics*, May, 321–39.

Bound, J. & Freeman, R.B. (1991). What went wrong? The erosion of relative earnings and employment among young black men in the 1980s. NBER Working Paper No. 3778, Cambridge, MA, July.

Borjas, G.J. (1994). The economics of immigration. *Journal of Economic Literature*, **32**(4), 1667–717.

Bowen, W. & Bok, D. (1998). *The Shape of the River: Long Term Consequences of Considering Race in College and University Admission*. Princeton, NJ: Princeton University Press.

Brown, C.C. (1982). The federal attack on labor market discrimination: The mouse that roared? In R. Ehrenberg (ed.), *Research in Labor Economics*, Vol. 5 (pp. 33–68). New York: JAI Press.

Brown, C. (1984). Black/white earnings ratios since the Civil Rights Act of 1964: The importance of labor market drop-outs. *Quarterly Journal of Economics*, 31–44.

Butcher, K.F. (1994). Black immigrants in the United States: A comparison with native blacks and other immigrants. *Industrial and Labor Relations Review*, **47**(2), 265–84.

Butler, R. & Heckman, J.J. (1978). The government's impact on the labor market status of black Americans: A critical review. In *Equal Rights and Industrial Relations*. 1977 Industrial Relations Research Association Series. Wisconsin.

Card, D. & Krueger, A.B. (1992). School quality and black-white relative earnings: A direct assessment. *Quarterly Journal of Economics*, **107**(1), 151–200.

Card, D. & Krueger, A.B. (1996). Labor market effects of school quality: Theory and evidence. In G. Burtless (ed.), *Does Money Matter? The Link between Schools, Student Achievement, and Adult Success*. Washington, DC: Brookings Institution.

Card, D. & Lemieux, T. (1994). Changing wage structure and black–white wage differentials. *American Economic Review Papers and Proceedings*, **84**(2), 29–33.

Card, D. & Rothstein, J. (2007). Racial segregation and the black-white test score gap. *Journal of Public Economics*, **91**(11–12), 2158–84.

Chandra, A. (2000). Labor-market dropouts and the racial wage gap: 1940–1990. *American Economic Review Papers and Proceedings*, **90**(2), 333–8.

Chay, K.Y. (1998). The impact of federal civil rights policy on black economic progress: Evidence from the Equal Employment Opportunity Act of 1972. *Industrial and Labor Relations Review*, **51**(4), 608–32.

Chiswick, B.R. (1973). Racial discrimination in the labor market: A test of alternative hypotheses. *Journal of Political Economy*, **81**(6), 1330–52.

Chiswick, B.R. (1978). The effect of Americanization on the earnings of foreign-born men. *Journal of Political Economy*, **86**, 897–921.

Clotfelter, C.T. (2004). *After Brown: The Rise and Retreat of School Desegregation*. Princeton, NJ: Princeton University Press.

Coleman, J. *et al.* (1966). *Equality of Educational Opportunity*. Washington, DC: Government Printing Office.

Congressional Budget Office (1977). *Inequalities in the Educational Experience of Black and White Americans*. Washington, DC: Government Printing Office.

Darity, W., Jr. & Myers Jr., S. (1998). *Persistent Disparity: Race and Economic Inequality in the United States since 1945*. Northampton, MA: Elgar.

Donohue, J.J. & Heckman, J.J. (1991). Continuous versus episodic change: The impact of civil rights policy on the economic status of blacks. *Journal of Economic Literature*, **24**, 1603–43.

Donohue, J.J., Heckman, J.J. & Todd, P.E. (2002). The schooling of southern blacks: The roles of legal activism and private philanthropy. *Quarterly Journal of Economics*, **117**, 225–68.

Duncan, G.J. & Hoffman, S.D. (1983). A new look at the causes of the improved economic status of black workers. *Journal of Human Resources*, **17**(2), 268–82.

Ellwood, D.T. & Crane, J. (1990). Family change among black Americans: What do we know?

Journal of Economic Perspectives, **4**(4), 65–84.

Fairlie, R.W. & Sundstrom, W.A. (1999). The emergence, persistence, and recent widening of the racial unemployment gap. *Industrial and Labor Relations Review*, **52**(2), 252–70.

Fosu, A.K. (1992). Occupational mobility of black women, 1959–1981: The impact of post-1964 antidiscrimination measures. *Industrial and Labor Relations Review*, **45**(2), 281–94.

Freeman, R.B. (1973a). Changes in the labor market for black Americans, 1948–72. *Brookings Papers*, **1**, 67–120.

Freeman, R.B. (1973b). Decline of labor market discrimination and economic analysis. *American Economic Review*, **63**, 280–6.

Freeman, R.B. (1974a). Labor market discrimination: Analysis, findings, and problems. In M.D. Intriligator & D.A. Kendrick (eds.), *Frontiers of Quantitative Economics*, Vol. II. New York: American Elsevier.

Freeman, R.B. (1974b). Alternative theories of labor-market discrimination: Individual and collective behavior. In G.M. von Furstenberg, A.R. Horowitz & B. Harrison (eds.), *Patterns of Racial Discrimination*, Vol. II. Lexington, MA: Lexington Books.

Freeman, R.B. (1981a). Black economic progress after 1964: Who has gained and why? In S. Rosen (ed.), *Studies in Labor Markets*, No. 31. Chicago: University of Chicago Press.

Freeman, R.B. (1981b). Have black labor market gains post-1964 been permanent or transitory? National Bureau of Economic Research Working Paper No. 751, September.

Gittleman, M. & Wolff, E.N. (2004). Racial differences in patterns of wealth accumulation. *Journal of Human Resources*, **39**(1), 193–227.

Gottschalk, P., Danziger, S. & Engberg, J. (1991). Decomposing changes in the black–white earnings gap: 1969 to 1979. *Research in Economic Inequality*, Vol. 1 (pp. 311–26). Greenwich, CT: JAI Press.

Grenier, G. (1984). The effect of language characteristics on the wages of Hispanic-American males. *Journal of Human Resources*, **19**, 25–52.

Grogger, J. (1996). Does school quality explain the recent black/white wage trend? *Journal of Labor Economics*, **14**, 231–53.

Guryan, J. (2004). Desegregation and black dropout rates. *American Economic Review*, **94**, 919–43.

Gwartney, J.D. (1970a). Discrimination and income differentials. *American Economic Review*, **60**, 396–408.

Gwartney, J.D. (1970b). Changes in the nonwhite/white income ratio: 1939–67. *American Economic Review*, **60**, 872–83.

Gwartney, J.D. & Long, J.E. (1978). The relative earnings of blacks and other minorities. *Industrial and Labor Relations Review*, **31**, 336–46.

Hacker, A. (1992). *Two Nations: Black and White, Separate, Hostile, Unequa.* New York: Scribner.

Hanoch, G. (1967). An economic analysis of earnings and schooling. *Journal of Human Resources*, **2**(3), 310–29.

Haworth, J.G., Gwartney, J. & Haworth, C.T. (1975). Earnings, productivity, and changes in employment discrimination during the 1960s. *American Economic Review*, **65**, 158–68.

Heckman, J.J. (1987). The impact of government on the economic status of black Americans. Department of Economics, University of Chicago, mimeo.

Heckman, J.J., Lyons, T.M. & Todd, P.E. (2000). Understanding black–white wage differentials, 1960–1990. *American Economic Review Papers and Proceedings*, **90**(2), 344–9.

Heckman, J.J. & Payner, B.S. (1989). Determining the impact of federal antidiscrimination policy on the economic status of blacks: A study of South Carolina. *American Economic Review*, **79**(1), 138–77.

Heckman, J.J. & Wolpin, K.I. (1976). Does the contract compliance program work? An analysis of Chicago data. *Industrial and Labor Relations Review*, **29**(4), 544–64.

Hirsch, B.T. & Schumacher, E.J. (1992). Labor earnings, discrimination, and the racial composition of jobs. *Journal of Human Resources*, **27**(4), 602–28.

Hoffman, S.D. (1979). Black–white life cycle earnings differences and the vintage hypothesis: A longitudinal analysis. *American Economic Review*, **69**, 855–67.

Holzer, H. & Neumark, D. (2000). Assessing affirmative action. *Journal of Economic Literature*, **38**, 483–568.

Hylton, K. (1984). Illusory wage differentials: Comment. *American Economic Review*, **74**(5), 1124–8.

Jaynes, G.D. (1990). The labor market status of black Americans: 1939–1985. *Journal of Economic Perspectives*, **4**(4), 9–24.

Jaynes, G.D. & Williams, R.M. (eds.) (1989). *A Common Destiny: Blacks and American Society.* Washington, DC: National Academy Press.

Johnson, W., Itamura, Y. & Neal, D. (2000). Evaluating a simple method for estimating black–white gaps in median wages. *American Economic Review Papers and Proceedings*, **90**(2), 339–43.

Jud, G.D. & Walker, J.L. (1982). Racial differences in the returns to schooling and experience among prime-age males, 1967–1975. *Journal of Human Resources*, **17**(4), 622–32.

Juhn, C. (2003). Labor market dropouts and trends in the wages of black and white men. *Industrial and Labor Relations Review*, **56**(4), 643–62.

Kennickell, A. & Shack-Marquez, J. (1992). Changes in family finances from 1983 to 1989: Evidence from the Survey of Consumer Finances. *Federal Reserve Bulletin*, **78**(1), 1–18.

Kennickell, A.B. & Starr-McCluer, M. (1994). Changes in family finances from 1989 to 1992: Evidence from the Survey of Consumer Finances. *Federal Reserve Bulletin*, **80**, 861–82.

Krueger, A., Rothstein, J. & Turner, S. (2005). Race, income and college in 25 years: The continuing legacy of segregation and discrimination. NBER Working Paper No. 11445, June.

La Ferrara, E. & Mele, A. (2006). Racial segregation and public school expenditure. CEPR Discussion Paper No. 5750, July.

Lazear, E. (1979). The narrowing of black–white wage differentials is illusory. *American Economic Review*, **69**(4), 553–64.

Leonard, J.S. (1984a). Employment and occupational advance under affirmative action. *Review of Economics and Statistics*, August, 377–85.

Leonard, J.S. (1984b). The impact of affirmative action on employment. *Journal of Labor Economics*, **2**, 439–63.

Leonard, J.S. (1984c). Antidiscrimination or reverse discrimination: The impact of changing demographics, title vii, and affirmative action on productivity. *Journal of Human Resources*, 19(2), 146–74.

Leonard, J.S. (1985a). Affirmative action as earnings redistribution: The targeting of compliance reviews. *Journal of Labor Economics*, **3**, 363–84.

Leonard, J.S. (1985b). What promises are worth: The impact of affirmative action goals. *Journal of Human Resources*, **20**, 3–20.

Leonard, J.S. (1986). What was affirmative action? *American Economic Review*, **76**(2), 359–63.

Leonard, J.S. (1990). The impact of affirmative action and equal employment law on black employment. *Journal of Economic Perspectives*, **4**(4), 47–63.

Leonard, J.S. (1996). Wage disparities and affirmative action in the 1980s. *American Economic Review Papers and Proceedings*, **86**(2), 285–9.

Link, C. & Ratledge, E. (1975). The influence of the quantity and quality of education on black–white earnings differentials: Some new evidence. *Review of Economics and Statistics*, **57**, 346–50.

Link, C., Ratledge, E. & Lewis, K. (1976). Black–white differences in returns to schooling: Some new evidence. *American Economic Review*, **66**, 221–3.

Link, C., Ratledge, E. & Lewis, K. (1980). The quality of education and cohort variation in black–white earnings differentials: Reply. *American Economic Review*, **70**, 196–203.

Margo, R.A. (1995). Explaining black–white wage convergence, 1940–1950. *Industrial and Labor Relations Review*, **48**(3), 470–81.

Mason, P.L. (2000). Persistent discrimination: Racial disparity in the United States, 1967–1988. *American Economic Review Papers and Proceedings*, **90**(2), 312–16.

Masters, S.H. (1975). *Black and White Income Differentials*. New York: Academic Press.

Maxwell, N. (1992). White–nonwhite income inequality: between-race and within-race changes, 1947–1985. *Research in Economic Inequality*, Vol. 2 (pp. 45–87). Greenwich, CT: JAI Press.

Maxwell, N. (1994). The effect on black–white wage differences of differences in the quantity and quality of education. *Industrial and Labor Relations Review*, **47**(2), 249–64.

McManus, W.S. (1985). Labor market costs of language disparity: An interpretation of Hispanic earnings differences. *American Economic Review*, **75**(4), 818–27.

McManus, W.S. (1990). Labor market effects of language enclaves: Hispanic men in the United States, *Journal of Human Resources*, **25**(2), 228–52.

McManus, W.S., Gould, W. & Welch, F. (1983). Earnings of Hispanic men: The role of proficiency in the English language. *Journal of Labor Economics*, **1**, 110–30.

Menchik, P.L. & Jianakoplos, N.A. (1997). Black–white wealth inequality: Is inheritance the reason? *Economic Inquiry*, **35**(2), 428–42.

Moss, P. & Tilly, C. (1991). *Why Black Men are Doing Worse in the Labor Market: A Review of Supply-Side and Demand-Side Explanations*. New York: Social Science Research Council.

Myrdal, G. (1944). *The American Dilemma: The Negro Problem and Modern Democracy*. New York: Harper & Row.

Neal, D. & Johnson, W. (1996). The role of pre-market factors in black–white wage differences. *Journal of Political Economy*, **104**, 869–95.

Neumark, D. (1988). Employers' discriminatory behavior and the estimation of wage discrimination. *Journal of Human Resources*, **23**(3), 279–95.

Oliver, M.L. & Shapiro, T.M. (1995). *Black Wealth/White Wealth: A New Perspective on Racial Inequality*. New York: Routledge.

Office of Policy Planning and Research (1965). *The Negro Family: The Case for National Action*. U.S. Department of Labor, March.

O'Neill, J. (1990). The role of human capital in earnings differences between black and white men. *Journal of Economic Perspectives*, **4**(4), 25–45.

O'Neill, J.E. & O'Neill, D.M. (2005). What do wage differentials tell us about labor market discrimination? NBER Working Paper No. 11240, March.

Orazem, P.F. (1987). Black–white differences in schooling investment and human capital production in segregated schools. *American Economic Review*, **77**(4), 714–23.

Rasmussen, D.W. (1970). A note on the relative income of nonwhite men, 1948–1964. *Quarterly Journal of Economics*, **84**(1), 168–72.

Reardon, E. (1997). Demand-side changes and the relative economic progress of black men: 1940–90. *Journal of Human Resources*, **32**(1), 69–97.

Reich, M. (1981). *Racial Inequality*. Princeton, NJ: Princeton University Press.

Reardon, E. (1997). Demand-side changes and black relative economic progress: 1940–1990. *Journal of Human Resources*, **32**(1), 69–97.

Reimers, C. (1983). Labor market discrimination against Hispanic and black men. *Review of Economics and Statistics*, **65**, 570–9.

Reimers, C. (1984). Sources of the family income differentials among Hispanics, blacks, and white non-Hispanic whites. *American Journal of Sociology*, **89**(4), 889–903.

Rivkin, S.G. (2000). School desegregation, academic attainment, and earnings. *Journal of Human Resources*, **35**, 333–46.

Schwartz, S. (1986). Earnings capacity and the trend in earnings among black men. *Journal of Human Resources*, **21**, 44–63.

Smith, J.P. (1978). The improving economic status of black Americans. *American Economic Review*, **68**(2), 171–8.

Smith, J.P. (1984). Race and human capital. *American Economic Review*, **74**(4), 685–98.

Smith, J.P. (1993). Affirmative action and the racial wage gap. *American Economic Review Papers and Proceedings*, **83**(2), 79–84.

Smith, J.P. & Welch, F.R. (1977). Black–white male wage ratios: 1960–1970. *American Economic Review*, **67**, 323–38.

Smith, J.P. & Welch, F.R. (1984). Affirmative action and labor markets. *Journal of Labor Economics*, **2**(3), 269–301.

Smith, J.P. & Welch, F.R. (1989). Black economic progress after Myrdal. *Journal of Economic Literature*, **27**(2), 519–64.

Stratton, L.S. (1993). Racial differences in men's unemployment. *Industrial and Labor Relations Review*, **46**(3), 451–63.

Strauss, R.F. & Horvath, F.W. (1976). Wage rate differences by race and sex in the U.S. labor market: 1960–1970. *Economica*, **43**, 287–98.

Taylor, D.E. (1981). Education, on-the-job training, and the black–white earnings gap. *Monthly Labor Review*, **104**, 28–34.

Thurow, L.C. (1969). *Poverty and Discrimination (Studies in Social Economics)*. Washington, DC: Brookings Institution.

Trejo, S. (1997). Why do Mexican Americans earn low wages? *Journal of Political Economy*, **105**(6), 1235–68.

Tobin, J. (1965). On the economic status of the negro. *Daedalus*, **94**(4), 878–98.

U.S. Census Bureau (1990a). Current Population Reports, Series P-60, No. 168, *Money Income and Poverty Status in the United States: 1989*. Washington, DC: U.S. Government Printing Office.

U.S. Census Bureau (1990b). Current Population Reports, Series P-60, No. 167, *Trends in Income by Selected Characteristics: 1947 to 1988*. Washington, DC: U.S. Government Printing Office.

U.S. Census Bureau (1993). Current Population Reports, Series P60, No. 184, *Money Income of Households, Families, and Persons in the United States: 1992*. Washington, DC: U.S. Government Printing Office.

Vigdor, J.L. (2006). The new promised land: Black–white convergence in the American south, 1960–2000. NBER Working Paper No. W12143, April.

Vroman, W. (1986). Transfer payments, sample selection, and male black–white earnings differences. *American Economic Review*, **76**(2), 351–4.

Weiss, L. & Williamson, J. (1972). Black education, earnings, and interregional migration: Some new evidence. *American Economic Review*, **62**, 372–83.

Weiss, L. & Williamson, J. (1975). Black education, earnings, and interregional migration: Even newer evidence. *American Economic Review*, **65**, 241–4.

Weiss, R.D. (1970). The effect of education on the earnings of blacks and whites. *Review of Economics and Statistics*, **52**, 150–9.

Welch, F.R. (1967). Labor market discrimination: An interpretation of income differences in the rural south. *Journal of Political Economy*, **75**, 225–40.

Welch, F.R. (1973a). Black–white differences in returns to schooling. *American Economic Review*, **63**, 893–907.

Welch, F.R. (1973b). Education and racial discrimination. In O. Ashenfelter & A. Rees (eds.), *Discrimination in Labor Markets*. Princeton, NJ: Princeton University Press.

Welch, F.R. (1975). Human capital theory: Education, discrimination, and life cycles. *American Economic Review*, **65**, 63–73.

Welch, F.R. (1980). The quality of education and cohort variation in black–white earnings differentials: Reply. *American Economic Review*, **70**, 192–5.

Wilson, W.J. (1978). *The Declining Significance of Race: Blacks and Changing American*

Institutions. Chicago: University of Chicago Press.

Wilson, W.J. (1987). *The Truly Disadvantaged: The Inner City, the Underclass, and Public Policy*. Chicago: University of Chicago Press.

13.9   DISCUSSION QUESTIONS AND PROBLEM SET

1   Describe the gains made by black men relative to white men in terms of labor market earnings. Some researchers have argued that these gains are overstated because of the reduction in the employment rate of black men. Explain this argument.

2   Discuss three reasons why outmigration from the South may have led to improvements in the economic status of black families.

3   Though blacks have made gains relative to whites in terms of labor earnings, relative gains have been much smaller in terms of median family income and poverty rates. How have changes in family structure in the black community accounted for this difference?

4   Explain the provisions of the Civil Rights Act of 1964. Was this legislation effective in reducing racial discrimination? Discuss the evidence which supports the effectiveness of this Act. What are the three arguments and supporting evidence for why the Civil Rights Act of 1964 was not effective?

5   Describe the origins of affirmative action plans. Evaluate the evidence with regard to the effectiveness of affirmative action.

6   (a)   Explain five reasons why the income of African Americans increased relative to white Americans from 1950 to 1975.

   (b)   Explain one reason why the income of African Americans failed to increase relative to white Americans from 1975 to 2000.

7   Suppose labor earnings for African American and white workers are given as follows:

	North	South
African Americans	30,000	20,000
Whites	50,000	50,000

Suppose half of white workers work in the North and half in the South. Compute the ratio of average earnings between African Americans and whites for the country as a whole if:

   (a)   60 percent of African American workers work in the South and 40 percent work in the North.

   (b)   40 percent of African American workers work in the South and 60 percent work in the North.

8   Suppose average labor earnings for African American and white workers are given as follows:

	North	South
African Americans	40,000	30,000
Whites	60,000	50,000

Compute the ratio of average earnings between African Americans and whites for the country as a whole if:

(a)   60 percent of white workers work in the North and 40 percent work in the South.

(b)   60 percent of African American workers work in the South and 40 percent work in the North.

NOTES

1   It might seem odd that the overall ratio of 0.68 is lower than that for any schooling group. The reason is that the table shows the ratio of *medians*, not means.

2   There is also a third dimension, the portion of employed persons who hold part-time jobs as opposed to full-time ones. Black males have done comparatively worse than white males in this respect also – that is, a higher percentage of black males hold part-time jobs than white males.

3   See Stratton (1993) for a telling analysis of differences in unemployment propensities between white and black males.

4   The employment rate is equal to one minus the unemployment rate multiplied by the labor force participation rate.

5   Before 1967, data on median family income are available only for nonwhite families. This should not bias the graph too much, because in 1967, the median income of black families differed from that of all nonwhite families by only 4 percent.

6   The relative poverty rate of black families (the ratio of poverty rates between blacks and whites) was as high as 3.7 in 1973 but fell to 2.3 in 2005.

7   This increase is connected in part to the issuance of so-called "sub-prime" mortgages discussed in the Chapter 12.

8   The source for these figures is the U.S. Census Bureau Current Population Survey, available at: http://www.census.gov/hhes/www/income/histinc/h02b.html.

9   The data shown here are based on the Current Population Survey. Since this is a household survey, it should, in principle, capture both documented (legal) and undocumented (illegal) workers. However, it is very likely that the undocumented workers and families are severely underrepresented in the CPS sampling frame.

10   The sources for the data are U.S. Census Bureau, *Statistical Abstract of the United States*, 1953, 1972, 1981, and 1994.

11   He also controlled for three other productivity-related factors: (i) age; (ii) region of the country; and (iii) city size. After controlling for these factors as well as educational attainment and scholastic achievement, he found that about one-third of the earnings gap was still unaccounted. He inferred that this remaining earnings gap may be the result of employment discrimination.

12   The cyclical adjustment was motivated by an argument put forward by Tobin (1965) that blacks do better relative to whites during periods of tight labor markets (low unemployment) and worse during periods of slack labor markets (high unemployment). The reason is that when labor markets are slack, employers are more likely to screen good jobs on the basis of race and unions are likely to discriminate more to preserve their control over scarce jobs.

13   In the following year, 1954, the famous Supreme Court case, *Brown v. Board of Education of Topeka, Kansas*, ruled that school desegregation was unlawful. See Section 13.6.

14   That is to say, the rate of return for black males who were 30 years old in 1967 was the same as it was for the same group or cohort who were 23 years old in 1960.

15   Technically, this consists of workers who left school less than 10 years before the sample date.

16   Interestingly, measures of the quality of schools attended by the individuals in the sample, such as student–teacher ratios and the percent of school faculty with advanced degrees, had no significant effects on the individual's earnings.

17   A similar conclusion was reached by Maxwell (1994) using the same data source and the same measure of scholastic achievement.

18   Moreover, since Hispanics can be either white or black, these studies also control for racial differences.

19 This report is often referred to as the "Moynihan Report" after its author.

20 The source for the poverty figures in this section is the March, 2006 Current Population Survey: http://www.census.gov/hhes/www/poverty/histpov/hstpov4.html.

21 The source for the poverty figures in this section is the March, 2006 Current Population Survey: http://pubdb3.census.gov/macro/032006/hhinc/new04_010.htm.

22 See Wilson (1987) for more discussion of these points.

23 Also, even if dollars spent per pupil on education were the same for whites and blacks, it may still not be the case that educational resources are the same. For example, inner-city schools may be forced to spend a much larger share of their budget on security measures and other nonclassroom functions than suburban or rural schools.

24 The source is SCOTUS, *Brown v. Board of Education of Topeka, Kansas, 1954*, page 473.

25 I would like to thank Spencer Wolff for providing the research for this section.

26 There is an indirect effect of an EEOC action – namely, the negative publicity given to a firm undergoing an investigation. This may induce compliance even though the EEOC might not take the employer to court or win a legal case against the employer.

27 For an extended assessment of the successes and failures of affirmative action, see Holzer and Neumark (2000).

Chapter 14

The Gender–Wage Gap and Occupational Segregation

14.1 INTRODUCTION

Chapter 13 revealed that black families made substantial progress relative to whites from 1940 to 1970. However, since 1970 they experienced only modest relative gains in labor earnings and no gains in family incomes and, indeed, black males suffered a sharp decrease in employment. Curiously, the story is almost the reverse for females. We find that the economic status of females actually deteriorated somewhat from the end of World War II to 1970, but they then showed significant improvement after 1970, particularly during the 1980s.

In Section 14.2 we present the basic evidence on the progress of female workers in the United States, both in terms of earnings and labor force participation rates. Section 14.3 raises the question of why females failed to make progress before 1970 and then showed significant gains thereafter. One reason is that women, particularly married women, have historically had interrupted work careers, especially during child-bearing and child-rearing ages. Section 14.3.1 considers the effects of experience differences on the earnings differentials between females and males. Occupational segregation is a second reason for the lower earnings of females, and Section 14.3.2 looks at changes in indices of occupational segregation.

Section 14.4 considers the role of civil rights programs that have been put into place to combat gender-based job discrimination. The principal programs are the Civil Rights Act of 1964 and Executive Order 11246 in 1965 authorizing affirmative action. Recent efforts have taken the form of comparable worth programs, which aim at creating pay parity between male and female jobs.

In Section 14.5 we look at how wives' earnings affect the distribution of *family income*. Have the earnings of wives led to greater equality in the distribution of family income or have they been disequalizing in effect? In this section, we also consider a new development in gender disparities, referred to as the "feminization of poverty." This is principally related to changes in the structure of the U.S. family. Some international comparisons are also presented in this section. A summary is provided in Section 14.6.

14.2 THE WAGE GAP AND LABOR FORCE PARTICIPATION TRENDS

We first look at the earnings or wage gap between female and male workers. Table 14.1 shows the ratio in annual earnings between male and female workers in 2004 by age and education group. The data are only for employees who worked full-time (35 or more hours per week) for

Table 14.1 The ratio of median annual earnings between male and female workers, by race, education, and age, 2004

Education	25–34	35–44	45–54	55–64	All ages (25+)
A. White females/White males					
Less than a high school graduate	0.75	0.72	0.69	0.63	0.70
High school graduate[a]	0.78	0.65	0.70	0.67	0.70
Some college, no B.A.	0.76	0.70	0.69	0.63	0.72
College, B.A. or more	0.80	0.69	0.68	0.70	0.70
All schooling levels	0.80	0.71	0.71	0.63	0.73
B. Black females/Black males					
Less than a high school graduate	0.99	0.80	0.64	—	0.80
High school graduate[a]	0.99	0.78	0.79	0.76	0.85
Some college, no B.A.	0.86	0.83	0.80	0.79	0.83
College, B.A. or more	0.93	0.76	0.96	0.91	0.82
All schooling levels	0.97	0.82	0.85	0.82	0.90

a   Includes equivalency (GED) degrees.
Earnings data are for year-round (defined as those who worked 50 or more weeks), full-time (defined as those who work 35 or more hours per week) employees. Hispanics are excluded from this table.
Source: http://pubdb3.census.gov/macro/032005/perinc/new03_139.htm.

the full year (50 or more weeks). The ratios are shown by racial group. Among all white persons who were full-time, full-year workers, women made, on average, only 73 percent the annual earnings of male workers.

Younger females did better than older ones. The average earnings of white females aged 25 to 34 was 80 percent that of males, whereas middle-aged white females (aged 35 to 54) earned only about 70 percent of males in the same age group and older females (aged 55 to 64) earned only 63 percent. Part of the explanation is that older females have had less continuous work experience than older males. In the past, at least, many married women typically worked until the birth of their first child, dropped out of the labor force, and then reentered the labor force when their children left home. As a result, the work experience of older women was typically interrupted and they had fewer years of actual work experience than men of the same age. We shall return to this point in Section 14.3.1.

The earnings ratio shows relatively little variation by educational status. Among younger workers (under 35), the female–male earnings ratio was slightly greater among college-educated workers than other educational groups. The same was true among workers 55 to 64.

The earnings gap between black females and males was smaller than that between white females and males. Black females earned, on average, 10 percent less than black males (an earnings ratio of 0.90). As with white workers, younger black females did better relative to younger black males than did older black females relative to older black males. The earnings ratio between black females and males in age group 25–34 was 0.97, compared to a ratio of 0.82 for black females and males in age group 55–64. There is again very little systematic variation in the earnings ratio by educational group. However, more educated black females tended to do slightly better relative to males than less educated black females.

The smaller gender–wage gap among black workers in comparison to white workers is *not* due to the higher earnings of black women relative to white women but rather to the lower earnings of black men relative to white men. Indeed, as we saw in the last chapter, white women

Table 14.2　The ratio of median annual income between females and males, by age group, 1947–2005

Year	25–34	35–44	45–54	55–64
1947	0.50	0.47	0.48	0.41
1957	0.39	0.38	0.40	0.36
1967	0.38	0.37	0.42	0.38
1970	0.39	0.36	0.40	0.38
1975	0.46	0.35	0.38	0.37
1980	0.45	0.32	0.32	0.31
1985	0.53	0.41	0.38	0.35
1988	0.56	0.44	0.41	0.37
1992	0.63	0.52	0.49	0.40
1995	0.66	0.55	0.50	0.43
2000	0.70	0.58	0.58	0.49
2005	0.73	0.62	0.61	0.54

Sources: U.S. Census Bureau (1993). Current Population Reports, Series P60, No. 184, *Money Income of Households, Families, and Persons in the United States: 1992*. Washington, DC: U.S. Government Printing Office; http://www.census.gov/hhes/www/income/histinc/p08ar.html.

and black women were close to parity in terms of earnings in the early 2000s. In a sense, the results suggest that black women are discriminated against solely for being women, rather than for being black. The reasons why black women are not subjected to racial discrimination in addition to gender discrimination may arise from the fact that black women have historically had more continuous participation in the labor force than white women (see below).

14.2.1　Time trends

Has the female–male wage gap declined since the end of World War II? Table 14.2 presents data on the earnings gap by age group from 1947 to 2005. The results are based on total annual income instead of labor earnings. Moreover, all men and women are included in the tabulation (as opposed to workers). Nonetheless, the results are quite dramatic. Among all age groups, the ratio of female to male income declined between 1947 and 1970. Among the youngest age group, the female–male ratio increased between 1970 and 2005, from 39 to 73 percent. Among the older three age groups, the female–male income ratio started to increase in 1980, rising from 0.32 in that year to 0.62 in 2005 for age group 35–44, from 0.32 to 0.61 for ages 45–54, and from 0.31 to 0.54 for age group 55–64.

Results using the same income concept by educational group reveal similar trends (Table 14.3). The gender–earnings ratio increased at all schooling levels between 1967 and 2005. Among those with 8 years of schooling or less, the ratio rose from 0.33 to 0.58; among high school graduates, from 0.40 to 0.55; and among college graduates, from 0.44 to 0.63. Among those with more than a B.A. degree, the increase in the wage ratio was more moderate, from 0.60 to 0.66.

Figure 14.1 shows the trend in the ratio of median annual labor earnings between female and male workers. Results are shown for all full-time, full-year workers and for all workers, including those who worked part time and those who worked only part of the year. Among all workers, the earnings ratio rose almost steadily from 1973 (a ratio of 0.38) to 2005 (a ratio of 0.63). Part of these gains was due to the fact that female employees were working more hours per year after 1973 (see below). When we consider only full-time, full-year workers, the gender–earnings ratio changed very little between 1967 and 1980 but then increased from 0.60 in 1980 to 0.77 in 2005.

Table 14.3   The ratio of median annual income between females and males, classified by education, 1967–2005

Year	*Elementary 8 years or less*	*High school 1 to 3 years*	*High school 4 years*	*College 1 to 3 years*	*College 4 years*	*College 5+ years*	*All*
1967	0.33	0.33	0.40	0.38	0.44	0.60	0.33
1970	0.35	0.33	0.39	0.38	0.44	0.59	0.33
1975	0.44	0.37	0.38	0.41	0.48	0.58	0.36
1980	0.47	0.37	0.36	0.42	0.44	0.55	0.35
1985	0.54	0.44	0.43	0.49	0.51	0.59	0.41
1988	0.52	0.45	0.46	0.53	0.57	0.59	0.46
1992	0.61	0.51	0.50	0.56	0.61	0.62	0.50
1995	0.61	0.51	0.52	0.58	0.62	0.64	0.52
2000	0.60	0.53	0.55	0.61	0.62	0.63	0.56
2005	0.58	0.53	0.55	0.60	0.63	0.66	0.58

The computations include only persons age 25 and older.
Sources: U.S. Census Bureau (1990). Current Population Reports, Series P-60, No. 167, *Trends in Income by Selected Characteristics: 1947 to 1988*. Washington, DC: U.S. Government Printing Office; U.S. Census Bureau (1993). Current Population Reports, Series P60, No. 184, *Money Income of Households, Families, and Persons in the United States: 1992*. Washington, DC: U.S. Government Printing Office.

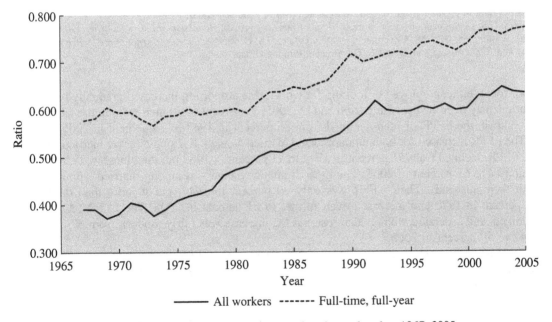

Figure 14.1   Ratio of median annual earnings between females and males, 1967–2005

14.2.2   Labor force participation patterns

Another major change in the postwar period is the labor force participation rate of females, which was steadily rising. We have already commented on this trend in Chapters 7 and 13. Table 14.4 highlights some of the changes. In 1947, 32 percent of all females (age 16 and over) were in the

Table 14.4 Labor force participation rates for females by marital status, 1947–2005

			Females who are			Women with children in age group:		Percent of female employees who work
Year	All males	All females	Never married	Married spouse, present	Widowed, divorced, separated	6–17	Under 6	FT-FY[a]
1947	86.4	31.8	51.2	20.0	37.4			
1950	86.4	33.9	50.5	23.8	37.8			36.8
1955	85.4	35.7	46.4	27.7	39.6			37.9
1960	83.3	38.1	44.1	30.5	40.0			36.9
1965	80.7	40.3	40.5	34.7	38.9			38.8
1970	79.7	43.4	53.0	40.8	39.1			40.7
1975	77.9	46.3	57.0	44.4	40.8	54.9	39.0	41.4
1980	77.4	51.5	61.5	50.1	44.0	64.3	46.8	44.7
1985	76.3	54.5	65.2	54.2	45.6	69.9	53.5	48.9
1988	76.2	56.6	65.2	56.5	46.1	73.3	56.1	50.7
1992	75.6	57.9	65.0	59.2	47.0	75.9	58.1	53.5
2000	74.8	59.9	68.6	61.1	50.2	79.1	65.6	59.8
2005	73.3	59.3	65.1	60.7	49.8	77.0	63.0	61.2

a FT-FY: full-time (35 hours or more per week), full-year (50 or more weeks per year).
Statistics refer to population age 16 and over (18 and over in 2000 and 2005).
Sources: U.S. Department of Labor, Bureau of Labor Statistics (1990). *Handbook of Labor Statistics 1989*, Bulletin 2340. Washington, DC: U.S. Government Printing Office; U.S. Census. *Statistical Abstract of the United States, 1994 and 2007*. Washington, DC: U.S. Government Printing Office.

labor force (either employed or looking for work). This proportion increased gradually but almost continuously over the postwar period and by 2005, 59 percent of women were in the labor force. In contrast, the LFPR of men declined from 86 percent in 1947 to 73 percent in 2005.

The LFPR increased for both unmarried and married women. For single (never married) women, the LFPR declined from 51 percent in 1947 to 41 percent in 1965 but then increased almost continuously to 65 percent in 2005. The most dramatic change was among married women (living with their husband). Their LFPR was only 20 percent in 1947, but it more than doubled to 40 percent in 1970 and increased even further to 61 percent in 2005. The LFPR of widowed, divorced, and separated women also rose but the increase was fairly modest, from 37 percent in 1947 to 50 percent in 2005.

What is, perhaps, even more telling is the increase in the LFPR of women with children. The LFPR of women with school-age children (6 to 17) was 55 percent in 1975 but increased sharply to 77 percent by 2005. A similar change occurred for mothers with young children, under the age of 6. Their LFPR rose from 39 to 63 percent over the same years.

Another important development was that the proportion of working women who were employed full time and full year was also on the rise. In 1950, only 37 percent of working women worked full time, full year. By 2005, this figure had risen to 61 percent.

14.2.3   Explanations of the rising LFPR of women*

There are two questions of immediate interest. First, why have females, particularly married women, historically had lower LFPR than men? Second, why has the LFPR of women been steadily increasing over the postwar period?

The human capital model, as developed by Ghez and Becker (1975), Becker (1981), and Mincer (1962a, 1962b), provides a framework to treat both these questions. The new household economics developed by these economists emphasizes the allocation of time within the household unit. According to this model, the market wage influences not only the allocation of time between market work and leisure but also that between market work and work in the home. An increase in the market wage relative to the wife's "household wage" would induce a substitution of market work (in the labor market) for home work. The strength of the effect would depend on the degree of substitutability between goods produced in the home and market goods. An increase in the husband's earnings or in family income generally would induce a substitution of leisure for total time worked. The degree to which hours of work in the labor market declined would depend on the income elasticity of market goods relative to that for goods produced in the home.

Another factor derives from the demand for children. Fuchs (1989) suggests the hypothesis that women have a stronger demand for children than do men and have a greater interest in children after they are born. Biological constraints on the age of child rearing for women may help account for this difference. Differences in the pattern of socialization may also help explain such difference in preference. According to this argument, both the lower wage of females relative to males in the labor market and the greater preference for child rearing of women may account for the lower rate of labor force participation of women than men.[1]

Several studies have applied this framework to explain the rising LFPR of women, particularly married women. Mincer (1962b) investigated the variation of LFPR of married women among 57 large Standard Metropolitan Statistical Areas (SMSAs) on the basis of the 1950 Census of Population data. He found that wives' wages had a strong positive effect on their LFPR, while husbands' earnings exerted a negative, but weaker, influence. The combination of wives' wages and husband's income explained about half of the variation in the labor supply of wives. Another factor that appeared important was the overall unemployment rate of the SMSA, which had a negative effect on the LFPR of married women. Mincer estimated that the change in women's earnings and family income explained about 70 percent of the rise in the LFPR of married women from 1920 to 1960.

Later studies by Cain (1966) and Bowen and Finegan (1969) on the basis of 1960 Census of Population data generally confirmed Mincer's findings, though the effects were smaller in magnitude. Fields (1976) found still weaker effects using the 1970 Census of Population data. Fields suggested that the weakening of the wage and income effects over time could reflect a change in the labor supply function of wives, as women were substantially changing their work role orientation. Cain and Dooley (1976) also incorporated the fertility rate (the number of births per 1,000 females) in their analysis and found that once this effect was included, the wife's wage and husband's income effects for the 1970 data were as strong as estimated by Mincer on the basis of the 1950 Census data. The Cain and Dooley results, as analyzed by O'Neill (1981), explained 86 percent of the increase in the LFPR of married women over the 1947 to 1957 period, 63 percent over the 1957 to 1967 period, and more than 100 percent of the change from 1967 to 1977.

Using time-series data from 1948 to 1978, O'Neill (1981) re-estimated the effects of both wives' wages and family income on the LFPR of married women. Her analysis included, besides women's wage rates and men's income, the unemployment rate, an index of industrial composition, the divorce rate (which she explained as a proxy for the risk of losing the "job" of housewife), and the fertility rate (the number of children born per woman). She found that the female wage and male income were important and statistically significant. The unemployment rate had the expected sign but was not generally statistically significant. The divorce rate was significant and had a positive effect on women's LFPR. Past fertility was found to be quite significant and exerted a positive effect on the labor force participation of older females. She concluded that the rising

LFPR of married women during the 1950s and 1960s was driven mainly by their rising wage earnings, while during the 1970s, it was largely due to the slowdown in the growth of husband's total income.

Smith and Ward (1985) also investigated time-series changes in the labor force participation of females. Their analysis covered the period from 1900 to 1981. They concluded that rising real wages accounted for 58 percent of the overall growth of the female labor force. Of this 58 percent, almost half can be traced to the reduction in child birth which stemmed from the rise in female wages.

14.3   EXPLANATIONS OF THE WAGE GAP

The evidence so far indicates that the earnings gap between females and males has historically been quite large in the United States. Females have typically earned between 60 and 75 percent that of males. However, the earnings gap has not been unchanged over time. After widening between the end of World War II and the early 1950s, it remained almost unchanged for 20 years. Beginning in the early 1970s, female earnings started to gain on male workers, and this process accelerated during the 1980s. Moreover, throughout the postwar period, the proportion of women in the labor force has been increasing dramatically. This has been true for all groups of women – singles and married, those with and without children. In addition, of those women working, the percentage working full time and full year has also been on the rise.

On the surface, these two trends appear to be inconsistent. If the relative supply of a factor increases over time, then, *ceteris paribus*, its relative price will fall. The only explanation for this apparent paradox is that the demand for female workers was also rising over time *relative to* the demand for male workers.

14.3.1   Human capital differences

14.3.1.1   Differences in experience

Many economists have emphasized the experience differential between men and women as an explanation of the gender–earnings gap. Women typically have fewer years of work experience than men of the same age and educational attainment. The reason is that, while men usually work continuously from the end of schooling, the labor force experience of women has historically been interrupted during child-bearing and child-rearing years. Though this pattern has changed recently, particularly among younger women who have entered the labor force since 1980, the experience differential will still exist between older men and women even today.

Evidence compiled by O'Neill (1985) and updated by Wolff illustrates the magnitude of the differences in work experience. Unfortunately, there are no comprehensive data available on total work experience for men and women of different ages. However, there is information available on the number of years worked with the same employer. These are shown in Table 14.5. There are three patterns that are evident from these figures. First, men have had, on average, greater work experience than women of the same age. This has been true for all years between 1951 and 2005. Second, the gender difference in work tenure increased rather sharply between 1951 and 1963 (or 1973) and then fell for all age groups. By 2005, gender differences in work experience had virtually vanished for age groups 25 to 34 and 35 to 44. Third, the difference in work experience was greater among older workers. In 2005, men in age group 25–34 had, on average, 0.2 years more of work tenure with the same employer than women in the same age group; the difference was 0.7 years among workers in the 35–44 age group, and 3.2 years for workers aged 45–54.

Table 14.5 Median years of work experience with current employer, for women and men by age group, 1951–2005

Age group	1951	1963	1973	1981	2005
A. All, 16 years and over[a]					
Men	3.9	5.7	4.6	4.0	4.4
Women	2.2	3.0	2.8	2.5	4.1
Difference	1.7	2.7	1.8	1.5	0.3
B. 25–34					
Men	2.8	3.5	3.2	2.9	3.0
Women	1.8	2.0	2.2	2.0	2.8
Difference	1.0	1.5	1.0	0.9	0.2
C. 35–44					
Men	4.5	7.6	6.7	6.6	5.2
Women	3.1	3.6	3.6	3.5	4.5
Difference	1.4	4.0	3.1	3.1	0.7
D. 45–54					
Men	7.6	11.4	11.5	11.0	9.6
Women	4.0	6.1	5.9	5.9	6.4
Difference	3.6	5.3	5.6	5.1	3.2

a   Age group 20 and over in 2005.
Sources: O'Neill, J. (1985). The trend in the male–female wage gap in the United States. *Journal of Labor Economics*, **3**(1), S91–S116; U.S. Census Bureau. *Statistical Abstract of the United States, 2007*. Washington, DC: U.S. Government Printing Office.

O'Neill also provided some estimates of the average number of years worked by age group for a more limited sample of female workers, based on the NLS. These data also show that the work experience of women has been generally rising over time. The average number of years worked by white female employees in age group 25–29 increased from 5.2 years in 1973 to 6.1 years in 1978; while for those in the 30–34 age bracket, it fell slightly from 8.9 years in 1967 to 8.4 years in 1978. For women aged 35–39, average work experience increased from 11.6 years in 1967 to 12.1 years in 1972; among women aged 40–44, it rose from 14.1 years in 1967 to 14.9 years in 1977; and for those aged 45–49, from 17.3 years in 1972 to 17.9 years in 1977.

Estimates provided by Smith and Ward (1989) show a similar pattern (see Table 14.6). The average years of work experience of working women aged 25 increased from 5.6 years in 1920 to 6.5 years in 1986. For women of age 30, the increase was from 8.7 years in 1920 to 10.4 years in 1990. Forty-year-old women saw their work experience rise from 14.0 years in 1950 to 17.0 years in 1990; and for 50-year-old women, from 19.3 years in 1950 to 22.5 years in 1990. Thus, by their calculations, gains in work experience occurred for working women in all age groups but the magnitude of the change since between 1920 and 1990 was relatively small.

Though the results of O'Neill (1985) and Smith and Ward (1989) generally show rising work experience of women over time, the trends are rather modest. This might seem surprising particularly in light of the dramatic increase in the LFPR of women over time. Yet, the relation between rising LFPR and the average experience level of women is rather complicated. As O'Neill, and Smith and Ward have argued, while an increase in the labor force participation of women

Table 14.6 Average number of years of women's labor market experience for employed women by age group, 1920–1990

Age group	1920	1950	1980	1986	1990
Working women, age 25	5.6	5.9	6.2	6.5	
Working women, age 30	8.7	8.0	9.5	10.5	10.4
Working women, age 40	—	14.0	14.4	15.5	17.0
Working women, age 50	—	19.3	20.6	21.5	22.5

Source: Smith, J.P. & Ward, M.P. (1989). Women in the labor market and in the family. *Journal of Economic Perspectives*, **3**(1), 9–23.

does result in an increase in the average work experience *among all women* (working and not working), it does not necessarily result in an increase in the average work experience among *employed* women. Consider two cases. In the first case, suppose that female workers in the labor force have a high propensity to continue working over time. Then, an increase in the overall LFPR of women must result from the fact that there are continually new female entrants into the labor force. Since the new entrants into the labor force have considerably less work experience than those women who are continuing to work, the *average* work experience of *working women* might actually go down.

In the second case, suppose that the female labor force is characterized by high turnover in employment. Then, the work experience of both women in the labor force and those not in the labor force would tend to be equal. An increase in the overall LFPR of women would then result from the *reentry* of women into the labor force who have already accumulated some work experience (but whose work experience had been interrupted). In this case, an increase in the LFPR of women would be associated with an increase in the average work experience of employed women.

The results of both O'Neill and Smith and Ward do show rising average work experience among employed women and seem to support the second case. Also, calculations made by Smith and Ward indicate that the average work experience among *all women* (both employed and not employed) increased much faster than the average experience of employed women. For example, the average experience of working women of age 50 increased by 3.2 years between 1950 and 1990 (from 19.3 to 22.5 years), while that of all women increased by 7.0 years (from 10.9 to 17.9 years). This difference held for every age group.

14.3.1.2 Schooling differences

Another surprising finding is that in the early 1950s male workers have typically had fewer years of schooling than female workers. However, this difference gradually eroded until sometime in the 1990s and then reversed. Table 14.7 shows median years of schooling for male and female workers by age group from 1952 to 2005. In 1952, the average female worker had 12.0 years of schooling (a high school graduate). We discussed in Chapter 13 how average schooling levels in the workforce have been rising. This was true for both male and female workers but the rate of increase was actually greater for men than for women. By 1969, the differential in favor of female workers had almost disappeared. Indeed, by 1983, the average male worker and the average female worker had completed 12.7 years of education. The situation then reversed again and in 2005 female workers had completed, on average, 13.7 years of schooling, 0.8 years more than the average male worker. The time trends are similar for the younger age groups, particularly age groups 25–34 and 35–44. For age group 45–54, there was virtually no difference in median

Table 14.7   Median years of schooling for male and female workers by age group, 1952–2005

Category	1952	1959	1969	1979	1983	2005
A. All, 18 and over						
Women	12.0	12.2	12.4	12.6	12.7	13.7
Men	10.4	11.5	12.3	12.6	12.7	12.9
Difference	1.6	0.7	0.1	0.0	0.0	0.8
B. 25–34						
Women	12.2	12.3	12.5	12.9	13.0	13.7
Men	12.1	12.3	12.6	13.1	13.0	12.6
Difference	0.1	0.0	−0.1	−0.2	0.0	1.1
C. 35–44						
Women	11.9	12.2	12.4	12.6	12.8	13.5
Men	11.2	12.1	12.4	12.8	12.9	12.8
Difference	0.7	0.1	0.0	−0.2	−0.1	0.7
D. 45–54						
Women		11.7	12.3	12.5	12.6	13.2
Men		10.4	12.2	12.5	12.7	13.0
Difference		1.3	0.1	0.0	−0.1	0.2
E. 55–64						
Women		10.0	12.1	12.4	12.5	13.0
Men		8.8	10.9	12.4	12.5	13.5
Difference		1.2	1.2	0.0	0.0	−0.5

Sources: O'Neill, J. (1985). The trend in the male–female wage gap in the United States. *Journal of Labor Economics*, **3**(1), S91–S116; and for 2005, http://www.census.gov/hhes/www/income/histinc/p20.html.

years of schooling in 2005, while for age group 55–64 male workers had, on average, more education than female workers.[2]

Why did men's schooling increase faster than women's? There are two reasons, according to O'Neill. First, during the 1950s, men entered college at a higher rate than women, aided in part by the educational benefits of the "GI bill," passed after World War II to provide benefits for veterans of the war. Second, the labor force participation of older, less educated females increased faster than younger, more educated women, thus reducing the *average* educational attainment among all female workers.

14.3.1.3   Effects of human capital differences on the gender–wage gap*

How much do differences in schooling and work experience help account for the earnings gap between men and women? As in the case of racial disparities in earnings, there have been numerous studies on the sources of the wage gap between men and women. These have usually taken the form of regression analysis, in which the individual wages of men and women are regressed on (that is, related to) the schooling and work experience of that individual, as well as other relevant labor market characteristics (see Section 12.2.1 for a discussion of the Blinder–Oaxaca decomposition using econometric analysis). In these studies, the unexplained difference (the "residual") is usually attributed to the presence of discrimination.

As noted in Section 14.2, the gender–wage gap has gone through three phases. In the early part of the postwar period, from the end of World War II to the early 1950s, the wage gap actually widened. Then, from the early 1950s to the early 1970s, the wage gap remained more or less stable. Finally, from the early 1970s to the mid-2000s, female wages have been increasing faster than male wages. The various studies summarized below tend to concentrate on different phases of the wage–gap trend.

Using U.S. Census of Population data, Gwartney and Stroup (1973) reported that the ratio of median income between females and males fell from 0.40 in 1949 to 0.32 in 1969 among all adults, and the ratio of median labor earnings declined from 0.58 to 0.47 among workers only. A large part of the gender difference in labor earnings was accounted for by differences in the amount of time worked. For example, in 1959, the ratio of annual earnings between females and males (including both full-time and part-time workers) was 0.49 but the ratio in hourly earnings (annual earnings divided by the number of hours worked) was 0.61. In 1969, the ratio in annual earnings for all workers was 0.47 but for full-time, year-round workers alone it was 0.56. They found that age and education explained very little of the remaining gender gap in earnings. In fact, female workers had, on average, greater schooling than male workers in 1949 and 1959 and about the same level of schooling in 1969. Thus about 40 percent of the difference in earnings between females and males in those years was left unexplained after controlling for human capital factors.

On further analysis, the authors found that the earnings gap between single males and females was substantially less than that between married males and females. In 1959, after adjustment for age, education, and time worked the female–male median income ratio was estimated to be between 0.91 and 0.96 for singles and to be 0.50 for those married. Gwartney and Stroup suggested that the large earnings gap between females and males may not necessarily reflect employer discrimination but may instead reflect the preference of married females for low-responsibility jobs which also carry with them lower pay.

Fuchs (1971), also analyzing 1960 Census of Population data, calculated an average hourly earnings ratio between nonfarm females and males of 0.60. He then adjusted the earnings data for differences in schooling, age, race, and city size and found that the resulting gender–earnings ratio increased to only 0.61. After further adjustments for differences in marital status, class of worker (whether self-employed, employed in private industry, or employed in the government), and commuting time,[3] the earnings ratio rose to 0.66. Thus, about 34 percent of the earnings gap was still left unaccounted for after controlling for productivity-related factors.

Fuchs also found that a large part of the earnings gap was due to gender differences in occupation of employment and, in particular, to the fact that women tended to be concentrated in the low-paying service occupations. Fuchs suggested that a large part of the earnings gap was due to gender differences in social roles. Role differentiation affected the choice of occupation, hours of work, and other variables that influence earnings. He speculated that role differences may themselves be a product of discrimination.

In a later paper, Fuchs (1974) compared the male–female earnings ratio using Census data over the decade between 1960 and 1970. In contrast to Gwartney and Stroup, he did find some relative gains made by females. The ratio of female to male hourly earnings adjusted for age and schooling increased from 0.61 to 0.64 over this decade, or by 5 percent. For some groups of females the gain was even larger. For college-educated females, the earnings ratio increased from 0.59 to 0.66 relative to college-educated men, or by 11 percent. For self-employed females, the ratio (relative to self-employed males) increased by 11 percent from 0.51 to 0.57. He also found that the earnings gap was smaller among workers under 35 years of age than older workers, considerably smaller for singles than married individuals (as Gwartney and Stroup had found), and smaller for government employees than nongovernment workers.

Oaxaca (1973) found substantial evidence of sex discrimination on the basis of the 1967 Survey of Economic Opportunity. Of the gross wage differential between white females and males of

0.54, he estimated that 0.40 points or 74 percent was due to discrimination, and of the gross wage differential between black females and males of 0.49, he estimated that 0.45 points or 92 percent was due to discrimination. In the absence of sex discrimination, he estimated that the average white female wage would have been 88 percent of the white male wage instead of the actual ratio of 54 percent and the average black female wage would have been 96 percent of the black male wage instead of the actual ratio of 67 percent.

In a follow-up study, Oaxaca (1977) found that the earnings ratio between year-round female and male workers actually fell between the mid-1950s and 1970s for whites, though it increased for blacks. He concluded that it was an increase in sex discrimination among white workers that accounted for the relative decline in the economic position of white female workers and a reduction in sex discrimination among black workers that accounted for the relative gain of black female workers.

O'Neill (1985) examined changes in the overall wage gap between males and females over the period from 1955 to 1982. She found a U-shaped pattern, with the gender pay gap (defined as one minus the ratio of female to male annual earnings adjusted for hours worked) first widening from 0.31 in 1955 to 0.37 in the early 1970s but subsequently narrowing to 0.33 in 1983. On net, there was very little change in the wage gap over the entire period.

O'Neill's analysis indicated that changes in productivity-related characteristics were primarily responsible for movements in the gender–wage gap. Male workers gained on females in educational attainment, from a difference of 1.6 years of schooling in favor of employed females in the 1950s to virtual parity in 1979. The rise in female labor force participation over the period tended to offset any increases in the average work experience of employed females. The work experience differential between women and men widened between 1952 and 1963 and then narrowed from 1963 to 1981. On net, there was little change in the experience differential between the early 1950s and the early 1980s. If anything, human capital of male workers increased relative to female workers between the 1950s and the 1980s. These changes should have resulted in an *increase* in the overall gender–wage gap, so that the fact that the overall wage gap did not increase may have reflected *reduced* labor market discrimination against females.

In a later study examining the gains made by females over the 1980s, O'Neill and Polachek (1993) concluded that increases in female human capital were the primary reason for the narrowing of the wage gap. Using data from the Panel Study of Income Dynamics (PSID) and the National Longitudinal Survey (NLS), they reported that the hourly wage gap between female and male workers declined by about 1 percent per year between 1976 and 1989. The two panel surveys allowed them to obtain good estimates of work experience for females, and they found that there was a significant increase in women's years of work experience over this period. Moreover, the return to female work experience (that is, the extra pay per year of experience) also rose over these years, presumably because of greater investment in on-the-job training. This latter effect may be due to increased effort on the part of female workers to obtain training, employer response to women's increased work attachment, or a decline in discrimination. O'Neill and Polachek also found that while the return to schooling increased for both men and women over this period, it increased faster for women and this also contributed to the narrowing of the wage gap.

Blau and Kahn (1997) also looked at the change in the female–male wage gap over the 1980s (in particular, from 1979 to 1988). They computed that the pay gap declined by 15.2 percentage points over this period. They estimated that less than 1 percentage point of this decline could be attributed to increases in the relative schooling of women. However, they found that 5.3 percentage points (over one-third) of the relative gains made by women were due to gains in the relative experience level of female workers.

Blau and Beller (1981) examined changes in the gender–wage gap between 1971 and 1981 on the basis of the Current Population Survey. They first analyzed changes in the gender–wage gap. They found that the usual measure of the gender–wage gap, the ratio in median earnings between full-time, year-round female and male workers, showed little change over this period – a 3 percent increase for whites and a 1 percent decline for blacks. However, when the earnings of all workers were adjusted for hours worked, the ratio in hourly wages between female and male workers increased by 9 percent for whites and 11 percent for blacks.

Blau and Beller then analyzed some of the factors contributing to the narrowing of the gender–wage gap over this period. They found that declining gender role specialization (as reflected in the occupational composition of employment) and declining discrimination explained a large part of the narrowing. They also found that the "marriage penalty" on female wages – the proclivity of employers to pay lower wages to married women than single women with the same human capital – declined over this period.

Hersch (1991a) used the 1986 Quality of Employment Survey to analyze the effects of marital status, the number of dependents, and housework responsibilities on female wages in the labor market. She found that household responsibilities (as measured by the amount of time spent in work at home) had a negative effect on female wages but little effect on male wages. For women, household responsibilities appeared to reduce the amount of their human capital investments (particularly in firm training) and also to reduce the amount of effort available for market work. On the basis of the PSID, Hersch (1995) reported the striking result that time spent in housework not only depressed female wages by reducing the time available for human capital investment but also had a direct negative effect on wages. This latter effect may reflect a lack of complete commitment to market work which women experience when they face burdensome household responsibilities in addition to market work.

Sorensen (1991) examined changes in the gender–wage gap over the 1980s. She first reported that women made tremendous gains relative to men over this period. Among full-time workers, the ratio of earnings between women and men increased from 61 percent in 1978 to 72 percent in 1990. Using the PSID, she estimated earnings equations for both males and females in 1979 and 1985 to analyze the sources of the narrowing of the wage gap. Her main conclusion was that most of the narrowing (77 percent among whites and 61 percent among blacks) was due to the unexplained residual, which she interpreted as a reduction in discrimination against females. There were three other contributing factors, whose effects were relatively small: (i) a modest convergence in the human capital of female and male workers; (ii) growing similarity in the occupational distributions of female and male workers; and (iii) industrial shifts in employment, in favor of the female-dominated service sectors and away from the male-dominated and heavily unionized goods-producing industries.

Ashraf (1996) also found a large reduction in the gender–pay gap between 1968 and 1989 on the basis of the PSID. Ashraf found a significant decline both in the portion of the wage gap due to human capital differences and in the "unexplained" component, which is usually attributed to discrimination.

Weinberger and Kuhn (2006), using Decennial Census and Current Population Survey data spanning 1959 through 1999, examined the relative contributions of two factors to the decline in the gender–wage gap: (i) changes across cohorts in the relative slopes of men's and women's age–earnings profiles; and (ii) changes in relative earnings levels at labor market entry. The first factor reflects the returns to years of experience and the second factor the starting salary of different age groups. They found that changes in the returns to experience accounted for about one-third of the narrowing of the gender wage over the years from 1959 to 1999. They surmised that this effect reflects the contribution of changes in work experience and other post-school investments to the decline of the gender–wage gap.

Blau and Kahn (2006) pointed to the slowing convergence of wages between women and men during the 1990s. They first noted that the female-to-male ratio of median annual earnings for year-round, full-time workers rose from 59.7 percent in 1979 to 68.7 percent in 1989, for a 9.0 percentage point gain over the 1980s, but only to 72.2 percent in 1999, for a 3.5 percentage point gain over the decade of the 1990s. They found that changes in human capital (schooling and experience) did not contribute to the slowdown because women's relative human capital improved comparably over the decades of the 1980s and 1990s. In particular, gains in the relative experience level of women relative to men were equally strong in the 1990s as in the 1980s. However, a reduction in occupational segregation and de-unionization had larger impacts in the 1980s than in the 1990s, which, in turn, explained part of the slower convergence in the 1990s. However, the biggest factor was a much faster reduction in the "unexplained" portion of the wage gap in the 1980s, which may partially reflect a greater decrease in gender discrimination in the 1980s than in the 1990s.

O'Neill and O'Neill (2005) analyzed the Decennial Census of Population data and the National Longitudinal Survey of Youth (NLSY79) for the year 2000. They found that differences in schooling levels and scholastic test scores as measured by the AFQT were quite small in 2000 and explained very little of the gender–pay gap. Instead, they concluded that the gender–pay gap stemmed largely from choices made by women and men concerning the amount of time and energy to devote to their career, as reflected in the amount of work experience, the choice of part-time versus full-time work, and other workplace and job characteristics.

Another important dimension to labor market compensation is the value of fringe benefits. Two studies examined gender differences in benefit coverage. Currie (1993) used the May 1988 Current Population Survey's Survey of Employee Benefits to examine differences in benefit structure. She reported that in 1988, pensions accounted for 5 percent of employee payrolls, health insurance and related expenditures for 8.1 percent, and sick leave and disability together for 1.9 percent. The preponderance of fringe benefits takes the form of pensions and health insurance. Using regression analysis, she concluded that after controlling for age, education, marital status, and number of children, male employees were more likely to have pensions, health coverage, and disability than women, though women were more likely to have paid sick leave. These differences were statistically significant. However, after controlling for wages, differences in benefit coverage disappeared, suggesting that much of the difference in benefit coverage between males and females was due to the fact that women, on average, were employed in jobs which paid lower wages.

A similar analysis was conducted by Currie and Chaykowski (1992) for Canada. Using establishment-level data for union contracts in Ontario over the period from 1980 to 1990 and individual data from the 1986 Canadian Labour Market Activities Survey, they found that, after controlling for job tenure, female workers were less likely to be covered by pension plans. This difference persisted even after wages were controlled for. On the other hand, among unionized workers, female workers had more generous leave provisions than male workers.

14.3.1.4   *Effects of work interruption on earnings**

A related but somewhat different concern is the impact of work disruptions on the relative earnings of females. The work surveyed in the preceding section generally sought to use years of experience as an explanatory variable in accounting for wage differences between men and women. However, the fact that women have experienced more interruptions in their work history than men may have an added (negative) effect on their labor earnings.

There are three reasons why the continuity or discontinuity of work experience may affect earnings. First, as Mincer and Polachek (1974) argued, the fact that women may expect discontinuous labor market participation and fewer total years at work than men provides less incentive for women to undertake human capital investments than men. This is particularly so for firm-specific training, since they will reap the rewards of such investment over fewer years. Second, employers will also have less incentive to train female workers, because the period for recapturing their investment is shorter. Third, withdrawals from the labor market may lead to depreciation of human capital, since the skills acquired may become obsolete.

Several studies have attempted to estimate the importance of work interruption on differences in earnings between males and females. Duncan and Hoffman (1979) were able to obtain direct measures of on-the-job training from the 1976 wave of the PSID. They found that men and women obtained the same return from on-the-job training. However, women systematically received less training than men with the same amount of past work experience. They noted that these results are consistent with the hypothesis that firms have different training and promotion policies for male and female employees. They concluded that the lower pay-offs to experience observed for women may reflect, in part, discrimination on the part of employers in providing job training.

Ragan and Smith (1981) pooled industry data on quit rates with 1970 Census of Population data on individual earnings and worker characteristics (including industry of employment) to estimate the effects of the likelihood of quitting on male–female wage differences. They argued that because of hiring and training costs, firms prefer, *ceteris paribus*, workers whose probability of leaving the firm is low. If an employer believes that the likelihood of a female leaving the company is greater than that of a male employee, the firm may hire female employees only if they accept a lower wage. They found that high-quit probabilities were associated with lower wages, and, in fact, the wage discount for female employees was greater than for male employees with the same quit rate. They concluded that differences in quit rates between males and females, together with other worker characteristics (schooling, experience, and socioeconomic characteristics) explained about half the wage gap between male and female workers in 1970.

The results reported so far suggest that the greater likelihood of female withdrawal from the labor force (or, at least, employer *perception* of a greater likelihood) is associated with less firm investment in female employees than male and thus a lower rate of return to female work experience than male work experience. A related issue is whether females are permanently penalized for labor market withdrawal when they reenter the labor force, due to the depreciation of their human capital while they are out of work. Several papers have analyzed the so-called "rebound effect." Mincer and Ofek (1982) argued that the restoration of past occupational skills is more efficient than the acquisition of new skills. As a result, we should expect to find that wages are low during the first year following a labor market interruption but that wages should quickly recover after several years of continuous work. Using data from the National Longitudinal Surveys for years 1966–1974, they found precisely this pattern: wages of female workers who had been out of the labor force for a period of time were lower on reentry than when they had last worked, but they soon recovered to their previous level.

Corcoran, Duncan, and Ponza (1983) used data covering the period 1967–1979 from the PSID to analyze the effects of female labor market withdrawals on future wages. They found the same pattern as Mincer and Ofek, and concluded that the net loss in earnings from labor market drop-out was small for females. However, they proposed a different explanation from the one advanced by Mincer and Ofek – namely that on reentry there is often a mismatch between worker skills and jobs. After a work interruption, women workers often lack complete information about job opportunities, and employers often lack complete information about the skills of the new worker. One common mechanism for this sorting process is to assign new workers to low-wage jobs on hiring and then to promote them as their skills become known.

Jacobsen and Levin (1992) reached a somewhat different conclusion on the basis of data from the 1984 wave of the Survey of Income and Program Participation. Like Mincer and Ofek (1982) and Corcoran, Duncan, and Ponza (1983), they found that when women reenter the labor force after a period of nonparticipation, their earnings were much lower than a comparable group of women with continuous labor market experience. Over time, the gap diminished between what they called the "gappers" and "non-gappers" because of the rebound effect. However, even after 20 years, the gap did not entirely disappear. Moreover, the effect of a gap on women's lifetime earnings was significantly greater than their foregone earnings alone during the period of non-participation.

Maxwell and D'Amico (1986), using data from the National Longitudinal Surveys over the period 1966–1983, looked at relative unemployment rates for males and females returning to the labor market. They found that unemployment rates among females who were reentering the labor force after a prolonged interruption were two and a half times greater than men reentering the labor market after a similar period of interruption. They concluded that women fare consider-ably worse than men after job interruption.

More recent work has tended to discount the importance of career interruptions on female earn-ings. Spivey (2005) used the National Longitudinal Survey of Youths over the period 1979–2000 to examine this issue. The author's main finding was that very little of the gender–wage gap was attributable to work interruptions for women. Wage profiles were affected by total amount of time out of work, by recent work interruptions, and by some past interruptions. Though women had, on average more work interruptions than men, the wage loss associated with any given inter-ruption was smaller for women. After controlling for the total amount of time out of work, the author found very little added effect from work interruptions *per se*.

14.3.2   Occupational segregation

Another important factor accounting for differences in female and male earnings is that female workers tend to be concentrated in the relatively low-paying occupations. This phenomenon is often referred to as *occupational segregation*. We have alluded to this factor before, in Section 12.8, in our discussion of the overcrowding model.

There are four questions of interest. First, what is the extent of occupational segregation between males and females? Second, how much does occupational segregation contribute to the female–male wage gap? Third, has occupational segregation lessened over time? Fourth, if so, how much has the abatement in occupational segregation contributed to the narrowing of the gender–wage gap?

We first show some figures on the composition of female employment by major occupational group over the period from 1900 to 2004 in Table 14.8. Panel A shows the distribution of total female employment among occupational groups. In 2004, the largest concentration of female employees was in clerical and sales jobs (35 percent); professional, technical, and kindred posi-tions (24 percent); and service jobs, including domestic servants (21 percent). Indeed, even as late as 1983, one-third of all female employees were found in only nine detailed occupations: secretaries (8.7 percent); bookkeepers and accounting clerks (5.0 percent); teachers, excluding college (5.4 percent); registered nurses (3.0 percent); waitresses (2.7 percent); information clerks (2.4 percent); health technicians (2.1 percent); private household workers (2.1 percent); and typists (2.0 percent).[4]

However, there have been significant changes over the twentieth century. The proportion of female workers employed in professional, technical, and kindred occupations rose rather steadily, from 8 percent in 1900 to 24 percent in 2004. The proportion in managerial and admin-istrative positions increased from only 1 percent in 1900 to 13 percent in 2004, with almost half of the increase occurring after 1977. The percentage in sales and clerical jobs grew from

Table 14.8 The percentage composition of female employment by occupation, 1900–2004

Occupational group	1900	1920	1940	1960	1970	1977	1988	1993	2004
A. Female employment by occupation as a percent of total female employment									
Professional & technical	8	12	13	12	14	15	18	20	24
Managers (exc. farm)	1	2	3	5	4	6	11	12	13
Clerical workers	4	19	22	30	34	34	28	27	} 35
Sales workers	4	6	7	8	7	7	13	13	
Craft & kindred	1	1	1	1	1	2	2	2	1
Operatives	24	20	20	16	15	12	7	6	7
Laborers, nonfarm	3	2	1	0	1	1	2	2	—
Private household	29	16	18	10	5	5	2	2	} 21
Service (exc. household)	7	8	11	15	17	18	16	16	
Farmers, farm managers and farm laborers	19	14	4	4	2	1	1	1	—
Total	100	100	100	100	100	100	100	100	100
B. Female occupational employment as a percent of total occupational employment									
Professional & technical	35	45	41	36	38	43	49	53	57
Managers (exc. farm)	4	7	11	16	16	22	39	42	44
Clerical workers	24	48	54	68	74	79	80	79	} 64
Sales workers	17	26	27	39	43	44	49	48	
Craft & kindred	2	2	2	3	3	5	9	9	5
Operatives	34	27	26	28	32	32	29	27	24
Laborers, nonfarm	4	4	3	2	4	4	17	18	—
Private household	97	98	95	98	97	97	93	95	} 57
Service (exc. household)	34	37	39	53	60	58	58	57	
Farmers, farm managers	5	4	3	4	5	5	} 17	15	—
Farm laborers	14	18	10	33	32	29			
Total	18	20	24	33	38	41	45	46	47
C. DD index	52	49	49	44	44	44	36	34	32

Sources: U.S. Census Bureau, Department of Commerce. *Historical Statistics of the U.S.: Colonial Times to 1970*, Bicentennial Edition, Part 2. Washington, DC: U.S. Government Printing Office; U.S. Bureau of Labor Statistics, Department of Labor (1979). *Handbook of Labor Statistics 1978*, Bulletin 2000. Washington, DC: U.S. Government Printing Office; U.S. Bureau of Labor Statistics, Department of Labor (1990). *Handbook of Labor Statistics 1989*, Bulletin 2340. Washington, DC: U.S. Government Printing Office; U.S. Census Bureau. *Statistical Abstract of the United States, 1994 and 1997*. Washington, DC: U.S. Government Printing Office.

8 percent in 1900 to 41 percent in 1977 but then declined to 35 percent in 2004.[5] The share of women employed in service jobs (excluding domestic servants) also grew, from 7 percent in 1900 to 16 percent in 1993.[6] In contrast, the proportion of women working as operatives (mainly machine operators) declined from 24 percent in 1900 to 7 percent in 2004 and the proportion in farming from 19 to 1 percent. The proportion working in craft and kindred jobs remained almost unchanged, at 1 percent in both 1900 and 2004.

Panel B presents figures on female employment in a particular occupational group as a percent of the total employment in that occupation. In 2004, females comprised 47 percent of overall employment but 64 percent of clerical and sales workers, 57 percent of service workers,[7] 57 percent of professional and technical employees, and 44 percent of managers and administrators. On the other hand, they made up only 5 percent of craft workers and 24 percent of operatives.

Table 14.9   Female occupational employment as a percent of total occupational employment for selected detailed occupations, 1979, 1986, 1993, and 2004

Occupation	1979	1986	1993	2004
Secretaries	98.8	99.2	98.9	
Registered nurses	94.6	92.7	94.4	92.4
Bookkeepers, accounting and auditing clerks	88.1	93.0	90.9	
Nursing aides, orderlies, and attendants	85.1	88.3	87.9	89.2
Cashiers	77.7	79.8	—	75.8
Computer operators	56.6	63.8	61.9	
Assemblers	47.2	42.1	32.7	
Accountants and auditors	34.0	44.7	49.2	
Computer programmers	28.0	39.7	31.5	
Supervisor and proprietors, sales occupations	22.4	26.6	36.4	37.8
Computer systems analysts	20.4	29.7	—	
Janitors and cleaners	15.3	21.0	30.7	
Lawyers	10.4	15.2	22.9	28.7
Sales representatives, mining, manufacturing, wholesale	10.1	13.4	21.0	
Electrical and electronic engineers	4.4	9.4	7.6	
Truck drivers, heavy	1.5	1.5	—	
Carpenters, except apprentices	1.1	0.5	0.9	2.3
Automotive mechanics, except apprentices	0.9	0.6	0.6	1.3

1979 and 1986 figures are for full-time workers.
Sources: U.S. Census Bureau (1987). Current Population Reports, Series P-70, No. 10, *Male-Female Differences in Work Experience, Occupations and Earnings: 1984*, August. Washington, DC: U.S. Government Printing Office; U.S. Census Bureau. *Statistical Abstract of the United States, 1994*. Washington, DC: U.S. Government Printing Office; 2005 CPS Annual Demographic Survey: http://pubdb3.census.gov/macro/032005/perinc/new06_019.htm.

Even though this aggregated classification shows substantial differences in the occupational employment patterns of female and male workers, employment data by detailed occupations show an even more extreme pattern of occupational segregation. As shown in Table 14.9, in 2004, females accounted for 92 percent of all registered nurses, 89 percent of nursing aides, and 76 percent of cashiers, while in 1993, females accounted for 99 percent of secretaries and 91 percent of bookkeepers. In contrast, they accounted for less than 1 percent of automotive mechanics and 2 percent of carpenters in 2004, and 2 percent of drivers of heavy trucks, and 8 percent of electrical and electronic engineers in 1993.

Despite the evidence of substantial occupational segregation in the latter part of the twentieth century, there have been dramatic gains over time. Females comprised only 4 percent of managerial and administrative positions in 1900 but 44 percent in 2004, with most of the change occurring after 1977 (Table 14.8); 24 percent of clerical positions in 1900 and 79 percent in 1993; 17 percent of sales jobs in 1900 and almost half in 1993; and 34 percent of service jobs in 1900 and 57 percent in 1993.

Even since 1979, women have made substantial inroads into traditional male occupations. Their share among accountants and auditors increased from 34 to 49 percent between 1979 and 1993 (Table 14.9); among computer systems analysts from 20 to 30 percent (in 1986); among lawyers from 10 percent in 1979 to 29 percent in 2004; and among electrical and electronic engineers from 4 to 8 percent between 1979 and 1993.

14.3.2.1   Duncan and Duncan index

A standard measure of occupation segregation is the Duncan and Duncan (DD) index, developed by Otis Dudley Duncan and Beverly Duncan in 1955. It is defined as follows:

$$DD = \sum_i |m_i - f_i|/2 \tag{14.1}$$

where m_i is the percent of total male employees working in occupation i, f_i is the percent of total females employees working in occupation i, and "|" is the sign for the absolute value of the difference. The index ranges from zero, if the occupational distributions of male and female workers are exactly the same (the same proportion of male and female employees in each occupation), to 100, if male and female workers do not overlap in any occupation (that is, there is complete occupational segregation).[8]

DD indices computed on the basis of the 11 occupational groups are shown in the last line of Table 14.8. Over the entire period from 1900 to 2004, the degree of occupational segregation declined by almost 40 percent, from a DD index of 52 to 32. However, there was almost no change in the degree of occupational segregation between 1900 to 1940, a noticeable reduction between 1940 and 1950, the effects of World War II on female employment;[9] almost no change between 1950 and 1977; and then a considerable decline between 1977 and 2004.

The DD indexes calculated in Table 14.8 are based on an aggregated occupational classification. Computations based on detailed occupations do show more change in the degree of occupational segregation. Beller (1985) calculated from Census of Population data that the DD index declined from 68.7 in 1960 to 65.9 in 1970, or by 2.8 points. Three studies were carried out for the 1970–1980 period on the basis of the 1970 and 1980 Census of Population data. Beller (1984) calculated a 4.2 point decline in the DD index over this period (65.9 to 61.7), Reskin and Hartmann (1988) an 8.4 point decline (67.7 to 59.3), and Fields and Wolff (1991) an 8.3 point decline (from 66.8 to 58.5). Blau (1989), using data from the Current Population Survey, calculated only a 2.4 point decline (59.1 to 56.7) in the DD index between 1983 and 1987.

Table 14.10 shows calculations of the DD indexes in 1960 and 1980 performed by Fuchs (1989) and updated by Wolff to 2004 on the basis of very detailed occupational categories for different demographic groups.[10] In 1980, the DD index stood at 57 among both whites and blacks. As Fuchs noted, a DD index of 57 suggests pervasive occupational segregation by gender, particularly when it is compared to the corresponding DD index by race: only 28 for black women versus white women and 33 for black men versus white men.

There was some reduction in occupational segregation by gender between 1960 and 1980. Among whites, the DD index declined by 8 percent (62 to 57) and among blacks by 20 percent (71 to 57).[11] The biggest reduction occurred among young adults, ages 25 to 34, for whom the DD index fell by 18 percent (from 67 to 55), and among college-educated workers (24 percent for those with a college degree and 23 percent for those with a graduate degree). Thus, younger and more educated female workers were penetrating traditionally male occupations, whereas there was relatively little change for older and less educated females.

Between 1980 and 2004, the overall DD index fell by another 23 percent, from 57 to 44. In this case, comparisons are available only by race. The decline was greater for black females (26 percent) than white females (19 percent).

14.3.2.2   Occupational segregation and the change in the gender–wage gap

Several studies have focused on the role of occupational segregation in explaining the gender–wage gap and its change over time. In this literature, there are two sources which account for the overall

Table 14.10 Duncan and Duncan indexes of occupational segregation by gender, 1960, 1980, and 2005

	1960	1980	2004	Change from 1960 to 1980	Change from 1980 to 2004
All	64	57	44	−7	−13
Whites	62	57	46	−5	−11
Blacks	71	57	42	−14	−15
25–34	67	55		−12	
35–44	63	58		−5	
45–54	63	60		−3	
55–64	65	61		−4	
Elementary school or less	66	60		−6	
High school 1–3 years	64	61		−3	
High school graduate	66	62		−4	
College degree	66	50		−16	
Graduate degree	56	43		−13	

Source: Fuchs, V. (1989). Women's quest for economic equality. *Journal of Economic Perspectives*, **3**(1), 25–41. The 1960 calculations are based on 291 occupations from the 1960 Census of Population 1 in 100 Public Use Sample; and the 1980 calculations are based on 503 occupations from the 1980 Census of Population 1 in 100 Public Use Sample. Both samples are restricted to full-time, full-year employees. The 2005 calculations are based on 73 occupations from the 2005 CPS Annual Demographic Survey: http://pubdb3.census.gov/macro/032005/perinc/new06_019.htm.

gender–wage gap. First, men and women are distributed differently among occupations, with women tending to be concentrated in the low-paying ones. Second, within occupations, women receive, on average, lower earnings than men. These studies have decomposed the overall gender–wage gap into these two effects.

Wolff (1976) calculated, on the basis of 33 occupational groups drawn from the 1960 and 1970 Census of Population, that in 1960, 74 percent of the overall gender–wage gap was due to the lower earnings of females within occupation and 26 percent was due to differences in their occupational distribution of employment; in 1970, the corresponding proportions were 69 percent and 31 percent. Using Current Population Surveys from 1967 to 1986, Orazem, Mattila, and Yu (1990) found that all of the narrowing of the male–female wage gap was due to increases in relative female wages within occupation and none to shifts in female occupational patterns. In these two studies, gender differences in pay within occupation were found to be more important than gender differences in the pattern of occupational employment in explaining both the overall gender–wage gap and its change over time.[12]

As noted above, Blau and Kahn (2006) used data from the PSID to study the slowdown in the reduction of the female–male pay gap in the 1990s relative to the 1980s. They estimated a greater decline in occupational segregation in the 1980s than in the 1990s. The slower reduction of occupational segregation in the 1990s explained part of the slower convergence in the 1990s.

14.3.2.3 Explanations of occupational segregation

Several arguments have been proposed to account for occupational segregation. First, Polachek (1981) argued that because women generally anticipate less continuous and shorter work lives than men, they will prefer "female occupations" which require smaller human capital investment and provide lower penalties for dropping out of the labor market. In this regard, women may also select occupations which are more compatible with their household responsibilities. Indeed, time budget studies have shown that women continue to perform the majority of household tasks even when they are working in the labor market (see Blau & Ferber, 1986, for example).

However, results reported by England (1982) on the basis of the 1967 National Longitudinal Sample seemed to contradict this interpretation. She found that the penalty faced by women for time spent out of the labor force was no smaller if they worked in female occupations than if they worked in mixed or predominantly male occupations. There was no evidence that anticipation of intermittent employment made the choice of a traditionally female occupation economically rational. In fact, after controlling for time worked in the labor market, women had higher wages if they were employed in an occupation containing mainly males. Moreover, women with more intermittent labor market experience were not more apt to be in a predominantly female occupation than women with more continuous work experience.

A second explanation hinges on differences in tastes between male and female workers. Killingsworth (1987) argued that differences in returns to job characteristics can arise in a non-discriminatory manner if tastes for job attributes differ, on average, between males and females. Filer (1983) obtained personnel records from a management consulting firm which had unique data on the tastes of their employees with regard to work attitudes. Individuals in the firm were asked to rank 11 factors in order of importance: job satisfaction, security, power, occupational prestige, social prestige, income, family life, religious activities, community activities, freedom for travel and recreation, and contribution of job to society. Using regression analysis, Filer found that a significant portion of the gender–earnings difference could be attributed to differences in job preferences, though there was still a large portion of the difference unexplained.

A third explanation rests on differences in socialization patterns. Fuchs (1989) argued that women's greater role in reproduction and smaller upper body strength probably played a large role in gender segregation in pre-industrial societies, but in modern society these differences have been amplified through socialization. The experiences of girls and boys in schools and families and their exposure to the media significantly affect their behavior as adults. This shows up in the choice of school subjects and extracurricular activities and the goals they set with respect to family and career. If boys and girls are exposed to different influences, training, and role models, it is likely that they will enter the labor market with different aptitudes, interests, and aspirations. Traditionally, socialization has tended to direct females to the role of wife, mother, and homemaker and men to the role of husband, father, and provider. Jobs taken by both men and women have historically been more compatible with their traditional role models.

These arguments suggest that the difference in the occupational distribution of male and female employment results from differences in tastes or choices – either because women prefer jobs with less training and responsibility due to household or childcare obligations or because they are socialized differently than men. An alternative view is that occupational segregation may result from unequal opportunities in the labor market – that is, discrimination. The model of statistical discrimination presented in Section 12.4 provides such a rationale.

It is rather difficult to distinguish empirically between choice on the one hand and discrimination on the other as the root cause of occupational segregation. Indeed, the two may reinforce each other if socialization leads women to prefer jobs that have traditionally been assigned to females because of discrimination. A study by Fields and Wolff (1991), based on Census of Population data for detailed occupations over the 1970–1980 period, does suggest that discrimination may be an important factor. They found clear evidence that high employment growth within an occupation was associated with declines in segregation within that occupation. They concluded that job barriers against women tended to be lower in sectors where labor demand was strong.[13] This result is consistent with the model of statistical discrimination, from which it can be inferred that discriminatory barriers against minorities and females will lessen when labor market shortages exist for white males.

14.4   THE ROLE OF PUBLIC POLICY

There are three major policy instruments which prohibit gender discrimination. The first is the Equal Pay Act of 1963. A 1963 amendment to the Fair Labor Standards Act of 1938 required that females receive the same pay as men for the same work. Known as the "Equal Pay Act," this amendment was designed to eliminate wage differentials based on sex. However, this Act did allow for differences in pay for the same work if it was based on seniority, merit, or some type of incentive plan. This Act is enforced by the Wage-Hour and Public Contracts Division of the Department of Labor.

Operationally, it is often difficult to determine whether equal work is being performed by a male and female worker, particularly if different job titles are used. Moreover, this Act does not address the critical problem of occupational segregation. Despite such difficulties, the Division has investigated thousands of complaints, sought voluntary compliance from employers, and, where this has failed, helped complainants bring cases to court.

As discussed in the last chapter (see Section 13.6), the two other major anti-discrimination regulations are the 1964 Civil Rights Act and Executive Order 11246. Title VII of the Civil Rights Act of 1964 prohibits employers from discriminating on the basis of gender in hiring or firing, compensation, terms and conditions of employment, and employer-provided training. The 1964 Civil Rights Act also set up the Equal Employment Opportunity Commission (EEOC) to enforce the provisions of Title VII. Executive Order 11246, originally issued in 1965 to prohibit race discrimination, was extended in 1968 to prohibit gender discrimination on the part of federal contractors. Executive Order 11246 also required federal contractors to take affirmative action to remedy any underrepresentation and set up the Office of Federal Contract Compliance (OFCC) to enforce this order.

14.4.1   The effectiveness of the anti-discrimination programs

The Equal Pay Act, Title VII of the Civil Rights Act of 1964, and Executive Order 11246 are the three major legal instruments implemented to combat employment discrimination. How effective have they been? A number of studies have been carried out to answer this question. As with studies on racial discrimination, they have generally been of two types. First, some have used time-series data to determine whether the passage of Title VII in 1964 affected the trends in the relative earnings of females – in particular, whether there has been a statistically significant break in the series after 1964. As Blau (1984) noted, the main problem with time-series analysis is the difficulty of including enough control variables so that it can be certain that the results isolate the effect of Title VII alone on the post-1964 trends. Second, other studies have used cross-sectional data to compare the progress of women in firms or industries covered by Executive Order 11246 (federal contractors) with those in sectors not covered. As Blau argues, the difficulty here is to identify correctly the covered and uncovered sectors.

Different studies have concentrated on different aspects of gender discrimination (see Gunderson, 1989, for a detailed review). Beller (1976, 1979, and 1980) used Current Population Surveys over the period from 1967 to 1975 to estimate the effects of the EEOC enforcements provisions on the female–male wage gap. She included measures of both the probability of an EEOC investigation and the probability of a successful settlement from an EEOC investigation in her analysis of the change in male and female earnings. She found that the female–male wage gap declined by almost 10 percent between 1967 and 1974 and that the rate of increase was faster after 1972, the date of the amendment to Title VII which provided for more effective enforcement. A higher probability of an investigation was found to be more important than a higher probability of a settlement in accounting for the increased earnings of female workers. She concluded that stricter enforcement of EEOC played an important role in the earnings gains made by females over this period.

In a later article, Beller (1992) used the same data to analyze the probability of a female worker entering a predominantly male occupation (defined as one in which at least two-thirds of the employees are males). She calculated that the probability of a female being employed in a male occupation relative to the probability of a male worker being found in such an occupation increased by 6.2 percent between 1967 and 1974. She found that both Title VII of the 1964 Civil Rights Act and the federal contract compliance program helped explain the inroads made by females into male-dominated occupations over this period. In this case, a higher probability of a settlement was found to be more important than a higher probability of an investigation in accounting for these gains.

Two other studies found no statistically significant effect of Title VII on the relative economic gains made by females after 1964. Leonard (1984c) used data on employment by manufacturing industry over the period between 1966 and 1978 to determine whether there was any significant connection between the proportion of females employed within an industry and the degree of Title VII compliance (as measured by the number of class action law suits). He failed to find a significant relation. Oaxaca (1977) used Census of Population data for 1960 and 1970 and Current Population Report figures over the period 1955–1971 to estimate whether the Civil Rights Act of 1964 had any significant effect on relative female earnings gains over these periods. He reported no statistically significant change in the discrimination (that is, unexplained) component of the gender–earnings gap before and after 1964.

The studies on the effects of affirmative action on the economic position of females are generally more positive. As noted above, Beller (1982), using Current Population Survey data, found that affirmative action efforts from the federal contract compliance program had a significant effect on the proportion of females entering male occupations over the 1967–1974 period. Osterman (1982), using data from the PSID in 1978 and 1979, found that the implementation of affirmative action plans significantly reduced the probability that female workers quit their job and that compliance reviews lowered the probability even more.

Four studies used EEO reports from individual establishments to assess the effects of affirmative action on female gains. Smith and Welch (1984) found that affirmative action had a positive effect on the employment of females, and the effect was quite large for black females though relatively small for white females. Leonard (1984a) constructed an index of occupational advance (that is, better jobs) and found that affirmative action had a significant positive effect on this index and that compliance reviews an even larger effect. Leonard (1984b) also reported that affirmative action spurred female employment growth, though compliance reviews did not augment these gains. In a 1985 article, Leonard further found that the establishment of targets by the OFCC exerted a separate effect in enhancing the employment growth of female employees.

As noted in Chapter 13, the 1980s saw a diminution in the enforcement of anti-discrimination programs by the federal government. Leonard (1990) pointed to a decrease in the federal budget devoted to affirmative action enforcement activity and the elimination of contract cancellation as a penalty for the failure to attain affirmative action goals. Moreover, both the executive branch of the federal government and the Supreme Court increased the requirements for plaintiffs to prove discrimination in Civil Rights Act lawsuits, and there was a decline in the number of class action lawsuits for employment discrimination during the 1980s. Leonard found in his study that the growth of female employment grew more slowly among federal contractors than noncontractors during the early 1980s, exactly the opposite of what occurred during the 1970s.

One other piece of evidence is provided by Blau and Kahn (2006) in their study of the factors that contributed to the slowing convergence of female and male earnings during the 1990s in comparison to the 1980s. In their econometric analysis, they found that the largest factor accounting for the slowing pay convergence was the trend in the "unexplained residual," which was by itself sufficient to more than fully account for the slowdown in wage convergence in the 1990s. They found evidence that the increase in the unexplained portion of the wage gap between the two decades was partly due to an increase in labor market discrimination against women. This, in turn, may be due to a further lessening of governmental anti-discrimination effort.

14.4.2 Comparable worth

Though federal anti-discrimination policy appears to have had some effect in reducing occupational segregation by gender, such segregation remains strong even today and still exerts a major influence on the male–female wage gap. One reason seems to be that women have been much more likely to file for grievances if they are paid less than men for doing the same work at the same place than if they are not hired for a particular job in the first place. As a result, women have tended to avail themselves more of the Equal Pay Act and of the equal compensation provisions of Title VII than of the equal employment opportunities of the latter. Since the primary source of earnings differences between males and females is still differences in occupation or employment, an emphasis on equal pay for the same work will not by itself do much to bring about earnings equality between the sexes. Affirmative action plans may, however, still result in some progress in breaking down occupational barriers and reducing occupational segregation. But insofar as occupational segregation is due to role selection and role stereotyping that is deeply embedded in the social fabric of our society, ending employment discrimination may not result in earnings equality between the sexes unless pre-labor market discrimination is reduced.

As a result, many economists and policy-makers have advocated a policy of "comparable worth" or the principle of equal pay for jobs that are determined to be of equal "value" to the employer. Unlike the provisions of the Equal Pay Act of 1963 or the equal compensation clause of the Civil Rights Act of 1964, which prohibit unequal pay for the *same* job, comparable worth allows comparisons among otherwise dissimilar jobs or occupations. These ratings are usually based on direct job evaluation procedures.

The rationale for comparable worth comes from the overcrowding model of occupational segregation, which we discussed in Section 12.8. The model assumes that there are separate male jobs and female jobs in the workplace and also that there are fewer female occupations than male occupations. The difference in the number of suitable occupations artificially raises the supply of workers to the female sector and correspondingly lowers the supply of workers to the male sector. The greater supply of workers to female occupations lowers the wages in female jobs, and the lower supply of workers in male jobs raises wages in male occupations. As a result, females with the same qualifications as male workers receive lower wages.

There are usually four steps involved in the development of a comparable worth program. First, jobs within an establishment are classified as either predominantly male or predominantly female (a cutoff of 70 percent of one gender is often used). Second, job evaluation experts assign job evaluation scores to each job based on various attributes of the work, such as educational requirements, skill, responsibility, effort, and working conditions. The point scores for each factor are then totaled to obtain the composite score for that job. Third, the total point scores are then compared to wages for each of the predominantly male jobs, and the same comparison is made for female jobs. The fourth step is to adjust female wages for a particular job to male wages of jobs that have the same point value.

As Gunderson (1989) noted, a number of criticisms have been made of the comparable worth procedure. First, the assignment of points is to some extent arbitrary, and a gender bias can still exist if a higher range of points is allocated for jobs that are performed more often by men than by women, or if compensating points are awarded for undesirable working conditions (noise, dirt, etc.) that are normally associated with male work as opposed to female jobs. Second, job evaluation systems that are typically in place in most establishments were designed to provide only an ordinal ranking of jobs, not a cardinal number on which to base an actual dollar value. Also, because of difficulties in comparability for different occupational groups, separate evaluation systems were traditionally designed for white-collar and blue-collar employment.

Third, for certain "benchmark jobs," market forces were often taken into account in the assignment of job evaluation scores, and these jobs were pegged at the market wage. The wages of other jobs were then set relative to that of the benchmark job. The evaluation system in many companies was also adjusted if the job evaluation scores suggested a wage that was out of line with the corresponding market wage.

Fourth, difficulties occur in the appropriate adjustment of the wages of the female jobs. Should they be set to the wages of the corresponding male jobs in terms of evaluation points or to the average wage of jobs (both male and female) with the same number of points? What if there are no male jobs that have the same score as a given female job? Fifth, according to the standard neoclassical model of wage determination, wages are set at the *margin*, according to the market supply and demand for a given factor, not according to the average value of the inputs required for the job. If the wage for a job is artificially set above its market value, then employment in that job will fall and there will be an excess supply of labor seeking that job.

So far, in the United States, comparable worth has been applied only to public sector jobs.[14] According to Gunderson (1989), as of 1984, 25 states had legislation relating to comparable worth, and 10 states had implemented or were planning to implement comparable worth programs. Also, as of 1987, 20 states had allocated money to use in adjusting female salaries for state government employees according to comparable worth principles (see Blau & Kahn, 1992b).[15] However, according to Killingsworth (2002), states with "comparable worth programs" vary considerably in the degree to which such policies are carried out. Minnesota, Iowa, and Washington (state) have to date the most developed systems of comparable worth for their state government employees.

Several studies have been made to test the effectiveness of the comparable worth programs in effect. Killingsworth (1990) looked at the effects of comparable worth in both Minnesota and the city of San Jose and found that comparable worth adjustments lowered the male–female wage gap by between 6 and 10 percentage points but at the same time lowered female employment by 4 to 7 percentage points. These two trends are, of course, not unconnected, since an increase in female wages will lead to reduced female employment as the firm moves up the labor demand curve.

O'Neill, Brien, and Cunningham (1989) did a similar study for Washington State and reached similar conclusions: relative female wages gained but female employment declined. Orazem and Mattila (1990) found that for the state of Iowa, comparable worth had the potential of closing the male–female wage gap by 9 percentage points but in actuality narrowed it by only 1.4 percentage points.

14.5   OTHER ISSUES*

14.5.1   Effects of wives' earnings on family income inequality

As discussed in Section 14.1 above, one of the most dramatic changes in the postwar U.S. economy has been the increasing labor force participation of women. This is particularly true for wives, whose LFPR increased from 20 percent in 1947 to 61 percent in 2005. In this section, we examine the effects of the increasing LFPR of wives on family income.

Figure 14.2 shows the median income of families in 1992 dollars over the period from 1967 to 2005. We have divided families into four types: (i) married couples, with wife working; (ii) married couples, with wife not working; (iii) male householders; and (iv) female householders. It is helpful to consider two subperiods: 1967–1973 and 1973–2005. During the 1967–1973 period, all four groups experienced an increase in their real family income. Median income grew by 18 percent for married couples with wives at work, 15 percent for married couples with wives not working, 21 percent for single males, and 4 percent for single females.

However, the situation changed radically over the 1973–2005 period. Over this time period, married couples with wives at work experienced by far the highest increase in real income – a 28 percent growth and single females saw a 16 percent increase in income. In contrast, married couples with wives not working saw their family income fall by 4 percent and single males by 6 percent.

How has the increased LFPR of wives affected the *inequality* of family income? There are two parts to this question. The first concerns its effect on the distribution of family income among married couples alone. Some have speculated that wives' earnings are disequalizing. This presumption is derived, at least in part, from the popular stereotype of "yuppie" couples in which both husband and wife are professionals earning high incomes. Two studies have shown that this

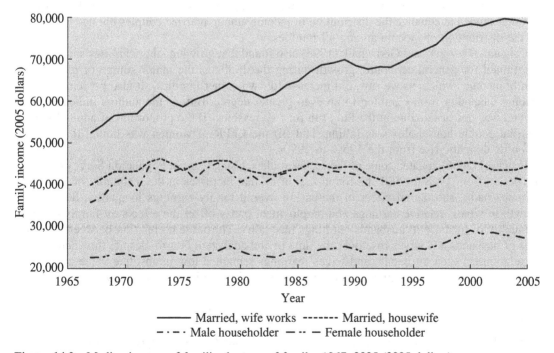

Figure 14.2   Median income of families by type of family, 1967–2005 (2005 dollars)

is generally not the case. Indeed, such a phenomenon remains quite rare and so has not had a major impact on the trend of family income inequality in recent years.

Blackburn and Bloom (1989) calculated the Gini coefficient for the distribution of family income among married couples over the period between 1967 and 1985 and then recalculated the Gini coefficient under the hypothetical assumption that wives had zero labor earnings. They found that the actual level of income inequality was uniformly less than the one estimated under the assumption that there were no working wives. In 1967, the Gini coefficient was 0.328 for the actual income distribution among married couples and 0.343 for the hypothetical one; in 1985, the corresponding Gini coefficients were 0.351 and 0.375. The explanation is a negative correlation between the hours worked by wives and the earnings of the husband – that is, wives are more apt to have a job and work more hours the less their husband earns.

Blackburn and Bloom also found that the equalizing effect of wives' earnings *increased* between 1967 and 1985.[16] In 1967, wives' earnings reduced the Gini coefficient by 0.015 points (from 0.343 to 0.328) and in 1985 by 0.024 points (from 0.375 to 0.351). Cancian, Danziger, and Gottschalk (1993) reported a similar result. They found that wives' earnings had a greater equalizing effect on the distribution of income of married couples in 1988 than in 1968. This was true despite the growing similarity of LFPR of wives with husbands who spanned the earnings spectrum. This finding was attributed to two factors: (i) wives' earnings were gaining ground on their husbands'; and (ii) the distribution of earnings among wives was becoming more equal, in part because of a decline in the number of nonworking wives.[17]

The second issue is the effect of wives' earnings on the distribution of income among *all* family units. Blackburn and Bloom, using the same comparisons between the actual distribution of family income and a hypothetical one, under the assumption that wives did not work, calculated that the effect of wives' earnings was neutral. In 1967, the Gini coefficient was 0.395 for the actual distribution of family income (among all families) and 0.397 for the hypothetical one; in 1985, the corresponding coefficients were 0.426 and 0.424. They concluded that wives' earnings tended to equalize the distribution of income among married couples but had little effect on the distribution of income among all families.

Cancian, Danziger, and Gottschalk (1993) also found that growing labor earnings among wives substituted for general economic growth during the 1980s as the major source of gain in real family income (which, as we saw, did increase for two-earner families). It also prevented family income inequality from climbing to an even greater degree. But, as the authors indicated, such a trend was not sustainable in the long run for two reasons: (i) the proportion of adults living in married couple households was falling; and (ii) the LFPR of women was bound to level off, given its dramatic rise from the 1950s to 1990s.

Pencavel (2006) updated some of the earlier studies. Using Current Population Survey data over the period from 1968 to 2001, he found first of all that increases in the inequality of husbands' earnings had a substantial effect in increasing overall family earnings inequality. Second, the growth in wives' relative earnings and employment partly offset the effects on family earnings inequality of increase in husbands' earnings inequality. Third, the correlation between the earnings of husbands and wives rose over the time period analyzed. Fourth, despite this increase, the correlation between husbands' and wives' earnings remained low in absolute value and played a negligible role in accounting for the increase in family earnings inequality over time.

14.5.2   The feminization of poverty

The evidence presented in this chapter indicates steady labor market progress for women in terms of access to the labor market and gains in earnings relative to male workers, particularly during

Table 14.11   Poverty rates for adults by gender, 1940–2005

	1940	*1950*	*1960*	*1970*	*1980*	*1989*	*1993*	*2005*
A. Poverty rate by gender								
Women	34	23	15	11	11	13	15	13
Men	34	22	13	8	7	8	10	9
B. Percentage composition of the poor								
Women	50	51	55	60	62	63	62	59
Men	50	49	45	40	38	37	38	41
Total	100	100	100	100	100	100	100	100

Adults refer to individuals 16 years or older (18 or over in 2005).
Sources: 1940–1980: Smith, J.P. & Ward, M.P. (1989). Women in the labor market and in the family. *Journal of Economic Perspectives*, **3**(1), 9–23; 1989: U.S. Census Bureau (1993). Current Population Reports, Series P-60, No. 168, *Money Income and Poverty Status in the United States: 1989*. Washington, DC: U.S. Government Printing Office; 1993: U.S. Census Bureau. Current Population Reports, Series P60, No. 188, *Income, Poverty, and Valuation of Noncash Benefits: 1993*. Washington, DC: U.S. Government Printing Office; 2005 Annual Demographic Survey: http://pubdb3.census.gov/macro/032005/pov/new01_100_01.htm.

the 1980s. However, the well-being of women in the whole population depends both on labor market activity *and* the structure of the family. Labor earnings by themselves do not directly indicate how well off people are. For intact families (husband and wife present), incomes are typically pooled among all family members so that all members share the common fortunes of the family. Wives may thus enjoy a high standard of living even if they are not employed in the labor market (and conversely for nonworking husbands). However, such is not the case for unmarried adults, who must generally rely only on themselves for their income. The growth in the relative number of female-headed households since 1970, which we also discussed in the last chapter, thus has direct implications for poverty among women.

Table 14.11 highlights some of these trends in poverty rates. At the outset it should be emphasized that poverty rates declined substantially for both females and males between 1940 and 1970, from 34 to 11 percent for the former and from 34 to 8 percent for the latter. Still, it is apparent that in 1940 poverty was gender-neutral. The poverty rates were the same for both adult males and females, and half the poor (adults) were female and half male. It is perhaps not coincidental that in 1940 over 90 percent of all families included both a husband and wife (see Smith & Ward, 1989, p. 19).

After 1940, particularly 1970 and after, poverty rates began to diverge between adult females and males. By 1993, the poverty rate among adult females was 15 percent and that among adult males only 10 percent, and by 2005 the respective figures were 13 and 9 percent. By 1993, females comprised 62 percent of the adult poor, while men made up the other 38 percent, and in 2005 females comprised 59 percent and males 41 percent of the adult poor. The growing feminization of poverty tracks almost exactly with the rising share of female-headed households in the population. By 1988, 13 percent of white families were headed by a female (up from 9 percent in 1960) and 44 percent of black families (up from 31 percent in 1970). Smith and Ward (1989) argued that the relative growth of poverty among females "has its origins exclusively in the growth of female-headed families" (p. 20). As long as families remained intact, the lower earnings capacity of females had no direct effect on the incidence of poverty by gender. However, with the break-up of the family, the relatively lower wages of females along with the presence of children in one-parent families made poverty far more likely for women than for men. The irony is that

Table 14.12 The ratio of female to male labor earnings for selected industrialized countries and years

Country	1960[a]	1980[a]	mid-1980s[b]	1994–2001[c]
Australia	0.59	0.75	0.75	
Austria			0.73	0.78
Belgium				0.89
Canada	0.59	0.64		
Denmark				0.89
Finland				0.82
France	0.64	0.71		0.86
Germany	0.65	0.72	0.69	0.76
Italy	0.73	0.83		0.94
Japan	0.46	0.54		
Netherlands				0.76
Norway			0.73	
Spain				0.88
Sweden	0.72	0.90	0.77	
Switzerland			0.62	
United Kingdom	0.61	0.79	0.63	0.70
United States	0.66	0.66	0.68	0.68
U.S.S.R.	0.70	0.70		

a *Source*: Gunderson, M. (1989). Male–female wage differentials and policy responses. *Journal of Economic Literature*, **27**, 46–72.

b *Source*: Blau, F.D. & Kahn, L.M. (1992a). The gender earnings gap: Learning from international comparisons. *American Economic Review Papers and Proceedings*, **82**, 533–8. Earnings differentials are adjusted for hours worked.

c *Source*: Olivetti, C. & Petrongolo, B. (2006). Unequal pay or unequal employment? A cross-country analysis of gender gaps. CEPR Discussion Paper 5506, London, February. Wage gaps are for workers aged 25–54.

the feminization of poverty was occurring while labor market opportunities were improving for women.

14.5.3   International comparisons

Though differences in male and female earnings continue to remain large in the United States, it is of interest to see how they compare to those of other countries. Some comparisons are shown in Table 14.12. In terms of male–female earnings inequality, the United States ranks in the middle of the pack among industrialized countries. In 1980, according to the Gunderson (1989) data, Japan had by far the largest male–female wage gap, a ratio of 0.54, and Sweden the narrowest, a ratio of 0.90. The female–male earnings ratio in the United States, according to these data, was 0.66. Interestingly, in the U.S.S.R., the earnings ratio was 0.70. Also, according to the Blau and Kahn (1992a) data, the female–male earnings ratio, adjusted for hours worked, in the mid-1980s ranged from a low of 0.62 in Switzerland and 0.63 in the United Kingdom, to a high of 0.77 in Sweden. The corresponding earnings ratio in the United States was 0.68.

More recent data for the 1994–2001 period compiled by Olivetti and Petrongolo (2006) are shown in the fourth column of the table. These are based on the PSID for the United States and comparable panel data called the European Community Household Panel Survey for the European countries. According to these data, the United States now had the highest gender–wage gap among their sample of countries (32 percent) for the late 1990s and Italy the lowest (only 6 percent).

The Gunderson data also showed changes in the earnings ratio between 1960 and 1980. According to these figures, all countries experienced a narrowing of the gender–wage gap, except the United States and the U.S.S.R., which had no change. Thus, it appears that most industrialized countries had made more progress than the United States in closing the gender–wage gap, at least over the period from 1960 to 1980.

14.6 SUMMARY

The gender–wage gap, the most direct measure of inequality between males and females in the labor market, shows a U-shaped trajectory between the end of World War II and the 1990s. It first widened between the late 1940s and the early 1950s, remained relatively unchanged between the early 1950s and the early 1970s, and then narrowed, particularly after 1980.

Over the same time, the labor force participation of females was steadily rising. The LFPR of all females increased from 32 percent in 1947 to 59 percent in 2005, while the LFPR of wives grew from 20 to 61 percent. For wives, the principal reasons for their increased participation rate were rising real earnings for women, a slowdown of income growth for men (particularly after 1970), and a reduced fertility rate. Moreover, the proportion of females working full-time, full-year increased from 37 percent in 1950 to 61 percent in 2005.

There are four principal reasons why the wage gap between male and female workers diminished over time in the United States. First, women gained on men in terms of years of experience. Second, occupational segregations waned over time. Third, women outdistanced men in terms of educational attainment. Fourth, public policy measures helped women obtain better jobs.

Historically, women typically had fewer years of work experience than men of the same age and educational attainment because of interrupted work careers. However, the average experience level of women of almost every age group rose between 1950 and 2005. With regard to education, in 1950, female workers had, on average, more years of schooling than male workers, by 1969 the schooling differential had all but disappeared, but in 2005 women once again exceeded men in terms of years of schooling.

There may also be a separate effect on earnings from career interruptions. Some economists argued that women will typically receive less on-the-job training than men of the same age because employers will have less incentive to invest in female employees. Several studies confirmed that women, on average, received less training than men with the same number of years of experience, and that the return to experience were smaller for women than for men. However, recent evidence seems to dispute whether work interruptions *per se* lead to lower wages for women.

The overall wage gap can be decomposed into one component due to differences in human capital and an "unexplained" residual, usually interpreted as a measure of discrimination. Because female schooling levels have now overtaken male levels and differences in experience levels have narrowed between males and females, there was little change in the relative quantities of human capital between working men and women from 1960 to 2005. As a result, many studies concluded that the decline in the gender–wage gap, particularly since 1980, was primarily due to a lessening of sex discrimination.

However, other studies found that while the return to schooling and experience increased for both male and female workers during the 1980s, it grew more for females than males. The rising pay-off to experience for women, in particular, presumably reflected more intensive job training. These studies attributed a large part of the declining wage gap during the 1980s to the fact that returns to human capital increased more for men than women over these years.

Another factor accounting for lower female pay is occupational segregation. Women tended to be concentrated in low-paying occupations. However, the degree of occupational segregation lessened over the postwar period, particularly after 1980, as female workers have penetrated traditionally male occupations. Two reasons have been cited for this development. The first was public policy, particularly affirmative action plans. The second was changes in cultural and social norms regarding the appropriate role of females in society. The role of the "women's liberation" movement beginning in the late 1960s is often cited as a factor behind changes in social norms.

Despite this, several studies have documented that the lower overall pay of female workers relative to male workers was due much more to the lower pay received by female workers than male workers in the same occupation than to the difference in their occupational distributions. Moreover, the narrowing of the gender–wage gap, particularly after 1980, was due almost exclusively to the increase in relative female wages within occupation, not to shifts in female occupational patterns.

Statistical analyses have also suggested that governmental anti-discrimination programs may played an important role in the improving economic status of female workers. The three major legal instruments are the Equal Pay Act of 1963, Title VII of the 1964 Civil Rights Act, and the 1965 Executive Order 11246. Results on the effectiveness of Title VII have been mixed. However, there is strong evidence that affirmative action programs have increased the proportion of females entering male occupations, the growth of female employment in general, and the occupational advance of female workers. These effects were much stronger in the 1970s than the 1980s, which saw a diminution in the enforcement of anti-discrimination programs by the federal government.

Another type of anti-discrimination initiative, comparable worth, has been undertaken at the state and local government level. Comparable worth programs aim at providing equal pay to jobs of equal "value." To date these programs have been directed exclusively at public employees. Studies have shown that such efforts have been successful in increasing relative female earnings but they have also been responsible for a loss of female employment.

Several other findings are worthy of note. First, the earnings of wives have tended to equalize the distribution of family income among married couples, and their equalizing effect has increased between the late 1960s and the late 1980s. Moreover, married couples with working wives had the highest real income growth of any family type between 1967 and 2005. Second, there has been a growing "feminization" of poverty in the United States. In 1950, half the adult poor were females, but by 2005 this fraction had grown to almost 60 percent. The growth in female poverty tracked almost exactly with the rising share of female-headed households in the population. Third, from an international perspective, in the late 1990s the United States ranked among the most unequal countries in terms of the gender–wage gap.

14.7   REFERENCES AND BIBLIOGRAPHY

Aldrich, M. & Buchele, R. (1986). *The Economics of Comparable Worth.* Cambridge, MA: Harper & Row, Ballinger.

Ames, L.J. (1995). Fixing women's wages: The effectiveness of comparable worth policies. *Industrial and Labor Relations Review,* **48**(4), 709–25.

Arulampalan, W., Booth, A.L. & Bryan, M.L. (2007). Is there a glass ceiling over Europe? Exploring the gender pay gap across the wage distribution. *Industrial and Labor Relations Review,* **60**(2), 163–86.

Ashraf, J. (1996). Is gender pay discrimination on the wane? Evidence from Panel Data, 1968–1989. *Industrial and Labor Relations Review,* **49**(3), 537–46.

Barbezat, D.A., & Hughes, J.W. & Kuhn, P. (1990). Sex discrimination in labor markets: The role of statistical evidence: Comment. *American Economic Review,* **80**(1), 277–86.

Barron, J.M., Black, D.A. & Lowenstein, M.A. (1993). Gender differences in training, capital, and wages. *Journal of Human Resources,* **28**(2), 343–64.

Bartlett, R.L. & Miller, T.I. (1985). Executive compensation: Female executives and networking. *American Economic Review*, **75**(2), 266–70.

Becker, G.S. (1981). *A Treatise on the Family*. Cambridge, MA: Harvard University Press.

Becker, G.S. (1985). Human capital, effort, and the sexual division of labor. *Journal of Labor Economics*, **3**, S33–S58.

Beller, A.H. (1976). EEO laws and the earnings of women. *Industrial Relations Research Association Proceedings* (pp. 190–8). Madison, WI: University of Wisconsin Press.

Beller, A.H. (1979). The impact of equal employment opportunity laws on the male–female earnings differential. In C.B. Lloyd, E.S. Andrews & C.L. Gilroy (eds.), *Women in the Labor Market* (pp. 304–30). New York: Columbia University Press.

Beller, A.H. (1980). The effect of economic conditions on the success of equal employment opportunity laws: an application to the sex differential in earnings. *Review of Economics and Statistics*, **62**(3), 370–87.

Beller, A.H. (1982). Occupational segregation by sex: Determinants and changes. *Journal of Human Resources*, **17**, 371–92.

Beller, A.H. (1984). Trends in occupational segregation by sex and race, 1960–1981. In B.F. Reskin (ed.), *Sex Segregation In The Workplace*. Washington, DC: National Academy Press.

Beller, A.H. (1985). Changes in the sex composition of U.S. occupations, 1960–81. *Journal of Human Resources*, **20**(2), 235–50.

Betson, D. & van der Gaag, J. (1984). Working married women and the distribution of income. *Journal of Human Resources*, **19**(4), 532–43.

Bielby, W.T. & Baron, J.N. (1986). Sex segregation within occupations. *American Economic Review Papers and Proceedings*, **76**, 43–7.

Black, S.E. & Juhn, C. (2000). The rise of female professionals: Are women responding to skill demand? *American Economic Review*, **90**, 450–5.

Blackburn, M.L. & Bloom, D.E. (1989). Income inequality, business cycles, and female labor supply. In D. Slottje (ed.), *Research in Economic Inequality*, Vol. 1. Greenwich, CT: JAI Press.

Blank, R.M. & Shierholz, H.S. (2006). Exploring gender differences in employment and wage trends among less-skilled workers. NBER Working Paper No. W12494, August.

Blau, F.D. (1972). Women's place in the labor market. *American Economic Review Papers and Proceedings*, **62**, 161–6.

Blau, F.D. (1977). *Equal Pay in the Office*. Lexington, MA: D.C. Heath.

Blau, F.D. (1984). Discrimination against women: Theory and evidence. In W. Darity, Jr. (ed.), *Labor Economics: Modern View* (pp. 53–89). Boston, MA: Kluwer-Hijhoff.

Blau, F.D. (1989). Occupational segregation by gender: A look at the 1980s. University of Illinois at Urbana-Champaign, mimeo, January.

Blau, F.D. (1998). Trends in the well-being of American women, 1970–1995. *Journal of Economic Literature*, **36**, 112–65.

Blau, F.D. & Beller, A. (1988). Trends in earnings differentials by gender, 1971–1981. *Industrial and Labor Relations Review*, **41**(4), 513–29.

Blau, F.D. & Ferber, M.A. (1986). *The Economics of Women, Men, and Work*. Englewood Cliffs, NJ: Prentice-Hall.

Blau, F.D. & Ferber, M.A. (1987). Discrimination: Empirical evidence from the United States. *American Economic Review Papers and Proceedings*, **77**, 246–50.

Blau, F.D. & Ferber, M.A. (1991). Career plans and expectations of young women and men. *Journal of Human Resources*, **26**(4), 581–607.

Blau, F.D. & Hendricks, W.E. (1979). Occupational segregation by sex: Trends and prospects. *Journal of Human Resources*, **14**(2), 197–210.

Blau, F.D. & Kahn, L.M. (1992a). The gender earnings gap: Learning from international comparisons. *American Economic Review Papers and Proceedings*, **82**, 533–8.

Blau, F.D. & Kahn, L.M. (1992b). Race and gender pay differentials. NBER Working paper No. 4120, July.

Blau, F.D. & Kahn, L.M. (1992c). The gender earnings gap: Some international evidence. NBER Working paper No. 4224, December.

Blau, F.D. & Kahn, L.M. (1994). Rising wage inequality and the U.S. gender wage gap. *American Economic Review Papers and Proceedings*, **84**(2), 23–8.

Blau, F.D. & Kahn, L.M. (1997). Swimming upstream: Trends in the gender wage gap differential in the 1980s. *Journal of Labor Economics*, **15**(1), 1–42.

Blau, F.D. & Kahn, L.M. (2003). Understanding international differences in the gender pay gap. *Journal of Labor Economics*, **21**(1), 106–44.

Blau, F.D. & Kahn, L.M. (2006). The US gender pay gap in the 1990s: Slowing convergence. *Industrial and Labor Relations Review*, **60**(1), 45–66.

Bowen, W.G. & Finegan, T.A. (1969). *The Economics of Labor Force Participation*. Princeton, NJ: Princeton University Press.

Brown, C. & Corcoran, M. (1997). Sex-based differences in school content and the male–female wage gap. *Journal of Labor Economics*, **15**, 431–65.

Brown, C. & Pechman, J.A. (eds.) (1987). *Gender in the Workplace*. Washington, DC: Brookings Institution.

Brown, R.S., Moon, M. & Zoloth, B.S. (1980). Incorporating occupational attainment in studies of male–female earnings differentials. *Journal of Human Resources*, **15**(1), 3–28.

Cain, G.C. (1966). *Married Women in the Labor Force: An Economic Analysis*. Chicago: University of Chicago Press.

Cain, G.C. & Dooley, M.D. (1976). Estimation of a model of labor supply, fertility and wages of married women. *Journal of Political Economy*, **84**, S177–S199.

Cancian, M., Danziger, S. & Gottschalk, P. (1993). The changing contributions of men and women to the level and distribution of family income, 1968–88. In D.B. Papadimitriou & E.N. Wolff (eds.), *Poverty and Prosperity in the USA in the Late Twentieth Century*. London: Macmillan.

Carlson, L.A. & Swartz, C. (1988). The earnings of women and ethnic minorities. *Industrial and Labor Relations Review*, **41**(4), 530–46.

Charles, K. & Luoh, M.-C. (2003). Gender differences in completed schooling. *Review of Economics and Statistics*, **83**(3), 559–77.

Coleman, M. & Pencavel, J. (1993). Trends in market work behavior of women since 1940. *Industrial and Labor Relations Review*, **46**(4), 653–79.

Corcoran, M. (1978). The structure of female wages. *American Economic Review*, **68**(2), 165–70.

Corcoran, M. & Courant, P.N. (1985). Sex role socialization and labor market outcomes. *American Economic Review Papers and Proceedings*, **75**(2), 275–8.

Corcoran, M. & Duncan, G.J. (1979). Work history, labor force attachment, and earnings differences between the races and sexes. *Journal of Human Resources*, **14**, 3–20.

Corcoran, M., Duncan, G.J. & Ponza, M. (1983). A longitudinal analysis of white women's wages. *Journal of Human Resources*, **18**, 497–520.

Cox, D. (1982). Inequality in the lifetime earnings of women. *Review of Economics and Statistics*, **64**(3), 501–4.

Cox, D. (1984). Panel estimates of the effects of career interruptions on the earnings of women. *Economic Inquiry*, **22**, 386–403.

Currie, J. (1993). Gender gaps in benefits coverage. NBER Working Paper No. 4265, January.

Currie, J. & Chaykowski, R. (1992). Male jobs, females jobs, and gender gaps in benefits coverage in Canada. MIT, mimeo, November.

Daly, A., Kawaguchi, A., Meng, X. & Mumford, K. (2006). The gender wage gap in four countries. IZA Discussion paper No. 1921, Bonn, Germany, January.

Dean, J. (1991). Sex-segregated employment, wage inequality and labor-intensive production. *Review of Radical Political Economy*, **23**(3&4), 244–68.

Devereux, P.J. (2005). Effects of industry growth and decline on gender and education wage gaps in the 1980s. *Industrial and Labor Relations Review*, **58**(4), 552–70.

Dolton, P., O'Neill, D. & Sweetman, O. (1996). Gender differences in a changing labor market. *Journal of Human Resources*, **31**(3), 549–65.

Dougherty, C. (2005). Why are the returns to schooling higher for women than for men? *Journal of Human Resources*, **50**(4), 969–88.

Duncan, G.C. & Hoffman, S. (1979). On-the-job training and earnings differences by race and sex. *Review of Economics and Statistics*, **61**(4), 594–603.

Duncan, O.D. & Duncan, B. (1955). A methodological analysis of segregation indexes. *American Sociological Review*, **20**, 210–17.

England, P. (1982). The failure of human capital theory to explain occupational segregation.

Journal of Human Resources, **17**(3), 358–70.

Even, W.E. (1990). Sex discrimination in labor markets: The role of statistical evidence: comment. *American Economic Review*, **80**(1), 287–9.

Even, W.E. & Macpherson, D. (1990). The gender gap in pensions and wages. *Review of Economics and Statistics*, **72**, 259–65.

Even, W.E. & Macpherson, D. (1993). The decline in private-sector unionism and the gender wage gap. *Journal of Human Resources*, **38**(2), 279–96.

Fields, J. (1976). A comparison of intercity differences in the labor force participation of married women in 1970 with 1940, 1950, and 1960. *Journal of Human Resources*, **11**, 568–77.

Fields, J. & Wolff, E.N. (1991). The decline of sex segregation and the wage gap, 1970–80. *Journal of Human Resources*, **26**(4), 608–22.

Fields, J. & Wolff, E.N. (1995). Industry wage differentials and the gender wage gap. *Industrial and Labor Relations Review*, **49**(1), 105–20.

Fields, J. & Wolff, E.N. (2000). Gender differentials in industry wage premia, affirmative action, and employment growth on the industry level. *Gender Issues*, **18**(4), 3–25.

Filer, R.K. (1983). Sexual differences in earnings: The role of individual personalities and tastes. *Journal of Human Resources*, **18**, 82–99.

Filer, R.K. (1985). Male–female wage differentials: The importance of compensating differentials. *Industrial and Labor Relations Review*, **38**(3), 426–37.

Fortin, N.M. & Lemieux, T. (1998). Rank regressions, wage distributions, and the gender gap. *Journal of Human Resources*, **33**(3), 610–43.

Frank, R.H. (1978). Why women earn less: The theory and estimation of differential overqualifications. *American Economic Review*, **68**, 360–73.

Fuchs, V. (1971). Differences in hourly earnings between men and women. *Monthly Labor Review*, **94**(5), 9–15.

Fuchs, V. (1974). Recent trends and long-run prospects for female earnings. *American Economic Review*, **64**(2), 236–42.

Fuchs, V. (1986). His and hers: Gender differences in work and income. *Journal of Labor Economics*, **4**(3), S245–S272.

Fuchs, V. (1988). *Women's Quest for Economic Equality*. Cambridge, MA: Harvard University Press.

Fuchs, V. (1989). Women's quest for economic equality. *Journal of Economic Perspectives*, **3**(1), 25–41.

Ghez, G. & Becker, G. (1975). *The Allocation of Goods and Time over the Life Cycle*. New York: Columbia University Press.

Goldin, C. (1986). Monitoring costs and occupational segregation by sex. *Journal of Labor Economics*, **4**(1), 1–27.

Goldin, C. (1989). Life-cycle labor force participation of married women: Historical evidence and implications. *Journal of Labor Economics*, **7**, 20–47.

Goldin, C. (1990). *Understanding the Gender Gap: An Economic History of American Women*. New York: Oxford University Press.

Goldin, C. (1991). The role of World War II in the rise of women's employment. *American Economic Review*, **81**(4), 741–56.

Goldin, C., Katz, L.F. & Kuzemko, I. (2006). The homecoming of American college women: The reversal of the college gender gap. *Journal of Economic Perspectives*, **20**(4), 133–56.

Goldin, C. & Katz, L.F. (2002). The power of the pill: Oral contraceptives and women's career and marriage decisions. *Journal of Political Economy*, **110**(4), 730–70.

Goldin, C. & Olachek, S. (1987). Residual differences by sex: Perspectives on the gender gap in earnings. *American Economic Review Papers and Proceedings*, **77**(2), 143–51.

Gronau, R. (1988). Sex-related differentials and women's interrupted labor careers – The chicken or the egg. *Journal of Labor Economics*, **6**(3), 277–301.

Groshen, E.L. (1991). The structure of the female–male wage differential. *Journal of Human Resources*, **26**(3), 457–72.

Gunderson, M. (1989). Male–female wage differentials and policy responses. *Journal of Economic Literature*, **27**, 46–72.

Gwartney, J.D. & Stroup, R. (1973). Measurement of employment discrimination according to sex. *Southern Economic Journal*, **39**(4), 575–87.

Hartmann, H. (ed.) (1985). *Comparable Worth: New Directions for Research*. Washington, DC: National Academy of Sciences.

Heckman, J.J. & MacCurdy, T.E. (1980). A life-cycle model of female labor supply. *Review of Economic Studies*, **47**, 47–74.

Hersch, J. (1991a). Male–female differences in hourly wages: The role of human capital, working conditions, and housework. *Industrial and Labor Relations Review*, **44**(4), 746–59.

Hersch, J. (1991b). EEO law and firm profitability. *Journal of Human Resources*, **26**(1), 139–53.

Hersch, J. (1991c). The impact of nonmarket work on market wages. *American Economic Review Papers and Proceedings*, **81**(2), 157–60.

Hersch, J. (1995). Housework, wages, and the division of housework time for employed spouses. *American Economic Review Papers and Proceedings*, **84**(2), 120–5.

Hill, M.S. (1979). The wage effect of marital status and children. *Journal of Human Resources*, **14**(4), 579–94.

Hodson, R. & England, P. (1986). Industrial structure and sex differences in earnings. *Industrial Relations*, Winter, 16–32.

Horrace, W.C. & Oaxaca, R.L. (2001). Inter-industry wage differentials and the gender wage gap: An identification problem. *Industrial and Labor Relations Review*, **54**(3), 611–18.

Hundley, G. (1993). The effects of comparable worth in the public sector on public/private occupational relative wages. *Journal of Human Resources*, **28**(2), 318–42.

Ishida, J. & Nosaka, H. (2007). Gender specialization of skill acquisition. *The B.E. Journal of Economic Analysis & Policy*, **7**(1) (Advances), Article 61. http://www.bepress.com/bejeap/vol7/iss1/art61.

Jacobs, J.A. (1983). The sex segregation of occupations and women's career patterns. Doctoral Dissertation, Department of Sociology, Harvard University.

Jacobsen, J.P. (2005). Occupational segregation and the tipping phenomenon: The contrary case of court reporting in the United States. Working Paper, Wesleyan University, August.

Jacobsen, J.P. & Levin, L.M. (1992). The effects of intermittent labor force attachment on female earnings. Paper presented at the 1992 American Economics Association Conference, New Orleans, January 3–5.

Jacobsen, J.P. & Rayack, W.L. (1996). Do men who's wives work really earn less? *American Economic Review Papers and Proceedings*, **86**(2), 268–73.

Killingsworth, M.R. (1987). Heterogeneous preferences, compensating wage differentials, and comparable worth. *Quarterly Journal of Economics*, **102**(4), 727–42.

Killingsworth, M.R. (1990). *The Economics of Comparable Worth*. Kalamazoo, MI: W.E. Upjohn Institute for Employment Research.

Killingsworth, M.R. (2002). Comparable worth and pay equity: Recent developments in the United States. *Canadian Public Policy*, **28**(1), S171–S185.

Kuhn, P. (1987). Sex discrimination in labor markets: The role of statistical evidence. *American Economic Review*, **77**(4), 567–83.

Lazear, E.P. & Rosen, S. (1990). Male–female wage differentials in job ladders. *Journal of Labor Economics*, **8**, S106–S123.

Leibowitz, A. (1977). Education and allocation of women's time. In F. Thomas Juster (ed.), *The Distribution of Economic Well-Being*. Cambridge, MA: Ballinger.

Leonard, J.S. (1984a). Employment and occupational advance under affirmative action. *Review of Economics and Statistics*, August, 377–85.

Leonard, J.S. (1984b). The impact of affirmative action on employment. *Journal of Labor Economics*, **2**, 439–63.

Leonard, J.S. (1984c). Antidiscrimination or reverse discrimination: The impact of changing demographics, Title VII, and affirmative action on productivity. *Journal of Human Resources*, **19**(2), 146–74.

Leonard, J.S. (1985). Affirmative action as earnings redistribution: The targeting of compliance reviews. *Journal of Labor Economics*, **3**, 363–84.

Leonard, J.S. (1990). The impact of affirmative action regulation and equal employment law on black employment. *Journal of Economic Perspectives*, **4**, 47–63.

Leonard, J.S. (1996). Affirmative action thirty years later: Wage disparities and affirmative action in the 1980s. *American Economic Review, Papers & Proceedings*, **86**(2), 285–301.

Levy, F. & Murnane, R. (1992). Earnings levels and earnings inequality. *Journal of Economic Literature*, **30**(3), 1331–81.

Lloyd, C.B. (ed.) (1975). *Sex, Discrimination, and the Division of Labor*. New York: Columbia University Press.

Lloyd, C.B., Andrews, E.S. & Gilroy, C.L. (eds.) (1979). *Women in the Labor Market*. New York: Columbia University Press.

Loury, L.D. (1997). The gender earnings gap among college-educated workers. *Industrial and Labor Relations Review*, **50**(4), 580–93.

MaCurdy, T.E. (1981). An empirical model of labor supply in a life-cycle setting. *Journal of Political Economy*, **89**(6), 1059–85.

Madden, J. (1985). The persistence of pay differentials: The economics of sex discrimination. *Women and Work*, **1**, 76–114.

Maxwell, N.L. & D'Amico, R.J. (1986). Employment and wage effects of involuntary job separation: Male–female differences. *American Economic Review Papers and Proceedings*, **76**(2), 373–7.

Mincer, J. (1962a). On-the-job training, costs, returns and some implications. *Journal of Political Economy*, Supplement, **70**, 50–79.

Mincer, J. (1962b). Labor force participation of married women. In G. Lewis (ed.), *Aspects of Labor Economics*, Universities-National Bureau Conference Series, 14. Princeton, NJ: Arno Press.

Mincer, J. & Ofek, H. (1982). Interrupted work careers: Depreciation and restoration of human capital. *Journal of Human Resources*, **17**, 3–24.

Mincer, J. & Polachek, S. (1974). Family investments in human capital: Earnings of women. *Journal of Political Economy*, **82**(2), S76–S108.

Mincer, J. & Polachek, S. (1978). Women's earnings reexamined. *Journal of Human Resources*, **13**, 118–33.

Nelson, R. & Bridges, W.P. (1999). *Legalizing Gender Inequality: Courts, Markets, and Unequal Pay for Women in America*. New York: Cambridge University Press.

Neumark, D. & McLennan, M. (1995). Sex discrimination of women's labor market outcomes. *Journal of Human Resources*, **30**(4), 713–40.

Oaxaca, R. (1973). Sex discrimination in wages. In O. Ashenfelter & A. Rees (eds.), *Discrimination in Labor Markets*. Princeton, NJ: Princeton University Press.

Oaxaca, R. (1977). The persistence of male–female earnings differentials. In F.T. Juster (ed.), *The Distribution of Economic Well-Being*. Cambridge, MA: Ballinger.

Olivetti, C. & Petrongolo, B. (2006). Unequal pay or unequal employment? A cross-country analysis of gender gaps. CEPR Discussion Paper 5506, London, February.

O'Neill, J. (1981). A time-series analysis of women's labor force participation. *American Economic Review Papers and Proceedings*, **71**(2), 76–81.

O'Neill, J. (1985). The trend in the male–female wage gap in the United States. *Journal of Labor Economics*, **3**(1), S91–S116.

O'Neill, J., Brien, M. & Cunningham, J. (1989). Effects of comparable worth policy: Evidence from Washington State. *American Economic Review Papers and Proceedings*, **79**, 305–9.

O'Neill, J. & O'Neill, D.M. (2005). What do wage differentials tell us about labor market discrimination? NBER Working Paper No. 11240, March.

O'Neill, J. & Polachek, S. (1993). Why the gender gap in wages narrowed in the 1980s? *Journal of Labor Economics*, **11**(1), 205–28.

Orazem, P.F. & Mattila, J.P. (1990). The implementation process of comparable worth: Winners and losers. *Journal of Political Economy*, **98**, 134–52.

Orazem, P.F., Mattila, J.P. & Yu, R.C. (1990). An index number approach to the measurement of wage differentials by sex. *Journal of Human Resources*, **25**(1), 125–36.

Osterman, P. (1982). Affirmative action and opportunity. *Review of Economics and Statistics*, **64**(2), 604–12.

Pencavel, J. (2006). A life cycle perspective on changes in earnings inequality among married men and women. *Review of Economics and Statistics*, **88**(2), 232–42.

Polachek, S. (1975a). Differences in expected post-school investment as a determinant of market wage differentials. *International Economic Review*, **16**, 451–70.

Polachek, S. (1975b). Potential biases in measuring male–female discrimination. *Journal of Human Resources*, **10**(2), 205–29.

Polachek, S. (1981). Occupational self-selection: A human capital approach to sex differences in occupational structure. *Review of Economics and Statistics*, **63**, 60–9.

Ragan, J.F. & Smith, S.P. (1981). The impact of differences in turnover rates on male/female pay differentials. *Journal of Human Resources*, **16**(3), 343–65.

Reskin, B.F. & Hartmann, H.I. (eds.) (1986). *Women's Work, Men's Work: Sex Segregation on the Job*. Washington DC: National Academy Press.

Reubens, B.G. & Reubens, E.P. (1979). Women workers, non-traditional occupations and full employment. In A.F. Cahn (ed.), *Women in The U.S. Labor Force*. New York: Praeger.

Roos, P.A. (1981). Sex stratification in the workplace, male–female differences in returns to occupation. *Social Sciences Research*, **10**(3), 195–224.

Royalty, A.B. (1996). The effects of job turnover on the training of men and women. *Industrial and Labor Relations Review*, **49**(3), 506–21.

Rytina, N.F. (1981). Occupational segregation and earnings differences by sex. *Monthly Labor Review*, **104**(1), 49–53.

Rytina, N.F. & Bianchi, S.M. (1984). Occupational reclassification and changes in distribution by gender. *Monthly Labor Review*, **107**, 11–17.

Schumann, P.L., Ahlburg, D.A. & Mahoney, C.B. (1994). The effects of human capital and job characteristics on pay. *Journal of Human Resources*, **29**(2), 481–503.

Shackett, J.R. & Trapani, J.M. (1987). Earnings differentials and market structure. *Journal of Human Resources*, **22**(4), 518–31.

Smith, J.P. & Ward, M.P. (1984). *Women's Wages and Work in the Twentieth Century*. Santa Monica, CA: Rand Corporation.

Smith, J.P. & Ward, M.P. (1985). Time-series growth in the female labor force. *Journal of Labor Economics*, **3**(1), S59–S90.

Smith, J.P. & Ward, M.P. (1989). Women in the labor market and in the family. *Journal of Economic Perspectives*, **3**(1), 9–23.

Sorensen, E. (1990). The crowding hypothesis and comparable worth." *Journal of Human Resources*, **25**(1), 55–89.

Sorensen, E. (1991). Exploring the reasons behind the narrowing gender gap in earnings. Urban Institute Report 91-2, Washington, DC.

Spivey, C. (2005). Time off at what price: The effects of career interruptions on earnings. *Industrial and Labor Relations Review*, **59**(1), 119–40.

Spriggs, W.E. & Williams, R.M. (1996). A logit decomposition analysis of occupational segregation: Results for the 1970s and 1980s. *Review of Economics and Statistics*, **73**(2), 348–55.

Stanley, T.D. & Jarrell, S.B. (1998). Gender wage discrimination bias? A meta-regression analysis. *Journal of Human Resources*, **33**(4), 947–73.

Terrell, K. (1992). Female–male earnings differentials and occupational structure. *International Labour Review*, **131**(4–5), 387–404.

Treiman, D.J. & Hartmann, H.I. (eds.) (1981). *Women, Work and Wages: Equal Pay for Jobs of Equal Value*. Washington DC: National Academy Press.

Welch, F. (2000). Growth in women's relative wages and in inequality among men: One phenomenon or two? *American Economic Review*, **90**(2), 444–9.

Weinberger, C. & Kuhn, P.J. (2006). The narrowing of the U.S. gender earnings gap, 1959–1999: A cohort-based analysis. NBER Working Paper No. W12115, March.

Weiss, Y. & Gronau, R. (1981). Expected interruptions in labor force participation and sex-related differences in earnings growth. *Review of Economic Studies*, **48**(4), 607–19.

Wellington, A.J. (1993). Changes in the male/female wage gap, 1976–85. *Journal of Human Resources*, **28**(2), 383–411.

Wolff, E.N. (1976). Occupational earnings behavior and the inequality of earnings by sex and race in the United States. *Review of Income and Wealth*, ser. 22, no. 2, 151–66.

Wooley, F.R. (1992). The feminist challenge to neoclassical economics. Carleton University, Ottawa, Canada, mimeo, October.

Wright, G. (1991). Understanding the gender gap: A review article. *Journal of Economic Literature*, **39**, 1153–63.

Zellner, H. (1972). Discrimination against women, occupational segregation, and the relative wage. *American Economic Review*, **62**(2), 157–60.

14.8 DISCUSSION QUESTIONS AND PROBLEM SET

1 Describe the trend in the LFPR of wives over the postwar period. Explain how changes in female earnings and male earnings helped account for the trend in their LFPR.

2 What has happened to the gender–wage gap in the United States since 1970? Explain the role of changes in women's schooling and experience on the change in the gender–wage gap.

3 Explain why the Duncan and Duncan index is a useful measure of occupational segregation. What do changes in the Duncan and Duncan index for female workers in the U.S. economy indicate about trends in occupational segregation over the postwar period?

4 Evaluate three explanations for the existence of occupational segregation in the U.S. labor force.

5 Summarize the evidence on the effects of affirmative action on the economic position of women in the labor force.

6 Discuss and evaluate the economic rationale for comparable worth initiatives.

7* Some economist have argued that total experience by itself might not be a good predictor of a woman's earnings because of the adverse effects of work interruption on human capital. Discuss the evidence that work interruptions might affect female earnings?

8 Define the Duncan and Duncan index of occupational segregation. Calculate the Duncan and Duncan index for the following distributions:

Occupation	Number of men employed in occupation	Number of women employed in occupation
1	10,000	6,000
2	20,000	6,000
3	10,000	8,000

9 Calculate the Duncan and Duncan index for the following distributions:

Occupation	Number of men employed in occupation	Number of women employed in occupation
1	15,000	6,000
2	20,000	6,000
3	10,000	8,000
4	5,000	5,000

NOTES

1 Another factor is a reduction in discrimination, emanating from the passage of the Equal Pay Act of 1963 and the Civil Rights Act of 1964. We shall discuss these effects in Section 14.4.

2 For male workers, this reflects, in part, the drop out from the labor force of less educated older male workers in recent years.

3 Commuting time was included as a variable because married females might have a preference for jobs close to home even if they are low paying.

4 Zellner (1972) reported that in 1960, 50 percent of employed women were concentrated in occupations where they represented 80 percent or more of the total employment in the occupation, whereas only 2 percent of total male employees were in these occupations. On the other hand, only 20 percent of female workers were employed in occupations where they represented a third or less of total employment in the occupation, whereas 90 percent of employed men were in these occupations. Indeed,

Blau (1972) found that in 1900, 30 percent of the female labor force was employed in just one occupational category, that of private household workers, while four of the detailed Census occupations in that year accounted for 46 percent of the female labor force.

5 The percent of females working in only sales jobs increased from 4 to 13 percent between 1900 and 1993, with the bulk of the change occurring between 1977 and 1988.

6 It is of interest that in 1900, 29 percent of all female workers were employed as domestic servants but this share shrank to 2 percent by 1993.

7 In 1993, females comprised 95 percent of all domestic servants.

8 As might be apparent, the magnitude of DD is very sensitive to the number of occupations used in the analysis. The measure is almost higher the more occupational classifications that are used. In time-series comparisons, the analyst tries to use the same number of occupations in each year.

9 See Goldin (1991) for an interesting analysis of the effects of wartime employment (World War II) on the structure of female employment.

10 There were 503 occupations used for the 1980 computations but only 291 occupations for the 1960 computations. Since the DD index usually rises as the number of occupations increases, the results are biased towards showing greater occupational segregation (a higher value of DD) in 1980 than in 1960. On the other hand, the DD index for 2004 was based on 73 occupations, so the bias runs the other way for the 1980–2004 period.

11 However, as Fuchs reported, there was an even greater reduction in occupational segregation by race. Between black women and white women, the DD index declined by 50 percent (from 56 to 28) and between black men and white men, the DD index declined by 34 percent (from 50 to 33).

12 A related point is that there may be a systematic relation between the male–female wage gap within occupation and the proportion of females employed within that occupation. Rytina (1981) found on the basis of 1976 Survey of Income and Education that the occupational female–male wage gap was negatively related to the percent of females in that occupation (that is, the wage gap was smaller in occupations with a higher percentage of females).

13 They also found that declines in industry segregation within occupation were associated with improvements in relative female earnings independently of other factors which affect relative pay and that high employment growth was associated with improvements in relative female earnings, independently of its effect on occupational segregation.

14 Australia has probably the most comprehensive system of comparable worth, covering the vast majority of both public and private workers. Canada and the United Kingdom also instituted comparable worth programs to some extent. See Gunderson (1989) for more details.

15 By 1987 there remained only four states which had not undertaken some comparable worth action such as data collection, creation of a task force, job evaluation studies, or salary adjustments.

16 Betson and van der Gaag (1984) reported the same trend for the 1968–1980 period.

17 A related topic is the debate over the impact of wives' work on the wages of their husbands. Earlier studies suggested that men with working wives, on average, earned less than men with nonworking wives. However, later studies found that, with proper controls for fixed effects, income effects, and marriage patterns, the work hours of wives had no significant effect on the wages of their husbands (see, for example, Jacobsen and Rayack, 1996).

Part IV
The Role of Public Policy on Poverty and Inequality

Chapter 15
Public Policy and Poverty Alleviation

15.1 INTRODUCTION

The last two chapters of the book investigate the impact of public policy on poverty and income inequality. This chapter focuses on the government transfer system and other programs aimed at alleviating poverty. Chapter 16 analyzes the effect of government taxes and expenditures on the overall distribution of income.

Section 15.2 presents a brief history of the development of the income maintenance system in the United States. The chapter then looks with more detail at three of the major income support systems in the United States today: (i) unemployment insurance (Section 15.3); (ii) the social security system (Section 15.4); and (iii) the welfare system, particularly, Temporary Assistance to Needy Families (Section 15.5) and related manpower programs (Section 15.6). The chapter describes the structure of each program, evaluates its effectiveness, and considers some of the incentive effects of the program. Section 15.7 discusses another government program that directly affects the low-income population, the minimum wage. The chapter ends with an overall assessment of these programs particularly with regard to the effectiveness of the various support systems in alleviating poverty (Section 15.8).

15.2 A BRIEF HISTORY OF INCOME MAINTENANCE PROGRAMS

The U.S. welfare system has developed in rather piecemeal fashion over the years. As a result, its effectiveness depends in large measure on which groups make up the poverty population and how the composition of the poor changes over time. Programs designed at one point of time to meet the needs of one population of the poor may become less effective over time if the structure of poverty changes. We will examine in the next few sections how the U.S. welfare system has met its challenges.

The development of the U.S. social welfare system has generally been dominated by two principles. The first is that work is the basis of income. The second is that the nuclear family is the principal unit in society. U.S. society has traditionally believed that all able-bodied men *should* work and support their wives and children.

The development of the income maintenance (transfer) programs has generally followed from these two ideas. This has led to two types of programs. The first is public assistance or welfare for unfortunate people who cannot provide for themselves. In this regard, the state is viewed as a charitable organization. The second is social insurance for the *working population*. Workers are viewed as taking out insurance in order to protect themselves in the event they are out of work.[1] The state is viewed as the insuring agency, and workers pay into various policies in the form of payroll taxes (such as social security or unemployment insurance).

15.2.1   Early developments

Several states and cities began implementing charitable assistance programs for their indigent population in the nineteenth century, particularly in light of mounting poverty in the cities. Despite the growth of federal programs that provide assistance to the poor, many states and localities continue to administer their own welfare programs, which are referred to as **general assistance**.[2]

The federal government's entry into welfare occurred in 1908 with the passage of **worker's compensation**. This program was developed to assist workers injured on the job. The law was designed to protect workers' families for income lost due to injury, both permanent and temporary, and also due to death. Though in theory an employee could sue his or her employer for an injury on the job, the tort system was not easily used for this purpose and judges were usually more sympathetic to the employers than the workers.

This is the earliest example of social insurance on the federal level. The justification for worker's compensation was that employment is the basis of income and the government should insure this source of income, at least from occupational hazards. If a person became disabled from a work-related injury, the government should provide at least some minimal income support until the person could get back on his or her feet and resume work. It is interesting that the scope of the intervention was limited to work interruptions resulting from injuries on the job. It would be another quarter-century before the idea of social insurance was extended to work interruptions due to job loss.

A second entry into the income support system came with the passage of **veteran's disability** in 1918. This act effectively extended worker's compensation to soldiers and sailors disabled during World War I. The rationale was that men who served in World War I should normally return to work as soon as they were discharged from service. However, if they were injured during service and could not return to work, this occurrence was similar to injury on the job and the government should step in and provide these veterans with basic income support. This act extended the notion of social insurance to a new group, the armed forces.

15.2.2   The New Deal

The Great Depression began in October 1929, with the stock market crash. By the early 1930s, the unemployment rate had soared to 25 percent. There was very little action taken by President Hoover to combat the effects of the Depression, and, partly as a result, Franklin Roosevelt was elected to office in 1932. He put together the first systematic attempt to provide a broad-based system of income support, called the New Deal. Three principal programs were formed: (i) unemployment insurance; (ii) the social security system; and (3) Aid to Families with Dependent Children. All three programs were set up under the **Social Security Act of 1935**, and the first two still form a major part of the U.S. income support system. These three programs were each established under the assumptions that: (i) the basic family unit is the nuclear family, a married couple with children; and (ii) the husband is the prime earner (if not the sole earner) in the family.

Unemployment insurance extended the notion of social insurance already embodied in worker's compensation and the veteran disability programs to a new class of individuals. Whereas the two older programs insured workers against the loss of jobs resulting from injuries sustained on the job (or in war), this new program extended it to loss of work resulting from *involuntary* unemployment. Employers were required to pay a special payroll tax on wages into an unemployment insurance fund. A worker who was laid off could collect a payment from the government, which was set at a fixed proportion of his or her wage. The program was intended to provide basic income support to unemployed workers while they were searching for a new job (or waiting to be recalled to their old job).

The social security system is technically referred to as the "old age, survivors, disability, and health insurance program, or **OASDHI** ("OA" for old age, "S" for survivors, "D" for disability, "H" for health, and "I" for insurance). In 1935, the system provided only old age (retirement) benefits. This was supplemented in 1939 by survivor's benefits (in the event that the husband died, the wife would still receive some income support); in 1957 by disability benefits (for injuries not sustained on the job, since these were already covered by worker's compensation); and in 1966 by medical benefits for persons 65 and over (Medicare). The social security system is financed by a payroll tax paid in equal amounts by employees and employers. There is a cap on the wage base.

The hallmark feature of the system is that retirees who have paid into the system receive an income payment when they retire. The benefit structure is based on the person's earnings history. However, the benefit levels are subject to legislative fiat and have been raised periodically by Congress.

The social security system has a dual character, both as a form of social insurance and as a pension plan. Poverty rates were very high among the elderly in the early 1930s, though specific estimates are hard to come by, because there was no official government estimate of the poverty rate. However, as we saw in Chapter 4, even in 1959, the incidence of poverty among the elderly was much higher than that among the general population. The labor market is not a good solution to the problem of elderly poverty for two reasons. First, many older people are unable to work due to physical limitations or health problems. Second, many firms are unwilling to hire older workers, because they do not feel that the worker's longevity in the firm would warrant making an investment in the person's training. Moreover, most firms have historically had mandatory retirement ages, and though mandatory retirement is no longer legal today, firms still provide very strong incentives to induce older workers to retire.

Before the advent of the social security system, retirees were generally forced to rely on the generosity of their children to maintain them in old age. There were some exceptions – people who had saved substantial sums and those with private pension plans – but this group was relatively small and tended to be limited to the wealthiest. With the massive unemployment of the 1930s, it was very difficult for workers to support their parents – workers were having a hard enough time making ends meet on their own.

The social security system was established as a form of social insurance – to insure workers against the loss of income in old age. The system establishes a minimum benefit level, to which all workers who contributed into the system are entitled regardless of the total amount of their contributions. This level is intended to provide elderly couples with the basic necessities. The system also provides higher benefits to workers with greater contributions, which is analogous to a pension scheme. However, the benefit level does not increase in proportion to contributions as it would in a normal pension plan. Benefits of low-income workers are set at a higher percentage of their contributions than high-income workers. In this way, the social security system redistributes income from higher to lower earners.

The third prong of the social safety net was Aid to Families with Dependent Children (AFDC).[3] Eligibility was restricted to families with children under the age of 18 living at home and with income and assets below pre-specified levels. The thresholds were set by each state according to general federal guidelines. Benefits were based on a schedule set by each state that provided a guaranteed amount depending on the number of children in the family. The benefit level was reduced as family income rose above the threshold level.

AFDC was intended for families that fell "between the cracks" of the first two programs. The unemployment insurance system was designed to take care of families whose husband was temporarily out of work. The social security system was set up to take care of the elderly. AFDC was supposed to provide basic support for nonelderly families with children who could not do so on their own. Who were these families? They were female-headed households, since it was assumed that husbands would be at work or collecting unemployment insurance while looking for work. In 1935, female-headed households were an unusual occurrence because both divorce and the birth of children to unmarried mothers were uncommon. As a result, the program was oriented toward widows and thought of as a form of social insurance to guard against the death of the prime wage earner – the husband. Viewing the nuclear family as the basic unit of society, the architects of this program could not have foreseen the huge increase in the number of female-headed households resulting from divorce and "out-of-wedlock" births (see Chapter 13).

15.2.3   Post-war developments

The New Deal was the first period of major social legislation. The second was the **Great Society** program of the mid-1960s. The reason for this is not altogether clear, because this was a period of general prosperity and rapid economic growth. However, it was also the period when poverty was "rediscovered" – partly a result of the publication of Michael Harrington's 1962 book, *The Other America*. It may also have resulted from the civil rights movement of the 1950s and early 1960s, which, as we saw in Chapter 13, provided impetus to the civil rights legislation of the 1960s. President Kennedy provided the initiative for much of the social legislation of the period. After his assassination in 1963, President Johnson was able to get enough support in Congress to enact three new programs: (i) **food stamps**, in 1964; (ii) **Medicaid**, in 1965; and (iii) **Medicare**, in 1966.

The Food Stamp program was designed to provide eligible low-income families with a nutritionally adequate low-cost diet. The program provides vouchers for qualifying families that can be used for the purchase of only foodstuffs (alcohol and tobacco products, for example, are excluded). Eligibility is limited to families whose income and assets fall below pre-specified levels. Since this is a federal program, the guidelines are set by the federal government and do not vary across states. In fact, almost all AFDC recipients were eligible for food stamps and almost all current Temporary Assistance to Needy Families (TANF) recipients are now eligible, as well as those covered by **Supplemental Security Income** or **SSI** (see below). The program is open to families with and without children, as long as they meet the income threshold. In 2007, the monthly income limit was set at $1,062 for a single-person household, $1,430 for a two-person household, and $2,167 for a four-person household.[4] There is also an asset limitation, such as a bank account. In 2007, it was $2,000 for a family, excluding the value of a home and vehicles owned by the family.[5]

The benefit level is determined by assuming that low-income families spend 30 percent of their cash income on food. The value of food stamps then makes up the difference between the cost of a nutritionally adequate low-cost diet (given the size of the family) estimated by the Department of Agriculture and 30 percent of the family's cash income. In 2007, the maximum monthly food stamp grant (for a family with no income) was $155 for a single-person household, $284 for a two-person household, and $518 for a four-person household. In fiscal year 2005, 11.2 million households received food stamp benefits, and the nationwide average monthly benefit per person was $92.56. The total cost of the programs was $31.1 billion. The food stamp allotment is reduced by $0.30 for each dollar of income earned.

Medicaid was established as an adjunct to AFDC. All families who qualified for AFDC and those who qualify for TANF and SSI automatically qualify for Medicaid. The program also covers low-income pregnant women and children in low-income families who may not be covered by AFDC or SSI.

Like AFDC, Medicaid is administered by the individual states under federal guidelines. The federal government establishes a minimal level of medical coverage for eligible families. These include basic inpatient and outpatient hospital services; laboratory and X-ray services; and some doctor office visits. The states must meet these minimal requirements but may also include additional medical services. The federal government reimburses each state for Medicaid expenses (reimbursement rates vary inversely to the level of per capita income of the state and typically range between 50 and 80 percent).

Medicare was enacted as an adjunct to the social security system (it forms the "H" in OASDHI). Anyone aged 65 or older who is receiving social security ("old age") benefits is automatically eligible for Medicare. Persons under the age of 65 who receive social security disability benefits can also qualify for this program. The Medicare program pays all "reasonable" expenses for inpatient hospital care minus a small deductible.[6] The program also pays for 80 percent of the reasonable charges for doctor services, though certain types of procedures are excluded and there is a nominal deductible per year. Hospitals and doctors who subscribe to this program usually agree to accept the reimbursement rates set by Medicare. The program is partially funded by monthly premiums paid for by individual beneficiaries which (as of 2007) were just under $100 per month.[7]

These three programs – food stamps, Medicaid, and Medicare – represent extensions of the basic income maintenance system put into place during the New Deal. The major change in philosophy is a movement away from cash income support to in-kind transfers of basic necessities. This may have reflected a paternalistic attitude on the part of the government to ensure that welfare benefits were used for "appropriate purposes." These programs provide low-income families directly with two of life's necessities, rather than with an additional cash allowance so that they can purchase these items. Together with direct housing assistance (see below), the programs provide the basic necessities of life – food, shelter, and medical care.

Since the 1960s, the only significant addition to the income support system was Supplemental Security Income (SSI), enacted in 1972, during the Nixon administration. SSI provides cash payments to needy aged, blind, and disabled persons. The guidelines are set by the federal government and are uniform across states. Elderly individuals (age 65 or over) who do not qualify for social security, as well as blind and disabled persons who meet the income and asset thresholds of this program, are eligible for benefits. The program is financed by general tax revenue.

During 1994, the Clinton administration attempted to develop some form of universal health care. Most workers and their families receive health insurance from their employer. Medicare provides health coverage to the elderly and Medicaid to the poor. In addition, health coverage is available through private health insurance plans for families rich enough to afford the premiums. However, that still leaves about 15 percent of U.S. families with no health coverage. These are mainly low-income working families employed in jobs which do not provide health insurance. Clinton's plan required employers to provide health insurance to all their employees, including low-wage workers. In August of 1994, this attempt was defeated in Congress.[8]

15.2.4   Housing assistance

Federal housing assistance programs have developed over the years, in a somewhat patch-quilt fashion. The objective of these programs is to reduce housing costs for low-income families and to improve the quality of housing they receive.

The earliest programs, dating from 1937, provided rental assistance to low-income families. These have been (and still are) of two forms. The first has been through the construction of special housing projects ("public housing") reserved for low-income families. Eligible families may qualify for an apartment in one of these housing units. The second is through household-based subsidies. Qualifying low-income families who rent standard apartments in the private housing market receive a rental subsidy from the federal government. In both cases (public housing and the private housing market), qualifying families are required to pay no more than a fixed percentage (generally 30 percent) of their income on rent. In the case of public housing, the rent is limited to this amount. In the case of the private housing market, the government pays directly to the landlord the difference between the market rent and the rental limit computed from the family income.

Besides rental assistance, the federal government also provides assistance to qualifying low- and moderate-income families to purchase homes. This usually takes the form of a long-term commitment to reduce the interest payments of the mortgage loan. In 1991, the federal government started making block grants to state and local governments to build more public housing for low-income families. In addition, state and local governments finance and administer public housing projects for their low-income populations.

15.2.5   Public expenditures on major federal programs

Table 15.1 highlights trends in spending on the principal federal income transfer programs. Both federal outlays as well as those provided by state and local governments are included in the table. The programs are separated into two groups, corresponding to the two principles of social welfare spending. The first consists of social insurance programs, which were set up to protect workers against job loss due to unemployment, disability, and old age. These programs are funded mainly through payroll taxes. The second group, referred to as public assistance or welfare, is intended to provide for families and individuals in need – irrespective of the circumstances that caused their poverty.

It is interesting to look at the 2005 figures first. The largest program in dollar terms was, by far, the social security system (OASDI). Government outlays on this program alone amounted to $513 billion, 36 percent of the total expenditures on the income transfer programs included in the table. Social security spending was 87 percent of the amount spent on defense in that year. Medicare was the second-largest program in dollar terms, at $333 billion. Public spending on the elderly from OASDHI (social security plus Medicare) summed to $845 billion, or 60 percent of the total for these income support programs.

The largest public assistance program is Medicaid, which amounted to $304 billion in 2005, or 22 percent of total income transfers. This amount was only slightly less than the outlays on Medicare. Expenditures on the other social insurance programs are much smaller. Outlays on unemployment insurance were 2 percent of total welfare spending, workers' compensation was 4 percent, and veteran's disability compensation was 2 percent. TANF outlays were $25 billion in 2005, 2 percent of total welfare spending. SSI, food stamps, and housing assistance each amounted to between 2 and 3 percent of total welfare expenditures.

Time trends are also striking. Social welfare spending increased from 3 percent of GDP in 1960 to 11 percent in 2005. In 1960, almost three times as much money was spent on national defense as on these programs. By 2005, income transfers were more than double national defense spending.

Spending on income transfer programs grew by 4.5 percent per year in real terms between 1970 and 2005. The annual growth in Medicaid topped the list, at 8.9 percent, followed by housing

Table 15.1 Public expenditures (outlays) on major federal income transfer programs, 1960–2005 (billions of 2005 dollars)

Program	Date enacted	1960	1970	1980	1990	2000	2005	Percent dist. 2005	Annual percent rate of growth 1970–2005
A. Social insurance									
1. Cash benefits									
a. Social security (OASDI)	1935	69.2	148.9	279.9	368.3	442.3	512.6	36	3.53
b. Unemployment insurance	1935	19.9	22.0	40.0	26.1	23.1	31.8	2	1.05
c. Workers' compensation	1908	8.5	15.4	31.9	55.0	54.3	55.4	4	3.66
d. Veterans' disability compensation	1917	0.0	34.2	27.7	22.8	24.8	32.6	2	−0.14
2. In-kind benefits									
a. Medicare	1965	0.0	34.2	80.6	160.4	223.5	332.8	24	6.50
B. Public assistance (welfare)									
1. Cash benefits									
a. AFDC and	1935								
TANF	1996	6.6	24.5	31.9	31.6	25.6	25.0	2	0.06
b. SSI[a]	1972	0.0	0.0	13.5	17.2	36.0	46.1	3	4.91[b]
2. In-kind benefits									
a. Medicaid	1965	0.0	13.7	33.2	61.4	226.3	304.4	22	8.87
b. Food stamps	1964	0.0	2.6	21.5	23.8	16.9	31.1	2	7.13
c. Housing assistance	1937	0.0	2.4	17.0	31.5	35.4	42.5	3	8.17
Total expenditures		104.3	297.9	577.4	798.2	1,108.4	1,414.3	100	4.45
Total expenditures as % of GDP		3.1	5.9	9.0	9.6	10.0	11.4		
Memo: National defense expenditures		298.8	386.5	338.2	469.3	420.0	588.7		1.20

a   Aid to the blind, to the permanently disabled and totally disabled, and old age assistance in 1965.
b   Growth rate is for 1980–2005.
Sources: U.S. House of Representatives (1994). Committee on Ways and Means, *Overview of Entitlement Programs: 1994 Green Book*. Washington, DC: U.S. Government Printing Office, July; U.S. House of Representatives (2004). Committee on Ways and Means, *Overview of Entitlement Programs: 2004 Green Book*. Washington, DC: U.S. Government Printing Office, July; Council of Economic Advisers, *Economic Report of the President, 1994, 1997, 2007*; National Income and Product Accounts, Table 3.12, at: http://www.bea.gov/national; *Social Security Bulletin Statistical Supplement, 2006*, at: http://www.ssa.gov/policy/docs/statcomps/supplement/2006/9b.pdf. The figures include benefits plus administrative expenses paid for by both the federal government and state and local governments.

assistance (8.2 percent), food stamps (7.1 percent), and Medicare (6.5 percent). Social security (OASDI) expenditures grew at 3.5 percent per year, unemployment insurance at 1.1 percent per year, and workers' compensation at 3.7 percent per year. AFDC/TANF expenditures in real terms remained virtually unchanged from 1970 to 2005. Spending on SSI grew much more rapidly, at 4.9 percent per year from 1980 to 1993. Spending on in-kind welfare benefits grew much faster than cash benefits over the period from 1970 to 2005.

15.3   UNEMPLOYMENT INSURANCE (UI)

The Social Security Act of 1935 created a combined federal/state system of unemployment insurance (UI). The federal legislation provided strong incentives for each state to set up its own system of unemployment insurance. Each state administers its own system and sets the important regulations of the system, such as minimum and maximum benefits, the rules for eligibility, and the UI tax rates. Originally, workers in only large companies in certain industries were covered by the system. However, federal legislation over the years, such as the Employment Security Act of 1970, has extended coverage of the system. In 2004, 99.7 percent of all wage and salary workers were covered by the UI system and about 90 percent of all employed persons.[9]

The stated objective of the 1935 Social Security Act was to provide temporary and partial wage replacement to involuntarily unemployed workers who were recently employed. There are a number of key elements to this statement. First, the worker had to be involuntarily unemployed. This means that unemployment must have occurred through job loss rather than discharge for cause (for example, being fired for lateness or absenteeism) or for voluntarily quitting. The most common cause of job loss is layoffs associated with a recession. Second, the worker must have been previously employed to qualify for UI. New workers, just entering the labor force, or reentrants who have been out for an extended period of time are not eligible. Third, the UI system guarantees only *partial* replacement of wages, not the level the worker earned before losing the job. Fourth, the relief is *temporary* so that UI benefits are provided for only a limited period of time, during which the worker is expected to search actively for another job.

Employers pay a payroll tax on wages and salaries into the UI fund. The rate is set by the federal government (it has recently been of the order of 0.8 percent). There is a rather low cap on the wage base (recently $7,000 to $8,000), and the UI tax is levied only on wages up to this level. As a result, the *effective* UI tax on wages (the ratio of UI taxes to total covered wages) has been about 0.2 to 0.3 percent since the 1960s.

15.3.1   A brief description of the UI system

Though the details of the system vary across states, the basic structure is very similar. The program provides unemployed workers a certain level of benefits depending on the reason for their joblessness and their previous weekly earnings. In most states, a worker must have previously worked two quarters (6 months) and have been laid off from his (her) job (not fired or voluntarily quit) to be eligible for UI benefits. In Rhode Island and New York, strikers are also eligible for benefits, and in some states those who voluntarily leave a job are also entitled to benefits. Those newly joining or returning to the labor force do not qualify for benefits.

In all states, there is a minimum weekly UI benefit (UI_1) and a maximum benefit (UI_2) for those who are eligible. The minimum and maximum vary considerably across states. The actual UI benefit depends on the worker's previous earnings, which in some states is based on the earnings of the last full week worked, in others on the worker's earnings over the last year, and in still others on the individual's earnings during his (her) best quarter over the last year. There is a minimum level of previous weekly earnings, W_1, needed to qualify for benefits. At W_1, the benefit is set at UI_1. Above W_1, the UI benefit increases in proportion to previous earnings W, though the rate is less than unity and typically about 50 percent (an additional dollar of benefit per two dollars of earnings). Benefits are capped at UI_2, corresponding to wage level W_2.

The replacement rate structure is shown in Figure 15.1, where the replacement rate is defined as the ratio of the individual's weekly UI benefit to previous weekly earnings W. At W_1, the replacement rate is equal to UI_1/W_1. From W_1 to W_2, the replacement rate remains at UI_1/W_1 (which, in

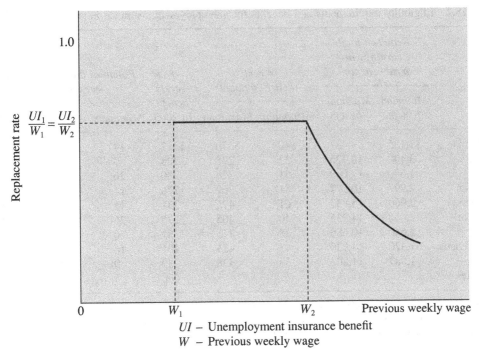

Figure 15.1   The replacement rate structure of the unemployment insurance system

turn, equals UI_2/W_2). Above W_2, the replacement rate declines inversely with W, since the benefit level is fixed at UI_2.

UI benefits generally last for a maximum of 26 weeks, as long as the individual shows evidence of actively looking for new work. During periods when the aggregate unemployment rate was particularly high, Congress has often enacted special legislation which extended the maximum number of weeks an individual can collect UI benefits (typically an extra 13 weeks). Up until 1978, UI benefits were not subject to federal income taxes. Since 1978, UI benefits have been treated as taxable income only if total family income exceeds a pre-specified maximum ($12,000 for single taxpayers and $18,000 for married couples).

Like social security, UI benefits are financed by a payroll tax, paid by the employer. An employer's UI tax rate is based on the employer's "experience rating." The rationale is that firms that lay off workers more frequently than others should pay a higher tax rate, since they place heavier demands on the UI system's finances. Like the benefit structure, there is both a minimum and a maximum UI tax rate that is assessed on the firm's total payroll. Firms that rarely lay off workers will pay the minimum rate. Firms that lay off workers frequently and for relatively long duration will pay the maximum rate. In between, the payroll tax rate is a step function of the firm's layoff record. Because of the structure of the system, firms that rarely lay off workers pay a greater amount into the system than the actual costs the system incurs from the firm (that is, the benefits the UI system pays to workers laid off by these firms). Conversely, firms that frequently lay off workers will pay less into the UI system than the system pays out in UI benefits to the firm's employees.

Table 15.2 shows relevant statistics on both eligibility requirements and benefit structure for a number of states in 2003. It is at once apparent that provisions vary considerably among states.

Table 15.2   Eligibility requirements and benefits for unemployment insurance in selected states, 2003

State	Required total earnings in base year for: Minimum benefit	Required total earnings in base year for: Maximum benefit	Weekly benefit amount Minimum	Weekly benefit amount Maximum	Average weekly benefit in 2003	Potential duration (weeks) Minimum	Potential duration (weeks) Maximum	Average duration of benefits (weeks) in 2002
California	$1,125	$9,487	$40	$370	$217	14	26	18
Florida	3,400	10,725	32	275	225	9	26	15
Illinois	1,600	17,069	51	326	280	26	26	19
Michigan	2,997	10,977	81	362	276	14	26	15
New Jersey	2,060	15,833	61	475	331	15	26	19
New York	2,400	14,235	40	405	275	26	26	19
Ohio	2,640	10,680	88	315	251	20	26	16
Pennsylvania	1,320	14,920	43	451	291	16	26	17
Texas	1,887	11,803	53	328	259	9	26	17
All states					260			

Sources: U.S. House of Representatives (2004). Committee on Ways and Means, *Overview of Entitlement Programs: 2004 Green Book*. Washington, DC: U.S. Government Printing Office, July; http://www.gpoaccess.gov/wmprints/green/2004.html.

The first column shows the minimum wage base, W_1, for eligibility. The minimum among these nine states varied from a low of $1,125 in California to $3,400 in Florida (the lowest minimum among the 50 states was $130 in Hawaii and the highest was $3,586 in North Carolina). The maximum wage base, W_2, ranged from a low of $9,487 in California to a high of $17,069 in Illinois (among the 50 states, from $7,000 in Arizona to $31,900 in West Virginia).

The minimum weekly UI benefit level, UI_1, corresponding to earnings level W_1, and the maximum benefit level, UI_2, corresponding to W_2, are shown in the third and fourth columns. Both minimum and maximum benefit levels differ considerably among the states (the minimum level of the states shown in Table 15.2 from $32 in Florida to $88 in Ohio and the maximum from $275 in Florida to $475 in New Jersey). The actual average weekly benefit paid to UI recipients in 2003 varied from $217 in California to $331 in New Jersey among the states shown in the table – more than a 50 percent difference.

Almost all states provide that an unemployed person can collect UI benefits for a maximum of 26 weeks (the exceptions are Massachusetts and Washington, which have a 30-week maximum). The actual number of weeks of eligibility is based on the person's previous earnings. New Jersey residents, for example, who just meet the New Jersey earnings requirement would be able to collect benefits for at most 15 weeks. The minimum potential duration varied from a low of 9 weeks in Florida and Texas (among the states shown in the table) to 26 weeks in all the states. The average number of weeks during which UI benefits were collected in 2003 ranged from 15 in Florida and Michigan to 19 in New Jersey and New York (among the states shown in the table).

15.3.2   Time trends in UI benefits

Though almost all wage and salary workers are covered by the UI system, the actual percentage of unemployed workers receiving UI benefits has typically ranged from 40 to 70 percent.

Table 15.3   Unemployment insurance (UI) coverage and benefit rates, selected years, 1967–2005

Year	Civilian unemployment rate (percent)[a]	Insured coverage rate (percent)[b]	Average weekly UI benefit[c] (2005 $)	Ratio of UI benefit to average wage[d]
1962	5.5		223	0.40
1967	3.8	43	241	0.41
1970	4.9	48	253	0.42
1975	8.5	76	254	0.43
1980	7.1	50	234	0.42
1985	7.2	34	232	0.43
1990	5.5	37	241	0.47
1993	6.8	48	242	0.48
2000	4.0	41	251	0.46
2005	5.1	40	267	0.49

a   *Source*: Council of Economic Advisers, *Economic Report of the President, 1994.*
b   Insured unemployment as a percent of total unemployment, average for year. *Source*: U.S. House of Representatives (1994). Committee on Ways and Means, *Overview of Entitlement Programs: 1994 Green Book.* Washington, DC: U.S. Government Printing Office, July; Council of Economic Advisers, *Economic Report of the President, 2007.*
c   *Source*: Council of Economic Advisers, *Economic Report of the President, 1994 and 2007.*
d   The average weekly wage is for the total private work force. *Source*: Council of Economic Advisers, *Economic Report of the President, 1994 and 2007.*

As we discussed above, there are two reasons for this. The first is that there are eligibility requirements for an unemployed person to receive UI benefits. These are of two forms: (i) a worker must have worked a certain number of weeks continuously or worked in a certain number of quarters before losing a job to qualify; and (ii) a worker is required to have earned a certain minimum level of wages to qualify. The second is that unemployment benefits are exhausted after a certain number of weeks (usually 26 weeks). At this point, the worker is no longer eligible for UI benefits.

Table 15.3 highlights these trends (see also Figure 15.2). The insured coverage rate, defined as the number of unemployed workers receiving benefits as a percent of total unemployment, has been as high as 76 percent (in 1975) and as low as 32 percent (1987 and 1988). Generally speaking, coverage rates declined rather sharply between the mid-1970s and the mid- to late 1980s, increased during the early 1990s, fell again in the mid-1990s, and then increased once again in the late 1990s and early 2000s. It is also interesting to note that there is no clear connection between the overall civilian unemployment rate (shown in the first column of Table 15.3) and the coverage rate. The reason is that during recessionary periods, when unemployment has been high, Congress has frequently added auxiliary UI benefits by increasing the number of weeks of eligibility.

The average weekly UI benefit check, in 2005 dollars, increased from $223 in 1962 to a peak of $267 in 2005. A more revealing statistic is the **replacement rate**, which is the ratio of the UI benefit to the earnings the worker received just before he or she became unemployed. Unfortunately, information on this statistic is relatively sparse. However, we do have reliable data on the ratio of the average UI benefit to the average wage of the total private workforce. Insofar as unemployed workers are a reasonably representative sample of the workforce, this

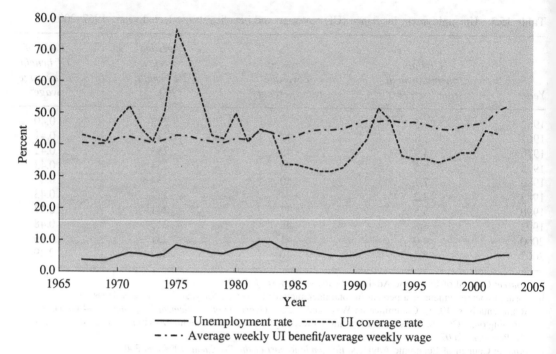

Figure 15.2   The unemployment rate, the UI coverage rate, and the UI replacement rate, 1967–2003

ratio is a good proxy of the actual replacement rate. The ratio of the average UI benefit to the average wage increased rather steadily over time since the early 1960s, from 0.40 in 1962 to 0.49 in 2005.

15.3.3   Incentive effects of the UI system

The UI system by its very nature may have an important effect on both the level of unemployment and its duration. In particular, by reducing the cost to an individual of being jobless, the UI system may actually prolong the duration of unemployment for many workers (see, for example, Feldstein, 1974). The original architects of the UI system explicitly recognized this and argued, in fact, that the added security individuals had while unemployed would enable them to select a job more compatible with their skills and interests. Rather than settling on the first position offered, an unemployed person could continue his (her) job search until a better match and higher wages were provided. In other words, UI provides a cushion during which search may be conducted. This, in turn, would prove socially beneficial, since better job matches should increase the national output by improving efficiency in the allocation of labor resources (see Haber & Murray, 1966, for related arguments).

The type of unemployment occasioned by the job search process is called *search unemployment*, which is a form of frictional unemployment (see Chapter 7). Since the UI system reduces the costs of remaining unemployed, the reservation wage – the minimum wage a person is willing to accept – for those searching for a new job will be higher on average than without UI benefits, and, as a result, so will be their average duration of unemployment. The higher the UI benefits, the longer will be the average unemployment spell. Most empirical studies have confirmed a positive relation between the UI replacement rate and the average duration of unemployment.

Typically, an increase in the replacement rate of 0.1 is associated with a half-week to a week increase in the average duration of unemployment. All told, the UI system may cause covered workers to remain unemployed 16 to 31 percent longer than those not covered.[10]

The UI system itself may also directly affect the layoff policies of firms. This is due to two features of the UI system. First, until 1978, UI benefits were not subject to federal income tax and after 1978 only if family income was above a certain critical level. As a result, if the (before-tax) UI replacement rate were 0.5, the after-tax replacement (the ratio of UI benefits to after-tax wages) would be higher. Feldstein (1974) estimated that in those states with higher UI benefits, the after-tax replacement rate could be as high as 80 percent for male workers and actually over 100 percent for some female workers. The loss of pay to many workers from being unemployed for short periods is relatively small. Indeed, since the probability of being recalled from temporary layoffs may be very high and since many workers on temporary layoffs treat this time as a vacation period, collective bargaining contracts may have "inverse seniority" provisions whereby the most senior workers are laid off first and rehired last (see Feldstein, 1978). As a result, some workers not only do not oppose temporary layoffs but even welcome them.

Second, because a firm's contribution to the UI system does not fully reflect the added costs to the system from laying off workers, a firm is not heavily penalized for temporarily laying off workers. Indeed, the added UI taxes it must pay from temporary layoffs may be quite minimal. As a result, firms also do not have much of a disincentive for laying off workers as a response to a decline in demand. In consequence, Feldstein and others argued that the UI system itself promotes a demand-deficient type of unemployment, since it discourages both firms and employees from reacting to declines in demand by wage reductions instead of layoffs. Topel (1983) estimated that more than one-quarter of layoffs and Anderson and Meyer (1994) estimated that about 20 percent of layoffs could be ascribed to the implicit subsidy of the UI system on layoff unemployment.

The UI system has also been shown to lead to increased seasonal unemployment. A study by Chiswick (1976) found that the extension of the coverage of the UI system to agricultural workers during the 1970s accounted for a sizable increase in the level of seasonal unemployment in that industry. Also, see Card and Levine (1994) for more recent evidence.

15.4   THE SOCIAL SECURITY SYSTEM

The old-age and survivors insurance (OASI) program provides benefits to retired workers and their dependents and to survivors of insured workers. The original Social Security Act of 1935 provided benefits to retired workers, and a 1939 amendment to the Act added benefits for dependents and survivors.

Workers become eligible for OASI benefits by working in covered employment (that is, in industries or occupations that are included within the social security system). In 2005, 96 percent of all jobs were covered by the social security system. Contributions to the social security system are made under the Federal Insurance Contributions Act (FICA for short). In 2005, employees contributed 7.65 percent of their wages and salaries to social security fund up to a maximum taxable wage base of $90,600. This is matched with an identical contribution from the employer, so that the effective social security tax rate on wages and salaries is 15.30 percent (see Chapter 16 for more details on the tax side).

When a person who is covered by the social security system retires, he or she is eligible to receive a monthly social security benefit. Under current rules, the person must have received covered earnings in at least 40 quarters to receive social security benefits.[11] In 2005, the person must have earned at least $980 during the quarter for it to qualify as a covered quarter. If a covered

Table 15.4 OASDI cash benefits to all recipients and new awards, 2002

Recipient class	All beneficiaries		New awards	
	Number of beneficiaries (1,000s)	Average monthly benefit ($)	Number of beneficiaries (1,000s)	Average monthly benefit ($)
All beneficiaries	46,444	815	4,336	736
Retired workers	29,190	895	1,813	914
Spouses of retired workers	2,681	451	318	345
Children of retired workers	477	426	116	408
Disabled workers	5,544	834	750	898
Widowed mothers and fathers	194	640	41	650
Widows and widowers	4,770	849	523	727
Surviving Children	1,908	585	310	605
Children and spouses of disabled workers	1,678	240	466	237

Source: U.S. House of Representatives (2004). Committee on Ways and Means, *Overview of Entitlement Programs: 2004 Green Book*. Washington, DC: U.S. Government Printing Office, July.

worker dies before retirement, the worker's spouse and/or children may also be entitled to receive social security benefits. In both cases, the award is based on the worker's earnings history.[12]

Table 15.4 shows average OASDI payments to various groups of beneficiaries in 2002. Over 46 million persons collected social security benefits of one form or another. The average monthly benefit was $815. Over 29 million retired workers received benefits in 2002, with an average monthly award of $895. Of this number, 1.8 million retired during 2002, and their average monthly benefit was $914. There were a total of 5.5 million disabled workers who were on the social security rolls, and their average benefit was $834. Widows and widowers collecting benefits amounted to a little under 5 million, and their average award was $849.

15.4.1   Determination of the social security benefit

The OASI benefit is calculated as follows:

1   A worker's earnings history is first converted into an average indexed monthly earnings (AIME) amount. This is the average monthly wage of the worker, adjusted for changes in the average wages of the total labor force. In effect, the indexing adjusts for both changes in the price level (inflation) and changes in real earnings. The computation of the AIME also reflects the number of quarters the person works in covered employment. A person must work (and receive a minimum amount of earnings) in at least 40 quarters to qualify for social security benefits. The maximum benefit is achieved at 140 quarters of covered work (35 full years). If fewer than 140 quarters are worked in covered employment, the AIME is reduced in proportion to the shortfall in the number of quarters (for example, the AIME for a person who works 70 quarters will be one-half of the AIME of a person who works 140 quarters or more with the same average index earnings). If a person works in covered employment for more than 35 years, the best (highest) 35 years of earnings are used in the computation of the person's AIME.

2   The AIME is then used to compute the monthly retirement benefit payable at the worker's normal retirement age. This is based on a progressive benefit formula to arrive at the primary insurance amount (PIA). The PIA is subject to both a minimum and maximum level. A retiree can qualify for a "special minimum benefit" which is not based on the amount of a worker's average earnings but instead on her number of years of covered employment.

The actual benefit received is a fixed proportion of the PIA. If the person retires at the normal retirement age of 65, the retiree receives the full amount of the PIA.[13] If the person retirees at age 62 (the earliest retirement age covered by the social security system), the person receives only 80 percent of the PIA. If the person retirees at age 67, the benefit is set at 110 percent of the PIA and, at age 70, 125 percent of the PIA.[14]

The different percentages are intended to make the benefits "actuarially fair." According to this formula, the discounted present value of the total social security benefit stream will be about equal for workers retiring at different ages. Since someone who retires at age 62 will, on average, collect social security benefits for three more years than someone retiring at age 65, the average monthly benefit is correspondingly reduced. Conversely, since someone retiring at age 70 will, on average, receive benefits for five fewer years than a worker retiring at 65, the average monthly benefits are higher.

Relative to the AIME, the PIA is redistributive. In other words, the system pays higher benefits relative to total social security contributions for lower income families than higher income ones. Computations shown in Table 15.5 indicate that low-income workers have a higher PIA relative to their AIME than middle- or high-income workers do.

A low-income worker, defined here as a person earning the minimum wage throughout working life, who retired at age 65 would receive a monthly benefit of $763.70, or 62 percent of the person's AIME, which is, roughly speaking, the person's average monthly earnings. A middle-income worker, defined as someone receiving the national average wage in each year, who retired at 65 would receive a benefit of $1,257.70, 46 percent of the person's AIME. A high-income worker, defined as someone who earned the maximum amount of wages that can be credited to the person's social security record, who retired at 65 would receive a benefit equal to only 33 percent of the person's AIME.

Another way of looking at social security benefits is in terms of what percent of the person's pre-retirement earnings the social security benefits represent or replace. Replacement rates are shown in Table 15.6 for retirement years 1940–2000, with projections made to the year 2080. It is again clear from this table that the social security benefit formula is redistributive in favor of low-income workers. Among persons retiring at age 65 in 1990, the social security benefit was equal to 52 percent of previous earnings for low-income workers, 39 percent for middle-income ones, and only 29 percent for the high earners. The social security system thus redistributes benefits

Table 15.5   Ratio of PIA to AIME for hypothetical low-, middle-, and high-income workers, 2003

	AIME ($)	*PIA ($)*	*Ratio of PIA/AIME*
Low-income worker	1,235.00	763.70	0.62
Middle-income worker	2,744.00	1,257.70	0.46
High-income worker	5,729.00	1,873.90	0.33

Source: U.S. House of Representatives (2004). Committee on Ways and Means, *Overview of Entitlement Programs: 2004 Green Book*. Washington, DC: U.S. Government Printing Office, July.

Table 15.6 Social security replacement rates, 1940–2080

Year of birth	Year attaining normal retirement age	Replacement rates		
		Low earner[a]	Average earner[b]	Maximum earner[c]
1875	1940	27.9	23.4	16.4
1885	1950	31.7	18.6	9.7
1895	1960	46.3	28.3	16.1
1905	1970	46.0	31.7	20.3
1915	1980	66.0	48.6	40.6
1925	1990	58.4	43.5	35.7
1935	2000	52.2	38.7	28.6
1944	2010[d]	55.4	41.1	28.1
1954	2020[d]	56.0	41.5	27.6
1963	2030[d]	55.3	41.0	27.3
1973	2040[d]	55.2	40.9	27.3
1983	2050[d]	55.2	41.0	27.3
1993	2060[d]	55.3	41.0	27.3
2003	2070[d]	55.2	41.0	27.3
2013	2080[d]	55.3	41.0	27.3

The replacement rate is defined as the social security benefit received at year of retirement as a percent of earnings in the year prior to retirement.

a   A worker earning 45 percent of the national average wage in each year.
b   A worker earning the average national wage in each year.
c   A worker earning the maximum taxable wage base in each year.
d   Projected by the Social Security Administration.
Source: U.S. House of Representatives (2004). Committee on Ways and Means, *Overview of Entitlement Programs: 2004 Green Book*. Washington, DC: U.S. Government Printing Office, July.

in favor of the poor, relative both to lifetime earnings and, as we saw in Section 10.4.1, relative to the social security contributions paid into the system.

Replacement rates have increased over time from the inception of the social security system through 1980. For the average retiree, the replacement rate rose from 26 percent in 1940 to 51 percent in 1980. However, replacement rates fell between 1980 and 2000 – for the average earner, from 49 to 39 percent. After 2000 and until the year 2080 at least, replacement rates are projected to stabilize at about 55 percent for low-income earners, 41 percent for average earners, and 27 percent for the high earners.

Since 1975, social security benefits have been automatically increased each year with changes in the cost of living.[15] This automatic cost-of-living adjustment, or COLA, is based on changes in the consumer price index (CPI-U). The reason for this adjustment was that poverty among the elderly was a big problem and the focus of public attention in the early 1970s as a result of the effects of inflation on real income (there were media stories about the elderly eating dog food). There was a big increase in support through social security benefit increases, which succeeded in reducing elderly poverty, though most of the funds went to people who were not in poverty.

Interestingly, since social security benefits are adjusted to keep up with inflation and real wages have been declining (see Chapter 1), social security benefits have been rising relative to real earnings. Since 1970, for example, while real earnings have fallen by 16 percent, the real value of social security benefits has been indexed upward through the COLA by 20 percent. This difference had the effect of redistributing income from the working population to retirees. Moreover, it had the somewhat perverse effect of making retirement more attractive relative to working, since retirement income is protected against inflation whereas wages are not, and this difference may induce people to retire at an earlier age.

Another provision of the social security system is the so-called *spousal benefit*. In the case when there is only one earner in a married couple, on retirement the family will receive a benefit equal to 1.5 times the amount that would normally be accorded to the retiree. In the case when both spouses worked in covered employment and subsequently retired, the family benefit is set equal to 1.5 times the amount of the higher benefit or the sum of the two social security benefits, whichever is greater.

Another provision of the original social security laws is that benefits were reduced if the retiree was still earning income at a job. The original architects of the social security law were concerned that social security benefits might not be sufficient to allow a family to attain a minimally desirable standard of living. As a result, they allowed retirees to earn outside income, usually at a part-time job, as long as the earnings did not exceed a pre-specified maximum. This was referred to as the "earnings test."

In 1994, the exempt amount was $8,040 for retirees under the age of 65 and $11,600 for retirees between 65 and 69. There was no restriction on the earnings of retirees over the age of 69. If earnings exceed the maximum, then social security benefits were reduced in proportion to the earnings above the maximum. For retirees between 62 and 64, their benefit level was reduced by one dollar for each two dollars of earnings over the exempt amount, while for retirees between 65 and 69, the benefits were reduced by one dollar for every three dollars of earnings over the exemption. However, under current law, there is now no earnings penalty for workers age 65 and over. They can earn as much as they want without losing social security benefits. However, the earnings test is still in place for workers between ages 62 and 64.

Before 1984, social security benefits were fully exempt from federal income taxation. However, beginning in 1984, a portion of the benefits became subject to taxation for high-income families. In 1984, half of the social security benefits were added to taxable income for individual taxpayers with an income of $25,000 or more and for married couples with an income of $32,000 or more. In 1994, the rules were changed so that 85 percent of social security benefits were included in taxable income for individual taxpayers with incomes of $34,000 or more and for married couples with incomes of $44,000 or more.

Another important issue concerns the fiscal viability of the so-called social security *trust fund*. Currently (as of 2008), the contribution rates and benefit formulas are set so that the total contributions received by the social security system are greater than the total benefits paid out. This surplus is accumulated in this "fictitious" trust fund. The interest on the value of the trust fund is also accumulated within the fund just like a normal investment account.

However, beginning in the year 2011, the so-called "baby boom" generation will begin to retire in large numbers. Since they are a much larger cohort than either preceding or succeeding ones, their retirement will create large financial pressures on the social security trust fund. In particular, the ratio of active workers to retirees will start to decline. It is now projected that by the year 2030 or so, the resulting social security benefits paid out by the system will start to exceed the contributions into the system. The social security trust fund will also reach a maximum value of about $7.5 trillion in or about the year 2030. After this point, the benefits paid out by the social security system will exceed the new contributions coming in and the social security trust fund will start to decline. Under current projections by the Social Security

Administration (and under current legislation), the trust fund will "run out of money" by the year 2050 or so.[16]

There are many ways to "fix the system" so that the trust fund does not become exhausted. These include modest increases in the social security contribution (tax) rate, raising the maximum taxable wage base (see Chapter 16), increasing the normal retirement age from its current legislated maximum of 67, modest lowering of social security benefits, and partial indexing of social security benefits to changes in the CPI. Changes in immigration law that favor younger workers might also help to restore balance to the social security trust fund. Moreover, even if the trust fund reaches a value of zero, this does not mean that social security benefits will terminate. Indeed, at this point benefits could be reduced to bring them in line with the current contributions into the system.

15.4.2   Incentive effects on labor supply

As might be expected, the availability of social security benefits starting at age 62 has had an important effect on the retirement behavior of older workers. A host of studies have tried to estimate the labor participation effects of various aspects of the social security system. Almost all studies have found a significant negative effect of the system as a whole on work effort.

Particular attention has focused on two aspects of the system. First, as we saw in Chapter 10, the future flow of social security benefits can be viewed as a form of wealth. Likewise, the future flow of social security contributions, in the form of a tax on future earnings, can be viewed as a liability to the worker. The difference between these two flows is the *net* value of social security wealth. In general, as a worker ages, his (her) net social security wealth increases. At some point, this *wealth effect* may discourage additional work. See, for example, Boskin (1977), Quinn (1977), Boskin and Hurd (1978), Reimers (1977), Gordon and Blinder (1980), Clark and Johnson (1980), and Burkhauser and Quinn (1983).

Danziger, Haveman, and Plotnick (1981) concluded that the social security system did induce earlier retirement and probably accounted for a 12 percentage point decline in the labor force participation of men aged 65 and older between 1950 and 1980. Since, as we saw in Chapter 7, the LFPR of this group fell by 25 percentage points over the period, rising social security eligibility and benefits would by itself explain about half of this decline. Also, see Blau (1997), Rust and Phelan (1997), Lee (1998), Anderson, Gustman, and Steinmeier (1999), Gruber and Orszag (2000), and Krueger and Meyer (2002).

Second, as we described above, there was an earnings test applied to wages and salaries received by retired workers collecting social security benefits. Once the threshold is passed, wages above this level reduced social security benefits. This may be viewed as an additional tax on labor earnings above the threshold, and this "tax" may also have discouraged work effort.[17] The existence of an earnings test appeared to reduce the work effort of workers aged 62 to 70 by about 10 percent. See, for example, the work of Pellechio (1980), and Friedberg (2000).

15.5   THE WELFARE SYSTEM

Perhaps, the most controversial and politically sensitive of the government transfer programs created by the Social Security Act of 1935 was Aid to Families with Dependent Children (AFDC), which was often referred to as "government welfare." Established in 1935, along with social security and unemployment insurance programs, it was about the same magnitude (as measured by actual expenditures) as unemployment insurance but considerably smaller than social security. Yet, despite its relatively small size, AFDC had often been singled out as a political target.

15.5.1   The Workings of AFDC and TANF

The key feature of AFDC was to provide cash assistance to children who are needy because their father or mother is absent from the home, disabled, deceased or unemployed. Eligibility in AFDC ended when the child reached the age of 18. The program was run by the individual states, which set benefit levels and established eligibility criteria within federal guidelines. Federal funds paid for a little over half of the costs of the program, with the rest contributed by the states.

The hallmark of AFDC and related programs such as food stamps is that they are **means-tested**. A family was eligible for AFDC benefits only if its income and assets fell below a predetermined threshold. The threshold was based on a "need standard." Each state was required to determine the amount of monthly income that was required to satisfy the basic needs of families of different sizes. Only families with incomes below this level could qualify for AFDC benefits.[18]

Because of the considerable political opposition to AFDC, this program was overhauled in 1996 under the Personal Responsibility and Work Opportunity Reconciliation Act (PRWORA) and replaced with a new program called Temporary Assistance to Needy Families (TANF) effective as of July 1, 1997. Under the AFDC program, no time limits were placed on welfare recipiency and a mother could stay on welfare indefinitely (as long as she had a child under the age of 18 living at home). The new program shifted the emphasis to *temporary assistance*. New time limits were imposed on the length of welfare recipiency. Under current rules, there is a maximum of 60 months of benefits within a person's lifetime (though there are some exceptions and some states issued shorter time periods). Moreover, in most states, there is a maximum of 24 months of continuous benefits.

TANF also imposes a work requirement. Recipients (with some exceptions) must work as soon as they are ready for a job or no later than two years after coming on assistance. Single parents are required to participate in work activities for at least 30 hours per week. Schooling or job training can count as a work activity in most, though not all, states. Failure to participate in work requirements can result in a reduction or termination of benefits to the family.

Another change was that the TANF program is financed through so-called block grants to individual states and individual states have much greater leeway in establishing eligibility. Under AFDC, eligibility was determined by state rules subject to overall guidelines issued by the federal government. As we shall see below, the switchover from AFDC to TANF resulted in a huge reduction in welfare caseloads.

Table 15.7 shows monthly income limits for selected states in 2003 under TANF. There was considerable variation in the income limitations. Monthly income thresholds varied from a low of $256 in Alabama to $1,993 in Alaska in 2003 (the lower the threshold the fewer the number of families who can qualify for TANF benefits). The median income limit among the 50 states was $1,011.

The asset limitation is based on the total value of all assets, excluding, in most states, the value of the home and one automobile, less the value of outstanding debt. There is relatively little variation in the asset test among states, and the threshold is typically $2,000.

The TANF benefit awarded to a qualifying family (one that meets both the income and asset limits) depends on the family size. Each state sets a maximum benefit amount for each family size. A family with no reported income receives the maximum benefit. The award is decreased as income rises, though by less than a dollar-for-dollar basis. For example, in the case of Pennsylvania in 2004, the award structure is as shown in Table 15.8.

Annual TANF benefits are reduced by $200 on the first $2,466 of income. Between $2,466 and $9,864, the award is decreased by about 65 cents for each additional dollar of income earned. Above $9,864 of income, there is no benefit.[19]

Table 15.7 Eligibility requirements and benefits for TANF in selected states, 2003

A. Family of three persons (one parent with two children)

State	Monthly income limit ($)	Maximum TANF grant ($)	Food stamp benefit ($)	Combined benefits ($)	TANF benefit as percent of 2003 poverty line	Combined benefit as percent of 2003 poverty line
Alabama	256	215	341	556	18	45
Alaska	1,933	923	234	1,157	75	95
California	1,531	679	191	870	56	71
Connecticut	1,252	636	215	851	52	70
Florida	786	303	315	618	25	51
Illinois	1,185	396	287	683	32	56
Indiana	1,112	288	319	607	24	50
Michigan	780	489	249	738	40	60
New Jersey	848	424	279	703	35	57
New York[a]	1,219	577	321	898	47	73
Ohio	976	373	294	667	30	55
Pennsylvania	822	421	279	700	34	57
Texas	1,723	201	345	546	16	45
Washington	1,072	546	242	788	45	64
Median, all states	1,011	421	283	702	35	57

B. Maximum TANF monthly benefit by family size, 2003

	1-person family ($)	2-person family ($)	3-person family ($)	4-person family ($)	5-person family ($)	6-person family ($)
Median, all states	230	330	424	495	552	619

a   New York City. Rules vary across counties.
Source: U.S. House of Representatives (2004). Committee on Ways and Means, *Overview of Entitlement Programs: 2004 Green Book*. Washington, DC: U.S. Government Printing Office, July.

Table 15.8 TANF benefit for a mother with two children by income level, Pennsylvania, 2004

Annual family income ($)	Annual TANF benefit ($)
0	5,052
2,466	4,892
4,932	3,292
6,165	2,492
7,398	1,692
8,631	892
9,864	0

Source: U.S. House of Representatives (2004). Committee on Ways and Means, *Overview of Entitlement Programs: 2004 Green Book*. Washington, DC: U.S. Government Printing Office, July.

There was also a very large variation in benefit levels among states in 2003. Table 15.7 shows the maximum TANF benefits for a family of three with no income. In 2004, this varied from a low of $201 per month in Texas to a high of $923 in Alaska (the high among the "Lower 48" was $679 in California). The median maximum monthly benefit among the 50 states was $421. It is interesting to note that the maximum benefit in almost all states is below the monthly income limit, which is supposed to represent the income required to meet the basic needs of families.

When the TANF benefit is compared to the 2003 poverty line for a family of three (fifth column), it is clear that no state provides a TANF grant sufficient to bring the family above the poverty threshold. On average, the TANF benefit was only 35 percent of the poverty threshold.[20] This ratio ranged from a low of 16 percent in Texas to a high of 75 percent in Alaska (56 percent in California among the "Lower 48").

Families receiving TANF are also automatically eligible for Medicaid and most are eligible for food stamps. Table 15.7 also shows the value of food stamps for families who receive TANF. The median value of food stamp benefits for these families among the 50 states was $283 in 2003. There was relatively little variation in the benefit among states.[21]

The fourth column shows the combined value of TANF and food stamps. This combined benefit ranged from a low of $546 in Texas to highs of $898 in New York and $1,157 in Alaska. If we count food stamps as part of family income when computing the poverty rate,[22] the combined value of TANF and food stamps in 2003 was still not sufficient to bring families over the poverty threshold in any state (column 6). Its median value was only 57 percent of the poverty threshold for a family of three in 2003.

Benefit levels also vary by family size to reflect different needs. As shown in Panel B of Table 15.7, the average monthly TANF benefit level in 2003 varied from $230 for a one-person family to $619 for a six-person family. The monthly benefit increased by about $65 for each additional family member.

Time trends are shown in Table 15.9. In 2002, a little over 2 million families (5 million individuals) were receiving TANF benefits. Between 1970 and 1975, the number of families on welfare increased by 1.36 million. From 1975 to 1990, only 0.71 million additional families were added to the welfare rolls, though the figure increased by another million between 1990 and 1993 (partly as a result of the 1992 recession). However, since the introduction of time limits and work requirements contained in the TANF program, caseloads dropped precipitously. Between 1993 and 1998, the number of families on welfare fell by 1.8 million and between 1998 and 2002 by another 1.1 million. Indeed, in 2002, the number of families collecting benefits was only 41 percent the number in 1993.

Another striking statistic is the change in the average monthly benefit level of welfare families. Though the average benefit level doubled in nominal terms between 1970 and 1993, it declined in real terms *by 45 percent*. From 1990 to 1993, it also declined in nominal terms, from $389 to $373 per month. Average benefit levels continued to decline from 1993 and 2002 not only in real terms but in nominal terms as well. The average TANF benefit in 2002 was $4,524 per year in 2005 dollars – a figure considerably below the poverty line for a single individual. In 2002, real average benefits were only 41 percent the level in 1970.

Another interesting statistic is provided by the average size of families on AFDC. This declined from 4.0 to 2.5 persons between 1970 and 2002. This trend will be relevant when we discuss the effects of AFDC and TANF on child-bearing behavior. This trend reflected, in part, behavioral responses in household formation. Research indicated that AFDC significantly increased the tendency for teen mothers to move out of their parents' households and set up their own households (see Blank, 1997). This behavior by itself would reduce average size of AFDC households.

Table 15.9 Number of beneficiaries and average monthly benefits per family from the AFDC and TANF programs, 1970–2002

Year	Number of families (1,000s)	Number of recipients (1,000s)	Average family size	Average monthly benefit per family (current $)	Average monthly benefit per family (2005 $)
1970	1,909	7,429	4.0	178	914
1975	3,269	11,067	3.2	208	778
1980	3,574	10,597	3.0	269	653
1985	3,692	10,813	3.0	329	599
1990	3,974	11,460	2.9	389	587
1993	4,981	14,144	2.9	373	504
1998	3,200	8,790	2.8	362	433
2002	2,064	5,146	2.5	348	377

Sources: U.S. House of Representatives (1994). Committee on Ways and Means, *Overview of Entitlement Programs: 1994 Green Book*. Washington, DC: U.S. Government Printing Office, July; U.S. House of Representatives (2004). Committee on Ways and Means, *Overview of Entitlement Programs: 2004 Green Book*. Washington, DC: U.S. Government Printing Office, July.

A further point of interest here is that TANF has included regulations to prevent this household formation by teens. Funds are provided only if teen moms remain with their own parent(s) unless abuse is an issue. This is a particularly interesting provision because it appears that the new TANF regulations resulted from legislators actually paying attention to the findings on household formation provided by the poverty-research community. The evidence seems to suggest that teen moms and their children are better off if they remain with the household of origin. Even more encouraging for researchers is that this TANF regulation appears to be having the desired effect of preventing the proliferation of smaller households consisting of teen moms living without the guidance of an adult family member.

15.5.2   Incentive effects of the welfare system

As noted above, the welfare system has been subject to much criticism by economists, sociologists, political scientists, the media, and public officials. A major controversy was ignited by Charles Murray in a provocative book entitled *Losing Ground*, published in 1984. He argued that the structure of the welfare system itself was in large measure responsible for the persistence of poverty in this country. Murray claimed that it has led to the development of "welfare dependency" by creating strong disincentives against working and causing a large rise in the number of female-headed households. The dismantling of AFDC and its replacement by TANF was, to some extent, an outgrowth of Murray's work.

15.5.2.1   Labor supply effects

Even before the appearance of Murray's book, considerable research had been devoted to analyzing the incentive effects of the welfare system. Much of the early work looked at the effects of the benefit structure of AFDC on labor supply. As the example for Pennsylvania illustrated in Table 15.8 demonstrates, TANF (and AFDC) benefits are reduced for each additional dollar earned from wages and salaries. This is equivalent to an implicit "tax" on earnings, or "benefit reduction rate," which can be quite substantial. In order to increase net family income by a dollar, the parent may have to earn anywhere from $1.40 to $1.80. This effect becomes magnified even more when the value of food stamps and Medicaid are included in the welfare benefit. Indeed, if additional earnings cause total family income to pass the Medicaid threshold so that the family loses that benefit, the implicit tax rate may be in excess of 100 percent.

Needless to say, almost all of these earlier empirical studies found a significant negative effect of both the AFDC benefit level and of the benefit reduction rate on labor supply (both hours of work and the LFPR). However, estimates of the magnitude of these effects did vary among studies. Danziger, Haveman, and Plotnick (1981), after surveying several major studies on the question,[23] concluded that the AFDC system probably reduced work effort among AFDC recipients by about 5 hours per week. Since AFDC recipients worked about 9 hours per week, on average, this implied about a 55 percent reduction in their work effort. Or, to put it another way, if the recipients earned the minimum wage, the extra 5 hours per week would have translated into an additional $1,000 per year (see Moffitt, 1992). This amount would have enabled only a small proportion of the AFDC families to escape poverty.

Another important implication of this literature, as reported by Moffitt (1992), was that the work disincentives of the AFDC program have had very little effect on the size of the welfare population. The empirical estimates indicated that only about 5 percent of AFDC recipients would have left the welfare rolls if the implicit tax on earnings were eliminated from the program. As Moffitt (p. 17) concluded: "Thus, the problem of 'welfare dependency' (i.e., participation in AFDC) cannot be ascribed to the work disincentives of the program."

In contrast, the work requirements and related sanctions of the TANF program appear to have increased the labor force participation of welfare recipients. Schoeni and Blank (2000), using March CPS data from 1977 through 1999, estimated that the changeover from AFDC to TANF increased the labor force participation of welfare recipients by 2 percentage points (or 3.7 percent). Grogger (2003), using March CPS data from 1978 through 1999, found that about 7 percent of the rise in employment among welfare recipients after 1993 could be traced due to the imposition of the 2-year time limit on welfare use.[24]

15.5.2.2 Welfare participation rates

A related issue is the effects of the AFDC/TANF benefit structure on both entry into and exit from the welfare rolls. Virtually all studies found that higher AFDC benefits led to higher participation rates in AFDC and lower exit rates (see, for example, Willis, 1980; Plotnick, 1983; Ellwood, 1986; Moffitt, 1986; and Blank, 1989).

One interesting tabulation of spell durations is provided by Ellwood (1986) and shown in Table 15.10. The first column of this table is based on the amount of time spent on AFDC from the time of entry to the time of first exit. This is referred to as the "duration of a single spell" of AFDC participation. The figures in the column show the percent of total AFDC recipients classified according to the duration of their spell. The numbers indicate that 27 percent of AFDC recipients left the AFDC rolls within 1 year, 47 percent leave within 2 years, and 70 percent leave within 4 years. However, 10 percent of AFDC recipients remained on the rolls for 10 or more years.

Since a person can leave the AFDC rolls and then return, the second column shows the total time spent by AFDC recipients over a fixed time length – in this case, 25 years. Here, it is clear, that many families leave AFDC only to return at a later date (this is also referred to as "recidivism"). The figures indicate that 16 percent of AFDC recipients were on the welfare rolls for less than 1 year over this 25-year period, and half were on welfare for 4 years or less. However, the disturbing finding is that almost one-quarter (23.4 percent) spent at least 10 of the 25 years on welfare.[25]

These figures indicate that the exit rate fell the longer the length of time spent on AFDC. In other words, the probability of leaving welfare decreased the more time a person was on the

Table 15.10   Percentage distribution of AFDC recipients by amount of time spent on AFDC

Amount of time on AFDC	Duration of single spell	Total time spent on AFDC over a 25-year period[a]
1 year	27.0	15.7
2 years	20.4	14.1
3 years	10.0	9.4
4 years	12.3	10.9
5 years	2.4	5.1
6 years	8.9	8.3
7 years	4.9	5.9
8 years	2.1	3.8
9 years	1.8	3.3
10 or more years	10.2	23.5
Total	100.0	100.0

a   Includes all spells of AFDC participation over the period.
Source: Ellwood, D. (1986). *Targeting "Would-Be" Long-Term Recipients of AFDC*. Princeton, NJ: Mathematica Policy Research. Calculations are made for women who entered the AFDC rolls during the period 1971–1982.

AFDC rolls. This phenomenon may have arisen from the fact that spending time on AFDC itself caused individuals to lose their incentive or motivation to leave the welfare system. However, it may also have arisen because an individual's human capital may have deteriorated while they were not working (see Chapter 8), because employers were less likely to hire someone who had spent considerable time on AFDC ("employer aversion"), or because long-term "stayers" on welfare had multiple barriers to self-sufficiency (see, for example, Danziger *et al.*, 2000, for a discussion of the "multiple barriers" hypothesis).[26]

In contrast, under TANF, the time limits imposed on benefit receipt resulted in a significant reduction in caseloads. Ribar, Edelhoch, and Liu (2008), using data from South Carolina from 1996 to 2003, which limited most families to 2 years of benefits in any 10-year period, found a significant number of welfare beneficiaries who exhausted their eligibility after the 2-year time limit. They estimated that the 2-year time limit resulted in about a 20 percent reduction in welfare caseloads. Grogger (2003), using March CPS data from 1978 through 1999, estimated that about 12 percent of the decline in welfare participation was due to the imposition of the 2-year time limit on welfare use. In contrast, Grogger, Haider, and Klerman (2003), using the Survey of Income and Program Participation from 1986 to 1999, found that fully half of the decline of caseloads from the inception of TANF could be traced to a decline of new entries onto welfare. This, in turn, was likely due to the stringency of the new TANF rules in comparison to AFDC. Moffitt (2003a), using data from a study of welfare families in Boston, Chicago, and San Antonio from 1999 to 2001, found that the new work requirements of TANF together with the new sanctions imposed by the program played a large role in explaining the increase of exits and the decline in entries into TANF over this period.

15.5.2.3   *Marital status and child bearing*

Perhaps, the most controversial indictment of the original AFDC welfare system was that it induced single women to have babies, unmarried mothers to remain unmarried, and mothers on the welfare rolls to have more children.

However, the basic time-series evidence on female headship would appear to contradict this hypothesis. As we saw in Chapter 13, there has been a steady growth in the percent of families headed by a female since 1960. However, while real welfare benefits grew from 1960 to the mid-1970s, there has been a steady deterioration of the real value of these benefits since the mid-1970s. Despite this, the rate of increase of female-headed families, if anything, accelerated after the mid-1970s rather than slowed down. The same is true for the illegitimacy rate, particularly among nonwhites. The percent of children born to unmarried black women actually increased faster after 1975 than before. The surface evidence does not appear to support this particular criticism of the welfare system.

The econometric studies generally found some evidence that both participation in AFDC/TANF and higher welfare benefits increased the probability of female headship and lowered the probability of marriage or remarriage (see, for example, Ellwood & Bane, 1985; Hoffman & Duncan, 1988; Hutchens, Jakubson, & Schwartz, 1989; Moffitt, 1990; Schoeni & Blank, 2000; Bitler, Gelbach, & Hoynes, 2002; and Moffitt, 2003b). However, the effects were not large enough to explain more than a small part of the growth in the number of female-headed families. AFDC/TANF seemed to have little effect on the likelihood that a married woman would become divorced in order to collect benefits (see Hoffman & Duncan, 1995, and Schoeni & Blank, 2000). The evidence of the effects of the welfare system on the illegitimacy rate was very mixed (see, for example, Plotnick, 1990; Lundberg & Plotnick, 1990; An, Haveman, & Wolfe, 1993; and Grogger & Bronars, 2001).

15.5.2.4   Other issues

Another controversial issue is that because of the wide variation of welfare benefits across states (even after adjusting for differences in the cost of living), the welfare system induces poor people to migrate to states which pay the best benefits. As might be expected, the argument would be based on the difference in welfare benefits between the current state of residence and prospective states. Thus, poor people from Alabama would be more likely to migrate to the north than poor people from Florida (see Table 15.7).

The statistical work confirmed the effects of welfare benefits on both residential location and migration patterns for low-income families. Female-headed households were found to have higher mobility rates from low-benefit states to high-benefit states than the reverse (Gramlich & Laren, 1984); were more likely to move to a high-benefit state (Blank, 1988); and were more likely to move out of a low-benefit states (Clark, 1990). However, here again, the effects were not very large in relation to the overall change in welfare rolls by state.

Another concern expressed by critics of the welfare system is that the system may induce welfare dependency across generations. In particular, daughters of mothers on welfare may be more likely to wind up on welfare when they are of age than daughters of nonwelfare mothers. The studies that examined this issue have used panel data (that is, a dataset that has followed a sample of families over time and that shows the connections between adults in one family unit and their parents in another family unit). These studies correlated the incidence of welfare recipiency in the parental unit with the later welfare incidence of the children in the family.

The earlier results showed consistent evidence that daughters from welfare families were much more likely to receive welfare themselves at a later date than those of nonwelfare parents, though sons are not (see, for example, McLanahan, 1988; Antel, 1988; and Gottschalk, 1990). Unfortunately, as Moffitt (1992) noted, these studies did not systematically control for other characteristics that might affect the poverty status of the daughters, such as the educational attainment of the parents. As a result, it was not clear that the welfare status of the parents was causally related to the welfare status of the daughter. In fact, the later literature indicated that once childhood poverty is controlled for, welfare daughters were no more likely to become welfare adults than poor daughters not raised on welfare (see Blank, 1997, for a review of this literature).

15.6   WORK PROGRAMS

The current welfare system, TANF, as discussed above has a work requirement for eligibility. The current system requires beneficiaries to obtain a job, to work in a government program, or to obtain training.

Despite the apparent novelty of this approach, there has been a long history of job and training programs attached to the AFDC system. The first major effort was the creation of a public jobs program called the Works Progress Administration (WPA) in 1935. This grew out of the unemployment crisis of the Great Depression and was instituted in order to alleviate unemployment. It was a massive job creation program and during its peak year, 1936, it employed more than 3 million workers. This program ended in 1943.

For the next 20 years or so there were no new formal programs enacted by the government to intervene directly in the labor market. However, in 1962, the Manpower Development and Training Act (MDTA) was created to provide vocational and on-the-job training for workers displaced by technological change. This program was principally targeted at unemployed male heads of household.

During the mid-1960s, a host of new job employment and training programs were created by the federal government in connection with the War on Poverty. These included the Job Corps, Neighborhood Youth Corps, Concentrated Employment Program, and Work Incentive Program, and they were targeted at welfare recipients, low-income youths, minorities, the elderly, and other disadvantaged groups. Motivated largely by human capital theory, their principal objective was to provide training (both on-the-job and in the classroom) and work experience with the stated intention of increasing the long-term employability and earnings of these groups.

In 1973, the Comprehensive Employment and Training Act (CETA) was passed, which consolidated many of the disparate programs of the 1960s. Its principal objective was also to provide training and work experience for disadvantaged groups. In addition, it provided public service jobs for depressed areas of the country. This program was well funded and also provided considerable experimentation with different forms of labor market intervention. In 1982, CETA was effectively replaced by the Job Training Partnership Act (JTPA). This program discontinued public service jobs and emphasized, instead, training for the disadvantaged population. This program was discontinued in 2000 and effectively replaced by the Workforce Investment Act of 1998 (WIA), which is still in place as of 2008.

The goal of the WIA was to fold JTPA and other employment and training and work-welfare programs into a single system designed to manage and develop the nation's human resources. Under WIA, each state may design its own employment and training program under guidelines provided by the federal government. Like JTPA, this program is primarily geared toward helping the economically disadvantaged (low-income) population to acquire necessary job training skills.

Several job programs have been targeted directly at welfare recipients. The first of these programs was the Work Incentive (WIN) program for AFDC recipients, established in 1968. Under this program, welfare recipients were referred by their welfare office to training or work programs operated by the state. The WIN program provided for on-the-job training, institutional and work experience training, and publicly provided work projects.

The passage of the Family Support Act of 1988 created the Job Opportunities and Basic Skills Training (JOBS) program, which supplanted the WIN program. Every state was required to have a JOBS program. The JOBS program required parents on AFDC whose youngest child was 3 years or older to enroll in a training or educational program. The purpose of the program was to provide welfare recipients with the tools to eventually leave the welfare rolls. The Family Support Act also required that states provide child care if it was decided that it was necessary for an individual's employment or participation in the JOBS program (though the Act failed to provide any extra funding for the mandated child care). However, despite these provisions, the JOBS program covered only a small percentage of the welfare caseload.

15.6.1   Effectiveness of the work programs

There are several underlying rationales for the various work programs that have been instituted. First, the training and educational programs have been geared to increasing the human capital of the participants. In principle, this should lead to long-term improvement in both their employability and their lifetime earnings. Second, public employment programs such as the WPA were implemented as a counter-cyclical measure to provide jobs to unemployed workers and keep them off the unemployment rolls. Third, the public service jobs programs were also designed, in part, with the belief that giving out-of-work individuals work experience would increase their attractiveness to private sector employers and thus provide them with more permanent jobs.

Fourth, requirements on welfare recipients to participate in a jobs program were implemented, in part, to reduce the welfare caseload. In this regard, as Moffitt (1992) noted, there were two offsetting effects. On the one hand, it was true that providing training and job experience to welfare recipients would increase their future employability and thus tend to reduce their time on the welfare rolls. On the other hand, the availability of a training or employment program attached to AFDC or TANF would make the welfare program more attractive and thus might draw more women onto the welfare rolls. *A priori*, it is not possible to say which effect would dominate.

Most of the statistical work on work programs concentrated on their effect on the long-term earnings of their participants. These studies attempted to compare the labor market success of individuals who "graduated" from these programs with a comparable group of individuals who were not enrolled in the programs. As Moffitt (1992) noted, there was a danger in this procedure that it might not be possible to find such a comparable control group. For example, participants in a program might be selected on the basis of their future employability in the first place. It was likely that the more able members of the eligible pool enrolled in training programs, so that the effectiveness of these programs could be overstated.

Even with this caution in mind, the evidence seemed to support overwhelmingly the success of these various training programs. A study by Ketron Inc. (1980) found that participants in WIN in 1974–1975 had higher earnings after 2 years than comparable nonparticipants. Similar result were reported by Bassi (1983) and Bassi *et al.* (1984) for AFDC recipients who were enrolled in CETA between 1976 and 1979; and by Hollister, Kemper, and Maynard (1984) and Grossman, Maynard, and Roberts (1985) for AFDC recipients who participated in various Work Support (WS) programs between 1977 and 1981. Similar effects were found for other governmental jobs programs (see, Moffitt, 1992; Lalonde, 2003; and Greenberg, Michalopoulos, & Robins, 2003, for more details).

These results might come as some surprise to the student, since the conventional wisdom has been that job training and employment programs have been notably ineffective in increasing employment or earnings. The evidence shows the opposite. However, the magnitude of the effect is not that large. Most results showed that annual earnings rose by between $500 and $1,000 from participation in these programs. This amount was not nearly enough to have had much effect on the poverty rate and AFDC or TANF participation rate among female heads.

15.7   THE MINIMUM WAGE

Another important piece of legislation that impacts directly on the low-income population is the minimum wage. The federal minimum wage was set up by the Fair Labor Standards Act of 1938.[27] Its purpose was to ensure that workers were paid a "living wage." The legislators of that time felt that market forces alone might not be sufficient to cause the market wage to reach a level that would provide a minimal subsistence standard of living to workers.

Figure 15.3 illustrates why this might be so. We have used the standard supply and demand schedules for labor derived for competitive product and labor markets. Without a minimum wage, the equilibrium employment for unskilled labor is L_e and the corresponding equilibrium wage is w_e. Suppose now that we impose a minimum wage of w_m, which is greater than the prevailing market wage. The equilibrium point now moves from A to B. The effect is to raise the wage of the unskilled workers to w_m. However, their employment also changes, falling to L_m. At the minimum wage w_m, there is now a surplus of unskilled workers, measured by the horizontal distance between points B and C. The minimum wage has thereby induced unemployment of workers to occur.

In contrast, if the minimum wage is set at $w_{m'}$, below the prevailing wage w_e, there is no effect on the labor market. The equilibrium wage remains at w_e, while equilibrium employment remains at L_e.

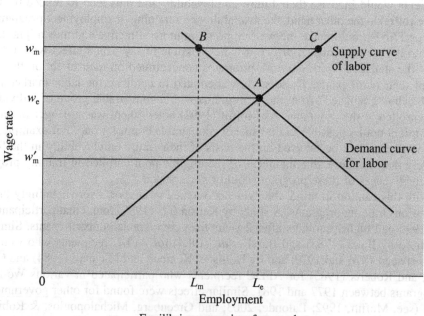

w_e – Equilibrium wage in a free market
w_m – Minimum wage (first alternative)
w_m' – Minimum wage (second alternative)
L_e – Equilibrium employment in a free market
L_m – Employment level with minimum wage w_m

Figure 15.3 Supply and demand curves for labor in competitive product and labor markets with a minimum wage

Most of the literature on the minimum wage has been concerned with its effects on employment and unemployment. The principal argument against the minimum wage is that it reduces the number of job opportunities and thereby decreases employment. Unskilled workers who remain at work do see their earnings increase, but this occurs at the expense of other unskilled workers who become unemployed. It is this trade-off that has occupied most of the policy discussion of the minimum wage.

As shown in Table 15.11, the minimum wage was set at $0.25 per hour in 1938, which was 40 percent of the average hourly earnings of production workers in that year. The federal law covered only workers engaged in interstate commerce or in the production of goods for interstate commerce. In essence, the law applied mainly to manufacturing and mining at its inception and covered less than half of all nonsupervisory workers.

Over time, the minimum wage has gradually increased and the coverage of the law extended to more and more workers. Table 15.11 shows the years in which the minimum wage was changed. The minimum wage has been raised over time on a rather sporadic basis. In real terms, the minimum increased between 1938 and 1968, when it peaked at $4.80 in 1983 dollars, almost three

Table 15.11 Minimum wage in current and constant prices and ratio of minimum wage to average hourly earnings, 1938–2009

Year	Minimum wage (current $)	Minimum wage (2005 $)	Ratio of minimum wage to average hourly earnings[a]
1938	0.25	3.47	0.40
1939	0.30	4.24	0.48
1945	0.40	4.35	0.39
1950	0.75	6.10	0.52
1956	1.00	7.22	0.51
1961	1.15	7.55	0.50
1963	1.25	8.00	0.51
1967	1.40	8.22	0.49
1968	1.60	9.02	0.53
1974	2.00	7.96	0.45
1975	2.10	7.65	0.43
1976	2.30	7.92	0.44
1978	2.65	7.96	0.43
1979	2.90	7.82	0.43
1980	3.10	7.37	0.43
1981	3.55	7.67	0.44
1987	3.55	6.14	0.36
1991	4.25	6.12	0.38
1996	4.75	5.91	0.37
1997	5.15	6.27	0.39
2007	5.85	—	—
2008[b]	6.55	—	—
2009[b]	7.25	—	—

a   Earnings are for production workers in manufacturing.
b   Scheduled as of November 2007.
Source: *Social Security Bulletin*, Annual Statistical Supplements, 1994 and 2007. Figures are for the *federal* minimum wage only.

times its original level in 1938. However, since that time, the minimum wage has eroded in real terms, particularly since 1981. In 1991, it was raised to $4.25, but this was almost identical to the 1987 level in real terms. It was increased in 1997 to $5.15 in nominal terms or $6.27 in 2005 dollars, a little higher than it was in 1987. By the most recent legislation, the minimum wage was raised to $5.85 in 2007 and scheduled to go up to $7.25 in 2009. Still, by 2009, the real minimum wage will be a lot lower than its peak value in 1968. The "collapse" of the minimum wage is one factor often cited in explaining the decline in the average real wage and the rise in poverty among working families.

Another way of looking at the minimum wage is in relation to the average hourly earnings of production workers. In 1938, it was set at 40 percent of average hourly earnings, and this gradually increased over time to 53 percent by 1968. Since that time, this ratio has also fallen, particularly since 1981. In 1987, the minimum wage stood at 36 percent of average earnings. Since that time, the ratio rose slightly to 39 percent in 1997.[28]

Coverage of workers has also widened over time. In 1961, the minimum wage was extended to employees in large retail and service trades, as well as local transit, construction, and gasoline stations. The 1966 amendments to the Fair Labor Standards Act further extended coverage to state and local government employees, small service establishments, such as restaurants and hotels, and, most notably, to agriculture. By 2005, about 90 percent of nonsupervisory workers were covered by the minimum wage.

Most of the empirical literature on the subject has failed to find much of an effect of the minimum wage on employment. As summarized in a lengthy review article by Brown, Gilroy, and Cohen (1982), the major effect of the minimum wage was on teenage employment. However, studies typically find that an increase in the minimum wage of 10 percent reduced teenage employment by only 1 to 3 percent (also see Brown, 1988; Wellington, 1991; Katz & Krueger, 1992; Card, 1992a, 1992b). The effect of the minimum wage on young adults (ages 20 to 24) was also negative but even smaller in magnitude than for teenagers (also, see Neumark & Wascher, 1992). Very little effect of changes in the minimum wage was found on adult employment overall, though in a few low-wage industries such as clothing and textiles, the effects were negative but still relatively small. However, it should be noted that most of these studies considered only relatively small changes in the minimum wage. A large change might induce considerable unemployment of low-skill workers.

An important study by Card and Krueger (1994), using a natural experiment methodology, examined the responses of firms on both sides of the New Jersey–Pennsylvania state border before and after the imposition of New Jersey's 1992 minimum wage increase. Card and Krueger focused their analysis on fast-food restaurants because these would be the most heavily affected by the minimum wage. By conducting a phone survey of a sample of over 400 establishments, Card and Krueger concluded that the increase in the New Jersey minimum wage did not lead to any measurable negative effect on employment but actually pointed to a slight positive effect on fast-food employment.

These results were challenged by Neumark and Wascher (2000). Using actual payroll records from restaurants, they reached the conclusion that the New Jersey minimum wage increase had a statistically significant negative employment effect (with an elasticity of −0.21 to −0.22). In response, Card and Krueger (2000) expanded their original research to include analysis of ES-202 data from the federal Bureau of Labor Statistics. These data are employer provided and collected by state employment security agencies for unemployment insurance tax purposes and, as such, represent a virtual census of employment. Using these data, Card and Krueger (2000) confirmed their earlier results that the minimum wage increase in New Jersey had no statistically significant effect on employment in the fast-food industry.

However, Neumark and Wascher (2006), in an extensive review of this literature both for the United States and other countries, concluded that there was a wide range of existing estimates and, as a result, a lack of consensus about the overall effects on low-wage employment of an increase in the minimum wage. The assertion that recent research failed to support the traditional view that the minimum wage reduced the employment of low-wage workers was clearly incorrect. A sizable majority of the studies surveyed gave a relatively consistent (although not always statistically significant) indication of negative employment effects of minimum wages. They also noted that very few studies provided convincing evidence of positive employment effects of minimum wages, especially those studies that focused on the broader groups (rather than a narrow industry) for which the competitive model predicts disemployment effects. Second, the studies that focused on the least-skilled groups provided almost overwhelming evidence of stronger disemployment effects for these groups.

Interestingly, there is little evidence that changes in the minimum wage affected overall family income inequality. The reason is that there is a weak relationship between low-wage workers and membership in low-income families, because many of the low-wage workers are teenagers or wives who work at secondary jobs in order to augment the income of the primary earner in the family (see Gramlich, 1976). A simulation analysis conducted by Johnson and Browning (1983) reached a similar conclusion. They simulated the effects of a 22 percent increase in the minimum wage under the (favorable) assumption that there was no loss of employment from the increase and computed that the average income of the bottom fifth of the income distribution would increase by only 1 percent. As a result, changes in the minimum wage have relatively little effect on the inequality of overall family income. Similar results were reported by Neumark, Schweitzer, and Wascher (2000, 2005).

15.8   CONCLUSION AND OVERALL ASSESSMENT OF GOVERNMENT PROGRAMS

Today over half of the poor are found in female-headed households. Children also have a very high poverty incidence, because many of them live in single-parent households. The aged population, on the other hand, has experienced a very sharp decline in their poverty rate. Poverty rates are also very high among nonworking families. However, almost half of poor families consist of the working poor. One reason is that members of the household may work only part time or part year. However, another reason is that family members may be earning low wages because they have minimal skills and low education, experience discrimination, or are employed in seasonal or service industries.

Spending on the major federal income transfer programs increased from 3 percent of GDP in 1960 to 11 percent in 2005. Outlays on these programs grew by 4.5 percent per year in real terms between 1970 and 2005. In 2005, public outlays on the major federal income transfer programs amounted to $1.4 trillion, or 11 percent of GDP. The major program in 2005 was, by far, the social security system (OASDI), with outlays of $513 billion. Medicare was the second largest, at $333 billion. Thus, public spending on the elderly from OASDHI amounted to $845 billion, or 60 percent of the total for the major federal income support programs. The other social insurance programs were, correspondingly, much smaller in value – unemployment insurance at 2 percent, workers' compensation at 4 percent, and veteran's disability compensation at 2 percent.

Public spending on the public assistance programs amounted to 32 percent of total social welfare spending in 2005. Much more money was spent on in-kind welfare benefits than cash benefits. Outlays on Medicaid alone amounted to $304 billion, or 22 percent of total public expenditures on federal transfer programs. Food stamps and housing assistance each constituted between 2 and 3 percent of total spending on the federal income support programs. Spending on the two cash benefit programs, TANF and SSI, was $74 billion, 5 percent of the total.

15.8.1 Effects on poverty

How effective has the government income support system been? One way of assessing this issue is to determine the extent to which the income transfer system has alleviated poverty. It should be noted at the outset that these estimates are based on computing family income with and without transfer income. There are no behavioral assumptions built into the analysis – for example, modeling how the family might change its labor market behavior in the absence of transfer payments. As a result, some caution must be used in interpreting these figures.

Panel A of Table 15.12 reports estimates that were prepared by Haveman (1988) on the effects of transfer income on the poverty rate. The first column provides the actual poverty rate for individuals in selected years between 1949 and 1983. For the second column, Haveman excluded reported transfer income from family income and recomputed the poverty rate on the basis of

Table 15.12   Effects of the government transfer system on poverty, 1949–2005

A. Effects on poverty, 1949–1983[a]

Year	Actual poverty rate (percent)	Pre-transfer poverty rate (percent)	Percentage point reduction in poverty due to government transfers
1949	41	44	3
1959	22	27	5
1969	12	18	6
1979	12	21	9
1983	15	24	9

B. Effects on poverty, 1979–2005[b]

Poverty rate (percent)	1979	1989	1992	2005
Actual poverty rate	11.7	12.8	14.5	12.6
Cash income before transfers	19.2	19.9	22.5	20.3
Plus social insurance (other than social security)	18.3	19.3	21.4	19.2
Plus social security	12.8	13.8	15.6	13.3
Plus means-tested cash transfers	11.7	12.8	14.5	12.6
Plus food and housing benefits	9.7	11.2	12.9	11.8
Less federal taxes[c]	10.0	11.8	13.0	11.1
Total reduction in the poverty rate	9.2	9.2	9.5	9.2

a *Source*: Haveman, R. (1988). *Starting Even: An Equal Opportunity Program to Combat the Nation's New Poverty*. New York: Simon and Schuster. Transfers include only government cash benefits.
b *Sources*: U.S. House of Representatives (1994). Committee on Ways and Means, *Overview of Entitlement Programs: 1994 Green Book*. Washington, DC: U.S. Government Printing Office, July; U.S. Census Bureau, Current Population Reports: http://pubdb3.census.gov/macro/032006/rdcall/2_000.htm.
c Includes federal Earned Income Tax Credit.

this new (smaller) family income. The difference between the two poverty rates gives an indication of the effect of transfer payments on poverty.

In 1949, the poverty rate was (a shocking!) 41 percent. If transfer income were excluded (that is, if we use pre-transfer income), the poverty rate would have been 44 percent – still very high but not much higher than the actual rate. In 1949, government transfers were still quite small. By 1959, pre-transfer poverty had fallen to 27 percent. If we include transfer income, the poverty rate fell still more, to 22 percent, or a 5 percentage point reduction. This larger reduction in the poverty rate reflects the growth in transfer payments during the 1950s.

A slightly larger reduction in the poverty rate from transfer payments was evident in 1969, a reflection of the beginnings of the War on Poverty. In this year, transfer income reduced the poverty rate by 6 percentage points. During the 1970s, pre-transfer poverty rose, from 18 to 21 percent. This reflected, in part, the growth in income inequality and the changing composition of poverty toward female-headed households, who had a much weaker labor force attachment than married couples. Yet, the post-transfer (actual) poverty rate remained unchanged at 12 percent. Indeed, in 1979, transfer income reduced the poverty rate by 9 percentage points. This was due to the continued growth in the transfer programs during the 1970s.

Pre-transfer poverty continued to rise during the early 1980s, from 21 percent in 1979 to 24 percent in 1983. However, the poverty-reducing effects of the transfer system remained unchanged, causing the poverty rate to fall by 9 percentage points again in 1983.

Panel B of Table 15.12 shows a similar set of statistics for 1979, 1989, 1992, and 2005. In addition, the effects of each of the major transfer programs on poverty are now isolated. In 2005, the actual (official) poverty rate among all individuals was 12.6 percent. Without any income transfers, the poverty rate would have been much higher, 20.3 percent. If we add in the cash benefits of unemployment insurance, workers' compensation, and other social insurance programs except social security, the poverty rate would fall only slightly, to 19.2 percent. If we next include social security benefits, the poverty rate would then fall quite considerably, to 13.3 percent. Adding means-tested cash transfers such as SSI and TANF caused only a further modest drop in the poverty rate, to 12.6 percent (equal to the official rate). If we next add in the value of food stamps and housing assistance to total family money income, the poverty rate would decline even further, to 11.8 percent. Finally, subtracting federal taxes from family income would have resulted in a modest further decline in the poverty rate to 11.1 percent. The fact that the poverty rate declined after taxes reflects the addition of the Earned Income Tax Credit (EITC) to the incomes of low-income families. This program provides supplementary wages to low-income families that qualify for the credit.[29]

All told, the transfer programs (including the effects of federal taxes) caused a 9.2 percentage point drop in the poverty rate in 2005. The largest effect comes from the social security system, which by itself reduced the poverty rate by 5.9 percentage points (63 percent of the total reduction). Public assistance (cash transfers, food benefits, and housing assistance) resulted in another 1.5 percentage point decline (17 percent of the total reduction).

The anti-poverty effect of the government transfer system was virtually unchanged between 1979 and 2005. The overall reduction in poverty from these programs was 9.2 percentage points in 1979, 1989, and 2005, and 9.5 percentage points in 1992 (the slight increase was mainly due to changes in federal income taxes).

How effective has the income transfer system been in reducing poverty? Without this "safety net," poverty rates would have been 50 to 70 percent higher during the 1980s, 1990s, and 2000s.[30] For the elderly, in particular, the poverty rate would have been *four to five times higher* without the income transfers (in 1992, for example, the pre-transfer poverty rate was 57.0 percent, compared to an actual poverty rate of 12.9 percent). For female-headed households, poverty rates would have been about 12 to 13 percentage points higher.

Unfortunately, given the continued growth of income transfers during the 1980s, 1990s, and 2000s both in real terms and as a percent of GDP, it is somewhat disappointing that their anti-poverty effects did not increase. As noted above, their poverty reduction effect remained virtually unchanged between 1979 and 2005. This trend was in large part due to the shift in the composition of the poor toward female-headed households, who rely heavily on AFDC/TANF and other forms of public assistance. This group was particularly hurt by the fact that average AFDC/TANF monthly benefits were declining in real terms since the late 1970s.

15.8.2   Proposals for reform

Each of the major federal income support programs has been the subject of lively (indeed, even acrimonious) debate over the years about how to reform the program. With regard to unemployment insurance, one of the chief problems is that the coverage rate (the percent of unemployed persons actually receiving UI benefits) has remained quite low since 1980. The coverage rate has been as low as one-third, and in 2005 was still only 40 percent. The main reason for this decline in coverage was an increase in the average duration of unemployment, so that a higher percent of the unemployed exhausted their benefits after 26 weeks. Another problem with the UI system is that new entrants into the labor force, who are not covered by UI, have also been experiencing longer spells of unemployment before finding a job. A common proposal for reform is to extend UI coverage to a full year for workers who have lost a job, and provide limited UI coverage for new entrants to the labor force. It should be noted that many European countries provide full unemployment benefits to new entrants.[31]

Social security reform has focused on the likely shortfall in social security revenue to cover the benefits of "baby-boom" workers who will begin to retire in the year 2010 or so. By the year 2025, the number of retired persons per worker will be greatly increased from its current level. Another problem with the social security system is that it is an uncomfortable mixture of a pension system and an entitlement program. Should it function as a pension system, providing higher benefits to those who contribute more into the system, or should it remain largely an entitlement program, providing retirement benefits mainly in proportion to need? Both problems are related.

Most proposals for reform have focused on the benefit structure, since social security tax rates were already substantially increased during the 1970s and 1980s (see Chapter 16). One proposal, currently in effect, is to extend the normal retirement age from 65 to 67. At age 67, the individual would receive 100 percent of his or her PIA, instead of at age 66, as the rules are currently structured (as of 2008). According to current legislation, the normal retirement age will increase to 67 by the year 2022. Proposals call for accelerating this change.

Another set of proposals calls for social security benefits to be treated as a means-tested benefit. Currently, both high-income and low-income retirees collect social security benefits, and the formula for the benefit depends only on their earnings history. As of 2007, the only difference in treatment of high-income retirees is that 85 percent of their social security income is treated as taxable income and hence subject to income tax. Some have proposed that the social security benefit should also depend on the retiree's other income, such as private pension income and property income, and that the benefit be reduced in stepwise fashion with the person's total income (in much the same way as TANF benefits are determined). This method would significantly reduce the total benefits paid out by the social security system. However, it would represent a major change in the rationale for the social security system, in that it would be viewed as public assistance program rather than as a pension scheme.

Perhaps, the most volatile focus of reform is the welfare system. Some have adopted the extreme position that the welfare system should be entirely dismantled. However, as noted above, the primary objective of welfare programs such as TANF is to ensure the well-being of children, irrespective of the merits of providing income support to "unworthy" parents.

In 1996, as discussed above, the welfare system was overhauled by Congress and the Clinton administration. During the debate over the system, Clinton proposed that greater resources be put into expanding the training, educational, and work programs for welfare mothers. (This proposed transition was termed a change from welfare to "workfare.") The proposal would also increase the amount of child care available for single parents to better enable them to participate in the training or work programs. The benefit structure would be modified to reduce the "earnings tax" on welfare benefits from increased labor earnings. Moreover, Medicaid benefits would be continued even if total family income exceeds the legal minimum.

The Republicans, in contrast, proposed imposing a limit on the length of time on welfare – 2 years in most cases. Welfare recipients would be required to enroll in training programs or have a job. Some extreme proposals called for eliminating welfare payments to unmarried teenage mothers and disallowing extra payments for additional births to mothers currently on welfare.

With regard to single mothers on welfare, both the Democrats and the Republicans put increasing emphasis on the role of the absentee father. Many of these single-parent households did not receive any financial assistance from the absent parent, which greatly increased the likelihood that the family would fall into poverty. The Family Support Act of 1988 required welfare applicants to reveal the name of the absent parent in order to qualify for government assistance. The aim was to shift part of the financial responsibilities for child rearing back to the absent parent and thus reduce government transfers. So far, these new requirements have failed to make much of a dent in the welfare roles. As a result, both political parties proposed that greater enforcement be used to increase the amount of child support provided by the father. For example, fathers who failed to make child support payments would have a portion of their earnings withheld by the federal government. However, these provisions were limited by the earnings capacity of the absentee fathers – many of whom were out of work or received wages that were too low to provide much in the way of child support.

The result of this debate, as we saw, was the passage of PRWORA. This was a compromise, which incorporated both the Clinton administration's proposal for training, educational, and work programs and the Republicans' insistence on time limits for welfare benefits. The upshot of this new program was a drastic reduction in the welfare caseload. Moreover, many former welfare mothers did obtain jobs. The bad news is that there was no further reduction in poverty rates among female-headed families and very little change in their median income.

The minimum wage is another policy issue that has received considerable attention during the 2000s. As noted above, the minimum wage was raised to $5.85 in 2007 and is scheduled to rise to $7.25 in 2009. Still, despite this latest increase, the main concern is that the minimum wage has dramatically declined in real terms, particularly since the late 1960s. Among other effects, this has greatly increased the number of full-time working families with incomes below the poverty line. One proposal is to keep the minimum wage constant in real terms (that is, indexed for inflation); another is to peg the minimum wage as a fixed percentage of the average hourly earnings of production workers. Both proposals would maintain the real earnings of low-income workers. However, such an increase of the minimum wage in 2007 (of the order of 50 percent!) might have serious dislocation consequences for the employment of low-skill workers.

On the other side of the spectrum, some economists have argued that the minimum wage should be completely abolished. Their argument is that the minimum wage may make it more difficult for a person with relatively little education or training to find a job and gain experience and human capital through on-the-job training and eventually escape poverty. This issue may be particularly germane to welfare mothers who lack work experience. One compromise is to have a subminimum wage for teenagers (set at, perhaps, 60 or 80 percent of the adult level). This might, at least, give young workers a better opportunity to acquire the necessary workplace skills to eventually move into well-paying jobs in the primary labor market.

15.9   REFERENCES AND BIBLIOGRAPHY

General

Barr, N. (1992). Economic theory and the welfare state: A survey and interpretation. *Journal of Economic Literature*, **30**, 741–803.

Blank, R.M. (1997). *It Takes a Nation*. Princeton, NJ: Princeton University Press.

Blank, R.M. (2000a). Fighting poverty: Lessons from recent U.S. history. *Journal of Economic Perspectives*, **14**(2), 3–19.

Caminada, K. & Goudsward, K. (2001). International trends in income inequality and social policy. *International Tax and Public Finance*, **8**, 395–415.

Danziger, S., Haveman, R. & Plotnick, R. (1981). How income transfer programs affect work, savings, and the income distribution: A critical review. *Journal of Economic Literature*, **19**, 975–1028.

Danziger, S. & Plotnick, R. (1977). Demographic change, government transfers, and income distribution. *Monthly Labor Review*, **51**(1), 7–11.

Engelhardt, G. & Gruber, J. (2004). Social security and the evolution of elderly poverty. NBER Working Paper No. 10466, May.

Gottschalk, P. & Danziger, S. (1985). A framework for evaluating the effects of economic growth and transfers on poverty. *American Economic Review*, **75**(1), 153–61.

Grogger, J. & Karoly, L.A. (2005). *Welfare Reform: Effects of a Decade of Change*. Cambridge, MA: Harvard University Press.

Harrington, M. (1962). *The Other America*, Revised Edition. New York: Macmillan.

Haveman, R. (1987). *Poverty Policy and Poverty Research: The Great Society and the Social Sciences*. Madison, WI: University of Wisconsin Press.

Haveman, R. (1988). *Starting Even: An Equal Opportunity Program to Combat the Nation's New Poverty*. New York: Simon and Schuster.

Jencks, C. (1992). *Rethinking Social Policy: Race, Poverty, and the Underclass*. Cambridge, MA: Harvard University Press.

Lampman, R.J. (1984). *Social Welfare Spending*. New York: Academic Press.

Lieberman, R. (1998). *Shifting the Color Line: Race and the American Welfare State*. Cambridge, MA: Harvard University Press.

Mead, L.M. (1992). *The New Politics of Poverty: The Nonworking Poor in America*. New York: Basic Books.

Moffitt, R. (2003a). Introduction. In R. Moffitt (ed.), *Means-Tested Transfer Programs in the United States* (pp. 1–14). Chicago: University of Chicago Press.

Moffitt, R. (ed.) (2003b). *Means-Tested Transfer Programs in the United States*. Chicago: University of Chicago Press.

Murray, C. (1984). *Losing Ground. American Social Policy 1950–1980*. New York: Basic Books.

Scholz, J.K. & Levine, K. (2001). The evolution of income support policies in recent decades. In S. Danziger & R. Haveman (eds.), *Understanding Poverty*. New York: Russell Sage Foundation.

Sinn, H.W. (1996). Social insurance, incentives, and risk taking. *International Tax and Public Finance*, **3**, 259–80.

Smeeding, T. (2005). Government programs and social outcomes: The United States in comparative perspective. Luxembourg Income Study Working Paper No. 426, May, http://www.lisproject.org/publications/liswps/426.pdf.

U.S. House of Representatives (1994). Committee on Ways and Means, *Overview of Entitlement Programs: 1994 Green Book*. Washington, DC: U.S. Government Printing Office, July.

U.S. House of Representatives (2004). Committee on Ways and Means, *Overview of Entitlement Programs: 2004 Green Book*. Washington, DC: U.S. Government Printing Office, July.

Valletta, R.G. (2006). The ins and outs of poverty in advanced economies: Government policy and poverty dynamics in Canada, Germany, Great Britain, and the United States. *Review of Income and Wealth*, ser. 52, no. 2, 261–84.

Unemployment insurance

Acemoglu, D. & Shimer, R. (1999). Efficient unemployment insurance. *Journal of Political Economy*, **107**(5), 893–928.

Anderson, P.M. & Meyer, B.D. (1993). Unemployment insurance in the United States: Layoff incentives and cross-subsidies. *Journal of Labor Economics*, **11**, S70–S95.

Anderson, P.M. & Meyer, B.D. (1994). The effects of unemployment insurance taxes and benefits on layoffs using firm and individual data. NBER Working Paper No. 4960, December.

Anderson, P.M. & Meyer, B.D. (1997a). Unemployment insurance takeup rates and the after-tax value of benefits. *Quarterly Journal of Economics*, **112**, 913–38.

Anderson, P.M. & Meyer, B.D. (1997b). The effects of firm specific taxes and government mandates with an application to the U.S. unemployment insurance program. *Journal of Public Economics*, **65**, 119–44.

Barron, J.M. & Mellow, W. (1981). Unemployment insurance: The recipients and its impact. *Southern Economic Journal*, **47**(3), 606–16.

Blank, R.M. & Card, D.E. (1990). Recent trends in insured and uninsured unemployment: Is there an explanation? *Quarterly Journal of Economics*, **106**, 1157–90.

Brechling, F. (1981). Layoffs and unemployment insurance. In S. Rosen (ed.), *Studies in Labor Markets*. Chicago: University of Chicago Press.

Burtless, G.S. (1990). Unemployment insurance and labor supply: A survey. In W.L. Hansen & J.F. Byers (eds.), *Unemployment Insurance*. Madison, WI: University of Wisconsin Press.

Card, D.E., Chetty, R. & Weber, A. (2007). The spike at benefit exhaustion: Leaving the unemployment system or starting a new job? *American Economic Review*, **97**(2), 113–18.

Card, D.E. & Levine, P.B. (1994). Unemployment insurance taxes and the cyclical and seasonal properties of unemployment. *Journal of Public Economics*, **53**, 1–29.

Card, D.E. & Levine, P.B. (2000). Extended benefits and the duration of UI spells: Evidence from the New Jersey extended benefit program. *Journal of Public Economics*, **78**, 107–38.

Chiswick, B. (1976). The effect of unemployment compensation on a seasonal industry: Agriculture. *Journal of Political Economy*, **84**, 591–602.

Classen, K.P. (1979). Unemployment insurance and job search. In S.A. Lippman & J.J. McCall (eds.), *Studies in the Economics of Search* (pp. 191–219). Amsterdam: North-Holland.

Ehrenberg, R.G. & Oaxaca, R. (1976). Unemployment insurance, duration of unemployment, and subsequent wage gains. *American Economic Review*, **66**, 754–66.

Feldstein, M. (1974). Unemployment compensation: Adverse incentives and distributional anomalies. *National Tax Journal*, **27**, 231–44.

Feldstein, M. (1978). The effect of unemployment insurance on temporary layoffs. *American Economic Review*, **68**, 834–40.

Feldstein, M. & Poterba, J. (1984). Unemployment insurance and reservation wages. *Journal of Public Economics*, **23**, 141–67.

Gustman, A. (1982). Analyzing the relation of unemployment insurance to unemployment. *Research in Labor Economics*, **5**, 69–114.

Haber, W. & Murray, M. (1966). *Unemployment Insurance in the American Economy*. Homewood, IL: Irwin.

Halpin, T. (1979). The effect of unemployment insurance on seasonal fluctuations in employment. *Industrial and Labor Relations Review*, **32**, 353–62.

Hopenhayn, H. & Nicolini, J.P. (1997). Optimal unemployment insurance. *Journal of Political Economy*, **105**(2), 412–38.

Jones, S.R.G. (2001). Reservation wages and job search behaviour: Evidence from the Survey on Repeat Use of Employment Insurance. In S. Schwartz & A. Aydermir (eds.), *Essays on the Repeat Use of Unemployment Insurance* (pp. 63–89). Ottawa: SRDC.

Katz, L.F. & Meyer, B.D. (1984). Unemployment insurance, recall expectations, and unemployment outcomes. *Quarterly Journal of Economics*, **19**, 118–26.

Katz, L.F. & Meyer, B.D. (1990). The impact of the potential duration of unemployment benefits on the duration of unemployment. *Journal of Public Economics*, **41**, 45–72.

Krueger, A. & Meyer, B.D. (2002). Labor supply effects of social insurance. In A. Auerbach & M. Feldstein (eds.), *Handbook of Public Economics* (pp. 2327–92). Amsterdam: Elsevier Science.

Lalive, R. (2007). Unemployment benefits, unemployment duration, and post-unemployment jobs: A regression-discontinuity approach. *American Economic Review*, **97**(2), 108–112.

Marston, S.T. (1975). The impact of unemployment insurance on job search. *Brookings Paper on Economic Activity*, **1**, 13–48.

Meyer, B.D. (1990). Unemployment insurance and unemployment spells. *Econometrica*, **58**(4), 757–82.

Meyer, B.D. (1995). Lessons from the US unemployment insurance experiments. *Journal of Economic Literature*, **33**(1), 91–131.

Moffitt, R. & Nicholson, W. (1982). The effects of unemployment insurance on unemployment: The case of federal supplemental benefits. *Review of Economics and Statistics*, **64**, 1–11.

Shimer, R. & Werning, I. (2006). Reservation wages and unemployment insurance. NBER Working Paper No. 12618, October.

Solon, G. (1979). Labor supply effects of extended unemployment benefits. *Journal of Human Resources*, **14**(2), 247–55.

Solon, G. (1985). Work incentive effects of taxing unemployment benefits. *Econometrica*, **53**, 295–306.

Topel, R.H. (1983). On layoffs and unemployment insurance. *American Economic Review*, **73**(3), 541–59.

Wolff, E.N. (2005). Computerization and rising unemployment duration. *Eastern Economic Journal*, **31**(4), 507–36.

Social security system

Anderson, P.M., Gustman, A.L. & Steinmeier, T.L. (1999). Trends in male labor force participation and retirement: Some evidence on the role of pensions and social security in the 1970s and 1980s. *Journal of Labor Economics*, **17**(4), 757–83.

Blau, D.M. (1997). Social security and the labor supply of older married couples. *Labour Economics*, **4**(4), 373–418.

Blinder, A.S., Gordon, R.H. & Wise, D.E. (1980). Reconsidering the work disincentive effects of social security. *National Tax Journal*, **33**(4), 431–42.

Boskin, M.J. (1977). Social security and retirement decisions. *Economic Inquiry*, **15**(1), 1–25.

Boskin, M.J. & Hurd, M.D. (1978). The effect of social security on early retirement. *Journal of Public Economics*, **10**(3), 361–77.

Burkhauser, R.V. & Quinn, J. (1983). Is mandatory retirement overrated? Evidence from the 1970s. *Journal of Human Resources*, **18**(3), 337–58.

Clark, R. & Johnson, T. (1980). Retirement in the dual career family. Final Report for the U.S. Social Security Administration. Raleigh, NC: North Carolina State University.

Crawford, V. & Lillien, D. (1981). Social security and the retirement decision. *Quarterly Journal of Economics*, **96**(3), 505–29.

Feldstein, M. & Liebman, J.B. (2001). Social security. NBER Working Paper No. 8451, September.

Friedberg, L. (2000). The labor supply effects of the social security earnings test. *Review of Economics and Statistics*, **82**(1), 48–63.

Gordon, R.H. & Blinder, A.S (1980). Market wages, reservation wages, and retirement decisions. *Journal of Public Economics*, **14**(2), 277–308.

Gruber, J. & Orszag, P. (2000). Does the social security earnings test affect labor supply and benefits receipt? National Bureau of Economic Research Working Paper No. 7923.

Kotlikoff, L.J., Marx, B. & Rizza, P. (2006). Americans' dependency on social security. NBER Working Paper No. 12696, November.

Lee, C. (1998). The rise of the welfare state and labor-force participation of older males: Evidence from the pre-social security era. *American Economic Review*, **88**(2), 222–6.

Pellechio, A. (1980). The social security earnings test, labor supply distortions and foregone payroll tax revenue. *Journal of Public Economics*, **14**(2).

Quinn, J.F. (1977). Microeconomic determinants of early retirement: A cross-sectional view of white, married men. *Journal of Human Resources*, **12**(3), 329–46.

Reimers, C.K.W. (1977). The timing of retirement of American men. Ph.D. Dissertation, Columbia University, New York.

Rust, J. & Phelan, C. (1997). How social security and Medicare affect retirement behavior in a world of incomplete markets. *Econometrica*, **65**(4), 781–831.

The welfare system and work programs

An, C.-B., Haveman, R. & Wolfe, B. (1993). Teen out of wedlock births and welfare receipt: The role of childhood events and economic circumstances. *Review of Economics and Statistics*, **75**(2), 195–208.

Antel, J. (1988). Mother's welfare dependency effects on daughter's early fertility and fertility out of wedlock, mimeo, University of Houston.

Bassi, L.J. (1983). The effect of CETA on the post-program earnings of participants. *Journal of Human Resources*, **18**(4), 539–56.

Bassi, L. *et al.* (1984). *Measuring the Effect of CETA on Youth and the Economically Disadvantaged*. Washington, DC: Urban Institute.

Bell, S.L. & Orr, L.L. (1994). Is subsidized employment cost effective for welfare recipients? *Journal of Human Resources*, **29**(1), 42–61.

Besley, T. & Coate, S. (1992). Workfare versus welfare: Incentive arguments for work requirements in poverty-alleviation programs. *American Economic Review*, **82**(1), 249–61.

Bitler, M.P., Gelbach, J.B. & Hoynes, H.W. (2002). The impact of welfare reform on living arrangements. NBER Working Paper No. 8784, February.

Blank, R. (1988). The effect of welfare and wage levels on the location decisions of female-headed households. *Journal of Urban Economics*, **24**(2), 186–211.

Blank, R. (1989). Analyzing the length of welfare spells. *Journal of Public Economics*, **39**(3), 245–73.

Blank, R. (2001). What causes public assistance caseloads to grow? *Journal of Human Resources*, **36**(1), 85–118.

Blank, R. (2002). Evaluating welfare reform in the United States. *Journal of Economic Literature*, **40**(4), 1105–66.

Burtless, G. (1990). The economists' lament: Public assistance in America. *Journal of Economic Perspectives*, **4**(1), 57–78.

Clark, R. (1990). Does welfare affect migration? Mimeo, Washington, DC: Urban Institute.

Danziger, S. *et al.* (2000). Barriers to the employment of welfare recipients. University of Michigan, February.

Danziger, S. & Weinberg, D.H. (1986). *Fighting Poverty: What Works and What Doesn't*. Cambridge, MA; Harvard University Press.

Danziger, S. & Gottschalk, P. (1986). Do rising tides life all boats? *American Economic Review*, **76**(2), 405–10.

Ellwood, D. (1986). *Targeting "Would-Be" Long-Term Recipients of AFDC*. Princeton, NJ: Mathematica Policy Research.

Ellwood, D. (1988). *Poor Support: Poverty in the American Family*. New York: Basic Books.

Ellwood, D. & Bane, M.-J. (1985). The impact of AFDC on family structure and living arrangements. In R. Ehrenberg (ed.), *Research in Labor Economics*, Vol. 7. Greenwich, CT: JAI Press.

Fitzgerald, J. (1991). Welfare durations and the marriage market: Evidence from the Survey of Income and Program Participation. *Journal of Human Resources*, **26**(3), 545–61.

Friedlander, D., Greenberg, D.H. & Robins, P.K. (1997). Evaluating government programs for the economically disadvantaged. *Journal of Economic Literature*, **35**(4), 1809–55.

Friedlander, D. & Robins, P.K. (1995). Evaluating program evaluations: New evidence on commonly used nonexperimental methods. *American Economic Review*, **85**(4), 923–37.

Garfinkel, I. & Orr, L.L. (1974). Welfare policy and employment rate of AFDC mothers. *National Tax Journal*, **27**(2), 275–84.

Gittleman, M. (2001). Declining caseloads: What do the dynamics of welfare participation reveal? *Industrial Relations*, **40**(4), 537–70.

Gottschalk, P. (1990). AFDC participation across generations. *American Economic Review*, **80**(21), 367–71.

Gottschalk, P. & Moffitt, R.A. (1994). Welfare dependence: Concepts, measures, and trends. *American Economic Review*, **84**(2), 38–53.

Gramlich, E. & Laren, D. (1984). Migration and income redistribution responsibilities. *Journal of Human Resources*, **19**(4), 489–511.

Greenberg, D.H., Michalopoulos, C. & Robins, P.K. (2003). A meta-analysis of government-sponsored training programs. *Industrial and Labor Relations Review*, **57**(1), 31–53.

Grogger, J. (2002). The behavioral effects of welfare time limits. *American Economic Review*, **92**(2), 385–9.

Grogger, J. (2003). The effects of time limits, the EITC and other policy changes on welfare use, work and income among female-headed families. *Review of Economics and Statistics*, **85**(2), 394–408.

Grogger, J. & Bronars, S.G. (2001). The effect of welfare payments on the marriage and fertility behavior of unwed mothers: Results from a twins experiment. *Journal of Political Economy*, **109**(3), 529–45.

Grogger, J., Haider, S.J. & Klerman, J. (2003). Why did welfare rolls fall during the 1990s? The importance of entry. *American Economic Review*, **93**(2), 288–92.

Grogger, J. & Michalopoulos, C. (2003). Welfare dynamics under time limits. *Journal of Political Economy*, **111**(3), 530–54.

Grossman, J., Maynard, R. & Roberts, J. (1985). *Reanalysis of the Effects of Selected Employment and Training Programs for Welfare Recipients*. Princeton, NJ: Mathematica Policy Research.

Gueron, J.M. (1990). Work and welfare: Lessons on employment programs. *Journal of Economic Perspectives*, **4**(1), 79–98.

Hausman, J.A. (1981). Labor supply. In H.J. Aaron & J.A. Pechman (eds.), *How Taxes Affect Economic Behavior* (pp. 27–72). Washington, DC: Brookings Institute.

Hoffman, S. & Duncan, G. (1988). A comparison of choice-based multinomial and nested logit models: The family structure and welfare use of decisions of divorced or separated women. *Journal of Human Resources*, **23**(4), 550–62.

Hoffman, S.D. & Duncan, G. (1995). The effect of incomes, wages and AFDC benefits on marital disruption. *Journal of Human Resources*, **30**(1), 19–41.

Hollister, R.G., Kemper, P. & Maynard, R.A. (1984). *The National Supported Work Demonstration*. Madison, WI: University of Wisconsin Press.

Hutchens, R.M., Jakubson, G. & Schwartz, S. (1989). AFDC and the formation of subfamilies. *Journal of Human Resources*, **24**(4), 599–628.

Ketron Inc. (1980). The long-term impact of WIN II: A longitudinal evaluation of the employment experiences of participants in the work incentive program. Wayne, PA.

LaLonde, R.J. (2003). Employment and training programs. In R. Moffitt (ed.), *Means-Tested Transfer Programs in the United States* (pp. 517–586). Chicago: University of Chicago Press.

Levy, F. (1979). The labor supply of female household heads, or AFDC work incentives don't work too well. *Journal of Human Resources*, **14**(1), 76–97.

Levy, F. (1986). Work for welfare: How much good will it do? *American Economic Review*, **76**(2), 399–404.

Lundberg, S. & Plotnick, R. (1990). Testing the opportunity cost hypothesis of adolescent premarital childbearing, mimeo, Paper presented at Meetings of Population Association of America, Toronto.

Masters, S.H. & Garfinkel, I. (1977). *Estimating the Labor Supply Effects of Income Maintenance Alternatives*. New York: Academic Press.

McLanahan, S. (1988). Family structure and dependency: Early transitions to female household headship. *Demography*, **25**(1), 1–16.

Meyer, B. & Rosenbaum, D. (2000). Making single mothers work: Recent tax and welfare policy and its effects. *National Tax Journal*, **53**(4).

Meyer, B. & Rosenbaum, D. (2001). Welfare, the earned income tax credit and the labor supply of single mothers. *Quarterly Journal of Economics*, **116**(3), 1063–114.

Moehling, C.M. (2007). The American welfare system and family structure: An historical perspective. *Journal of Human Resources*, **44**(1), 117–55.

Moffitt, R. (1983). An economic model of welfare stigma. *American Economic Review*, **73**(5), 1023–35.

Moffitt, R. (1986). Work incentives in transfer programs (revisited): A study of the AFDC program. In R. Ehrenberg (ed.), *Research in Labor Economics*, Vol. 8 (pp. 389–439). Greenwich, CT: JAI Press.

Moffitt, R. (1990). The effect of the U.S. welfare system on marital status. *Journal of Public Economics*, **41**(1), 101–24.

Moffitt, R. (1992). Incentive effects of the U.S. welfare system: A review. *Journal of Economic Literature*, **30**, 1–61.

Moffitt, R. (2003a). The role of nonfinancial factors in exit and entry in the TANF program. *Journal of Human Resources*, **38**, 1221–54.

Moffitt, R. (2003b). The Temporary Assistance for Needy Families Program. In R. Moffitt (ed.), *Means-Tested Transfer Programs in the United States* (pp. 291–364). Chicago: University of Chicago Press.

Plotnick, R. (1983). Turnover in the AFDC population: An event history analysis, *Journal of Human Resources*, **18**(1), 65–81.

Plotnick, R. (1990). Welfare and out-of-wedlock childbearing: Evidence from the 1980s. *Journal of Marriage and the Family*, **52**, 735–46.

Ribar, D.C., Edelhoch, M. & Liu, Q. (2008). Watching the clocks: The role of food stamp recertification and TANF time limits in caseload dynamics, *Journal of Human Resources*, **43**(1), 208–39.

Saks, D.H. (1975). *Public Assistance for Mothers in an Urban Labor Market*. Princeton, NJ: Industrial Relations Section, Princeton University.

Schoeni, R.G. & Blank, R.M. (2000). What has welfare reform accomplished? Impacts on welfare participation, employment, income, poverty & family structure. NBER Working Paper 7627, March.

Swann, C. (2005). Welfare reform when recipients are forward-looking. *Journal of Human Resources*, **40**(1), 31–56.

Weinberg, D.H. (1985). Filling the poverty "gap": multiple transfer program participation. *Journal of Human Resources*, **20**(1), 64–97.

Williams, R. (1975). *Public Assistance and Work Effort*. Princeton, NJ: Industrial Relations Section, Princeton University.

Willis, P. (1980). Participation rages in the aid to families with dependent children program, part III. Working Paper 1387-04. Washington, DC: Urban Institute.

The minimum wage

Addison, J.T. & Blackburn, M.L. (1999). Minimum wages and poverty. *Industrial and Labor Relations Review*, **52**(3), 393–409.

Brown, C. (1988). Minimum wage laws: Are they overrated? *Journal of Economic Perspectives*, **2**(3), 133–46.

Brown, C., Gilroy, C. & Kohen, A. (1982). The effect of the minimum wage on employment and unemployment. *Journal of Economic Literature*, **20**(2), 487–528.

Brown, C., Gilroy, C. & Kohen, A. (1983). Time-series evidence of the effect of the minimum wage on youth employment and unemployment. *Journal of Human Resources*, **18**(1), 3–31.

Card, D.E. (1992a). Using regional variation in wages to measure the effects of the federal minimum wage. *Industrial and Labor Relations Review*, **46**(1), 22–37.

Card, D.E. (1992b). Do minimum wages reduce employment? A case study of California, 1987–89. *Industrial and Labor Relations Review*, **46**(1), 38–54.

Card, D.E. & Krueger, A.B. (1994). Minimum wages and employment: A case study of the fast-food industry in New Jersey and Pennsylvania. *American Economic Review*, **84**(4), 772–93.

Card, D.E. & Krueger, A.B. (1994). Minimum wages and employment: A case study of the fast-food industry in New Jersey and Pennsylvania: Reply. *American Economic Review*, **90**(5), 1397–420.

Card, D.E. & Krueger, A.B. (1995a) *Myth and Measurement: The New Economics of the Minimum Wage*. Princeton, NJ: Princeton University Press.

Card, D.E. & Krueger, A.B. (1995b). Time-series minimum-wage studies: A meta-analysis. *American Economic Review Papers and Proceedings*, **85**(2), 238–43.

Carrington, W.J. & Fallick, B.C. (2001). Do some workers have minimum wage careers? *Monthly Labor Review*, 17–27.

Ehrenberg, R.G. (1992). New minimum wage research: Symposium introduction. *Industrial and Labor Relations Review*, **46**(1), 3–5.

Gramlich, E.M. (1976). Impact of minimum wages on other wages, employment, and family incomes. *Brookings Papers on Economic Activity*, **2**, 409–61.

Hammermesh, D.S. (1982). Minimum wages and the demand for labor. *Economic Inquiry*, **20**, 365–80.

Hashimoto, M. (1982). Minimum wage effects on training on the job. *American Economic Review*, **72**(5), 1070–87.

Johnson, W.R. & Browning, E.K. (1983). The distributional and efficiency effects of increasing the minimum wage: A simulation. *American Economic Review*, **73**(1), 204–11.

Katz, L.F. & Krueger, A.B. (1992). The effect of the minimum wage on the fast-food industry. *Industrial and Labor Relations Review*, **46**(1), 6–21.

Linneman, P. (1982). The economic impacts of minimum wage laws: A new look at an old question. *Journal of Political Economy*, **90**(3), 443–69.

Mincer, J. (1976). Unemployment effects of minimum wages. *Journal of Political Economy*, **84**(4), S87–S104.

Neumark, D., Schwitzeer, M. & Wascher, W. (2000). The effects of minimum wages throughout the wage distribution. NBER Working Paper No. 7519, February.

Neumark, D., Schwitzeer, M. & Wascher, W. (2005). The effects of minimum wages on the distribution of family incomes. *Journal of Human Resources*, **40**(4), 867–94.

Neumark, D. & Wascher, W. (1992). Employment effects of minimum and subminimum wages: Panel data on state minimum wage laws. *Industrial and Labor Relations Review*, **46**(1), 55–81.

Neumark, D. & Wascher, W. (2000). The effect of New Jersey's minimum wage increase on fast-food employment: A reevaluation using payroll records. *American Economic Review*, **90**(5), 1362–96.

Neumark, D. & Wascher, W. (2006). Minimum wages and employment: A review of evidence from the new minimum wage research. Unpublished manuscript.

Smith, R.E. & Vavrichek, B. (1992). The wage mobility of minimum wage workers. *Industrial and Labor Relations Review*, **46**(1), 82–8.

Wellington, A.J. (1991). Effects of the minimum wage on the employment status of youths: An update. *Journal of Human Resources*, **26**(1), 27–46.

15.10   DISCUSSION QUESTIONS AND PROBLEM SET

1   Briefly describe the trend in the coverage rate (the percent of unemployed workers receiving benefits) of the UI system since 1970. Discuss the factors that account for this trend.

2   Why might an increase in the UI replacement rate lead to an increased average duration of unemployment?

3   Define the social security replacement rate. Explain why the replacement rate is higher for a low-income earner than a high-income earner.

4   Discuss two reasons why the social security benefit structure might reduce the LFPR of older individuals.

5   The welfare (AFDC/TANF) system has often been criticized for discouraging work and creating "welfare dependency." Evaluate the evidence on the disincentive effects of welfare on work effort.

6   Summarize the effects of the government transfer system on the overall poverty rate. What components of the income transfer system have the largest effects in reducing poverty and which have relatively small effects?

7   Explain three ways in which TANF differs from AFDC.

8   The social security trust fund is projected to run out of money by about the year 2050. Explain why this is the case. Describe three policies that could be implemented to prevent the social security trust fund from going broke.

9   Suppose that UI benefits are set according to the following rules: (i) minimum weekly earnings in last week of employment of $200.00 is needed to qualify; (ii) the maximum UI weekly benefit is $1,000; and (iii) UI benefits are set equal to 50% of the last week's earnings between the minimum and maximum levels.
   (a)   Show the structure of the UI benefit system on a diagram.
   (b)   Compute both the UI benefit level and the replacement rate if weekly earnings in the last week of employment is: (i) $100; (ii) $500; and (iii) $3,000.

10   Suppose that welfare (TANF) benefits are structured in the following way in a state:

Annual family income ($)	Annual TANF benefit ($)
0	5,000
2,000	4,500
4,000	4,000
6,000	3,000
8,000	2,000
10,000	1,000
12,000	0

(a)   Show the structure of the TANF benefit system on a diagram.
(b)   Compute both the TANF benefit level and the implicit tax rate if annual family income is: (i) $1,000; and (ii) $9,000.

11   Suppose that welfare (TANF) benefits are structured in the following way in a state:

Annual family income ($)	Annual TANF benefit ($)
0	5,052
2,000	4,892
4,000	3,292
5,000	2,492
6,000	1,692
7,000	892
8,000	0

(a)   Show the structure of the TANF benefit system on a diagram.
(b)   Compute both the TANF benefit level and the implicit tax rate if annual family income is: (i) $1,000; and (ii) $6,500.

NOTES

1   This concept of insurance is similar to home, property, or automobile insurance. Individuals pay a premium for a policy which protects them against unforeseen and undesirable occurrences (fire, burglary, a car accident, etc.). Like home insurance, a social insurance program reduces the risk and increases the certainty equivalent income of the covered population. Like home insurance, social insurance programs will pay benefits at any given time to those policy holders who have experience adverse events. Thus, in an *ex post* sense, there will be a redistribution from the lucky to the unlucky but in an *ex ante* sense the entire covered population receives an insurance benefit. The risk-pooling argument can also be said to apply to the public provision of basic goods. See Sinn (1996) for more discussion of this point.

2   England has a much longer history of support for its poor. England's "Poor Law" was the system for the provision of social security in operation in England from the sixteenth century (as early as 1552) until the establishment of the welfare state in the twentieth century. The Poor Law is made up a series of Acts of parliament and subsequent amendments that spanned this period of history, which aimed at providing support for the country's indigent population (see http://en.wikipedia.org/wiki/Poor_Law for more information on the English Poor Law). The Poor Law became a source of considerable dissension in England when it proved to be very expensive in the industrial revolution. Attitudes towards people on welfare go way back in time – see, for example, *David Copperfield* by Charles Dickens. There were early debates about workhouses, and the trickle-down theory, and whether support just

allowed the poor to expand until they died off. (Thomas Malthus' argument that man is destined to return to subsistence-level conditions as a result of population growth outpacing agricultural production led him to oppose any kind of support programs for the poor.)

3   Technically speaking, the Social Security Act of 1935 created Aid to Dependent Children (ADC). In the 1960s, the program was expanded to AFDC to include the parents as well.

4   The source for the data on food stamps is from the U.S. Department of Agriculture: http://www.fns.usda.gov/fsp/.

5   Households may have $3,000 if at least one person is age 60 or older, or is disabled.

6   This is the case for the first 60 days of hospital care. After that, the patient must pay a small co-insurance amount.

7   While deductibles in the program may be "nominal," many low-income individuals in the program may find the premiums fairly steep.

8   Actually, one of the earliest state proposals to develop universal health care was made in 1945 by California (Republican) Governor Earl Warren. President Harry Truman tried and failed in 1949 to get a nationwide universal health care proposal passed. In 1971 President Richard Nixon proposed to provide universal coverage. He was also unsuccessful. For more information on health care proposals, see www.cmanet.org/upload/health_coverage_history.pdf.

9   *Source*: U.S. House of Representatives (2004), http://frwebgate.access.gpo.gov/cgi-bin/getdoc.cgi?dbname=108_green_book&docid=f:wm006_04.pdf.

10   See, for example, Ehrenberg and Oaxaca (1976), Classen (1979), Solon (1979), Barron and Mellow (1981), Moffitt and Nicholson (1982), Feldstein and Poterba (1984), Meyer (1990), Katz and Meyer (1990), Meyer (1995), Jones (2001), Krueger and Meyer (2002), Shimer and Werning (2006), and Lalive (2007).

11   Technically speaking, the minimum number of quarters needed to be eligible for benefits depends on the worker's age.

12   Current figures on the basics of the social security system (taxes, taxable maximums, average benefits, etc.) are available at: http://www.ssa.gov/cola/.

13   Under current legislation, the normal retirement age will be gradually raised to age 67 by the year 2022.

14   Under current law, any retiree covered by the social security system is now eligible for full benefits at normal retirement age even if he (she) continues to work after that age.

15   Prior to 1975, social security benefits were periodically raised by the U.S. Congress. These upward adjustments were usually greater than the inflation rate.

16   This projection is based on the so-called "intermediate assumptions" used by the Social Security Administration concerning future rates of growth of output and wages and future inflation rates. For more current information on the Social Security Administration's Annual Trustee Reports, information about what the "intermediate assumptions" are, and for projections of OASDI solvency, see http://www.socialsecurity.gov/OACT/TR/.

17   However, there is a subtle offset to the tax effect. The calculation of the AIME is based on the best 35 years of earnings. If an elderly person has a job that pays more than the lowest year of earnings used to calculate the person's AIME, then continuing to work at the job will allow a substitution of the new year of earnings for the lowest. The worker's AIME will then be recalculated, and his or her prospective social security benefit thereby increased. See Blinder, Gordon, and Wise (1980) for more details.

18   Technically, this was true for most states. However, in some, the income limitation actually lay below the need standard.

19   Actually, in some states (for example, Connecticut), TANF recipients are allowed a 100 percent earned income disregard for the first several months on a job.

20   This is true despite the fact that the poverty line itself has deteriorated over time as a percent of median family income (see Chapter 4 for more details).

21   Food stamp benefits differ among states because the benefit is computed on the basis of an income concept which includes wages and salaries, other income, and TANF. Families who otherwise have

no reported income and live in states which have a high TANF benefit (like Connecticut) will receive a relatively low food stamp benefit. The converse is true for a state like Alabama which pays a very low TANF benefit. There is also some variation in food stamp benefits across states due to state rules.

22 Recall from Chapter 4 that food stamps and other noncash government benefits are not included in family income when calculating the official poverty rate.

23 See, for example, Garfinkel and Orr (1974), Williams (1975), Saks (1975), Masters and Garfinkel (1977), Levy (1979), and Hausman (1981).

24 The data for both the Schoeni and Blank and the Grogger studies ended in 1999 and this year might be too close to the start of TANF to yield definitive results. This is particularly true because the TANF program was typically quite generous in terms of the earned-income disregards in the first several years of the program.

25 There is a technical problem with these calculations that may lead to an overestimation of both spell duration and total time spent on AFDC. Because of data limitations, it was necessary to define a year of "AFDC receipt" as receiving at least one month of benefits sometime over the year. However, an examination of monthly data indicates that many families were on welfare for only part of a year (see Fitzgerald, 1991, for example), so that both spell durations and total time spent on AFDC may be less than the figures in Table 15.11 suggest.

26 Another explanation is based on a spurious statistical correlation arising from "unobserved heterogeneity" in the AFDC population. The argument is that the AFDC population may have differed in their level of human capital and hence their probable employability. In particular, those with lower human capital were likely to remain on the welfare rolls longer than those with greater skills and education. Thus, the finding that the exit rate increased as duration on AFDC rose may have been due to the fact that the more skilled AFDC recipients left the welfare rolls faster than the less skilled, even though exit rates for each group remained constant over time. See Moffitt (1992) for more details.

27 Actually, some states had enacted a minimum wage standard before 1938. The earliest was Massachusetts in 1912.

28 It is still too early to ascertain the corresponding ratio for 2007 and 2009.

29 See Chapter 16 for a detailed discussion of the EITC.

30 Once again it should be emphasized that these estimates are based on computing family income with and without transfer income. There are no behavioral assumptions built into the analysis – for example, modeling how the family might change its labor market behavior in the absence of transfer payments. As a result, caution must be used in interpreting these figures.

31 On the negative side, the higher unemployment benefits in Europe are often cited as one reason why the unemployment rate is so much higher in Europe than in the United States.

Chapter 16

The Redistributional Effects of Public Policy

16.1 INTRODUCTION

In the last chapter, we analyzed the array of income support systems and other programs aimed primarily at helping the poor in the United States. In this chapter, we consider the overall effects of the government fiscal system on income inequality.

Section 16.2 raises the issue of why social equity may be an important social concern. It considers several philosophical positions, both for and against the proposition that the state should pursue equality as an independent social goal. Section 16.3 considers general properties of tax systems and their overall effects on income inequality.

Section 16.4 first provides a description of the system of taxation currently in place in the United States. It then considers the redistributional effects of government tax policy. Is the tax system progressive, regressive, or neutral? Does the system reduce or exacerbate overall income inequality? This section also presents statistics on the extent of taxation in the United States and some comparisons with other advanced economies.

Section 16.5 considers proposals for a so-called **negative income** tax. This program is designed to replace all other government transfer programs and to provide an income subsidy to low-income households. It looks at one particular aspect of the tax system, the **Earned Income Tax Credit** (or **EITC**). This program, which is actually in place in the U.S. tax system, resembles in many ways a negative income tax.

Section 16.6 looks at the other side of the ledger, the effects of government disbursements. There are two main types of disbursements: transfer payments to individuals and actual expenditures on goods and services. This section first investigates how the government spends its revenue – that is, the relative magnitudes of the different government programs. It then takes up the question of which groups benefit from government expenditures and their distributional consequences. A summary of the chapter is provided in Section 16.7.

16.2 EQUALITY AS A SOCIAL GOAL

16.2.1 Arguments in favor of promoting equality

Why should we be concerned about inequality? To what should inequality refer – incomes, total resources, other measures of outcomes, or opportunity? Why should equality be viewed as a social or political objective? Perhaps, the most compelling reason is that it is indicative of the consumption possibilities of different groups within society. Consider a simple example. Suppose there are two countries with the same average incomes. The first is an oil-rich sheikdom ruled by a royal family who own all the oil rights. The second is a country like Sweden with very high tax rates and generous transfer programs available to the population. In the first country it is possible that the vast majority of the population is poor, while in the second country only a small fraction of the population may be poor. Thus, even though the average incomes are the same in the two countries, only a small fraction of the population in the first country will have very high incomes, whereas the vast majority of the population in the second country will have medium to high incomes. This difference will be reflected only in comparative measures of income inequality between the two countries.

Another reason to be concerned about the level of income inequality of a country is that income equality is often considered an important social goal of a nation. Equality is often included as a basic public policy objective along with such other goals such as allocative efficiency, economic growth, and economic and political freedom. Five distinct grounds are often cited as reasons for trying to achieve equality in a society.[1]

The first is based on a notion of *fairness*. If a country happens to be rich in oil or other natural resources, is it fair for a small number of individuals to receive all the benefits from this "gift of nature"? If a nation's economy is very productive because of the accumulation of capital stock and technology, should not all the citizens of a nation share in the rewards of past history? Such a judgment can, of course, only be made on *normative* (that is, ethical) grounds. Indeed, the underlying notion behind the concept of fairness is that members of a society are *entitled* to certain rights and privileges, simply for being members of a society. One of these rights is an "adequate" standard of living and a "just" share of society's benefits. This is a position that cannot be proved or disproved on scientific grounds but rests on philosophical beliefs. However, much social and economic policy in the United States, particularly since World War II, has been made with this goal in mind.

In opposition to this line of reasoning, some have argued (as we shall see below) that fairness should concern only *opportunity*, not outcomes. Moreover, the guarantee of a certain level of income may destroy incentives to work and to save.

A second ground for striving for economic equality is based on **utilitarianism**. This philosophical doctrine was set forth by the English philosopher Jeremy Bentham some 200 years ago, and its major precept is that society's goal should be to maximize the total *utility* (that is, happiness or satisfaction) of its members. This, too, is a normative judgment and depends on a person's philosophical bent. Given the objective of maximizing total utility, we still need an additional assumption to arrive at equality of income as a social goal. One fairly plausible assumption is that income has diminishing marginal utility. Income is first used to buy necessities, but beyond some income level, additional dollars are used to buy conveniences and luxuries. Figure 16.1 provides a schematic illustration of this assumption. As income rises, total utility also increases but the added utility from an additional dollar declines.

If we make this assumption and, in addition, assume that everyone has the same utility function, it follows that distributing income equally among individuals will maximize total utility.[2] To show this, consider the case where incomes are distributed unequally. In particular, suppose that individual A receives $2,000 more income than individual B ($18,000 versus $16,000). Then, if we redistribute $1,000 from A to B (so that each now receives $17,000), then B's gain in utility will be greater than A's loss, so that total social welfare is increased. Thus, total utility will reach its highest value when everyone receives the same income.

This is also an argument for redistributing income in an equitable fashion. However, if income is perfectly equal and everyone is guaranteed the same income level, then what is the incentive to work? Too much equality may reduce work effort (and investment) and thereby the total

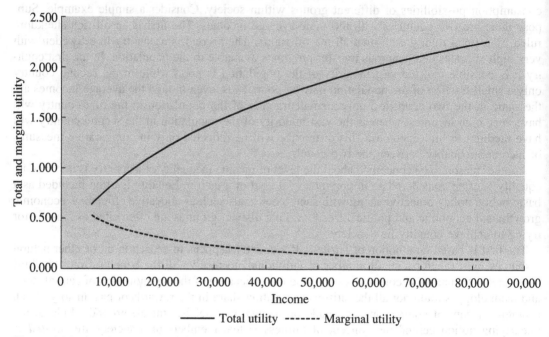

Figure 16.1   Total and marginal utility with diminishing marginal utility of income

product of society. The utilitarian argument thus implicitly assumes that labor supply and investment are unaffected by the rewards individuals receive for their activity. Maximizing the total utility of society may require a distribution that is more equal than that prevailing from market incomes but less equal than perfect equality.

A third line of argument derives from a theory of fairness developed by John Rawls in his 1971 book entitled *A Theory of Justice*. Rawls argues that a sense of fairness or social justice can be developed only if an individual is unaware of his or her particular circumstances. This circumstance Rawls calls "the original position." In such a situation, when the person does not know his or her own income, wealth, or level of well-being, the individual is said to be behind a "veil of ignorance." The rationale is that for a person to recommend what is best for society, she must be unaware of her position (otherwise she would recommend what is in her own best interest). Rawls argues that such an individual would favor a society that provided a minimal level of well-being (or income) to all members of society. This is also referred to as a **maximin** solution – that is, a system of distribution that would maximize the minimum level of income that would be available to every individual in a society.

Here it is interesting that the theory of fairness that devolves from such a philosophical system says nothing directly about the overall level of inequality that a "just society" would sustain. Rather, the theory implies that a just social order would ensure that all members of society would receive some minimal level of support. This view is more consistent with a "social safety net" conception of the role of the state in promoting equity. It would imply that the government would provide a range of transfer programs, including welfare payments, and social programs that would enable each member of a country to secure a level of income at least at the poverty line.

A criticism of the Rawlsian position is that the veil of ignorance implicitly assumes that people have a very high (indeed, infinite) *risk aversion*. Risk aversion refers to the reluctance of a person to accept a bargain with an uncertain payoff rather than another bargain with a more certain, but possibly lower, expected payoff. Rawls' theory of justice assumes that people are "naturally" risk averse, whereas some (perhaps, most) people would prefer some risk if the expected reward was on average higher.

A fourth argument is based on self-interest. Too much inequality and, in particular, poverty may lead to an excessive amount of violence and crime in a society. Moreover, individuals may prefer not to be confronted with beggars and homeless people on a continual basis, as sometimes happens in the major cities of the United States today. The average citizen in a country like the United States may thus feel better off with less poverty and lower inequality.

A fifth line of reasoning derives from Sen's (1992) emphasis of basic capabilities or "functionings." The Sen framework is a natural progression from that of Rawls but it goes beyond Rawls' emphasis on fair process. As an alternative, Sen suggests a new focus on the equalization of basic capabilities or, as he calls them, *functionings*, that all have reason to value in life (also see Section 4.2.4).

Functionings are of two kinds: elementary ones such as having good health, nourishment, and shelter; and more complex social ones such as having self-respect, taking part in the life of the community etc. An individual's achievement in life is the set of these realized functionings. Nevertheless, inequalities related to class, gender, and race among others can hinder the extent of human freedom and thus decrease a person's capability to function. That is the reason that a "good society" ought to mitigate discrimination and promote the freedom of individuals, which, according to Sen, is the most valuable element of a satisfactory life. The same criticism can be made of Sen's argument as that of Rawls – namely, that Sen assumes that people are "naturally" risk averse, whereas people may prefer some risk if the overall payoff is greater.

16.2.2 Arguments against promoting greater equality

These views do not imply that all economists (or individuals) agree that income equality is in itself a desirable social goal. There are three common arguments that have been proposed against seeking greater equality in income distribution.

The first derives from the *libertarian* viewpoint, which is also based on a notion of fairness. We must distinguish between the equality of *rights* or *opportunities*, on the one hand, and income equality or equality of *outcomes*, on the other hand. The doctrine of fairness simply guarantees that each individual has the same basic political rights and economic opportunities, particularly in access to jobs and for the acquisition of education and training. This notion of equal opportunity is, of course, the cornerstone of much current public policy-making. However, beyond this, according to this argument, society has no further obligation. Indeed, if one individual has greater drive and puts forth more work effort than a second individual, who may have greater preference for leisure, then the first individual should be entitled to greater income. Moreover, if one individual has greater ability and produces more than a second, then he should receive more compensation. If one worker is older and more experienced than a second, then it is also fair for that worker to receive a higher wage or salary than the younger worker.

Yet, it is often argued in opposition to the libertarian position that complete equality of opportunity is impossible to achieve. Consider disabled, blind, or elderly individuals, who, through no fault of their own, are unable to participate in the labor market. Should they be completely ignored by the state and made to depend on relatives or charities for their bare necessities?

Also, consider the difference in opportunities between children of rich families and those of poor ones. Rich children have greater access to education and training and potentially to jobs through family connections (see Chapter 6 on intergenerational mobility). Moreover, children of wealthy parents are likely to receive greater inheritances than those from poor families, and, as we saw in Section 10.4, inheritances play a major role in explaining inequality in household wealth. Such differences are particularly acute between white families and minorities, and, as a result, the federal government has enacted special programs to remedy the lack of equal opportunity (see Section 13.6 for a description of these programs).

The counter-argument to the libertarian view is that equal opportunity does not exist in society without some form of government intervention. Life is not a fair game and, to use the expression of Haveman (1988), children are not "starting even." As a result, society must take specific remedial steps to counter inequality in the distribution of income. This is also an argument for combating nonmarket discrimination because it can restrict opportunities as well.

The second argument against promoting greater income equality is related to the first. This is that paying higher wages and salaries to individuals who produce more serves as an *incentive* for everyone to work harder and to acquire new productive abilities and skills. As a result, the *total product* of the economy will be greater if workers are rewarded according to what they produce rather than being guaranteed an income that is not directly related to their productivity. This argument concludes that even those at the bottom of the income distribution will be better off since the total product will be so much greater than if people received equal incomes.

This view is often referred to as the "trickle-down" effect, because the higher incomes of the upper part of the income distribution will eventually cause incomes at the bottom of the distribution to rise. Briefly stated, it is that growth leads to a bigger "pie" to divide among a nation's citizens. Promoting growth will be more effective in the long run in making the poor better off than promoting current redistribution, since an expanding pie makes more income available for all, including the poor, while giving a larger slice of a fixed pie to the poor makes them better off only in the short run.[3]

This argument hinges on the belief that a smaller piece of a larger pie will be greater in *absolute terms* than a larger slice of a smaller pie. This is, of course, an *empirical* question – that is, has history shown this belief to be true? However, even if this view is correct and the poor do experience an increase in real income even though income inequality goes up, there may still be reason to oppose the growth position. Some, for example, have argued that a person's utility may depend not only on the person's absolute income but on his or her relative income as well (see, for example, the provocative 1985 book by Robert Frank). That is, a person's satisfaction may depend, in part, on that person's relative standing in the community – that is, on "keeping up with the Joneses." So even if a person's income is rising in absolute terms over time, if it is declining *relative* to other people's income (or the median income of the country), then the person's utility level may actually decline.[4] This counter-argument would thus favor greater income equality even if the trickle-down effect were occurring, since greater equality would raise the *average* level of utility in society.

The third argument accepts the basic utilitarian objective of maximizing the common good but the assumption of equal needs for everyone is disputed. There are in fact two variants of this position. The Marxist principle of "to each according to his needs" assumes that people's needs differ according to their circumstances. The disabled or aged may require greater health care; a large family requires more food than a small one; and so on. Therefore, income should be redistributed in favor of those whose *needs* are greatest. This will then lead to the greatest overall satisfaction. Interestingly, as we saw in the last chapter, most welfare programs implicitly adopt this position, since transfer payments such as TANF are based on number of children in the family, as well as disability and other special circumstances.

The second variant also assumes that people differ in their utility function, but here the assumption is that some people are much "harder to please" than others. The emphasis here is on how to please those hardest to please, and this may be referred to as the "elitist position." For example, some people may require a very expensive house and rare art works to have a minimal level of happiness in life. According to the utilitarian position, these people should receive greater income than those who are more easily satisfied with the simpler (and cheaper) pleasures of life. Fortunately, this view is not widely held (except, perhaps, in bankruptcy court), since it would suggest that we should transfer income from the poor to the rich.[5]

16.3 THE STRUCTURE OF TAX SYSTEMS

Whether we believe that the government should or should not be involved in the job of promoting greater equality in society, in point of fact, government fiscal policy does affect the *actual* distribution of income. In this section, we discuss the general distributional properties of tax systems. In Section 16.4, we look in particular at the distributional effects of the overall tax system in the United States. In Section 16.6, we discuss the distributional effects of the government's expenditure side.

16.3.1 Proportional, progressive, and regressive tax structures

The tax rate (or **average tax rate**) t is defined as the ratio of taxes paid T to income Y:

$$t = T/Y \tag{16.1}$$

Taxes are classified into three types: (i) proportional; (ii) progressive; and (iii) regressive. These three types of taxes are illustrated in Figure 16.2 (where we have arbitrarily chosen the same starting point – 10 percent – in each case for reasons of illustration).

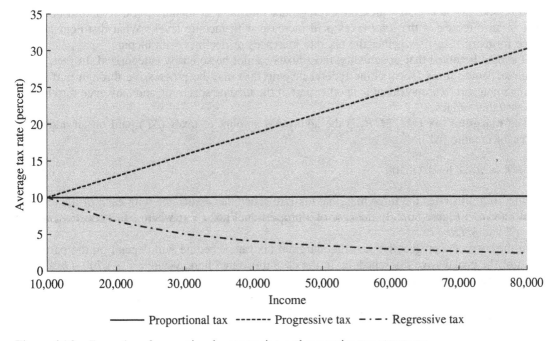

Figure 16.2 Examples of proportional, progressive and regressive tax structures

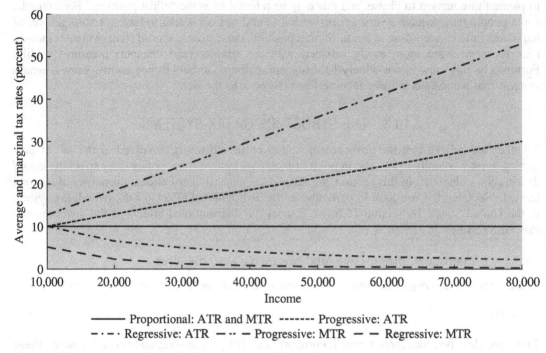

Figure 16.3   Average and marginal tax rates for different illustrative tax systems

A proportional tax is defined as one in which the average tax rate remains constant over income levels. A progressive tax is one in which the average tax rate increases with income level. And a regressive tax is one in which the average tax rate falls as income rises. It should be noted that in all three cases the *total* taxes paid increase with income level.[6] What distinguishes the three forms of taxes is whether the tax rate increases or declines with income.

It should be noted that in actuality, most taxes cannot be so easily categorized. In fact, as we shall see, some taxes (such as the federal income tax) may be progressive through part of the income range, turn proportional in another part of the income spectrum, and may even turn regressive at other ranges.

The **marginal tax rate**, *MTR*, is the additional amount of taxes (ΔT) paid on an additional dollar of income (ΔY):

$$MTR = \Delta T/\Delta Y \text{ [or } dT(Y)/dY] \tag{16.2}$$

Figure 16.3 illustrates the three marginal tax rate schedules associated with each of the tax systems shown in Figure 16.2. In the case of a proportional tax, $t = c$, where c is a constant, so that $T = cY$ and $MTR = c$.

In the case of a progressive tax, the marginal tax rate schedule will depend on the particular form of the progressive tax schedule. In the case illustrated here, where $t = a + bY$, $a,b > 0$ and a and b are constant, then $MTR = a + 2bY$.[7]

In this case, the marginal tax rate rises with income. An analogous derivation can be made for the regressive tax. In the case illustrated here, $t = b/(a + Y)$, $a,b > 0$ and a and b are constant, then $MTR = ab/(a + Y)^2$.

In the case of a regressive tax, the marginal tax rate declines with the income level.[8]

Average tax rates are more relevant when considering the effects of the tax system on income inequality. However, most of the public policy debate centers on the marginal tax rate because it is more crucial when considering the incentive effects of the tax system. The marginal tax rate determines the net gain for an additional dollar of income and therefore directly affects labor supply and investment behavior.

In actuality, most tax schedules are not formed as simple functions of income. Figures 16.4(a) and (b) illustrate the 2005 federal personal income tax scheme, both for single filers and married couples (joint tax returns).[9] The marginal tax system is, in effect, a step function, with the marginal tax rate remaining constant along a range of incomes and then jumping up to a new level at the end of the range. These income ranges are referred to as **tax brackets**.[10]

As shown in Table 16.1, the marginal tax rate starts out at 10 percent for singles up to a taxable income of $7,300 and up to $14,600 for married couples filing jointly. Marginal tax rates then increase to 15 percent, 25 percent, 28 percent, 33 percent, and 35 percent for over $326,450 in income.

Table 16.1 also shows the average tax rates by income level. There are four important points to note. First, the average tax rate rises with income. Second, the average tax rate rises smoothly with income (there are no "discontinuities" as there are in the marginal tax schedule). Third, the average tax rate is uniformly lower than the marginal tax rate. For example, at $182,800 of taxable income for couples, the marginal tax rate is 33 percent while the average tax rate is only 22.4 percent. This is a consequence of the step function structure of the marginal tax rates. Fourth, as income rises, the average tax rate approaches the top marginal tax rate (35 percent in 2005) in the limit.[11]

It should be apparent that the federal personal income tax schedule is a *progressive tax*, since the average tax rate increases with income. This, in turn, is due to the marginal tax structure, which increases in stepwise fashion with income. However, it should be emphasized, even at this point, that the actual or *effective* tax rates by income level do, indeed, differ from the tax schedule as it appears on paper. This is due the availability of deductions, exclusions, tax preference items, and other so-called "tax loopholes." We will have more to say about this in the next section.

Table 16.1 Marginal and average tax rates based on the 2005 federal personal income tax code

Income brackets		Marginal tax rate (percent)	Average tax rate (percent) (at lower limit of range)	Total taxes paid
Over	*But less than*			
A. Singles				
0	7,300	10	0.0	0
7,300	29,700	15	10.0	730
29,700	71,950	25	13.8	4,090
71,950	150,150	28	20.4	14,653
150,150	326,450	33	24.3	36,549
326,450	—	35	29.0	94,728
B. Married couples, filing jointly				
0	14,600	10	0.0	0
14,600	59,400	15	10.0	1,460
59,400	119,950	25	13.8	8,180
119,950	182,800	28	19.4	23,318
182,800	326,450	33	22.4	40,916
326,450	—	35	27.1	88,320

Source: http://www.irs.gov/pub/irs-prior/i1040–2005.pdf. Income levels are based on taxable income.

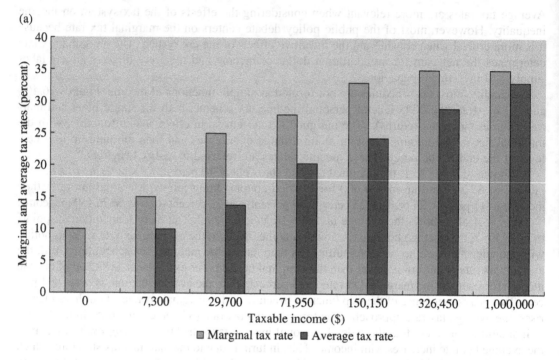

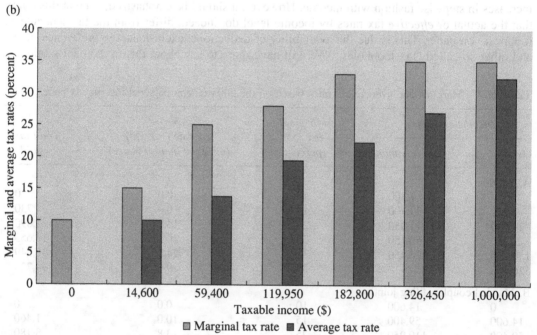

Figure 16.4 Marginal and average tax rates. (a) Singles. (b) Married couples, filing jointly (the 2005 Federal Tax Code)

16.3.2   Inequality measures and the tax system

How does the tax system affect overall income inequality in an economy? This requires a comparison of the distribution of before-tax income with that of after-tax income. The effect is typically summarized using one of the standard measures of inequality, such as the Gini coefficient or the coefficient of variation. We already broached this subject in Section 3.5.1, in which we discussed studies which compared before-tax and after-tax measures of inequality. Here, we treat the subject theoretically.

The standard measures of inequality, such as the Gini coefficient, are designed in such a way that they are *scale-free*. That is to say, a proportionate change in income (every family's income changes by the same percentage) will leave the inequality measure unchanged. This, we suggested, made intuitive sense, since inequality depends on *relative* income and a proportionate change in income leaves everyone's relative income unchanged.

An analysis of the effect of the tax system on inequality thus depends on the structure of *average* tax rates. Let us define after-tax income as Y^*,

$$Y^* = (1 - t)Y \tag{16.3}$$

where Y is before-tax income. It should, perhaps, be apparent that a proportional tax system will leave inequality unchanged because everyone's income will decline by the same percentage. In the example above, $t = c$, a constant, and $Y^* = (1 - c)Y$. In this case, we simply have a change in scale of our income measure.

We can demonstrate this formally for the Gini coefficient. In Section 3.3.4, we defined the Gini coefficient, G, as:

$$G = 1 - \sum_{i=1}^{t} f_i(z_{i-1} + z_i) \tag{3.5}$$

for t income classes, where f_i is the percent frequency of income recipients in income class i, y_i is the percent of total income received by income class i, and z_i is the cumulative percentage of income up through income class i given by

$$z_i = y_1 + y_2 + \ldots + y_i$$

and z_0 is defined as equal to zero.

What happens when a proportional tax is imposed on income? It should first be clear that the percent frequency of families in each income class remains *unchanged*. In a sense, we are just redefining the income class boundaries. The income side is a bit less obvious. Let us consider income class i. After-tax mean income in income class i, $\bar{Y}^*$, becomes

$$\bar{Y}^*_i = (1 - c)\bar{Y}_i$$

and the overall average after-tax income becomes

$$\bar{Y}^* = (1 - c)\bar{Y}$$

The percent of after-tax total income in income class i, y^*_i, then becomes

$$y^*_i = (1 - c)n_i\bar{Y}_i/(1 - c)N\bar{Y} = n_i\bar{Y}_i/N\bar{Y} = y_i$$

where n_i is the number of taxpayers in income class i and N is the total number of taxpayers. As a result, y_i remains unchanged, because total income and income in income class i both change by the same percentage (they both decline by a factor of $(1 - c)$). It also follows that z_i remains unchanged. Since both f_i and z_i are unchanged, the after-tax Gini coefficient must equal the before-tax Gini coefficient.[12]

Another point is that the Lorenz curve for after-tax income is identical to the one based on before-tax income. From Chapter 3, the Lorenz curve graphs the cumulative percentage of income, z_i, against the cumulative percentage of families, P_i. Since the imposition of a proportional tax leaves both z_i and P_i unchanged, the after-tax Lorenz curve is the same as the before-tax Lorenz curve.

What about progressive and regressive tax structures? There is no straightforward analytical demonstration of their effect on the Gini coefficient or the coefficient of variation, because the forms of these taxes may vary and, in most cases, the resulting equations do not admit to tractable solutions. However, we can use the Lorenz curve technique to assess their effects. For this, we need to impose one important condition – namely, that the *rank order* of families remains the same on the basis of after-tax income as before-tax income. In other words, the tax must be imposed in such a way that family A with more (before-tax) income than family B must also have more after-tax income than family B. In this case, we can still classify after-tax income families in the same before-tax income classes by simply redefining the income class bracket. As a result, the tax will leave f_i unchanged for each income class i.[13]

In the case of a progressive tax, income class i will, by definition, pay a higher percentage tax than lower income class $i - 1$. Consider the first (lowest) income tax. Its tax rate, t_1, must be less than the average tax rate, $\bar{t}$ for the population as a whole. Its after-tax mean income is

$$\bar{Y}^*_1 = (1 - t_1)/\bar{Y}_1$$

Its share of total after-tax income is

$$y^*_1 = (1 - t_1)n_1\bar{Y}_1/[(1 - \bar{t})N\bar{Y}]$$

and, as a result,

$$y^*_1 = (1 - t_1)n_1\bar{Y}_1/[(1 - \bar{t})N\bar{Y}] > n_1\bar{Y}_1/[N\bar{Y}] = y_1$$

since $(1 - t_1)/(1 - \bar{t})$ is greater than unity. It is clear that this relation will hold for all the bottom income classes whose tax rate is below the average tax rate in the economy. As a result, for all such income classes i below the average tax rate,

$$z^*_1 = y^*_1 + \ldots + y^*_i > y_1 + \ldots + y_i = z_i$$

As a result, for the bottom part of the income distribution, the after-tax Lorenz curve must lie *above* the before-tax Lorenz curve. This is illustrated in Figure 16.5.

To look at the income classes above the mean tax rate, we "flip" the Lorenz curve around. Recall from Section 3.2 that we can read the Lorenz curve from the upper right point of the square as the cumulative percentage of income received by the *top* percentiles of the income distribution. In this regard, let us consider the highest income class, k. Its after-tax mean income is

$$\bar{Y}^*_k = (1 - t_k)\bar{Y}_k$$

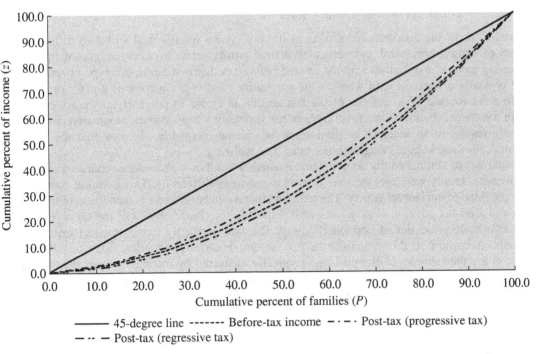

Figure 16.5 Lorenz curves for before-tax and after-tax income (with a progressive and regressive tax structure)

Its share of total after-tax income is

$$y^*_k = (1 - t_k)n_k\bar{Y}_k/[(1 - \bar{t})N\bar{Y}]$$

and, as a result,

$$y^*_k = (1 - t_k)n_k\bar{Y}_k/[(1 - \bar{t})N\bar{Y}] > n_k\bar{Y}_k/[N\bar{Y}] = y_k$$

since $(1 - t_k)/(1 - \bar{t})$ is less than unity. This relation holds for all the top income classes, above the average tax rate in the economy. As a result, for all such income classes j above the average tax rate, the share of total after-tax income received by the top income classes through j, s^*_j (the *concentration of income*), is given by

$$s^*_j = y^*_k + \ldots + y^*_j < y_k + \ldots + y_j = s_j$$

In other words, the top part of the after-tax Lorenz curve, above the mean tax rate, must also lie above the before-tax Lorenz curve. As a result, a progressive tax, subject to maintaining the rank order of income recipients, must lower income inequality.

An analogous proof demonstrates that in the case of a regressive tax, the after-tax Lorenz curve must lie completely below the before-tax Lorenz curve. As a result, a regressive tax must increase income inequality.

16.3.3   Vertical versus horizontal equity

Discussions of the distributional effects of the tax system usually deal with two different concepts of equity: horizontal and vertical. **Vertical equity** refers to a comparison of the overall after-tax income distribution with the overall before-tax distribution. In this type of analysis, we are typically concerned with whether the inequality of after-tax income is greater or less than before-tax income. The analysis of the last section is a case in point. Here, we are concerned with whether each of the three main types of tax structures – proportional, progressive, and regressive – results in an increase or diminution in income inequality. We saw that the first was neutral, the second equalizing, and the third disequalizing.

Analyses of vertical equity do not concern whether families with the same characteristics (such as income, family size, age, etc.) are treated the same or differently. This question comes under the province of **horizontal equity**. The term horizontal equity refers to a comparison of the before-tax and after-tax position of taxpayers with respect to the characteristics of the taxpayers. There are two basic principles of horizontal equity. The first is usually stated as equal treatments of equals. According to this principle, the tax system should levy identical taxes on all families who enjoy the same level of well-being (typically measured by income or equivalent income).

The second principle is referred to as **rank preservation**. The notion here is that an equitable tax system should leave the rank order of tax units unaltered. If family A was better off than family B before taxes, it should remain better off after taxes. It should be apparent that this principle incorporates the first principle but is more general. If equals are treated equally, then their relative rank will remain unchanged. However, this principle is broader, since it asserts that all *relative* positions must be maintained – there can be no reranking.

How do the three types of tax systems measure up with respect to this second principle of horizontal equity (assuming that the tax depends only on the income of the family)? A proportional tax, as indicated above, must be rank preserving, since all tax units experience the same percentage loss in income. Perhaps surprisingly, a regressive tax is rank preserving because a higher income family cannot slip below a lower income unit. Indeed, the feature of a regressive system is that the after-tax income of a higher income family will *increase* relative to that of a lower income unit. Thus, even though a *regressive tax violates the principle of vertical equity*, it will fulfill the second principle of horizontal equity.

Of the three, only the progressive tax is ambiguous. It is not too hard to imagine an example which will cause a higher pre-tax income family to slip below a lower pre-tax family (to take an extreme example, a 50% tax on middle-income families and a 100% tax on rich families). In actuality, most progressive tax schedules also fulfill the second principle of horizontal equity. The 2005 U.S. federal tax schedule does so with respect to *taxable income*.[14] Indeed, any progressive tax schedule in which marginal tax rates increase with income level in stepwise fashion will fulfill the second principle as long as the marginal rate is less than 100 percent. The reason is that after-tax income must increase monotonically (that is, in direct relation with) before-tax income. Once the marginal tax rate hits 100 percent, this relation no longer holds. If the 100 percent limitation condition is met, the post-tax income of taxpayer i will always be greater than that of taxpayer j as long as i's pre-tax income is greater.[15] Thus, a progressive tax fulfills the principle of vertical equity and will generally satisfy the second principle of horizontal equity, except in perverse cases.[16]

Both dimensions of equity are relevant for policy making. With regard to vertical equity, the notion that the tax system should reduce the overall inequality in the distribution of income accords with many arguments in favor of social justice. A somewhat different justification is based on the principle of the "ability to pay," which holds that taxpayers with greater resources should contribute a higher proportion of their resources to the maintenance of the state. This condition also derives ultimately from a sense of fair play.

With regard to horizontal equity, the unequal treatment of equals and rank reversals may generate social conflict in a society such as ours that generally views market incomes (and therefore individual ranking in the income distribution) as deserved. Tax policies that allow one family to have greater after-tax income than another family that has the same before-tax income goes against our usual notion of fairness. Likewise, a tax system that elevates a lower before-tax individual above a higher before-tax person may create considerable resentment. Thus, both equal treatment of equals and rank preservation appear to form part of the general notion of social justice.[17]

16.4   DISTRIBUTIONAL CONSEQUENCES OF THE U.S. TAX SYSTEM

Does the U.S. tax system help to reduce overall income inequality, increase it, or leave it basically unaltered? This is the subject of this section of the chapter. We shall begin by looking at the structure of personal income tax and then consider other forms of taxes, including the social security tax, the corporate income tax, and sales taxes. Though the income tax is often at the center of political debates on taxation, it will become apparent that these other forms of taxation also play an important role when considering the overall distributional effects of the tax system.[18]

16.4.1   Tax schedules for the personal income tax

The federal individual income tax was enacted in 1913. There is an interesting history associated with this tax. The first federal tax on personal income was enacted during the Civil War and lasted from 1862 through 1871. Support for an income tax languished during the next 20 years but because of the large fortunes made during the 1880s and 1890s a new income tax law was passed in 1894. However, in the following year, the Supreme Court declared this law unconstitutional. The reason is that the Constitution of the United States originally forbade the federal government from levying taxes directly on individuals. Thus, an amendment to the Constitution was necessary for the enactment of a federal income tax. In 1913, the Sixteenth Amendment was ratified, which provided Congress the power "to lay and collect taxes on income, from whatever source derived . . ."[19] The income tax was enacted shortly thereafter in 1913.

For almost 30 years since its passage, the individual income tax applied to only a small percentage of families, since the income exemptions were very high. However, during World War II, the revenue needs of the federal government were enormously expanded, and exemptions were drastically cut. Today, over 90 percent of families are subject to the federal personal income tax and it is the largest source of federal government revenue.

The income concept used in the federal personal income tax system is **adjusted gross income** or **AGI**. AGI differs in several ways from ordinary income. First, AGI includes realized capital gains – that is, the appreciation (or loss) of assets owned by the family that are sold during the year. This is defined as the difference between the selling price and the purchase price.[20] Second, for most retirees, social security income is excluded from AGI.[21] Third, welfare payments, food stamps, veterans' benefits, and fringe benefits received by employees from their employer (such as health insurance and pension contributions) are also excluded. Fourth, interest earned on certain state and local government bonds is, by law, exempt from federal income tax (appropriately enough, these bonds are referred to as *tax-exempt issues*). Fifth, investments made in individual retirement accounts (IRAs), Keogh plans, and 401(k) retirement plans as well as the income on these plans are excluded from income. Sixth, other technical adjustments are made to the income base to obtain AGI.

The actual tax schedule is applied not to AGI but to a concept called **taxable income**. This is defined as AGI less **deductions** less **exemptions**. In 2007, the principal deductions were health expenditures (exceeding 7.5 percent of AGI), state and local income tax, local property tax, mortgage interest payments, and charitable contributions. A filer may choose between the sum of these deductions and the standard deduction provided in the tax schedule (in 2007, $5,350 for a single filer and $10,700 for a married couple filing jointly). Generally, the number of exemptions a family can claim equals the number of individuals in the family. An additional exemption is given for each person in the family over the age of 65 and for blindness. In the 2007 tax schedule, the number of exemptions is multiplied by $3,400 and this total is subtracted from AGI.[22] In 2007, a single person would pay income taxes only on ordinary income above $8,750 and a married couple filing jointly on income above $17,500.

The personal income tax system implicitly adopts an "ability to pay" criterion as the basis of tax payments. This is reflected in two ways. First, the marginal tax rates are progressive with respect to taxable income. Thus, families with more income generally pay higher tax *rates* (see Table 16.1). Second, the tax schedule also adjusts for family size and composition. In Chapter 4, in our discussion of poverty, we argued that needs are based on family size (and, to a lesser extent, composition). Larger families require more income to attain the same living standard as a smaller one. This feature is captured in the use of equivalence classes to define the official poverty line by family size.

A similar notion is embodied in the tax code. This is reflected in two ways. First, the number of exemptions is equal to the size of the taxpaying unit. Larger families have more exemptions. Moreover, there are additional exemptions for the elderly and for blindness. Second, there are basically three different tax schedules provided in the tax code depending on the filing status of the taxpaying unit: (i) singles; (ii) married couples;[23] and (iii) single adults who are heads of households (that is, have children or other dependents living with them). Single individuals pay a higher tax on the same taxable income than married couples, even after adjusting for the greater number of exemptions that can be claimed by the latter. The rationale is that single adults should be more heavily taxed, since they do not bear the same costs and responsibilities of supporting children. Heads of households pay a tax rate that is about halfway between that of singles and married couples with the same taxable income.

The federal tax schedule has been changed frequently over time since its inception in 1913. Table 16.2 shows a history of the federal personal income tax structure from 1913 to 2005,

Table 16.2 The structure of the federal personal income tax, 1913–2005 (for married couples filing jointly with two children)

A. Personal exemptions and bottom and top bracket rates in current dollars

		Marginal tax rates				
		Bottom bracket		Top bracket		
Year	Personal exemptions	Rate (percent)	Taxable income up to	Rate (percent)	Taxable income over	Maximum effective rate (percent)
1913	4,000	1.0	20,000	7.0	50,000	
1917	2,400	2.0	2,000	67.0	2,000,000	
1921	3,300	4.0	4,000	73.0	1,000,000	
1924	3,300	1.5	4,000	46.0	500,000	
1929	4,300	0.4	4,000	24.0	100,000	
1936	3,300	4.0	4,000	79.0	5,000,000	

Table 16.2 (*Continued*)

A. Personal exemptions and bottom and top bracket rates in current dollars

		Marginal tax rates				
		Bottom bracket		Top bracket		Maximum
Year	Personal exemptions	Rate (percent)	Taxable income up to	Rate (percent)	Taxable income over	effective rate (percent)
1941	2,300	10.0	2,000	81.0	5,000,000	
1944	2,000	23.0	2,000	94.0	200,000	90.0
1946	2,000	19.0	2,000	86.5	200,000	85.5
1948	2,400	16.6	4,000	82.1	400,000	77.0
1950	2,400	17.4	4,000	91.0	400,000	87.0
1953	2,400	22.2	4,000	92.0	400,000	88.0
1960	2,400	20.0	4,000	91.0	400,000	
1966	2,400	14.0	1,000	70.0	200,000	
1969	2,400	14.0	1,000	77.0	200,000	
1975	3,000	14.0	1,000	70.0	200,000	
1980	4,000	14.0	2,100	70.0	212,000	
1983	4,000	12.0	2,100	50.0	106,000	
1986	8,000	15.0	32,400	28.0	208,560	
1991	8,600	15.0	34,000	31.0	82,150	
1993	9,400	15.0	36,900	39.6	250,000	
2001	11,600	15.0	45,200	39.1	297,350	
2005	12,800	10.0	14,600	35.0	326,450	

B. Marginal tax rate (in percent) by level of taxable income in 1987 dollars

	Taxable income							
Year	5,000	10,000	25,000	50,000	75,000	100,000	250,000	1,000,000
1944	23.0	23.0	29.0	37.0	50.0	56.0	75.0	93.0
1946	19.0	20.9	24.7	36.1	47.5	53.2	71.3	86.5
1948	16.6	16.6	19.4	26.4	33.4	37.8	57.2	78.3
1950	17.4	17.4	20.0	27.3	34.6	39.1	59.2	82.5
1953	22.2	22.2	24.6	34.0	42.0	53.0	68.0	91.0
1960	20.0	20.0	26.0	34.0	43.0	50.0	69.0	90.0
1966	15.0	17.0	22.0	28.0	36.0	45.0	60.0	70.0
1969	17.6	20.9	24.2	35.2	42.9	52.8	68.2	77.0
1975	17.0	19.0	25.0	39.0	50.0	53.0	66.0	70.0
1980	14.0	18.0	28.0	49.0	54.0	59.0	70.0	70.0
1983	13.0	15.0	26.0	40.0	44.0	50.0	50.0	50.0
1986	15.0	15.0	15.0	28.0	33.0	33.0	28.0	28.0
1991	15.0	15.0	28.0	28.0	31.0	31.0	31.0	31.0
1993	15.0	15.0	28.0	28.0	31.0	36.0	39.6	39.6
2001	15.0	15.0	15.0	27.5	30.5	30.5	39.1	39.1
2005	10.0	15.0	15.0	25.0	28.0	28.0	35.0	35.0
Addendum: Ratio of 2005 rate to 1944 rate:								
	0.43	0.65	0.52	0.68	0.56	0.50	0.47	0.38

Sources: 1913–1983: Pechman, J.A. (1983). *Federal Tax Policy*, 4th edition. Washington, DC: Brookings Institution; 1986–2005: Federal income tax return, Form 1040, 1986, 1991, 1993, 2001, and 2005.

featuring the years in which there was a change in the tax laws. The first panel shows the marginal tax rates of the lowest and top income brackets, as well as the personal exemptions for a family of four. In 1913, the marginal tax rates ranged from a low of 1 percent to a high of 7 percent, with the top bracket beginning at $50,000 (Panel A). By 1917, during World War I, the top marginal rate had been increased to 67 percent, for a bracket of $2,000,000 or more.

The top marginal rate declined during the 1920s, reaching a low of 24 percent in 1929. During the 1930s the marginal rates increased again and by 1944, in the midst of World War II, reached a high of *94 percent*. The top marginal rate then declined during the late 1940s (falling to 82 percent in 1948) but was again over 90 percent during the Korean War (reaching 92 percent in 1953). During the 1960s and 1970s, the top marginal rate dropped to 70 percent (though it was raised to 77 percent in 1969, during the Vietnam War).

During the Reagan years, there was a substantial reduction in the top marginal rate. The 1981 Tax Act lowered it to 50 percent; and the rather famous Tax Reform Act of 1986 reduced it still further to 28 percent.[24] However, in the Tax Act of 1991, during the George Bush administration, the top marginal rate was raised to 31 percent, and the first year of the Clinton administration saw the top marginal rate rising again, to 39.6 percent in 1993. During George W. Bush's administration, the top marginal tax rate was first lowered to 39.1 percent and then to 35.0 percent in 2005, where it is scheduled to remain until 2010 (under current law).[25]

Students today might be astonished at how high marginal tax rates have been in the past in the United States. From 1936 to 1964, the highest marginal rate never fell below 77 percent and during periods of war hovered around 90 percent. Even during the late 1960s and the 1970s, it tended to be in the 70–75 percent range. It was not until Reagan's second term of office that the top rate returned to the 30 percent range, though in 1993 it rose back close to 40 percent but subsequently fell back to the mid-30 percent range.

The top marginal rate is one indicator of the progressivity of the tax system, since the higher it is the greater the range in the marginal and hence average tax rates by income class. However, it is difficult to compare the relative progressivity of the tax structure across years from Panel A for three reasons. First, only the bottom and top marginal rates are shown, rather than the whole structure of marginal rates. Second, the income brackets are changing over time (compare the cut-off points for the lowest and highest tax brackets), so that the range of marginal rates by themselves do not give a full indication of the degree of progressivity of the tax system.

Third, even if the tax brackets were unchanging over time in *nominal* terms (that is, current dollars), they might still be changing in *real* terms. That is to say, with inflation occurring, a family with the same real income over time would be forced into higher and higher marginal tax brackets, even if the tax schedule remain unaltered in nominal terms. This phenomenon is referred to as "bracket creep."[26] However, tax brackets are now indexed for inflation.

To correct for inflation, Panel B of Table 16.2 shows the marginal rate schedule at constant dollar (1987 dollars) levels of taxable income for selected years between 1944 and 2005. Marginal tax rates have generally fallen at all real income levels since the end of World War II. At the bottom income level, $5,000, the marginal tax rate fell from 23 to 10 percent between 1944 and 2005, at the next lowest level, $10,000, from 23 to 15 percent, and at the next level, $25,000, from 29 to 15 percent, though the declines were not continuous over time and in some years, such as 1953, the tax rates were raised rather sharply.

At the $50,000 level, the marginal tax rate also fluctuated over time, falling from 37 percent in 1944 to 26 percent in 1948, rising to 49 percent in 1980, falling to 28 percent in 1986 and then to 25 percent in 2005. Similar patterns are evident at the next three income levels. The pattern is slightly different at a million dollars of taxable income. The marginal rate declined from 93 to 78 percent between 1944 and 1948, returned to 90 percent in 1960, fell to 70 percent in

1966, 50 percent in 1983, and 28 percent in 1986.[27] Since then, it first increased to 39.6 percent in 1993 but fell back to 35 percent in 2005.

Though tax rates have fallen at all real income levels between 1944 and 2005, the *relative* decline has been greater at the lowest and upper two income levels. At the lowest income level, the marginal tax rate fell by 57 percent; while at the middle-income level of $50,000, it was down by 32 percent. At both the $75,000 and $100,000 levels, the marginal tax rate was down by about a half, while at $250,000 of taxable income, the 1993 rate was down by slightly more than half and at a million dollars, it was down by 62 percent. Thus, the successive waves of tax reform and tax reduction acts since the end of World War II have generally benefited the rich more than the poor and middle class, with the possible exception of the Earned Income Tax Credit (EITC), which we will discuss in Section 16.5 below.

16.4.2   Effective tax rates for the personal income tax

The tax schedule records the relation between tax liability and taxable income. As such, it is also referred to as the *nominal tax rate*. The **effective tax rate** is defined as the ratio of actual tax payments to total taxpayer income. The difference in the two concepts reflects primarily the difference between total income and taxable income.

We have already indicated two sources of difference in the two concepts of income. The first is based on the number of exemptions a taxpayer can claim, which depends primarily on the number of individuals in the family. The second is based on either the standard deduction or itemized deductions. For higher income taxpayers, the latter can be a source of considerable reduction in taxable income, particularly with regard to state and local tax payments, interest payments,[28] and charitable deductions.

A third source is exclusions to ordinary income – mainly, social security benefits, interest income on tax-exempt state and local government bonds, contributions to and income on IRAs, 401(k) plans, and other retirement accounts,[29] and unemployment insurance receipts (in some years). Other income exclusions come from "tax preference items" such as accelerated depreciation on certain kinds of investments and depletion allowances for oil and gas drilling. A fourth source is tax limitations on long-term capital gains and dividends. In 2007, both were subject to a *maximum* tax rate of 15 percent.[30]

A fifth source is **tax credits** that can be used to offset the amount of taxes owed. These include the EITC, which applies to low-income individuals with children (see Section 16.5 for more details); a child tax credit, which applies mainly to low- and middle-income families who have children living in the home; a tax credit for child care expenses, which applies mainly to low- and middle-income families who pay for child care; and an investment tax credit (applicable in some years), which applies to self-employed workers who purchase capital goods used in their business.[31]

Table 16.3 presents estimates for 1985 showing the relation between nominal and effective tax rates by level of ordinary income.[32] Average nominal tax rates were highly progressive, ranging from 11.6 to 48.7 percent. The next four columns show how exemptions, deductions, and tax preference items reduce the actual tax burden. Personal exemptions reduced the effective tax rate by 7.3 percentage points for the lowest income class but by only 0.1 percentage points for the top income class. This is not too surprising, since in 1985 the dollar value of exemptions depended only on family characteristics, not family income.[33]

The tax offset of deductions generally rises with the level of income. Deductions reduced the effective tax rate by 4.3 percentage points for the lowest income and 8.0 percentage points for the highest. The reason is that lower income families usually claim the standard deduction whereas

Table 16.3 Effective and nominal tax rates of the federal personal income tax system, 1985 (percent of ordinary income)

Total ordinary income[a]	Average nominal tax rate	Reduction due to:				Effective tax rate	Difference between nominal and effective tax rate
		Personal exemptions	Deductions	Tax preference items[b]	Others[c]		
0–3,000	11.6	7.3	4.3	—	1.0	−1.0	12.6
3–5,000	12.6	4.7	6.7	—	1.7	−0.5	13.1
5–7,000	13.6	4.1	5.6	0.2	2.5	1.2	12.4
7–10,000	14.8	3.5	4.8	0.1	3.0	3.4	11.4
10–15,000	17.3	3.5	4.8	0.2	3.4	5.4	11.9
15–20,000	20.3	4.0	5.0	0.3	4.2	6.8	13.5
20–25,000	23.2	4.0	5.7	0.5	5.0	8.0	15.2
25–35,000	26.9	4.0	7.0	0.7	6.0	9.2	17.7
35–50,000	31.2	3.5	8.4	1.6	6.7	11.0	20.2
50–75,000	35.4	2.8	9.1	1.5	8.1	13.9	21.5
75–100,000	39.5	2.0	9.5	2.5	8.4	17.1	22.4
100–150,000	42.2	1.5	9.4	3.4	8.1	19.8	22.4
150–200,000	44.3	1.1	9.0	4.2	7.1	22.9	21.4
200–500,000	46.1	0.7	8.6	6.0	5.2	25.6	20.5
500–1,000,000	47.8	0.3	8.6	9.8	3.0	26.1	21.7
1,000,000 +	48.7	0.1	8.0	16.4	1.4	22.8	25.9
Average	30.1	3.3	7.6	1.5	6.2	11.5	18.6

a   Defined as the sum of adjusted gross income; excluded dividends, capital gains, and other tax preference items; tax-exempt state and local government bond interest; social security benefits, unemployment compensation, and workmen's compensation insurance; employer-provided health insurance, life insurance, and other tax exempt benefits; and other miscellaneous items.
b   Includes capital gains exclusion, IRA and Keogh accounts, accelerated depreciation, and other tax preference items.
c   Includes excluded social security benefits and other transfer payments; EITC, investment outlays, and child care expenses; and the tax advantages of income splitting.
Source: Pechman, J.A. (1983). *Federal Tax Policy*, 4th edition. Washington, DC: Brookings Institution. The figures are based on averages for married couples, filing separately.

richer families can generally claim more itemized deductions, because they pay higher state and local taxes and mortgage interest and give larger charitable contributions.

The effect of tax preference items such as excluded capital gains, accelerated depreciation, and the various tax shelters described above on the effective tax rate was very dramatic. The tax offset was almost nonexistent for incomes below $100,000 and then increased sharply with income level, to 16.4 percentage points for incomes above $1 million.

The other tax provisions benefited different income classes. Income splitting in 1985 helped families with incomes ranging between $35,000 and $200,000. The exclusion of social security income aided income classes $10,000 to $30,000, reducing their effective tax rate by about 3 percentage points. Tax credits from the EITC helped income classes below $10,000 (1.0–1.5 percentage point reduction in their effective tax rate), while the investment tax credit benefited the wealthy, above $100,000 of income (1.1–1.7 percentage point reduction in the effective tax rate).

On average, the result of these special provisions of the tax code reduced the average tax rate by about two-thirds, from its nominal level of 30 percent to only 12 percent. The biggest effect came from deductions, which reduced the effective tax rate by 7.6 percentage points. Exemptions lessened the tax burden by another 3.3 percentage point. The exclusion of transfer payments accounted for an additional 2.1 percentage points, tax preference items for 1.5 percentage points, income splitting for 3.6 percentage points, and tax credits for 0.5 percentage points.

Overall, the higher income classes benefited more from the tax reduction provisions of the tax code. The tax burden of the lowest income class was reduced by 13 percentage points, whereas that of the highest income class fell by 26 percentage points (last column of Table 16.3). The tax reduction effect rose almost monotonically with the income level of the taxpayer. The resulting effective tax rate schedule was still progressive, ranging from −1.0 to 23 percent. However, it was less progressive than the nominal tax rate schedule. We shall return to effective tax rates when we consider the effects of the total tax system.

16.4.3   The payroll tax

The second-largest source of federal government revenue is now the payroll tax. It was first introduced by the Social Security Act of 1935 and has grown enormously since the end of World War II. Unlike most other taxes, payroll taxes are "earmarked" to finance specific programs of the government, notably the social security system.

We have talked at some length about the social security system in the previous chapter from its standpoint as a transfer system. In this chapter, we consider the system from its tax side. The 1935 Social Security Act set up two different programs – old-age benefits and unemployment insurance. The former is technically referred to as the "old age, survivors, disability, and health insurance program, or OASDHI, though it is more commonly referred to as the "social security system." In 1935, the system provided only old-age (retirement) benefits. This was supplemented in 1939 by survivor's benefits, in 1957 by disability benefits, and in 1966 by medical benefits for persons 65 and over (also called Medicare).

Table 16.4 highlights the tremendous increase in the social security tax since 1937. There are two dimensions to the tax. The first is the tax rate, which is imposed only on wages, salaries, and other forms of employee remuneration, such as tips for waiters and self-employment income. The tax is imposed equally on employee and employers, so that the total tax rate is actually double the amount shown in Table 16.4. The second is referred to as the maximum taxable wage base. The social security tax is imposed on employee compensation only up to this amount.[34]

In 1937, the social security tax was 1.0 percent on wages and salaries for both the employee and employer, and the tax was levied on earnings up to $3,000. This rate remained in effect until 1950, when it was raised to 1.5 percent. After that point, both the tax rate and the maximum taxable wage base were steadily raised. The tax rate rose to 3.0 percent in 1960, 4.8 percent in 1970, 6.13 percent in 1980, 7.0 percent in 1985, and 7.65 percent in 1990, where it is scheduled to remain for the foreseeable future. Even more dramatic is the rise in the maximum earnings level, from $3,000 in 1950 to $4,200 in 1960, $7,800 in 1970, $25,900 in 1980, and $60,600 in 1994. Since 1982, the top limit on earnings has been increased annually at the same rate as the growth in average wages, and this provision is still in effect today. Between 1937 and 1993, the tax rate has increased more than seven-fold and the maximum earnings limit by a factor of 20.

It should be clear that with respect to wages and salaries, the social security tax is proportional up to the maximum taxable earnings, and then turns regressive. This is so because the marginal tax rate is constant up to maximum earnings and then becomes zero. As a result, the average tax rate also remains constant up to the maximum base level, and then declines with

Table 16.4   Social security (OASDHI) tax rates and maximum taxable earnings, selected years, 1937–2008

Year	Employee tax rate (percent)	Maximum taxable wage base
1937–49	1.00	3,000
1950	1.50	3,000
1955	2.00	4,200
1960	3.00	4,200
1965	3.625	4,200
1970	4.80	7,800
1975	5.85	14,100
1980	6.13	25,900
1985	7.05	39,600
1990	7.65	51,300
1994	7.65	60,600
2000	7.65	76,200
2005	7.65	90,000
2008[a]	7.65	102,000

The tax rate is shown for the employee portion only. The employer also pays the same amount, so that the total tax rate is double this amount.
a   Under current law.
Sources: U.S. House of Representatives (1994). Committee on Ways and Means, *Overview of Entitlement Programs: 1994 Green Book*. Washington, DC: U.S. Government Printing Office, July; U.S. House of Representatives (2004). Committee on Ways and Means, *Overview of Entitlement Programs: 2004 Green Book*. Washington, DC: U.S. Government Printing Office, July.

earnings, asymptotically approaching zero. We shall discuss the structure of the social security tax system with respect to family income in Section 16.4.6 below.

Unemployment insurance is a much smaller tax. Though it is a federally mandated tax, it is administered separately by each state under federal guidelines and therefore the exact tax structure varies across states. It is generally levied only on the employer. In 1937, the federal unemployment insurance tax rate was set at 1.0 percent of payrolls on all wages. It has also been periodically raised, to 3.0 percent in 1939 (on earnings up to $3,000), 3.5 percent in 1983 (on earnings up to $7,000), 6.2 percent in 1985 (on earnings up to $7,000), 5.4 percent in 1993 (on earnings up to $8,000 to $10,000 in most states), and 6.2 percent of earnings up to $7,000 in 2007. Though the tax rates look high (5 to 6 percent), the earnings base is so low that the proceeds from this tax are quite small – 0.6 percent of total wages in 2003.[35]

16.4.4   Other federal taxes

Another large source of federal revenue is the **corporation income tax**. Established in 1909, this is levied directly on businesses and is based on their reported profits. The top marginal tax rate was raised from 38 percent in 1946 to 52 percent in 1952, where it generally remained until 1969. It was since been lowered to 48 percent in 1971, 46 percent in 1979, 34 percent in 1986, and 35 percent in 1993, where it has remained through 2007.

Like the personal income tax, the marginal corporate tax increases with the income (profits) of the company. The federal corporate income tax schedule looks quite progressive. In 2007, the lowest marginal tax rate was 15 percent on taxable income up to $50,000, 25 percent in the next bracket up to $75,000, 34 percent up to $100,000, and then between 34 and 39 percent for income above $100,000. The progressivity of this schedule is generally regarded as a concession to small businesses, and since many corporations earn incomes in the millions and billions, the vast majority of corporate taxable income (over 80 percent) is subject to the top rate of 35 percent. However, as with the personal income tax, there is a gulf between the nominal corporate tax rates and the actual (effective) rates paid by corporations. Most of the difference is due to tax preference items, such as accelerated depreciation.[36] The Center on Budget and Policy Priorities estimates an average effective corporate tax rate (corporate tax receipts as a percent of corporate profits) of 27 percent in 2002, compared to a nominal maximum rate of 35 percent.[37]

There are several other sources of federal revenue. One is the *excise tax*. This is like a sales tax, except that it is levied on a small number of items, including alcohol and tobacco products (these are sometimes referred to as "sin taxes"), gasoline and other oil products, automobiles and other vehicles, and jewelry, furs, and other luxury goods. A second is the **customs duty**, which is levied on imports. The structure of customs duties, or tariffs, is quite complex and reflects, among other considerations, the degree to which different industries can achieve protection, the tariff and other export restrictions of countries with which the United States trades, and international rules and regulations (such as the General Agreement on Trade and Tariffs – GATT) regarding tariffs.

The third is the **estate tax**, which is levied on inheritances. Federal estate taxes were first introduced in 1916, with major revisions in 1976 and 1981. The current system provides for the taxation of the value of an estate at the time of death of an individual. Moreover, the estate tax system is integrated with the gift tax, which refers to the (*inter-vivos*) voluntary transfer of assets from one individual to another. In principle, gifts are aggregated over the lifetime of an individual, and the lifetime aggregate of gifts are combined with the value of an estate at death. The estate tax applies to the full value of gifts and estates.

As of 2007, each individual is exempted from estate taxes on net worth up to $2,000,000. Wealth above that amount is levied at marginal tax rates, which begin at 18 percent and reach as high as 46 percent (for estates over $4,000,000). All forms of wealth are included in the tax base for calculating the gift-estate tax except pension annuities and life insurance. Though on the books the estate tax might appear to be an effective way of limiting inheritances, in fact collections from this tax are very small, about $20 billion in 2005 or about 1 percent of total federal tax receipts.[38] There are also many loopholes and avoidance mechanisms such as special trust fund arrangements associated with the estate tax.[39]

16.4.5 State and local government taxes

State governments rely on two major sources of revenues – income taxes and general sales taxes. The vast majority of states today now have an income tax. State personal income taxes are usually modeled directly on the federal tax structure. In some states, the marginal tax rates can be quite high (in New York State, the top marginal tax rate in 2005 was 7.7 percent on $500,000 or more of taxable income for married couples). A few localities, such as New York City, also enact a personal income tax. In addition, almost all states follow the federal government by enacting a separate income tax on corporations. In addition, all states except Nevada have an estate tax.[40]

The main source of state revenue is the general sales tax. Almost all states today have such a tax, with rates varying from 2 to 9 percent. This tax is levied on retail sales only and is therefore paid directly by the individual consumer. Most states exempt food and medicines from the tax base.

The principal source of revenue for local governments is the property tax. This is levied on real estate owned by individuals and businesses (that owned by nonprofit organizations such as churches and universities is usually exempt). Some localities also enact a general sales tax. In addition, there are often "user fees" for specific services provided by local governments, such as water and sewerage and sanitation collection.

16.4.6   The overall tax bite?

What are the overall distributional consequences of the tax system in the United States? This is a consequence of two factors. The first is the progressivity or regressivity of the individual taxes that make up the tax system. The second is the relative magnitude of the various taxes. Together, they determine the overall regressivity or progressivity of the tax system.

Let us first begin with the magnitudes of the different taxes. Table 16.5 (also see Figure 16.6) shows the share of the receipts from each of the major taxes in federal government income, state and local government income, and total government income between 1955 and 2005. Payments of federal individual income taxes are the principal source of federal government revenue, ranging from 42 to 46 percent. Generally speaking, this share remained fairly constant between 1955 and 2005. Revenue from state and local individual income taxes increased rather sharply, from 4 to 15 percent of total state and local government revenue over this period. However, together, personal income taxes made up a relatively constant share of about one-third of total government revenue between 1955 and 2005.[41]

In contrast, receipts from the federal corporate income tax fell sharply, from 27 percent of total federal revenue in 1955 to only 8 percent in 1985 but then rose back to 13 percent in 2005. In the 1950s, this was the second principal source of federal income but by the 2000s, it had

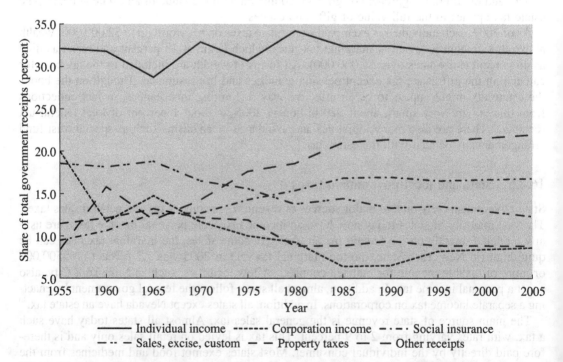

Figure 16.6   Percentage distribution of total government receipts by source, 1955–2005

Table 16.5 Distribution of government receipts by source, 1955–2005 (percent)

Source	1955	1965	1975	1985	1995	2005
A. Total federal government[a]	100	100	100	100	100	100
Individual income taxes	44	42	44	46	44	43
Corporation income taxes	27	22	15	8	12	13
Excise taxes	14	12	6	5	4	3
Customs duties and fees	1	1	1	2	1	1
Social insurance taxes and contributions[b]	12	19	30	36	36	37
Estate and gift taxes	1	2	2	1	1	1
Other receipts[c]	1	1	2	3	3	2
B. Total state and local government receipts[d]	100	100	100	100	100	100
Individual income taxes	4	7	12	14	15	15
Corporation income taxes	3	3	4	4	3	2
Sales and gross receipts taxes	27	27	27	26	25	25
Property taxes	38	35	28	21	22	22
All other[e]	27	28	29	35	35	37
C. Total government receipts[f]	100	100	100	100	100	100
Individual income taxes	32	29	31	32	32	32
Corporation income taxes	20	15	10	6	8	9
Sales and gross receipts taxes, excise taxes, and customs duty	19	19	16	15	14	12
Social insurance taxes and contributions[b]	8	12	18	21	21	22
Property taxes	11	13	12	9	9	9
Other[g]	9	13	14	17	16	17
D. Total government receipts as a percent of GDP[h]						
Total	24.3	27.8	31.8	31.8	31.0	29.1
Federal government	17.0	17.4	18.5	18.5	18.3	17.3
State and local government	7.3	10.4	13.3	13.3	12.7	11.8

a   *Sources*: 1955–1980: Pechman, J.A. (1983). *Federal Tax Policy*, 4th edition. Washington, DC: Brookings Institution; 1981–2005: *Economic Report of the President, 2007*. The total includes both on-budget and off-budget items.
b   Includes employee and employer contributions to OASDHI and payroll taxes for unemployment insurance.
c   Includes earnings of Federal Reserve banks and other miscellaneous receipts.
d   *Source: Economic Report of the President, 2007*. Total excludes revenues or expenditures of publicly owned utilities and liquor stores, and of insurance trust activities. Revenue from the federal government, other intergovernmental receipts and payments between state and local governments are also excluded.
e   Includes other taxes and charges and miscellaneous revenues.
f   Includes miscellaneous receipts and user charges and excludes all intergovernmental transfers.
g   Includes other taxes and charges and miscellaneous revenues as well as estate and gift taxes and earnings of Federal Reserve banks.
h   *Source: Economic Report of the President, 2007*.

declined to a distant third. On the state level, corporate income taxes remained rather steady at 2 to 4 percent of total state and local government revenue. Together, corporate income taxes declined from 20 percent of total government revenue in 1955 to only 9 percent in 2005.

Federal excise taxes also showed a sharp decline as a source of federal government revenue, from 14 to only 3 percent over the years from 1955 to 2005. Customs duties and fees have remained small, accounting for only 1 to 2 percent of total federal income. Among state and local governments, sales taxes accounted for 25 to 27 percent of their receipts, with the share remaining fairly constant over time. Together, sales, excise, and customs taxes diminished as a source of total government receipts, from 19 percent in 1955 to 12 percent in 2005.

With corporate income and excise taxes declining in importance on the federal level, what source of revenue made up the difference? The most dramatic growth occurred in social insurance (mainly social security) taxes, which rose from 12 percent of federal revenue in 1955 to 37 percent in 2005. It also increased from 8 percent of total government income to 22 percent. In 1955, it was fourth in importance as a source of federal receipts but by 1970 it had climbed into second place, where it has since remained. Today, collections from social insurance are only slightly behind those from federal personal income taxes (37 versus 43 percent). By the year 2015, social insurance payments may be the main source of federal government receipts.

On the state and local government level, the two other principal sources of revenue are property taxes and an "other" category, which principally includes user fees (for example, special taxes for garbage collection, water and sewer usage, and fees for parks, mass transit, and the like). Property taxes were the most important source of state and local government revenue in 1955, accounting for 38 percent, but by 2005 its share had dropped to 22 percent. Other taxes, in contrast, have risen from 27 to 37 percent. On the federal level, estate and gift taxes and other sources have remained relatively minor as a source of revenue.

Panel D of Table 16.5 shows the share of government receipts in GDP. This is another factor in determining the distributional effect of the tax system on family income. If total taxes represent only a small percent of personal income, then their distributional impact will be small, irrespective of how progressive or regressive the tax structure is.[42]

Government receipts as a percent of GDP increased between 1955 and 1970, from 24 to 32 percent. The share remained fairly steady until 1990 but actually came down a bit to 29 percent by 2005. Moreover, even between 1955 and 1985, federal receipts increased rather modestly as a share of GDP, from 17.0 to 18.5 percent but then fell back to 17.3 percent in 2005. The biggest growth was on the state and local government level, whose income rose from 7.3 to 11.8 percent of GDP between 1955 and 2005. In 1955, the federal budget was much bigger than the total budget of state and local governments (about two and a half times larger) but by 2005, it was only 47 percent larger. However, it should be stressed even at this point that governmental receipts include income (principally, social security taxes) that is merely transferred from one set of individuals to another. When we "net" this out of the government account and look at the real expenditure side of the government sector, the size of the government sector appears much smaller (see Section 16.6)!

16.4.7   International comparisons of taxation

Before we examine the effective tax rate structure in the United States, it might be elucidating to compare tax burdens in the United States with those of other industrialized countries. There is often the sense that the United States is a very heavily taxed society. We, of course, just saw that total taxes paid in the United States as a percent of GDP has remained fairly constant since 1970. However, how does the U.S. tax rate compare to that of other advanced economies?

Comparisons with other OECD countries are shown for 1981, 1990, and 2004 in Table 16.6 (also see Figure 16.7). In 2004, the United States had the third lowest overall tax rate among OECD countries (only Korea and Mexico were lower), at 26 percent of GDP.[43] The highest was Sweden, at 50 percent. Eight countries (including Sweden) paid more than 40 percent of their national income in the form of taxes, and all except Mexico, Korea, the United States,

Table 16.6 Tax revenues as a percentage of GDP among OECD countries, 1981, 1990, and 2004

Country	Total	2004 Individual income	Corporate income	Social security contributions	Taxes on goods and services[a]	Other taxes	1981 total	1990 total
Sweden	50.4	15.8	3.2	14.2	13.0	4.3	51.3	56.9
Denmark	48.8	24.7	3.2	1.2	16.0	3.8	45.3	48.6
Belgium	45.0	13.8	3.6	12.8	11.3	3.5	45.4	44.9
Finland	44.2	13.5	3.6	11.1	14.0	2.0		38.0
Norway	44.0	10.3	9.9	8.9	13.1	1.7	48.5	46.3
France	43.4	7.4	2.7	15.0	11.1	7.2	43.0	43.7
Austria	42.6	9.7	2.3	12.6	12.0	6.0	42.6	41.6
Italy	41.1	10.4	2.8	10.9	10.9	6.0	33.7	39.1
Iceland	38.7	14.3	1.3	3.2	15.9	4.0		
Czech Republic	38.4	4.9	4.8	14.0	12.0	2.8		
Hungary	38.1	6.8	2.2	11.3	15.5	2.2		
Luxembourg	37.8	6.7	5.8	9.5	11.5	4.3		50.3
Netherlands	37.5	6.2	3.1	11.1	12.0	5.3	45.5	45.2
United Kingdom	36.0	10.3	2.9	6.5	11.5	4.7	37.4	36.7
New Zealand	35.6	14.6	5.5	0.0	12.0	3.5		38.2
Greece	35.0	4.8	3.3	10.5	13.0	3.4		36.5
Spain	34.8	6.2	3.4	10.4	9.7	5.1		34.4
Germany	34.7	7.9	1.6	13.0	10.1	2.1	37.4	37.7
Portugal	34.5	5.5	2.9	10.6	13.3	2.2		34.6
Poland	34.4	4.1	2.0	14.1	12.4	1.8		
Canada	33.5	11.8	3.5	4.9	8.7	4.7	34.8	37.1
Turkey	31.3	4.7	2.3	6.0	14.9	3.5		27.8
Australia	31.2	12.5	5.7	0.0	8.9	4.1	31.5	30.8
Slovak Republic	30.3	2.8	2.5	11.3	12.1	1.6		
Ireland	30.1	8.2	3.6	4.2	11.4	2.6		37.2
Switzerland	29.2	10.2	2.5	6.5	6.9	3.1	30.2	31.7
Japan	26.4	4.7	3.7	8.8	5.3	3.9	26.9	31.3
United States	25.5	8.8	2.2	6.3	4.7	3.4	31.3	29.9
Korea	24.6	3.3	3.5	5.1	8.9	3.7		
Mexico	19.0	4.7	0.0	3.1	10.5	0.6		
EU average	39.7	9.8	3.3	10.3	12.2	4.2		
OECD average	35.9	8.8	3.4	8.4	11.6	3.6	39.0	39.1

Countries are ranked according to their 2004 ratio of taxes to GDP.
a Includes national and local taxes.
Sources: 1981: Pechman, J.A. (1983). *Federal Tax Policy*, 4th edition. Washington, DC: Brookings Institution.
1990: U.S. Census Bureau (1993). *Statistical Abstract of the United States: 1993*, 113th edition. Washington, DC:
U.S. Government Printing Office; 2004: *OECD in Figures, 2007*.

Japan, Switzerland, Ireland, the Slovak Republic, Australia, and Turkey paid more than a third. Interestingly, Japan, the U.S.'s chief economic rival, had a somewhat higher overall tax rate than the United States in 2004 (though it was lower in 1981). Canada's average tax rate in 2004 was 34 percent, compared to 26 percent in the United States.

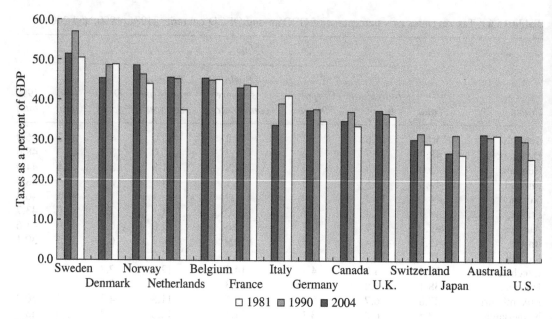

Figure 16.7   Tax revenues as a percent of GDP, selected OECD countries, 1981, 1990, and 2004

Table 16.6 also shows a breakdown of the sources of taxes for 2004. The United States was about average in terms of individual income taxes as a percent of GDP. However, it was below average in the share of corporate income taxes, social security contributions, and sales taxes in GDP. In particular, it was substantially below average in sales taxes – 3.4 percent of GDP compared to an average OECD share of 11.6 percent.

The United States thus appears to be one of the most lightly taxed countries in OECD. However, this does not mean that other countries are worse off than the United States. Indeed, other countries receive much more in the way of publicly provided services from the state – particularly in regard to health care, which is almost entirely paid by the government in most other OECD countries, college tuition, which is almost completely provided for by the government, and an array of income support programs.

16.4.8   The overall effective tax structure in the United States

We now consider the effective tax rates by type of tax. These are shown in Table 16.7 by percentile level of the population, based on the work of Pechman (1985). It should be noted at the outset that these calculations are based on statistical estimates. The raw data come from the Brookings MERGE file, which is a statistical match between household survey data from the Current Population Survey and actual federal tax returns provided by the Internal Revenue Service. The figures on federal individual income taxes paid are computed directly from the federal income tax returns. However, the estimates of payments of other taxes, such as payroll, property, and sales taxes, are simulated on the basis of the available data in the file (for example, sales taxes are estimated on the basis of personal consumption expenditures reported in the raw data, as well as sales tax rates by state of residence).[44]

Moreover, assumptions have to be made regarding the **incidence** of each type of tax. For example, in the case of the corporate income tax, part of the tax is borne by stock holders in the

Table 16.7 Effective tax rates by specific kinds of federal, state, and local taxes, for each population decile and top 5 and 1 percent, 1985

Income group	Individual income tax	Corporate income tax	Payroll taxes	Sales & excise taxes[a]	Property tax	Total taxes
A. Most progressive incidence assumptions used in simulation						
Bottom decile	4.3	0.5	9.4	7.1	0.7	21.9
2nd decile	5.5	0.5	8.7	6.0	0.7	21.3
3rd decile	6.9	0.6	7.9	5.1	0.9	21.4
4th decile	8.2	0.6	7.9	4.8	0.9	22.5
5th decile	9.1	0.7	7.8	4.5	1.0	23.1
6th decile	9.8	0.8	7.5	4.3	1.2	23.5
7th decile	10.3	0.8	7.2	4.1	1.3	23.7
8th decile	11.4	0.9	7.0	3.9	1.3	24.6
9th decile	12.2	1.2	6.4	3.5	1.7	25.1
Top decile	12.7	3.6	3.6	2.0	3.3	25.3
Top 5 percent	12.7	4.5	2.6	1.6	3.8	25.2
Top 1 percent	12.8	5.7	1.4	1.2	4.4	25.5
All deciles	10.9	1.8	6.2	3.6	2.0	24.5
B. Least progressive incidence assumptions used in simulation						
Bottom decile	4.1	2.8	10.8	7.3	3.3	28.2
2nd decile	5.4	2.3	9.5	5.8	2.5	25.6
3rd decile	6.8	2.0	8.6	5.0	2.1	24.6
4th decile	8.1	1.9	8.4	4.8	2.1	25.2
5th decile	8.9	1.9	8.1	4.4	2.1	25.3
6th decile	9.6	1.9	7.8	4.2	2.1	25.6
7th decile	10.0	1.9	7.4	4.0	2.1	25.4
8th decile	11.2	1.8	7.2	3.9	2.2	26.3
9th decile	12.0	1.9	6.5	3.4	2.3	26.1
Top decile	12.9	2.3	3.8	2.0	2.3	23.3
Top 5 percent	13.1	2.4	2.9	1.7	2.3	22.4
Top 1 percent	13.4	2.6	1.8	1.2	2.2	21.2

a   Includes personal property and motor vehicle tax.
Source: Pechman, J.A. (1985). *Who Paid the Taxes, 1966–85?* Washington, DC: Brookings Institution. The figures are based on statistical estimates from the Brookings MERGE file.

company in the form of reduced profits (and hence reduced dividend payments and capital gains) but part of the tax may be "shifted forward" to consumers in the form of higher prices for products of corporate enterprises, so that a portion of the tax is distributed among consumers of corporate products. Different assumptions can be made with regard to the relative proportions of the tax borne by each group. Similar problems exist with other kinds of taxes, principally sales taxes, property taxes, and payroll taxes

The two panels in Table 16.7 show the results of these simulations on the basis of incidence assumptions which lead to the most progressive tax schedules and the least progressive tax schedules (also see Figures 16.8(a) and (b)). It is likely that the true effective tax structure lies in between these two extremes. However, with the exception of the corporate income tax and property tax, the results are quite similar in the two simulations.

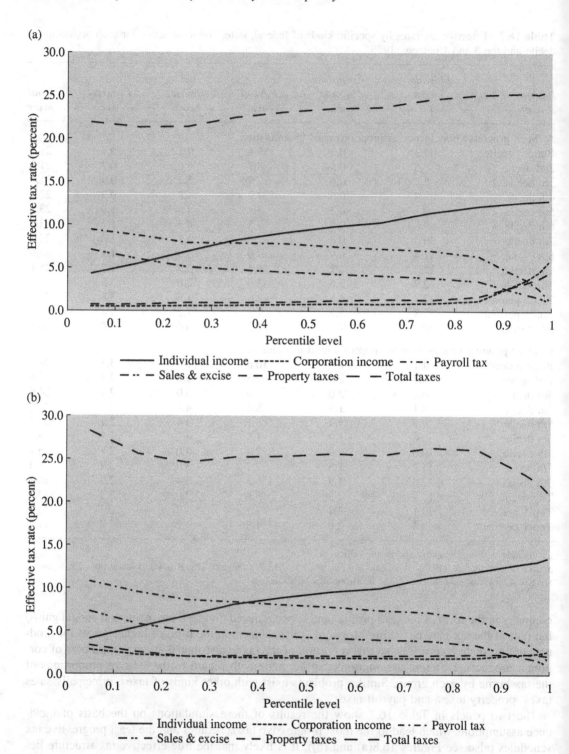

Figure 16.8   Effective tax rates by income percentile, 1985. (a) Most progressive assumption.
(b) Least progressive assumption

The individual income tax was the most progressive tax, with effective tax rates varying from 4 percent for the lowest decile (10 percent of families) to 13 percent for the richest decile in 1985.[45] On average, the individual income tax amounted to 11 percent of family income in that year. The pattern of the corporate income tax was very sensitive to the incidence assumption used. If it is assumed that most of the corporate tax is borne by stock holders, then, as shown in Panel A, the effective tax rate was 1 percent or less for the bottom 90 percent of the income distribution and 3.6 percent for the top 10 percent (even higher for the top percentile). This result reflects the extreme concentration of stock ownership (see Section 5.4.3). On the other hand, if it is assumed that the tax is generally borne by consumers of products of corporations, then the tax was generally a flat (proportional) tax. In both cases, the average effective tax rate was quite small, about 2 percent.

The payroll (mainly, social security) tax was mildly regressive over the bottom nine deciles, and then turned extremely regressive at the top. This pattern reflects two factors. First, low-income families relied almost exclusively on wages and salaries as their source of income. As income increases, other sources of income, such as interest and dividends, became increasingly more important as a source of support. Second, in 1985, the maximum taxable wage base was $39,600. Wages and salaries above this level were not subject to the social security tax. On average, payroll taxes amounted to about 6 percent of total income.

General sales and excise taxes were steeply regressive, with effective tax rates varying from 7 percent for the poorest 10 percent of the population to 2 percent for the richest 10 percent. The reason is that the percentage of family income spent on goods and services subject to these taxes fell with family income. On average, the effective tax rate for sales and excise taxes was 3.6 percent in 1985. Property taxes were either highly progressive if it is assumed that they are fully borne by property owners (Panel A) or proportional if it is assumed that they are shifted to consumers in general (Panel B). Its average effective tax rate was about 2 percent.

Perhaps, the main point of interest is the total effect of all taxes on the distribution of income. This can be calculated by summing up the effective tax rates for the individual taxes. On average, in 1985, total taxes amounted to about 25 percent of personal income. Under the most progressive incidence assumptions, the total tax system was mildly progressive, with effective tax rates rising from 22 percent for the poorest decile to 25 percent for the richest. However, under the least progressive incidence assumptions, the total tax system was mildly regressive, with effective tax rates falling from 28 percent for the poorest decile to 21 percent for the richest. In all likelihood, the actual tax structure was generally a proportional tax on income.

How has the structure of effective tax rates changed over time? Estimates for 3 years – 1966, 1975, and 1988 – made by Pechman (1990) using the same methodology are shown in Table 16.8 (also see Figure 16.9). These are based on the most progressive incidence assumptions – namely, that all corporate taxes are borne by owners of corporate stock and all property taxes by owners of property. The average tax burden appeared to have been about the same in these 3 years, about 25 percent of total income. However, it appears that the tax structure became more progressive at the bottom of the income distribution but less progressive at the top.

In 1966, the effective tax rate was estimated to be 17 percent for the bottom decile, 19 percent for the second decile, between 22 and 23 percent for the third through ninth deciles, 30 percent for the top decile, and 40 percent for the richest 1 percent. In 1988, the effective tax rate for the bottom decile was almost the same as in 1966, but the effective rate for the second and third deciles was lower (16 percent). Tax rates for deciles 4 to 9 were slightly higher in 1988 but lower for the top decile (28 percent). Indeed, the effective tax rate for the top 1 percent in 1988 was 27 percent, compared to 40 percent in 1966. This change reflected in part, the provisions of the 1986 Tax Reform Act.

Table 16.8   Effective tax rates: Total of federal, state, and local taxes, by population percentiles, 1966, 1975, and 1988

Percentile	1966	1975	1988
Bottom decile	16.8	19.7	16.4
2nd decile	18.9	17.6	15.8
3rd decile	21.7	18.9	18.0
4th decile	22.6	21.7	21.5
5th decile	22.8	23.5	23.9
6th decile	22.7	23.9	24.3
7th decile	22.7	24.2	25.2
8th decile	23.1	24.7	25.6
9th decile	23.3	25.4	26.8
Top decile	30.1	27.8	27.7
Top 5 percent	32.7	28.4	27.4
Top 1 percent	39.6	29.0	26.8
All deciles	25.2	25.0	25.4

Source: Pechman, J.A. (1990). The future of the income tax. *American Economic Review*, **80**(1), 1–20. The figures are based on statistical estimates from the Brookings MERGE file. These estimates assume that all corporate income taxes and property taxes are borne by owners of these assets.

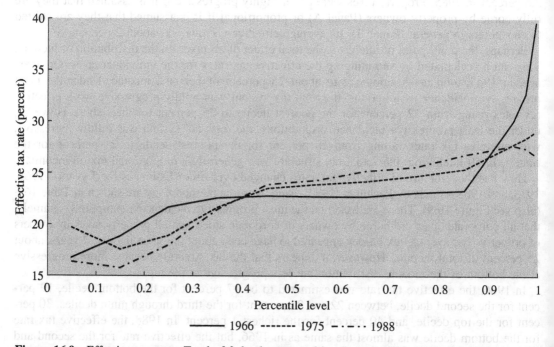

Figure 16.9   Effective tax rates: Total of federal, state, and local taxes, 1966, 1975, and 1988

Table 16.9 Federal tax rates by population percentile, 2004

| | | | | | | Income shares | |
| | | | | | | Pre-tax | Post-tax |
Percentile	*Federal individual*	*Payroll*[a]	*Federal corporate*	*Fed. estate & gifts*	*Total federal*	*income*	*income*
Second quintile	−3.2	10.6	2.0	0.0	9.4	6.1	7.2
Third quintile	3.2	11.2	1.7	0.0	16.1	11.5	12.6
Fourth quintile	7.3	11.6	1.6	0.0	20.5	20.0	20.8
P80–90	9.2	11.9	1.6	0.0	22.7	15.9	16.1
P90–95	11.6	11.5	1.8	0.0	24.9	11.3	11.1
P95–99	16.4	8.1	2.5	0.1	27.2	15.3	14.5
P99–99.9	22.6	3.8	4.0	1.7	32.1	10.7	9.5
P99.9–100	25.2	1.6	4.9	2.4	34.2	9.0	7.7
All	11.5	9.3	2.3	0.4	23.4	100.0	100.0
Memo:							
Gini coefficient						0.601	0.565

a   Includes employee and employer social security and Medicare taxes only.
Source: Piketty, T. & Saez, E. (2007). How progressive is the U.S. federal tax system? A historical and international perspective. *Journal of Economic Perspectives*, **21**(1), 3–24. The figures are based on tax return statistics and the NBER TAXSIM calculator.

Table 16.9 shows the effective *federal* tax rate structure in 2004. The data are from the Internal Revenue Service's *Statistics of Income* (these are based on actual federal tax returns filed for tax year 2004) and provide detail on the very top of the income distribution. According to the analysis of Piketty and Saez (2007), the effective federal income tax was quite progressive, with income tax rates rising from −3.2 percent for the second quintile of taxpayers to 25.2 percent for the *top one-hundredth of 1 percent*.[46] The payroll tax was largely proportional from the second quintile through percentiles 90 to 95 and then became regressive after that. Both the corporate income tax and the federal estate and gift tax were progressive but they were relatively small compared to the other two taxes. Altogether, the effective federal tax structure was progressive, with overall tax rates rising from 9.4 percent for the second quintile of taxpayers to 34.2 percent for the top one-hundredth of 1 percent. The last two columns of Table 16.9 show the pre-tax and post-tax income shares. In 2004, federal taxes increased the income share of the bottom income groups and reduced the share of the upper income groups (for example, the share of the second quintile rose from 6.1 to 7.2 percent and that of the top one-hundredth of 1 percent fell from 9.0 to 7.7 percent). The federal tax system was quite equalizing, causing a sizable reduction in the Gini coefficient, from 0.601 to 0.565.

Table 16.10 (and Figure 16.10) show the changes in the federal tax structure between 1960 and 2004 on the basis of the same data source. Here it is clear that the degree of progressivity of the federal tax system declined markedly over time. The very top tax rate (on the top one-hundredth of 1 percent) fell from 56.9 percent in 1960 to 34.2 percent in 2004 and that paid by P99–P99.9 fell from 37.7 to 32.1 percent. The tax rate paid by the second quintile also fell, from 13.9 to 9.4 percent, but the tax rates paid by percentiles 40 through 99 all rose.

Another way of posing the question of the degree of progressivity of the tax system is to compare Gini coefficients based on before-tax and after-tax income. If the difference between the

Table 16.10   Federal tax rates by income class, 1960–2004

Percentile	1960	1970	1980	1990	2000	2004
Second quintile	13.9	18.5	16.3	16.2	13.1	9.4
Third quintile	15.9	20.2	21.4	21.0	20.0	16.1
Fourth quintile	16.7	20.7	24.5	24.3	23.9	20.5
P80–90	17.4	20.5	26.7	26.2	26.4	22.7
P90–95	18.7	21.4	27.9	27.9	28.7	24.9
P95–99	23.5	25.6	31.0	28.6	31.1	27.2
P99–99.9	37.7	40.3	40.3	32.2	37.0	32.1
P99.9–100	56.9	60.7	51.8	34.4	40.3	34.2
All	21.4	23.3	26.6	25.8	27.4	23.4

Source: Piketty, T. & Saez, E. (2007). How progressive is the U.S. federal tax system? A historical and international perspective. *Journal of Economic Perspectives*, **21**(1), 3–24. The figures are based on tax return statistics and the NBER TAXSIM calculator. Federal taxes include individual, corporate, payroll, and estate taxes.

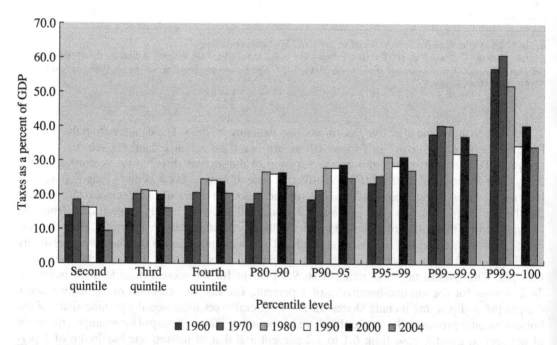

Figure 16.10   Total federal tax rates by income percentile, 1960–2004

before-tax and after-tax Gini coefficient increases over time, this implies that the tax structure has become more progressive; if the difference declines, it has become less progressive (or more regressive).

Three sets of estimates are shown in Table 16.11. The first (Panel A), from the Congressional Budget Office (CBO), was calculated from only federal taxes. In 1977, the Gini coefficient for before-tax income was 0.45 and that for after-federal tax income was 0.42, for a difference of 0.03. The difference was almost the same in 1980. However, in 1984 and 1988, the difference fell to 0.02, despite a large increase in before-tax inequality between 1980 and 1988. The

Table 16.11   Gini coefficients of before-tax and after-tax income, selected years, 1977–2004

Year	Before-tax inequality	After-tax inequality	Difference
A. Before and after federal taxes[a]			
1977	0.450	0.419	0.032
1980	0.463	0.432	0.031
1984	0.488	0.470	0.018
1988	0.494	0.472	0.022
B. Before and after federal taxes[b]			
1988	0.322	0.290	0.032
1992	0.317	0.282	0.036
1996	0.334	0.286	0.048
2000	0.378	0.331	0.046
2004	0.357	0.315	0.042
C. Before and after federal income taxes[c]			
1972	0.468	0.445	0.023
1976	0.485	0.458	0.027
1980	0.496	0.467	0.029
1984	0.524	0.502	0.022
1988	0.567	0.544	0.023

a   *Source*: U.S. Congressional Budget Office (1988). *The Changing Distribution of Federal Taxes: A Closer Look at 1980*, July. Washington, DC: The Congress of the United States.
b   *Source*: Congressional Budget Office, http://www.cbo.gov/ftpdocs/77xx/doc7718/EffectiveTaxRates.pdf. Calculations are based on "comprehensive income," which includes noncash government benefits.
c   *Source*: Slemrod, J. (1992). Taxation and inequality: A time-exposure perspective. In J.M. Poterba (ed.), *Tax Policy and the Economy*. Cambridge, MA: MIT Press.

federal tax structure, which was only mildly progressive in 1977 and 1980, had become even less progressive in 1984 and 1988, a result, in part, of the declining top marginal tax rates from the 1981 and 1986 Tax Acts.

Panel B updates the CBO estimates to 2004. It also uses a difference income concept called "comprehensive income," which includes the value of noncash governmental benefits. These results show the progressivity of the federal tax system increasing from 1988 to 1996, with the difference between the before-tax and after-tax Gini coefficients widening from 0.032 to 0.048. However, with the reductions of the top marginal tax rates after 2001, the difference between the before-tax and after-tax Gini coefficients contracted from 0.048 in 1996 to 0.042 in 2004.

Panel C, from Slemrod (1992), is based only on federal income taxes. Slemrod also used an "expanded" concept of income, which is equal to the sum of AGI, excluded capital gains and dividends, and other income adjustments. The trends are very similar to those shown in Panel A. The difference in the before-tax and after-tax Gini coefficient fell from 0.029 in 1980 to 0.022 in 1984. The 1988 difference was almost the same in 1988 as in 1984. Interestingly, Slemrod's results also show a widening gap between 1972 and 1980, from 0.023 to 0.029. According to the Slemrod figures, the redistributional effect of the federal income tax system increased during the 1970s and then declined during the 1980s, so that the difference in before-tax and after-tax inequality was almost the same in 1988 as in 1972.

16.5   THE NEGATIVE INCOME TAX AND THE EITC

One proposal for helping the low-income population is the **negative income tax**. While reducing the income tax burdens on low-income families would obviously benefit them, there are two reasons why the effect would be relatively limited. First, most families with incomes below the poverty line do not pay any income taxes at all. Second, when poor individuals do pay income tax, the amounts are relatively small. Thus, even fully eliminating income taxes for this group (by, for example, raising the exemption level or standard deduction) would add little to their after-tax income.

As we discussed in the last chapter, the current method of helping poor families is through direct public transfers, such as TANF, food stamps, Medicare, and housing subsidies. These programs target very specific subgroups of the poor (for example, TANF is limited to families with children). Moreover, low-income families with working parents do not generally benefit from these transfer programs.

The negative income tax can be seen as an extension of the progressive structure of the income tax system to existing transfer programs. The major difference is that low-income taxpayers will now pay *negative* rates instead of low positive ones (that is, they will receive a payment from the federal government instead of making one). This is similar to the current workings of the EITC, in which a low-income family with labor earnings below a certain amount will receive a credit from the government. If they owe no income tax, the federal government will still refund the credit to the family (a refundable credit). See below for more discussion of the EITC.

A negative income tax could thus substitute for the patchwork-quilt system of income transfers now in place. As a result, the system would be fairer and more comprehensive than the current transfer system. The administrative costs could also be substantially lower.

There have been different proposals for how such a tax would be structured. The simplest would work something like the following: All individuals or families would now file a federal tax return, including those whose income falls below the current minimum taxable level. As in the current system, taxpayers would compute their taxable income by subtracting the value of their exemptions and deductions from their AGI. The difference now is that if taxable income is negative, the taxpayer would be entitled to a payment from the federal government. The payment is computed by multiplying their (negative) taxable income by a new prespecified tax rate, say −50 percent.

Suppose that personal exemptions are each worth $2,000 and the standard deduction is $3,000 (see Figure 16.11). Then, a family of four with an AGI of $11,000 and taking the standard deduction would have a taxable income of exactly zero ($11,000 − 4 × $2,000 − $3,000). Such a family would pay no income taxes and receive no payment from the government. With these rates, $11,000 would be the "break-even" level. With a negative tax rate of 50 percent, a family with zero income would have a taxable income of −$11,000 and receive a payment from the government of $5,500 (half of $11,000). The $5,500 is referred to as the *basic allowance*, since it is the minimum post-tax income that would be allowed for a family of four.

As is apparent, the payment from the government would decline as income rises between zero and $11,000. For a family of four with $5,000 income, their taxable income would be −$6,000 and their payment from the government $3,000, so that their "post-tax" income would be $8,000. If their income were $6,000, their post-tax income would be $8,500 ($6,000 + $2,500). As a result, their post-tax income would rise with pre-tax income but the marginal gain would be only 50 cents for each additional dollar of income earned. For incomes above $11,000, positive tax rates would then go into effect.

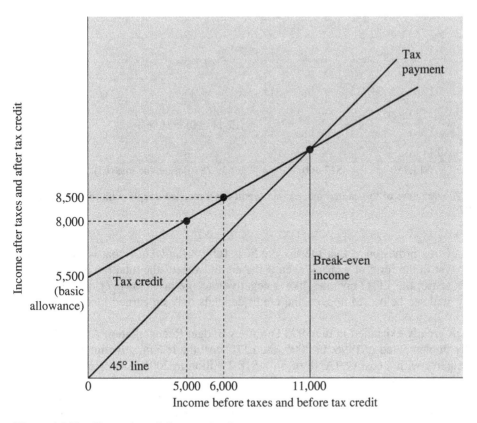

Figure 16.11 Illustration of the negative income tax

As might be apparent, one criticism of the negative income tax is that it creates a disincentive for working.[47] In this example, with an implicit tax rate of 50 percent, each additional dollar earned by a low-income family, below the break-even income level, will net it only 50 cents. The effective wage is thus reduced by half.

Between 1968 and 1982, the federal government sponsored four negative income tax experiments – New Jersey (1968–1972), Rural Iowa and North Carolina (1969–1973), Gary, Indiana (1971–1974), and Seattle and Denver (1971–1982). The experiments varied in their break-even level of income but in all of them, the negative tax rate averaged about 50 percent. The results were remarkably consistent. All the experiments found a negative effect on labor supply associated with the introduction of a negative income tax, but the effects were relatively small. On average, husbands reduced their labor supply by about 2 weeks, wives and single females by about 3 weeks, and youths by about 4 weeks (see Robins, 1985, for a good summary of these results.)[48]

The EITC was introduced into the federal tax code in 1975, mainly as a way of offsetting increased social security taxes for low-income households. The credit operates as a fixed percentage (originally 10 percent in 1975) of earned income (wages, salaries, and tips) up to a pre-specified ceiling ($5,000 originally), which is phased down to zero up to another fixed ceiling ($10,000 originally). The credit applies only to families who have *earned income* below a certain threshold. Moreover, the credit originally pertained only to families with children, though in 1993 it was expanded to include those without children as well.

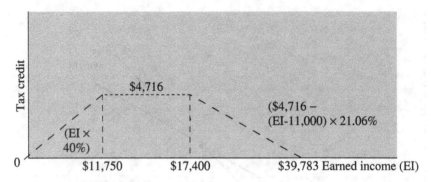

Figure 16.12   The structure of the earned income tax credit for a married couple with two or more children in 2007

One feature of this provision is that the tax credit is fully *refundable* – that is, the credit is sent to the taxpayer in the form of a check even if the credit exceeds the total tax liability of the tax filer. In this sense, the EITC operates like a negative income tax. However, its structure is different, as we will see below. Moreover, the credit depends only on earned income, not total family income.

The EITC was greatly expanded in the 1993 Omnibus Budget Reconciliation Act (OBRA93), which was fully implemented in 1996. In 2005, the EITC cost the federal government $49.2 billion.[49] This compares with a cost of TANF of only $18.2 billion in 2005. The credit depends on the number of children in the family. In 2007, the maximum credit is $4,716 for a family with two or more children, $2,853 for a family with one child, and $428 for those with no children.

The EITC is calculated in three income ranges: the phase-in range; the stationary range; and the phase-out range (see Figure 16.12). In 2007, a married couple with two or more children received a credit equal to 40 percent of the first $11,750 of earned income and $4,716 for earned income between $11,750 and $17,400 (hence the term "stationary range").[50] For earned income above $17,400, the credit declines by 21.06 percent for each dollar earned above $17,400. The credit becomes zero for incomes above $39,783. A family with an earned income of $6,000 (and two children), for example, will receive a credit of $2,400 (6,000 × 0.4); one with an earned income of $13,000 will receive a credit of $4,716; and one with earned income of $20,000 will receive $4,168 [4,716 – (20,000 – 17,400) × 0.2106].

One advantage of the EITC over a pure negative income tax is that the credit is tied to work. As a result, it provides less of a disincentive effect on work. Moreover, it might actually encourage greater labor force participation on the part of low-income families, since the marginal benefit at the beginning of the schedule exceeds the marginal wage (the total gain from an additional hour of work is 1.4 times the actual wage received). In fact, in the phase-in range, the EITC effectively provides a 40 percent increase in wages.

As Dickert, Houser, and Scholz (1995) noted, for those not in the labor force, the substitution effect associated with higher wages will provide an incentive to enter the labor market. In the phase-in range, the substitution effect provides an incentive to increase hours of work, while the income effect provides an incentive to decrease hours of work. In the stationary phase, only the income effect is operative, which leads to reduced hours of work. Finally, in the phase-out range, the net wage is now reduced by 21.06 percent for each additional dollar earned, so that both the substitution and income effect lead to reduced working hours.

According to calculations by Levin-Waldman (1995), in 1994, only 28 percent of all EITC recipients had incomes in the phase-in range, 19 percent had incomes in the stationary range, and 53 percent had incomes in the phase-out range. As a result, most of the EITC recipients were in the income ranges where EITC created a disincentive to work. However, Dickert, Houser, and Scholz (1995) estimated that the overall effect on work hours was quite small: EITC reduced hours worked by less than 1 percent. Moreover, when they included the positive effect of EITC on entry into the labor market, the net effect of EITC was to increase total hours worked. A similar conclusion was reached in a very recent study by Trampe (2007). He also found a small but statistically significant negative effect on work by those in the phase-out range of EITC (a reduction of 2.7 hours of work per week for families with two children). However, the effect appears much smaller than the positive effects on workforce participation in the phase-in range, so that on net EITC seems to encourage work.

16.6 THE DISTRIBUTIONAL EFFECTS OF GOVERNMENT EXPENDITURES

So far this chapter has been concerned with who pays the taxes. However, government taxes do not simply enter a "black hole" but are returned to individuals and families in two forms. The first are government transfers, which are payments made by the government to individuals. We discussed the government transfer system in Chapter 15. In this regard, the government can be viewed as a holding company or "trust fund," which receives payments from individuals and disburses these funds to other individuals. (The social security system is, in fact, officially set up as a trust fund, which collects social security contributions from workers and employers and provides benefits to retirees.) As noted in Chapter 15, such transfer payments entail administrative costs, some of which can be quite high.[51]

The second consists of actual expenditures on goods and services made by the government which directly or indirectly benefit individuals. Examples include education, highway construction and maintenance, hospitals, and sewerage treatment. In this sense, the government can be viewed as an enterprise which provides services to individual "clients." The major difference between the government and private enterprises (that is, corporations and small businesses) is that for most services the government does not charge fees directly to the user of the services. Rather, the costs are covered by general tax revenue, which may be collected from people who do not make use of the service. For example, public schools are usually financed through a local property tax, which is paid both by families with children and families without children. There may thus be little relation between taxes paid by individuals and the services they receive from the government.[52]

To get a complete picture of how the government affects the distribution of well-being in a country, it is necessary to look not only on the tax side but also on the transfer and expenditure side. In fact, taxes and expenditures are just two sides of the same ledger, so that the net impact of the government is the incidence of **net government expenditures**, which is defined as government expenditures on goods and services plus government transfers minus taxes. Chapter 15 considered the distribution of government transfers. Here, we look at the distributional effects of government expenditures. Which groups benefit from government expenditures and how does this relate to the taxes paid by the group?[53]

We begin by considering the functional structure of government expenditure (Table 16.12).[54] The biggest federal government outlay was for income security, which includes social security, disability insurance, TANF, workmen's compensation, veteran's benefits, and unemployment insurance. This amounted to 22 percent of total government expenditures in 1980 and 19 percent in 2005. In 2005, the next largest was health (mainly Medicare and Medicaid), which amounted to 14 percent of total government spending, up from 7 percent in 1980. The third largest expenditure made by the federal government in 2005 was for national defense, 12 percent of all government outlays, down from 16 percent in 1980. Federal net interest (mainly interest payments on the national

Table 16.12   Percent distribution of government outlays by function, 1980–2005

Government outlay	1980	1995	2005
Federal government outlays	64.0	62.1	60.2
General public service	2.6	1.5	1.9
Interest payments	7.6	11.2	6.0
National defense	15.9	11.6	12.2
Public order and safety: Police, fire, etc.	0.4	0.6	0.9
Transportation	1.0	0.6	0.7
Space	0.6	0.5	0.4
Other economic affairs	3.5	1.8	1.9
Housing and community services	1.2	1.2	1.1
Health	7.6	12.3	14.3
Recreation and culture	0.2	0.1	0.1
Education	1.7	1.3	1.6
Income security: Total	21.7	19.4	18.9
Disability	3.3	2.4	2.9
Retirement	11.9	11.5	10.3
Welfare and social services	3.9	3.7	3.2
Unemployment	2.2	1.0	0.8
Other	0.4	0.8	1.7
State and local government outlays	36.0	37.9	39.8
General public service	3.4	3.3	3.2
Interest payments	2.1	2.5	2.1
Public order and safety: Police, fire, etc.	3.6	4.6	5.0
Transportation	2.8	2.2	2.2
Other economic affairs	1.3	1.0	0.9
Housing and community services	0.3	0.2	0.2
Health	4.5	6.9	8.4
Recreation and culture	0.5	0.5	0.6
Education	14.1	13.3	13.9
Income security	3.6	3.5	3.2
Total	100.0	100.0	100.0

a   *Source*: Bureau of Economic Analysis, National Income and Product Accounts, Table 3.16, http://www.bea.gov/national/nipaweb/.

debt) ate up 6 percent of total government spending in 2005, down from 11 percent in 1995 and 8 percent in 1980. The other federal government programs were relatively small, in contrast. In 2005, for example, international affairs; science, space, and technology; natural resources and the environment; agriculture; the administration of justice; housing and community services; and general government each comprised about 1 to 2 percent of the total budget.

On the state and local government level, the largest budget item was education, which made up 14 percent of total government spending in both 1980 and 2005. Income security, including welfare payments and social services, workmen's compensation, and disability insurance comprised another 3 to 4 percent in the 3 years, while health care way was up from its 4 percent share in 1980 to 8 percent in 2005. Highways and other transportation made up 2 percent in 2005, and police, fire, and other public safety another 5 percent. The other state and local government functions were relatively small.

The question of who benefits from government expenditures is not an easy one to answer. The general procedure is to take each government program and allocate the expenditures on those programs to the individuals who directly benefit from them. For some government expenditures, this allocation is relatively easy. For example, educational expenses can be allotted in direct proportion to the number of school children a family has. However, the beneficiaries of others, such as national defense, international affairs, and science and technology, are more difficult to determine.

One of the first studies for the United States was conducted by Ruggles and O'Higgins (1981) on 1970 data. In many cases, the beneficiaries of government programs could be directly identified. On the federal level, social security benefits were allocated directly to their beneficiaries; veteran health benefits to disabled veterans; educational expenditures to households with students enrolled in colleges; and public assistance to welfare recipients. Agricultural expenditures were divided on the basis of farm insurance. Labor department expenditures were distributed on the basis of wages and salaries. For highway expenditures, it was assumed that two-thirds of the benefits accrued to individual car owners and one-third to trucking. The first portion was allocated on the basis of household car ownership and the second share was distributed in proportion to household consumption, since the goods carried by truckers were eventually consumed by families. Expenditures on general federal programs, such as national defense, international affairs, justice, science, energy, environment, were divided among families in proportion to the number of individuals in the family.

On the state and local government level, school expenditures were allocated on the basis of the number of school-age children in the household; higher education expenditures on the basis of the number of college students; health and hospital expenditures on the basis of the number of patients in the family; and unemployment insurance on the basis of employment status. Police and fire expenses were divided among families according to family size.

Their results indicated that the average benefits received from the programs of the federal government amounted to $2,917 in 1970. The average federal tax burden in 1970 was $3,251, so that the *net* benefits received (the difference between the benefit level and the taxes paid) from the federal government was negative, −$334 ($2,917 − $3,251). On the state and local government level, the average family benefit was $2,515. The biggest source was education. Average taxes paid to state and local governments were $2,099, so that the net benefit received by families was $416. Combining both the federal and state and local government levels, the authors calculated an average net benefit of $83, because government expenditures were slightly greater than tax receipts.

The most interesting results were obtained by comparing the benefits and taxes of the different income deciles. On the federal level, average benefits were almost twice as great for the second decile as the first ($2,640 versus $1,450) and somewhat greater for the third than the second decile ($3,250 versus $2,620) but very similar for the third through top decile. The reason was that average social security benefits were much higher for the second and third income deciles than for the first but then tapered off with income among the upper income deciles, whereas the benefits from other government expenditures generally increased with income level. On the other hand, benefits from state and local government expenditures did tend to rise with income level, though the difference in average benefits was rather small among deciles. The main reason for this was that average benefits from public schooling expenditures were greater for richer families. In contrast, the benefits from public assistance, health and hospitals, and housing expenditures were higher at the lower income levels.

As we saw in Section 16.4.6, taxes paid tended to rise more or less in proportion to family income. As a result, net government benefits (the difference between benefits received and taxes paid) fell off rather precipitously with income level (at least after the third decile of income), from a high of $3,068 for families in the third decile to a low of –$6,400. Net benefits were positive for the bottom six deciles but negative for the top four deciles. Moreover, in relation to before-tax income, the bottom deciles were the clear winners from government expenditures. If we add government benefits and subtract out taxes from original income, then the average income of the bottom decile more than triples, that of the second decile doubles, that of the third decile rises by about three-quarters, and that of the fourth decile by a third. The fifth through eighth deciles saw little change in their income. The ninth decile suffered a 16 percent reduction in their income level, and the highest decile a 23 percent reduction.

A more recent study was conducted by Wolff and Zacharias (2007) based on 2000 income data. The methodology was similar. However, in the Wolff–Zacharias study, certain government expenditures such as defense spending and general administrative expenses were excluded in the imputation schema since they were considered general overhead expenses of the government, which do not benefit individuals directly. Certain taxes were also excluded such as corporate income tax and other business taxes, since these were not paid for directly by individuals and families.

Results are shown in Figure 16.13. The income concept used here is "wealth-adjusted" income (WI), which included an annuity flow from nonhome wealth as well as imputed rent to owner-occupied housing (see Section 5.4.3.4 for details on the income concept). They first reported that total government transfers were extremely progressive, falling monotonically from 50 percent of WI for the lowest decile to 2.6 percent for the top decile in 2000. The same pattern held for the largest government transfers, social security and medical benefits (Medicare plus Medicaid). Similar patterns could be observed for other transfers too, with one or two exceptions.

Public consumption was also highly progressive, though not quite as strongly as transfers. Unlike transfers, the absolute amount of public consumption did not fall between the lower and higher income deciles. Only the ratio of public consumption to income fell, reflecting the fact that the disparity in income was far bigger than the disparity in public consumption. Total public consumption fell monotonically from 34 percent of WI for the lowest decile to 3 percent for the top decile in 2000. The same pattern could be observed for the largest source of public consumption, educational expenditures, as well as other types of public consumption.

The federal income tax was generally progressive in 2000. The average federal income tax increased steadily from 2.2 percent of WI in the first decile to 13.8 percent in the ninth but then dropped a bit to 13.5 percent in the top decile. State income taxes were also progressive (with two exceptions). Payroll tax rates increased modestly between the first and eighth deciles and then declined over the top two deciles. State consumption taxes were (not unexpectedly) regressive in the 2 years, with average tax rates falling across deciles from 3.7 to 0.8 percent in 2000. Property taxes were generally regressive in the 2 years. This reflected the fact that though house values rise with income, they declined as a *percent* of income across income classes.

Overall, total personal taxes by decile were generally progressive. In 2000, the average personal tax rate rose continuously from 13.6 percent in the lowest decile to 28.3 percent in the ninth decile but then fell to 22.0 percent in the top decile. The sharp drop off in the average tax rate between the ninth and tenth deciles was largely a reflection of the correspondingly sharp decline in the average payroll tax between these two deciles.

Net government spending was extremely progressive. Net government spending as a percent of WI plummeted from 70 percent for the lowest decile to –16 percent for the top in 2000. Net government expenditure was positive for the lowest six deciles (and at the median) and negative for the top four deciles. A comparison of the tax schedule and the net government expenditure schedule showed that the latter yielded a much more progressive view of the fiscal system,

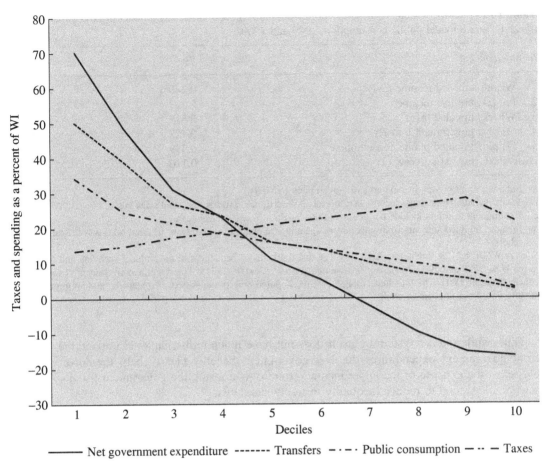

Figure 16.13   Net government expenditure as a percent of wealth-adjusted income (WI) by WI decile, 2000

thus confirming Musgrave's (1994, p. 354) observation that the distribution of net fiscal burden is more "pro-poor" than is the distribution of tax burden "anti-rich."

Table 16.13 confirms these results by considering the impact of each of these three components on the overall Gini coefficient. The analysis begins with inequality of WI, the basic income concept. In 2000, its Gini coefficient was 0.48. It next looked at pre-fisc income, which was defined as WI minus all government transfers. Its Gini coefficient in 2000 was quite a bit larger, at 0.54 because transfers are highly progressive, so that their exclusion results in a higher level of measured inequality (pre-fisc income versus WI). Next, taxes were subtracted from pre-fisc income, and the Gini coefficient actually increased a small amount because the overall tax system with respect to WI was slightly regressive (line 3). Then all government transfers were added back, including cash and noncash, to line 3 (line 4). The Gini coefficient fell sharply, by 0.087 in 1989 and by 0.080 in 2000. Finally, public consumption was added to line 4, resulting in a further drop in the Gini coefficient of 0.029 in 1989 and 0.030 in 2000. Altogether, the total effect of net government expenditures was to reduce the Gini coefficient from its pre-tax, pre-fisc value by 0.11 in both years.

Table 16.13   Gini coefficients of before-tax income and income after taxes, noncash government transfers, and imputed public consumption, 1989 and 2000

Income concept	1989	2000
1. Wealth-adjusted income (WI)	0.440	0.477
2. Pre-tax, pre-fisc income[a]	0.509	0.542
3. WI less imputed taxes[b]	0.515	0.550
4. (3) plus government transfers[c]	0.428	0.470
5. (4) plus imputed public consumption[d]	0.399	0.440
Difference: row (1) less row (4)	0.110	0.102

a   Subtracts from pre-tax income all cash government transfers.
b   Taxes include the personal income tax, the social security tax, property tax, and sales tax.
c   Government transfers include both cash and noncash transfers (like Medicare).
d   Includes imputed amounts from government spending on education, highways, health, police and fire, and others.
Source: Wolff, E.N. & Zacharias, A. (2007). The distributional consequences of government spending and taxation in the U.S., 1989 and 2000. *Review of Income and Wealth*, **53**(4), 692–715. The basic income concept is wealth-adjusted income (WI), which includes money income, imputed rent to owner-occupied housing, and an imputed annuity flow from nonhome wealth.

Thus, while the tax system by itself does not have much redistributional impact, the benefits from government expenditures do. Net government benefits clearly help the lower income classes at the expense of the upper income groups. As a result, the government fiscal system as a whole does tend to reduce inequality in living standards.

16.7   SUMMARY AND CONCLUSION

Income equality is often included as a basic public policy objective. Three distinct grounds are often used to justify this position: (i) The first, based on a notion of fairness, argues that individuals in a society are *entitled* to certain rights and privileges based on their citizenship, including a share of society's output. (ii) The second is derived from utilitarianism. If it is assumed that there is a diminishing marginal utility of income and everyone's utility function is identical, then equality will maximize the total utility of individuals in a society. (iii) The third is a maximin or Rawlsian position, which advocates a system of distribution that would maximize the minimum level of income that would be available to each individual in a society.

There are also two common arguments against promoting greater income equality in society. (i) The first is based on a concept of fairness which guarantees that each individual has the same basic political rights and economic opportunities but not necessarily the same economic incomes. (ii) The second is the growth position, which maintains that paying higher wages to workers who are more productive serves as an *incentive* for everyone to work harder and thus increases total output.

Government affects income inequality both by its tax system and the distribution of its expenditures. With regard to the tax system, we generally distinguish among three types: (i) a proportional tax, in which the average tax rate remains constant over income levels; (ii) a progressive tax, in which the average tax rate rises with income; and (iii) a regressive tax, in which the average tax rate falls with income. We also distinguish between the average tax rate, the ratio of tax payments to income, and the marginal tax rate, the taxes paid on an additional dollar of income.

A proportional tax leaves income inequality unchanged (that is, the level of after-tax inequality is the same as that of before-tax inequality), a progressive tax reduces income inequality, and a regressive tax increases income inequality.

Comparisons of the overall distribution of before-tax and after-tax income come under the province of vertical equity. A different consideration is horizontal equity, which refers to a comparison of the before-tax and after-tax position of individual taxpayers. There are two basic principles: The first is that the tax system should levy identical taxes on taxpayers with the same income. The second principle, called "rank preservation," maintains that the tax system should not change the rank order of taxpayers.

The federal individual income tax has been in effect since 1913. The basic income concept is adjusted gross income (AGI), which is equal to ordinary money income plus realized capital gains less interest from state and local government bonds, most of social security income, welfare payments, and other excluded items. Tax payments are based on taxable income, which equals AGI less exemptions and deductions. Different tax schedules are provided for married couples, single individuals, and heads of households.

The tax schedule is progressive, with marginal tax rates rising in stepwise fashion with AGI. The tax structure has changed frequently over time. The top marginal rate was set at 7 percent in 1913, rose to 67 percent in 1917, was reduced during the 1930s, increased to 94 percent in 1944, fell to 70 percent during the 1960s and 1970s, was lowered to 50 percent in 1981 and to 28 percent in 1986, It was then raised to 39.6 percent in 1993 but lowered to 35 percent in 2005. The reduction in marginal tax rates since the end of World War II benefited the rich more than the middle class or the poor.

The tax schedule shows the nominal tax rates, the ratio between tax liability and taxable income. The effective tax rate is the ratio of actual tax payments to total taxpayer income. For the personal income tax, there are several sources of difference between the two: (i) the number of exemptions a taxpayer can claim; (ii) income deductions; (iii) exclusions to ordinary income; (iv) income adjustments; (v) the use of tax preference items; (vi) the availability of tax credits; and (vii) the imposition of the alternative minimum tax.

Differences between nominal and effective tax rates are quite large. The result of these special provisions of the tax code reduced the average tax rate by about two-thirds in 1985, from its nominal level of 30 percent to only 12 percent. The biggest effect came from deductions. Overall, the rich benefited more from the availability of tax reduction provisions of the tax code. Tax liability was reduced by 13 percentage points in 1985 for the lowest income class and 26 percentage points for the highest.

The payroll tax is now the second-largest source of federal government revenue. When first introduced in 1937, the social security tax was 1.0 percent on wages and salaries for both the employee and employer, and the tax was levied on earnings up to $3,000. By 2005, the tax rate had been raised to 7.65 percent on each, and the earnings limit to $90,000. Unemployment insurance is a second form of payroll tax but is considerably smaller.

Another source of federal revenue is the corporation income tax, established in 1909. The basic tax rate was raised from 38 percent in 1946 to 52 percent in 1952, where it generally remained until 1969. It was then lowered to 48 percent in 1971, 46 percent in 1979, 34 percent in 1986, and 35 percent in 1993, where it has remained through 2007. Other federal levies include the excise tax, customs duties, and the estate and gift tax.

State governments rely on two major sources of revenues – income taxes and general sales taxes. The principal source of revenue for local governments is the property tax. In addition, there are often "user fees" for specific services provided by local governments, such as water and sewerage and sanitation collection.

Federal individual income taxes are the main source of federal government revenue, comprising anywhere from 42 to 47 percent between 1955 and 2005. Revenue from state and local individual income taxes increased rather sharply, from 4 to 15 percent of total state and local government receipts between 1955 and 2005. However, together, personal income taxes made up a relatively constant share of about one-third of total government revenue between 1955 and 2005.

In contrast, federal corporate income tax proceeds have fallen sharply, from 27 percent of total federal revenue in 1955 to 13 percent in 2005. On the state level, corporate taxes remained rather steady at 2 to 4 percent of total state and local government revenue. Together, corporate income taxes fell from 20 percent of total government revenue in 1955 to only 9 percent in 2005.

Federal excise taxes also showed a sharp decline as a source of federal government revenue, from 14 to only 3 percent over the years from 1955 to 2005. Customs duties and fees have remained small, accounting for only 1 to 2 percent of total federal income. Among state and local governments, sales taxes comprised between 25 and 27 percent of their income, with the share staying relatively constant over time. Together, sales, excise, and customs taxes diminished as a source of total government receipts, from 19 percent in 1955 to 12 percent in 2005.

The most dramatic growth occurred in payroll (mainly social security) taxes, which rose from 12 percent of federal revenue in 1955 to 37 percent in 2005. It also increased from 8 percent of total government income to 22 percent. Property taxes were the most important source of state and local government revenue in 1955, accounting for 38 percent, but by 2005 its share had dropped to 22 percent. Other taxes and special user fees, in contrast, have risen from 27 to 37 percent.

Government receipts as a percent of GDP grew from 24 to 32 percent between 1955 and 1970. Its share has remained almost unchanged between 1970 and 1985, at a little less than a third, but then fell to 29 percent in 2005. Moreover, federal receipts remained relatively constant as a share of GDP between 1955 and 2005, at 17 to 18 percent, while state and local government income surged from 7 to 12 percent of GDP.

Comparisons with other OECD countries show that the United States has been one of the least taxed countries among the advanced economies. In 2005, the United States had the third-lowest overall tax rate among OECD countries (only Korea and Mexico were lower), at about 25 percent of GDP. The highest was Sweden, at 50 percent. Eight countries (including Sweden) paid more than 40 percent of their national income in the form of taxes, and only five paid less than 30 percent.

Analysis of the overall effective tax rate structure in the United States revealed that the individual income tax was the most progressive tax, with effective tax rates varying from 4 percent for the lowest decile to 13 percent for the richest decile in 1985. The payroll (mainly, social security) tax was mildly regressive over the bottom nine deciles, and then turned extremely regressive at the top. Sales taxes were highly regressive, with effective tax rates varying from 7 percent for the poorest 10 percent of the population to 2 percent for the richest 10 percent. Under the most progressive incidence assumptions, the total tax system was mildly progressive, with effective tax rates increasing from 22 percent for the poorest decile to 25 percent for the richest. However, under the least progressive incidence assumptions, the total tax system was mildly regressive, with effective tax rates declining from 28 percent for the poorest decile to 21 percent for the richest. In actuality, the total tax system was likely to be a basically proportional tax on income.

Has the effective tax structure changed over time? In 1966, the effective tax rates ranged from 17 percent for the bottom decile to 30 percent for the top decile and 40 percentile for the richest 1 percent. In 1988, the effective tax rate for the bottom decile was almost the same as in 1966, but the effective rate for the top 1 percent was 27 percent. More recent work also shows that the degree of progressivity of the federal tax system declined markedly between 1960 and 2004. The very top tax rate (on the top one-hundredth of 1 percent) fell from 57 percent in 1960 to 34 percent in 2004 and that paid by P99 to P99.9 fell from 37.7 to 32.1 percent. The tax rate paid by the second quintile also fell, from 13.9 to 9.4 percent, but the tax rates paid by percentiles 40 through 99 all rose.

A comparison of before-tax income and after-tax income Gini coefficients also indicated that the federal tax structure, which was only mildly progressive in 1977 and 1980, became even less progressive in 1984 and 1988. CBO estimates, on the other hand, show the progressivity of the federal tax system increasing from 1988 to 1996, with the difference between the before-tax and after-tax Gini coefficients widening from 0.032 to 0.048. However, with the reductions of the top marginal tax rates after 2001, the difference between the before-tax and after-tax Gini coefficients contracted from 0.048 in 1996 to 0.042 in 2004.

The government provides benefits to individuals and families in two forms: transfer payments and expenditures on goods and services. To obtain a full picture of the role of the government on the distribution of well-being in a country, it is necessary to look not only on the tax collection side but also on the transfer and expenditure side. The largest expenditure made by the federal government in 2005 was for income security at 19 percent of total government expenditures, followed by health at 14 percent, national defense at 12 percent, and net interest, at 6 percent. The other federal government programs were relatively small. On the state and local government level, the largest budget item was education, which made up 14 percent of total government spending in 2005. Income security comprised another 3 percent, while health care made up 8 percent. The other state and local government functions were small.

The question of who benefits from government expenditures involves allocating the expenditures of each government program to the individuals who directly benefit from them. An analysis on 2000 data indicates that net benefits from government (the difference between benefits received and taxes paid) as a percent of income fell rather precipitously with income level, from 70 percent for the lowest decile to −16 percent for the top decile in 2000. Net government expenditure was positive for the lowest six deciles (and at the median) and negative for the top four deciles. A comparison of the tax schedule and the net government expenditure schedule showed that the latter yielded a much more progressive view of the fiscal system. Thus, while the tax system by itself does not have much redistributional impact, net government benefits clearly help the lower income classes relative to the upper income groups.

16.8   REFERENCES AND BIBLIOGRAPHY

Aaron, H.J. & Galper, H. (1985). *Assessing the Income Tax*. Washington, DC: Brookings Institution.

Atkinson, A. (1983). *The Economics of Inequality*, 2nd edition. Oxford: Clarendon Press.

Berliant, M.C. & Strauss, R.P. (1985). The horizontal and vertical equity characteristics of the federal individual income tax, 1966–1977. In M. David & T. Smeeding (eds.), *Horizontal Equity, Uncertainty, and Economic Well-Being*, Studies in Income and Wealth, Vol. 50, National Bureau of Economic Research. Chicago: Chicago University Press.

Berliant, M.C. & Strauss, R.P. (1993). State and federal tax equity: Estimates before and after the Tax Reform Act of 1986. *Journal of Policy Analysis and Management*, **12**(1), 9–43.

Blum, W.J. & Kalven, H. (1953). *The Uneasy Case for Progressive Taxation*. Chicago: Chicago University Press.

Blumenthal, M., Erard, B. & Ho, C.-C. (2005). Participation and compliance with the Earned Income Tax Credit. *National Tax Journal*, **58**(2), 189–213.

Boskin, M.J. (1988). Tax policy and economic growth: Lessons from the 1980s. *Journal of Economic Perspectives*, **2**(4), 71–97.

Bosworth, B. & Burtless, G. (1992). Effects of tax reform on labor supply, investment, and saving. *Journal of Economic Perspectives*, 6(1), 3–25.

Bradford, D.F. (1986). *Untangling the Income Tax*. Cambridge, MA: Harvard University Press.

David, M. & Smeeding, T. (eds.) (1985). *Horizontal Equity, Uncertainty, and Economic Well-Being*, Studies in Income and Wealth, Vol. 50, National Bureau of Economic Research. Chicago: Chicago University Press.

Davies, J., St-Hilaire, F. & Whalley, J. (1984). Some calculations of lifetime tax incidence. *American Economic Review*, 74(4), 633–49.

Dickert, S., Houser, S. & Scholz, J.K. (1995). The Earned Income Tax Credit and transfer programs: A study of labor market and program participation. In J.M. Poterba (ed.), *Tax Policy and the Economy*, Vol. 9 (pp. 1–50). Cambridge, MA: MIT Press.

Eissa, N. & Hoynes, H. (2004). Taxes and the labor market participation of married couples: The Earned Income Tax Credit. *Journal of Public Economics*, 88(9–10), 1931–58.

Eissa, N. & Hoynes, H. (2006). Behavioral responses to taxes: Lessons from the EITC and labor supply. In J.M. Poterba (ed.), *Tax Policy and the Economy*, Vol. 20 (pp. 74–110). Cambridge, MA: MIT Press.

Eissa, N. & Liebman, J. (1996). Labor supply response to the Earned Income Tax Credit. *Quarterly Journal of Economics*, 111(2), 605–37.

Ellwood, D. (2000). The impact of the Earned Income Tax Credit and social policy reforms on work, marriage and living arrangements. *National Tax Journal*, 53(4), 1063–105.

Feenberg, D.R. & Poterba, J.M. (2000). The income and tax share of very high-income households, 1960–1995. *American Economic Review Papers and Proceedings*, 90(2), 264–70.

Frank, R.H. (1985). *Choosing the Right Pond*. New York: Oxford University Press.

Fullerton, D. & Metcalf, G.E. (2002). Tax incidence. NBER Working Paper No. 8829, March.

Fullerton, D. & Rogers, D.L. (1993). *Who Bears the Lifetime Tax Burden?* Washington, DC: Brookings Institution.

Gramlich, E.M., Kasten, R. & Sammartino, F. (1991). Growing inequality in the 1980s: The role of federal taxes and cash transfers. In S. Danziger & P. Gottschalk (eds.), *Uneven Tides: Rising Inequality in the 1980s*. New York: Russell Sage.

Gravelle, J.G. (1992). Equity effects of the Tax Reform Act of 1986. *Journal of Economic Perspectives*, 6(1), 27–44.

Haveman, R.H. (1988). *Starting Even: An Equal Opportunity Program to Combat the Nation's New Poverty*. New York: Simon and Schuster.

Hicks, U.K. (1946). The terminology of tax analysis. *The Economic Journal*, 56(221), 38–50.

Hotz, V.J. & Scholz, J.K. (2003). The Earned Income Tax Credit. In R. Moffitt (ed.), *Means-Tested Transfer Programs in the United States*. Chicago: University of Chicago Press.

Jenkins, S.P. (1988). Empirical measurement of horizontal equity. *Journal of Public Economics*, 37(3), 305–30.

Kaplow, L. (1989). Horizontal equity: Measures in search of a principle. *National Tax Journal*, 42(2), 139–54.

Kern, B.B. (1990). The Tax Reform Act of 1986 and progressivity of the individual income tax. *Public Finance Quarterly*, 18(3), 259–72.

Kiefer, D.W. (1984). Distributional tax progressivity indexes. *National Tax Journal*, 37(4), 487–514.

King, M.A. (1980). How effective have fiscal policies been in changing the distribution of income and wealth. *American Economic Review*, 70(2), 72–6.

King, M.A. (1983). An index of inequality: With applications to horizontal equity and social mobility. *Econometrica*, 51(1), 99–115.

Kurz, M. (1978). Negative income taxation. *Federal Tax Reform: Myths and Realities*. San Francisco, CA: Institute for Contemporary Studies.

Lambert, P.J. (2001). *The Distribution and Redistribution of Income*, 3rd Edition. Manchester: Manchester University Press.

Lambert, P.J. & Pfahler, W. (1988). On aggregate measures of the net redistributive impact of taxation and government expenditure. *Public Finance Quarterly*, 16(2), 178–202.

Lampman, R.J. (1971). *Ends and Means of Reducing Income Poverty*. Chicago: Markham.

Lerman, R.I. (1999). How do income sources affect income inequaqlity? In J. Silber (ed.), *Handbook on Income Inequality Measure-*

ment (pp. 341–58). Boston, MA: Kluwer Academic.

Lerman, R.I. & Yitzhaki, S. (1995). Changing ranks and the inequality impacts of taxes and transfers. *National Tax Journal*, **48**(1), 45–59.

Levin-Waldman, O.M. (1995). The consolidated assistance program. Jerome Levy Economics Institute Public Policy Brief, No. 21.

Liebman, J. (1998). The impact of the Earned Income Tax Credit on incentives and income distribution. In J. Poterba (ed.), *Tax Policy and the Economy*, Vol. 12 (pp. 97–107). Cambridge, MA: MIT Press.

Marx, K. & Engels, F. (1968). *The Manifesto of the Communist Party*, 1848. In K. Marx & F. Engels (eds.), *Selected Works*. New York: International Publishers.

McIntyre, R.S. *et al.* (2003). *Who Pays? A Distributional Analysis of the Tax Systems in all 50 States*, 2nd Edition. Washington, DC: Institute on Taxation and Economic Policy.

Meyer, B. (2002). Labor supply at the extensive and intensive margins: The EITC, welfare, and hours worked. *American Economic Review*, **92**(2), 373–9.

Meyer, B. & Rosenbaum, D. (2001). Welfare, the Earned Income Tax Credit, and the labor supply of single mothers. *Quarterly Journal of Economics*, **116**(3), 1063–114.

Minarik, J.K. (1980). Who doesn't bear the tax burden? In H.J. Aaron & M.J. Boskin (eds.), *The Economics of Taxation* (pp. 55–68). Washington, DC: Brookings Institution.

Moffitt, R. (2003). The negative income tax and the evolution of U.S. welfare policy. *Journal of Economic Perspectives*, **17**(3), 119–40.

Musgrave, R.A. (1994). Progressive taxation, equity and tax design. In J. Slemrod (ed.), *Tax Progressivity and Income Inequality* (pp. 341–56). Cambridge: Cambridge University Press.

Musgrave, R., Case, K.E. & Leonard, H. (1974). The distribution of fiscal burdens and benefits. *Public Finance Quarterly*, **2**(3), 259–311.

Musgrave, R.A. & Musgrave, P.B. (1989). *Public Finance in Theory and Practice* 5th edition. New York: McGraw-Hill.

Neumark, D. & Wascher, W. (2000). Using the EITC to help poor families: New evidence and a comparison with the minimum wage. NBER Working Paper No. 7599, March.

OECD (Organization of Economic Co-operation and Development) (1984). *Tax Expenditures: A Review of the Issues and Country Practices*. Paris: OECD Committee on Fiscal Affairs.

OECD (Organization for Economic Co-Operation and Development) (1988). *Taxation of Net Wealth, Capital Transfers and Capital Gains of Individuals*. Paris: OECD.

O'Higgins, M. & Ruggles, P. (1981). The distribution of public expenditures and taxes among households in the United Kingdom. *Review of Income and Wealth*, ser. 27, 298–326.

Okner, B.A. (1980). Total U.S. taxes and their effect on the distribution of family income in 1966 and 1970 In H.J. Aaron & M.J. Boskin (eds.), *The Economics of Taxation*. Washington, DC: Brookings Institution.

Okner, B.A. & Pechman, J.A. (1974). *Who Bears the Tax Burden?* Washington, DC: Brookings Institution.

Pechman, J.A. (1983). *Federal Tax Policy*, 4th edition. Washington, DC: Brookings Institution.

Pechman, J.A. (1985). *Who Paid the Taxes, 1966–85?* Washington, DC: Brookings Institution.

Pechman, J.A. (1990). The future of the income tax. *American Economic Review*, **80**(1), 1–20.

Pechman, J.A. & Okner, B. (1974). *Who Bears the Tax Burden?* Washington, DC: Brookings Institution.

Phelps-Brown, E.H. (1988). *Egalitarianism and the Generation of Inequality*. Oxford: Oxford University Press.

Piggott, J. & Whalley, J. (1987). Interpreting net fiscal incidence calculations. *Review of Economics and Statistics*, **69**(4), 685–94.

Piketty, T. & Saez, E. (2007). How progressive is the U.S. federal tax system? A historical and international perspective. *Journal of Economic Perspectives*, **21**(1), 3–24.

Plotnick, R. (1982). The concept and measurement of horizontal inequity. *Journal of Public Economics*, **17**, 373–91.

Plotnick, R. (1985). A comparison of measures of horizontal inequity. In M. David & T. Smeeding (eds.), *Horizontal Equity, Uncertainty. and Economic Well-Being*, Studies in Income and Wealth, Vol. 50, National Bureau of Economic Research. Chicago: Chicago University Press.

Quigley, J.M. & Smolensky, E. (1990). Redistribution with several levels of government: The recent US experience. In R. Prud'homme (ed.), *Public Finance with Several Levels of Government*, Proceedings of the 46th Congress of the International Institute of Public Finance (pp. 125–36). Brussels.

Rawls, J. (1971). *A Theory of Justice*. Cambridge, MA: Harvard University Press.

Reynolds, M. & Smolensky, E. (1977). *Public Expenditures, Taxes, and the Distribution of Income: The United States, 1950, 1961, 1970*. New York: Academic Press.

Robins, P.K. (1985). A comparison of the labor supply findings from the four negative income tax experiments. *Journal of Human Resources*, **20**(4), 567–82.

Roemer, J.E. (1988). *Free to Lose: An Introduction to Marxist Economic Philosophy*. Cambridge, MA: Harvard University Press.

Ruggles, P. & O'Higgins, M. (1981). The distribution of public expenditure among households in the United States. *Review of Income and Wealth*, ser. 27, 137–63.

Scholz, J.K. (1996). In-work benefits in the United States: The Earned Income Tax Credit. *Economic Journal*, **106**(434), 159–69.

Sen, A. (1992). *Inequality Reexamined*. Cambridge, MA: Harvard University Press.

Slemrod, J. (1992). Taxation and inequality: A time-exposure perspective. In J.M. Poterba (ed.), *Tax Policy and the Economy*. Cambridge, MA: MIT Press.

Trampe, P. (2007). The EITC disincentive: The effects on hours worked from the phase-out of the Earned Income Tax Credit. *Econ Journal Watch*, **4**(3), 308–20.

U.S. Census Bureau (1993). *Statistical Abstract of the United States: 1993*, 113th edition.

Washington, DC: U.S. Government Printing Office.

U.S. Congress (2006). Joint Economic Committee, *Costs and Consequences of the Federal Estate Tax*. May. http://www.house.gov/jec/publications/109/05-01-06estatetax.pdf.

U.S. Congressional Budget Office (1988). *The Changing Distribution of Federal Taxes: A Closer Look at 1980*, July. Washington, DC: The Congress of the United States.

U.S. Congressional Budget Office (2003). Effective tax rates, 1997–2000. Washington, DC: The Congress of the United States. http://www.cbo.gov/doc.cfm?index=4514.

U.S. House of Representatives (1994). Committee on Ways and Means, *Overview of Entitlement Programs: 1994 Green Book*. Washington, DC: U.S. Government Printing Office, July.

U.S. House of Representatives (2004). Committee on Ways and Means, *Overview of Entitlement Programs: 2004 Green Book*. Washington, DC: U.S. Government Printing Office, July.

Whalley, J. (1984). Regression or progression: The taxing question of incidence analysis. *The Canadian Journal of Economics*, **17**(4), 654–82.

Wolff, E.N. & Zacharias, A. (2007). The distributional consequences of government spending and taxation in the U.S., 1989 and 2000. *Review of Income and Wealth*, **53**(4), 692–715.

Wu, X. & Perloff, J.M. (2006). Effects of government policies on urban and rural income inequality. *Review of Income and Wealth*, **52**(2), 213–35.

Young, H.P. (1990). Progressive taxation and equal sacrifice. *American Economic Review*, **80**, 253–66.

16.9   DISCUSSION QUESTIONS AND PROBLEM SET

1   Discuss the difference between regressive, progressive, and proportional taxes. How do average and marginal tax rates vary with income for each type of tax?

2   Define the effective tax rate. Why is the effective tax structure of the personal income tax less progressive than the actual IRS tax schedule?

3   Give two reasons why the social security tax is mildly regressive with respect to family income.

4   What is the effect of total personal taxes on the size distribution of family income in the United States?

5   What advantages does a negative income tax have over current income transfer programs? What are the disadvantages? In what sense is the EITC a negative income tax?

6   Discuss why the net benefits from government expenditure have a more progressive effect on the distribution of family well-being than taxes do.

7 Suppose a country has the following income distribution:

Income class	Number of families	Average income ($)
1.	6,000	20,000
2.	4,000	70,000

(a) Draw the Lorenz curve (show all computations).
(b) Suppose a proportional tax of 10% is levied. Draw the new Lorenz curve (show all computations).
(c) Suppose a progressive tax of 10% is imposed on income class 1 and a tax of 30% is imposed on income class 2. Draw the new Lorenz curve (show all computations).
(d) Suppose a regressive tax of 30% is imposed on income class 1 and a tax of 10% is imposed on income class 2. Draw the new Lorenz curve (show all computations).

8 Suppose a negative income tax is designed as follows: (i) The basic allowance is set at $8,000. (ii) The break-even income is $16,000. (iii) The slope of the after-tax income line is constant.
(a) Show the structure of the negative income tax on a diagram.
(b) Compute both the tax credit and the total after-tax income if before-tax income is: (i) $10,000; (ii) $20,000.

9 Suppose the EITC is designed as follows: (i) The maximum tax credit is $5,000, which is given on earned income between $15,000 and $30,000. (ii) The EITC becomes zero at $50,000 of earned income.
(a) Show the structure of the EITC on a diagram.
(b) Compute the EITC if earned income is (i) $9,000; (ii) $40,000.

NOTES

1 For further arguments for and against inequality, see Atkinson (1983, Chapter 1); Lampman (1971); Sen (1992, Chapter 1); and Roemer (1988).
2 We must also assume that individual utilities are additive and that total social welfare is the sum of individual utility levels – that is, there are no externalities present.
3 There is another side to this argument, which rests on the assumption that the rich save more of their income than the poor. Thus, the argument goes, redistributing income from the rich to the poor will reduce the overall savings rate and hence the investment rate and the rate of economic growth. This will cause the overall pie to grow more slowly and, everyone, including the poor, will be made worse off in the long run. However, it should be noted that aggregate capital formation depends on national savings, the sum of household, corporate, and government saving, so that any adverse effect on personal savings can, in principle be offset by increased corporate or government savings.
4 There is a very close connection between this position and arguments in favor of using a relative poverty line (see Section 4.1). In the case of the latter, the central notion is that the collection of goods that constitutes a minimally decent standard of living depends itself on the average living standard. As the standard of living grows, what the general populace considers necessities also rises. The argument here is even broader in that everyone's utility is seen to depend on the standard of living of the other individuals living in the community.
5 For more discussion of these issues, see Phelps-Brown (1988).
6 An exception is the regressive tax, in which it is possible that after a certain income level there are no additional taxes paid.
7 The derivation is as follows: Since $T/Y = a + bY$, then $T = aY + bY^2$ and $dT/dY = a + 2bY$.
8 The derivation is as follows. Since $T/Y = b/(a + Y)$, then $T = bY/(a + Y)$ and $dT/dY = ab/(a + Y)^2$.

9   Current information on the federal tax schedule can be found at: http://www.irs.gov/instructions/index.html.

10   The tax brackets are based on "taxable income" (see Section 16.4.1 for details on the definition of taxable income).

11   For married couples, the slope of the average tax rate with respect to income above $326,450 is given by: $d(ATR/Y) = 25,938/Y^2$. The increase in the ATR for each additional dollar earned therefore declines as income increases.

12   The proof is also straightforward for the coefficient of variation. Recall from Section 3.2 that the measure is defined as: $CV(Y) = STD(Y)/\bar{Y}$.
   Then, $CV(Y^*) = STD(Y^*)/\bar{Y}^* = STD[(1 - c)Y)]/[(1 - c)\bar{Y}] = (1 - c)STD(Y)/[(1 - c)\bar{Y}] = CV(Y)$.

13   See Section 16.3.3 for more discussion of this ranking criterion. It should be noted that a proportional and a regressive tax will always fulfill this rank order criterion. A progressive tax will also meet this criterion as long as the marginal tax rate is always less than 100 percent.

14   However, the U.S. system may very well violate the second principle and even the first principle with respect to ordinary income or even adjusted gross income, since exemptions and deductions may not be the same for tax units with the same ordinary income or AGI.

15   Actually, in the Swedish tax system of the 1980s, there were cases in which the marginal tax rate exceeded 100 percent. One famous case involved the Swedish film director Ingmar Bergmann.

16   See Berliant and Strauss (1985) and Plotnick (1985) for further discussion of these points.

17   However, this notion of fairness rest very heavily on the belief that the pre-tax income distribution is deserved. A Marxist, for example, may feel that the high incomes of capitalists are the result of the exploitation of workers and therefore undeserved.

18   Because of the technical nature of most measures of horizontal equity, our discussion here will focus mainly on issues of vertical equity. See the excellent papers contained in the volume, *Horizontal Equity, Uncertainty, and Economic Well-Being*, edited by David and Smeeding (1985), as well as Jenkins (1988) and Kaplow (1989) for analyses of horizontal equity in the U.S. tax system.

19   This is not to say that there was unanimous support in Congress for an income tax. Indeed, there was staunch opposition from many conservative legislators. One apparent reason is that Karl Marx and Frederic Engels proposed a progressive income tax in the *Communist Manifesto*. As a result, many conservatives associated an income tax with communism and opposed it on this ground.

20   In the case of tangible assets, like a home, the total value of capital improvements are also added to the purchase price in the calculating capital gains. Moreover, in the case of a primary residence owned by a married couple, as of 2007 only capital gains greater than $250,000 are subject to the capital gains tax.

21   In the 2007 tax code, up to 85 percent of social security income is added back into AGI if the sum of the other components of AGI exceed a prespecified limit.

22   As in most of the tax code, things are not quite as simple as this. In the case of both deductions and exemptions, there are limitations imposed on the total value of each for higher income returns.

23   Actually, there are two separate categories for married couples: (i) married couples filing joint returns and (ii) married couples filing separate returns. For many years, there was an advantage for a married couple to "split" their income and file two separate tax returns, since both parts would be subject to lower marginal tax rates and therefore a lower overall average tax rate. However, current provisions of the tax code have eliminated most of the advantage of income splitting.

24   There was a slight peculiarity in the 1986 tax schedule. The top rate was actually 33 percent, for income bracket $78,400–$208,560. The marginal tax rate then fell to 28 percent, for taxable income over $208,560. The reason is that the allowable value of exemptions and deductions was gradually phased out above $208,560 of income. The lower marginal tax rate of this bracket in a sense compensated for the reduction of allowable exemptions and deductions.

25   Panel A of Table 16.2 also shows maximum effective tax rates for the years 1944–1953. The effective tax rate, as we shall discuss in more detail, shows the ratio of actual taxes paid to AGI. During this period, the effective tax rate was capped at the indicated levels.

26   This is the principal reason why an increasing percentage of the poverty population were paying federal income taxes during the 1970s and 1980s (see Section 4.6.3).

27 The increase between 1966 and 1969, from 70 to 77 percent, was due to a tax surcharge placed on high incomes, stemming from the Vietnam War.

28 Until the Tax Reform Act of 1986, all interest payments, including those for car loans, credit card debt, and other forms of consumer debt, were fully deductible. Between 1986 and 1991, deductions for non-mortgage interest payments were phased out. Today, only mortgage interest payments are deductible.

29 However, withdrawals from pension accounts *are* subject to income tax. That is the reason why pension accounts are referred to as *tax-deferred* accounts.

30 In some prior years, a portion of long-term capital gains were excluded from ordinary income instead of being subject to a special income tax rate. This provision was effective in most years, though the percentage exclusion has varied over time.

31 A relatively recent addition to the tax code is the alternative minimum tax (AMT) which provides for the payment of a minimum percentage of ordinary income for taxpayers who include tax preference items in their tax return. This provision has been quite effective in closing tax loopholes used by wealthy taxpayers.

32 Though the table is somewhat dated, it still provides the most complete analysis of this subject.

33 Since the Tax Reform Act of 1986, the dollar value of personal exemptions actually declines with income when AGI exceeds a prespecified level.

34 Actually, the health portion of OASDHI has no earnings limit today.

35 Source: U.S. House of Representatives (2004). Committee on Ways and Means, *Overview of Entitlement Programs: 2004 Green Book*. Washington, DC: U.S. Government Printing Office, July.

36 As we discussed in Chapter 2, depreciation, or more technically, the "capital consumption allowance," refers to the loss of economic value of capital goods (plant, machinery, and equipment) which comes about through wear and tear and age. Corporations are allowed to "write off" the value of their capital at rates that are probably much above the actual loss in their value. This capital consumption allowance is subtracted from the gross profits of the company to obtain net profits, and the corporate income tax is levied on the net profit figure.

37 Source: http://www.cbpp.org/10-16-03tax.htm.

38 Technically, this amount is for the unified estate and gift tax.

39 As of February 2008, the federal estate tax is scheduled to disappear entirely in 2010 and then revert back it its 2001 structure in 2011. It is unlikely that the newly elected Congress in 2009 will maintain these provisions. Also, see U.S. Congress (2006) for a detailed analysis of the federal estate tax, as well as arguments for and against the estate tax.

40 Many states had an estate tax in place before the federal government established a permanent one in 1916. Pennsylvania had established one in 1825 and Wisconsin had a progressive estate tax system in operation in 1903.

41 This is not an arithmetic error! The reason is that state and local government receipts have been increasing *relative* to federal receipts over this period.

42 Ideally, we would like to show total tax collections as a share of personal income. Unfortunately, it is not possible to identify whether the sources of some taxes, such as sales and property taxes, are individuals or businesses.

43 Note that these figures for the United States differ somewhat from those in Table 16.6 because of differences in concepts.

44 Unfortunately, the Pechman study has yet to be updated.

45 It should be noted that these results differ from those reported in Table 16.4 because of the use of the family unit here as opposed to the tax unit in Table 16.3, differences in income concepts, and other technical differences. See Pechman (1983) and Pechman (1985) for more discussion.

46 The tax rate is negative at the bottom because EITC provides a tax credit. (See Section 16.5 for a description of the EITC.)

47 A similar criticism was made about AFDC and TANF. See Section 15.5.

48 Though a negative income tax has never been implemented as such, the idea is still very much alive. There is a new group called "the U.S. Basic Income Guarantee Network" that is still promoting the idea (see http://www.usbig.net/).

49   The source is the National Income and Product Accounts, Table 3.12.
50   These schedules differ for a family with only one child and a family with no children.
51   This is particularly true of programs that require the monitoring of recipients such as TANF and unemployment insurance.
52   Many services provided by governments are paid for directly by the consumer in the form of user fees. Examples of these include toll highways, meter charges for water, local transit such as buses and subways, park admissions, and motor vehicle charges. Local governments are shifting more and more to user fees and away from general tax collection as a source of financing their activities.
53   Government expenditures also have an indirect effect on households through the so-called "multiplier effect" of government spending on output and employment. Individuals can potentially benefit from the employment that is generated by government expenditures. Indeed, a potential anti-poverty policy of the government is to increase government expenditure which thereby increases labor demand and therefore wages and employment. This is another avenue through which government expenditure might affect redistribution. We look at only the direct effects of government spending here.
54   The analysis of government expenditures and taxes presented here implicitly uses an annual time frame. However, fiscal incidence can look very different on a lifetime income basis. See Chapter 10 (Section 10.4.3) for a discussion of "generational accounting" of government taxes and benefits.

Index

ability
  definition, 274
  earnings and, 273–8, 396
  effect estimates, 275–6
  nature vs. nurture controversy, 276–8
ability adjustment, 261–2
ability to pay, 586–7, 588
absentee fathers, 563
absolute mobility, 181
accounting period, effect on poverty measures,
    121–2
Adamson Act (1916), 304
Adarand v. Pena (1995), 473
adjusted gross income (AGI), 587–8, 608
AFDC *see* Aid to Families with Dependent
    Children
affirmative action, 435, 437, 473–4
  effects, 477, 510
AFL, 304–5
AFL-CIO, 305, 311
AFQT, 268, 275, 329, 464–5, 467
Africa, rates of return to education, 265–6
age–earnings profiles, 248–9, 258–60
age–wealth profiles, 356–60
  augmented household wealth, 359–60
  as cross-sectional, 357
AGI, 587–8, 608
agricultural employment
  decline, 219, 326–7
  and regional income levels, 328
  seasonal changes, 233, 541
agriculture, government expenditures, 613
Aid to Families with Dependent Children
    (AFDC), 117, 531–2, 546–53
  average family size, 549–50
  child bearing effects, 552–3

expenditure trends, 535
  job programs for recipients, 554–5
  labor supply effects, 550–1
  marital status effects, 552–3
  means-testing, 547
  welfare participation rates, 551–2
  workings, 547–50
AIME, 542–3, 572
air traffic controllers' strike, 309
Alabama, TANF, 547–8, 573
Alaska
  TANF, 547–9
  unemployment rates, 231–2
alternative maximum tax, 625
altruism model, 375–6
American Federation of Labor (AFL), 304–5
Annual Social and Economic Supplement
    (ASEC), 178
Annual Survey of Manufactures, 388
annuities, 140, 359, 364
  wealth, 164–6
Appalachia, unemployment, 234
Arizona
  unemployment insurance, 538
  unemployment rates, 231–2
Armed Forces Qualification Test (AFQT), 268,
    275, 329, 464–5, 467
ASEC, 178
Asia, rates of return to education, 265–6
asset poverty, 120
assortative mating, 178
asymmetrical distribution, 59
Atkinson's measure, 69–70
augmented wealth, 140–1, 359
  trends, 142–3, 159
  see also share of augmented wealth

Australia
  comparable worth, 526
  gender–wage gap, 516
  income distribution
    around 1980, 81
    around 2000, 83
  income inequality
    around 1970, 75
    around 1980, 77
    P90/P10 ratio, 78–9
  taxation, 599–600
  union density, 310
Australian Twin Register, 276
Austria
  gender–wage gap, 516
  poverty rates, around 2000, 111
  regional income differences, 328
  taxation, 599
  union density, 310
auto glass company study, 281
automobiles, value, 140
average family income *see* mean family
      income
average indexed monthly earnings (AIME),
      542–3, 572
average tax rate
  definition, 579
  federal personal income tax scheme,
      581–2

B index, 184
baby boom generation, 213, 263, 264, 545
baby dearth generation, 213, 264
Bangladesh
  income distribution
    around 1980, 81
    around 2000, 83
bank deposits, trends, 145
bargaining unit, 311
baseball, 435
basic allowance, 608
Becker, Gary, 247
Belgium
  gender–wage gap, 516
  income distribution
    around 1980, 81
    around 2000, 83
  income inequality, P90/P10 ratio, 78–9
  poverty rates, around 2000, 111
  taxation, 599–600
  union density, 310
Bentham, Jeremy, 575

bequest motive, 366–71
black Americans
  educational attainment progress, 461–7
  family structure changes, 469–71
  migration, 226, 460–1
Blinder–Oaxaca decomposition, 424–5
block grants, 547
BLS, 114, 208, 209
bonds, tax-exempt issues, 587
Botswana, income distribution, around 1980,
      81
boycotts, 312
bracket creep, 115, 590
Brazil
  income distribution
    around 1980, 81–2
    around 2000, 83–4
  regional income differences, 328
Bretton Woods agreement, 390
Brookings MERGE file, 600
Brookings studies, 367
Brooklyn Dodgers, 435
Brown v. Board of Education of Topeka, Kansas
      (1954), 472–3
"buffer-stock" model, 372
Bureau of Economic Analysis, 44
Bureau of Labor Statistics (BLS), 114, 208,
      209
Burt, Cyril, 276
Bush, George H., 590
Bush, George W., 590
business cycle theory, 235
business equity
  by age class, 162
  by wealth class, 159
  unincorporated, 137
business income, 21
  see also proprietors' earnings

California
  TANF, 548–9
  unemployment insurance, 538
  unemployment rates, 232
Canada
  comparable worth, 526
  fringe benefits, 501
  gender–wage gap, 516
  household wealth inequality, 168–70
  Human Development Index, 35
  income distribution
    around 1980, 75–6, 82
    around 2000, 83

income inequality, 395
    around 1970, 75
    around 1980, 77
    P90/P10 ratio, 78–9
industry mix by province, 328
inheritances, 369
intergenerational mobility, 196–7
labor share, 31
poverty gap ratio, around 1980, 110
poverty rates
    around 1980, 110
    around 2000, 110–11
regional income differences, 328
skill margins, 339
taxation, 599–600
union density, 309–10, 395
capability approach, 99, 577
capital consumption allowances, 46
capital gains
    definition, 51, 587
    inclusion in AGI, 587
    treatment in national accounting, 51–2
capital markets, perfect, 254
cardinal utility function, 97
Caribbean
    poverty rates (1987 and 1998), 112
    rates of return to education, 266
"causation story", 195
CBO, 606–7
censuring argument, 476
Census of Manufactures, 329, 332, 335
Census of Population data
    in DD index studies, 506
    in earnings function estimation, 271, 273
    educational attainment data, 429
    in gender–wage gap studies, 498, 500–2, 507,
        510
    in immigration studies, 392–3, 417
    in income inequality studies, 327–30, 334,
        393
    in intergenerational mobility studies, 194
    in labor demand studies, 388–9
    in LFPR studies, 493
    in racial earnings gap studies, 463–6, 469,
        476
    in returns to schooling studies, 260, 261
Center on Budget and Policy Priorities, 595
Central Asia, poverty rates (1987 and 1998),
    112
CEO compensation, 342–3
CETA, 554, 555
child tax credit, 591

children
    demand for, 493
    poverty rate, 103–4
chronic poverty, 107–8
CIO, 305
Civil Rights Act (1964), 217, 473, 474, 509, 511
    effects, 474–5, 509–10
civil rights movement, 471, 532
Civil War, effects, 464
class distribution of income definition, 29
    see also factor shares
class struggle, 437–8
Clayton Act (1914), 304
Clinton, Bill, 533, 563, 590
close-ended classes, 58
coefficient of immobility, 197
coefficient of variation (CV), 61–3, 341
    definition, 61
cognitive response, 286
COLA, 544–5
Coleman Report, 464
collective bargaining, 236, 311–12
college education, rates of return, 263–5
Colombia
    income distribution
        around 1980, 81
        around 2000, 83
comparable worth, 511–12
competition, perfect, 254
competitive imports, 54
compliance reviews, 477, 510
Comprehensive Employment and Training Act
    (CETA) (1973), 554, 555
comprehensive income, 607
computerization, 389–90
    coefficient of, 389
    see also information technology
Concentrated Employment Program, 554
concentration of income, 585
concentration measures, 61
concentration ratio, 61
Congress of Industrial Organizations (CIO), 305
Congressional Budget Office (CBO), 606–7
Connecticut, TANF, 548, 572–3
construction
    seasonal changes, 233
    wage effects of unions, 343
consumer durables, 135, 140
    trends, 144–5
Consumer Expenditure Survey, 121, 361, 369,
    372
consumer price index *see* CPI-U; CPI-U-RS

consumption
  after retirement, 361
  "buffer-stock" model, 372
contingent workers, 344
corporate stock, 138
  by age class, 162
  by wealth class, 159–60
  ratio of prices to housing prices, 153
  trends, 145–6
corporation income tax, 594–5
  effective tax rates, 600–3, 605
  receipts trends, 596–7
corporations, oligopolistic, 323–4
correlation coefficient, 182
  see also intergenerational correlation coefficient;
    Spearman correlation coefficient
cost-of-living adjustment (COLA), 544–5
Costa Rica
  income distribution
    around 1980, 81
    around 2000, 83
Cote d'Ivoire
  income distribution
    around 1980, 81
    around 2000, 83
coverage rate, unemployment insurance, 539–40,
    562
covered employment, 541
CPI-U, 17–18, 114–15, 544
CPI-U-RS, 115
craft unions, 311
credit
  discrimination in provision, 427
  lines of, 135
cross-sectional samples, 298
culture of poverty, 108
Current Population Survey (CPS), 147, 209–10
  data deflation, 115
  in DD index calculations, 506
  in earnings mobility studies, 188
  in earnings and schooling studies, 258, 262,
    264–5, 283, 388–9
  educational attainment data, 462–3
  in gender–wage gap studies, 500–1, 507,
    509–10
  history, 210
  in immigration studies, 392–3
  in income inequality studies, 393–6, 416–17,
    514
  in industry wage differentials studies, 335, 338
  in labor demand and supply studies, 388–9
  in labor earnings studies, 397

  in labor force participation rate studies, 551
  in occupational wage differentials studies, 341
  poverty rate data, 228, 229
  in racial inequality studies, 457, 476–7
  schooling variance trends, 401
  in taxation studies, 600
  in trade union effects studies, 318
custom, 321
customs duty, 595, 597–8
CV *see* coefficient of variation
cyclical unemployment *see* Keynesian
    unemployment
Czech Republic
  taxation, 599
  union density, 310

Danbury Hatters' Union, 304
DC plans, 366
DD index, 506–7
debt
  household *see* household debt
  ratio to net worth *see* debt–equity ratio
debt–equity ratio, 6, 138
  by age class, 162
  trends, 162
debt–income ratio, 138
  by age class, 162
Defined Benefit (DB) wealth, 366
Defined Contribution (DC) plans, 366
degree of inequality aversion, 69
deindustrialization, 220, 393
Delaware, unemployment rates, 232
demand curves
  elastic, 314–15
  inelastic, 314–15
  labor, 313–15, 556
    for minority workers, 432
  product, 315
  schooling, 257–8
demand-deficient unemployment *see* Keynesian
    unemployment
Denmark
  gender–wage gap, 516
  household production, 39
  income distribution
    around 1980, 82
    around 2000, 83
  income mobility indices, 186–7
  intergenerational mobility, 196–7
  taxation, 599–600
  union density, 309–10
Denver, negative income tax, 609

Department of Agriculture, 532
Department of Defense, performance rating
    scheme, 280
Department of Labor, 509
deposits, by wealth class, 159
depreciation, 46, 595, 625
    of human capital, 260
deregulation, industrial, 309
desegregation, of schools, 217, 467
deskilling, 341
Detroit schools, 473
deviation, 56
    see also standard deviation
direct coefficient matrix, 53
disability, incidence, non-white males, 215
discipline, 286
discount rate, 249
"discouraged workers", 209, 224, 424, 452
    poverty frequency, 225
discrimination
    in credit provision, 427
    definition, 421
    meaning, 423–9
    in mortgage provision, 427
    pre-labor market, 427–9, 511
    public policy programs, 472–4
        effectiveness, 474–6
    reverse, 474
    statistical, 430, 434–6, 508–9
    taste for, 430–4
    theories, 429–40
        overview, 429–30
    see also gender discrimination
discrimination coefficients, 431
disorder, 68
dispersion, 56
dissimilarity index, 426
distributions *see* frequency distributions
divide and conquer model, 430, 437–8
dividends
    definition, 22
    trends, 23
divorce rate, 493
doctors, entry restrictions, 254
domestic servants, housemakers vs., 209
downsizing, 13–14, 344, 395
drop-out argument, 476
dual labor market model, 322–5
    challenges to, 326
    extensions, 323–5
Duncan and Duncan (DD) index, 506–7
duration of poverty, 108

Earned Income Tax Credit (EITC), 116, 117,
    561, 591, 608–11
    phase-in range, 610–11
    phase-out range, 610–11
    stationary range, 610
earnings
    ability and, 273–8, 396
    age and *see* age–earnings profile
    productivity and, 279–86
    schooling and, 258–9, 281–6, 395–6,
        401–2
    see also income; labor earnings; schooling-
        earnings function; wages
earnings capacity, 123
earnings differentials, 256, 264
    racial differences, 264
    see also discrimination
earnings functions, 269–73, 401
    regional, 329
earnings inequality *see* income inequality
earnings test, 545, 546
East Asia, poverty rates (1987 and 1998),
    112
Eastern Europe, poverty rates (1987 and 1998),
    112
economic mobility *see* intergenerational
    mobility; lifetime mobility; mobility
economic status, intergenerational transmission
    mechanisms, 194–5
economies of consumption, 95
economy food plan, 94
education
    consumption component, 254
    government expenditures, 612, 613
    see also schooling
education index, 35
educational attainment
    and annual earnings, 10–11
    intergenerational correlation, 195
    of labor force, 217–19
    and poverty incidence, 105, 107
    racial differences, 217, 429, 461–9
    socioeconomic status and, 284
    trends, 8–10, 217–19, 461–3
    see also schooling
EEOC, 473, 475, 509–10
efficiency wage theory, 336–9
eigenvalues, 184
EITC *see* Earned Income Tax Credit
elasticity of demand, 314
elderly persons, poverty rate, 104, 531, 561–2
elitist position, 579

employment
  definition, 208
  growth
    by industry, 331
    wages and, 333
  industrial composition, 219–20
  occupational composition, 220–1
  see also labor force; unemployment
employment rate, trends, 452
Employment Security Act (1970), 536
employment statistics, estimation, 209–10
employment status, and poverty incidence,
    105–6
Engels, Frederic, 624
English proficiency, 468–9
entertainment, 342
entropy, 68
entropy index, 68
entry ports, 319–20, 326
Equal Employment Opportunity Act (EEOA)
    (1972), 477
Equal Employment Opportunity Commission
    (EEOC), 473, 475, 509–10
Equal Pay Act (1963), 473, 509, 511
equal treatment of equals, 586–7
equality
  as social goal, 574–9
    arguments against, 577–9
    arguments in favor, 574–7
equipment investment, trends, 398–400,
    405–8
equities, 138
equivalence classes/scales, 95, 113–14, 588
equivalent income, 95, 114
  definition, 25
  trends, 4–5
ES-202 data, 558
estate division, 375
estate tax, 595, 598
  data, 148–9, 197–8
  effective tax rates, 605
  state, 595
eugenics, 278
Europe, rates of return to education, 266
European Community Household Panel Survey,
    516
excise tax, 595, 597–8
  effective tax rates, 601–3
Executive Order 10925 (1961), 473
Executive Order 11246 (1965), 473–4, 477,
    509
exit ports, 319–20, 326
experience, work *see* work experience

exports
  definition, 49
  treatment in national accounting, 49–50
  see also international trade
extended earnings function, 272–3

factor content of trade model, 390, 391
factor prices, output prices and, 391
factor shares
  definition, 29
  derivation, 48–9
  historical studies, 31–2
  see also class distribution of income
factors of production, 46
Fair Labor Standards Act (1938), 473, 509, 556
  amendments (1966), 558
fairness, 575–7
family assistance payments, 22
family background, screening, 283–5
family composition, trends, 469–71
family income
  augmented measure, 164–6
  correlation with technological, structural, and
    institutional variables, 399
  distribution of gains, 158–9
  Lorenz curve (2004), 157–8
  and wealth, correlation, 163–4
  see also income inequality; mean family
    income; median equivalent family
    income; median family income
family size
  and poverty incidence, 105–6
  trend, 215
Family Support Act (1988), 554–5, 563
family unit
  definition, 52
  in poverty measurement, 122–3
  as welfare measure, 25
farm business equity, trends, 145
farm families, poverty rate, 105, 107
fast-food industry, 558
Federal Housing Administration (FHA), 427
Federal Insurance Contributions Act (FICA), 541
federal personal income tax, 581–2, 587–93
  deductions, 588, 591–3
  effective tax rates, 591–3, 600–3, 605
  exemptions, 588–93
  government receipts trends, 596–7
  as progressive, 614
  structure history, 588–91
    marginal tax rates, 588–91
    personal exemptions, 588–90
  tax schedules, 587–91

federal tax
    effective tax rates, 605–6
    trends, 605–6
federations, labor, 303
feedback cycle, 323
female employment
    by detailed occupations, 505
    by occupational group, 503–5
    World War II effects, 506
female-headed families
    AFDC set up for, 532
    as percentage of total families, 404, 407,
        553
    poverty rate, 104–6, 471, 562
feminization of poverty, 106, 514–16
fertility rate, 493
FHA, 427
Fields–Ok index, 182–3
final goods, 45
final output, 46
final users, 44
financial assets, 137
financial securities, 138
    by wealth class, 159
    trends, 145–6
financial wealth, 140
    distribution of gains, 158
    see also share of financial wealth
Finland
    gender–wage gap, 516
    household wealth inequality, 169–70
    income distribution
        around 1980, 82
        around 2000, 83
    income inequality, P90/P10 ratio, 78–9
    intergenerational mobility, 196–7
    poverty rates, around 2000, 110–11
    regional income differences, 328
    taxation, 599
    union density, 309–10
firm size, and wages, 335–6
fixed coefficient manpower model, 302
Florida
    TANF, 548
    unemployment insurance, 538
    unemployment rates, 231–2
Flow of Funds Accounts, 141
Food Stamp program, 116, 532
    benefits, 549, 572–3
    expenditure trends, 534–5
    poverty rate effects, 561
Forbes 400, 166–7, 198
Ford Motor Company study, 338

forgone earnings, 248
45° line, 63
France
    estate division, 375
    gender–wage gap, 516
    household wealth inequality, 168–9
    income distribution
        around 1980, 82
        around 2000, 83
    income inequality, 395
        around 1970, 74–5
        P90/P10 ratio, 78–9
    intergenerational mobility, 196–7
    intergenerational transfers, 367
    minimum wage, 395
    skill margins, 339
    taxation, 599–600
    union density, 309–10, 395
frequency distributions, 56–60
fringe benefits
    gender differences, 501
    trends, 24
    unionization effect, 353
"full employment" unemployment rate, 234–5
functional capabilities, 99
functional distribution of income definition,
        29
    trends, 29–31
functional securities
    by age class, 162
    by wealth class, 159
functionings, 577
fungibility, 116

Gary (Indiana), negative income tax, 609
Gates, Bill, 166
GATT, 595
GDP *see* gross domestic product
GDP index, 35
gender discrimination, 498–501, 508–9
    overcrowding model, 430, 438–40, 511
    public policy programs, 509–13
        effectiveness, 509–11
gender–wage gap, 422–3
    earnings ratios, 488–9
        by age group, 489, 490
        by education, 489, 490–1
        trends, 490–1, 498–501
    explanations, 494–509
        human capital differences, 494–503
        see also occupational segregation
    international comparisons, 516–17
    occupational segregation and, 506–7

General Agreement on Trade and Tariffs
    (GATT), 595
general assistance, 530
general sales tax, 595–6
    effective tax rates, 600–3
General Social Survey (GSS), 193
generalized entropy mobility measure, 187
generational accounting, 376–7
genetic transmission, 194
geometric series, 297
Germany
    gender–wage gap, 516
    household wealth inequality, 169–70
    income distribution, around 2000, 83
    income inequality, P90/P10 ratio, 79
    income mobility indices, 187–8
    intergenerational mobility, 196–7
    poverty rates, around 2000, 111
    savings patterns, 361
    skill margins, 339
    taxation, 599–600
    unemployment rates, 233
    union density, 309–10
    wealth tax, 149
    see also West Germany
Ghana
    income distribution
        around 1980, 81
        around 2000, 83
"GI bill", 497
gift tax, 595, 598
    effective tax rates, 605
gifts, 367, 370–1
Gini, Corrado, 64
Gini coefficient, 64–6
    computation, 65–6
    proportional tax system, 583–4
    trends, 4, 72–3, 605–7, 615–16
globalization, 13, 234, 390
GNP, 50
    trends, 142–3
Gompers, Samuel, 304
government debt, 375, 376–7
government expenditures, 46
    beneficiaries, 613
    distributional effects, 611–16
    functional structure, 611–12
    net, 611, 614–15
government transfer systems *see* income
    maintenance programs
Great Depression, 304, 530
    unemployment rate, 221, 235, 304, 530

Great Society program, 532
Greece, taxation, 599
gross domestic product (GDP)
    definition, 24, 50
    from national accounts, 46
    government receipts as percentage of, 597–8
    national income and, 51
    per capita
        trends, 26–8
        see also RGDPL
    see also GDP index
gross house value, trends, 144–5
gross output, 46
gross profits, 45
growth, promotion, 578
GSOEP, 187
GSS, 193
Guatemala
    income distribution
        around 1980, 81
        around 2000, 83

Harrington, Michael, 108, 532
Harvard University, 428
Hawaii, unemployment insurance, 538
head count ratio, 99
health care
    government expenditures, 611–12, 613
    universal, 533, 572
health expenses, uncertainty over, 371
health insurance, 533
Health and Retirement Survey (HRS), 366
Heckscher–Ohlin model, 390
highways, government expenditures, 612, 613
Hispanics, 457–9
    earnings, 457–8
    educational attainment progress, 462–3,
        468–9
    immigration effects, 468
    labor force participation rates, 458–9
    median family income, 457
    poverty rate trends, 102, 454, 457
    unemployment rates, 458–9
home equity, 138
    by age class, 162
    trends, 145
homeless, 133
homeownership rates, 139
    by race, 146–7, 454–5
    trends, 146–7, 454–5
Hong Kong, income distribution, around 1980,
        81

Hoover, Herbert, 530
horizontal equity, 586
household, definition, 52
household consumption, 46
household debt
  by age class, 162
  by wealth class, 159–60
  composition, 138
  trends, 145
household income *see* family income; mean
      family income; median equivalent family
      income; median family income
household production, 35–9
  definition, 37
  empirical work on, 38–9
  income inequality and, 39
  market cost approach, 37
  opportunity cost approach, 38
household responsibilities, 500, 508
household survey data, 149
household wealth
  augmented *see* augmented wealth
  average wealth trends, 142–3, 154–5,
    455–6
    by race, 455–6
  composition, 136–40
    by age class, 162–3
    by wealth class, 159–62
    trends, 139–40, 143–6, 159–63
  definitions, 136, 140–1
  distribution of gains, 158
  financial *see* financial wealth
  and income, correlation, 163–4
  Lorenz curve (2004), 157–8
  marketable *see* marketable wealth
  median wealth trends, 154–5
  sources of accumulation, 369–70
  treatment in poverty measurement, 119–20
  trends, 5–6
  and well-being, 135–6
  see also personal savings
household wealth inequality, 147–67
  changes 1962–2004, 154–66
    average wealth holdings, 154–5
    trends analysis, 155–9
  estimation methods, 148–50
  income inequality vs., 151–3
  international comparisons, 167–70
    long-term trends, 167–8
    recent trends, 168–70
  long-term trends in U.S., 150–3
  see also share of wealth

housemakers, domestic servants vs., 209
housing assistance, 533–4
  expenditure trends, 534–5
  poverty rate effects, 561
housing price index, 114
housing prices, 139
  ratio of stock prices to, 153
housing segregation, 425–7
HRS, 366
human capital model, 247–58
  basic assumptions, 254
  depreciation of human capital, 260
  earnings inequality and, 286–8
  equilibrium formation, 255–8
  as indeterminate, 256
  and LFPR of women, 493
  policy implications, 255
  rate of return to human capital, 248–51
    regional differences, 329
  relative earnings theory, 255
  screening model vs., 282–3
  structural models vs., 302
  see also on-the-job training
Human Development Index (HDI), 33, 35
  international comparison, 35–6
Hungary
  income distribution
    around 1980, 81
    around 2000, 83
  taxation, 599
  union density, 310
hysteresis, 235

Iceland, taxation, 599
illegitimacy rates, 553
Illinois
  TANF, 548
  unemployment insurance, 538
  unemployment rates, 232
immigration, 13
  and earnings inequality, 392–3, 468
  law, 546
  trends, 399, 401, 405–7
immobility coefficient, 197
immobility index, 182
implicit contract theory, 236
imports
  competitive, 54
  definition, 49
  noncompetitive, 54
  treatment in national accounting, 49–50
  see also international trade

incarceration rates, 471
incentives
    structures, 436
    to work, 578
income
    in constant dollars *see* real income
    in current dollars *see* nominal income
    marginal utility, 575–6
income capitalization, 149–50
income classes, 57
income deficiency index *see* poverty gap ratio
income deficit, definition, 107
Income Evaluation Question, 97
income inequality
    causes of rise, 12–14, 386–96
        data sources, 416–17
        econometric results, 405–8
    household production and, 39
    human capital and, 286–8
    industrial composition and, 326–31
        inter-industry employment shifts effects,
            330
    international comparisons, 74–85
        among high-income countries, 74–9
        for countries at various development levels,
            80–4
        world income distribution, 84–5
    minimum wage effect, 559
    racial differences, 457
        see also racial inequality
    regional differences, 326–8
    state differences, 327–8
    time trends in U.S., 70–4, 396–7, 403–4
        in key explanatory variables, 396–404
    trade unionism effect, 318
    wealth inequality vs., 151–3
    wives' earnings effects, 513–14
    see also industry wage differentials; labor
        earnings; occupational wage differentials;
        share of total income
income inequality measures, 60–74
    concentration measures, 61
    as scale-free, 583
    see also Atkinson's measure; coefficient of
        variation; Gini coefficient; log variance
        of income; Lorenz curve; Lorenz
        dominance; Theil entropy index
income levels, regional differences, 328–9
income maintenance programs
    effects on poverty, 117–19, 560–2
    history, 529–35
        early developments, 530
        post-war developments, 532–3

    public expenditures on major programs,
        534–5, 559–60
    see also housing assistance; New Deal
    reform proposals, 562–4
income security, government expenditures,
    611–12
income shares *see* share of total income
income splitting, 592–3
income spread, trends, 4–5
Income Survey and Development Program
    (ISDP), 150
income taxes
    computation, 51
    negative, 608–11
    progressive systems, 75
    state personal, 595
        see also corporation income tax; federal
            personal income tax
independent jobs, 323
India
    income distribution
        around 1980, 81
        around 2000, 83
    poverty rates (1987 and 1998), 112
Indiana
    negative income tax, 609
    TANF, 548
indirect business taxes, 45
Indonesia
    income distribution
        around 1980, 81
        around 2000, 83
industrial composition
    income inequality and, 326–31
        inter-industry employment shifts effects,
            330
industrial mobility, 189
industrial unions, 311
industry concentration, 332, 334
industry profitability, 334
industry wage differentials, 331–9
    explanations, 331–6
    plant and firm size effects, 335–6
    recent trends, 336–9
inequality, income *see* income inequality
inflation, unemployment and, 235
"inflation-threshold" unemployment rate, 234–5
inflection point, 59
information, perfect, 254
information technology (IT)
    diffusion, 387, 389–90
    labor market effects, 265, 389–90
information theory, 67

inheritances, 367–8, 375–6
  appreciation, 370
  racial differences, 455–6
  see also estate tax
input–output analysis, 44–6
  and national accounts, 46–7
insurance value, 116
insured coverage rate, 539–40, 562
intelligence
  socioeconomic class and, 277
  see also ability
inter vivos transfers *see* gifts
interest income
  definition, 22
  trends, 23–4
interest rates
  market/real, 248, 297
    adjustments, 255
  nominal, 297
intergenerational altruism, 367
intergenerational correlation
    coefficient, 181
intergenerational elasticity, 181, 191, 193–4
intergenerational equity, 372–7
intergenerational mobility, 180, 189–97
  continuous time trends, 193
  international comparisons, 195–7
  measurement error, 190
  measures, 180–1
  occupational, 193
  racial differences, 191, 192, 195
  transmission mechanisms, 194–5
  United States results, 190–4
  wealth, 197–8
intergenerational transfers, 367, 375–6
  trends, 368
  see also gifts; inheritances
intermediate goods, 44–5
intermediate users, 44
internal labor markets, 236, 302, 319–22, 395
  in corporations, 324
  criticisms, 326
  definition, 319
  rationale, 320–2
  structure, 319–20
internal rate of return, 255, 298
  definition, 251
Internal Revenue Service (IRS), tax return data, 185, 600, 605
international trade
  and earnings inequality, 390–2
  intensity trends, 399, 401, 405–8
  treatment in national accounting, 49–50

interspousal transfers, 367
inventories, 53
investment, 46
investment banking, 342
investment tax credit, 591
Iowa
  comparable worth system, 512
  negative income tax, 609
Ireland
  income inequality, P90/P10 ratio, 79
  poverty rates, around 2000, 110–11
  taxation, 599
  union density, 310
IRS *see* Internal Revenue Service
ISDP, 150
Israel
  income distribution
    around 1980, 75–6, 81
    around 2000, 83
  income inequality
    around 1980, 77
    P90/P10 ratio, 79
  poverty gap ratio, around 1980, 110
  poverty rates, around 1980, 110
IT *see* information technology
Italy
  gender–wage gap, 516
  household wealth inequality, 169–70
  income distribution
    around 1980, 81
    around 2000, 83
  income inequality
    around 1970, 75
    P90/P10 ratio, 79
  poverty rates, around 2000, 110–11
  regional income differences, 328
  taxation, 599–600
  union density, 309–10

Jamaica
  income distribution
    around 1980, 81
    around 2000, 83
Japan
  gender–wage gap, 516
  Human Development Index, 35
  income distribution
    around 1980, 82
    around 2000, 83
  income inequality, 395
    around 1970, 75
  taxation, 599–600
  union density, 310

Jim Crow laws, 426
Job Corps, 554
job evaluation, 511–12
job leavers, 209, 222–3
job losers, 209, 222–3
Job Opportunities and Basic Skills Training
    (JOBS) program, 554–5
job preferences, gender differences, 508
job security, 321
Job Training Partnership Act (JTPA), 554
job vacancies, unemployment and, 225
JOBS program, 554–5
Johnson, Lyndon B., 473, 532
JTPA, 554
"just sufficient" income level, 97

Kennedy, John F., 427, 473, 532
Kerr, Clark, 319
Keynesian unemployment (demand-deficient
    unemployment), 225, 235–6, 237–8
Korea, taxation, 598–9
Korean War, 590
Kuznets, Simon, 44, 80
Kuznets curve, 80

labor
    demand trends, 265
    elasticity of demand, 314
    see also demand curves; supply curves
labor earnings
    definition, 22
    indices, trends, 3, 7
    trends, 22, 26–8, 397
    see also earnings; income; wages
labor force
    definitions
        civilian labor force, 209
        total labor force, 209
    trends, 211
        educational attainment, 217–19
    see also employment
labor force participation rate (LFPR), 210–19
    definition, 210
    trends, 211
        by age, 211–16, 449–51
        by educational attainment, 449–50
        by gender, 211–16, 449–50
        by race, 212–13, 215–16, 449–53, 458–9
        females by marital status, 491–4
        married women, 3, 215–17, 492–4,
            513–14
        two-earner households, 216–17

labor market segmentation, 319–26
    development, 323–4
    evaluation, 325–6
    see also internal labor markets; secondary
        labor market
labor market twist, 237
labor productivity, trends, 7–8
labor unions see trade unions
Latin America
    poverty rates (1987 and 1998), 112
    rates of return to education, 265–6
lawyers, 342
layoffs
    policies of firms, 541
    wage reduction vs., 236
LCM see lifecycle model
LE see lifetime earnings
leisure time, value, 123
Leontief, Wassily, 44
Lewis, John, 305
Leyden poverty line, 96–7
    derivation, 97–9
LFPR see labor force participation rate
libertarianism, 577–8
life expectancy index, 35
life insurance, by wealth class, 159
lifecycle model (LCM), 356, 363
    extensions, 363–72
        bequest motive, 366–71
        liquidity constraints, 371–2
        pension and social security wealth role,
            364–6
        precautionary savings, 371–2
        uncertainty, 364
    longitudinal analyses, 359–61
    regression analysis, 362–3
    simulation analysis, 361–3
    and top wealth classes, 363
    see also age–wealth profiles
lifetime earnings (LE), 256, 267–9
    by schooling group, 267–9
    in lifecycle model, 363
lifetime mobility, 180, 184–9
    earnings, 188–9
    income, 184–8
        international comparisons, 186–7
    industrial, 189
    measures, 181–4
    occupational, 189
liquid assets, 137–8
    by age class, 162
    trends, 145

liquidity constraints, 371–2
literacy rates, importance of raising, 266
living standards *see* standard of living
local government taxes, 595–6, 597–8
log-normal distribution, 67
log variance of income, 66–7
longevity, uncertainty about, 364
longitudinal samples, 298
Lorenz curve, 63–4
   progressive tax structure, 584–5
   proportional tax structure, 583–4
   regressive tax structure, 584–5
Lorenz dominance, 70
Louisiana, unemployment rates, 231
low-wage workers, characteristics, 325
Luxembourg
   income inequality, P90/P10 ratio, 79
   RGDPL, 33
   taxation, 599
Luxembourg Income Study (LIS), 75, 109

macroeconomic policy, unemployment rate and, 238
macro-economy, poverty and, 125
Malaysia
   income distribution
      around 1980, 81
      around 2000, 83
male–female wage gap *see* gender–wage gap
Malthus, Thomas, 572
Manpower Development and Training Act (MDTA) (1962), 554
manufacturing
   employment decline, 219–20
   regional wage differences, 329
   skill-bias, 387–8
   union organization, 311
marginal rate of return, 257
marginal revenue product, 252
marginal tax rate, 580–1
   definition, 580
   federal personal income tax scheme, 581–2
   trends, 6–7
marital customs, 148
marital status, and LFPR, 215
market power, 332–4
market value, 116
marketable wealth, 136–40
   international comparisons, 168–9
   trends, 142–3, 155–6
"marriage penalty", 500

Marshall, Alfred, 314
Marshall's rules, 314–15
Marx, Karl, 624
Marxian model, 430, 437–8
Massachusetts
   minimum wage, 573
   unemployment insurance, 538
   unemployment rates, 231–2
maximin solution, 576
maximum taxable wage base, 593–4
MDTA, 554
mean, definition, 56
mean family income
   bottom quintile, trends, 2–3
   median income vs., 60
   trends, 1–2, 154
      by race, 421–2, 455–6
mean income deficit, 106, 107
mean squared proportionate poverty gap, 101
mechanization, 340
median, definition, 59
median equivalent family income, trends, 26–7, 29
median family income
   by household type, 471, 513
   mean income vs., 60
   trends, 1–2, 26–8, 155
      by household type, 513
      by race, 453–4
Medicaid, 116, 117, 532–3, 611
   expenditure trends, 534–5
Medicare, 116, 117, 531, 532–3, 611
   expenditure trends, 534–5
MESP file, 150, 373
Mexico
   income inequality, P90/P10 ratio, 79
   taxation, 598–9
Michigan
   TANF, 548
   unemployment insurance, 538
   unemployment rates, 232
Middle East
   poverty rates (1987 and 1998), 112
   rates of return to education, 266
migration
   black American, 226, 460–1
   welfare benefits and, 553
Milken v. Bradley (1974), 473
Mill, John Stuart, 322
minimum wage, 345, 556–9
   coverage, 558
   decline in real terms, 394–5, 558, 563

minimum wage (*cont'd*)
  reform proposals, 563–4
  trends, 401–2, 405–8, 557–8
mining, employment decline, 219
Minnesota, comparable worth system, 512
mobility, 180–99
  absolute, 181
  measures, 180–4
  over time *see* lifetime mobility
  relative, 181
  see also intergenerational mobility
mobility *M* index, 187
modal class, 58
mode, definition, 58
Monthly Report on the Labor Force, 210
Monthly Report on Unemployment, 210
Morocco
  income distribution
    around 1980, 81
    around 2000, 83
mortality multipliers, 148
mortgages, 138
  debt trends, 145
  discrimination in provision, 427
  "sub-prime", 133, 178, 443
motivation, by external reward, 286
Moynihan, Patrick, 469
multiplier effect, 626
Murray, Charles, 550
mutual funds, 138
  by wealth class, 160
Myrdal, Gunnar, 445

NAEP, 396, 429, 465
NAIRU, 235
National Academy of Sciences, 114
national accounts *see* National Income and
    Product Accounts
National Assessment of Educational Progress
    (NAEP), 396, 429, 465
National Bureau of Economic Research, 275
  see also NBER-Thorndike sample
National Center for Education Sciences (NCES),
    429
  Common Core of Data, 428
National Compensation Survey (2003), 318
national defense, government expenditures,
    611–12, 613
national income (NI)
  definition, 48, 51
  GDP and, 51
  sources, 49

National Income and Product Accounts (NIPA),
    44–52, 416–17
  capital gains treatment, 51–2
  factor shares derivation, 48–9
  input–output analysis and, 46–7
  international trade treatment, 49–50
  personal income sources, 47–8
National Industrial Recovery Act (1933), 304
National Labor Relations Act, 304–5
National Labor Relations Board (NLRB), 304,
    311
National Longitudinal Surveys (NLS)
  in gender–wage gap studies, 499, 502–3, 508
  in intergenerational mobility studies, 191, 193
  in lifecycle model studies, 372
  in lifetime earnings studies, 475
  of Mature Men, 197
  of older men, 360, 365
  in racial inequality studies, 455–6
  in return to schooling studies, 284–5
  in work experience studies, 495
  of Youth (NLSY)
    in earnings mobility studies, 188
    in educational attainment studies, 464, 467,
        469
    in gender–wage gap studies, 500, 503
    in return to education studies, 396
national poverty line, 98
National Science Foundation, 416
National Trades' Union, 303
National Typographical Union, 303
natural rate of unemployment, 234–5, 238
nature vs. nurture controversy, 276–8
NBER Manufacturing Productivity Database,
    392
NBER–Thorndike sample, 267, 275–6, 282
Nebraska, unemployment rates, 231–2
need standard, 547
needs, redistribution according to, 578
negative income tax, 608–11
neighborhood effects, 465
Neighborhood Youth Corps, 554
net equity, 140
net government benefits, 613–14
net government expenditures, 611, 614–15
net investment, 47
net national product (NNP), 24–5
  from national accounts, 46–7
net profit rate, trends, 8
net profit share, trends, 8
net profits, 46
net worth *see* marketable wealth

Netherlands
  gender–wage gap, 516
  income distribution
    around 1980, 82
    around 2000, 83
  income inequality
    around 1970, 75
    around 1980, 77
    P90/P10 ratio, 78–9
  poverty rates, around 2000, 111
  taxation, 599–600
  union density, 310
New Deal, 304, 530–1
new entrants, 209, 222–3
New Hampshire, unemployment rates, 231–2
New Jersey
  minimum wage, 558
  negative income tax, 609
  TANF, 548
  unemployment insurance, 538
New York (city)
  personal income tax, 595
  TANF, 548–9
New York (state)
  personal income tax, 595
  unemployment insurance, 536, 538
  unemployment rates, 232
New Zealand
  income distribution
    around 1980, 81
    around 2000, 83
  income inequality, P90/P10 ratio, 78
  taxation, 599
  union density, 310
NI *see* national income
Nigeria, income distribution, around 2000, 83
NIPA *see* National Income and Product
        Accounts
Nixon, Richard, 533, 572
NLRB, 304, 311
NLS *see* National Longitudinal Surveys
NLSY *see* National Longitudinal Surveys (NLS),
        of Youth
NNP *see* net national product
nominal income, definition, 25
nominal tax rate, 591–2
non-accelerating inflation rate of unemployment
        (NAIRU), 235
noncash government benefits, treatment in
        poverty measurement, 116–19
noncognitive skills, development, 286
noncompeting groups, 322

noncompetitive imports, 54
nonmarket time, value, 123
normative judgments, 575
North Africa
  poverty rates (1987 and 1998), 112
  rates of return to education, 266
North Carolina
  negative income tax, 609
  unemployment insurance, 538
North Dakota, unemployment rates, 231–2
Norway
  gender–wage gap, 516
  Human Development Index, 35
  income distribution
    around 1980, 75–6, 82
    around 2000, 83
  income inequality
    around 1970, 75
    around 1980, 77
    P90/P10 ratio, 78–9
  income mobility indices, 186–7
  intergenerational mobility, 196–7
  poverty gap ratio, around 1980, 110
  poverty rates, around 1980, 110
  taxation, 599–600
  union density, 310
Nussbaum, Martha, 99

OASDHI, 531, 593–4
  expenditure trends, 534
  tax trends, 593–4
  see also social security system
OASDI *see* social security system
OASI *see* Old Age and Survivors Insurance
OCA investment, trends, 398–400, 405–8
occupational mobility
  intergenerational, 193
  lifetime, 189
occupational segregation, 429, 503–9
  Duncan and Duncan (DD) index, 506–7
  explanations, 507–9
  and gender–wage gap change, 506–7
  overcrowding model, 430, 438–40, 511
  persistence, 439–40
occupational wage differentials, 339–43
  historical studies, 339
  skewness at top, 342–3
  trends, 340–1
occupations, classification, 324
OECD countries
  income inequality, 395
  rates of return to education, 266

Office of Education, 429
Office of Federal Contract Compliance (OFCC), 474, 475, 477, 509–10
Ohio
  TANF, 548
  unemployment insurance, 538
Oklahoma, unemployment rates, 232
Old Age and Survivors Insurance (OASI), 21, 372–4, 541
  see also social security system
Omnibus Budget Reconciliation Act (1993), 610
on-the-job training, 251–3, 320–1, 475, 502
  direct costs, 251
  effect on age–earnings profile, 259–60
  formal, 251
  general, 252–3, 255, 320
  indirect costs, 251
  informal, 251
  specific, 252–3, 320, 502
open-ended classes, 58
opportunity, equality of, 474, 575, 577–8
Orshansky, Mollie, 94
outcomes, equality of, 577
output prices, factor prices and, 391
outsourcing, 13–14, 395
overcrowding model, 430, 438–40, 511
owner-occupied housing, 136–7
  by age class, 162
  by wealth class, 159
  trends, 144–5

Pakistan
  income distribution
    around 1980, 81
    around 2000, 83
Panel Study of Income Dynamics (PSID), 107–8, 122
  in altruism model testing, 376
  in gender–wage gap studies, 499–500, 502, 507, 510, 516
  in intergenerational mobility studies, 190–6, 198, 284
  in interracial earnings gap studies, 467
  in interracial wealth gap studies, 456
  in lifetime mobility studies, 184, 185, 187–9
  in productivity studies, 280–1
  in schooling and earnings studies, 283
parabolic earnings function, 272
parental resources, 284
partnerships, 23
patenting, 388

path dependency, 235
payroll taxes, 593–4
  distributional effects, 614
  effective tax rates, 600–3, 605
peer effects, 284, 428
Penn World Tables, 32–3
Pennsylvania
  TANF, 548
  unemployment insurance, 538
  unemployment rates, 232
pension accounts, 138
  by wealth class, 159–60
pension benefits, 22
pension wealth (PW), 136, 140–1, 359
  effect on savings, 364–6
  trends, 143, 159
per capita measures, 25
percentile ranking, 59–60
permanent income, 121
permanent income hypothesis, 121
personal disposable income
  definition, 25
  trends, 26–8, 142–3
personal income, 22
  composition, 22–4
  sources, 47–8
  see also personal disposable income; total personal income
personal property income, trends, 404, 407
Personal Responsibility and Work Opportunity Reconciliation Act (PRWORA), 547, 563
personal savings, 48
  pension and social security wealth effect, 364–6
  see also household wealth
personality traits
  inculcation, 285
  intergenerational transmission, 194
Peru
  income distribution
    around 1980, 81
    around 2000, 83
Philippines
  income distribution
    around 1980, 81
    around 2000, 83
Philips curve, 235
PIA, 543
piece-rate incentive schemes, 332
Pigou–Dalton transfer principle, 60–1
plant size, and wages, 335

Plessy v. Ferguson (1896), 472
Poland
  income distribution
    around 1980, 81
    around 2000, 83
  income inequality, P90/P10 ratio, 79
  taxation, 599
  union density, 310
poor *see* poverty population
Poor Law, 571
ports of entry, 319–20, 326
ports of exit, 319–20, 326
Portugal, taxation, 599
post-schooling investment, 260
poverty
  as capability-deprivation, 99
  composite measures, 100–1
  consumption-based measures, 120–1
  feminization of, 106, 514–16
  macro-economy and, 125
  measurement, 93–9
    issues in, 112–23
  movements into, 108
  movements out of, 108
  needs-based definition, 95
  permanence, 107–8
  severe, definition, 111
  temporary, 107–8
  unemployment and, 225
  World Bank definitions, 111
poverty gap ratio
  definition, 99–100
  trends, 106–7
poverty gap squared, 133
poverty lines
  absolute, 95–6
  official definition, 94–5
    by size of family (2005), 94
  relative, 95, 96
  subjective, 96–9
poverty population, composition, 103–7
poverty rate
  definition, 99
  government transfer program effects, 117–19, 560–2
  international comparisons, 109–12
  trends, 1–2, 85, 101–7, 454, 515
    all persons, 101–2
    blacks, 102, 454, 471
    by age group, 103–4
    by family type, 103, 471
    by gender, 515

    Hispanics, 102, 454, 457
    whites, 102–3, 454, 471
  poverty spells, duration, 108
PPP, 33
precautionary savings, 371–2
pre-fisc income, 615–16
prejudice
  definition, 421
  in economic terms, 430
pre-labor market discrimination, 427–9, 511
present values, 248
President's Commission on Pension Policy, 365
price index, choice, 114
primary insurance amount (PIA), 543
primary labor market, 322, 324
  see also internal labor market
probate records, 197, 365
product demand curves, 315
productivity
  direct measures, 279–81
  earnings and, 279–86
  wages growth and, 332–3, 335–6
  work experience and, 279–81
profit share, trends, 32
promotion, seniority and, 280
promotional ladders, 320
property tax, 596, 598
  effective tax rates, 600–3
  as regressive, 614
proprietors' earnings
  definition, 22
  trends, 22–3
PRWORA, 547, 563
PSID *see* Panel Study of Income Dynamics
public housing, 534
Public Housing Administration, 426
public order and safety, government
    expenditures, 612, 613
public policy
  changes, 14
  programs, 472–4
    effectiveness, 474–6
purchasing power parity (PPP), 33
PW *see* pension wealth

Quality of Employment Survey, 500
quintile, definition, 60
quit rates, 502

R&D
  activity measures, 398–400
  trends, 398–400, 405–7

racial inequality
  causes, 135–6
  earnings ratios, 446–9, 457–8
    educational gains role, 463–4
    trends, 447–9
  family income, trends, 421–2, 455–6
  household wealth, trends, 455–6
  labor force participation, trends, 212–13,
      215–16, 449–53, 458–9
  unemployment rate, trends, 226–7, 231,
      449–52, 458–9
  see also poverty rate
racial stigma model, 430, 436–7
racism, 421
rank order, 584
rank preservation, 586–7
rationality, perfect, 254
Rawls, John, 576
Reagan, Ronald, 590
real estate (nonhome), 137
  by age class, 162
  by wealth class, 159
real income, definition, 25
rebound effect, 502–3
recipient value, 117
redistribution of income, 61
redlining, 427
reentrants, 209, 222–3
regional income differentials, 328–9
regression to the mean, 181
relative earnings theory, 255
relative mobility, 181
"rent sharing", 338
rental income
  definition, 22
  trends, 23
replacement investment, 47
replacement rate
  social security, 543–4
  unemployment insurance, 536–7, 539–40
re-segregation, 428
reservation wage, 540
residence, and poverty incidence, 106–7
retirement age, 562
Retirement History Survey (RHS), 360–1, 365,
      366, 368, 373
retirement wealth, 141
  trends, 159
return on capital, 45
reverse discrimination, 474
RGDPL, international comparisons, 33–4
Rhode Island, unemployment insurance, 536
RHS, 360–1, 365, 366, 368, 373

rigidity index, 182
risk aversion, 576–7
Robinson, Jackie, 435
Roosevelt, Franklin D., 530
Russia, income inequality, P90/P10 ratio, 79

salaries, 21
  see also labor earnings
sales tax *see* general sales tax
sample, 55
  random, 55
  stratified, 91
sample selection bias, 385
SAT scores, 396, 465
savings *see* household wealth; personal savings
"scabs", 312
scale independence, 60
SCF *see* Survey of Consumer Finances
school busing, 427, 472
schooling
  coefficient of, 271
  demand curve, 257–8
  desegregation, 217, 467
  direct costs, 248
  earnings and, 258–9, 281–6, 395–6, 401–2
  as family background transmitter, 283–5
  gender differences, 496–7
  job-related, 289
  median years of, by age group, 497
  opportunity/indirect costs, 248
  as productivity-augmenting, 282
  quality, 464–5
  rates of return, 260–7, 386, 396
    by world region, 265–6
    fluctuation over time, 262–3
    policy implications, 266–7
    private, 265–6, 282
    racial differences, 465–7
    social, 265–6, 282
    trends, 287–8, 403, 405–8
  as screening device, 281–3
  segregation, 427–8, 472
  size distribution trends, 403–4
  as socializing mechanism, 285–6
  supply curve, 256–8
  variance trends, 401–3, 405–8
  see also education; educational attainment
schooling attainment *see* educational attainment
schooling–earnings function, 269–72
Schultz, Theodore, 247
screening model, human capital model vs.,
      282–3
search unemployment, 540

Seattle, negative income tax, 609
secondary labor market, 319, 322
  consequences, 323
  make-up, 323
  rationale for, 322–3
segmented labor markets *see* labor market
    segmentation
segregation, 425–9, 472
  imperfect information and, 436
  see also occupational segregation
selection model, 336–7
"selection story", 195
selectivity bias, 299, 452
self-interest, 577
self-reinforcing mechanisms, 437
Sen, Amartya, 96, 99, 577
Sen index, 100
SEO, 165–6, 324, 498
"separate but equal", 471
service sectors
  employment growth, 220, 407
  union impact on wages, 316
services, shift to, 13, 393–4
sex discrimination *see* gender discrimination
sex stereotyping, 429
SFCC *see* Survey of Financial Characteristics of
    Consumers
share of augmented wealth, trends, top 1
    percentile, 151
share of financial wealth
  trends
    bottom 80 percentile, 157
    top quintile, 157
    top 1 percentile, 157
    top 5 percentile, 157
share of total income
  trends
    by type of income, 72
    bottom quintile, 2–5, 71
    second quintile, 71
    third quintile, 71
    fourth quintile, 71
    top quintile, 71, 157
    top 1 percentile, 71, 72, 73–4, 157
    top 5 percentile, 4–5, 71, 73, 151–2, 157
    top 10 percentile, 71
share of wealth
  international comparisons, 168–70
  trends
    bottom quintile, 156–7
    second quintile, 156–7
    third quintile, 156–7

    fourth quintile, 156–7
    top quintile, 156–7
    top 1 percentile, 150–1, 155–7
    top 5 percentile, 157
Sherman Antitrust Act (1890), 304
ship maintenance study, 279
shirking model, 336–7
Shorrocks index, 183
Shorrocks R measure, 182
"sin taxes", 595
Singapore
  income distribution
    around 1980, 81
    around 2000, 83
SIPP *see* Survey of Income and Program
    Participation
Sixteenth Amendment, 587
size distribution of income, 57–9
  definition, 29
skewed distribution, 59
skewness, direction, 59
skill margins, 339
  see also occupational wage differentials
skill specificity, 320–1
skilled labor, demand trends, 265
Slovak Republic
  taxation, 599
  union density, 310
Slovenia, income distribution, around 2000, 83
"slowdowns", 312
SMSA level data, 392
social capital, 284
social insurance, 530, 531, 598
social roles, gender differences, 498
social safety net, 576
Social Security Act (1935), 530, 536, 541, 546,
    593
Social Security Administration (SSA),
    longitudinal earnings data, 189, 191
Social Security Exact Match file, 373
social security system, 530–1, 541–6, 593–4
  benefits, 22
    by recipient class, 542
    determination, 542–3
    exclusion from AGI, 587
    taxation, 545
  earnings test, 545, 546
  establishment, 531
  expenditure trends, 534–5
  labor supply incentive effects, 546
  means-testing, 562
  poverty rate effects, 561

social security system (*cont'd*)
  reform proposals, 562
  replacement rates, 543–4
  spousal benefit, 545
  tax trends, 593–4
  see also OASDHI; Old Age and Survivors
    Insurance
social security trust fund, 545–6, 611
social security wealth (SSW), 136, 140–1, 359,
    546
  annuity value, 372–4
  by age group, 373–5
  effect on savings, 364–6
  transfer value, 372–4
  trends, 143, 159
socialization patterns, 508
socioeconomic class
  intelligence and, 277
  preserving, 283–5
sociological model, 337–8
South, migration from, 226, 460–1
South Asia, poverty rates (1987 and 1998), 112
South Carolina, TANF, 552
South Korea, union density, 310
Spain
  gender–wage gap, 516
  income distribution
    around 1980, 81
    around 2000, 83
  income inequality, around 1970, 75
  taxation, 599
  union density, 310
Spearman correlation coefficient, 182
specific training, 252–3, 320, 502
specification bias, 274, 299
sports, 342
spousal benefit, 545
Sri Lanka
  income distribution
    around 1980, 81
    around 2000, 83
SSA *see* Social Security Administration
SSI *see* Supplemental Security Income
SSW *see* social security wealth
standard deviation, definition, 56
standard of living
  international comparisons, 32–5
  measurement options, 24–6
  trends, 1–12, 26–9
state personal income taxes, 595
state taxes, 595–6, 597–8
statistical discrimination, 430, 434–6, 508–9

statistics, review, 55–60
stochastic dominance, 70
  first-order, 70
stock *see* corporate stock
Stolper–Samuelson theorem, 390–1, 392
Stone, Richard, 44
strikes, 312
structural models, human capital model vs.,
    302
subordinancy, 285–6
subordinate jobs, 323
Sub-Saharan Africa
  poverty rates (1987 and 1998), 112
  rates of return to education, 266
substantive freedoms, 99
superstars, 342
Supplemental Security Income (SSI), 532, 533,
    561
  expenditure trends, 534–5
supply curves, 313–14, 556
  for minority workers, 432
Survey of Consumer Finances (SCF)
  in household wealth studies, 136, 154, 165–6
  in interracial wealth gap studies, 456
  in lifecycle model studies, 357–9, 362, 365,
    367–8, 373
  lifetime earnings calculations from, 268–9
  in poverty rate studies, 120
Survey on the Economic Behavior of the
    Affluent, 367
Survey of Economic Opportunity (SEO), 165–6,
    324, 498
Survey of Financial Characteristics of
    Consumers (SFCC)
  in household wealth studies, 154
  in household well-being studies, 164
  in lifecycle model studies, 357, 360, 365, 367,
    369
Survey of Income and Education, 468, 526
Survey of Income and Program Participation
    (SIPP)
  in gender–wage gap studies, 502–3
  in generational accounting studies, 376
  in labor market studies, 325
  in lifecycle model studies, 366
  in poverty studies, 108, 122
  in welfare system studies, 552
Survey Research Center National Sample, 267
Sussex, University of, 389
Sweden
  gender–wage gap, 516
  household wealth inequality, 167–70

income distribution
    around 1980, 75–6, 82
    around 2000, 83
income inequality
    around 1970, 75
    around 1980, 77
    P90/P10 ratio, 78–9
income mobility indices, 186–7
industry wage differentials, 339
intergenerational mobility, 195–7
poverty gap ratio, around 1980, 110
poverty rates
    around 1980, 110
    around 2000, 110–11
regional income differences, 328
taxation, 598–600
union density, 309–10
wealth tax, 149
Swedish Level of Living Survey, 196
Swedish Twin Registry, 195
Switzerland
    gender–wage gap, 516
    income distribution
        around 1980, 82
        around 2000, 83
    income inequality, around 1980, 77
    taxation, 599–600
    union density, 309–10
    wealth tax, 149
symbolic analysis, 390
symmetrical distribution, 59

Taft–Hartley Labor–Management Relations Act
        (1947), 305
TANF *see* Temporary Assistance to Needy
        Families
tangible assets, 136
Tax Acts, 590
tax avoidance, 148
tax brackets, 581
tax credits, 591, 593
tax-deferred accounts, 625
"tax loopholes", 581
tax preference items, 591–3, 595
tax rate
    definition, 579
    effective, 581, 591–3, 600–7
        corporation income tax, 600–3, 605
        estate tax, 605
        excise tax, 601–3
        federal personal income tax, 591–3, 600–3,
            605

federal tax, 605–6
general sales tax, 600–3
gift tax, 605
incidence assumptions, 600–1
payroll taxes, 600–3, 605
property tax, 600–3
trends, 603–6
nominal, 591–2
see also average tax rate; marginal tax rate
Tax Reform Act (1986), 115, 590, 603
tax systems
    structure, 579–87
        inequality measures, 583–5
        vertical versus horizontal equity, 586–7
    see also United States tax system
taxable income, 588
taxes
    effect on poverty rate, 117, 119, 561
    international comparisons, 598–600
    progressive, 579–80, 581, 584–6
    proportional, 579–80, 583–4, 586
    regressive, 579–80, 584–6
    treatment in poverty measurement, 115–16
"teaser rate", 443
"techno-economic" paradigm, 386, 389
technology
    effect of changes, 234, 237
    skill-biased change, 12–13, 265, 387–9,
        397–8, 409–10
    and skill margins, 340–1
teen mothers, 549–50
teenage employment, minimum wage and,
        558
temporary assistance, 547
Temporary Assistance to Needy Families
        (TANF), 122, 532
    benefits, 547–9
        trends, 549–50
    cost, 610
    eligibility requirements, 547–8, 554
    expenditure trends, 534–5
    labor supply effects, 550–1
    poverty rate effects, 561
    welfare participation rates, 552
    workings, 547–50
temporary poverty, 107–8
Texas
    TANF, 548–9
    unemployment insurance, 538
    unemployment rates, 231–2
TFP growth, 397–8, 405–8
Theil entropy index, 67–9

threat effect, 317–18
time use studies, 37, 38–9
total factor productivity (TFP) growth, 397–8,
    405–8
total personal income, 25
trace, of matrix, 183–4
trade unions, 303–14
    economic role, 310–15
    history in United States, 303–5
    labor market impact, 312–14
    membership trends, 305–10
        by industry, 307–9
        by occupational group, 306–7
        decline, 309–10
        international comparisons, 309–10
    organization, 311
    wage effects, 315–18
        by industry, 316–17
        by occupation, 316
        earnings inequality, 318
        threat effect, 317–18
training, on-the-job *see* on-the-job training
transfer payments
    definition, 22
    trends, 24
transfer principle, 60–1
transition matrices, 183
    by earnings quartile, 188
    by income quartile, 185–6
    parents' and children's income quintiles,
        192
transitory income, 121
transportation, government expenditures, 612
trends, 22
"trickle-down" effect, 578
Truman, Harry, 572
trust funds, 138
trusts
    by age class, 162
    by wealth class, 159
Turkey
    income distribution, around 2000, 83
    taxation, 599
turnover model, 336–7
"twin peaks", 191, 192
twins, studies of, 276–8
Twinsburg Twins Festival, 276

UI *see* unemployment insurance
underclass, 108–9
    definition, 109
"underemployed", 224

unemployment
    categories, 209, 222
    causes debate, 236–8
    definition, 209
    "disguised", 244
    duration, 223
        family income effect, 225–6
        mean, 224
        median, 224
    frictional, 225, 232–3, 237–8, 540
    hidden, 224–5
    incidence, 226–32
        see also unemployment rate
    inflation and, 235
    job vacancies and, 225
    Keynesian (demand-deficient), 225, 235–6,
        237–8
    poverty and, 225
    search, 540
    seasonal, 233, 237, 541
    structural, 225, 234–5, 237–8
    trends, 404, 405–7
    types, 232–8
    youth, effects, 228, 244
unemployment benefits, 22
unemployment insurance (UI), 530–1, 536–41,
    594
    benefits structure, 537–8
    benefits trends, 538–40
    description, 536–8
    eligibility requirements, 537–8
    expenditure trends, 534–5
    incentive effects, 540–1
    poverty rate effects, 561
    reform proposals, 562
    replacement rate, 536–7, 539–40
    tax rate, 594
unemployment rate
    cyclical pattern, 221–2, 237
    definition, 209
    "full employment", 234–5
    macroeconomic policy and, 238
    natural, 234–5, 238
    for reentrants to labor market, 503
    trends, 221–3, 449–52, 539–40
        adjusted for hidden unemployment, 224–5
        by age, 226–8, 450–2, 459
        by gender, 226–7, 450–2, 459
        by industry, 229–30
        by marital status, 228–9
        by occupation, 230–1
        by race, 226–7, 231, 449–52, 458–9

by reason for unemployment, 222–3
   by region, 231–2
union labels, 312, 315
unionization
   decline, 13, 394–5, 410
   and market power, 332
   rate trends, 401–2, 405–8
unions *see* trade unions
unit of analysis, in poverty measurement, 122–3
unitary elasticity, 353
United Farm Workers, 312
United Kingdom
   comparable worth, 526
   estate division, 375
   gender–wage gap, 516
   household production, 39
   household wealth inequality, 167–9
   income distribution
      around 1980, 75–6, 81
      around 2000, 83
   income inequality, 395
      around 1970, 75
      around 1980, 77
      P90/P10 ratio, 78–9
   intergenerational elasticity, 196–7
   intergenerational mobility, 196–7
   lifecycle model analysis, 361–2
   poverty gap ratio, around 1980, 110
   poverty rates
      around 1980, 110
      around 2000, 110–11
   regional income differences, 328
   skill margins, 339
   taxation, 599–600
   unemployment rates, 233
   union density, 309–10
   welfare system, 571–2
United States in international comparisons
   estate division, 375
   gender–wage gap, 516–17
   income distribution
      around 1980, 75–6, 82
      around 2000, 83
   income inequality
      around 1970, 74–5
      around 1980, 77
      P90/P10 ratio, 78–9
   income mobility indices, 186–8
   poverty gap ratio, around 1980, 110
   poverty rates
      around 1980, 109–10
      around 2000, 110–11

skill margins, 339–43
taxation, 598–600
union density, 309–10
United States tax system
   customs duty, 595, 597–8
   distributional consequences, 587–607
      overall trends, 596–8
   local government taxes, 595–6, 597–8
   overall effective tax structure, 600–7
      see also tax rate, effective
   state taxes, 595–6, 597–8
   see also corporation income tax; estate
      tax; excise tax; federal personal
      income tax; federal tax; general
      sales tax; gift tax; payroll taxes;
      property tax
unskilled labor, demand trends, 265
upper tail, 59
user fees, 596, 598, 626
U.S.S.R., gender–wage gap, 516–17
utilitarianism, 575–6

value added, 46
   relation to income, 47
value productivity, 333
variance, definition, 56
veil of ignorance, 576
Venezuela
   income distribution
      around 1980, 81
      around 2000, 83
vertical equity, 586
veterans' benefits, 22
veterans' disability compensation, 530
   expenditure trends, 534–5
Vietnam War, 590
vintage effect, 466–7, 475
virtual social identity, 436

wage claims investigations studies,
   280
wage reduction, layoffs vs., 236
wage structures, rigid, 320, 321–2
wages, 21
   employment growth and, 333
   firm size and, 335–6
   plant size and, 335
   see also income; labor earnings; minimum
      wage
Wagner Act, 304–5
War on Poverty, 473, 554, 561
Warren, Earl, 472, 572

Washington (state)
  comparable worth system, 512
  TANF, 548
  unemployment insurance, 538
wealth
  definition, 134
  household *see* household wealth
wealth-adjusted income (WI), 614–16
wealth annuities, 164–6
wealth inequality *see* household wealth
      inequality
wealth mobility, 197–8
wealth tax data, 149
weighted averages, 460
weights, population, 91
welfare dependency, 550–1, 553–4
welfare programs, expansion, 476
welfare system, 546–54
  incentive effects, 550–4
    child bearing, 552–3
    labor supply, 550–1
    marital status, 552–3
    migration, 553
    welfare participation rates, 551–2
  payments, 21
  reform proposals, 563
  see also Aid to Families with Dependent
      Children; Temporary Assistance to Needy
      Families
well-being, wealth and, 135–6
West Germany
  income distribution, around 1980, 75–6, 82
  income inequality
    around 1970, 74–5
    around 1980, 77
  poverty gap ratio, around 1980, 110
  poverty rates, around 1980, 110
  unemployment rates, 233
West Virginia, unemployment insurance, 538
"white flight", 426
WI, 614–16
WIA, 554
"wildcat strikes", 312

Wilson, William Julius, 108–9
WIN program, 554, 555
winner-take-all markets, 342
Wisconsin Longitudinal Study (WLS), 285
wives, labor force participation, trends, 3,
      215–17, 492, 513–14
women's liberation movement, 518
Woodrow Wilson Fellows, 275
work experience
  age as proxy for, 258
  gender differences, 494–6
  and poverty incidence, 105–6
  productivity and, 279–81
  returns to, 500
Work Incentive (WIN) program, 554, 555
work interruption, effects on earnings, 501–3
work programs, 554–5
  effectiveness, 555
work week, decline in, 215
Worker-Establishment Characteristic Database,
      336
workers' compensation, 530
  expenditure trends, 534–5
  poverty rate effects, 561
Workforce Investment Act (WIA) (1998), 554
Works Progress Administration (WPA), 210,
      554
World Bank, poverty measurement standards,
      111–12
world income distribution, 84–5
world prices, computable general equilibrium
      (CGE) model, 392
World War I, disability compensation, 530
World War II
  effects on female employment, 506
  tax rates, 590
WPA, 210, 554
Wyoming, unemployment rates, 231–2

Yugoslavia, income distribution, around 1980,
      81

zoning regulations, 426